"*The superiority of Emerson's writing is in their character—they mean something. He may be obscure, but he is certain. Any other of the best American writers has in general a clearer style, has more of the received grace and ease, is less questioned and forbidden than he, makes a handsomer appearance in the society of the books, sells better, passes his time more apparently in the popular understanding; yet there is something in the solitary specimen of New England that outvies them all. He has what none else has; he does what none else does. He pierces the crusts that envelope the secrets of life. He joins on equal terms the few great sages and original seers. He represents the freeman, America, the individual. He represents the gentleman. No teacher or poet of old times or modern times has made a better report of manly and womanly qualities, heroism, chastity, temperance, friendship, fortitude. None has given more beautiful accounts of truth and justice. His words shed light to the best souls; they do not admit of argument. As a sprig from the pine tree or a glimpse anywhere into the daylight belittles all artificial flower work and all the painted scenery of theatres, so are live words in a book compared to cunningly composed words. A few among men (soon perhaps to become many) will enter easily into Emerson's meanings; by those he will be well-beloved. The flippant writer, the orthodox critic, the numbers of good or indifferent imitators, will not comprehend him; to them he will indeed be a transcendentalist, a writer of sunbeams and moonbeams, a strange and unapproachable person.*"

Walt Whitman, "The Superiority of Emerson's Writing"

Estimating Emerson

An Anthology of Criticism from Carlyle to Cavell

Edited by
David LaRocca

B L O O M S B U R Y
NEW YORK · LONDON · NEW DELHI · SYDNEY

Bloomsbury Academic

An imprint of Bloomsbury Publishing Plc

175 Fifth Avenue
New York
NY 10010
USA

50 Bedford Square
London
WC1B 3DP
UK

www.bloomsbury.com

First published 2013

ISBN: HB: 978-1-4411-9938-6
PB: 978-1-4411-6486-5

Library of Congress Cataloging-in-Publication Data
Estimating Emerson: an anthology of criticism from Carlyle to
Cavell/edited by David LaRocca.
p. cm.
Includes bibliographical references and index.
ISBN 978-1-4411-6486-5 (pbk.) –
ISBN 978-1-4411-9938-6 (hardback)
1. Emerson, Ralph Waldo, 1803–1882–Criticism and interpretation.
I. LaRocca, David, 1975–
PS1638.E88 2012
814'.3–dc23
2012031991

Typeset by Deanta Global Publishing Services, Chennai, India

Contents

Introduction

David LaRocca

A Conversation Among Critics

Why have so many notable writers taken their interest in Ralph Waldo Emerson's work beyond private admiration—or irritation—and chosen to write essays, critical remarks, and other forms of prose as well as poetry that name, engage, correct and clarify, and often celebrate his writing? The present volume may form a partial reply, or by the sheer extent and diversity of comments on Emerson it may create a deeper mystery, a more pressing desire to understand how Emerson's writing provoked and persuaded so many exceptional writers to single out his work for approbation and critique, to fathom the pleasure and difficulty of inheriting his work, and more generally to estimate Emerson's singular contribution. A quick scan of the authors in the table of contents—given their illustrious intellectual pedigrees and histories of influence—suggests why the value of their opinions on Emerson is self-evident. We have before us 67 writers composing work on Emerson over the course of 174 years. But not just any writers—*these* writers: some of the finest and most celebrated contributors to prose in the last few centuries. And that all these remarkable writers, scholars, critics, and poets have had something to say about Emerson creates a kind of consensus, across time, of his enduring significance. No matter what is said, *that* these many excellent writers said anything at all seems in itself a sufficient impetus to explore their common subject.

If there has ever been a question about the inheritance of Emerson's prose—that it is (still) worth reading, that it is perpetually relevant—then this book offers a response to that doubt; if there was ever an interest in the varied effects Emerson's writing had upon writers (seduction, incitement, or allergic reaction—among other effects), or in some cases a worry that his intellectual legacy was not sufficiently or appropriately acknowledged, then this book should offer a response to that interest or that worry as well. Indeed, we might ask ourselves—if not from the best writers, then from whom should we learn to read Emerson? Even if one has had little interest in or familiarity with Emerson's writing, then the present collection will be a pleasant excuse to read these great writers. That they all have something to say about Emerson is a startling facet of an unintended and circuitous history of critical interpretation. "Because the critical remarks of one author concerning another are rarely without interest," as William Braswell writes in this volume, we all take notice when discovering so many critical remarks on Emerson by esteemed authors. For instance, a critical description of Emerson's writing style—either to mark the achievements or failures of his work—is not objective but interestingly revelatory of the critic's values and preferences, and sense of what accomplished and meaningful prose looks like, or might be. Is the critic comfortable with metaphor, allegory, ellipsis, and allusion? What are the implied criteria he imputes to notions of rigor and structure and clarity? It is partly the critic's admission of these values and preferences that not only imbues a particular tone or mood to his criticism but also by turns and degrees returns us to Emerson's prose with a renewed sense of intrigue, asking ourselves: do I see what the critic—even this legendary, celebrated critic—sees? If not, am I in a position to articulate why I feel differently, read Emerson differently?

The contents of the volume reveal a long, but of course not exhaustive, sweep from classical to contemporary views, and not strictly from America but also from Great Britain, Europe, and Latin America. Since the criticism begins in 1834, one reads for decades—indeed, for nearly half-a-century—in prose written by Emerson's living contemporaries, both friends and detractors, before one reaches, at the time of his death in 1882, the effort to understand and evaluate the significance of his legacy. And thereafter for the next century and a quarter, the criticism continues through a range of literary and philosophical movements: from symbolism to modernism to post-modernism; in poetry, literary theory, and film studies; and in the varied and variable engagements with what F. O. Matthiessen called "The American Renaissance"—that crucial period of mid-nineteenth century American letters that Emerson so strongly defined and influenced.

Pamela Schirmeister has said that Emerson "remains one of the single most influential figures in the American cultural imagination. We may argue with him, as Hawthorne, Melville, Robert Penn Warren, and Ivor Winters have done, or embrace his thought with Kate Chopin, Hemingway, and Bart Giamatti, but we are all Emerson's heirs, willingly, knowingly, or not."[1] So we find a worthy portrait of all the contributors to the volume as well as all its readers: we are all heirs of Emerson, whether we like it or not. As heirs, then, having an opinion of Emerson—and becoming familiar with the opinions others have of his work, especially when those others are among the finest prose stylists of the nineteenth and twentieth centuries—seems not just a worthy aspiration but a sort of intellectual obligation. And with these writers at work, there is a chance it might also be an intellectual pleasure. The present volume should make us better informed heirs—more capable of fielding the range of criticism and more competent in rendering our own opinions of this ineluctable, and at times ineffable, force in American thinking.

I. The Criteria and Conundrums of Selection and Sequencing

There are many factors that inform what gets included in an anthology. In this case, I began with the ambition to collect as much compelling criticism on Emerson as possible—most of it focused directly on Emerson and occasionally with him and his work as the oblique subject—by some of the most accomplished, influential, and celebrated writers since Thomas Carlyle penned his first letters to Emerson in 1834. Once these works were assembled I sought permission to reproduce them; in this last phase, the denial of rights or the demand for prohibitive fees has led to the absence of some texts or a great diminishment of reproduction from the original. I draft this narrative of selection criteria and production factors as a brief account for not only those readers who may ask "Why was this writer included and not that one?" but also to follow after the further questions "Why was this piece by this writer included and not this other work" or "Why is this fine selection excerpted and not offered in its complete form?"

That a famous writer has written on Emerson may at first blush seem an odd criterion for a collection. Yet the sheer accumulation of celebrated writers writing on Emerson—sometimes at length and with great nuance, at other times more briefly and obliquely but with no less sense of a deep connection—is, as the table of contents should attest, a little overwhelming. A different criterion for selection might be simply "the best writing" on Emerson, but then I would be the judge of what matches that subjective criterion. And even here, the idea that a writer is famous is a bit difficult to hold down since fame can come and go. Many of the nineteenth century writers in the table of contents may be unfamiliar names to contemporary readers, and yet most of them were literary celebrities in their own day. I have relied, then, on a criterion that blends an author's prominence-at-the-time-of-composition with the impression his criticism made on the forms and features of criticism that followed his work. In this respect, I may echo M. H. Abrams' sentiment from the preface to his *The Mirror and the Lamp*: "The book deals, for the most part, with the original and enduring critics of the time, rather than with the run-of-the-mill reviewers who often had a more immediate, though shorter-lived influence on the general reading public."[2] Furthermore, trying to quantify the fame of intellectuals is not always an indication or prediction of their literary and philosophical effects, nor is it necessarily interesting to make such an assessment. But it is of interest that such minds have thought of Emerson—thought his work worthy of having considered opinions about.

The pieces included in this volume are neither of uniform opinion nor of uniform length or style. Here you will find oration, address, epistle, lecture, note, diatribe, poem, essay, review, journal entry, conversation, stump speech, among other forms. I should prefer that we make the disparate nature of the pieces something we critically explore instead of something I should, as editor, be obliged to apologize for. The inclusion of fragmentary elements in the anthology (e.g., by Dickens, Ruskin, Nietzsche, Proust, Musil, Peirce, et al.) may place the book on the path of censure, but I think the net benefit for imaginative reading—and the stimulation of new generations of Emerson readers—will be worth the risk. Thus the volume should not be expected to comprise a totality or a last word, but rather should provide a provocation to further reading and research—both in Emerson's work and the writers who address it. An encounter with a brief text, such as Jorge Luis Borges' poem on Emerson, or his remarks on Emerson drawn from interviews, might be enough to reframe one's thinking about the vast extent of Borges' fiction. If some entries may seem too short or out of balance with longer pieces, I wish to asseverate—if it is not already taken for granted—that masterful, affecting, and abiding criticism and poetry can be written in just a few lines.

Just as the entries in this collection are not uniform, so are their styles variable, and true to the original sources. This is especially evident in the work from the nineteenth century. I have retained the original—in some cases now archaic—grammar, punctuation, and spelling in order to present the prose and poetry in the form Emerson and his contemporaries would have found it. For example, in many cases among Emerson's contemporaries, we find spelling deviations such as Shakspeare for Shakespeare, subtile for subtle, labour for labor, sceptical for skeptical, fulfil for fulfill, to-day for today, etc. That said, very slight errors and omissions have been normalized to improve flow and clarity; there is no reason to needlessly replicate an obvious typographical error for the sake of being true to the original. Also, when annotations—footnotes or endnotes—appear in the original piece, they are reproduced here according to their original formatting. When I add editorial annotations to pieces, and I do so as infrequently as possible, the interventions and custodial notes appear in curly brackets { }.

In an effort to provide some order and sense of sequence to the vast number of entries collected here, selections are grouped into 20-year segments (save the first and final 30-plus-year terms), roughly reflecting the criticism of cascading generations. Within the segments, entries are for the most part presented in chronological order but are occasionally placed according to conceptual and content affiliations—an order that will hopefully amplify the flow of the texts, and their interrelation, especially if read consecutively from piece to piece. For example, P. Adam Sitney's essay appeared in 2008, and therefore should technically be placed after Cavell's most recent entry from 2004, but Cavell's work on Emerson featured here begins in 1979, which (also technically) throws his contribution back into the previous time segment (1961–1980). Cavell's presence at the end of the volume is not just for the fortuitous alliteration of the subtitle, but is an intentional editorial decision to showcase a philosopher who has written consistently, originally, and influentially on Emerson for more than three decades. Cavell could have been featured at the end of the 1961–1980 period as a kind of seminal interpreter, but it seems more fitting to see his work as presiding retrospectively—or belatedly, as he might say—across the previous range of critics, given what he has to say about their inheritance of Emerson. For most selections, however, a more straightforward chronological approach is highly effective—as for example when we find a sequence of American philosophers taking stock not just of Emerson's work but of each other's opinions of Emerson's work. Consider, for instance, how regularly and variously George Santayana's "The Genteel Tradition in American Philosophy" is invoked in works that follow it.

II. Brief Introductions to Each Contributor

While most of the names on the roster of 67 contributors are well known—name-brand stars of intellectual and international renown—it was suggested that a header introduction for each author might be of service to readers, if only as a reminder of accomplishments and some pertinent biographical and intellectual facts. I have tried to add a further valence of help by saying, very briefly, how the contributor or his/her work is connected to Emerson. The headers thus tend to skew toward facts and accomplishments that may best amplify lines of relation to Emerson—and were intentionally written with this kind of distorting lens. Of course, such connections are not uniform, as people are not, so the headers naturally reflect this unevenness—a variability that I hope will interest readers in its own right.

The brief introductions are meant to be deliberate and functional. Each one is a kind of prompt to the reader—inviting him or her to come closer, to take an interest in the specific work collected while also finding ways into other pieces in the volume. The headers are, then, neither strict biographical summaries of the author nor dedicated analysis of the text; they are not uniform or generated according to a preassigned formula but differ according to my sense of what might prove heuristic in the reader's approach to a given piece of work. As the reputations of the writers and their relationship to Emerson's writing vary, so must the account given of their accomplishments or relevance to this gathered community of critics. The anthologized writing should be the ultimate gauge of criteria for inclusion, but the headers form an initial, accessible, and I hope generative introduction to the excerpt. I have aimed to note quickly and pointedly how the writer is connected to Emerson—to isolate and emphasize some aspect of what brings the writer together with Emerson, and why he or she might have come to have opinions on his work—and then make way for the writer to state his or her own case. If I have succeeded, the brief headers should provide a coruscating snapshot or vignette instead of a portentous, encyclopedic portrait.

III. Criticism and the Field of Interpretation

The subtitle of the present volume denotes, and promises, "criticism," but the name—used in the title partly for the sake of economy—must hold a broad range of forms, meanings, and allusions. Something, then, must be said about the nature and variety of criticism as it is gathered on this occasion.

Estimating Emerson is, among other things, a collection of a wide range of literary forms and genres: essays, journal articles, newspaper reports, book reviews, chapters from monographs, lectures, eulogies, orations, addresses, poetry, letters, interviews, journal entries, and an equally wide range of pertinent literary, philosophical, and religious miscellany. The inclusion of so many disparate forms and genres, in which some comment or criticism of Emerson takes place, is directly correlated to the curious fact of Emerson's presence in the work of so many writers—often part of the writers' effort to understand his influence—and the variety of occasions we find his work invoked. It seemed unfair and imbalanced to include *only* literary criticism since that would deprive readers of the unexpected moments of encounter we find with his work among other kinds of intellectual engagement.

Once we recognize the variety of literary forms and genres, we must address the spirit of commentary and criticism. Fame does not, of course, entail universal acclaim. And likewise in Emerson's case of international literary celebrity, we find a good deal of negative criticism, which is nevertheless very finely written by some of the world's best prose stylists.

It may be useful to think of the works in the present volume, and the many works that are elsewhere collected by others, as if they live on a graph with two axes: from Praise (x) to Rebuke ($-x$) and from Explicit (y) to Implicit ($-y$) reference. Call this a matrix of inheritance and influence. Everything in *Estimating Emerson* falls somewhere on this schematic—the location of any particular piece of writing, of course, being largely determined by the work with which it is compared. (Is this account more or less full of praise? Is this mention more or less explicit?) Identifying the relative location of these works on the matrix is, therefore, an interpretive activity, and readers of the present volume will naturally be drawn into a consideration of both the individual quality of a work and its effect on a field of other contributions.

To speak more directly to the meaning of the axes and the coordinates they imply, I might describe the top extreme of the x-axis as an area of positive criticism, or the sort of criticism that seeks to praise Emerson's work. Such positive criticism customarily includes points of admiration, genuine interest, close reading, and overt efforts to acknowledge or in some cases rehabilitate Emerson's credentials as a philosopher and poet. At the other, bottom end of the x-axis, we find what might be called negative criticism, or the sort of criticism that seeks to qualify, rebut, or find fault with Emerson's work, or otherwise reprimand his writing—its opinions and outlook. This work tends to proceed with condescension about the merit of Emerson as a thinker, skepticism about his value to America and its literary culture, impatience with his prose style and his chosen subjects, and other forms of mocking assessment—from playful to severe, from high-minded to crude and flagrantly insulting.

Importantly, the nature of this spectrum or continuum—from high praise to severe rebuke—does not always mean that a writer is trying to come to terms with Emerson's influence on his or her work. Much of the writing is conducted as some variant of literary criticism, an art that seeks to properly understand the terms, conditions, and consequences of reading an author a certain way; even the philosophers tend to dedicate considerable attention to the way Emerson's literary qualities (or liabilities) relate to the work of philosophy and the generation of philosophical ideas and texts. Clearly, the mere appearance of the name "Emerson" in an author's work hardly necessitates the judgment that Emerson was an influence, significant or not. The more intriguing cases, in fact, may be those when the influence is felt but not stated; this is also part of the larger purview of literary criticism and philosophical analysis.

Thus praise and rebuke are complicated by a further inflection of the traits of inheritance—namely, the degree to which either is made explicit or instead remains implied. The introduction of this continuum requires another axis of interpretation, where the highest end of the y-axis means an overt and undisputed acknowledgement of Emerson's work and the lowest end of the y-axis means there is a barely discernable, and perhaps contestable, link to his work.

IV. Varieties and Permutations of Influence

When P. Adams Sitney, in the penultimate position of this volume, charts the "transmission of Emersonian aesthetics" into the realm of American *avant-garde* cinema, he writes: "American artists—poets, composers, painters, filmmakers—have largely perpetuated Emerson's transformation of the homiletic tradition in their polemical position papers. Sometimes they have even implicitly acknowledged their awareness of that tradition, as when Charles Ives published his *Essays Before a Sonata* (1920) to accompany his 'Concord Sonata.' More often they have been unwitting Emersonians, or even Emersonians in spite of themselves. Gertrude Stein is an example of the former, John Cage and Charles Olson of the latter." While the table of contents quickly attests to the capacious panorama of writers who have intentionally chosen to write on Emerson, either with praise or rebuke (and sometimes, as with Santayana, a blend of both), there are many who, as Sitney says, remain "unwitting Emersonians, or even Emersonians in spite of themselves." Tracing Emerson's influence on writing where he is not explicitly or directly mentioned is fascinating, but it is the work of the interpretive and speculative scholar, and would necessarily give rise to a different kind of anthology.

There are many, perhaps untold and unknown, who owe a debt or an allegiance to Emerson. In some cases, the writer may keep Emerson close but only allow his influence to appear transformed or transmuted—much as Friedrich Nietzsche does, though even he occasionally names Emerson, or lovingly imitates him, in the mainstream of his philosophical writing (as we find in the excerpts presented in this volume). But there are a surprising number of writers who only afford a glimpse of their interest in Emerson, the depth of which ranges from intriguing but vague to definitive but undeveloped; these works are not included here, but some notice of their type should be made.

In the *The Ball and the Cross*, G. K. Chesterton once remarked: "All the rational philosophers have gone along different roads, so it is impossible to say which has gone furthest. Who can discuss whether Emerson was a better optimist than Schopenhauer was pessimist? It is like asking if this corn is as yellow as that hill is steep."[3] The extent to which Chesterton read Emerson, or to which Emerson can be said to have contributed to his work, is one of many occasions that prompt further scholarly attention. Likewise, Rainier Maria Rilke, also a steady reader of Emerson, does not, in his published work, explicitly offer remarks on Emerson's significance or influence, but there is strong scholarly evidence to suggest that a poem such as "Notes on the Melody of Things" owes a great deal to close readings of "The Poet," "Circles," and other essays.[4] The philosopher George Herbert Mead was a contemporary—and admirer—of Josiah Royce, William James, and John Dewey, all of them, in turn, admirers of Emerson (and some of their remarks are included in this volume), but Mead himself did not have much to say directly on Emerson. Even in his essay "The Philosophies of Royce, James, and Dewey in their American Setting," which would seem to provide a natural occasion to reflect on Emerson as part of that context, Mead makes only a passing reference to him.[5] When F. Max Müller published his *Introduction to the Science of Religion* in 1873, he placed this note at the front of the book: "Dedicated to Ralph Waldo Emerson in memory of his visit to Oxford in May, M DCCC LXXIII, and in acknowledgment of constant refreshment of head and heart derived from his writings during the last twenty-five years."[6] While Müller made occasional reference to Emerson in his published work, for instance in a lecture on Sufism, he by and large does not write extensively on a figure whose work reliably supported him for a quarter century.[7] When the Pre-Raphaelites—among them Holman Hunt, John Millais, and Dante Gabriel Rossetti—set out to name the figures who "constitute the whole of our creed," they concurred on four: Washington, Poe, Longfellow . . . and Emerson.[8] In a memoir-cum-biographical portrait published the year after Emerson's death, Moncure Daniel Conway writes of this admiration with elements of first-person reportage: "It is a notable fact [. . .] that when Emerson's works appeared in England, among the first to welcome them were the Rossettis, both William and Dante. The Pre-raphaelist Brothers especially admired his poetry, as one of them tells me, 'for its august, seer-like qualities, notwithstanding some rustiness on the hinges of verse.' Emerson is mentioned with honour in 'The Germ.' William Rossetti was present at a lecture in Exeter Hall on 'Napoleon,' and tells me that he well remembers Emerson's 'upright figure, clear-cut physiognomy, clear elocution, resolved self-possession.'"[9] In his essay in this volume, William H. Gass asks of Emerson "Doesn't he dimly seem, sometimes, an Ayn Rand beforehand?" And yet Rand herself had very little patience for Emerson. She mentions him by name in the essay "Philosophy: Who Needs It" only to anoint him "a very little mind" and blame him for her poor reading of a line of his she misquotes—"Consistency is the hobgoblin of little minds." It is of course a *foolish* consistency that he chides.

There are times when what we might call a private admiration becomes public, or perhaps in posterity finds its way to printed form. These remarks are among the works I have chosen to include here, since they are—if fragmentary, and often allusive—also meaningfully suggestive of careful reading and the integration of ideas in further work. For instance, in his private journals (later edited and published), Robert Musil makes brief allusions to Emerson, and these remarks seem to provide the ground for exploring a significant influence in the wider work of the posthumously celebrated author of *The Man Without Qualities*. A few of these journal passages are excerpted below. Some scholars have claimed that Musil's novel is imbued with many Emersonian sentiments, even as Emerson is not explicitly mentioned anywhere in that two-volume masterwork. Still, Musil was familiar with Maurice Maeterlinck's essay on Emerson (included in this volume) and read Emerson directly.[10] On page one of his introduction to the *Diaries*, editor Mark Mirsky notes that at the *fin de siecle* Musil was reading Emerson (along with Nietzsche), and points out how Musil was greatly influenced by the work of Ellen Key that draws on Emerson—for instance, her book *The Unfolding of the Soul Through the Art of Living*.[11] Similarly, Jorge Luis Borges, when in conversation with writers and journalists (in selections below), points out the prominence of Emerson in his reading and thinking, and yet the only published work by Borges that names Emerson is an eponymous poem (also included, and in two translations). John Ruskin, whom Emerson met in 1873, was a close reader of Emerson and yet the latter's influence was only glancingly mentioned in Ruskin's published works (some of those passages are included here). Marcel Proust was an avid, dedicated reader of Ruskin and familiar with Emerson's work; when Proust translated Ruskin's *The Bible of Amiens*, he quoted from Emerson in the preface (and some of those remarks are collected below). The dispersed references and allusions to Emerson in Proust's other writing also suggest both that he read widely in Emerson's work and admired what he read.

In the list of those influential writers who would have been familiar with Emerson's work but did not register that influence in prose we might look in poetry to Emily Dickinson or in political and social philosophy to John Stuart Mill. Emerson and Mill met when Emerson made his first visit to England in 1833, and it was Mill who provided the personal introduction to Carlyle that meant so much to the young American and his Scottish hero. While Mill did not write on or about Emerson, he did write in his intellectual vicinity; there is much in their work to recommend them as sharing intellectual projects, preoccupations, and outlooks.[12]

John Jay Chapman said Emerson "is the chief poet of that school of which Emily Dickinson is a minor poet." We know that Dickinson attended a lecture presented by Emerson, and there is evidence to suggest that Dickinson relied on him both in practical and spiritual matters; as Tejvan Pettinger has written: "The works of other poets, in particular Emerson, were important for Emily Dickinson in opening up spiritual ideas beyond the strict Calvinism. Emily had innovative views and unorthodox beliefs, but she often doubted her own convictions; thus influences of Emerson and other poets were of great importance."[13] In the article "Dickinson's Emerson: A Critique of American Identity," featured in *The Emily Dickinson Journal*, Shira Wolosky writes: "Dickinson's work, in its recalcitrant selfhood, specifically recalls Emerson's writings, and it also more broadly refers to the general and looming concern with autonomy and individualism so central to American culture."[14]

Emerson would likely have been gratified by the degree to which he attracted poets, and perhaps even aided their own poetic expressions. After all, he said: "I am in all my theory, ethics and politics a poet."

While there are many twentieth-century poets who appear to read and admire Emerson's work, there are also many poets, especially among the Southern Agrarians and New Critics, who have consistently ridiculed his work. So, as we see in literary criticism, philosophy, and other fields of inheritance, there is a range of explicit mention—and from positive to negative—of Emerson among poets, and within their poetical work. Appearing somewhere in the domain of poetical composition and analytical judgment are William Carlos Williams, Wallace Stevens, Robert Penn Warren, Robert Duncan, Robert Creeley, Charles Olson, Charles Bernstein, Susan Howe, Ronald Johnson, Gary Snyder, Mark Strand, Mary Oliver, and Ann Lauterbach. Wallace Stevens, for example, is what Harold Bloom calls a "less candid Emersonian" (e.g., as contrasted with Mary Oliver who boldly confesses her allegiance to Emerson).

As we trace degrees of candor, we also discover increments from adoration to vitriol. On the latter end of the spectrum, Yvor Winters proposed this peculiar syllogism to summarize Emerson's work: "Immediate inspiration amounts to the same thing as unrevised reactions to stimuli," and such reactions are mechanistic; as a result "man in a state of perfection is an automaton," and "an automatic man is insane." Following this line of thinking, Winters concludes that "Emerson's perfect man is a madman."[15] After World War II, as the agents of New Criticism increased their attacks on Emerson,

Winters added another dire judgment to his reprimand: "the doctrine of Emerson and Whitman, if really put into practice, should naturally lead to suicide."[16] Southern Agrarian poet and New Critic Allen Tate also castigated Emerson for claiming that each individual, in "being himself the Over-Soul, is innately perfect." In his angry exasperation over Emerson, Tate transforms the often saccharine appellation "Sage of Concord" into a new, contemptuous epithet: "the Lucifer of Concord."[17] As Bloom points out, Winters and Tate "blamed Emerson for everything they disliked in American literature, and even to some extent in American life" (See "Mr. America"). Other Southern Agrarians such as Cleanth Brooks, John Crowe Ransom, and Robert Penn Warren could reasonably be added to the crowd of dissenting critics. One way to disclose one's suspicion and distrust of a writer is to exclude him from the reading list; when Warren and Brooks, joined by John Thibaut Purser, edited the massive anthology *An Approach to Literature* (1939), they made sure it contained no work (or mention of) Emerson—a sure sign that he does not register in their conception of the American canon, what it was or should be.

Leslie Fiedler said "the self-styled 'New Critics' condemned [Emerson] for having denied the reality of Evil and the fallen nature of mankind." Some readers get nervous, even indignant, when they read lines such as this by Emerson from the Address to the Divinity School at Harvard: "Good is positive. Evil is merely privative, not absolute: it is like cold, which is the privation of heat. All evil is so much death and nonentity. Benevolence is absolute and real." Or, as in "Spiritual Laws," when he claims we "miscreate our own evils. We interfere with the optimism of nature." Emerson's essay "The Tragic" has also been a touchstone for readers worried about his appreciation of human suffering, as when he writes "But the essence of tragedy does not seem to me to lie in any list of particular evils." A point of recognizable interest in Emerson (and controversy) is his understanding of evil. Of course, the secondary literature— including what is collected in this volume—reflects many other topics one could choose to identify and explore, among them: his adolescent experience with Calvinism; growing up with Unitarianism; abdicating from the Church and his subsequent effort to articulate religious views that are not "mere antinomianism"; his provocation to American scholars; his reading and interpretation of ancient Greek and Roman writers, English literature and poetry, and Continental Transcendentalism; his friendship with Carlyle and Thoreau; his capacity for political agitation and social reform (abolition, the treatment of Native Americans, women's rights); his understanding and use of natural science; his engagement with the history of philosophy and his treatment by philosophers; his poetry; and his prose style—this last one being among the most debated points of critical engagement in the work of celebrated writers collected here. Is Emerson's writing style novel, vigorous, and revelatory of penetrating insight, or is it a fog, a mist, and suffused with contradiction? Can it sustain all of these claims and charges?

Denigrating remarks about Emerson's lack of awareness of, or belief in, the existence of evil are usually paired with, or obscured by, condescending descriptions of his unflappable optimism. While the New Critics, and critics who followed after them, have launched these twin critiques (often in tandem), there have been a variety of contentious debates—some supplementing the censorious early readings, some aiming to revise and overturn them. And the critiques reach back into the nineteenth century—in fact to Emerson's own time, among his contemporaries, as for example with John Ruskin, who we find in *Time and Tide* (1867) censuring both "great teachers" (as he called them) Carlyle and Emerson, among others: "none of them seem to me yet to have enough insisted on the inevitable power and infectiousness of all evil, and the easy and utter extinguishableness of good. Medicine often fails of its effect—but poison never." Augustine Birrell, an English politician and author, sustained the complaint about this alleged feature of Emerson's work in the late 1880s, for example, when he noted: "For authors and books his affection, real as it was, was singularly impersonal. In his treatment of literary subjects, we miss the purely human touch, the grip of affection, the accent of scorn, that so pleasantly characterise the writings of Mr. Lowell" (See Birrell's "Emerson"). Years earlier, Amos Bronson Alcott was among the earliest critics to register dismay (though reluctantly) at Emerson's "pains to be impersonal"; and while admitting his context was "cold New England," Alcott could not help but wish that Emerson was "capable of abandonment sometimes" (See Alcott's "Essay"). By 1911, the judgment had spread and taken hold, as when George Santayana inflamed the situation by saying Emerson "was a cheery, child-like soul, impervious to the evidence of evil [. . .] detached, unworldly, contemplative" (See "The Genteel Tradition in American Philosophy"). Throughout the twentieth century, critics remain both captivated and concerned by the legacy of Emerson's understanding of evil; we find Newton Arvin at mid-century, drawing his essay title from the first line of Emerson's essay "The Tragic," and (as Cavell says in "Thinking of Emerson") collecting "the chorus of charges against Emerson":

> They all mount up—judgments like these, and there are a hundred of them— to what sometimes seems like not only a damaging but a fatal indictment of Emerson as a writer whom we can ever again listen to with the old reverential attention. A writer who lacks the Vision of Evil, who has no great sense of wrong—how can he be read with respect, or perhaps read at all, in a time when we all seem agreed that anguish, inquietude, the experience of guilt, and the knowledge of the Abyss are the essential substance of which admissible literature is made? It is a painful question to any reader who cannot suppress his sense of a deep debt to Emerson. But it is a question that must be asked, and one has to confess that, as one turns the pages of his essays, the reasons stare one in the face why Hawthorne and Melville, Eliot and Yeats, should have answered it negatively.[18]

And the procession of scholars worried about this dimension of Emerson's thinking continued to the end of the twentieth century. For instance, in the 1980s, John Updike refers to Emerson's worldview as "optimistic cosmology" and asks rhetorically: "Is not a world of suffering scandalously excluded from such an equation?" (See "Emersonianism"). Updike tells us how Emerson's "'can do' optimism [. . .] encourages the magnificent sprawl we see on all sides—the parking lots and skyscrapers, the voracious tracts of single-family homes, the heaped supermarket aisles and crowded ribbons of highway [. . .]." And to this list of offenses, Updike further claims that totalitarianism is "self-reliance gone amok," a "distorted" understanding of genius.

And having concluded that he has the measure of what Emerson means by optimism, Updike relates both sincerely and sensationally: "The extermination camps are one of the things that come between us and Emerson's optimism." A few years later, Cornel West wrote, "mysticism did not encourage Emerson to invest too much of himself—his time, energies, or hopes—in the immediate results of human efforts. It allows him to downplay injustice, suffering, and impotence in the world and rest content with inaction or minimal resistance to evil" (See "The Emersonian Prehistory of American Pragmatism"). At the end of the next decade, Sharon Cameron contributes to this tradition of critique by considering the related charge of Emerson's coldness or "impersonal" qualities (seen earlier in Alcott's and Birrell's commentary) and scrutinizes "a series of concerns that threaten to produce a devastating critique of Emerson in any serious reading of him. Someone might reasonably feel that Emerson's idea of the impersonal is ethically illegitimate if not indeed simply delusional. If it is neither of these, what keeps it from being so?"[19] Cameron concludes, in part, that "Emerson does not take the responsibility a person should take for his words and therefore betrays the complexity of a person's response to their desirability."[20] In her view, "one of the reasons Emerson fails to acknowledge others' suffering, which is never very real to him, is that he fails to acknowledge his own suffering, which is never very real to him."[21] What reading these critics together encourages is an impression that they are not so much reading Emerson as reading other critics *on* Emerson—responding to existing interpretations rather than fashioning their own.

So, even as Newton Arvin claims there are "a hundred" damaging critiques of Emerson's optimism and the alleged deleterious effects of his understanding of evil, and his impersonal ethics, "a hundred reasons" (as Mary Oliver writes) or counterinstances could be adduced. Beginning randomly, take, for example, Charles Ives who said: "If Emerson must be dubbed an optimist—then an optimist fighting pessimism, but not wallowing in it; an optimist who does not study pessimism by learning to enjoy it. [. . .] This strength of optimism—indeed the strength we find always underlying his tolerance, his radicalism, his searches, prophecies, and revelations—is heightened and made efficient by 'imagination-penetrative,' a thing concerned not with the combining but the apprehending of things" (See the selection from *Essays Before a Sonata*). Lewis Mumford even reframes the critical assessment of Emerson as cool, "chilly" (as Perry Miller later remarks), or cold, saying that we forget that his "coldness is not that of an impotence, but of an inner intensity: it burns!" (See "The Morning Star"). In the mid-1950s, Alfred Kazin said his "preoccupation" with Emerson was tied up with trying to "come to terms with that whole set of miserable, reactionary literary philosophers, Eliot and the Southerners"—that is, the New Critics, the Southern Agrarians, and other sympathetic modernists.

Readers such as Ives, Mumford, and Kazin suggest to us the degree to which these New Critical interpretations of Emerson should be considered vulgarized readings of his texts. The New Critics, among other readers, do not seem to take Emerson seriously enough to take him seriously; they are, as it were, predisposed to deride his outlook, and thereby do not so much read as judge, even ridicule, in order to embarrass Emerson rather than understand his work. For them, Emerson is a caricatured object of their intellectual fears and an affront to their critical aspirations. Contrast this condescension with the confidence expressed by Cornel West (who, admittedly, has just above leveled his own sanction) when he offers the following corrective of "interpretative blindness" that comes from "situating Emerson in the age of the American literary renaissance (along with Hawthorne, Melville, Thoreau, and Whitman) rather than relating him to the European explosions (both intellectual and social) that produced Karl Marx, John Stuart Mill, Thomas Carlyle, and Friedrich Nietzsche." And West continues by insisting that "We can no longer afford or justify confirming Emerson to the American terrain. He belongs to that highbrow cast of North Atlantic cultural critics who set the agenda and the terms for understanding the modern world. We must not overlook the parochialism implicit in his call for American cosmopolitanism, but we can no longer view his call through present-day parochial lenses."

Candid mention of Emerson's influence among poets also moves in the direction Ives, Mumford, Kazin, and West point us—that is, askew from the one we find among the just-noted post-War literary critics. For instance, Mary Oliver describes Emerson as "one of the mentors" of our time and offers a remark both personal and relevant to her professional achievements: "There are, for myself, a hundred reasons why I would find my life—not only my literary, thoughtful life but my emotional, responsive life—impoverished by Emerson's absence, but none is greater than this uncloseting of thought into the world's brilliant, perilous present. I think of him whenever I set to work on something worthy. And there he is also, avuncular and sweet, but firm and corrective, when I am below the mark. What we bring forth, he has taught me as deeply as any writer could, is predictable."[22] Like Oliver, poet Ann Lauterbach has also given attention in prose to Emerson, and like Oliver has confided something of Emerson's mentorship in expression. Addressing inductees of Phi Beta Kappa at the City College of New York, as Emerson once did at Harvard, Lauterbach's remarks sustain a quotation from Emerson ("I unsettle all things"): "This idea of being unsettled resonates now, as it must have when Emerson first wrote it. [. . .] I took this contrary, unsettled path: the precarious was, for me, more dependable than the secure. As time went on, an at times reckless commitment to instability and uncertainty migrated into a form of perception, and from perception into an interest in the limits of order, the outer rims of sense. These became the basis for a poetics."[23] Some results of Lauterbach's poetics as informed by Emerson include *In the Night Sky: Writings on the Poetics of Experience*, the poem "N/est," and the collection of poems, *On a Stair*.

There are also characters in prominent works of literature that some scholars believe were generated, in part, from an understanding of Emerson's temperament as a person and as a writer. Leslie Fiedler, for example, has noted that the character Mark Winsome in Melville's *The Confidence-Man* is a "wicked caricature of Emerson" (See Fiedler's preface); John Updike also supports this judgment and identifies the character of "the cosmopolitan" as a representative for Melville's critique of Emerson; as Updike understands the complaint, Winsome is "too mystical and also too practical. His philosophy is unreal, yet at the same time it serves the world's base purposes." And again, according to Fiedler, "Melville calls him [viz., Winsome] '[. . .] purely and coldly radiant as a prism. It seemed as if one could almost hear him vitreously chime and ring.'" Other scholars, as well as Melville himself (see his letters included below), appear to disagree that Winsome is based on Emerson, much less that the character reflects *Melville's* opinion of Emerson.

Nathanial Hawthorne's *The Blithedale Romance* is another work of American literature that commonly comes in for speculation about its depiction not of Blithedale Farm but of Brook Farm, a community experiment led by Amos Bronson Alcott in the early 1840s. In *Hawthorne in Concord*, Philip McFarland says that in the novel "components of Brook Farm have been invested with symbolic value that disclose meanings below the surface."[24] One of those components is the character Mr. Hollingsworth who is often noted for bearing a resemblance to Emerson. That he is a blacksmith by trade is not, for example, one of the features interpreters tend to dwell on. Rather, scholars such as Thomas R. Mitchell point out the way the "Emerson in Hollingsworth" possesses the "power to attract a Zenobia as well as a Priscilla."[25] Mitchell has also suggested that Hollingsworth is meant to be a hybrid, where he "functions at different levels as a representative of both Hawthorne and Emerson in the autobiographical dimensions of the romance."[26] And yet as Melville has a clear sense of the difference between historical figures and his literary creations, so too is Hawthorne at pains—in his preface to *The Blithedale Romance*—to emphasize his sense of literary reality, or in his words, "begs it to be understood" that the events at Blithedale Farm exist "without exposing them to a close comparison with the actual events of real lives."[27]

To conclude this brief sketch of Emerson's apparent presence as transformed by literary masters, I mention an English work—*A Room With a View*—in which E. M. Forster features a character (in fact, two—a father and a son) by the name Emerson: Mr. Emerson and George Emerson, respectively. The doubleness invites a reader to wonder whether both characters are meant to represent aspects of the historical Emerson—perhaps his thoughtfulness and generosity on the one hand, and his passion and unpredictability on the other. Or it may be that in calling his characters Emerson, father, and son, Forster has enhanced their *difference* from the historical Emerson; in this way, these Emersons do not constitute an homage or a reference but a pair of pseudonyms.

The foregoing explicit/implicit range of references and allusions to Emerson—for example, when an author notes a point of admiration, pleasure, or dismay in one of Emerson's lines by quoting or paraphrasing his work—may transform a reader's relationship both with the author's work and with Emerson, lead to an interest in the ways Emerson's work affected the author, and raise questions about what precisely in Emerson's writing attracted the author. Such an inquiry, as in the above cases, raises anew a reader's sense of what it means for an author to be influenced at all. Just because a writer notes reverence, respect, or regard—or as the case may be, disappointment, disillusionment, or disdain—in Emerson's work does not necessarily mean the writer will incorporate elements of such approbation or critique into future work of the writer's own. A necessary, much less a pervasive, connection is not part of the suggestion here. Rather, one may appreciate the instances of reference and quotation as part of a speculative kind of research—that is, as a matter not of reading literally but instead literarily—noting confluences, resemblances, and moments of affinity.

There are clearly what might be called the attackers of Emerson, as illustrated above: critics who, according to the proposed x/y matrix sketched earlier, populate the $-x$ field. Starting immediately, in the first years of Emerson's public life as a published intellectual, writers began to register their deep suspicion of his work—not just what he wrote about (content) but also how he wrote about it (style)—and their doubts over his influence on American literary and cultural experience, a tradition that continues in the present day. Though Emerson achieved instant literary celebrity upon the publication of his first book *Nature* (1836), and accumulated rafts of positive criticism, his work is hardly immune from harsh, penetrating, and ongoing assault.

Emerson's Address to the Divinity School at Harvard in 1838 placed a great strain on the tolerance of the entrenched Unitarian community. While Andrews Norton's attack is famous—noted by many biographers and included in this volume—there were many other voices full of concern and negative critique. J. W. Alexander, Albert Dod, and Charles Hodge (all theologians at Princeton Theological Seminary) took issue with the "nonsense and impiety" of the address, saying that in it "there is no ratiocination; there is endless assertion, not merely of unproved, but of unreasonable, of contradictory, of absurd propositions.[28] Worrying about the influence of "French declaimers" (such as Victor Cousin) and German philosophers—with their "impious temerity"—on American minds, the three Princeton theologians scorn Emerson's attempt to inherit these traditions from a Scotsman familiar with both strains of Continental thinking: "It is rhapsody, obviously in imitation of Thomas Carlyle, and possessing as much of the vice of his mannerism as the author could borrow, but without his genius."[29]

Richard Monckton Milnes, Lord Houghton, writing in the *Westminster Review* is nowhere near as panicked as the Princetonians, yet comments on Emerson's derivativeness from European thinking, again especially from Carlyle: "The utterances of Mr. Carlyle are in the streets and schools of experienced and studious Europe, but this voice has come to us over the broad Atlantic, full of the same tender complaint, the same indignant exhortation, the same trust and distrust, faith and incredulity, yet all sufficiently modified by circumstances of personality and place to show that the plant is assimilated to the climate and the soil, although the seed may have been brought from elsewhere."[30] Yet it is precisely the familiarity of Emerson's ideas—despite their occasionally strange recommendations—that gives Milnes comfort: "to the general English reader there is much that would appear extravagantly, absurdly original; and we believe that no one, however well read, would feel anything but gratification at reading thoughts already familiar to him, arrayed in language so freshly vigorous, so eloquently true."[31]

Other critics—of different strains and temperaments, across a wide swath of time—are included in the present volume. Andrews Norton and D. H. Lawrence, for example, exhibit impatience with Emerson's claims, Theodore Parker and Matthew Arnold with his style, and James Truslow Adams with the possibility that a reader can successfully mature with his ideas—thus relegating Emerson's work to the naïve adoration of adolescents.[32] Charles William Eliot, by contrast, notes: "As a young man I found the writings of Emerson unattractive, and not seldom unintelligible." Eliot thereafter emphasizes how in maturity he "discovered in Emerson's poems and essays all the fundamental motives and principles of my own hourly struggle [. . .]." And there is James Russell Lowell's poetic satire of poets, *A Fable for Critics*—in a section of which, included in this volume, he focuses on Emerson—where Emerson, who leads the pack of his contemporaries, fares pretty well. Lowell comments on Emerson's "rich words" and "grand verse" and compliments "rare depths of soul that have ne'er been excelled"; Emerson escapes Lowell's much graver critique of Poe ("Three-fifths of him genius and two-fifths sheer fudge").

Then there are times when a reader cannot be immediately sure whether a comment is full of commendation or censure. We seem to hear it differently depending on our appreciation of context, and also, of course, what we value generally and what we think we value in Emerson. For instance, the English critic Joseph Forster collected several of his lectures into the book *Four Great Teachers: John Ruskin, Thomas Carlyle, Ralph Waldo Emerson, and Robert Browning* (1890). Many of Forster's remarks about Emerson are squirm-inducing, for they seem to miss attributes of seriousness, depth, and even melancholy that were evident while Emerson was still alive—for example, when Forster speaks of "the moral purity and simple childlike goodness and sweetness of the man."[33] Yet even aside from what may be called moments of hagiographic excess, there are claims that are made based on a reading of Emerson's work, interpretations that may seem peculiar, out of phase, and at odds with the spirit of the work itself.

Do we agree with Forster, for example, who claimed: "The peculiar note of Emerson's style is its elevation and simplicity. He did not think of pleasing or displeasing any one; and therefore succeeded in delighting every one worth pleasing."[34] Forster continues: "It is not by pleasing the vulgar that a man succeeds. It is by pleasing the wise and discriminating, who dictate to the vulgar what to admire. Genius can only be thoroughly appreciated by genius."[35] How then do we explain Emerson's widespread appreciation by the young? Are they preternatural geniuses who later lose, which is to say grow out of, their powers of perception—as if educated into ignorance? Stanley Cavell has, in fact, observed that it is precisely Emerson's attention to the everyday— the common, the familiar, the low, and even the vulgar—that is part of his intellectual legacy. Emerson wrote in "The American Scholar" "I ask not for the great, the remote, the romantic; [. . .] I embrace the common, I sit at the feet of the familiar, the low," "a claim," writes Cavell, "I have taken as underwriting ordinary language philosophy's devotion to the ordinary, surely one inheritance of the Enlightenment."[36]

In an earlier essay, "An Emerson Mood," a companion to "Thinking of Emerson" (included in this volume), Cavell said: "By 'embracing the common,' by 'sitting at the feet of the low,' Emerson surely takes his stand on the side of what philosophers such as Berkeley and Hume would have called the vulgar. [. . . Emerson] takes the familiar and the low to be his study, his guide, his guru. In this he joins his thinking with the new poetry and art of his times, whose topics he characterizes as 'the literature of the poor, the feelings of the child, the philosophy of the street, the meaning of household life.'"[37] When Forster described himself (and his audience) as "we little people" who "may pick up some little thoughts and ideas, suitable to our size," he may have missed what Cavell believes to be something Emerson shares with English philosophers (viz., Berkeley and Hume), namely, that it is "internal to their philosophical ambitions to reconcile their philosophical discoveries with the views of the vulgar."[38] Forster's belief that Emerson's work required, in effect, spiritual and intellectual aristocracy to be fully apprehended rides in the other direction of Cavell's observation that Emerson is a student of the everyday—studying it and contributing to its philosophy.

As a reader might expect from a book such as this—a collection that contains so many critics on a shared *oeuvre*—there is a steady repetition, recursion, and re-invocation of the same lines from Emerson. But the fact that critics refer to a shared text, much as they would a scripture, is nothing compared with the pleasures, often experienced as moments of insight as well as disorientation that come from reading so many writers who generate so many different—often conflicting—readings of the same sequence of words. (Of course, someone familiar with the existence of Emerson's expansive corpus—16 volumes of journals, 12 volumes of collected writing, 6 volumes of letters, plus myriad volumes of sermons, lectures, and other miscellany—will wonder why critics do in fact tend to quote from such a narrow bandwidth of his work.) Emerson writes: "In all my lectures, I have taught one doctrine, namely, the infinitude of the private man," and over the decades and the generations critics have made their glosses on this claim apparent, using it as evidence for whatever approach they sought to bolster. If Emerson's claim is arresting—a provocation—so also are the disparate interpretations it and so many others have stimulated in his critical inheritors.

Even as there is abundant work that lands on the matrix of inheritance proposed above, we find instances in the literature of famed authors where work might be dubbed a false positive—work that, in short, doesn't belong anywhere on the *x/y* field. While G. K. Chesterton's contrast between Emerson and Schopenhauer noted above counts as a legitimate reference to the American, we cannot say the same for the other Emerson—Professor Emerson Eames, a character in Chesterton's *Man Alive* (1912). Is it possible, however, that Chesterton intended to borrow the name to refract some trait of Emerson's character, or Chesterton's perception of it? It is unlikely that Chesterton could have known that the name "Eames" appears in Emerson's *Journals* in 1862, or could have been familiar with Emerson's knowledge of a person by that name. If it were shown to be a legitimate invocation, the example of Emerson Eames would have to be grouped among the literary references as we find them noted above in Melville, Hawthorne, and E. M. Forster, and not regarded as a confusion among historical Emersons. To offer but one conspicuous example of that latter sort of case, I direct the reader to a poem by Elizabeth Barrett Browning that acknowledges "Emerson's Journals" as the source of her literary inspiration in composing the work. The attribution misguides insofar as the Mr. Emerson of her attention is not the one we may think it is.[39] Rest assured that the work collected in *Estimating Emerson* achieves an authentic match with its subject. That the authors have trained their attention on *our* Emerson, however, does not displace the chance that the reader may be surprised by the interpretations of his work—left to wonder if this is in fact the same Mr. Emerson the reader has signed on to read about, and not someone altogether unknown. It is a gift, some may say, to be given back familiar and influential thinking in uncanny and unknown ways, but the gift can also be bewildering and estranging. Who have I been reading all these years? *Estimating Emerson* presents an invitation to ask and respond to such a question anew.

V. Further Notes on What is Included and What is Left Out, and Why

John J. McDermott, writing in 1986, noted: "It is striking that in the vast secondary literature on Emerson, distinctively philosophical considerations are virtually absent." McDermott has in mind criticism collected in anthologies edited by professors of English in the 1960s and 70s.[40] Since then, however, an appreciable amount of new philosophical scholarship has grown up around Emerson. Fortunately, much of that impressive catalogue of books and journal articles is for the most part available—both in print, and accessible through digital archives; understandably, many of these works are not collected here. One aim of the present collection is, instead, to gather a few of these "distinctively philosophical" works and place them in the (not always hospitable) company of other criticism—thereby offering a new aggregation of works in a convenient and accessible form.

Selections for the present volume were made on objective and subjective criteria, the objective encouraging the assembly of works that are out of print, undercirculated, or otherwise hard to find, and the subjective affording the inclusion of pieces that are written by prominent, influential, and accomplished writers, or who (if not household names) offer some important contribution to the continuing conversation about—and necessary correctives to—Emerson's inheritance in, as Cavell says, "the culture he helped to found."

Some of the selections indicate a well-known, name-brand writer who has written something rarely read; in these cases, our curiosity is piqued by the very fact that such and such a writer had something—anything—to say about Emerson. Other selections are by writers who may have once been well-known but are now largely part of intellectual history, and yet their writing on Emerson seems distinctive—constitutive of a voice we might be better off remembering; with these selections the hope is to recover (in the sense of returning to the ground of, going over again, and not hiding once more) their work for a new season of reading. Often the most peculiar and wonderful readerly experience occurs when these various selections are read according to one's interests (either by title or author)—when the distinct voices begin to share a space, share in Emerson a text of reference, and yet rarely render the same verdict by the same methods.

Of course, there are many cases when, among many fine intellects who have written on Emerson, we are faced with an embarrassment of riches; indeed, the abundance of similarly high-quality criticism of Emerson could easily fill several more volumes of the present size. Cavell, to be sure, stands out in having produced a tremendous library of essential essays, but then his *Emerson's Transcendental Etudes* was meant to address this fact by collecting a career's worth of critical work on Emerson into a single, chronological volume supplemented by annotations and indices. But we also find intriguing remarks by Emma Lazarus in her essay "Emerson's Personality,"[41] by Frederick Ives Carpenter when he compares Emerson and William James,[42] and by Paul Elmer More—in his "Emerson" chapter in *A New England Group and Others* (1921), the last installment of his 11-volume *Shelburne Essays*. And even among writers who are customarily regarded as harsh and unyielding critics of Emerson, such as Santayana, we discover several long essays worthy of inclusion (and not incidentally, along the way, encounter moments of Santayana's appreciation, even admiration of his subject). These few examples are meant to suggest some of the ways in which I was forced to choose between fascinating and compelling options. As essays have a way of speaking with one another—directly and indirectly, and across time—I chose essays that not only were meritorious on their own terms, but also were meaningfully engaged and reinforced by the presence of the essays that surround them, early and late. The selections should read well independently—for those who dip randomly into the book; and provide genuine satisfaction when read consecutively from one entry to the next (as topics, temperaments, and even plots emerge); and also function synoptically, for those who venture organically through a self-selected course of reading.

Given the variety of contributors in this collection, it is not immediately evident if they share a name or description above "contributor"—perhaps author or writer or critic might work. Partly the variety of titles is a function of the breadth of time covered by the entries—174 years, from 1834 to 2008; in that temporal expanse, we might acknowledge a tremendous shift in our expectations for what writers do and a formidable transformation in academic life—its professionalization. For example, Richard Rorty, in his essay in this volume, points to an always evolving sense of what we mean by "philosopher" and "critic." So, as we attempt to give our writers and thinkers a proper assignation— or orient ourselves in relation to the kind of writing they offer—we can keep in mind what Rorty says: "Possibly they will be given a name which would seem as odd to us as our use of 'critic' would have seemed to Dr. Johnson, or our use of 'philosopher' to Socrates." But such oddness in naming, as Cavell reminds us, is an essential aspect of the interpretation. "Perhaps," Cavell notes, "I will be taken as struggling merely over labels; but sometimes labels should be struggled over." Thus, as editor and as reader, we may be best served to find commonality in the quality of the prose (admitting differences even on this criterion) and the shared object of their attentions, namely, Emerson.

A further aspiration for collecting the volume as I have is to illustrate both the temporal range and temperamental variety of criticism on Emerson. When reviewing Lawrence Buell's *Emerson* (2003), John Updike wrote: "Buell's solicitous, corrective slant has the unintended effect of showing how thoroughly Emerson, who spoke to wake up the democratic masses to the power within them, is now captive to the contentious, incestuous circles of academe" (See "Big Dead White Male"). If this is true, one hope is that *Estimating Emerson* will also be a corrective, making evident the long, varied, intellectually vigorous, and multivocal conversation dedicated to understanding Emerson's work and its effects. One crucial aspect of Emerson's legacy is that he has prompted many academics—whether contentious and incestuous or not—to explore the meaning of academic discourse and the role the academy plays in intellectual and everyday life. Several of the most prominent academic critics of Emerson's work undertake metacritical reflections of the academic profession— including its conceptual categories, assigned titles, and accepted disciplines and fields of inquiry. In this way, Emerson's writing retains its ongoing challenge—truly a perpetual provocation—to any mode of complacency over the meaning and relevance of the academy. For this reason, a reader of *Estimating Emerson* may become aware of the "contentious, incestuous circles of academe," but will by no means be entrapped by them. The collection, instead, draws a new circle.

Meanwhile, many other works stand as useful and fitting complements to the present volume, among them monographs whose authors have aimed to contextualize, narrativize, and otherwise make more accessible the inheritance of Emerson in American culture; see, for example, Charles E. Mitchell's *Individualism and Its Discontents: Appropriations of Emerson, 1880–1950* and Sarah Ann Wider's *The Critical Reception of Emerson: Unsettling All Things*. In *Building Their Own Waldos: Emerson's First Biographers and the Politics of Life-Writing in the Gilded Age*, Robert Habich's historiographical work helps us understand the nature and variety of Emerson biographies—how Emerson's story is not unified, authorized, and evident but rather is shaped by the intentions, temperament, values, and ambitions of each biographer, and therein seems to provide strong evidence for Emerson's claim that "all biography is autobiography." Alan M. Levine and Daniel S. Malachuk's *A Political Companion to Ralph Waldo Emerson* offers a fresh engagement with Emerson's impact on American political thought by coupling established and influential texts with new essays. Much as Joseph Blau's essay does in the present volume, *A Political Companion* provides a robust corrective to the "pernicious myth" of Emerson's apolitical individualism. Similarly, Arthur Lothstein and Michael Brodrick's *New Morning: Emerson in the Twenty-First Century* reclaims important scholarship (such as Robert C. Pollock's "The Single Vision"), adds new voices, and expands the range of engagement with Emerson's work to include poetry and essays by poets.[43] Anthologies such as *New Morning*, and the several collections of critical literature that have been published in the last few decades—incorporating "distinctively philosophical considerations"—provide the most obvious reason why the contributions of some important scholars have been left out here. To discover who these scholars are, and how their work relates to the present volume, simply refer to the existing anthologies that collect their crucial scholarship.[44]

If there are perceived gaps or lacunae in the final phase of the collection—say in the last 20 to 30 years, where it could be said certain essential and influential contributions are set aside—I wish to clarify immediately and emphatically that the absence of important work is not owing to lack of esteem but rather should indicate an effort to gather work that forms a coherent conversation of criticism. Attempted coherence is complicated—and enriched—by the simultaneous fact of variability in the styles and sentiments of these chosen authors and the unrehearsed effects of their intimate cohabitation between the same covers; the physical proximity, in turns, illuminates both intellectual distance and intellectual affinity. Consequently these works generate a conversation featuring compliments and quarrels, negotiations and evasions, rapprochements and neglect; in short, they should reflect an authentic occasion of shared investigation—one full of cacophony and contention. In this final and most professionalized period, we find writers, critics, poets, activists, and academics inexorably drawn to a common subject of inquiry, though seldom claiming a unified, uniform, univocal, or settled opinion of it. There are, admittedly, many other worthy and ongoing conversations in recent decades, but the present one—as represented by these writers and these selections—is intended both to suggest the richness of the field of Emerson criticism and to highlight these aspects of the critical inheritance of Emerson's intellectual legacy.

VI. Last Words ... at the Beginning

One of the great pleasures of this volume should be a growing perception by readers of the ways the essays are interrelated—especially insofar as the later essays form a perpetual, helical commentary on the earlier works. There are beautiful, intriguing, perplexing cascades of criticism, where one writer prompts the interest of another whose work is then mentioned by a third, and the consolidating work of the third finds new treatment by a fourth, and so on. No matter where a reader begins reading in the volume, he or she will be rewarded with an implied invitation to explore a related entry; the brief header introductions are intended to facilitate this hoped-for eventuality. Though the entries are for the most part chronologically arranged, one need not begin at the beginning in order to enter the conversation.

If a reader were to start reading *Estimating Emerson* at the end of the book, she would find Stanley Cavell, in a contribution from *Cities of Words*, reminding us to turn or return to Emerson's text—to read and reread Emerson in the wake of or in tandem with these many remarks by remarkable writers. The spirit that concludes Cavell's chapter, and that appropriately closes this volume, is one of inquiry conducted in and out of school. At this threshold, Cavell is poised to begin a "pedagogical lesson on a register of the moral life," and if a reader has been surprised and stimulated, dismayed and reconfirmed after reading *Estimating Emerson*, he or she will likely feel—at the end—a new impetus for beginning, and for going further with Emerson.

What *Estimating Emerson* should ideally make evident is how, despite the accumulation of critical prose on Emerson's writing—even by these celebrated writers, critics, philosophers, and poets—there is yet so much left to say, to write, and to read about Emerson. As a collection of commentaries and criticisms, a sort of midrash, *Estimating Emerson* reconfirms our sense of awe at the source text—Emerson's prose— and its inexhaustible capacity to form and inform our thinking.

David LaRocca
New York

Notes

1 Ralph Waldo Emerson, *Representative Men*, ed. Pamela Schirmeister (New York: Marsilio Publishers, 1995), ix–x.
2 M. H. Abrams, *The Mirror and the Lamp: Romantic Theory and the Critical Tradition* (Oxford: Oxford University Press, 1953).

3 G. K. Chesterton, *The Ball and the Cross* (1910), in *The Collected Works of G. K. Chesterton* (San Francisco: Ignatius Press, 2004), Vol. VII, 118.

4 See Jan Wojcik, "Emerson and Rilke: A Significant Influence?" *MLN*, Vol. 91, No. 3, German Issue (Apr., 1976), 565–574; and Marilyn Vogler Urion, "Emerson's Presence in Rilke's Imagery: Shadows of Early Influence," *Monatshefte*, Vol. 85, No. 2 (Summer, 1993), 153–169.

5 "The Philosophies of Royce, James, and Dewey in their American Setting" in *Selected Writings*, ed. Andrew J. Reck (Chicago: University of Chicago Press, 1964), 377.

6 Four Lectures Delivered at the Royal Institution in February and May 1870.

7 See F. Max Müller, *Theosophy or Psychological Religion*: The Gifford Lectures delivered before the University of Glasgow in 1892 (Cambridge: Cambridge University Press, 2011), 349.

8 Robert D. Richardson, Jr., *Emerson: The Mind on Fire* (Berkeley: University of California Press, 1995), 444.

9 Moncure Daniel Conway, *Emerson at Home and Abroad* (London: Trübner & Co., Ludgate Hill, 1883), 271.

10 Robert Musil, *Diaries, 1899–1941*, ed., trans., Philip Payne (New York: Basic Books, 1998), xxviii.

11 See Musil, *Diaries*, n93 and n94, 545.

12 See for example, David Justin Hodge, "The Opacity of the Initial: Deciphering the Terms of Agency and Identity in 'Self-Reliance' and *On Liberty*," in *Ralph Waldo Emerson: Bicentenary Appraisals*, ed. Barry Tharaud (Mosaic: Studien und Texte zur Amerikanischen Kultur und Geschichte, Wissenshaftlicher Verlag Trier, 2007); and Alex Zakaras, *Individuality and Mass Democracy: Emerson, Mill, and the Burdens of Citizenship* (Oxford: Oxford University Press, 2009).

13 Tejvan Pettinger, "Biography of Emily Dickinson," (Oxford: <biographyonline.net>, 2006).

14 Shira Wolosky, "Dickinson's Emerson: A Critique of American Identity," *The Emily Dickinson Journal*, Vol. 9, No. 2 (2000), 134–141.

15 Yvor Winters, "The Experimental School in American Poetry," *In Defense of Reason* (Denver: Alan Swallow, 1947), 54–5.

16 Yvor Winters, "The Significance of 'The Bridge' by Hart Crane, or What Are We to Think of Professor X?" *In Defense of Reason* (Athens, Ohio: Swallow Press, 1987), 589.

17 Allen Tate, "Four American Poets," *Reactionary Essays in Poetry and Ideas* (New York: Scribners, 1936), 7–8.

18 Newton Arvin, "The House of Pain: Emerson and the Tragic Sense," *The Hudson Review*, Vol. 12, No. 1 (Spring 1959), 38–9.

19 Sharon Cameron, "The Way of Life by Abandonment: Emerson's Impersonal," *Critical Inquiry* 25 (Autumn 1998), 4.

20 Ibid., 31.

21 Ibid.

22 Mary Oliver, *Long Life: Essays and Other Writing* (Cambridge, Massachusetts: Da Capo Press, 2004), 51.

23 Ann Lauterbach, "After Emerson: Of General Knowledge and the Common Good" (2004), *New Morning: Emerson in the Twenty-First Century*, eds. Arthur S. Lothstein and Michael Brodrick (Albany: State University of New York Press, 2008).

24 Philip McFarland, *Hawthorne in Concord* (New York: Grove Press, 2004), 150.

25 Thomas R. Mitchell, *Hawthorne's Fuller Mystery* (Amherst: University of Massachusetts Press, 1998), 195.

26 Thomas R. Mitchell, "In the Whale's Wake," *Hawthorne and Melville: Writing a Relationship*, eds. Jana Argersinger and Leland S. Person (Athens: University of Georgia Press, 2008), 263; see also Mitchell, *Hawthorne's Fuller Mystery*, 190–198.

27 Nathanial Hawthorne, *The Blithedale Romance* (New York: W.W. Norton & Company, 1958/1998) 27.

28 J. W. Alexander, Albert Dod, and Charles Hodge, "Transcendentalism of the Germans and of Cousin and Its Influence on Opinion in this Country," *The Biblical Repertory and Princeton Review* (1839); reprinted in *The Recognition of Ralph Waldo Emerson*, ed. Milton R. Konvitz (Ann Arbor: University of Michigan Press, 1972), 13–15.

29 Ibid., 13.

30 Ibid., 16. Richard Monckton Milnes, *Westminster Review*, March 1840.

31 Ibid.

32 See also Theodore Gross' chapter "Under the Shadow of Our Swords: Emerson and the Heroic Ideal" in *The Heroic Ideal in American Literature* (New York: The Free Press, 1971).

33 Joseph Forster, *Four Great Teachers: John Ruskin, Thomas Carlyle, Ralph Waldo Emerson, and Robert Browning* (London, George Allen; and New York, Scribner and Welford, 1890), 72.

34 Ibid., 73.

35 Ibid., 74.

36 Stanley Cavell, "Aversive Thinking," *Emerson's Transcendental Etudes*, ed. David Justin Hodge (Stanford: Stanford University Press, 2003), 142.

37 Cavell, "An Emerson Mood," *Emerson's Transcendental Etudes*, 24.

38 Ibid.

39 Since Elizabeth Barrett Browning (1806–1861) was a prominent Victorian poet, author of *Poems* (1844), and wife of poet Robert Browning, it is highly likely that she was acquainted with Emerson's work. Thus as a contemporary of Emerson, it is understandable that even a literary historian would assume that Browning's Emerson was the same figure who occupies our present attention. However, Browning wrote the following poem—"Stanzas Occasioned by a Passage in Mr. Emerson's Journal"—in 1826, which should immediately seize the reader with a perception of her influence by Emerson *avant la lettre*. Indeed the "Mr. Emerson" of her title is not our Mr. Emerson, but one Mr. James Emerson, Esq. a traveler in 1820s Greece. The poem is therefore not occasioned by a passage in the journals of the American philosopher. For the sake of scholarly clarification and disambiguation, then—that is, to align the poem with its proper Mr. Emerson—I include here both James Emerson's journal passage, and following it, Browning's poem.

In *The Literary Gazette; and Journal of Belles Lettres, Arts, Sciences, & c. for the year 1825* (published on the Strand in London by Whiting and Branston), we find a review of the same journals that Browning refers to as collected in *A Picture of Greece in 1825; as exhibited in the personal Narratives of James Emerson, Esq., Count Pecchio, and W. H. Humphrey's, Esq., comprising a detailed Account of the Events of the late Campaign, and Sketches of the principal Military, Naval, and Political Chiefs in*

Two Volumes (London, Colburn, 1826; as cited in the *Museum of Foreign Literature and Science*, April 1826, Vol., VIII, No. 46, 20). A passage from James Emerson's journal reads:

> Having this morning removed, with Count Gamba, to apartments assigned us by the Government in the palace of the late Pacha, we had, shortly after, a visit from an old Roumeliot, Captain Demetrius, who had been attached to Lord Byron. On seeing Gamba, he embraced him with sincere affection; and immediately, on mentioning Byron, burst into tears; saying, that in him he had lost a father, and Greece her truest friend. His language, in speaking of him, was at once feeling and poetical. In describing the hopes which Byron's fame had created in the heart of the Greeks, he said, that as soon as they understood that a great English effendi was coming to assist them, they waited his arrival like young swallows for their mother" (*The London Literary Gazette and Journal of Belles Lettres, Arts, and Sciences, etc.*, No. 465, December 17, 1825, 807).
>
> Stanzas Occasioned by a Passage in Mr. Emerson's Journal, Which States, That on The Mention of Lord Byron's Name, Captain Demetrius, An Old Roumeliot Burst Into Tears

> NAME not his name, or look afar—
>   For when my spirit hears
> That name, its strength is turned to woe—
>   My voice is turned to tears.
>
> Name me the host and battle-storm,
>   Mine own good sword shall stem;
> Name me the foeman and the block,
>   I have a smile for *them!*
>
> But name *him* not, or cease to mark
>   This brow where passions sweep—
> Behold, a warrior is a man,
>   And as a man may weep!
>
> I could not scorn my Country's foes,
>   Did not these tears descend—
> I could not love my Country's fame,
>   And not my Country's Friend.
>
> Deem not his memory e'er can be
>   Upon our spirits dim—
> Name us the generous and the free,
>   And we must think of *him!*

40 Anthologies that illustrate McDermott's point include *Emerson: A Collection of Critical Essays*, eds. Milton R. Konvitz and Stephen E. Whicher (Englewood Cliffs: Prentice Hall, 1962) and *The Recognition of Ralph Waldo Emerson: Selected Criticism since 1837*, ed. Milton R. Konvitz (Ann Arbor: University of Michigan Press, 1972).

41 Emma Lazarus, "Emerson's Personality" in *Emma Lazarus: Selected Poems and Other Writings* (Orchard Park, NY: Broadview Press, 2002).

42 Frederick Ives Carpenter, "Points of Comparison between Emerson and William James," *New England Quarterly*, Vol. 2 (1929), 458–74; and "William James and Emerson," *American Literature*, Vol. 11 (1939), 39–57. Carpenter is also the author of *Emerson and Asia* (1930), *Ralph Waldo Emerson* (1934), editor of *The Emerson Handbook* (1953).

43 Charles E. Mitchell, *Individualism and Its Discontents: Appropriations of Emerson, 1880–1950* (Amherst: University of Massachusetts Press, 1997); Sarah Ann Wider, *The Critical Reception of Emerson: Unsettling All Things* (Rochester: Camden House, 2000); Robert Habich, *Building Their Own Waldos: Emerson's First Biographers and the Politics of Life-Writing in the Gilded Age* (Iowa City: University of Iowa Press, 2011); *A Political Companion to Ralph Waldo Emerson*, eds. Alan M. Levine and Daniel S. Malachuk, (Lexington: University Press of Kentucky, 2011); *New Morning: Emerson for the Twenty-First Century*, eds. Arthur Lothstein and Michael Brodrick (Albany: State University of New York Press, 2008).

44 See for example, *Emerson Centenary Essays*, ed. Joel Myerson (Carbondale: Southern Illinois University, 1982); *Ralph Waldo Emerson: A Collection of Critical Essays*, ed. Lawrence Buell (Englewood Cliffs: Prentice Hall, 1993); *On Emerson*, eds. Edwin Cady and Louis J. Budd (Durham: Duke University Press, 1988); *The Cambridge Companion to Ralph Waldo Emerson*, eds. Joel Porte and Saundra Morris (Cambridge: Cambridge University Press, 1999); *Ralph Waldo Emerson: Bicentenary Appraisals*, ed. Barry Tharaud (Wissenschaftlicher Verlag Trier, 2006); *Ralph Waldo Emerson*, ed. Harold Bloom (New York: Chelsea House, 2007); and *Emerson for the Twenty-First Century: Global Perspectives on an American Icon*, ed. Barry Tharaud (Newark: University of Delaware Press, 2010).

Thomas Carlyle (1795–1881)

Scottish philosopher, biographer, social critic, and historian who moved to London in 1834, the year after Emerson (with a note of introduction by John Stuart Mill) visited him at Craigenputtock. Emerson, disappointed after his visits with Coleridge and Wordsworth the same year, found relief and inspiration with Carlyle. Emerson arranged to have Carlyle's Sartor Resartus published in America in 1836 and wrote a supportive preface for the new work, and Carlyle reciprocated by prefacing Emerson's Essays, First Series *when the book was published in England. Carlyle's preface to* Essays, *which was published in London by James Fraser in 1841, commences the present volume. The two men effectively introduced one another to their respective native countries and by the force of their judgment created audiences and interest in both directions. Thereafter, Emerson and Carlyle maintained a transatlantic correspondence for the rest of their lives, and died within a year of one another. Though there were moments of tension in their relationship, resulting in occasional lapses, even breaches, it is evident from the vitality of their letters—full of unvarnished critique of their personal and professional lives—that they were committed intellectual help-meets. Some of Carlyle's letters to Emerson are included below. One of the running themes of their lengthy correspondence is Carlyle's near-comedic flirtation with the prospect of visiting America—an idea that, he tells Emerson, "occasionally rises like a mad prophetic dream in me." Emerson visited Carlyle on the three occasions he traveled to England (1833–34, 1847–48, and 1872–73), but Carlyle never made it to New England. When Carlyle died in 1881, Emerson, already fading mentally and a little more than a year from his own death, eulogized his friend as the "best of all men in England," in part by drawing from reflections made after his second visit with Carlyle in 1848: "His guiding genius is his moral sense, his perception of the sole importance of truth and justice; but that is a truth of a character, not of catechisms."*

Preface by the Editor to *Essays, First Series*

Thomas Carlyle

To the great reading public entering Mr. Fraser's and other shops in quest of daily provender, it may be as well to state, on the very threshold, that this little Reprint of an American Book of Essays is in no wise the thing suited for them; that not the great reading public, but only the small thinking public, and perhaps only a portion of these, have any question to ask concerning it. No Editor or Reprinter can expect such a Book ever to become popular here. But, thank Heaven, the small thinking public has now also a visible existence among us, is visibly enlarging itself. At the present time it can be predicted, what some years ago it could not be, that a certain number of human creatures will be found extant in England to whom the words of a man speaking from the heart of him, in what fashion soever, under what obstructions soever, will be welcome;—welcome, perhaps, as a brother's voice, to 'wanderers in the labyrinthic Night!' For these, and not for any other class of persons, is this little Book reprinted and recommended. Let such read, and try; ascertain for themselves, whether this *is* a kind of articulate human voice speaking words, or only another of the thousand thousand ventriloquisms, mimetic echoes, hysteric shrieks, hollow laughters, and mere inarticulate mechanical babblements, the soul-confusing din of which already fills all places? I will not anticipate their verdict; but I reckon it safe enough, and even a kind of duty in these circumstances, to invite them to *try*.

The name of Ralph Waldo Emerson is not entirely new in England: distinguished Travelers bring us tidings of such a man; fractions of his writings have found their way into the hands of the curious here; fitful hints that there is, in New England, some spiritual Notability called Emerson, glide through Reviews and Magazines. Whether these hints were true or not true, readers are now to judge for themselves a little better.

Emerson's writings and speakings amount to something:—and yet hitherto, as seems to me, this Emerson is perhaps far less notable for what he has spoken or done, than for the many things he has not spoken and has forborne to do. With uncommon interest I have learned that this, and in such a never-resting locomotive country too, is one of those rare men who have withal the invaluable talent of sitting still! That an educated man of good gifts and opportunities, after looking at the public arena, and even trying, not with ill success, what its tasks and its prizes might amount to. Should retire for long years into rustic obscurity; and, amid the all-pervading jingle of dollars and loud chaffering of ambitions and promotions, should quietly, with cheerful deliberateness, sit down to spend *his* life not in Mammon-worship, or the hunt for reputation, influence, place or any outward advantage whatsoever: this, when we get notice of it, is a thing really worth noting. As Paul Louis Courrier said: *"Ce qui me distingue de tous mes contemporains c'est que je nai pas la prétention d'être roi."* 'All my contemporaries;'—poor contemporaries! It is as if the man said: Yes, ye contemporaries, be it known to you, or let it remain unknown, There is one man who does not need to be a king; king neither of nations, nor of parishes or cliques, nor even of *cent-per-annums*; nor indeed of anything at all save of himself only. 'Realities?' Yes, your dollars are real, your cotton and molasses are real; so are Presidentships, Senatorships, celebrations, reputations, and the wealth of Rothschild: but to me, on the whole, they are not the reality that will suffice. To me, without some other reality, they are mockery, and amount to *zero*, nay to a negative quantity. ETERNITIES surround this god-given Life of mine: what will all the dollars in creation do for me? Dollars, dignities, senate-addresses, review-articles, gilt coaches or cavalcades, with world-wide huzzaings and particoloured beef-eaters never so many: O Heaven, what were all these? Behold, ye shall have all these, and I will endeavour for a thing other than these. Behold, we will entirely agree to differ in this matter; I to be in your eyes nothing, you to be something, to be much, to be all things:—wherefore, adieu in God's name; go ye that way, I go this! Pity that a man, for such cause, should be so distinguished from *all* his contemporaries! It is a misfortune partly of these our peculiar times. Times and nations of any strength have always privately held in them many such men. Times and nations that hold none or few of such, may indeed seem to themselves strong and great, but are only bulky, loud; no heart or solidity in them;—*great*, as the blown bladder is, which by and by will collapse and become small enough!

For myself I have looked over with no common feeling to this brave Emerson, seated by his rustic hearth, on the other side of the Ocean (yet not altogether parted from me either), silently communing with his own soul, and with the God's World it finds itself alive in yonder. Pleasures of Virtue, Progress of the Species, Black Emancipation, New Tarif, Eclecticism, Locofocoism, ghost of Improved-Socinianism: these with many other ghosts and substances are squeaking, jabbering, according to their capabilities, round this man; to one man among the sixteen millions their jabber is all unmusical. The silent voices of the Stars above, and of the green Earth beneath, are profitable to him,—tell him gradually that these others are but ghosts, which will shortly have to vanish; that the Life-Fountain these proceeded out of does not vanish! The words of such a man, what words he finds good to speak, are worth attending to. By degrees a small circle of living souls eager to hear is gathered. The silence of this man has to become speech: may this too, in its due season, prosper for him!—Emerson has gone to lecture, various times, to special audiences, in Boston, and occasionally elsewhere. Three of those Lectures, already printed, are known to some here; as is the little Pamphlet called *Nature*, of somewhat earlier date. It may be said, a great meaning lies in these pieces, which as yet finds no adequate expression for itself. A noteworthy though very unattractive work, moreover, is that new Periodical they call *The Dial*, in which he occasionally writes; which appears indeed generally to be imbued with his way of thinking, and to proceed from the circle that learns of him. This present little Volume of *Essays*, printed in Boston a few months ago, is Emerson's first Book. An unpretending little Book, composed probably, in good part, from mere Lectures which already lay written. It affords us, on several sides, in such manner as it can, a direct glimpse into the man and that spiritual world of his.

Emerson, I understand, was bred to Theology; of which primary bent his latest way of thought still bears traces. In a very enigmatic way, we hear much of the 'universal soul,' of the &c. &c.: flickering like bright bodiless Northern Streamers, notions and half-notions of a metaphysic, theosophic, theologic kind are seldom long wanting in these *Essays*. I do not advise the British Public to trouble itself much with all that; still less, to take offence at it. Whether this Emerson be 'a Pantheist,' or what land of Theist or *Ist* he may be, can perhaps as well remain undecided. If he prove a devout-minded, veritable, original man, this for the present will suffice. *Ists* and *Isms* are rather growing a weariness. Such a man does not readily range himself under *Isms*. A man to whom the 'open secret of the universe' is no longer a closed one, what can his *speech* of it be in these days? All human speech, in the best days, all human thought that can or could articulate itself in reference to such things, what is it but the eager stammering and struggling as of a wondering infant,—in view of the Un-nameable! That this little Book has no 'system,' and points or stretches far beyond all systems, is one of its merits. We will call it the soliloquy of a true soul, alone under the stars, in this day. In England as elsewhere the voice of a true soul, *any* voice of such, may be welcome to some. For in England as elsewhere old dialects and formulas are mostly lying dead: some dim suspicion, or clear knowledge, indicates on all hands that they are as good as dead;—and how can the skilfullest *galvanizing* make them any more live? For they are dead: and their galvanic motions, O Heavens, are not of a pleasant sort!—That one man more, in the most modern dialect of this year 1841, recognises the oldest everlasting truths: here is a thing worth seeing, among the others. One man more who knows, and believes of very certainty, that Man's Soul is still alive, that God's Universe is still godlike, that of all Ages of Miracles ever seen, or dreamt of, by far the most miraculous is this age in this hour; and who with all these devout beliefs has dared, like a valiant man, to bid chimeras, "*Be* chimerical; disappear, and let us have an end of you!"—is not this worth something? In a word, while so many Benthamisms, Socialisms, Fourrierisms, *professing* to have no soul, go staggering and lowing like monstrous mooncalves, the product of a heavy-laden moonstruck age; and, in this same baleful 'twelfth hour of the night,' even galvanic Puseyisms, as we say, are visible, and dancings of the sheeted dead,—shall not any voice of a living man be welcome to us, even because it is alive?

For the rest, what degree of mere literary talent lies in these utterances, is but a secondary question; which every reader may gradually answer for himself. What Emerson's talent is, we will not altogether estimate by this Book. The utterance is abrupt, fitful; the great idea not yet embodied struggles towards an embodiment. Yet everywhere there is the true heart of a man; which is the parent of all talent; which without much talent cannot exist. A breath as of the green country,—all the welcomer that it is *New*-England country, not second-hand but first-hand country,—meets us wholesomely everywhere in these *Essays*: the authentic green Earth is there, with her mountains, rivers, with her mills and farms. Sharp gleams of insight arrest us by their pure intellectuality; here and there, in heroic rusticism, a tone of modest manfulness, of mild invincibility, low-voiced but lion-strong, makes us too thrill with a noble pride, Talent? Such ideas as dwell in this man, how can they ever speak themselves with *enough* of talent? The talent is not the chief question here. The idea, that is the chief question. Of the living acorn you do not ask first, How *large* an acorn art thou? The smallest living acorn is fit to be the parent of oaktrees without end,—could clothe all New England with oaktrees by and by. You ask it, first of all: Art thou a living acorn? Certain, now, that thou art not a dead mushroom, as the most are?—

But, on the whole, our Book is short; the Preface should not grow too long. Closing these questionable parables and intimations, let me in plain English recommend this little Book as the Book of an original veridical man, worthy the acquaintance of those who delight in such; and so: Welcome to it whom it may concern!

Letters to Emerson

Thomas Carlyle

5 Great Cheyne Row, Chelsea, London
12 August, 1834

MY DEAR SIR,

Some two weeks ago I received your kind gift from Fraser. To say that it was welcome would be saying little: is it not as a voice of affectionate remembrance, coming from beyond the Ocean waters, first decisively announcing for me that a whole New Continent *exists*,—that I too have part and lot there! "Not till we can think that here and there one is thinking of us, one is loving us, does this waste Earth become a peopled Garden." Among the figures I can recollect as visiting our Nithsdale hermitage,—all like *Apparitions* now, bringing with them airs from Heaven or else blasts from the other region,—there is perhaps not one of a more undoubtedly supernal character than yourself: so pure and still, with intents so charitable; and then vanishing too so soon into the azure Inane, as an Apparition should! Never has your Address in my Notebook met my eye but with a friendly influence. Judge if I am glad to know that there, in Infinite Space, you still hold by me.

I have read in both your books at leisure times, and now nearly finished the smaller one. He is a faithful thinker, that Swedenborgian Druggist {viz., Sampson Reed} of yours, with really deep ideas, who makes me too pause and think, were it only to consider what manner of man he must be, and what manner of thing, after all, Swedenborgianism must be. "Through the smallest window look well, and you can look out into the Infinite." {Daniel} Webster also I can recognize a sufficient, effectual man, whom one must wish well to, and prophesy well of. The sound of him is nowise poetic-rhythmic; it is clear, one-toned, you might say metallic, yet distinct, significant, not without melody. In his face, above all, I discern that "indignation" which, if it do not make "verses," makes *useful* way in the world. The higher such a man rises, the better pleased I shall be. And so here, looking over the water, let me repeat once more what I believe is already dimly the sentiment of all Englishmen, Cisoceanic and Transoceanic, that we and you are not two countries, and cannot for the life of us be; but only two *parishes* of one country, with such wholesome parish hospitalities, and dirty temporary parish feuds, as we see; both of which brave parishes *Vivant! vivant!* And among the glories of *both* be Yankee-doodle-doo, and the Felling of the Western Forest, proudly remembered; and for the rest, by way of parish constable, let each cheerfully take such George Washington or George Guelph as it can get, and bless Heaven! I am weary of hearing it said, "We love the Americans," "We wish well," &c., &c. What in God's name should we do else?

You thank me for *Teufelsdrockh*; how much more ought I to thank you for your hearty, genuine, though extravagant acknowledgment of it! Blessed is the voice that amid dispiritment, stupidity, and contradiction proclaims to us, *Euge!* Nothing ever was more ungenial than the soil this poor Teufelsdrockhish seed-corn has been thrown on here; none cries, Good speed to it; the sorriest nettle or hemlock seed, one would think, had been more welcome. For indeed our British periodical critics, and especially the public of *Fraser's* Magazine (which I believe I have now done with), exceed all speech; require not even contempt, only oblivion. Poor Teufelsdrockh!—Creature of mischance, miscalculation, and thousand-fold obstruction! Here nevertheless he is, as you see; has struggled across the Stygian marshes, and now, as a stitched pamphlet "for Friends," cannot be *burnt* or lost before his time. I send you one copy for your own behoof; three others you yourself can perhaps find fit readers for: as you spoke in the plural number, I thought there might be three; more would rather surprise me. From the British side of the water I have met simply one intelligent response,—clear, true, though almost enthusiastic as your own. My British Friend too is utterly a stranger, whose very name I know not, who did not print, but only write, and to an unknown third party. Shall I say then, "In the mouth of two witnesses"? In any case, God be thanked, I am done with it; can wash my hands of it, and send it forth; sure that the Devil will get his full share of it, and not a whit more, clutch as he may. But as for you, my Transoceanic brothers, read this earnestly, for it *was* earnestly meant and written, and contains no *voluntary* falsehood of mine. For the rest, if you dislike it, say that I wrote it four years ago, and could not now so write it, and on the whole (as Fritz the Only said) "will do better another time." With regard to style and so forth, what you call your "saucy" objections are not only most intelligible to me, but welcome and instructive. You say well that I take up that attitude because I have no known public, am alone under the heavens, speaking into friendly or unfriendly space; add only, that I will not defend such attitude, that I call it questionable, tentative, and only the best that I, in these mad times, could conveniently hit upon. For you are to know, my view is that now at last we have lived to see all manner of Poetics and Rhetorics and Sermonics, and one may say generally all manner of *Pulpits* for addressing mankind from, as good as broken and abolished: alas, yes! if you have any earnest meaning which demands to be not only listened to, but *believed* and *done*, you cannot (at least I cannot) utter it *there*, but the sound sticks in my throat, as when a solemnity were *felt* to have become a mummery; and so one leaves the pasteboard coulisses, and three unities, and Blair's Lectures, quite behind; and feels only that there is *nothing sacred*, then, but the *Speech of Man* to believing Men! This, come what will, was, is, and forever must be *sacred*; and will one day, doubtless, anew environ itself with fit modes; with solemnities that are *not* mummeries. Meanwhile, however, is it not pitiable? For though Teufelsdrockh exclaims, "Pulpit! canst thou not make a pulpit by simply *inverting the nearest tub*?" yet, alas! he does not sufficiently reflect that it is still only a tub, that the most inspired utterance will come from *it*, inconceivable, misconceivable, to the million; questionable (not of *ascertained* significance) even to the few. Pity us therefore; and with your just shake of the head join a sympathetic, even a hopeful smile. Since I saw you I have been trying, am still trying, other methods, and shall surely get nearer the truth, as I honestly strive for it. Meanwhile, I know no method of much consequence, except that of *believing*, of being *sincere*: from Homer and the Bible down to the poorest Burns's Song, I find no other Art that promises to be perennial.

But now quitting theoretics, let me explain what you long to know, how it is that I date from London. Yes, my friend, it is even so: Craigenputtock now stands solitary in the wilderness, with none but an old woman and foolish grouse-destroyers in it; and we for the last ten weeks, after a fierce universal disruption, are here with our household gods. Censure not; I came to London for the best of all reasons,—to seek bread and work. So it literally stands; and so do I literally stand with the hugest, gloomiest Future before me, which in all sane moments I good-humoredly defy. A strange element this, and I as good as an Alien in it. I care not for Radicalism, for Toryism, for Church, Tithes, or the "Confusion" of useful Knowledge. Much as I can speak and hear, I am alone, alone. My brave Father, now victorious from his toil, was wont to pray in evening worship: "Might we say, We are not alone, for God is with us!" Amen! Amen!

I brought a manuscript with me of another curious sort, entitled *The Diamond Necklace*. Perhaps it will be printed soon as an Article, or even as a separate Booklet,—a *queer* production, which you shall see. Finally, I am busy, constantly studying with my whole might for a Book on the French Revolution. It is part of my creed that the Only Poetry is History, could we tell it right. This truth (if it prove one) I have not yet got to the limitations of; and shall in no way except by *trying* it in practice. The story of the Necklace was the first attempt at an experiment.

My sheet is nearly done; and I have still to complain of you for telling me nothing of yourself except that you are in the country. Believe that I want to know much and all. My wife too remembers you with unmixed friendliness; bids me send you her kindest wishes. Understand too that your old bed stands in a new room here, and the old welcome at the door. Surely we shall see you in London one day. Or who knows but Mahomet may go to the mountain? It occasionally rises like a mad prophetic dream in me, that I might end in the Western Woods!

From Germany I get letters, messages, and even visits; but now no tidings, no influences, of moment. Goethe's Posthumous Works are all published; and Radicalism (poor hungry, yet inevitable Radicalism!) is the order of the day. The like, and even more, from France. Gustave d'Eichthal (did you hear?) has gone over to Greece, and become some kind of Manager under King Otho.

Continue to love me, you and my other friends; and as packets sail so swiftly, let me know it frequently. All good be with you!

Most faithfully,
T. CARLYLE

Coleridge, as you doubtless hear, is gone. How great a Possibility, how small a realized Result! They are delivering Orations about him, and emitting other kinds of froth, *ut mos est*. What hurt can it do?

5 Cheyne Row, Chelsea, London,
13 February, 1837

MY DEAR EMERSON,

You had promise of a letter to be despatched you about New-year's-day; which promise I was myself in a condition to fulfil at the time set, but delayed it, owing to delays of printers and certain "Articles" that were to go with it. Six weeks have not yet entirely brought up these laggard animals: however, I will delay no longer for them. Nay, it seems the Articles, were they never so ready, cannot go with the Letter; but must fare round by Liverpool or Portsmouth, in a separate conveyance. We will leave them to the bounty of Time.

Your little Book and the Copy of *Teufelsdrockh* came safely; soon after I had written. The *Teufelsdrockh* I instantaneously despatched to Hamburg, to a Scottish merchant there, to whom there is an allusion in the Book; who used to be my *Speditor* (one of the politest extant though totally a stranger) in my missions and packages to and from Weimar. The other, former Copy, more specially yours, had already been, as I think I told you, delivered out of durance; and got itself placed in the bookshelf, as *the* Teufelsdrockh. George Ripley tells me you are printing another edition; much good may it do you! There is now also a kind of whisper and whimper rising *here* about printing one. I said to myself once, when Bookseller Fraser shrieked so loud at a certain message you sent him: "Perhaps after all they will print this poor rag of a thing into a Book, after I am dead it may be,—if so seem good to them. *Either* way!" As it is, we leave the poor orphan to its destiny, all the more cheerfully. Ripley says farther he has sent me a critique of it by a better hand than the *North American*: I expect it, but have not got it Yet {an article by N. L. Frothingham in the *Christian Examiner*}. The *North American* seems to say that he too sent me one. It never came to hand, nor any hint of it,—except I think once before through you. It was not at all an unfriendly review; but had an opacity, of matter-of-fact in it that filled one with amazement. Since the Irish Bishop who said there were some things in *Gulliver* on which he for one would keep his belief *suspended*, nothing equal to it, on that side, has come athwart me. However, he *has* made out that Teufelsdrockh is, in all human probability, a fictitious character; which is always something, for an Inquirer into Truth.—Will you, finally, thank Friend Ripley in my name, till I have time to write to him and thank him.

Your little azure-colored Nature gave me true satisfaction. I read it, and then lent it about to all my acquaintance that had a sense for such things; from whom a similar verdict always came back. You say it is the first chapter of something greater. I call it rather the Foundation and Ground-plan on which you may build whatsoever of great and true has been given you to build. It is the true Apocalypse, this when the "Open Secret" becomes revealed to a man. I rejoice much in the glad serenity of soul with which you look out on this wondrous Dwelling-place of yours and mine—with an ear for the *Ewigen Melodien*, which pipe in the winds round us, and utter themselves forth in all sounds and sights and things: not to be written down by gamut-machinery; but which all right writing is a kind of attempt to write down. You will see what the years will bring you. It is not one of your smallest qualities in my mind, that you can wait so quietly and let the years do their best. He that cannot keep himself quiet is of a morbid nature; and the thing he yields us will be like him in that, whatever else it be.

Miss Martineau (for I have seen her since I wrote) tells me you "are the only man in America" who has quietly set himself down on a competency to follow his own path, and do the work his own will prescribes for him. Pity that you were the only one! But be one, nevertheless; be the first, and there will come a second and a third. It is a poor country where all men are *sold* to Mammon, and can make nothing but Railways and Bursts of Parliamentary Eloquence! And yet your New England here too has the upper hand of our Old England, of our Old Europe: we too are sold to Mammon, soul, body, and spirit; but (mark that, I pray you, with double pity) Mammon will not *pay* us,—we, are "Two Million three hundred thousand in Ireland that have not potatoes enough"! I declare, in History I find nothing more tragical. I find also that it will alter; that for me as one it has altered. Me Mammon will *pay* or not as he finds convenient; buy me he will not.—In fine, I say, sit still at Concord, with such spirit as you are of; under the blessed skyey influences, with an open sense, with the great Book of Existence open round you: we shall see whether you too get not something blessed to read us from it.

The Paper is declining fast, and all is yet speculation. Along with these two "Articles" (to be sent by Liverpool; there are two of them, *Diamond Necklace* and *Mirabeau*), you will very probably get some stray Proofsheet—of the unutterable *French Revolution!* It is actually at Press; two Printers working at separate Volumes of it,—though still too slow. In not many weeks, my hands will be washed of it! You, I hope, can have little conception of the feeling with which I wrote the last word of it, one night in early January, when the clock was striking ten, and our frugal Scotch supper coming in! I did not cry; nor I did not pray but could have done both. No such *spell* shall get itself fixed on me for some while to come! A beggarly Distortion; that will please no mortal, not even myself; of which I know not whether the fire were not after all the due place! And yet I ought not to say so: there is a great blessing in a man's doing what he utterly can, in the case he is in. Perhaps great quantities of dross are burnt out of me by this calcination I have had; perhaps I shall be far quieter and healthier of mind and body than I have ever been since boyhood. The world, though no man had ever less empire in it, seems to me a thing lying *under* my feet; a mean imbroglio, which I never more shall fear, or court, or disturb myself with: welcome and welcome to go wholly *its own way*; I wholly clear for going mine. Through the summer months I am, somewhere or other, to rest myself, in the deepest possible sleep. The residue is vague as the wind,—unheeded as the wind. Some way it will turn out that a poor, well-meaning Son of Adam has bread growing for him too, better or worse: *any* way,—or even *no* way, if that be it,—I shall be content. There is a scheme here among Friends for my Lecturing in a thing they call Royal Institution; but it will not do there, I think. The instant two or three are gathered together under any terms, who want to learn something I can teach them,—then we will, most readily, as Burns says, "loose our tinkler jaw"; but not I think till then; were the Institution even Imperial.

America has faded considerably into the background of late: indeed, to say truth, whenever I think of myself in America, it is as in the Backwoods, with a rifle in my hand, God's sky over my head, and this accursed Lazar-house of quacks and blockheads, and sin and misery (now near ahead) lying all behind me forevermore. A thing, you see, which is and can be at bottom but a daydream! To rest through the summer: that is my only fixed wisdom; a resolution taken; only the place where uncertain.—What a pity this poor sheet is done! I had innumerable things to tell you about people whom I have seen, about books,—Miss Harriet Martineau, Mrs. Butler, Southey, Influenza,

Parliament, Literature and the Life of Man,—the whole of which must lie over till next time. Write to me; do not forget me. My Wife, who is sitting by me, in very poor health (this long while), sends "kindest remembrances," "compliments" she expressly does not send. Good be with you always, my dear Friend!

T. CARLYLE

We send our felicitation to the Mother and little Boy, which latter you had better tell us the name of.

Chelsea, London,
8 May, 1841

MY DEAR EMERSON,

Your last letter found me on the southern border of Yorkshire, whither Richard Milnes had persuaded me with him, for the time they call "Easter Holidays" here. I was to shake off the remnants of an ugly *Influenza* which still hung about me; my little portmanteau, unexpectedly driven in again by perverse accidents, had stood packed, its cowardly owner, the worst of all travelers, standing dubious the while, for two weeks or more; Milnes offering to take me as under his cloak, I went with Milnes. The mild, cordial, though something dilettante nature of the man distinguishes him for me among men, as men go. For ten days I rode or sauntered among Yorkshire fields and knolls; the sight of the young Spring, new to me these seven years, was beautiful, or better than beauty. Solitude itself, the great Silence of the Earth, was as balm to this weary, sick heart of mine; not Dragons of Wantley (so they call Lord Wharncliffe, the wooden Tory man), not babbling itinerant Barrister people, fox-hunting Aristocracy, nor Yeomanry Captains cultivating milk-white mustachios, nor the perpetual racket, and "dinner at eight o'clock," could altogether countervail the fact that green Earth was around one and unadulterated sky overhead, and the voice of water sand birds,—not the foolish speech of Cockneys at *all* times!—On the last morning, as Richard and I drove off towards the railway, your Letter came in, just in time; and Richard, who loves you well, hearing from whom it was, asked with such an air to see it that I could not refuse him. We parted at the "station," flying each his several way on the wings of Steam; and have not yet met again. I went over to Leeds, staid two days with its steeple-chimneys and smoke-volcano still in view; then hurried over to native Annandale, to see my aged excellent Mother yet again in this world while she is spared to me. My birth-land is always as the Cave of Trophonius to me; I return from it with a haste to which the speed of Steam is slow,—with no smile on my face; avoiding all speech with men! It is not yet eight-and-forty hours since I got back; your Letter is among the first I answer, even with a line; your new Book—But we will not yet speak of that....

My Friend, I *thank* you for this Volume of yours; not for the copy alone which you send to me, but for writing and printing such a Book. *Euge!* say I, from afar. The voice of one crying in the desert;—it is once more the voice of a *man*. Ah me! I feel as if in the wide world there were still but this one voice that responded intelligently to my own; as if the rest were all hearsays, melodious or unmelodious echoes; as if this alone were true and alive. My blessing on you, good Ralph Waldo! I read the Book all yesterday; my Wife scarcely yet done with telling me her news. It has rebuked me, it has aroused and comforted me. Objections of all kinds I might make, how many objections to superficies and detail, to a dialect of thought and speech as yet imperfect enough, a hundred-fold too narrow for the Infinitude it strives to speak: but what were all that? It is an Infinitude, the real vision and belief of one, seen face to face: a "voice of the heart of Nature" is here once more. This is the one fact for me, which absorbs all others whatsoever. Persist, persist; you have much to say and to do. These voices of yours which I likened to unembodied souls, and censure sometimes for having nobody,—how can they have a body? They are light-rays darting upwards in the East; they will yet make much and much to have a body! You are a new era, my man, in your new huge country: God give you strength, and speaking and silent faculty, to do such a work as seems possible now for you! And if the Devil will be pleased to set all the Popularities *against* you and evermore against you,—perhaps that is of all things the very kindest any *Angel* could do.

Of myself I have nothing good to report. Years of sick idleness and barrenness have grown wearisome to me. I do nothing. I waver and hover, and painfully speculate even now as to health, and where I shall spend the summer out of London! I am a very poor fellow;—but hope to grow better by and by. Then this *alluvies* of foul lazy stuff that has long swum over me may perhaps yield the better harvest. *Esperons!*—Hail to all of you from both of us.

> *Yours ever,*
> T. CARLYLE

> *Chelsea, London,*
> *29 August, 1842*

MY DEAR EMERSON,

This, morning your new Letter, of the 15th August, has arrived; exactly one fortnight old: thanks to the gods and steam-demons! I already, perhaps six weeks ago, answered your former Letter,—acknowledging the manna-gift of the L51, and other things; nor do I think the Letter can have been lost, for I remember putting it into the Post-Office myself. Today I am on the eve of an expedition into Suffolk, and full of petty business: however, I will throw you one word, were it only to lighten my own heart a little. You are a kind friend to me, and a precious;—and when I mourn over the impotence of Human Speech, and how each of us, speak or write as he will, has to stand *dumb*, cased up in his own unutterabilities, before his unutterable Brother, I feel always as if Emerson were the man I could soonest *try* to speak with,—were I within reach of him! Well; we must be content. A pen is a pen, and worth something; though it expresses about as much of a *man's* meaning perhaps as the stamping of a hoof will express of a horse's meaning; a very poor expression indeed!

Your bibliopolic advice about Cromwell or my next Book shall be carefully attended, if I live ever to write another Book! But I have again got down into primeval Night; and live alone and mute with the *Manes*, as you say; uncertain whether I shall ever more see day. I am partly ashamed of myself; but cannot help it. One of my grand difficulties I suspect to be that I cannot write *two Books at once*; cannot be in the seventeenth century and in the nineteenth at one and the same moment; a feat which excels even that of the Irishman's bird: "Nobody but a bird can be in two places at once!" For my heart is sick and sore in behalf of my own poor generation; nay, I feel withal as if the one hope of help for it consisted in the possibility of new Cromwells and new Puritans: thus do the two centuries stand related to me, the seventeenth *worthless* except precisely in so far as it can be made the nineteenth; and yet let anybody try that enterprise! Heaven help me.—I believe at least that I ought *to hold my tongue*; more especially at present.

Thanks for asking me to write you a word in the *Dial*. Had such a purpose struck me long ago, there have been many things passing through my head,—march-marching as they ever do, in long drawn, scandalous Falstaff-regiments (a man ashamed to be seen passing through Coventry with such a set!)—some one of which, snatched out of the ragged rank, and dressed and drilled a little, might perhaps fitly have been saved from Chaos, and sent to the *Dial*. In future we shall be on the outlook. I love your *Dial*, and yet it is with a kind of shudder. You seem to me in danger of dividing yourselves from the Fact of this present Universe, in which alone, ugly as it is, can I find any anchorage, and soaring away after Ideas, Beliefs, Revelations, and such like,—into perilous altitudes, as I think; beyond the curve of perpetual frost, for one thing! I know not how to utter what impression you give me; take the above as some stamping of the fore-hoof. Surely I could wish you *returned* into your own poor nineteenth century, its follies and maladies, its blind or half-blind, but gigantic toilings, its laughter and its tears, and trying to evolve in some measure the hidden Godlike that lies in it;—that seems to me the kind of feat for literary men. Alas, it is so easy to screw one's self up into high and ever higher altitudes of Transcendentalism, and see nothing under one but the everlasting snows of Himmalayah, the Earth shrinking to a Planet, and the indigo firmament sowing itself with daylight stars; easy for *you*, for me: but whither does it lead? I dread always, To inanity and mere injuring of the lungs!—"Stamp, Stamp, Stamp!"—Well, I do believe, for one thing, a man has no right to say to his own generation, turning quite away from it, "Be damned!" It is the whole Past and the whole Future, this same cotton-spinning, dollar-hunting, canting and shrieking, very wretched generation of ours. Come back into it, I tell you;—and so for the present will "stamp" no more....

Adieu, my friend; I must not add a word more. My Wife is out on a visit; it is to bring her back that I am now setting forth for Suffolk. I hope to see Ely too, and St. Ives, and Huntingdon, and various *Cromwelliana*. My blessings on the Concord Household now and always. Commend me expressly to your Wife and your Mother. Farewell, dear friend.

T. CARLYLE

Chelsea,
18 May, 1847

DEAR EMERSON,

.... My time is nearly up today; but I write a word to acknowledge your last Letter (30 April), and various other things. For example, you must tell Mr. Thoreau (is that the exact name? for I have lent away the printed pages) that his Philadelphia Magazine with the *Lecture* in two pieces was faithfully delivered here, about a fortnight ago; and carefully read, as beseemed, with due entertainment and recognition {"On Carlyle" in *Graham's Magazine*, March and April 1847}. A vigorous Mr. Thoreau,—who has formed himself a good deal upon one Emerson, but does not want abundant fire and stamina of his own;—recognizes us, and various other things, in a most admiring great-hearted manner; for which, as for *part* of the confused voice from the jury bog (not yet summed into a verdict, nor likely to be summed till Doomsday, nor needful to sum), the poor prisoner at the bar may justly express himself thankful! In plain prose, I like Mr. Thoreau very well; and hope yet to hear good and better news of him:—only let him not "turn to foolishness"; which seems to me to be terribly easy, at present, both in New England and Old! May the Lord deliver us all from *Cant*; may the Lord, whatever else he do or forbear, teach us to look Facts honestly in the face, and to beware (with a kind of shudder) of smearing *them* over with our despicable and damnable palaver, into irrecognizability, and so *falsifying* the Lord's own Gospels to his unhappy blockheads of children, all staggering down to Gehenna and the everlasting Swine's-trough for *want* of Gospels.—O Heaven, it is the most accursed sin of man; and done everywhere, at present, on the streets and high places, at noonday! Very seriously I say, and pray as my chief orison, May the Lord deliver us from it.—

About a week ago there came your neighbor {Ebenezer R.} Hoar; a solid, sensible, effectual-looking man, of whom I hope to see much more. So soon as possible I got him under way for Oxford, where I suppose he was, last week;—*both* Universities was too much for the limits of his time; so he preferred Oxford;—and now, this very day, I think, he was to set out for the Continent; not to return till the beginning of July, when he promises to call here again. There was something really pleasant to me in this Mr. Hoar: and I had innumerable things to ask him about Concord, concerning which topic we had hardly got a word said when our first interview had to end. I sincerely hope he will not fail to keep his time in returning.

You do very well, my Friend, to plant orchards; and fair fruit shall they grow (if it please Heaven) for your grandchildren to pluck;—a beautiful occupation for the son of man, in all patriarchal and paternal times (which latter are patriarchal too)! But you are to understand withal that your coming hither to lecture is taken as a settled point by all your friends here; and for my share I do not reckon upon the smallest doubt about the *essential* fact of it, simply on some calculation and adjustment about the circumstantials. Of {Alexander} Ireland, who I surmise is busy in the problem even now, you will hear by and by, probably in more definite terms: I did not see him again after my first notice of him to you; but there is no doubt concerning his determinations (for all manner of reasons) to get you to Lancashire, to England;—and in fact it is an adventure which I think you ought to contemplate as *fixed*,—say for this year and the beginning of next? Ireland will help you to fix the dates; and there is nothing else, I think, which should need fixing.—Unquestionably you would get an immense quantity of food for ideas, though perhaps not at all in the way you anticipate, in looking about among us: nay, if you even thought us *stupid*, there is something in the godlike indifference with which London will accept and sanction even that verdict,—something highly instructive at least! And in short, for the truth must be told, London is properly your Mother City too,—verily you have about as much to do with it, in spite of Polk and Q. Victory, as I had! And you ought to come and look at it, beyond doubt; and say to this land, "Old Mother, how are you getting on at all?" To which the Mother will answer, "Thankee, young son, and you?"—in a way useful to both parties! That is truth.

Adieu, dear Emerson; good be with you always. Hoar gave me your *American Poems*: thanks. *Vale et me ama.*

T. CARLYLE

Henry David Thoreau (1817–1862)

Thoreau's family resided in Concord, Massachusetts, not far from Emerson's home, and the two contemporaries—fourteen years apart—became close, lifelong friends and intellectual companions. Emerson recognized in Thoreau many appealing and representative qualities, and admired his writing and his mode of life. When Thoreau died, Emerson eulogized him: "He was a speaker and actor of the truth, born such, and was ever running into dramatic situations from this cause." And Emerson summarized the results of those efforts and expenditures: "No truer American existed than Thoreau." To get some sense of Thoreau's relationship with Emerson, and Thoreau's opinion of him, a letter from 1843 is included below; the letters from Horace Greeley in this volume add another valence of suggestion about Thoreau's friendship with Emerson—for instance, Thoreau's unwillingness to exploit Emerson for personal gain, including literary celebrity. In 1845, when Thoreau wanted to make an experiment in the woods to examine the kind of life he was living, and wanted to live, he asked Emerson for permission to settle on his land at Walden Pond. In mid-1846, Thoreau was summoned to pay a poll tax, which he refused in protest of the Mexican American War and slavery, and served a night in jail. Thoreau's response to the incident, inspired in part by Percy Shelley's The Mask of Anarchy *(1819), led to the speech "The Rights and Duties of the Individual in Relation to Government," presented in Concord (1848), later revised to the now-canonical "Civil Disobedience." Two years, two months, and two days after Thoreau began his experiment at the pond, Emerson's call for a favor—that Thoreau stay with his family while he traveled to England—prompted Thoreau's return to Concord to live with the Emersons. And now, even at our distance from their lives, they remain neighbors: at Sleepy Hollow Cemetery in Concord, the Thoreau family plot is not far from the Emersons'.*

Letter to Emerson

Henry David Thoreau

February 12, 1843.

Dear Friend,—

As the packet still tarries, I will send you some thoughts, which I have lately relearned, as the latest public and private news.

How mean are our relations to one another! Let us pause till they are nobler. A little silence, a little rest, is good. It would be sufficient employment only to cultivate true ones.

The richest gifts we can bestow are the least marketable. We hate the kindness which we understand. A noble person confers no such gift as his whole confidence: none so exalts the giver and the receiver; it produces the truest gratitude. Perhaps it is only essential to friendship that some vital trust should have been reposed by the one in the other. I feel addressed and probed even to the remote parts of my being when one nobly shows, even in trivial things, an implicit faith in me. When such divine commodities are so near and cheap, how strange that it should have to be each day's discovery! A threat or a curse may be forgotten, but this mild trust translates me. I am no more of this earth; it acts dynamically; it changes my very substance. I cannot do what before I did. I cannot be what before I was. Other chains may be broken, but in the darkest night, in the remotest place, I trail this thread. Then things cannot *happen*. What if God were to confide in us for a moment! Should we not then be gods?

How subtle a thing is this confidence! Nothing sensible passes between; never any consequences are to be apprehended should it be misplaced. Yet something has transpired. A new behavior springs; the ship carries new ballast in her hold. A sufficiently great and generous trust could never be abused. It should be cause to lay down one's life,—which would not be to lose it. Can there be any mistake up there? Don't the gods know where to invest their wealth? Such confidence, too, would be reciprocal. When one confides greatly in you, he will feel the roots of an equal trust fastening themselves in him. When such trust has been received or reposed, we dare not speak, hardly to see each other; our voices sound harsh and untrustworthy. We are as instruments which the Powers have dealt with. Through what straits would we not carry this little burden of a magnanimous trust! Yet no harm could possibly come, but simply faithlessness. Not a feather, not a straw, is entrusted; that packet is empty. It is only *committed* to us, and, as it were, all things are committed to us.

The kindness I have longest remembered has been of this sort,—the sort unsaid; so far behind the speaker's lips that almost it already lay in my heart. It did not have far to go to be communicated. The gods cannot misunderstand, man cannot explain. We communicate like the burrows of foxes, in silence and darkness, under ground. We are undermined by faith and love. How much more full is Nature where we think the empty space is than where we place the solids!—full of fluid influences. Should we ever communicate but by these? The spirit abhors a vacuum more than Nature. There is a tide which pierces the pores of the air. These aerial rivers, let us not pollute their currents. What meadows do they course through? How many fine mails there are which traverse their routes! He is privileged who gets his letter franked by them.

I believe these things.

Henry D. Thoreau.

Nathaniel Hawthorne (1804–1864)

A native of Salem, Massachusetts, Hawthorne was educated at Bowdoin College, and thereafter worked at a number of jobs, including the editorship of the American Magazine of Useful and Entertaining Knowledge *(1836), and by the end of the decade he earned an appointment at the Boston Custom House (1839). All the while, however, he was writing. In a letter to his friend and Bowdoin classmate, Henry Wadsworth Longfellow, he wrote of this time "I have not lived, but only dreamed of living" (June 4, 1837). In the same year he published* Twice-Told Tales, *and in 1841 joined George Ripley's Brook Farm—mainly as a way to save money to marry Sophia Peabody, which he did in 1842. The newlyweds moved into The Old Manse in Concord, an ancestral Emerson home, where Emerson himself once lived. Hawthorne's writings from his residency were collected under the title* Mosses from an Old Manse *(1846). Soon after the publication and success of* The Scarlet Letter *(1850), Hawthorne, with wife and three children, moved to Lenox, Massachusetts where he became friends with Oliver Wendell Holmes, Sr. and Herman Melville (who would soon after dedicate his in-progress work,* Moby-Dick, *to Hawthorne). While he was in the Berkshires his other celebrated books appeared, including* The House of the Seven Gables *(1851) and* The Blithedale Romance *(1852). Hawthorne's college friend Franklin Peirce, now newly elected President of the United States, appointed him consul in Liverpool. In the letter included below, Hawthorne writes from England about Emerson's* English Traits, *published the month before. Hawthorne returned to America in 1860 and died two years later. "We buried Hawthorne in Sleepy Hollow, in a pomp of sunshine & verdure, & gentle winds," Emerson wrote in his journal. Yet while serving as one of his pallbearers, he remarked "I thought there was a tragic element in the event, that might be more fully rendered—in the painful solitude of the man—which, I suppose, could no longer be endured, & he died of it" (May 24, 1864). Estimating his response to Hawthorne's death and his legacy, Emerson writes: "I have found in his death a surprise & disappointment. I thought him a greater man than any of his works betray, that there was still a great deal of work in him, & that he might one day show a purer power." Regretting that they never became intimate friends, Emerson writes: "It would have been a happiness, doubtless to both of us, to have come into habits of unreserved intercourse. It was easy to talk with him,—there were no barriers,—only, he said so little, that I talked too much. [. . .] Now it appears that I waited too long."*

Letter to Emerson

Nathaniel Hawthorne

Liverpool, Septr 10th 1856.

My dear Emerson,

I thank you for your book, which reached me a week or two ago, just as I was about starting on a journey to London; so I made it my travelling companion, and compared it all the way with the England actually before my eyes.

Undoubtedly, these are the truest pages that have yet been written, about this country. Some of them seem to me absolutely true; as regards others, the truth has not been made apparent to me by my own observations. If I had time—and a higher opinion of my own fitness—I should be glad to write notes on the book.

I am afraid it will please the English only too well; for you give them credit for the possession, in very large measure, of all the qualities that they value, or pride themselves upon; and they never will comprehend that what you deny is far greater and higher than what you concede. In fact, you deny them only what they would be ashamed of, if they possessed it.

But perhaps I am no fair judge of Englishmen, just now. Individually, they suit me well; it is very comfortable to live among them. But yet I am not unconscious of a certain malevolence and hostility in my own breast, such as a man must necessarily feel, who lives in England without melting entirely into the mass of Englishmen. I must confess to have sympathized with Russia more than England, in the late war; and nothing has given me quite so much pleasure, since I left home, as the stoop which I saw in every Englishman's shoulders, after the settlement of the Enlistment question.

Sincerely Yours,
Nathl Hawthorne.

Edgar Allan Poe (1809–1849)

Harold Bloom once placed Poe—author of Tamerlane *(1827) and* The Raven
*(1845)—for an audience of readers by saying: "Poe, a true Southerner, abominated
Emerson, plainly perceiving that Emerson (like Whitman, like Lincoln) was not a
Christian, not a royalist, not a classicist. [. . .] If you dislike Emerson, you probably
will like Poe. [. . .] Emerson, for better and for worse, was and is the mind of America, but Poe was and is our hysteria, our uncanny unanimity in our repressions."[1] The
passage by Poe presented here bears out Bloom's assessment, and leaves no ambiguity
regarding Poe's opinion of his literary contemporary; it appeared in "An Appendix of
Autographs,"* Graham's Magazine, *January 1842.*

R. W. Emerson

Edgar Allan Poe

MR. RALPH WALDO EMERSON belongs to a class of gentlemen with whom we have no
patience whatever—the mystics for mysticism's sake. Quintilian mentions a pedant who
taught obscurity, and who once said to a pupil "this is excellent, for I do not understand
it myself." How the good man would have chuckled over Mr. E! His present *rôle* seems
to be out-Carlyling Carlyle. *Lycophron Tenebrosus* is a fool to him. The best answer to
his twaddle is *cui bono?*—a very little Latin phrase very generally mistranslated and
misunderstood—*cui bono?*—to whom is it a benefit? If not to Mr. Emerson individually,
then surely to no man living.

His love of the obscure does not prevent him, nevertheless, from the composition
of occasional poems in which beauty is apparent *by flashes*. Several of his effusions
appeared in the "Western Messenger"—more in the "Dial," of which he is the soul—or
the sun—or the shadow. We remember the "Sphynx," the "Problem," the "Snow Storm,"
and some fine old-fashioned verses entitled "Oh fair and stately maid whose eye."

His MS. is bad, sprawling, illegible and irregular—although sufficiently bold. This
latter trait may be, and no doubt is, only a portion of his general affectation.

Note

1   *Edgar Allan Poe*, Bloom's Modern Critical Views, ed. Harold Bloom, updated edition
(New York: Chelsea House, 2006), 1.

Charles Dickens (1812–1870)

After Emerson read Dickens' American Notes for General Circulation *in November 1842—the month it arrived in America—he said of the work that it is marked by "the broadest caricature," and that "monstrous exaggeration is an easy secret of romance."[1] On this occasion, at least, Emerson contrasts "romance" with "truth," noting that the work "answers its end very well, which plainly was to make a readable book, nothing more. Truth is not his object for a single instant, but merely to make good points in a lively sequence, and he proceeds very well. As an account of America it is not to be considered for a moment: it is too short, too narrow, too superficial, and too ignorant, too slight, and too fabulous, and the man totally unequal to the work." Dickens, nevertheless, appears to have been pleased with his experience in New England as he writes in the pages of the work that "[I]f I were a Bostonian, I think I would be a Transcendentalist." The paragraph included below is from the "Boston" chapter in* American Notes. *Dickens didn't meet Emerson until years later at a dinner given by John Forster in London on April 25, 1848. When Dickens presented the inaugural reading for his second American tour in Boston on December 2, 1867, Emerson was in the audience.*

Boston

Charles Dickens

The fruits of the earth have their growth in corruption. Out of the rottenness of these things, there has sprung up in Boston a sect of philosophers known as Transcendentalists. On inquiring what this appellation might be supposed to signify, I was given to understand that whatever was unintelligible would be certainly transcendental. Not deriving much comfort from this elucidation, I pursued the inquiry still further, and found that the Transcendentalists are followers of my friend Mr. Carlyle, or I should rather say, of a follower of his, Mr. Ralph Waldo Emerson. This gentleman has written a volume of Essays, in which, among much that is dreamy and fanciful (if he will pardon me for saying so) there is much more that is true and manly, honest and bold. Transcendentalism has its occasional vagaries (what school has not?) but it has good healthful qualities in spite of them; not least among the number a hearty disgust of Cant, and an aptitude to detect her in all the million varieties of her everlasting wardrobe. And therefore if I were a Bostonian, I think I would be a Transcendentalist.

Note

1   Ralph Waldo Emerson, *The Journals and Miscellaneous Notebooks of Ralph Waldo Emerson*, ed. William H. Gilman, et al. (Cambridge: Belknap Press of Harvard University Press, 1982), Vol. XVI, 222.

Elizabeth Palmer Peabody (1804–1894)

A neighbor, friend, and intellectual collaborator of Emerson's (and his former pupil in Greek), Peabody closely allied herself to his projects. She wrote the following review, published in the United States Magazine and Democratic Review *(February 1838), in a mode of sympathetic or advocatory exegesis, as if to make Emerson's first book* Nature *available to a wider audience who she believed needed to comprehend it. "But whoever reads Reviews," she writes below, "whoever can understand our diluted English, can understand still better this concentrated and severely correct expression of what every child of civilization experiences every day." Peabody, the sister of Sophia (wife of Nathanial Hawthorne), was an assistant teacher at Amos Bronson Alcott's Temple School in Boston, and later contributed crucially to the development of early childhood education in America and labored for American Indian rights. For a dozen years, she was the proprietor of West Street Bookstore in Boston, where Margaret Fuller hosted "Conversations" with leading female intellectuals and women's rights advocates such as Sophia Dana Ripley, Maria White Lowell, and Caroline Sturgis.*

Nature—A Prose Poem

Elizabeth Palmer Peabody

Minds of the highest order of genius draw their thoughts most immediately from the Supreme Mind, which is the fountain of all finite natures. And hence they clothe the truths they see and feel, in those forms of nature which are generally intelligible to all ages of the world. With this poetic instinct, they have a natural tendency to withdraw from the *conventions* of their own day; and strive to forget, as much as possible, the arbitrary associations created by temporary institutions and local peculiarities. Since the higher laws of suggestion operate in proportion as the lower laws are made subordinate, suggestions of thought by mere proximity of time and place must be subtracted from the habits of the mind that would cultivate the principle of analogy; and this principle of suggestion, in its turn, must be made to give place to the higher law of cause and effect; and at times even this must be set aside, and Reason, from the top of the being, look into the higher nature of original truth, by Intuition,—no unreal function of our nature:

> Nor less I deem that there are powers,
>   Which, of themselves, our minds impress;
> That we can feed these minds of ours,
>   In a wise passiveness.

But if it is precisely because the most creative minds take the symbols of their thoughts and feelings from the venerable imagery of external nature, or from that condition of society which is most transparent in its simplicity, that, when they utter themselves, they speak to all ages, it is also no less true, that this is the reason why the greatest men, those of the highest order of intellect, often do not appear very great to their contemporaries. Their most precious sayings are naked, if not invisible, to the eyes of the conventional, precisely because they are free of the thousand circumstances and fashions which interest the acting and unthinking many. The greatest minds take no cognizance of the local interests, the party spirit, and the pet subjects of the literary coteries of particular times and places. Their phraseology is pure from the ornament which is the passing fashion of the day. As, however, they do not think and speak for their own order only, as they desire to address and receive a response from the great majority of minds—even from those that doubt their own power of going into the holy of holies of thought for themselves—there is needed the office of an intermediate class of minds, which are the natural critics of the human race. For criticism, in its worthiest meaning, is not, as is too often supposed, fault-finding, but interpretation of the oracles of genius. Critics are the priests of literature. How often, like other priests, they abuse their place and privilege, is but too obvious. They receive into their ranks the self-interested, the partisan, the lover of power, besides the stupid and frivolous; and thus the periodical literature of the day is in the rear, rather than in advance of the public mind.

After this preamble, which we trust has suitably impressed the minds of our readers with the dignity of the critical office, we would call those together who have feared that the spirit of poetry was dead, to rejoice that such a *poem* as "Nature" is written. It grows upon us as we reperuse it. It proves to us, that the only true and perfect mind is the poetic. Other minds are not to be despised, indeed; they are germs of humanity; but the poet alone is the man—meaning by the poet, not the versifier, nor the painter of outward nature merely, but the total soul, grasping truth, and expressing it melodiously, equally to the eye and heart.

The want of apprehension with which this *poem* has been received, speaks ill for the taste of our literary priesthood. Its title seems to have suggested to many persons the notion of some elementary treatise on physics, as physics; and when it has been found that it treats of the *metaphysics* of nature—in other words, of the highest designs of God, in forming nature and man in relations with each other—it seems to have been laid down with a kind of disgust, as if it were a cheat; and some reviewers have spoken of it with a stupidity that is disgraceful alike to their sense, taste, and feeling.

It has, however, found its readers and lovers, and those not a few; the highest intellectual culture and the simplest instinctive innocence have alike received it, and felt it to be a divine Thought, borne on a stream of 'English undefiled,' such as we had almost despaired could flow in this our world of grist and saw mills, whose utilitarian din has all but drowned the melodies of nature. The time will come, when it will be more universally seen to be "a gem of purest ray serene," and be dived after, into the dark unfathomed caves of that ocean of frivolity, which the literary productions of the present age spread out to the eyes of despair.

We have said that "Nature" is a poem; but it is written in prose. The author, though "wanting the accomplishment of verse," is a devoted child of the great Mother; and comes forward bravely in the midst of the dust of business and the din of machinery; and naming her venerable name, believes that there is a reverence for it left, in the bottom of every heart, of power to check the innumerable wheels for a short Sabbath, that all may listen to her praises.

In his introduction, he expresses his purpose. He tells us, that we concede too much to the sceptic, when we allow every thing venerable in religion to belong to history. He tells us that were there no past, yet nature would tell us great truths; and, rightly read, would prove the prophecies of revelation to be "a very present God;" and also, that the past itself, involving its prophets, divine lawgivers, and the human life of Him of Nazareth, is comparatively a dead letter to us, if we do not freshen these traditions in our souls, by opening our ears to the living nature which for-evermore prepares for, and re-echoes, their sublime teachings.

"The foregoing generations," he says, "beheld God face to face: we, through their eyes. Why should not *we* also enjoy an original relation to the Universe?"

Why should we not indeed? for *we* not only have the Universe, which the foregoing generations had, but *themselves* also. Why are we less wise than they? Why has our wisdom less of the certainty of intuition than theirs? Is it because we have more channels of truth? It may be so. The garden of Eden, before the fall of man, and when God walked in its midst, was found to be a less effective school of virtue, than the workshop of a carpenter, in a miserable town of Judea, of which 'an Israelite without guile' could ask, "*Can* any good come out of Nazareth?" And is not this, by the way, a grave warning to the happily circumstanced of all time to tremble—lest they grow morally passive, just in proportion to their means of an effective activity? With the religion of history must always be combined the religion of experience, in order to a true apprehension of God. The poet of "Nature" is a preacher of the latter. Let us "hear him gladly," for such are rare.

The first Canto of this song respects the outward form of Nature. He sketches it in bold strokes. The stars of Heaven above—the landscape below—the breathing atmosphere around—and the living forms and sounds—are brought up to us, by the loving spirit of the singer; who recognizes in this drapery of the world without, the same Disposer that arranged the elements of his own conscious soul. Thus, in his first recognition of Nature's superficies, he brings us to Theism. There is a God. Our Father is the author of Nature. The brotherly "nod" of companionship assures us of it.

But wherefore is Nature? The next Canto of our Poem answers this question in the most obvious relation. It is an answer that "all men apprehend." Nature's superficies is for the well-being of man's body, and the advantage of his material interests. This part of the book requires no interpretation from the critic. Men are active enough concerning commodity, to understand whatever is addressed to them on this head. At least there is no exception but in the case of the savage of the tropics, if is mind has not explored his wants even to the extent of his body. He does not comprehend the necessities of the narrowest civilization. But whoever reads Reviews, whoever can understand our diluted English, can understand still better this concentrated and severely correct expression of what every child of civilization experiences every day. There is but one sentence here that the veriest materialist can mistake. He may not measure all that the poet means when he says, man is thus conveniently waited upon in order "that he may work." He may possibly think that "work" relates to the physical operations of manufacture or agriculture. But what is really meant is no less than this; "man is fed that he may work" with his mind; add to the treasures of thought; elaborate the substantial life of the spiritual world. This is a beautiful doctrine, and worthy to be sung to the harp, with a song of thanksgiving. Undoubtedly Nature, by working for man with all her elements, is adequate to supply him with so much "commodity" that the time may be anticipated when all men will have leisure to be artists, poets, philosophers,—in short, to live through life in the exercise of their proper humanity. God speed to the machinery and application of science to the arts which is to bring this about!

The third Song is of Nature's Beauty, and we only wonder why it was not sung first; for surely the singer found out that Nature was beautiful, before he discovered that it was convenient. Some children, we know, have asked what was the use of flowers, and, like little monkeys, endeavoring to imitate the grown-up, the bearings of whose movements they could not appreciate, have planted their gardens with potatoes and beans, instead of sweet-briar and cupid's-delights. But the poet never made this mistake. In the fullness of his first love for his "beautiful mother," and his "gentle nest," he did not even find out those wants, which the commodity of Nature supplies....

The second passage on Beauty, is one of those which recalls the critic to the office of interpreter, for it is one which the world has called mystical, To say the same thing in worse English, the oracle here tells us, that if we look on Nature with pleasurable emotions only, and without, at the same time, exerting our moral powers, the mind grows effeminate, and thus becomes incapable of perceiving the highest beauty of whose original type the external forms are but the varied reflections or shadows. When man's moral power is in action, the mind spontaneously traces relations between itself and surrounding things, and there forms with Nature one whole, combining the moral delight which human excellence inspires, with that suggested by Nature's forms.

The next passage rises a step higher in the praise of Beauty. It recognizes the cherishing influence of Nature's forms upon the faculties. Nature not only calls out taste, not only glorifies virtue, and is in its turn by virtue glorified, but it awakens the creative impulse—God's image in man. Hence Art, or "Nature in miniature." And the works of Art lead back to Nature again. Thus Beauty circulates, and becomes an aspect of Eternity.

The next chapter, showing that Language is founded on material Nature, is quite didactic. But even here one critic[1] quotes a sentence, of which he says, he cannot understand "what it means."

This relation between the mind and matter is not fancied by some poet, but stands in the will of God, and so is free to be known by all men. It appears to men, or it does not appear.

Where lies the obscurity? We have heard some men say that they did not believe that the forms of Nature bore any relation to the being of God, which his children could appreciate; but even these men could not understand the simple proposition of the opposite theory. Men may think that all nations, whose language has yet been discovered, have called youth *the morning of life*, by accident; but it is inconceivable that they should not understand the simple words in which other men say that there is *no accident in the world*, but all things relate to the spirit of God to which man also has relation and access. Perhaps, however, it is the second sentence which is unintelligible, "it appears to men, or it does not appear." In other words, *to people with open eyes there are colors; to people with shut eyes, at least, to those born blind, there are no colors.*

But having come to this fact, viz: that "the relation between mind and matter stands in the will of God," our poet grows silent with wonder and worship. The nature of this relation he acknowledges to be the yet unsolved problem. He names some of the principal men who have attempted a solution. Many readers of his book would have been glad, had he paused to tell us, in his brief comprehensive way, what was the solution of Pythagoras, and Plato, Bacon, Leibnitz, and Swedenborg, with remarks of his own upon each.

And to his own solution, some say he is unintelligible, talks darkly, They do not seem to have observed that he says nothing in the way of solution, so that nothing can be darkly said. This is what has disappointed the best lovers of his book. But if he does not give his own solution of the enigma, he does what is next best, he tells us the condition of solving it ourselves.

> A life in harmony with nature, the love of truth and virtue, will purge the eyes to understand her text. By degrees we may come to know the primitive sense of the permanent objects of Nature, so that the world shall be to us an open book, and every form significant of the hidden life and final cause.

The chapter on Discipline is still more didactic than the one on Language. The first portion treats of the formation of the Understanding by the ministry of Nature to the senses, and faculty of deduction. The second section is in a higher strain. It treats of the development of the Reason and Conscience, by means of that relation between matter and mind, which "appears" so clearly to some men, and to all in a degree...,

In the last part of this chapter on Discipline, the author makes a bold sally at the cause of the analogy between the external world and the moral nature. He implies that causes (the spiritual seeds of external things) are identical with the principles that constitute our being; and that *virtues* (the creations of our own heaven-aided wills) correspond to God's creations in matter; the former being the natural growth in the moral world, the latter the natural growth in the material world; or to vary the expression once more, Goodness being the projection inward—Beauty the projection outward—of the same all-pervading Spirit.

Our author here leaves the didactic, and "the solemn harp's harmonious sound" comes full upon the ear and the heart from the next Canto of his poem—Idealism. No part of the book has been so mistaken as this. Some readers affect to doubt his Practical

Reason, because he acknowledges, that we have no evidence of there being essential outlying beings, to that which we certainly see, by consciousness, by looking inward, *except 'a constant faith' which God gives us of this truth*. But why should 'the noble doubt,' which marks the limit of the understanding, be so alarming, when it is found to be but an introduction of the mind to the *superior certainty* residing in that 'constant faith?' Do we not advance in truth, when we learn to change the childish feeling by which we ascribe reality to the 'shows of things,' for a feeling involving a sense of GOD, as the only real—immutable—the All in All?

The theory of Idealism has doubtless been carried to absurdity by individuals who but half understood it; and has still more often been represented in a way which was not only useless but injurious to minds entirely dependent on what others say: for, to borrow two good compounds from Coleridge, the *half-Ideas* of many would-be Idealist writers, have passed, perforce, into the *no-Ideas* of many would-be Idealist readers. But Mr. Emerson has sufficiently guarded his Idealism by rigorous and careful expression, to leave little excuse for cavilling at his words or thoughts, except, indeed, by professed materialists and atheists, to whom he gives no ground.

> "The frivolous make themselves merry," he says, "with the Ideal theory, as if its consequences were burlesque; as if it affected the stability of nature. It surely does not. God never jests with us, and will not compromise the end of Nature, by permitting any inconsequence in its procession. Any distrust of the permanence of laws, would paralyse the faculties of man. Their permanence is sacredly respected, and his faith therein is perfect. The wheels and springs of man are all set to the hypothesis of the permanence of Nature. We are not built like a ship to be tossed, but like a house to stand."

He proceeds to give the progressive appearances of Nature, as the mind advances, through the ministry of the senses, to "the best and the happiest moments of life, those delicious awakenings of the higher powers,—the withdrawing of Nature before its God." The means by which Nature herself, Poetic genius, Philosophy, both natural and intellectual—and, above all, Religion and Ethics, work, to idealize our thought and being, are then minutely pointed out. No careful thinker can dispute a step of the process.

We are tempted to quote all these pages and defy the materialist to answer them. But for those sober Christians, who ignorantly and inconsistently fear Idealism, one paragraph will answer the purpose:

> "The first and last lesson in religion is, *the things that are seen are temporal, the things that are unseen are eternal*. It puts an affront upon Nature. It does that for the unschooled, which philosophy does for Berkely and Viasa. The uniform language that may be heard in the churches of the most ignorant sects is, *contemn the unsubstantial shows of the world; they are vanities, dreams, shadows, unrealities; seek the realities of religion*. The devotee flouts Nature. * * * * * * They might all better say of matter, what Michael Angelo said of external beauty, it is the frail and weary weed in which God dresses the soul, which he has called into time."

Many philosophers have stopped at Idealism. But, as Mr. Emerson says, this hypothesis, if it only deny, or question the existence of matter "does not satisfy the demands of the Spirit. It leaves God out of me. It leaves me in the splendid labyrinth of my perceptions, to wander without end. Then the heart resists it, because it baulks the affections, in denying substantive being to men and women."

Mr. Emerson then proceeds to his chapter on Spirit, by which he means to suggest to us the substantial essence of which Idealism is the intellectual form. But this chapter is not full enough, for the purposes of instruction. One passage is indeed of great significance:

> But when, following the invisible steps of thought, we come to inquire, Whence
> is matter? and whereto?—many truths arise out of the depths of consciousness.
> We learn that the highest is present to the soul of man; that the great universal
> essence which is not wisdom, or love, or beauty, or power, but all in one and each
> entirely, is that for which all things exist, and that by which what they are; *that
> Spirit creates*; that behind Nature, throughout Nature, *Spirit is present*, that Spirit
> is one and not compound; that Spirit does not act upon us from without, that
> is, in space or time, but spiritually or through ourselves. Therefore, that Spirit,
> that is the Supreme Being, does not build up Nature around us, but puts it forth
> through us, as the life of the tree puts forth new branches and leaves through the
> pores of the old. As a plant upon the bosom of God, he is nourished by unfailing
> fountains, and draws at his need inexhaustible power. Who can set bounds to
> the possibilities of Man? Once inspire the infinite, by being admitted to behold
> the absolute natures of justice and truth, and we learn that man has access to the
> entire mind of the Creator in the finite. This view, which admonishes me where
> the sources of wisdom and power lie, and points to virtue as
>
> > 'The golden key
> > Which opes the palace of Eternity,'
>
> carries upon its face, the highest certificate of truth, because it animates me to
> create my own world through the purification of my soul.

This is not only of refreshing moral *aura*, but it is a passage of the highest imaginative power, (taking the word *imaginative* in that true signification which farthest removes it from *fanciful*,) the mind must become purified indeed which can take this point of view, to look at "the great shadow pointing to the sun behind us." Sitting thus at the footstool of God, it may realise that all that we see is created by the light that shines through ourselves. Not until thus purified, can it realise that those through whose being more light flows, see more than we do; and that others, who admit less light, see less. What assistance in human culture would the application of this test give us! How would our classifications of men and women be changed, did the positive pure enjoyment of Nature become the standard of judgment! But who may apply the standard? Not every mawkish raver about the moon, surely, but only a comprehender of Nature. And has there yet been any one in human form, who could be called a comprehender of Nature, save Him who had its secret, and in whose hands it was plastic, even to the raising of the dead?

Mr. Emerson must not accuse us of ingratitude, in that after he had led his readers to this high point of view, they crave more, and accuse him of stopping short, where the world most desires and needs farther guidance. We want him to write another book, in which he will give us the philosophy of his "orphic strains," whose meaning is felt, but can only be understood by glimpses.

He does, indeed, tell us that "the problem of restoring to the world original and eternal beauty," (in other words, of seeing Nature and Life in their wholeness), "is solved by the redemption of the soul." It is not unnecessary for the philosopher thus to bring his disciples round, through the highest flights of speculation, to the primitive faith of the humblest disciple, who sits, in the spirit of a child, at the feet of Jesus. But we should like to hear Mr. Emerson's philosophy of Redemption. It is very plain that it consists of broad and comprehensive views of human culture; worthy to employ the whole mind of one who seeks reproduction of Christ within himself, by such meditations as the following, which must be our last extract:

Is not Prayer also a study of truth—a sally of the soul into the unfound infinite? No man ever prayed heartily without learning something. But when a faithful thinker, resolute to detach every object from personal relations, and see it in the light of thought, shall, at the same time, kindle science with the fire of the holiest affections, then will God go forth anew into the creation.

Orestes Augustus Brownson (1803–1876)

Born a Presbyterian, Brownson shifted his attention to the more liberal Christianity of Universalism, and preached on its behalf. His religious faith continued to evolve during a time in Ithaca where he was pastor to a Unitarian community. And later he was part of the founding of The Transcendentalist Club (1836), the same year Emerson's first book, Nature, *was published. In Chelsea, Massachusetts, he established his own church, The Society for Christian Union and Progress, and published his first book:* New Views of Christianity, Society, and the Church *(1836), which offered a radical critique of wealth inequality, and a call for egalitarianism. His claims were substantiated by Transcendentalist philosophy and ideas imported from Constant and Schleiermacher: "the religious sentiment is universal, permanent and indestructible; religious institutions depend on transient causes." In 1838, Brownson founded the* Boston Quarterly Review, *and wrote the following review of Emerson's Address to the Divinity School at Harvard, presented four months earlier. Given Brownson's dedication to the contemporary understanding of religious thinking, it is not surprising that he is here eager to explain how his audience should understand Emerson's comment on religion, and institutional Christianity in particular. Brownson would be responsible for his own shock to the community when in 1844 he converted to Catholicism, and thereafter spent his life dedicated to a rigorous defense of the Roman Catholic Church. He renounced his former advocacy of Transcendentalist thinking and renamed his journal the* Brownson Quarterly Review, *now aimed at converting his audience to his latest views. Emerson's "Man the Reformer" is a reply to Brownson's critique of Transcendentalism and George Ripley's utopian socialist initiative, Brook Farm. Brownson's "Nature" appeared in the* Boston Reformer, *September 10, 1836; "Mr. Emerson's Address" in the* Boston Quarterly Review, *October 1838; and "Emerson's Essays" in the* Boston Quarterly Review, *July 1841.*

Nature

Orestes Augustus Brownson

This is a singular book. It is the creation of a mind that lives and moves in the Beautiful, and has the power of assimilating to itself whatever it sees, hears or touches. We cannot analyze it; whoever would form an idea of it must read it.

We welcome it however as an index to the spirit which is silently at work among us, as a proof that mind is about to receive a new and a more glorious manifestation; that higher problems and holier speculations than those which have hitherto engrossed us, are to engage our attention; and that the inquiries, what is perfect in Art, and what is true in Philosophy, are to surpass in interest those which concern the best place to locate a city, construct a rail road, or become suddenly rich. We prophesy that it is the forerunner of a new class of books, the harbinger of a new Literature as much superior to whatever has been, as our political institutions are superior to those of the Old World.

This book is aesthetical rather than philosophical. It inquires what is the Beautiful rather than what is the True. Yet it touches some of the gravest problems in metaphysical science, and may perhaps be called philosophy in its poetical aspect. It uniformly subordinates nature to spirit, the understanding to the reason, and mere hand-actions to ideas, and believes that ideas are one day to disenthrall the world from the dominion of semi-shadows, and make it the abode of peace and love, a meet Temple in which to enshrine the Spirit of universal and everlasting Beauty.

The author is a genuine lover of nature, and in a few instances he carries his regard for woods and fields so far as to be in danger of forgetting his socialities, and that all nature combined is infinitely inferior to the mind that contemplates it, and invests it with all its charms. And what seems singular to us is, that with all this love for nature, with this passion for solitary woods and varied landscapes, he seems seriously to doubt the existence of the external world except as a picture which God stamps on the mind. He all but worships what his senses seem to present him, and yet is not certain that all that which his senses place out of him, is not after all the mere subjective laws of his own being, existing only to the eye, not of a necessary, but of an irresistible Faith.

Some great minds have, we know had this doubt. This was the case with the acute and amiable Bishop Berkeley, the audacious Fichte and several others we could mention. Taking their stand-point in the creative power of the human soul, and observing the landscape to change in its coloring as the hues of their own souls change, they have thought the landscape was nothing but themselves projected, and made an object of contemplation. The notion is easily accounted for, but we confess that we should think so acute a philosopher as our author would easily discover its fallacy.

The Reason is undoubtedly our only light, our only criterion of certainty; but we think the Reason vouches for the truth of the senses as decidedly and as immediately as it does for its own conceptions. He who denies the testimony of his senses, seems to us to have no ground for believing the apperceptions of consciousness; and to deny those is to set oneself afloat upon the ocean of universal scepticism. The whole difficulty seems to us to be in not duly understanding the report of the senses. The senses are the windows of the soul through which it looks out upon a world existing as really and as substantially as itself; but what the external world is, or what it is the senses report it to be, we do not at first understand. The result of all culture, we think will not be as our author thinks, to lead to Idealism, but to make us understand what it is we say, when we say, there is an external world.

The author calls the external world phenomenal, that is, an Appearance; but he needs not to be told that the appearance really exists, though it exists as an appearance, as that which appears, as the Absolute. Man is phenomenal in the same sense as is the universe, but man exists. The author calls him "the apparition of God." The apparition exists as certainly as God exists, though it exists as an apparition, not as absolute being. God is absolute being.—Whatever is absolute is God; but God is not the universe, God is not man; man and the universe exist as manifestations of God. His existence is absolute, theirs is relative, but real.

But we are plunging too deeply into metaphysics for our readers and perhaps for ourselves.—In conclusion, we are happy to say that however the author may deviate from what we call sound philosophy, on his road, he always comes to the truth at last. In this little book he has done an important service to his fellow men.—He has clothed nature with a poetic garb, and interpenetrated her with the living spirit of Beauty and Goodness, showed us how we ought to look upon the world round and about us, set us an example of a calm, morally independent, and devout spirit discoursing on the highest and holiest topics which can occupy the human soul, and produced a book which must ever be admired as a perfect specimen of Art. We thank him for what he has done and commend his book—his poem we might say—to every lover of the True, the Beautiful and the Good.

Mr. Emerson's Address

Orestes Augustus Brownson

This is in some respects a remarkable address,—remarkable for its own character and for the place where and the occasion on which it was delivered. It is not often, we fancy, that such an address is delivered by a clergyman in a Divinity College to a class of young men just ready to go forth into the churches as preachers of the Gospel of Jesus Christ. Indeed it is not often that a discourse teaching doctrines like the leading doctrines of this, is delivered by a professedly religious man, anywhere or on any occasion.

We are not surprised that this address should have produced some excitement and called forth some severe censures upon its author; for we have long known that there are comparatively few who can hear with calmness the utterance of opinions to which they do not subscribe. Yet we regret to see the abuse which has been heaped upon Mr. Emerson. We ought to learn to tolerate all opinions, to respect every man's right to form and to utter his own opinions whatever they may be. If we regard the opinions as unsound, false, or dangerous, we should meet them calmly, refute them if we can; but be careful to respect, and to treat with all Christian meekness and love, him who entertains them.

There are many things in this address we heartily approve; there is much that we admire and thank the author for having uttered. We like its life and freshness, its freedom and independence, its richness and beauty. But we cannot help regarding its tone as somewhat arrogant, its spirit is quite too censorious and desponding, its philosophy as indigested, and its reasoning as inconclusive. We do not like its mistiness, its vagueness, and its perpetual use of old words in new senses. Its meaning too often escapes us; and we find it next to impossible to seize its dominant doctrine and determine what it is or what it is not. Moreover, it does not appear to us to be all of the same piece. It is made up of parts borrowed from different and hostile systems, which "baulk and baffle" the author's power to form into a consistent and harmonious whole. {...}

In dismissing this address, we can only say that we have spoken of it freely, but with no improper feeling to its author. We love bold speculation; we are pleased to find a man who dares tell us what and precisely what he thinks, however unpopular his views may be. We have no disposition to check his utterance, by giving his views a bad name, although we deem them unsound. We love progress, and progress cannot be effected without freedom. Still we wish to see a certain sobriety, a certain reserve in all speculations, something like timidity about rushing off into an unknown universe, and some little regret in departing from the faith of our fathers.

Nevertheless, let not the tenor of our remarks be mistaken. Mr. Emerson is the last man in the world we should suspect of conscious hostility to religion and morality. No one can know him or read his productions without feeling a profound respect for the singular purity and uprightness of his character and motives. The great object he is laboring to accomplish is one in which he should receive the hearty coöperation of every American scholar, of every friend of truth, freedom, piety, and virtue. Whatever may be the character of his speculations, whatever may be the moral, philosophical, or theological system which forms the basis of his speculations, his real object is not the inculcation of any new theory on man, nature, or God; but to induce men to think for themselves on all subjects, and to speak from their own full hearts and earnest convictions. His object is to make men scorn to be slaves to routine, to custom, to established creeds, to public opinion, to the great names of this age, of this country, or of any other. He cannot bear the idea that a man comes into the world to-day with the field of truth monopolized and foreclosed. To every man lies open the whole field of truth, in morals, in politics, in science, in theology, in philosophy. The labors of past ages, the revelations of prophets and bards, the discoveries of the scientific and the philosophic, are not to be regarded as superseding our own exertions and inquiries, as impediments to the free action of our own minds, but merely as helps, as provocations to the freest and fullest spiritual action of which God has made us capable.

This is the real end he has in view, and it is a good end. To call forth the free spirit, to produce the conviction here implied, to provoke men to be men, self-moving, self-subsisting men, not mere puppets, moving but as moved by the reigning mode, the reigning dogma, the reigning school, is a grand and praiseworthy work, and we should reverence and aid, not abuse and hinder him who gives himself up soul and body to its accomplishment. So far as the author of the address before us is true to this object, earnest in executing this work, he has our hearty sympathy, and all the aid we, in our humble sphere, can give him. In laboring for this object, he proves himself worthy of his age and his country, true to religion and to morals. In calling, as he does, upon the literary men of our community, in the silver tones of his rich and eloquent voice, and above all by the quickening influence of his example, to assert and maintain their independence throughout the whole domain of thought, against every species of tyranny that would encroach upon it, he is doing his duty"; he is doing a work the effects of which will be felt for good far and wide, long after men shall have forgotten the puerility of his conceits, the affectations of his style, and the unphilosophical character of his speculations. The doctrines he puts forth, the positive instructions, for which he is now censured, will soon be classed where they belong: but the influence of his free spirit, and free utterance, the literature of this country will long feel and hold in grateful remembrance.

Emerson's *Essays*

Orestes Augustus Brownson

In this Journal for April last, we called attention to these Essays, and promised that we would take an early opportunity to speak of them more at large. The promise we then made, we proceed now to redeem. And yet we hardly know how to do it. The Essays are good and significant, but exceedingly troublesome to reviewers, for whose especial ease and convenience they seem by no means to have been written. They contain no doctrine or system of doctrines, logically drawn out, and presented to the understanding of the reader. They consist of detached observations, independent propositions, distinct, enigmatical, oracular sayings, each of which is to be taken by itself, and judged of by its own merits. Consequently, it is impossible to reduce their teachings to a few general propositions, and to sum up their worth in a single sentence.

To most persons, who read these Essays, they will seem to be wanting in unity and coherence. They will always strike as beautiful, often as just, and sometimes as profound; but the reader will be puzzled to round their teachings into a whole, or to discover their practical bearing on life or thought. Yet they have unity and coherence, but of the transcendental sort. The author seems to us to have taken, as far as possible, his stand in the Eternal, above time and space, and tried to present things as they appear from that point of vision,—not in their relation to each other as seen in the world of the senses, but in their relation to the spectator, who views them from above the world of the senses.

This fact should be borne in mind. Mr. Emerson, to speak scientifically, is no philosopher. He is a philosopher neither in the order of his mind, nor in his method of investigation. He explains nothing, accounts for nothing, solves no intellectual problem, and affords no practical instruction. He proposes nothing of all this, and, therefore, is not to be censured for not doing it. He is to be regarded as a Seer, who rises into the regions of the Transcendental, and reports what he sees, and in the order in which he sees it. His worth can be determined, that is, the accuracy of his reports can be properly judged of, by none except those who rise to the same regions, and behold the universe from the same point of view.

Writers like Mr. Emerson are seldom to be consulted for clear, logical, systematic expositions of any subject or doctrine, never for the purpose of taking them as teachers or guides in the formation of opinions; but for the suggestions, the incentives to thought they furnish, and the life they kindle up within us. They are thought by some to be writers without any practical value for mankind; but they have, in fact, a very high practical value; only not of the every day sort, only not that of dogmatic teachers or scientific expositors. They present new aspects of things, or at least old familiar objects in new dresses, the various subjects of thought and inquiry in new relations, break up old associations, and excite to greater and fresher mental activity. After having read them, we cannot say that we are wiser or more learned than we were before; we cannot say that we have become acquainted with any new facts in the history of man or of the universe, or that we have any new ideas in regard to the human soul or its Creator; but we feel, that somehow or other new virtue has been imparted to us, that a change has come over us, and that we are no longer what we were, but greater and better.

These are not the only writers we need; but they have their place, and one of high trust, and of no slight influence. Their influence is not sudden, noisy, obvious to all senses, but slow, silent, subtle, permanent, entering into and becoming an integrant part of the life of the age, sometimes of the ages. They live and exert a power over the souls of men, long after their names are forgotten, and their works have ceased to be read. They are never in vogue with the multitude, but they are admired in select circles, who inhale their spirit, and breathe it into other and larger circles, who in their turn breathe it into the souls of all men. Though they may seem to have no practical aim, and no reference to every-day life, they have in the end a most important practical bearing, and exert a controlling influence over even the business concerns of the world. Let no one, then, regard them as mere idle dreamers, as mere literary toys, with whose glitter we may amuse ourselves, but without significance for the world of reality. They appear always for good or evil, and their appearance usually marks an epoch.

Mr. Emerson's book is a sincere production. It could have been produced only in this community at the present moment, and only by a man who had been placed in the relations he has to society and the Church. Such a book could never have emanated from a man, who had not been bred a clergyman, nor from one, who, having been bred a clergyman, had not ceased to be one. We may also say, that it could have been produced by no man, who had not been bred in a creed, which he had found insufficient to meet the wants of his intellect and heart, and who had not, in some measure, deserted it, without having found another in all respects satisfactory. We may say again, he must have been bred a unitarian, and having found unitarianism defective in consequence of its materialism, have felt and yielded to the reaction of spiritualism, and yet not sufficiently to return to any of the standard forms of orthodoxy.

We would speak respectfully of unitarianism, as we would always of the dead. It had its mission, and it has, in the providence of God, done great good in our community. But unitarianism was not, strictly speaking, a religion, could not become a religion; and it is well known, that almost always persons brought up under its influence, desert it as soon as they become seriously impressed, and desirous of leading religious lives. Men never embraced unitarianism because they were pious, but because they would dispense with being pious. Unitarianism never spoke to the heart, to the soul; never waked any real enthusiasm, or called forth any religious energy of character. It is in its nature *un*spiritual, merely intellectual and material, a sort of baptized atheism. The same causes, at bottom, which produced deism and atheism in France, produced unitarianism in New England. If the American mind had been as consequent as the French, as bold to push a doctrine to its last results, and had the Church here been organized as it was in France, and been as oppressive, our unitarians would have been avowed deists or atheists. We can find no more to feed our piety in the "*Statement of Reasons,*" than in the "*Système de la Nature.*" Indeed, the author of the latter seems the more pious worshipper of the two, and betrays altogether more of peculiar religious emotion; and reverence is more readily yielded to d'Holbach's Nature than to Norton's Divinity. The one is living, plastic, active; the other is a stern, old mechanic, placed on the outside of nature, and troubling himself rarely with its operations; wrapping himself in night and silence, neither seen nor needed by men, and would be unconceived of, did he not charitably send us now and then a messenger to inform us that he really is, and no fiction,—a piece of information altogether gratuitous, as it serves no useful purpose in either the economy of nature or of salvation. With this "Statement of Reasons," unitarianism died, and there are few mourners to go about the streets, albeit there is for it no resurrection.

The old forms of faith had ceased to satisfy the minds of the generation preceding us. Calvinism could not be explained on the principles of Locke's philosophy, and the asceticism which puritanism had enjoined could not but be distasteful and offensive to the growing aristocracy of a prosperous country. Men politely educated, sumptuously clad, fond of good eating and drinking, full of hilarity and mirth, feeling in themselves an exuberance of life, and finding the world very well adapted to their tastes, and being, therefore, in no hurry to exchange it for another, were ill prepared to embrace the ascetic doctrines and practices of their stern old fathers, who never suffered their rigid features to relax with a smile, who thought to please God only by marring the beauty of his works, and by trampling under foot the choicest of his blessings. We do not blame them much. These old puritans are a very unpoetic race of beings, and neither so pious nor so ascetic, so ungiven to the flesh withal, as their admirers would fain have us believe, as may be learned by whomsoever will take the trouble to consult our old church records. They were a strong race, and able to do much; but they attempted altogether more than they could do. They undertook to demolish both the flesh and the devil, and to live on earth as they expected to live in heaven; that is, in surly communion with their own thoughts, and in singing psalms, with no better accompaniment than a jews-harp. Peace to their ashes. They were not without their mission, and have left their track on the ages. Perhaps, with less sourness, surliness, less rigidity, and with more of the amiable, the gentle, the attractive, they could not have done their work.

But the asceticism, which our puritan fathers insisted on, can be really practised by a people only while in the wilderness; while poor, exposed to a thousand hardships, and finding earth no resting place, but a weary land, from which any deliverance may be accounted a blessing. In proportion as the wilderness is peopled, the barren waste converted into the fruitful garden, as grow the ornamental shrubs, and blossoms the rose, and delights are multiplied around us, we take more cheerful views of the world, and of life, and seek not to mortify ourselves, but to enjoy. Asceticism must, then, give way in practice, if not in theory. It did give way in practice, and for years all New England presented the spectacle of a people professing one faith, and living according to another. Some saw this, and being honest, were shocked at it. These became unitarians. Unitarianism was with us a protest against asceticism, even more than against the absurdity of Calvinism, as contemplated from the point of view of the Lockian philosophy. It was an effort of those who could not live in a perpetual lie, to reconcile their theology and their religion to their philosophy and their mode of living.

For a time it could do very well; and as long as controversy could be maintained with opposing sects, it could apparently sustain some degree of intellectual life; but no longer. As soon as the orthodox ceased to controvert, threw it back on itself, left it to its own resources, it ceased to live.

Inasmuch as it was a dissent from the popular faith, unitarianism appealed to freedom of thought and inquiry. It asserted the rights of the individual reason. They who became unitarians, then, were not bound to continue such. They had a right to examine unitarianism, as well as the doctrines opposed to it. Such, again, was its own intrinsic deficiency, its utter inadequacy, as a religion, that the moment its own friends began to investigate it, they found they had outgrown it. They found elements in their nature it did not and could not accept, wants it did not and could not meet. They revolted against its materialism, its dryness, coldness, deadness. They fell back on the religious element of their natures, and sought refuge in a more spiritual philosophy. In this state of transition from materialism to spiritualism, from unitarianism to a modified orthodoxy, if we may be allowed the expression, our unitarian community now is. This transition is represented, in certain of its phases, in the book before us. It marks a movement of the unitarian mind towards a higher, a broader, a more truly religious faith and life. In this consists its significance, and if our orthodox friends were aware of this, they would read it with avidity and profit by it.

This revolt against materialism, and this return towards spiritualism, we regard as among the chief glories of our epoch, as a proof that the reign of infidelity is well nigh over, and that we are preparing a religious future. In this point of view, the men among us who represent this movement, and are for the present condemned, in no measured terms, as was to be expected, by both unitarians and the representatives of the old trinitarian asceticism, the old Calvinistic spiritualism, are the real benefactors of their age and country; the men, who, instead of abuse and discouragement, deserve honor and coöperation. But we never recognise our redeemers till we have crucified them. We cannot say of a truth, that they are sons of God, till we perceive the darkness which comes over the earth as they leave it.

These Essays mark among us the reaction of spiritualism. This constitutes their historical value. How far they represent truly the spiritualism that should become dominant, is another question, and one which can be answered only by determining their positive value. This last can be done only by entering into a critical examination of their merits, a thing which it seems to us almost sacrilegious to attempt. They do not seem to us legitimate subjects of criticism. There is a sacredness about them, a mystic divinity, a voice issuing from them, saying to critics, "Procul, O procul, este, profani." To do them justice, they should be read with reverence, with a yielding spirit, an open heart, ready to receive with thankfulness whatever meets its wants or can be appropriated to its use. The rest, what is not congenial, should be left with pious respect; perhaps there are souls which will find it wholesome food. Why should we deprive others of appropriate nutriment, because it is no nutriment to us?

But Mr. Emerson sometimes descends from the Seer, and assumes the Reasoner. He sometimes touches on dogmas and systems, and if he adopts rarely a philosophical form, a system of philosophy lies back of his poetic utterances, and constitutes even for him the ground on which they are to be legitimated. This system we may examine without profanity. It will, moreover, be ultimately drawn out and formally taught by his disciples. His book will give it currency, and be appealed to as its authority. There can, then, be no impropriety in asking if it be true or false, complete or incomplete.

This system, we say distinctly, is not scientifically taught in the book before us. We are not sure that Mr. Emerson himself is always conscious of it. We are inclined to believe, that he thinks that he eschews all systems, and entangles himself in the meshes of no theory. But every man who speaks at all implies a theory, and in general the greatest theorizers are those who profess to abjure all theory. Every man has his own point of view, from which he contemplates the universe, and whence all his reports are drawn. The question may, then, always come up, is this the true point of view, the point from which the universe may be seen as it really is, and represented in all its unity and diversity? The moment this question is asked, and we undertake to answer it, we plunge into metaphysics, and avail ourselves of system, of theory.

Mr. Emerson's point of view is, we have said, the transcendental. Can the universe, seen from this point of view alone, be truly represented? The answer to this question will enable us to determine the philosophic value of his Essays.

In the philosophy against which there is, in our times, a decided movement, there is no recognition of a transcendental world, of aught that transcends time and space. Immensity is merely space that cannot be measured; eternity is merely time without end. God, as well as man, exists in time and space, and differs from man only in the fact that he fills all space, and continues through all time. Eternal life is a life in time, but merely time endlessly continued. This philosophy never, therefore, carries us out of time and space. To all persons embracing this philosophy, transcendentalists must appear mere dreamers, endeavoring to give to airy nothing, a local habitation and a name.

Now, transcendentalism recognises a world lying back of and above the world of time and space. Time and space belong merely to the world of the senses; but the reason,—not as the principle of logic, but as the principle of intelligence,—rises immediately into a region where there is no time, no space. Immensity is not space infinitely extended, but the negation of all space; eternity is not time endlessly continued, but the negation of all time. God does not exist in space. We cannot say that he is here, there, somewhere, but that he is everywhere, which is only saying again, in other words, that he is Nowhere. He exists not in, but out of time. We cannot say God was, God will be, but simply that he is, as the Hebrew name of God, I AM, plainly implies. To him there is no time. He has no past, no future. He inhabiteth eternity, dwells not in time, but in NO-time, as Watts implies, when he says, with God "all is one eternal NOW."

All our ideas of truth, justice, love, beauty, goodness, are transcendental. Truth is truth, independent of time and place. The just is the just at one epoch, in one country, as much as in another. The beautiful never varies; its laws, we all say, are eternal. Goodness is ever the same. The great principles of the Christian religion inhabit eternity. Hence Jesus says, "before Abraham was I am," and hence he is called "the Lamb slain from the foundations of the world," meaning thereby, that the principles of truth and duty he represented, and by which alone man can come into harmony with his Maker, were no principles of modern creation, but principles existing in the very Principle of things,—principles that have no dependence on time and space, but were in the beginning with God, and were God.

These remarks will help us to understand what is meant by transcendentalism. Transcendentalism, in its good sense, as used in our community, means the recognition of an order of existences, which transcend time and space, and are in no sense dependent on them, or affected by them. Transcendental means very nearly what our old writers, in Shakespeare's time, meant by the word *metaphysical*, from μετα, *beyond*, and φύσιχος, *physical*, natural, belonging to the outward, visible, material world. Transcendentalists recognise a world lying beyond or above the world of the senses, and in man the power of seeing or knowing this transcendental world immediately, by direct cognition, or intuition.

All persons, who believe in God, in the reality of a spiritual world, and contend that their belief has any legitimate basis, are transcendentalists. Whoever is not a transcendentalist, must, if consequent, needs be a skeptic, or a materialist and an atheist. The early Christian fathers were transcendentalists, so were the distinguished English writers of the seventeenth century; so were Descartes, Malebranche, George Fox, William Penn, and our own Edwards; so were Price, and to a feeble extent, the Scottish School; so are nearly all the Germans, and the French Eclectics. Locke and his followers were not, nor were Condillac and the old French school. In fact, all real faith implies the Transcendental, and religion is an idle dream unless we admit the reality of an order of existences, a spiritual world transcending this outward, material, sensible world; and also unless we admit in man the means of attaining legitimately to faith in that reality.

Mr. Emerson, by taking his stand in this transcendental region, evidently asserts its existence, and our power to take cognizance of it. So far his philosophy is eminently religious, and as we have demonstrated over and over again in the pages of this Journal, as well as elsewhere, is sound, and worthy of all acceptation. In this consists his chief philosophical merit. In this too consists his departure from Locke and the unitarian school proper, and his approach to orthodoxy. Thus far we go with him heart and hand, and recognise him as a fellow-laborer in that school of which we profess to be a disciple, though it may be an unworthy one.

But the transcendental, or, if you please, metaphysical, or spiritual world, exists not for the senses, nor can it be inferred from data furnished by the senses. It exists only for the reason. It is ideal, as opposed to sensible, spiritual as opposed to material, but real and substantial. Its existence is indeed involved in all the perceptions of the senses, and asserted in every thought and affirmation; but we rise to the cognition of it only by means of reason, taken, as we have said, not as the principle of logic, but as the principle of intelligence.

Now, by taking our stand on the reason as the principle of intelligence, which is partly analogous to what Mr. Emerson calls the "Over-Soul," and attending exclusively to what it reveals, we are in danger of losing sight of the world of the senses, and therefore of suffering one aspect of the universe to escape us. The moment we rise into the world of reason, we find it altogether richer, sublimer, more beautiful, than this outward visible world. This outward visible world gradually loses its charms for us, disappears from the horizon of our vision, and is therefore very naturally denied to have any existence. We thus fall into Idealism.

Again; the world of the senses is manifold and diverse, while the world of the reason is one and identical. In the transcendental world we rise to the principles of things. The principle of a thing is after all, in a certain sense, the thing itself. All principles proceed from and centre in one common principle, the principle of all things,—God. The diversity noted by the senses is then no real diversity, but merely phenominal and illusory, and deserving no account from him who has risen to the perception of absolute unity, into which all is resolved at last. Diversity is therefore rejected, denied. The distinction between cause and effect ceases then to be intelligible; all difference between God and the universe to be perceptible. The universe is identical with God. God and the universe are one and the same; this is Pantheism.

Whoever then takes his stand exclusively in the Transcendental must fall into ideal Pantheism. From the transcendental point of view alone, a correct report of the universe cannot be made out, any more than from the point of view of the senses alone.

Now Mr. Emerson seems to us to verify in his own case the truth of this deduction. He falls in his philosophy, so far as philosophy he has, into ideal Pantheism. He is so charmed with the world of ideas, that he contemns the sensible, so struck with the unity and identity revealed by the reason, that he is led to overlook and occasionally to deny the manifold and the diverse, revealed by the senses. We cannot read a page of these Essays without perceiving that the tendency of his mind is to seek unity and identity. He brings together in the same sentence perpetually persons and things, events and transactions, apparently the most diverse, by a law of association which most readers are unable to discover, and the point of resemblance between which very few are able to perceive. Yet is he in general just. The resemblance, the identity he asserts is there. His power of detecting the identical in the diverse, the analogous in the dissimilar, the uniform in the manifold, the permanent in the transitory, is remarkable, and unsurpassed in any writer of our acquaintance. He is ever surprising us by unexpected resemblances. To him all things are the same. In all this he is right. He uttered a great truth when he declared the identity of the power by which Lazarus was raised from the dead, and that by which falls the rain or blows the clover; also when he so shocked some of our pious people by declaring the identity of gravitation and purity of heart. This identity does run through all nature, and he has not true insight into the universe who cannot detect it.

But diversity, dissimilarity, multiplicity, are no less obvious and real in the universe than unity and identity. They have their origin too in the same source. God, the cause and principle of the universe, is not a mere unity, but a unity that has in itself the principle of multiplicity,—not pure identity, but at once identity and diversity,—a fact shadowed forth in the doctrine of a Triune God, which runs through all religious philosophies ever promulgated. Whoever overlooks this fact must fall into Pantheism. Mr. Emerson has a tendency to overlook it; and his disciples, for disciples always exaggerate the tendencies of their masters, will most assuredly overlook it. Some of them even now avow themselves Pantheists, and most of the young men and maidens who listened with so much delight to these Essays when they were delivered as lectures, virtually run into Pantheism, whether they know it or not.

The outward visible world is not the only world into which we are admitted, but it is a real world; that is, it really exists, and is no more an illusion than the world of reason; and the idealist is as exclusive and as erroneous as the materialist. The one denies the Transcendental, the other the Sensible. Both are wrong in what they deny, both are right in what they assert; and this fact, it strikes us, does not lie at the basis of Mr. Emerson's philosophy. Hence the wrong tendency of his speculations.

We are not prone to be frightened or shocked at mere words. Thank Heaven, we have strong nerves, and can bear much; but we regard Pantheism as an error of no less magnitude than Atheism itself, and consequently must earnestly protest against every tendency to it. God and the universe are in the most intimate relation, but that relation is one of cause and effect, not of identity; and while we admit that there is this identity running through all nature, to which Mr. Emerson points us, we also contend that there is a corresponding diversity to which he does not point us. We complain not of him for not doing this, but we note the fact in order to warn our readers against taking his utterances as complete expositions of the universe. He brings up one pole of truth, the one which has been too much depressed; but in bringing up that he is not sufficiently heedful not to depress equally the other. We have revolted against exclusive materialism; let us be careful not to fall now into exclusive spiritualism; we have protested against Atheism and irreligion, or the forms of religion which were in fact no religion, and we should look to it that we do not now swallow up all diversity in unity, and man and the universe in God. The latter error would turn out to be as fatal to piety and morals as the former.

But after all, we have no serious apprehensions on this score. Ideal Pantheism, though a fatal error, is not one into which our countrymen are likely to fall, at least to any great extent. Only a few of the cultivated, the refined, the speculative, the idle, and contemplative, are exposed to it. Men in active business, taking their part in the rough and tumble of life, coming in daily contact with one another in the market, the husting, the legislative halls, scrambling for power or place, wealth or distinction, have little leisure, less inclination, and still less aptitude for that order of thought which ends in the denial of matter, and of the universe as distinguished from its Creator. The cast of their minds is too practical, and they are of too sturdy, too robust a make to find anything satisfactory in so refined a spiritualism. Their daily habits and pursuits demand a solid earth on which to work, a providence to protect them, a sovereign to rule over them, a real God to curb their headstrong violence, and to reduce them to order and peace, to chastise them for their errors, and to solace them in their afflictions. The practical tendencies of our countrymen will save them from all danger they would be likely to incur from speculative refinements like those we have pointed out; and we are not sure but Mr. Emerson's strong statements are needed to rectify their over-attachment to the material order.

As it concerns the ethical doctrines implied rather than set forth in these Essays, we have nothing to add to the remarks we have heretofore made on the same subject.[1]

Mr. Emerson's moral philosophy, reduced to its systematic element, belongs to the egoistical school; but we presume, after all, that he means little more by those expressions which imply it, and which have given so much offence, than that just self-reliance, that fidelity to one's own nature and conscience, without which it is impossible to reach or maintain a true manly worth. In this view of the case, his Essay on Self-Reliance is a noble and unexceptionable performance, and inculcates a lesson, which it were well for us all to learn and practise,—a lesson which is perhaps more appropriate to the American people than to any other Christian nation, for no other Christian nation is so timid in its speculations, so afraid of solving for itself, independently, the problem of the destiny of man and society. We regard it as decidedly one of the best Essays in the collection.

We did intend to quote from the book itself, in order to justify our criticisms, but it is not a book from which quotations can be made with much satisfaction. We could not select a paragraph that would not at once confirm and refute our general criticisms. We content ourselves, therefore, with speaking merely of its dominant tendency, as it appears to us. The book cannot be judged of without being read, and the best way to read it, will be to forget its metaphysics, and to take it up as we would a collection of poems, or of proverbs.

Of the Essays we cannot speak particularly. The one on Heroism is inferior to what we expected from its author, and falls far below the general average of the book. Those on Love and Friendship are beautiful and often true, but their truth and beauty proceed from the intellect and imagination rather than the heart and soul. They read not like the confessions of a lover or a friend. There are depths in the affections, into which the author does not descend, deeper experiences than any he discloses, The Essays we have liked the best are those on the Over-Soul, Self-Reliance, and History.

These Essays are, to a certain extent, democratic; they condemn all ordinary aristocracies, and breathe much respect for labor and the laborer; but it is evident, at a single glance, that the author is at best only an amateur workingman, one who has never himself wielded spade or mattock to any great extent, and who has viewed labor with the eye of a poet, rather than with the feelings of an actual laborer. His book, though apparently radical, contains nothing more likely to give offence to the capitalist than to the proletary.

One of the most serious objections, we have to urge against these Essays, is the little importance they assign to the state, and the low rank they allow to patriotism as a virtue. This is an error of our transcendental school generally, and results, we suppose, chiefly from the fact, that its principal masters are or have been churchmen, and, therefore, not over and above acquainted with practical life. Their studies lead them to rely on preaching, persuasion, advice, appeals to the reason and conscience. Their habits and position remove them from the actual world, and its necessities, and keep them ignorant of no small part of the actual developments of human nature. Clergymen are usually able to give wholesome advice, at least, advice which will generally be regarded as canonical; but they are rarely gifted with much practical skill or sagacity. A deliberative assembly, composed entirely of clergymen, is usually a very disorderly body, and ill adapted to the speedy despatch of business. The members are all so enlightened, so wise, so good, so meek, and so conscientious, that ordinary parliamentary rules are rarely thought to be necessary; and the result is not seldom confusion, angry, disorderly debate, and no little ill feeling and ill speaking. This anti-political tendency of our transcendentalists is, therefore, easily accounted for. Nevertheless, it is a false tendency. Man, as we have endeavored to prove in a foregoing article, is to be perfected in society, and society is to be perfected by government. More, than even politicians themselves usually imagine, depends on the right organization of the commonwealth. The science of politics, when rightly viewed, is a grand and an essential science, and needs always to be held in honor. Much is lost by not making it a subject of more serious study. Everybody talks about politics, and yet there is scarcely a man among us acquainted with the simplest principles of politics, regarded as a science. The proper organization of the state, the true exposition of the constitution, and the proper administration, so as to secure the true end of government, are matters with which we, as a people, rarely trouble ourselves; and scarcely a man can be found, who can speak on them five minutes in succession, without betraying gross ignorance, both theoretical and practical. In this state of political science, our scholars are doing us great disservice by sneering at politics and the state.

As mere literary productions, these Essays must take rank with the best in the language. There is now and then an affectation of quaintness, a puerile conceit, not precisely to our taste, but it detracts not much from their general beauty. In compactness of style, in the felicitous choice of words, in variety, aptness, and wealth of illustration, they are unrivalled. They have a freshness, a vigor, a freedom from old hacknied forms of speech, and from the conventionalisms of the schools, worthy of the highest praise, and which cannot fail to exert a salutary influence on our growing literature. They often remind us of Montaigne, especially in the little personal allusions, which the author introduces with inimitable grace, delicacy, and effect.

In conclusion, we will simply add, that notwithstanding the metaphysical errors to which we have referred, the Essays make up a volume unique in its character, and which all competent judges will agree in regarding as among the most creditable productions of the American press. It must secure to the author a distinguished rank among the more distinguished writers of the age. We feel ourselves deeply indebted for his present. We receive his utterances with thankfulness and reverence, and shall wait impatiently till he permits us to hear from him again. It is not often, that in our profession as a critic, we meet with a work of fewer faults, nor one that can better bear to have its faults pointed out; for it is rare that we meet with one with its positive excellencies. It is no ephemeral production; it will survive the day; for it is full of sincerity, truth, beauty. Whoso pores over its pages will find his soul quickened, his vision enlarged, his heart warmed, and his life made better.

Note

1   See in this volume Brownson's "Mr. Emerson's Address" (first published in the *Boston Quarterly Review*, October 1838).

Andrews Norton (1786–1853)

The Dexter Professor of Sacred Literature at Harvard Divinity School from 1819 to 1830, a tenure that included the time when Emerson matriculated in the mid-1820s, Norton was celebrated for The Evidences of the Genuineness of the Gospels *(1837–1844), a three-volume work of New Testament historicism. With William Ellery Channing, he was a leader in New England Unitarianism, the form of Christianity that Emerson preached at the Second Church in Boston in the late 1820s until his resignation in 1832. Though Norton began his career in a liberal strain that resisted inherited forms of Calvinism and Trinitarianism, liberal thinking in George Ripley, Emerson, and the Transcendentalists more generally led Norton to take up increasingly conservative approaches to challenges made to orthodoxy—even the liberal orthodoxies of the Unitarians. Norton worried that Emerson's emphasis on intuition, individual self-knowledge, and doubt in religious institutions entailed a kind of anti-intellectualism, and—worse—would become provocations that undermine religious truth, including faith in miracles. After publishing an attack on George Ripley's views in late 1836—amid an unprecedented flurry of new work by Transcendentalists, including Emerson's* Nature—*Norton continued his critique following Emerson's presentation of an* Address *to the Divinity School at Harvard in 1838. Norton's response, first printed in* The Boston Daily Advertiser *on August 27, 1838 and included below, helped to solidify his place as a chief critic of Transcendentalism, but also, perhaps unfairly, led to a caricature of his concerns and the seriousness of his claims. (For a corrective to the popular reading of Norton in much of the critical literature, including the "dangers of reducing the transcendental controversy" to "strict polarities," see Robert Habich's "Emerson's Reluctant Foe: Andrews Norton and the Transcendental Controversy"*[1]*). It is worth dwelling on the fact that Norton nearly missed his appointment as Dexter Professor on account of what was perceived in his work as a "want of orthodoxy." For his part, Emerson did not engage Norton in print (as Ripley did in a counter-essay, "'The Latest Form of Infidelity' Examined" (1839)), though Emerson noted in his journal: "It is a poor-spirited age. [. . .] The feminine vehemence with which the A. N. of the Daily Advertiser beseeches the dear people to whip that naughty heretic is the natural feeling in the mind whose religion is external."*[2]

On the Divinity School Address

Andrews Norton

There is a strange state of things existing about us in the literary and religious world, of which none of our larger periodicals has yet taken notice. It is the result of that restless craving for notoriety and excitement, which in one way or another, is keeping our community in a perpetual stir. {...}

The characteristics of this school are the most extraordinary assumption, united with great ignorance, and incapacity for reasoning. There is indeed a general tendency among its disciples to disavow learning and reasoning as sources of their higher knowledge.—The mind must be its own unassisted teacher. It discerns transcendental truths by immediate vision, and these truths can no more be communicated to another by addressing his understanding, than the power of clairvoyance can be given to one not magnetized. They announce themselves as the prophets and priests of a new future, in which all is to be changed, all old opinions done away, and all present forms of society abolished. But by what process this joyful revolution is to be effected we are not told; nor how human happiness and virtue is to be saved from the universal wreck, and regenerated in their Medea's caldron. There are great truths with which they are laboring, but they are unutterable in words to be understood by common minds. To such minds they seem nonsense, oracles as obscure as those of Delphi.

The rejection of reasoning is accompanied with an equal contempt for good taste. All modesty is laid aside. The writer of an article for an obscure periodical, or a religious newspaper, assumes a tone as if he were one of the chosen enlighteners of a dark age.— He continually obtrudes himself upon his reader, and announces his own convictions, as if from their haying that character, they were necessarily indisputable. {...}

The state of things described might seem a matter of no great concern, a mere insurrection of folly, a sort of Jack Cade rebellion, which in the nature of things must soon be put down, if those engaged in it were not gathering confidence from neglect, and had not proceeded to attack principles which are the foundation of human society and human happiness. "Silly women," it has been said, and silly young men, it is to be feared, have been drawn away from their Christian faith, if not divorced from all that can properly be called religion. The evil is becoming, for the time, disastrous and alarming; and of this fact there could hardly be a more extraordinary and ill boding evidence, than is afforded by a publication, which has just appeared, entitled, an "Address, delivered before the Senior Class in Divinity College, Cambridge," upon the occasion of that class taking leave of the Institution—"By Ralph Waldo Emerson."

It is not necessary to remark particularly on this composition. It will be sufficient to state generally, that the author professes to reject all belief in Christianity as a revelation, that he makes a general attack upon the Clergy, on the ground that they preach what he calls "Historical Christianity," and that if he believe in God in the proper sense of the term, which one passage might have led his hearers to suppose, his language elsewhere is very ill-judged and indecorous. But what *his* opinions may be is a matter of minor concern; the main question is how it has happened, that religion has been insulted by the delivery of these opinions in the Chapel of the Divinity College of Cambridge, as the last instruction which those were to receive, who were going forth from it, bearing the name of Christian preachers. This is a question in which the community is deeply interested. No one can doubt for a moment of the disgust and strong disapprobation with which it must have been heard by the highly respectable officers of that Institution. They must have felt it not only as an insult to religion, but as personal insult to themselves. But this renders the fact of its having been so delivered only the more remarkable. We can proceed but a step in accounting for it. The preacher was invited to occupy the place he did, not by the officers of the Divinity College, but by the members of the graduating class. These gentlemen, therefore, have become accessories, perhaps innocent accessories, to the commission of a great offence; and the public must be desirous of learning what exculpation or excuse they can offer.

It is difficult to believe that they thought this incoherent rhapsody a specimen of fine writing, that they listened with admiration, for instance, when they were told that the religious sentiment "is myrrh, and storax and chlorine and rosemary;" or that they wondered at the profound views of their present Teacher, when he announced to them that "the new Teacher," for whom he is looking, would "see the identity of the law of gravitation with purity of heart;" or that they had not some suspicion of inconsistency, when a new Teacher was talked of, after it had been declared to them, that religious truth "is an intuition," and "cannot be received at second hand."

But the subject is to be viewed under a far more serious aspect. The words God, Religion, Christianity, have a definite meaning, well understood. They express conceptions and truths of unutterable moment to the present and future happiness of man. We well know how shamefully they have been abused in modern times by infidels and pantheists; but their meaning remains the same; the truths which they express are unchanged and unchangeable. The community know what they require when they ask for a Christian Teacher; and should any one approving the doctrines of this discourse assume that character, he would deceive his hearers; he would be guilty of a practical falsehood for the most paltry of temptations; he would consent to live a lie, for the sake of being maintained by those whom he had cheated. It is not, however, to be supposed that his vanity would suffer him long to keep his philosophy wholly to himself. This would break out in obscure intimations, ambiguous words, and false and mischievous speculations. But should such preachers abound, and grow confident in their folly, we can hardly overestimate the disastrous effect upon the religion and moral state of the community.

Notes

1   Robert Habich, "Emerson's Reluctant Foe: Andrews Norton and the Transcendental Controversy," *The New England Quarterly*, Vol. 65, No. 2 (June 1992), 208–237.

2   Ralph Waldo Emerson, *The Journals and Miscellaneous Notebooks of Ralph Waldo Emerson*, ed. William H. Gilman, et al. (Cambridge: Belknap Press of Harvard University Press, 1969), Vol. VII, 110–111.

William Henry Channing (1810–1884)

The nephew of the founder of the Unitarian Church, William Ellery Channing,
W. H. Channing was raised in Boston and, like Emerson, attended Harvard College
(1829) and Harvard Divinity School (1833), and was approbated to preach in
the Unitarian church, taking up a pulpit in Cincinnati in 1835. Though Emerson
remained wary of socialist experiments such as Brook Farm, Channing regularly
visited Alcott's commune and was committed to the implications for social reform in
the work of Charles Fourier (1772–1837). Channing was critical of Emerson for not
being more involved in the reform movements of the day, including abolitionism, but
praised Emerson's intellectual work, as for instance in his remarks on "The American
Scholar," published in Boston Quarterly Review *(January 1838) and included*
below. While Emerson became a vocal and public supporter of emancipation in
the mid-1840s—he delivered the rousing and castigating anniversary speech "An
Address . . . on . . . the Emancipation of the Negroes in the British West Indies"—he
also wrote in his journal in the same year "I do not & can not forsake my vocation
for abolitionism."[1] In 1847, Emerson published "Ode," a poem inscribed to Channing,
"the evil time's sole patriot." A couple of years later, after Margaret Fuller died at sea,
Channing asked Emerson to write her biography. Emerson worried that the task
"might turn out to be a work above our courage," and that Channing was "too much
her friend to leave him quite free enough" to write, but the three friends of Fuller—
James Freeman Clarke joined the project—collaborated on a lasting work in her
honor, two volumes of Memoirs of Margaret Fuller Ossoli *(1852).*

Emerson's Phi Beta Kappa Oration

William Henry Channing

We have been not a little amused and somewhat edified by the various criticisms on this address, which we have seen and heard of all kinds, from kindling admiration to gaping wonder, shrewd caviling, sneering doubt, and even offended dignity. We wish for ourselves, to express our hearty thanks to the author, to disburden our minds of a small load of censure, and utter some thoughts on the subject-matter of the address.

There are writers whom we should designate as in the twilight state, walking ever in an opposite direction to the motion of the earth—following with longing admiration the descending glory of the past—delighting in each tall peak, each floating cloud, which reflects the lustre of a fading day. To them the present is weary and worn, and the darkness and vapors steam up from the sunken vales of common life. There is a second class, in the midnight season of thought, lone and abstracted—watching the truths of eternity as they smile through far space on a darkened world. To them the present is the gleaming lights, the snatches of music, the distasteful clamor of foolish revelry, breaking harshly in upon their hour of rapt and solemn meditation. There is a third class, in morning wakefulness. Their gaze is on the brightening orient. They stand as *muezzins* on the mosques, as watchmen on the towers, summoning to prayer and work;—for the streaks of the dawning, and the golden flushes, are heralding the sun. The present is bright to them with hope; and the dewy incense promises fruitfulness, and the rising race are going forth to husband the garden of life. There is a fourth class, in the noonday and sunny cheerfulness, and clear light, of God's providence in the present time, on whose useful the *spirit of the age* shines down to ripen and to bless.

When we read a former production by the author of this address, we feared from its tone of somewhat exclusive and unsympathising contemplativeness, that he was of the second class. But we hail him now as one of the youthful expectants of a coming brighter hour of social life. Shall we not indeed say, that in his industry, and the unreserved communication of his best nature, as a preacher and lecturer, we gratefully recognize him as one of the working men of this generation? And yet would we see him more fully warmed with the great social idea of our era,—the great idea, which he has hinted at in this very address—of human brotherhood, of son-ship to God. We have full faith that in this land is this ideal to be manifested in individual character, in social life, in art, in literature, as for the last eighteen hundred years it has been in religion. We echo with joy the language of the orator.[2]

Why did Providence veil our land till the fulness of time, and then gather upon it an elect people from all nations of the earth, under institutions the most favorable to individual development, if not, that in a recovered Eden of freedom, love and peace, the products of all by-gone civilization, might blossom together? And shall not such a social state of Humanity utter itself, and is not that utterance a Literature?

We see, in Mr. Emerson, many traits befitting an American, that is, a Christian, free writer. He has deep faith in a heavenly Father of souls, reverence for each brother as a child of God,—respect for his own reason as a divine inspiration,—too much love for men to fear them,—a conscientious hungering and thirsting for truth,—and a serene trust in the triumph of good. He seems to us true, reverent, free, and loving. We cheerfully tolerate therefore any quaint trappings in which a peculiar taste may lead him to deck his thoughts; and we pity the purists, who cannot see a manly spirit through a mantle not wholly courtly. At the same time we will freely express our regret that Mr. Emerson's style is so little a transparent one. There are no thoughts which may not be simply expressed. Raphael's pictures with their profound beauty are simple as a family group in a peasant's cottage, or a crowd in a market place. The author of this address, we feel assured, does not willingly hide his thoughts from the poor vanity of being understood only by the initiated; and we have no doubt endeavors to be intelligible. He loves truth and respects man too well for such folly. His faith that man's very holy of holies enshrines no ideas too pure for popular worship, is thus beautifully expressed.[3]

Why then should he not open himself freely, simply? We think he means to do so. He cordially welcomes us to his high summits of speculation, and to the prospect they command, in full faith that our sight is keen as his. But he forgets that he has not pointed out the way by which he climbed. His conclusions are hinted, without the progressive reasonings through which he was led to them. Perhaps he does not come at them by any consecutive processes. They rather come to him unasked. To use his own language.[4]

There are no developments of thought, there is no continuous flow in his writings. We gaze as through crevices on a stream of subterranean course, which sparkles here and there in the light, and then is lost. The style is in the extreme aphoristic. But again, another cause of his obscurity is a fondness for various illustrations. He has a quick eye for analogies, and finds in all nature symbols of spiritual facts. His figures are occasionally so exquisitely felicitous, that we have hardly the heart to complain of this habit of mind, though, we confess, that not seldom we are attracted from the feature of his thoughts to the splendid jewelry of their attire, and yet oftener annoyed by the masquerade of rural or civic plainness, in which they see fit to march.

The subject of this Address is "The American Scholar," his training, duties, and prospects; and we cannot but wish that there had been more unity and order observed in treating it. The division is good—and the thoughts are apparently cast in a form. But the truth is, there is no progress, no onward stream. The best thoughts are not the leading but the incidental ones, and their arrangement might be varied without much altering the effect of the whole. But then these thoughts are fine ones, and there is a mass of them. And they might easily be run into shape, or rather built into a beautiful composition; or yet again grow naturally forth from the root of his central idea. This idea is variously expressed:

> "There is One Man—present to all particular men only partially; you must take the whole of society to find the whole man." "Man is one." "It is one soul which animates all men." "In a century—in a millennium one or two men; that is to say, one or two approximations to the right state of every man. All the rest behold in the hero or the poet their own green and crude being ripened." "A man rightly viewed comprehendeth the particular natures of all men. Each philosopher, each bard, each actor, has only done for me as by a delegate what I can one day do for myself." "The one thing of value in the world is the active soul,—the soul free, sovereign, active." "A nation of men, because each believes himself inspired, by the Divine Soul which also inspires all men."

This fundamental truth, which Jesus felt, uttered, and lived as no disciple has ever faintly dreamed of, our author has apprehended with awe. It is a thought to open the fountains of the soul. As the orator says. {Summary of the address omitted}

Now to our thinking this is high doctrine—timely, and well put. We trust all who have heard or read will lay it to heart, and go forth in the brightening day of a Christian, free literature with solemn purpose, patient resolve, cheerful hope, and forgiving tolerance; filled with the thought that, "God is working in them to will and do of his good pleasure"; and greeting each brother heir of immortality with a reverence and a benediction.

We have endeavored to give a skeleton of this, to us deeply interesting address, and now would proceed to remark upon the subject-matter itself. The theme proposed by the orator is the "American Scholar." Why did he not say Author? Every man is or should be a "student," "man thinking." On every mind Nature, the Past, and Action, pour their influences. Some of the most active souls—the freest, bravest thinkers of our time and country, communicate their observations, make their instincts prevalent, embody their highest spiritual vision; but it is only in their lives—their manners—their public acts—their social talk. They fill up the idea of the orator's "scholar." But they are not authors; they do not utter the spirit that is in them. They are the seers, but not the poets—the teachers, but not the artists of the time. Their influence is falling on the mountains and in the vales, instilling through the mass of the universal mind the waters of life, which one day shall well forth in crystal gleams and musical trillings to swell the stream of a truly American literature, and pour along a fertilizing stream of thought. When and how shall our *Authors* be formed? They are forming. When the idea of human brotherhood, of sonship to God—of eternal reason in each human soul—of respect for man—shall be assimilated and organized in our social frame, then shall American Literature go forth in vigor, symmetry, and graceful action. Men will utter when they are filled with the spirit. Our manners, our tone of life, our habits of thought, our social garniture, are a worn out casing, and the new robes of nature's handiwork to clothe a higher form of life as yet but imperfectly grown. Many a poet is walking now our green hill sides, toiling in our mechanic shops, ay, bartering in the bustling mart, even jostling in the caucus and voting at the polls, living a poem in the round of professional duties and the ever fresh romance of quiet homes. And wherever they are, the forms—the castes—the trappings—the badges—the fashion and parade of life, are seen by them as thin disguises, and the purity and vigor of the soul in each brother, the true spiritual experiences of man beneath God's sky upon God's earth, are the only things of worth. When shall they utter the music which swells sweetly in the chambers of their own spirits? When the standard of man's measure is changed, and persons are prized for what they *are*, not for what they *have*. And whenever and however any one is filled to overflowing with this grand idea of God in the soul of man, he will utter it—he must utter it. He will be an American Author. He may prophesy from the pulpit, at the Lyceum, in the schoolhouse, in the daily press, in books, in public addresses. But the burden of the prophecy will be the same: "Man measures man the world over:" Man's spirit is from God: We are brethren.

In speaking therefore of the training of American authors—we should place first, second, and third, action, or rather *Life*. A man to utter the American spirit, which is now in embryo, and will sooner or later be born into life, should walk in the noonday brightness of the great Idea of our era and land, till he is quickened by its beams. The great author is he who embodies in language the spirit of his time. The great American author will be he who lives out the American idea—the Christian—the Divine idea of *Brotherhood*.

He must study "Nature." Yes! open his inmost soul to this beautiful smile of God's perfections, that the spirit of God may abide in him as a temple. But nowhere does nature respond to the call within, nowhere do the floods of being answer to the floods of will, as in the form and presence, the ways and deeds and will of man; nowhere, as in the mighty social movement, which ever sweeps along through a silent eternity the ever new present age. The nature of man, and the cycle of that nature, which even now is revolving, is God's voice to us—a new-born creation which angels hymn.

The author must study the "Past." Yes! For every genius, every martyr, every hero, every living soul, has been a hue of promise, which Humanity has caught from the day-spring from on high. And silently through the tide of roving hordes and the storms of desolating revolutions—in calm hours of bright prosperity—and the wide hush of peaceful eras—in the uprising of downtrodden millions—and the fervent hopings and prayers of philanthropy, has the present time been slowly preparing—the aloes sometime to bloom.

And the Author must "act." Yes! but chiefly, not "subordinately." He must throw himself heartily into the moving army of the time, and serve an unnoticed private or a followed leader, as his strength may be—willing to be trampled down, so the powers of good triumph. And he must go out into life too, not to build up himself and complete his being only; not to gain wisdom, to gather raw material only—not to stock a vocabulary, not to recreate only—but from a deep insight into the sublimity of daily, hourly, common life, from awe of the force of Providence stirring in the deep springs of the present generation. Not as a scholar, not with a view to literary labor, not as an artist, must he go out among men—but as a brother man, all unconscious that he has uttered any thing, all purposeless of future utterance till it is given. We rejoiced with sympathetic joy when we read that sentence in this address, "I ask not for the great, the remote, the romantic, what is doing in Italy or Arabia; what is Greek Art or Provencal Minstrelsy; I embrace the common, I explore and sit at the feet of the familiar, the low." A distinguished sculptor was asked, "where when the gods had returned to Olympus, and the iconoclastic spirit of the time had overturned the Madonnas and the martyrs, he would look for subjects for his chisel?" "To the grace and poetry of the simple acts of life," was his answer. The greatest painter of the age has breathed his purest ideal beauty through the unpicturesque attire, the easy attitude, the homely plainness, of peasant girlhood. And perfectly true is it, as our orator says, that this idea has inspired the genius of the finest authors of our day. A man must live the life of Jesus, according to his power, would he be a truly American author; yes! he must live a self-forgetting minister to men, in the charities of home and acquaintance—in thankless and unnoticed sympathy,—in painful toil amid great enterprises,—among interests of the day—sacrificing notoriety, relinquishing unfavorite tastes, penetrated through his habitual thoughts with the prayer, that the kingdom of God may come— the kingdom of truth, love, beauty, and happiness—of fresh minds and warm hearts and clear consciences, the kingdom of brother souls in their Father's mansion. And he must do this because he feels the worth of man as man—because he sees the infinite in the finite—the spiritual in the material—the eternal in the present—the divine in man.

When his heart is tuned to unison with every chord that vibrates through the moral universe, and responds to the music of love through his whole being, let him pour out the joy of a spirit communing with the All Holy, of an Immoral stepping onward hand in hand with growing spirits on a brightening pathway to heaven.

All this may seem extravagant and enthusiastic. We say it with the calmest conviction. We look for a high-toned literature in this Christian, free land, where the vine of truth is not overgrown with the weeds of past civilization. We fully expect to see *American* authors. And yet more, we feel sure they will form a most numerous class, or rather be *so numerous as not to form a class*. The benefits of the existence of a literary caste have been vaunted. We have no faith in them. The change which has for years been going on, by which more and more minds have been incited to produce their store for the public good—in reviews, miscellanies, essays, fictions, lectures, is we believe auspicious. Literature has become less monkish, more manly. The days of astrology and alchemy in the world of books is over; and those of its astronomy and chemistry have come; and our bark of life will ride the safer, and our comforts be multiplied by the change. Literature should be the reflection of an age upon itself, the self-converse of the race, and the more expressions of its consciousness, the better; or again literature should be the challenge and answer of "all's well," as each generation takes its stand in time. The more minds that light up their tapers, the better. All men have genius, if they will be true to the inward voice. Let them serve God and not men, and bear what testimony they can. We cannot spare them. Literature will thus assume a more conversational, a heartier tone; and no man will be ashamed, afraid, or vain, or proud, to be an author. The age is superficial, it is said—the attention is dissipated by variety—there is a slip-shod style in vogue—thinkers are rare. We doubt much the justice of all this. The energy of the time, perhaps the genius of the time, is chiefly turned to the business of life. But never, we believe, was there a period of healthier intellectual action. The people—the public, crave thought. They passionately follow a strong man who utters his deepest self healthily, naturally; the higher, the purer his message, the better prized by them. And compare the thoughts and style of expression too of our reviews, yes even of light novels, and of newspaper pieces, dashed off as they are by ordinary minds, with what was written by the select few of earlier time, and do they not prove really a wonderful development of the thinking faculties? All writers are to some degree thinkers, if not thinking men. For their own sakes, composition is salutary; it reveals to themselves what force they have in them. The next stage will be the casting off of authority; yes, even that public opinion which now enslaves, and the rising up of an immense class of independent thinkers, to declare what they too have seen of heavenly light through the telescopes in high observatories, or with the naked eye on the bare hills. We sometimes think that the profusion, with which the knowledge of the most interesting facts, laws, and phenomena of nature, of the great miracles of art and invention, of the mighty events of history, of the original characters who have made history,—that the profusion, we say with which a knowledge of these has been diffused to readers and hearers—though done merely to amuse, will produce a fine result. Men seek novelties, something to animate and awake; where will they find them, if not in the infinity of their own spiritual natures and experiences,—in the marvels and wonders of the quite familiar and common? The crowd of authors even now has broken down the aristocracy of literature. Men are no longer notorious for being writers. Poor vanity no longer, or in a less degree, impels fools to ape sages. But yet the instinct of utterance remains. And we need not fear, that minds, which through the deep caverns of their own spirit have passed to Elysian fields, will be hindered from declaring their bright visions, because the air is full of the murmur of voices. Literature must become what it ought to be, the *best* thoughts of *all*, given out in the grand school room, debating hall, and conversazione of the world, rather let us say in the grand family group of God's children. Inspired prophets and apostles of truth will easily be recognised,—and listened to all the more eagerly by those, to whom all past utterances are familiar, and who seek something new. No Paul will be neglected at Athens. And the temptation lessens every day for a man to desert the field which heaven appointed him to till, by running into the mart to speculate in buying up popular applause. The public are tired of parrots. They want men. We feel convinced that our best minds and all minds, instead of being frittered away and dissipated by chasing the butterflies, and hunting the bright shells, and gathering the choice flowers of thoughts, to amuse or be amused with, will confine themselves more and more to laborious working in their own peculiar mines; that our public lectures will lose their desultory and take a systematic character; that private teachers will appear of higher and higher branches of knowledge. And this will prepare the way for independent, thorough, original action of the American mind. And we long to see what will be produced in that democratic age of literature, where no clan of Authors are tolerated longer as the dictators of fashion and the judges of caste in the world of books, but where appeal is only to the spirit of truth; where the court garment is always sincerity's work-day dress.

But we must bring these remarks to a close. We look, we say, for an American literature. We feel as if the old strata of thought, in the old world, had been broken up, with the old manners which clothed them and grew out from them; and as if the fused and melted mass had settled here to form a new world of higher beauty. And the rock basis of a new era will be a philosophy, which recognises the divinity of reason in every soul; which sees the identity of reason and faith, and honors common sense as the voice of truth; which feels the mystery of moral freedom in every man of that perfect liberty of the entire obedience to right, and which bows with awe before the conviction that God is in each human soul, that never is the individual so entirely himself as when at one with the indwelling Spirit. And the life, which will pervade this new world of thought, will be a poetry of love and sympathy for the commonest familiar feeling, as well as the higher and holier, and for every human tie and relation. Science is always liberal, for nature is no respecter of persons or of forms. She will speak to the humblest or highest of her children through the light which covers the heavens, as with a canopy for angels, through the swift flashes which rend the mountain, or the unseen influence which follows down the string of the paper kite. And shall not it be, is the world never to see a system of social manners too, growing out from this Christian idea of brotherhood, which shall embody the principles of this philosophy—the spirit of this poetry? Our manners will ever be the leaves to clothe with beauty the trunk and branches of our faith; but through them it must imbibe from the sun of God's love, and the atmosphere of human kindness, a purifying, a vital influence. We shall never have a healthy American Literature, unless we have an American Spirit, an American Manner of Life.

Notes

1 Ralph Waldo Emerson, *The Journals and Miscellaneous Notebooks of Ralph Waldo Emerson*, ed. William H. Gilman, et al. (Cambridge: Belknap Press of Harvard University Press, 1971), Vol. IX, 64n (1844).
2 Reference to original source given as 52.22–25, 69.11–12, 70.5–7.
3 Ibid., 63.27–34.
4 Ibid., 60.6–9.

Margaret Fuller (1810–1850)

A path-breaking figure and member of Emerson's inner circle, Fuller wrote the still-crucial Woman in the Nineteenth Century *(1845), a seminal articulation of women's rights. She oversaw an educational initiative for women called "Conversations," was among the best-read people in New England, and was the first woman granted access to Harvard College Library. She co-edited the literary magazine* The Dial *along with George Ripley and Emerson, and was on staff at Horace Greeley's* New-York Tribune, *where the following review of Emerson's* Essays, Second Series *appeared on December 7, 1844. She was a dedicated reader of Emerson's writing and had access to drafts of his work, including* Nature, *which she directed Emerson to conclude differently. He heeded her recommendation with the chapter "Prospects," and continued to rely on her considered judgment of his work. She died tragically at sea, with her son and husband, off the coast of Long Island, returning from Italy. Of her death, Emerson wrote in his journal: "I have lost in her my audience."[1]*

Essays, Second Series

Margaret Fuller

At the distance of three years this volume follows the first series of Essays, which have already made to themselves a circle of readers, attentive, thoughtful, more and more intelligent, and this circle is a large one if we consider the circumstances of this country, and of England, also, at this time.

In England it would seem there are a larger number of persons waiting for an invitation to calm thought and sincere intercourse than among ourselves. Copies of Mr. Emerson's first published little volume called "Nature," have there been sold by thousands in a short time, while one edition has needed seven years to get circulated here. Several of his Orations and Essays from "The Dial" have also been republished there, and met with a reverent and earnest response.

We suppose that while in England the want of such a voice is as great as here, a larger number are at leisure to recognize that want; a far larger number have set foot in the speculative region and have ears refined to appreciate these melodious accents.

Our people, heated by a partisan spirit, necessarily occupied in these first stages by bringing out the material resources of the land, not generally prepared by early training for the enjoyment of books that require attention and reflection, are still more injured by a large majority of writers and speakers, who lend all their efforts to flatter corrupt tastes and mental indolence, instead of feeling it their prerogative and their duty to admonish the community of the danger and arouse it to nobler energy. The aim of the writer or lecturer is not to say the best he knows in as few and well-chosen words as he can, making it his first aim to do justice to the subject. Rather he seeks to beat out a thought as thin as possible, and to consider what the audience will be most willing to receive.

The result of such a course is inevitable. Literature and Art must become daily more degraded; Philosophy cannot exist. A man who feels within his mind some spark of genius, or a capacity for the exercises of talent, should consider himself as endowed with a sacred commission. He is the natural priest, the shepherd of the people. He must raise his mind as high as he can toward the heaven of truth, and try to draw up with him those less gifted by nature with ethereal lightness. If he does not so, but rather employs his powers to flatter them in their poverty, and to hinder aspiration by useless words, and a mere seeming of activity, his sin is great, he is false to God, and false to man.

Much of this sin indeed is done ignorantly. The idea that literature calls men to the genuine hierarchy is almost forgotten. One, who finds himself able, uses his pen, as he might a trowel, solely to procure himself bread, without having reflected on the position in which he thereby places himself.

Apart from the troop of mercenaries, there is one, still larger, of those who use their powers merely for local and temporary ends, aiming at no excellence other than may conduce to these. Among these, rank persons of honor and the best intentions, but they neglect the lasting for the transient, as a man neglects to furnish his mind that he may provide the better for the house in which his body is to dwell for a few years.

When these sins and errors are prevalent, and threaten to become more so, how can we sufficiently prize and honor a mind which is quite pure from such? When, as in the present case, we find a man whose only aim is the discernment and interpretation of the spiritual laws by which we live and move and have our being, all whose objects are permanent, and whose every word stands for a fact.

If only as a representative of the claims of individual culture in a nation which tends to lay such stress on artificial organization and external results, Mr. Emerson would be invaluable here. History will inscribe his name as a father of the country, for he is one who pleads her cause against herself.

If New-England may be regarded as a chief mental focus to the New World, and many symptoms seem to give her this place, as to other centres the characteristics of heart and lungs to the body politic; if we may believe, as the writer does believe, that what is to be acted out in the country at large is, most frequently, first indicated there, as all the phenomena of the nervous system in the fantasies of the brain, we may hail as an auspicious omen the influence Mr. Emerson has there obtained, which is deep-rooted, increasing, and, over the younger portion of the community, far greater than that of any other person.

His books are received there with a more ready intelligence than elsewhere, partly because his range of personal experience and illustration applies to that region, partly because he has prepared the way for his books to be read by his great powers as a speaker.

The audience that waited for years upon the lectures, a part of which is incorporated into these volumes of Essays, was never large, but it was select, and it was constant. Among the hearers were some, who though, attracted by the beauty of character and manner, they were willing to hear the speaker through, always went away discontented. They were accustomed to an artificial method, whose scaffolding could easily be retraced, and desired an obvious sequence of logical inferences. They insisted there was nothing in what they had heard, because they could not give a clear account of its course and purport. They did not see that Pindar's odes might be very well arranged for their own purpose, and yet not bear translating into the methods of Mr. Locke.

Others were content to be benefitted by a good influence without a strict analysis of its means. "My wife says it is about the elevation of human nature, and so it seems to me;" was a fit reply to some of the critics. Many were satisfied to find themselves excited to congenial thought and nobler life, without an exact catalogue of the thoughts of the speaker.

Those who believed no truth could exist, unless encased by the burrs of opinion, went away utterly baffled. Sometimes they thought he was on their side, then presently would come something on the other. He really seemed to believe there were two sides to every subject, and even to intimate higher ground from which each might be seen to have an infinite number of sides or bearings, an impertinence not to be endured! The partisan heard but once and returned no more.

But some there were, simple souls, whose life had been, perhaps, without clear light, yet still a search after truth for its own sake, who were able to receive what followed on the suggestion of a subject in a natural manner, as a stream of thought. These recognized, beneath the veil of words, the still small voice of conscience, the vestal fires of lone religious hours, and the mild teachings of the summer woods.

The charm of the elocution, too, was great. His general manner was that of the reader, occasionally rising into direct address or invocation in passages where tenderness or majesty demanded more energy. At such times both eye and voice called on a remote future to give a worthy reply. A future which shall manifest more largely the universal soul as it was then manifest to this soul. The tone of the voice was a grave body tone, full and sweet rather than sonorous, yet flexible and haunted by many modulations, as even instruments of wood and brass seem to become after they have been long played on with skill and taste; how much more so the human voice! In the more expressive passages it uttered notes of silvery clearness, winning, yet still more commanding. The words uttered in those tones, floated awhile above us, then took root in the memory like winged seed.

In the union of an even rustic plainness with lyric inspirations, religious dignity with philosophic calmness, keen sagacity in details with boldness of view, we saw what brought to mind the early poets and legislators of Greece—men who taught their fellows to plow and avoid moral evil, sing hymns to the gods and watch the metamorphoses of nature. Here in civic Boston was such a man—one who could see man in his original grandeur and his original childishness, rooted in simple nature, raising to the heavens the brow and eyes of a poet.

And these lectures seemed not so much lectures as grave didactic poems, theogonies, perhaps, adorned by odes when some Power was in question whom the poet had best learned to serve, and with eclogues wisely portraying in familiar tongue the duties of man to man and "harmless animals."

Such was the attitude in which the speaker appeared to that portion of the audience who have remained permanently attached to him.—They value his words as the signets of reality; receive his influence as a help and incentive to a nobler discipline than the age, in its general aspect, appears to require; and do not fear to anticipate the verdict of posterity in claiming for him the honors of greatness, and, in some respects, of a Master.

In New-England he thus formed for himself a class of readers, who rejoice to study in his books what they already know by heart. For, though the thought has become familiar, its beautiful garb is always fresh and bright in hue.

A similar circle of like-minded the books must and do form for themselves, though with a movement less directly powerful, as more distant from its source.

The Essays have also been obnoxious to many charges. To that of obscurity, or want of perfect articulation. Of 'Euphuism,' as an excess of fancy in proportion to imagination, and an inclination, at times, to subtlety at the expense of strength, has been styled. The human heart complains of inadequacy, either in the nature or experience of the writer, to represent its full vocation and its deeper needs. Sometimes it speaks of this want as "under-development" or a want of expansion which may yet be remedied; sometimes doubts whether "in this mansion there be either hall or portal to receive the loftier of the Passions." Sometimes the soul is deified at the expense of nature, then again nature at that of man, and we are not quite sure that we can make a true harmony by balance of the statements.—This writer has never written one good work, if such a work be one where the whole commands more attention than the parts. If such an one be produced only where, after an accumulation of materials, fire enough be applied to fuse the whole into one new substance. This second series is superior in this respect to the former, yet in no one essay is the main stress so obvious as to produce on the mind the harmonious effect of a noble river or a tree in full leaf. Single passages and sentences engage our attention too much in proportion. These essays, it has been justly said, tire like a string of mosaics or a house built of medals. We miss what we expect in the work of the great poet, or the great philosopher, the liberal air of all the zones: the glow, uniform yet various in tint, which is given to a body by free circulation of the heart's blood from the hour of birth. Here is, undoubtedly, the man of ideas, but we want the ideal man also; want the heart and genius of human life to interpret it, and here our satisfaction is not so perfect. We doubt this friend raised himself too early to the perpendicular and did not lie along the ground long enough to hear the secret whispers of our parent life. We could wish he might be thrown by conflicts on the lap of mother earth, to see if he would not rise again with added powers.

All this we may say, but it cannot excuse us from benefitting by the great gifts that have been given, and assigning them their due place.

Some painters paint on a red ground. And this color may be supposed to represent the ground work most immediately congenial to most men, as it is the color of blood and represents human vitality. The figures traced upon it are instinct with life in its fulness and depth.

But other painters paint on a gold ground. And a very different, but no less natural, because also a celestial beauty, is given to their works who choose for their foundation the color of the sunbeam, which nature has preferred for her most precious product, and that which will best bear the test of purification, gold.

If another simile may be allowed, another no less apt is at hand. Wine is the most brilliant and intense expression of the powers of earth.—It is her potable fire, her answer to the sun. It exhilarates, it inspires, but then it is liable to fever and intoxicate too the careless partaker.

Mead was the chosen drink of the Northern gods. And this essence of the honey of the mountain bee was not thought unworthy to revive the souls of the valiant who had left their bodies on the fields of strife below.

Nectar should combine the virtues of the ruby wine, the golden mead, without their defects or dangers.

Two high claims our writer can vindicate on the attention of his contemporaries. One from his sincerity. You have his thought just as it found place in the life of his own soul. Thus, however near or relatively distant its approximation to absolute truth, its action on you cannot fail to be healthful. It is a part of the free air.

He belongs to that band of whom there may be found a few in every age, and who now in known human history may be counted by hundreds, who worship the one God only, the God of Truth. They worship, not saints, nor creeds, nor churches, nor reliques, nor idols in any form. The mind is kept open to truth, and life only valued as a tendency toward it. This must be illustrated by acts and words of love, purity and intelligence. Such are the salt of the earth; let the minutest crystal of that salt be willingly by us held in solution.

The other is through that part of his life, which, if sometimes obstructed or chilled by the critical intellect, is yet the prevalent and the main source of his power. It is that by which he imprisons his hearer only to free him again as a "liberating God" (to use his own words). But indeed let us use them altogether, for none other, ancient or modern, can more worthily express how, making present to us the courses and destinies of nature, he invests himself with her serenity and animates us with her joy.

"Poetry was all written before time was, and whenever we are so finely organized that we can penetrate into that region where the air is music, we hear those primal warblings, and attempt to write them down, but we lose ever and anon a word, or a verse, and substitute something of our own, and thus miswrite the poem. The men of more delicate ear write down these cadences more faithfully, and these transcripts, though imperfect, become the songs of the nations."

"As the eyes of Lyncæus were said to see through the earth, so the poet turns the world to glass, and shows us all things in their right series and procession. For, through that better perception, he stands one step nearer to things, and sees the flowing or metamorphosis; perceives that thought is multiform; that within the form of every creature is a force impelling it to ascend into a higher form; and following with his eyes the life, uses the forms which express that life, and so the speech flows with the flowing of nature."

Thus have we in a brief and unworthy manner indicated some views of these books. The only true criticism of these, or any good books, may be gained by making them the companions of our lives. Does every accession of knowledge or a juster sense of beauty make us prize them more? Then they are good, indeed, and more immortal than mortal. Let that test be applied to these; essays which will lead to great and complete poems—somewhere.

Note

1   Ralph Waldo Emerson, *The Journals and Miscellaneous Notebooks of Ralph Waldo Emerson*, ed. William H. Gilman, et al. (Cambridge: Belknap Press of Harvard University Press, 1975), Vol. XI, 258 (1850).

Amos Bronson Alcott (1799–1888)

An education and social reformer who was a longtime friend and sometimes
neighbor of Emerson's, Alcott taught at the Temple School in Boston (1834–1838),
along with Elizabeth Palmer Peabody and Margaret Fuller, and later reflected
on his experiences teaching young children in two works: Records of a School:
Exemplifying the General Principles of Spiritual Culture *and* Conversations with
Children on the Gospels *(in two volumes, 1836, 1837). In "Psyche," Alcott wrote of*
his experience teaching his four daughters, which Emerson tried, apparently with
difficulty, to help him edit into publishable form. Alcott contributed to The Dial,
though with work that Fuller was not pleased with. After a visit to England (funded
by Emerson), Alcott became friends with Charles Lane who was already a fan of
Alcott's educational initiatives. The following year, Lane purchased land in Harvard
Massachusetts where the men, their families, and others could join a utopian
experiment called Fruitlands. Unlike George Ripley's Brook Farm, the members of
the Fruitlands "consociate family" isolated themselves; the community that peaked at
thirteen members ended after seven months. One of Alcott's daughters, Louisa May,
later wrote Transcendental Wild Oats *(1873) based on her months at Fruitlands. In*
the year of Emerson's death, Alcott published Ralph Waldo Emerson, Philosopher
and Seer: An Estimate of his Character and Genius in Prose and Verse *that*
included an essay "without material alteration or addition"—reprinted below—that
he had presented to Emerson on his birthday in 1865.

Essay

Amos Bronson Alcott

The ancients entertained noble notions of the poet. He was an enthusiast and a
rhapsodist. His work was done in surprise and delight. And all good epic poets were
thought to compose, not by choice, but by inspiration; and so, too, the good lyric poets
drew, they tell us, "from fountains flowing with nectar, and gathered flowers from the
gardens and glades of the Muses; they, like bees, being ever on the wing. For the poet
was a thing light-winged and sacred, unable to compose until he became inspired, and
the imagination was no longer under his control. For as long as he was in complete
possession of it, he was unable to compose verses or to speak oracularly." And hence
all noble numbers were credited by them, not to the poet whom they knew, but to the
Power working in and through him, and making him the most delighted of auditors

whenever he chanted his verses, because he did not conceive them to be his. He was the Voice, the favored of the Nine. Hence the value they set upon discipline as the means of poetic divination. The poet, they conceived, must be most virtuous. It was essential to his accomplishment that he be chaste, that he be gentle, that he be noble in his generation, that his endowment be older than himself; that he descend from a race of pure souls,—bring centuries of culture in his descent among men, ideas of ages in his brain,—enabling him to conceive by instinct, and speak his experiences unconsciously, as a child opens his lips, in his most rapturous accents. Therefore, any pretence of ownership in the gift was esteemed an impiety. For a prayer, a song, a tender tone, a glance of the eye, all those magnetic attractions known to friendship, had a like ancestry; were ours personally, primarily, as we became worthy of being their organs.

Is it an egotism in us to claim for New England and for a contemporary of ours parts and antecedents like these? or shall such endowments, admirable always, and awakening enthusiasm, be the less prized when represented in a countryman of ours, and when we have so frequently partaken of the pleasure which his books, his lectures especially, excite? I allude, of course, to Emerson. A rhapsodist by genius, and the chief of his class, his utterances are ever a surprise as they are a delight to his audiences; select though these are, and not all unworthy of him.

Hear how Goethe describes him, where in his letters to Schiller, he calls the rhapsodist—

A wise man, who, in calm thoughtfulness, shows what has happened; his discourse aiming less to excite than to calm his auditors, in order that they shall listen to him with contentment and long. He apportions the interest equally, because it is not in his power to balance a too lively impression. He grasps backwards and forwards at pleasure. He is followed, because he has only to do with the imagination, which of itself produces images, and up to a certain degree, it is indifferent what kind he calls up. He does not appear to his auditors, but recites, as it were behind a curtain; so there is a total abstraction from himself, and it seems to them as though they heard only the voice of the Muses.

See our Ion standing there,—his audience, his manuscript, before him,—himself an auditor, as he reads, of the Genius sitting behind him, and to whom he defers, eagerly catching the words,—the words,—as if the accents were first reaching his ears too, and entrancing alike oracle and auditor. We admire the stately sense, the splendor of diction, and are surprised as we listen. Even his hesitancy between the delivery of his periods, his perilous passages from paragraph to paragraph of manuscript, we have almost learned to like, as if he were but sorting his keys meanwhile for opening his cabinets; the spring of locks following, himself seeming as eager as any of us to get sight of his specimens, as they come forth from their proper drawers ; and we wait willingly till his gem is out glittering; admire the setting, too, scarcely less than the jewel itself. The magic minstrel and speaker! whose rhetoric, voiced as by organ-stops, delivers the sentiment from his breast in cadences peculiar to himself; now hurling it forth on the ear, echoing; then, as his mood and matter invite it, dying like

> Music of mild lutes
> Or silver coated flutes,
> Or the concealing winds that can convey
> Never their tone to the rude ear of day.

He works his miracles with it, as Hermes did, his voice conducting the sense alike to eye and ear by its lyrical movement and refraining melody. So his compositions affect us, not as logic linked in syllogisms, but as voluntaries rather, or preludes, in which one is not tied to any design of air, but may vary his key or note at pleasure, as if improvised without any particular scope of argument; each period, each paragraph, being a perfect note in itself, however it may chance chime with its accompaniments in the piece; as a waltz of wandering stars, a dance of Hesperus with Orion. His rhetoric dazzles by circuits, contrasts, antitheses; Imagination, as in all sprightly minds, being his wand of power. He comes along his own paths, too, and always in his own fashion. What though he build his piers downwards from the firmament to the tumbling tides, and so throw his radiant span across the fissures of his argument, and himself pass over the frolic arches,—Ariel-wise,—is the skill less admirable, the masonry less secure for its singularity? So his books are best read as irregular writings, in which the sentiment is, by his enthusiasm, transfused throughout the piece, telling on the mind in cadences of a current under-song, and giving the impression of a connected whole—which it seldom is,—such is the rhapsodist's cunning in its structure and delivery.

The highest compliment we can pay to the scholar is that of having edified and instructed us, we know not how, unless by the pleasure his words have given us. Conceive how much the Lyceum owes to his presence and teachings; how great the debt of many to him for their hour's entertainment. His, if any one's, let the institution pass into history,— since his art, more than another's, has clothed it with beauty, and made it the place of popular resort, our purest organ of intellectual entertainment for New England and the Western cities. And, besides this, its immediate value to his auditors everywhere, it has been serviceable in ways they least suspect; most of his works, having had their first readings on its platform, were here fashioned and polished in good part, like Plutarch's Morals, to become the more acceptable to readers of his published books.

And is not the omen auspicious, that just now, during these winter evenings, at the opening of this victorious year, *his* Sundays have come round again; the metropolis, eager, as of old, to hear his words. Does it matter what topic he touches? He adorns all with a severe sententious beauty, a freshness and sanction next to that of godliness, if not that in spirit and effect.

> The princely mind, that can
> Teach man to keep a God in man;
> And when wise poets would search out to see
> Good men, behold them all in thee.

'Tis near thirty years since his first book, entitled *Nature*, was printed. Then followed volumes of Essays, Poems, Orations, Addresses and during all the intervening period down to the present, he has read briefs of his lectures through a wide range, from Canada to the Capitol; in most of the Free States; in the large cities, East and West, before large audiences; in the smallest towns and to the humblest companies. Such has been his appeal to the mind of his countrymen, such his acceptance by them. He has read lectures in the principal cities of England also. A poet, speaking to individuals as few others can speak, and to persons in their privileged moments, he must be heard as none others are. The more personal he is, the more prevailing, if not the more popular.

Because the poet, accosting the heart of man, speaks to him personally, he is one with all mankind. And if he speak eloquent words, these words must be cherished by mankind,—belonging as they do to the essence of man's personality, and, partaking of the qualities of his Creator, they are of spiritual significance. While, in so far as he is individual only,—unlike any other man,—his verses address special aptitudes in separate persons ; and he will belong, not to all times, but to one time only, and will pass away,—except to those who delight in that special manifestation of his gifts.

Now were Emerson less individual, according to our distinction, that is, more personal and national,—as American as America,—then were his influence so much the more diffusive, and he the Priest of the Faith earnest hearts are seeking. Not that religion is wanting here in New England; but that its seekers are, for the most part, too exclusive to seek it independent of some human leader,—religion being a personal oneness with the Person of Persons; a partaking of Him by putting off the individualism which distracts and separates man from man. Hence differing sects, persuasions, creeds, bibles, for separate peoples, prevail all over the earth; religions, being still many, not one and universal, not personal; similar only as yet in their differences. Still the religious sentiment, in binding all souls to the Personal One, makes the many partake of him in degrees lesser or greater. Thus far, the poets in largest measure; mankind receiving through them its purest revelations, they having been its inspired oracles and teachers from the beginning till now. The Sacred Books,—are not these Poems in spirit, if not in form? their authors inspired bards of divinity? Meant for all men in all ages and states, they appeal forever to the springing faiths of every age, and so are permanent and perennial, as the heart itself and its everlasting hopes.

See how the Christian Theism, for instance, has held itself high above most men's heads till now; its tender truths above all cavil and debate by their transcendent purity and ideal beauty! How these truths still survive in all their freshness, keeping verdant the Founder's memory! and shall to distant generations; churches, peoples, persons, a widening Christendom, flourishing or fading as they spring forth, or fall away from this living stem.

> The Son of Man, at last the son of woman,
> Brother of all men, and the Prince of Peace,
> Grafts, on the solemn valor of the Roman,
> *Fresh Saxon service,* and the wit of Greece.

Now, am I saying that our poet is inspiring this fresher Faith? Certainly I mean to be so understood; he, the chiefest of its bards and heralds. Not spoken always, 'tis implied, nevertheless, in his teachings; defective, it is admitted, as colored by his temperament, which trenches on Personal Theism not a little by the stress he lays on Nature, on Fate; yet more nearly complementing the New England Puritanism than aught we have, and coming nearest to satisfying the aspirations of our time.

But it were the last thought of his, this conceiving himself the oracle of any Faith, the leader of any school, any sect of religionists. His genius is ethical, literary; he speaks to the moral sentiments through the imagination, insinuating the virtues so, as poets and moralists of his class are wont. The Sacred Class, the Priests, differ in this,— they address the moral sentiment directly, thus enforcing the sanctions of personal righteousness, and celebrating moral excellence in prophetic strain.

'Tis everything to have a true believer in the world, dealing with men and matters as if they were divine in idea and real in fact; meeting persons and events at a glance directly, not at a million removes, and so passing fair and fresh into life and literature, the delight and ornament of the race.

Pure literatures are personal inspirations, springing fresh from the Genius of a people. They are original; their first fruits being verses, essays, tales, biographies— productions as often of obscure as of illustrious persons. And such, so far as we have a literature, is ours. Of the rest, how much is foreign both in substance and style, and might have been produced elsewhere! His, I consider original and American; the earliest, purest our country has produced,—best answering the needs of the American mind. Consider how largely our letters have been enriched by his contributions. Consider, too, the change his views have wrought in our methods of thinking; how he has won over the bigot, the unbeliever, at least to tolerance and moderation, if not to acknowledgment, by his circumspection and candor of statement.

> His shining armor
> A perfect charmer;
> Even the hornets of divinity
> Allow him a brief space,
> And his thought has a place
> Upon the well-bound library's chaste shelves,
> Where man of various wisdom rarely delves.

Am I extravagant in believing that our people are more indebted to his teachings than to any other person who has spoken or written on his themes during the last twenty years,—are more indebted than they know, becoming still more so? and that, as his thoughts pass into the brain of the coming generation, it will be seen that we have had at least one mind of home growth, if not independent of the old country? I consider his genius the measure and present expansion of the American mind. And it is plain that he is to be read and prized for years to come. Poet and moralist, he has beauty and truth for all men's edification and delight. His works are studies. And any youth of free senses and fresh affections shall be spared years of tedious toil,—in which wisdom and fair learning are, for the most part, held at arm's length, planet's width, from his grasp,—by graduating from this college. His books are surcharged with vigorous thoughts, a sprightly wit. They abound in strong sense, happy humor, keen criticisms, subtile insights, noble morals, clothed in a chaste and manly diction, and fresh with the breath of health and progress.

We characterize and class him with the moralists who surprise us with an accidental wisdom, strokes of wit, felicities of phrase,—as Plutarch, Seneca, Epictetus, Marcus Antoninus, Saadi, Montaigne, Bacon, Sir Thomas Browne, Goethe, Coleridge,—with whose delightful essays, notwithstanding all the pleasure they give us, we still plead our disappointment at not having been admitted to the closer intimacy which these loyal leaves had with their owner's mind before torn from his notebook; jealous, even, at not having been taken into his confidence in the editing itself.

We read, never as if he were the dogmatist, but a fair-speaking mind, frankly declaring his convictions, and committing these to our consideration, hoping we may have thought like things ourselves; oftenest, indeed, taking this for granted as he wrote. There is nothing of the spirit of proselyting, but the delightful deference ever to our free sense and right of opinion. He might take for his motto the sentiment of Henry More, where, speaking of himself, he says: "Exquisite disquisition begets diffidence; diffidence in knowledge, humility; humility, good manners and meek conversation. For my part, I desire no man to take anything I write or speak upon trust without canvassing, and would be thought rather to propound than to assert what I have here or elsewhere written or spoken. But continually to have expressed my diffidence in the very tractates and colloquies themselves, had been languid and ridiculous."

Then he has chosen a proper time and manner for saying his good things; has spoken to almost every great interest as it rose. Nor has he let the good opportunities pass unheeded, or failed to make them for himself. He has taken discretion along as his constant attendant and ally; has shown how the gentlest temper ever deals the surest blows. His method is that of the sun against his rival for the cloak, and so he is free from any madness of those, who, forgetting the strength of the solar ray, go blustering against men's prejudices, as if the wearers would run at once against these winds of opposition into their arms for shelter. What higher praise can we bestow on any one than to say of him, that he harbors another's prejudices with a hospitality so cordial as to give him, for the time, the sympathy next best to, if, indeed, it be not edification in, charity itself? For what disturbs and distracts mankind more than the uncivil manners that cleave man from man? Yet for his amendment letters, love, Christianity, were all given!

How different is he in temper and manners from Carlyle, with whom he is popularly associated! but who, for the most part, is the polemic, the sophist, the scorner: whose books, opened anywhere, show him berating the wrong he sees, but seeing, shows never the means of removing. Ever the same melancholy advocacy of work to be done under the dread master; force of stroke, the right to rule and be ruled, ever the dismal burden. Doomsday books are all save his earliest—Rhadamanthus sitting and the arbiter. He rides his Leviathan as fiercely as did his countryman, Hobbes, and can be as truculent and abusive; the British Taurus, and a mad one. Were he not thus possessed and fearfully in earnest, we should take him for the harlequin he seems, nor see the sorrowing sadness playing off its load in this grotesque mirth, this scornful irony of his; he painting in spite of himself his portraits in the warmth of admiration, the fire of wrath, and giving mythology for history; all the while distorting the facts into grimace in his grim moods. Yet, what breadth of perspective, strength of outline! the realism how appalling, the egotism how enormous,—all history showing in the background of the one figure, Carlyle. Burns, Goethe, Richter, Mira-beau, Luther, Cromwell, Frederick,—all dashed from his flashing pen, heads of himself, alike in their unlikeness, prodigiously individual, willful, some of them monstrous; all Englishmen with their egregious prejudices and pride; no patience, no repose in any. He still brandishes his truncheon through his pages with an adroitness that renders it unsafe for any, save the few that wield weapons of celestial temper, to do battle against this Abaddon. Silenced he will not be; talking terribly against all talking but his own; agreeing, disagreeing, all the same; he, the Jove, permitting none, none to mount Olympus, till the god deigns silence and invites. Curious to see him, his chin aloft, the pent thunders rolling, lightnings darting from under the bold brows, words that tell of the wail within, accents not meant for music, yet made lyrical in the cadences of his Caledonian refrain ; his mirth mad as Lear's, his humor as willful as the wind's. Not himself is approachable by himself even. And Emerson is the one only American deserving a moment's consideration in his eyes. Him he honors and owns the better, giving him the precedence and the manners:

> Had wolves and lions seen but thee,
> They must have paused to learn civility.

Of Emerson's books I am not here designing to speak critically, but of his genius and personal influence rather. Yet, in passing, I may say, that his book of "Traits" deserves to be honored as one in which England, Old and New, may take honest pride, as being the liveliest portraiture of British genius and accomplishments,—a book, like Tacitus, to be quoted as a masterpiece of historical painting, and perpetuating the New Englander's fame with that of his race. 'Tis a victory of eyes over hands, a triumph of ideas. Nor, in my judgment, has there been for some time any criticism of a people so characteristic and complete. It remains for him to do like justice to New England. Not a metaphysician, and rightly discarding any claims to systematic thinking; a poet in spirit, if not always in form; the consistent idealist, yet the realist none the less, he has illustrated the learning and thought of former times on the noblest themes, and come nearest of any to emancipating the mind of his own time from the errors and dreams of past ages.

> Why nibble longer there,
> Where nothing fresh ye find,
>   Upon those rocks?

Lo! meadows green and fair
Come pasture here your mind,
   Ye bleating flocks.

There is a virtuous curiosity felt by readers of remarkable books to learn something more of their author's literary tastes, habits and dispositions than these ordinarily furnish. Yet, to gratify this is a task as difficult as delicate, requiring a diffidency akin to that with which one would accost the author himself, and without which graceful armor it were impertinent for a friend even to undertake it. We may venture but a stroke or two here.

All men love the country who love mankind with a wholesome love, and have poetry and company in them. Our essayist makes good this preference. If city bred, he has been for the best part of his life a villager and countryman. Only a traveller at times professionally, he prefers home-keeping; is a student of the landscape; is no recluse misanthrope, but a lover of his neighborhood, of mankind, of rugged strength wherever found; liking plain persons, plain ways, plain clothes; prefers earnest people, hates egotists, shuns publicity, likes solitude, and knows its uses. He courts society as a spectacle not less than a pleasure, and so carries off the spoils. Delighting in the broadest views of men and things, he seeks all accessible displays of both for draping his thoughts and works. And how is his page produced? Is it imaginable that he conceives his piece as a whole, and then sits down to execute his task at a heat? Is not this imaginable rather, and the key to the comprehension of his works? Living for composition as few authors can, and holding company, studies, sleep, exercise, affairs, subservient to thought, his products are gathered as they ripen, and stored in his commonplaces; the contents transcribed at intervals, and classified. The order of ideas, of imagination, is observed in the arrangement, not that of logical sequence. You may begin at the last paragraph and read backwards. 'Tis Iris-built. Each period is self-poised; there may be a chasm of years between the opening passage and the last written, and there is endless time in the composition. Jewels all! separate stars. You may have them in a galaxy, if you like, or view them separate and apart. But every one knows that, if he take an essay or verses, however the writer may have pleased himself with the cunning workmanship, 'tis all cloud-fashioned, and there is no pathway for any one else. Cross as you can, or not cross, it matters not; you may climb or leap, move in circles, turn somersaults;

In sympathetic sorrow sweep the ground,

like his swallow in Merlin. Dissolving views, projects, vistas open wide and far,—yet earth, sky, realities all, not illusions. Here is substance, sod, sun; much fair weather in the seer as in his leaves. The whole quarternion of the seasons, the sidereal year, has been poured into these periods. Afternoon walks furnished the perspectives, rounded and melodized them. These good things have all been talked and slept over, meditated standing and sitting, read and polished in the utterance, submitted to all various tests, and, so accepted, they pass into print. Light fancies, dreams, moods, refrains, were set on foot, and sent jaunting about the fields, along wood-paths, by Walden shores, by hill and brook-sides,—to come home and claim their rank and honors too in his pages. Composed of surrounding matters, populous with thoughts, brisk with images, these books are wholesome, homelike, and could have been written only in New England, in Concord, and by our poet.

> Because I was content with these poor fields,
> Low, open meads, slender and sluggish streams,
> And found a home in haunts which others
>   scorned,
> The partial wood-gods overpaid my love,
> And granted me the freedom of their state;
> And in their secret senate have prevailed
> With the dear, dangerous lords that rule our life,
> Made moon and planets parties to their bond,
> And through my rock-like, solitary wont
> Shot million rays of thought and tenderness.
> For me, in showers, in sweeping showers, the
>   spring,
> Visits the valley;—break away the clouds,—
> I bathe in the morn's soft and silvered air,
> And loiter willing by yon loitering stream.
> Sparrows far off, and nearer, April's bird,
> Blue-coated, flying before from tree to tree,
> Courageous, sing a delicate overture
> To lead the tardy concert of the year.
> Onward and nearer rides the sun of May;
> And wide around, the marriage of the plants
> Is sweetly solemnized. Then flows amain
> The surge of summer's beauty ; dell and crag,
> Hollow and Jake, hillside, and pine arcade,
> Are touched with Genius. Yonder ragged cliff
> Has thousand faces in a thousand hours.
>
> . . . . The gentle deities
> Showed me the lore of colors and of sounds,
> The innumerable tenements of beauty,
> The miracle of generative force,
> Far-reaching concords of astronomy
> Felt in the plants and in the punctual birds;
> Better, the linked purpose of the whole,
> And, chiefest prize, found I true liberty

In the glad home plain-dealing nature gave.
The polite found me impolite; the great
Would mortify me, but in vain; for still
I am a willow of the wilderness,
Loving the wind that bent me. All my hurts
My garden spade can heal. A woodland walk,
A quest of river-grapes, a mocking thrush,
A wild-rose, or rock-loving columbine,
Salve my worst wounds.
For thus the wood-gods murmured in my ear:
'Dost love our manners? Canst thou silent lie?
Canst thou, thy pride forgot, like nature pass
Into the winter night's extinguished mood?
Canst thou shine now, then darkle,
And being latent feel thyself no less?
As, when the all-worshipped moon attracts the eye,
The river, hill, stems, foliage, are obscure;
Yet envies none, none are unenviable.'

I know of but one subtraction from the pleasure the reading of his books—shall I say his conversation?—gives me, his pains to be impersonal or discrete, as if he feared any the least intrusion of himself were an offence offered to self-respect the courtesy due to intercourse and authorship; thus depriving his page, his company, of attractions the great masters of both knew how to insinuate into their text and talk, without overstepping the bounds of social or literary decorum. What is more delightful than personal magnetism? 'Tis the charm of good fellowship as of good writing. To get and to give the largest measures of satisfaction, to fill ourselves with the nectar of select experiences, not without some intertinctures of egotism so charming in a companion, is what we seek in books of the class of his, as in their authors. We associate diffidence properly with learning, frankness with fellowship, and owe a certain blushing reverence to both. For though our companion be a bashful man,—and he is the worse if wanting this grace,—we yet wish him to be an enthusiast behind all reserves, and capable of abandonment sometimes in his books. I know how rare this genial humor is, this frankness of the blood, and how surpassing is the gift of good spirits, especially here in cold New England, where, for the most part,

Our virtues grow
Beneath our humors, and at seasons show.

And yet, under our east winds of reserve, there hides an obscure courtesy in the best natures, which neither temperament nor breeding can spoil. Sometimes manners the most distant are friendly foils for holding eager dispositions subject to the measure of right behavior. 'Tis not every New Englander that dares venture upon the frankness, the plain speaking, commended by the Greek poet.

> Caress me not with words, while far away
> Thy heart is absent, and thy feelings stray;
> But if thou love me with a faithful breast,
> Be that pure love with zeal sincere exprest;
> And if thou hate, the bold aversion show
> With open face avowed, and known my foe.

Fortunate the visitor who is admitted of a morning for the high discourse, or permitted to join the poet in his afternoon walks to Walden, the Cliffs, or elsewhere,—hours likely to be remembered, as unlike any others in his calendar of experiences. I may say, for me they have made ideas possible, by hospitalities given to a fellowship so enjoyable. Shall I describe them as sallies oftenest into the cloud-lands, into scenes and intimacies ever new? none the less novel nor remote than when first experienced; colloquies, in favored moments, on themes, perchance

> Of fate, free-will, foreknowledge absolute;

nor yet

> In wand'ring mazes lost,

as in Milton's page;

> But pathways plain through starry alcoves high,
> Or thence descending to the level plains.

Interviews, however, bringing their trail of perplexing thoughts, costing some days' duties, several nights' sleep oftentimes, to restore one to his place and poise for customary employment; half a dozen annually being full as many as the stoutest heads may well undertake without detriment.

Certainly safer not to venture without the sure credentials, unless one will have his pretensions pricked, his conceits reduced in their vague dimensions.

> Fools have no means to meet
> But by their feet.

But to the modest, the ingenuous, the gifted, welcome! Nor can any bearing be more poetic and polite than his to all such, to youth and accomplished women especially. I may not intrude farther than to say, that, beyond any I have known, his is a faith approaching to superstition concerning admirable persons; the divinity of friendship come down from childhood, and surviving yet in memory if not in expectation; the rumor of excellence of any sort, being like the arrival of a new gift to mankind, and he the first to proffer his recognition and hope. His affection for conversation, for clubs, is a lively intimation of the religion of fellowship. He, shall we say? if any, must have taken the census of the admirable people of his time, numbering as many among his friends, perhaps, as most living Americans; while he is already recognized as the representative mind of his country, to whom distinguished foreigners are especially commended on visiting us.

Extraordinary persons may be forgiven some querulousness about their company, when we remember that ordinary people often complain of theirs. Impossible for such to comprehend the scholar's code of civilities,—disposed as men are to hold all persons to their special standard. Yet dedicated to high labors, so much the more strict is the scholar with himself, as his hindrances are the less appreciable, and he has, besides, his own moods to humor.

Askest how long thou shalt stay,
Devastator of the day?
Heartily know,
When half-gods go,
The Gods arrive.

Companionableness comes by nature. We meet magically, and pass with sounding manners; else we encounter repulses, strokes of fate; temperament telling against temperament, precipitating us into vortices from which the nimblest finds no escape. We pity the person who shows himself unequal to such occasions; the scholar, for example, whose intellect is so exacting, so precise, that he cannot meet his company otherwise than critically; cannot descend through the senses or the sentiments to that common level where intercourse is possible with men; but we pity him the more, who, from caprice or confusion, can meet through these only. Still worse the case of him who can meet men neither as sentimentalist nor idealist, or, rather not at all in a human way. Intellect interblends with sentiment in the companionable mind, and wit with humor. We detain the flowing tide at the cost of lapsing out of perception into memory, into the limbo of fools. Excellent people wonder why they cannot meet and converse. They cannot,—no—their wits have ebbed away, and left them helpless. Why, but because of hostile temperaments, different states of animation? The personal magnetism finds no conductor, when one is individual, and the other individual no less. Individuals repel; persons meet; and only as one's personality is sufficiently overpowering to dissolve the other's individualism, can the parties flow together and become one. But individuals have no power of this sort. They are two, not one, perhaps many. Prisoned within themselves by reason of their egotism, like animals, they stand aloof; are separate even when they touch; are solitary in any company, having no company in themselves. But the free personal mind meets all, is apprehended by all; by the least cultivated, the most gifted; magnetizes all; is the spellbinder, the liberator of every one. We speak of sympathies, antipathies, fascinations, fates, for this reason.

Here we have the key to literary composition, to eloquence, to fellowship. Let us apply it, for the moment, to Emerson's genius. We forbear entering into the precincts of genesis, and complexions, wherein sleep the secrets of character and manners. Eloquent in trope and utterance when his vaulting intelligence frees itself for the instant, yet see his loaded eye, his volleyed period; jets of wit, sallies of sense, breaks, inconsequences, all betraying the pent personality from which his rare accomplishments have not yet liberated his gifts, nor given him unreservedly to the Muse and mankind.

Take his own account of the matter.

> When I was born,
> From all the seas of strength Fate filled a chalice,
> Saying: 'This be thy portion, child: this chalice,
> Less than a lily's, thou shalt daily draw
> From my great arteries,—not less nor more.'
> All substances the cunning chemist, Time,
> Melts down into the liquor of my life,—
> Friends, foes, joys, fortunes, beauty and disgust;
> And whether I am angry or content,
> Indebted or insulted, loved or hurt,
> All he distils into sidereal wine,
> And brims my little cup, heedless, alas!
> Of all he sheds, how little it will hold,
> How much runs over on the desert sands.
> If a new Muse draw me with splendid ray,
> And I uplift myself into its heaven,
> The needs of the first sight absorb my blood;
> And all the following hours of the day
> Drag a ridiculous age.
> To-day, when friends approach, and every hour
> Brings book, or star-bright scroll of Genius,
> The little cup will hold not a bead more,
> And all the costly liquor runs to waste;
> Nor gives the jealous lord one diamond drop
> So to be husbanded for poorer days.
> Why need I volumes, if one word suffice?
> Why need I galleries, when a pupil's draught,
> After the master's sketch, fills and o'erfills
> My apprehension? Why seek Italy,
> Who cannot circumnavigate the sea
> Of thoughts and things at home, but still adjourn
> The nearest matter for a thousand days?

Plutarch tells us that of old they were wont to call men φῶτα, which imports light, not only for the vehement desire man has to know, but to communicate also. And the

Platonists fancied that the gods, being above men, had something whereof man did not partake, pure intellect and knowledge, and thus kept on their way quietly. The beasts, being below men, had something whereof man had less, sense and growth, so they lived quietly in their way. While man had something in him whereof neither gods nor beasts had any trace, which gave him all the trouble, and made all the confusion in the world,—and that was egotism and opinion.

A finer discrimination of gifts might show that Genius ranges through this threefold dominion, partaking in turn of each essence and degree.

Was our poet planted so fast in intellect, so firmly rooted in the mind, so dazzled with light, yet so cleft withal by duplicity of gifts, that, thus forced to traverse the mid-world of contrast and contrariety, he was ever glancing forth from his coverts at life as reflected through his dividing prism,—resident never long in the tracts he surveyed, yet their persistent Muse nevertheless? And so, housed in the Mind, and thence sallying forth in quest of his game, whether of persons or things, he was the Mercury, the merchantman of ideas to his century. Nor was he left alone in life and thinking. Beside him stood his townsman {Thoreau}, whose sylvan intelligence, fast rooted in sense and Nature, was yet armed with a sagacity, a subtlety and strength, that penetrated while divining the essences of the creatures and things he studied, and of which he seemed both Atlas and Head.

Forcible protestants against the materialism of their own, as of preceding times, these masterly Idealists substantiated beyond all question their right to the empires they swayed,—the rich estates of an original genius.

Herman Melville (1819–1891)

Author of Moby-Dick; or, the Whale, *and perhaps the most sublime of American writers, Melville admired Emerson but did not claim him for a mentor or an advocate. "Nay, I do not oscillate in Emerson's rainbow," Melville remarked in a letter to his friend Evert Duyckinck (March 3, 1849)—an allusion to a satirical cartoon of Emerson swinging in an inverted rainbow, published in Horace Greeley's* New-York Tribune *on February 6th—the day after Emerson delivered a lecture from his series* Mind and Manners of the Nineteenth Century, *likely "Natural Aristocracy," which Melville attended. For his part in the audience, Melville was "very agreeably disappointed"—that is to say, pleased—by what Emerson said since it diverged so widely from the writer reputed to be "full of transcendentalisms, myths, & oracular gibberish." "I have heard Emerson since I have been here," Melville wrote again to Duyckinck, and concluded: "Say what they will, he's a great man" (February 24, 1849). Both of these letters are reproduced here, along with a third addressed to his father in law, Lemuel Shaw, written by Melville ahead of sailing for England on October 11, 1849; it appears that Shaw never solicited the requested letters on his son in law's behalf. During his travels, Melville did not meet Carlyle. For further inquiry into Melville's reception of Emerson, see in this volume William Braswell's "Melville as a Critic of Emerson."*

Letters to Evert Duyckinck and Lemuel Shaw

Herman Melville

Feb 24th [1849, Boston]

Dear Duyckinck

Thank you for satisfying my curiosity. Mr Butler's a genius, but between you & me, I have a presentiment that he never will surprise me more.—I have been passing my time very pleasurably here. But chiefly in lounging on a sofa (a la the poet Grey) & reading Shakspeare. It is an edition in glorious great type, every letter whereof is a soldier, & the top of every "t" like a musket barrel. Dolt & ass that I am I have lived more than 29 years, & until a few days ago, never made close acquaintance with the divine William. Ah, he's full of sermons-on-the-mount, and gentle, aye, almost as Jesus. I take such men to be inspired. I fancy that this moment Shakspeare in heaven ranks with Gabriel Raphael and Michael. And if another Messiah ever comes twill be in Shakespere's person.—I am mad to think how minute a cause has prevented me hitherto from reading Shakspeare. But until now, every copy that was come-atable to me, happened to be in a vile small print unendurable to my eyes which are tender as young sparrows. But chancing to fall in with this glorious edition, I now exult over it, page after page.—

I have heard Emerson since I have been here. Say what they will, he's a great man. Mrs [Fanny Kemble] Butler too I have heard at her Readings. She makes a glorious Lady Macbeth, but her Desdemona seems like a boarding school miss.—She's so unfemininely masculine that had she not, on unimpeachable authority, borne children, I should be curious to learn the result of a surgical examination of her person in private. The Lord help Butler—not the poet—I marvel not he seeks being amputated off from his matrimonial half.

My respects to Mrs Duyckinck & your brother

Yours
H Melville

Evert A Duyckinck Esq

Mount Vernon Street
Saturday, [March] 3d [1849, Boston]

Nay, I do not oscillate in Emerson's rainbow, but prefer rather to hang myself in mine own halter than swing in any other man's swing. Yet I think Emerson is more than a brilliant fellow. Be his stuff begged, borrowed, or stolen, or of his own domestic manufacture he is an uncommon man. Swear he is a humbug—then is he no common humbug. Lay it down that had not Sir Thomas Browne lived, Emerson would not have mystified—I will answer, that had not Old Zack's father begot him, Old Zack would never have been the hero of Palo Alto. The truth is that we are all sons, grandsons, or nephews or great-nephews of those who go before us. No one is his own sire.—I was very agreeably disappointed in Mr Emerson. I had heard of him as full of transcendentalisms, myths & oracular gibberish; I had only glanced at a book of his once in Putnam's store—that was all I knew of him, till I heard him lecture.—To my surprise, I found him quite intelligible, tho' to say truth, they told me that that night he was unusually plain.—Now, there is a something about every man elevated above mediocrity, which is, for the most part, instinctively perceptible. This I see in Mr Emerson. And, frankly, for the sake of the argument, let us call him a fool;—then had I rather be a fool than a wise man.—I love all men who *dive.* Any fish can swim near the surface, but it takes a great whale to go down stairs five miles or more; & if he dont attain the bottom, why, all the lead in Galena can't fashion the plummet that will. I'm not talking of Mr Emerson now—but of the whole corps of thought-divers, that have been diving & coming up again with blood-shot eyes since the world began.

I could readily see in Emerson, notwithstanding his merit, a gaping flaw. It was, the insinuation, that had he lived in those days when the world was made, he might have offered some valuable suggestions. These men are all cracked right across the brow. And never will the pullers-down be able to cope with the builders-up. And this pulling down is easy enough—a keg of powder blew up Brock's Monument—but the man who applied the match, could not, alone, build such a pile to save his soul from the shark-maw of the Devil. But enough of this Plato who talks thro' his nose. To one of your habits of thought, I confess that in my last, I seemed, but only *seemed* irreverent. And do not think, my boy, that because I impulsively broke forth in jubilations over Shakspeare, that, therefore, I am of the number of the *snobs* who burn their tuns of rancid fat at his shrine. No, I would stand afar off & alone, & burn some pure Palm oil, the product of some overtopping trunk.

—I would to God Shakspeare had lived later, & promenaded in Broadway. Not that I might have had the pleasure of leaving my card for him at the Astor, or made merry with him over a bowl of the fine Duyckinck punch; but that the muzzle which all men wore on their souls in the Elizebethan day, might not have intercepted Shakspere's full articulations. For I hold it a verity, that even Shakspeare, was not a frank man to the uttermost. And, indeed, who in this intolerant Universe is, or can be? But the Declaration of Independence makes a difference.—There, I have driven my horse so hard that I have made my inn before sundown. I was going to say something more—It was this.—You complain that Emerson tho' a denizen of the land of gingerbread, is above munching, a plain cake in company of jolly fellows, & swiging off his ale like you & me. Ah, my dear sir, that's his misfortune, not his fault. His belly, sir, is in his chest, & his brains descend down into his neck, & offer an obstacle to a draught of ale or a mouthful of cake. But here I am. Good bye—

H. M.

Monday Sept 10th [1849, New York]

My Dear Sir—In writing you the other day concerning the letters of introduction, I forgot to say, that could you conveniently procure me one from Mr Emerson to Mr Carlyle, I should be obliged to you.—We were concerned to hear that you were not entirely well, some days ago; but I hope you will bring the intelligence of your better health along with you, when you come here on that promised visit, upon which you set out the day after tomorrow. Lizzie is most anxiously expecting you—but Malcolm seems to await the event with the utmost philosophy.—The weather here at present is exceedingly agreeable—quite cool, & in the morning, bracing.

My best remembrances to Mrs Shaw & all.

Most Sincerely Yours
H Melville

If, besides a letter to Mr Carlyle, Mr Emerson could give you *other* letters, I should be pleased.

The Board of Health have ceased making reports—the Cholera having almost entirely departed from the city.

Theodore Parker (1810–1860)

A graduate of Harvard Divinity School in 1836, Parker was deeply sympathetic to and inspired by Emerson's Address in 1838—a speech that ignited diametric responses from the religious community and led to Emerson's twenty-nine year exile from his alma mater. Parker became part of the wider circle of Transcendentalists, maintained friendships with Bronson Alcott and William Henry Channing, and was closely linked to various reform movements, including abolition, women's rights, and educational reform. He authored a landmark text that antagonized established religious orthodoxy, "A Discourse on the Permanent and Transitory in Christianity" (1841), which echoes some claims and sentiments from Emerson's "The Lord's Supper" (1832). In 1847 Parker founded the Massachusetts Quarterly Review, *and in the March 1850 issue endeavored to offer a lengthy critical assessment of Emerson's work in the context of New England Transcendentalism, including questions about American intellectual identity and Emerson's contribution to it. In his effort to provide a critical review of Emerson's writing between* Nature *(1836) and* Representative Men *(1850), Parker quotes liberally, and there is much to learn not just from what he selects—what Parker might put in his own commonplace book—but that he must choose from first editions, which in turn reveal occasional differences from our familiar versions. Parker's more-than-ample quotations also provide a picture of a certain inductive method of literary criticism, where one makes a case not through paraphrase but through the artful ordering, arrangement, and display of gathered examples from source texts. In the excerpt below, drawn mainly from the beginning and end of the essay, we find Parker addressing the style of Emerson's writing—a topic that is by 1850 already a hallmark of serious criticism on his prose and his intellectual credentials.*

The Writings of Ralph Waldo Emerson

Theodore Parker

{...} It is now almost fourteen years since Mr. Emerson published his first book: *Nature.* A beautiful work it was, and will be deemed for many a year to come. In this old world of literature, with more memory than wit, with much tradition and little invention, with more fear than love, and a great deal of criticism upon very little poetry, there came forward this young David, a shepherd, but to be a king, "with his garlands and singing robes about him"; one note upon his new and fresh-strung lyre was "worth a thousand men." Men were looking for something original, they always are; when it came some said it thundered, others that an angel had spoke. How men wondered at the little book! It took nearly twelve years to sell the five hundred copies of *Nature*. Since that time Mr. Emerson has said much, and if he has not printed many books, at least has printed much; some things far surpassing the first essay, in richness of material, in perfection of form, in continuity of thought; but nothing which has the same youthful freshness, and the same tender beauty as this early violet, blooming out of Unitarian and Calvinistic sand or snow. *Poems* and *Essays* of a later date are there, which show that he has had more time and woven it into life; works which present us with thought deeper, wider, richer, and more complete, but not surpassing the simplicity and loveliness of that maiden flower of his poetic spring.

We know how true it is, that a man cannot criticise what he cannot comprehend, nor comprehend either a man or a work greater than himself. Let him get on a Quarterly never so high, it avails him nothing; "pyramids are pyramids in vales," and emmets are emmets even in a Review. Critics often afford an involuntary proof of this adage, yet grow no wiser by the experience. Few of our tribe can make the simple shrift of the old Hebrew poet, and say, "*we* have not exercised ourselves in great matters, nor in things too high for *us*." Sundry Icarian critics have we seen, wending their wearying way on waxen wing to overtake the eagle flight of Emerson; some of them have we known getting near enough to see a fault, to overtake a feather falling from his wing, and with that tumbling to give name to a sea, if one cared to notice to what depth they fell.

Some of the criticisms on Mr. Emerson, transatlantic and cisatlantic, have been very remarkable, not to speak more definitely. "What of this new book?" said Mr. Public to the reviewer, who was not "seized and tied down to judge," but of his own free will stood up and answered: "Oh! 'tis out of all plumb, my lord—quite an irregular thing! not one of the angles at the four corners is a right angle. I had my rule and compasses, my lord, in my pocket. And for the poem; your lordship bid me look at it—upon taking the length, breadth, height, and depth of it, and trying them at home, upon an exact scale of Bossu's—they are out, my lord, in every one of their dimensions."

Oh, gentle reader, we have looked on these efforts of our brother critics not without pity. There is an excellent bird, terrene, marine, and semi-aerial; a broad-footed bird, broad-beaked, broad-backed, broad-tailed; a notable bird she is, and a long-lived; a useful bird, once indispensable to writers, as furnishing the pen, now frutiful in many a hint. But when she undertakes to criticise the music of the thrush, or the movement of the humming-bird, why, she oversteps the modesty of her nature, and if she essays the flight of the eagle—she is fortunate if she falls only upon the water. "No man," says the law, "may stultify himself." Does not this canon apply to critics? No, the critic may do so. Suicide is a felony, but if a critic only slay himself critically, dooming himself to "hoise with his own petard," why, 'tis to be forgiven

> That in our aspirations to be great,
> Our destinies o'erleap our mortal state. {…}

We are warned by the fate of our predecessors, when their example does not guide us; we confess not only our inferiority to Mr. Emerson, but our consciousness of the fact, and believe that they should "judge others who themselves excel," and that authors, like others on trial, should be judged by their peers. So we will not call this a criticism, which we are about to write on Mr. Emerson, only an attempt at a contribution towards a criticism, hoping that, in due time, some one will come and do faithfully and completely, what it is not yet time to accomplish, still less within our power to do.

All of Mr. Emerson's literary works, with the exception of the *Poems*, were published before they were printed; delivered by word of mouth to audiences. In frequently reading his pieces, he had an opportunity to see any defect of form and amend it. Mr. Emerson has won by his writings a more desirable reputation than any other man of letters in America has yet attained. It is not the reputation which bring him money or academic honours, or membership of learned societies; nor does it appear conspicuously in the literary journals as yet. But he has a high place among thinking men, on both sides of the water; we think no man who writes the English tongue has now so much influence in forming the opinions and character of young men and women. His audience steadily increases, at home and abroad, more rapidly in England than America. It is now with him as it was, at first, with Dr. Channing; the fairest criticism has come from the other side of the water; the reason is that he, like his predecessor, offended the sectarian and party spirit, the personal prejudices of the men about him; his life was a reproach to them, his words an offence, or his doctrines alarmed their sectarian, their party, or their personal pride, and they accordingly condemned the man. A writer who should bear the same relation to the English mind as Emerson to ours, for the same reason would be more acceptable here than at home. Emerson is neither a sectarian nor a partisan, no man less so; yet few men in America have been visited with more hatred,—private personal hatred, which the authors poorly endeavoured to conceal, and perhaps did hide from themselves. The spite we have heard expressed against him, by men of the common morality, would strike a stranger with amazement, especially when it is remembered that his personal character and daily life are of such extraordinary loveliness. This hatred has not proceeded merely from ignorant men, in whom it could easily be excused; but more often from men who have had opportunities of obtaining as good a culture as men commonly get in this country. Yet while he has been the theme of vulgar abuse, of sneers and ridicule in public and in private; while critics, more remarkable for the venom of their poison than the strength of their bow, have shot at him their little shafts, barbed more than pointed, he has also drawn about him some of what old Drayton called "the idle smoke of praise." Let us see what he has thrown into the public fire to cause this incense; what he has done to provoke the immedicable rage of certain other men; let us see what there is in his works, of old or new, true or false, what American and what cosmopolitan; let us weigh his works with such imperfect scales as we have, weigh them by the universal standard of beauty, truth, and love, and make an attempt to see what he is worth.

American literature may be distributed into two grand divisions: namely, the permanent literature, consisting of books not written for a special occasion, books which are bound between hard covers; and the transient literature, written for some special occasion and not designed to last beyond that. Our permanent literature is almost wholly an imitation of old models. The substance is old, and the form old. There is nothing American about it. But as our writers are commonly quite deficient in literary culture and scientific discipline, their productions seem poor when compared with the imitative portion of the permanent literature in older countries, where the writers start with a better discipline and a better acquaintance with letters and art. This inferiority of culture is one of the misfortunes incident to a new country, especially to one where practical talent is so much and so justly preferred to merely literary accomplishment and skill. This lack of culture is yet more apparent, in general, in the transient literature which is produced mainly by men who have had few advantages for intellectual discipline in early life, and few to make acquaintance with books at a later period. That portion of our literature is commonly stronger and more American, but it is often coarse and rude. The permanent literature is imitative; the other is rowdy. But we have now no time to dwell upon this theme, which demands a separate paper.

Mr. Emerson is the most American of our writers. The idea of America, which lies at the bottom of our original institutions, appears in him with great prominence. We mean the idea of personal freedom, of the dignity and value of human nature, the superiority of a man to the accidents of a man. Emerson is the most republican of republicans, the most protestant of the dissenters. Serene as a July sun, he is equally fearless. He looks everything in the face modestly, but with earnest scrutiny, and passes judgment upon its merits. Nothing is too high for his examination; nothing too sacred. On earth only one thing he finds which is thoroughly venerable, and that is the nature of man; not the accidents, which make a man rich or famous, but the substance, which makes him a man. The man is before the institutions of man; his nature superior to his history. All finite things are only appendages of man, useful, convenient, or beautiful. Man is master, and nature his slave, serving for many a varied use. The results of human experience—the State, the Church, society, the family, business, literature, science, art—all of these are subordinate to man: if they serve the individual, he is to foster them, if not, to abandon them and seek better things. He looks at all things, the past and the present, the State and the Church, Christianity and the market-house, in the daylight of the intellect. Nothing is allowed to stand between him and his manhood. Hence there is an apparent irreverence; he does not bow to any hat which Gessler has set up for public adoration, but to every man, canonical or profane, who bears the mark of native manliness. He eats show-bread, if he is hungry. While he is the most American, he is almost the most cosmopolitan of our writers, the least restrained and belittled by the popular follies of the nation or the age.

In America, writers are commonly kept in awe and subdued by fear of the richer class, or that of the mass of men. Mr. Emerson has small respect for either; would bow as low to a lackey as a lord, to a clown as a scholar, to one man as a million. He spurns all constitutions but the law of his own nature, rejecting them with manly scorn. The traditions of the churches are no hindrances to his thought; Jesus or Judas were the same to him, if either stood in his way and hindered the proportionate development of his individual life. The forms of society and the ritual of scholarship are no more effectual restraints. His thought of to-day is no barrier to freedom of thought tomorrow, for his own nature is not to be subordinated, either to the history of man, or his own history. "Tomorrow to fresh fields and pastures new," is his motto.

Yet, with all this freedom, there is no willful display of it. He is so confident of his freedom, so perfectly possessed of his rights, that he does not talk of them. They appear, but are not spoken of. With the hopefulness and buoyant liberty of America, he has none of our ill-mannered boasting. He criticises America often; he always appreciates it; he seldom praises, and never brags of our country. The most democratic of democrats, no disciple of the old regime is better mannered, for it is only the vulgar democrat or aristocrat who flings his follies in your face. While it would be difficult to find a writer so uncompromising in his adhesion to just principles, there is not in all his works a single jeer or ill-natured sarcasm. None is less addicted to the common forms of reverence, but who is more truly reverential?

While his idea is American, the form of his literature is not less so. It is a form which suits the substance, and is modified by the institutions and natural objects about him. You see that the author lives in a land with free institutions, with town-meetings and ballot-boxes; in the vicinity of a decaying church; amongst men whose terrible devils are poverty and social neglect, the only devils whose damnation is much cared for. His geography is American. Katskill and the Alleghanies, Monadnock, Wachusett, and the uplands of New Hampshire, appear in poetry or prose; Contocook and Agiochook are better than the Ilyssus, or Pactolus, or "smooth-sliding Mincius, crowned with vocal reeds." New York, Fall River, and Lowell have a place in his writings, where a vulgar Yankee would put Thebes or Paestum. His men and women are American—John and Jane, not Coriolanus and Persephone. He tells of the rhodora, the club-moss, the blooming clover, not of the hibiscus and the asphodel. He knows the humblebee, the blackbird, the bat, and the wren, and is not ashamed to say or sing of the things under his own eyes. He illustrates his high thought by common things out of our plain New-England life—the meeting in the church, the Sunday school, the dancing-school, a huckleberry party, the boys and girls hastening home from school, the youth in the shop, beginning an unconscious courtship with his unheeding customer, the farmers about their work in the fields, the bustling trader in the city, the cattle, the new hay, the voters at a town-meeting, the village brawler in a tavern full of tipsy riot, the conservative who thinks the nation is lost if his ticket chance to miscarry, the bigot worshipping the knot hole through which a dusty beam of light has looked in upon his darkness, the radical who declares that nothing is good if established, and the patent reformer who screams in your ears that he can finish the world with a single touch,—and out of all these he makes his poetry, or illustrates his philosophy. Now and then he wanders off to other lands, reports what he has seen, but it is always an American report of what an American eye saw. Even Mr. Emerson's recent exaggerated praise of England is such a panegyric as none but an American could bestow.

We know an American artist who is full of American scenery. He makes good drawings of Tivoli and Subiaco, but, to colour them, he dips his pencil in the tints of the American heaven, and over his olive trees and sempervives, his asses and his priests, he sheds the light only of his native sky. So is it with Mr. Emerson. Give him the range of the globe, it is still an American who travels.

Yet with this indomitable nationality, he has a culture quite cosmopolitan and extraordinary in a young nation like our own. Here is a man familiar with books, not with many, but the best books, which he knows intimately. He has kept good company. Two things impress you powerfully and continually—the man has seen nature, and been familiar with books. His literary culture is not a varnish on the surface; not a mere polish of the outside; it has penetrated deep into his consciousness. The salutary effect of literary culture is more perceptible in Emerson than in any American that we know, save one, a far younger man, and of great promise, of whom we shall speak at some other time.

We just now mentioned that our writers were sorely deficient in literary culture. Most of them have only a smattering of learning, but some have read enough, read and remembered with ability to quote. Here is one who has evidently read much, his subject required it, or his disposition, or some accident in his history furnished the occasion; but his reading appears only in his quotations, or references in the margin. His literature has not penetrated his soul and got incorporated with his whole consciousness. You see that he has been on Parnassus, by the huge bouquet, pedantic in its complexity, that he affronts you with; not by the odour of the flowers he has trampled or gathered in his pilgrimage, not by Parnassian dust clinging to his shoes, or mountain vigour in his eye. The rose gatherer smells of his sweets, and needs not prick you with the thorn to apprize you of what he has dealt in.

Here is another writer who has studied much in the various literatures of the world, but has lost himself there-in. Books supersede things, art stands between him and nature, his figures are from literature not from the green world. Nationality is gone. A traveller on the ocean of letters, he has a mistress in every port, and a lodging-place where the night overtakes him; all flags are the same to him, all climes; he has no wife, no home, no country. He has dropped nationality, and in becoming a cosmopolitan, has lost his citizenship everywhere. So, with all Christendom and heathendom for his metropolis, he is an alien everywhere in the wide world. He has no literary inhabitiveness. Now he studies one author, and is the penumbra thereof for a time; now another, with the same result. Trojan or Tyrian is the same to him, and he is Trojan or Tyrian as occasion demands. A thin vapoury comet, with small momentum of its own, he is continually deflected from his natural course by the attraction of other and more substantial bodies, till he has forgotten that he ever had any orbit of his own, and dangles in the literary sky, now this way drawn, now that, his only certain movement an oscillation. With a chameleon variability, he attaches himself to this or the other writer, and for the time his own colour disappears and he along with it.

With Emerson all is very different; his literary culture is of him, and not merely on him. His learning appears not in his quotations, but in his talk. It is the wine itself, and not the vintner's brand on the cask, which shows its quality. In his reading and his study, he is still his own master. He has not purchased his education with the loss of his identity, not of his manhood; nay, he has not forgotten his kindred in getting his culture. He is still the master of himself; no man provokes him even into a momentary imitation. He keeps his individuality with maidenly asceticism, and with a conscience rarely found amongst literary men. Virgil Homerizes, Hesiodizes, and plays Theocritus now and then. Emerson plays Emerson, always Emerson. He honours Greece, and is not a stranger with her noblest sons; he pauses as a learner before the lovely muse of Germany; he bows low with exaggerating reverence before the practical skill of England; but no one, nor all of these, have power to subdue that serene and upright intellect. He rises from the oracle he stooped to consult just as erect as before. His reading gives a certain richness to his style, which is more literary than that of any American writer that we remember; as much so as that of Jeremy Taylor. He takes much for granted in his reader, as if he were addressing men who had read everything, and wished to be reminded of what they had read. In classic times, there was no reading public, only a select audience of highly cultivated men. It was so in England once; the literature of that period, indicates the fact. Only religious and dramatic works were designed for pit, box, and gallery. Nobody can speak more clearly and more plainly than Emerson, but take any one of his essays or orations, and you see that he does not write in the language of the mass of men, more than Thucydides or Tacitus. His style is allusive, as an ode of Horace or Pindar, and the allusions are to literature which is known to but few. Hence, while his thought is human in substance, and American in its modifications, and therefore easily grasped, comprehended, and welcomed by men of the commonest culture, it is but few who understand the entire meaning of the sentences which he writes. His style reflects American scenery, and is dimpled into rare beauty as it flows by, and so has a pleasing fascination, but it reflects also the literary scenery of his own mind, and so half of his thought is lost on half his readers. Accordingly no writer or lecturer finds a readier access for his thoughts to the mind of the people at large, but no American author is less intelligible to the people in all his manifold meaning and beauty of allusion. He has not completely learned to think with the sagest sages and then put his thoughts into the plain speech of plain men. Every word is intelligible in the massive speech of Mr. Webster, and has its effect, while Emerson has still something of the imbecility of the scholar, as compared to the power of the man of action, whose words fall like the notes of the wood-thrush, each in its time and place, yet without picking and choosing. "Blacksmiths and teamsters do not trip in their speech," says he, "it is a shower of bullets. It is Cambridge men who correct themselves, and begin again at every half sentence; and moreover, will pun and refine too much, and swerve from the matter to the expression." But of the peculiarities of his style we shall speak again. {...}

No writer in our language is more rich in ideas, none more suggestive of noble thought and noble life. {...}

His works abound also with the most genial wit; he clearly sees and sharply states the halfnesses of things and men, but his wit is never coarse, and wholly without that grain of malice so often the accompaniment thereof.

Let us now say a word of the artistic style and rhetorical form of these remarkable books. Mr. Emerson always gravitates towards first principles, but never sets them in a row, groups them into a system, or makes of them a whole. Hence the form of all his prose writings is very defective, and much of his rare power is lost. He never fires by companies, nor even by platoons, only man by man; nay, his soldiers are never ranked into line, but stand scattered, sundered and individual, each serving on his own account, and "fighting on his own hook." Things are huddled and lumped together; diamonds, pearls, bits of chalk and cranberries, thrown pell-mell together. You can

No joints and no contexture find.
Nor their loose parts to any method bring.

Here is a specimen of the Lucretian "fortuitous concourse of atoms," for things are joined by a casual connection, or else by mere caprice. This is so in the Orations, which were designed to be heard, not read, where order is the more needful. His separate thoughts are each a growth. Now and then it is so with a sentence, seldom with a paragraph; but his essay is always a piece of composition, carpentry, and not growth. {…}

His marked love of individuality appears in his style. His thoughts are seldom vague, all is distinct; the outlines are sharply drawn, things are always discrete from one another. He loves to particularize. He talks not of flowers, but of the violet, the clover, the cowslip and anemone; not of birds, but the nuthatch, and the wren; not of insects, but of the Volvex Globator; not of men and maids, but of Adam, John, and Jane. Things are kept from things, each surrounded by its own atmosphere. This gives great distinctness and animation to his works, though latterly he seems to imitate himself a little in this respect. It is remarkable to what an extent this individualization is carried. The essays in his books are separate, and stand apart from one another, only mechanically bound by the lids of the volume; his paragraphs in each essay are distinct and disconnected, or but loosely bound to one another; it is so with sentences in the paragraph, and propositions in the sentence. Take for example his essay on Experience; it is distributed into seven parts, which treat respectively of Illusion, Temperament, Succession, Surface, Surprise, Reality, and Subjectiveness. These seven brigadiers are put in one army with as little unity of action as any seven Mexican officers; not subject to one head, nor fighting on the same side. The subordinates under these generals are in no better order and discipline; sometimes the corporal commands the king. But this very lack of order gives variety of form. You can never anticipate him. One half of the essay never suggests the rest. If he have no order, he never sets his method a going, and himself with his audience goes to sleep, trusting that he, they, and the logical conclusion will all come out alive and waking at the last. He trusts nothing to the discipline of his camp; all to the fidelity of the individual soldiers.

His style is one of the rarest beauty; there is no affectation, no conceit, no effort at effect. He alludes to everybody and imitates nobody. No writer that we remember, except Jean Paul Richter, is so rich in beautiful imagery; there are no blank walls in his building. But Richter's temple of poesy is a Hindoo pagoda, rich, elaborate, of costly stone, adorned with costly work, but as a whole, rather grotesque than sublime, and more queer than beautiful; you wonder how any one could have brought such wealth together, and still more that any one could combine things so oddly together. Emerson builds a rambling Gothic church, with an irregular outline, a chapel here, and a tower there, you do not see why; but all parts are beautiful, and the whole constrains the soul to love and trust. His manifold images come from his own sight, not from the testimony of other men. His words are pictures of the things daguerreotyped from nature. Like Homer, Aristotle, and Tacitus, he describes the thing, and not the effect of the thing. This quality he has in common with the great writers of classic antiquity, while his wealth of sentiment puts him with the classics of modern times. Like Burke he lays all literature under contribution, and presses the facts of every-day life into his service. He seems to keep the sun and moon as his retainers, and levy black-mail on the cricket and the titmouse, on the dawdling preacher and the snow-storm which seemed to rebuke his unnatural whine. His works teem with beauty. {…}

Emerson is a great master of language; therewith he sculptures, therewith he paints; he thunders and lightens in his speech, and in his speech also he sings. In Greece, Plato and Aristophanes were mighty masters of the pen, and have not left their equals in ancient literary art; so in Rome were Virgil and Tacitus; four men so marked in individuality, so unlike and withal so skilful in the use of speech, it were not easy to find; four mighty masters of the art to write. In later times there have been in England Shakespeare, Bacon, Milton, Taylor, Swift, and Carlyle; on the Continent, Voltaire, Rousseau, and Goethe; all masters in this art, skilful to work in human speech. Each of them possessed some qualities which Emerson has not. In Bacon, Milton, and Carlyle, there is a majesty, a dignity and giant strength, not to be claimed for him. Yet separating the beautiful from what men call sublime, no one of all that we have named, ancient or modern, has passages so beautiful as he. From what is called sublime if we separate what is simply vast, or merely grand, or only wide, it is in vain that we seek in all those men for anything to rival Emerson. {…}

From what has been said, notwithstanding the faults we have found in Emerson, it is plain that we assign him a very high rank in the literature of mankind. He is a very extraordinary man. To no English writer since Milton can we assign so high a place; even Milton himself, great genius though he was, and great architect of beauty, has not added so many thoughts to the treasury of the race; no, nor been the author of so much loveliness. Emerson is a man of genius such as does not often appear, such as has never appeared before in America, and but seldom in the world. He learns from all sorts of men, but no English writer, we think, is so original. We sincerely lament the want of logic in his method, and his exaggeration of the intuitive powers, the unhappy consequences of which we see in some of his followers and admirers. They will be more faithful than he to the false principle which he lays down, and will think themselves wise because they do not study, learned because they are ignorant of books, and inspired because they say what outrages common sense. In Emerson's poetry there is often a ruggedness and want of finish which seems wilful in a man like him. This fault is very obvious in those pieces he has put before his several essays. Sometimes there is a seed-corn of thought in the piece, but the piece itself seems like a pile of rubbish shot out of a cart which hinders the seed from germinating. His admirers and imitators not unfrequently give us only the rubbish and probably justify themselves by the example of their master. Spite of these defects, Mr. Emerson, on the whole, speaks with a holy power which no other man possesses who now writes the English tongue.

Others have more readers, are never sneered at by respectable men, are oftener praised in the journals, have greater weight in the pulpits, the cabinets, and the councils of the nation; but there is none whose words so sink into the mind and heart of young men and maids; none who work so powerfully to fashion the character of the coming age. Seeing the power which he exercises, and the influence he is likely to have on generations to come, we are jealous of any fault in his matter, or its form, and have allowed no private and foolish friendship to hinder us from speaking of his faults.

This is his source of strength: his intellectual and moral sincerity. He looks after Truth, Justice, and Beauty. He has not uttered a word that is false to his own mind or conscience; has not suppressed a word because he thought it too high for men's comprehension, and therefore dangerous to the repose of men. He never compromises. He sees the chasm between the ideas which come of man's nature and the institutions which represent only his history; he does not seek to cover up the chasm, which daily grows wider between Truth and Public Opinion, between Justice and the State, between Christianity and the Church; he does not seek to fill it up, but he asks men to step over and build institutions commensurate with their ideas. He trusts himself, trusts man, and trusts God. He has confidence in all the attributes of infinity. Hence he is serene; nothing disturbs the even poise of his character, and he walks erect. Nothing impedes him in his search for the true, the lovely, and the good; no private hope, no private fear, no love of wife or child, or gold, or ease, or fame. He never seeks his own reputation; he takes care of his Being, and leaves his seeming to take care of itself. Fame may seek him; he never goes out of his way a single inch for her.

He has not written a line which is not conceived in the interest of mankind. He never writes in the interest of a section, of a party, of a church, of a man always in the interest of mankind. Hence comes the ennobling influence of his works. Most of the literary men of America, most of the men of superior education, represent the ideas and interest of some party: in all that concerns the welfare of the human race, they are proportionably behind the mass who have only the common culture; so while the thought of the people is democratic, putting man before the accidents of a man, the literature of the nation is aristocratic, and opposed to the welfare of mankind. Emerson belongs to the exceptional literature of the times—and while his culture joins him to the history of man, his ideas and his whole life enable him to represent also the nature of man, and so to write for the future. He is one of the rare exceptions amongst our educated men, and helps redeem American literature from reproach of imitation, conformity, meanness of aim, and hostility to the progress of mankind. No faithful man is too low for his approval and encouragement; no faithless man too high and popular for his rebuke.

A good test of the comparative value of books, is the state they leave you in. Emerson leaves you tranquil, resolved on noble manhood, fearless of the consequences; he gives men to mankind, and mankind to the laws of God. His position is a striking one. Eminently a child of Christianity and of the American idea, he is out of the Church and out of the State. In the midst of Calvinistic and Unitarian superstition, he does not fear God, but loves and trusts Him. He does not worship the idols of our time—wealth and respectability, the two calves set up by our modern Jeroboam. He fears not the damnation these idols have the power to inflict—neither poverty nor social disgrace. In busy and bustling New England comes out this man serene and beautiful as a star, and shining like "a good deed in a naughty world." Reproached as an idler, he is active as the sun, and pours out his radiant truth on Lyceums at Chelmsford, at Waltham, at Lowell, and all over the land. Out of a cold Unitarian Church rose this most lovely light. Here is Boston, perhaps the most humane city in America, with its few noble men and women, its beautiful charities, its material vigour, and its hardy enterprise; commercial Boston, where honour is weighed in the public scales, and justice reckoned by the dollars it brings; conservative Boston, the grave of the Revolution, wallowing in its wealth, yet grovelling for more, seeking only money, careless of justice, stuffed with cotton yet hungry for tariffs, sick with the greedy worm of avarice, loving money as the end of life, and bigots as the means of preserving it; Boston with toryism in its parlours, toryism in its pulpits, toryism in its press, itself a tory town, preferring the accidents of man to man himself—and amidst it all there comes Emerson, graceful as Phoebus-Apollo, fearless and tranquil as the sun he was supposed to guide, and pours down the enchantment of his light, which falls where'er it may, on dust, on diamonds, on decaying heaps to hasten their rapid rot, on seeds new sown to quicken their ambitious germ, on virgin minds of youths and maids to waken the natural seed of nobleness therein, and make it grow to beauty and to manliness. Such is the beauty of his speech, such the majesty of his ideas, such the power of the moral sentiment in men, and such the impression which his whole character makes on them, that they lend him, everywhere, their ears, and thousands bless his manly thoughts.

Walter Savage Landor (1775–1864)

After visiting England twice, Emerson recalls at the opening of English Traits *that it was "the wish to see the faces of three or four writers" that prompted his first visit to the island, and in the illustrious company of Coleridge, Wordsworth, and De Quincey, Emerson includes Landor. In Florence, Emerson was welcomed by the American sculptor Horatio Greenough who later helped his compatriot find an audience with Landor who was living in his nearby villa in Fiesole. In 1856 Emerson recounts his visit of 1833 and finds much to praise about Landor—a poet of renown for* Rose Aylmer *and the author of* Imaginary Conversations, *which appeared in six volumes beginning in 1824. In* English Traits *Emerson reflected on their own conversation, his esteem for the poet and the poet's reception, and concluded that his host is "strangely undervalued in England; usually ignored; and sometimes savagely attacked in the Reviews." Despite mention of some disagreement in their tastes, Emerson remained full of praise and interest more than two decades after their visit. (And Emerson had written a near-hagiographic portrait of Landor—with unequivocal and undiluted awe—that was published in* The Dial *(1841), where for instance he wrote: "Mr. Landor is one of the foremost of that small class who make good in the nineteenth-century the claims of pure literature. [. . .] We do not recollect an example of more complete independence in literary history.") To Emerson's surprise, then, Landor took the brief account in* English Traits *poorly and responded with a vitriolic open letter, which is reproduced below. In the letter, which amounted to dozens of pages that he personally had published at Bath in 1856, Landor complains of slights, errors, and injuries. Samuel Arthur Jones reminds us that Landor was "imperial, imperious, impetuous, and irascible" and therefore that his ire and injured pride over Emerson's sketch was out of proportion and unjustified.[1] Emerson's notes on their meeting in* English Traits *and Landor's response in the form of a public epistolary reprimand create a remarkable occasion to consider the nature—and conflicts—of memory, perspective, and evaluation.*

Landor's Letter to Emerson

Walter Savage Landor

My Dear Sir,

Your *English Traits* have given me great pleasure; and they would have done so even if I had been treated by you with less favour. The short conversations we held at my Tuscan

Villa were insufficient for an estimate of my character and opinions. A few of these, and only a few, of the least important, I may have modified since. Let me run briefly over them as I find them stated in your pages. Twenty-three years have not obliterated from my memory the traces of your visit, in company with that intelligent man and glorious sculptor, who was delegated to erect a statue in your capital to the tutelary genius of America. I share with him my enthusiastic love of ancient art; but I am no *exclusive*, as you seem to hint I am. In my hall at Fiesole there are two busts, if you remember, by two artists very unlike the ancients, and equally unlike each other; Donatello and Fiamingo; surveying them at a distance is the sorrowful countenance of Germanicus. Sculpture at the present day flourishes more than it ever did since the age of Pericles; and America is not cast into the shade by Europe. I do prefer Giovanni da Bologna to Michael Angelo, who indeed in his conceptions is sublime, but often incorrect, and sometimes extravagant, both in sculpture and painting. I confess I have no relish for his prodigious *giblet pie* in the Capella Sistina, known throughout the world as his *Last Judgment*. Grand in architecture, he was no ordinary poet, no lukewarm patriot. Deplorable, that the inheritor of his house and name is so vile a sycophant, that even the blast of the Michael's trumpet could not rouse his abject soul.

I am an admirer of Pietro Perugino, and more than an admirer of Raffaelle; but I could never rank the Madonna della Seggiola among the higher of his works; I see no divinity in the child, and no such purity in the Virgin as he often expressed in her. I have given my opinion as freely on the *Transfiguration*. The cartoons are his noblest works: they place him as high as is Correggio in the Dome of Parma: nothing has been, or is likely to be, higher.

Among my *cloud of pictures* you did not observe a little Masaccio (one of his easel-pieces) representing Saint Jerome. The idea of it is truer than Domenichino's.

The last of the Medici Grandukes, Giovanni Gaston, sent to the vicinity of Parma and Correggio an old Florentine, who was reputed to be an excellent judge of painting. He returned with several small pieces on canvass, which the painters at that time in Florence turned into ridicule, and which were immediately thrown into the Palazzo Vecchio. About a quarter of a century ago, the chambers of this Palazzo were cleared of their lumber, and I met in the Via degli Archibugieri a tailor who had two small canvases under his arms, and two others in his hands. He had given a few paoli for each; I offered him as many francesconi. He thought me a madmen; an opinion which I also heard expressed as I sat under the shade of a vast old fig tree, while about twenty labourers were extirpating three or four acres of vines and olives, in order to make somewhat like a meadow before my windows. The words we "*Matti sono tutti gli Inglesi, ma questo poi*" followed by a shrug and an aposiopesis. I acquired two more *cerotti*, as they had been called, painted by the same master; three I have at Bath, and three remain at my villa in Tuscany. Mr. George Wallis, who accompanied Soult in that Marshal's *Eclectic Review* of the Spanish Galleries, pronounced them to be Correggios. What is remarkable, one is a landscape. It would indeed be strange if he, who painted better than any before or since, should have produced no greater number of works than are attributed to him by Mengs. I have seen several of which I entertain no doubt. Raffaelle is copied more easily; so perhaps is Titian, if not Giorgione. On this subject the least fallible authority is Morris More, who however could not save our National Gallery from devastation.

Curious as I was in collecting specimens of the earlier painters, I do not prefer them to the works either of their nearer successors or to those of the present day. My Domenichino, about which I doubted, has been authenticated by M. Cosveldt; my Raffaelle is by M. Dennistoune, who was wrong only in believing it had been called a portrait of the painter. It is in fact the portrait of the only son of that Doni whose wife's is in the Tribuna at Florence. He died in boyhood; and the picture was long retained in his mother's family, the Strozzi, and thrown into a bedchamber of the domestics as a piece of *robaccia* and *anticaglia*.

We will now walk a little way out of the gallery. Let me say, before we go further, that I do not think "the Greek historians the only good ones." Davila, Machiavelli, Voltaire, Michelet, have afforded me much instruction and much delighted. Gibbon is worthy of a name among the most enlightened and eloquent of the ancients. I find no fault in his language; on the contrary, I find the most exact propriety. The grave, and somewhat austere, becomes the historian of the Roman Republic; the grand, and somewhat gorgeous, finds its proper place in the palace of Byzantium. Am I indifferent to the merits of our own historians? indifferent to the merits of him who balanced with equal hand Wellington and Napoleon? No; I glory in my countryman and friend. It is certain that I am indiscriminating in my judgment of Charron? Never have I compared him with Montaigne; but there is much of wisdom, and, what is remarkable in their earlier French authors, much of sincerity in him.

I am sorry to have "*pestered you with Southey*," and to have excited the inquiry, "*Who is Southey?*" I will answer the question. Southey is the poet who has written the most imaginative poem of any in our own times, English or Continental; such is the *Curse of Kahama*. Southey is the proseman who has written the purest prose; Southey is the critic the most cordial and the least invidious. Show me another, of any note, without captiousness, without arrogance, and without malignity.

"Slow rises worth by poverty deprest,"

But Southey raised it.

Certainly you could not make me praise Mackintosh. What is there eminently to praise in him? Are there not twenty men and women at the present hour who excell him in style and genius? His reading was extensive: he had much capacity, less comprehensiveness and concentration. I know not who may be the "others of your recent friends" who you could not excite me to applaud. I am more addicted to praise than censure. We English are generally as fierce partizans in literary as in parliamentary elections, and we cheer or jostle a candidate of whom we know nothing. I always kept clear of both quarters. I have votes in three countries, I believe I have in four, and never gave one. I would rather buy than solicit or canvass, but preferably neither. Nor am I less abstinent in the turbulent contest for literary honors. Among the many authors you have conversed with in England, did you find above a couple who spoke not ill of nearly all the rest? Even the most liberal of them, they who concede the most, subtract at last the greater part of what they have conceded, together with somewhat beside. And this is done, forsooth, out of fairness, truthfulness, &c.!

The nearest the kennel are the most disposed to splash the polished boot.

I never envied any man anything but waltzing, for which I would have given all the little talents I had acquired. I dared not attempt to learn it; for, although I was active and my ear was accurate, I felt certain I should have been unsuccessful. Even the shameless (and I am not among those) have somewhat of shame in one part of other; and here lay mine.

We now come to Carlyle, of who you tell us "he worships a man that will manifest any truth to him." Would he have patience for the truth to be manifested? or would he accept it then? Certainly the face of truth is very lovely, and we take especial care that it shall never lose its charms by familiarity. He declares that "*Landor's principle is mere rebellion.*"

Quite the contrary is apparent and prominent in many of my writings. I always was a Conservative; but I would eradicate any species of evil, political, moral, or religious, as soon as it springs up, with no reference to the blockheads who cry out "*What would you substitute in its place?*" When I pluck up a dock or a thistle, do I ask any such a question? I have said plainly, more than once, and in many quarters, that I would not alter or greatly modify the English Constitution. I denounced at the time of its enactment the fallacy of the Reform Bill. And here I beg pardon for the word *fallacy*, instead of *humbug*, which entered into our phraseology with two other sister graces, *Sham* and *Pluck*. I applaud the admission of new peers; and I think it well that a large body of them should be hereditary. But it is worse than mere popery that we should be encumbered by a costly and heavy bench of Cardinals, under the title of Bishops, and that their revenues should exceed those in the Roman States. I would send a beadel after every Bishop who left his diocese, without the case of his Sovran, the head of the Church, for some peculiar and urgent purpose relating to it solely. I would surround the throne with splendour and magnificence, and grant as large a sum as a thousand pounds weekly for it, with two palaces; no land but what should be rented. The highest of the nobility would be proud of service under it, without the pay of menials. I approve the expansion of our peerage; but never let its members, adscititious or older, think themselves the only nobility; else peradventure some of them may be reminded that there are among us men whose ancestors stood in high places, and who did good service to the country, when theirs were cooped up within borough-walls, or called on duty from the field as serfs and villains.

Democracy, such as yours in America, is my abhorrence. Republicanism far from it; but there are few nations capable of receiving, fewer of retaining, this pure and efficient form. Democracy is lax and disjointed; and whatever is loose wears out the machine. The nations on the Ebro, and the mountaineers of Biscay, enjoyed it substantially for century after century. Holland, Ragusa, Genoa, Venice, were deprived of it is by that *Holy Alliance* whose influence is now withering the Continent, and changing the features of England. We are losing our tensity of sinew; we are germanizing into a flabby and effete indifference. It appears to me that the worst calamity the world has ever undergone, is the prostration of Venice at the feet of Austria. The oldest and truest nobility in the world was swept away by Napoleon. How happily were the Venetian States governed for a thousand years, by the brave and circumspect gentlemen of the island city! All who did not conspire against its security were secure. Look at the palaces they erected! Look at the Arts they cultivated! Look, on the other side, at the damp and decaying walls; enter; and there behold such countenances as you will never see elsewhere. These are not among the creatures whom God will permit any Deluge to sweep away. Heretofore, a better race of beings has uniformly succeeded to a viler though a vaster; and it will be so again.

Rise, Manin! rise, Garibaldi! rise, Mazzini! Compose your petty differences, quell your discordances, and stand united! Strike and spare not; strike high. "*Miles, faciem feri*," cried the wisest and most valiant of the Roman race.

I have enjoyed the conversation of Carlyle within the room where I am writing. It appeared at that time less evidently than now that his energy goes far beyond his discretion. Perverseness is often mistaken for strength, and obstinacy for consistency. There is only one thing in which he resembles other writers, namely, in saying that which he can say best, and with most point. You tell us, "he does not read Plato." Perhaps there may be a sufficient reason for it.

Resolved to find out what there is in this remarkable philosopher, I went daily for several weeks into the Magliabechian library at Florence, and thus refreshing my neglected Greek, I continued the reading of his works in the original from beginning to end. The result of this reading may be found in several of the *Imaginary Conversations*. That one of them between Lord Chesterfield and Lord Chatham contains observations on the cacophony of some sentences; and many more could have been added quite as exceptionable. Even Attic honey hath its impurities.

"He (Carlyle) took despairing or satirical views of literature at this moment."

I am little fond of satire, and less addicted to despair. It seems to me that never in this country was there a greater number of good writers than now; and some are excellent. Our epic is the novel or romance. I dare not praise the seven or eight of both sexes who have written these admirably; if I do, the *ignavum fuci pecus* would settle on me. All are glad to hear the censure, few the praise, of those who labor in the same vineyard.

We are now at Rydal Mount.

Wordsworth's bile is less fervid than Carlyle's: it comes with more saliva about it, and with a hoarser expectoration. "Lucretius he esteems a far *higher* poet than Virgil."

The more fool he! "not in his system, which is nothing, but in his power of illustration."

Does a power of illustration imply the *high* poet? It is in his system (which, according to Wordsworth, *is nothing*) that the power of Lucretius consists. Where then is its use? But what has Virgil in his Eclogues, in his Georgics, or in his Æneid, requiring illustration? Lucretius does indeed well illustrate his subject; and few even in prose among the philosophers have written so intelligibly; but the quantity of his poetry does not much exceed three hundred lines in the whole: one of the noblest specimens of it is a scornful expostulation against the fear of death. Robert Smith, brother of Sidney, wrote in the style of Lucretius such latin poetry as is fairly worth all the rest in that language since the banishment of Ovid. Even Lucretius himself nowhere hath exhibited such a continuation of manly thought and of lofty harmony.

We must now descend to Wordsworth once again.

He often gave an opinion on authors which he never had red, and on some which he could not read; Plato for instance. He speaks contemptuously of the Scotch. The first time I ever met him, and the only time I ever conversed with him longer than a few minutes, he spoke contemptuously of Scott, and violently of Byron. He chattered about them incoherently and indiscriminately. In reality, Scott had singularly the power of imagination and of construction: Byron little of either; but this is what Wordsworth neither said nor knew. His censure was hardened froth. I praised a line of Scott's on the dog of a traveller lost in the snow (if I remember) on Skiddaw. He said it was the only good one in the poem, and began instantly to recite a whole one of his own upon the same subject. This induced me afterward to write as follows on a flyleaf in Scott's poems,

> Yet who have lungs to mount the Muse's hill,
> Here slake your thirst aside their liveliest rill:
> Asthmatic Wordsworth, Byron piping hot,
> Leave in the rear, and march with manly Scott.

I was thought unfriendly to Scott for one of the friendliest things I ever did toward an author. Having noted all the faults of grammar and expression in two or three of his volumes, I calculated that the number of them, in all, must amount to above a thousand. Mr. Lockhart, who married his daughter, was indignant at this, and announced, at the same time (to prove how very wrong I was) that they were corrected in the next edition.

Poor Scott! he bowed his high intellect and abased the illustrious rank conferred on him by the unanimous acclaim of nations, before a prince who was the opprobrium of his country for enduring so quietly and contentedly his Neronianism.

Scott's reading was extensive, but chiefly within the range of Great Britain and France; Wordsworth's lay, almost entirely, between the near grammar school and Rydal Mount. He would not have scorned, although he might have reviled, the Scotch authors, if he ever red Archibald Bower, or Hume, or Smollet or Adam Smith; he would have indeed hated Burns; he would never have forgiven Beattie that incomparable stanza,

> O, how canst thou renounce the boundless store
>   Of charms that Nature to her votary yields,
> The warbling woodland, the resounding shore,
>   The pomp of groves and garniture of fields,
> All that the genial ray of morning gilds,
>   And all that echoes to the song of even,
> All that the mountain's sheltering bosom shields,
>   And all the dream magnificence of heaven:
> O how canst thou renounce, and hope to be forgiven?

Nor would he have endured that song of Burns, more animated than the odes of Pindar,

> Scots wha ha' wi' Wallace bled.

He would have been horrified at the Doric-Scotch of "*wha' ha'*;" yet what wool in the mouth were *have* and *with*! Gerald Massey too much have fared ill with him; and the gentle and graceful Tennyson's dress-shoes might have stood in danger of being trodden on by the wooden. Wordsworth's walk was in the lowlands of poetry, where the wooden shoe is most commodious. The vigorous and animated ascend their high battle-field neither in that nor in the slipper, but press on, and breathe hard, $ευκνημιδες$.

When Hazlitt was in Tuscany he often called on me, and once asked me whether I had ever seen Wordsworth. I answered in the negative, and expressed a wish to know something of his appearance.

"Sir," said Hazlitt, "have you ever seen a horse?" "Assuredly." "Then, Sir, you have seen Wordsworth."

When I met him some years after at a friend's on the lake of Waswater, I found him extremely civil. There was *equinity* in the lower part of his face: in the upper was much of the contemplative, and no little of the calculating. This induced me, when, at a breakfast where many were present, he said he "would not give five shillings for all Southey's poetry," to tell a friend of his that he might safely make such an investment of his money and throw all his own in. Perhaps I was too ill-humoured; but my spirit rose against his ingratitude toward the man who first, and with incessant effort and great difficulty, brought him into notice. He ought to have appreciated his poetical benefactor as he did the

> illustrious peer,
> With high respect and gratitude sincere.

Southey would have been more pleased by the friendliness of the sentiment than by the intensity of the poetry in which it is expressed; for Southey was the most equitable, the most candid, the most indulgent of mankind. I was unacquainted with him for many years after he had commended, in the *Critical Review*, my early poem, "Gebir." In the letters now edited by Mr. Warter, I find that in the *Whitehaven Journal* there was inserted a criticism, in which, on the strength of this poem, I am compared and preferred to Göthe. I am not too much elated. Neither in my youthful days nor in any other have I thrown upon the world such trash as "Werter" and "Wilhelm Meister," nor flavoured my poetry with the corrugated spicery of metaphysics. Nor could he have written in a lifetime any twenty, in a hundred or thereabout, of my "Imaginary Conversations." My poetry I throw to the Scotch terriers growling at my feet. Fifty pages of Shelley contain more of pure poetry than a hundred of Göthe, who spent the better part of his time in contriving a puzzle, and in spinning out a yarn for a labyrinth. How different in features, both personal and poetical, are Göthe and Wordsworth! In the countenance of Göthe there was something of the elevated and august; less of it in his poetry; Wordsworth's physiognomy was entirely rural. With a rambling pen he wrote admirable paragraphs in his longer poem, and sonnets worthy of Milton: for example:

Two voices are there, & c.,

which is far above the highest pitch of Göthe. But his unbraced and unbuttoned impudence in presence of our grand historians, Gibbon and Napier, must be reprehended and scouted. Of Gibbon I have delivered my opinion; of Napier too, on whom I shall add nothing more at present than that he superseded the Duke, who intended to write the history of his campaigns, and who (his nephew Capt. William Wellesley tells me) has left behind him "Memoirs."

I never *glorified* Lord Chesterfield; yet he surely is among the best of our writers in regard to style, and appears to have formed Horace Walpole's and Sterne's, a style purely English. His Letters were placed by Beresford, Archbishop of Tuam, in the hands of his daughters. This I remember to have been stated to me by his son. A polished courtier and a virtuous prelate knew their value; and perhaps the neglect of them at the present day is one reason why a gentleman is almost as rare as a man of genius.

I am not conscious that I underrate Burke: never have I placed any of his parliamentary contemporaries in the same rank with him. His language is brilliant, but not always elegant; which induced me once to attribute to him the *Letters of Junius*. I am now more inclined to General Lee as author. Lord Nugent, an inquisitive and intelligent reader, told me he never could "worm out the secret" from his uncle Mr. Thomas Grenville, who, he believed, knew it. Surely it is hardly worth the trouble of a single hour's research. We have better things weekly in the *Examiner*, and daily in the *Times*.

I do not "undervalue Socrates." Being the cleverest of the Sophists, he turned the fraternity into ridicule: he eluded the grasp of his antagonist by anointing with the oil of quibble all that was tangible and prominent. To compare his philosophy (if indeed you can catch it) with the philosophy of Epicurus and Epictetus, whose systems meet, is insanity.

I do not "despise entomology." I am ignorant of it; as indeed I am of almost all science.

I love also flowers and plants; but I know less about them than is known by a beetle or a butterfly.

I must have been misunderstood, or have been culpably inattentive, if I said "I knew not Herschell by name." The father's I knew well, from his giving to a star the baptismal one of that pernicious madman who tore America from England, and who rubbed his hands when the despatches announced to him the battle of Bunker's Hill, in which he told his equerry that his soldiers had "*got well peppered.*" Probably I had not then received in Italy the admirable writings of the great Herschell's greater son.

Phocion, who excites as much of pity as of admiration, was excellent as a commander and as an orator, but was deficient and faulty as a politician. No Athenian had, for so long a period, rendered to his country so many and such great services. He should have died a short time earlier; he should have entered the temple with Demosthenes. On the whole, I greatly prefer this last consistent man, although he could not have his country like Epaminondas and like Washington.

I make no complaint of what is stated in the following page, that "Landor is strangely undervalued in England." I have heard it before, but I never have taken the trouble to ascertain it. Here I find that I am "savagely attacked in the Reviews." Nothing more likely; I never see them; my acquaintances lie in a different and far distant quarter. Some honors have, however, been conferred on me in the literary world. Southey dedicated to me his *Kehama*; James his *Attila*; he and Dickens invited me to be godfather to their sons. Moreover, I think as many have offered me the flatteries of verse as were offered to any one but Louis the Fourteenth.

P. 19. I think oftener with Alfieri than with any other writer, and quite agree with him that "Italy and England are the only countries worth living in." The only time I ever saw Alfieri, was just before he left this country for ever. I accompanied my Italian master, Parachinetti, to a bookseller's, to order the Works of Alfieri and Metastasio, and was enthusiastic, as most young men were, about the French Revolution. "Sir," said Alfieri, "you are a very young man; you are yet to learn that nothing good ever came out of France, or ever will. The ferocious monsters are about to devour one another; and they can do nothing better. They have always been the curse of Italy; yet we too have fools among us who trust them."

Such were the expressions of the most classical and animated poet existing in the present or past century, of him who could at once be a true patriot and a true gentleman. There was nothing of the ruffianly in his vigour; nothing of the vulgar in his resentment; he could scorn without a scoff; he could deride without a grimace. Had he been living in these latter days, his bitterness would have overflowed, not on France alone, nor Austria in addition, the two beasts that have torn Italy in pieces, and are growling over her bones; but more, and more justly, on those constitutional governments which, by abetting, have aided them in their aggressions and incursions. We English are the most censurable of all. Forbear, in pity forbear, to say, what I am afraid is too true, that we are a litter of blind lickspittles, waiting to be thrown with a stone about the neck into the next horsepond. Will historians be credited, some centuries hence, when they related what our countrymen in the present have done against the progress of freedom throughout Europe? The ministers of England have signed that *Holy Alliance* which delivered every free State to the domination of arbitrary and irresponsible despots. The ministers of England have entered more recently into treaties with usurpers and assassins. And now, forsooth, it is called *assassination* to remove from the earth an assassin; the assassin of thousands; an outlaw, the subverter of his country's, and even of his own, laws. The valiant and the wise of old thought differently. Even now there are some, and they not devoid of intellect, who are of opinion that the removal of an evil at the least possible cost is best. They would not expose an army when one brave man could do the thing effectually: they would not impoverish a nation, nor maim and decimate the strong supports, nor leave destitute and desolate the fathers of its families, rather than strike a single blow which would sound the hour of their deliverance and security.

Impressed by these sentiments, which never have varied a tittle in the long course of my existence, I openly avowed that I had reserved insurance money, to a small extent, in favour of the first tyrannicide. My words are circulated in America and on our continent, and well received and widely echoed. I regret that here in England are some professing to be the friends of liberty and justice, who stand forward as shields and bucklers to the enemies of both. Surely wit and wisdom might be better employed. Permit me to repeat my words, written in a letter to Mr. White.

"Sir, I have only one hundred pounds of ready money, and am never likely to have at my disposal as much in future. Of this I transmit five to you, toward the acquisition of the ten thousand muskets to be given, in accordance with your manifesto, 'to the first Italian province which shall rise.' The remaining ninety-five I reserve for the family of the first patriot who asserts by action the dignity of tyrannicide. Abject men have cried out against me for my commendation of this ancient virtue, the highest of which a man is capable, and now the most important and urgent.

"Is it not an absurdity to remind us that usurpers will rise up afresh? Do not all transgressors? And must we therefor lay aside the terrors of chastisement, or give a ticket of leave to the most atrocious criminals? Shall one enslave millions? Shall laws be subverted, and we then be told that we act against them, or without their sanction, when none are left us, and we lay prostrate the subverter? Three or four blows, instantaneously and simultaneously given, may save the world many years of warfare, of discord, and of degradation. It is everywhere unsafe to rob a citizen; shall it be safe anywhere to rob a people? Impelled unconsciously by a hand invisible, the hand of eternal Justice, even the priest teaches the schoolboy the glory that always hath accompanied the tyrannicide. At the recital, he strikes the desk with his ferule, and the boy springs up at once into the man."

Such are the sentiments I last avowed on reading how a brave man, with his two inoffensive children, were murdered by the usurper of the Hungarian crown, the abolitionist of Hungarian laws, and the persecutor and hangman of Hungarian patriots. Bearing these cruelties in memory, and seeing many more such daily before his eyes, let any true Englishman read the narrative of Colonel Türr, and then ask his own heart whether the atrocities there detailed can fail to excite the execration of every honourable man, and the chastisement of the perpetrator. There was a time, and I should be sorry to think it ended with Sydney, when the man who upheld the dignity of his fellow man, and who would strike down a felon in feathers and bedizened with stars and crosses, experienced far other treatment than contumely and buffoonery. Poerio and Kossuth and Türr, it seems to me, are greatly more deserving of our sympathy than their oppressors; yet these oppressors, being Potentates, we connive at them and coax them, and at last say, "*Now, pray! pray! don't! our own people will get angry with us, and force us into demonstrations.*" Meanwhile, it is only in set speeches to gain popularity, that a few of the ministry, and other members of parliament, warm up again a stale side-dish of pity for the exiled and imprisoned.

We once taught other nations; may other nations soon teach *us*! There is no great man in existence; shall it be said there is no brave one? The Crimea contradicts this, even to the face of our commanders. In the *Athenæum* you will find a paragraph, well worthy of notice, on the best of these.

"While our readers were admiring the modesty which led 'the heroes of Kars' to ignore all merits *except their own*, a letter was on its way from the Bosphorus, and has been this week printed in the *Times*, from General Kmety, in which the aged soldier addresses Sir W. F. Williams, in a tone of calm remonstrance worthy of his fame, on the historical suppression under which he, in common with others, is made to labor. Injustice of this sort, however, works its own cure. We hear with satisfaction that a subscription is being raised in the name of General Guyon, with a view to present that distinguished officer with a sword of honour."

The sword of honour was the sword he carried; the other may be laid across his coffin. The valiant and virtuous Guyon is no more. It is now a year since I red a letter from the most affectionate of wives, announcing that his heart was broken. Even her love could no longer support it. What then must be the weight of grief under which it at last was crushed! But he had fought against Austria; and Austria is German; German is England too. We may now expect that Orsini be demanded from us, and delivered up to the perjured Apostolic Majesty. No intercession was made by our Court for the cousin of our Queen; he had committed the heinous crime of asserting the cause of freedom.

And we are now called sticklers for assassination, who by one sweep of the arm would deliver a nation from its oppressor, and hurl down the tower that overhangs the dungeon! It was the lictor who carried the axe; he was no assassin; he bore before magistrate the symbol of unity and of law.

Only one man worthy of notice reprehends me. Ah Manin! Manin! when he of ebullient blood sits down again after exertion, he is apt to take cold so as to keep him room.

No one is more averse than I am to interference with other governments; but it is our duty to insist on the observance of the treaties they have made with us. Let the people of each be their own defenders and avengers. I must repeat what already is declared in several of my writings, that I have no fondness for innovation. Whatever is changed should rest, if possible, on what has been tried. Edifices are corroded and crumble first in their exterior and ornamental parts, leaving the foundation, if ever solid, the more solid the longer it hath stood. Far as our English Constitution is from absolute perfection, farther is it from that region of earthquakes where chance and change are causing by their indomitable fire incessant eruptions and oscillations. Certain it is, however, that we shall not rest where we are; but uncertain is it whether, when Enceladus hath shaken his shoulder and turned his side, we shall then rest long.

Accept this memorial, which your name will render of less brief duration, of the esteem in which you are held by

Walter Landor.

P.S. If you have not received our *Morning Advertiser,* you will ask for it, and will read with indignation the conduct of Lord Clarendon toward Colonel Türr. It was hoped that the family of Villiers had left its earlier titles in abeyance. Here is evidence of the contrary.

Note

1 Walter Savage Landor, *Landor's Letter to Emerson,* ed. Samuel Arthur Jones (Cleveland: The Rowfant Club, 1895), 11.

Arthur Hugh Clough (1819–1861)

While Emerson was traveling in England in 1847 he received an invitation to visit
Oxford from Clough, who was a Fellow at Oriel. Emerson took up the invitation
to meet Clough, noting, "There are few objects in England so attractive to me as
Oxford." Perhaps he could not have expected that Clough himself would become
more attractive than the university he represented. The next year Emerson wrote in
his journal, "'Tis, I think, the most real benefit I have had from my English visit, this
genius of Clough. [. . .] I have a new friend, and the world has a new poet." Emerson
esteemed Clough's poetry as "a high gift from angels that are very rare in our mortal
state" and noted in Clough's work "all this wealth of expression, this wealth of
imagery, this joyful heart of youth, this temperate continuity, that belongs only to
high masters." After their initial engagement in Oxford, they saw each other again
in London, and spent weeks together walking, dining, and talking in Revolutionary
Paris in the spring of 1848. When Emerson was at Liverpool, set to disembark for
America, Clough said to him mournfully, "Think where we are. Carlyle has led us
all out into the desert, and he has left us there." To which Emerson replied, as if in
benediction, with his hand upon Clough's head: "Clough, I consecrate you Bishop of
all England. It shall be your part to go up and down through the desert to find out
these wanderers and to lead them into the promised land." Even as Clough praised
Emerson's "perfect intellectual cultivation," he noted that "One thing that struck
everybody is that he is much less Emersonian than his essays. There is no dogmatism
or arbitrariness, or positiveness about him." At Emerson's invitation, Clough lived in
America for a while and was his neighbor, residing in nearby Cambridge. The final
decade of their relationship was however spent at its original distance, with Clough
writing from London (as he does in the following two letters), often making reference
to his days in New England.

Letters to Emerson

Arthur Hugh Clough

My dear Emerson

Fragments amounting to a whole letter are somewhere in my drawer written in
the autumn & withheld because correspondence seemed chimerical—It is now
nearly a twelvemonth since I fled in that precipitate half-voluntary manner from

Massachusetts—another fortnight will I think complete the year, and another two days from this will in all probability see me married—

You in the meantime are in all the turmoil of a renewed Slavery Contest—I was quite astonished to see after all that the Bill was passed by the Representatives—I had imagined it had already been virtually defeated there—

From this distance it almost looks as if this aggression wo^d be of more use in breaking down the idea of compromise than of harm in its actual results—

I heard of your lecture or speech whichever it was in New York, but saw no report of it.

I am going on here working in the Office in the ordinary routine—which however after years of Greek tuition is really a very great relief—All education is in England & I think in America so horribly mixed up with religious matters that it is a great difficulty—One does not want to parade opinions which indeed one cannot very well define—and yet it seems a treachery to the parents to teach their boys what they did not count upon—

I always think of coming out to you again, but this will stand in the way of it—Having got work which leaves me independent in all these respects, & which moreover has no competition in it & may be done in, I sho^d think, as unmercenary a way as any daily labour at any rate in England—I don't doubt it will be difficult to quit it—So I don't plan anything—

Farewell—

I often look into Thoreau's River Book with gratification now because it brings up your country—I hope to see it again some day one way or other—

I dont think there is any news worth the telling—

Give my love to your young people please—specially my particular friend, if she is not grown too old to accept it—

Ever Your's faithfully,
A H Clough

Council Office,
Downing St
June 10th—[1854]
R. W. Emerson Esq

Council Office, Whitehall
Augt 22n [1854]

My dear Emerson

Your letter, about a week ago, was very welcome, and the silver candlestick which came in Felton's box of treasures was very much appreciated and I am to send the kindest possible thanks for it—I only hope fortune may indeed some day waft us over at least for a visit to your Northern Vinland & give my wife the opportunity of being made familiar with Concord—

I haven't seen Carlyle for an age—He is I believe ruralizing at Addiscombe, a few miles out of London, which always does him a great deal of good—I dare say we shall not meet till London begins to consider itself alive again in October—This country has as you say, its concentrated civilisation to hold one to it—it seems waste of opportunity to leave such a mass of old knowledge—But I think you are better & more happily off in America, where the vastness of the machinery does not destroy the sense of individual moral purpose—The ship here is really so big that one cannot see that it moves, or that any one of the little petty services which people are for the dear head's sake set to do, can have any effect one way or other on its motion. If one has a place or business here, one is only standing in some other person's shoes, who really could very likely do the thing as well—

You are so infinitely more plastic again, as to opinion than, except in talk, the English are—

As for your politics, certainly they do not look well at present—& one is half afraid that New York may after all acquiesce in the fait accompli, & go back to its farm & its counting house without concerning itself further—I am afraid the English theory is when one has Done a wrong thing, to forget it as soon as possible—

farewell—

With kindest remembrances at Concord

Ever Yours

A H Clough.

Herman Grimm (1828–1901)

As indicated by the candid letters reproduced here, Herman Grimm was a devoted reader of Emerson's writing and among the first to read him in Germany. Grimm—the son of philologist and folktale archivist Wilhelm Grimm (1786–1859), half of the Brothers Grimm—was a scholar of Raphael and Michelangelo. Grimm was familiar with Emerson's essay "Michelangelo" (first published in the North American Review, *January 1837), and praised its author for his "wise and generous" views of the painter; when it was published in 1868, Grimm sent Emerson the first volume of his* The Life of Michelangelo. *Grimm told Emerson, "I have endeavored to write my book about Michelangelo in this sense—every page, so that it would stand the test if I could read it aloud to you" (October 25, 1860). Emerson and Grimm would often make introductions for their fellow countrymen traveling abroad; Emerson wrote to Grimm in April 1867 with such a request: "Will you allow me the pleasure of introducing to you a young friend of mine, Mr. William James, a student of medicine at Cambridge. [. . .] His father, Henry James, Esq., an old friend of mine, is a man of rare insight and of brilliant conversation, and I doubt not you will find the son the valued companion that we hold him" (April 14, 1867).[1] Grimm reported that he was "greatly pleased" with his young American visitor. Herewith are three letters from an admiring Grimm, who over the course of the eleven years that elapse between these lines begins to add "and friend" to his salutation.*

Letters to Emerson

Herman Grimm

BERLIN, *April 5, 1856.*

HONORED SIR,—The departure of Mr. Alexander Thayer gives me the opportunity of addressing a few words to you. A year ago I first became acquainted with your writings, which since that time have been read by me repeatedly, with ever recurring admiration. Everywhere I seem to find my own secret thoughts,—even the words in which I would prefer to have expressed them. Of all the writers of our day you seem to me to understand the genius of the time most profoundly, to anticipate our future most clearly. It makes me happy to be permitted to say this to you.

I have permitted myself to enclose with this letter some of my essays and poems. I do it, not in order to receive thanks from you,—indeed, I do not even think of your reading them, but it is, nevertheless, a great satisfaction to me to send them to you. The thought makes me proud that they will come into your house and into your hands.

With true veneration and esteem,

Yours, HERMAN GRIMM.

BERLIN, *October* 25, 1860.

HONORED SIR,—Had I written you as often as I intended to do so, you would have many letters from me. Primarily, when more than a year ago I received yours, I wanted to thank you for it, for I was proud that you had thought of me and had written to me; but I omitted to do so because too many things seemed to crowd in, of which I would have had to speak, and of which, nevertheless, had I wanted to do so, it would have been impossible for me to speak. The illness of my departed mother-in-law showed even then its dangerous character, which brought about the end; then her death followed; then came my own physical collapse. After that, the illness and death of my father, coming soon after I had married Gisela von Arnim, of whom you did not know that she was to become my wife, and since then one prevention followed the other. All this made me so incapable of sending you the letter which I wanted to write, that I even sent you my book about Michelangelo, without an accompanying greeting.

Even now there is really no change for the better. It seems that I am not to attain the rest for which I am longing so greatly, for my Uncle Jacob is in indifferent health since the death of his brother, and into all that I think and do there enters care for the future which is facing me inexorably. At the moment he is better; he has convalesced somewhat from the chills and fever from which he suffered during the summer, but there is no reliance to be placed upon this convalescence, for he is old. He is in his seventy-seventh year, and even if he were healthy and vigorous it would be necessary to be resigned to his loss.

Thus the last years have been an exceptional period for me. I only wish to tell you how often during this time I have opened your books and how much comforting ease of mind I have drawn from them. You write so that everyone reading your words must think that you had thought of him alone. The love which you have for all mankind is felt so strongly that one thinks it impossible that you should not have thought of single preferred persons, among whom the reader counts himself. What a happiness for a country to possess such a man! When I think of America I think of you, and America appears to me as the first country of the world. You well know I would not say this if it were not really my innermost conviction. When I read your words, the course of years and events appears to me like the rhythm of a beautiful poem, and even the most commonplace is dissolved into necessary beauty through your observation.

I have endeavored to write my book about Michelangelo in this sense—every page, so that it would stand the test if I could read it aloud to you. I sent the book to you in August, and hope that it has reached your address. I know how imperfect it is, but please take the good will for the deed, and if you ever have time let me know what you find to censure. I should like to utilize your remarks for a second volume upon which I am now engaged. {...}

Farewell. My wife greets you a thousand times. If you wish to make us happy, please do send us a very good portrait of yourself. I have succeeded in getting some which do not, however, seem to me to be good likenesses.

With esteem and gratitude,

Your HERMAN GRIMM.

(Yesterday we had been married just one year.)

BERLIN, *October* 19, 1867.

HONORED SIR AND FRIEND,—Instead of all the letters which I have for years written to you in my thoughts, without ever putting them to paper, I now send you brief news through Mr. Foote. Why I wanted to write so often I hardly need tell you. In all the heavy hours through which I have passed in the last years—when my wife's mother died, when my Uncle Jacob followed her, and my father, and last summer, hardly two months ago, my mother—it was almost my only comfort to formulate the thoughts which filled me into letters to you, in which I expressed that which was cutting my heart in twain.

Then again however I omitted to write out what I had thought, but I had the feeling that you knew it nevertheless.

What else is there that I could write,—that I read your books again and again, that your letters made me happy, and that I like nothing better than to hear talk about you? I can mention no one whom I wish to know except yourself. If I did not dread the sea voyage on account of my wife, I should have come over long ago; but she would not be able to bear the voyage over to you. {...}

Mr. {William} James has arrived here, and we are greatly pleased with him. To-morrow evening he will become acquainted at our house with Joachim, the celebrated violinist,—at the same time my best friend, and also the man who was among the first in Germany to become acquainted with your thoughts in the fullness of their importance. Joachim and I read your works at the time in Germany when besides us perhaps no one knew them. Now indeed many know them, and more and more are becoming acquainted with you. {...}

I conclude my letter as though I had written yesterday and expected to write again to-morrow.

With most cordial regards,

Yours, HERMAN GRIMM.

Note

1 *Correspondence between Ralph Waldo Emerson and Herman Grimm*, ed. Frederick William Holls (Boston and New York: Houghton, Mifflin and Company, 1903), 67.

Charles Baudelaire (1821–1867)

Influential French poet, essayist, art critic, and translator of work by Edgar Allan Poe, Baudelaire was the author of The Flowers of Evil *(*Les Fleur du mal, *1857).*
T. S. Eliot, who quoted Baudelaire in The Waste Land, *said that his "technical mastery [. . .] can hardly be overpraised." Below, following a brief passage from Baudelaire's essay on Delacroix, "The Painter of Modern Life"[1] (1863), featuring a quotation from Emerson's "Considerations by the Way" (an essay from* The Conduct of Life *(1860)), is an excerpt from Baudelaire's poem* My Heart Laid Bare—*a title drawn from a remark by Poe. In the poem, Baudelaire suggests Emerson might have improved* Representative Men *by adding a French author—perhaps as a complement and contrast to Napoleon? Baudelaire likely already noticed that no American appears on Emerson's list. Several scholars have addressed Baudelaire's reading of Emerson, including Margaret Gilman,* Baudelaire and Emerson *(1943); Bernard Howells,* Baudelaire: Individualism, Dandyism, and the Philosophy of History—*with a chapter "On the Meaning of Great Men: Baudelaire and Emerson Revisited" (1996); and Dudley M. Marchi,* Baudelaire, Emerson, and the French-American Connection: Contrary Affinities *(2011). On the basis of documentary sources, Marchi posits that Emerson and Baudelaire were both likely to be seen in the crowd at political rallies in mid-May 1848, though they never met. Branka Arsić suggests that Baudelaire's notion of "the wearisome Bostonian school" is traceable to Baudelaire's awareness of Poe's opinion of Emerson.[2]*

from *The Painter of Modern Life*

Charles Baudelaire

"The hero is he who is immovably centered," says the transatlantic moralist, Emerson, who, in spite of reputation as the leader of the wearisome Bostonian school, has nevertheless a certain flavor of Seneca about him, which effectively stimulates meditation. . . . But this maxim, which the leader of American *Transcendentalism* applies to the conduct of life and the sphere of business, can equally well be applied to the sphere of poetry and art.

from *My Heart Laid Bare*

XXIV

I am bored in France, especially as every one resembles Voltaire.

Emerson forgot Voltaire in his "Representative Men." He could have made a fine chapter entitled Voltaire or The Antipoet, the king of boobies, the prince of the shallow, the anti-artist, the preacher of innkeepers, the father who "lived in a shoe" of the editors of the century.

Notes

1 Charles Baudelaire, "The Life and Work of Eugene Delacroix" in *The Painter of Modern Life and Other Essays*, ed. and trans. Jonathan Mayne (London: Phaidon Press, 2003), 53.
2 Branka Arsić, *On Leaving* (Cambridge: Harvard University Press, 2010), 78.

John Greenleaf Whittier (1807–1892)

*Quaker, poet, and vigorous abolitionist, Whittier is customarily noted as belonging
to the Fireside Poets, in company with H. W. Longfellow, O. W. Holmes, Sr.,
W. C. Bryant, and J. R. Lowell. Scholars have noted that Emerson's poem
"The Snow-Storm" may have inspired one of Whittier's most celebrated poems,
"Snow-Bound" (1866). Whittier, for his part, motivated Emerson to write more
publically against the institution of American slavery. In 1880, Whittier, along
with Walt Whitman, G. W. Curtis, T. W. Higginson, and others, wrote the following
remarks in* The Literary World *(May 22) to celebrate Emerson's birthday.*

Emerson's Birthday

John Greenleaf Whittier

No words of mine can overstate my respect and admiration for the great poet and
essayist whose seventy-seventh birthday the *Literary World* does well to honor.
Standing as he does at the head of our literature, and foremost among the philosophical
thinkers of our age, it needs no gift of prophecy to foresee that his reputation will lose
nothing by the lapse of time. No living poet of the English-speaking tongue has written
verses bearing more distinctly than his the mark of immortality. In his prose works
all must recognize his keen insight, wisdom, fine sense of humor, large tolerance, and
love of nature in her simplest as well as grandest aspects—an inimitable combination
of practical sagacity, profound reflection and mystical intuition. May his days be long
in the land!

John G. Whittier
Boston, May 22, 1880

James Russell Lowell (1819–1891)

Editor of the first four volumes of the Atlantic Monthly *(1857–1861), Lowell was a highly respected editor, critic, translator, essayist, poet, diplomat, and Professor of Belles-Lettres at Harvard College. He was linked with the Fireside Poets, among them H. W. Longfellow, O. W. Holmes, Sr., and J. G. Whittier. Lowell wrote poetry that criticized slavery, and came to widespread fame with the book-length poem* A Fable for Critics *(1848) in which he satirized noted critics and poets, including Emerson. In the wake of Lincoln's assassination, Lowell presented poetic work at Harvard along with Emerson and Holmes. Emerson praised Lowell's effort, which it appears Lowell despaired over, as full of "high thought & sentiment."[1] Emerson noted that in his poetry Lowell "rather expresses his wish, his ambition, than the uncontrollable interior impulse which is the authentic mark of a new poem [. . .] and which is felt in the pervading tone, rather than in brilliant parts or lines."[2] Lowell once assessed Emerson's impact on a generation of thinkers: "We were still socially and intellectually moored to English thought, till Emerson cut the cable and gave us a chance at the dangers and the glories of blue water." The range of the following work, poetic and polemical, attests to Lowell's appraisal of Emerson's effect. The reader will find below Section I of* A Fable for Critics *(1848), remarks on Emerson's* The Conduct of Life *from the* Atlantic Monthly Magazine *(February 1861), and the essay "Mr. Emerson's New Course of Lectures" from the* Nation *(November 12, 1868). For disambiguation, the 1861 and 1868 pieces are combined and published as "Emerson, the Lecturer" in Lowell's book of essays,* My Study Windows *(1871).*

from *A Fable for Critics*

James Russell Lowell

I. Emerson

There comes Emerson first, whose rich words, every one,
Are like gold nails in temples to hang trophies on,
Whose prose is grand verse, while his verse, the Lord knows,
Is some of it pr—No, 'tis not even prose;
I'm speaking of metres; some poems have welled

From those rare depths of soul that have ne'er been excelled;
They're not epics, but that doesn't matter a pin,
In creating, the only hard thing's to begin;
A grass-blade's no easier to make than an oak,
If you've once found the way you've achieved the grand stroke;
In the worst of his poems are mines of rich matter,
But thrown in a heap with a crash and a clatter
Now it is not one thing nor another alone
Makes a poem, but rather the general tone,
The something pervading, uniting, the whole,
The before unconceived, unconceivable soul,
So that just in removing this trifle or that, you
Take away, as it were, a chief limb of the statue;
Roots, wood, bark, and leaves, singly perfect may be,
But, clapt hodge-podge together, they don't make a tree.

But, to come back to Emerson, (whom by the way,
I believe we left waiting,)—his is, we may say,
A Greek head on right Yankee shoulders, whose range
Has Olympus for one pole, for t' other the Exchange;
He seems, to my thinking, (although I'm afraid
The comparison must, long ere this, have been made,)
A Plotinus-Montaigne, where the Egyptians gold mist
And the Gascon's shrewd wit cheek-by-jowl coexist;
All admire, and yet scarcely six converts he's got
To I don't (nor they either) exactly know what;
For though he builds glorious temples, 'tis odd
He leaves never a doorway to get in a god.
'Tis refreshing to old-fashioned people like me,
To meet such a primitive Pagan as he,
In whose mind all creation is duly respected
As part of himself—just a little projected;
And who's willing to worship the stars and the sun,
A convert to—nothing but Emerson.
So perfect a balance there is in his head,
That he talks of things sometimes as if they were dead;
Life, nature, love, God, and affairs of that sort,
He looks at as merely ideas; in short,
As if they were fossils stuck round in a cabinet,
Of such vast extent that our earth's a mere dab in it;
Composed just as he is inclined to conjecture her,
Namely, one part pure earth, ninety-nine parts pure lecturer;
You are filled with delight at his clear demonstration,

Each figure, word, gesture, just fits the occasion,
With the quiet precision of science he'll sort 'em,
But you can't help suspecting the whole a *post mortem*.

Notes

1   Martin Duberman, *James Russell Lowell* (Boston: Houghton Mifflin Company, 1966), 224–225.
2   Wilson Sullivan, *New England Men of Letters* (New York: The Macmillan Company, 1972), 220.

The Conduct of Life

James Russell Lowell

It is a singular fact, that Mr. Emerson is the most steadily attractive lecturer in America. Into that somewhat cold-waterish region, adventurers of the sensation kind come down now and then with a splash, to become disregarded King Logs before the next season. But Mr. Emerson always draws. A lecturer now for something like a quarter of a century, one of the pioneers of the lecturing system, the charm of his voice, his manner, and his matter has never lost its power over his earlier hearers, and continually winds new ones in its enchanting meshes. What they do not fully understand they take on trust, and listen, saying to themselves, as the old poet of Sir Philip Sidney,—

"A sweet, attractive, kind of grace,
    A full assurance given by looks,
Continual comfort in a face,
    The lineaments of gospel books."

We call it a singular fact, because we Yankees are thought to be fond of the spread-eagle style, and nothing can be more remote from that than his. We are reckoned a practical folk, who would rather hear about a new air-tight stove than about Plato; yet our favorite teacher's practicality is not in the least of the Poor Richard variety. If he have any Buncombe constituency, it is that unrealized commonwealth of philosophers which Plotinus proposed to establish; and if he were to make an almanac, his directions to farmers would be something like this:—"OCTOBER: *Indian Summer;* now is the time to get in your early Vedas." What, then, is his secret? Is it not that he out-Yankees us all? that his range includes us all? that he is equally at home with the potato-disease and original sin, with pegging shoes and the Over-soul? that, as we try all trades, so has he tried all cultures? and above all, that his mysticism gives us a counterpoise to our super-practicality?

There is no man living to whom, as a writer, so many of us feel and thankfully acknowledge so great an indebtedness for ennobling impulses,—none whom so many cannot abide. What does he mean? ask these last. Where is his system? What is the use of it all? What the deuse have we to do with Brahma? Well, we do not propose to write an essay on Emerson at the fag-end of a February "Atlantic," with Secession longing for somebody to hold it, and Chaos come again in the South Carolina teapot. We will only say that we have found grandeur and consolation in a starlit night without caring to ask what it meant, save grandeur and consolation; we have liked Montaigne, as some ten generations before us have done, without thinking him so systematic as some more eminently tedious (or shall we say tediously eminent?) authors; we have thought roses as good in their way as cabbages, though the latter would have made a better show in the witness-box, if cross-examined as to their usefulness; and as for Brahma, why, he can take care of himself, and won't bite us at any rate.

The bother with Mr. Emerson is, that, though he writes in prose, he is essentially a poet. If you undertake to paraphrase what he says, and to reduce it to words of one syllable for infant minds, you will make as sad work of it as the good monk with his analysis of Homer in the "Epistolæ Obscurorum Virorum." We look upon him as one of the few men of genius whom our age has produced, and there needs no better proof of it meanwhile you will find that it has kindled all your thoughts. For choice and pith of language he belongs to a better age than ours, and might rub shoulders with Fuller and Browne,—though he does use that abominable word, *reliable.* His eye for a fine, telling phrase that will carry true is like that of a backwoodsman for a rifle; and he will dredge you up a choice word from the ooze of Cotton Mather himself. A diction at once so rich and so homely as his we know not where to match in these days of writing by the page; it is like homespun cloth-of-gold. The many cannot miss his meaning, and only the few can find it. It is the open secret of all true genius. What does he mean, quotha? He means inspiring hints, a divining-rod to your deeper nature, "plain living and high thinking."

We meant only to welcome this book, and not to review it. Doubtless we might pick our quarrel with it here and there; but all that our readers care to know is, that it contains essays on Fate, Power, Wealth, Culture, Behavior, Worship, Considerations by the Way, Beauty, and Illusions. They need no invitation to Emerson. "Would you know," says Goethe, "the ripest cherries? Ask the boys and the blackbirds." He does not advise you to inquire of the crows.

Mr. Emerson's New Course of Lectures

James Russell Lowell

The readers of the *Nation*, who are interested in all good things, will perhaps like to hear a word of Mr. Emerson's new course of lectures now going on in Boston. The announcement that such a pleasure is coming, to people as old as I am, is something like those forebodings of spring that prepare us every year for a familiar novelty, none the less novel, when it arrives, because it is familiar. We know perfectly well what we are to expect from Mr. Emerson, and yet what he says always penetrates and stirs us, as is apt to be the case with genius, in a very unlooked-for fashion. Perhaps genius is one of the few things which we gladly allow to repeat itself,—one of the few that multiply rather than weaken the force of their impression by iteration? Perhaps some of us hear more than the mere words, are moved by something deeper than the thoughts? If it be so, we are quite right, for it is thirty years and more of "plain living and high thinking" that speak to us in this altogether unique lay-preacher. We have shared in the beneficence of this varied culture, this fearless impartiality in criticism and speculation, this masculine sincerity, this sweetness of nature which rather stimulates than cloys, for a generation long. If ever there was a standing testimonial to the cumulative power and value of Character (and we need it sadly in these days), we have it in this gracious and dignified presence. What an antiseptic is a pure life! At sixty-five (or two years beyond his grand climacteric, as he would prefer to call it) he has that privilege of soul which abolishes the calendar, and presents him to us always the unwasted contemporary of his own prime. I do not know if he seem old to his younger hearers, but we who have known him so long wonder at the tenacity with which he maintains himself even in the outposts of youth. I suppose it is not the Emerson of 1868 to whom we listen. For us the whole life of the man is distilled in the clear drop of every sentence, and behind each word we divine the force of a noble character, the weight of a large capital of thinking and being. We do not go to hear what Emerson says so much as to hear Emerson. Not that we perceive any falling-off in anything that ever was essential to the charm of Mr. Emerson's peculiar style of thought or phrase. The first lecture, to be sure, was more disjointed even than common. It was as if, after vainly trying to get his paragraphs into sequence and order, he had at last tried the desperate expedient of *shuffling* them. It was chaos come again, but it was a chaos full of shooting-stars, a jumble of creative forces. The second lecture, on "Criticism and Poetry," was quite up to the level of old times, full of that power of strangely subtle association whose indirect approaches startle the mind into almost painful attention, of those flashes of mutual understanding between speaker and hearer that are gone ere one can say it lightens. The vice of Emerson's criticism seems to be, that while no man is so sensitive to what is poetical, few men are less sensible than he of what makes a poem. He values the solid meaning of thought above the subtler meaning of style. He would prefer Donne, I suspect, to Spenser, and sometimes mistakes the queer for the original.

To be young is surely the best, if the most precarious, gift of life; yet there are some of us who would hardly consent to be young again, if it were at the cost of our recollection of Mr. Emerson's first lectures during the consulate of Van Buren. We used to walk in from the country to the Masonic Temple (I think it was), through the crisp winter night, and listen to that thrilling voice of his, so charged with subtle meaning and subtle music, as shipwrecked men on a raft to the hail of a ship that came with unhoped-for food and rescue. Cynics might say what they liked. Did our own imaginations transfigure dry remainder-biscuit into ambrosia? At any rate, he brought us *life,* which, on the whole, is no bad thing. Was it all transcendentalism? magic-lantern pictures, on mist? As you will. Those, then, were just what we wanted. But it was not so. The delight and the benefit were that he put us in communication with a larger style of thought, sharpened our wits with a more pungent phrase, gave us ravishing glimpses of an ideal under the dry husk of our New England; made us conscious of the supreme and everlasting originality of whatever bit of soul might be in any of us; freed us, in short, from the stocks of prose in which we had sat so long that we had grown well-nigh contented in our cramps. And who that saw the audience will ever forget it, where every one still capable of fire, or longing to renew in himself the half-forgotten sense of it, was gathered? Those faces, young and old, a-gleam with pale intellectual light, eager with pleased attention, flash upon me once more from the deep recesses of the years with an exquisite pathos. Ah, beautiful young eyes, brimming with love and hope, wholly vanished now in that other world we call the Past, or peering doubtfully through the pensive gloaming of memory, your light impoverishes these cheaper days! I hear again that rustle of sensation, as they turned to exchange glances over some pithier thought, some keener flash of that humor which always played about the horizon of his mind like heat-lightning, and it seems now like the sad whisper of the autumn leaves that are whirling around me. But would my picture be complete if I forgot that ample and vegete countenance of Mr. R____ of W____,—how, from its regular post at the corner of the front bench, it turned in ruddy triumph to the profaner audience as if he were the inexplicably appointed fugleman of appreciation? I was reminded of him by those hearty cherubs in Titian's Assumption that look at you as who should say, "Did you ever see a Madonna like *that?* Did you ever behold one hundred and fifty pounds of womanhood mount heavenward before like a rocket?"

To some of us that long-past experience remains as the most marvellous and fruitful we have ever had. Emerson awakened us, saved us from the body of this death. It is the sound of the trumpet that the young soul longs for, careless, what breath may fill it. Sidney heard it in the ballad of "Chevy Chase," and we in Emerson. Nor did it blow retreat, but called to us with assurance of victory. Did they say he was disconnected? So were the stars, that seemed larger to our eyes, still keen with that excitement, as we walked homeward with prouder stride over the creaking snow. And were *they* not knit together by a higher logic than our mere sense could master? Were we enthusiasts? I hope and believe we were, and am thankful to the man who made us worth something for once in our lives. If asked what was left? what we carried home? we should not have been careful for an answer. It would have been enough if we had said that something beautiful had passed that way. Or we might have asked in return what one brought away from a symphony of Beethoven? Enough that he had set that ferment of wholesome discontent at work in us. There is one, at least, of those old hearers, so many of whom are now in the fruition of that intellectual beauty of which Emerson gave them both the desire and the foretaste, who will always love to repeat:—

"Che in la mente m'è fitta, ed or m'accuora
La cara e buona immagine paterna
Di voi, quando nel mondo ad ora ad ora
M'insegnavaste come l'uom s'eterna."

I am unconsciously thinking, as I write, of the third lecture of the present course, in which Mr. Emerson gave some delightful reminiscences of the intellectual influences in whose movement he had shared. It was like hearing Goethe read some passages of the "Wahrheit aus seinem Leben." Not that there was not a little *Dichtung,* too, here and there, as the lecturer built up so lofty a pedestal under certain figures as to lift them into a prominence of obscurity, and seem to masthead them there. Everybody was asking his neighbor who this or that recondite great man was, in the faint hope that somebody might once have heard of him. There are those who call Mr. Emerson cold. Let them revise their judgment in presence of this loyalty of his that can keep warm for half a century, that never forgets a friendship, or fails to pay even a fancied obligation to the uttermost farthing. This substantiation of shadows was but incidental, and pleasantly characteristic of the man to those who know and love him. The greater part of the lecture was devoted to reminiscences of things substantial in themselves. He spoke of Everett, fresh from Greece and Germany; of Channing; of the translations of Margaret Fuller, Ripley, and Dwight; of the "Dial" and Brook Farm. To what he said of the latter an undertone of good-humored irony gave special zest. But what every one of his hearers felt was that the protagonist in the drama was left out. The lecturer was no Æneas to babble the *quorum magna pars fui,* and, as one of his listeners, I cannot help wishing to say how each of them was commenting the story as it went along, and filling up the necessary gaps in it from his own private store of memories. His younger hearers could not know how much they owed to the benign impersonality, the quiet scorn of everything ignoble, the never-sated hunger of self-culture, that were personified in the man before them. But the older knew how much the country's intellectual emancipation was due to the stimulus of his teaching and example, how constantly he had kept burning the beacon of an ideal life above our lower region of turmoil. To him more than to all other causes together did the young martyrs of our civil war owe the sustaining strength of thoughtful heroism that is so touching in every record of their lives. Those who are grateful to Mr. Emerson, as many of us are, for what they feel to be most valuable in their culture, or perhaps I should say their impulse, are grateful not so much for any direct teachings of his as for that inspiring lift which only genius can give, and without which all doctrine is chaff.

This was something like the *caret* which some of us older boys wished to fill up on the margin of the master's lecture. Few men have been so much to so many, and through so large a range of aptitudes and temperaments, and this simply because all of us value manhood beyond any or all other qualities of character. We may suspect in him, here and there, a certain thinness and vagueness of quality, but let the waters go over him as they list, this masculine fibre of his will keep its lively color and its toughness of texture. I have heard some great speakers and some accomplished orators, but never any that so moved and persuaded men as he. There is a kind of undertow in that rich baritone of his that sweeps our minds from their foothold into deeper waters with a drift we cannot and would not resist. And how artfully (for Emerson is a long-studied artist in these things) does the deliberate utterance, that seems waiting for the fit word, appear to admit us partners in the labor of thought and make us feel as if the glance of humor were a sudden suggestion, as if the perfect phrase lying written there on the desk were as unexpected to him as to us! In that closely filed speech of his at the Burns centenary dinner, every word seemed to have just dropped down to him from the clouds. He looked far away over the heads of his hearers, with a vague kind of expectation, as into some private heaven of invention, and the winged period came at last obedient to his spell. "My dainty Ariel!" he seemed murmuring to himself as he cast down his eyes as if in deprecation of the frenzy of approval and caught another sentence from the Sibylline leaves that lay before him, ambushed behind a dish of fruit and seen only by nearest neighbors. Every sentence brought down the house, as I never saw one brought down before,— and it is not so easy to hit Scotsmen with a sentiment that has no hint of native brogue in it. I watched, for it was an interesting study, how the quick sympathy ran flashing from face to face down the long tables, like an electric spark thrilling as it went, and then exploded in a thunder of plaudits. I watched till tables and faces vanished, for I, too, found myself caught up in the common enthusiasm, and my excited fancy set me under the *bema* listening to him who fulmined over Greece. I can never help applying to him what Ben Jonson said of Bacon: "There happened in my time one noble speaker, who was full of gravity in his speaking. His language was nobly censorious. No man ever spake more neatly, more pressly, more weightily, or suffered less emptiness, less idleness, in what he uttered. No member of his speech but consisted of his own graces. His hearers could not cough, or look aside from him, without loss. He commanded where he spoke." Those who heard him while their natures were yet plastic, and their mental nerves trembled under the slightest breath of divine air, will never cease to feel and say—

"Was never eye did see that face,
    Was never ear did hear that tongue,
Was never mind did mind his grace,
    That ever thought the travail long;
But eyes, and ears, and every thought,
Were with his sweet perfections caught."

Horace Greeley (1811–1872)

Perhaps the most influential newspaper editor in mid-nineteenth century America, Greeley founded and edited the New-York Tribune, *and was a prominent and outspoken advocate for the abolition of slavery. Given Greeley's talent and power as an editor, it is meaningful to read his opinion of the journal* The Dial, *which was edited by Margaret Fuller (who worked for Greeley), and later by Emerson. In his* Autobiography; or Recollections of a Busy Life (1868), *Greeley wrote: "I presume the circulation of The Dial never reached two thousand copies and that it hardly averaged one thousand. But its influence and results are nowise measured by the number of its patrons, nor even of its readers. To the 'fit audience, though few,' who had long awaited and needed its advent, without clearly comprehending their need, it was like manna in the wilderness."[1] In the essay "Literature as a Vocation," Greeley says there are "men decidedly in advance of their time,—who come to their own, and not recognized and made welcome,—who write, like Wordsworth or Emerson, for a public which their genius must create or their patience await,—authors whose works would sell better if they were less profoundly good."[2] In the following letters from Greeley to Thoreau, the latter's lack of response to Greeley's request creates an enthymeme from which readers can quickly deduce that Thoreau would not exploit his friendship with Emerson to satisfy either the demands of an editor or those of his curious public.*

Letters to Thoreau

Horace Greeley

[April 3, 1852]

Friend Thoreau,—

I wish you to write me an article on Ralph Waldo Emerson, his Works and Ways, extending to one hundred pages, or so, of letter sheet like this, to take the form of a review of his writings, but to give some idea of the Poet, the Genius, the Man,—with some idea of the New England scenery and home influence, which have combined to make him what he is. Let it be calm, searching, and impartial; nothing like adulation, but a just summing up of what he is and what he has done. I mean to get this into the "Westminster Review," but if not acceptable there, I will publish it elsewhere. I will pay you fifty dollars for the article when delivered; in advance, if you desire it. Say the word, and I will send the money at once. It is perfectly convenient to do so. Your

"Carlyle" article is my model, but you can give us Emerson better than you did Carlyle. I presume he would allow you to write extracts for this purpose from his lectures not yet published. I would delay the publication of the article to suit his publishing arrangements, should that be requested.

Yours,
Horace Greeley.

New York, April 20, 1852

Dear Sir:

I have yours of the 17th. I am rather sorry you will not do the Works and Ways; but glad that you are able to employ your time to better purpose.

But your Quebeck notes don't reach me yet, and I fear the 'good time' is passing. They ought to have appeared in the June Nos. of the Monthlies, but now cannot before July. If you choose to send them to me all in a bunch, I will try to get them printed in that way. I don't care about them if you choose to reserve or to print them elsewhere; but I can better make a use for them at this season than at any other.

Yours,
Horace Greeley.

H. D. Thoreau, Concord, Mass.

Notes

1   Horace Greeley, *The Autobiography of Horace Greeley; or Recollections of a Busy Life* (New York: E. B. Treat, 1868), 170.

2   Ibid., 444.

John Ruskin (1819–1900)

A prominent art critic in Victorian England, Ruskin wrote Modern Painters *(1843),
a lengthy defense of J. M. W. Turner. While visiting England for the second time
in 1848, Emerson read the second volume of* Modern Painters, *and when Emerson
saw Turner's paintings in person, he recorded in his journal that the works "justify
Ruskin's praise."[1] When Emerson visited Turner's painting studio (though the artist
was absent at the time), he was told by his guide, none other than the anatomist
Robert Owen (who also showed him the Hunterian Museum), that "in his earlier
pictures, he painted conventionally, painted what he knew was there; finished the
coat & hat & buttons; in the later he paints only what the eye really sees, & gets
the genius of the city or landscape."[2] And as Owen's description and Ruskin's art
criticism appealed to Emerson, so decades later, in 1871, Emerson re-read Ruskin's*
The Two Paths *(from lectures delivered in 1858 and 1859) and found the writer's
sentiments on art remained agreeable. (The two met in Oxford in 1873.) Ruskin, in
turn, appears to have read Emerson closely, as suggested by the following selection
of varied excerpts from "Plagiarism" (chapter three of the Appendix in* Modern
Painters, *Vol. III, 1856), "Dictatorship" (Letter XII of* Time and Tide, *1867), and*
Fors Clavigera *(pamphlets written from 1871–84; this piece from 1872 is one in
which he quotes from Emerson's* English Traits*). "And, next to Carlyle," Ruskin
wrote, "for my own immediate help and teaching, I nearly always look to Emerson."
Emerson is for Ruskin, along with Carlyle, one of our "great teachers."[3]*

from Plagiarism in *Modern Painters III*

John Ruskin

Some time after I had written the concluding chapter of this work, the interesting and
powerful poems of Emerson were brought under my notice by one of the members
of my class at the Working Men's College. There is much in some of these poems so
like parts of the chapter in question, even in turn of expression, that though I do not
usually care to justify myself from the charge of plagiarism, I felt that a few words were
necessary in this instance.

I do not, as aforesaid, justify myself, in general, because I know there is internal
evidence in my work of its originality, if people care to examine it; and if they do not,
or have not skill enough to know genuine from borrowed work, my simple assertion
would not convince them, especially as the charge of plagiarism is hardly ever made
but by plagiarists, and persons of the unhappy class who do not believe in honesty but

on evidence. Nevertheless, as my work is so much out of doors, and among pictures, that I have time to read few modern books, and am therefore in more danger than most people of repeating, as if it were new, what others have said, it may be well to note, once for all, that any such apparent plagiarism results in fact from my writings being more original than I wish them to be, from my having worked out my whole subject in unavoidable, but to myself hurtful, ignorance of the labours of others. On the other hand, I should be very sorry if I had not been continually taught and influenced by the writers whom I love; and am quite unable to say to what extent my thoughts have been guided by Wordsworth, Carlyle, and Helps; to whom (with Dante and George Herbert, in olden time) I owe more than to any other writers;—most of all, perhaps to Carlyle, whom I read so constantly, that, without willfully setting myself to imitate him, I find myself perpetually falling into his modes of expression, and saying many things in a "quite other," and, I hope, stronger, way, than I should have adopted some years ago; as also there are things which I hope are said more clearly and simply than before, owing to the influence upon me of the beautiful *quiet* English of Helps. It would be both foolish and wrong to struggle to cast off influences of this kind; for they consist mainly in a real and healthy help;—the master, in writing as in painting, showing certain methods of language which it would be ridiculous, and even affected, not to employ, when once shown; just as it would have been ridiculous in Bonifazio to refuse to employ Titian's way of laying on colour, if he felt it the best, because he had not himself discovered it. There is all the difference in the world between this receiving of guidance, or allowing of influence, and wilful imitation, much more, plagiarism; nay, the guidance may even innocently reach into local tones of thought, and most do so to some extent; so that I find Carlyle's stronger thinking colouring mine continually; and should be very sorry if I did not; otherwise I should have read him to little purpose. But what I have of my own is still all there, and I believe, better brought out, by far, than it would have been otherwise. Thus, if we glance over the wit and satire of the popular writers of the day, we shall find that the *manner* of it, so far as it is distinctive, is always owing to Dickens; and that out of his first exquisite ironies branched innumerable other forms of wit, varying with the disposition of the writers; original in the matter and substance of them, yet never to have been expressed as they now are, but for Dickens. {...}

from Dictatorship in *Time and Tide*

It is true, of course, that, in the end of ends, nothing but the right conquers: the prevalent thorns of wrong, at last, crackle away in indiscriminate flame: and of the good seed sown, one grain in a thousand, at last, verily comes up—and somebody lives by it; but most of our great teachers, not excepting Carlyle and Emerson themselves, are a little too encouraging in their proclamation of this comfort, not, to my mind, very sufficient, when for the present our fields are full of nothing but nettles and thistles, instead of wheat; and none of them seem to me yet to have enough insisted on the inevitable power and infectiousness of all evil, and the easy and utter extinguishableness of good. Medicine often fails of its effect—but poison never: and while, in summing the observation of past life, not unwatchfully spent, I can truly say that I have a thousand times seen patience disappointed of her hope, and wisdom of her aim, I have never yet seen folly fruitless of mischief, nor vice conclude but in calamity.

from *Fors Clavigera*

PROPOSITION I. (I. 3, 4).—The English nation is beginning another group of ten years, empty in purse, empty in stomach, and in a state of terrified hostility to every other nation under the sun.

I assert this very firmly and seriously. But in the course of these papers every important assertion on the opposite side shall be fairly inserted; so that you may consider of them at your leisure. Here is one, for instance, from the 'Morning Post' of Saturday, August 31, of this year [1872]:—"The country is at the present moment in a state of such unexampled prosperity that it is actually suffering from the very superabundance of its riches. ... Coals and meat are at famine prices, we are threatened with a strike among the bakers, and there is hardly a single department of industry in which the cost of production has not been enhanced."

This is exceedingly true; the 'Morning Post' ought to have congratulated you further on the fact that the things produced by this greater cost are now usually good for nothing: Hear on this head, what Mr. Emerson said of us, even so far back as 1856 {in *English Traits*} (and we have made much inferior articles since then), "England is aghast at the disclosure of her fraud in the adulteration of food, of drugs, and of almost every fabric in her mills and shops; finding that milk will not nourish, nor sugar sweeten, nor bread satisfy, nor pepper bite the tongue, nor glue stick. In true England all is false and forged. ... It is rare to find a merchant who knows why a crisis occurs in trade,—why prices rise or fall, or who knows the mischief of paper money (or the use of it, Mr. Emerson should have added). In the culmination of National Prosperity, in the annexation of countries; building of ships, depôts, towns; in the influx of tons of gold and silver; amid the chuckle of chancellors and financiers, it was found that bread rose to famine prices, that the yeoman was forced to sell his cow and pig, his tools, and his acre of land; and the dreadful barometer of the poor-rates was touching the point of ruin."

Notes

1   Ralph Waldo Emerson, *The Journals and Miscellaneous Notebooks of Ralph Waldo Emerson*, ed. William H. Gilman, et al. (Cambridge: Belknap Press of Harvard University Press, 1973), Vol. X, 273.

2   Ibid., Vol. X, 277.

3   John Ruskin, *The Complete Works of John Ruskin*, ed. E. T. Cook and Alexander Wedderburn (London: George Allen, 1905), Vol. XVII, 477, 374.

Frederick Douglass (1818–1895)

Born into slavery, Douglass escaped to freedom and became one of the leading intellects of the antislavery movement. The most prominent and influential African-American male abolitionist, Douglass wrote several versions of his autobiography, continually revising and adding to the narrative of his life. His unceasing endeavor to write appears coextensive with his effort to achieve full humanity as a man and as a citizen. In the following speech, first delivered in 1859, and in this version presented at the Carlisle School for Indians in Carlisle, Pennsylvania in 1872, Douglass contributes to the literature on the subject of how one becomes a man, and more particularly, becomes oneself. (The talk opens with an introduction; Douglass' remarks begin with, "The subject announced for this evening's entertainment is not new.") In the history of American letters this topic has invited a range of postulations and responses, and the phrase "self-made man" is often associated with the likes of Benjamin Franklin and Horatio Alger, and (somewhat misleadingly) with Emerson. For Douglass, as for Alger, being self-made is a fairly literal process of energetic, disciplined, and progressive self-improvement; the self-made man is described by Douglass as "the man of work." And Douglass clearly privileges such men and their achievement. Yet he lends some qualification to the term when he says "there is, in more respects than one, something like a solecism in this title," since "properly speaking, there are in the world no such men as self-made-men." In the following address, Douglass begins with an invocation of terms Emerson helped make famous—great men, representative men, men of genius, men of the world—and writes: "Mr. Emerson has declared that it is natural to believe in great men. Whether this is a fact, or not, we do believe in them and worship them." As intimated by the title, Douglass' lecture is profitably read alongside Emerson's "The American Scholar," "Self-Reliance," and Representative Men. Douglass and Emerson lived in an age preoccupied with genealogies and origins, necessarily fixated on race and pedigree, and so their remarks—occasionally aligned, sometimes disparate—on the meaning and implications of self-creation remain apt and elucidatory.

Self-Made Men

Frederick Douglass

Before entering upon his address to the students of the Indian School at Carlisle, Pa., Mr. Douglass remarked that it was impossible for him to fully or adequately express the sentiments awakened in him by what he had, that day and evening, seen and heard.

He had been surprised, gratified and astonished by the order and aptitude displayed in the drill witnessed, and by the concord of sweet sounds to which he had that evening listened. What he had seen and heard had filled him with admiration and with the hope that the Indian will yet do his full share towards the civilization of our composite nation. He rejoiced, beyond expression, at what he had seen and heard at the Carlisle School for Indians. He had himself been known as a negro, but for then and there, he wished to be known as an Indian.

After these sentiments had been heartily applauded, Mr. Douglass proceeded with the following lecture, entitled

SELF-MADE MEN.

The subject announced for this evening's entertainment is not new. Man in one form or another, has been a frequent and fruitful subject for the press, the pulpit and the platform. This subject has come up for consideration under a variety of attractive titles, such as "Great Men," "Representative Men," "Peculiar Men," "Scientific Men," "Literary Men," "Successful Men," "Men of Genius," and "Men of the World," but under whatever name or designation, the vital point of interest in the discussion has ever been the same, and that is, manhood itself, and this in its broadest and most comprehensive sense.

This tendency to the universal, in such discussion, is altogether natural and all controlling: for when we consider what man, as a whole, is; what he has been; what he aspires to be, and what, by a wise and vigorous cultivation of his faculties, he may yet become, we see that it leads irresistibly to this broad view of him as a subject of thought and inquiry.

The saying of the poet that "The proper study of mankind is man," and which has been the starting point of so many lectures, essays and speeches, holds its place, like all other great utterances, because it contains a great truth and a truth alike for every age and generation of men. It is always new and can never grow old. It is neither dimmed by time nor tarnished by repetition; for man, both in respect of himself and of his species, is now, and evermore will be, the center of unsatisfied human curiosity.

The pleasure we derive from any department of knowledge is largely due to the glimpse which it gives to us of our own nature. We may travel far over land and sea, brave all climates, dare all dangers, endure all hardships, try all latitudes and longitudes; we may penetrate the earth, sound the ocean's depths and sweep the hollow sky with our glasses, in the pursuit of other knowledge; we may contemplate the glorious landscape gemmed by forest, lake and river and dotted with peaceful homes and quiet herds; we may whirl away to the great cities, all aglow with life and enterprise; we may mingle with the imposing assemblages of wealth and power; we may visit the halls where Art works her miracles in music, speech and color, and where Science unbars the gates to higher planes of civilization; but no matter how radiant the colors, how enchanting the melody, how gorgeous and splendid the pageant; man himself, with eyes turned inward upon his own wondrous attributes and powers surpasses them all. A single human soul standing here upon the margin we call TIME, overlooking, in the vastness of its range, the solemn past which can neither be recalled nor remodeled, ever chafing against finite limitations, entangled with interminable contradictions, eagerly seeking to scan the invisible past in to pierce the clouds and darkness of the ever mysterious future, has attractions for thought and study, more numerous and powerful than all other objects beneath the sky. To human thought and inquiry he is broader than all visible worlds, loftier than all heights and deeper than all depths. Were I called upon to point out the broadest and most permanent distinction between mankind and other animals, it would be this; their earnest desire for the fullest knowledge of human nature on all its many sides. The importance of this knowledge is immeasurable, and by no other is human life so affected and colored. Nothing can bring to man so much of happiness or so much of misery as man himself. Today he exalts himself to heaven by his virtues and achievements; to-morrow he smites with sadness and pain, by his crimes and follies. But whether exalted or debased, charitable or wicked; whether saint or villain, priest or prize fighter; if only he be great in his line, he is an unfailing source of interest, as one of a common brotherhood; for the best man finds in his breast, the evidence of kinship with the worst, and the worst with the best. Confront us with either extreme and you will rivet our attention and fix us in earnest contemplation, for our chief desire is to know what there is in man and to know him at all extremes and ends and opposites, and for this knowledge, or for the want of it, we will follow him from the gates of life to the gates of death, and beyond them.

As this subject can never become old, so it can never be exhausted. Man is too closely related to the Infinite to be divided, weighed, measured and reduced to fixed standards, and thus adjusted to finite comprehension. No two of anything are exactly alike, and what is true of man in one generation may lack some degree of truth in another, but his distinctive qualities as man, are inherent and remain forever. Progressive in his nature, he defies power of progress to overtake him to make known, definitely, the limits of his marvelous powers and possibilities.

From man comes all that we know or can imagine of heaven and earth, of time and eternity. He is the prolific constituter of manners, morals, religions and governments. He spins them out as the spider spins his web, and they are coarse or fine, kind or cruel, according to the degree of intelligence reached by him at the period of their establishment. He compels us to contemplate his past with wonder and to survey his future with much the same feelings as those with which Columbus is supposed to have gazed westward over the sea. It is the faith of the race that in man there exists far outlying continents of power, thought and feeling, which remain to be discovered, explored, cultivated, made practical and glorified.

Mr. Emerson has declared that it is natural to believe in great men. Whether this is a fact, or not, we do believe in them and worship them. The Visible God of the New Testament is revealed to us as a man of like passions with ourselves. We seek out our wisest and best man, the man who, by eloquence or the sword compels us to believe him such, and make him our leader, prophet, preacher and law giver. We do this, not because he essentially different from us, but because of his identity with us. He is our best representative and reflects, on a colossal scale, the scale to which we would aspire, our highest aims, objects, powers and possibilities.

This natural reverence for all that is great in man, and this tendency to deify and worship him, though natural and the source of man's elevation, has not always shown itself wise but has often shown itself far otherwise than wise. It has often given us a wicked ruler for a righteous one, a false prophet for a true one, a corrupt preacher for a pure one, a man of war for a man of peace, and a distorted and vengeful image of God for an image of justice and mercy.

But it is not my purpose to attempt here any comprehensive and exhaustive theory or philosophy of the nature of manhood in all the range I have indicated. I am here to speak to you of a peculiar type of manhood under the title of

Self-Made Men.

That there is, in more respects than one, something like a solecism in this title, I freely admit. Properly speaking, there are in the world no such men as self-made men. That term implies and individual independence of the past and present which can never exist.

Our best and most valued acquisitions have been obtained either from our contemporaries or from those who have preceded us in the field of thought and discovery. We have all either begged, borrowed or stolen. We have reaped where others have sown, and that which others have strown, we have gathered. It must in truth be said though it may not accord well with self-conscious individuality and self-concept, that no possible native force of character, and no depth or wealth of originality, can lift a man into absolute independence of his fellowmen, and no generation of men can be independent of the preceding generation. The brotherhood and inter-dependence of mankind are guarded and defended at all points. I believe in individuality, but individuals are, to the mass, like waves to the ocean. The highest order of genius is as dependent as is the lowest. It, like the loftiest waves of the sea, derives its power and greatness from the grandeur and vastness of the ocean of which it forms a part. We differ as the waves, but are one as the sea. To do something well does not necessarily imply the ability to do everything else equally well. If you can do in one direction that which I cannot do, I may in another direction, be able to do that which you cannot do. Thus the balance of power is kept comparatively even, and a self-acting brotherhood and inter-dependence is maintained.

Nevertheless, the title of my lecture is eminently descriptive of a class and is, moreover, a fit and convenient one for my purpose, in illustrating the idea which I have in view. In the order of discussion I shall adopt the style of an old-fashioned preacher and have a "firstly," a "secondly," a "thirdly," a "fourthly" and, possibly, a "conclusion."

My first is, "Who are self-made men?" My second is, "What is the true theory of their success?" My third is, "The advantages which self-made men derive from the manners and institutions of their surroundings," and my fourth is, "The grounds of the criticism to which they are, as a class, especially exposed."

On the first point I may say that, by the term "self-made men," I mean especially what, to the popular mind, the term itself imports. Self-made men are the men who, under peculiar difficulties and without the ordinary helps of favoring circumstances, have attained knowledge, usefulness, power and position and have learned from themselves the best uses to which life can be put in this world, in the exercises of these uses to build up worthy character. They are the men who owe little or nothing to birth, relationship, friendly surroundings; to wealth inherited or to early approved means of education; who are what they are, without the aid of any of the favoring conditions by which other men usually rise in the world and achieve great results. In fact they are the men who are not brought up but who are obliged to come up, not only without the voluntary assistance or friendly co-operation of society, but often in open and derisive defiance of all the efforts of society and the tendency of circumstances to repress, retard and keep them down. They are the men who, in a world of schools, academies, colleges and other institutions of learning, are often compelled by unfriendly circumstances to acquire their education elsewhere and, amidst unfavorable conditions, to hew out for themselves a way to success, and thus to become the architects of their own good fortunes. They are in a peculiar sense, indebted to themselves for themselves. If they have travelled far, they have made the road on which they traveled. If they have ascended high, they have built their own ladder. From the depths of poverty such as these have often come. From the heartless pavements of large and crowded cities; barefooted, homeless, and friendless, they have come. From hunger, rags and destitution, they have come; motherless and fatherless, they have come, and may come. Flung overboard in the midnight storm on the broad and tempest-tossed ocean of life; left without ropes, planks, oars or life-preservers, they have bravely buffeted the frowning billows and have risen in safety and life where others, supplied with the best appliances for safety and success, have fainted, despaired and gone down forever.

Such men as these, whether found in one position or another, whether in the colleges or in the factory; whether professors or plowmen; whether Caucasian or Indian; whether Anglo-Saxon or Anglo-Africa, are self-made men and are entitled to a certain measure of respect for their success and for proving to the world the grandest possibilities of human nature, of whatever variety of race or color.

Though a man of this class need not claim to be a hero or to be worshiped as such, there is genuine heroism in his struggle and something of sublimity and glory in his triumph. Every instance of such success is an example and a help to humanity. It, better than any mere assertion, give us assurance of the latent powers and resources of simple and unaided manhood. It dignifies labor, honors application, lessens pain and depression, dispels gloom from the brow of the destitute and weariness from the heart of him about to faint, and enables man to take hold of the roughest and flintiest hardships incident to the battle of life, with a lighter heart, with higher hopes and a larger courage.

But I come at once to the second part of my subject, which respects the

THEORY OF SELF-MADE MEN.

"Upon what meat doth this, our CÆSAR, feed, he hath grown so great?" How happens it that the cottager is often found equal to the lord, and that, in the race of life, the sons of the poor often get even with, and surpass even, the sons of the rich? How happens it from the field often come statesmen equal to those from the college? I am sorry to say that, upon this interesting point, I can promise nothing absolute nor anything which will be entirely satisfactory and conclusive. Burns says:

"I see how folks live that hae riches,
But surely poor folks maun be witches."

The various conditions of men and the different uses they make of their powers and opportunities in life, are full of puzzling contrasts and contradictions. Here, as elsewhere, it is easy to dogmatize, but it is not so easy to define, explain and demonstrate. The natural laws for the government, well-being and progress of mankind, seem to be equal and are equal; but the subjects of these laws everywhere abound in inequalities, discords and contrasts. We cannot have fruit without flowers, but we often have flowers without fruit. The promise of youth often breaks down in manhood, and real excellence often comes unheralded and from unexpected quarters.

The scene presented from this view is as a thousand arrows shot from the same point and aimed at the same object. United in aim, they are divided in flight. Some fly too high, others too low. Some go to the right, others to the left. Some fly too far and others, not far enough, and only a few hit the mark. Such is life. United in the quiver, they are divided in the air. Matched when dormant, they are unmatched in action.

When we attempt to account for greatness we never get nearer to the truth than did the greatest of poets and philosophers when he classified the conditions of greatness: "Some are born great, some achieve greatness and some have greatness thrust upon them." We may take our choice of these three separate explanations and make which of them we please, most prominent in our discussion. Much can certainly be said of superior mental endowments, and I should on some accounts, lean strongly to that theory, but for numerous examples which seem to, and do, contradict it, and but for the depressing tendency such a theory must have upon humanity generally.

This theory has truth in it, but it is not the whole truth. Men of very ordinary faculties have, nevertheless, made a very respectable way in the world and have sometimes presented even brilliant examples of success. On the other hand, what is called genius is often found by the wayside, a miserable wreck; the more deplorable and shocking because from the height from which it has fallen and the loss and ruin involved in the fall. There is, perhaps, a compensation in disappointment and in the contradiction of means to ends and promise to performance. These imply a constant effort on the part of nature to hold the balance evenly between all her children and to bring success within the reach of the humblest as well as of the most exalted.

From apparently the basest metals we have the finest toned bells, and we are taught respect from simple manhood when we see how, from the various dregs of society, there come men who may well be regarded as the pride and as the watch towers of the race.

Steel is improved by laying on damp ground, and the rusty razor gets a keener edge after giving its dross to the dirt in which it has been allowed to lie neglected and forgotten. In like manner, too, humanity, though it lay among the pots, covered with the dust of neglect and poverty, may still retain the divine impulse and the element of improvement and progress. It is natural to revolt at squalor, but we may well relax our lip of scorn and contempt when we stand among the lowly and despised, for out of the rags of the meanest cradle there may come a great man and this is a treasure richer than all the wealth the Orient.

I do not think much of the accident or good luck theory of self-made men. It is worth but little attention and has no practical value. An apple carelessly flung into a crowd may hit one person, or it may hit another, or it may hit nobody. The probabilities are precisely the same in this accident theory of self-made men. It divorces a man from his own achievements, contemplates him as a being of chance and leaves him without will, motive, ambition and aspiration. Yet the accident theory is among the most popular theories of individual success. It has about it the air of mystery which the multitude so well like, and withal, it does something to mar the complacency of the successful.

It is one of the easiest and commonest things in the world for a successful man to be followed in his career through life and to have constantly pointed out this or that particular stroke of good fortune which fixed his destiny and made him successful. If not ourselves great, we like to explain why others are so. We are stingy in our praise to merit, but generous in our praise to chance. Besides, a man feels himself measurably great when he can point out the precise moment and circumstance which made his neighbor great. He easily fancies that the sight difference between himself and his friend is simply one of luck. It was his friend who was lucky but it might easily have been himself. Then too, the next best thing to success is a valid apology for non-success. Detraction is, to many, a delicious morsel. The excellence which it loudly denies to others it silently claims for itself. It possesses the means of covering the small with the glory of the great. It adds to failure that which it takes from success and shortens the distance between those in front and those in the rear. Even here there is an upward tendency worthy of notice and respect. The kitchen is ever the critic of the parlor. The talk of those below is of those above. We imitate those we revere and admire.

But the main objection to this very comfortable theory is that, like most other theories, it is made to explain too much. While it ascribes success to chance and friendly circumstances, it is apt to take no cognizance of the very different uses to which different men put their circumstances and their chances.

Fortune may crowd a man's life with favorable circumstances and happy opportunities, but they will, as all know, avail him nothing unless he makes a wise and vigorous use of them. It does not matter that the wind is fair and the tide at its flood, if the mariner refuses to weigh his anchor and spread his canvas to the breeze. The golden harvest is ripe in vain if the farmer refuses to reap. Opportunity is important but exertion is indispensable. "There is a tide in the affairs of men which, taken at its flood, leads on to fortune;" but it must be taken at its flood.

Within this realm of man's being, as elsewhere, Science is diffusing its broad, beneficent light. As this light increases, dependence upon chance or luck is destined to vanish and the wisdom of adapting means to ends, to become more manifest.

It was once more common than it is now, to hear men religiously ascribing their good or ill fortune directly to supernatural intervention. Success and failure, wealth and poverty, intelligence and ignorance, liberty and slavery, happiness and misery, were all bestowed or inflicted upon individual men by a divine hand and for all-wise purposes. Man was, by such reasoners, made a very insignificant agent in his own affairs. It was all the Lord's doings and marvelous to human eyes. Of course along with this superstition came the fortune teller, the pretender to divination and the miracle working priest who could save from famine by praying easier than by under-draining and deep plowing.

In such matter a wise man has little use for altars or oracle. He knows that the laws of God are perfect and unchangeable. He knows that health is maintained by right living; that disease is cured by the right use of remedies; that bread is produced by tilling the soil; that knowledge is obtained by study; that wealth is secured by saving and that battles are won by fighting. To him, the lazy man is the unlucky man and the man of luck is the man of work.

> "The fault, dear Brutus, is not in our stars,
> But in ourselves, that we are underlings."

When we find a man who has ascended heights beyond ourselves; who has a broader range of vision than we and a sky with more stars in it than we have in ours, we may know that he has worked harder, better and more wisely than we. He was awake while we slept. He was busy while we were idle and he was wisely improving his time and talents while we were wasting ours. Paul Dunbar, the colored poet, has well said:

> "There are not beaten paths to glory's height,
> There are no rules to compass greatness known;
> Each for himself must cleave a path alone.
> And press his own way forward in the fight.
> Smooth is the way to ease and calm delight.
> And soft the road Sloth chooseth for her own;
> But he who craves the flow'r of life full-blown
> Must struggle up in all his armor dight.
> What tho' the burden bear him sorely down,
> And crush to dust the mountain of his pride.
> Oh! then with strong heart let him still abide
> For rugged is the roadway to renown.
> Nor may he hope to gain the envied crown
> Till he hath thrust the looming rocks aside."

I am certain that there is nothing good, great or desirable which man can possess in this world, that does not come by some kind of labor, either physical or mental, moral or spiritual. A man may, at times, get something for nothing, but it will, in his hands, amount to nothing. What is true in the world of matter, is equally true in the world of mind. Without culture there can be no growth; without exertion, no acquisition; without friction, no polish; without labor, no knowledge; without action, no progress and without conflict, no victory. The man who lies down a fool at night, hoping that he will waken wise in the morning, will rise up in the morning as he laid down in the evening.

Faith, in the absence of work, seems to be worth little, if anything. The preacher who finds it easier to pray for knowledge than to tax his brain with study and application will find his congregation growing beautifully less and his flock looking elsewhere for their spiritual and mental food. In the old slave times colored ministers were somewhat remarkable for the fervor with which they prayed for knowledge, but it did not appear that they were remarkable for any wonderful success. In fact, they who prayed loudest seemed to get least. They thought if they opened their mouths they would be filled. The result was an abundance of sound with a great destitution of sense.

Not only in man's experience, but also in nature do we find exemplified the truth upon which I have been insisting. My father worketh, said the Savior, and I also work. In every view which we obtain of the perfections of the universe; whether we look to the bright stars in the peaceful blue dome above us, or to the long shore line of the ocean, where land and water maintain eternal conflict; the lesson taught is the same; that of endless action and reaction. Those beautifully rounded pebbles which you gather on the sand and which you hold in your hand and marvel at their exceeding smoothness, were chiseled into their varied and graceful forms by the ceaseless action of countless waves. Nature is herself a great worker and never tolerates, without certain rebuke, and contradiction to her wise example. Inaction is followed by stagnation. Stagnation is followed by pestilence and pestilence is followed by death. General Butler, busy with his broom, could sweep yellow fever out of New Orleans, but this dread destroyer returned when the General and his broom were withdrawn, and the people, neglecting sanitary wisdom, went on ascribing to Divinity what was simply due to dirt.

From these remarks it will be evident that, allowing only ordinary ability and opportunity, we many explain success mainly by one word and that word is WORK! WORK!! WORK!!! WORK!!!! Not transient and fitful effort, but patient, enduring, honest, unremitting and indefatigable work, into which the whole heart is put, and which, in both temporal and spiritual affairs, is the true miracle worker. Every one may avail himself of this marvelous power, if he will. There is no royal road to perfection. Certainly no one must wait for some kind friend to put a springing board under his feet, upon which he may easily bound from the first round of the ladder onward and upward to its highest round. If he waits for this, he may wait long and perhaps forever. He who does not think himself worth saving from poverty and ignorance, by his own efforts, will hardly be thought worth the efforts of anybody else.

The lesson taught at this point by human experience is simply this, that the man who will get up will be helped up; and that the man who will not get up will be allowed to stay down. This rule may appear somewhat harsh, but in its general application and operation it is wise, just and beneficent. I know of no other rule which can be substituted for it without bringing social chaos. Personal independence is a virtue and it is the soul out of which comes the sturdiest manhood. But there can be no independence without a large share of self-dependence, and this virtue cannot be bestowed. It must be developed from within.

I have been asked "How will this theory affect the negro?" and "What shall be done in his case?" My general answer is "Give the negro fair play and let him alone. If he lives, well. If he dies, equally well. If he cannot stand up, let him fall down."

The apple must have strength and vitality enough in itself to hold on, or it will fall to the ground where it belongs. The strongest influence prevails and should prevail. If the vital relation of the fruit is severed, it is folly to tie the stem to the branch or the branch to the tree or to shelter the fruit from the wind. So, too, there is no wisdom in lifting from the earth a head which must only fall the more heavily when the help is withdrawn. Do right, though the heavens fall; but they will not fall.

I have said "Give the negro fair play and let him alone." I meant all that I said and a good deal more than some understand by fair play. It is not fair play to start the negro out in life, from nothing and with nothing, while others start with the advantage of a thousand years behind them. He should be measured, not by the heights others have obtained, but from the depths from which he has come. For any adjustment of the scale of comparison, fair play demands that to the barbarism from which the negro started shall be added two hundred years heavy with human bondage. Should the American people put a school house in every valley of the South and a church on every hill side and supply the one with teachers and the other with preachers, for a hundred years to come, they would not then have given fair play to the negro.

The nearest approach to justice to the negro for the past is to do him justice in the present. Throw open to him the doors of the schools, the factories, the workshops, and of all mechanical industries. For his own welfare, give him a chance to do whatever he can do well. If he fails then, let him fail: I can, however, assure you that he will not fail. Already has he proven it. As a soldier he proved it. He has since proved it by industry and sobriety and by the acquisition of knowledge and property. He is almost the only successful tiller of the soil of the South, and is fast becoming the owner of land formerly owned by his old master and by the old master class. In a thousand instances has he verified my theory of self-made men. He well performed the task of making bricks without straw; now give him straw. Give him all the facilities for honest and successful livelihood, and in all honorable avocations receive him as a man among men.

I have by implication admitted that work alone is not the only explanation of self-made men, or of the secret of success. Industry, to be sure, is the superficial and visible cause of success, put what is the cause of industry? In the answer to this question one element is easily pointed out, and that element is necessity. Thackeray very wisely remarks that, "All men are about as lazy as they can afford to be." Men cannot be depended upon to work when they are asked to work for nothing. They are not only as lazy as they can afford to be, but I have found many who were great deal more so. We all hate the task master, but all men, however industrious, are either lured or lashed through the world, and we should be a lazy, good-for-nothing set, if we were not so lured and lashed.

Necessity is not only the mother of invention, but the mainspring of exertion. The presence of some urgent, pinching, imperious necessity, will often not only sting a man into marvelous exertion, but into a sense of the possession, within himself, of powers and resources which else had slumbered on through a long life, unknown to himself and never suspected by others. A man never knows the strength of his grip till life and limb depend upon it. Something is likely to be done when something must be done.

If you wish to make your son helpless, you need not cripple him with bullet or bludgeon, but simply place him beyond the reach of necessity and surround him with ease and luxury. This experiment has often been tried and has seldom failed. As a general rule, where circumstances do most for men, there man will do least for him self; and where man does least, he himself is least. His doing or not doing makes or unmakes him.

Under the palm trees of Africa man finds, without effort, food, raiment and shelter. For him, there, Nature has done all and he has done nothing. The result is that the glory of Africa is in her palms,—and not in her men.

In your search after manhood go not to those delightful latitudes where "summer is blossoming all the year long," but rather to the hardy North, to Maine, New Hampshire and Vermont, to the coldest and flintiest parts of New England, where men work gardens with gunpowder, blast rocks to find places to plant potatoes, where, for six months of the year, the earth is covered with snow and ice. Go to the states which Daniel Webster thought good enough to emigrate from, and there you will find the highest type of American physical and intellectual manhood.

Happily for mankind, labor not only supplies the good things for which it is exerted, but it increases its own resources and improves, sharpens and strengthens its own instruments.

The primary condition upon which men have and retain power and skill is exertion. Nature has no use for unused power. She abhors a vacuum. She permits no preemption without occupation. Every organ of body and mind has its use and improves by use. "Better to wear out than to rust out," is sound philosophy as well as common sense. The eye of the watch-maker is severely taxed by the intense light and effort necessary in order to see minute objects, yet it remains clear and keen long after those of other men have failed. I was told at the Remington Rifle Works, by the workmen there employed who have to straighten the rifle barrels by flashing intense light through them, that, by this practice, severe as it seems, their eyes were made stronger.

But what the hands find to do must be done in earnest. Nature tolerates no halfness. He who wants hard hands must not, at sight of the first blister, fling away the spade, the rake, the broad axe or the hoe; for the blister is a primary condition to the needed hardness. To abandon work is not only to throw away the means of success, but it is also to part with the ability to work. To be able to walk well, one must walk on, and to work with ease and effect, one must work on.

Thus the law of labor is self-acting, beneficent and perfect; increasing skill and ability according to exertion. Faithful, earnest and protracted industry gives strength to the mind and facility to the hand. Within certain limits, the more that a man does, the more he can do.

Few men ever reach, in any one direction, the limits of their possibilities. As in commerce, so here, the relation of supply to demand rules. Our mechanical and intellectual forces increase or decrease according to the demands made upon them. He who uses most will have most to use. This is the philosophy of the parable of the ten talents. It applies here as elsewhere. "To him that hath shall be given and from him that hath not shall be taken even that which he hath."

Exertion to muscle or mind, for pleasure and amusement alone, cannot bring anything like the good results of earnest labor. Such exertion lacks the element attached to duty. To play perfectly upon and complicated instrument, one must play long, laboriously and with earnest purpose. Though it be an amusement at first, it must be labor at the end, if any proficiency is reached. If one plays for one's own pleasure alone, the performance will give little pleasure to any one else and will finally become a rather hard and dry pleasure to one's self.

In this respect one cannot receive much more than one gives. Men may cheat their neighbors and may cheat themselves but they cannot cheat nature. She will only pay the wages one honestly earns.

In the idea or exertion, of course fortitude and perseverance are included. We have all met a class of men, very remarkable for their activity, and who yet make but little headway in life; men who, in their noisy and impulsive pursuit of knowledge, never get beyond the outer bark of an idea, from a lack of patience and perseverance to dig to the core; men who begin everything and complete nothing; who see, but do not perceive; who read, but forget what they read, and are as if they had not read; who travel, but go nowhere in particular, and have nothing of value to impart when they return. Such men may have greatness thrust upon them but they never achieve greatness.

As the gold in the mountain is concealed in huge and flinty rocks, so the most valuable ideas and inventions are often enveloped in doubt and uncertainty. The printing press, the sewing machine, the railroad, the telegraph and the locomotive, are all simple enough now, but who can measure the patience, the persistence, the fortitude, the wearing labor and the brain sweat, which produced these wonderful and indispensable additions to our modern civilization.

My theory of self-made men is, then, simply this; that they are men of work. Whether or not such men have acquired material, moral or intellectual excellence, honest labor faithfully, steadily and persistently pursued, is the best, if not the only, explanation of their success. But in thus awarding praise to industry, as the main agency in the production and culture of self-made men, I do not exclude other factors of the problem. I only make them subordinate. Other agencies co-operate, but this is the principal one and the one without which all others would fail.

Indolence and failure can give a thousand excuses for themselves. How often do we hear men say, "If I had the head of this one, or the hands of that one; the health of this one, or the strength of that one; the chances of this or of that one, I might have been this, that, or the other;" and much more of the same sort.

Sound bodily health and mental faculties unimpaired are very desirable, if not absolutely indispensable. But a man need not be a physical giant or an intellectual prodigy, in order to make a tolerable way in the world. The health and strength of the soul is of far more importance than is that of the body, even when viewed as a means of mundane results. The soul is the main thing. Man can do a great many things; some easily and some with difficulty, but he cannot build a sound ship with rotten timber. Her model may be faultless; her spars may be the finest and her canvas the whitest and the flags of all nations may be displayed at her masthead, but she will go down in the first storm. So it is with the soul. Whatever its assumptions, if it be lacking in the principles of honor, integrity and affection, it, too will go down in the first storm. And when the soul is lost, all is lost. All human experience proves over and over again, that any success which comes through meanness, trickery, fraud and dishonor, is but emptiness and will only be a torment to its possessor.

Let not the morally strong, though the physically weak abandon the struggle of life. For such happily, there is both place and chance in the world. The highest services to man and the richest rewards to the worker are not conditioned entirely upon physical power. The higher the plane of civilization, the more abundant the opportunities of the weak and infirm. Society and civilization move according to celestial order. "Not that which is spiritual is first, but that which is natural. After that, that which is spiritual." The order of progress, is, first, barbarism; afterward, civilization. Barbarism represents physical force. Civilization represents spiritual power. The primary condition, that of barbarism, knows no other law than that of force; not right, but might. In this condition of society or rather of no society, the man of mind is pushed aside by the man of muscle. A Kit Carson, far out on the borders of civilization, dexterously handling his bowie knife, rifle and bludgeon, easily gets himself taken for a hero; but the waves of science and civilization rolling out over the Western prairies, soon leave him no room for his barbarous accomplishment. Kit is shorn of his glory. A higher type of manhood is required.

Where ferocious beasts and savage inhabitants have been dispersed and the rudeness of nature has been subdued, we welcome milder methods and gentler instrumentalities for the service of mankind. Here the race is not to the swift nor the battle to the strong, but the prize is brought within the reach of those who are neither swift nor strong. None need despair. There is room and work for all: for the weak as well as the strong. Activity is the law for all and its rewards are open to all. Vast acquirements and splendid achievements stand to the credit of men of feeble frames and slender constitutions. Channing was physically weak. Milton was blind. Montgomery was small and effeminate. But these men were more to the world than a thousand Sampsons. Mrs Stowe would be nothing among the grizzly bears of the Rocky mountains. We should not be likely to ask for her help at a barn raising, or a ship launch; but when a great national evil was to be removed; when a nation's heart was to be touched; when a whole country was to be redeemed and regenerated and millions of slaves converted into free men, the civilized world knew no earthly power equal to hers.

But another element of the secret of success demands a word. That element is order, systematic endeavor. We succeed, not alone by the laborious exertion of our faculties, be they small or great, but by the regular, thoughtful and systematic exercise of them. Order, the first law of heaven, is itself a power. The battle is nearly lost when your lines are in disorder. Regular order and systematic effort which moves without friction and needless loss of time or power; which has a place for everything and everything in its place; which knows just where to begin, how to proceed and where to end, though marked by no extraordinary outlay of energy or activity, will work wonders, not only in the matter of accomplishment, but also in the increase of the ability of the individual. It will make the weak man strong and the strong man stronger; the simple man wise and the wise men, wiser, and will insure success by the power and influence that belong to habit.

On the other hand, no matter what gifts and what aptitudes a man may possess; no matter though his mind be of the highest order and fitted for the noblest achievements; yet, without this systematic effort, his genius will only serve as a fire of shavings, soon in blaze and soon out.

Spontaneity has a special charm, and the fitful outcroppings of genius are, in speech or action, delightful; but the success attained by these is neither solid nor lasting. A man who, for nearly forty years, was the foremost orator in New England, was asked by me, if his speeches were extemporaneous? They flowed so smoothly that I had my doubts about it. He answered, "No, I carefully think out and write my speeches, before I utter them." When such a man rises to speak, he knows what he is going to say. When he speaks, he knows what he is saying. When he retires from the platform, he knows what he *has* said.

There is still another element essential to success, and that is, a commanding object and a sense of its importance. The vigor of the action depends upon the power of the motive. The wheels of the locomotive lie idle upon the rail until they feel the impelling force of the steam; but when that is applied, the whole ponderous train is set in motion. But energy ought not to be wasted. A man may dispose of his life as Paddy did of his powder,—aim at nothing, and hit it every time.

If each man in the world did his share of honest work, we should have no need of a millennium. The world would teem with abundance, and the temptation to evil in a thousand directions, would disappear. But work is not often undertaken for its own sake. The worker is conscious of an object worthy of effort, and works for that object; not for what he is to it, but for what it is to him. All are not moved by the same objects. Happiness is the object of some. Wealth and fame are the objects of others. But wealth and fame are beyond the reach of the majority of men, and thus, to them, these are not motive-impelling objects. Happily, however, personal, family and neighborhood well-being stand near to us all and are full of lofty inspirations to earnest endeavor, if we would but respond to their influence.

I do not desire my lecture to become a sermon; but, were this allowable, I would rebuke the growing tendency to sport and pleasure. The time, money and strength devoted to these phantoms, would banish darkness and hunger from every hearthstone in our land. Multitudes, unconscious of any controlling object in life, flit, like birds, from point to point; now here, now there; and so accomplish nothing, either here or there.

"For pleasures are like poppies spread.
You seize the flower, its bloom is shed!
Or like the snow-falls in the river,
A moment white—then melts forever;

Or like the borealis race,
That flit ere you can point their place;
Or like the rainbow's lovely form
Evanishing amid the storm.—"

They know most of pleasure who seek it least, and they least who seek it most. The cushion is soft to him who sits on it but seldom. The men behind the chairs at Saratoga and Newport, get better dinners than the men in them. We cannot serve two masters. When here, we cannot be there. If we accept ease, we must part with appetite. A pound of feathers is as heavy as a pound of iron,—and about as hard, if you sit on it long enough. Music is delightful, but too much of it wounds the ear like the filing of a saw. The lounge, to the lazy, becomes like flint; and to him, the most savory dishes lose their flavor.

"It's true, they need na starve or sweat,
Thro' winter's cauld or simmer's heat;
But human bodies are sic fools,
For all their colleges an' schools,
That when na real ills perplex them,
They mak enow, themselves to vex them."

But the industrious man does find real pleasure. He finds it in qualities and quantities to which the baffled pleasure seeker is a perpetual stranger. He finds it in the house well built, in the farm well tilled, in the books well kept, in the page well written, in the thought well expressed, in all the improved conditions of life around him and in whatsoever useful work may, for the moment, engage his time and energies.

I will give you, in one simple statement, my idea, my observation and my experience of the chief agent in the success of self-made men. It is not luck, nor is it great mental endowments, but it is well directed, honest toll. "Toll and Trust!" was the motto of John Quincy Adams, and his Presidency of the Republic proved its wisdom as well as its truth. Great in his opportunities, great in his mental endowments and great in his relationships, he was still greater in persevering and indefatigable industry.

Examples of successful self-culture and self-help under great difficulties and discouragements, are abundant, and they vindicate the theory of success thus feebly and with homely common sense, presented. For example: Hugh Miller, whose lamented death mantled the mountains and valleys of his native land with a broad shadow of sorrow, scarcely yet lifted, was a grand example of the success of persistent devotion, under great difficulties, to work and to the acquisition of knowledge. In a country justly distinguished for its schools and college, he, like Robert Burns, Scotia's matchless son of song, was the true child of science, as Burns was of song. He was his own college. The earth was his school and the rocks were his school master. Outside of all the learned institutions of his country, and while employed with his chisel and hammer, as a stone mason, this man literally killed two birds with one stone; for he earned his daily bread and at the same time made himself an eminent geologist, and gave to the world books which are found in all public libraries and which are full of inspiration to the truth seeker.

Not unlike the case of Hugh Miller, is that of our own Elihu Burritt. The true heart warms with admiration for the energy and perseverance displayed in this man's pursuit of knowledge. We call him "The learned blacksmith," and the distinction was fairly earned and fitly worn. Over the polished anvil and glowing forge; amidst the smoke, dust and din of the blacksmith's shop; amidst its blazing fires and hissing sparks, and while hammering the red-hot steel, this brave son of toil is said to have mastered twenty different languages, living and dead.

It is surprising with what small means, in the field of earnest effort, great results have been achieved. That neither costly apparatus nor packed libraries are necessarily required by the earnest student in self-culture, was demonstrated in a remarkable manner by Louis Kossuth. That illustrious patriot, scholar and statesman, came to our country from the far east of Europe, a complete master of the English language. He spoke our difficult tongue with an eloquence as stately and grand as that of the best American orators. When asked how he obtained this mastery of language so foreign to him, he told us that his school house was an Austrian prison, and his school books, the Bible, Shakespeare, and an old English dictionary.

Side by side with the great Hungarian, let me name the King of American self-made men; the man who rose highest and will be remembered longest as the most popular and beloved President since Washington—ABRAHAM LINCOLN. This man came to us, not from the schools or from the mansions of ease and luxury, but from the back woods. He mastered his grammar by the light of a pine wood torch. The fortitude and industry which could split rails by day, and learn grammar at night at the hearthstone of a log hut and by the unsteady glare of a pine wood knot, prepared this man for a service to his country and to mankind, which only the most exalted could have performed.

The examples thus far given, belong to the Caucassian race; but to the African race, as well, we are indebted for examples equally worthy and inspiring. Benjamin Bannecker, a man of African descent, born and reared in the state of Maryland, and a contemporary with the great men of the revolution, is worthy to be mentioned with the highest of his class. He was a slave, withheld from all those inspiring motives which freedom, honor and distinction furnish to exertion; and yet this man secured an English education; became a learned mathematician, was an excellent surveyor, assisted to lay out the city of Washington, and compelled honorable recognition from some of the most distinguished scholars and statesmen of that early day of the Republic.

The intellect of the negro was then, as now, the subject of learned inquiry. Mr. Jefferson, among other statesmen and philosophers, while he considered slavery an evil, entertained a rather low estimate of the negro's mental ability. He thought that the negro might become learned in music and in language, but that mathematics were quite out of the question with him.

In this debate Benjamin Bannecker came upon the scene and materially assisted in lifting his race to a higher consideration than that in which it had been previously held. Bannecker was not only proficient as a writer, but, like Jefferson, he was a philosopher. Hearing of Mr. Jefferson's opinion of negro intellect, he took no offense but calmly addressed that statesman a letter and a copy of an almanac for which he had made the astronomical calculations. The reply of Mr. Jefferson is the highest praise I wish to bestow upon this black self-made man. It is brief and I take great pleasure in presenting it.

PHILADELPHIA, August 30, 1790.

SIR:

I thank you sincerely for your letter and the almanac it contains. Nobody more than I do, wishes to see such proofs as you exhibit, that nature has given our black brethren talents equal to those of other colors of men, and that the appearance of the want of them, is owing mainly to the degrading conditions of their existence in Africa and America. I have taken the liberty of sending your almanac to Monsieur Cordozett, Secretary of the Academy of Science at Paris, and a member of the Philanthropic Society, because I considered it a document of which your whole race had a right, for their justification against the doubts entertained of them.

I am, with great esteem, sir,
Your most obedient servant,
THOMAS JEFFERSON.

This was the impression made by an intelligent negro upon the father of American Democracy, in the earlier and better years of the Republic. I wish that it were possible to make a similar impression upon the children of the American Democracy of this generation. Jefferson was not ashamed to call the black man his brother and to address him as a gentleman.

I am sorry that Bannecker was not entirely black, because in the United States, the slightest infusion of Teutonic blood is thought to be sufficient to account for any considerable degree of intelligence found under any possible color of the skin.

But Bannecker is not the only colored example that I can give. While I turn with honest pride to Bannecker, who lived a hundred years ago, and invoke his aid to roll back the tide of disparagement and contempt which pride and prejudice have poured out against the colored race, I can also cite examples of like energy in our own day.

William Dietz, a black man of Albany, New York, with whom I was personally acquainted and of whom I can speak from actual knowledge, is one such. This man by industry, fidelity and general aptitude for business affairs, rose from the humble calling of house servant in the Dudley family of that city, to become the sole manager of the family estate valued at three millions of dollars.

It is customary to assert that the negro never invented anything, and that, if he were today struck out of life, there would, in twenty years, be nothing left to tell of his existence. Well, this black man; for he was positively and perfectly black; not partially, but WHOLLY black; a man whom a few years ago, some of our learned ethnologists would have read out of the human family and whom a certain Chief Justice would have turned out of court as a creature having no rights which white men are bound to respect, was one of the very best draftsmen and designers in the state of New York. Mr. Dietz was not only an architect, but he was also an inventor. In this he was a direct contradiction to the maligners of his race. The noble railroad bridge now spanning the Hudson river at Albany, was, in all essential features, designed by William Dietz. The main objection against a bridge across that highway of commerce had been that of its interference with navigation. Of all the designs presented, that of Dietz was the least objectionable on that score, and was, in its essential features, accepted. Mr. Dietz also devised a plan for an elevated railway to be built in Broadway, New York. The great objection to a railway in that famous thoroughfare was then, as now, that of the noise, dust, smoke, obstruction and danger to life and limb, thereby involved. Dietz undertook to remove all these objections by suggesting an elevated railway, the plan of which was, at the time, published in the *Scientific American* and highly commended by the editor of that journal. The then readers of the *Scientific American* read this account of the inventions of William Dietz, but did not know, as I did, that Mr. Dietz was a black man. There was certainly nothing in his name or in his works to suggest the American idea of color.

Among my dark examples I can name no man with more satisfaction than I can Toussaint L'Overture, the hero of Santo Domingo. Though born a slave and held a slave till he was fifty years of age; though, like Bannecker, he was black and showed no trace of Caucassian admixture, history hands him down to us as a brave and generous soldier, a wise and powerful statesmen, and ardent patriot and a successful liberator of his people and of his country.

The cotemporaries of this Haitien Chief paint him as without a single moral blemish; while friends and foes alike, accord him the highest ability. In his eulogists no modern hero has been more fortunate than Toussaint L'Overture. History, poetry and eloquence have vied with each other to do him reverence. Wordsworth and Whittier have, in characteristic verse, encircled his brow with a halo of fadeless glory, while Phillips has borne him among the gods in something like Elijah's chariot of fire.

The testimony of these and a thousand others who have come up from depths of society, confirms the theory that industry is the most potent factor in the success of self-made men, and thus raises the dignity of labor; for whatever may be one's natural gifts, success, as I have said, is due mainly to this great means, open and free to all.

A word now upon the third point suggested at the beginning of this paper; namely, The friendly relation and influence of American ideas and institutions to this class of men.

America is said, and not without reason, to be preeminently the home and patron of self-made men. Here, all doors fly open to them. They may aspire to any position. Courts, Senates and Cabinets, spread rich carpets for their feet, and they stand among our foremost men in every honorable service. Many causes have made it easy, here, for this class to rise and flourish, and first among these causes is the general respectability of labor. Search where you will, there is no country on the globe where labor is so respected and the laborer so honored, as in this country. The conditions in which American society originated; the free spirit which framed its independence and created its government based upon the will of the people exalted both labor and laborer. The strife between capital and labor is, here, comparatively equal. The one is not the haughty and powerful master and the other the weak and abject slave as is the ease in some parts of Europe. Here, the man of toil is not bowed, but erect and strong. He feels that capital is not more indispensable than labor, and he can therefore meet the capitalist as the representative of an equal power.

Of course these remarks are not intended to apply to the states where slavery has but recently existed. That system was the extreme degradation of labor, and though happily now abolished its consequences still linger and may not disappear for a century. To-day, in the presence of the capitalist, the Southern black laborer stands abashed, confused and intimidated. He is compelled to beg his fellow worm to give him leave to toil. Labor can never be respected where the laborer is despised. This is today, the great trouble at the South. The land owners still resent emancipation and oppose the elevation of labor. They have yet to learn that a condition of affairs well suited to a time of slavery may not be well suited to a time of freedom. They will one day learn that large farms and ignorant laborers are as little suited to the South as to the North.

But the respectability of labor is not, as already intimated, the only or the most powerful cause of the facility with which men rise from humble conditions to affluence and importance in the United States. A more subtile and powerful influence is exerted by the fact that the principle of measuring and valuing men according to their respective merits and without regard to their antecedents, is better established and more generally enforced here than in any other country. In Europe, greatness is often thrust upon men. They are made legislators by birth.

> "A king can make a belted knight,
> A marquis, duke and a' that."

But here, wealth and greatness are forced by no such capricious and arbitrary power. Equality of rights brings equality of positions and dignities. Here society very properly saves itself the trouble of looking up a man's kinsfolks in order to determine his grade in life and the measure of respect due him. It cares very little who was his father or grandfather. The boast of the Jews, "We have Abraham for our father," has no practical significance here. He who demands consideration on the strength of a reputation of a dead father, is, properly enough, rewarded with derision. We have no reverence to throw away in this wise.

As a people, we have only a decent respect for our seniors. We cannot be beguiled into accepting empty-headed sons for full-headed fathers. As some one has said, we dispense with the smoke when the candle is out. In popular phrase we exhort every man as he comes upon the stage of active life, "Now do your level best!" "Help yourself!" "Put your shoulder to the wheel!" "Make your own record!" "Paddle your own canoe!" "Bet the architect of your own fortune!"

The sons of illustrious men are put upon trial like the sons of common people. They must prove themselves real CLAYS, WEBSTERS and LINCOLNS, if they would attract to themselves the cordial respect and admiration generally awarded to their brilliant fathers. There is, here, no law of entail or primogeniture.

Our great men drop out from their various groups and circles of greatness as bright meteors vanish from the blue overhanging sky bearing away their own slivery light and leaving the places where they once shone so brightly, robed in darkness till relighted in turn by the glory of succeeding ones.

I would not assume that we are entirely devoid of affection for families and for great names. We have this feeling, but it is a feeling qualified and limited by the popular thought; a thought which springs from the heart of free institutions and is destined to grow stronger the longer these institutions shall endure. George Washington, Jr., or Andrew Jackson, Jr., stand no better chance of being future Presidents than do the sons of Smith or Jones, or the sons of anybody else.

We are in this, as Edmund Quincy once said of the rapping spirits, willing to have done with people when they are done with us. We reject living pretenders if they come only in the old clothes of the dead.

We have as a people no past and very little present, but a boundless and glorious future. With us, it is not so much what has been, or what is now, but what is to be in the good time coming. Our mottoes are "Look ahead!" and "Go ahead!" and especially the latter. Our moral atmosphere is full of the inspiration of hope and courage. Every man has his chance. If he cannot be President he can, at least, be prosperous. In this respect, America is not only the exception to the general rule, but the social wonder of the world. Europe, with her divine-right governments and ultra-montane doctrines; with her sharply defined and firmly fixed classes; each class content if it can hold its own against the others, inspires little of individual hope or courage. Men, on all sides, endeavor to continue from youth to old age in their several callings and to abide in their several stations. They seldom hope for anything more or better than this. Once in a while, it is true, men of extraordinary energy and industry, like the Honorable John Bright and the Honorable Lord Brougham, (men whose capacity and disposition for work always left their associates little or nothing to do) rise even in England. Such men would rise to distinction anywhere. They do not disprove the general rule, but confirm it.

What is, in this respect, difficult and uncommon in the Old World, is quite easy and common in the New. To the people of Europe, this eager, ever moving mass which we call American society and in which life is not only a race, but a battle, and everybody trying to get just a little ahead of everybody else, looks very much like anarchy.

The remark is often made abroad that there is no repose in America. We are said to be like the troubled sea, and in some sense this is true. If it is a fact it is also one not without its compensation. If we resemble the sea in its troubles, we also resemble the sea in its power and grandeur, and in the equalities of its particles.

It is said, that in the course of centuries, I dare not say how many, all the oceans of this great globe go through the purifying process of filtration. All their parts are at work and their relations are ever changing. They are, in obedience to ever varying atmospheric forces, lifted from their lowly condition and are borne away by gentle winds or furious storms to far off islands, capes and continents; visiting in their course, mountain, valley and plain; thus fulfilling a beneficent mission and leaving the grateful earth refreshed, enriched, invigorated, beautiful and blooming. Each pearly drop has its fair chance to rise and contribute its share to the health and happiness of the world.

Such, in some sort, is a true picture of the restless activity and ever-changing relations of American Society. Like the sea, we are constantly rising above, and returning to, the common level. A small son follows a great father, and a poor son, a rich father. To my mind we have no reason to fear that either wealth, knowledge or power will here be monopolized by the few as against the many.

These causes which make America the home and foster-mother of self-made men, combined with universal suffrage, will, I hope, preserve us from this danger. With equal suffrage in our hands, we are beyond the power of families, nationalities or races.

Then, too, our national genius welcomes humanity from every quarter and grants to all an equal chance in the race of life.

"We ask not for his lineage,
We ask not for his name;
If manliness be in his heart,
He noble birth may claim.
We ask not from what land he came,
Nor where his youth was nursed;
If pure the stream, it matters not
The spot from whence it burst."

Under the shadow of a great name, Louis Napoleon could strike down the liberties of France and erect the throne of a despot; but among a people so jealous of liberty as to revolt at the idea of electing, for a third term, one of our best Presidents, no such experiment as Napoleon's could ever be attempted here.

We are sometimes dazzled by the gilded show of aristocratic and monarchical institutions, and run wild to see a prince. We are willing that the nations which enjoy these superstitions and follies shall enjoy them in peace. But, for ourselves, we want none of them and will have none of them and can have none of them while the spirit of liberty and equality animates the Republic.

A word in conclusion, as to the criticisms and embarrassments to which self-made men are exposed, even in this highly favored country. A traveler through the monarchies of Europe in annoyed at every turn by a demand for his passport. Our government has imposed no such burden, either upon the traveler or upon itself. But citizens and private individuals, in their relation to each other and the world, demand of every one the equivalent of a passport to recognition, in the possession of some quality or acquirement which shall commend its possessor to favor. We believe in making ourselves pretty well acquainted with the character, business and history of all comers. We say to all such, "Stand and deliver!" And to this demand self-made men are especially subject.

There is a small class of very small men who turn their backs upon any one who presumes to be anybody, independent of Harvard, Yale, Princeton or other similar institutions of learning. These individuals cannot believe that any good can come out of Nazareth. With them, the diploma is more than the man. To that moral energy upon which depends the lifting of humanity, which is the world's true advancement, these are utter strangers. To them the world is never indebted for progress, and they may safely be left to the gentle oblivion which will surely overtake them.

By these remarks, however, there is meant no disparagement of learning. With all my admiration for self-made men, I am far from considering them the best made men. Their symmetry is often marred by the effects of their extra exertion. The hot rays of the sun and the long and rugged road over which they have been compelled to travel, have left their marks, sometimes quite visibly and unpleasantly, upon them.

While the world values skill and power, it values beauty and polish, as well. It was not alone the hard good sense and honest heart of Horace Greeley, the self-made man, that made the *New York Tribune*; but likewise the brilliant and thoroughly educated men silently associated with him.

There never was a self-educated man, however well-educated, who, with the same exertion, would not have been better educated by the aid of schools and colleges. The charge is made and well sustained, that self-made men are not generally over modest or self-forgetful men. It was said of Horace Greeley, that he was a self-made man and worshipped his maker. Perhaps the strong resistance which such men meet in maintaining their claim, may account for much of their self-assertion.

The country knows by heart, and from his own lips, the story of Andrew Jackson. In many cases, the very energies employed, the obstacles overcome the heights attained and the broad contrasts at every step forced upon the attention, tend to incite and strengthen egotism. A man indebted for himself to himself may naturally think well of himself.

But this is apt to be far overdone. That a man has been able to make his own way in the world, is an humble fact as well as an honorable one. It is, however, possible to state a very humble fact in a very haughty manner, and self-made men are, as a class, much addicted to this habit. By this peculiarity they make themselves much less agreeable to society than they would otherwise be.

One other criticism upon these men is often very properly made. Having never enjoyed the benefits of schools, colleges and other like institutions of learning, they display for them a contempt which is quite ridiculous and which also makes them appear so. A man may know much about educating himself, and but little about the proper means for educating others. A self-made man is also liable to be full of contrarieties. He may be large, but at the same time, awkward; swift, but ungraceful; a man of power, but deficient in the polish and amiable proportions of the affluent and regularly educated man. I think that, generally, self-made men answer more or less closely to this description.

For practical benefit we are often about as much indebted to our enemies, as to our friends, as much to the men who hiss, as to those who applaud; for it may be with men as some one has said about tea; that if you wish to get its strength, you must put it into hot water. Criticism took Theodore Parker from a village pupil and gave him the whole country for a platform and the whole nation for an audience. England laughed at American authorship and we send her Emerson and Uncle Tom's Cabin. From its destitution of trees, Scotland was once a by-word; now it is a garden of beauty. Five generations ago, Britain was ashamed to write books in her own tongue. Now her language is spoken in all quarters of the globe. The Jim Crow Minstrels have, in many cases, led the negro to the study of music; while the doubt cast upon the negro's tongue has sent him to the lexicon and grammar and to the study of Greek orators and orations.

Thus detraction paves the way for the very perfections which it doubts and denies.

Ladies and gentlemen: Accept my thanks for your patient attention. I will detain you no longer. If, by statement, argument, sentiment or example, I have awakened in any, a sense of the dignity of labor or the value of manhood, or have stirred in any mind, a courageous resolution to make one more effort towards self-improvement and higher usefulness, I have not spoken altogether in vain, and your patience is justified.

Walt Whitman (1819–1892)

Harold Bloom has claimed that Whitman is "the greatest poet since the High Romantics," perhaps the greatest poet America has ever produced, judgments most recently heralded anew in The Anatomy of Influence *(2011). And even as early as 1855, Emerson recorded similarly prominent praise for the poet. When* Leaves of Grass *was published, the young Whitman sent a copy to Emerson, who responded to the 12 poems with the oft-quoted lines: "I find it the most extraordinary piece of wit and wisdom that America has yet contributed." Whitman is also frequently quoted for having said, "I was simmering, simmering, simmering. Emerson brought me to a boil." The two writers clearly admired each other's work and were not shy to express their sentiments, though both were also made nervous by each other. In a letter to Carlyle, Emerson described* Leaves of Grass *as a "nondescript monster which yet has terrible eyes & buffalo strength, & was indisputably American" (May 6, 1856). In 1881, the year before he died, Emerson hosted a dinner in Whitman's honor at his home in Concord, Massachusetts. Over the next couple of years, Whitman composed the following critical reading of the man he once addressed in a letter as "friend and Master" with what appears to be a sincere attempt to avoid the hyperbole that is expected from hero worship. Instead, Whitman aims to say precisely what Emerson makes possible for us despite or because of the way he wrote. Even as Whitman claims Emerson was most pleased with "superb verbal polish," Whitman's remarks reflect an unvarnished look at his mentor's qualities. The selections include: "The Superiority of Emerson's Writing" (c.1847–55); Emerson's Books, (the Shadows of Them) (May 22, 1880), portions of which were reprinted in "A Democratic Criticism," * New York Tribune, *May 15, 1882; "How I Still Get Around the Take Notes (No. 5)" printed in the* Critic, *December 3, 1881 and based on his visits with Emerson in September and October 1881 (as Whitman says "in his 79th year," what would end up being about a half-dozen months before Emerson died); and lastly "By Emerson's Grave," from an article Whitman published on May 6, 1882 in the* Critic—*ten days after Emerson's death.*

The Superiority of Emerson's Writing

Walt Whitman

The superiority of Emerson's writing is in their character—they mean something. He may be obscure, but he is certain. Any other of the best American writers has in general a clearer style, has more of the received grace and ease, is less questioned and forbidden than he, makes a handsomer appearance in the society of the books, sells better, passes his time more apparently in the popular understanding; yet there is something in the solitary specimen of New England that outvies them all. He has what none else has; he does what none else does. He pierces the crusts that envelope the secrets of life. He joins on equal terms the few great sages and original seers. He represents the freeman, America, the individual. He represents the gentleman. No teacher or poet of old times or modern times has made a better report of manly and womanly qualities, heroism, chastity, temperance, friendship, fortitude. None has given more beautiful accounts of truth and justice. His words shed light to the best souls; they do not admit of argument. As a sprig from the pine tree or a glimpse anywhere into the daylight belittles all artificial flower work and all the painted scenery of theatres, so are live words in a book compared to cunningly composed words. A few among men (soon perhaps to become many) will enter easily into Emerson's meanings; by those he will be well-beloved. The flippant writer, the orthodox critic, the numbers of good or indifferent imitators, will not comprehend him; to them he will indeed be a transcendentalist, a writer of sunbeams and moonbeams, a strange and unapproachable person.

Emerson's Books, (the Shadows of Them)

Walt Whitman

Democracy (like Christianity) is not served best by its own most brawling advocates, but often far, far better, finally, by those who are outside its ranks. I should say that such men as Carlyle and Emerson and Tennyson—to say nothing of Shakspere or Walter Scott—have done more for popular political and social progress and liberalization, and for individuality and freedom, than all the pronounced democrats one could name.

The foregoing assumptions on Emerson and his books may seem—perhaps are—paradoxical; but, as before intimated, is not every first-class artist, himself, and are not all real works of art, themselves, paradoxical? and is not the world itself so? As also intimated in the beginning, I have written my criticism in the unflinching spirit of the man's own inner teachings. As I understand him, the truest honor you can pay him is to try his own rules, his own heroic treatment, on the greatest themes, even his own works.

It remains to be distinctly avowed by me that Emerson's books form the tallest and finest growth yet of the literature of the New World. They bring, with miraculous opportuneness, exactly what America needs, to begin at the head, to radically sever her (not too apparently at first) from the fossilism and feudalism of Europe.

How I Still Get Around and Take Notes (No. 5)

Walt Whitman

Camden, N. J., Dec. 1, '81—During my late three or four months' jaunt to Boston and through New England, I spent such good days at Concord, and with Emerson, seeing him under such propitious circumstances, in the calm, peaceful, but most radiant, twilight of his old age (nothing in the height of his literary action and expression so becoming and impressive), that I must give a few impromptu notes of it all. So I devote this cluster entirely to the man, to the place, the past, and all leading up to, and forming, that memorable and peculiar Personality, now near his 80th year—as I have just seen him there, in his home, silent, sunny, surrounded by a beautiful family.

AN EARLY AUTUMN SIDE-BIT.

Concord, Mass., Sept. 17.—Out here on a visit—elastic, mellow, Indian-summery weather. Came to-day from Boston (a pleasant ride of 40 minutes by steam, through Somerville, Belmont, Waltham, Stony Brook, and other lively towns), convoyed by my friend F. B. Sanborn, and to his ample house, and the kindness and hospitality of Mrs. S. and their fine family. Am writing this under the shade of some old hickories and elms, just after 4 P.M., on the porch, within stone's throw of the Concord river. Off against me, across stream, on a meadow and side-hill, haymakers are gathering and wagoning-in probably their second or third crop. The spread of emerald-green and brown, the knolls, the score or two of little hay-cocks dotting the meadow, the loaded-up wagons, the patient horses, the slow-strong action of the men and pitch-forks—all in the just-waning afternoon, with patches of yellow sun-sheen, mottled by long shadows—a cricket shrilly chirping, herald of the dusk—a boat with two figures noiselessly gliding along the little river, passing under the stone bridge-arch—the slight settling haze of aerial moisture, the sky and the peacefulness expanding in all directions, and overhead—fill and soothe me.

EMERSON AS HE LOOKS TO-DAY.

Same Evening.—Never had I a better piece of luck befall me: a long and blessed evening with Emerson, in a way I couldn't have wished better or different. For nearly two hours he has been placidly sitting where I could see his face in the best light near me. Mrs. S.'s back parlor well fill'd with people, neighbors, many fresh and charming faces, women, mostly young, but some old. My friend A. B. Alcott and his daughter Louisa were there early. A good deal of talk, the subject Henry Thoreau—some new glints of his life and fortunes, with letters to and from him—one of the best by Margaret Fuller, others by Horace Greeley, Channing, etc.—one from Thoreau himself, most quaint and interesting. (No doubt I seemed very stupid to the room-full of company, taking hardly any part in the conversation; but I had "my own pail to milk in," as the Swiss proverb puts it.) My seat and the relative arrangement were such that, without being rude or anything of the kind, I could just look squarely at E., which I did a good part of the two hours. On entering he had spoken very briefly, easily and politely to several of the company, then settled himself in his chair, a trifle pushed back, and, though a listener and apparently an alert one, remained silent through the whole talk and discussion. A lady friend quietly took a seat next him to give special attention,

And so, there Emerson sat, and I looking at him. A good color in his face, eyes clear, with the well-known expression of sweetness and the old clear-peering aspect quite the same.

Next Day.—Several hours at E.'s house, and dinner there. An old familiar house (he has been in it thirty-five years), with the surroundings furnishment, roominess, and plain elegance and fulness signifying democratic ease, sufficient opulence, and an admirable old-fashioned simplicity—modern luxury, with its mere sumptuousness and affectation, either touched lightly upon, or ignored altogether. Dinner the same. (It was not my first dinner with Emerson. In 1857, and along there, when he came to New York to lecture, we two would dine together at the Astor House. And some years after, I living for a while in Boston, we would occasionally meet for the same purpose at the American or Parker's. Before I get through these notes I will allude to one of our dinners, following a pretty vehement discussion.)

Of course the best of the present occasion (Sunday, September 18, '81) was the sight of E. himself. As just said, a healthy color in the cheeks and good light in the eyes, cheery expression, and just the amount of talking that best suited, namely, a word or short phrase only where needed, and almost always with a smile. Besides Emerson himself, Mrs. E., with their daughter Ellen, the son Edward and his wife, with my friend F. S. and Mrs. S., and others, relatives and intimates. Mrs. Emerson, resuming the subject of the evening before (I sat next to her), gave me further and fuller information about Thoreau, who years ago, during Mr. E.'s absence in Europe, had lived for some time in the family, by invitation.

But I suppose I must glide lightly over these interiors. (Some will say I ought to have skipped them entirely.) It is certain that E. does not like his friends to make him and his the subjects of publication-gossip. I write as I do because I feel that what I say *is* justified not only in itself, and my own respect and love, but by the fact that thousands of good men and women, here and abroad, have a right to know it, and that it will comfort them to know it. Besides, why should the finest critic of our land condemn the last best means and finish of criticism?

FINALES OF LITERATURE.

If Taine, the French critic, had done no other good, it would be enough that he has brought to the fore the first, last, and all-illuminating point, with respect to any grand production of literature, that the only way to finally understand it is to minutely study the personality of the one who shaped it—his origin, times, surroundings, and his actual fortunes, life, and ways. All this supplies not only the glass through which to look, but is the atmosphere, the very light itself. Who can profoundly get at Byron or Burns without such help? Would I apply the rule to Shakspere? Yes, unhesitatingly; the plays of the great poet are not only the concentration of all that lambently played in the best fancies of those times—not only the gathered sunset of the stirring days of feudalism, but the particular life that the poet led, the kind of man he was, and what his individual experience absorbed. I don't wonder the theory is broached that other brains and fingers (Bacon's, Raleigh's, and more,) had to do with the Shaksperian work—planned main parts of it, and built it. The singular absence of information about the *person* Shakspere leaves unsolved many a riddle, and prevents the last and dearest descriptive touches and dicta of criticism.

Accordingly, I doubt whether general readers and students of Emerson will get the innermost flavor and appositeness of his utterances, as not only precious in the abstract, but needing (to scientific taste and inquiry, and complete appreciation), those hereditary, local, biographic, even domestic statements and items he is so shy of having any one print. Probably no man lives too, who could so well bear such inquiry and statement to the minutest and fullest degree. This is all just as it must be—and the paradox is that that is the worst of it.

A Life-Outline.

Emerson, born May 25, 1803, and now of course in his 79th year, is the native and raised fruit of New England Puritanism, and the fullest justification of it I know. His ancestry on both sides forms an indispensable explanation and background of every page of his writings. "The Emerson family," says his latest biographer, speaking of his father, "were intellectual, eloquent, with a strong individuality of character, robust and vigorous in their thinking—practical and philanthropic. His mother (Ruth Haskins her maiden name) was a woman of great sensibility, modest, serene, and very devout. She was possessed of a thoroughly sincere nature, devoid of all sentimentalism, and of a temper the most even and placid—(one of her sons said that in his boyhood, when she came from her room in the morning, it seemed to him as if she always came from communion with God)—knew how to guide the affairs of her house, of the sweetest authority—always manners of natural grace and dignity. Her dark, liquid eyes, from which old age did not take away the expression, were among the remembrances of all on whom they ever rested."

As lad and young man his teachers were Channing, Ticknor, Everett, President Kirkland of Harvard, and Caleb Cushing. His favorite study was Greek; and his chosen readings, as he grew to manhood, were Montaigne, Shakspere, and old poets and dramatists. He assisted his brother William at school-teaching. Soon he studied theology. In 1826 he was "approbated to preach"—failed in strength and health—went south to Florida and South Carolina—preached in Charleston several times—returned to New England—seems to have had some pensive and even sombre times—wrote

"Good bye proud world, I'm going home,"

—in 1829 was married, ordained, and called to the Second Unitarian Church of Boston—was acceptable, yet in 1832 resigned his post (the immediate cause was his repugnance to serving the conventional communion service)—his wife died this year— he went off on a European tour, and saw Coleridge, Wordsworth, and Carlyle, the latter quite intimately—back home—in 1834 had a call to settle as pastor in New Bedford, but declined—in 1835 began lecturing in Boston (themes, Luther, Milton, Burke, Michel Angelo, and George Fox)—married the present Mrs. E. this year—absorbed Plotinus and the mystics and (under the influence of them, but living at the Old Manse, and in the midst of New England landscape and life), wrote and launched out "Nature" as his formal entrance into highest authorship—(with poor publishing success, however, only about 500 copies being sold or got rid of in twelve years).

Soon afterward he entered the regular lecture field, and with speeches, poems, essays and books, began, matured, and duly maintained for forty years, and holds to this hour, and in my opinion, fully deserves, the first literary and critical reputation in America.

Other Concord Notations.

Though the evening at Mr. and Mrs. Sanborn's, and the memorable family dinner at Mr. and Mrs. Emerson's, have most pleasantly and permanently filled my memory, I must not slight other notations of Concord. I went to the Old Manse, walked through the ancient garden, and entered the rooms. Here Emerson wrote his principal poems. (The spot, I see as I look around, serves the understanding of them like a frame does a picture. The same of Hawthorne's "Mosses.") One notes the quaintness, the unkempt grass and bushes, the little panes in the windows, the low ceilings, the spicy smell, the creepers embowering the light, a certain severity, precision, and melancholy, even a *twist* to all, notwithstanding the pervading calmness and normality of the scene. The house, too, gives out the aroma of generations of buried New England Puritanism and its ministers.

I went to the Concord Battle Ground, which is close by, scanned French's statue, "the Minute Man," read Emerson's poetic inscription on the base, lingered a long while on the Bridge, and stopt by the grave of the unnamed British soldiers buried there the day after the fight in April, '75.

Then riding on, (thanks to my friend Miss M. and her spirited white ponies, she driving them), a half hour at Hawthorne's and Thoreau's graves. I got out and went up of course on foot, and stood a long while and pondered. They lay close together in a pleasant wooded spot well up the Cemetery Hill, "Sleepy Hollow." The flat surface of the first was densely covered by myrtle, with a border of arbor-vitæ, and the other had a brown head-stone, moderately elaborate, with inscriptions. By Henry's side lies his brother John, of whom much was expected, but he died young.

Also to Walden Pond, that beautifully embowered sheet of water, and spent over an hour there. On the spot in the woods where Thoreau had his solitary house is now quite a cairn of stones, to mark the place; I too carried one and deposited on the heap. As we drove back, saw the "School of Philosophy," but it was shut up, and I would not have it opened for me. Near by stopped at the house of W. T. Harris, the Hegelian, who came out, and we had a pleasant chat while I sat in the wagon.

I shall not soon forget my Concord drives, and especially that charming Sunday forenoon one with my friend Miss M., and the white ponies. The town deserves its name, has nothing stunning about it, no mountains, and I should think no malaria—ample in fields, grass, grain, orchards, shade trees—comfortable, roomy, opulent-enough houses in all directions—but I saw neither any thing very ambitious indeed, nor any low quarter; reminiscences of '76, the cemeteries, sturdy old names, brown and mossy stone fences, lanes and linings and clumps of oaks, sunny areas of land, everywhere signs of thrift, comfort, ease—with the locomotives and trains of the Fitchburg road rolling and piercingly whistling every hour through the whole scene. I dwell on it here because I couldn't better suggest the background atmospheres and influences of the Emerson cultus than by Concord town itself, its past for several generations, what it has been in our time, and what it is to-day.

BOSTON COMMON—MORE OF EMERSON.

Oct. 10–13, '81.—I spend a good deal of time on the Common, these delicious days and nights—every mid-day from 11.30 to about 1—and almost every sunset another hour. I know all the big trees, especially the old elms along Tremont and Beacon Streets, and have come to a sociable-silent understanding with most of them, in the sunlit air (yet crispy-cool enough); as I saunter along the wide unpaved walks.

Up and down this breadth by Beacon Street, between these same old elms, I walked for two hours, of a bright sharp February midday twenty-one years ago, with Emerson, then in his prime, keen, physically and morally magnetic, armed at every point, and when he chose, wielding the emotional just as well as the intellectual. During those two hours, he was the talker and I the listener. It was an argument-statement, reconnoitering, review, attack, and pressing home (like an army corps, in order, artillery, cavalry, infantry), of all that could be said against that part (and a main part) in the construction of my poems, "Children of Adam." More precious than gold to me that dissertation—(I only wish I had it now, verbatim). It afforded me, ever after, this strange and paradoxical lesson; each point of E.'s statement was unanswerable, no judge's charge ever more complete or convincing. I could never hear the points better put—and then I felt down in my soul the clear and unmistakable conviction to disobey all, and pursue my own way. "What have you to say then to such things?" said E., pausing in conclusion. "Only that while I can't answer them at all, I feel more settled than ever to adhere to my own theory, and exemplify it," was my candid response. Whereupon we went and had a good dinner at the American House.

And thenceforward I never wavered or was touched with qualms, (as I confess I had been two or three times before).

A Concluding Thought.

Which hurried notes, scribbled off here at the eleventh hour, let me conclude by the thought, after all the rest is said, that most impresses me about Emerson. Amid the utter delirium-disease called book-making, its feverish cohorts filling our world with every form of dislocation, morbidity, and special type of anemia or exceptionalism (with the propelling idea of getting the most possible money, first of all), how comforting to know of an author who has, through a long life, and in spirit, written as honestly, spontaneously and innocently, as the sun shines or the wheat grows—the truest, sanest, most moral, sweetest literary man on record—unsoiled by pecuniary or any other warp—ever teaching the law within—ever loyally outcropping his own self only—his own poetic and devout soul! If there be a Spirit above that looks down and scans authors, here is one at least in whom It might be well pleased.

By Emerson's Grave

Walt Whitman

May 6, '82.—We stand by Emerson's new-made grave without sadness—indeed a solemn joy and faith, almost hauteur—our soul-benison no mere

"Warrior, rest, thy task is done,"

for one beyond the warriors of the world lies surely symboll'd here. A just man, poised on himself, all-loving, all-inclosing, and sane and clear as the sun. Nor does it seem so much Emerson himself we are here to honor—it is conscience, simplicity, culture, humanity's attributes at their best, yet applicable if need be to average affairs, and eligible to all. So used are we to suppose a heroic death can only come from out of battle or storm, or mighty personal contest, or amid dramatic incidents or danger, (have we not been taught so for ages by all the plays and poems?) that few even of those who most sympathizingly mourn Emerson's late departure will fully appreciate the ripen'd grandeur of that event, with its play of calm and fitness, like evening light on the sea.

How I shall henceforth dwell on the blessed hours when, not long since, I saw that benignant face, the clear eyes, the silently smiling mouth, the form yet upright in its great age—to the very last, with so much spring and cheeriness, and such an absence of decrepitude, that even the term *venerable* hardly seem'd fitting.

Perhaps the life now rounded and completed in its mortal development, and which nothing can change or harm more, has its most illustrious halo, not in its splendid intellectual or esthetic products, but as forming in its entirety one of the few, (alas! how few!) perfect and flawless excuses for being, of the entire literary class.

We can say, as Abraham Lincoln at Gettysburg, It is not we who come to consecrate the dead—we reverently come to receive, if so it may be, some consecration to ourselves and daily work from him.

Oliver Wendell Holmes, Sr. (1809–1894)

While Holmes studied medicine in Paris he was visited by Emerson, who was in the midst of his first European tour. The two, who had earlier met in Massachusetts, remained lifelong friends despite strong points of disagreement, especially on slavery. It was Holmes who first described "The American Scholar" as "our Intellectual Declaration of Independence," and Holmes would go on to shape Emerson's posthumous reception, sometimes in unhelpful ways. Len Gougeon has described in Virtue's Hero *how in writing a major biography of Emerson in 1884, two years after his death, Holmes cast Emerson as a fellow conservative. As Gougeon describes it, Holmes states flatly that "Emerson had never been identified with the abolitionists," and consequently implies that Emerson's sympathies for their cause were not strong.[1] Holmes thereby downplayed claims made by previous biographers George Willis Cooke, Moncure Daniel Conway, and Alexander Ireland about Emerson's committed, ongoing agitation for the destruction of American slavery, and his active involvement with and contribution to the abolition movement. In 1855, Emerson himself voiced a "sad but severe rebuke" of Holmes for "his apparent support of slaveholders." Later biographers such as Ralph Rusk emphasize Emerson's activity, while Stephen Whicher re-affirms Emerson's withdrawal, reluctance, and reticence; more recently Robert Richardson and Robert Habich, along with Gougeon and others, have provided useful, often corrective, histories of this contentious narrative. One biographer, John McAleer, appears to reclaim Holmes' doubts over the extent of Emerson's credentials as an abolitionist. McAleer writes: "Holmes assessed Emerson's role [as a reformer] correctly when he said: 'Nothing is plainer than that it was Emerson's calling to supply impulses and not methods. He was not an organizer, but a power behind many organizers, inspiring them with lofty motive, giving breath to their views.'"[2] The following tribute—from May 8, 1882, a couple of weeks after Emerson's death—begins with remarks by George E. Ellis (Vice-President of the Massachusetts Historical Society), is followed by a note from Ebenezer R. Hoar (brother of Elizabeth Hoar), continues with Holmes' "pebble upon the cairn," and concludes with James Freeman Clarke's resolution to the members of the society. The letter Ellis quotes at length is by Emerson, written on October 8, 1838 in response to Henry Ware's recent sermon in which he meditated on the content and some implications of Emerson's Address presented to the Divinity School at Harvard on July 15.*

A Tribute on the Occasion of Emerson's Death

Oliver Wendell Holmes, et al.

May Meeting, 1882.

The regular monthly meeting was held on Thursday, the 11th instant, at 3 o'clock P. M.; the senior Vice-President, Dr. GEORGE E. ELLIS, in the chair.

The record of the previous meeting was read and accepted.

The Librarian read the monthly list of donors to the Library.

The Corresponding Secretary reported that Judge Morris, of Springfield, had accepted his election as a Resident Member.

The VICE-PRESIDENT then announced the death of a Resident Member, Mr. Ralph Waldo Emerson, as follows:—

Many of us who meet in this Library to-day are doubtless recalling vividly the memory of the impressive scene here when, fifteen months ago, Mr. Emerson, appearing among us for the last time, read his characteristic paper upon Thomas Carlyle. It was the very hour in which the remains of that remarkable man were committed to his Scotch grave. There was much to give the occasion here a deep and tender interest. We could not but feel that it was the last utterance to which we should listen from our beloved and venerated associate, if not, as it proved to be, the last of his presence among us. So we listened greedily and fondly. The paper had been lying in manuscript more than thirty years, but it had kept its freshness and fidelity. The matter of it, its tone and utterance, were singularly suggestive. Not the least of the crowding reflections with which we listened was the puzzling wonder, to some of us, as to the tie of sympathy and warm personal attachment, of nearly half a century's continuance, between the serene and gentle spirit of our poet-philosopher and the stormy and aggressive spirit of Mr. Carlyle.

There are those immediately to follow me who, with acute and appreciative minds, in closeness of intercourse and sympathy with Mr. Emerson, will interpret to you the form and significance of his genius, the richness of his fine and rare endowments, and account to you for the admiring and loving estimate of his power and influence and world-wide fame in the lofty realms of thought, with insight and vision and revealings of the central mysteries of being. They must share largely in those rare gifts of his who undertake to be the channel of them from him to others. For it is no secret, but a free confession, that the quality, methods, and fruits of his genius are so peculiar, unique, obscure, and remote from the appreciation of a large class of those of logical, argumentative, and prosaic minds, as to invest them with the ill-understood and the inexplicable. He was signally one of those, rare in our race, in the duality of our human elementary composition, in whom the dust of the ground contributed its least proportion, while the ethereal inspiration from above contributed the greatest.

The words which I would add, prompted as in keeping with this place and occasion, shall be in reminiscence of years long past. Those whose memories are clear and strong, and who forty-five years ago in their professional, literary, or social fellowships were intent upon all that quickened thought and converse in this peculiar centre of Boston and its neighborhoods, will recall with what can hardly be other than pensive retrospects the charms and fervors, the surprises, and perhaps the shocks, certainly the bewilderment and the apprehension, which signalled the announcement here of what was called Transcendentalism. Though the word was from the first wrongfully applied, there was an aptness in its use, as in keeping with the mistiness and cloudiness of the dispensation to which it was attached. The excitement here was adjusted to the size, the composition, the tone and spirit, and the unassimilated elements of this community. The movement had the quickening zest of mystery. It was long before those who were not a part of it could reach to any intelligible idea of what it might signify, or promise, or portend. There were a score, a hundred, persons craving to have explained to them what it all meant, to each one who seemed ready or able in volunteering to throw light upon it. And this intended light was often but an adumbration. Mr. Emerson gained nothing from his interpreters. Nor does he now. The key which they offered did not fit the wards of the lock. The vagueness of the oracle seemed to be deepened when repeated by any other lips than those which gave it first utterance. In most of the recent references in the newspapers and magazines to the opening of Mr. Emerson's career in high philosophy, emphatic statements are made as to the ridicule and satire and banter evoked by the first utterances of this transcendentalism. It is not impressed upon my memory that any of this triviality was ever spent upon Mr. Emerson himself. The modest, serene, unaggressive attitude, and personal phenomena of bearing and utterance which were so winningly characteristic of his presence and speech, as he dropped the sparkles and nuggets of his fragmentary revelations, were his ample security against all such disrespect. The fun, as I remember, was spent upon the first circle of repeaters, and so-called disciples, a small but lively company of both sexes, who seemed to patent him as their oracle, as an inner fellowship who would be the medium between him and the unillumined. Nor was it strange that explanations, or demonstrative and argumentative expositions of the Emersonian philosophy proffered by its interpreters did not open it clearly to inquirers, inasmuch as he himself assured us that it was not to be learned or tested by old-fashioned familiar methods. I know of but one piece from his pen now in print, and dating from the first year of his publicity, in which he appears, not in self-defence under challenge,—for he never did that,—but in attempted and baffled self-exposition. Nor have lines ever been written, by himself or by his interpreters, so apt, so characteristic, so exquisitely phrased and toned, so exhaustively descriptive of the style and spirit of his philosophy as those which I will quote.

The younger Henry Ware, whose colleague he had been during his brief pastorship of a church, disturbed by something in a discourse which Mr. Emerson, after leaving the pulpit, had delivered in Cambridge in 1838, had preached in the college chapel a sermon dealing in part with a position which had startled himself and others in his friend's address, and, in part, with a breeze of excitement which it had raised in a tinderish community. The sermon being printed, Mr. Ware sent a copy of it to

Mr. Emerson, with a letter, which the latter says "was right manly and noble." The letter expressed a little disturbance, puzzle, and anxiety of mind, and put some questions hinting at desired explanations and arguments.

In reply Mr. Emerson interprets himself thus:—

"If the sermon assails any doctrines of mine,—perhaps I am not so quick to see it as writers generally,—certainly I did not feel any disposition to depart from my habitual contentment, that you should say your thought whilst I say mine. I believe I must tell you what I think of my new position. It strikes me very oddly that good and wise men at Cambridge and Boston should think of raising me into an object of criticism. I have always been—from my very incapacity of methodical writing—'a chartered libertine,' free to worship and free to rail, lucky when I could make myself understood, but never esteemed near enough to the institutions and mind of society to deserve the notice of the masters of literature and religion. I have appreciated fully the advantages of my position, for I well know that there is no scholar less able or willing to be a polemic. I could not give accounts of myself if challenged. I could not possibly give you one of the 'arguments' you cruelly hint at, on which any doctrine of mine stands. For I do not know what arguments mean, in reference to any expression of a thought. I delight in telling what I think; but, if you ask me how I dare say so, or why it is so, I am the most helpless of mortal men. I do not even see that either of these questions admits of an answer. So that in the present droll posture of my affairs, when I see myself suddenly raised into the importance of a heretic, I am very uneasy when I advert to the supposed duties of such a personage, who is to make good his thesis against all comers. I certainly shall do no such thing. I shall read what you and other good men write, as I have always done,—glad when you speak my thoughts, and skipping the page that has nothing for me. I shall go on, just as before, seeing whatever I can, and telling what I see; and, I suppose, with the same fortune that has hitherto attended me,—the joy of finding that my abler and better brothers, who work with the sympathy of society, loving and beloved, do now and then unexpectedly confirm my perceptions, and find my nonsense is only their own thought in motley."

No one in comment, essay, or criticism upon Mr. Emerson has improved upon his own revealing of his philosophy of intuition, insight, eye, and thought, as distinguished from that of logic and argument. It needed some considerable lapse of time, with much wondering, questioning, and debating in this community, to clear the understanding, that the new and hopeful message brought to us was something like this,—that those who were overfed, or starved, or wearied with didactic, prosaic lessons of truth for life and conduct, through formal teaching, by reasoning, arguings, and provings, might turn to their own inner furnishings, to their thinkings as processes, not results, and to the free revealings and inspirings from without as interpreted from within.

But whatever was the baffling secret of Mr. Emerson's philosophy, there was no mystery save that to the charm and power of which we all love to yield ourselves, in the poise and repose of his placid spirit, in the grace and felicity of his utterance, in the crowding of sense and suggestiveness into his short, terse sentences, in his high reachings for all truth as its disciple, and in the persuasiveness with which he communicated to others what was disclosed to him. He never answered to a challenge by apology or controversy.

At the conclusion of his address, Dr. ELLIS read the following letter from Judge Hoar:—

CONCORD, May 8, 1882.

MY DEAR DR. ELLIS,—I find that it will be out of my power to attend the meeting of the Historical Society on Thursday next, and I am sorry to lose the opportunity of hearing the tributes which its members will pay to the memory of Mr. Emerson, than whose name none more worthy of honor is found on its roll. His place in literature, as poet, philosopher, seer, and thinker, will find much more adequate statement than any which I could offer. But there are two things which the Proceedings of our Society may appropriately record concerning him, one of them likely to be lost sight of in the lustre of his later and more famous achievements, and the other of a quality so evanescent as to be preserved only by contemporary evidence and tradition.

The first relates to his address in September, 1835, at the celebration of the two hundredth anniversary of the settlement of Concord; which seems to me to contain the most complete and exquisite picture of the origin, history, and peculiar characteristics of a New England town that has ever been produced.

The second is his *power as an orator*, rare and peculiar, and in its way unequalled among our contemporaries. Many of us can recall instances of it, and there are several prominent in my recollection; but perhaps the most striking was his address at the Burns centennial, in Boston, on the 25th of January, 1859.

The company that he addressed was a queer mixture. First, there were the Burns club,—grave, critical, and long-headed Scotchmen, jealous of the fame of their countryman, and doubtful of the capacity to appreciate him in men of other blood. There were the scholars and poets of Boston and its neighborhood, and professors and undergraduates from Harvard College. Then there were state and city officials, aldermen and common councilmen, brokers and bank directors, ministers and deacons, doctors, lawyers, and "carnal self-seekers" of every grade.

I have had the good fortune to hear many of the chief orators of our time, among them Henry Clay, John Quincy Adams, Ogden Hoffman, S. S. Prentiss, William H. Seward, Charles Sumner, Wendell Phillips, George William Curtis, some of the great preachers, and Webster, Everett, Choate, and Winthrop at their best. But I never witnessed such an effect of speech upon men as Mr. Emerson apparently then attained. It reached at once to his own definition of eloquence,—"a taking sovereign possession of the audience." He had uttered but a few sentences before he seemed to have welded together the whole mass of discordant material and lifted them to the same height of sympathy and passion. He excited them to smiles, to tears, to the wildest enthusiasm. His tribute to Burns is beautiful to read, perhaps the best which the occasion produced on either side of the ocean. But the clear articulation, the ringing emphasis, the musical modulation of tone and voice, the loftiness of bearing, and the radiance of his face, all made a part of the consummate charm.

When he closed, the company could hardly tolerate any other speaker, though good ones were to follow.

I am confident that every one who was present on that evening would agree with me as to the splendor of that eloquence.

Very truly yours,
E. R. Hoar.

Rev. George E. Ellis, D. D.,
  Vice-President of the Massachusetts Historical Society.

Dr. Oliver Wendell Holmes then addressed the Society as follows:—

It is a privilege which any of us may claim, as we pass each of these last and newly raised mounds, to throw our pebble upon the cairn. For our own sakes we must be indulged in the gratification of paying our slender tribute. So soon, alas, after bidding farewell to our cherished poet to lose the earthly presence of the loftiest, the divinest of our thinkers! The language of eulogy seemed to have exhausted itself in celebrating him who was the darling of two English worlds, the singer of Acadian and Pilgrim and Indian story, of human affections and aspirations, of sweet, wholesome life from its lullaby to its requiem. And now we hardly know what measure to observe in our praises of him who was singularly averse to over-statement, who never listened approvingly to flattery when living, and whose memory asks only the white roses of truth for its funeral garlands.

The work of his life is before us all, and will have full justice done it by those who are worthy of the task and equal to its demands. But, as out of a score of photographs each gives us something of a friend's familiar face, though all taken together do not give us the whole of it, so each glimpse of reminiscence, each hint of momentary impression, may help to make a portrait which shall remind us of the original, though it is, at best, but an imperfect resemblance.

When a life so exceptional as that which has just left our earthly companionship appears in any group of our fellow-creatures, we naturally ask how such a well-recognized superiority came into being. We look for the reason of such an existence among its antecedents, some of which we can reach, as, for instance, the characteristics of the race, the tribe, the family. The forces of innumerable generations are represented in the individual, more especially those of the last century or two. Involved with these, inextricable, insoluble, is the mystery of mysteries, the mechanism of personality. No such personality as this which was lately present with us is the outcome of cheap paternity and shallow motherhood.

I may seem to utter an Hibernian absurdity; I may recall a lively couplet which has often brought a smile at the expense of our good city; I may—I hope I shall not—offend the guardians of ancient formulæ, vigilant still as watch-dogs over the bones of their fleshless symbols, but I must be permitted to say that I believe the second birth may precede that which we consider as the first. The divine renovation which changes the half-human animal, the cave-dweller, the cannibal, into the servant of God, the friend, the benefactor, the lawgiver of his kind, may, I believe, be wrought in the race before it is incarnated in the individual. It may take many generations of chosen births to work the transformation, but what the old chemists called *cohobation* is not without its meaning for vital chemistry; life must pass through an alembic of gold or of silver many times before its current can possibly run quite clear.

A New Englander has a right to feel happy, if not proud, if he can quarter his coat-of-arms with the bands of an ancestry of clergymen. Eight generations of ministers preceded the advent of this prophet of our time. There is no better flint to strike fire from than the old nodule of Puritanism. Strike it against the steel of self-asserting civil freedom, and we get a flash and a flame such as showed our three-hilled town to the lovers of liberty all over the world. An ancestry of ministers, softened out of their old-world dogmas by the same influences which set free the colonies, is the true Brahminism of New England.

Children of the same parentage, as we well know, do not alike manifest the best qualities belonging to the race. But those of the two brothers of Ralph Waldo Emerson whom I can remember were of exceptional and superior natural endowments. Edward, next to him in order of birth, was of the highest promise, only one evidence of which was his standing at the head of his college class at graduation. I recall a tender and most impressive tribute of Mr. Everett's to his memory, at one of our annual Phi Beta Kappa meetings. He spoke of the blow which had jarred the strings of his fine intellect and made them return a sound

"Like sweet bells jangled out of tune and harsh,"

in the saddened tones of that rich sonorous voice still thrilling in the ears of many whose hearing is dulled for all the music, all the eloquence of to-day.

Of Charles Chauncy, the youngest brother, I knew something in my college days. A beautiful, high-souled, pure, exquisitely delicate nature in a slight but finely wrought mortal frame, he was for me the very ideal of an embodied celestial intelligence. I may venture to mention a trivial circumstance, because it points to the character of his favorite reading, which was likely to be guided by the same tastes as his brother's, and may have been specially directed by him. Coming into my room one day, he took up a copy of Hazlitt's British Poets. He opened it to the poem of Andrew Marvell's, entitled "The Nymph Complaining for the Death of her Fawn," which he read to me with delight irradiating his expressive features. The lines remained with me, or many of them, from that hour,—

"Had it lived long, it would have been
Lilies without, roses within."

I felt as many have felt after being with his brother, Ralph Waldo, that I had entertained an angel visitant. The Fawn of Marvell's imagination survives in my memory as the fitting image to recall this beautiful youth; a soul glowing like the rose of morning with enthusiasm, a character white as the lilies in its purity.

Such was the family nature lived out to its full development in Ralph Waldo Emerson. Add to this the special differentiating quality, indefinable as the tone of a voice, which we should know not the less, from that of every other of articulately speaking mortals, and we have the Emerson of our recollections.

A person who by force of natural gifts is entitled to be called a personage is always a surprise in the order of appearances, sometimes, as in the case of Shakespeare, of Goethe, a marvel, if not a miracle. The new phenomenon has to be studied like the young growth that sprang up between the stones in the story of Picciola. Is it a common weed, or a plant with virtues and beauties of its own? Is it a cryptogam that can never flower, or shall we wait and see it blossom by and by? Is it an endogen or an exogen,—did the seed it springs from drop from a neighboring bough, or was it wafted hither on the wings of the wind from some far-off shore?

Time taught us what to make of this human growth. It was not an annual or a biennial, but a perennial; not an herbaceous plant, but a towering tree; not an oak or an elm like those around it, but rather a lofty and spreading palm, which acclimated itself out of its latitude, as the little group of Southern magnolias has done in the woods of our northern county of Essex. For Emerson's was an Asiatic mind, drawing its sustenance partly from the hard soil of our New England, partly, too, from the air that has known Himalaya and the Ganges. So impressed with this character of his mind was Mr. Burlingame, as I saw him, after his return from his mission, that he said to me, in a freshet of hyperbole, which was the overflow of a channel with a thread of truth running in it, "There are twenty thousand Ralph Waldo Emersons in China."

What could we do with this unexpected, unprovided for, unclassified, half unwelcome new-comer, who had been for a while potted, as it were, in our Unitarian cold greenhouse, but had taken to growing so fast that he was lifting off its glass roof and letting in the hailstorms? Here was a protest that outflanked the extreme left of liberalism, yet so calm and serene that its radicalism had the accents of the gospel of peace. Here was an iconoclast without a hammer, who took down our idols from their pedestals so tenderly that it seemed like an act of worship.

The scribes and pharisees made light of his oracular sayings. The lawyers could not find the witnesses to subpoena and the documents to refer to when his case came before them, and turned him over to their wives and daughters. The ministers denounced his heresies, and handled his writings as if they were packages of dynamite, and the grandmothers were as much afraid of his new teachings as old Mrs. Piozzi was of geology. We had had revolutionary orators, reformers, martyrs; it was but a few years since Abner Kneeland had been sent to jail for expressing an opinion about the great First Cause; but we had had nothing like this man, with his seraphic voice and countenance, his choice vocabulary, his refined utterance, his gentle courage, which, with a different manner, might have been called audacity, his temperate statement of opinions which threatened to shake the existing order of thought like an earthquake.

His peculiarities of style and of thinking became fertile parents of mannerisms, which were fair game for ridicule as they appeared in his imitators. For one who talks like Emerson or like Carlyle soon finds himself surrounded by a crowd of walking phonographs, who mechanically reproduce his mental and vocal accents. Emerson was before long talking in the midst of a babbling Simonetta of echoes, and not unnaturally was now and then himself a mark for the small shot of criticism. He had soon reached that height in the "cold thin atmosphere" of thought where

> "Vainly the fowler's eye
> Might mark his distant flight to do wrong."

I shall add a few words, of necessity almost epigrammatic, upon his work and character. He dealt with life, and life with him was not merely this particular air-breathing phase of being, but the spiritual existence which included it like a parenthesis between the two infinities. He wanted his daily draughts of oxygen like his neighbors, and was as thoroughly human as the plain people he mentions who had successively owned or thought they owned the house-lot on which he planted his hearthstone. But he was at home no less in the interstellar spaces outside of all the atmospheres. The semi-materialistic idealism of Milton was a gross and clumsy medium compared to the imponderable ether of "The Over-soul" and the unimaginable vacuum of "Brahma." He followed in the shining and daring track of the *Graius homo* of Lucretius:—

> "Vivida vis animi pervicit, et extra
> Processit longe flammantia mœnia mundi."

It always seemed to me as if he looked at this earth very much as a visitor from another planet would look upon it. He was interested, and to some extent curious about it, but it was not the first spheroid he had been acquainted with, by any means. I have amused myself with comparing his descriptions of natural objects with those of the Angel Raphael in the seventh book of Paradise Lost. Emerson talks of his titmouse as Raphael talks of his emmet. Angels and poets never deal with nature after the manner of those whom we call naturalists.

To judge of him as a thinker, Emerson should have been heard as a lecturer, for his manner was an illustration of his way of thinking. He would lose his place just as his mind would drop its thought and pick up another, twentieth cousin or no relation at all to it. This went so far at times that one could hardly tell whether he was putting together a mosaic of colored fragments, or only turning a kaleidoscope where the pieces tumbled about as they best might. It was as if he had been looking in at a cosmic peep-show, and turning from it at brief intervals to tell us what he saw. But what fragments these colored sentences were, and what pictures they often placed before us, as if we too saw them! Never has this city known such audiences as he gathered; never was such an Olympian entertainment as that which he gave them.

It is very hard to speak of Mr. Emerson's poetry; not to do it injustice, still more to do it justice. It seems to me like the robe of a monarch patched by a New England housewife. The royal tint and stuff are unmistakable, but here and there the gray worsted from the darning-needle crosses and ekes out the Tyrian purple. Few poets who have written so little in verse have dropped so many of those "jewels five words long" which fall from their setting only to be more choicely treasured. *E pluribus unum* is hardly more familiar to our ears than "He builded better than he knew," and Keats's "thing of beauty" is little better known than Emerson's "beauty is its own excuse for being." One may not like to read Emerson's poetry because it is sometimes careless, almost as if carefully so, though never undignified even when slipshod; spotted with quaint archaisms and strange expressions that sound like the affectation of negligence, or with plain, homely phrases, such as the self-made scholar is always afraid of. But if one likes Emerson's poetry he will be sure to love it; if he loves it, its phrases will cling to him as hardly any others do. It may not be for the multitude, but it finds its place like pollen-dust and penetrates to the consciousness it is to fertilize and bring to flower and fruit.

I have known something of Emerson as a talker, not nearly so much as many others who can speak and write of him. It is unsafe to tell how a great thinker talks, for perhaps, like a city dealer with a village customer, he has not shown his best goods to the innocent reporter of his sayings. However that may be in this case, let me contrast in a single glance the momentary effect in conversation of the two neighbors, Hawthorne and Emerson. Speech seemed like a kind of travail to Hawthorne. One must harpoon him like a cetacean with questions to make him talk at all. Then the words came from him at last, with bashful manifestations, like those of a young girl, almost,—words that gasped themselves forth, seeming to leave a great deal more behind them than they told, and died out, discontented with themselves, like the monologue of thunder in the sky, which always goes off mumbling and grumbling as if it had not said half it wanted to, and meant to, and ought to say.

Emerson was sparing of words, but used them with great precision and nicety. If he had been followed about by a short-hand writing Boswell, every sentence he ever uttered might have been preserved. To hear him talk was like watching one crossing a brook on stepping-stones. His noun had to wait for its verb or its adjective until he was ready; then his speech would come down upon the word he wanted, and not Worcester and Webster could better it from all the wealth of their huge vocabularies.

These are only slender rays of side-light on a personality which is interesting in every aspect and will be fully illustrated by those who knew him best. One glimpse of him as a listener may be worth recalling. He was always courteous and bland to a remarkable degree; his smile was the well-remembered line of Terence written out in living features. But when anything said specially interested him he would lean toward the speaker, with a look never to be forgotten, his head stretched forward, his shoulders raised like the wings of an eagle, and his eye watching the flight of the thought which had attracted his attention as if it were his prey to be seized in mid-air and carried up to his eyry.

To sum up briefly what would, as it seems to me, be the text to be unfolded in his biography, he was a man of excellent common-sense, with a genius so uncommon that he seemed like an exotic transplanted from some angelic nursery. His character was so blameless, so beautiful, that it was rather a standard to judge others by than to find a place for on the scale of comparison. Looking at life with the profoundest sense of its infinite significance, he was yet a cheerful optimist, almost too hopeful, peeping into every cradle to see if it did not hold a babe with the halo of a new Messiah about it.

He enriched the treasure house of literature, but, what was far more, he enlarged the boundaries of thought for the few that followed him, and the many who never knew, and do not know to-day, what hand it was which took down their prison walls. He was a preacher who taught that the religion of humanity included both those of Palestine, nor those alone, and taught it with such consecrated lips that the narrowest bigot was ashamed to pray for him, as from a footstool nearer to the throne. "Hitch your wagon to a star"; this was his version of the divine lesson taught by that holy George Herbert whose words he loved. Give him whatever place belongs to him in our literature, in the literature of our language, of the world, but remember this: the end and aim of his being was to make truth lovely and manhood valorous, and to bring our daily life nearer and nearer to the eternal, immortal, invisible.

After the address of Dr. Holmes, the Rev. James Freeman Clarke, D. D., spoke of his long acquaintance with Mr. Emerson, and read several interesting extracts from letters which he had received from him at an early period of his career. At the close of his remarks Dr. Clarke presented the following Resolution, which was adopted by a rising vote:—

Resolved, That this Society unites in the wide-spread expression of esteem, gratitude, and affectionate reverence paid to the memory of our late associate, Ralph Waldo Emerson, and recognizes the great influence exercised by his character and writings to elevate, purify, and quicken the thought of our time.

Notes

1 Len Gougeon, *Virtue's Hero: Emerson, Antislavery, and Reform* (Athens: University of Georgia Press, 1990), 7–8.
2 John McAleer, *Ralph Waldo Emerson: Days of Encounter* (Boston: Little, Brown, 1984), 518.

Matthew Arnold (1822–1888)

Renowned English poet, literary critic, and social commentator, Arnold was elected Professor of Poetry at Oxford in 1857, having published works of poetry, including Empedocles on Etna and Other Poems *(1852). His influential work of social criticism,* Culture and Anarchy *(1869), was followed by a major work of religious criticism,* Literature and Dogma *(1873). Arnold's two volumes* Essays in Criticism: First Series *(1865) and* Essays in Criticism: Second Series *(1888) suggest an affinity for the structure of Emerson's own "series" of essays. Arnold began a lecture tour in the United States in 1883, the year after Emerson's death. His remarks during that visit culminated in the appearance of* Discourses in America *(1885), which was comprised of three chapters or "discourses": "Numbers; or the Majority and the Remnant," "Literature and Science," and "Emerson," which was delivered in Boston and is presented below. In his Preface, Arnold writes: "I cannot think that what I have said of Emerson will finally be accounted scant praise, although praise universal and unmixed it certainly is not." Arnold's "discourse" on Emerson is followed by the fourth sonnet in his* Dramatic and Early Poems *(1902) entitled "Written in Emerson's Essays."*

Emerson

Matthew Arnold

Forty years ago, when I was an undergraduate at Oxford, voices were in the air there which haunt my memory still. Happy the man who in that susceptible season of youth hears such voices! they are a possession to him for ever. No such voices as those which we heard in our youth at Oxford are sounding there now. Oxford has more criticism now, more knowledge, more light; but such voices as those of our youth it has no longer. The name of Cardinal Newman is a great name to the imagination still; his genius and his style are still things of power. But he is over eighty years old; he is in the Oratory at Birmingham; he has adopted, for the doubts and difficulties which beset men's minds to-day, a solution which, to speak frankly, is impossible. Forty years ago he was in the very prime of life; he was close at hand to us at Oxford; he was preaching in St. Mary's pulpit every Sunday; he seemed about to transform and to renew what was for us the most national and natural institution in the world, the Church of England. Who could resist the charm of that spiritual apparition, gliding in the dim afternoon light through the aisles of St. Mary's, rising into the pulpit, and then, in the most entrancing of voices, breaking the silence with words and thoughts which were a religious music,—subtle, sweet, mournful? I seem to hear him still, saying: 'After the fever of life, after wearinesses and sicknesses, fightings and despondings, languor and fretfulness, struggling and succeeding; after all the changes and chances of this troubled, unhealthy state,—at length comes death, at length the white throne of God, at length the beatific vision.' Or, if we followed him back to his seclusion at Littlemore, that dreary village by the London road, and to the house of retreat and the church which he built there,—a mean house such as Paul might have lived in when he was tent-making at Ephesus, a church plain and thinly sown with worshippers,—who could resist him there either, welcoming back to the severe joys of church-fellowship, and of daily worship and prayer, the firstlings of a generation which had well-nigh forgotten them? Again I seem to hear him: 'The season is chill and dark, and the breath of the morning is damp, and worshippers are few; but all this befits those who are by their profession penitents and mourners, watchers and pilgrims. More dear to them that loneliness, more cheerful that severity, and more bright that gloom, than all those aids and appliances of luxury by which men nowadays attempt to make prayer less disagreeable to them. True faith does not covet comforts; they who realise that awful day, when they shall see Him face to face whose eyes are as a flame of fire, will as little bargain to pray pleasantly now as they will think of doing so then.'

Somewhere or other I have spoken of those 'last enchantments of the Middle Age' which Oxford sheds around us, and here they were! But there were other voices sounding in our ear besides Newman's. There was the puissant voice of Carlyle; so sorely strained, over-used, and misused since, but then fresh, comparatively sound, and reaching our hearts with true, pathetic eloquence. Who can forget the emotion of receiving in its first freshness such a sentence as that sentence of Carlyle upon Edward Irving, then just dead: 'Scotland sent him forth a herculean man; our mad Babylon wore and wasted him with all her engines,—and it took her twelve years!' A greater voice still,—the greatest voice of the century,—came to us in those youthful years through Carlyle: the voice of Goethe. To this day,—such is the force of youthful associations,—I read the *Wilhelm Meister* with more pleasure in Carlyle's translation than in the original. The large, liberal view of human life in *Wilhelm Meister,* how novel it was to the Englishman in those days! and it was salutary, too, and educative for him, doubtless, as well as novel. But what moved us most in *Wilhelm Meister* was that which, after all, will always move the young most,—the poetry, the eloquence. Never, surely, was Carlyle's prose so beautiful and pure as in his rendering of the Youths' dirge over Mignon!—'Well is our treasure now laid up, the fair image of the past. Here sleeps it in the marble, undecaying; in your hearts, also, it lives, it works. Travel, travel, back into life! Take along with you this holy earnestness, for earnestness alone makes life eternity.' Here we had the voice of the great Goethe;—not the stiff, and hindered, and frigid, and factitious Goethe who speaks to us too often from those sixty volumes of his, but of the great Goethe, and the true one.

And besides those voices, there came to us in that old Oxford time a voice also from this side of the Atlantic,—a clear and pure voice, which for my ear, at any rate, brought a strain as new, and moving, and unforgettable, as the strain of Newman, or Carlyle, or Goethe. Mr. Lowell has well described the apparition of Emerson to your young generation here, in that distant time of which I am speaking, and of his workings upon them. He was your Newman, your man of soul and genius visible to you in the flesh, speaking to your bodily ears, a present object for your heart and imagination. That is surely the most potent of all influences! nothing can come up to it. To us at Oxford Emerson was but a voice speaking from three thousand miles away. But so well he spoke, that from that time forth Boston Bay and Concord were names invested to my ear with a sentiment akin to that which invests for me the names of Oxford and of Weimar; and snatches of Emerson's strain fixed themselves in my mind as imperishably as any of the eloquent words which I have been just now quoting. 'Then dies the man in you; then once more perish the buds of art, poetry, and science, as they have died already in a thousand thousand men.' 'What Plato has thought, he may think; what a saint has felt, he may feel; what at any time has befallen any man, he can understand.' 'Trust thyself! every heart vibrates to that iron string. Accept the place the Divine Providence has found for you, the society of your contemporaries, the connexion of events. Great men have always done so, and confided themselves childlike to the genius of their age; betraying their perception that the Eternal was stirring at their heart, working through their hands, predominating in all their being. And we are now men, and must accept in the highest spirit the same transcendent destiny; and not pinched in a corner, not cowards fleeing before a revolution, but redeemers and benefactors, pious aspirants to be noble clay plastic under the Almighty effort, let us advance and advance on chaos and the dark!' These lofty sentences of Emerson, and a hundred others of like strain, I never have lost out of my memory; I never *can* lose them.

At last I find myself in Emerson's own country, and looking upon Boston Bay. Naturally I revert to the friend of my youth. It is not always pleasant to ask oneself questions about the friends of one's youth; they cannot always well support it. Carlyle, for instance, in my judgment, cannot well support such a return upon him. Yet we should make the return; we should part with our illusions, we should know the truth. When I come to this country, where Emerson now counts for so much, and where such high claims are made for him, I pull myself together, and ask myself what the truth about this object of my youthful admiration really is. Improper elements often come into our estimate of men. We have lately seen a German critic make Goethe the greatest of all poets, because Germany is now the greatest of military powers, and wants a poet to match. Then, too, America is a young, country; and young countries, like young persons, are apt sometimes to evince in their literary judgments a want of scale and measure. I set myself, therefore, resolutely to come at a real estimate of Emerson, and with a leaning even to strictness rather than to indulgence. That is the safer course. Time has no indulgence; any veils of illusion which we may have left around an object because we loved it, Time is sure to strip away.

I was reading the other day a notice of Emerson by a serious and interesting American critic. Fifty or sixty passages in Emerson's poems, says this critic,—who had doubtless himself been nourished on Emerson's writings, and held them justly dear,—fifty or sixty passages from Emerson's poems have already entered into English speech as matter of familiar and universally current quotation. Here is a specimen of that personal sort of estimate which, for my part, even in speaking of authors dear to me, I would try to avoid. What is the kind of phrase of which we may fairly say that it has entered into English speech as matter of familiar quotation? Such a phrase, surely, as the 'Patience on a monument' of Shakespeare; as the 'Darkness visible' of Milton; as the 'Where ignorance is bliss' of Gray. Of not one single passage in Emerson's poetry can it be truly said that it has become a familiar quotation like phrases of this kind. It is not enough that it should be familiar to his admirers, familiar in New England, familiar even throughout the United States; it must be familiar to all readers and lovers of English poetry. Of not more than one or two passages in Emerson's poetry can it, I think, be truly said, that they stand ever-present in the memory of even many lovers of English poetry. A great number of passages from his poetry are no doubt perfectly familiar to the mind and lips of the critic whom I have mentioned, and perhaps a wide circle of American readers. But this is a very different thing from being matter of universal quotation, like the phrases of the legitimate poets.

And, in truth, one of the legitimate poets, Emerson, in my opinion, is not. His poetry is interesting, it makes one think; but it is not the poetry of one of the born poets. I say it of him with reluctance, although I am sure that he would have said it of himself; but I say it with reluctance, because I dislike giving pain to his admirers, and because all my own wish, too, is to say of him what is favourable. But I regard myself, not as speaking to please Emerson's admirers, not as speaking to please myself; but rather, I repeat, as communing with Time and Nature concerning the productions of this beautiful and rare spirit, and as resigning what of him is by their unalterable decree touched with caducity, in order the better to mark and secure that in him which is immortal.

Milton says that poetry ought to be simple, sensuous, impassioned. Well, Emerson's poetry is seldom either simple, or sensuous, or impassioned. In general it lacks directness; it lacks concreteness; it lacks energy. His grammar is often embarrassed; in particular, the want of clearly-marked distinction between the subject and the object of his sentence is a frequent cause of obscurity in him. A poem which shall be a plain, forcible, inevitable whole he hardly ever produces. Such good work as the noble lines graven on the Concord Monument is the exception with him; such ineffective work as the 'Fourth of July Ode' or the 'Boston Hymn' is the rule. Even passages and single lines of thorough plainness and commanding force are rare in his poetry. They exist, of course; but when we meet with them they give us a slight shock of surprise, so little has Emerson accustomed us to them. Let me have the pleasure of quoting one or two of these exceptional passages:—

'So nigh is grandeur to our dust,
     So near is God to man,
When Duty whispers low, *Thou must,*
     The youth replies, *I can.*'

Or again this:—

'Though love repine and reason chafe,
There came a voice without reply;

"'Tis man's perdition to be safe,
When for the truth he ought to die."

Excellent! but how seldom do we get from him a strain blown so clearly and firmly! Take another passage where his strain has not only clearness, it has also grace and beauty:—

'And ever, when the happy child
In May beholds the blooming wild,
And hears in heaven the bluebird sing,
"Onward," he cries, "your baskets bring!
In the next field is air more mild,
And in yon hazy west is Eden's balmier spring."'

In the style and cadence here there is a reminiscence, I think, of Gray; at any rate the pureness, grace, and beauty of these lines are worthy even of Gray. But Gray holds his high rank as a poet, not merely by the beauty and grace of passages in his poems; not merely by a diction generally pure in an age of impure diction: he holds it, above all, by the power and skill with which the evolution of his poems is conducted. Here is his grand superiority to Collins, whose diction in his best poem, the 'Ode to Evening,' is purer than Gray's; but then the 'Ode to Evening' is like a river which loses itself in the sand, whereas Gray's best poems have an evolution sure and satisfying. Emerson's 'Mayday,' from which I just now quoted, has no real evolution at all; it is a series of observations. And, in general, his poems have no evolution. Take, for example, his 'Titmouse.' Here he has an excellent subject; and his observation of Nature, moreover, is always marvellously close and fine. But compare what he makes of his meeting with his titmouse with what Cowper or Burns makes of the like kind of incident! One never quite arrives at learning what the titmouse actually did for him at all, though one feels a strong interest and desire to learn it; but one is reduced to guessing, and cannot be quite sure that after all one has guessed right. He is not plain and concrete enough,—in other words, not poet enough,—to be able to tell us. And a failure of this kind goes through almost all his verse, keeps him amid symbolism and allusion and the fringes of things, and, in spite of his spiritual power, deeply impairs his poetic value. Through the inestimable virtue of concreteness, a simple poem like 'The Bridge' of Longfellow, or the 'School Days' of Mr. Whittier, is of more poetic worth, perhaps, than all the verse of Emerson.

I do not, then, place Emerson, among the great poets. But I go further, and say that I do not place him among the great writers, the great men of letters. Who are the great men of letters? They are men like Cicero, Plato, Bacon, Pascal, Swift, Voltaire,— writers with, in the first place, a genius and instinct for style; writers whose prose is by a kind of native necessity true and sound. Now the style of Emerson, like the style of his transcendentalist friends and of the 'Dial' so continually,—the style of Emerson is capable of falling into a strain like this, which I take from the beginning of his 'Essay on Love': 'Every soul is a celestial being to every other soul. The heart has its sabbaths and jubilees, in which the world appears as a hymeneal feast, and all natural sounds and the circle of the seasons are erotic odes and dances.' Emerson altered this sentence in the later editions. Like Wordsworth, he was in later life fond of altering; and in general his later alterations, like those of Wordsworth, are not improvements. He softened the passage in question, however, though without really mending it. I quote it in its original and strongly-marked form. Arthur Stanley used to relate that about the year 1840, being in conversation with some Americans in quarantine at Malta, and thinking to please them, he declared his warm admiration for Emerson's 'Essays', then recently published. However, the Americans shook their heads, and told him that for home taste Emerson was decidedly too *greeny*. We will hope, for their sakes, that the sort of thing they had in their heads was such writing as I have just quoted. Unsound it is, indeed, and in a style almost impossible to a born man of letters.

It is a curious thing, that quality of style which marks the great writer, the born man of letters. It resides in the whole tissue of his work, and of his work regarded as a composition for literary purposes. Brilliant and powerful passages in a man's writings do not prove his possession of it; it lies in their whole tissue. Emerson has passages of noble and pathetic eloquence, such as those which I quoted at the beginning; he has passages of shrewd and felicitous wit; he has crisp epigram; he has passages of exquisitely touched observation of nature. Yet he is not a great writer; his style has not the requisite wholeness of good tissue. Even Carlyle is not, in my judgment, a great writer. He has surpassingly powerful qualities of expression, far more powerful than Emerson's, and reminding one of the gifts of expression of the great poets,—of even Shakespeare himself. What Emerson so admirably says of Carlyle's 'devouring eyes and portraying hand', 'those thirsty eyes, those portrait-eating, portrait-painting eyes of thine, those fatal perceptions', is thoroughly true. What a description is Carlyle's of the first publisher of *Sartor Resartus,* 'to whom the idea of a new edition of *Sartor* is frightful, or rather ludicrous, unimaginable'; of this poor Fraser, in whose 'wonderful world of Tory pamphleteers, conservative Younger-brothers, Regent Street loungers, Crockford gamblers, Irish Jesuits, drunken reporters, and miscellaneous unclean persons (whom nitre and much soap will not wash clean), not a soul has expressed the smallest wish that way!' What a portrait, again, of the well-beloved John Sterling! 'One, and the best, of a small class extant here, who, nigh drowning in a black wreck of Infidelity (lighted up by some glare of Radicalism only, now growing *dim* too), and about to perish, saved themselves into a Coleridgian Shovel-Hattedness.' What touches in the invitation of Emerson to London! 'You shall see blockheads by the million; Pickwick himself shall be visible,—innocent young Dickens, reserved for a questionable fate. The great Wordsworth shall talk till you yourself pronounce him to be a bore. Southey's complexion is still healthy mahogany brown, with a fleece of white hair, and eyes that seem running at full gallop. Leigh Hunt, man of genius in the shape of a cockney, is my near neighbour, with good humour and no commonsense; old Rogers with his pale head, white, bare, and cold as snow, with those large blue eyes, cruel, sorrowful, and that sardonic shelf chin.' How inimitable it all is! And finally, for one must not go on for ever, this version of a London Sunday, with the public-houses closed during the hours of divine service! 'It is silent Sunday; the populace not yet admitted to their beer-shops, till the respectabilities conclude their rubric mummeries,—a much more audacious feat than beer.' Yet even Carlyle is not, in my judgment, to be called a great writer; one cannot think of ranking him with men like Cicero and Plato and Swift and Voltaire. Emerson freely promises to Carlyle immortality for his histories. They will not have it. Why? Because the materials furnished to him by that devouring eye of his, and that portraying hand, were not wrought in and subdued by him to what his work, regarded as a composition for literary purposes, required. Occurring in conversation, breaking out in familiar correspondence, they are magnificent, inimitable; nothing more is required of them; thus thrown out anyhow, they serve their turn and fulfil their function. And, therefore, I should not wonder if really Carlyle lived, in the long run, by such an invaluable record as that correspondence between him and Emerson, of which we owe the publication to Mr. Charles Norton,—by this and not by his works, as Johnson lives in Boswell, not by his works. For Carlyle's sallies, as the staple of a literary work, become wearisome; and as time more and more applies to Carlyle's works its stringent test, this will be felt more and more. Shakespeare, Molière, Swift,— they, too, had, like Carlyle, the devouring eye and the portraying hand. But they are great literary masters, they are supreme writers, because they knew how to work into a literary composition their materials, and to subdue them to the purposes of literary effect. Carlyle is too wilful for this, too turbid, too vehement.

You will think I deal in nothing but negatives. I have been saying that Emerson is not one of the great poets, the great writers. He has not their quality of style. He is, however, the propounder of a philosophy. The Platonic dialogues afford us the example of exquisite literary form and treatment given to philosophical ideas. Plato is at once a great literary man and a great philosopher. If we speak carefully, we cannot call Aristotle or Spinoza or Kant great literary men, or their productions great literary works. But their work is arranged with such constructive power that they build a philosophy, and are justly called great philosophical writers. Emerson cannot, I think, be called with justice a great philosophical writer. He cannot build; his arrangement of philosophical ideas has no progress in it, no evolution; he does not construct a philosophy. Emerson himself knew the defects of his method, or rather want of method, very well; indeed, he and Carlyle criticise themselves and one another in a way which leaves little for any one else to do in the way of formulating their defects. Carlyle formulates perfectly the defects of his friend's poetic and literary production when he says of the 'Dial': 'For me it is too ethereal, speculative, theoretic; I will have all things condense themselves, take shape and body, if they are to have my sympathy.' And, speaking of Emerson's orations, he says: 'I long to see some concrete Thing, some Event, Man's Life, American Forest, or piece of Creation, which this Emerson loves and wonders at, well *Emersonised*,— depictured by Emerson, filled with the life of Emerson, and cast forth from him, then to live by itself. If these orations balk me of this, how profitable soever they may be for others, I will not love them.' Emerson himself formulates perfectly the defect of his own philosophical productions when he speaks of his 'formidable tendency to the lapidary style. I build my house of boulders.' 'Here I sit and read and write,' he says again, 'with very little system, and, as far as regards composition, with the most fragmentary result; paragraphs incomprehensible, each sentence an infinitely repellent particle.' Nothing can be truer; and the work of a Spinoza or Kant, of the men who stand as great philosophical writers, does not proceed in this wise.

Some people will tell you that Emerson's poetry, indeed, is too abstract, and his philosophy too vague, but that his best work is his *English Traits*. The *English Traits* are beyond question very pleasant reading. It is easy to praise them, easy to commend the author of them. But I insist on always trying Emerson's work by the highest standards. I esteem him too much to try his work by any other. Tried by the highest standards, and compared with the work of the excellent markers and recorders of the traits of human life,—of writers like Montaigne, La Bruyere, Addison,—the *English Traits* will not stand the comparison. Emerson's observation has not the disinterested quality of the observation of these masters. It is the observation of a man systematically benevolent, as Hawthorne's observation in *Our Old Home* is the work of a man chagrined. Hawthorne's literary talent is of the first order. His subjects are generally not to me subjects of the highest interest; but his literary talent is of the first order, the finest, I think, which America has yet produced,—finer, by much, than, Emerson's. Yet *Our Old Home* is not a masterpiece any more than *English Traits*. In neither of them is the observer disinterested enough. The author's attitude in each of these cases can easily be understood and defended. Hawthorne was a sensitive man, so situated in England that he was perpetually in contact with the British Philistine; and the British Philistine is a trying personage. Emerson's systematic benevolence comes from what he himself calls somewhere his 'persistent optimism'; and his persistent optimism is the root of his greatness and the source of his charm. But still let us keep our literary conscience true, and judge every kind of literary work by the laws really proper to it. The kind of work attempted in the *English Traits* and in *Our Old Home* is work which cannot be done perfectly with a bias such as that given by Emerson's optimism or by Hawthorne's chagrin. Consequently, neither *English Traits* nor *Our Old Home* is a work of perfection in its kind.

Not with the Miltons and Grays, not with the Platos and Spinozas, not with the Swifts and Voltaires, not with the Montaignes and Addisons, can we rank Emerson. His work of various kinds, when one compares it with the work done in a corresponding kind by these masters, fails to stand the comparison. No man could see this clearer than Emerson himself. It is hard not to feel despondency when we contemplate our failures and shortcomings: and Emerson, the least self-flattering and the most modest of men, saw so plainly what was lacking to him that he had his moments of despondency. 'Alas, my friend,' he writes in reply to Carlyle, who had exhorted him to creative work,— 'Alas, my friend, I can do no such gay thing as you say. I do not belong to the poets, but only to a low department of literature,—the reporters; suburban men.' He deprecated his friend's praise; praise 'generous to a fault,' he calls it; praise 'generous to the shaming of me,—cold, fastidious, ebbing person that I am. Already in a former letter you had said too much good of my poor little arid book, which is as sand to my eyes. I can only say that I heartily wish the book were better; and I must try and deserve so much favour from the kind gods by a bolder and truer living in the months to come,—such as may perchance one day release and invigorate this cramp hand of mine. When I see how much work is to be done; what room for a poet, for any spiritualist, in this great, intelligent, sensual, and avaricious America,—I lament my fumbling fingers and stammering tongue.' Again, as late as 1870, he writes to Carlyle: 'There is no example of constancy like yours, and it always stings my stupor into temporary recovery and wonderful resolution to accept the noble challenge. But "the strong hours conquer us;" and I am the victim of miscellany,—miscellany of designs, vast debility, and procrastination.' The forlorn note, belonging to the phrase, 'vast debility,' recalls that saddest and most discouraged of writers, the author of *Obermann,* Senancour, with whom Emerson has in truth a certain kinship. He has, in common with Senancour, his pureness, his passion for nature, his single eye; and here we find him confessing, like Senancour, a sense in himself of sterility and impotence.

And now I think I have cleared the ground. I have given up to envious Time as much of Emerson as Time can fairly expect ever to obtain. We have not in Emerson a great poet, a great writer, a great philosophy-maker. His relation to us is not that of one of those personages; yet it is a relation of, I think, even superior importance. His relation to us is more like that of the Roman Emperor Marcus Aurelius. Marcus Aurelius is not a great writer, a great philosophy-maker; he is the friend and aider of those who would live in the spirit. Emerson is the same. He is the friend and aider of those who would live in the spirit. All the points in thinking which are necessary for this purpose he takes; but he does not combine them into a system, or present them as a regular philosophy. Combined in a system by a man with the requisite talent for this kind of thing, they would be less useful than as Emerson gives them to us; and the man with the talent so to systematise them would be less impressive than Emerson. They do very well as they now stand;—like 'boulders,' as he says;—in 'paragraphs incompressible, each sentence an infinitely repellent particle.' In such sentences his main points recur again and again, and become fixed in the memory.

We all know them. First and foremost, character. Character is everything. 'That which all things tend to educe,—which freedom, cultivation, intercourse, revolutions, go to form and deliver,—is character.' Character and self-reliance. 'Trust thyself! every heart vibrates to that iron string.' And yet we have our being in a *not ourselves.* 'There is a power above and behind us, and we are the channels of its communications.' But our lives must be pitched higher. 'Life must be lived on a higher plane; we must go up to a higher platform, to which we are always invited to ascend; there the whole scene changes.' The good we need is for ever close to us, though we attain it not. 'On the brink of the waters of life and truth, we are miserably dying.' This good is close to us, moreover, in our daily life, and in the familiar, homely places. 'The unremitting retention of simple and high sentiments in obscure duties,—that is the maxim for us. Let us be poised and wise, and our own today. Let us treat the men and women well,—treat them as if they were real; perhaps they are. Men live in their fancy, like drunkards whose hands are too soft and tremulous for successful labour. I settle myself ever firmer in the creed, that we should not postpone and refer and wish, but do broad justice where we are, by whomsoever we deal with; accepting our actual companions and circumstances, however humble or odious, as the mystic officials to whom the universe has delegated its whole pleasure for us. Massachusetts, Connecticut River, and Boston Bay, you think paltry places, and the ear loves names of foreign and classic topography. But here we are; and if we will tarry a little we may come to learn that here is best. See to it only that thyself is here.' Furthermore, the good is close to us *all*. 'I resist the scepticism of our education and of our educated men. I do not believe that the differences of opinion and character in men are organic. I do not recognise, besides the class of the good and the wise, a permanent class of sceptics, or a class of conservatives, or of malignants, or of materialists. I do not believe in the classes. Every man has a call of the power to do something unique.' Exclusiveness is deadly. 'The exclusive in social life does not see that he excludes himself from enjoyment in the attempt to appropriate it. The exclusionist in religion does not see that he shuts the door of heaven on himself in striving to shut out others. Treat men as pawns and ninepins, and you shall suffer as well as they. If you leave out their heart you shall lose your own. The selfish man suffers more from his selfishness than he from whom that selfishness withholds some important benefit.' A sound nature will be inclined to refuse ease and self-indulgence. 'To live with some rigour of temperance, or some extreme of generosity, seems to be an asceticism which common good-nature would appoint to those who are at ease and in plenty, in sign that they feel a brotherhood with the great multitude of suffering men.' Compensation, finally, is the great law of life; it is everywhere, it is sure, and there is no escape from it. This is that 'law alive and beautiful, which works over our heads and under our feet. Pitiless, it avails itself of our success when we obey it, and of our ruin when we contravene it. We are all secret believers in it. It rewards actions after their nature. The reward of a thing well done is to have done it. The thief steals from himself, the swindler swindles himself. You must pay at last your own debt.'

This is tonic indeed! And let no one object that it is too general; that more practical, positive direction is what we want; that Emerson's optimism, self-reliance, and indifference to favourable conditions for our life and growth have in them something of danger. 'Trust thyself;' 'what attracts my attention shall have it;' 'though thou shouldst walk the world over thou shalt not be able to find a condition inopportune or ignoble;' 'what we call vulgar society is that society whose poetry is not yet written, but which you shall presently make as enviable and renowned as any.' With maxims like these, we surely, it may be said, run some risk of being made too well satisfied with our own actual self and state, however crude and imperfect they may be. 'Trust thyself?' It may be said that the common American or Englishman is more than enough disposed already to trust himself. I often reply, when our sectarians are praised for following conscience: Our people are very good in following their conscience; where they are not so good is in ascertaining whether their conscience tells them right. 'What attracts my attention shall have it?' Well, that is our people's plea when they run after the Salvation Army, and desire Messrs. Moody and Sankey. 'Thou shalt not be able to find a condition inopportune or ignoble?' But think of the turn of the good people of our race for producing a life of hideousness and immense ennui; think of that specimen of your own New England life which Mr. Howells gives us in one of his charming stories which I was reading lately; think of the life of that ragged New England farm in the *Lady of the Aroostook*; think of Deacon Blood, and Aunt Maria, and the straight-backed chairs with black horse-hair seats, and Ezra Perkins with perfect self-reliance depositing his travellers in the snow! I can truly say that in the little which I have seen of the life of

New England, I am more struck with what has been achieved than with the crudeness and failure. But no doubt there is still a great deal of crudeness also. Your own novelists say there is, and I suppose they say true. In the New England, as in the Old, our people have to learn, I suppose, not that their modes of life are beautiful and excellent already; they have rather to learn that they must transform them.

To adopt this line of objection to Emerson's deliverances would, however, be unjust. In the first place, Emerson's points are in themselves true, if understood in a certain high sense; they are true and fruitful. And the right work to be done, at the hour when he appeared, was to affirm them generally and absolutely. Only thus could he break through the hard and fast barrier of narrow, fixed ideas, which he found confronting him, and win an entrance for new ideas. Had he attempted developments which may now strike us as expedient, he would have excited fierce antagonism, and probably effected little or nothing. The time might come for doing other work later, but the work which Emerson did was the right work to be done then.

In the second place, strong as was Emerson's optimism, and unconquerable as was his belief in a good result to emerge from all which he saw going on around him, no misanthropical satirist ever saw shortcomings and absurdities more clearly than he did, or exposed them more courageously. When he sees 'the meanness,' as he calls it, 'of American politics,' he congratulates Washington on being 'long already happily dead,' on being 'wrapt in his shroud and for ever safe.' With how firm a touch he delineates the faults of your two great political parties of forty years ago! The Democrats, he says, 'have not at heart the ends which give to the name of democracy what hope and virtue are in it. The spirit of our American radicalism is destructive and aimless; it is not loving; it has no ulterior and divine ends, but is destructive only out of hatred and selfishness. On the other side, the conservative party, composed of the most moderate, able, and cultivated part of the population, is timid, and merely defensive of property. It vindicates no right, it aspires to no real good, it brands no crime, it proposes no generous policy. From neither party, when in power, has the world any benefit to expect in science, art, or humanity, at all commensurate with the resources of the nation.' Then with what subtle though kindly irony he follows the gradual withdrawal in New England, in the last half century, of tender consciences from the social organisations,— the bent for experiments such as that of Brook Farm and the like,—follows it in all its 'dissidence of dissent and Protestantism of the Protestant religion!' He even loves to rally the New Englander on his philanthropical activity, and to find his beneficence and its institutions a bore! 'Your miscellaneous popular charities, the education at college of fools, the building of meeting-houses to the vain end to which many of these now stand, alms to sots, and the thousand-fold relief societies,—though I confess with shame that I sometimes succumb and give the dollar, yet it is a wicked dollar, which by and by I shall have the manhood to withhold.' 'Our Sunday schools and churches and pauper societies are yokes to the neck. We pain ourselves to please nobody. There are natural ways of arriving at the same ends at which these aim, but do not arrive.' 'Nature does not like our benevolence or our learning much better than she likes our frauds and wars. When we come out of the caucus, or the bank, or the Abolition convention, or the Temperance meeting, or the Transcendental club, into the fields and woods, she says to us: "So hot, my little sir?"'

Yes, truly, his insight is admirable; his truth is precious. Yet the secret of his effect is not even in these; it is in his temper. It is in the hopeful, serene, beautiful temper wherewith these, in Emerson, are indissolubly joined; in which they work, and have their being. He says himself: 'We judge of a man's wisdom by his hope, knowing that the perception of the inexhaustibleness of nature is an immortal youth.' If this be so, how wise is Emerson! for never had man such a sense of the inexhaustibleness of nature, and such hope. It was the ground of his being; it never failed him. Even when he is sadly avowing the imperfection of his literary power and resources, lamenting his fumbling fingers and stammering tongue, he adds: 'Yet, as I tell you, I am very easy in my mind and never dream of suicide. My whole philosophy, which is very real, teaches acquiescence and optimism. Sure I am that the right word will be spoken, though I cut out my tongue.' In his old age, with friends dying and life failing, his tone of cheerful, forward-looking hope is still the same. 'A multitude of young men are growing up here of high promise, and I compare gladly the social poverty of my youth with the power on which these draw.' His abiding word for us, the word by which being dead he yet speaks to us, is this: 'That which befits us, embosomed in beauty and wonder as we are, is cheerfulness and courage, and the endeavour to realise our aspirations. Shall not the heart, which has received so much, trust the Power by which it lives?'

One can scarcely overrate the importance of thus holding fast to happiness and hope. It gives to Emerson's work an invaluable virtue. As Wordsworth's poetry is, in my judgment, the most important work done in verse, in our language, during the present century, so Emerson's *Essays* are, I think, the most important work done in prose. His work is more important than Carlyle's. Let us be just to Carlyle, provoking though he often is. Not only has he that genius of his which makes Emerson say truly of his letters, that 'they savour always of eternity.' More than this may be said of him. The scope and upshot of his teaching are true; 'his guiding genius,' to quote Emerson again, is really 'his moral sense, his perception of the sole importance of truth and justice.' But consider Carlyle's temper, as we have been considering Emerson's! take his own account of it! 'Perhaps London is the proper place for me after all, seeing all places are *im*proper: who knows? Meanwhile, I lead a most dyspeptic, solitary, self-shrouded life; consuming, if possible in silence, my considerable daily allotment of pain; glad when any strength is left in me for writing, which is the only use I can see in myself,—too rare a case of late. The ground of my existence is black as death; too black, when all *void* too; but at times there paint themselves on it pictures of gold, and rainbow, and lightning; all the brighter for the black ground, I suppose. Withal, I am very much of a fool.'—No, not a fool, but turbid and morbid, wilful and perverse. 'We judge of a man's wisdom by his hope.'

Carlyle's perverse attitude towards happiness cuts him off from hope. He fiercely attacks the desire for happiness; his grand point in *Sartor*, his secret in which the soul may find rest, is that one shall cease to desire happiness, that one should learn to say to oneself: 'What if thou wert born and predestined not to be happy, but to be unhappy!' He is wrong; Saint Augustine is the better philosopher, who says: 'Act we *must* in pursuance of what gives us most delight.' Epictetus and Augustine can be severe moralists enough; but both of them know and frankly say that the desire for happiness is the root and ground of man's being. Tell him and show him that he places his happiness wrong, that he seeks for delight where delight will never be really found; then you illumine and further him. But you only confuse him by telling him to cease to desire happiness: and you will not tell him this unless you are already confused yourself.

Carlyle preached the dignity of labour, the necessity of righteousness, the love of veracity, the hatred of shams. He is said by many people to be a great teacher, a great helper for us, because he does so. But what is the due and eternal result of labour, righteousness, veracity?—Happiness. And how are we drawn to them by one who, instead of making us feel that with them is happiness, tells us that perhaps we were predestined not to be happy but to be unhappy?

You will find, in especial, many earnest preachers of our popular religion to be fervent in their praise and admiration of Carlyle. His insistence on labour, righteousness, and veracity, pleases them; his contempt for happiness pleases them too. I read the other day a tract against smoking, although I do not happen to be a smoker myself. 'Smoking,' said the tract, 'is liked because it gives agreeable sensations. Now it is a positive objection to a thing that it gives agreeable sensations. An earnest man will expressly avoid what gives agreeable sensations.' Shortly afterwards I was inspecting a school, and I found the children reading a piece of poetry on the common theme that we are here to-day and gone to-morrow. I shall soon be gone, the speaker in this poem was made to say,—

'And I shall be glad to go,
  For the world at best is a dreary place,
  And my life is getting low.'

How usual a language of popular religion that is, on our side of the Atlantic at any rate! But then our popular religion, in disparaging happiness here below, knows very well what it is after. It has its eye on a happiness in a future life above the clouds, in the New Jerusalem, to be won by disliking and rejecting happiness here on earth. And so long as this ideal stands fast, it is very well. But for very many it now stands fast no longer; for Carlyle, at any rate, it had failed and vanished. Happiness in labour, righteousness, and veracity,—in the life of the spirit,—here was a gospel still for Carlyle to preach, and to help others by preaching. But he baffled them and himself by preferring the paradox that we are not born for happiness at all.

Happiness in labour, righteousness, and veracity; in all the life of the spirit; happiness and eternal hope;—that was Emerson's gospel. I hear it said that Emerson was too sanguine; that the actual generation in America is not turning out so well as he expected. Very likely he was too sanguine as to the near future; in this country it is difficult not to be too sanguine. Very possibly the present generation may prove unworthy of his high hopes; even several generations succeeding this may prove unworthy of them. But by his conviction that in the life of the spirit is happiness, and by his hope that this life of the spirit will come more and more to be sanely understood, and to prevail, and to work for happiness,—by this conviction and hope Emerson was great, and he will surely prove in the end to have been right in them. In this country it is difficult, as I said, not to be sanguine. Very many of your writers are over-sanguine, and on the wrong grounds. But you have two men who in what they have written show their sanguineness in a line where courage and hope are just, where they are also infinitely important, but where they are not easy. The two men are Franklin and Emerson.[1]

These two are, I think, the most distinctively and honourably American of your writers; they are the most original and the most valuable. Wise men everywhere know that we must keep up our courage and hope; they know that hope is, as Wordsworth well says,—

'The paramount *duty* which Heaven lays,
For its own honour, on man's suffering heart.'

But the very word *duty* points to an effort and a struggle to maintain our hope unbroken. Franklin and Emerson maintained theirs with a convincing ease, an inspiring joy. Franklin's confidence in the happiness with which industry, honesty, and economy will crown the life of this work-day world, is such that he runs over with felicity. With a like felicity does Emerson run over, when he contemplates the happiness eternally attached to the true life in the spirit. You cannot prize him too much, nor heed him too diligently. He has lessons for both the branches of our race. I figure him to my mind as visible upon earth still, as still standing here by Boston Bay, or at his own Concord, in his habit as he lived, but of heightened stature and shining feature, with one hand stretched out towards the East, to our laden and labouring England; the other towards the ever-growing West, to his own dearly-loved America,—'great, intelligent, sensual, avaricious America.' To us he shows for guidance his lucid freedom, his cheerfulness and hope; to you his dignity, delicacy, serenity, elevation.

---

1 I found with pleasure that this conjunction of Emerson's name with Franklin's had already occurred to an accomplished writer and delightful man, a friend of Emerson, left almost the sole survivor, alas! of the famous literary generation of Boston,—Dr. Oliver Wendell Holmes. Dr. Holmes has kindly allowed me to print here the ingenious and interesting lines, hitherto unpublished, in which he speaks of Emerson thus:—

'Where in the realm of thought, whose air is song,
Does he, the Buddha of the West, belong?
He seems a winged Franklin, sweetly wise,
Born to unlock the secret of the skies;
And which the nobler calling—if 'tis fair
Terrestrial with celestial to compare—
To guide the storm-cloud's elemental flame,
Or walk the chambers whence the lightning came
Amidst the sources of its subtile fire,
And steal their effluence for his lips and lyre?'

Written in Emerson's Essays

Matthew Arnold

"O monstrous, dead, unprofitable world,
That thou canst hear, and hearing, hold thy way!
A voice oracular hath peal'd to-day,
To-day a hero's banner is unfurl'd.

Hast thou no lip for welcome?"—So I said.
Man after man, the world smiled and pass'd by;
A smile of wistful incredulity
As though one spake of life unto the dead:

Scornful, and strange, and sorrowful; and full
Of bitter knowledge. Yet the will is free;
Strong is the Soul, and wise, and beautiful;

The seeds of godlike power are in us still;
Gods are we, Bards, Saints, Heroes, if we will!—
Dumb judges, answer, truth or mockery?

Augustine Birrell (1850–1933)

English politician and author, Birrell published Obiter Dicta, Second Series *(1887),
a volume of essays following a first series from 1884; like Matthew Arnold, Birrell
appears to adopt an Emersonian approach by presenting his work as a series of
essays. Birrell's essay on Emerson is preceded by essays on Milton, Pope, Johnson,
Burke, and Charles Lamb—an illustrious and exclusively English procession.
Emerson is the only American author who captures a starring role in this volume,
though Birrell's interest in Emerson, one discovers, is mainly pronounced as a
series of corrections, depreciations, and disappointments. Birrell is irritated with
the "unmeasured praise" of O. W. Holmes' biography of Emerson, and surprised by
Matthew Arnold's estimation that Emerson's essays "are the most valuable prose
contributions to English literature of the century." Hoping to exempt himself from
being a mere disparager, Birrell notes: "He would, indeed, be a churl who grudged
Emerson his fame." And yet Birrell seems to suggest that the fame is misplaced,
empty, or otherwise undeserved. Emerson's reputation might be something Americans
are better suited to assess, Birrell recommends, since "here at home, where we are
sorely pressed for room, it is certain he must be content with a small allotment."
Birrell concludes reluctantly that Emerson is fine in measured doses, and counsels
that if we "read Emerson at the right times and in small quantities, we shall not be
strangers to his charm." Given the title of Birrell's book, readers are left to wonder
whether these remarks are meant to count in our, as it were, official judgment of
Emerson, or whether they are rather "said in passing,"—to be treated as beyond
the scope of proper jurisdiction. Then again, the title can also be taken as a sign of
English reserve, Birrell's sense of humor, or—less generously—his false modesty.*

Emerson

Augustine Birrell

There are men whose charm is in their entirety. Their words occasionally utter what
their looks invariably express. We read their thoughts by the light of their smiles.
Not to see and hear these men is not to know them, and criticism without personal
knowledge is in their case mutilation. Those who did know them listen in despair to
the half-hearted praise and clumsy disparagement of critical strangers, and are apt to
exclaim, as did the younger Pitt, when some extraneous person was expressing wonder
at the enormous reputation of Fox, 'Ah! you have never been under the wand of the
magician.'

Of such was Ralph Waldo Emerson. When we find so cool-brained a critic as Mr. Lowell writing and quoting thus of Emerson:—'Those who heard him while their natures were yet plastic, and their mental nerves trembled under the slightest breath of divine air, will never cease to feel and say:—

'"Was never eye did see that face,
    Was never ear did hear that tongue,
Was never mind did mind his grace
    That ever thought the travail long;
But eyes, and ears, and every thought
    Were with his sweet perfections caught;"'

we recognise at once that the sooner we take off our shoes the better, for that the ground upon which we are standing is holy. How can we sufficiently honour the men who, in this secular, work-a-day world, habitually breathe

'An ampler ether, a diviner air',

than ours!

But testimony of this kind, conclusive as it is upon the question of Emerson's personal influence, will not always be admissible in support of his claims as an author. In the long run an author's only witnesses are his own books.

In Dr. Holmes's estimate of Emerson's books every one must wish to concur.[1] These are not the days, nor is this dry and thirsty land of ours the place, when or where we can afford to pass by any well of spiritual influence. It is matter, therefore, for rejoicing that, in the opinion of so many good judges, Emerson's well can never be choked up. His essays, so at least we are told by no less a critic than Mr. Arnold, are the most valuable prose contributions to English literature of the century; his letters to Mr. Carlyle carried into all our homes the charm of a most delightful personality; the quaint melody of his poems abides in many ears. He would, indeed, be a churl who grudged Emerson his fame.

But when we are considering a writer so full of intelligence as Emerson—one so remote and detached from the world's bluster and brag—it is especially incumbent upon us to charge our own language with intelligence, and to make sure that what we say is at least truth for us.

Were we at liberty to agree with Dr. Holmes, in his unmeasured praise—did we, in short, find Emerson full of inspiration—our task would be as easy as it would be pleasant; but not entirely agreeing with Dr. Holmes, and somehow missing the inspiration, the difficulty we began by mentioning presses heavily upon us.

Pleasant reading as the introductory thirty-five pages of Dr. Holmes's book make, we doubt the wisdom of so very sketchy an account of Emerson's lineage and intellectual environment. Attracted towards Emerson everybody must be; but there are many who have never been able to get quit of an uneasy fear as to his 'staying power.' He has seemed to some of us a little thin and vague. A really great author dissipates all such fears. Read a page and they are gone. To inquire after the intellectual health of such a one would be an impertinence. Emerson hardly succeeds in inspiring this confidence, but is more like a clever invalid who says, and is encouraged by his friends to say, brilliant things, but of whom it would be cruel to expect prolonger mental exertion. A man, he himself has said, 'should give us a sense of mass.' He perhaps does not do so. This gloomy and possibly distorted view is fostered rather than discouraged by Dr. Holmes's introductory pages about Boston life and intellect. It does not seem to have been a very strong place. We lack performance. It is of small avail to write, as Dr. Holmes does, about 'brilliant circles,' and 'literary luminaries,' and then to pass on, and leave the circles circulating and the luminaries shining *in vacuo*. We want to know how they were brilliant, and what they illuminated. If you wish me to believe that you are witty I must really trouble you to make a joke. Dr. Holmes's own wit, for example, is as certain as the law of gravitation, but over all these pages of his hangs vagueness, and we scan them in vain for reassuring details.

'Mild orthodoxy, ripened in Unitarian sunshine,' does not sound very appetising, though we are assured by Dr. Holmes that it is 'a very agreeable aspect of Christianity.' Emerson himself does not seem to have found it very lively, for in 1832, after three years' experience of the ministry of the 'Second Church' of Boston, he retires from it, not tumultuously or with any deep feeling, but with something very like a yawn. He concludes his farewell sermon to his people as follows:—

'Having said this I have said all. I have no hostility to this institution. I am only stating my want of sympathy with it.'

Dr. Holmes makes short work of Emerson's childhood. He was born in Boston on the 25th May, 1803, and used to sit upon a wall and drive his mother's cow to pasture. In fact, Dr. Holmes adds nothing to what we already knew of the quiet and blameless life that came to its appointed end on the 27th April, 1882. On the completion of his college education, Emerson became a student of theology, and after a turn at teaching, was ordained, in March 1829, minister of the 'Second Church' in Boston. In September of the same year he married; and the death of his young wife, in February 1832, perhaps quickened the doubts and disinclinations which severed his connection with his 'Institution' on the 9th September, 1832. The following year he visited Europe for the first time, and made his celebrated call upon Carlyle at Craigenputtock, and laid the keel of a famous friendship. In the summer of 1834 he settled at Concord. He married again, visited England again, wrote essays, delivered lectures, made orations, published poems, carried on a long and most remarkable correspondence with Carlyle, enjoyed after the most temperate and serene of fashions many things and much happiness. And then he died.

'Can you emit sparks?' said the cat to the ugly duckling in the fairy tale, and the poor abashed creature had to admit that it could not. Emerson could emit sparks with the most electrical of cats. He is all sparks and shocks. If one were required to name the most non-sequacious author one had ever read, I do not see how we could help nominating Emerson. But, say some of his warmest admirers, 'What then?' 'It does not matter!' It appears to me to matter a great deal.

A wise author never allows his reader's mind to be at large, but casts about from the very first how to secure it all for himself. He takes you (seemingly) into his confidence, perhaps pretends to consult you as to the best route, but at all events points out to you the road, lying far ahead, which you are to travel in his company. How carefully does a really great writer, like Dr. Newman or M. Rénan, explain to you what he is going to do and how he is going to do it! His humour, wit, and fancy, however abundant they may be, spring up like wayside flowers, and do but adorn and render more attractive the path along which it is his object to conduct you. The reader's mind, interested from the beginning, and desirous of ascertaining whether the author keeps his word, and adheres to his plan, feels the glow of healthy exercise, and pays a real though unconscious attention. But Emerson makes no terms with his readers—he gives them neither thread nor clue, and thus robs them of one of the keenest pleasures of reading,—the being beforehand with your author, and going shares with him in his own thoughts.

If it be said that it is manifestly unfair to compare a mystical writer like Emerson with a polemical or historical one, I am not concerned to answer the objection, for let the comparison be made with whom you will, the unparalleled non-sequaciousness of Emerson is as certain as the Correggiosity of Correggio. You never know what he will be at. His sentences fall over you in glittering cascades, beautiful and bright, and for the moment refreshing, but after a very brief while the mind, having nothing to do on its own account but to remain wide open, and see what Emerson sends it, grows first restive and then torpid. Admiration gives way to astonishment, astonishment to bewilderment, and bewilderment to stupefaction.

'Napoleon is not a man, but a system,' once said, in her most impressive tones, Madame de Staël to Sir James Mackintosh, across a dinner-table. 'Magnificent!' murmured Sir James. 'But what does she mean?' whispered one of those helplessly commonplace creatures who, like the present writer, go about spoiling everything. 'Mass! I cannot tell!' was the frank acknowledgment and apt Shaksperian quotation of Mackintosh. Emerson's meaning, owing to his non-sequacious style, is often very difficult to apprehend. Hear him for a moment on 'Experience':—

'I gossip for my hour concerning the eternal politic. I have seen many fair pictures, not in vain. A wonderful time I have lived in. I am not the novice I was fourteen, not yet seven years ago. Let who will ask, Where is the fruit? I find a private fruit sufficient. This is a fruit, that I should not ask for a rash effect from meditations, counsels, and the hiving of truths.'

This surely is an odd way of hiving truths. It follows from it that Emerson is more striking than suggestive. He likes things on a large scale—he is fond of ethnical remarks and typical persons. Notwithstanding his habit of introducing the names of common things into his discourses and poetry ('Hay, corn, roots, hemp, flax, apples, wool, and wood,' is a line from one his poems), his familiarity therewith is evidently not great. 'Take care, papa,' cried his little son, seeing him at work with his spade, 'you will dig your leg.'

His essay on *Friendship* will not be found satisfactory. Here is a subject on which surely we are entitled to 'body.' The *Over Soul* was different, *there* it was easy to agree with Carlyle, who, writing to Emerson, says: 'Those voices of yours which I likened to unembodied souls and censure sometimes for having no body,—how *can* they have a body? They are light rays darting upwards in the east!' But friendship is a word the very sight of which in print makes the heart warm. One remembers Elia: 'Oh! it is pleasant as it is rare to find the same arm linked in yours at forty which at thirteen helped it to turn over the Cicero *De Amicitiâ*, or some other tale of antique friendship which the young heart even then was burning to anticipate.' With this in your ear it is rather chilling to read, 'I do, then, with my friends as I do with my books. I would have them where I can find them, but I seldom use them. We must have society on our own terms, and admit or exclude it on the slightest cause. I cannot afford to speak much with my friend.' These are not genial terms.

For authors and books his affection, real as it was, was singularly impersonal. In his treatment of literary subjects, we miss the purely human touch, the grip of affection, the accent of scorn, that so pleasantly characterise the writings of Mr. Lowell. Emerson, it is to be feared, regarded a company of books but as a congeries of ideas. For one idea he is indebted to Plato, for another to Dr. Channing. *Sartor Resartus*, so Emerson writes, is a noble philosophical poem, but 'have you read Sampson Reed's *Growth of the Mind*?' We read somewhere of 'Pindar, Raphael, Angelo, Dryden, and De Staël.' Emerson's notions of literary perspective are certainly 'very early.' Dr. Holmes himself is every bit as bad. In this very book of his, speaking about the dangerous liberty some poets—Emerson amongst the number—take of crowding a redundant syllable into a line, he reminds us 'that Shakspeare and Milton knew how to use it effectively; Shelley employed it freely; Bryant indulged in it; Willis was fond of it.' One has heard of the *Republic of Letters*, but this surely does not mean that one author is as good as another. 'Willis was fond of it.' I daresay he was, but we are not fond of Willis, and cannot help regarding the citation of his poetical example as an outrage.

None the less, if we will have but a little patience, and bid our occasional wonderment be still, and read Emerson at the right times and in small quantities, we shall not remain strangers to his charm. He bathes the universe in his thoughts. Nothing less than the Whole ever contented Emerson. His was no parochial spirit. He cries out—

'From air and ocean bring me foods,
From all zones and altitudes.'

How beautiful, too, are some of his sentences. Here is a bit from his essay on Shakspeare in *Representative Men*:—

'It is the essence of poetry to spring like the rainbow daughter of Wonder from the invisible, to abolish the past, and refuse all history. Malone, Warburton, Dyce, and Collier have wasted their life. The famed theatres have vainly assisted. Betterton, Garrick, Kemble, Kean, and Macready dedicate their lives to his genius—him they crown, elucidate, obey, and express,—the genius knows them not. The recitation begins, *one golden word leaps out immortal from all this painful pedantry, and sweetly torments us with invitations to his own inaccessible homes.*'

The words we have ventured to italicise seem to us to be of surpassing beauty, and to express what many a play-goer of late years must often have dimly felt.

Patience should indeed be the motto for any Emerson reader who is not by nature 'author's kin.' For example, in the essay on *Character*, after reading, 'Everything in nature is bipolar, or has a positive and negative pole. There is a male and female, a spirit and a fact, a north and a south. Spirit is the positive, the event is the negative; will is the north, action the south pole. Character may be ranked as having its natural place in the north,'—how easy to lay the book down and read no more that day; but a moment's patience is amply rewarded, for but sixteen lines farther on we may read as follows: 'We boast our emancipation from many superstitions, but if we have broken any idols it is through a transfer of the idolatry. What have I gained that I no longer immolate a bull to Jove or to Neptune, or a mouse to Hecate; that I do not tremble before the Eumenides or the Catholic Purgatory, or the Calvinistic Judgment Day,—if I quake at opinion, the public opinion as we call it, or the threat of assault or contumely, or bad neighbours, or poverty, or mutilation, or at the rumour of revolution or of wonder! If I quake, what matters it what I quake at?' Well and truly did Carlyle write to Emerson, 'You are a new era, my man, in your huge country.'

Emerson's poetry has at least one of the qualities of true poetry—it always pleases and occasionally delights. Great poetry it may not be, but it has the happy knack of slipping in between our fancies, and of clinging like ivy to the masonry of the thought-structure beneath which each one of us has his dwelling. I must be allowed room for two quotations, one from the stanzas called *Give all to Love*, the other from *Wood Notes*.

'Cling with life to maid;
But when the surprise,
First shadow of surmise,
Flits across her bosom young
Of a joy apart from thee,
Free be she, fancy-free,
Nor though detain her vesture's hem,
Nor the palest rose she flung
From her summer's diadem.
Though thou loved her as thyself,
As a self of purer clay,
Tho' her parting dims the day,
Stealing grace from all alive;
   Heartily know
   When the half-gods go,
The gods arrive.'

The lines from *Wood Notes* run as follows:—

'Come learn with me the fatal song
Which knits the world in music strong,

Whereto every bosom dances,
Kindled with courageous fancies;
Come lift thine eyes to lofty rhymes
Of things with things, of times with times,
Primal chimes of sun and shade,
Of sound and echo, man and maid;
The land reflected in the flood;
Body with shadow still pursued.
For nature beats in perfect tune
And rounds with rhyme her every rune
Whether she work in land or sea
Or hide underground her alchemy,
Thou canst not wave thy staff in air,
Or dip they paddle in the lake,
But it carves the bow of beauty there,
And the ripples in rhymes the oar forsake.
Not unrelated, unaffied,
But to each thought and thing allied,
Is perfect nature's every part,
Rooted in the mighty heart.'

What place Emerson is to occupy in American literature is for America to determine. Some authoritative remarks on this subject are to be found in Mr. Lowell's essay on 'Thoreau,' in *My Study Windows*; but here at home, where we are sorely pressed for room, it is certain he must be content with a small allotment, where, however, he may for ever sit beneath his own vine and fig-tree, none daring to make him afraid. Emerson will always be the favourite author of somebody; and to be always read by somebody is better than to be read first by everybody and then by nobody. Indeed, it is hard to fancy a pleasanter destiny than to join the company of lesser authors. All their readers are sworn friends. They are spared the harsh discords of ill-judged praise and feigned rapture. Once or twice in a century some enthusiastic and expansive admirer insists upon dragging them from their shy retreats, and trumpeting their fame in the market-place, asserting, possibly with loud asseverations (after the fashion of Mr. Swinburne), that they are precisely as much as Otway and Collins and George Eliot as they are below Shakspeare and Hugo and Emily Brontë. The great world looks on good-humouredly for a moment or two, and then proceeds as before, and the disconcerted author is left free to scuttle back to his corner, where he is all the happier, sharing the raptures of lonely student, for his brief experience of publicity.

Let us bid farewell to Emerson, who has bidden farewell to the world, in the words of his own *Good-bye*.

'Good-bye to flattery's fawning face,
To grandeur with his wise grimace,
To upstart wealth's averted eye,

To supple office low and high,
To crowded halls, to court and street,
To frozen hearts and hasting feet,
To those who go and those who come,—
Good-bye, proud world, I'm going home,
I am going to my own hearth-stone
Bosomed in yon green hills, alone,
A secret nook in a pleasant land,
Whose groves the frolic fairies planned;
Where arches green the livelong day
Echo the blackbird's roundelay,
And vulgar feet have never trod,
A spot that is sacred to thought and God.'

Note

1   See *Life of Emerson*, by O. W. Holmes.

Henry James, Sr. (1811–1882)

The patriarch of the James family—father of William, Henry, and Alice—Henry, Sr. was a devout follower of Emanuel Swedenborg (1688–1772). James and Emerson were friends, sharing at the very least an interest in Swedenborg's mysticism; Emerson devoted a chapter of his Representative Men *to the Swedish philosopher, theologian, and Christian mystic. After Thoreau met Henry, Sr. at Emerson's house he wrote with customary candor and what seemed to him fitting opprobrium: "He utters quasi-philanthropic dogmas in a metaphysic dress; but they are, for all practical purposes, very crude."[1] When Emerson wrote to his wife, Lidian, from New York City upon meeting Henry, Sr. for the first time, his impression was quite different: Emerson counted him "the best apple on the tree thus far," and writing soon after to Margaret Fuller he described him as "an independent right minded man."[2] In the present volume, the James family represents an unique occasion of commentary on Emerson—indeed F. O. Matthiessen once claimed that "the comments" of Henry, Sr., Henry, Jr., and William "upon Emerson compose by themselves a chapter of American intellectual history."[3] So in the following remarks by the father (drawn from* The Literary Remains of the Late Henry James, *ed. William James, 1885), thereafter followed by reflections from his two sons, we may come to appreciate both the variety of their impressions of Emerson and their consequence.*

Mr. Emerson

Henry James, Sr.

At all events, if we are still to go on cherishing any such luxury as a private conscience towards God, I greatly prefer for my own part that it should be an evil conscience. Conscience was always intended as a rebuke and never as an exhilaration to the private citizen; and so let it flourish till the end of our wearisome civilization. There are many signs, however, that this end is near. My recently deceased friend Mr. Emerson, for example, was all his days an arch traitor to our existing civilized regimen, inasmuch as he unconsciously managed to set aside its fundamental principle in doing without conscience, which was the entire secret of his very exceptional interest to men's speculation. He betrayed it to be sure without being at all aware of what he was doing; but this was really all that he distinctively did to my observation. His nature had always been so innocent, so unaffectedly innocent, that when in later life he began to cultivate a club consciousness, and to sip a glass of wine or smoke a cigar, I felt very much outraged by it. I felt very much as if some renowned Boston belle had suddenly collapsed and undertaken to sell newspapers at a street corner. "Why, Emerson, is this *you* doing such things?" I exclaimed. "What profanation! Do throw the unclean things behind your back!" But, no; he was actually proud of his accomplishments! This came from his never knowing (intellectually) what he stood for in the evolution of New England life. He was lineally descended to begin with, from a half-score of comatose New England clergymen, in whose behalf probably the religious instinct had been used up. Or, what to their experience had been religion, became in that of their descendant *life*. The actual truth, at any rate, was that he never felt a movement of the life of conscience from the day of his birth till that of his death. I could never see any signs of such a life in him. I remember, to be sure, that he had a great gift of friendship, and that he was very plucky in behalf of his friends whenever they felt themselves assailed—as plucky as a woman. For instance, whenever Wendell Phillips ventilated his not untimely wit at the expense of our club-house politicians, Emerson, hearing his friends among these latter complain, grew indignant, and for several days you would hear nothing from his lips but excessive eulogies of Mr. Garrison, which sounded like nothing else in the world but revilings of Mr. Phillips. But, bless your heart! there was not a bit of conscience in a bushel of such experiences, but only wounded friendship, which is a totally different and much lower thing.

The infallible mark of conscience is that it is always a subjective judgment couched in some such language as this: "God be merciful to *me* a sinner!" and never an objective judgment such as this: *God damn Wendell Phillips, or some other of my friends!* This latter judgment is always an outbreak of ungovernable temper on our part, and was never known to reach the ear of God save in this guise: *God* BLESS *W. P. or any other friend implicated!* Now Emerson was seriously incapable of a subjective judgment upon himself; he did not know the inward difference between good and evil, so far as he was himself concerned. No doubt he perfectly comprehended the outward or moral difference between these things; but I insist upon it that he never so much as dreamed of any inward or spiritual difference between them. For this difference is vitally seen only when oneself seems unchangeably evil to his own sight, and one's neighbor unchangeably good in the comparison. How could Emerson ever have known this difference? I am satisfied that he never in his life had felt a temptation *to bear false-witness* against his neighbor, *to steal, to commit adultery, or to murder*; how then should he have ever experienced what is technically called a conviction of sin?—that is, a conviction of himself as *evil* before God, and all other men as *good*. One gets a conviction of the evil that attaches to the natural selfhood in man in no other way than—as I can myself attest—by this growing acquaintance with his own moral infirmity, and the consequent gradual decline of his self-respect. For I myself had known all these temptations—in forms of course more or less modified—by the time I was fourteen or fifteen years old; so that by the time I had got to be twenty-five or thirty (which was the date of my first acquaintance with Emerson) I was saturated with a sense of spiritual evil—no man ever more so possibly, since I felt thoroughly *self*-condemned before God. Good heavens! how soothed and comforted I was by the innocent lovely look of my new acquaintance, by his tender courtesy, his generous laudatory appreciation of my crude literary ventures! and how I used to lock myself up with him in his bed-room, swearing that before the door was opened I would arrive at the secret of his immense superiority to the common herd of literary men! I might just as well have locked myself up with a handful of diamonds, so far as any capacity of self-cognizance existed in him. I found in fact, before I had been with him a week, that the immense superiority I ascribed to him was altogether personal or practical—by no means intellectual; that it came to him by birth or genius like a woman's beauty or charm of manners; that no other account was to be given of it in truth than that Emerson himself was an unsexed woman, a veritable fruit of almighty power in the sphere of our *nature*.

This after a while grew to be a great discovery to me; but I was always more or less provoked to think that Emerson himself should take no intellectual stock in it. On the whole I may say that at first I was greatly disappointed in him, because his intellect never kept the promise which his lovely face and manners held out to me. He was to my senses a literal divine presence in the house with me; and we cannot recognize literal divine presences in our houses without feeling sure that they will be able to say something of critical importance to one's intellect. It turned out that any average old dame in a horse-car would have satisfied my intellectual rapacity just as well as Emerson. My standing intellectual embarrassment for years had been to get at the bottom of the difference between law and gospel in humanity—between the head and the heart of things—between the great God almighty, in short, and the intensely wooden and ridiculous gods of the nations. Emerson, I discovered immediately, had never been the least of an expert in this sort of knowledge; and though his immense personal fascination always kept up, he at once lost all intellectual prestige to my regard. I even thought that I had never seen a man more profoundly devoid of spiritual understanding. This prejudice grew, of course, out of my having inherited an altogether narrow ecclesiastical notion of what spiritual understanding was. I supposed it consisted unmistakably in some doctrinal lore concerning man's regeneration, to which, however, my new friend was plainly and signally incompetent. Emerson, in fact, derided this doctrine, smiling benignly whenever it was mentioned. I could make neither head nor tail of him according to men's ordinary standards—the only thing that I was sure of being that he, like Christ, was somehow divinely begotten. He seemed to me unmistakably virgin-born whenever I looked at him, and reminded me of nothing so much as of those persons dear to Christ's heart who should come after him professing no allegiance to him—having never heard his name pronounced, and yet perfectly fulfilling his will. He never seemed for a moment to antagonize the church of his own consent, but only out of condescension to his interlocutor's weakness. In fact he was to all appearance entirely ignorant of the church's existence until you recalled it to his imagination; and even then I never knew anything so implacably and uniformly mild as his judgments of it were. He had apparently lived all his life in a world where it was only subterraneously known; and, try as you would, you could never persuade him that any the least living power attached to it. The same profound incredulity characterized him in regard to the State; and it was only in his enfeebled later years that he ever lent himself to the idea of society as its destined divine form. I am not sure indeed that the lending was ever very serious. But he was always greedy, with all a Yankee's greediness, after facts, and would at least appear to listen to you with earnest respect and sympathy whenever you plead for society as the redeemed form of our nature.

In short he was, as I have said before, fundamentally treacherous to civilization, without being at all aware himself of the fact. He himself, I venture to say, was peculiarly unaware of the fact. He appeared to me utterly unconscious of himself as either good or evil. He had no conscience, in fact, and lived by perception, which is an altogether lower or less spiritual faculty. The more universalized a man is by genius or natural birth, the less is he spiritually individualized, making up in breadth of endowment what he lacks in depth. This was remarkably the case with Emerson. In his books or public capacity he was constantly electrifying you by sayings full of divine inspiration. In his talk or private capacity he was one of the least remunerative men I ever encountered. No man could look at him speaking (or when he was silent either, for that matter) without having a vision of the divinest beauty. But when you went to him to hold discourse about the wondrous phenomenon, you found him absolutely destitute of reflective power. He had apparently no private personality; and if any visitor thought he discerned traces of such a thing, you may take for granted that the visitor himself was a man of large imaginative resources. He was nothing else than a show-figure of almighty power in our nature; and that he was destitute of all the apparatus of humbuggery that goes to eke out more or less the private pretension in humanity, only completed and confirmed the extraordinary fascination that belonged to him. He was full of living inspiration to me whenever I saw him; and yet I could find in him no trivial sign of the selfhood which I found in other men. He was like a vestal virgin, indeed, always in ministry upon the altar; but the vestal virgin had doubtless a prosaic side also, which related her to commonplace people. Now Emerson was so far *unlike* the virgin: he had no prosaic side relating him to ordinary people. Judge Hoar and Mr. John Forbes constituted his spontaneous political conscience; and his domestic one (equally spontaneous) was supplied by loving members of his own family—so that he only connected with the race at second-hand, and found all the material business of life such as voting and the payment of taxes transacted for *him* with marvellous lack of friction.

Incontestably the main thing about him, however, as I have already said, was that he unconsciously brought you face to face with the infinite in humanity. When I looked upon myself, or upon the ordinary rabble of ecclesiastics and politicians, everything in us seemed ridiculously undivine. When I looked upon Emerson, these same undivine things were what gave *him* his manifest divine charm. The reason was that in him everything seemed innocent by the transparent absence of selfhood, and in us everything seemed foul and false by its preternatural activity. The difference between us was made by innocence altogether. I never thought it was a real or spiritual difference, but only a natural or apparent one. But such as it was, it gave me my first living impression of the great God almighty who alone is at work in human affairs, avouching his awful and adorable spiritual infinitude only through the death and hell wrapped up in our finite experience. This was Emerson's incontestable virtue to everyone who appreciated him, that he recognized no God outside of himself and his interlocutor, and recognized him there only as the *liaison* between the two, taking care that all their intercourse should be holy with a holiness undreamed of before by man or angel. For it is not a holiness taught by books or the example of tiresome, diseased, self-conscious saints, but simply by one's own redeemed flesh and blood. In short, the only holiness which Emerson recognized, and for which he consistently lived, was innocence. And innocence—glory be to God's spiritual incarnation in our nature!—has no other root in us than our unconscious flesh and bones. That is to say, it attaches only to what is definitively universal or natural in our experience, and hence appropriates itself to individuals only in so far as they learn to denude themselves of personality or self-consciousness; which reminds one of Christ's mystical saying: *He that findeth his life (in himself) shall lose it, and he that loseth his life for my sake shall find it.*

Notes

1 Ralph Barton Perry, *The Thought and Character of William James* (Boston: Little, Brown, 1936), Vol. I, 149–50.
2 Ralph Waldo Emerson, *The Letters of Ralph Waldo Emerson*, ed. Ralph Rusk (New York: Columbia University Press, 1939), Vol. III, 26, 30 (1842).
3 F. O. Matthiessen, *The James Family* (New York: A. A. Knopf, 1947), 428.

Henry James, Jr. (1843–1916)

The son of Emerson's friend, Henry James, Sr., a sibling of the philosopher-psychologist, William, and the diarist, Alice, the younger Henry James was educated mainly in the intellectual capitals of Europe. A prolific novelist celebrated both for his renditions of American encounters with European culture and for his development of literary realism and core elements of literary modernism, James authored The American *(1877),* The Europeans *(1878),* The Portrait of a Lady *(1881),* The Bostonians *(1886),* The Wings of the Dove *(1902),* The Ambassadors *(1903), and* The Golden Bowl *(1904), among many other novels and works of criticism and short fiction. After 53 years as an émigré in England, he became a British subject the year before his death. In his youth, James knew Emerson as a family friend and later, in his maturity, wrote of Emerson as a thinker, principally represented by the following selections, which include: his review of* The Correspondence of Thomas Carlyle and Ralph Waldo Emerson, 1834–1872 *in the* Century Magazine *(June 1883); and a reading of James Elliot Cabot's two-volume* A Memoir of Ralph Waldo Emerson *(1887), a biography that James finds "incontestable" and yet wanting. This review of Cabot's biography, excerpted below, from* Macmillan's Magazine *(December 1887), is reprinted the following year as the chapter "Emerson" in* Partial Portraits *(1888). James read Cabot's* Memoir *with an intimate knowledge of Emerson's personal and social life, and anticipates a fuller portrait of Emerson in the context of his times and relations—a desire that will not be answered until the next century, though James himself contributes meaningfully to that project. The selections from James begin, however, with a brief extract from* Hawthorne *(1879) where he writes nostalgically about the days when Emerson's "orations poured forth in their early newness" and at that point "were the most poetical, the most beautiful productions of the American mind."*

The Emersonian Philosophy

Henry James, Jr.

A biographer of Hawthorne might well regret that his hero had not been more mixed up with the reforming and free-thinking class, so that he might find a pretext for writing a chapter upon the state of Boston society forty years ago. A needful warrant for such regret should be, properly, that the biographer's own personal reminiscences should stretch back to that period and to the persons who animated it. This would be a guarantee of fulness of knowledge and, presumably, of kindness of tone. It is difficult to see, indeed, how the generation of which Hawthorne has given us, in *Blithedale,* a few portraits, should not, at this time of day, bespoken of very tenderly and sympathetically. If irony enter into the allusion, it should be of the lightest and gentlest. Certainly, for a brief and imperfect chronicler of these things, a writer just touching them as he passes, and who has not the advantage of having been a contemporary, there is only one possible tone. The compiler of these pages, though his recollections date only from a later period, has a memory of a certain number of persons who had been intimately connected, as Hawthorne was not, with the agitations of that interesting time. Something of its interest adhered to them still—something of its aroma clung to their garments; there was something about them which seemed to say that when they were young and enthusiastic, they had been initiated into moral mysteries, they had played at a wonderful game. Their usual mark (it is true I can think of exceptions) was that they seemed excellently good. They appeared unstained by the world, unfamiliar with worldly desires and standards, and with those various forms of human depravity which flourish in some high phases of civilisation; inclined to simple and democratic ways, destitute of pretensions and affectations, of jealousies, of cynicisms, of snobbishness. This little epoch of fermentation has three or four drawbacks for the critics—drawbacks, however, that may be overlooked by a person for whom it has an interest of association. It bore, intellectually, the stamp of provincialism; it was a beginning without a fruition, a dawn without a noon; and it produced, with a single exception, no great talents. It produced a great deal of writing, but (always putting Hawthorne aside, as a contemporary but not a sharer) only one writer in whom the world at large has interested itself. The situation was summed up and transfigured in the admirable and exquisite Emerson. He expressed all that it contained, and a good deal more, doubtless, besides; he was the man of genius of the moment; he was the Transcendentalist *par excellence*. Emerson expressed, before all things, as was extremely natural at the hour and in the place, the value and importance of the individual, the duty of making the most of one's self, of living by one's own personal light, and carrying out one's own disposition. He reflected with beautiful irony upon the exquisite impudence of those institutions which claim to have appropriated the truth and to dole it out, in proportionate morsels, in exchange for a subscription. He talked about the beauty and dignity of life, and about every one who is born into the world being born to the whole, having an interest and a stake in the whole. He said "all that is clearly due to-day is not to lie," and a great many other things which it would be still easier to present in a ridiculous light. He insisted upon sincerity and independence and spontaneity, upon acting in harmony with one's nature, and not conforming and compromising for the sake of being more comfortable. He urged that a man should await his call, his finding the thing to do which he should really believe in doing, and not be urged by the world's opinion to do simply the world's work. "If no call should come for years, for centuries, then I know that the want of the Universe is the attestation of faith by my abstinence.... If I cannot work, at least I need not lie." The doctrine of the supremacy of the individual to himself, of his originality, and, as regards his own character, *unique* quality, must have had a great charm for people living in a society in which introspection—thanks to the want of other entertainment—played almost the part of a social resource.

In the United States, in those days, there were no great things to look out at (save forests and rivers); life was not in the least spectacular; society was not brilliant; the country was given up to a great material prosperity, a homely *bourgeois* activity, a diffusion of primary education and the common luxuries. There was, therefore, among the cultivated classes, much relish for the utterances of a writer who would help one to take a picturesque view of one's internal responsibilities, and to find in the landscape of the soul all sorts of fine sun-rise and moonlight effects. "Mean-time, while the doors of the temple stand open, night and day, before every man, and the oracles of this truth cease never, it is guarded by one stern condition; this, namely—it is an intuition. It cannot be received at second hand. Truly speaking, it is not instruction but provocation that I can receive from another soul." To make one's self so much more interesting would help to make life interesting, and life was probably, to many of this aspiring congregation, a dream of freedom and fortitude. There were faulty parts in the Emersonian philosophy; but the general tone was magnificent; and I can easily believe that, coming when it did and where it did, it should have been drunk in by a great many fine moral appetites with a sense of intoxication. One envies, even, I will not say the illusions, of that keenly sentient period, but the convictions and interests— the moral passion. One certainly envies the privilege of having heard the finest of Emerson's orations poured forth in their early newness. They were the most poetical, the most beautiful productions of the American mind, and they were thoroughly local and national. They had a music and a magic, and when one remembers the remarkable charm of the speaker, the beautiful modulation of his utterance, one regrets in especial that one might not have been present on a certain occasion which made a sensation, an era—the delivery of an address to the Divinity School of Harvard University, on a summer evening in 1838. In the light, fresh American air, unthickened and undarkened by customs and institutions established, these things, as the phrase is, told.

Carlyle and Emerson

Henry James, Jr.

IN THE DELUGE of "new books," in which so many of us at present are occupied in swimming for our lives, it is not often that there floats toward us a pair of volumes so well deserving to be arrested in their passage as this substantial record of a beautiful and distinguished friendship. The book has a high interest, and we have found it even more absorbing than we expected. It is only superficially, indeed, that it may be spoken of as new; for the persons and things it commemorates have already receded—so fast we move to-day—into a kind of historical perspective. The last letter that passed between the correspondents is of the date only of 1872; Carlyle died nine and Emerson ten years later. But we seem to see them from a distance; the united pair presents itself in something of the uplifted relief of a group on canvas or in marble. They have become, as I say, historical: so many of their emotions, their discussions, their interests, their allusions belong to a past which is already remote. It was, in fact, in the current of an earlier world that the Correspondence began. The first letter, which is from Emerson as the last is from Carlyle, is of the date of 1834. Emerson was the voice of New England in those days, and New England has changed not a little. There is something peculiarly young and tender in the social scene in which we see him engaged; for, in the interval that separates us from the period included in the whole of the first of these volumes and in the greater part of the second, a great many things have come and gone. The questions of those years are not the questions of these. There were more questions then, perhaps; at least, they made more show. It may seem to the reader of Emerson's early letters that at that time there was nothing in New England but questions. There were very few things, and even few persons. Emerson's personal references are rare. Bronson Alcott, W. E. Channing, Margaret Fuller, Thoreau, an occasional American about to go to Europe, carrying a letter or a book to Carlyle, constitute in this direction the chief objects of mention. Transcendentalism has come and gone, and the abolition of slavery, and the novelty of the Unitarian creed, and the revelation of Goethe, and the doctrine of a vegetable diet, and a great many other reforms then deemed urgent. Carlyle's extraordinary personality has, moreover, thanks to recent publications, revealed itself with unlooked-for vividness. Of few distinguished men has the public come into such complete possession so soon after death has unlocked the cabinets. The deeply interesting volumes given to the world so promptly by Mr. Froude, have transmuted the great Scotch humorist from a remote and mysterious personage—however portentous, disclosing himself in dusky, smoky ejaculations and rumblings—into a definite and measurable, an almost familiar figure, with every feature marked and every peculiarity demonstrated. We know Carlyle, in short; we may look at him at our ease, and the advantage, though we have enjoyed it but for a year or two, has become part of our modern illumination. When we receive new contributions accordingly, we know what to do with them, and where, as the phrase is, to fit them in; they find us prepared. I should add that if we know Carlyle, we know him in a great measure because he was so rich, so original a letter writer. The letters in Mr. Froude's volumes constituted the highest value of those memorials and led us to look for entertainment as great in the Correspondence which Mr. Charles Eliot Norton had had for some time in his keeping, and which, though his name does not appear on the title page, he has now edited with all needful judgment and care. Carlyle takes his place among the first of English, among the very first of all letter writers. All his great merits come out in this form of expression; and his defects are not felt as defects, but only as striking characteristics and as tones in the picture. Originality, nature, humor, imagination, freedom, the disposition to talk, the play of mood, the touch of confidence—these qualities, of which the letters are full, will, with the aid of an inimitable use of language—a style which glances at nothing that it does not render grotesque—preserve their life for readers even further removed from the occasion than ourselves, and for whom possibly the vogue of Carlyle's published writings in his day will be to a certain degree a subject of wonder. The light thrown upon his character by the mass of evidence edited by Mr. Froude had not embellished the image nor made the reader's sympathy advance at the same pace as his curiosity. But the volumes that lie before us seemed to promise a more genial sort of testimony, and the promise has been partly kept. Carlyle is here in intercourse with a friend for whom, almost alone among the persons with whom he had dealings, he appears to have entertained a sentiment of respect—a constancy of affection untinged by that humorous contempt in which (in most cases) he indulges when he wishes to be kind, and which was the best refuge open to him from his other alternative of absolutely savage mockery. Of the character, the sincerity, the genius, the many good offices of his American correspondent, he appears to have had an appreciation which, even in his most invidious hours, never belied itself. It is singular, indeed, that throughout his intercourse with Emerson, he never appears to have known the satiric fury which he directed at so many other objects—accepting his friend *en bloc*, once for all, with reservations and protests so light that, as addressed to Emerson's own character, they are only a finer form of consideration. Emerson, on the other hand, who was so much more kindly a judge, so much more luminous a nature, holds off, as the phrase is, comparatively, and expresses, at times, at least, the disapprobation of silence. Carlyle was the more constant writer of the two, especially toward the end of their correspondence; he constantly expresses the desire to hear from Emerson oftener. The latter had not an abundant epistolary impulse; the form and style of his letters, charming as they are, is in itself a proof of that. But there were evidently certain directions in which he could not go with his friend, who has likewise sundry tricks of style which act at times even upon the placid nerves of the inventor of Transcendentalism. He thinks, for instance, that Carlyle's satire of the "gigmania" has been overdone; and this, although Emerson himself was as little as possible of a gigmaniac. I must add that it would be wrong to suppose that the element of reserve, or of calculated silence, plays in the least a striking part in the letters of either. There is nothing more striking, and nothing finer, than their confident frankness. Altogether the charm of the book is that as one reads it one is in excellent company. Two men of rare and beautiful genius converse with each other, and the conversation is a kind of exhibition.

There was something almost dramatic in the beginning of their friendship. Emerson, a young Bostonian, then unknown, went to Europe for the first time in 1833. He had read Carlyle's contributions to the "Edinburgh Review," and on his return from Italy, spending the summer in England, had no greater care than to become acquainted with the author. Carlyle, hardly better known then than Emerson—poor, struggling, lonely, discouraged, but pregnant with all his future eloquence—was spending at the farm of Craigenputtock, in the south of Scotland, those melancholy, those almost savage years of which we have so rich a report in the letters and journals published by Mr. Froude. "I found the house amid desolate, heathery hills, where the lonely scholar nourished his mighty heart." So writes Emerson in the first chapter of the "English Traits." The two spent a day of early autumn together, walking over the moors, and when they separated it was with a presentiment of the future and a conviction on the part of each that he had made a rare acquisition. Carlyle has commemorated in several places the apparition of the generous young American,—"one of the most lovable creatures in himself that we had ever looked upon," he wrote to his mother; and toward the end of his life, in one of these letters, he glances back at it in the tenderest manner, across the years. "I shall never forget the visitor," at a later date, too, Mrs. Carlyle wrote, "who years ago, in the desert, descended on us out of the clouds, as it were, and made one day there look like enchantment for us, and left me weeping that it was only one day." Emerson went back to America, and the first letter in this collection is of the date of nine months later—May, 1834. This letter contains, by the way, an allusion to Carlyle's situation at that time, which, in the light thrown upon his state of mind and circumstances at Craigenputtock by the "lonely scholar's" own letters, journals, and reminiscences, may provoke a smile. "I remembered with joy the favored condition of my lonely philosopher, his happiest wedlock, his fortunate temper, his steadfast simplicity, his all means of happiness—not," Emerson indeed adds, "that I had the remotest hope that he should so far depart from his theories as to expect happiness." Carlyle's fortunate temper and steadfast simplicity sound to-day like bold touches of satire. It is true that his idiosyncrasies were as yet more or less undeveloped. The Correspondence speedily became brisk, the more so that, in the winter of 1834–5, Carlyle had settled himself in London, that life and work had opened to him with a somewhat better promise, and that the transmission to his American disciple of his new compositions offered repeated occasion for letters.

They pass with frequency for the following fifteen years, when there is an interruption of a twelvemonth. They begin again in 1850, and continue at the rate of two or three a year, till 1856. After this they are less frequent, though the mutual regard of the writers evidently knew no diminution. In 1872, Emerson went abroad again (he had visited England for a second time in 1847); and after his return the letters cease. Many of the early ones are occupied with the question of the republication of Carlyle's writings in America. Emerson took upon himself to present "Sartor Resartus" and some of its successors to the American public, and he constantly reports to the author upon the progress of this enterprise. He transmits a great many booksellers' accounts as well as a considerable number of bills of exchange, and among the American publishers is a most faithful and zealous representative of his friend. Some of these details, which are very numerous, are tedious; but they are interesting at the same time, and Mr. Norton has done well to print them all. In the light of the present relations of British authors to the American public, they are curious reading. There appears to have been a fortunate moment (it was not of long duration) when it was possible for the British author to reap something of a harvest here. It would appear that, between 1838 and 1847, Emerson sent Carlyle some five hundred and thirty pounds, the proceeds of the sale of several of his works in this country. The sum is not large, but it must be measured by the profit that he had up to that time derived in England. It was in Boston that "Sartor Resartus," with which the English publishers would have so little to do, first made its way into the light, after a precarious and abbreviated transit through "Fraser's Magazine." "It will be a very brave day," Carlyle wrote in 1838, after Emerson had made arrangements for the issue of the "French Revolution" in Boston, "it will be a very brave day when cash actually reaches me, no matter what the *number* of the coins, whether seven or seven hundred, out of Yankee-land; and strange enough, what is not unlikely, if it be the *first* cash I realize for that piece of work—Angle-land continuing still *in*solvent to me." Six years later, in 1844, he writes, on the occasion of a remittance from Emerson of thirty-six pounds, "America, I think, is like an amiable family tea-pot; you think it is all out long since, and lo, the valuable implement yields you another cup, and another!" Encouragement had come to him from America as well as money; and there is something touching in the care with which Emerson assures him of the growth of his public on this side of the ocean, and of there being many ingenuous young persons of both sexes to whom his writings are as meat and drink. We had learned from Mr. Froude's publications that his beginnings were difficult; but this Correspondence throws a new light upon those grim years—I mean in exposing more definitely the fact that he was for some time on the point of coming to seek his fortune in this country. Both his own and Emerson's early letters are full of allusions to this possible voyage: for Emerson, in particular, the idea appears to have a fascination; he returns to it again and again, keeps it constantly before his correspondent, never ceases to express his desire that Carlyle should embark for Boston. There was a plan of his giving lectures in the United States, and Emerson, at Carlyle's request, collects all possible information as to the expenses and the rewards of such an attempt. It would appear that the rewards of the lecturer's art, fifty years ago, were extremely slender in comparison of what they have since become; though it must be added that Emerson gives a truly touching description of the cost of living. One might have entertainment at the best hotels for the sum of eight dollars a week. It is true that he gives us no reassurance as to what the best hotels in America, fifty years ago, may have been. Emerson offers his friend the most generous hospitality; on his return from Europe, he had married and settled himself at Concord. To Concord he entreats Mr. and Mrs. Carlyle to take their way; their room is ready and their fire is made. The reader at this point of the correspondence feels a certain suspense: he knows that Carlyle never did come to America, but like a good novel the letters produce an illusion. He holds his breath, for the terrible Scotchman may after all have embarked, and there is something really almost heart-shaking in the thought of his transporting that tremendous imagination and those vessels of wrath and sarcasm to an innocent New England village. The situation becomes dramatic, like the other incident I have mentioned, in the presence of Emerson's serene good faith, his eagerness for the arrival of such a cloud-compelling host. The catastrophe never came off, however, and the air of Concord was disturbed by no fumes more irritating than the tonic emanations of Emerson's own genius. It is impossible to imagine what the historian of the French Revolution, of the iron-fisted Cromwell, and the Voltairean Frederick, would have made of that sensitive spot, or what Concord would have made of Carlyle.

Emerson, indeed, throughout had no hesitations on this score, and talked of the New England culture to his lurid correspondent without the least fear that his delicate specimens would be scorched. He sends him Mr. Alcott, he sends him Margaret Fuller, and others besides, who have a varying fortune at the little house in Cheyne Walk. It is true that Carlyle gave him constantly the encouragement of a high and eloquent esteem for his own utterances. He was evidently a great and genuine admirer of the genius, the spirit of his American friend, and he expresses this feeling on a dozen occasions.

> "My friend! you know not what you have done for me there [in the oration of 'The American Scholar']. It was long decades of years that I had heard nothing but the infinite jangling and jabbering, and inarticulate twittering and screeching, and my soul had sunk down sorrowful and said there is no articulate speaking then any more, and thou art solitary among stranger-creatures; and lo, out of the West comes a clear utterance, clearly recognizable as a *man's* voice, and I *have* a kinsman and brother: God be thanked for it! I could have *wept* to read that speech; the clear high melody of it went tingling through my heart; I said to my wife, 'There, woman!' * * * My brave Emerson! And all this has been lying silent, quite tranquil in him, these seven years, and the 'vociferous platitude' dinning his ears on all sides, and he quietly answering no word; and a whole world of thought has silently built itself in these calm depths, and, the day having come, says quite softly, as if it were a common thing, 'Yes, I *am* here, too.' Miss Martineau tells me, 'Some say it is inspired; some say it is mad.' Exactly so; no *say* could be suitabler."

That is from a letter of 1837, and though at a later date (in 1850) he speaks of seeing "well enough what a great deep cleft divides us in our ways of practically looking at this world"; though, too (in 1842), he had already uttered a warning against Emerson's danger (with his fellow-transcendentalists) of "soaring away * * * into perilous altitudes, beyond the curve of perpetual frost * * * and seeing nothing under one but the everlasting snows of Himmalayah"—the danger of "inanity and mere injuring of the lungs!"—though, as I say, he threw out his reflections upon certain inevitable disparities, his attitude toward the Concord philosopher remained (I have already noted it) an eminently hospitable one. "The rock-strata, miles deep, unite again; and the two poor souls are at one," he adds in the letter written in 1850, from which I have just quoted. When "English Traits" came out, Carlyle wrote, "Not for seven years and more have I got hold of such a Book;—Book by a real *man*, with eyes in his head; nobleness, wisdom, humor, and many other things in the heart of him. Such Books do not turn up often in the decade, in the century." He adds, indeed, rather unexpectedly: "In fact, I believe it to be worth all the Books ever written by New England upon Old." Carlyle speaks as if there had been an appreciable literature of that kind. It is faint praise to say that "English Traits" was the authority on the subject. He declares in another letter that "My Friend Emerson, alone of all voices out of America, has sphere-music in him for me." These words, written in 1843, are part of a paragraph in which Carlyle expresses his feelings with regard to the American "reforming" class at large. The high esteem in which he held his correspondent did not impel him to take an enthusiastic view of certain persons with whom, apparently, he supposed his correspondent to be in some degree associated. "Another Channing, whom I once saw here, sends me a 'Progress-of-the-Species' Periodical from New York. *Ach Gott!* These people and their affairs seem all 'melting' rapidly enough into thaw-slush, or one knows not what. Considerable madness is visible in them * * * I am terribly sick of all that;—and wish it would stay at home at Fruitland, or where there is good pasture for it, * * * a bottomless hubbub, which is not all cheering." Several of the wanderers from "Fruitland" knocked at his door, and he speaks of them to Emerson with a humorous irreverence that contrasts characteristically with Emerson's own tone of consideration (that beautiful courtesy which he never lost) for the same persons. One of them, "all bent on saving the world by a return to acorns and the golden age," he desires to be suffered to love him as he can, "and live on vegetables in peace; as I, living *partly* on vegetables, will continue to love him!" But he warns Emerson against the "English Tail" of the same visitor, who, arrived in London, apparently had given away his confidence on terms too easy. "Bottomless imbeciles ought not to be seen in company with Ralph Waldo Emerson, who has already *men* listening to him on this side of the water." Of Margaret Fuller, however,—one of those who had attempted "the flight of the unwinged," as he calls it,—Carlyle speaks in the most affectionate though the most discriminating manner:

> "Poor Margaret, that is a strange tragedy that history of hers, and has many traits of the Heroic in it, though it is wild as the prophecy of a Sybil. Such a predetermination to *eat* this big Universe as her oyster or her egg, and to be absolute empress of all height and glory in it that her heart could conceive, I have not before seen in any human soul. Her 'mountain *me*' indeed:—but her courage too is high and clear, her chivalrous nobleness indeed is great; her veracity, in its deepest sense, *à toute épreuve.*"

It is difficult to resist quoting, where so much is quotable; but the better way is to urge the reader to go straight to the book. Then he will find himself interested, even more than in the happy passages of characterization in which it abounds, in the reflection it offers of two contrasted characters of men of genius. With several qualities in common, Carlyle and Emerson diverged, in their total expression, with a completeness which is full of suggestion as to their differences of circumstance, race, association, temper. Both were men of the poetic quality, men of imagination; both were Puritans; both of them looked, instinctively, at the world, at life, as a great total, full of far-reaching relations; both of them set above everything else the importance of conduct—of what

Carlyle called veracity and Emerson called harmony with the universe. Both of them had the desire, the passion, for something better—the reforming spirit, an interest in the destiny of mankind. But their variations of feeling were the widest, and the temperament of the one was absolutely opposed to the temperament of the other. Both were men of the greatest purity and, in the usual sense, simplicity of life; each had a high ideal, each kept himself unspotted from the world. Their Correspondence is to an extraordinary degree the record, on either side, of a career with which nothing base, nothing interested, no worldly avidity, no vulgar vanity or personal error, was ever mingled—a career of public distinction and private honor. But with these things what disparities of tone, of manner, of inspiration! "Yet I think I shall never be killed by my ambition," Emerson writes in a letter of the date of 1841. "I behold my failures and shortcomings there in writing, wherein it would give me much joy to thrive, with an equanimity which my worst enemy might be glad to see. * * * My whole philosophy—which is very real—teaches acquiescence and optimism. Only when I see how much work is to be done, what room for a poet—for any spiritualist—in this great, intelligent, sensual and avaricious America, I lament my fumbling fingers and stammering tongue." Emerson speaks the word in that passage; he was an optimist, and this in spite of the fact that he was the inspiration of the considerable body of persons who at that time, in New England, were seeking a better way. Carlyle, on the other hand, was a pessimist—a pessimist of pessimists—and this great difference between them includes many of the others. The American public has little more to learn in regard to the extreme amenity of Emerson, his eminently gentle spirit, his almost touching tolerance, his deference toward every sort of human manifestation; but many of his letters remind us afresh of his singular modesty of attitude and of his extreme consideration for that blundering human family whom he believed to be in want of light. His optimism makes us wonder at times where he discovered the errors that it would seem well to set right, and what there was in his view of the world on which the spirit of criticism could feed. He had a high and noble conception of good, without having, as it would appear, a definite conception of evil. The few words I have just quoted in regard to the America of 1841, "intelligent, sensual, and avaricious," have as sharp an ironical ring in them as any that I remember to have noticed in his part of the Correspondence. He has not a grain of current contempt; one feels, at times, that he has not enough. This salt is wanting in his taste of things. Carlyle, on the other hand, who has fearfully little amenity (save in his direct relation to Emerson, where he is admirable), has a vivid conception of evil without a corresponding conception of good. Curiously narrow and special, at least, were the forms in which he saw this latter spirit embodied. "For my heart is sick and sore on behalf of my own poor generation," he writes in 1842. "Nay, I feel withal as if the one hope of help for it consisted in the possibility of new Cromwells and new Puritans." Eleven years later, returning from a visit to Germany, he writes that "truly and really the Prussian soldiers, with their intelligent *silence,* with the touches of effective Spartanism I saw or fancied in them, were the class of people that pleased me best." There could be nothing more characteristic of Carlyle than this confession that such an impression as that was the most agreeable that he had brought back from a Continental tour. Emerson, by tradition and temperament, was as deeply rooted a

Puritan as Carlyle; but he was a Puritan refined and sublimated, and a certain delicacy, a certain good taste would have prevented him from desiring (for the amelioration of mankind) so crude an occurrence as a return of the regiments of Oliver. Full of a local quality, with a narrow social horizon, he yet never would have ventured to plead so undisguisedly (in pretending to speak for the world at large) the cause of his own parish. Of that "current contempt" of which I just now spoke, Carlyle had more than enough. If it is humorous and half-compassionate in his moments of comparative tolerance, it is savage in his melancholy ones; and, in either case, it is full of the entertainment which comes from great expression. "Man, all men, seem radically dumb, jabbering mere jargons and noises from the teeth outward; the inner meaning of them—of them and of me, poor devils—remaining shut, buried forever. * * * Certainly could one generation of men be forced to live without rhetoric, babblement, hearsay, in short with the tongue well cut out of them altogether, their fortunate successors would find a most improved world to start upon!" Carlyle's pessimism was not only deep, but loud; not of the serene, but of the irritable sort. It is one of the strangest of things to find such an appreciation of silence in a mind that in itself was, before all things, expressive. Carlyle's expression was never more rich than when he declared that things were immeasurable, unutterable, not to be formulated. "The gospel of silence, in thirty volumes," that was a happy epigram of one of his critics; but it does not prevent us from believing that, after all, he really loved, as it were, the inarticulate. And we believe it for this reason, that the working of his own genius must have been accompanied with an extraordinary internal uproar, sensible to himself, and from which, in a kind of agony, he was forced to appeal. With the spectacle of human things resounding and reverberating in his head, awaking extraordinary echoes, it is no wonder that he had an ideal of the speechless. But his irritation communed happily for fifty years with Emerson's serenity; and the fact is very honorable to both.

"I have sometimes fancied I was to catch sympathetic activity from contact with noble persons," Emerson writes in a letter from which I have already quoted; "that you would come and see me; that I should form stricter habits of love and conversation with some men and women here who are already dear to me." That is the tone in which he speaks, for the most part, of his own life; and that was the tone which doubtless used to be natural in Concord. His letters are especially interesting for the impression they give us of what we may call the thinness of the New England atmosphere in those days—the thinness, and, it must be added, the purity. An almost touching lightness, sparseness, transparency marked the social scenery in those days; and this impression, in Emerson's pages, is the greater by contrast with the echoes of the dense, warm life of London that are transmitted by his correspondent. One is reminded, as we remember being reminded in the perusal of Hawthorne's "American Notebooks," of the importance of the individual in that simple social economy—of almost any individual who was not simply engaged in buying and selling. It must be remembered, of course, that the importance of the individual was Emerson's great doctrine; every one had a kingdom within himself—was potential sovereign, by divine right, over a multitude of inspirations and virtues. No one maintained a more hospitable attitude than his toward anything that anyone might have to say. There was no presumption against even the humblest, and the ear of the universe was open to any articulate voice. In this respect the opposition to Carlyle was complete. The great Scotchman thought *all* talk a jabbering of apes; whereas Emerson, who was the perfection of a listener, stood always in a posture of hopeful expectancy and regarded each delivery of a personal view as a new fact, to be estimated on its merits. In a genuine democracy all things are democratic; and this spirit of general deference, on the part of a beautiful poet who might have availed himself of the poetic license to be fastidious, was the natural product of a society in which it was held that every one was equal to everyone else. It was as natural on the other side that Carlyle's philosophy should have aristocratic premises, and that he should call aloud for that imperial master, of the necessity for whom the New England mind was so serenely unconscious. Nothing is more striking in Emerson's letters than the way in which people are measured exclusively by their moral standards, designated by moral terms, described according to their morality. There was nothing else to describe them by. "A man named Bronson Alcott is great, and one of the jewels we have to show you. * * * A man named Bronson Alcott is a majestic soul, with whom conversation is possible. He is capable of the truth, and gives one the same glad astonishment that he should exist which the world does. * * * The man Alcott bides his time.——is a beautiful and noble youth, of a most subtle and magnetic nature. * * * I have a young poet in the village named Thoreau, who writes the truest verses. I pine to show you my treasures. * * * One reader and friend of yours dwells now in my house, Henry Thoreau, a poet whom you may one day be proud of, a noble, manly youth, full of melodies and inventions." Carlyle, who held melodies and inventions so cheap, was probably not a little irritated (though, faithful to his constant consideration for Emerson, he shows it but mildly) by this enumeration of characters so vaguely constituted. "In fact, I do again desiderate some *concretion* of these beautiful *abstracta.*" That remark which he makes in regard to one of Emerson's discourses might have been applied to certain of his friends. "The *Dial,* too, it is all spirit-like, aëriform, aurora-borealis-like. Will no *Angel* body himself out of that; no stalwart Yankee *man,* with color in the cheeks of him and a coat on his back?" Emerson speaks of his friends too much as if they were disembodied spirits. One doesn't see the color in the cheeks of them and the coats on their back. The fine touch in his letters, as in his other writings, is always the spiritual touch. For the rest, felicitous as they are, for the most part they suffer a little by comparison with Carlyle's; they are less natural, more composed, have too studied a quaintness. It was his practice, apparently, to make two drafts of these communications. The violent color, the large, avalanche-movement of Carlyle's style— as if a mass of earth and rock and vegetation had detached itself and came bouncing and bumping forward—make the efforts of his correspondent appear a little pale and stiff. There is always something high and pure in Emerson's speech, however, and it has often a perfect propriety—seeming, in answer to Carlyle's extravagances, the note of reason and justice. "Faith and love are apt to be spasmodic in the best minds. Men live on the brink of mysteries and harmonies into which they never enter, and with their hand on the door-latch they die outside."

Emerson's views of the world were what the world at all times thought highly peculiar; he neither believed nor thought nor spoke in the most apprehensible manner. He says himself (in 1840) that he is "gently mad"—surrounded, too, by a number of persons in the same condition. "I am gently mad myself and am resolved to live cleanly. George

Ripley is talking up a colony of agriculturists and scholars, with whom he threatens to take the field and the book. One man renounces the use of animal food; and another of coin; and another of domestic hired service; and another of the State; and on the whole, we have a commendable share of reason and hope." But Emerson's "madness" was as mild as moonlight, compared with the strange commixture of the nature of his friend. If the main interest of these letters is, as I have said, their illustration of the character of the writers, the effect of Carlyle's portion of them is to deepen our sense, already sufficiently lively, of his enormous incongruities. Considerably sad, as he would have said himself, is the picture they present of a man of genius. One must allow, of course, for his extraordinary gift of expression, which set a premium on every sort of exaggeration; but even when one has done so, darkness and horror reside in every line of them. He is like a man hovering on the edge of insanity—hanging over a black gulf and wearing the reflection of its bottomless deeps in his face. His physical digestion was of the worst, but it was nothing compared with his moral digestion. Truly, he was not genial, and he was not gracious, as how should he have been in such conditions? He was born out of humor with life, he came into the world with an insurmountable prejudice, and to be genial and gracious naturally seemed of small importance in the face of the eternal veracities—veracities of such a grim and implacable sort. The strangest thing, among so many that were strange, was that his magnificent humor— that saving grace which has eased off the troubles of life for so many people who have been blessed with it—did so little to lighten his burden. Of this humor these volumes contain some admirable specimens—as in the description of "the brave Gambardella," the Neapolitan artist who comes to him with an introduction from Emerson; of the fish-eating Rio, historian of Christian Art; of the "loquacious, scriblacious" Heraud; of the "buckramed and mummy-swathed" Miss Martineau, and many more besides. His humor was in truth not of comic but of tragic intention, and not so much a flame as an all-enveloping smoke. His treatment of all things is the humorous—unfortunately in too many cases, the ill-humorous. He even hated his work—hated his subjects. These volumes are a sort of record of the long weariness and anguish (as one may indeed call it) with which he struggled through his "Cromwell," his "French Revolution," and the history of Frederick. He thought, after all, very little of Frederick, and he detested the age in which he lived, the "putrid eighteenth century—an ocean of sordid nothingness, shams, and scandalous hypocrisies." He achieved a noble quantity of work, but all the while he found no inspiration in it. "The reason that I tell you nothing about Cromwell is, alas, that there is nothing to be told. I am, day and night, these long months and years, very miserable about it—nigh broken-hearted often. * * * No history of it *can* be written to this wretched, fleering, sneering, canting, twaddling, God-forgetting generation. How can I explain men to Apes by the Dead Sea?" Other persons have enjoyed life as little as Carlyle; other men have been pessimists and cynics; but few men have rioted so in their disenchantments, or thumped so perpetually upon the hollowness of things with the view of making it resound. Pessimism, cynicism, usually imply a certain amount of indifference and resignation; but in Carlyle these forces were nothing if not querulous and vocal. It must be remembered that he had an imagination which made acquiescence difficult—an imagination haunted with theological and apocalyptic visions. We have no occasion here to attempt to estimate his position in literature, but we may be permitted to say that it is mainly to this splendid imagination that he owes it. Both the moral and the physical world were full of pictures for him, and it would seem to be by his great pictorial energy that he will live. To get an idea of the solidity and sincerity of this gift one must read his notes on a tour in Ireland in 1849;[1] it is a revelation of his attention to external things and his perception of the internal states that they express. His doctrine, reduced to the fewest words, is that life is very serious and that everyone should do his work honestly. This is the gist of the matter; all the rest is magnificent vocalization. We call it magnificent, in spite of the fact that many people find him unreadable on account of his unprecedented form. His extemporized, empirical style, however, seems to us the very substance of his thought. If the merit of a style lies in complete correspondence with the feeling of the writer, Carlyle's is one of the best. It is not defensible, but it is victorious; and if it is neither homogeneous, nor, at times, coherent, it bristles with all manner of felicities. It is true, nevertheless, that he had invented a manner, and that his manner had swallowed him up. To look at realities and not at imitations is what he constantly and sternly enjoins; but all the while he gives us the sense that it is not at things themselves, but straight into this abysmal manner of his own that he is looking.

All this, of course, is a very incomplete account of him. So large a genius is full of interest of detail, and in the application in special cases of that doctrine of his which seems so simple there is often the greatest suggestiveness. When he does look *through* his own manner into the vivid spots of history, then he sees more in them than almost any one else. We may add that no account of him would have even a slight completeness which should fail to cite him as a signal instance of the force of local influences, of the qualities of race and soil. Carlyle was intensely of the stock of which he sprang, and he remained so to the end. No man of equal genius was probably ever less of a man of the world at large—more exclusively a product of his locality, his clan, his family. Readers of his "Reminiscences" and of Mr. Froude's memoir will remember how the peasant-group in which he was born—his parents, his brothers and sisters— appeared to constitute one of the great facts of the universe for him; and we mean not as a son and a brother simply, but as a student of human affairs. He was impressed, as it were, with the historical importance of his kinsfolk. And as one finds a little of everything in a man of genius, we find a great deal of tenderness even in the grimness of Carlyle; so that we may say, as the last word of all (for it qualifies our implication that he was narrow), that his tenderness was never greater than when, in spite of the local limitation, he stretched across the ocean, in gratitude for early sympathy, for early services, and held fast to the friendship of Emerson. His family was predominant for him, as we say, and he cleaved to his relations, to his brothers. But it was as a brother that he addressed Emerson.

Note

1 See *The Century* for May, June, and July 1882.

Cabot's Emerson

Henry James, Jr.

MR. ELLIOT CABOT has made a very interesting contribution to a class of books of which our literature, more than any other, offers admirable examples: he has given us a biography intelligently and carefully composed. These two volumes are a model of responsible editing—I use that term because they consist largely of letters and extracts from letters: nothing could resemble less the manner in which the mere bookmaker strings together his frequently questionable pearls and shovels the heap into the presence of the public. Mr. Cabot has selected, compared, discriminated, steered an even course between meagreness and redundancy, and managed to be constantly and happily illustrative. And his work, moreover, strikes us as the better done from the fact that it stands for one of the two things that make an absorbing memoir a good deal more than for the other. If these two things be the conscience of the writer and the career of his hero, it is not difficult to see on which side the biographer of Emerson has found himself strongest. Ralph Waldo Emerson was a man of genius, but he led for nearly eighty years a life in which the sequence of events had little of the rapidity, or the complexity, that a spectator loves. There is something we miss very much as we turn these pages—something that has a kind of accidental, inevitable presence in almost any personal record—something that may be most definitely indicated under the name of colour. We lay down the book with a singular impression of paleness—an impression that comes partly from the tone of the biographer and partly from the moral complexion of his subject, but mainly from the vacancy of the page itself. That of Emerson's personal history is condensed into the single word Concord, and all the condensation in the world will not make it look rich. It presents a most continuous surface. Mr. Matthew Arnold, in his *Discourses in America,* contests Emerson's complete right to the title of a man of letters; yet letters surely were the very texture of his history. Passions, alternations, affairs, adventures had absolutely no part in it. It stretched itself out in enviable quiet—a quiet in which we hear the jotting of the pencil in the notebook. It is the very life for literature (I mean for one's own, not that of another): fifty years of residence in the home of one's forefathers, pervaded by reading, by walking in the woods and the daily addition of sentence to sentence.

If the interest of Mr. Cabot's pencilled portrait is incontestable and yet does not spring from variety, it owes nothing either to a source from which it might have borrowed much and which it is impossible not to regret a little that he has so completely neglected: I mean a greater reference to the social conditions in which Emerson moved, the company he lived in, the moral air he breathed. If his biographer had allowed himself a little more of the ironic touch, had put himself once in a way under the protection of Sainte-Beuve and had attempted something of a general picture, we should have felt that he only went with the occasion. I may over-estimate the latent treasures of the field, but it seems to me there was distinctly an opportunity—an opportunity to make up moreover in some degree for the white tint of Emerson's career considered simply in itself. We know a man imperfectly until we know his society, and we but half know a society until we know its manners. This is especially true of a man of letters, for manners lie very close to literature. From those of the New England world in which Emerson's character formed itself Mr. Cabot almost averts his lantern, though we feel sure that there would have been delightful glimpses to be had and that he would have been in a position—that is that he has all the knowledge that would enable him—to help us to them. It is as if he could not trust himself, knowing the subject only too well. This adds to the effect of extreme discretion that we find in his volumes, but it is the cause of our not finding certain things, certain figures and scenes, evoked. What is evoked is Emerson's pure spirit, by a copious, sifted series of citations and comments. But we must read as much as possible between the lines, and the picture of the transcendental time (to mention simply one corner) has yet to be painted—the lines have yet to be bitten in. Meanwhile we are held and charmed by the image of Emerson's mind and the extreme appeal which his physiognomy makes to our art of discrimination. It is so fair, so uniform and impersonal, that its features are simply fine shades, the gradations of tone of a surface whose proper quality was of the smoothest and on which nothing was reflected with violence. It is a pleasure of the critical sense to find, with Mr. Cabot's extremely intelligent help, a notation for such delicacies.

We seem to see the circumstances of our author's origin, immediate and remote, in a kind of high, vertical moral light, the brightness of a society at once very simple and very responsible. The rare singleness that was in his nature (so that he was *all* the warning moral voice, without distraction or counter-solicitation), was also in the stock he sprang from, clerical for generations, on both sides, and clerical in the Puritan sense. His ancestors had lived long (for nearly two centuries) in the same corner of New England, and during that period had preached and studied and prayed and practised. It is impossible to imagine a spirit better prepared in advance to be exactly what it was—better educated for its office in its far-away unconscious beginnings. There is an inner satisfaction in seeing so straight, although so patient, a connection between the stem and the flower, and such a proof that when life wishes to produce something exquisite in quality she takes her measures many years in advance. A conscience like Emerson's could not have been turned off, as it were, from one generation to another: a succession of attempts, a long process of refining, was required. His perfection, in his own line, comes largely from the non-interruption of the process.

As most of us are made up of ill-assorted pieces, his reader, and Mr. Cabot's, envies him this transmitted unity, in which there was no mutual hustling or crowding of elements. It must have been a kind of luxury to be—that is to feel—so homogeneous, and it helps to account for his serenity, his power of acceptance, and that absence of personal passion which makes his private correspondence read like a series of beautiful circulars or expanded cards *pour prendre congé*. He had the equanimity of a result; nature had taken care of him and he had only to speak. He accepted himself as he accepted others, accepted everything; and his absence of eagerness, or in other words his modesty, was that of a man with whom it is not a question of success, who has nothing invested or at stake. The investment, the stake, was that of the race, of all the past Emersons and Bulkeleys and Waldos. There is much that makes us smile, to-day, in the commotion produced by his secession from the mild Unitarian pulpit: we wonder at a condition of opinion in which any utterance of his should appear to be wanting in superior piety—in the essence of good instruction. All that is changed: the great difference has become the infinitely small, and we admire a state of society in which scandal and schism took on no darker hue; but there is even yet a sort of drollery in the spectacle of a body of people among whom the author of *The American Scholar* and of the Address of 1838 at the Harvard Divinity College passed for profane, and who failed to see that he only gave his plea for the spiritual life the advantage of a brilliant expression. They were so provincial as to think that brilliancy came ill-recommended, and they were shocked at his ceasing to care for the prayer and the sermon. They might have perceived that he *was* the prayer and the sermon: not in the least a seculariser, but in his own subtle insinuating way a sanctifier.

Of the three periods into which his life divides itself, the first was (as in the case of most men) that of movement, experiment and selection—that of effort too and painful probation. Emerson had his message, but he was a good while looking for his form—the form which, as he himself would have said, he never completely found and of which it was rather characteristic of him that his later years (with their growing refusal to give him the *word*), wishing to attack him in his most vulnerable point, where his tenure was least complete, had in some degree the effect of despoiling him. It all sounds rather bare and stern, Mr. Cabot's account of his youth and early manhood, and we get an impression of a terrible paucity of alternatives. If he would be neither a farmer nor a trader he could "teach school"; that was the main resource and a part of the general educative process of the young New Englander who proposed to devote himself to the things of the mind. There was an advantage in the nudity, however, which was that, in Emerson's case at least, the things of the mind did get themselves admirably well considered. If it be his great distinction and his special sign that he had a more vivid conception of the moral life than any one else, it is probably not fanciful to say that he owed it in part to the limited way in which he saw our capacity for living illustrated. The plain, God-fearing, practical society which surrounded him was not fertile in variations: it had great intelligence and energy, but it moved altogether in the straight-forward direction. On three occasions later—three journeys to Europe—he was introduced to a more complicated world; but his spirit, his moral taste, as it were, abode always within the undecorated walls of his youth. There he could dwell with that ripe unconsciousness of evil which is one of the most beautiful signs by which we know him. His early writings are full of quaint animadversion upon the vices of the place and time, but there is something charmingly vague, light and general in the arraignment. Almost the worst he can say is that these vices are negative and that his fellow-townsmen are not heroic. We feel that his first impressions were gathered in a community from which misery and extravagance, and either extreme, of any sort, were equally absent. What the life of New England fifty years ago offered to the observer was the common lot, in a kind of achromatic picture, without particular intensifications. It was from this table of the usual, the merely typical joys and sorrows that he proceeded to generalise—a fact that accounts in some degree for a certain inadequacy and thinness in his enumerations. But it helps to account also for his direct, intimate vision of the soul itself—not in its emotions, its contortions and perversions, but in its passive, exposed, yet healthy form. He knows the nature of man and the long tradition of its dangers; but we feel that where as he can put his finger on the remedies, lying for the most part, as they do, in the deep recesses of virtue, of the spirit, he has only a kind of hearsay, uninformed acquaintance with the disorders. It would require some ingenuity, the reader may say too much, to trace closely this correspondence between his genius and the frugal, dutiful, happy but decidedly lean Boston of the past, where there was a great deal of will but very little fulcrum—like a ministry without an opposition.

The genius itself it seems to me impossible to contest—I mean the genius for seeing character as a real and supreme thing. Other writers have arrived at a more complete expression: Wordsworth and Goethe, for instance, give one a sense of having found their form, whereas with Emerson we never lose the sense that he is still seeking it. But no one has had so steady and constant, and above all so natural, a vision of what we require and what we are capable of in the way of aspiration and independence. With Emerson it is ever the special capacity for moral experience—always that and only that. We have the impression, somehow, that life had never bribed him to look at anything but the soul; and indeed in the world in which he grew up and lived the bribes and lures, the beguilements and prizes, were few. He was in an admirable position for showing, what he constantly endeavoured to show, that the prize was within. Any one who in New England at that time could do that was sure of success, of listeners and sympathy: most of all, of course, when it was a question of doing it with such a divine persuasiveness. Moreover, the way in which Emerson did it added to the charm—by word of mouth, face to face, with a rare, irresistible voice and a beautiful mild, modest authority. If Mr. Arnold is struck with the limited degree in which he was a man of letters I suppose it is because he is more struck with his having been, as it were, a man of lectures. But the lecture surely was never more purged of its grossness—the quality in it that suggests a strong light and a big brush—than as it issued from Emerson's lips; so far from being a vulgarisation, it was simply the esoteric made audible, and instead of treating the few as the many, after the usual fashion of gentlemen on platforms, he treated the many as the few. There was probably no other society at that time in which he would have got so many persons to understand that; for we think the better of his audience as we read him, and wonder where else people would have had so much moral attention to give. {...}

It has not, however, been the ambition of these remarks to account for everything, and I have arrived at the end without even pointing to the grounds on which Emerson justifies the honours of biography, discussion and illustration. I have assumed his importance and continuance, and shall probably not be gainsaid by those who read him. Those who do not will hardly rub him out. Such a book as Mr. Cabot's subjects a reputation to a test—leads people to look it over and hold it up to the light, to see whether it is worth keeping in use or even putting away in a cabinet. Such a revision of Emerson has no relegating consequences. The result of it is once more the impression that he serves and will not wear out, and that indeed we cannot afford to drop him. His instrument makes him precious. He did something better than any one else; he had a particular faculty, which has not been surpassed, for speaking to the soul in a voice of direction and authority. There have been many spiritual voices appealing, consoling, reassuring, exhorting, or even denouncing and terrifying, but none has had just that firmness and just that purity. It penetrates further, it seems to go back to the roots of our feelings, to where conduct and manhood begin; and moreover, to us today, there is something in it that says that it is connected somehow with the virtue of the world, has wrought and achieved, lived in thousands of minds, produced a mass of character and life. And there is this further sign of Emerson's singular power, that he is a striking exception to the general rule that writings live in the last resort by their form; that they owe a large part of their fortune to the art with which they have been composed. It is hardly too much, or too little, to say of Emerson's writings in general that they were not composed at all. Many and many things are beautifully said; he had felicities, inspirations, unforgettable phrases; he had frequently an exquisite eloquence.

> "O my friends, there are resources in us on which we have not yet drawn. There are men who rise refreshed on hearing a threat; men to whom a crisis which intimidates and paralyses the majority—demanding not the faculties of prudence and thrift, but comprehension, immovableness, the readiness of sacrifice, come graceful and beloved as a bride.... But these are heights that we can scarce look up to and remember without contrition and shame. Let us thank God that such things exist."

None the less we have the impression that that search for a fashion and a manner on which he was always engaged never really came to a conclusion; it draws itself out through his later writings—it drew itself out through his later lectures, like a sort of renunciation of success. It is not on these, however, but on their predecessors, that his reputation will rest. Of course the way he spoke was the way that was on the whole most convenient to him; but he differs from most men of letters of the same degree of credit in failing to strike us as having achieved a style. This achievement is, as I say, usually the bribe or toll-money on the journey to posterity; and if Emerson goes his way, as he clearly appears to be doing, on the strength of his message alone, the case will be rare, the exception striking, and the honour great.

John Jay Chapman (1862–1933)

*Born in New York and educated at Harvard, Chapman practiced law until 1898, the year his first major book—*Emerson and Other Essays*—was published (the source of the present essay). From then on he was an active and celebrated essayist. Chapman heralded Emerson as "the great radical of America, the arch-radical of the world," as a figure who "represents a protest against the tyranny of democracy," and much of the essay is written in a spirit of agitation and intended to address the sort of tyranny Emerson came of age in and responded to. Chapman describes the America of Emerson's youth as a pitiable place, a "time of humiliation, when there was no free speech, no literature, little manliness, no reality, no simplicity, no accomplishment." According to Chapman, it is Emerson's "revulsion" against this world—his "Promethean antagonism" to it—that informs the direction of his thought. Chapman also raises some alarm about the manner of Emerson's protest: "There is an implication of a fundamental falsehood in every bit of Transcendentalism, including Emerson. That falsehood consists in the theory of the self-sufficiency of each individual, men and women alike." In the complete version of the essay, Chapman's attention ranges from assessments of Emerson's contribution to political and social reform, his impact on transcendentalism, his understanding of mysticism, and his talents as a poet. In the excerpt from his essay included below, we find Chapman usefully contrasting the energies directed to promoting and protecting the individual from society that may also, inadvertently, do too much on behalf of the individual.*

Emerson

John Jay Chapman

I

"LEAVE this hypocritical prating about the masses. Masses are rude, lame, unmade, pernicious in their demands and influence, and need not to be flattered, but to be schooled. I wish not to concede anything to them, but to tame, drill, divide, and break them up, and draw individuals out of them. The worst of charity is that the lives you are asked to preserve are not worth preserving. Masses! The calamity is the masses. I do not wish any mass at all, but honest men only, lovely, sweet, accomplished women only, and no shovel-handed, narrow-brained, gin-drinking million stockingers or lazzaroni at all. If government knew how, I should like to see it check, not multiply the population. When it reaches its true law of action, every man that is born will be hailed as essential. Away with this hurrah of masses, and let us have the considerate vote of single men spoken on their honor and their conscience."

This extract from The Conduct of Life gives fairly enough the leading thought of Emerson's life. The unending warfare between the individual and society shows us in each generation a poet or two, a dramatist or a musician who exalts and deifies the individual, and leads us back again to the only object which is really worthy of enthusiasm or which can permanently excite it,—the character of a man. It is surprising to find this identity of content in all great deliverances. The only thing we really admire is personal liberty. Those who fought for it and those who enjoyed it are our heroes.

But the hero may enslave his race by bringing in a system of tyranny; the battle-cry of freedom may become a dogma which crushes the soul; one good custom may corrupt the world. And so the inspiration of one age becomes the damnation of the next. This crystallizing of life into death has occurred so often that it may almost be regarded as one of the laws of progress.

Emerson represents a protest against the tyranny of democracy. He is the most recent example of elemental hero-worship. His opinions are absolutely unqualified except by his temperament. He expresses a form of belief in the importance of the individual which is independent of any personal relations he has with the world. It is as if a man had been withdrawn from the earth and dedicated to condensing and embodying this eternal idea—the value of the individual soul—so vividly, so vitally, that his words could not die, yet in such illusive and abstract forms that by no chance and by no power could his creed be used for purposes of tyranny. Dogma cannot be extracted from it. Schools cannot be built on it. It either lives as the spirit lives, or else it evaporates and leaves nothing. Emerson was so afraid of the letter that killeth that he would hardly trust his words to print. He was assured there was no such thing as literal truth, but only literal falsehood. He therefore resorted to metaphors which could by no chance be taken literally. And he has probably succeeded in leaving a body of work which cannot be made to operate to any other end than that for which he designed it. If this be true, he has accomplished the inconceivable feat of eluding misconception. If it be true, he stands alone in the history of teachers; he has circumvented fate, he has left an unmixed blessing behind him.

The signs of those times which brought forth Emerson are not wholly undecipherable. They are the same times which gave rise to every character of significance during the period before the war. Emerson is indeed the easiest to understand of all the men of his time, because his life is freest from the tangles and qualifications of circumstance. He is a sheer and pure type and creature of destiny, and the unconsciousness that marks his development allies him to the deepest phenomena. It is convenient, in describing him, to use language which implies consciousness on his part, but he himself had no purpose, no theory of himself; he was a product.

The years between 1820 and 1830 were the most pitiable through which this country has ever passed. The conscience of the North was pledged to the Missouri Compromise, and that Compromise neither slumbered nor slept. In New England, where the old theocratical oligarchy of the colonies had survived the Revolution and kept under its own water-locks the new flood of trade, the conservatism of politics reinforced the conservatism of religion; and as if these two inquisitions were not enough to stifle the soul of man, the conservatism of business self-interest was superimposed. The history of the conflicts which followed has been written by the radicals, who negligently charge up to self-interest all the resistance which establishments offer to change. But it was not solely self-interest, it was conscience that backed the Missouri Compromise, nowhere else, naturally, so strongly as in New England. It was conscience that made cowards of us all. The white-lipped generation of Edward Everett were victims, one might even say martyrs, to conscience. They suffered the most terrible martyrdom that can fall to man, a martyrdom which injured their immortal volition and dried up the springs of life. If it were not that our poets have too seldom deigned to dip into real life, I do not know what more awful subject for a poem could have been found than that of the New England judge enforcing the fugitive slave law. For lack of such a poem the heroism of these men has been forgotten, the losing heroism of conservatism. It was this spiritual power of a committed conscience which met the new forces as they arose, and it deserves a better name than these new forces afterward gave it. In 1830 the social fruits of these heavy conditions could be seen in the life of the people. Free speech was lost.

"I know no country," says Tocqueville, who was here in 1831, "in which there is so little independence of mind and freedom of discussion as in America." Tocqueville recurs to the point again and again. He cannot disguise his surprise at it, and it tinged his whole philosophy and his book. The timidity of the Americans of this era was a thing which intelligent foreigners could not understand. Miss Martineau wrote in her Autobiography: "It was not till months afterwards that I was told that there were two reasons why I was not invited there [Chelsea] as elsewhere. One reason was that I had avowed, in reply to urgent questions, that I was disappointed in an oration of Mr. Everett's; and another was that I had publicly condemned the institution of slavery. I hope the Boston people have outgrown the childishness of sulking at opinions not in either case volunteered, but obtained by pressure. But really, the subservience to opinion at that time seemed a sort of mania."

The mania was by no means confined to Boston, but qualified this period of our history throughout the Northern States. There was no literature. "If great writers have not at present existed in America, the reason is very simply given in the fact that there can be no literary genius without freedom of opinion, and freedom of opinion does not exist in America," wrote Tocqueville. There were no amusements, neither music nor sport nor pastime, indoors or out of doors. The whole life of the community was a life of the intelligence, and upon the intelligence lay the weight of intellectual tyranny. The pressure kept on increasing, and the suppressed forces kept on increasing, till at last, as if to show what gigantic power was needed to keep conservatism dominant, the Merchant Province put forward Daniel Webster.

The worst period of panic seems to have preceded the anti-slavery agitations of 1831, because these agitations soon demonstrated that the sky did not fall nor the earth yawn and swallow Massachusetts because of Mr. Garrison's opinions, as most people had sincerely believed would be the case. Some semblance of free speech was therefore gradually regained.

Let us remember the world upon which the young Emerson's eyes opened. The South was a plantation. The North crooked the hinges of the knee where thrift might follow fawning. It was the era of Martin Chuzzlewit, a malicious caricature,—founded on fact. This time of humiliation, when there was no free speech, no literature, little manliness, no reality, no simplicity, no accomplishment, was the era of American brag. We flattered the foreigner and we boasted of ourselves. We were over-sensitive, insolent, and cringing. As late as 1845, G. P. Putnam, a most sensible and modest man, published a book to show what the country had done in the field of culture. The book is a monument of the age. With all its good sense and good humor, it justifies foreign contempt because it is explanatory. Underneath everything lay a feeling of unrest, an instinct,—"this country cannot permanently endure half slave and half free,"—which was the truth, but which could not be uttered.

So long as there is any subject which men may not freely discuss, they are timid upon all subjects. They wear an iron crown and talk in whispers. Such social conditions crush and maim the individual, and throughout New England, as throughout the whole North, the individual was crushed and maimed.

The generous youths who came to manhood between 1820 and 1830, while this deadly era was maturing, seem to have undergone a revulsion against the world almost before touching it; at least two of them suffered, revolted, and condemned, while still boys sitting on benches in school, and came forth advancing upon this old society like gladiators. The activity of William Lloyd Garrison, the man of action, preceded by several years that of Emerson, who is his prophet. Both of them were parts of one revolution. One of Emerson's articles of faith was that a man's thoughts spring from his actions rather than his actions from his thoughts, and possibly the same thing holds good for society at large. Perhaps all truths, whether moral or economic, must be worked out in real life before they are discovered by the student, and it was therefore necessary that Garrison should be evolved earlier than Emerson.

The silent years of early manhood, during which Emerson passed through the Divinity School and to his ministry, known by few, understood by none, least of all by himself, were years in which the revolting spirit of an archangel thought out his creed. He came forth perfect, with that serenity of which we have scarce another example in history,—that union of the man himself, his beliefs, and his vehicle of expression that makes men great because it makes them comprehensible. The philosophy into which he had already transmuted all his earlier theology at the time we first meet him consisted of a very simple drawing together of a few ideas, all of which had long been familiar to the world. It is the wonderful use he made of these ideas, the closeness with which they fitted his soul, the tact with which he took what he needed, like a bird building its nest, that make the originality, the man.

The conclusion of Berkeley, that the external world is known to us only through our impressions, and that therefore, for aught we know, the whole universe exists only in our own consciousness, cannot be disproved. It is so simple a conception that a child may understand it; and it has probably been passed before the attention of every thinking man since Plato's time. The notion is in itself a mere philosophical catch or crux to which there is no answer. It may be true. The mystics made this doctrine useful. They were not content to doubt the independent existence of the external world. They imagined that this external world, the earth, the planets, the phenomena of nature, bore some relation to the emotions and destiny of the soul. The soul and the cosmos were somehow related, and related so intimately that the cosmos might be regarded as a sort of projection or diagram of the soul.

Plato was the first man who perceived that this idea could be made to provide the philosopher with a vehicle of expression more powerful than any other. If a man will once plant himself firmly on the proposition that *he is* the universe, that every emotion or expression of his mind is correlated in some way to phenomena in the external world, and that he shall say how correlated, he is in a position where the power of speech is at a maximum. His figures of speech, his tropes, his witticisms, take rank with the law of gravity and the precession of the equinoxes. Philosophical exaltation of the individual cannot go beyond this point. It is the climax.

This is the school of thought to which Emerson belonged. The sun and moon, the planets, are mere symbols. They signify whatever the poet chooses. The planets for the most part stay in conjunction just long enough to flash his thought through their symbolism, and no permanent relation is established between the soul and the zodiac. There is, however, one link of correlation between the external and internal worlds which Emerson considered established, and in which he believed almost literally, namely, the moral law. This idea he drew from Kant through Coleridge and Wordsworth, and it is so familiar to us all that it hardly needs stating. The fancy that the good, the true, the beautiful,—all things of which we instinctively approve,—are somehow connected together and are really one thing; that our appreciation of them is in its essence the recognition of a law; that this law, in fact all law and the very idea of law, is a mere subjective experience; and that hence any external sequence which we coordinate and name, like the law of gravity, is really intimately connected with our moral nature,—this fancy has probably some basis of truth. Emerson adopted it as a corner-stone of his thought.

Such are the ideas at the basis of Emerson's philosophy, and it is fair to speak of them in this place because they antedate everything else which we know of him. They had been for years in his mind before he spoke at all. It was in the armor of this invulnerable idealism and with weapons like shafts of light that he came forth to fight. {...}

It is unnecessary to go, one by one, through the familiar essays and lectures which Emerson published between 1838 and 1875. They are in everybody's hands and in everybody's thoughts. In 1840 he wrote in his diary: "In all my lectures I have taught one doctrine, namely, the infinitude of the private man. This the people accept readily enough, and even with commendation, as long as I call the lecture Art or Politics, or Literature or the Household; but the moment I call it Religion they are shocked, though it be only the application of the same truth which they receive elsewhere to a new class of facts." To the platform he returned, and left it only once or twice during the remainder of his life.

His writings vary in coherence. In his early occasional pieces, like the Phi Beta Kappa address, coherence is at a maximum. They were written for a purpose, and were perhaps struck off all at once. But he earned his living by lecturing, and a lecturer is always recasting his work and using it in different forms. A lecturer has no prejudice against repetition. It is noticeable that in some of Emerson's important lectures the logical scheme is more perfect than in his essays. The truth seems to be that in the process of working up and perfecting his writings, in revising and filing his sentences, the logical scheme became more and more obliterated. Another circumstance helped make his style fragmentary. He was by nature a man of inspirations and exalted moods. He was subject to ecstasies, during which his mind worked with phenomenal brilliancy. Throughout his works and in his diary we find constant reference to these moods, and to his own inability to control or recover them. "But what we want is consecutiveness. 'Tis with us a flash of light, then a long darkness, then a flash again. Ah! could we turn these fugitive sparkles into an astronomy of Copernican worlds!"

In order to take advantage of these periods of divination, he used to write down the thoughts that came to him at such times. From boyhood onward he kept journals and commonplace books, and in the course of his reading and meditation he collected innumerable notes and quotations which he indexed for ready use. In these mines he "quarried," as Mr. Cabot says, for his lectures and essays. When he needed a lecture he went to the repository, threw together what seemed to have a bearing on some subject, and gave it a title. If any other man should adopt this method of composition, the result would be incomprehensible chaos; because most men have many interests, many moods, many and conflicting ideas. But with Emerson it was otherwise. There was only one thought which could set him aflame, and that was the thought of the unfathomed might of man. This thought was his religion, his politics, his ethics, his philosophy. One moment of inspiration was in him own brother to the next moment of inspiration, although they might be separated by six weeks. When he came to put together his star-born ideas, they fitted well, no matter in what order he placed them, because they were all part of the same idea.

His works are all one single attack on the vice of the age, moral cowardice. He assails it not by railings and scorn, but by positive and stimulating suggestion. The imagination of the reader is touched by every device which can awake the admiration for heroism, the consciousness of moral courage. Wit, quotation, anecdote, eloquence, exhortation, rhetoric, sarcasm, and very rarely denunciation, are launched at the reader, till he feels little lambent flames beginning to kindle in him. He is perhaps unable to see the exact logical connection between two paragraphs of an essay, yet he feels they are germane. He takes up Emerson tired and apathetic, but presently he feels himself growing heady and truculent, strengthened in his most inward vitality, surprised to find himself again master in his own house.

The difference between Emerson and the other moralists is that all these stimulating pictures and suggestions are not given by him in illustration of a general proposition. They have never been through the mill of generalization in his own mind. He himself could not have told you their logical bearing on one another. They have all the vividness of disconnected fragments of life, and yet they all throw light on one another, like the facets of a jewel. But whatever cause it was that led him to adopt his method of writing, it is certain that he succeeded in delivering himself of his thought with an initial velocity and carrying power such as few men ever attained. He has the force at his command of the thrower of the discus.

His style is American, and beats with the pulse of the climate. He is the only writer we have had who writes as he speaks, who makes no literary parade, has no pretensions of any sort. He is the only writer we have had who has wholly subdued his vehicle to his temperament. It is impossible to name his style without naming his character: they are one thing.

Both in language and in elocution Emerson was a practised and consummate artist, who knew how both to command his effects and to conceal his means. The casual, practical, disarming directness with which he writes puts any honest man at his mercy. What difference does it make whether a man who can talk like this is following an argument or not? You cannot always see Emerson clearly; he is hidden by a high wall; but you always know exactly on what spot he is standing. You judge it by the flight of the objects he throws over the wall,—a bootjack, an apple, a crown, a razor, a volume of verse. With one or other of these missiles, all delivered with a very tolerable aim, he is pretty sure to hit you. These catchwords stick in the mind. People are not in general influenced by long books or discourses, but by odd fragments of observation which they overhear, sentences or head-lines which they read while turning over a book at random or while waiting for dinner to be announced. These are the oracles and orphic words that get lodged in the mind and bend a man's most stubborn will. Emerson called them the Police of the Universe. His works are a treasury of such things. They sparkle in the mind, or you may carry them off in your pocket. They get driven into your mind like nails, and on them catch and hang your own experiences, till what was once his thought has become your character.

"God offers to every mind its choice between truth and repose. Take which you please; you can never have both." "Discontent is want of self-reliance; it is infirmity of will." "It is impossible for a man to be cheated by any one but himself."

The orchestration with which Emerson introduces and sustains these notes from the spheres is as remarkable as the winged things themselves. Open his works at a hazard. You hear a man talking. {...}

Your attention is arrested by the reality of this gentleman in his garden, by the first-hand quality of his mind. It matters not on what subject he talks. While you are musing, still pleased and patronizing, he has picked up the bow of Ulysses, bent it with the ease of Ulysses, and sent a shaft clear through the twelve axes, nor missed one of them. But this, it seems, was mere byplay and marksmanship; for before you have done wondering, Ulysses rises to his feet in anger, and pours flight after flight, arrow after arrow, from the great bow. The shafts sing and strike, the suitors fall in heaps. The brow of Ulysses shines with unearthly splendor. The air is filled with lightning. After a little, without shock or transition, without apparent change of tone, Mr. Emerson is offering you a biscuit before you leave, and bidding you mind the last step at the garden end. If the man who can do these things be not an artist, then must we have a new vocabulary and rename the professions.

There is, in all this effectiveness of Emerson, no pose, no literary art; nothing that corresponds even remotely to the pretended modesty and ignorance with which Socrates lays pitfalls for our admiration in Plato's dialogues.

It was the platform which determined Emerson's style. He was not a writer, but a speaker. On the platform his manner of speech was a living part of his words. The pauses and hesitation, the abstraction, the searching, the balancing, the turning forward and back of the leaves of his lecture, and then the discovery, the illumination, the gleam of lightning which you saw before your eyes descend into a man of genius,—all this was Emerson. He invented this style of speaking, and made it express the supersensuous, the incommunicable. {...}

It has been necessary to reduce the living soul of Emerson to mere dead attributes like "moral courage" in order that we might talk about him at all. His effectiveness comes from his character; not from his philosophy, nor from his rhetoric nor his wit, nor from any of the accidents of his education. He might never have heard of Berkeley or Plato. A slightly different education might have led him to throw his teaching into the form of historical essays or of stump speeches. He might, perhaps, have been bred a stonemason, and have done his work in the world by travelling with a panorama. But he would always have been Emerson. His weight and his power would always have been the same. It is solely as character that he is important. He discovered nothing; he bears no relation whatever to the history of philosophy. We must regard him and deal with him simply as a man.

Strangely enough, the world has always insisted upon accepting him as a thinker: and hence a great coil of misunderstanding. As a thinker, Emerson is difficult to classify. Before you begin to assign him a place, you must clear the ground by a disquisition as to what is meant by "a thinker," and how Emerson differs from other thinkers. As a man, Emerson is as plain as Ben Franklin.

People have accused him of inconsistency; they say that he teaches one thing one day, and another the next day. But from the point of view of Emerson there is no such thing as inconsistency. Every man is each day a new man. Let him be to-day what he is to-day. It is immaterial and waste of time to consider what he once was or what he may be.

His picturesque speech delights in fact and anecdote, and a public which is used to treatises and deduction cares always to be told the moral. It wants everything reduced to a generalization. All generalizations are partial truths, but we are used to them, and we ourselves mentally make the proper allowance. Emerson's method is, not to give a generalization and trust to our making the allowance, but to give two conflicting statements and leave the balance of truth to be struck in our own minds on the facts. There is no inconsistency in this. It is a vivid and very legitimate method of procedure. But he is much more than a theorist: he is a practitioner. He does not merely state a theory of agitation: he proceeds to agitate. "Do not," he says, "set the least value on what I do, or the least discredit on what I do not, as if I pretended to settle anything as false or true. I unsettle all things. No facts are to me sacred, none are profane. I simply experiment, an endless seeker with no past at my back." He was not engaged in teaching many things, but one thing,—Courage. Sometimes he inspires it by pointing to great characters,—Fox, Milton, Alcibiades; sometimes he inspires it by bidding us beware of imitating such men, and, in the ardor of his rhetoric, even seems to regard them as hindrances and dangers to our development. There is no inconsistency here. Emerson might logically have gone one step further and raised inconsistency into a jewel. For what is so useful, so educational, so inspiring, to a timid and conservative man, as to do something inconsistent and regrettable? It lends character to him at once. He breathes freer and is stronger for the experience.

Emerson is no cosmopolitan. He is a patriot. He is not like Goethe, whose sympathies did not run on national lines. Emerson has America in his mind's eye all the time. There is to be a new religion, and it is to come from America; a new and better type of man, and he is to be an American. He not only cared little or nothing for Europe, but he cared not much for the world at large. His thought was for the future of this country. You cannot get into any chamber in his mind which is below this chamber of patriotism. He loves the valor of Alexander and the grace of the Oxford athlete; but he loves them not for themselves. He has a use for them. They are grist to his mill and powder to his gun. His admiration of them he subordinates to his main purpose,—they are his blackboard and diagrams. His patriotism is the backbone of his significance. He came to his countrymen at a time when they lacked, not thoughts, but manliness. The needs of his own particular public are always before him. {. . .}

It is the same wherever we open his books. He must spur on, feed up, bring forward the dormant character of his countrymen. When he goes to England, he sees in English life nothing except those elements which are deficient in American life. If you wish a catalogue of what America has not, read English Traits. Emerson's patriotism had the effect of expanding his philosophy. To-day we know the value of physique, for science has taught it, but it was hardly discovered in his day, and his philosophy affords no basis for it. Emerson in this matter transcends his philosophy. {. . .}

No convulsion could shake Emerson or make his view unsteady even for an instant. What no one else saw, he saw, and he saw nothing else. Not a boy in the land welcomed the outbreak of the war so fiercely as did this shy village philosopher, then at the age of fifty-eight. He saw that war was the cure for cowardice, moral as well as physical. It was not the cause of the slave that moved him; it was not the cause of the Union for which he cared a farthing. It was something deeper than either of these things for which he had been battling all his life. It was the cause of character against convention. Whatever else the war might bring, it was sure to bring in character, to leave behind it a file of heroes; if not heroes, then villains, but in any case strong men. On the 9th of April, 1861, three days before Fort Sumter was bombarded, he had spoken with equanimity of "the downfall of our character-destroying civilization. . . . We find that civilization crowed too soon, that our triumphs were treacheries; we had opened the wrong door and let the enemy into the castle." {. . .}

The place which Emerson forever occupies as a great critic is defined by the same sharp outlines that mark his work, in whatever light and from whatever side we approach it. A critic in the modern sense he was not, for his point of view is fixed, and he reviews the world like a search-light placed on the top of a tall tower. He lived too early and at too great a distance from the forum of European thought to absorb the ideas of evolution and give place to them in his philosophy. Evolution does not graft well upon the Platonic Idealism, nor are physiology and the kindred sciences sympathetic. Nothing aroused Emerson's indignation more than the attempts of the medical faculty and of phrenologists to classify, and therefore limit individuals. "The grossest ignorance does not disgust me like this ignorant knowingness."

We miss in Emerson the underlying conception of growth, of development, so characteristic of the thought of our own day, and which, for instance, is found everywhere latent in Browning's poetry. Browning regards character as the result of experience and as an ever changing growth. To Emerson, character is rather an entity complete and eternal from the beginning. He is probably the last great writer to look at life from a stationary standpoint. There is a certain lack of the historic sense in all he has written. The ethical assumption that all men are exactly alike permeates his work. In his mind, Socrates, Marco Polo, and General Jackson stand surrounded by the same atmosphere, or rather stand as mere naked characters surrounded by no atmosphere at all. He is probably the last great writer who will fling about classic anecdotes as if they were club gossip. In the discussion of morals, this assumption does little harm. The stories and proverbs which illustrate the thought of the moralist generally concern only those simple relations of life which are common to all ages. There is charm in this familiar dealing with antiquity. The classics are thus domesticated and made real to us. What matter if Æsop appear a little too much like an American citizen, so long as his points tell?

It is in Emerson's treatment of the fine arts that we begin to notice his want of historic sense. Art endeavors to express subtle and ever changing feelings by means of conventions which are as protean as the forms of a cloud; and the man who in speaking on the plastic arts makes the assumption that all men are alike will reveal before he has uttered three sentences that he does not know what art is, that he has never experienced any form of sensation from it. Emerson lived in a time and clime where there was no plastic art, and he was obliged to arrive at his ideas about art by means of a highly complex process of reasoning. He dwelt constantly in a spiritual place which was the very focus of high moral fervor. This was his enthusiasm, this was his revelation, and from it he reasoned out the probable meaning of the fine arts. "This," thought Emerson, his eye rolling in a fine frenzy of moral feeling, "this must be what Apelles experienced, this fervor is the passion of Bramante. I understand the Parthenon." And so he projected his feelings about morality into the field of the plastic arts. He deals very freely and rather indiscriminately with the names of artists,—Phidias, Raphael, Salvator Rosa,—and he speaks always in such a way that it is impossible to connect what he says with any impression we have ever received from the works of those masters.

In fact, Emerson has never in his life felt the normal appeal of any painting, or any sculpture, or any architecture, or any music. These things, of which he does not know the meaning in real life, he yet uses, and uses constantly, as symbols to convey ethical truths. The result is that his books are full of blind places, like the notes which will not strike on a sick piano.

It is interesting to find that the one art of which Emerson did have a direct understanding, the art of poetry, gave him some insight into the relation of the artist to his vehicle. In his essay on Shakespeare there is a full recognition of the debt of

Shakespeare to his times. This essay is filled with the historic sense. We ought not to accuse Emerson because he lacked appreciation of the fine arts, but rather admire the truly Goethean spirit in which he insisted upon the reality of arts of which he had no understanding. This is the same spirit which led him to insist on the value of the Eastern poets. Perhaps there exist a few scholars who can tell us how far Emerson understood or misunderstood Saadi and Firdusi and the Koran. But we need not be disturbed for his learning. It is enough that he makes us recognize that these men were men too, and that their writings mean something not unknowable to us. The East added nothing to Emerson, but gave him a few trappings of speech. The whole of his mysticism is to be found in *Nature*, written before he knew the sages of the Orient, and it is not improbable that there is some real connection between his own mysticism and the mysticism of the Eastern poets. {...}

II

{...} Much of what Emerson wrote about the United States in 1850 is true of the United States to-day. It would be hard to find a civilized people who are more timid, more cowed in spirit, more illiberal, than we. It is easy to-day for the educated man who has read Bryce and Tocqueville to account for the mediocrity of American literature. The merit of Emerson was that he felt the atmospheric pressure without knowing its reason. He felt he was a cabined, cribbed, confined creature, although every man about him was celebrating Liberty and Democracy, and every day was Fourth of July. He taxes language to its limits in order to express his revolt. He says that no man should write except what he has discovered in the process of satisfying his own curiosity, and that every man will write well in proportion as he has contempt for the public.

Emerson seems really to have believed that if any man would only resolutely be himself, he would turn out to be as great as Shakespeare. He will not have it that anything of value can be monopolized. His review of the world, whether under the title of Manners, Self-Reliance, Fate, Experience, or what-not, leads him to the same thought. His conclusion is always the finding of eloquence, courage, art, intellect, in the breast of the humblest reader. He knows that we are full of genius and surrounded by genius, and that we have only to throw something off, not to acquire any new thing, in order to be bards, prophets, Napoleons, and Goethes. This belief is the secret of his stimulating power. It is this which gives his writings a radiance like that which shone from his personality.

The deep truth shadowed forth by Emerson when he said that "all the American geniuses lacked nerve and dagger" was illustrated by our best scholar. Lowell had the soul of the Yankee, but in his habits of writing he continued English tradition. His literary essays are full of charm. The Commemoration Ode is the high-water mark of the attempt to do the impossible. It is a fine thing, but it is imitative and secondary. It has paid the inheritance tax. Twice, however, at a crisis of pressure, Lowell assumed his real self under the guise of a pseudonym; and with his own hand he rescued a language, a type, a whole era of civilization from oblivion. Here gleams the dagger and here is Lowell revealed. His limitations as a poet, his too much wit, his too much morality, his mixture of shrewdness and religion, are seen to be the very elements of power. The novelty of the Biglow Papers is as wonderful as their world-old naturalness. They take rank with greatness, and they were the strongest political tracts of their time. They imitate nothing; they are real.

Emerson himself was the only man of his times who consistently and utterly expressed himself, never measuring himself for a moment with the ideals of others, never troubling himself for a moment with what literature was or how literature should be created. The other men of his epoch, and among whom he lived, believed that literature was a very desirable article, a thing you could create if you were only smart enough. But Emerson had no literary ambition. He cared nothing for belles-lettres. The consequence is that he stands above his age like a colossus. While he lived his figure could be seen from Europe towering like Atlas over the culture of the United States.

Great men are not always like wax which their age imprints. They are often the mere negation and opposite of their age. They give it the lie. They become by revolt the very essence of all the age is not, and that part of the spirit which is suppressed in ten thousand breasts gets lodged, isolated, and breaks into utterance in one. Through Emerson spoke the fractional spirits of a multitude. He had not time, he had not energy left over to understand himself; he was a mouthpiece.

If a soul be taken and crushed by democracy till it utter a cry, that cry will be Emerson. The region of thought he lived in, the figures of speech he uses, are of an intellectual plane so high that the circumstances which produced them may be forgotten; they are indifferent. The Constitution, Slavery, the War itself, are seen as mere circumstances. They did not confuse him while he lived; they are not necessary to support his work now that it is finished. Hence comes it that Emerson is one of the world's voices. He was heard afar off. His foreign influence might deserve a chapter by itself. Conservatism is not confined to this country. It is the very basis of all government. The bolts Emerson forged, his thought, his wit, his perception, are not provincial. They were found to carry inspiration to England and Germany. Many of the important men of the last half-century owe him a debt. It is not yet possible to give any account of his influence abroad, because the memoirs which will show it are only beginning to be published. We shall have them in due time; for Emerson was an outcome of the world's progress. His appearance marks the turning-point in the history of that enthusiasm for pure democracy which has tinged the political thought of the world for the past one hundred and fifty years. The youths of England and Germany may have been surprised at hearing from America a piercing voice of protest against the very influences which were crushing them at home. They could not realize that the chief difference between Europe and America is a difference in the rate of speed with which revolutions in thought are worked out.

While the radicals of Europe were revolting in 1848 against the abuses of a tyranny whose roots were in feudalism, Emerson, the great radical of America, the arch-radical of the world, was revolting against the evils whose roots were in universal suffrage. By showing the identity in essence of all tyranny, and by bringing back the attention of political thinkers to its starting-point, the value of human character, he has advanced the political thought of the world by one step. He has pointed out for us in this country to what end our efforts must be bent.

Charles Sanders Peirce (1839–1914)

In the brief passage included here, Peirce writes his own intellectual biography as it relates to the presence of Emerson in his life. Now a celebrated logician, semiotician, and founder of pragmatism, Peirce was a career scientist for the United States Coast Survey, taught briefly at Johns Hopkins, and died destitute in the remote woods of Pennsylvania. While Peirce mentions below a physical proximity to Emerson, Frederick Ives Carpenter describes Peirce as sharing an intellectual proximity as well: "In the realm of the mind, Peirce was neighbor to Emerson also. Particularly when he most disagreed with the pragmatism of his friend William James, he most completely agreed with the transcendentalism of Concord."[1] Carpenter adds that Peirce "valued instinctive insights as the source of all intellection, and translated the Emersonian 'intuitions' into the 'hypotheses' of modern science."[2] Peirce's wife, Zina (Harriet Melusina Fay Peirce) was a close friend of Emerson's, and "carried on a brief but intense correspondence" with him.[3] She once wrote to Emerson: "I love you too much, however, for some things in that book of yours. [. . .] I can see no Christianity in your book from one end of it to the other. [. . .] If I have said anything impertinent or self-conceited, I beg your pardon mostly humbly since next after Religion I bow to Intellect."[4] At fifty-two, Peirce wrote the following candid but circumspect lines at the beginning of his essay, a selection from "The Law of Mind" (1892), published as part of a series of his work in the prominent journal The Monist.

from The Law of Mind

Charles Sanders Peirce

I may mention, for the benefit of those who are curious in studying mental biographies, that I was born and reared in the neighbourhood of Concord—I mean Cambridge—at the time when Emerson, Hedge, and their friends were disseminating the ideas that they had caught from Schelling, and Schelling from Plotinus, from Boehm, or from God knows what minds stricken with the monstrous mysticism of the East. But the atmosphere of Cambridge held many an antiseptic against Concord transcendentalism; and I am not conscious of having contracted any of that virus. Nevertheless, it is probable that some cultured bacilli, some benignant form of the disease was implanted in my soul, unawares, and that now, after long incubation, then it comes to the surface, modified by mathematical conceptions and by training in physical investigations.

Notes

1 Frederick Ives Carpenter, "Charles Sanders Peirce: Pragmatic Transcendentalist,"
   The New England Quarterly, Vol. 14 (1941), 36.

2 Ibid.

3 Joseph Brent, *Charles Sanders Peirce: A Life* (Bloomington: Indiana University Press,
   1993), 64.

4 Letter from Zina Peirce to Emerson, October 5, 1856, as quoted in Norma Pereira
   Atkinson, *An Examination of the Life and Thought of Zina Fay Peirce, an American
   Reformer and Feminist*, dissertation (Ball State University, Muncie, Indiana, 1983), 17.

Josiah Royce (1855–1916)

Born in Grass Valley during Gold Rush-era California, Royce earned one of the first doctorate degrees in philosophy at Johns Hopkins, and later at the invitation of William James took up a professorship at Harvard in the year Emerson died. In his last year out west, Royce wrote the following article, which was published in the Californian *(1881). In this essay and the excerpt from a letter to George Buchanan Coale (September 23, 1880) that precedes it, Royce conducts an inquiry into a generational shift in consciousness. He writes to his friend: "I fear we younger men have so much else to read and believe and puzzle over, that this heritage from the age of the Idealists comes to our minds in a very diluted, perhaps even polluted form." He seemed convinced that Emerson and his age, for all their prominence, were being eclipsed by the rise of modern science: "It is the theory of Evolution," he notes in "The Decay of Earnestness," "that, with its magnificent triumphs, its wonderful ingenuity and insight, has put them out of sight." Royce did not perhaps have a sense for the degree to which Emerson's work is adaptable to the onward rush of late nineteenth-century science. As scholar Laura Dassow Walls claims, when Emerson "came to read Darwin, which he did in 1860, he saw nothing he had not seen before—a fact that reveals little about Darwin and a great deal about Emerson."[1] When Royce delivered a Phi Beta Kappa oration at Harvard's Sanders Theatre on June 29, 1911, entitled "William James and the Philosophy of Life," he aimed to nominate James the "third representative American philosopher"; the oration becomes chapter one of Royce's* William James and Other Essays on the Philosophy of Life *(1911). In an excerpt presented below, Royce begins his remarks by reminding us of the first two: Jonathan Edwards and Emerson.[2]*

Letter to George Buchanan Coale

September 23, 1880

The men of your generation are now rare, and we young men meet you but seldom. By your generation I mean the men with the vivid sense and faith of and in the ideal value of life, as Carlyle and Emerson once taught that faith and sense, and as the whole generation of the Transcendentalists received it. We young men hear from our time no such doctrines preached. I know, as you used to say, that may be because there is no longer the need to preach and repeat what through Carlyle and Emerson has been made the common property of all; but I fear that we younger men have so much else to read and believe and puzzle over, that this heritage from the age of the Idealists comes to our minds in a very diluted, perhaps even polluted form. For my part I have needed the living man to help me in appreciating the meaning of this pure and hopeful spirit of faith, and in this way I owe you personally a good deal. Not that I am a disciple myself. The condition whose presence saves you, as you say, from Pessimism, is unfortunately lacking in my case; and though I am not properly a Pessimist, I am a dabbler in dangerous problems; and a very extensive doubter. But you emphasized, or it least greatly helped to emphasize for me one moment or element of the truth of which I sincerely hope never to lose sight. And for this I shall always thank you.

Notes

1   Laura Dassow Walls, *Emerson's Life in Science: The Culture of Truth* (Ithaca: Cornell University Press, 2003), 167.
2   For more on Jonathan Edwards and Emerson see Perry Miller's "From Edwards to Emerson," *Errand into the Wilderness* (Cambridge: Harvard University Press, 1956), 184–203. The chapter appears with an informative preface by the author, who responds in part to the reception of the work since it was first published in *The New England Quarterly*, December 1940, Vol. XIII, 589–617.

The Decay of Earnestness

Josiah Royce

Every animal, when not frightened, shows in its own way a certain quiet self-complacency, a confidence in the supreme worth of its individual existence, an exalted egotism, which is often not a little amusing if we reflect on the shortness, the insignificance, and the misery of most creatures' lives. This animal self-complacency characterizes, also, as we know, all naturally-minded men. We know, too, that most men are nearly as much in error as the beasts, in the degree of importance that they attach to their lives. But what I have just now most in mind is that the same kind of blunder is frequently found in the judgment that any one age passes upon itself and its own work. Every active period of history thinks its activity of prodigious importance, and its advance beyond its predecessors very admirable. So the eighteenth century thought that the English poetry of past times had been far surpassed in form and in matter by the poetry of the age of Dryden and of Pope. Long since the blindness of the eighteenth century upon this point has been fully exposed. The Neoplatonic philosophy, the Crusades, the First French Empire, are familiar instances from the multitudes of cases where men utterly failed to perform the permanent work which they were very earnestly trying to do, and where they were, at most, doing for the world that which they least of all wished or expected to do. Like individuals, then, whole eras of history go by, sublimely confident in their own significance, yet often unable to make their claims even interesting in the sight of posterity.

The same lesson may be drawn both here and in the case of individuals. The man is vain; so is the age. The man ought to correct his vanity first by negative criticism; so ought the time. But the disillusioning process is a cruel one in both cases. It is hard for the man to bear the thought that, perhaps, after all, he is a useless enthusiast. So it is hard for an age to bear the thought that its dearest worship may be only idolatry, and its best work only a fighting of shadows. But for both the lesson is the same. Let them find some higher aim than this merely natural one of self-satisfaction. Let their work be done, not that it may seem grand to them alone, but so that it must have an element of grandeur in it, whatever be the success of its particular purposes. Grandeur does not depend upon success alone, nor need illusions always be devoid of a higher truth. The problem is to find out what is the right spirit, and to work in that. If the matter of the work is bad, that must perish, but the spirit need not.

Now, in our age we are especially engaged upon certain problems of thought. We discuss the origin of the present forms of things in the physical and in the moral universe. Evolution is our watchword; "everything grew," is the interpretation. Our method of inquiry is the historical. We want to see how, out of certain simple elements, the most complex structures about us were built up. Now, in the enormous thought-activity thus involved, two things especially strike one who pauses to watch. The first is, that in studying Evolution men have come to neglect other important matters that used to be a good deal talked about. The true end of life, the nature and grounds of human certitude, the problems of Goethe's *Faust* and of Kant's *Critique*—these disappear from the view of many representative men. The age finds room to talk about these things, but not to enter upon them with a whole-souled enthusiasm. Yet these are eternally valuable matters of thought. The age for which they are not in the very front rank of problems is a one-sided age, destined to be severely criticized within a century. The other fact that strikes us in this age is that the result of our one-sidedness is an unhappy division, productive of no little misery, between the demands of modern thought and the demands of the whole indivisible nature of man. The ethical finds not enough room in the philosophy of the time. The world is studied, but not the active human will, without whose interference the world is wholly void of human significance. The matter of thinking overwhelms us; we forget to study the form, and so we accept, with a blank wonder, the results of our thinking as if they were self-existent entities that had walked into our souls of themselves. For example, we make molecules by reasoning about facts of sensation, and by grouping these facts in the simplest and easiest fashion possible; then we fall into a fear lest the molecules have, after all, made us, and we write countless volumes on a stupid theme called materialism. This unreflective fashion of regarding the products of our thought as the conditions and source of our thought, is largely responsible for the strife between the ethical and the scientific tendencies of the time. The scientific tendency stops in one direction at a certain point, content with having made a theory of evolution, and fearing, or, at any rate, neglecting, any further analysis of fundamental ideas. The ethical tendency, on the other hand, rests on a rooted feeling that, after all, conscious life is of more worth than anything else in the universe. But this is, nowadays, commonly a mere feeling, which, finding nothing to justify it in current scientific opinion, becomes morose, and results in books against science. The books are wrong, but the feeling, when not morose, is right. The world is of importance only because of the conscious life in it, and the Evolution theory is one-sided because of the subordinate place it gives to consciousness. But the cure is not in writing books against science, but solely in such a broad philosophy as shall correct the narrowness of the day, and bring back to the first rank of interest once more the problems of Goethe's *Faust* and of Kant's *Critique*. We want not less talk about evolution, but more study of human life and destiny, of the nature of men's thought, and the true goal of men's actions. Send us the thinker that can show us just what in life is most worthy of our toil, just what makes men's destiny more than poor and comic, just what is the ideal that we ought to serve; let such a thinker point out to us plainly that ideal, and then say, in a voice that we must hear, "Work, work for that; it is the highest"—then such a thinker will have saved our age from one-sidedness, and have given it eternal significance. Now, to talk about those problems of thought which concern the destiny, the significance, and the conduct of human life, is to talk about what I have termed "the ethical aspect of thought." Some study we must give to these things if we are not to remain, once for all, hopelessly one-sided.

In looking for the view of the world which shall restore unity to our divided age, we must first not forget the fact that very lately all these now neglected matters have been much talked about. It is the theory of Evolution that, with its magnificent triumphs, its wonderful ingenuity and insight, has put them out of sight. Only within twenty years has there been a general inattention to the study of the purposes and the hopes of human life—a study that, embodied in German Idealism, or in American Transcendentalism, in Goethe, in Schiller, in Fichte, in Wordsworth, in Shelley, in Carlyle, in Emerson, had been filling men's thoughts since the outset of the great Revolution. But since the end of the period referred to our knowledge of the origin of the forms of life has driven from popular thought matters of the worth and of the conduct of life, so that one might grow up nowadays well taught in the learning of the age, and when asked, "Hast thou as yet received into thy heart any Ideal?" might respond very truthfully, "I have not heard so much as whether there be any Ideal."

Yet, I repeat, the fault in our time is negative rather than positive. We have to enlarge, not to condemn. Evolution is a great truth, but it is not all truth. We need more, not less, of science. We need a more thorough-going, a more searching—yes, a more critical and skeptical—thought than any now current. For current thought is, in fact, *naïf* and dogmatic, accepting without criticism a whole army of ideas because they happen to be useful as bases for scientific work. We need, then, in the interests of higher thought, an addition to our present philosophy—an addition that makes use of the neglected thought of the last three generations. But as preliminary to all this, it becomes us to inquire: Why was modern thought so suddenly turned from the contemplation of the ethical aspect of reality to this present absorbing study of the material side of the world? How came we to break with Transcendentalism, and to begin this search after the laws of the redistribution of matter and of force? To this question I want to devote the rest of the present study; for just here is the whole problem in a nut shell. Transcendentalism, the distinctly ethical thought-movement of the century, failed to keep a strong hold on the life of the century. Why? In the answer to this question lies at once the relative justification, and at the same time the understanding, of the incompleteness of our present mode of thinking.

By Transcendentalism, I mean a movement that began in Germany in the last thirty years of the eighteenth century, and that afterward spread, in one form or another, all over Europe, and even into our own country—a movement that answered in the moral and mental world to the French Revolution in the political world. Everywhere this movement expressed, through a multitude of forms, a single great idea: the idea that in the free growth and expression of the highest and strongest emotions of the civilized man might be found the true solution of the problem of life. Herein was embodied a reaction against the characteristic notions of the eighteenth century. In the conventional, in submission to the external forms of government, religion, and society, joined with a total indifference to the spiritual, and with a general tendency to free but shallow speculation, the average popular thought of the last century had sought to attain repose, rather than perfection. The great thinkers rose far above this level; but, on the whole, we look to the age of the rationalists rather for ingenuity than for profundity, rather for good sense than for grand ideas. The prophetic, the emotional, the sublime, are absent from the typical eighteenth century mind-life. Instead, we find cultivation, criticism, skepticism, and at times, as a sort of relief, a mild sentimentality. The Transcendental movement expressed a rebound from this state of things. With the so-called Storm and

Stress Period of German literature the protest against conventionality and in favor of a higher life began. Love, enthusiasm, devotion, the affection for humanity, the search after the ideal, the faith in a spiritual life—these became objects of the first interest. A grand new era of history seemed opening. Men felt themselves on the verge of great discoveries. The highest hopes were formed. A movement was begun that lasted through three generations, and far into a fourth. It was, to be sure, in nature a young men's movement; but as the men of one generation lost their early enthusiasm, others arose to follow in their footsteps—blunderingly, perhaps, but earnestly. When Goethe had outgrown his youthful extravagances, behold there were the young Romanticists to undertake the old work once more. When they crystallized with time, and lost hold on the German national life, there came Heine and the Young Germany to pursue with new vigor the old path. In England, Wordsworth grows very sober with age, when there come Byron and Shelley; Coleridge fails, and Carlyle is sent; Shelley and Bryon pass away, but Tennyson arises. And with us in America Emerson and his helpers renew the spirit of a half century before their time. This movement now seems a thing of the past. There is no Emerson among the younger men, no Tennyson among the new school of poets, no Heine in Germany—much less, then, a Fichte or a Schiller. Not merely is genius lacking, but the general public interest, the soil from which a genius draws nourishment, is unfavorable. The literary taste of the age is represented by George Eliot's later novels, where everything is made subordinate to analysis, by the poetry of several skillful masters of melody, by the cold critical work of the authors of the series on "English Men of Letters." Men of wonderful power there are among our writers—men like William Morris in poetry, or Matthew Arnold in both criticism and poetry; but their work is chiefly esoteric, appealing to a limited class. Widely popular writers we have upon many subjects; but they are either great men of abstract thought, like Spencer and Huxley; or else, alas! mere superficial scribblers like Mr. Mallock, or rhetoricians like Rev. Joseph Cook. The moral leader, the seer, the man to awaken deep interest in human life as human life, no longer belongs to the active soldiers of the army of today; and, what is worse, the public mind no longer inquires after such a leader. There must surely be a cause for this state of public sentiment. Neglect of such vital questions must have sprung from some error in their treatment. Let us look in history for that error.

The Storm and Stress Period in Germany began with the simplest and most unaffected desire possible to get back from conventionality and from shallow thought to the purity and richness of natural emotion. There was at first no set philosophy or creed about the universe common to those engaged in the movement. The young poets worshipped genius, and desired to feel intensely and to express emotion worthily. To this end they discarded the traditions as to form which they found embodied in French poetry and in learned textbooks. Lessing had furnished them critical authority. He had shown the need of appealing to Nature for instruction, both in the matter and in the manner of poetry. Popular ballads suggested to some of the young school their models. Their own overflowing hearts, their warm, ideal friendships with one another, their passion for freedom, their full personal experiences, gave them material. Together they broke down conventions, and opened a new era in literary life, as the

French Revolution, twenty years later, did in national life. Every one knows that Goethe's famous *Werther* is the result of this time of ferment. Now, if one reads *Werther* attentively, and with an effort (for it needs an effort) to sympathize with the mood that produced and enjoyed it, one will see in it the characteristic idea that the aim of life is to have as remarkable and exalted emotional experiences as possible, and those of a purely personal character; that is, not the emotion that men feel in common when they engage in great causes, not the devotion to sublime impersonal objects, not surrender to unworldly ideals, but simply the overwhelming sense of the magnitude and worth of one's own loves and longings, of one's own precious soul-experiences—this, and not the other, is to be sought. Werther cannot resist the fate that drives him to load his heart down with emotion until it breaks. He feels how far asunder from the rest of mankind all this drives him. But he insists upon despising mankind, and upon reveling in the dangerous wealth of his inspiration. Now surely such a state of mind as this must injure men if they remain long in it. Men need work in life, and so long as they undertake to dig into their own bowels for the wonderful inner experiences that they may find by digging, so long must their lives be bad dreams. The purpose of these young men was the highest, but only those of them who, following this purpose, passed far beyond the simplicity of their youth, did work of lasting merit. The others stayed in a state of passionate formlessness, or died early. The result of remaining long in this region, where nothing was of worth but a violent emotion or an incredible deed, one sees in such a man as Klinger, who lived long enough to reap what he had sown, but did not progress sufficiently to succeed in sowing anything but the wind. I remember once spending an idle hour on one of his later romances, written years after the time of Storm and Stress had passed by, which well expresses the state of mind, the sort of *katzenjammer* resulting from a long life of literary dissipation. It is Klinger's *Faustus*—the same subject as Goethe's masterpiece, but how differently treated! Faustus is a man desperately anxious to act. He wants to reform the world, to be sure, but that only by the way. His main object is to satisfy a vague, restless craving for tremendous excitement. The contract with the devil once made, he plunges into a course of reckless adventure. Where he undertakes to do good he only makes bad worse. Admirable about him is merely the magnitude of his projects, the vigor of his actions, the desperate courage wherewith he defies the universe. Brought to hell at last, he ends his career by cursing all things that are with such fearless and shocking plainness of speech that the devils themselves are horrified. Satan has to invent a new place of torment for him. He is banished, if I remember rightly, into horrible darkness, where he is to pass eternity perfectly alone. Thus terribly the poet expresses the despair in which ends for him, as for all, this self-adoration of the man whose highest object is violent emotional experiences, enjoyed merely because they are his own, not because by having them one serves the Ideal. As a mere beginning, then, the Storm and Stress Period expressed a great awakening of the world to new life. But an abiding place in this state of mind there was none. What then followed?

The two masters of German literature who passed through and rose above this period of beginnings, and created the great works of the classical period, were Goethe and Schiller. As poets, we are not now specially concerned with them. As moral teachers, what have they to tell us about the conduct and the worth of life? The answer is they bear not altogether the same message. There is a striking contrast, well recognized by themselves and by all subsequent critics, between their views of life. Both aim at the highest, but seek in different paths. Goethe's mature ideal seems to be a man of finely appreciative powers, who follows his life-calling quietly and with such diligence as to gain for himself independence and leisure, who so cultivates his mind that it is open to receive all noble impressions, and who then waits with a sublime resignation, gained through years of self-discipline, for such experiences of what is grand in life and in the universe as the Spirit of Nature sees fit to grant to him. Wilhelm Meister, who works eagerly for success in a direction where success is impossible, and who afterward finds bliss where he least expected to find it, seems to teach this lesson. Faust, at first eagerly demanding indefinite breadth and grandeur of life, and then coming to see what the limitations of human nature are, "that to man nothing perfect is given," and so at last finding the highest good of life in the thought that he and posterity must daily earn anew freedom, never be done with progressing, seems to illustrate the same thought. Do not go beyond or behind Nature, Goethe always teaches. Live submissively the highest that it is given you to live, and neither cease quietly working, nor despair, nor rebel, but be open to every new and worthy experience. For Goethe this was a perfect solution of the problem of life. He needed no fixed system of dogmas to content him. In the divine serenity of one of the most perfect of minds, Goethe put in practice this maxim: Live thy life out to the full, earnestly but submissively, demanding what attainment thy nature makes possible, but not pining for more.

Now, this of course is a selfish maxim. If the highest life is to be unselfish, Goethe cannot have given us the final solution to the problem. His selfishness was not of a low order. It was like the selfishness in the face of the Apollo Belvedere, the simple consciousness of vast personal worth. But it was selfishness for all that. We see how it grew for him out of his early enthusiasm. The Storm and Stress Period had been full of the thought that there is something grand in the emotional nature of man, and that this something must be cultivated. Now, Goethe, absorbed in the faith of the time—himself, in fact, its high priest—learned after a while that all these much sought treasures of emotion were there already, in his own being, and that they needed no long search, no storming at all. He had but to be still and watch them. He needed no anxious brooding to find ideals; he went about quietly, meeting the ideal everywhere. The object of search thus attained, in so far as any mortal could attain it, Goethe the poet was in perfect harmony with the Goethe of practical life; and so was formed the creed of the greatest man of the century. But it was a creed of little more than personal significance. For us the grand example remains, but the attainment of like perfection is impossible, and we must look for another rule of living. For those sensitive and earnest people who learn, as many learn while yet mere school boys or school girls, that there is a great wealth of splendid emotional life, of affection and aspiration and devotion, shut up in their own hearts; for those who, feeling this, want to develop this inner nature, to enjoy these high gifts, to order their lives accordingly, to avoid shams and shows, and to possess the real light of life—for such natural Transcendentalists, what shall Goethe's precept avail? Alas! their little lives are not Olympian, like his.

They cannot meet the Ideal everywhere. Poetry does not come to express their every feeling. No Grand Duke calls them to his court. No hosts of followers worship them. Of all this they are not worthy. Yet they ought to find some path, be it never so steep a one, to a truly higher life. Resignation may be the best mood, but Goethe's reason for resignation such souls have not.

Perhaps Schiller's creed may have more meaning for men in general. In fact, Schiller, though no common man, had much more in him that common men may, without trouble, appreciate. His origin was humble, and the way up steep and rough. In his earlier writings the Storm and Stress tendency takes a simpler and cruder form than that of Werther. What Schiller accomplished was for a long time the result of very hard work, done in the midst of great doubt and perplexity. Schiller's ideal is, therefore, to use his own figure, the laborious, oppressed, and finally victorious Hercules—*i. e.*, the man who fears no toil in the service of the highest, who knows that there is something of the divine in him, who restlessly strives to fulfill his destiny, and who at last ascends to the sight and knowledge of the truly perfect. Schiller's maxim, therefore, is: Toil ceaselessly to give thy natural powers their full development, knowing that nothing is worth having but a full consciousness of all that thou hast of good, now latent and unknown within thee. Resignation, therefore, though it is the title of one of Schiller's poems, is never his normal active mood. He retains to the end a good deal of the old Storm and Stress. He is always a sentimental poet, to use the epithet in his own sense; that is, he is always toiling for the ideal, never quite sure that he is possessed of it. He dreams sometimes, that he soon will know the perfect state of mind; but he never does attain, nor does he seem, like Goethe, content with the eternal progress. There is an under-current of complaint and despair in Schiller, which only the splendid enthusiasm of the man keeps, for the most part, out of sight. Some of his poems are largely under its influence.

Now, this creed, in so far as it is earnest and full of faith in the ideal, appeals very much more immediately than does Goethe's creed to the average sensitive mind. Given a soul that is awake to the higher emotions, and if you tell such a one to work earnestly and without rest to develop this better self, you will help him more than if you bid him contemplate the grand attainment of a Goethe, and be resigned to his own experiences as Goethe was to his. For most of us the higher life is to be gained only through weary labor, if at all. But what seems to be lacking in Schiller's creed is a sufficiently concrete definition of the ideal that he seeks. Any attentive reader of *Faust* feels strongly, if vaguely, what it is that Faust is looking for. But one may read Schiller's "Das Ideal und das Leben" a good many times without really seeing what it is that the poor Hercules, or his earthly representative, is seeking. Schiller is no doubt, on the whole, the simpler poet, yet I must say that if I wanted to give any one his first idea of what perfection of mind and character is most worthy of search, I should send such a one to Goethe rather than to Schiller. Schiller talks nobly about the way to perfection, but he defines perfection quite abstractly. Goethe is not very practical in his directions about the road, but surely no higher or clearer ideals of what is good in emotion and action can be put into our minds than those he suggests in almost any passage you please, if he is in a serious mood, and is talking about good and evil at all.

But neither of the classical poets satisfied his readers merely as a moral teacher. As poets, they remain what they always seemed—classics, indeed; but as thinkers they did little more than state a problem. Here is a higher life, and they tell us about it. But wherein consists its significance, how it is to be preached to the race, how sought by each one of us—these questions remain still open.

And open they are, the constant theme for eager discussion and for song all through the early part of the nineteenth century. Close upon the classical period followed the German Romantic school. Young men again, full of earnestness and of glorious experience! On they come, confident that they at least are called to be apostles, determined to reform life and poetry—the one through the other. Surely they will solve the problem, and tell us how to cultivate this all important higher nature. Fichte, the great idealist, whose words set men's hearts afire, or else, alas! make men laugh at him; young Friedrich Schlegel, versatile, liberal in conduct even beyond the bounds that may not safely be passed, bold in spirit even to insolence; the wonderful Novalis, so profound, and yet so unaffected and childlike, so tender in emotion and yet so daring in speculation; Schelling, full of vast philosophic projects; Tieck, skillful weaver of romantic fancies; Schleiermacher, gifted theologian and yet disciple of Spinoza; surely, these are the men to complete the work that will be left unfinished when Schiller dies and Goethe grows older. So at least, they thought and their friends. Never were young men more confident; and yet never did learned and really talented men, to the most of whom was granted long life with vigor, more completely fail to accomplish anything of permanent value in the direction of their early efforts. As mature men, some of them were very influential and useful, but not in the way in which they first sought to be useful. There is to my mind a great and sad fascination in studying the lives and thoughts of this school, in whose fate seems to be exemplified the tragedy of our century. Such aspirations, such talents, and such a failure! Fragments of inspired verse and prose, splendid plans, earnest private letters to friends, prophetic visions and nothing more of enduring worth. Further and further goes the movement, in its worship of the emotional, away from the actual needs of human life. Dramatic art, the test of the poet that has a deep insight into the problems of our nature, is tried, with almost complete failure. The greatest dramatic poet of the new era, one that, if he had lived, might have rivaled Schiller, was Heinrich von Kleist, author of the *Prinz von Homburg*. Driven to despair by unsolved problems and by loneliness, this poet shot himself before his life-work was more than fairly begun. There remain a few dramas, hardly finished, a few powerful tales, and a bundle of fragments to tell us what he was. His fate is typical of the work of the younger school between the 1805 and 1815. There was a keen sense of the worth of emotional experience, and an inability to come into unity with one's aspirations. Life and poetry, as the critics have it, were at variance.

Now, in all this, these men were not merely fighting shadows. What they sought to do is eternally valuable, They felt, and felt nobly, as all generous-minded, warm-hearted youths and maidens at some time do feel. They were not looking for fame alone; they wanted to be and to produce the highest that mortals may. It is a pity that we have not just now more like them. Yet their efforts failed. What problems Goethe and Schiller, men of genius and of good fortune, had solved for themselves alone, men of lesser genius or of less happy lives could only puzzle over. The poetry of the next following age is largely the poetry of melancholy. The emotional movement spread all over Europe; men everywhere strove to make life richer and worthier; and most men grew sad at their little success. Alfred de Musset, in a well known book, has told in the gloomiest strain the story of the unrest, the despair, the impotency of the youth of the Restoration.

Wordsworth and Shelley represent in very much contrasted ways the efforts of English poets to carry on the work of Transcendentalism, and these men succeeded, in this respect, better than their fellows. Wordsworth is full of a sense of the deep meaning of little things and of the most common life. Healthy men, that work like heroes, that have lungs full of mountain air, and that yet retain the simplicity of shepherd life, or children, whose eyes and words teach purity and depth of feeling, are to him the most direct suggestions of the ideal. Life is, for Wordsworth, everywhere an effort to be at once simple and full of meaning; in harmony with nature, and yet not barbarous. But Wordsworth, if he has very much to teach us, seems to lack the persuasive enthusiasm of the poetic leader of men. At all events, his appeal has reached, so far, only a class. He can be all in all to them, his followers, but he did not reform the world. Shelley, is, perhaps, the one of all English poets in this century to whom was given the purest ideal delight in the higher affections. If you want to be eager to act out the best that is in you, read Shelley. If you want to cultivate a sense for the best in the feelings of all human hearts, read Shelley. He has taught very many to long for a worthy life and for purity of spirit. But, alas! Shelley, again, knows not how to teach the way to the acquirement of the end that he so enthusiastically describes. If you can feel with him, he does you good. If you fail to understand him, he is no systematic teacher. At best, he will arouse a longing. He can never wholly satisfy it. Shelley wanted to be no mere writer. He had in him a desire to reform the world. But when he speaks of reform one sees how vague an idea he had of the means. Prometheus, the Titan, who represents in Shelley's poem oppressed humanity, is bound on the mountain. The poem is to tell us of his deliverance. But how is this accomplished? Why, simply when a certain fated hour comes, foreordained, but by nobody in particular, up comes Demogorgon, the spirit of eternity, stalks before the throne of Jupiter, the tyrant, and orders him out into the abyss; and thereupon Prometheus is unchained, and the earth is happy. Why did not all this happen before? Apparently, because Demogorgon did not sooner leave the underworld. What a motive is this for an allegoric account of the deliverance of humanity! Mere accident rules everything, and yet apparently, there is a coming triumph to work for. The poet of lofty emotions is but an eager child when he is to advise us to act.

The melancholy side of the literary era that extends from 1815 to 1840 is represented especially by two poets, Byron and Heine. Both treat the same great problem, What is this life, and what in it is of most worth? Both recognize the need there is for something more than mere existence. Both know the value of emotion, and both would wish to lead men to an understanding of this value, if only they thought that men could be led. Despairing themselves, of ever attaining an ideal peace of mind, they give themselves over to melancholy. Despairing of raising men even to their own level, they become scornful, and spend far too much time in merely negative criticism. The contrast between them is not a little instructive. Byron is too often viewed by superficial readers merely in the light of his early sentimental poems. Those, for our present purpose, may be disregarded. It is the Byron of *Manfred* and *Cain* that I now have in mind. As for Heine, Matthew Arnold long since said the highest in praise of his ethical significance that we may dare to say. Surely both men have great defects. They are one-sided, and often insincere. But they are children of the ideal. Byron has, I think, the greater force of character, but the gift of seeing well what is beautiful and pathetic in life fell to the lot of Heine. The one is great in spirit, the other in experience. Byron is, by nature, combative, a hater of wrong, one often searching for the highest truth; but his experience is petty and heart-sickening, his real world is miserably unworthy of his ideal world, and he seems driven on into the darkness like his own Cain and Manfred. Heine has more the faculty of vision. The perfect delight in a moment of emotion is given to him as it has seldom been given to any man since the unknown makers of the popular ballads. Hence, his frequent use of ballad forms and incidents. Surely, Byron could never have given us that picture of Edith of the Swan's Neck searching for the dead King Harold on the field of Hastings, which Heine has painted in one of the ballads of the *Romancero*. But, on the other hand, Heine lacks the force to put into active life the meaning and beauty that he can so well appreciate. He sees in dreams, but he cannot create in the world the ideal of perfection. So he is bitter and despairing. He takes a cruel delight in pointing out the shams of the actual world. Naturally romantic, he attacks romantic tendencies, ever fresh with hate and scorn. In brief, to live the higher life, and to teach others to live it also, one would have to be heroic in action, like Byron, and gifted with the power to see, as Heine saw, what is precious, and in all its simplicity, noble, about human experience. The union of Byron and Heine would have been a new, and, I think, a higher, sort of Goethe.

Since these have passed away we have had our Emerson, our Carlyle, our Tennyson. Upon these men we cannot dwell now. I pass to the result of the whole long struggle. Humanity was seeking, in these its chosen representative men, to attain to a fuller emotional life. A conflict resulted with the petty and ignoble in human nature, and with the dead resistance of material forces. Men grew old and died in this conflict, did wonderful things, and—did not conquer. And now, at last, Europe gave up the whole effort, and fell to thinking about physical science and about great national movements. The men of the last age are gone, or are fast going, and we are left face to face with a dangerous practical materialism. The time is one of unrest, but not of great moral leaders. Action is called for, and, vigorous as we are, spiritual activity is not one of the specialties of the modern world.

So much, then, for the reasons why what I have for brevity's sake called Transcendentalism lost its hold on the life of the century. The reasons were briefly these: First, the ideal sought by the men of the age of which we have spoken was too selfish, not broad and human enough. Goethe might save himself, but he could not teach us the road. Secondly, men did not strive long and earnestly enough. Surely, if the problems of human conduct are to be solved, if life is to be made full of emotion, strong, heroic, and yet not cold, we must all unite, men, women, and children, in the common cause of living ourselves as best we can, and of helping others, by spoken and by written word, to do the same. We lack perseverance and leaders. Thirdly, the splendid successes of certain modern investigations have led away men's minds from the study of the conduct of life to a study of the evolution of life. I respect the latter study, but I do not believe it fills the place of the former. I wish there were time in our hurried modern life, for both. I know there must be found time, and that right quickly, for the study of the old problems of the Faust of Goethe.

With this conclusion, the present study arrives at the goal set at the beginning. How we are to renew these old discussions, what solution of them we are to hope for, whether we shall ever finally solve them, what the true ideal of life is—of all such matters I would not presume to write further at this present. But let us not forget that if our Evolution textbooks contain much of solid—yes, of inspiring—truth, they do not contain all the knowledge that is essential to a perfect life or to the needs of humanity. A philosophy made possible by the deliberate neglect of that thought-movement, whose literary expression was the poetry of our century, cannot itself be broad enough and deep enough finally to do away with the needs embodied in that thought-movement. Let one, knowing this fact, be therefore, earnest in the search for whatever may make human life more truly worth living. Let him read again, if he has read before, or begin to read, if he has never read, our Emerson, our Carlyle, our Tennyson, or the men of years ago, who so aroused the ardent souls of the best among our fathers. Let him study Goethe, Schiller, Heine, Wordsworth, anything and everything that can arouse in him a sense of our true spiritual needs. And having read, let him work in the search after the ideal—work not for praise but for the good of his time.

And then, perhaps, some day a new and a mightier Transcendental Movement may begin—a great river, that shall not run to waste and be lost in the deserts of sentimental melancholy.

Edwards and Emerson

Josiah Royce

Fifty years since, if competent judges were asked to name the American thinkers from whom there had come novel and notable and typical contributions to general philosophy, they could in reply mention only two men—Jonathan Edwards and Ralph Waldo Emerson. For the conditions that determine a fair answer to the question, "Who are your representative American philosophers?" are obvious. The philosopher who can fitly represent the contribution of his nation to the world's treasury of philosophical ideas must first be one who thinks for himself, fruitfully, with true independence, and with successful inventiveness, about problems of philosophy. And, secondly, he must be a man who gives utterance to philosophical ideas which are characteristic of some stage and of some aspect of the spiritual life of his own people. In Edwards and in Emerson, and only in these men, had these two conditions found their fulfillment, so far as our American civilization had yet expressed itself in the years that had preceded our civil war. {. . .} Therefore {Edwards} was, in order of time, the first of our nationally representative philosophers.

Another stage of our civilization—a later phase of our national ideals—found its representative in Emerson. He too was in close touch with many of the world's deepest thoughts concerning ultimate problems. Some of the ideas that most influenced him have their far-off historical origins in oriental as well as in Greek thought, and also their nearer foreign sources in modern European philosophy, but he transformed what ever he assimilated. He invented upon the basis of his personal experience, and so he was himself no disciple of the orient, or of Greece, still less of England and Germany. He thought, felt, and spoke as an American.

Fifty years ago, I say, our nation had so far found these two men to express each his own stage of the philosophy of our national civilization. The essence of a philosophy, in case you look at it solely from a historical point of view, always appears to you thus: A great philosophy expresses an interpretation of the life of man and a view of the universe, which is at once personal, and, if the thinker is representative of his people, national in its significance. Edwards and Emerson had given tongue to the meaning of two different stages of our American culture. And these were thus far our only philosophical voices. {. . .}

Friedrich Nietzsche (1844–1900)

Lionel Trilling remarked, in an essay included in this volume, that Nietzsche's "admiration of Emerson is always an engaging surprise." Harold Bloom notes, also in the present collection, that "Nietzsche, who could tolerate so few of his own contemporaries, delighted in Emerson, and seems to have understood Emerson very well." An appreciable amount of scholarship has been devoted to the ways in which Emerson is, as Pamela Schirmeister puts it, Nietzsche's "true intellectual father,"[1] or as Nietzsche himself characterized his relation to the American in 1883: "I feel in Emerson a brother soul." The following year, while writing Thus Spoke Zarathustra, *have having had some of Emerson's work translated, Nietzsche noted: "I don't know how much I would give to effect retroactively the strict disciplining, the real scholarly education of so great and splendid a nature, with its spiritual and intellectual wealth. As it is, we have lost a philosopher in Emerson." Since Hermann Hummel wrote in 1946 that "the relation between Nietzsche and Emerson has been the subject of much suggestive comment, but never of exhaustive research" many scholars have contributed brilliantly to accounts of Emerson's substantive influence on Nietzsche— and even, as Stanley Cavell has argued, how Nietzsche's affirmation of Emerson helped to rehabilitate Emerson in America through a sort of foreign legitimation. The vast literature on the influence and effects of Nietzsche's love of Emerson—he carried a copy of Emerson's* Essays *with him for twenty-five years—includes essential contributions from Stanley Cavell, George Kateb, Lawrence Buell, George Stack, David Mikics, and Jennifer Ratner-Rosenhagen. In the following extracts from* Untimely Mediations *(1876), the* Gay Science *(1882), and* Twilight of the Idols *(1888) we encounter first-hand some of the more overt ways in which Nietzsche acknowledged and incorporated Emerson into his own writing.[2]*

from Schopenhauer as Educator in *Untimely Meditations*

Friedrich Nietzsche

These, then, are some of the conditions under which the philosophical genius can at any rate come into existence in our time despite the forces working against it: free manliness of character, early knowledge of mankind, no scholarly education, no narrow patriotism, no necessity for bread-winning, no ties with the state—in short, freedom and again freedom: that wonderful and perilous element in which the Greek philosophers were able to grow up. Whoever wants to reproach him, as

Niebuhr reproached Plato, with being a bad citizen, let him do so and be a good citizen himself: thus he will be in the right and so will Plato. Another will see this great freedom as a piece of presumption: he too is right, for he himself would do nothing with it and it would be very presumptuous in him to claim it for himself. That freedom is in fact a heavy debt which can be discharged only by means of great deeds. In truth, every ordinary son of earth has the right to regard with resentment a man favoured in this way: only may some god guard him from being thus favoured himself, that is from becoming so fearfully indebted. For he would at once perish of his freedom and solitude, and become a fool, and a malicious fool at that, out of boredom.—

From what we have discussed perhaps some father or other may be able to learn something and apply it in some way to the private education of his son; though it is truly not to be expected that fathers will want only philosophers for sons. It is probable that fathers in every age have put up the most determined resistance to their sons' being philosophers, as though it were extremely perverse; as is well known, Socrates fell victim to the wrath of the fathers over his 'seduction of youth', and Plato for that reason considered it necessary to institute a whole new state if the existence of the philosopher was not to be imperiled by the unreason of the fathers. It almost looks now as though Plato really did achieve something. For the modern state regards the promotion of philosophy as among *its* tasks and seeks at all times to bless a number of men with that 'freedom' which we understand as the most essential condition for the genesis of the philosopher. But historically speaking Plato has been singularly unfortunate: as soon as a structure has appeared which has essentially corresponded to his proposals, it has always turned out on close examination to be a changeling, an ugly elf-child; such as the medieval priestly state was by comparison with the rule of the 'sons of god' he had dreamed of. The last thing the modern state wants to do, of course, is to install philosophers as rulers—God be praised! every Christian will add—: but even promotion of philosophy as the state understands it will one day have to be inspected to see whether the state understands it *Platonically*, which is to say as seriously and honestly as though its highest objective were to produce new Platos. If the philosopher as a rule appears in his age by chance—does the state now really set itself the task of consciously translating this fortuitousness into necessity and here too rendering assistance to nature?

Experience unfortunately teaches us better—or rather, worse: it tells us that nothing stands so much in the way of the production and propagation of the great philosopher by nature as does the bad philosopher who works for the state. A painful fact, is it not?—recognizably the same as that to which Schopenhauer first directed attention in his celebrated treatise on university philosophy. I shall return to it later: for one has to compel men to take it seriously, that is to say to let it inspire them to action, and I consider every word behind which there does not stand such a challenge to action to have been written in vain; and it is in any event a good thing again to demonstrate the truth of Schopenhauer's always valid propositions, and to do so by direct reference to our closest contemporaries, since a well-disposed man might think that since he launched his accusations everything has taken a turn for the better in Germany. Even on this point, minor though it is, his work is not yet done.

Considered more closely, that 'freedom' with which, as I have said, the state now blesses some men for the good of philosophy is no freedom at all but an office of profit. The promotion of philosophy nowadays consists, it seems, only in the state's enabling a number of men to *live* from their philosophy by making of it a means of livelihood: whereas the sages of ancient Greece were not paid by the state but at most were, like Zeno, honoured with a gold crown and a monument in the Ceramicus. Whether truth is served when one is shown a way of living off it I cannot say in general, because here it all depends on the quality of the individual who is shown it. I could well envisage a degree of pride and self-esteem which would lead a man to say to his fellow-men: look after me, for I have something better to do, namely to look after you. In the case of Plato or Schopenhauer, such grandeur of disposition and expression would not alienate one; which is why precisely they could even be university philosophers, as Plato was for a time a court philosopher, without demeaning the dignity of philosophy. But even Kant was, as we scholars are accustomed to be, cautious, subservient and, in his attitude towards the state, without greatness: so that, if university philosophy should ever be called to account, he at any rate could not justify it. And if there are natures capable of justifying it—such natures as those of Schopenhauer and Plato—I fear they will never have occasion for doing so, since no state would ever dare to favour such men and install them in university posts. Why is that so? Because every state fears them and will favour only philosophers it does not fear. For it does happen that the state is afraid of philosophy as such, and when this is the case it will try all the more to draw to it philosophers who will give it the appearance of having philosophy on its side—because it has on its side those men who bear the name of philosopher and yet are patently nothing to inspire fear. If, however, a man should arise who really gave the impression of intending to apply the scalpel of truth to all things, including the body of the state, then the state would, since it affirms its own existence before all else, be justified in expelling such a man and treating him as an enemy: just as it expels and treats as an enemy a religion which sets itself above the state and desires to be its judge. So if anyone is to tolerate being a philosopher in the employ of the state, he will also have to tolerate being regarded as having abandoned any attempt to pursue truth into all its hideouts. At the very least he is obliged, so long as he is the recipient of favours and offices, to recognize something as being higher than truth, namely the state. And not merely the state but at the same time everything the state considers necessary for its wellbeing: a certain form of religion, for example, or of social order, or of army regulations—a *noli me tangere [do not touch me]* is inscribed upon everything of this sort. Can a university philosopher ever have realized to the full the whole gamut of duties and limitations imposed upon him? I do not know; if he has done so and has nonetheless remained an official of the state he has been a bad friend of truth; if he has never done so—well, I would say he would still be no friend of truth.

This is the most general objection: to people as they are now, however, it is of course the weakest objection and the one to which they are most indifferent. Most will be content to shrug their shoulders and say: 'as though anything great and pure has ever been able to maintain itself on this earth without making concessions to human baseness! Would you prefer it if the state persecuted the philosopher rather than paid him and took him into service?' Without immediately replying to this question, I shall only observe that these concessions to the state on the part of philosophy go very far at the present time. Firstly: it is the state which selects its philosophical servants, and which selects just the number it needs to supply its institutions; it therefore takes on the appearance of being able to distinguish between good philosophers and bad ones and, even worse, it presupposes that there must always be a sufficiency of *good* philosophers to fill all its academic chairs. It is now the authority, not only with regard to the quality of philosophers, but also in regard to how many good philosophers are needed. Secondly: it compels those it has chosen to reside in a certain place, to live among certain people, to undertake a certain activity; they are obliged to instruct every academic youth who desires instruction, and to do so daily at certain fixed hours. Question: can a philosopher really undertake with a good conscience to have something to teach every day? And to teach it to anyone who cares to listen? Will he not be obliged to give the impression of knowing more than he does know? Will he not be obliged to speak before an audience of strangers of things which he can safely speak of only among his nearest friends? And speaking generally: is he not robbing himself of his freedom to follow his genius whenever and wherever it calls him?—through being obligated to think in public about predetermined subjects at predetermined hours? And to do so before youths! Is such thinking not as it were emasculated from the first! Supposing one day he said to himself: I can't think of anything today, at least not of anything worthwhile—he would still have to present himself and pretend to think!

But, you will object, he is not supposed to be a thinker at all, but at most a learned presenter of what others have thought: and as to that, he will always have something to say his pupils do not already know.—But precisely this—to undertake to appear first and foremost as scholarliness—is the third perilous concession which philosophy makes to the state. Above all when it appears as knowledge of the history of philosophy: for to the genius, who gazes upon things as a poet does, with pure and loving eyes, and cannot immerse himself too deeply in them, grubbing around in countless strange and perverse opinions is the most repugnant and inappropriate occupation imaginable. The learned history of the past has never been the business of a true philosopher, neither in India nor in Greece; and if a professor of philosophy involves himself in such work he must at best be content to have it said of him: he is a fine classical scholar, antiquary, linguist, historian—but never: he is a philosopher. And that, as remarked, is only at best: for most of the learned work done by university philosophers seems to a classicist to be done badly, without scientific rigour and mostly with a detestable tediousness. Who, for example, can clear the history of the Greek philosophers of the soporific miasma spread over it by the learned, though not particularly scientific and unfortunately all too tedious, labours of Ritter, Brandis and Zeller? I for one prefer reading Laertius Diogenes to Zeller, because the former at least breathes the spirit of the philosophers of antiquity, while the latter breathes neither that nor any other spirit. And finally, what in the world have our young men to do with the history of philosophy? Is the confusion of opinions supposed to discourage them from having opinions of their own? Are they supposed to learn how to join in the rejoicing at how wonderfully far we ourselves have come? Are they supposed even to learn to hate philosophy or to despise it? One might almost think so when one knows how students have to torment themselves for the sake of their philosophical examinations so as to cram into their poor brain the maddest and most caustic notions of the human spirit together with the greatest and hardest to grasp. The only critique of a philosophy that is possible and that proves something, namely trying to see whether one can live in accordance with it, has never been taught at universities: all that has ever been taught is a critique of words by means of other words. And now imagine a youthful head, not very experienced in living, in which fifty systems in the form of words and fifty critiques of them are preserved side-by-side and intermingled—what a desert, what a return to barbarism, what a mockery of an education in philosophy! But of course it is admittedly no such thing; it is a training in passing philosophical examinations, the usual outcome of which is well known to be that the youth to be tested—tested all too severely, alas!—admits to himself with a sigh of relief: 'Thank God I am no philosopher, but a Christian and a citizen of my country!'

What if this sigh of relief were the state's actual objective and 'education in philosophy' only a means of deterring from philosophy? Let one ask oneself this question.— If it really is so, however, there is only one thing to be feared: that youth may one day finally come to realize to what end philosophy is here being misused. The supreme objective, the production of the philosophical genius, nothing but a pretext? The goal perhaps the prevention of his production? The meaning of it all reversed into its opposite? In that case—woe to the whole complex of state and professorial policy!—

And is something of the sort not supposed to have transpired already? I do not know; but I do know that university philosophy is now the object of universal disrespect and scepticism. This is in part due to the fact that a feebler race now holds sway over the lecture-room; and if Schopenhauer had to write his treatise on university philosophy now, he would no longer have need of the club but would conquer with a reed. They are the heirs and progeny of those pseudo-thinkers whose much-turned heads he battered: their appearance is sufficiently infantile and dwarfish for us to be reminded of the Indian saying: 'Men are born, in accordance with their deeds, stupid, dumb, deaf, misshapen.' Their fathers deserved such a progeny by virtue of their 'deeds', as the saying has it. That is why it is quite indisputable that academic youth will very soon be able to manage without the philosophy taught at their universities, and that unacademic men are already able to manage without it. One has only to recall one's own student days; in my case, for example, academic philosophers were men towards whom I was perfectly indifferent: I counted them as people who raked together something for themselves out of the results of the other sciences and employed their leisure time in reading newspapers and going to concerts, and for the rest were treated by their own academic comrades with a politely masked contempt. They were credited with knowing little and with never being at a loss for some obscure expression with which to conceal this lack of knowledge. They thus preferred to dwell in gloomy places where the clear-eyed cannot endure to be for long. One of them urged it against the natural sciences: none of them can completely explain to me the simplest process of becoming, so what have any of them to do with me? Another said of history: to him who has ideas it has nothing new to say—in short, they always discovered reasons why it was more philosophical to know nothing than to learn something. If they did engage in learning, their secret motive in doing so was to elude science and to found a dark domain in one or other of its lacunae. Thus they went on ahead of the sciences only in the sense that the deer is ahead of the huntsmen who are after it. Lately they have been content to assert that they are really no more than the frontier guards and spies of the sciences; to which end they are especially served by the teachings of Kant, out of which they are intent upon fashioning an idle scepticism that will soon be of no interest to anybody. Only now and then does one of them still hoist himself up to a little system of metaphysics, with the consequences that usually follow, namely dizziness, headache and nosebleed. After having so often enjoyed no success on this trip into the mist and clouds, after some rude, hard-headed disciple of the real sciences has again and again seized them by the pigtail and pulled them back down, their face habitually assumes an expression of primness and of having been found out. They have lost their confidence, so that none of them lives even a moment for the sake of his philosophy. Formerly some of them believed themselves capable of inventing new religions or of replacing old ones with their philosophical systems; nowadays they have lost all this old arrogance and are as a rule pious, timid and uncertain folk, never brave like Lucretius or wrathful at human oppression. Neither can one any longer learn from them how to think logically and, with a correct estimation of their powers, they have ceased the formal disputations they used to practise. It is indisputable that the individual sciences are now pursued more logically, cautiously, modestly, inventively, in short more philosophically, than is the case with so-called philosophers: so that everyone will agree with the impartial Englishman Bagehot when he says of our contemporary system-builders: 'Who is not almost sure beforehand that they will contain a strange mixture of truth and error, and therefore that it will not be worthwhile to spend life in reasoning over their consequences? The mass of a system attracts the young and impresses the unwary; but cultivated people are very dubious about it. They are ready to receive hints and suggestions and the smallest real truth is ever welcome. But a large book of deductive philosophy is much to be suspected. Unproved abstract principles without number have been eagerly caught up by sanguine men and then carefully spun out into books and theories which were to explain the whole world. The world goes totally against these abstractions, and it must do so since they require it to go in antagonistic directions.' If formerly philosophers, especially in Germany, used to be sunk in such profound reflection that they were in constant danger of hitting their head on a beam, they are now supplied with a whole regiment of flappers, such as Swift describes in the Voyage to Laputa, to give them a gentle blow now and then on the eyes or elsewhere. Sometimes these blows may be a little too heavy, on which occasions the enraptured thinker can easily forget himself and hit back—something that always results in his discomfiture. Can't you see the beam, you sleepy-head! the flapper then says—and often the philosopher really does see the beam and becomes tractable again. These flappers are history and the natural sciences; they have gradually come so to overawe the German dream- and thought-business which was for long confused with philosophy that these thought-mongers would be only too glad to abandon any attempt at an independent existence; if however they should happen to impede the former or try to fasten leading-strings on to them, the flappers at once start to flap as violently as they can—as though they wanted to say: 'For a thought-monger like this to profane our history or natural sciences would be the last straw! Away with him!' Then they totter back into their own uncertainty and perplexity: they really do want to get a little natural science into their possession, perhaps like the Herbartians in the shape of empirical psychology, they really do want a little history as well—then they can act, at least in public, as though they were engaged in scientific undertakings, even though in private they would like to consign all philosophy and science to the devil.

But granted that this troop of bad philosophers is ludicrous—and who will not grant it?—to what extent are they also *harmful*? The answer, in brief, is: *to the extent that they make philosophy itself ludicrous*. As long as this officially recognized guild of pseudo-thinkers continues to exist, any effectiveness of a true philosophy will be brought to naught or at least obstructed, and it will suffer this fate through nothing other than the curse of the ludicrous which the representatives of that philosophy have called down upon themselves but which also strikes at philosophy itself. That is why I say it is a demand of culture that philosophy should be deprived of any kind of official academic recognition and that state and academy be relieved of the task, which they cannot encompass, of distinguishing between real and apparent philosophy. Let the philosophers grow untended, deny them all prospect of place and position within the bourgeois professions, cease to entice them with salaries, more, persecute them, show them disfavour—you will behold miracles! The poor seeming philosophers will flee apart and seek a roof wherever they can find it; one will become a parson, another a schoolmaster, a third will creep into the shelter of an editorial job on a newspaper, a fourth will write instruction manuals for girls' high schools, the most sensible of them will take up the plough and the vainest will go to court. Suddenly it will all be empty, everyone will have flown the nest: for it is easy to get rid of bad philosophers, one only has to cease rewarding them. And that is in any event more advisable than for the state publicly to patronize any philosophy, *whichever it may be*.

The state never has any use for truth as such, but only for truth which is useful to it, more precisely for anything whatever useful to it whether it be truth, half-truth or error. A union of state and philosophy can therefore make sense only if philosophy can promise to be unconditionally useful to the state, that is to say, to set usefulness to the state higher than truth. It would of course be splendid for the state if it also had truth in its pay and service; but the state itself well knows that it is part of the *essence* of truth that it never accepts pay or stands in anyone's service. Thus what the state has is only false 'truth', a person in a mask; and unfortunately this cannot do for it what it so much desires genuine truth to do: validate and sanctify it. It is true that if a medieval prince wanted to be crowned by the Pope but the Pope refused to do it, he nominated an anti-Pope who then performed for him this service. This might have worked then to some extent; but for a modern state to nominate an anti-philosophy to legitimatize it will not work: for it will still have philosophy against it as before, and now more than before. I believe in all seriousness that it is more useful to the state to have nothing at all to do with philosophy, to desire nothing from it and for as long as possible to regard it as something to which it is completely indifferent. If this condition of indifference does not endure, if it becomes dangerous and hostile to the state, then let the state persecute it.—Since the state can have no interest in the university other than seeing it raise useful and devoted citizens of the state, it should hesitate to place this usefulness and devotion in jeopardy by demanding that these young men should sit an examination in philosophy: it could well be, of course, that the dull and incompetent would be frightened off university study altogether by this spectre of a philosophy examination; but this gain could not compensate for the harm done to rash and restless youth by this enforced drudgery; they get to know books forbidden them, begin to criticize their teachers and finally even become aware of the objective of university philosophy and its examinations—not to speak of the misgivings which this circumstance can excite in young theologians and as a result of which they are beginning to die out in Germany, as the ibex is in the Tyrol.—I understand well enough the objections the state could have raised against this whole way of looking at things so long as the fair green shoots of Hegelianism were sprouting up in every field: but now that this harvest has come to nothing, all the expectations built upon it have proved vain and all the barns remained empty—one prefers no longer to raise objections but to turn away from philosophy altogether. One now possesses power: formerly, in Hegel's time, one wanted to possess it—that is a vast distinction. Philosophy has become superfluous to the state because the state no longer needs its sanction. If the state no longer maintains its professors or, as I foresee in the near future, appears to maintain them but in fact neglects them, it derives advantage from doing so—yet it appears to me of more importance that the universities should see that it is to their benefit too. At least I would think that an institution for the real sciences must see it is good for it no longer to have to keep company with a semi-science. The universities enjoy so little regard, moreover, they must on principle desire the exclusion of disciplines which academics themselves hold in low esteem. For non-academics have good reason for a certain general disrespect for universities; they reproach them with being cowardly, since the small ones fear the big ones and the big ones fear public opinion; with failing to take the lead in questions of higher culture but limping slowly and tardily in the rear, with ceasing to maintain the respected sciences on their true course. Linguistic studies, for example, are pursued more zealously than ever, but no one considers it necessary to educate himself in correct writing and speaking. Indian antiquity is opening its gates, yet the relationship of those who study it to the imperishable works of the Indians, to their philosophies, hardly differs from that of an animal to a lyre: even though Schopenhauer considered its acquaintance with Indian philosophy the greatest advantage our century possessed over all others. Classical antiquity has become a take-it-or-leave-it antiquity and has ceased to produce a classic and exemplary effect; a fact demonstrated by its disciples, who are truly not exemplary. Whither has the spirit of Friedrich August Wolf departed, of which Franz Passow could say it appeared a genuinely patriotic, genuinely human spirit which, if it needed to, possessed the force to set a continent on fire and in ferment—where has this spirit gone? On the other hand, the spirit of the journalist is penetrating the universities more and more, and not seldom under the name of philosophy; a smooth, highly coloured mode of address, Faust and Nathan the Wise constantly invoked, the language and views of our nauseating literary journals, lately even chattering about our sacred German music and the demand for chairs for the study of Goethe and Schiller—all signs that the spirit of the university is beginning to confuse itself with the *Zeitgeist*. It thus seems to me of the first importance that there should be created outside the universities a higher tribunal whose function would be to supervise and judge these institutions in regard to the education they are promoting; and as soon as philosophy departs from the universities, and therewith purifies itself of all unworthy considerations and prejudices, it must constitute precisely such a tribunal: devoid of official authority, without salaries or honours, it will know how to perform its duty free of the *Zeitgeist* and free from fear of it—in short, as Schopenhauer lived, as the judge of the so-called culture around him. In this way the philosopher, if instead of amalgamating with it he supervises it from a dignified distance, is able to be of use to the university.

Finally, however—of what concern to us is the existence of the state, the promotion of universities, when what matters above all is the existence of philosophy on earth! or—to leave absolutely no doubt as to what I think—if it is so unspeakably more vital that a philosopher should appear on earth than that a state or a university should continue to exist. The dignity of philosophy can increase in the measure that servitude to public opinion and the danger to freedom increases; it was at its greatest during the earthquake attending the fall of the Roman republic and during the imperial era, when its name and that of history became *ingrata principibus nomina [names displeasing to princes]*. Brutus demonstrates more for its dignity than does Plato; he belonged to an age in which ethics ceased to be platitudinous. If philosophy is little regarded at present, one ought only to ask why it is that no great general or statesman at present has anything to do with it—the answer is simply that at the time he sought it he encountered a feeble phantom bearing the name of philosophy, a scholarly lecture-hall wisdom and lecture-hall cautiousness; in short, it is because in his early years philosophy became to him something ludicrous. What it ought to be to him, however, is something fearsome, and men called to the search for power ought to know what a source of the heroic wells within it. Let an American tell them what a great thinker who arrives on this earth signifies as a new centre of tremendous forces. 'Beware', says Emerson, 'when the great God lets loose a thinker on this planet. Then all things are at risk. It is as when a conflagration has broken out in a great city, and no man knows what is safe, or where it will end. There is not a piece of science but its flank may be turned tomorrow; there is not any literary reputation, not the so-called eternal names of fame, that may not be revised and condemned; the things which are dear to men at this hour are so on account of the ideas which have emerged on their mental horizon, and which cause the present order of things, as a tree bears its apples. *A new degree of culture would instantly revolutionize the entire system of human pursuits*.[3] Now, if such thinkers are dangerous, it is of course clear why our academic thinkers are not dangerous; for their thoughts grow as peacefully out of tradition as any tree ever bore its apples: they cause no alarm, they remove nothing from its hinges; and of all their art and aims there could be said what Diogenes said when someone praised a philosopher in his presence: 'How can he be considered great, since he has been a philosopher for so long and has never yet *disturbed* anybody?' That, indeed, ought to be the epitaph of university philosophy: 'it disturbed nobody'. But this, of course, is praise of an old woman rather than of the goddess of truth, and it is not to be wondered at if those who know that goddess only as an old woman are themselves very unmanly and thus, as might be expected, completely ignored by the men of power.

But if this is how things stand in our time, then the dignity of philosophy is trampled into the dust; it has even become something ludicrous, it would seem, or a matter of complete indifference to anyone: so that it is the duty of all its true friends to bear witness against this confusion, and at the least to show that it is only its false and unworthy servants who are ludicrous or a matter of indifference. It would be better still if they demonstrated by their deeds that love of truth is something fearsome and mighty.

Schopenhauer demonstrated both these things—and will demonstrate them more and more as day succeeds day.

Notes

1   Ralph Waldo Emerson, *Representative Men*, ed. Pamela Schirmeister (New York: Marsilio Publishers, 1995), ix.
2   Selections from Nietzsche's works are drawn from the following editions and translations: "Schopenhauer as Educator," *Untimely Meditations*, trans. R. J. Hollingdale (Cambridge: Cambridge University Press, 1983), 182–194; Section 92, *The Gay Science: with a Prelude of Rhymes and an Appendix of Songs*, trans. Walter Kaufmann (New York: Random House, 1974), 145–146; and, "Raids of an Untimely Man," *Twilight of the Idols: Or, How to Philosophize with a Hammer*, trans. Richard Polt (Indianapolis: Hackett Publishing Company, Inc., 1997), 58–59.
3   Ralph Waldo Emerson, "Circles" in *The Complete Works of Ralph Waldo Emerson*, Concord Edition (Boston: Houghton, Mifflin and Company, 1903–4), Vol. II.

from *The Gay Science*

Friedrich Nietzsche

§ 92

Prose and poetry.—It is noteworthy that the great masters of prose have almost always been poets, too—if not publicly than at least secretly, in the "closet." Good prose is written only face to face with poetry. For it is an uninterrupted, well-mannered war with poetry: all of its attractions depend on the way in which poetry is continually avoided and contradicted. Everything abstract wants to be read as a prank against poetry and as with a mocking voice; everything dry and cool is meant to drive the lovely goddess into lovely despair. Often there are *rapprochements*, reconciliations for a moment—and then a sudden leap back and laughter. Often the curtain is raised and harsh light let in just as the goddess is enjoying her dusks and muted colors. Often the words are taken out of her mouth and sung to a tune that drives her to cover her refined ears with her refined hands. Thus there are thousands of delights in this war, including the defeats of which the unpoetic souls, the so-called prose-men, do not know a thing; hence they write and speak only *bad* prose. *War is the father of all good things*; war is also the father of good prose.

Four very strange and truly poetic human beings in this century have attained mastery in prose, for which this century was not made otherwise—for lack of poetry, as I have suggested. Not including Goethe, who may fairly be claimed by the century that produced him, I regard only Giacomo Leopardi, Prosper Mérimée, Ralph Waldo Emerson, and Walter Savage Landor, the author of *Imaginary Conversations*, as worthy of being called masters of prose.

from Raids of an Untimely Man in *Twilight of the Idols*

Friedrich Nietzsche

Emerson.—Much more enlightened, venturesome, complex, refined than Carlyle; above all, happier . . . The sort of man who instinctively feeds only on ambrosia, who leaves behind whatever is indigestible in things. In comparison to Carlyle, a man of taste.—Carlyle, who loved him very much, nevertheless said of him: "he does not give *us* enough to chew on"—which he may have been right to say, but not to Emerson's disadvantage.—Emerson has that good-natured and brilliant cheerfulness that deters all seriousness; he simply does not know how old he already is and how young he will still be—he could say of himself, in the words of Lope de Vega, *"yo me sucedo a mi mismo"* [*"I am my own successor"*]. His spirit always finds reasons to be content and even thankful; and on occasion he approaches the cheerful transcendence of that worthy man who came back from an amorous tryst *tamquam re bene gesta [as if the deed had been well done].* "*Ut desint vires,*" he said thankfully, "*tamen est laudanda voluptas*" [*"Though the power is lacking, the lust is to be praised"*].

William James (1842–1910)

James was an infant in 1842 when Emerson met his father in New York City while lecturing on "The Times" at The New York Society Library. The bonds were immediately and strongly felt: Emerson was named James' godfather, and became part of the Jameses' family life; the guest room of the Washington Square house was referred to as "Mr. Emerson's Room." As James matured, he read more closely in Emerson's work, and proved both temperamentally and intellectually receptive to Emerson: "James had the same optative ebullience, the same metaphorical panache, the same bedrock faith in the individual," notes biographer Robert D. Richardson.[1] When James gave the following address in 1903, marking the centenary of Emerson's birth—a work that fittingly reads at times like a eulogy for a family member—he was already the author of Principles of Psychology *(1890),* The Will to Believe *(1897), and the just-published* Varieties of Religious Experience *(1902). When James sketched what he called a "motto for my philosophy," he selected from Emerson: "We are born believing. A man bears beliefs as a tree bears apples." The re-reading of Emerson that James undertook to prepare this address appears to have convinced him, as he wrote to his brother Henry, to transition from "University business" to "a different manner," a simpler, more contemplative phase in which to write "such impressions as my own intellect has received from the universe."*

Address at the Emerson Centenary in Concord

William James

The pathos of death is this, that when the days of one's life are ended, those days that were so crowded with business and felt so heavy in their passing, what remains of one in memory should usually be so slight a thing. The phantom of an attitude, the echo of a certain mode of thought, a few pages of print, some invention, or some victory we gained in a brief critical hour, are all that can survive the best of us. It is as if the whole of a man's significance had now shrunk into the phantom of an attitude, into a mere musical note or phrase suggestive of his singularity—happy are those whose singularity gives a note so clear as to be victorious over the inevitable pity of such a diminution and abridgment.

An ideal wraith like this, of Emerson's personality, hovers over all Concord to-day, taking, in the minds of those of you who were his neighbors and intimates a somewhat fuller shape, remaining more abstract in the younger generation, but bringing home to all of us the notion of a spirit indescribably precious. The form that so lately moved upon these streets and country roads, or awaited in these fields and woods the beloved Muse's visits, is now dust; but the soul's note, the spiritual voice, rises strong and clear above the uproar of the times, and seems securely destined to exert an ennobling influence over future generations.

What gave a flavor so matchless to Emerson's individuality was, even more than his rich mental gifts, their singularly harmonious combination. Rarely has a man so accurately known the limits of his genius or so unfailingly kept within them. "Stand by your order," he used to say to youthful students; and perhaps the paramount impression one gets of his life is of his loyalty to his own personal type and mission. The type was that of what he liked to call the scholar, the perceiver of pure truth; and the mission was that of the reporter in worthy form of each perception. The day is good, he said, in which we have the most perceptions. There are times when the cawing of a crow, a weed, a snowflake, or a farmer planting in his field become symbols to the intellect of truths equal to those which the most majestic phenomena can open. Let me mind my own charge, then, walk alone, consult the sky, the field and forest, sedulously waiting every morning for the news concerning the structure of the universe which the good Spirit will give me.

This was the first half of Emerson, but only half; for genius, as he said, is insatiate for expression, and truth has to be clad in the right verbal garment. The form of the garment was so vital with Emerson that it is impossible to separate it from the matter. They form a chemical combination—thoughts which would be trivial expressed otherwise, are important through the nouns and verbs to which he married them. The style is the man, it has been said; the man Emerson's mission culminated in his style, and if we must define him in one word, we have to call him Artist. He was an artist whose medium was verbal and who wrought in spiritual material.

This duty of spiritual seeing and reporting determined the whole tenor of his life. It was to shield this duty from invasion and distraction that he dwelt in the country, that he consistently declined to entangle himself with associations or to encumber himself with functions which, however he might believe in them, he felt were duties for other men and not for him. Even the care of his garden, "with its stoopings and fingerings in a few yards of space," he found "narrowing and poisoning," and took to long free walks and saunterings instead, without apology. "Causes" innumerable sought to enlist him as their "worker"—all got his smile and word of sympathy, but none entrapped him into service. The struggle against slavery itself, deeply as it appealed to him, found him firm:

> God must govern his own world, and knows his way out of this pit without my desertion of my post, which has none to guard it but me. I have quite other slaves to face than those Negroes, to wit, imprisoned thoughts far back in the brain of man, and which have no watchman or lover or defender but me.

This in reply to the possible questions of his own conscience. To hot-blooded moralists with more objective ideas of duty, such a fidelity to the limits of his genius must often have made him seem provokingly remote and unavailable; but we, who can see things in more liberal perspective, must unqualifiably approve the results. The faultless tact with which he kept his safe limits while he so dauntlessly asserted himself within them, is an example fitted to give heart to other theorists and artists the world over.

The insight and creed from which Emerson's life followed can be best summed up in his own verses:

> So nigh is grandeur to our dust,
> So near is God to man!

Through the individual fact there ever shone for him the effulgence of the Universal Reason. The great Cosmic Intellect terminates and houses itself in mortal men and passing hours. Each of us is an angle of its eternal vision, and the only way to be true to our Maker is to be loyal to ourselves. "O rich and various Man!" he cries, "thou palace of sight and sound, carrying in thy senses the morning and the night and the unfathomable galaxy; in thy brain the geometry of the city of God; in thy heart the bower of love and the realms of right and wrong."

If the individual open thus directly into the Absolute, it follows that there is something in each and all of us, even the lowliest, that ought not to consent to borrowing traditions and living at second hand. "If John was perfect, why are you and I alive?" Emerson writes; "As long as any man exists there is some need of him: let him fight for his own." This faith that in a life at first hand there is something sacred is perhaps the most characteristic note in Emerson's writings. The hottest side of him is this non-conformist persuasion, and if his temper could ever verge on common irascibility, it would be by reason of the passionate character of his feelings on this point. The world is still new and untried. In seeing freshly, and not in hearing of what others saw, shall a man find what truth is. "Each one of us can bask in the great morning which rises out of the Eastern Sea, and be himself one of the children of the light." "Trust thyself, every heart vibrates to that iron string. There is a time in each man's education when he must arrive at the conviction that imitation is suicide; when he must take himself for better or worse as his portion; and know that though the wide universe is full of good, no kernel of nourishing corn can come to him but through his toil bestowed on that plot of ground which it was given him to till."

The matchless eloquence with which Emerson proclaimed the sovereignty of the living individual electrified and emancipated his generation, and this bugle-blast will doubtless be regarded by future critics as the soul of his message. The present man is the aboriginal reality, the Institution is derivative, and the past man is irrelevant and obliterate for present issues. "If anyone would lay an axe to your tree with a text from I John, vs. 7, or a sentence from Saint Paul, say to him," Emerson wrote, "'My tree is Yggdrasil, the tree of life.' Let him know by your security that your conviction is clear and sufficient, and, if he were Paul himself, that you also are here and with your Creator." "Cleave ever to God," he insisted, "against the name of God";—and so, in spite of the intensely religious character of his total thought, when he began his career it seemed to many of his brethren in the clerical profession that he was little more than an iconoclast and desecrator.

Emerson's belief that the individual must in reason be adequate to the vocation for which the Spirit of the world has called him into being, is the source of those sublime pages, hearteners, and sustainers of our youth, in which he urges his hearers to be incorruptibly true to their own private conscience. Nothing can harm the man who rests in his appointed place and character. Such a man is invulnerable; he balances the universe, balances it as much by keeping small when he is small, as by being great and spreading when he is great. "I love and honor Epaminondas," said Emerson, "but I do not wish to be Epaminondas. I hold it more just to love the world of this hour than the world of his hour. Nor can you, if I am true, excite me to the least uneasiness by saying, 'He acted and thou sittest still.' I see action to be good when the need is, and sitting still to be also good. Epaminondas, if he was the man I take him for, would have sat still with joy and peace, if his lot had been mine. Heaven is large, and affords space for all modes of love and fortitude." "The fact that I am here certainly shows me that the Soul has need of an organ here, and shall I not assume the post?"

The vanity of all superserviceableness and pretence was never more happily set forth than by Emerson in the many passages in which he develops this aspect of his philosophy. Character infallibly proclaims itself. "Hide your thoughts!—hide the sun and moon. They publish themselves to the universe. They will speak through you though you were dumb. They will flow out of your actions, your manners and your face. . . . Don't say things: What you are stands over you the while and thunders so that I cannot hear what you say to the contrary. . . . What a man *is* engraves itself upon him in letters of light. Concealment avails him nothing, boasting nothing. There is confession in the glances of our eyes; in our smiles; in salutations; and the grasp of hands. His sin bedaubs him, mars all his good impression. Men know not why they do not trust him, but they do not trust him. His vice glasses the eye, casts lines of mean expression in the cheek, pinches the nose, sets the mark of the beast upon the back of the head, and writes, O fool! fool! on the forehead of a king. If you would not be known to do a thing, never do it; a man may play the fool in the drifts of a desert, but every grain of sand shall seem to see—How can a man be concealed? How can he be concealed?"

On the other hand, never was a sincere word or a sincere thought utterly lost. "Never a magnanimity fell to the ground but there is some heart to greet and accept it unexpectedly. . . . The hero fears not that if he withstood the avowal of a just and brave act, it will go unwitnessed and unloved. One knows it,—himself—and is pledged by it to sweetness of peace and to nobleness of aim, which will prove in the end a better proclamation than the relating of the incident."

The same indefeasible right to be exactly what one is, provided one only be authentic, spreads itself, in Emerson's way of thinking, from persons to things and to times and places. No date, no position is insignificant, if the life that fills it out be only genuine:

In solitude, in a remote village, the ardent youth loiters and mourns. With inflamed eye, in this sleeping wilderness, he has read the story of the Emperor, Charles the Fifth, until his fancy has brought home to the surrounding woods the faint roar of cannonades in the Milanese, and marches in Germany. He is curious concerning that man's day. What filled it? The crowded orders, the stern

decisions, the foreign despatches, the Castilian etiquette? The soul answers—
Behold his day here! In the sighing of these woods, in the quiet of these gray
fields, in the cool breeze that sings out of these northern mountains; in the
workmen, the boys, the maidens you meet,—in the hopes of the morning, the
ennui of noon, and sauntering of the afternoon; in the disquieting comparisons;
in the regrets at want of vigor; in the great idea and the puny execution,—behold
Charles the Fifth's day; another, yet the same; behold Chatham's, Hampden's,
Bayard's, Alfred's, Scipio's, Pericles's day,—day of all that are born of women. The
difference of circumstance is merely costume. I am tasting the selfsame life,—
its sweetness, its greatness, its pain, which I so admire in other men. Do not
foolishly ask of the inscrutable, obliterated past what it cannot tell,—the details
of that nature, of that day, called Byron or Burke;—but ask it of the enveloping
Now.... Be lord of a day, and you can put up your history books.

"The deep to-day which all men scorn" receives thus from Emerson superb revindication. "Other world! there is no other world." All God's life opens into the individual
particular, and here and now, or nowhere, is reality. "The present hour is the decisive
hour, and every day is doomsday."

Such a conviction that Divinity is everywhere may easily make of one an optimist of
the sentimental type that refuses to speak ill of anything. Emerson's drastic perception
of differences kept him at the opposite pole from this weakness. After you have seen
men a few times, he could say, you find most of them as alike as their barns and pantries,
and soon as musty and as dreary. Never was such a fastidious lover of significance
and distinction, and never an eye so keen for their discovery. His optimism had
nothing in common with that indiscriminate hurrahing for the Universe with which
Walt Whitman has made us familiar. For Emerson, the individual fact and moment
were indeed suffused with absolute radiance, but it was upon a condition that saved
the situation—they must be worthy specimens,—sincere, authentic, archetypal; they
must have made connection with what he calls the Moral Sentiment, they must in
some way act as symbolic mouthpieces of the Universe's meaning. To know just which
thing does act in this way, and which thing fails to make the true connection, is the
secret (somewhat incommunicable, it must be confessed) of seership, and doubtless
we must not expect of the seer too rigorous a consistency. Emerson himself was a real
seer. He could perceive the full squalor of the individual fact, but he could also see
the transfiguration. He might easily have found himself saying of some present-day
agitator against our Philippine conquest what he said of this or that reformer of his
own time. He might have called him, as a private person, a tedious bore and canter.
But he would infallibly have added what he then added: "It is strange and horrible to
say this, for I feel that under him and his partiality and exclusiveness is the earth and
the sea, and all that in them is, and the axis round which the Universe revolves passes
through his body where he stands."

Be it how it may, then, this is Emerson's revelation: The point of any pen can be an
epitome of reality; the commonest person's act, if genuinely actuated, can lay hold on
eternity. This vision is the head-spring of all his outpourings; and it is for this truth,

given to no previous literary artist to express in such penetratingly persuasive tones, that posterity will reckon him a prophet, and, perhaps neglecting other pages, piously turn to those that convey this message. His life was one long conversation with the invisible divine, expressing itself through individuals and particulars: "So nigh is grandeur to our dust, so near is God to man!"

I spoke of how shrunken the wraith, how thin the echo, of men is after they are departed. Emerson's wraith comes to me now as if it were but the very voice of this victorious argument. His words to this effect are certain to be quoted and extracted more and more as time goes on, and to take their place among the Scriptures of humanity. "'Gainst death and all oblivious enmity, shall you pace forth," beloved Master. As long as our English language lasts men's hearts will be cheered and their souls strengthened and liberated by the noble and musical pages with which you have enriched it.

Note

1   Robert D. Richardson, *William James: In the Maelstrom of American Modernism* (Boston: Houghton Mifflin, 2006), 157.

John Dewey (1859–1952)

American philosopher, pragmatist, and educational reformer, Dewey studied at Johns Hopkins and later became the Head of the Department of Philosophy, Psychology, and Pedagogy at the University of Chicago, where he established the Laboratory School. Dewey was among the first scholars to explore critically the meaning and significance of Emerson as a philosopher. Dewey perceived that "philosopher" was not just a simple or descriptive assignation but a title that carried with it crucial cultural insinuations and consequential intellectual implications. In the following remarks presented at a centenary celebration of Emerson's birth at the University of Chicago on May 25, 1903, first published in the International Journal of Ethics *(1903), and later reprinted in* Characters and Events *(1929), Dewey set out to make his position on the matter evident—especially the degree to which Emerson's philosophical thinking contributes to the existence and persistence of democracy. "Plato's own generation would, I think, have found it difficult to class Plato," writes Dewey, acknowledging a tradition of critics who don't know how to class or categorize Emerson, and doubt especially his philosophical credentials. Dewey then suggests: "But at least, thinking of Emerson as the one citizen of the New World fit to have his name uttered in the same breath with that of Plato, one may without presumption believe that even if Emerson has no system, none the less he is the prophet and herald of any system which democracy may henceforth construct and hold by, and that when democracy has articulated itself, it will have no difficulty in finding itself already proposed in Emerson."*

Emerson—The Philosopher of Democracy

John Dewey

It is said that Emerson is not a philosopher. I find this denegation false or true according as it is said in blame or praise—according to the reasons proffered. When the critic writes of lack of method, of the absence of continuity, of coherent logic, and, with the old story of the string of pearls loosely strung, puts Emerson away as a writer of maxims and proverbs, a recorder of brilliant insights and abrupt aphorisms, the critic, to my mind, but writes down his own incapacity to follow a logic that is finely wrought. "We want in every man a long logic; we cannot pardon the absence of it, but it must not be spoken. Logic is the procession or proportionate unfolding of the intuition; but its virtue is as silent method; the moment it would appear as propositions and have a separate value, it is worthless." Emerson fulfills his own requisition. The critic needs the method separately propounded, and not finding his wonted leading-string is all lost. Again, says Emerson, "There is no compliment like the addressing to the human being thoughts out of certain heights and presupposing his intelligence"—a compliment which Emerson's critics have mostly hastened to avert. But to make this short, I am not acquainted with any writer, no matter how assured his position in treatises upon the history of philosophy, whose movement of thought is more compact and unified, nor one who combines more adequately diversity of intellectual attack with concentration of form and effect. I recently read a letter from a gentleman, himself a distinguished writer of philosophy, in which he remarked that philosophers are a stupid class, since they want every reason carefully pointed out and labelled, and are incapable of taking anything for granted. The condescending patronage by literary critics of Emerson's lack of cohesiveness may remind us that philosophers have no monopoly of this particular form of stupidity.

Perhaps those are nearer right, however, who deny that Emerson is a philosopher, because he is more than a philosopher. He would work, he says, by art, not by metaphysics, finding truth "in the sonnet and the play." "I am," to quote him again, "in all my theories, ethics and politics, a poet"; and we may, I think, safely take his word for it that he meant to be a maker rather than a reflector. His own preference was to be ranked with the seers rather than with the reasoners of the race, for he says, "I think that philosophy is still rude and elementary; it will one day be taught by poets. The poet is in the natural attitude; he is believing; the philosopher, after some struggle, having only reasons for believing." Nor do I regard it as impertinent to place by the side of this utterance, that other in which he said "We have yet to learn that the thing uttered in words is not therefore affirmed. It must affirm itself or no forms of grammar and no plausibility can give it evidence and no array of arguments." To Emerson, perception was more potent than reasoning; the deliverances of intercourse more to be desired than the chains of discourse; the surprise of reception more demonstrative than the conclusions of intentional proof. As he said "Good as is discourse, silence is better, and shames it. The length of discourse indicates the distance of thought betwixt the speaker and the hearer." And again, "If I speak, I define and confine, and am less." "Silence is a solvent that destroys personality and gives us leave to be great and universal."

I would not make hard and fast lines between philosopher and poet, yet there is some distinction of accent in thought and of rhythm in speech. The desire for an articulate, not for silent, logic is intrinsic with philosophy. The unfolding of the perception must be stated, not merely followed and understood. Such conscious method is, one might say, the only thing of ultimate concern to the abstract thinker. Not thought, but reasoned thought, not things, but the ways of things, interest him; not even truth, but the paths by which truth is sought. He construes elaborately the symbols of thinking. He is given over to manufacturing and sharpening the weapons of the spirit. Outcomes, interpretations, victories, are indifferent. Otherwise is it with art. That, as Emerson says, is "the path of the creator to his work"; and again "a habitual respect to the whole by an eye loving beauty in detail." Affection is towards the meaning of the symbol, not to its constitution. Only as he wields them, does the artist forge the sword and buckler of the spirit. His affair is to uncover rather than to analyze; to discern rather than to classify. He reads but does not compose.

One, however, has no sooner drawn such lines than one is ashamed and begins to retract. Euripides and Plato, Dante and Bruno, Bacon and Milton, Spinoza and Goethe, rise in rebuke. The spirit of Emerson rises to protest against exaggerating his ultimate value by trying to place him upon a plane of art higher than a philosophic platform. Literary critics admit his philosophy and deny his literature. And if philosophers extol his keen, calm art and speak with some depreciation of his metaphysic, it also is perhaps because Emerson knew something deeper than our conventional definitions. It is indeed true that reflective thinkers have taken the way to truth for their truth; the method of life for the conduct of life—in short, have taken means for end. But it is also assured that in the completeness of their devotion, they have expiated their transgression; means become identified with end, thought turns to life, and wisdom is justified not of herself but of her children. Language justly preserves the difference between philosopher and sophist. It is no more possible to eliminate love and generation from the definition of the thinker than it is thought and limits from the conception of the artist. It is interest, concern, caring, which makes the one as it makes the other. It is significant irony that the old quarrel of philosopher and poet was brought off by one who united in himself more than has another individual the qualities of both artist and metaphysician. At bottom the quarrel is not one of objectives nor yet of methods, but of the affections. And in the divisions of love, there always abides the unity of him who loves. Because Plato was so great he was divided in his affections. A lesser man could not brook that torn love, because of which he set poet and philosopher over against one another. Looked at in the open, our fences between literature and metaphysics appear petty—signs of an attempt to affix the legalities and formularies of property to the things of the spirit. If ever there lived not only a metaphysician but a professor of metaphysics it was Immanuel Kant. Yet he declares that he should account himself more unworthy than the day laborer in the field if he did not believe that somehow, even in his technical classifications and remote distinctions, he too, was carrying forward the struggle of humanity for freedom—that is for illumination.

And for Emerson of all others, there is a one-sidedness and exaggeration, which he would have been the first to scorn, in exalting overmuch his creative substance at the expense of his reflective procedure. He says in effect somewhere that the individual man is only a method, a plan of arrangement. The saying is amply descriptive of Emerson. His idealism is the faith of the thinker in his thought raised to its nth power. "History," he says, "and the state of the world at any one time is directly dependent on the intellectual classification then existing in the minds of men." Again, "Beware when the great God lets loose a thinker on this planet. Then all things are at risk. The very hopes of man, the thoughts of his heart, the religion of nations, the manners and morals of mankind are all at the mercy of a new generalization." And again, "Everything looks permanent until its secret is known. Nature looks provokingly stable and secular, but it has a cause like all the rest; and when once I comprehend that, will these fields stretch so immovably wide, these leaves hang so individually considerable?" And finally, "In history an idea always overhangs like a moon and rules the tide which rises simultaneously in all the souls of a generation." There are times, indeed, when one is inclined to regard Emerson's whole work as a hymn to intelligence, a paean to the all-creating, all-disturbing power of thought.

And so, with an expiatory offering to the Manes of Emerson, one may proceed to characterize his thought, his method, yea, even his system. I find it in the fact that he takes the distinctions and classifications which to most philosophers are true in and of and because of their systems, and makes them true of life, of the common experience of the everyday man. To take his own words for it, "There are degrees in idealism. We learn first to play with it academically, as the magnet was once a toy. Then we see, in the heyday of youth and poetry, that it may be true, that it is true in gleams and fragments. Then, its countenance waxes stern and grand, and we see that it must be true. It now shows itself ethical and practical." The idealism which is a thing of the academic intellect to the professor, a hope to the generous youth, an inspiration to the genial projector, is to Emerson a narrowly accurate description of the facts of the most real world in which all earn their living.

Such reference to the immediate life is the text by which he tries every philosopher. "Each new mind we approach seems to require," he says, "an abdication of all our past and present possessions. A new doctrine seems at first a subversion of all our opinions, tastes and manner of living." But while one gives himself "up unreservedly to that which draws him, because that is his own, he is to refuse himself to that which draws him not, because it is not his own. I were a fool not to sacrifice a thousand Aeschyluses to my intellectual integrity. Especially take the same ground in regard to abstract truth, the science of the mind. The Bacon, the Spinoza, the Hume, Schelling, Kant, is only a more or less awkward translator of things in your consciousness. Say, then, instead of too timidly poring into his obscure sense, that he has not succeeded in rendering back to you your consciousness. Anyhow, when at last, it is done, you will find it is not recondite, but a simple, natural state which the writer restores to you." And again, take this other saying, "Aristotle or Bacon or Kant propound some maxim which is the key-note of philosophy thenceforward, but I am more interested to know that when at last they have hurled out their grand word, it is only some familiar experience of every man on the street." I fancy he reads the so-called eclecticism of Emerson wrongly who does not see that it is reduction of all the philosophers of the race, even the prophets like Plato and Proclus whom Emerson holds most dear, to the test of trial by the service rendered the present and immediate experience. As for those who contemn Emerson for superficial pedantry because of the strings of names he is wont to flash like beads before our eyes, they but voice their own pedantry, not seeing, in their literalness, that all such things are with Emerson symbols of various uses administered to the common soul.

As Emerson treated the philosophers, so he treats their doctrines. The Platonist teaches the immanence of absolute ideas in the World and in Man, that every thing and every man participates in an absolute Meaning, individualized in him and through which one has community with others. Yet by the time this truth of the universe has become proper and fit for teaching, it has somehow become a truth of philosophy, a truth of private interpretation, reached by some men, not others, and consequently true for some, but not true for all, and hence not wholly true for any. But to Emerson all "truth lies on the highway." Emerson says, "We lie in the lap of immense intelligence which makes us organs of its activity and receivers of its truth," and the Idea is no longer either an academic toy nor even a gleam of poetry, but a literal report of the experience of the hour as that is enriched and reinforced for the individual through the tale of history, the appliance of science, the gossip of conversation and the exchange of commerce. That every individual is at once the focus and the channel of mankind's long and wide endeavor, that all nature exists for the education of the human soul— such things, as we read Emerson, cease to be statements of a separated philosophy and become natural transcripts of the course of events and of the rights of man.

Emerson's philosophy has this in common with that of the transcendentalists; he prefers to borrow from them rather than from others certain pigments and delineations. But he finds truth in the highway, in the untaught endeavor, the unexpected idea, and this removes him from their remotenesses. His ideas are not fixed upon any Reality that is beyond or behind or in any way apart, and hence they do not have to be bent. They are versions of the Here and the Now, and flow freely. The reputed transcendental worth of an overweening Beyond and Away, Emerson, jealous for spiritual democracy, finds to be the possession of the unquestionable Present. When Emerson, speaking of the chronology of history, designated the There and Then as "wild, savage and preposterous," he also drew the line which marks him off from transcendentalism— which is the idealism of a Class. In sorry truth, the idealist has too frequently conspired with the sensualist to deprive the pressing and so the passing Now of value which is spiritual. Through the joint work of such malign conspiracy, the common man is not, or at least does not know himself for, an idealist. It is such disinherited of the earth that Emerson summons to their own. "If man is sick, is unable, is mean-spirited and odious, it is because there is so much of his nature which is unlawfully withholden from him."

Against creed and system, convention and institution, Emerson stands for restoring to the common man that which in the name of religion, of philosophy, of art and of morality, has been embezzled from the common store and appropriated to sectarian and class use. Beyond anyone we know of, Emerson has comprehended and declared how such malversation makes truth decline from its simplicity, and in becoming partial and owned, become a puzzle of and trick for theologian, metaphysician and litterateur—a puzzle of an imposed law, of an unwished for and refused goodness, of a romantic ideal gleaming only from afar, and a trick of manipular skill, of specialized performance.

For such reasons, the coming century may well make evident what is just now dawning, that Emerson is not only a philosopher, but that he is the Philosopher of Democracy. Plato's own generation would, I think, have found it difficult to class Plato. Was he an inept visionary or a subtle dialectician? A political reformer or a founder of the new type of literary art? Was he a moral exhorter, or an instructor in an Academy? Was he a theorist upon education, or the inventor of a method of knowledge? We, looking at Plato through the centuries of exposition and interpretation, find no difficulty in placing Plato as a philosopher and in attributing to him a system of thought. We dispute about the nature and content of this system, but we do not doubt it is there. It is the intervening centuries which have furnished Plato with his technique and which have developed and wrought Plato to a system. One century bears but a slender ratio to twenty-five; it is not safe to predict. But at least, thinking of Emerson as the one citizen of the New World fit to have his name uttered in the same breath with that of Plato, one may without presumption believe that even if Emerson has no system, none the less he is the prophet and herald of any system which democracy may henceforth construct and hold by, and that when democracy has articulated itself, it will have no difficulty in finding itself already proposed in Emerson. It is as true to-day as when he said it: "It is not propositions, not new dogmas and the logical exposition of the world that are our first need, but to watch and tenderly cherish the intellectual and moral sensibilities and woo them to stay and make their home with us. Whilst they abide with us, we shall not think amiss." We are moved to say that Emerson is the first and as yet almost the only Christian of the Intellect. From out such reverence for the instinct and impulse of our common nature shall emerge in their due season propositions, systems and logical expositions of the world. Then shall we have a philosophy which religion has no call to chide and which knows its friendship with science and with art.

Emerson wrote of a certain type of mind: "This tranquil, well-founded, wide-seeing soul is no express-rider, no attorney, no magistrate. It lies in the sun and broods on the world." It is the soul of Emerson which these words describe. Yet this is no private merit nor personal credit. For thousands of earth's children, Emerson has taken away the barriers that shut out the sun and has secured the unimpeded, cheerful circulation of the light of heaven, and the wholesome air of day. For such, content to endure without contriving and contending, at the last all express-riders journey, since to them comes the final service of all commodity. For them, careless to make out their own case, all attorneys plead in the day of final judgment; for though falsehoods pile mountain high, truth is the only deposit that nature tolerates. To them who refuse to be called "master, master," all magistracies in the end defer, for theirs is the common cause for which dominion, power and principality is put under foot. Before such successes, even the worshipers of that which to-day goes by the name of success, those who bend to millions and incline to imperialisms, may lower their standard, and give at least a passing assent to the final word of Emerson's philosophy, the identity of Being, unqualified and immutable, with Character.

George Santayana (1863–1952)

Born in Madrid but educated at Boston Latin School and Harvard (where his teachers included William James and Josiah Royce), Santayana became a prominent contributor to American Pragmatism. He was a member of the Department of Philosophy at Harvard from 1889 until 1912—James and Royce now colleagues, along with Hugo Münsterberg and George Herbert Palmer—but resigned his professorship and exiled himself to Europe where he wrote 19 books over the course of 40 years. Like Dewey, Santayana, writing here first in work drawn from Interpretations of Poetry and Religion *(1900), was aware of questions raised about Emerson's reputation as a philosopher. Should he be regarded as one? What consequences follow if he is? Or isn't? As categories change over time, and their relative promise or scandal, so will the reader have to assess Santayana's impression of Emerson as a thinker who "was not primarily a philosopher, but a Puritan mystic with a poetic fancy and a gift for observation and epigram. [. . .]" In the second selection, "The Genteel Tradition in American Philosophy," first delivered before the Philosophical Union on August 25, 1911 in Berkeley (and later printed in* Winds of Doctrine *(1913)), Santayana remains skeptical of Emerson's philosophical status, and situates him in a tradition of thinkers who were "employed on a sort of inner play, or digestion of vacancy"—a tradition that Santayana wishes to distinguish himself from. Santayana's remarks on Emerson from this occasion have been taken seriously and widely invoked, as is indicated from the many times, among a range of critics, the piece is quoted in this volume—both as having gotten something right about Emerson and as having offered a flawed judgment of his work, as the readings variously elucidate. In short, it is a controversial text, and one that may seem a foil or a bulwark depending on your opinion of Emerson and the American philosophical tradition. While Santayana's address is often selectively quoted (usually to disparage Emerson), reading the work in its entirety shows that Santayana's deep critique of Emerson is complemented by ample and evident esteem. Though Santayana is often an ungenerous critic of Emerson, and sometimes at pains to distinguish himself from Emerson's approach to writing and thinking, John Crowe Ransom points out that "In fact, in 1886, Santayana submitted "The Optimism of Ralph Waldo Emerson" as his senior essay while an undergraduate at Harvard College." Henry S. Levinson says this early work illustrated "the academic preoccupations, assumptions, motives, and aims of a student in philosophy typically impressed with the teachings of professors like Francis Bowen, George Herbert Palmer, Josiah Royce, and William James. It also reveals Santayana making his own first effort to come to grips in prose with Emersonian romanticism."[1] On May 22, 1903, Santayana presented "Emerson's*

*Poems Proclaim the Divinity of Nature, with Freedom as His Profoundest Ideal" at
a centenary celebration convened at Harvard.*[2] *Santayana's criticism of Emerson
is obviously pointed; whether it is also accurate, enriching, or unfounded is part
of what scholars such as Richard Rorty and John J. McDermott undertake in their
contributions to the present collection.*

Emerson

George Santayana

Those who knew Emerson, or who stood so near to his time and to his circle that
they caught some echo of his personal influence, did not judge him merely as a poet
or philosopher, nor identify his efficacy with that of his writings. His friends and
neighbors, the congregations he preached to in his younger days, the audiences that
afterward listened to his lectures, all agreed in a veneration for his person which had
nothing to do with their understanding or acceptance of his opinions. They flocked to
him and listened to his word, not so much for the sake of its absolute meaning as for the
atmosphere of candor, purity, and serenity that hung about it, as about a sort of sacred
music. They felt themselves in the presence of a rare and beautiful spirit, who was in
communion with a higher world. More than the truth his teaching might express, they
valued the sense it gave them of a truth that was inexpressible. They became aware, if
we may say so, of the ultra-violet rays of his spectrum, of the inaudible highest notes of
his gamut, too pure and thin for common ears.

The effect was by no means due to the possession on the part of Emerson of the
secret of the universe, or even of a definite conception of ultimate truth. He was not a
prophet who had once for all climbed his Sinai or his Tabor, and having there beheld
the transfigured reality, descended again to make authoritative report of it to the world.
Far from it. At bottom he had no doctrine at all. The deeper he went and the more
he tried to grapple with fundamental conceptions, the vaguer and more elusive they
became in his hands. Did he know what he meant by Spirit or the "Over-Soul"? Could
he say what he understood by the terms, so constantly on his lips, Nature, Law, God,
Benefit, or Beauty? He could not, and the consciousness of that incapacity was so lively
within him that he never attempted to give articulation to his philosophy. His finer
instinct kept him from doing that violence to his inspiration.

The source of his power lay not in his doctrine, but in his temperament, and the
rare quality of his wisdom was due less to his reason than to his imagination. Reality
eluded him; he had neither diligence nor constancy enough to master and possess it;
but his mind was open to all philosophic influences, from whatever quarter they might
blow; the lessons of science and the hints of poetry worked themselves out in him to a
free and personal religion. He differed from the plodding many, not in knowing things
better, but in having more ways of knowing them. His grasp was not particularly firm,
he was far from being, like a Plato or an Aristotle, past master in the art and the science
of life. But his mind was endowed with unusual plasticity, with unusual spontaneity

and liberty of movement—it was a fairyland of thoughts and fancies. He was like a young god making experiments in creation: he blotched the work, and always began again on a new and better plan. Every day he said, "Let there be light," and every day the light was new. His sun, like that of Heraclitus, was different every morning.

What seemed, then, to the more earnest and less critical of his hearers a revelation from above was in truth rather an insurrection from beneath, a shaking loose from convention, a disintegration of the normal categories of reason in favor of various imaginative principles, on which the world might have been built, if it had been built differently. This gift of revolutionary thinking allowed new aspects, hints of wider laws, premonitions of unthought-of fundamental unities to spring constantly into view. But such visions were necessarily fleeting, because the human mind had long before settled its grammar, and discovered, after much groping and many defeats, the general forms in which experience will allow itself to be stated. These general forms are the principles of common sense and positive science, no less imaginative in their origin than those notions which we now call transcendental, but grown prosaic, like the metaphors of common speech, by dint of repetition.

Yet authority, even of this rational kind, sat lightly upon Emerson. To reject tradition and think as one might have thought if no man had ever existed before was indeed the aspiration of the Transcendentalists, and although Emerson hardly regarded himself as a member of that school, he largely shared its tendency and passed for its spokesman. Without protesting against tradition, he smilingly eluded it in his thoughts, untamable in their quiet irresponsibility. He fled to his woods or to his "pleachèd garden," to be the creator of his own worlds in solitude and freedom. No wonder that he brought thence to the tightly conventional minds of his contemporaries a breath as if from paradise. His simplicity in novelty, his profundity, his ingenuous ardor must have seemed to them something heavenly, and they may be excused if they thought they detected inspiration even in his occasional thin paradoxes and guileless whims. They were stifled with conscience and he brought them a breath of Nature; they were surfeited with shallow controversies and he gave them poetic truth.

Imagination, indeed, is his single theme. As a preacher might under every text enforce the same lessons of the gospel, so Emerson traces in every sphere the same spiritual laws of experience—compensation, continuity, the self-expression of the Soul in the forms of Nature and of society, until she finally recognizes herself in her own work and sees its beneficence and beauty. His constant refrain is the omnipotence of imaginative thought; its power first to make the world, then to understand it, and finally to rise above it. All Nature is an embodiment of our native fancy, all history a drama in which the innate possibilities of the spirit are enacted and realized. While the conflict of life and the shocks of experience seem to bring us face to face with an alien and overwhelming power, reflection can humanize and rationalize that power by conceiving its laws; and with this recognition of the rationality of all things comes the sense of their beauty and order. The destruction which Nature seems to prepare for our special hopes is thus seen to be the victory of our impersonal interests. To awaken in us this spiritual insight, an elevation of mind which is at once an act of comprehension and of worship, to substitute it for lower passions and more servile forms of intelligence—that is Emerson's constant effort. All his resources of illustration, observation, and rhetoric are used to deepen and clarify this sort of wisdom.

Such thought is essentially the same that is found in the German romantic or idealistic philosophers, with whom Emerson's affinity is remarkable, all the more as he seems to have borrowed little or nothing from their works. The critics of human nature, in the eighteenth century, had shown how much men's ideas depend on their predispositions, on the character of their senses and the habits of their intelligence. Seizing upon this thought and exaggerating it, the romantic philosophers attributed to the spirit of man the omnipotence which had belonged to God, and felt that in this way they were reasserting the supremacy of mind over matter and establishing it upon a safe and rational basis.

The Germans were great system-makers, and Emerson cannot rival them in the sustained effort of thought by which they sought to reinterpret every sphere of being according to their chosen principles. But he surpassed them in an instinctive sense of what he was doing. He never represented his poetry as science, nor countenanced the formation of a new sect that should nurse the sense of a private and mysterious illumination, and re-light the fagots of passion and prejudice. He never tried to seek out and defend the universal implications of his ideas, and never wrote the book he had once planned on the law of compensation, foreseeing, we may well believe, the sophistries in which he would have been directly involved. He fortunately preferred a fresh statement on a fresh subject. A suggestion once given, the spirit once aroused to speculation, a glimpse once gained of some ideal harmony, he chose to descend again to common sense and to touch the earth for a moment before another flight. The faculty of idealization was itself what he valued. Philosophy for him was rather a moral energy flowering into sprightliness of thought than a body of serious and defensible doctrines. In practicing transcendental speculation only in this poetic and sporadic fashion, Emerson retained its true value and avoided its greatest danger. He secured the freedom and fertility of his thought and did not allow one conception of law or one hint of harmony to sterilize the mind and prevent the subsequent birth within it of other ideas, no less just and imposing than their predecessors. For we are not dealing at all in such a philosophy with matters of fact or with such verifiable truths as exclude their opposites. We are dealing only with imagination, with the art of conception, and with the various forms in which reflection, like a poet, may compose and recompose human experience.

A certain disquiet mingled, however, in the minds of Emerson's contemporaries with the admiration they felt for his purity and genius. They saw that he had forsaken the doctrines of the Church; and they were not sure whether he held quite unequivocally any doctrine whatever. We may not all of us share the concern for orthodoxy which usually caused this puzzled alarm: we may understand that it was not Emerson's vocation to be definite and dogmatic in religion any more than in philosophy. Yet that disquiet will not, even for us, wholly disappear. It is produced by a defect which naturally accompanies imagination in all but the greatest minds. I mean disorganization. Emerson not only conceived things in new ways, but he seemed to think the new ways might cancel and supersede the old. His imagination was to invalidate the understanding. That inspiration which should come to fulfil seemed too often to come to destroy. If he was able so constantly to stimulate us to fresh thoughts, was it not because he demolished the labor of long ages of reflection? Was not the startling effect of much of his writing due to its contradiction to tradition and to common sense?

So long as he is a poet and in the enjoyment of his poetic license, we can blame this play of mind only by a misunderstanding. It is possible to think otherwise than as common sense thinks; there are other categories beside those of science. When we employ them we enlarge our lives. We add to the world of fact any number of worlds of the imagination in which human nature and the eternal relations of ideas may be nobly expressed. So far our imaginative fertility is only a benefit: it surrounds us with the congenial and necessary radiation of art and religion. It manifests our moral vitality in the bosom of Nature.

But sometimes imagination invades the sphere of understanding and seems to discredit its indispensable work. Common sense, we are allowed to infer, is a shallow affair: true insight changes all that. When so applied, poetic activity is not an unmixed good. It loosens our hold on fact and confuses our intelligence, so that we forget that intelligence has itself every prerogative of imagination, and has besides the sanction of practical validity. We are made to believe that since the understanding is something human and conditioned, something which might have been different, as the senses might have been different, and which we may yet, so to speak, get behind—therefore the understanding ought to be abandoned. We long for higher faculties, neglecting those we have, we yearn for intuition, closing our eyes upon experience. We become mystical.

Mysticism, as we have said, is the surrender of a category of thought because we divine its relativity. As every new category, however, must share this reproach, the mystic is obliged in the end to give them all up, the poetic and moral categories no less than the physical, so that the end of his purification is the atrophy of his whole nature, the emptying of his whole heart and mind to make room, as he thinks, for God. By attacking the authority of the understanding as the organon of knowledge, by substituting itself for it as the herald of a deeper truth, the imagination thus prepares its own destruction. For if the understanding is rejected because it cannot grasp the absolute, the imagination and all its works—art, dogma, worship—must presently be rejected for the same reason. Common sense and poetry must both go by the board, and conscience must follow after: for all these are human and relative. Mysticism will be satisfied only with the absolute, and as the absolute, by its very definition, is not representable by any specific faculty, it must be approached through the abandonment of all. The lights of life must be extinguished that the light of the absolute may shine, and the possession of everything in general must be secured by the surrender of everything in particular.

The same diffidence, however, the same constant renewal of sincerity which kept Emerson's flights of imagination near to experience, kept his mysticism also within bounds. A certain mystical tendency is pervasive with him, but there are only one or two subjects on which he dwells with enough constancy and energy of attention to make his mystical treatment of them pronounced. One of these is the question of the unity of all minds in the single soul of the universe, which is the same in all creatures; another is the question of evil and of its evaporation in the universal harmony of things. Both these ideas suggest themselves at certain turns in every man's experience, and might receive a rational formulation. But they are intricate subjects, obscured by many emotional prejudices, so that the labor, impartiality, and precision which would be needed to elucidate them are to be looked for in scholastic rather than in inspired thinkers, and in Emerson least of all. Before these problems he is alternately ingenuous and rhapsodical, and in both moods equally helpless. Individuals no doubt exist, he says to himself. But, ah! Napoleon is in every schoolboy. In every squatter in the western prairies we shall find an owner—

Of Caesar's hand and Plato's brain,
Of Lord Christ's heart, and Shakespeare's strain.

But how? we may ask. Potentially? Is it because any mind, were it given the right body and the right experience, were it made over, in a word, into another mind, would resemble that other mind to the point of identity? Or is it that our souls are already so largely similar that we are subject to many kindred promptings and share many ideals unrealizable in our particular circumstances? But then we should simply be saying that if what makes men different were removed, men would be indistinguishable, or that, in so far as they are now alike, they can understand one another by summoning up their respective experiences in the fancy. There would be no mysticism in that, but at the same time, alas, no eloquence, no paradox, and, if we must say the word, no nonsense.

On the question of evil, Emerson's position is of the same kind. There is evil, of course, he tells us. Experience is sad. There is a crack in everything that God has made. But, ah! the laws of the universe are sacred and beneficent. Without them nothing good could arise. All things, then, are in their right places and the universe is perfect above our querulous tears. Perfect? we may ask. But perfect from what point of view, in reference to what ideal? To its own? To that of a man who renouncing himself and all naturally dear to him, ignoring the injustice, suffering, and impotence in the world, allows his will and his conscience to be hypnotized by the spectacle of a necessary evolution, and lulled into cruelty by the pomp and music of a tragic show? In that case the evil is not explained, it is forgotten; it is not cured, but condoned. We have surrendered the category of the better and the worse, the deepest foundation of life and reason; we have become mystics on the one subject on which, above all others, we ought to be men.

Two forces may be said to have carried Emerson in this mystical direction; one, that freedom of his imagination which we have already noted, and which kept him from the fear of self-contradiction; the other the habit of worship inherited from his clerical ancestors and enforced by his religious education. The spirit of conformity, the unction, the loyalty even unto death inspired by the religion of Jehovah, were dispositions acquired by too long a discipline and rooted in too many forms of speech, of thought, and of worship for a man like Emerson, who had felt their full force, ever to be able to lose them. The evolutions of his abstract opinions left that habit unchanged. Unless we keep this circumstance in mind, we shall not be able to understand the kind of elation and sacred joy, so characteristic of his eloquence, with which he propounds laws of Nature and aspects of experience which, viewed in themselves, afford but an equivocal support to moral enthusiasm. An optimism so persistent and unclouded as his will seem at variance with the description he himself gives of human life, a description colored by a poetic idealism, but hardly by an optimistic bias.

We must remember, therefore, that this optimism is a pious tradition, originally justified by the belief in a personal God and in a providential government of affairs for the ultimate and positive good of the elect, and that the habit of worship survived in Emerson as an instinct after those positive beliefs had faded into a recognition of "spiritual laws." We must remember that Calvinism had known how to combine an awestruck devotion to the Supreme Being with no very roseate picture of the destinies of mankind, and for more than two hundred years had been breeding in the stock from which Emerson came a willingness to be, as the phrase is, "damned for the glory of God."

What wonder, then, that when, for the former inexorable dispensation of Providence, Emerson substituted his general spiritual and natural laws, he should not have felt the spirit of worship fail within him? On the contrary, his thought moved in the presence of moral harmonies which seemed to him truer, more beautiful, and more beneficent than those of the old theology. An independent philosopher would not have seen in those harmonies an object of worship or a sufficient basis for optimism. But he was not an independent philosopher, in spite of his belief in independence. He inherited the problems and the preoccupations of the theology from which he started, being in this respect like the German idealists, who, with all their pretence of absolute metaphysics, were in reality only giving elusive and abstract forms to traditional theology. Emerson, too, was not primarily a philosopher, but a Puritan mystic with a poetic fancy and a gift for observation and epigram, and he saw in the laws of Nature, idealized by his imagination, only a more intelligible form of the divinity he had always recognized and adored. His was not a philosophy passing into a religion, but a religion expressing itself as a philosophy and veiled, as at its setting it descended the heavens, in various tints of poetry and science.

If we ask ourselves what was Emerson's relation to the scientific and religious movements of his time, and what place he may claim in the history of opinion, we must answer that he belonged very little to the past, very little to the present, and almost wholly to that abstract sphere into which mystical or philosophic aspiration has carried a few men in all ages. The religious tradition in which he was reared was that of Puritanism, but of a Puritanism which, retaining its moral intensity and metaphysical abstraction, had minimized its doctrinal expression and become Unitarian. Emerson was indeed the Psyche of Puritanism, "the latest-born and fairest vision far" of all that "faded hierarchy." A Puritan whose religion was all poetry, a poet whose only pleasure was thought, he showed in his life and personality the meagerness, the constraint, the frigid and conscious consecration which belonged to his clerical ancestors, while his inmost impersonal spirit ranged abroad over the fields of history and Nature, gathering what ideas it might, and singing its little snatches of inspired song.

The traditional element was thus rather an external and unessential contribution to Emerson's mind; he had the professional tinge, the decorum, the distinction of an old-fashioned divine; he had also the habit of writing sermons, and he had the national pride and hope of a religious people that felt itself providentially chosen to establish a free and godly commonwealth in a new world. For the rest, he separated himself from the ancient creed of the community with a sense rather of relief than of regret. A literal belief in Christian doctrines repelled him as unspiritual, as manifesting no understanding of the meaning which, as allegories, those doctrines might have to a philosophic and poetical spirit. Although as a clergyman he was at first in the habit of referring to the Bible and its lessons as to a supreme authority, he had no instinctive sympathy with the inspiration of either the Old or the New Testament; in Hafiz or Plutarch, in Plato or Shakespeare, he found more congenial stuff.

While he thus preferred to withdraw, without rancor and without contempt, from the ancient fellowship of the church, he assumed an attitude hardly less cool and deprecatory toward the enthusiasms of the new era. The national ideal of democracy and freedom had his entire sympathy; he allowed himself to be drawn into the movement against slavery; he took a curious and smiling interest in the discoveries of natural science and in the material progress of the age. But he could go no farther. His contemplative nature, his religious training, his dispersed reading, made him stand aside from the life of the world, even while he studied it with benevolent attention. His heart was fixed on eternal things, and he was in no sense a prophet for his age or country. He belonged by nature to that mystical company of devout souls that recognize no particular home and are dispersed throughout history, although not without intercommunication. He felt his affinity to the Hindus and the Persians, to the Platonists and the Stoics. Like them he remains "a friend and aider of those who would live in the spirit." If not a star of the first magnitude, he is certainly a fixed star in the firmament of philosophy. Alone as yet among Americans, he may be said to have won a place there, if not by the originality of his thought, at least by the originality and beauty of the expression he gave to thoughts that are old and imperishable.

Notes

1   Henry S. Levinson, *Santayana, Pragmatism, and the Spiritual Life* (Chapel Hill: University of North Carolina Press, 1992), 46.
2   Santayana's address first appeared in the Boston *Daily Advertiser*, May 23, 1903 and was reprinted in *George Santayana's America: Essays on Literature and Culture*, ed. James Ballowe (Champaign: University of Illinois Press, 1967).

The Genteel Tradition in American Philosophy

George Santayana

Ladies and Gentlemen: The privilege of addressing you to-day is very welcome to me, not merely for the honor of it, which is great, nor for the pleasures of travel, which are many, when it is California that one is visiting for the first time, but also because there is something I have long wanted to say which this occasion seems particularly favorable for saying. America is still a young country, and this part of it is especially so; and it would have been nothing extraordinary if, in this young country, material preoccupations had altogether absorbed people's minds, and they had been too much engrossed in living to reflect upon life, or to have any philosophy. The opposite, however, is the case. Not only have you already found time to philosophize in California, as your society proves, but the eastern colonists from the very beginning were a sophisticated race. As much as in clearing the land and fighting the Indians they were occupied, as they expressed it, in wrestling with the Lord. The country was new, but the race was tried, chastened, and full of solemn memories. It was an old wine in new bottles; and America did not have to wait for its present universities, with their departments of academic philosophy, in order to possess a living philosophy,—to have a distinct vision of the universe and definite convictions about human destiny.

Now this situation is a singular and remarkable one, and has many consequences, not all of which are equally fortunate. America is a young country with an old mentality: it has enjoyed the advantages of a child carefully brought up, and thoroughly indoctrinated; it has been a wise child. But a wise child, an old head on young shoulders, always has a comic and unpromising side. The wisdom is a little thin and verbal, not aware of its full meaning and grounds; and physical and emotional growth may be stunted by it, or even deranged. Or when the child is too vigorous from that, he will develop a fresh mentality of his own, out of his observations and actual instincts; and this fresh mentality will interfere with the traditional mentality, and tend to reduce it to something perfunctory, conventional, and perhaps secretly despised. A philosophy is not genuine unless it inspires and expresses the life of those who cherish it. I do not think the hereditary philosophy of America has done much to atrophy the natural activities of the inhabitants; the wise child has not missed the joys of youth or of manhood; but what has happened is that the hereditary philosophy has grown stale, and that the academic philosophy afterwards developed has caught the stale odor from it. America is not simply, as I said a moment ago, a young country with an old mentality: it is a country with two mentalities, one a survival of the beliefs and standards of the fathers, the other an expression of the instincts, practice, and discoveries of the younger generations. In all the higher things of the mind—in religion, in literature, in the moral emotions—it is the hereditary spirit that still prevails, so much so that Mr. Bernard Shaw finds that America is a hundred years behind the times. The truth is that one-half of the American mind, that not occupied intensely in practical affairs, has remained, I will not say high-and-dry, but slightly becalmed; it has floated gently in the backwater, which, alongside, in invention and industry and social organization the other half of the mind was leaping down a sort of Niagara Rapids. This division may be found symbolized in American architecture: a neat reproduction of the colonial mansion—with some modern comforts introduced surreptitiously—stands beside the sky-scraper. The American Will inhabits the sky-scraper; the American Intellect inhabits the colonial mansion. The one is the sphere of the American man; the other, at least predominantly, of the American woman. The one is all aggressive enterprise; the other is all genteel tradition.

Now, with your permission, I should like to analyze more fully how this interesting situation has arisen, how it is qualified, and whither it tends. And in the first place we should remember what, precisely, that philosophy was which the first settlers brought with them into the country. In strictness there was more than one; but we may confine our attention to what I will call Calvinism, since it is on this that the current academic philosophy has been grafted. I do not meant exactly the Calvinism of Calvin, or even of Jonathan Edwards; for in their systems there was much that was not pure philosophy, but rather faith in the externals and history of revelation. Jewish and Christian revelation was interpreted by these men, however, in the spirit of a particular philosophy, which might have arisen under any sky, and been associated with any other religion as well as with Protestant Christianity. In fact, the philosophical principle of Calvinism appears also in the Koran, in Spinoza, and in Cardinal Newman; and persons with no very distinctive Christian belief, like Carlyle or like Professor Royce, may be nevertheless, philosophically, perfect Calvinists. Calvinism, taken in this sense, is an expression of the agonized conscience. It is a view of the world which an agonized conscience readily embraces, if it takes itself seriously, as, being agonized, of course it must. Calvinism, essentially, asserts three things: that sin exists, that sin is punished, and that it is beautiful that sin should exist to be punished. The heart of the Calvinist is therefore divided between tragic concern at his own miserable condition, and tragic exultation about the universe at large. He oscillates between a profound abasement and a paradoxical elation of the spirit. To be a Calvinist philosophically is to feel a fierce pleasure in the existence of misery, especially of one's own, in that this misery seems to manifest the fact that the Absolute is irresponsible or infinite or holy. Human nature, it feels, is totally depraved: to have the instincts and motives that we necessarily have is a great scandal, and we must suffer for it; but that scandal is requisite, since otherwise the serious importance of being as we ought to be would not have been vindicated.

To those of us who have not an agonized conscience this system may seem fantastic and even unintelligible; yet it is logically and intently thought out from its emotional premises. It can take permanent possession of a deep mind here and there, and under certain conditions it can become epidemic. Imagine, for instance, a small nation with an intense vitality, but on the verge of ruin, ecstatic and distressful, having a strict and minute code of laws, that paint life in sharp and violent chiaroscuro, all pure righteousness and black abominations, and exaggerating the consequences of both perhaps to infinity. Such a people were the Jews after the exile, and again the early Protestants. If such a people is philosophical at all, it will not improbably be

Calvinistic. Even in the early American communities many of these conditions were fulfilled. The nation was small and isolated; it lived under pressure and constant trial; it was acquainted with but a small range of goods and evils. Vigilance over conduct and an absolute demand for personal integrity were not merely traditional things, but things that practical sages, like Franklin and Washington, recommended to their countrymen, because they were virtues that justified themselves visibly by their fruits. But soon these happy results themselves helped to relax the pressure of external circumstances, and indirectly the pressure of the agonized conscience within. The nation became numerous; it ceased to be either ecstatic or distressful; the high social morality which on the whole it preserved took another color; people remained honest and helpful out of good sense and good will rather than out of scrupulous adherence to any fixed principles. They retained their instinct for order, and often created order with surprising quickness; but the sanctity of law, to be obeyed for its own sake, began to escape them; it seemed too unpractical a notion, and not quite serious. In fact, the second and native-born American mentality began to take shape. The sense of sin totally evaporated. Nature, in the words of Emerson, was all beauty and commodity; and while operating on it laboriously, and drawing quick returns, the American began to drink in inspiration from it aesthetically. At the same time, in so broad a continent, he had elbow-room. His neighbors helped more than they hindered him; he wished their number to increase. Good-will became the great American virtue; and a passion arose for counting heads, and square miles, and cubic feet, and minutes saved—as if there had been anything to save them for. How strange to the American now that saying of Jonathan Edwards, that men are naturally God's enemies! Yet that is an axiom to any intelligent Calvinist, though the words he uses may be different. If you told the modern American that he is totally depraved, he would think you were joking, as he himself usually is. He is convinced that he always has been, and always will be, victorious and blameless.

Calvinism thus lost its basis in American life. Some emotional natures, indeed, reverted in their religious revivals or private searchings of heart to the sources of the tradition; for any of the radical points of view in philosophy may cease to be prevalent, but none can cease to be possible. Other natures, more sensitive to the moral and literary influences of the world, preferred to abandon parts of their philosophy, hoping thus to reduce the distance which should separate the remainder from real life.

Meantime, if anybody arose with a special sensibility or a technical genius, he was in great straits; not being fed sufficiently by the world, he was driven in upon his own resources. The three American writers whose personal endowment was perhaps the finest—Poe, Hawthorne, and Emerson—had all a certain starved and abstract quality. They could not retail the genteel tradition; they were too keen, too perceptive, and too independent for that. But life offered them little digestible material, nor were they naturally voracious. They were fastidious, and under the circumstances they were starved. Emerson, to be sure, fed on books. There was a great catholicity in his reading; and he showed a fine tact in his comments, and in his way of appropriating what he read. But he read transcendentally, not historically, to learn what he himself felt, not what others might have felt before him. And to feed on books, for a philosopher or a poet, is still to starve. Books can help him acquire form, or to avoid pitfalls; they cannot supply him with substance, if he is to have any. Therefore the genius of Poe and Hawthorne, and even of Emerson, was employed on a sort of inner play, or digestion of vacancy. It was a refined labor, but it was in danger of being morbid, or tinkling, or self-indulgent. It was a play of intra-mental rhymes. Their mind was like an old music-box, full of tender echoes and quaint fancies. These fancies expressed their personal genius sincerely, as dreams may; but they were arbitrary fancies in comparison with what a real observer would have said in the premises. Their manner, in a word, was subjective. In their own persons they escaped the mediocrity of the genteel tradition, but they supplied nothing to supplant it in other minds.

The churches, likewise, although they modified their spirit, had no philosophy to offer save a selection or a new emphasis on parts of what Calvinism contained. The theology of Calvin, we must remember, had much in it besides philosophical Calvinism. A Christian tenderness, and a hope of grace for the individual, came to mitigate its sardonic optimism; and it was these evangelical elements that the Calvinistic churches now emphasized, seldom and with blushes referring to the hell-fire or infant damnation. Yet philosophic Calvinism, with a theory of life that would perfectly justify hell-fire and instant damnation if they happened to exist, still dominates the traditional metaphysics. It is an ingredient, and the decisive ingredient, in what calls itself idealism. But in order to see just what part Calvinism plays in current idealism, it will be necessary to distinguish the other chief element in that complex system, namely, transcendentalism.

Transcendentalism is the philosophy which the romantic era produced in Germany, and independently, I believe, in America also. Transcendentalism proper, like romanticism, is not any particular set of dogmas about what things exist; it is not a system of the universe regarded as a fact, or as a collection of facts. It is a method, a point of view, from which any world, no matter what it might contain, could be approached by a self-conscious observer. Transcendentalism is systematic subjectivism. It studies the perspectives of knowledge, as they radiate from the self; it is a plan of those avenues of inference by which our ideas of things must be reached, if they are to afford any systematic or distant vistas. In other words, transcendentalism is the critical logic of science. Knowledge, it says, has a station, as in a watch-tower; it is always seated here and now, in the self of the moment. The past and the future, things inferred and things conceived, lie around it, painted as upon a panorama. They cannot be lighted up save by some centrifugal ray of attention and present interest, by some active operation of the mind.

This is hardly the occasion for developing or explaining this delicate insight; suffice it to say, lest you think later that I disparage transcendentalism, that as a method I regard it as correct and, when once suggested unforgettable. I regard it as the chief contribution made in modern times to speculation. But it is a method only, an attitude we may always assume if we like and that will always be legitimate. It is no answer, and involves no particular answer, to the question: What exists; in what order is what exists produced; what is to exist in the future? This question must be answered by observing the object, and tracing humbly the movement of the object. It cannot be answered at all by harping on the fact that this object, if discovered, must be discovered by somebody, and by somebody who has an interest in discovering it. Yet the Germans who first gained the full transcendental insight were romantic people; they were more or less frankly poets; they were colossal egotists, and wished to make not only their own knowledge but the whole universe center about themselves. And full as they were of their romantic isolation and romantic liberty, it occurred to them to imagine that all reality might be a transcendental self and a romantic dream like themselves; nay, that it might be just their own transcendental self and their own romantic dreams extended indefinitely. Transcendental logic, the method of discovery for the mind, was to become also the method of evolution in nature and history. Transcendental method, so abused, produced transcendental myth. A conscientious critique of knowledge was turned into a sham system of nature. We must therefore distinguish sharply the transcendental grammar of the intellect, which is significant and potentially correct, from the various transcendental systems of the universe, which are chimeras.

In both its parts, however, transcendentalism had much to recommend it to American philosophers, for the transcendental method appealed to the individualistic and revolutionary temper of their youth, while transcendental myths enabled them to find a new status for their inherited theology, and to given what parts of it they cared to preserve some semblance of philosophical backing. This last was the use to which the transcendental method was put by Kant himself, who first brought it into vogue, before the terrible weapon had got out of hand, and become the instrument of pure romanticism. Kant came, he himself said, to removed knowledge in order to make room for faith, which in his case meant faith in Calvinism. In other words, he applied the transcendental method to matters of fact, reducing them thereby to human ideas, in order to give to the Calvinistic postulates of conscience a metaphysical validity. For Kant had a genteel tradition of his own, which he wished to remove to a place of safety, feeling that the empirical world had become too hot for it; and this place of safety was the region of transcendental myth. I need hardly say how perfectly this expedient suited the needs of philosophers in America, and it is no accident if the influence of Kant soon became dominant here. To embrace this philosophy was regarded as a sign of profound metaphysical insight, although the most mediocre minds found no difficult in embracing it. In truth it was a sign of having been brought up in the genteel tradition, of feeling it weak, and of wishing to save it.

But the transcendental method, in its way, was also sympathetic to the American mind. It embodied, in a radical form, the spirit of Protestantism as distinguished from its inherited doctrines; it was autonomous, undismayed, calmly revolutionary; it felt that Will was deeper than Intellect; it focused everything here and now, and asked all things to show their credentials at the bar of the young self, and to prove their value for this latest born moment. These things are truly American; they would be characteristic of any young society with a keen and discursive intelligence, and they are strikingly exemplified in the thought and in the person of Emerson. They constitute what he called self-trust. Self-trust, like other transcendental attitudes, may be expressed in metaphysical fables. The romantic spirit may imagine itself to be an absolute force, evoking and molding the plastic world to express its varying moods. But for a pioneer who is actually a world-builder this metaphysical illusion has a partial warrant in historical fact; far more warrant than it could boast of in the fixed and articulated society of Europe, among the moonstruck rebels and sulking poets of the romantic era. Emerson was a shrewd Yankee, by instinct on the winning side; he was a cheery, child-like soul, impervious to the evidence of evil, as of everything that it did not suit his transcendental individuality to appreciate or notice. More, perhaps, than anybody that has ever lived, he practiced the transcendental method in all its purity. He had no system. He opened his eyes on the world every morning with a fresh sincerity, marking how things seemed to him then, or what they suggested to his spontaneous fancy. This fancy, for being spontaneous, was not always novel; it was guided by the habits and training of his mind, which were those of a preacher. Yet he never insisted on his notions so as to turn them into settled dogmas; he felt in his bones that they were myths. Sometimes, indeed, the bad example of other transcendentalists, less true than he to their method, or the pressing questions of unintelligent people, or the instinct we all have to think our ideals final, led him to the very verge of system-making; but he stopped short. Had he made a system out of his notion of compensation, or the over-soul, or spiritual laws, the result would have been as thin and forced as it is in other transcendental systems. But he coveted truth; and he returned to experience, to history, to poetry, to the natural science of his day, for new starting-points and hints toward fresh transcendental musings.

To covet truth is a very distinguished passion. Every philosopher says he is pursuing the truth, but this is seldom the case. As Mr. Bertrand Russell has observed, one reason why philosophers often fail to reach the truth is that they often do not desire to reach it. Those who are genuinely concerned in discovering what happens to be true are rather the men of science, the naturalists, the historians; and ordinarily they discover it, according to their lights. The truths they find are never complete, and are not always important; but they are integral parts of the truth, facts and circumstances that help to fill in the picture, and that no later interpretation can invalidate or afford to contradict. But professional philosophers are usually only scholastics: that is, they are absorbed in defending some vested illusion or some eloquent idea. Like lawyers or detectives, they study the case for which they are retained, to see how much evidence or semblance of evidence they can gathered for the defense, and how much prejudice they can raise against the witnesses for the prosecution; for they know they are defending prisoners suspected by the world, and perhaps by their own good sense, of falsification. They do no covet truth, but victory and the dispelling of their own doubts. What they defend is some system, that is, some view about the totality of things, of which men are actually ignorant. No system would have ever been framed if people had been simply interested in knowing what is true, whatever it may be. What produces systems is the interest in maintaining against all comers that some favorite or inherited idea of ours is sufficient and right. A system may contain an account of many things which, in detail, are true enough; but as a system, covering infinite possibilities that neither our experience nor our logic can prejudge, it must be a work of imagination, and a piece of human soliloquy. It may be expressive of human experience, it may be poetical; but how should any one who really coveted truth suppose that it was true?

Emerson had no system; and his coveting truth had another exceptional consequence: he was detached, unworldly, contemplative. When he came out of the conventicle or the reform meeting, or out of the rapturous close atmosphere of the lecture-room, he heard nature whispering to him: "Why so hot, little sir?" No doubt the spirit or energy of the world is what is acting in us, as the sea is what rises in every little wave; but it passes through us, and cry out as we may, it will move on. Our privilege is to have perceived it as it moves. Our dignity is not in what we do, but in what we understand. The whole world is doing things. We are turning in that vortex; yet within us is silent observation, the speculative eye before which all passes, which bridges the distances and compares the combatants. On this side of his genius Emerson broke away from all conditions of age or country and represented nothing except intelligence itself.

There was another element in Emerson, curiously combined with transcendentalism, namely, his love and respect for Nature. Nature, for the transcendentalist, is precious because it is his own work, a mirror in which he looks at himself and says (like a poet relishing his own verses), "What a genius I am! Who would have thought there was stuff in me?" And the philosophical egotist finds in his doctrine a ready explanation of whatever beauty and commodity nature actual has. No wonder, he says to himself, that nature is sympathetic, since I made it. And such a view, one-sided and even fatuous as it may be, undoubtedly sharpens the vision of a poet and a moralist to all that is inspiriting and symbolic in the natural world. Emerson was particularly ingenious and clear-sighted in feeling the spiritual uses of fellowship with the elements. This is something in which all Teutonic poetry is rich and which forms, I think, the most genuine and spontaneous part of modern taste, and especially of American taste. Just as some people are naturally enthralled and refreshed by music, so others are by landscape. Music and landscape make up the spiritual resources of those who cannot or dare not express their unfulfilled ideals in words. Serious poetry, profound religion (Calvinism, for instance) are the joys of an unhappiness that confesses itself; but when a genteel tradition forbids people to confess that they are unhappy, serious poetry and profound religion are closed to them by that; and since human life, in its depths, cannot then express itself openly, imagination is driven for comfort into abstract arts, where human circumstances are lost sight of, and human problems dissolve in a purer medium. The pressure of care is thus relieved, without its quietus being found in intelligence. To understand oneself is the classic form of consolation; to elude oneself is the romantic. In the presence of music or landscape human experience eludes itself; and thus romanticism is the bond between transcendental and naturalistic sentiment.

Have there been, we may ask, any successful efforts to escape from the genteel tradition, and to express something worth expressing behind its back? This might well not have occurred as yet; but America is so precocious, it has been trained by the genteel tradition to be so wise for its years, that some indications of a truly native philosophy and poetry are already to be found. I might mention the humorists, of whom you here in California have had your share. The humorists, however, only half escape the genteel tradition; their humor would lose its savor if they had wholly escaped it. They point to what contradicts it in the facts; but not in order to abandon the genteel tradition, for they have nothing solid to put in its place. When they point out how ill many facts fit into it, they do no clearly conceive that this militates against the standard, but think it a funny perversity in the facts. Of course, did they earnestly respect the genteel tradition, such incongruity would seem to them sad, rather than ludicrous. Perhaps the prevalence of humor in America, in and out of season, may be taken as one more evidence that the genteel tradition is present pervasively, but everywhere weak. Similarly in Italy, during the Renaissance, the Catholic tradition could not be banished from the intellect, since there was nothing articulate to take its place; yet its hold on the heart was singularly relaxed. The consequence was that humorists could regale themselves with the foibles of monks and of cardinals, with the credulity of fools, and the bogus miracles of the saints; not intending to deny the theory of the church, but caring for it so little at heart, that they could find it infinitely amusing that it should be contradicted in men's lives, and that no harm should come of it. So when Mark Twain says, "I was born of poor but dishonest parents," the humor depends on the parody of the genteel Anglo-Saxon convention that it is disreputable to be poor; but to hint at the hollowness of it would not be amusing if it did not remain at bottom one's habitual conviction.

The one American writer who has left the genteel tradition entirely behind is perhaps Walt Whitman. For this reason educated Americans find him rather an unpalatable person, who they sincerely protest ought not to be taken for a representative of their culture; and he certainly should not, because their culture is so genteel and traditional. But the foreigner may sometimes think otherwise, since he is looking for what may have arisen in America to express, not the polite and conventional American mind, but the spirit and inarticulate principles that animate the community, on which its own genteel mentality seems to sit rather lightly. When the foreigner opens the pages of Walt Whitman, he thinks that he has come at last upon something representative and original. In Walt Whitman democracy is carried into psychology and morals. The various sights, moods, and emotions are given each one vote; they are declared to be all free and equal, and the innumerable commonplace moments of life are suffered to speak like the others. Those moments formerly reputed great are not excluded, but they are made to march in the ranks with their companions,—plain foot-soldiers and servants of the hour. Nor does the refusal to discriminate stop there; we must carry our principle further down, to the animals, to inanimate nature, to the cosmos as a whole. Whitman became a pantheist; but his pantheism, unlike that of the Stoics and of Spinoza, was unintellectual, lazy, self-indulgent; for he simply felt jovially that everything real was good enough, and that he was good enough himself. In him Bohemia rebelled against the genteel tradition; but the reconstruction that alone can justify revolution did not ensue. His attitude, in principle, was utterly disintegrating; his poetic genius fell back to the lowest level, perhaps, to which it is possible for poetic genius to fall. He reduced his imagination to a passive sensorium for the registering of impressions. No element of construction remained in it, and therefore no element of penetration. But his scope was wide; and his lazy, desultory apprehension was poetical. His work, for the very reason that it is so rudimentary, contains a beginning, or rather many beginnings, that might possibly grow into a noble moral imagination, a worthy filling for the human mind. An American in the nineteenth century who completely disregarded the genteel tradition could hardly have done more.

But there is another distinguished man, lately lost to this country, who has given some rude shocks to this tradition and who, as much as Whitman, may be regarded as representing the genuine, the long silent American mind—I mean William James. He and his brother Henry were tightly swaddled in the genteel tradition as any infant geniuses could be, for they were born in Cambridge, and in a Swedenborgian household. Yet they burst those bands almost entirely. The ways in which the two brothers freed themselves, however, are interestingly different. Mr. Henry James has done it by adopting the point of view of the outer world, and by turning the genteel American tradition, as he turns everything else, into a subject-matter for analysis. For him it is a curious habit of mind, intimately comprehended, to be compared with the genteel tradition in the classic way, by understanding it. With William James too this infusion of worldly insight and European sympathies was a potent influence, especially in his earlier days; but the chief source of his liberty was another. It was his personal spontaneity, similar to that of Emerson, and his personal vitality, similar to that of nobody else. Convictions and ideas came to him, so to speak, from the subsoil. He had a prophetic sympathy with the dawning sentiments of the age, with the moods of the dumb majority. His scattered words caught fire in many parts of the world. His way of thinking and feeling represented the true America, and represented in a measure the whole ultra-modern, radical world. Thus he eluded the genteel tradition in the romantic way, by continuing it into its opposite. The romantic mind, glorified in Hegel's dialectic (which is not dialectic at all, but a sort of tragi-comic history of experience), is always rendering its thoughts unrecognizable through the infusion of new insights, and through the insensible transformation of the moral feeling that accompanies them, till at last it has completely reversed its old judgments under cover of expanding them. Thus the genteel tradition was led a merry dance when it fell again into the hands of a genuine and vigorous romanticist, like William James. He restored their revolutionary force to its neutralized elements, by picking them out afresh, and emphasizing them separately, according to his personal predilections.

For one thing, William James kept his mind and heart wide open to all that might seem, to polite minds, odd, personal, or visionary in religion and philosophy. He gave a sincerely respectful hearing to sentimentalists, mystics, spiritualists, wizards, cranks, quacks, and imposters—for it is hard to draw the line, and James was not willing to draw it prematurely. He thought, with his usual modesty, that any of these might have something to teach him. The lame, the halt, the blind, and those speaking with tongues could come to him with the certainty of finding sympathy; and if they were not healed, at least they were comforted, that a famous professor should take them so seriously; and they began to feel that after all to have only one leg, or one hand, or one eye, or to have three, might be in itself no less beauteous than to have just two, like the stolid majority. Thus William James became the friend and helper of those groping, nervous, half-educated, spiritually disinherited, emotionally hungry individuals of which America is full. He became, at the same time, their spokesman and representative before the learned world; and he made it a chief part of his vocation to recast what the learned world has to offer, so that as far as possible it might serve the needs and interests of these people.

Yet the normal practical masculine American, too, had a friend in William James. There is a feeling abroad now, to which biology and Darwinism lend some color, that theory is simply an instrument for practice, and intelligence merely a help toward material survival. Bears, it is said, have fur and claws, but poor naked man is condemned to be intelligent, or he will perish. This feeling William James embodied in that theory of thought and of truth which he called pragmatism. Intelligence, he thought, is no miraculous, idle faculty, by which we mirror passively any or every thing that happens to be true, reduplicating the real world to no purpose. Intelligence has its roots and its issue in the context of events; it is one kind of practical adjustment, and experimental act, a form of vital tension. It does not essentially serve to picture other parts of reality, but to connect them. This view was not worked out by William James in its psychological and historical details; unfortunately he developed it chiefly in controversy against its opposite, which he called transcendentalism, and which he hated with all the hatred of which his kind heart was capable. Intellectualism, as he conceived it, was pure pedantry; it impoverished and verbalized everything, and tied up nature in red tape. Ideas and rules that may have been occasionally useful, it put in the place of the full-blooded irrational movement of life which had called them into being; and these abstractions, so soon obsolete, it strove to fix and to worship forever. Thus all creeds and theories and all formal precepts sink in the estimation of the pragmatist to a local and temporary grammar of action; a grammar that must be changed slowly by time, and may be changed quickly by genius. To know things as a whole, or as they are eternally, if there is anything eternal in them, is not only beyond our powers, but would prove worthless, and perhaps even fatal to our lives. Ideas are not mirrors, they are weapons; their function is to prepare us to meet events, as future experience may unroll them. Those ideas that disappoint us are false ideas; those to which events are true are true themselves.

This may seem a very utilitarian view of the mind; and I confess I think it a partial one, since the logical force of beliefs and ideas, their truth or falsehood as assertions, has been overlooked altogether, or confused with the vital force of the material processes which these ideas express. It is an external view only, which marks the place and conditions of the mind in nature, but neglects its specific essence; as if a jewel were defined as a round hole in a ring. Nevertheless, the more materialistically we interpret the pragmatist theory of what the mind is, the more vitalistic our theory of nature will have to become. If the intellect is a device produced in organic bodies to expedite their processes, these organic bodies must have interests and a chosen direction in their life; otherwise their life could not be expedited, nor could anything be useful to it. In other words—and this is a third point at which the philosophy of William James has played havoc with the genteel tradition, while ostensibly defending it—nature must be conceived anthropomorphically and in psychological terms. Its purposes are not to be static harmonies, self-unfolding destinies, the logic of spirit, the spirit of logic, or any other formal method and abstract law; its purposes are to be concrete endeavors, finite efforts of souls living in an environment which they transform and by which they, too, are affected. A spirit, the divine spirit as much as the human, as this new animism conceives it, is a romantic adventurer. Its future is undetermined. Its scope, its duration, and the quality of its life, are all contingent. The spirit grows; it buds and sends forth feelers, sounding the depths around for such other centers of force or life as may exist there. It has a vital momentum, but no predetermined goal. It uses its past as a stepping-stone, or rather as a diving-board, but has an absolutely fresh will at each moment to plunge this way or that into the unknown. The universe is an experiment; it is unfinished. It has no ultimate or total nature, because it has no end. It embodies no formula or statable law; any formula is at best a poor abstraction, describing what, in some region and for some time, may be the most striking characteristic of existence; the law is a description *a posteriori* of the habit things have chosen to acquire, and which they may possibly throw off altogether. What a day may bring forth is uncertain; uncertain even to God. Omniscience is impossible; time is real; what had been omniscience hitherto might discover something more to-day. "There shall be news," William James was fond of saying with rapture, quoting from the unpublished poem of an obscure friend, "there shall be news in heaven!" There is almost certainly, he thought, a God now; there may be several gods, who might exist together, or one after the other. We might, by our conspiring sympathies, help to make a new one. Much in us in doubtless immortal; we survive death for some time in a recognizable form; but what our career and transformations may be in the sequel, we cannot tell, although we may help to determine them by our daily choices. Observation must be continual, if our ideas are to remain true. Eternal vigilance is the price of knowledge; perpetual hazard, perpetual experiment keep quick the edge of life.

This is, so far as I know, a new philosophical vista; it is a conception never before presented, although implied, perhaps, in various quarters, as in Norse and even Greek mythology. It is a vision radically empirical and radically romantic; and as William James himself used to say, the vision and not the arguments of a philosopher is the interesting and influential thing about him. William James, rather too generously, attributed this vision to M. Bergson, and regarded him in consequence as a philosopher of the first rank, whose thought was to be one of the turning-points in history. M. Bergson had killed intellectualism. It was his book on creative evolution, said James with humorous emphasis, that had come at last to "*écraser l'infâme.*" We may suspect, notwithstanding, that intellectualism, infamous and crushed, will survive the blow; and if the author of the Book of Ecclesiastes were now alive, and heard that there shall be news in heaven, he would doubtless say that there may possibly be news there, but that under the sun there is nothing new—not even radical empiricism or radical romanticism, which from the beginning of the world has been the philosophy of those who as yet had had little experience; for to the blinking little child it is not merely something in the world that is new daily, but everything is new all day.

I am not concerned with the rights and wrongs of that controversy; my point is only that William James, in this genial evolutionary view of the world, has given a rude shock to the genteel tradition. What! The world a gradual improvization? Creation unpremeditated? God a sort of young poet or struggling artist? William James is an advocate of theism; pragmatism adds one to the evidences of religion; that is excellent. But is not the cool abstract piety of the genteel getting more than it asks for? This empirical naturalistic God is too crude and positive a force; he will work miracles, he will answer prayers, he may inhabit distinct places, and have distinct conditions under which alone he can operate; he is a neighboring being, whom we can act upon, and rely upon for specific aids, as upon a personal friend, or a physician, or an insurance company. How disconcerting! Is not this new theology a little like superstition? And yet how interesting, how exciting, if it should happen to be true! I am far from wishing to suggest that such a view seems to me more probable than conventional idealism or than Christian orthodoxy. All three are in the region of dramatic system-making and myth, to which probabilities are irrelevant. If one man says the moon is sister to the sun, and another that she is his daughter, the question is not which notion is more probable, but whether either of them is at all expressive. The so-called evidences are devised afterwards, when faith and imagination have prejudged the issue. The force of William James's new theology, or romantic cosmology, lies only in this: that it has broken the spell of the genteel tradition, and enticed faith in a new direction, which on second thoughts may prove no less alluring than the old. The important fact is not that the new fancy might possibly be true—who shall know that?—but that it has entered the heart of a leading American to conceive and to cherish it. The genteel tradition cannot be dislodged by these insurrections; there are circles to which it is still congenial, and where it will be preserved. But it has been challenged and (what is perhaps more insidious) it has been discovered. No one need be brow-beaten any longer into accepting it. No one need be afraid, for instance, that his fate is sealed because some young prig may call him a dualist; the pint would call the quart a dualist, if you tried to pour the quart into him. The intellectual world may be traversed in many directions; the whole has not been surveyed; there is a great career in it open to talent. That is a sort of knell, that tolls the passing of the genteel tradition. Something else is now in the field; something else can appeal to the imagination, and be a thousand times more idealistic than academic idealism, which is often simply a way of white-washing and adoring things as they are. The illegitimate monopoly which the genteel tradition had established over what ought to be assumed and what ought to be hoped for has been broken down by the first-born of the family, by the genius of the race. Henceforth there can hardly be the same peace and the same pleasure in hugging the old properties. Hegel will be to the next generation what Sir William Hamilton was to the last. Nothing will have been disproved, but everything will have been abandoned. An honest man has spoken, and the cant of the genteel tradition has become harder for young lips to repeat.

With this I have finished such a sketch as I am here able to offer you of the genteel tradition in American philosophy. The subject is complex, and calls for many an excursus and qualifying footnote; yet I think the main outlines are clear enough. The chief foundations of this tradition were Calvinism and transcendentalism. Both were living fountains; but to keep them alive they required, one an agonized conscience, and the other a radical subjective criticism of knowledge. When these rare metaphysical preoccupations disappeared—and the American atmosphere is not favorable to either of them—the two systems ceased to be inwardly understood; they subsisted as sacred mysteries only; and the combination of the two in some transcendental system of the universe (a contradiction in principle) was doubly artificial. Besides, it could hardly be held with a single mind. Natural science, history, the beliefs implied in labor and invention, could not be disregarded altogether; so that the transcendental philosopher was condemned to a double allegiance, and to not letting his left hand know the bluff that his right hand was putting up. Nevertheless, the difficulty in bringing practical inarticulate convictions to expression is very great, and the genteel tradition has subsisted in the academic mind, for want of anything equally academic to take its place.

The academic mind, however, has had its flanks turned. On the one side came the revolt of the Bohemian temperament, with its poetry of crude naturalism; on the other side came an impassioned empiricism, welcoming popular religious witnesses to the unseen, reducing science to an instrument of success in action, and declaring the universe to be wild and young, and not to be harnessed by the logic of any school.

This revolution, I should think, might well find an echo among you, who live in a thriving society, and in the presence of a virgin and prodigious world. When you transform nature to your uses, when you experiment with her forces, and reduce them to industrial agents, you cannot feel that nature was made by you or for you, for then these adjustments would have been pre-established. You must feel, that you are an offshoot of her life; one brave little force among her immense forces. When you escape, as you love to do, to your forests and your Sierras, I am sure again that you do not feel you made them, or that they were made for you. They have grown, as you have grown, only more massively and more slowly. In their non-human beauty and peace they stir the sub-human depths and the superhuman possibilities of your own spirit. It is no transcendental logic that they teach; and they give no sign of any deliberate morality seated in the world. It is rather the vanity and superficiality of all logic, the needlessness of argument, the finitude of morals, the strength of time, the fertility of matter, the variety, the unspeakable variety, of possible life. Everything is measurable and conditioned, indefinitely repeated, yet, in repetition, twisted somewhat from its old form. Everywhere is beauty and nowhere permanence, everywhere an incipient harmony, nowhere an intention, nor a responsibility, nor a plan. It is the irresistible suasion of this daily spectacle, it is the daily discipline of contact with things, so different from the verbal discipline of the schools, that will, I trust, inspire the philosophy of your children. A Californian whom I had recently the pleasure of meeting observed that, if the philosophers had lived among your mountains their systems would have been different from what they are. Certainly, I should say, very different from what those systems are from which the European genteel tradition has handed down since Socrates; for these systems are egotistical; directly or indirectly they are anthropocentric, and inspired by the conceited notion that man, or human reason, or the human distinction between good and evil, is the center and pivot of the universe. That is what the mountains and the woods should make you at last ashamed to assert. From what, indeed, does the society of nature liberate you, that you find it so sweet? It is hardly (is it?) that you wish to forget your past, or your friends, or that you have any secret contempt for your present ambitions. You respect these, you respect them perhaps too much; you are not suffered by the genteel tradition to criticize or to reform them at all radically. No; it is the yoke of this genteel tradition itself, your tyrant from the cradle to the grave, that these primeval solitudes lift from your shoulders. They suspend your forced sense of your own importance not merely as individuals, but even as men. They allow you, in one happy moment, at once to play and to worship, to take yourselves simply, humbly, for what you are, and to salute the wild, indifferent, non-censorious infinity of nature. You are admonished that what you can do avails little materially, and in the end nothing. At the same time, through wonder and pleasure, you are taught speculation. You learn what you are really fitted to do, and where lie your natural dignity and joy, namely, in representing many things, without being them, and in letting your imagination, through sympathy, celebrate and echo their life. Because the peculiarity of man is that his machinery for reaction on external things has involved an imaginative transcript of these things, which is preserved and suspended in his fancy; and the interest and beauty of this inward landscape, rather than any fortunes that may await his body in the outer world, constitute his happiness. By their mind, its scope, quality, and temper, we estimate men, for by the mind only do we exist as men, and are more than so many storage-batteries for material energy. Let us therefore be frankly human. Let us be content to live in the mind.

Charles William Eliot (1834–1926)

Eliot served as President of Harvard University from 1869 to 1909, still the longest tenure in that position and a duration that reflects his influence in magnifying the school's academic prominence. The innovations he brought to Harvard were imported from 2 years spent researching a range of educational forms in Europe, both inside and outside the university system. His article "The New Education" published in The Atlantic Monthly *upon his return promptly inspired the invitation to assume the presidency, and made him, at 35, the youngest leader of the oldest college in the United States. Eliot's candidacy was supported by Emerson, and in turn Eliot invited Emerson to become a lecturer in Philosophy—29 years after his Address to the Divinity School effectively forced Emerson into exile from the institution. Though Eliot gleaned much from European modes of education, his pedagogical touchstone was American Unitarianism and especially Emerson's writing as he understood it. In the following selection from* Four American Leaders *(1906), Eliot places Emerson at the end of a series of chapters on Benjamin Franklin, George Washington, and William Ellery Channing (1780–1842, founder of the Unitarian movement), an address that he originally presented at the Emerson centenary celebration in Boston, May 24, 1903. Eliot, who came late to an appreciation of Emerson, is at pains to illustrate "how many of the sober, practical undertakings of to-day had been anticipated in all their principles by this solitary, shrewd, independent thinker." Fittingly, Eliot begins by addressing what he calls "the prophetic teachings of Emerson with regard to education," and subsequently broadens his sense of Emerson's prophetic achievements in other aspects of American life in the new century: from transformations in social conditions to the emergence of landscape design to, above all, the evolving status of religion.*

Emerson

Charles William Eliot

EMERSON was not a logician or reasoner, and not a rhetorician, in the common sense. He was a poet, who wrote chiefly in prose, but also in verse. His verse was usually rough, but sometimes finished and melodious; it was always extraordinarily concise and expressive. During his engagement to the lady who became his second wife, he wrote thus to her: "I am born a poet,—of a low class without doubt, yet a poet; that is my nature and vocation. My singing, be sure, is very husky, and is, for the most part, in prose. Still, I am a poet in the sense of a perceiver and dear lover of the harmonies that are in the soul and in matter, and specially of the correspondences between these and those."

This husky poet had his living to get. His occupations in life were those of the teacher, minister, lecturer, and author. He was a teacher at various times between 1818 and 1826; but he never liked teaching. He was a preacher at intervals from 1826 to 1847, but a settled minister only from 1829 to 1832. His career as a lecturer began in the autumn of 1833; and his first book, "Nature," was published in 1836, when he was thirty-three years old. His lectures for money were given as a rule during the winter and early spring; and for thirty years the travelling he was obliged to do in search of audiences was often extremely fatiguing, and not without serious hardships and exposures. These occupations usually gave him an income sufficient for his simple wants; but there were times when outgo exceeded income. The little property his first wife left him ($1200 a year) relieved him from serious pecuniary anxiety by 1834; although it did not relieve him from earning by his own labor the livelihood of his family.

In 1834 he went to live in Concord, where his grandfather had been the minister at the time of the Revolution, and in 1835 he bought the house and grounds there which were his home for the rest of his days. Before settling in Concord, he had spent one winter and spring (1826–27) in the Southern states, and seven months of 1833 in Europe. Both of these absences were necessitated by the state of his health, which was precarious during his young manhood. With these exceptions, he had lived in Boston or its immediate neighborhood, until he settled in Concord. His progenitors on both sides were chiefly New England ministers. His formal education was received in the Boston Latin School and Harvard College, and was therefore purely local. How narrow and provincial seems his experience of life! A little city, an isolated society, a country village! Yet through books, and through intercourse with intelligent persons, he was really "set in a large place." The proof of this largeness, and of the keenness of his mental and moral vision, is that, in regard to some of the chief concerns of mankind, he was a seer and a fore-seer. This prophetic quality of his I hope to demonstrate to-night in three great fields of thought,—education, social organization, and religion.

Although a prophet and inspirer of reform, Emerson was not a reformer. He was but a halting supporter of the reforms of his day; and the eager experimenters and combatants in actual reforms found him a disappointing sort of sympathizer. His visions were far-reaching, his doctrines often radical, and his exhortations fervid; but when it came to action, particularly to habitual action, he was surprisingly conservative. With an exquisite candor, and a gentle resolution of rarest quality he broke his strong ties to the Second Church of Boston before he was thirty years old, abandoning the profession for which he had been trained, and which, in many of its aspects, he honored and enjoyed; yet he attended church on Sundays all his life with uncommon regularity. He refused to conduct public prayer, and had many things to say against it; but when he was an Overseer of Harvard College, he twice voted to maintain the traditional policy of compelling all the students to attend morning prayers, in spite of the fact that a large majority of the Faculty urgently advocated abandoning that policy. He manifested a good deal of theoretical sympathy with the community experiments at Brook Farm and Fruitlands; but he declined to take part in them himself. He was intimate with many of the leading abolitionists; but no one has described more vividly their grave intellectual and social defects. He laid down principles which, when applied, would inevitably lead to progress and reform; but he took little part in the imperfect step-by-step process of actual reforming. He probably would have been an ineffective worker in any field of reform; and, at any rate, strenuous labor on applications of his philosophy would have prevented him from maintaining the flow of his philosophic and prophetic visions. The work of giving practical effect to his thought was left for other men to do,—indeed for generations of other serviceable men, who, filled with his ideals, will slowly work them out into institutions, customs, and other practical values.

When we think of Emerson as a prophet, we at once become interested in the dates at which he uttered certain doctrines, or wrote certain pregnant sentences; but just here the inquirer meets a serious difficulty. He can sometimes ascertain that a given doctrine or sentence was published at a given date; but he may be quite unable to ascertain how much earlier the doctrine was really formulated, or the sentence written. Emerson has been dead twenty-one years, and it is thirty years since he wrote anything new; but his whole philosophy of life was developed by the time he was forty years old, and it may be doubted if he wrote anything after 1843, the germinal expression of which may not be found in his journals, sermons, or lectures written before that date. If, therefore, we find in the accepted thought, or established institutions, of to-day recent developments of principles and maxims laid down by Emerson, we may fairly say that his thought outran his times certainly by one, and probably by two generations of men.

I take up now the prophetic teachings of Emerson with regard to education. In the first place, he saw, with a clearness to which very few people have yet attained, the fundamental necessity of the school as the best civilizing agency, next to steady labor, and the only sure means of permanent and progressive reform. He says outright: "We shall one day learn to supersede politics by education. What we call our root-and-branch reforms, of slavery, war, gambling, intemperance, is only medicating the symptoms. We must begin higher up—namely, in education." He taught that if we hope to reform mankind, we must begin not with adults, but with children: we must begin in the school. There are some signs that this doctrine has now at last entered the minds of the so-called practical men. The Cubans are to be raised in the scale of civilization and public happiness; so both they and we think they must have more and better schools. The Filipinos, too, are to be developed after the American fashion; so we send them a thousand teachers of English. The Southern states are to be rescued from the persistent poison of slavery; and, after forty years of failure with political methods, we at last accept Emerson's doctrine, and say: We must begin earlier,—at school. The city slums are to be redeemed; and the scientific charity workers find the best way is to get the children into kindergartens and manual training schools.

Since the Civil War, a whole generation of educational administrators has been steadily at work developing what is called the elective system in the institutions of education which deal with the ages above twelve. It has been a slow, step-by-step process, carried on against much active opposition and more sluggish obstruction. The system is a method of educational organization which recognizes the immense expansion of knowledge during the nineteenth century, and takes account of the needs and capacities of the individual child and youth. Now, Emerson laid down in plain terms the fundamental doctrines on which this elective system rests. He taught that the one prudence in life is concentration; the one evil, dissipation. He said: "You must elect your work: you shall take what your brain can, and drop all the rest." To this exhortation he added the educational reason for it,—only by concentration can the youth arrive at the stage of doing something with his knowledge, or get beyond the stage of absorbing, and arrive at the capacity for producing. As Emerson puts it, "Only so can that amount of vital force accumulate which can make the step from knowing to doing." The educational institutions of to-day have not yet fully appreciated this all-important step from knowing to doing. They are only beginning to perceive that, all along the course of education, the child and the youth should be doing something as well as learning something; should be stimulated and trained by achievement; should be constantly encouraged to take the step beyond seeing and memorizing to doing,— the step, as Emerson says, "out of a chalk circle of imbecility into fruitfulness." Emerson carried this doctrine right on into mature life. He taught that nature arms each man with some faculty, large or small, which enables him to do easily some feat impossible to any other, and thus makes him necessary to society; and that this faculty should determine the man's career. The advocates of the elective system have insisted that its results were advantageous for society as a whole, as well as for the individual Emerson put this argument in a nutshell at least fifty years ago: "Society can never prosper, but must always be bankrupt, until every man does that which he was created to do."

Education used to be given almost exclusively through books. In recent years there has come in another sort of education through tools, machines, gardens, drawings, casts, and pictures. Manual training, shop-work, sloyd, and gardening have come into use for the school ages; the teaching of trades has been admitted to some public school systems; and, in general, the use of the hands and eyes in productive labor has been recognized as having good educational effects. The education of men by manual labor was a favorite doctrine with Emerson. He had fully developed it as early as 1837, and he frequently recurred to it afterwards. In December of that year, in a course of lectures on Human Culture, he devoted one lecture to The Hands. He saw clearly that manual labor might be made to develop not only good mental qualities, but good moral qualities. Today, it is frequently necessary for practical teachers, who are urging measures of improvement, to point this out, and to say, just as Emerson said two generations ago, that any falseness in mechanical work immediately appears; that a teacher can judge of the moral quality of each boy in the class before him better and sooner from manual work than from book-work. Emerson taught that manual labor is the study of the external world; that the use of manual labor never grows obsolete, and is inapplicable to no person. He said explicitly that "a man should have a farm or a mechanical craft for his culture"; that there is not only health, but education in garden work; that when a man gets sugar, hominy, cotton, buckets, crockery ware, and letter paper by simply signing his name to a cheque, it is the producers and carriers of these articles that have got the education they yield, he only the commodity; and that labor is God's education. This was Emerson's doctrine more than sixty years ago. It is only ten years since the Mechanic Arts High School was opened in Boston.

We are all of us aware that within the last twenty years there has been a determined movement of the American people toward the cultivation of art, and toward the public provision of objects which open the sense of beauty and increase public enjoyment. It is curious to see how literally Emerson prophesied the actual direction of these efforts:—

> "On the city's paved street
> Plant gardens lined with lilac sweet;
> Let spouting fountains cool the air,
> Singing in the sun-baked square;
> Let statue, picture, park, and ball,
> Ballad, flag, and festival
> The past restore, the day adorn,
> And make to-morrow a new morn!"

We have introduced into our schools, of late years, lessons in drawing, modeling, and designing,—not sufficiently, but in a promising and hopeful way. Emerson taught that it is the office of art to educate the perception of beauty; and he precisely describes one of the most recent of the new tendencies in American education and social life, when he says: "Beauty must come back to the useful arts, and the distinction between the fine and the useful arts be forgotten." That sentence is the inspiration of one of the most recent of the efforts to improve the arts and crafts, and to restore to society the artistic craftsman. But how slow is the institutional realization of this ideal of art education! We are still struggling in our elementary and secondary schools to get a reasonable amount of instruction in drawing and music, and to transfer from other subjects a fair allotment of time to these invaluable elements of true culture, which speak a universal language. Yet the ultimate object of art in education is to teach men to see nature to be beautiful and at the same time useful, beautiful because alive and reproductive, useful while symmetrical and fair. Take up to-day the last essays on education, the last book on landscape architecture, or the freshest teachings of the principles of design, and you will find them penetrated with Emerson's doctrine of art as teacher of mankind. Emerson insists again and again that true culture must open the sense of beauty; that "a man is a beggar who only lives to the useful." It will probably require several generations yet to induce the American people to accept his doctrine that all moments and objects can be embellished, and that cheerfulness, serenity, and repose in energy are the "end of culture and success enough."

It has been clearly perceived of late that a leading object in education is the cultivation of fine manners. On this point the teachings of Emerson are fundamental; but the American institutions of education are only beginning to appreciate their significance. He teaches that genius or love invents fine manners, "which the baron and the baroness copy very fast, and by the advantage of a palace better the instruction. They stereotype the lesson they have learned into a mode." There is much in that phrase, "by the advantage of a palace." For generations, American institutions of education were content with the humblest sort of shelters, with plain wooden huts and brick barracks, and unkempt grounds about the buildings. They are only lately beginning to acquire fine buildings with pleasing surroundings; that is, they are just beginning to carry into practice Emerson's wisdom of sixty years ago. The American cities are beginning to build handsome houses for their High Schools. Columbia University builds a noble temple for its library. The graduates and friends of Harvard like to provide her with a handsome fence round the Yard, with a fair array of shrubs within the fence, with a handsome stadium instead of shabby, wooden seats round the football gridiron, and to take steps for securing in the future broad connections between the grounds of the University and the Cambridge parks by the river. They are just now carrying into practice Emerson's teaching; by the advantage of a palace they mean to better Harvard's instruction in manners. They are accepting his doctrine that "manners make the fortune of the ambitious youth; that for the most part his manners marry him, and, for the most part, he marries manners. When we think what keys they are, and to what secrets; what high lessons, and inspiring tokens of character they convey, and what divination is required in us for the reading of this fine telegraph,—we see what range the subject has, and what relations to convenience, power, and beauty."

In Emerson's early days there was nothing in our schools and colleges which at all corresponded to what we now know too much about under the name of athletic sports. The elaborate organization of these sports is a development of the last thirty years in our schools and colleges; but I find in Emerson the true reason for the athletic cult, given a generation before it existed among us. Your boy "hates the grammar and Gradus, and loves guns, fishing-rods, horses, and boats. Well, the boy is right, and you are not fit to direct his bringing-up, if your theory leaves out his gymnastic training.... Football, cricket, archery, swimming, skating, climbing, fencing, riding are lessons in the art of power, which it is his main business to learn.... Besides, the gun, fishing-rod, boat, and horse constitute, among all who use them, secret free-masonries." We shall never find a completer justification of athletic sports than that.

In his memorable address on The American Scholar, which was given at Cambridge in 1837, Emerson pointed out that the function of the scholar should include creative action, or, as we call it in these days, research, or the search for new truth. He says: "The soul active ... utters truth, or creates.... In its essence it is progressive. The book, the college, the school of art, the institution of any kind, stop with some past utterance of genius. ... They look backward and not forward. But genius looks forward. Man hopes: genius creates. Whatever talents may be, if the man create not, the pure efflux of the Deity is not his;—cinders and smoke there may be, but not yet flame." And more explicitly still, he says: "Colleges have their indispensable office,—to teach elements. But they can only highly serve us when they aim not to drill, but to create." When Emerson wrote this passage, the spirit of research, or discovery, or creation had not yet breathed life into the higher institutions of learning in our country; and to-day they have much to do and to acquire before they will conform to Emerson's ideal.

There are innumerable details in which Emerson anticipated the educational experiences of later generations. I can cite but two of them. He taught that each age must write its own books; "or rather, each generation for the next succeeding. The books of an older period will not fit this." How true that is in our own day when eighty thousand new books come from the press of the civilized world in a single year! Witness the incessant remaking or re-casting of the books of the preceding generation! Emerson himself has gone into thousands of books in which his name is never mentioned. Even history has to be re-written every few years, the long-surviving histories being rather monuments of style and method than accepted treasuries of facts. Again, contrary to the prevailing impression that the press has, in large measure, stripped eloquence of its former influence, Emerson taught that "if there ever was a country where eloquence was a power, it is the United States." He included under eloquence the useful speech, all sorts of political persuasion in the great arena of the Republic, and the lessons of science, art, and religion which should be "brought home to the instant practice of thirty millions of people," now become eighty. The colleges and universities have now answered in the affirmative Emerson's question, "Is it not worth the ambition of every generous youth to train and arm his mind with all the resources of knowledge, of method, of grace, and of character to serve such a constituency?" But then Emerson's definition of eloquence is simple, and foretells the practice of to-day rather than describes the practice of Webster, Everett, Choate, and Winthrop, his contemporaries: "Know your fact; hug your fact For the essential thing is heat, and heat comes of sincerity. . . . Eloquence is the power to translate a truth into language perfectly intelligible to the person to whom you speak."

I turn next to some examples of Emerson's anticipation of social conditions, visible to him as seer in his own day, and since become plain to the sight of the ordinary millions. When he accumulated in his journals the original materials of his essay on Worship, there were no large cities in the United States in the present sense of that term. The great experiment of democracy was not far advanced, and had not developed many of its sins and dangers; yet how justly he presented them in the following description; "In our large cities, the population is godless, materialized,—no bond, no fellow-feeling, no enthusiasm. These are not men, but hungers, thirsts, fevers, and appetites walking. How is it people manage to live on, so aimless as they are? . . . There is faith in chemistry, in meat and wine, in wealth, in machinery, in the steam-engine, galvanic battery, turbine wheels, sewing-machines, and in public opinion, but not in divine causes."

In Emerson's day, luxury in the present sense had hardly been developed in our country; but he foresaw its coming, and its insidious destructiveness. "We spend our incomes for paint and paper, for a hundred trifles, I know not what, and not for the things of a man. Our expense is almost all for conformity. It is for cake that we run in debt; it is not the intellect, not the heart, not beauty, not worship, that costs us so much. Why needs any man be rich? Why must he have horses, fine garments, handsome apartments, access to public houses and places of amusement? Only for want of thought. . . . We are first thoughtless, and then find that we are moneyless. We are first sensual and then must be rich." He foresaw the young man's state of mind to-day about marriage—I must have money before I can marry; and deals with it thus: "Give us wealth and the home shall exist. But that is a very imperfect and inglorious solution of the problem, and therefore no solution. Give us wealth! You ask too much. Few have wealth; but all must have a home. Men are not born rich; in getting wealth the man is generally sacrificed, and often is sacrificed without acquiring wealth at last."

We have come to understand by experience that the opinion of masses of men is a formidable power which can be made safe and useful. In earlier days this massed opinion was either despised or dreaded; and it is dreadful, if either confined or misdirected. Emerson compares it to steam. Studied, economized, and directed, steam has become the power by which all great labors are done. Like steam is the opinion of political masses! If crushed by castles, armies, and police, dangerously explosive; but if furnished with schools and the ballot, developing "the most harmless and energetic form of a state." His eyes were wide open to some of the evil intellectual effects of democracy. The individual is too apt to wear the time-worn yoke of the multitude's opinions. No multiplying of contemptible units can produce an admirable mass. "If I see nothing to admire in a unit, shall I admire a million units?" The habit of submitting to majority rule cultivates individual subserviency. He pointed out two generations ago that the action of violent political parties in a democracy might provide for the individual citizen a systematic training in moral cowardice.

It is interesting, at the stage of industrial warfare which the world has now reached, to observe how Emerson, sixty years ago, discerned clearly the absurdity of paying all sorts of service at one rate, now a favorite notion with some labor unions. He points out that even when all labor is temporarily paid at one rate, differences in possessions will instantly arise: "In one hand the dime became an eagle as it fell, and in another hand a copper cent. For the whole value of the dime is in knowing what to do with it." Emerson was never deceived by a specious philanthropy, or by claims of equality which find no support in the nature of things. He was a true democrat, but still could say: "I think I see place and duties for a nobleman in every society; but it is not to drink wine and ride in a fine coach, but to guide and adorn life for the multitude by forethought, by elegant studies, by perseverance, self-devotion, and the remembrance of the humble old friend,—by making his life secretly beautiful." How fine a picture of the democratic nobility is that!

In his lecture on Man the Reformer, which was read before the Mechanics' Apprentices' Association in Boston in January, 1841, Emerson described in the clearest manner the approaching strife between laborers and employers, between poor and rich, and pointed out the cause of this strife in the selfishness, unkindness, and mutual distrust which ran through the community. He also described, with perfect precision, the only ultimate remedy,—namely, the sentiment of love. "Love would put a new face on this weary old world in which we dwell as pagans and enemies too long. . . . The virtue of this principle in human society in application to great interests is obsolete and forgotten. But one day all men will be lovers; and every calamity will be dissolved in the universal sunshine." It is more than sixty years since those words were uttered, and in those years society has had large experience of industrial and social strife, of its causes and consequences, and of many attempts to remedy or soften it; but all this experience only goes to show that there is but one remedy for these ills. It is to be found in kindness, good fellowship, and the affections. In Emerson's words, "We must be lovers, and at once the impossible becomes possible." The world will wait long for this remedy, but there is no other.

Like every real seer and prophet whose testimony is recorded, Emerson had intense sympathy with the poor, laborious dumb masses of mankind, and being a wide reader in history and biography, he early arrived at the conviction that history needed to be written in a new manner. It was long before Green's History of the English People that Emerson wrote: "Hence it happens that the whole interest of history lies in the fortunes of the poor." In recent years this view of history has come to prevail, and we are given the stories of institutions, industries, commerce, crafts, arts, and beliefs, instead of the stories of dynasties and wars. For Emerson it is always feats of liberty and wit which make epochs of history. Commerce is civilizing because "the power which the sea requires in the sailor makes a man of him very fast." The invention of a house, safe against wild animals, frost, and heat, gives play to the finer faculties, and introduces art, manners, and social delights. The discovery of the post office is a fine metre of civilization. The seagoing steamer marks an epoch; the subjection of electricity to take messages and turn wheels marks another. But, after all, the vital stages of human progress are marked by steps toward personal, individual freedom. The love of liberty was Emerson's fundamental passion:—

"For He that ruleth high and wise,
    Nor pauseth in His plan,
Will take the sun out of the skies
    Ere freedom out of man."

The new National League of Independent Workmen of America has very appropriately taken its motto from Emerson:—

"For what avail the plough or sail
    Or land or life, if freedom fail?"

The sympathetic reader of Emerson comes often upon passages written long ago which are positively startling in their anticipation of sentiments common today and apparently awakened by very recent events. One would suppose that the following passage was written yesterday. It was written fifty-six years ago. "And so, gentlemen, I feel in regard to this aged England, with the possessions, honors, and trophies, and also with the infirmities of a thousand years gathering around her, irretrievably committed as she now is to many old customs which cannot be suddenly changed; pressed upon by the transitions of trade, and new and all incalculable modes, fabrics, arts, machines, and competing populations,—I see her not dispirited, not weak, but well remembering that she has seen dark days before;—indeed with a kind of instinct that she sees a little better in a cloudy day, and that in storm of battle and calamity, she has a secret vigor and a pulse like a cannon."

Before the Civil War the Jew had no such place in society as he holds to-day. He was by no means so familiar to Americans as he is now. Emerson speaks twice of the Jew in his essay on Fate, in terms precisely similar to those we commonly hear to-day: "We see how much will has been expended to extinguish the Jew, in vain. . . . The sufferance which is the badge of the Jew has made him in these days the ruler of the rulers of the earth." Those keen observations were made certainly more than forty years ago, and probably more than fifty.

Landscape architecture is not yet an established profession among us, in spite of the achievements of Downing, Cleveland, and Olmsted and their disciples; yet much has been accomplished within the last twenty-five years to realize the predictions on this subject made by Emerson in his lecture on The Young American. He pointed out in that lecture that the beautiful gardens of Europe are unknown among us, but might be easily imitated here, and said that the landscape art "is the Fine Art which is left for us. . . . The whole force of all arts goes to facilitate the decoration of lands and dwellings. . . . I look on such improvement as directly tending to endear the land to the inhabitant." The following sentence might have been written yesterday, so consistent is it with the thought of to-day: "Whatever events in progress shall go to disgust men with cities, and infuse into them the passion for country life and country pleasures, will render a service to the whole face of this continent, and will further the most poetic of all the occupations of real life, the bringing out by art the native but hidden graces of the landscape." In regard to books, pictures, statues, collections in natural history, and all such refining objects of nature and art, which heretofore only the opulent could enjoy, Emerson pointed out that in America the public should provide these means of culture and inspiration for every citizen. He thus anticipated the present ownership by cities, or by endowed trustees, of parks, gardens, and museums of art or science, as well as of baths and orchestras. Of music in particular he said: "I think sometimes could I only have music on my own terms; could I . . . know where I could go whenever I wished the ablution and inundation of musical waves,—that were a bath and a medicine." It has been a long road from that sentence, written probably in the forties, to the Symphony Orchestra in this Hall, and to the new singing classes on the East Side of New York City.

For those of us who have attended to the outburst of novels and treatises on humble or squalid life, to the copious discussions on child-study, to the masses of slum literature, and to the numerous writings on home economics, how true to-day seems the following sentence written in 1837: "The literature of the poor, the feelings of the child, the philosophy of the street, the meaning of household life are the topics of the time."

I pass now to the last of the three topics which time permits me to discuss,—Emerson's religion. In no field of thought was Emerson more prophetic, more truly a prophet of coming states of human opinion, than in religion. In the first place, he taught that religion is absolutely natural,—not supernatural, but natural:—

"Out from the heart of Nature rolled
The burdens of the Bible old."

He believed that revelation is natural and continuous, and that in all ages prophets are born. Those souls out of time proclaim truth, which may be momentarily received with reverence, but is nevertheless quickly dragged down into some savage interpretation which by and by a new prophet will purge away. He believed that man is guided by the same power that guides beast and flower. "The selfsame power that brought me here brought you," he says to beautiful Rhodora. For him worship is the attitude of those "who see that against all appearances the nature of things works for truth and right forever." He saw good not only in what we call beauty, grace, and light, but in what we call foul and ugly. For him a sky-born music sounds "from all that's fair; from all that's foul:"—

> "'Tis not in the high stars alone,
>   Nor in the cups of budding flowers,
> Nor in the redbreast's mellow tone,
>   Nor in the bow that smiles in showers,
> But in the mud and scum of things
> There alway, alway something sings."

The universe was ever new and fresh in his eyes, not spent, or fallen, or degraded, but eternally tending upward:—

> "No ray is dimmed, no atom worn,
>   My oldest force is good as new,
> And the fresh rose on yonder thorn
>   Gives back the bending heavens in dew."

When we come to his interpretation of historical Christianity, we find that in his view the life and works of Jesus fell entirely within the field of human experience. He sees in the deification of Jesus an evidence of lack of faith in the infinitude of the individual human soul. He sees in every gleam of human virtue not only the presence of God, but some atom of His nature. As a preacher he had no tone of authority. A true nonconformist himself, he had no desire to impose his views on anybody. Religious truth, like all other truth, was to his thought an unrolling picture, not a deposit made once for all in some sacred vessel. When people who were sure they had drained that vessel, and assimilated its contents, attacked him, he was irresponsive or impassive, and yielded to them no juicy thought; so they pronounced him dry or empty. Yet all of Emerson's religious teaching led straight to God,—not to a withdrawn creator, or anthropomorphic judge or king, but to the all-informing, all-sustaining soul of the universe.

It was a prophetic quality of Emerson's religious teaching that he sought to obliterate the distinction between secular and sacred. For him all things were sacred, just as the universe was religious. We see an interesting fruition of Emerson's sowing in the nature of the means of influence, which organized churches and devout people have, in these later days, been compelled to resort to. Thus the Catholic Church keeps its hold on its natural constituency quite as much by schools, gymnasiums, hospitals, entertainments, and social parades as it does by its rites and sacraments. The Protestant Churches maintain in city slums "settlements," which use the secular rather than the so-called sacred methods. The fight against drunkenness, and the sexual vice and crimes of violence which follow in its train, is most successfully maintained by eliminating its physical causes and providing mechanical and social protections.

For Emerson inspiration meant not the rare conveyance of supernatural power to an individual, but the constant incoming into each man of the "divine soul which also inspires all men." He believed in the worth of the present hour:—

"Future or Past no richer secret folds,
O friendless Present! than thy bosom holds."

He believed that the spiritual force of human character imaged the divine:—

"The sun set, but set not his hope:
Stars rose; his faith was earlier up:
Fixed on the enormous galaxy,
Deeper and older seemed his eye,"

Yet man is not an order of nature, but a stupendous antagonism, because he chooses and acts in his soul. "So far as a man thinks, he is free." It is interesting to-day, after all the long discussion of the doctrine of evolution, to see how the much earlier conceptions of Emerson match the thoughts of the latest exponents of the philosophic results of evolution.

The present generation of scholars and ministers has been passing through an important crisis in regard to the sacred books of Judaism and Christianity. All the features of the contest over "the higher criticism" are foretold by Emerson in "The American Scholar." "The poet chanting was felt to be a divine man; henceforth the chant is divine also. The writer was a just and wise spirit: henceforward it is settled the book is perfect. Colleges are built on it; books are written on it . . . Instantly the book becomes noxious; the guide is a tyrant." This is exactly what has happened to Protestantism, which substituted for infallible Pope and Church an infallible Book; and this is precisely the evil from which modern scholarship is delivering the world.

In religion Emerson was only a nineteenth-century non-conformist instead of a fifteenth or seventeenth century one. It was a fundamental article in his creed that, although conformity is the virtue in most request, "Whoso would be a man must be a non-conformist." In the midst of increasing luxury, and of that easygoing, unbelieving conformity which is itself a form of luxury, Boston, the birthplace of Emerson, may well remember with honor the generations of non-conformists who made her, and created the intellectual and moral climate in which Emerson grew up. Inevitably, to conformists and to persons who still accept doctrines and opinions which he rejected, he seems presumptuous and consequential. In recent days we have even seen the word "insolent" applied to this quietest and most retiring of seers. But have not all prophets and ethical teachers had something of this aspect to their conservative contemporaries? We hardly expect the messages of prophets to be welcome; they imply too much dissatisfaction with the present.

The essence of Emerson's teaching concerning man's nature is compressed into the famous verse:—

"So nigh is grandeur to our dust,
　So near is God to man,
When Duty whispers low, Thou must,
　The youth replies, I can."

The cynic or the fall-of-man theologian replies—Grandeur indeed, say rather squalor and shame. To this ancient pessimism Emerson makes answer with a hard question—"We grant that human life is mean, but how did we find out that it was mean?" To this question no straight answer has been found, the common answer running in a circle. It is hard indeed to conceive of a measure which will measure depths but not heights; and besides, every measure implies a standard.

I have endeavored to set before you some of the practical results of Emerson's visions and intuitions, because, though quite unfit to expound his philosophical views, I am capable of appreciating some of the many instances in which his words have come true in the practical experience of my own generation. My own work has been a contribution to the prosaic, concrete work of building, brick by brick, the new walls of old American institutions of education. As a young man I found the writings of Emerson unattractive, and not seldom unintelligible. I was concerned with physical science, and with routine teaching and discipline; and Emerson's thinking seemed to me speculative and visionary. In regard to religious belief, I was brought up in the old-fashioned Unitarian conservatism of Boston, which was rudely shocked by Emerson's excursions beyond its well-fenced precincts. But when I had got at what proved to be my lifework for education, I discovered in Emerson's poems and essays all the fundamental motives and principles of my own hourly struggle against educational routine and tradition, and against the prevailing notions of discipline for the young; so when I was asked to speak to you to-night about him, although I realized my unfitness in many respects for such a function, I could not refuse the opportunity to point out how many of the sober, practical undertakings of to-day had been anticipated in all their principles by this solitary, shrewd, independent thinker, who, in an inconsecutive and almost ejaculatory way, wrought out many sentences and verses which will travel far down the generations.

I was also interested in studying in this example the quality of prophets in general. We know a good deal about the intellectual ancestors and inspirers of Emerson; and we are sure that he drank deep at many springs of idealism and poetry. Plato, Confucius, Shakespeare, and Milton were his teachers; Oken, Lamarck, and Lyell lent him their scientific theories; and Channing stirred the residuum which came down to him through his forbears from Luther, Calvin, and Edwards. All these materials he transmuted and moulded into lessons which have his own individual quality and bear his stamp. The precise limits of his individuality are indeterminable, and inquiry into them would be unprofitable. In all probability the case would prove to be much the same with most of the men that the world has named prophets, if we knew as much of their mental history as we know of Emerson's. With regard to the Semitic prophets and seers, it is reasonable to expect that as Semitic exploration and discovery advance, the world will learn much about the historical and poetical sources of their inspiration. Then the Jewish and Christian peoples may come nearer than they do now to Emerson's conceptions of inspiration and worship, of the naturalness of revelation and religion, and of the infinite capacities of man. Meantime, it is an indisputable fact that Emerson's thought has proved to be consonant with the most progressive and fruitful thinking and acting of two generations since his working time. This fact, and the sweetness, fragrance, and loftiness of his spirit, prophesy for him an enduring power in the hearts and lives of spiritually-minded men.

Hugo Münsterberg (1863–1916)

A German-educated psychologist, Münsterberg caught the attention of William James at an international conference in 1891 and was invited by James to chair the psychology laboratory at Harvard. Münsterberg became a prominent part of academic psychology in America and contributed to emerging fields such as forensic psychology (On the Witness Stand *(1908))* and industrial psychology *(Psychology and Industrial Efficiency *(1913))*. As an émigré, Münsterberg was interested in America's relations with his homeland and wrote* American Traits from the Point of View of a German *(1901) as a bid for understanding and rapprochement between the two cultures. In 1904, he authored* The Americans, *which was a more direct and extended analysis of his adopted nation. Münsterberg also wrote a still-admired work of film theory,* The Photoplay: A Psychological Study *(1916). In the selections by Münsterberg that follow here, the first address was delivered at a centenary celebration at Harvard in May 1903—part of a ceremony that included anointing Harvard's home for philosophy, Emerson Hall—and finds him, like Dewey and Santayana, interested in Emerson's status as a philosopher. Münsterberg writes of his American subject with "German eyes" (as he says in* American Traits*) and works to contextualize what it should mean to understand Emerson as a philosopher in the age of Science and Positivism, at the dawn of the twentieth century. In the second address, which was presented on May 25, 1903 to the Social Circle in Concord, Münsterberg reminds his audience what Emerson said some 60 years prior to that occasion: "Harvard University is thin like a wafer compared with the solid land of our Social Circle in Concord." Münsterberg, along with colleague Josiah Royce (who makes a cameo appearance), pledges to build Emerson Hall on solid land; and as Royce notes: "that the founding of this new building may mean the beginning of a new life for philosophical study in our country."*

Emerson as Philosopher

Hugo Münsterberg

At the hundredth anniversary of Emerson's birthday, Harvard University is to take a noble share in the celebration. For years it has been one of the deepest desires of the Harvard community to erect in the college yard a building devoted to philosophy only. To-day this building is secured. To be sure, the good-will of the community must still do much before the funds allow the erection of a building spacious enough to fulfil our hopes; but whether the hall shall be small or large, we know to-day that it will soon stand under the Harvard elms and that over its door will be inscribed the name: Ralph Waldo Emerson. No worthier memorial could have been selected. Orations may be helpful, but the living word flows away; a statue may be lasting, but it does not awaken new thought. We shall have orations and we shall have a statue, but we shall have now, above all, a memorial which will last longer than a monument and speak louder than an oration: Emerson Hall will be a fountain of inspiration forever. The philosophical work of Harvard has been too long scattered in scores of places; there was no unity, philosophy had no real home. But Emerson Hall will be not only the workshop of the professional students of philosophy, will be not only the background for all that manifold activity in ethics and psychology, in logic and metaphysics, in aesthetics and sociology, it will become a new centre for the whole University, embodying in outer form the mission of philosophy to connect the scattered specialistic knowledge of the sciences. Harvard could not have offered a more glorious gift to Emerson's memorial.

But the spirit of such a memorial hour demands, more than all, sincerity. Can we sincerely say that the choice was wise, when we look at it from the point of view of the philosophical interests? It was beautiful to devote the building to Emerson. Was it wise, yes, was it morally right to devote Emerson's name to the Philosophy Building? Again and again has such a doubt found expression. Your building, we have heard from some of the best, belongs to scientific philosophy; the men who are to teach under its roof are known in the world as serious scholars, who have no sympathy with the vague pseudo-philosophy of popular sentimentalists; between the walls of your hall you will have the apparatus of experimental psychology, and you will be expected to do there the most critical and most consistent work in methodology and epistemology. Is it not irony to put over the door, through which daily hundreds of students are to enter, the name of a man who may be a poet and a prophet, a leader in literature and a leader in life, but who certainly was a mystic and not a thinker, an enthusiast but not a philosopher? Not only those who belittle him to-day and who shortsightedly deny even his immense religious influence, but even many of Emerson's warmest admirers hold such an opinion. They love him, they are inspired by the superb beauty of his intuitions, but they cannot respect the content of his ideas, if they do not wish to deny all their modern knowledge and scientific insight. Yes, for the most part they deny that his ideas form at all a connected whole; they are aphorisms, beautiful sparks. Did he not himself say: "With consistency a great soul has simply nothing to do. He may as well concern himself with his shadow on the wall." And yet how can there be philosophy without consistency; how can we interpret reality if we contradict ourselves? If Emerson's views of the world did really not aim at consistency and did really ignore our modern knowledge, then it would be better to go on with our philosophical work in Harvard without shelter and roof than to have a hall whose name symbolizes both the greatest foe of philosophy, the spirit of inconsistency, and the greatest danger for philosophy, the mystic vagueness which ignores real science.

But Emerson stands smiling behind this group of admirers and says, "To be great is to be misunderstood." Yes, he did say, "A foolish consistency is the hobgoblin of little minds, adored by little statesmen and philosophers and divines;" but he soon adds, "Of one will the actions will be harmonious however unlike they seem." Emerson despises the consistency of the surface because he holds to the consistency of the depths, and every sentence he speaks is an action of the one will, and however unlike they seem they are harmonious, and, we can add, they are philosophical; and, what may seem to these anxious friends more daring, they are not only in harmony with each other, they are in deepest harmony with the spirit of modern philosophy, with a creed which ought to be taught by the most critical scholars of Harvard's Philosophy Hall.

What is the essence of Emerson's doctrine in the realm of philosophy? It seems like sacrilege to formulate anything he said in the dry terms of technical philosophy. We must tear from it all the richness and splendor of his style, we must throw off the glory of his metaphor, and we must leave out his practical wisdom and his religious emotion. It seems as if we must lose all we love. It is as if we were to take a painting of Raphael and abstract not only from the richly colored gowns of the persons in it, but from their flesh and blood, till only the skeletons of the figures remained. All beauty would be gone, and yet we know that Raphael himself drew at first the skeletons of his figures, knowing too well that no pose and no gesture is convincing, and no drapery beautiful if the bones and joints fit not correctly together. And such a skeleton of theoretical ideas appears not only without charm, it appears necessarily also uninteresting, without originality, commonplace. All the philosophies, from Plato to Hegel, brought down to their technical formulas, sound merely like new combinations of trivial elements, and yet they have made the world, have made revolutions and wars, have led to freedom and peace, have been mightier than traditions and customs; and it is true for every one of them that, as Emerson said, "A philosopher must be more than a philosopher."

There are, it seems, three principles of a philosophical character without which Emerson's life-work cannot be conceived. To bring them to the shortest expression we might say, Nature speaks to us; Freedom speaks in us; the Oversoul speaks through us. There is no word in Emerson's twelve volumes which is inconsistent with this threefold conviction, and everything else in his system either follows immediately from this belief or is a non-essential supplement. But that threefold faith is a courageous creed indeed. The first, we said, refers to Nature; he knew Nature in its intimacy, he knew Nature in its glory; "Give me health and a day and I will make the pomp of emperors ridiculous." And this Nature, that is the assertion, is not what natural sciences teach it to be. The Nature of the physicist, the dead world of atoms controlled by the laws of a dead causality, is not really the Nature we live in; the reality of Nature cannot be expressed by the record of its phenomena, but merely by the understanding of its meaning. Natural science leads us away from Nature as it really is. We must try to understand the thoughts of Nature. "Nature stretches out her arms to embrace man; only let his thoughts be of equal greatness;" and again Emerson says, "All the facts of natural history taken by themselves have no value, but are barren like a single sex; but marry it to human history and it is full of life;"

and finally, "The philosopher postpones the apparent order of things to the empire of Thought."

And in the midst of Nature, of the living Nature, we breathe in freedom; man is free. Take that away and Emerson is not. Man is free. He does not mean the freedom of the Declaration of Independence, a document so anti-Emersonian in its conception of man; and he does not mean the liberty after which, as he says, the slaves are crowing while most men are slaves. No, we are free as responsible agents of our morality. We are free with that freedom which annuls fate; and if there is fate, then freedom is its most necessary part. "Forever wells up the impulse of choosing and acting in the soul." "So far as a man thinks, he is free." "Before the revelations of the soul, time, space, and nature shrink away." "Events are grown on the same stem with the personality; they are sub-personalities." "We are not built like a ship to be tossed, but like a house to stand." This freedom alone gives meaning to our life with its duties, and puts the accent of the world's history on the individual, on the personality: "All history resolves itself very easily into the biography of a few stout and earnest persons," and "An institution is the lengthened shadow of a man."

Nature speaks to us, Freedom speaks in us, but through us speaks a Soul that is more than individual, an over-individual soul, an "Over-soul, within which every man is contained and made one with all others." Now even "Nature is a great shadow, pointing always to the sun behind her." Every one of us belongs to an absolute consciousness which in us and through us wills its will; "Men descend to meet" and "Jove nods to Jove from behind each of us." Yes, "Man is conscious of a universal soul within or behind his individual life, wherein as in a firmament justice, truth, love, freedom arise and shine." The ideals, the duties, the obligations, are not man's will but the will of an Absolute.

Does not all this sound like a wilful denial of all that has been fixed by the sciences of our time? Does not every Sophomore who has had his courses in Physics, Psychology, and Sociology know better? He knows, we all know, that the processes of Nature stand under physical laws, that the will of man is the necessary outcome of psychological laws, that the ideals of man are the products of human civilization and sociological laws. And if every atom in the universe moves according to the laws which physics and chemistry, astronomy and geology, have discovered, is it not anti-scientific sentimentality to seek a meaning and thoughts in the mechanical motions of the dead world of substance? So the poet may speak, but we ought not to say that his fanciful dreams have value for scholarly philosophers. The philosophy of the scientist ought to be the acknowledgment that matter and energy, and space and time are eternal, and that the smallest grain of sand and the largest solar system move meaningless by blind causality.

And emptier still is the naive belief that man is free. Do we not profit from decades of psychological labor, whereby the finest structure of the brain has been discovered, wherein the psychological laws have been studied with the exactitude of a natural science, wherein we have studied the mental life of animals and children, and have observed the illusions of freedom in the hypnotized man and in the insane? Yes, we know to-day that every mental act, that every psychological process is the absolutely necessary outcome of the given circumstances; that the functions of the cells in the cortex of the brain determine every decision and volition, and that man's deed is as necessary as the falling of the stone when its support is taken away. Yes, modern psychology does not even allow the will as an experience of its own kind; it has shown with all the means of its subtle analysis that all which we feel as our will is only a special combination of sensations which accompany certain movement-impulses in our body. Can we still take it seriously, when the philosopher steps in and pushes sovereignly aside all the exact knowledge of mankind, and declares simply "Man's will is free!"

Finally, the claim for the over-personal, absolute consciousness in man. It is a triumph of modern science to understand how the duties and ideals have grown up in the history of civilization. What one nation calls moral is perhaps indifferent or immoral for another people or for another time; what the one calls beautiful is ugly for the other; what one period admires as truth is absurdity for another; there is no absolute truth, no absolute beauty, no absolute religion, no absolute morality; and sociology shows how it was necessary that just these ideals and just these obligations should have grown up under a given climate and soil, a given temperament of the race, a given set of economical conditions, a given accumulation of technical achievements. Man has made his Absolute, not the Absolute made man, and whatever hopes and fears make men believe, the scholarly mind cannot doubt that these beliefs and idealizations are merely the products of the feelings and emotions of individuals bound together by equal conditions of life. Leave it to the raptures of the mystic to ignore all scientific truth, to get over-soul connection beyond all experience. In short, to accept Emerson's philosophy, the scientist would say, means to be a poet where Nature is concerned, means to be ignorant where man is concerned, and means to be a mystic where moral and religious, aesthetic and logical ideals are concerned. Can such be the herald of modern philosophy?

But those who are so proud and so quick are not aware that the times have changed and that their speech is the wisdom of yesterday. In the history of human knowledge the periods alternate. Great waves follow each other, and while one tendency of scientific thought is ebbing, another is rising; and there is no greater alternation than that between positivism and idealism. The positivistic period of natural science has ebbed for ten or fifteen years; an idealistic one is rising. Emerson once said here in Harvard that the Church has periods when it has wooden chalices and golden priests, and others when it has golden chalices and wooden priests. That is true for the churches of human knowledge too, and for knowledge of all denominations. Forty, fifty years ago, in the great period when Helmholtz discovered the conservation of energy and Darwin the origin of species, one naturalistic triumph followed the other, golden high priests of natural science were working with wooden chalices in narrow, awkward laboratories; to-day natural science has golden chalices provided in luxurious institutions, but there are too many wooden priests. The fullest energies of our time are pressing on to an idealistic revival, are bringing about a new idealistic view of the world, and turning in sympathy to that last foregoing period of idealism of which Ralph Waldo Emerson was perhaps the last original exponent. But also with his period idealism was not new.

When he came to speak on the Transcendentalist, he began, "The first thing we have to say respecting the new views here in New England is that they are not new." Yes, indeed; since the beginnings of Greek philosophy, more than two thousand years ago, the two great tendencies have constantly followed each other. Each one must have its time of development, must reach its climax, must go over into undue exaggeration, and thus destroy itself to make room for the other, which then begins in its turn to grow, to win, to overdo, and to be defeated.

Glorious had been the triumph of Positivism in the middle of the eighteenth century when the French encyclopædists were at work, those men who wrote the decrees for the French Revolution. But before the last consequences of the Positivism of the eighteenth century were drawn, the idealistic counter-movement had started. Immanuel Kant gave the signal, he fired the shot heard round the world; and Fichte followed, whose ethical Idealism changed the map of Europe, and his spirit went over the Channel to Carlyle, and finally over the ocean to these shores of New England and spoke with the lips of Emerson. It is unimportant whether Emerson studied the great transcendental systems in the original; he knew Kant and Schelling probably at first through Coleridge, and Fichte through Carlyle. But in the meantime Idealism too had exaggerated its claims, it had gone forward to Hegel, and while Hegelian thought, about 1830, held in an iron grasp the deepest knowledge of his time, his neglect of positive experience demanded reaction, a counter-movement became necessary, and in the midst of the nineteenth century the great idealistic movement with all its philosophical and historical energies went down, and a new Positivism, full of enthusiasm for natural science and technique and full of contempt for philosophy, gained the day. With logical consistency, the spirit of empiricism went from realm to realm. It began with the inorganic world, passed into physics, then forward to chemistry, became more ambitious and conquered the world of organisms, and when biology had said its positivistic say, turned from the outer nature of being to the inner nature. The mind of man was scrutinized with positivistic methods; we came to experimental psychology, and finally, as the highest possible aim of naturalism, to the positivistic treatment of society as a whole, to sociology. But naturalism again has overdone its mission, the world has begun to feel that all the technique and all the naturalistic knowledge makes life not more worth living, that comfort and bigness do not really mean progress, that naturalism cannot give us an ultimate view of the world. And above all, the reaction has come from the midst of the sciences themselves. Twenty years ago scientific work received its fullest applause for the neglect of philosophical demands. Ten years ago the feeling came up that there are after all problems which need philosophy, and today philosophers, with good or bad philosophy, are at work everywhere. The physicists, the chemists and the biologists, the astronomers and the mathematicians, the psychologists and the sociologists, the historians and the economists, the linguists and the jurists, all are to-day busily engaged in philosophical enquiries, in enquiries into the conditions of their knowledge, into the presuppositions and methods of their sciences, into their ultimate principles and conceptions; in short, without a word of sudden command, the front has changed its direction. We are moving again towards philosophy, towards Idealism, towards Emerson.

Does all this mean that we are to forget the achievements of natural science, and ignore the results of empirical labor, of labor which has given us all invincible mastery of stubborn nature and an undreamed-of power to calculate all processes of the physical and of the psychical world? No sane man can entertain such a notion. Yes, such ideas would contradict the laws which have controlled the alternation of Idealism and Positivism through the ages of the past. Whenever Positivism returned, it always showed a new face, and the teaching of the intervening period of Idealism was never lost. The naturalism of the middle of the nineteenth century was not at all identical with the naturalism of the middle of the eighteenth; and so Idealism too, as often as it returned to mankind after periods of neglect and contempt, had every time gained in meaning, had every time found increased responsibilities, had every time to do justice to the new problems which the preceding period of Positivism had raised. If Idealism to-day wants to gain new strength, nothing must be lost of all that the last fifty years have brought us, no step must be taken backward, the careful scientific work of the specialists must be encouraged and strengthened, and yet the totality of this work must be brought under new aspects which allow a higher synthesis; yes, a higher synthesis is the problem of the philosopher of to-day. He does not want to be ignorant of natural science and simply to substitute idealistic demands in the place of solid, substantial facts; and he should feel ashamed of the foul compromise with which half-thinkers are easily satisfied, a compromise which allows science its own way till it comes over the boundaries of human emotions, a compromise which accepts rigid causality but pierces little holes in the causal world, making little exceptions here and there that human freedom may be saved in the midst of a world-machinery; a compromise which accepts the social origin of ideals, but claims a mystic knowledge that just our own private pattern will remain in fashion for eternity. No philosophy can live by compromises. If natural science is to be accepted and Idealism is to hold its own, they must be combined, they must form a synthesis in which the one no longer contradicts the other, just such synthetic harmonization, and not at all a stubborn ignorance of the other side or a compromise with cheap concessions, was the aim of the period from Kant to Emerson. It is merely the naturalistic period which ignores its idealistic counterpart, which delights in its one-sidedness, which is afraid of harmony because it is suspicious of demands for concessions. It is naturalism only which thinks that mankind can walk on one leg.

If we ask where such harmonization can be found, where the great Idealists of the beginning of the last century have sought it, and where our modern philosophy is seeking it again, well aware that by the progress of science in the mean time the difficulties have been multiplied, the logical responsibilities have become gigantic, we cannot do more here than to point out the direction; we cannot go the way. And it is clear, of course, too, that such an answer has its individual shape, and that no one can promise to give a bird's-eye view of the marching movement while he is himself marching among his comrades. But the individual differences are non-essential. The one great tendency, the Emersonian spirit, if it is rightly understood, is common to them all. What has modern philosophy all over the world to say about that threefold claim concerning Nature, Freedom, and Oversoul? What has it to say when natural science has fully said its say and had its fair hearing, and has been approved as sound and welcome?

A philosopher might answer, perhaps, as follows: You Positivists have done wonderfully with your microscopes and your telescopes, with your chronoscopes and spectroscopes; you have measured and weighed and analyzed and described, and finally explained the whole world which you perceive, and there is nothing in space and time and causality which can escape your search. But did not all that work of yours involve certain presuppositions which you had accepted and which it was not your business to look on critically, but which, nevertheless, may be open to enquiry? Your first claims granted, all may follow; but how is it with the first claims? You examine all that is in space and time, but what are space and time? You examine the material substances and the contents of consciousness, but what is consciousness, and what is matter? You seek the special applications of causality, but what is causality? Well, you reply, you give the facts just as you find them; but do you do that really? And what do you mean by saying that you find the facts? Let us look, at least for a moment, at the very simplest facts with which your work begins. You say there are physical objects made up of atoms, and you describe them as a physicist; and there are mental ideas in consciousness made up of sensations, and you describe them as a psychologist; and both, you say, you are finding. But what does it mean, that you find the physical object outside there and the mental idea of the object inside in you; is that really a statement of your immediate experience? The physicist speaks of this table here before me, outside of me; and the psychologist speaks of my idea of this table, enclosed in my consciousness. Both may do well to speak so; but will you make me believe that I find that doubleness in my experience? If I see this table and want to use it, I am not aware of one table of wooden stuff and another in me of mental stuff. I am not aware of a two-ness at all, and if the physicist says that this wooden table is made up of molecules and has in itself no color and no continuity, and that the mental idea in me furnishes all those qualities of color and smoothness, but has no solidity, then they speak of two interesting worlds about which I am anxious to know, but certainly neither of them is the world I live in. If I lean on this table I am not aware of a table in my mind at all. I know the one table only, and this one table has its color and its smoothness.

I know what you will answer. You will say, in your immediate experience there are indeed not two worlds of objects, a physical and a psychical; the real thing to which our interests in life refer is not differentiated into a molecular object outside of us and a sensational object in us, but it is clear that every real thing allows a kind of double aspect; we can consider this table in so far as it is common to all of us, in so far as it is a possible object for every one of us, and in so far as it becomes an object for the individual, and we can then call the objects, in so far as they are common property, physical; and in so far as we take the aspect of individual relations, psychical; and as it must be of the highest importance for our practical purposes to discriminate between those two aspects, we have clearly the right to consider the world from the point of view of both the physicist and the psychologist. It is, of course, an abstraction if we leave out in the one case the one side, in the other case the other side of our objective experience; but we gain by that the possibility of constructing two closed causal systems of which each one must have its special conditions of existence, inasmuch as the one is conceived as related to individuals and the other as independent of individuals.

Very true, we should answer. Something like that saves you completely, justifies fully your claim to separate the physical and the psychical worlds of objects, the world of matter and the world of ideas; but can you deny that you have lost your case, are you not now yourself in the midst of philosophical, methodological discussions, which your physics and psychology themselves cannot settle, yet which must be settled before they can enter into their rights; and above all, do you not yourself see now that your whole physics, for instance, is not at all an account of reality, but merely a certain logical transformation of reality; that you do not find the world of physics at all, just as little as you find the psychical ideas, but that you can merely work over and reshape the reality which you find till you construct out of it your world of matter and your world of consciousness? What you believed you would find you have never found, while your construction of physical things may have been most necessary for your purposes; but do not deny that you have left reality far behind you.

And so it is with all your doings. You tell us proudly, for instance, that you show us the deepest nature of the world by showing us the elements which the object contains, and that you thus bring us at least nearer to the essence of things; and yet if we begin to look into your real achievements, we are disappointed again to find that you are far away from even attempting anything of the kind. You tell us that water is hydrogen and oxygen, and if we say "Prove it," you show us simply that you can transform the water into hydrogen and oxygen, and that you can transform these two elements again into water. Is that really what you promise? We want to know what the thing is, and you show us simply how the one thing can be transformed into another thing; and whenever we turn to your wisdom, it is always the same story. You show us always, and most nicely, how the one goes over into the other, but you never show us what the one or the other really is in itself. For your practical purposes the first may be the most important aspect, but do not make us believe, therefore, that it is the only possible aspect. In short, whether science describes or explains, it never gives us what we find in reality, but makes out of reality a new ideal construction in the service of certain purposes, and never gives us the things as they are, but merely the effects and changes which they produce. Are we still, then, to be deeply impressed with the claim of the naturalist that he alone has the monopoly of knowing reality, while we see now that every step of his leads us away from reality? And have we still to be afraid to raise the voice as philosophers with the claim that reality itself must find its expression, that there must be a science which shall give account of reality as we really find it, of nature before it is made up and repolished for the purposes of the physicist? Only if we have such other account of nature, then only do we speak of that nature in which we live and in which we act, and compared with such an account of the fuller reality, the constructed schematism of the physicist must appear, indeed, as Emerson said, "barren like a single sex." Not the slightest result of natural science is depreciated, not the slightest discovery ignored, if we insist that all these so-called facts have a meaning only under certain artificial conditions which set them apart from the reality of our life; and in this reality lies the interest of the philosopher. We have thus no reason to reproach the scientist so long as the scientist does not fancy that his science gives an account of nature as it really is. Both kinds of work are necessary, and the scientist may well speak, as the squirrel in Emerson's poem:

"Talents differ,
All is well and wisely put;
If I cannot carry forests on my back,
Neither can you crack a nut."

Natural science has to crack our nuts, but philosophy has to carry on its back the flourishing forests of life, in which we wander and breathe. And if Emerson is right, to-day and forever, in claiming that the facts of natural science are not expressions of reality, it is only a small step to see that he was not less right in saying that man is free. Consider man as a particle in the physical universe, consider his actions from the point of view of a causal science, and there is no possibility of escaping materialism and fatalism. We must understand every activity as a necessary outcome of foregoing conditions. Psychology must do so, and physics must do the same. The empirical sciences would be disloyal to their own principles if they allowed the slightest exception. The noblest gesture, the greatest word, the bravest action, must be considered by them under the category of causality. They are necessary effects of all the preceding causes. It may be interesting, it may be fascinating to follow such lines with the enthusiastic energy of scholarly research. But are we really obliged to accept the outcome as an ultimate word concerning the meaning of our freedom? "Forever wells up the impulse of choosing and acting in the soul." Is it really merely an illusion? Has responsibility still its moral value, are we the actors of our actions, are we still good, are we still guilty, when every deed follows as necessary effect? Is not, then, the whole constitution of the world, which has made us, responsible whenever we move our hand for good or for bad?

But we know now where we are standing; we know now that the world of objects, of psychical as well as of physical, is a constructed world, constructed for the purpose of satisfying our demand for causal connection; for that world holds causality because it is the world seen from the point of view of causality; and just as there cannot be anything in that world of physical and psychical objects which is not causally connected, just so it cannot have any meaning at all to ask for causal connection before the world is conceived in the service of this artificial construction. Reality in itself is not causal, and to ask for the causes of the real experience of our inner life has not more meaning than to ask how many pounds is the weight of a virtue, and how many inches is the length of our hopes. But we must go farther. To apply the question of cause and effect to our real will means not only that we apply to the real object a standard which belongs to the artificial or constructed object, but it means above all that we consider as an object something which in reality is not an object at all. The will which the psychologist describes and must describe, the will which has causes and which is thus not free, is a will conceived as an object found in our mind like an idea, something of which we are aware, something whose happening we perceive, and yet if anything is sure it is the immediate experience that we are aware of our will in a way which is absolutely different from the way in which we perceive objects. We do not perceive our will at all, we will it, we strive it, we fight it; yes, we feel ourselves, only in so far as we are the subjects of will. Our will is our personality, which we do not find but which we are, and which stands opposed and separated by the deepest gulf from the world of objects. Those objects are means and purposes of our will, are ends and aims and instruments; but they come in question for us only as we will them, as we like and dislike them, as we approve and reject them. And if we take this world of objects and reconstruct it into the artificial world of physical and psychical things connected by causality, in this very act of reconstruction we feel ourselves as willing, deciding, approving, aiming personalities, whose wills decide, who think the world as causally connected, whose freedom guarantees the value of our conception of a world not free. There is no knowledge but in our judgments; there is no judgment but in our affirming and denying; there is no affirming and denying but in our will. Our will chooses for its purposes to conceive reality as if it were unfree. What a climax of confusion to think that this conception of an unfree world, the conception of science, can itself now condemn the freedom of the will which has chosen. "Freedom is necessary," said Emerson. We can add, necessity itself is merely a purpose determined by freedom. "Intellect annuls fate," Emerson says. We may add, fate is merely an idea of intellect. Let us be psychologists if we want to analyze, to calculate, to explain the unfree man; but let us be philosophers to understand what it means to be a psychologist. Now the synthesis is reached; the real world is free, but we choose for our purposes to conceive the world as unfree, and thus to construct causal sciences.

And if we understand that in reality man is free and that the psychological aspect of man as unfree is a special way of looking on man for special purposes, then suddenly there opens itself before us the vast field of history, and the historical life, which seemed deprived of all interest by the psychological, iconoclastic mood, suddenly wins again a new importance. We feel instinctively that this free man of reality, this man who is a responsible actor of his actions, he only is the agent of history; and history is falsified and cheapened when it is brought down to a causal explanation of psychological man instead of real man. History had become an appendix of sociology, and what great historians aimed at in the interpretation of the few "stout and earnest personalities" seemed lost in favor of a construction in which the great man and the genius rank with the fool as mere extreme variations of psychological averages. Now suddenly do we understand that history has to deal with the world of freedom, that it has not to explain, but to interpret, that it has not to connect the facts by linking causes and effects, but by understanding the meaning of purposes, their agreement and disagreement, their growth and liberty. Now we understand why Fichte, why Carlyle, why Emerson believes in heroes and hero-worship, why Idealism has been at all times the fertile ground for writing history and for making history, while Naturalism has made technique, and thought in an anti-historical spirit. Our time begins again to think historically. It can do so because it again begins to emancipate itself from its positivistic disbelief in man's freedom and from its unphilosophic superstition that causal science alone is science, that we know only when we explain.

And when we at last stand man to man in full freedom, no longer as psycho-physical constructions but as free personalities, and when we debate and try to convince each other, will you deny that Jove stands behind each of us and Jove nods to Jove when we meet? Would it even have a meaning for us to go on with our talk, should we try at all to convince each other if you thought and I thought, each one for himself, that our will is only our personal will, that there is no over-individual will, no Oversoul behind us? Can we discuss at all if we do not presuppose that there is really a truth which we are seeking in common, that there are certain judgments which we are bound to will, which we are obliged to affirm, which we will, but not as individuals, and of which we take for granted that every one whom we acknowledge at all as a personality must will them too; and if you come with the flippant air of the sceptic and tell me, "No, there is no truth, all is only as it appears to me, there is no objective truth," do you not contradict yourself, are you not saying that at least this, your own statement, expresses objective truth; that you will this with a faith and belief that this will of yours is an over-individual will which is, as such, a duty, an obligation for every one who thinks? Every escape is futile. And all the over-individuality that lives in our will towards truth comes to us again in our will towards morality. Do not say sceptically that there is no absolute obligation, that you do not feel bound by an over-individual will in your action, that you will do in every moment what pleases you individually. You cannot even speak this sceptical word without contradicting yourself again, as you demand through the fact of your saying it that we believe that you speak the truth and that you thus feel yourself bound not to lie. If you leave us doubtful whether your word was not a lie, the word itself cannot have any meaning. Do not try to dodge the Oversoul. Men live and fight in its purposes, and men descend to meet. It is as Emerson said, "At first delighted with the triumph of the intellect, we are like hunters on the scent and soldiers who rush to battle; but when the game is run down, when the enemy lies cold in his blood at our feet, we are alarmed at our solitude." Let the sociologists triumphantly reduce the ideals to necessary social products of evolution in the same spirit in which the psychologist eliminates the freedom of the individual; but let us never forget that such a social mechanism is as much an artificial construction necessary for its purposes as is the psycho-physical mechanism of individuality. In that reality with which history deals, in which our freedom lies, there our over-individual will comes from deeper ground than from the soil and the food and the climate. Our logical obligations, our ethical duties, our aesthetic appreciations, our religious revelations, in reality they do not come from without, they come from within; but from within as far as we are souls in the Oversoul. There is no duty in the world but the duty which we will ourselves; no outer force, no training, no custom, no punishment can make us have duties. Duty is our will, it may be the duty to think for the ideal of truth, the duty to feel for the ideal of aesthetics, the duty to act for the idea of morality, the duty to have faith in the ideal of religion; but it is always our own will, and yet not our fanciful, personal, individual will. It is a system of purposes upon whose reality all knowledge of the world, and thus the world as we know it, is dependent forever. The wave of Idealism is rising. The short-sighted superstition of Positivism will not lurk under the roof of a new hall of philosophy. To be a true student of the most scientific, of the most scholarly, of the most insistent philosophy means to respect and to study the sciences, the physical and the psychical sciences, but at the same time to understand that natural science is not the science of reality, that psychology does not touch the freedom of man, that no life has a meaning without the relation to the Oversoul. We cannot write a whole system and a whole text-book on the front of the new building. It must be enough to write there a symbolic word; happy, forever happy, the university which can write over the door of its temple of philosophy the name: Ralph Waldo Emerson.

Address to the Social Circle in Concord

Hugo Münsterberg

The Chairman {William Lorenzo Eaton}:—The gentleman who has perhaps honored the memory of Emerson by the grandest and most lasting memorial, and who proposed the plan for the Emerson Hall of Philosophy at Cambridge, at an expense of $150,000, which sum he has already raised, is with us to-night, and we desire to thank him in this manner for the great service he has done for the memory of Emerson. I have pleasure in introducing to you Professor Münsterberg, of Harvard University.

Mr. Chairman, Ladies and Gentlemen:—The overwhelming kindness of your generous words, Mr. Chairman, adds much to the embarrassment with which I stand before you. I am deeply embarrassed indeed,—how can I, a foreigner, an outsider, rise at this occasion to speak to a circle of women and men, inspired from childhood by the atmosphere of Emerson's New England? I have been brought up near the Baltic Sea, and in my childhood the waves of the ocean seldom brought greetings from these New England shores to the shores of Germany. And yet my youth was not untouched by Emerson's genius. I am glad to mention this Emersonian influence abroad, because in the rich chord of the joyful enthusiasm of this day I missed only one overtone: a tone bringing out the grateful appreciation which Emerson found in the not-English speaking foreign countries. As far as I remember, I had only three American books, in German translation, in my little schoolday library. At ten I got a boys' edition of Cooper's *Leatherstocking*; at twelve I enjoyed Longfellow's poems, but at fourteen I had Emerson's Essays. And they accompanied me through my student days; I read and reread them, and he became thus the star to which I hitched my little wagon when it was to carry me to the new world from the fatherland. This was not without effect on my own American experiences. Emerson's work had so often represented to me the spirit of the new world which I entered that my mental eye became so sensitive as to recognize the Emersonian lines and curves and forms everywhere in the background of American life. Most Europeans, and especially Germans, who come over, see everywhere the features of commercialism and practical utilitarianism. I was impressed by the idealism of this young, healthful community, and in the first essay which I published on America, in a German paper, only a few months after my first visit, I wrote with most sincere conviction: "If you really want to understand the deepest energies of this glorious country, do not consult the editorials of the yellow press of New York, but read the golden books of the wise man of Concord."

But, Mr. Chairman, I feel that I have no right to speak here as a German, since you have assured us that foreign scholars have been invited for tonight, with the understanding that they are not allowed to come—if a cover has been laid for me, nevertheless, I take it that I was expected not to forget that I am here as the representative of the Harvard Philosophy Department. But, Mr. Chairman, the Philosophy Department of Harvard has not to report any new facts to-night. The Emerson story is very simple, very short, and completely known to you. We saw a year ago that the time had come to place an Emerson Hall for Philosophy on the Harvard Yard, and that it was necessary for that purpose to collect $150,000 before the 25th of May, 1903; we began thus to collect, and when we counted the contents of our purse, on the 23rd of May, 1903, we found there $150,250. That is the whole simple story indeed, and yet some connotations to it may be in order, and I am most happy to make them in this company.

First, do not misunderstand the report of our treasurer; the sum I mentioned was meant from the beginning merely as a fund sufficient to secure a building,—not at all sufficient to secure the building for which we were hoping from the start. We want a spacious, noble, monumental hall—the architectural plans are drawn. To build it as the plans suggest it we need $100,000 more; and while we highly appreciate any small gifts toward this additional sum we are firmly determined not to reject even the largest contributions.

But all this refers to the externals, to the newspaper side of our memorial work; let me speak in this narrower circle of some more internal points. Seen from such an exoteric point of view, it may look as though we Harvard philosophers had said through all the year: "Happy public, you are fortunate in being allowed to build a fine building for our splendid philosophy instruction, and now that the checks are written, the public may kindly remove itself and the students may fill their fountain pens to write down in the new building our glorious effusion of wisdom." Well, over there in Cambridge, we must impose on the freshmen and sophomores, but here let me say at once, we know exactly that the generous contributions of the community were not given to us but to Emerson. And if we ever forgot it, our benefactors reminded us of it. I asked, for instance, the help of Andrew Carnegie, and he gave generously, but when I replied that there would be rejoicing in Harvard that at last he had given to Harvard University,—I saw in the far background the big Harvard Library building we need so badly,—he left me not the slightest doubt that his pledge was for the Emerson Memorial, but not for Harvard as Harvard. Yes, it is thoroughly an Emerson building, a late expression of Harvard's gratitude for her greatest son.

But we know also that the value of this memorial gift lies not in its walls and roof, but in the kind of work which will develop within those walls. It will be a true Emerson memorial only if the words and work in that hall become help and guidance, wisdom and inspiration for new and new generations of Harvard men. There would be no hope of such influence if we instructors really entered into it with an air of self-satisfaction and self-complacency. Let me assure you that it is exactly the opposite feeling with which we look into the future, and this conviction that we must fulfill our duty better, much better, than heretofore, is common to all of us in the whole large Department of Philosophy. A lucky chance brought to me this morning, when I left for Concord, a letter from our colleague, Professor Royce, who is spending his sabbatical year in the country of his childhood, in California. He finds the fit word better than I could hope to do; let me read from his letter. I had written to him that the success seems near, and he replies:—

> "I feel very deeply how great are the responsibilities which the new gift places upon the shoulders of each teacher of the department which is thus endowed. I do not know how much I shall be able to do to live up to these new responsibilities. I only know that the news of the success of the Emerson Hall endowment fills me with a desire not only to improve here and there, but quite to make over afresh, and to change throughout for the better, my methods of work as a teacher of philosophy; and with a determination to devote myself as never before to the task of offering to philosophy and to Harvard my best services. That the founding of this new building may mean the beginning of a new life for philosophical study in our country, and the dawning of a new day for the interests of higher thought in our national affairs, is the earnest wish of your absent colleague."

This is the feeling of our common department's soul. We shall not enter the new Philosophy Hall with the feeling that we can sit there on our laurels, but with the firm promise that we will live up to the duties which the single word above its door demands from us. We all are united by the ideal to make our work in Emerson Hall worthy of the name that honors it.

Mr. Chairman, I see from your pretty menu-card that Emerson once said, "Harvard University is thin like a wafer compared with the solid land of our Social Circle in Concord." That was sixty years ago, and there has not been much change since that time, indeed. But now the change will come, believe us. Emerson Hall in Harvard University will be built on solid land, too, on the solid land of our best will and effort, and we will work that it may prove perhaps even not less solid than the Social Circle,— solid land on which to stand to-night gave me the greatest possible pleasure.

Robert Musil (1880–1942)

Musil's unfinished novel The Man Without Qualities *(1930–42,* Der Mann ohne Eigenschaften*) has been heralded by fellow Austrian-born writer Frederic Morton as "the third member of the trinity in twentieth century literature, complementing* Ulysses *and* Remembrance of Things Past." *As a young man, while studying engineering by day at Brünn, Musil read literature and philosophy by night, including works by Nietzsche, Dostoyevsky, Mach, and Emerson. Philip Payne, a translator of Musil's diaries, notes that Emerson (along with Maurice Maeterlinck and a few others) was "vital to his understanding of the dimensions of human experience."[1] One of the entries in his journal, included below, begins with Emerson's book title* Conduct of Life. *Christian Rogowski has noted that Musil's "narrative works involve efforts to apply ideas drawn from diverse and heterogeneous sources of discourse (including Emerson, Nietzsche, Kant,* Gestalt *theory and, covertly, Freudian psychoanalysis) to narration."[2] Burton Pike tells us that "Musil's view of morality revolves around the problem of how eternal notions and ethical laws can be reconciled with individual thoughts and feelings that are fluid and ever changing. The explorations of this paradox by Emerson, Nietzsche, Mach, William James, and Husserl formed an important basis of Musil's thought."[3] In his Introduction to the novel, Pike claims that "Musil's purpose in writing [*Der Mann ohne Eigenschaften*] was a moral one. He had set out to explore the possibilities for the right life in a culture that had lost both its center and its bearings. [. . .] Musil equated ethics and aesthetics, and was convinced that a union of 'precision and soul,' the language and discoveries of science with one's inner life of perceptions and feelings, could be and must be achieved. He meant this novel as a moral lever to move the world, as Emerson and Nietzsche intended their writing to be experienced."[4] Such attestations suggest Emerson's pervasive impact on Musil, though the evidence of the influence must by and large be inferred from Musil's transformation of the influence in less overt ways. The following few passages from his* Diaries *offer a glimpse of Musil's reading in Emerson. For example, when Musil writes below of the Emersonian meaning of "deeds"—"transform insight into 'deeds'"—he might have the last line of "Experience" in mind: "true romance which the world exists to realize will be the transformation of genius into practical power."*

selections from *Diaries*

Robert Musil

[*Notebook 4*: 1899? to 1904 or later]

4. III. An hour of our Sundays belongs to God, the rest to pleasure that has no relation to God whatsoever.

Religion has quite forgotten its base.

Why do I love so much the illogical products from the early phase of the *Vienna Review* era?

—They have the royal freedom of fantasy—after Emerson—

Their authors are often mediocre human beings but are appealing because they are so possessed.

* * *

"Art is a form of sickness. Or rather it would be possible to treat art as a kind of sickness"—this was roughly how I put it in my *Paraphrases*.

And today, one year later, this idea is reborn within me—so I can see that it really did die in me—just like the whole of that beautiful period.

This sensation of dying—that once led to the abrupt break with Valerie—is evil.

We cannot hold fast to a wonderful insight within us, it withers away, petrifies and then we find that all that is left in our hands is the impoverished logical framework of the idea.

The possession of an insight is of no consequence whatsoever—even if it was the greatest expression of genius since the world began (and the world doesn't exist, by the way). We have to make anxious attempts to transform insight into "deeds" (in terms of the terminology of either Emerson or Maeterlinck). Then we possess it.

(This contrast between insight and deed is, by the way, not without a certain psychological interest.)

* * *

Conduct of life. At the age of thirty, in terms of high culture, one is a beginner, a child. One has to learn to see, one has to learn to think, one has to learn to speak and to write: the goal of all these is an aristocratic culture. To learn to see—to accustom the eye to be calm, patient, to be practiced in "waiting-for-things-to-approach-one"; to defer judgment, to learn to examine, to comprehend the individual case from all sides. This is the first schooling in spirituality: not to react immediately to a stimulus but to get a hold on those instincts that stall and inhibit. To learn to see, as I understand it, is almost the same as what is called—in non-philosophical terminology—"strength of will." The essential thing here is, precisely, not "wanting," suspending the decision. All lack of spirituality, all baseness, rests on the inability to resist a stimulus: one is compelled to react, one follows each and every impulse. In many cases such a necessity is, in itself, a susceptibility to illness, decline, a symptom of exhaustion. Almost everything that is crudely and unphilosophically branded with the name "vice" is nothing but the physiological inability *not* to react. One use to which one can put "having-learned-to-see": as a learner one becomes slow, suspicious, reluctant in all things. Anything alien or new one first, with hostile composure, allows to approach—one pulls back one's hand from them. (Doesn't this image vaguely remind one of the little dog whose hair stands on end and that puffs itself up when it faces a big one? M[usil]) Standing there with all doors open, the obsequious "lying-down-on-one's belly" before every petty fact, the all-too obliging "putting-oneself-out-for," "putting-oneself-into," other people and other things, in short that famous modern attitude, objectivity, is in bad taste, it's non-aristocratic in the extreme.

Path to Express[ionism]

***

[*Notebook 11*: 1905 to 1908 (or later, circa 1918–19)]

25. VII. In *Essays,* I, Emerson says: "A human being belongs only half to himself—the other half is expression. For all people who, in their anguish of soul, demand to express themselves. In love, in art, in greed, in politics, in work, in play we all seek to give voice to our painful mystery." {from "The Poet": "For all men live by truth, and stand in need of expression. In love, in art, in avarice, in politics, in labor, in games, we study to utter our painful secret. The man is only half himself, the other half is his expression."}

Notes

1 Robert Musil, *Diaries, 1899–1941*, ed., trans., Philip Payne (New York: Basic Books, 1998), xxviii.
2 Christian Rogowski, "'Shifts in Emphasis': Robert Musil's *Die Schwärmer* and Twentieth-Century Drama" in *A Companion to the Works of Robert Musil*, ed. Philip Payne, Graham Bartram, and Galin Tihanov (Rochester: Camden House, 2007), 215.
3 Burton Pike, chapter 12 of *A Companion to the Works of Robert Musil*, 357.
4 Robert Musil, *The Man Without Qualities*, trans. Sophie Wilkins and Burton Pike (New York: Vintage, 1996) in two volumes.

Marcel Proust (1871–1922)

Author of the seven-volume masterwork In Search of Lost Time (À la recherche du temps perdu *(1913–1927)), one of the most celebrated works of literature ever written, Proust read Emerson's writing in a French translation beginning in 1895— including* Essais de philosophie américaine *(1851) and* Sept Essais d'Emerson *(1894)—along with work by Thomas Carlyle and John Ruskin. Scholars and critics have noted, sometimes anecdotally and occasionally with sweeping research, some effects of Proust's reading of Emerson. A book-length study such as Michael Murphy's* Proust and America *gives credence to the ways Emerson's influence was present in Proust's writing in both obvious and oblique ways, among them that "Emerson gave Proust a mandate to take his own life as the subject matter of his fiction."[1] But as Proust scholar Reino Virtanen has written in the essay "Proust and Emerson," "let us review the objective facts" of Proust's reading "before venturing on to the more uncertain ground of parallels and affinities."[2]*

In Pleasures and Days (Les Plaisirs et les jours *(1896)), Proust's first collection of writing, quotations from* Essays, First Series *serve as the mottos to four of the pieces. In 1907, Proust quotes from Emerson's work and comments on it in the course of a book review. In letters from 1899, 1900, 1901, 1909, and 1919, Proust makes reference to Emerson; for instance, writing to friend Robert de Billy in December 1909, he says: "It is curious that in all the different genres, from George Eliot to Hardy, from Stevenson to Emerson, there is no literature which has as much hold on me as English and American literature. Germany, Italy, very often France, leave me indifferent." In* Pastiches and Mixtures (Pastiches et mélanges *(1919)) and* The Guermantes Way (Le Côté de Guermantes *(1920/21)), Proust mentions Emerson half a dozen times. As Virtanen assesses these 16 instances: "none of these references is extensive, but most of the comments express esteem and two of them come close to eulogy." Everett Carter, who claims in his essay "The Emersonian Proust" that Emerson was one of Proust's favorite philosophers, located two further "significant passages" in the unfinished novel* Jean Santeuil, *which Proust began in 1896, the year after first reading Emerson, and which was posthumously published in 1952.[3] As Carter notes: "In one, the narrator with a rhetorical question asserts that he would feel 'comme en présence d'un ami' with anyone whose room held "les poésies d'Alfred de Vigny, les* Essais *d'Emerson et le Rouge et le Noir." Furthermore, Carter says "a close reading of* À la Recherche *shows that the basic elements of Emersonian transcendental idealism, which stressed the significance of the quotidian material world, formed the philosophical underpinning for Proust's devotion to the commonplace world of his own experience as the proper subject for his art." Virtanen suggests that Proust's attraction to Emerson likely lies in the latter's* "spontaneity in thought, of his suggestive passages on memory, his penetrating *'aperçus' on morals, his lesson of self-reliance, his cloudily luminous utterances on time and eternity."*

More recently, in his epistolary memoir Little Did I Know: Excerpts from Memory, *Stanley Cavell writes:*

> Proust's early admiration of Emerson is not exactly announced in the one mention of Emerson I recall in *À la recherche du temps perdu*, but it is explicit in Proust's notes to his early translations of Ruskin. (Evidently I am not quite beyond the defensiveness of authorizing my gratitude for Emerson's achievement by appealing to the grandeur of earlier readers of his who have sensed something of the sort.)[4]

* * *

> I am not prepared at this late stage of recounting to take much of a further step beyond, but I must pause to record a lovely discovery in the past year or so (like so many I prize in myself it is one that has come to me terribly, I dare say shamefully, belatedly, namely, that Proust, in the preface to his early translation of John Ruskin's *The Bible of Amiens*, cites Emerson from his late essay "Civilization," whose subject is evidently our needing to be reminded of our relation to what in reading Wittgenstein's *Investigations* I have called the farther shore of human existence and its language [...]; I have sometimes called it the transcendental shore. "Civilization" is the essay in which Emerson announces the central, focal image of the text in his summary words, "Hitch your wagon to a star." Proust responds to Emerson's point, if not quite his method, accurately and richly: "[In such a cathedral as that at Amiens] men of the thirteenth century came to seek [...] a teaching which, with a useless and bizarre luxury, it continues to offer in a kind of open book, written in a solemn language where each letter is a work of art, a language no longer understood. Giving it meaning less literally religious than during the Middle Ages or even an aesthetic meaning only, you have been able, nevertheless, to relate it to one of those feelings that appear to us as the true reality beyond our lives, to one of 'those stars to which it is well that we hitch our wagon.'" Whether this phrase of Emerson's, perhaps slightly modified, was already famous in 1910, when Proust made his Ruskin translation, or whether Proust spotted its distinction for himself in his reading of Emerson, are to my mind equally credible possibilities.[5]

While there is much interest in the variety and extensiveness of Proust's explicit and implicit references to Emerson noted above, in the following excerpts I have chosen to concentrate on a specific scene of Proust's engagement with Emerson that Cavell describes, namely, excerpts from the preface Proust wrote in 1904 for his French translation of John Ruskin's The Bible of Amiens (La Bible d'Amiens *(1885)), later reprinted as the chapter "John Ruskin" in* Pastiches et mélanges *(1919). Here, in selections from an English translation by Jean Autret, William Burford, and*

Phillip J. Wolfe, Proust's reading of Ruskin reflects Proust's understanding of Emerson's work—how it bears on Ruskin's ideas, and also how it amplifies and complements Proust's reading of The Bible of Amiens.[6]

from the Preface to *The Bible of Amiens*

Marcel Proust

Here ends the teaching that men of the thirteenth century came to seek at the cathedral, a teaching which, with a useless and bizarre luxury, it continues to offer in a kind of open book, written in a solemn language where each letter is a work of art, a language no longer understood. Giving it a meaning less literally religious than during the Middle Ages or even an aesthetic meaning only, you have been able, nevertheless, to relate it to one of those feelings that appear to us as the true reality beyond our lives, to one of "those stars to which it is well that we hitch our wagon." Not appreciating until then the import of religious art in the Middle Ages, I had said to myself, in my enthusiasm for Ruskin: He will teach me, for he too, in some portion at least, is he not the truth? He will make my spirit enter where it had no access, for he is the door. He will purify me, for his inspiration is like the lily of the valley. He will intoxicate me and will give me life, for he is the vine and the life. Indeed, I have felt that the mystic perfume of the rose trees of Sharon has not vanished forever, since one still breathes it, at least his words. And now indeed the stones of Amiens have acquired for me the dignity of the stones of Venice, and almost the grandeur the Bible had, when it was still the truth in the hearts of men and solemn beauty in their works. *The Bible of Amiens* was intended by Ruskin to be but the first book of a series entitled *Our Fathers Have Told Us*, and in fact if the old prophets of the porch of Amiens were sacred for Ruskin, it was because the soul of the thirteenth-century artists was still in them. Even before knowing whether I would find it, it was the soul of Ruskin I went to seek there, which he imparted to the stones of Amiens as deeply as their sculptors had imparted theirs, for the words of genius can give, as well as does the chisel, an immortal form to things. Literature, too, is a "lamp of sacrifice," consuming itself to light the coming generations. I was complying unconsciously with the spirit of the title, *Our Fathers Have Told Us*, when I went to Amiens with these thoughts and with the desire to read the Bible of Ruskin there. For Ruskin, having believed in those men of another time because in them was faith and beauty, also happened to write his Bible as they had written theirs, believing in the prophets and apostles. For Ruskin, the statues of Jeremiah, Ezekiel, and Amos perhaps no longer had exactly the same meaning as they had for the sculptors of the past; yet they were at least works full of instruction from great artists and men of faith, and the eternal meaning of forgotten prophecies. For us, if their being the work of those artists and the meaning of these words are no longer sufficient to make them precious, let them at least be for us the things in which Ruskin found this spirit, the brother of his own and father of ours. Before we arrived at the cathedral, was it not for us above all the one he had loved? And did we not feel that there were such things as the Holy Scriptures, since we were reverently looking for Truth in his books? And now we stop in vain before the statues of Isaiah, Jeremiah, Ezekiel, and Daniel, saying to ourselves, "Here are the four great prophets, and the other prophets after them are minor, for there are only four great prophets," there is one more who is not here and of whom, moreover, we cannot say that he is absent, for we see him everywhere. It is Ruskin: if his statue is not at the cathedral door, it is at the entrance to our heart. That prophet's voice is no longer heard. But it is because he has finished uttering his words. It is for the coming generations to take them up again in chorus. {...}

You will then understand that, the poet being for Ruskin, as for Carlyle, a sort of scribe writing at nature's dictation a more or less important part of its secret, the artist's first duty is to add nothing of his own to the sublime message. From this eminence you will see vanish, like low-lying mists, the accusations of realism as well as of intellectualism levelled at Ruskin. If these objections are off the mark, it is because they do not aim high enough. There is an error of altitude in these criticisms. The reality that the artist must record is both material and intellectual. Matter is real because it is an expression of the mind. As for mere appearance, no one has ridiculed better than Ruskin those who see in its imitation the aim of art. "The simple pleasure in the imitation would be precisely of the same degree (if the accuracy could be equal), whether the subject of it were the hero or his horse. We may consider tears as the result of agony or of art, whichever we please, but not of both at the same moment. If we are surprised by them as an attainment of the one, it is impossible we can be moved by them as a sign of the other." If he attaches so much importance to the aspect of things, it is because this alone reveals their deep nature. Mr. de la Sizeranne has admirably translated a page in which Ruskin shows that the principle lines of a tree indicate what other pernicious trees have come in its way and pushed it aside, what winds have tormented it, etc. The configuration of an object is not merely the image of its nature, it is the expression of its destiny and the outline of its history.

 Another outcome of this conception of art is this: if reality is one and if the man of genius is he who sees it, what does it matter what medium he represents it in, be it in paintings, statues, symphonies, laws, or acts? In his *Heroes*, Carlyle does not discriminate between Shakespeare and Cromwell, between Mohammed and Burns. Emerson counts Swedenborg as well as Montaigne among his *Representative Men of Humanity*. The weakness of the system is that, because of the unity of the reality expressed, it does not differentiate deeply enough between the various modes of expression. Carlyle says it was inevitable that Boccaccio and Petrarch should be good diplomats, since they were good poets. Ruskin commits the same error when he says that "a painting is beautiful in the measure the ideas it translates into images are independent of the language of the images." It seems to me that if Ruskin's system errs in any direction, it is in this. For painting can attain the unique reality of things, and thus rival literature only so long as it is not literary itself. {...}

It is certain that when I read the first pages, feeling their power and their charm, I tried not to resist them, not to argue too much within myself, because I felt that if one day the charm of Ruskin's thought should, for me, permeate everything it had touched upon, in a word, if I were entirely captivated by his thought, the universe would become enriched by all that I had not known until then, Gothic cathedrals, and innumerable paintings of England and Italy, which had not yet roused in me that longing without which there is never true knowledge. For Ruskin's thought is not like that of Emerson, for example, which is entirely contained in a book, that is to say, an abstract thing, a pure sign of itself. The object to which thought such as Ruskin's is applied, and from which it is inseparable, is not immaterial, it is scattered here and there over the surface of the earth. One must seek it where it is, in Pisa, Florence, Venice, the National Gallery, Rouen, Amiens, the mountains of Switzerland. Such thought which has an object other than itself, which has materialized in space, which is no longer infinite and free, but limited and subdued, which is incarnated in bodies of sculptured marble, in snowy mountains, in painted countenances, is perhaps less sublime than pure thought. But it makes the universe more beautiful for us, or at least certain individual parts, certain specifically named parts of the universe, because it touched upon them, and because it introduced us to them by obliging us, if we want to understand it, to love them. {...}

Notes

1   Michael Murphy, *Proust and America* (Liverpool: Liverpool University Press, 2007), 83.
2   Reino Virtanen, "Proust and Emerson," *Yale French Studies* 55–56 (1977): 123; originally published in *Symposium* 6:1 (May 1952).
3   Everett Carter, "The Emersonian Proust," *Comparative Literature Studies*, Vol. 29, No. 1 (1992): 39–53.
4   Stanley Cavell, *Little Did I Know: Excerpts from Memory* (Stanford: Stanford University Press, 2010), July 12, 2003, 31.
5   Ibid., August 27, 2004, 533.
6   Marcel Proust, *On Reading Ruskin*, trans. and eds. Jean Autret, William Burford, and Phillip J. Wolfe (New Haven: Yale University Press, 1987), 27–28, 34–35, 58–59.

Virginia Woolf (1882–1941)

Born a few months before Emerson's death, Woolf's acclaim arrived between the wars with the novels Mrs. Dalloway *(1925),* To the Lighthouse *(1927), and* Orlando *(1928), and a book-length essay* A Room of One's Own *(1929). In the following book review of the* Journals of Ralph Waldo Emerson, 1820–1832 *(edited by Edward Waldo Emerson and Waldo Emerson Forbes, 1909), Woolf writes about "twelve most important years" in young Emerson's life—a period of time that ends when her subject and she were about the same age. In her review, originally published in* The Times Literary Supplement *(March 3, 1910), Woolf interweaves her retelling of events in Emerson's life with her appraisal of their significance. She does not find the young Emerson particularly vain or smug, and yet dwells on what seems his apparent divide from the social world. Emerson was preoccupied with the "distempers of his spirit," she says, and "often in company and in solitude he was absorbed in regulating his sensations." In her account, Woolf lends praise and finds fault in the same lines, lines often laced with ambiguous, unfinished judgments: if he is a "schoolmaster" who makes things "very simple for his scholars," such "simplicity" emerges from "concentration upon a few things." She concludes that there is a problem in knowing what to do with Emerson's work, seemingly both his published and private writing. For her, Emerson's penetrating vision is coupled with his blindness—something we can appreciate but that also leaves us, as it left Woolf, with questions.*

Emerson's Journals

Virginia Woolf

Emerson's Journals have little in common with other journals. They might have been written by starlight in a cave if the sides of the rock had been lined with books. In reality they cover twelve most important years—when he was at college, when he was a clergyman, and when he was married for the first time. But circumstances as well as nature made him peculiar. The Emerson family was now threadbare, but it had noble traditions in the past. His widowed mother and his eccentric aunt were possessed with the fierce Puritan pride of family which insisted upon intellectual distinction and coveted with a pride that was not wholly of the other world a high place for their name among the select families of Boston. They stinted themselves and stinted the boys that they might afford learning. The creed of the enthusiastic women was but too acceptable to children "born to be educated." They chopped the firewood, read classics in their spare time, and lay bare in all their sensitiveness to the "pressure of I know not how many literary influences" with which the Emerson household was charged. The influence of Aunt Mary, their father's sister, was clearly the most powerful. There are general rough sketches of men of genius in the family, and Miss Emerson rudely represented her nephew. She possessed the intense faith of the first Americans, together with a poetic imagination which made her doubt it. Her soul was always in conflict. She did not know whether she could suffer her nephews to reform the precious fabric, and yet was so full of new ideas herself that she could not help imparting them. But, unlike them, she was only self-taught, and her fervour boiled within her, scalding those she loved best. "I love to be a vessel of cumbersomeness to society," she remarked. But the strange correspondence which she kept up with Ralph, although it is but half intelligible from difficulty of thought and inadequacy of language, shows us what an intense and crabbed business life was to a serious American.

With such voices urging him on Emerson went to school fully impressed with the importance of the intellect. But his journals do not show vanity so much as a painful desire to get the most out of himself and a precocious recognition of ends to be aimed at. His first object was to learn how to write. The early pages are written to the echo of great prose long before he could fit words that gave his meaning into the rhythm. "He studied nature with a classical enthusiasm, and the constant activity of his mind endowed him with an energy of thought little short of inspiration." Then he began to collect rare words out of the books he read:—"Ill conditioned, Cameleon, Zeal, Whortleberry." The frigid exercises upon "The Drama," "Death," "Providence" were useful also to decide the anxious question whether he belonged to the society of distinguished men or not. But it was the responsibility and the labour of being great and not the joy that impressed him. His upbringing had early made him conscious that he was exceptional, and school no doubt confirmed him. At any rate he could not share his thoughts with friends. Their arguments and views are never quoted beside his own in the diary. The face of one Freshman attracted him, but "it would seem that this was an imaginary friendship. There is no evidence that the elder student ever brought himself to risk disenchantment by active advances." To make up for the absence of human interest we have the annals of the Pythologian Club. But although they show that Emerson occasionally read and listened to papers comparing love and ambition, marriage and celibacy, town-life and country life, they give no impression of intimacy. Compared with the contemporary life of an Englishman at Oxford or Cambridge, the life of an American undergraduate seems unfortunately raw. Shelley took the world seriously enough, but Oxford was so full of prejudices that he could never settle into complacent self-improvement; Cambridge made even Wordsworth drunk. But the great bare building at Harvard, which looks (in an engraving of 1823) like a reformatory in the middle of a desert, had no such traditions; its pupils were profoundly conscious that they had to make them. Several volumes of the Journals are dedicated to "America," as though to a cause.

A weaker mind, shut up with its finger on its pulse, would have used a diary to revile its own unworthiness. But Emerson's diary merely confirms the impression he made on

his friends; he appeared "kindly, affable, but self-contained . . . apart, as if in a tower";
nor was he more emotional writing at midnight for his own eye; but we can guess the
reason. It was because he had convictions. His indefatigable brain raised a problem out
of every sight and incident; but they could be solved if he applied his intellect. Safe in
this knowledge, which time assured, he could live alone, registering the development,
relying more and more on his sufficiency, and coming to believe that by close scrutiny
he could devise a system. Life at twenty-one made him ponder thoughts like these:
"Books and Men; Civilization; Society and Solitude; Time; God within." Novels,
romances, and plays seemed for the most part written for "coxcombs and deficient
persons." The only voice that reached him from without was the voice of his Aunt
Mary, tumultuous in fear lest he should lose his belief in original sin. Before he had
developed his theory of compensation, he was sometimes harassed by the existence of
evil; occasionally he accused himself of wasting time. But his composure is best proved
by an elaborate essay headed "Myself." There one quality is weighed with another, so
that the character seems to balance scrupulously. Yet he was conscious of a "signal
defect," which troubled him because it could destroy this balance more completely
than its importance seemed to justify. Either he was without "address," or there was a
"levity of the understanding" or there was an "absence of common sympathies." At any
rate, he felt a "sore uneasiness in the company of most men and women . . . even before
women and children I am compelled to remember the poor boy who cried, 'I told you,
Father, they would find me out'." To be a sage in one's study, and a stumbling schoolboy
out of it—that was the irony he had to face.

Instead, however, of slipping into easier views, he went on with his speculations;
nor was he bitter against the world because it puzzled him. What he did was to assert
that he could not be rejected because he held the universe within him. Each man,
by finding out what he feels, discovers the laws of the universe; the essential thing,
therefore, is to be as conscious of yourself as possible.

> He that explores the principles of architecture and detects the beauty of the
> proportions of a column, what doth he but ascertain one of the laws of his own
> mind? . . . The Kingdom of God is within you . . . I hold fast to my old faith: that
> to each soul is a solitary law, a several universe.
>
> Every man is a new creation: can do something best, has some intellectual
> modes or forms, or a character the general result of all, such as no other in the
> universe has.

But this is different from selfishness; praise or blame or a reflection in the face of
society—anything that made him remember himself discomfited him; a solitude as
empty as possible, in which he could feel most acutely his contact with the universe,
rejoiced him. "The more exclusively idiosyncratic a man is, the more general and
infinite he is"—that was the justification of solitude, but the fruits depend upon the
worth of the man. Small minds, imbibing this doctrine, turn their possessors into
cranks and egoists, and a delicate mind is strained until it is too pure to act: there was
Mr. Bradford, for example, who, "too modest and sensitive" to be a clergyman, became

a "teacher of classes for young ladies," and was a "devoted gardener." In Emerson the reason was strong enough to lift him beyond the temptation of purifying his own soul. Yet it did not free him, in youth at least, from an interest in the distempers of his spirit which is unpleasantly professional. Often in company and in solitude he was absorbed in regulating his sensations. "When I stamp through the mud in dirty boots, I hug myself with the feeling of my immortality." Only the bland and impersonal spirit which never left him makes such reflections other than smug; they are often dismal enough. But the wonder is that, treating as he does of platitudes and expounding them for our good, he yet contrives to make them glow so frequently, as if, next minute, they would illumine the world. He had the poet's gift of turning far, abstract thoughts, if not into flesh and blood, at least into something firm and glittering. In the pages of his diary one can see how his style slowly emerged from its wrappings, and became more definite and so strong that we can still read it even when the thought is too remote to hold us. He discovered that "No man can write well who thinks there is any choice of words for him. . . . In good writing, every word means something. In good writing, words become one with things." But the theory has something priggish about it. All good writing is honest in the sense that it says what the writer means; but Emerson did not see that one can write with phrases as well as with words. His sentences are made up of hard fragments each of which has been matched separately with the vision in his head. It is far rarer to find sentences which, lacking emphasis because the joins are perfect and the words common, yet grow together so that you cannot dismember them, and are steeped in meaning and suggestion.

But what is true of his style is true of his mind. An austere life, spent in generalizing from one's own emotions and in keeping their edges sharp, will not yield rich romantic pages, so deep that the more you gaze into them the more you see. Isolated, one loses the power of understanding why men and women do not live by rule, and the confusion of their feelings merely distresses one. Emerson, born among half-taught people, in a new land, kept always the immature habit of conceiving that a man is made up of separate qualities, which can be separately developed and praised. It is a belief necessary to schoolmasters; and to some extent Emerson is always a schoolmaster, making the world very simple for his scholars, a place of discipline and reward. But this simplicity, which is in his diaries as well as in his finished works—for he was not to be "found out"—is the result not only of ignoring so much, but of such concentration upon a few things. By means of it he can produce an extraordinary effect of exaltation, as though the disembodied mind were staring at the truth. He takes us to a peak above the world, and all familiar things have shrunk into pinheads and faint greys and pinks upon the flat. There, with beating hearts, we enjoy the sensation of our own dizziness; there he is natural and benign. But these exaltations are not practicable; they will not stand interruption. Where shall we lay the blame? Is he too simple, or are we too worn? But the beauty of his view is great, because it can rebuke us, even while we feel that he does not understand.

Maurice Maeterlinck (1862–1949)

Born in Belgium, Maeterlinck wrote poetry, essays, and dramatic works in French,
including the play Pelléas and Mélisande *(1892). Conceptually intrigued by the*
metaphorical implications of the marionette theatre for live actors—that humans
are but puppets on the strings of fate—he innovated stage dialogue to create what
he called "static drama," a notion he explained in "The Tragic in Daily Life" in The
Treasure of the Humble *(1896), an account that went on to influence the Symbolist*
movement. Three of the essays in that book—on Emerson, Novalis (1772–1801), and
the Flemish mystic John of Ruysbroeck (1293/4–1381)—became an independent
volume, Emerson and Other Essays, *when the work was translated into English by*
Montrose J. Moses in 1912. The chapter on Emerson reflects Maeterlinck's fascination
with interpretable objects and Emerson's unique role in emphasizing the symbolic
nature of existence: he is someone who has "succeeded in fixing some few of the
eternal allusions which we encounter at every instant in life, in a gesture, a sign, a
look, a word,—in silence and in the events which surround us."

Emerson

Maurice Maeterlinck

"Only one thing matters," says Novalis, "and that is the search for our transcendental
self." This self we discern at moments in the words of God, of poets, and of sages; in
the depths of certain joys and sorrows; in sleep, in love and sickness, and in unforeseen
crises where it signals us from afar, and points out our relations with the universe.
Some philosophers devote themselves solely to this investigation, and they write those
books in which only the extraordinary prevails. "What is there of value in books," says
our author, "if it be not the transcendental and the extraordinary?" These philosophers
are as painters striving to seize a likeness in the dark. Some trace abstract images for
us, very remarkable but almost indistinct. There are others who succeed in fixing an
attitude or an habitual gesture of the superior life. A number exist who imagine strange
beings. There are not many of these images. They are never alike. Some of them are
very beautiful, and those who have not seen them dwell all their lives through like
unto men who have never come forth into broad daylight. The lines of these images
are purer than the lines of heaven; but then these figures appear to us so very distant
that we know not if they be alive, or if they were created in our mind's eye. They are
the work of pure mystics, and man does not as yet recognise himself in them. Others

there are whom we call poets, and who speak to us indirectly of these things. A third class of thinkers, elevating by one degree the myth of the old centaurs, has given us an image of this occult identity more easy of access—by blending the characteristics of our apparent self with those of our superior self. The countenance of our divine soul smiles at times over the shoulder of the human soul, her sister, bent to the humble labours of thought; and this smile, which gives us a fleeting glimpse of all that lies beyond thought, alone matters in the works of men. . . .

There are not many who have shown us that man is greater and more profound than man, and who have thus succeeded in fixing some few of the eternal allusions which we encounter at every instant of life, in a gesture, a sign, a look, a word,—in silence and in the events which surround us. The science of human greatness is the strangest of sciences. None among us is ignorant of it; but most of us do not know that we possess it. The child that meets me will not be able to tell his mother what he has seen; however, as soon as his eyes have sensed my presence, he knows all that I am, all that I have been, all that I shall be, even as well as my brother, and thrice better than myself. He knows me immediately in the past and in the future, in this world here, and in the other worlds, and, in turn, his eyes reveal to me the rôle I assume in the universe and in eternity.

Our infallible souls discern each other, and as soon as the child's glance has met mine,—my face, my attitude and the infinite which surrounds them and of which they are the interpreters,—he knows what to cling to; and though he cannot as yet distinguish the crown of an emperor from the wallet of a beggar, he has known me for one instant as exactly as God knows me.

It is true that we already act like gods, and our entire life passes amidst certitudes and infinite infallibilities. But we are blind men who play with precious stones along the roadway; and that man who knocks at my door expends, at the very moment he greets me, as many marvellous spiritual treasures as the prince whom I have wrested from death. I open to him, and in an instant he sees at his feet, as though from the height of a tower, all that takes place between two souls. I judge the country woman of whom I ask the way as profoundly as though I had asked of her the life of my mother, and her soul has spoken to me as intimately as that of my betrothed. She rises rapidly to the very greatest mysteries before answering me; then she tells me quietly, knowing on a sudden what I am, that it will be necessary for me to take the foot-path to the left for the village. If I pass an hour amidst a crowd, without saying anything and without giving it a single thought, I have judged a thousand times the living and the dead. And which of these judgments will be altered on the last day? There are in this room some five or six beings who speak of rain and of pleasant weather; but above this miserable conversation, six souls carry on a conversation which no human wisdom could approach without danger. And though they speak through their glances, their hands, their faces, and their assembled presence, they shall ever be ignorant of what they have said. However, they must wait the end of their elusive converse, and that is why they have an undefinable mysterious joy in their *ennui*, without knowing what hearkens within them to all the laws of life, of death, of love,—laws which pass like inexhaustible rivers around the house.

Thus is it everywhere and always. We live only by virtue of our transcendental being, whose actions and thoughts momentarily pierce the envelope which surrounds us. I go to-day to see a friend whom I have never seen before, but I know his work, and I know that his soul is extraordinary, and that he has passed his life expressing it as exactly as possible, and in accordance with the duty of superior intellects. I am full of uncertainty, and it is a solemn hour. He enters, and at the opening of the door which reveals his presence, every explanation of himself that he has given us during a number of years falls into dust. He is not what he believes himself to be. He is of another nature than his thoughts. Once more we prove that the emissaries of the spirit are ever faithless. He has said many profound things of his soul; but in that small time which divides a glance that pauses from a glance that vanishes, I have learned all that he could never say, and all that he was never able to cultivate in his spirit. Henceforward, he belongs to me forever. Formerly we were united by thought. To-day, something a myriad times more mysterious than thought gives us to each other. For years and years we had waited this moment; and, behold, we feel that all is useless, and, for fear of silence, we, who were prepared to show each other secret and amazing treasures, talk about the time of day or about the setting sun, so as to give our souls an opportunity to wonder at each other and to bind themselves in another silence which the murmur of lips and of thought will not be able to disturb. . . .

In reality, we live only from soul to soul, and we are gods who do not know each other. If it is impossible for me this evening to bear my solitude, and if I should go among men, they will only tell me that the storm has beaten down their pears or that the late frost has closed the port. Is it for this that I have come? And yet, I shall soon go away from it, my soul as satisfied and as full of new richness and power as though I had passed these hours with Plato, Socrates, and Marcus Aurelius. What their mouth utters signifies nought besides what their presence declares, and it is impossible for man not to be great and admirable. What the mind thinks is of no importance beside the truth that we are,—a truth which silently affirms itself; and if, after fifty years of solitude, Epictetus, Goethe, and St. Paul should come to my island, they could tell me only what the smallest cabin-boy on their ship would say to me at the same time, and perhaps more directly.

In truth, what is strangest about man are his gravity and his hidden wisdom. The most frivolous amongst us never really laughs, and in spite of his efforts, never succeeds in losing a minute, for the human soul is attentive and does nothing useless. *Ernst ist das Leben*: Life is grave, and in the depths of our being, our soul has not yet smiled. On the other side of our involuntary emotions, we lead a marvellous life, still, very pure, and very certain, to which our hands which are outstretched, our eyes which are opened, and our unexpected glances which meet, make continual allusion. All our organs are the mystical accomplices of a superior being; and it is never a man,—but a soul that we have known. I did not see that poor wretch who begged for alms on the steps before my door. But I perceived some other thing: in our eyes two identical destinies saluted each other and loved each other, and, just when he stretched forth his hand, the small door of the house opened for an instant upon the sea.

"In my dealing with my child," writes Emerson [in "Over-Soul"], "my Latin and Greek, my accomplishments and my money stead me nothing. They are all lost on him; but as much soul as I have avails. If I am merely wilful, he gives me a Rowland for an Oliver, sets his will against mine, one for one, and leaves me, if I please, the degradation of beating him by my superiority of strength. But if I renounce my will, and act for the soul, setting that up as umpire between us two, out of his young eyes looks the same soul; he reveres and loves with me."

But if it be true that the least amongst us is not able to make the slightest gesture without reckoning with the soul and with the spiritual kingdoms wherein the soul reigns, it is also true that the wisest scarcely ever thinks of the infinite which is moved by the opening of an eyelid, by the bending of the head, and by the closing of a hand. We live so far from ourselves that we are ignorant of nearly everything that occurs at the horizon of our being. We wander at random in the valley, without suspecting that all our actions are reproduced and gain their significance on the mountain top, and it is necessary at times for some one to come to us and say: Raise your eyes, see what you are, see what you do; it is not here that we live; it is up yonder, high above us, that we are. This glance exchanged in the dark; these words which had no meaning at the foot of the mountain—see what they become and what they signify further on the snowy summits; and how our hands, which we believe so feeble and so small, unknowingly reach God every moment.

Some there are who have come to us, and who have touched us in this manner on the shoulder, revealing to us yonder what takes place upon the glaciers of mystery. They are not many. There are three or four in this century! There were five or six in centuries past! And all that they have been able to say to us is nought in comparison with what has taken place and with that of which our soul is not ignorant. But what does it matter! Are we not like unto a man who has lost his eyesight during the first years of his childhood? He has seen the endless spectacle of beings. He has noted the sun, the sea, and the forest. Now, and always, these marvels are ever-present in his make-up; and should you speak of them, what will you be able to say to him, and what will your poor words be beside the glade, the tempest, and the dawn which still live in the depths of his spirit, and are made part of his flesh? He will listen to you, however, with an intense and astonished joy, and though he know all, and though your words represent what he knows more imperfectly than a glass of water represents a broad river,—the small, ineffective phrases which fall from the lips of man will illumine for a moment the ocean, and the light and shadow which dwell amidst the darkness beneath his dead lids.

The faces of this "transcendental me," of which Novalis speaks, are probably innumerable, and not one of the mystic moralists has succeeded in studying the same. Swedenborg, Pascal, Novalis, Hello, and several others examine our relations with an abstract, subtle, and very remote infinite. They lead us upon mountains whose summits do not seem natural or habitable to us, and where we often breathe with difficulty. Goethe accompanies our soul upon the shores of the sea of Serenity. Marcus Aurelius places our soul on the hill-side of an ideal humanity, its perfect excellence somewhat tiresome, and beneath too heavy a foliage of hopeless resignation. Carlyle, the spiritual brother of Emerson, who in this century has given us warning from the other end of the valley, has brought before us in lightning strokes, upon a background of shadow and storm, of an unknown, relentlessly strange, the only heroic moments of our being. He leads us like a flock frightened by the tempest, toward unknown and sulphurous pastures. He drives us into the profoundest depths of darkness, which he has discovered with joy, and where shines alone the intermittent and passionate star of heroes, and there he abandons us, with a mischievous laugh, to the vast reprisals of mysteries.

But at the same time, behold Emerson, the good morning shepherd of pale meadows, green with a new optimism, both natural and plausible. He does not lead us to the edge of a precipice. He does not make us go from the humble and familiar close, because the glacier, the sea, the eternal snows, the palace, the stable, the cheerless hearth of the poor, and the cot of the sick,—all are found beneath the same heaven, purified by the same stars, and subjected to the same infinite powers.

He came for many just when he should have come, and just when they had extreme need of new explanations. Heroic hours are less apparent, those of abnegation have not yet returned; there remains to us only our daily life; and even then we are not able to live without greatness. He has given an almost acceptable meaning to this life which no longer has its traditional horizons, and perhaps he has been able to show us that it is strange enough, profound enough, and great enough to have need of no other end than itself. He has no more knowledge of it than the others, but he affirms with more courage, and he has confidence in mystery. You must live—all of you who pass through days and years, without actions, without thoughts, without light, because, in spite, of everything, your life is incomprehensible. You must live because no one has the right to avoid spiritual events in commonplace weeks. You must live because there are no hours without innermost miracles and without ineffable significance. You must live because there is not an act, there is not a word, there is not a gesture which escapes inexplicable claims in a world "where there are many things to do and few things to know."

There is neither a great nor a small life, and a deed of Regulus or Leonidas has no significance when I compare it with a moment of my soul's secret life. They might have done what they did, or they might not have done it—these things do not touch the soul; and the soul of Regulus, while he was returning to Carthage, was probably as absorbed and as indifferent as that of the mechanic going toward the factory. The soul is far removed from all our deeds; it is too far from all our thoughts. Deep within us it lives alone a life of which, it does not speak; and on the heights where it exists, variety of being is no longer discerned. We move, weighted down beneath the burdens of our soul, and there is no symmetry between it and us. It probably never thinks deeply of what we do, and this can itself be read on our face. If one could ask an intelligence from another world what is the composite expression of the faces of all men, it would without doubt reply, after having seen all men in their joys, in their sorrows, and in their perturbations, "They seem as though thinking of other things." Be great, be wise and eloquent. The soul of the poor man who holds forth his hand at the corner of the bridge will not be jealous, but yours perhaps will envy him his silence. The hero has need of approbation from ordinary men, but the ordinary man does not ask the approbation of heroes, and he pursues his life without uneasiness, as one who has all his treasures in a safe place.

> "When Socrates speaks," writes Emerson, "Lysis and Menexenus are afflicted by no shame that they do not speak. They also are good. He likewise defers to them, loves them whilst he speaks. Because a true and natural man contains and is the same truth which an eloquent man articulates, but in the eloquent man, because he can articulate it, it seems something the less to reside, and he turns to these silent, beautiful, with the more inclination and respect."

Man is eager for explanations. His life must be shown to him. He rejoices when he somewhere finds the exact interpretation of a small gesture which he has been making for some twenty-five years. Here on earth there is no trivial gesture; there are in great proportion the attitudes of our quotidian soul. You will not find in this life the eternal character of the thought of Marcus Aurelius. Yet Marcus Aurelius *is* thought par excellence. Besides, who among us leads the life of a Marcus Aurelius? Here, it is the man and nothing more. He is not arbitrarily exalted; he is merely nearer us than usual. It is John who prunes his tree; it is Peter who builds his house; it is you who speaks to me of the harvest; it is I who give you my hand. But we are so situated that we touch the gods, and we are astonished by what we do. We did not know that all the forces of the soul were present; we did not know that all the laws of the universe were about us, and we turn dumbfounded, like people who have seen a miracle.

Emerson has come to affirm simply this equal and secret grandeur of our life. He has encompassed us with silence and with wonder. He has placed a shaft of light beneath the feet of the workman who leaves the workshop. He has shown us all the powers of heaven and of earth, at the same time intent on sustaining the threshold upon which two neighbours speak of the rain that falls or of the wind that blows. And above these two passers-by who accost each other, he has made us see the countenance of God who smiles with the countenance of God. He is nearer than any other to our common life. He is the most attentive, the most assiduous, the most honest, the most scrupulous, and probably the most human of guides. He is the sage of commonplace days, and commonplace days are in sum the substance of our being. More than a year passes by without passions, without virtues, without miracles. Teach us to respect the little hours of life. If this morning I have been able to act with the spirit of Marcus Aurelius, do not over-emphasise my actions, for I know, even I myself, that something has happened. But if I believe I have sacrificed my day to wretched enterprises, and if you are able to prove to me that I have lived meanwhile as profoundly as a hero, and that my soul has not lost its rights, then you will have done more than if you had persuaded me to save my enemy to-day, for you have increased within me the amount, the greatness, and the desire of life; and tomorrow, in all likelihood, I shall know how to live with respect.

T. S. Eliot (1888–1965)

Poet, playwright, and literary critic, Eliot is esteemed for The Waste Land *(1922),*
Ash Wednesday *(1930), and* Four Quartets *(1945), among other celebrated works.*
In his late twenties, Eliot became well known for the poem "The Love Song of J.
Alfred Prufrock" (1910–15), which was printed as the lead poem in Prufrock and
Other Observations *(1917) and featured one of the two poems presented below,*
"Cousin Nancy." Eliot appears to offer the poem as an ironic revision of George
Meredith's (1828–1909) poem "Lucifer in Starlight," both works ending with the same
line but getting there very differently. Eliot includes a reference to "Matthew and
Waldo, guardians of the faith"—likely allusions to Emerson and Matthew Arnold
(1822–1888), who died in Liverpool a few months before Eliot was born in Missouri.
In "Sweeney Erect," collected in Poems *(1920) and included below, Eliot adapted*
a line from Emerson's "Self-Reliance"—"an institution is the lengthened shadow of
one man." The title of the poem may also reference, from the same essay, Emerson's
description of a figure who "throws himself unhesitatingly on his thought, instantly
rights himself, stands in the erect position, commands his limbs, works miracles."
For a glimpse into personal history, also included are three letters Eliot wrote to
his mother from London in September 1917, aged 29, as he returned to reading
Emerson in preparation for giving a series of 25 lectures on Victorian literature
(to be presented at the County Secondary School in Sydenham beginning on the
28th). At the time he was working at Lloyds Bank, and expected to be paid one
pound sterling for each lecture. As an anecdote of family history, Eliot's grandfather,
William Greenleaf Eliot, trained at Harvard Divinity School in the 1830s, was
a friend of Margaret Fuller and William Henry Channing, and later became a
Unitarian minister in St. Louis. When Emerson visited the city in 1852, the elder
Eliot was among the hosts Emerson most appreciated.

Cousin Nancy

T. S. Eliot

Miss Nancy Ellicott
Strode across the hills and broke them,
Rode across the hills and broke them—
The barren New England hills—
Riding to hounds
Over the cow-pasture.

Miss Nancy Ellicott smoked
And danced all the modern dances;
And her aunts were not quite sure how they felt about it,
But they knew that it was modern.

Upon the glazen shelves kept watch
Matthew and Waldo, guardians of the faith,
The army of unalterable law.

Sweeney Erect

T. S. Eliot

And the trees about me,
Let them be dry and leafless; let the rocks
Groan with continual surges; and behind me
Make all a desolation. Look, look, wenches!

Paint me a cavernous waste shore
    Cast in the unstilled Cyclades,
Paint me the bold anfractuous rocks
    Faced by the snarled and yelping seas.

Display me Aeolus above
    Reviewing the insurgent gales
Which tangle Ariadne's hair
    And swell with haste the perjured sails.

Morning stirs the feet and hands
    (Nausicaa and Polypheme).
Gesture of orang-outang
    Rises from the sheets in steam.

This withered root of knots of hair
    Slitted below and gashed with eyes,
This oval O cropped out with teeth:
    The sickle motion from the thighs

Jackknifes upward at the knees
    Then straightens out from heel to hip
Pushing the framework of the bed
    And clawing at the pillow slip.

Sweeney addressed full length to shave
    Broadbottomed, pink from nape to base.
Knows the female temperament
    And wipes the suds around his face.

(The lengthened shadow of a man
    Is history, said Emerson
Who had not seen the silhouette
    Of Sweeney straddled in the sun)

Tests the razor on his leg
    Waiting until the shriek subsides.
The epileptic on the bed
    Curves backward, clutching at her sides.

The ladies of the corridor
    Find themselves involved, disgraced,
Call witness to their principles
    And deprecate the lack of taste

Observing that hysteria
    Might easily be misunderstood;
Mrs. Turner intimates
    It does the house no sort of good.

But Doris, towelled from the bath,
    Enters padding on broad feet.
Bringing sal volatile
    And a glass of brandy neat.

selections from *Letters*

T. S. Eliot

Sunday 2 September 1917
[London]

My dearest mother,

It is a long time since I have written. I have thought of you all the oftener for not writing, however. I have in the last two weeks—I think it is ten days or more since I wrote—done two articles for the *Egoist*, and two for the *New Statesman*, and have nearly finished a longer one. I must now begin at once to prepare my two sets of lectures; which will involve reading a number of authors of whom I know very little: Brontë, George Eliot, Emerson, Charles Reade, Kingsley, Huxley, Spencer, Samuel Butler. I should slip a prospectus of one of my two sets of lectures into this letter, but I know that enclosures are not allowed. While I enjoy these lectures very much in a way, I shall be very glad when I can give them up altogether, for they take a great deal of time that I want to devote to work of a more permanent nature. Just at present they form a very important addition to my income, but at my present rate of increase of salary I can reasonably look forward to a time when they will be unnecessary, and I shall be able to spend *all* my spare time exactly as I please. When I can earn all the money I need out of one thing, and be able to read and write in the rest of my time without thinking of the financial reward for what I do, then I shall be satisfied. The lecturing really takes more out of me than the bank work during the day. Vivien is staying on for a few days more at Bosham; and I have been for the past five days with my friends the Dakyns's, who live about ten minutes walk from us. It is an economy, and they leave me quite to myself for working, and going out or coming in when I like; and they have a large house with a good library, so that I am quite comfortable. I shall go home again in a day or two, not to abuse their hospitality too long.

I wonder how much longer you are staying at Gloucester. I like to think of you being there until October, but perhaps it will be cold by then. I see that the first draft is being called up soon.

I must get back to work. It is Sunday, and I must make the most of it. After all, without working very hard, I think the times we live in would be unendurable.

Always your very devoted son,
Tom

12 September 1917
[18 Crawford Mansions]

My dearest Mother,

I have begun to be very busy the last few days preparing my lectures. One set covers very much the same ground as my lectures at Southall last year, but more broadly, beginning with 'The Makers of 19th Century Ideas', lectures on Carlyle, Mill, Arnold, Huxley, Spencer, Ruskin, Morris—then the poets, and then the novelists. I have never read much of George Eliot, the Brontës, Charles Reade, or the Kingsleys. I have read *The Mill on the Floss* and *Wuthering Heights* last week. The other course is a continuation of last year's; they want me to start with Emerson, go on to Samuel Butler and Wm. Morris, then the Pre-Raphaelites, and so on. Both of these courses depend for their continuance upon the enrolment at the first few lectures, so I am waiting anxiously. The first lecture is on the 28th. The preparation keeps me fairly well occupied, along with the *Egoist*, the *New Statesman*, the Spanish Irregular verbs, and the subject of Foreign Exchange, which I find very knotty in the books on the subject. I am behindhand with Jourdain too. I have been trying to read May Sinclair's *Defence of Idealism* to review for the *Statesman* and Jourdain. She is better known as a novelist. Did you ever hear of her? She is a pleasant little person; I have met her several times.

Vivien will be back in a day or two, and will no doubt begin cleaning at once. I have been looking after myself, and the rooms have not been cleaned for ever so long. I make oatmeal overnight and warm it in the morning. She is going to bring up quantities of blackberries to make jam.

London has been having perfect weather lately; I only hope you have had as good. I am sorry you intend to leave Gloucester early, but I suppose as you say it is very expensive. You have had Charlotte and the children for a long time; it must be fatiguing at times. I should like to know what Theodora is like now. I suppose very tall.

When I was at Bosham I wished that I could take you out sailing there. I don't regret all the sailing that you and I and father did together, I assure you!

Your devoted son
Tom

I am sorry Henry does not get away.
I should like some ice cream.

19 September 1917
[London]

Dearest Mother,

I shall send this to St Louis, as I am sure that you will be there by the time this arrives. It has seemed like winter here today. The clocks have been put back to solar time, so that what *was* half past six last week is half past five now; so it seems dark much earlier; and today has been a rainy dark day like winter. Saturday still seemed summer; it was hot and cloudless; I spent the afternoon on the river with a man in the bank who owns a 'sailing canoe'; they are tiny little boats like toys. You sit on the edge of the cockpit with your knees up to your chin. A breath makes them move, but they are very steady. There was no wind, and the water was covered with rowboats and punts and canoes; still, it seemed like sailing.

Vivien came back Monday afternoon, after a very crowded and tiring journey; with a quantity of blackberries, which she has made into delicious jam, working all day yesterday; so she is now quite exhausted. She is better on the whole, I think, but she had a severe migraine today in consequence of her efforts.

I had a pleasant evening with Professor {William Ernest} Hocking of Harvard a few days ago. He was just returning. He is a very nice man, but not very intelligent. He had been invited (among others) to come over and inspect conditions here and report them in America—saying of course whatever he likes. He did not impress me as having learned much. I should like to see [James] Woods. He is much more alert.

I am busy reading Emerson. He strikes me as very wordy. He has something to say often, but he spreads it out and uses very general terms; it seems more oratory than literature. His biography is interesting, and contains many familiar names.

I must stop now. It is late.

Your very devoted son
Tom

No letter from you so far this week.

H. L. Mencken (1880–1956)

Journalist, essayist, editor, and critic whose choice of subjects, often fraught in his time—Nietzsche, Jews, democracy, evolutionary theory—were complicated by his controversial interpretations of them. Noted, and now famous, as an acerbic critic of American culture and ideas, Mencken had already written two books on Nietzsche— The Philosophy of Friedrich Nietzsche *(1907) and* The Gist of Nietzsche *(1910)—by the time he wrote "The Unheeded Law-Giver." This essay, featured below, is included in the collection* Prejudices *(1919), published with what appears to be an Emerson-inspired subtitle:* First Series. *Mencken would go on to write a total of six volumes in the* Prejudices *series between 1919 and 1927. Mencken begins by saying that "despite the vast mass of writing about" Emerson, "he remains to be worked out critically," and Mencken's essay is meant, a reader assumes, to be part of that effort. If Mencken disparages "practically all the existing criticism" on Emerson, he is not easy on Emerson either. Given Mencken's familiarity with Nietzsche, it is expected (and fitting) that he would find Emerson's ideas "ratified" by his German reader, but also by what was once referred to as New Thought (or what William James, in* The Varieties of Religious Experience *(1901–02) calls the "Mind-cure movement," where he cites "Emersonianism and New England transcendentalism" as one of the "doctrinal sources" of the outlook). Mencken's evisceration of the critical literature aims, in part, to unseat its confidence in the centrality of Emerson's influence on American thought. At the very end, Mencken's allusion to an "elsewhere" suggests that he has some notion that Emerson's work could be better understood and put to better use than it has been up until 1919.*

An Unheeded Law-Giver

H. L. Mencken

One discerns, in all right-thinking American criticism, the doctrine that Ralph Waldo Emerson was a great man, but the specifications supporting that doctrine are seldom displayed with any clarity. Despite the vast mass of writing about him, he remains to be worked out critically; practically all the existing criticism of him is marked by his own mellifluous obscurity. Perhaps a good deal of this obscurity is due to contradictions inherent in the man's character. He was dualism ambulant. What he actually *was* was seldom identical with what he represented himself to be or what his admirers thought him to be. Universally greeted, in his own day, as a revolutionary, he was, in point of fact, imitative and cautious—an importer of stale German elixirs, sometimes direct and sometimes through the Carlylean branch house, who took good care to dilute them with buttermilk before merchanting them. The theoretical spokesman, all his life long, of bold and forthright thinking, of the unafraid statement of ideas, he started his own so muggily that they were ratified on the one hand by Nietzsche and on the other hand by the messiahs of the New Thought, that lavender buncombe.

What one notices about him chiefly is his lack of influence upon the main stream of American thought, such as it is. He had admirers and even worshipers, but no apprentices. Nietzscheism and the New Thought are alike tremendous violations of orthodox American doctrine. The one makes a headlong attack upon egalitarianism, the corner-stone of American politics; the other substitutes mysticism, which is the notion that the true realities are all concealed, for the prevailing American notion that the only true realities lie upon the surface, and are easily discerned by Congressmen, newspaper editorial writers and members of the Junior Order of United American Mechanics. The Emerson cult, in America, has been an affectation from the start. Not many of the chautauqua orators, literary professors, vassarized old maids and other such bogus *intelligentsia* who devote themselves to it have any intelligible understanding of the Transcendentalism at the heart of it, and not one of them, so far as I can make out, has ever executed Emerson's command to "defer never to the popular cry." On the contrary, it is precisely within the circle of Emersonian adulation that one finds the greatest tendency to test all ideas by their respectability, to combat free thought as something intrinsically vicious, and to yield placidly to "some great decorum, some fetish of a government, some ephemeral trade, or war, or man." It is surely not unworthy of notice that the country of this prophet of Man Thinking is precisely the country in which every sort of dissent from the current pishposh is combated most ferociously, and in which there is the most vigorous existing tendency to suppress free speech altogether.

Thus Emerson, on the side of ideas, has left but faint tracks behind him. His quest was for "facts amidst appearances," and his whole metaphysic revolved around a doctrine of transcendental first causes, a conception of interior and immutable realities, distinct from and superior to mere transient phenomena. But the philosophy that actually prevails among his countrymen—a philosophy put into caressing terms by William James—teaches an almost exactly contrary doctrine: its central idea is that whatever satisfies the immediate need is substantially true, that appearance is the only form of fact worthy the consideration of a man with money in the bank, and the old flag floating over him, and hair on his chest. Nor has Emerson had any ponderable influence as a literary artist in the technical sense, or as the prophet of a culture—that is, at home. Despite the feeble imitations of campus critics, his manner has vanished with his matter. There is, in the true sense, no Emersonian school of American writers. Current American writing, with its cocksureness, its somewhat hard competence, its air of selling goods, is utterly at war with his loose, impressionistic method, his often mystifying groping for ideas, his relentless pursuit of phrases. In the same way, one searches the country in vain for any general reaction to the cultural ideal that he set up. When one casts about for salient men whom he moved profoundly, men who got light from his torch, one thinks first and last, not of Americans, but of such men as

Nietzsche and Hermann Grimm, the Germans, and Tyndall and Matthew Arnold, the Englishmen. What remains of him at home, as I have said, is no more than, on the one hand, a somewhat absurd affectation of intellectual fastidiousness, now almost extinct even in New England, and, on the other hand, a debased Transcendentalism rolled into pills for fat women with vague pains and inattentive husbands—in brief, the New Thought—in brief, imbecility. This New Thought, a decadent end-product of American superficiality, now almost monopolizes him. One hears of him in its preposterous literature and one hears of him in text-books for the young, but not often elsewhere. Allowing everything, it would surely be absurd to hold that he has colored and conditioned the main stream of American thought as Goethe colored and conditioned the thought of Germany, or Pushkin that of Russia, or Voltaire that of France....

Charles Ives (1874–1954)

*An American modernist composer who also transformed his interest in Emerson
and the Transcendentalists into what would become his most well-known and
celebrated piece of music, Second Pianoforte Sonata—"Concord, Mass., 1840–60"
(1909–1915), more commonly referred to as the* Concord Sonata. *The work
includes four movements: Emerson, Hawthorne, The Alcotts (Bronson and Louisa
May), and Thoreau. Immediately preceding the premiere of the* Concord Sonata
*in 1920, Ives paid Knickerbocker Press of New York to print a companion book
of essays fittingly entitled* Essays Before a Sonata *in which he said the music was
meant to form his "impression of the spirit of transcendentalism that is associated
in the minds of many with Concord, Mass., of over a half century ago," to create
"impressionistic pictures of Emerson and Thoreau, a sketch of the Alcotts, and a*
scherzo *supposed to reflect a lighter quality which is often found in the fantastic
side of Hawthorne." Editor Howard Boatwright notes that Ives is regularly casual
in his quotation from Emerson's work—sometimes revising it, sometimes adding
new phrases and lines to it. Since Ives is not an academic, it should be of interest
how Ives remembers, integrates, and even invents such writing; even a well-trained
Emerson scholar may have trouble generating prose that resembles the content and
cadence of Emerson's writing. In this respect, Ives presents a novel case of quotation
and originality, of appropriation and transformation. If his use of Emerson's
writing is inexact or imprecise, it nevertheless stands as a sign of Ives' memory of
Emerson's work and his interpretation of it. And given what Emerson has to say
about quotation as a basis for creative work, Ives' practice of quoting from other
music—in this case from Beethoven's Symphony No. 5,* Hammerklavier Sonata, *and
other works—makes the* Concord Sonata *an Emersonian work in an additional
sense. Though an audio file from Ives' work is not included here (now widely
available in many recorded performances), a sheet of music from the beginning
of the* Concord Sonata *is reproduced. Ives's own opening question contextualizes
the* Concord Sonata, *and his relation to it as an innovative musician: "How far is
anyone justified, be he an authority or a layman, in expressing or trying to express
in terms of music (in sounds, if you like) the value of anything, material, moral,
intellectual, or spiritual, which is usually expressed in terms other than music?"
While it is a common question, it is a rare case when the artist himself strikes out
to make a formal prose response to it, as we find in what follows: the "Emerson"
chapter of* Essays Before a Sonata.

I. "Emerson"

Essays Before a Sonata (Emerson)

Charles Ives

It has seemed to the writer that Emerson is greater—his identity more complete, perhaps—in the realms or revelation—natural disclosure—than in those of poetry, philosophy, or prophecy. Though a great poet and prophet, he is greater, possibly, as an invader of the unknown—America's deepest explorer of the spiritual immensities—a seer painting his discoveries in masses and with any color that may lie at hand—cosmic, religious, human, even sensuous; a recorder freely describing the inevitable struggle in the soul's uprise, perceiving from this inward source alone that "every ultimate fact is only the first of a new series"; a discoverer, whose heart knows, with Voltaire, that "man seriously reflects when left alone" and who would then discover, if he can, that "wondrous chain which links the heavens with earth—the world of beings subject to one law." In *his* reflections Emerson, unlike Plato, is not afraid to ride Arion's Dolphin, and to go wherever he is carried—to Parnassus or to Musketaquid.

We see him—standing on a summit at the door of the infinite, where many men do not care to climb, peering into the mysteries of life, contemplating the eternities, hurling back whatever he discovers there—now thunderbolts for us to grasp, if we can, and translate—now placing quietly, even tenderly, in our hands things that we may see without effort, if we won't see them, so much the worse for us.

We see him—a mountain guide so intensely on the lookout for the trail of his star that he has no time to stop and retrace his footprints, which may often seem indistinct to his followers, who find it easier and perhaps safer to keep their eyes on the ground. And there is a chance that this guide could not always retrace his steps if he tried—and why should he! He is on the road, conscious only that, though his star may not lie within walking distance, he must reach it before his wagon can be hitched to it—a Prometheus illuminating a privilege of the Gods—lighting a fuse that is laid towards men. Emerson reveals the lesser not by an analysis of itself, but by bringing men towards the greater. He does not try to reveal, personally, but leads, rather, to a field where revelation is a harvest-part—where it is known by the perceptions of the soul towards the absolute law. He leads us towards this law, which is a realization of what experience has suggested and philosophy has hoped for. He leads us, conscious that the aspects of truth as he sees them may change as often as truth remains constant. Revelation, perhaps, is but prophecy intensified—the intensifying of its mason-work as well as its steeple. Simple prophecy, while concerned with the past, reveals but the future, while revelation is concerned with all time. The power in Emerson's prophecy confuses it with—or at least makes it seem to approach—revelation. It is prophecy with no time element, Emerson tells, as few bards could, of what will happen in the past, for his future is eternity, and the past is a part of that. And so, like all true prophets, he is always modern, and will grow modern with the years—for his substance is not relative but a measure of eternal truths, determined rather by a universalist than by a partialist. He measured, as Michelangelo said true artists should, "with the eye and not the hand." But to attribute modernism to his substance, though not to his expression, is an anachronism, and is as futile as calling today's sunset modern.

As revelation and prophecy, in their common acceptance, are resolved by man from the absolute and universal to the relative and personal, and as Emerson's tendency is fundamentally the opposite, it is easier, safer, and, so, apparently clearer to think of him as a poet of natural and revealed philosophy. And, as such, a prophet—but not one to be confused with those singing soothsayers whose pockets are filled, as are the pockets of conservative reaction and radical demagoguery in pulpit, street-corner, and bank and columns, with dogmatic fortune-tellings. Emerson as a prophet in these lower heights was a conservative in that he seldom lost his head, and a radical in that he seldom cared whether he lost it or not. He was a born radical, as are all true conservatives. He was too much "absorbed by the absolute," too much of the universalist to be either—though he could be both at once. To Cotton Mather he would have been a demagogue; to a real demagogue he would not be understood, as it was with no self-interest that he laid his hand on reality. The nearer any subject or an attribute of it approaches to the perfect truth at its base, the more does qualification become necessary. Radicalism must always qualify itself. Emerson clarifies as he qualifies, by plunging into rather than emerging from Carlyle's "soul-confusing labyrinths of speculative radicalism." The radicalism that we hear much about today is not Emerson's kind, but of thinner fiber; it qualifies itself by going to "A root" and often cutting other roots in the process. It is usually as impotent as dynamite in its cause, and sometimes as harmful to the wholesome progress of all causes; it is qualified by its failure. But the radicalism of Emerson plunges to all roots; it becomes greater than itself—greater than all its formal or informal doctrines, too advanced and too conservative for any specific result, too catholic for all the churches—for the nearer it is to truth, the farther it is from a truth, and the more it is qualified by its future possibilities.

Hence comes the difficulty—the futility of attempting to fasten on Emerson any particular doctrine, philosophic, or religious theory. Emerson wrings the neck of any law that would become exclusive and arrogant, whether a definite one of metaphysics or an indefinite one of mechanics. He hacks his way up and down, as near as he can to the absolute, the oneness of all nature, both human and spiritual, and to God's benevolence. To him the ultimate of a conception is its vastness, and it is probably this rather than the "blind-spots" in his expression that makes us incline to go with him but half-way, and then stand and build dogmas. But if we cannot follow all the way—if we do not always clearly perceive the whole picture—we are at least free to imagine it; he makes us feel that we are free to do so. Perhaps that is the most he asks. For he is but reaching out through and beyond mankind, trying to see what he can of the infinite and its immensities, throwing back to us whatever he can, but ever conscious that he but occasionally catches a glimpse; conscious that, if he would contemplate the greater, he must wrestle with the lesser, even though it dims an outline; that he must struggle if he would hurl back anything—even a broken fragment for men to examine and perchance in it find a germ of some part of truth; conscious at times of the futility of his effort and its message; conscious of its vagueness but ever hopeful for it, and confident that its foundation, if not its medium, is somewhere near the eventual and absolute good—the divine truth underlying all life. If Emerson must be dubbed an optimist—then an optimist fighting pessimism, but not wallowing in it; an optimist who does not study pessimism by learning to enjoy it; whose imagination is greater than his curiosity; who, seeing the signpost to Erebus is strong enough to go the other way. This strength of optimism—indeed the strength we find always underlying his tolerance, his radicalism, his searches, prophecies, and revelations—is heightened and made efficient by "imagination-penetrative," a thing concerned not with the combining but the apprehending of things. A possession akin to the power Ruskin says all great pictures have, which "depends on the penetration of the imagination into the *true* nature of the thing represented, and on the utter scorn of the imagination for all shackles and fetters of mere external fact that stand in the way of its suggestiveness"—a possession which gives the strength of distance to his eyes and the strength of muscle to his soul. With this he slashes down through the loam—nor would he have us rest there. If we would dig deep enough only to plant a doctrine from one part of him, he would show us the quick-silver in that furrow. If we would creed his "Compensation," there is hardly a sentence that could not wreck it, or could not show that the idea is no tenet of a philosophy, but a clear (though perhaps not clearly hurled on the canvas) illustration of universal justice—of God's perfect balances; a story of the analogy, or, better, the identity of polarity and duality in Nature with that in morality. The essay is no more a doctrine than the law of gravitation is. If we would stop and attribute too much to genius, he shows us that "what is best written or done by genius in the world, was no one man's work, but came by wide social labor, when a thousand wrought like one, sharing the same impulse." If we would find in his essay on Montaigne a biography, we are shown a biography of scepticism—and in reducing this to a relation between sensation and the morals, we are shown a true Montaigne; we know the man better, perhaps, by this lesser presentation. If we would stop and trust heavily on the harvest of originality, he shows us that this plant—this part of the garden—is but a relative thing. It is dependent also on the richness that ages have put into the soil. "Every thinker is retrospective."

Thus is Emerson always beating down through the crust towards the first fire of life, of death, and of eternity. Read where you will, each sentence seems not to point to the next but to the undercurrent of all. If you should label his a religion of ethics or of morals, he shames you at the outset, "for ethics is but a reflection of a divine personality." All the religions this world has ever known have been but the aftermath of the ethics of one or another holy person; "as soon as character appears be sure, love will"; "the intuition of the moral sentiment is an insight of the perfection of the laws of the soul"; but these laws cannot be catalogued.

If a versatilist—a modern Goethe, for instance—could put all of Emerson's admonitions into practice, a constant permanence would result—an eternal short-circuit—a focus of equal X-rays. Even the value or success of but one precept is dependent, like that of a ballgame, as much on the batting-eye as on the pitching arm. The inactivity of permanence is what Emerson will not permit. He will not accept repose against the activity of truth. But this almost constant resolution of every insight towards the absolute may get a little on one's nerves, if one is at all partial-wise to the specific. One begins to ask, what is the absolute, anyway, and why try to look clear through the eternities and the unknowable—even out of the other end? Emerson's fondness for flying to definite heights on indefinite wings, and the tendency to over-resolve, becomes unsatisfying to the impatient, who want results to come as they walk. Probably this is a reason that it is occasionally said that Emerson has no vital message for the rank and file. He has no definite message, perhaps, for the literal, but his messages are all vital, as much by reason of his indefiniteness as in spite of it.

There is a suggestion of irony in the thought that the power of his vague but compelling vitality, which ever sweeps us on in spite of ourselves, might not have been his if it had not been for those definite religious doctrines of the old New England theologians. For almost two centuries, Emerson's mental and spiritual muscles had been in training for him in the moral and intellectual contentions, a part of the religious exercises of his forebears. A kind of higher sensitiveness seems to culminate in him. It gives him a power of searching for a wider freedom of soul than theirs. The religion of Puritanism was based to a great extent on a search for the unknowable, limited only by the dogma of its theology—a search for a path, so that the soul could better be conducted to the next world—while Emerson's transcendentalism was based on the wider search for the unknowable, unlimited in any way or by anything except the vast bounds of innate goodness, as it might be revealed to him in any phenomena of Man, Nature, or God. This distinction, tenuous in spite of the definite *sounding* words, we like to believe has something peculiar to Emerson in it. We like to feel that it superimposes the one that makes all transcendentalism but an intellectual state based on the theory of innate ideas, the reality of thought, and the necessity of its freedom. For the philosophy of the religion (or whatever you will call it) of the Concord Transcendentalists is at least more than an intellectual state. It has even some of the functions of the Puritan church; it is a spiritual state in which both soul *and* mind can better conduct themselves in this world, and also in the next—when the time comes. The search of the Puritan was rather along the path of logic spiritualized, and the Transcendentalist, of reason spiritualized—a difference, in a broad sense, between objective and subjective contemplation.

The dislike of inactivity, repose, and barter drives one to the indefinite subjective. Emerson's lack of interest in permanence may cause him to present a subjectivity harsher on the outside than is essential. His very universalism occasionally seems a limitation. Somewhere here may lie a weakness, real to some, apparent to others; a weakness insofar as his revelation becomes less vivid—to the many, insofar as he over-disregards the personal unit in the universal. If Genius is the most indebted, how much does it owe to those who would but do not easily ride with it? If there is a weakness here, is it the fault of substance, or only of manner? If of the former, there is organic error somewhere, and Emerson will become less and less valuable to man. But this seems impossible, at least to us. Without considering his manner or expression here (it forms the general subject of the second section of this paper), let us ask if Emerson's substance needs an affinity, a supplement or even a complement or a gangplank. And if so, of what will it be composed?

Perhaps Emerson could not have risen to his own if it had not been for his Unitarian training and association with the churchmen emancipators. "Christianity is founded on and supposes the authority of reason, and cannot therefore oppose it without subverting itself. . . . Its office is to discern universal truths, great and eternal principles . . . the highest power of the soul." Thus preached Channing. Who knows but that this pulpit aroused the younger Emerson to the possibilities of intuitive reasoning in spiritual realms? The influence of men like Channing—in his fight for the dignity of human nature against the arbitrary revelations that Calvinism had strapped on the church, and for the belief in the divine in human reason—doubtless encouraged Emerson in his unshackled search for the infinite, and gave him premises which he later took for granted instead of carrying them around with him. An overinterest, not an underinterest, in Christian ideal aims may have caused him to feel that the definite paths were well established and doing their share, and that for some to reach the same infinite ends, *more* paths might be opened—paths which would in themselves, and in a more transcendent way, partake of the spiritual nature of the land in quest—another expression of God's Kingdom in Man. Would you have the indefinite paths *always* supplemented by the shadow of the definite one—of the first influence?

A characteristic of rebellion is that its results are often deepest when the rebel breaks not from the worst to the greatest, but from the great to the greater. The youth of the rebel increases this characteristic. The innate rebellious spirit in young men is active and buoyant. They could rebel against and improve the millennium. This excess of enthusiasm at the inception of a movement causes loss of perspective, and a natural tendency to undervalue the great in that which is being taken as a base of departure. A "youthful sedition" of Emerson was his withdrawal from the communion, perhaps, the most socialistic doctrine (or rather symbol) of the church—a "commune" above property or class.

Picking up an essay on religion of a rather remarkable-minded boy—perhaps with a touch of genius—written when he was still in college, and so serving as a good illustration in point, we read: "Every thinking man knows that the church is dead." But every thinking man knows that the church part of the church always has been dead—that part seen by candle-light, not Christ-light. Enthusiasm is restless, and hasn't time to see that if the church holds itself as nothing but the symbol of the greater light, it is life itself; as a symbol of a symbol, it is dead. Many of the sincerest followers of Christ never heard of Him. It is the better influence of an institution that arouses in the deep and earnest souls a feeling of rebellion to make its aims more certain. It is their very sincerity that causes these seekers for a freer vision to strike down for more fundamental, universal, and perfect truths, but with such feverish enthusiasm that they appear to overthink themselves—a subconscious way of going Godward, perhaps. The rebel of the twentieth century says: "Let us discard God, immortality, miracle—but be not untrue to ourselves." Here he, no doubt, in a sincere and exalted moment, confuses God with a name. He apparently feels that there is a separatable difference between natural and revealed religion. He mistakes the powers behind them to be fundamentally separate. In the excessive keenness of his search, he forgets that "being true to ourselves" *is* God, that the faintest thought of immortality *is* God, and that God is "miracle." Overenthusiasm keeps one from letting a common experience of a day translate what is stirring the soul. The same inspiring force that arouses the young rebel brings, later in life, a kind of "experience-afterglow"—a realization that the soul cannot discard or limit anything. Would you have the youthful enthusiasm of rebellion, which Emerson carried beyond his youth, *always* supplemented by the shadow of experience?

Perhaps it is not the narrow-minded alone that have no interest in anything but in its relation to their personality. Is the Christian religion, to which Emerson owes embryo ideals, anything but the revelation of God in a personality—a revelation so that the narrow mind could become opened? But the tendency to over-personalize personality may also have suggested to Emerson the necessity for more universal and impersonal paths, though they be indefinite of outline and vague of ascent. Could you journey with equal benefit if they were less so? Would you have the universal always supplemented by the shadow of the personal? If this view is accepted, and we doubt that it can be by the majority, Emerson's substance could well bear a supplement, perhaps an affinity; something that will support that which some conceive he does not offer; something that will help answer Alton Locke's question: "What has Emerson for the working-man?" and questions of others who look for the gangplank before the ship comes in sight; something that will supply the definite banister to the infinite, which it is said he keeps invisible; something that will point a crossroad from "his person" to "his nature"; something that may be in Thoreau or Wordsworth, or in another poet whose songs "breathe of a new morning of a higher life through a definite beauty in Nature"; or something that will show the birth of his ideals and hold out a background of revealed religion as a perspective to his transcendent religion—a counterpoise in his rebellion which we feel Channing or Dr. Bushnell, or other saints, known and unknown, might supply.

If the arc must be completed, if there are those who would have the great, dim outlines of Emerson fulfilled, it is fortunate that there are Bushnells and Wordsworths to whom they may appeal—to say nothing of the Vedas, the Bible, or their own souls. But such possibilities and conceptions, the deeper they are received, the more they seem to reduce their need. Emerson's "circle" may be a better whole without its complement. Perhaps his "insatiable demand for unity, the need to recognize one nature in all variety of objects" would have been impaired if something should make it simpler for men to find the identity they at first want in his substance. "Draw if thou canst the mystic line severing rightly his from thine, which is human, which divine." Whatever means one would use to personalize Emerson's natural revelation, whether by a vision or a board walk, the vastness of his aims and the dignity of his tolerance would doubtless cause him to accept, or at least try to accept, and use these means "magically as part of his fortune." He would modestly say, perhaps, that the world is enlarged for him not by finding new objects, but by more affinities, and potencies than those he already has." But, indeed, is not enough manifestation already there? Is not the asking that it be made more manifest forgetting that "we are not strong by our power to penetrate, but by our relatedness?" Will more signs create a greater sympathy? Is not our weak suggestion needed only for those content with their own hopelessness?

Others may lead others to him, but he finds his problem in making "gladness, hope, and fortitude flow from his page," rather than in arranging that our hearts be there to receive it. The first is his duty—the last ours!

II

A devotion to an end tends to undervalue the means. A power of revelation may make one more concerned about his perceptions of the soul's nature than the way of their disclosure. Emerson is more interested in what he perceives than in his expression of it. He is a creator whose intensity is consumed more with the substance of his creation than with the manner by which he shows it to others. Like Petrarch, he seems more a discoverer of beauty than an imparter of it. But these discoveries, these devotions to aims, these struggles toward the absolute—do not these in themselves impart something, if not all, of their own unity and coherence which is not received as such at first, nor is foremost in their expression? It must be remembered that truth was what Emerson was after—not strength of outline or even beauty, except insofar as they might reveal themselves naturally in his explorations towards the infinite. To think hard and deeply and to say what is thought regardless of consequences may produce a first impression either of great translucence or of great muddiness—but in the latter there may be hidden possibilities. Some accuse Brahms' orchestration of being muddy. This may be a good name for a first impression of it. But if it should seem less so, he might not be saying what he thought. The mud may be a form of sincerity which demands that the heart be translated rather than handed around through the pit. A clearer scoring might have lowered the thought. Carlyle told Emerson that some of his paragraphs didn't cohere. Emerson wrote by sentences or phrases rather than by logical sequence. His underlying plan of work seems based on the large unity of a series of particular aspects of a subject rather than on the continuity of its expression. As thoughts surge to his mind, he fills the heavens with them, crowds them in, if necessary, but seldom arranges them along the ground first. Among class-room excuses for Emerson's imperfect coherence and lack of unity is one that remembers that his essays were made from lecture notes. His habit, often, in lecturing was to compile his ideas as they came to him on a general subject in scattered notes, and, when on the platform, to trust to the mood of the occasion to assemble them. This seems a specious explanation, though true to fact. Vagueness is at times an indication of nearness to a perfect truth. The definite glory of Bernard of Cluny's "Celestial City" is more beautiful than true—probably. Orderly reason does not always have to be a visible part of all great things. Logic may possibly require that unity mean something ascending in self-evident relation to the parts and to the whole, with no ellipsis in the ascent. But reason may permit, even demand, an ellipsis, and genius may not need the self-evident parts. In fact, these parts may be the "blind-spots" in the progress of unity. They may be filled with little but repetition. "Nature loves analogy and hates repetition." Botany reveals evolution, not permanence. An apparent confusion, if lived with long enough, may become orderly. Emerson was not writing for lazy minds, though one of the keenest of his academic friends said that he (Emerson) could not explain many of his own pages. But why should he! He explained them when he discovered them, the moment before he spoke or wrote them. A rare experience of a moment at daybreak, when something in nature seems to reveal all consciousness, cannot be explained at noon. Yet it is a part of the day's unity. At evening, nature is absorbed by another experience. She dislikes to explain as much as to repeat. It is conceivable that what is unified form to the author or composer may of necessity be formless to his audience. A home run will cause more unity in the grandstand than in the season's batting average. If a composer once starts to compromise, his work will begin to drag on *him*. Before the end is reached, his inspiration has all gone up in sounds pleasing to his audience, ugly to him—sacrificed for the first acoustic—an opaque clarity—a picture painted for its hanging. Easy unity, like easy virtue, is easier to describe when judged from its lapses than from its constancy. When the infidel admits God is great, he means only: "I am lazy—it is easier to talk than live." Ruskin also says: "Suppose I like the finite curves best, who shall say which of us is right? No one. It is simply a question of experience." You may not be able to experience a symphony, even after twenty performances. Initial coherence today may be dullness tomorrow, probably because formal or outward unity depends so much on repetition, sequences, antitheses, paragraphs, with inductions and summaries. Macaulay had that kind of unity. Can you read him today? Emerson rather goes out and shouts: "I'm thinking of the sun's glory today and I'll let his light shine through me. I'll say any damn thing that this inspires me with." Perhaps there are flashes of light, still in cipher, kept there by unity, the code of which the world has not yet discovered. The unity of one sentence inspires the unity of the whole—though its physique is as ragged as the Dolomites.

Intense lights, vague shadows, great pillars in a horizon are difficult things to nail signboards to. Emerson's outward-inward qualities make him hard to classify—but easy for some. There are many who like to say that he—even all the Concord men—are intellectuals. Perhaps—but intellectuals who wear their brains nearer the heart than some of their critics. It is as dangerous to determine a characteristic by manner, as by mood. Emerson is a pure intellectual to those who prefer to take him as literally as they can. There are reformers—and in the "form" lies their interest—who prefer to stand on the plain, and then insist they see from the summit. Indolent legs supply the strength of eye for their inspiration. The intellect is never a whole. It is where the soul finds things. It is often the only track to the over-values. It appears a whole—but never becomes one, even in the stock exchange or the convent or the laboratory. In the cleverest criminal, it is but a way to a low ideal. It can never discard the other part of its duality—the soul, or the void where the soul ought to be. So why classify a quality always so relative that it is more an agency than substance—a quality that disappears when classified "The life of the All must stream through us to make the man and the moment great." A sailor with a precious cargo doesn't, analyze the water.

Because Emerson had generations of Calvinistic sermons in his blood, some cataloguers would localize or provincialize him with the sternness of the old Puritan mind. They make him *that*, hold him *there*. They lean heavily on what they find of the above influence in him. They won't follow the rivers in his thought and the play of his soul. And their cousin cataloguers put him in another pigeonhole. They label him "ascetic." They translate his outward serenity into an impression of severity. But truth keeps one from being hysterical. Is a demagogue a friend of the people because he will lie to them to make them cry and raise false hopes? A search for perfect truths throws out a beauty more spiritual than sensuous. A somber dignity of style is often confused by under-imagination, and by surface-sentiment, with austerity. If Emerson's manner is not always beautiful in accordance with accepted standards, why not accept a few other standards? He is an ascetic, in that he refuses to compromise content with manner. But a real ascetic is an extremist who has but one height. Thus may come the confusion of one who says that Emerson carries him high, but then leaves him always at *that* height, no higher—a confusion mistaking a latent exultation for an ascetic reserve. The rules of thorough-bass can be applied to his scale of flight no more than they can to the planetary system. [Salomon] Jadassohn, if Emerson were literally a composer, could no more analyze his harmony than a Guide-to-Boston could. A microscope might show that he uses chords of the ninth, eleventh, or the ninety-ninth, but a lens far different tells us they are used with different aims from those of Debussy. Emerson is definite, in that his art is based on something stronger than the amusing, or, at its best, the beguiling of a few mortals. If he uses a sensuous chord, it is not for sensual ears. His harmonies may float, if the wind blows in that direction, through a voluptuous atmosphere, but he has not Debussy's fondness for trying to blow a sensuous atmosphere from his own voluptuous cheeks. And so he is an ascetic! There is a distance between jowl and soul—and it is not measured by the fraction of an inch between Concord and Paris. On the other hand, if one thinks that his harmony contains no dramatic chords, because no theatrical sound is heard, let him listen to the finale of "Success," or of "Spiritual Laws," or to some of the poems—"Brahma" or "Sursum Corda," for example. Of a truth, his codas often seem to crystallize in a dramatic though serene and sustained way the truths of his subject—they become more active and intense, but quieter and deeper.

Then there comes along another set of cataloguers. They put him down as a classicist or a romanticist or an eclectic. Because a prophet is a child of romanticism, because revelation is classic, because eclecticism quotes from eclectic Hindu philosophy, a more sympathetic cataloguer may say that Emerson inspires courage of the quieter kind, and delight of the higher kind.

The same well-bound school teacher who told the boys that Thoreau was a naturalist because he didn't like to work puts down Emerson as a "classic," and Hawthorne as a "romantic." A loud voice made this doubly *true*, and *sure* to be on the examination paper. But this teacher of "truth *and* dogma" apparently forgot that there is no such thing as "classicism or romanticism." One has but to go to the various definitions of these to know that. If you go to a classic definition you know what a true classic is, and similarly a true romantic. But if you go to both, you have an algebraic formula, $x = x$, a cancellation, an *aperçu*, and hence satisfying; if you go to all definitions you have another formula $x > x$, a destruction, another *aperçu*, and hence satisfying. Professor {Henry Augustin} Beers goes to the dictionary (you wouldn't think a college professor would be as reckless as that). And so he can say that "romantic" is "pertaining to the style of the Christian and popular literature of the Middle Ages"—a Roman Catholic mode of salvation (not this definition, but having a definition). And so Prof. B. can say that Walter Scott is a romanticist (and Billy Phelps a classic—sometimes). But for our part Dick Croker is a classic and Job a romanticist. Another professor, {Irving} Babbitt by name, links up romanticism with Rousseau and charges against it many of man's troubles. He somehow likes to mix it up with sin. He throws saucers at it, but in a scholarly, interesting, sincere, and accurate way. He uncovers a deformed foot, gives it a name, from which we are allowed to infer that the covered foot is healthy and named "classicism." But no Christian Scientist can prove that Christ never had a stomach ache. The *Architecture of Humanism* {Geoffrey Scott, 1914} tells us that "romanticism may be said to consist in a high development of poetic sensibility towards the remote, as such." But is Plato a classic, or towards the remote? Is classicism a poor relation of time—not of man? Is a thing classic or romantic because it is or is not passed by that biologic—that indescribable stream-of-change going on in all life? Let us settle the point "for good," and say that a thing is classic if it is thought of in terms of the past and romantic if thought of in terms of the future—and a thing thought of in terms of the present is—well, that is impossible! Hence, we allow ourselves to say that Emerson is neither a classic or romantic but both—and both not only at different times in one essay, but at the same time in one sentence—in one word. And must we admit it, so is everyone. If you don't believe it, there must be some true definition you haven't seen. Chopin shows a few things that Bach forgot—but he is not eclectic, they say. Brahms shows many things that Bach did remember, so he is an eclectic, they say. Leoncavallo writes pretty verses, and Palestrina is a priest, and Confucius inspires Scriabin. A choice is freedom. Natural selection is but one of Nature's tunes. "All melodious poets shall be hoarse as street ballads, when once the penetrating keynote of nature and spirit is sounded—the earth-beat, sea-beat, heart-beat, which make the tune to which the sun rolls, and the globule of blood and the sap of the trees."

An intuitive sense of values tends to make Emerson use social, political, and even economic phenomena as means of expression—as the accidental notes in his scale, rather than as ends, even lesser ends. In the realization that they are essential parts of the greater values, he does not confuse them with each other. He remains undisturbed except in rare instances when the lower parts invade and seek to displace the higher. He was not afraid to say that "there are laws which should not be too well obeyed." To him, slavery was *not* a social or a political or an economic question, nor even one of morals or of ethics, but one of universal spiritual freedom only. It mattered little what party or what platform or what law of commerce governed men. Was man governing himself? Social error and virtue were but relative.

This habit of not being hindered by using, but still going beyond, the great truths of living to the greater truths of life gave force to his influence over the materialists. Thus he seems to us more a regenerator than a reformer—more an interpreter of life's reflexes than of life's "facts," perhaps. Here he appears greater than Voltaire or Rousseau, and helped, perhaps, by the centrality of his conceptions; he could arouse the deeper spiritual and moral emotions without causing his listeners to distort their physical ones. To prove that mind is over matter, he doesn't place matter over mind. He is not like the man who, because he couldn't afford both, gave up metaphysics for an automobile, and when he ran over a man, blamed metaphysics. He would not have us get overexcited about physical disturbance, but have it accepted as a part of any progress in culture—moral, spiritual or æsthetic. If a poet retires to the mountainside, to avoid the vulgar unculture of men and their physical disturbance, so that he may better catch a nobler theme for his symphony, Emerson tells him: "Man's culture can spare nothing, wants all the material. He is to convert all impediments into instruments, all enemies into power." The latest product of man's culture, the aeroplane, then sails o'er the mountain, and instead of an inspiration—a spray of tobacco-juice falls on the poet. "Calm yourself, Poet!" says Emerson. "Culture will convert Furies into Muses and hells into benefit. This wouldn't have befallen you if it hadn't been for the latest transcendent product of the genius of culture (we won't say that kind), a consummation of the dreams of poets, from David to Tennyson." Material progress is but a means of expression. Realize that man's coarseness has its future and will also be refined in the gradual uprise. Turning the world upside down may be one of its lesser incidents. It is the cause, seldom the effect, that interests Emerson. He can help the cause—the effect must help itself. He might have said to those who talk knowingly about the cause of war—or of the last war, and who would trace it down through long vistas of cosmic, political, moral evolution and what not—he might say that the cause of it was as simple as that of any dog-fight—the "hog-mind" of the minority against the universal mind, the majority. The un-courage of the former fears to believe in the innate goodness of mankind. The cause is always the same; the effect different by chance. It is as easy for a hog, even a stupid one, to step on a box of matches under a tenement with a thousand souls as under an empty bird-house. The many kindly burn up for the few; for the minority is selfish and the majority generous. The minority has ruled the world for physical reasons. The physical reasons are being removed by this "converting culture." Webster will not much longer have to grope for the mind of his constituency. The majority—the people—will need no intermediary. Governments will pass from the representative to the direct. The hog-mind is the principal thing that is making this transition slow. The biggest prop to the hog-mind is pride—pride in property and the power property gives. Ruskin backs this up—"it is at the bottom of all great mistakes; other passions do occasional good, but whenever pride puts in its word . . . it is all over with the artist." The hog-mind and its handmaidens in disorder—superficial brightness, fundamental dullness, then cowardice and suspicion; all a part of the minority (the non-people); the antithesis of everything called "soul," "spirit," "Christianity," "truth," "freedom"—will give way more and more to the great primal truths: that there is more good than evil, that God is on the side of the majority (the people), that he is not enthusiastic about the minority (the non-people), that he has made men greater than man, that he has made the universal mind and the over-soul greater and a part of the individual mind and soul, that he has made the Divine a part of all.

Again, if a picture in economics is before him, Emerson plunges down to the things that *are* because they are *better* than they are. If there is a row (which there usually is between the ebb and flood tide in the material ocean), for example, between the theory of the present order of competition and of attractive and associated labor, he would sympathize with Ricardo, perhaps, that labor is the measure of value, but "embrace, as do generous minds, the proposition of labor shared by all." He would go deeper than political economics, strain out the self-factor from both theories, and make the measure of each pretty much the same, so that the natural (the majority) would win, but not to the disadvantage of the minority (the artificial) because this has disappeared—it is of the majority. John Stuart Mill's political economy is losing value because it was written by a mind more a banker's than a poet's. The poet knows that there is no such thing as the perpetual law of supply and demand—perhaps not of demand and supply, or of the wage-fund, or price-level, or increments earned or unearned—and that the existence of personal or public property may not prove the existence of God.

Emerson seems to use the great definite interests of humanity to express the greater, indefinite, spiritual values—to fulfill what he can in his realms of revelation. Thus, it seems that so close a relation exists between his content and expression, his substance and manner, that if he were more definite in the latter he would lose power in the former.

Perhaps some of those occasional flashes would have been unexpressed—flashes that have gone down through the world and will flame on through the ages—flashes that approach as near the divine as Beethoven in his most inspired moments—flashes of transcendent beauty, of such universal import, that they may bring, of a sudden, some intimate personal experience, and produce the same indescribable effect that comes in rare instances to men from some common sensation.

In the early morning of a Memorial Day, a boy is awakened by martial music—a village band is marching down the street—and as the strains of Reeves' majestic *Seventh Regiment March* come nearer and nearer—he seems of a sudden translated—a moment of vivid power comes, a consciousness of material nobility—an exultant something gleaning with the possibilities of this life—an assurance that nothing is impossible, and that the whole world lies at his feet. But, as the band turns the corner, at the soldiers' monument, and the march steps of the Grand Army become fainter and fainter, the boy's vision slowly vanishes—his "world" becomes less and less probable—but the experience ever lies within him in its reality.

Later in life, the same boy hears the Sabbath morning bell ringing out from the white steeple at the "Center," and as it draws him to it, through the autumn fields of sumach and asters, a Gospel hymn of simple devotion comes out to him—"There's a wideness in God's mercy"—an instant suggestion of that Memorial Day morning comes—but the moment is of deeper import—there is no personal exultation—no intimate world vision—no magnified personal hope—and in their place a profound sense of a spiritual truth—a sin within reach of forgiveness. And as the hymn voices die away, there lies at his feet—not the world, but the figure of the Saviour—he sees an unfathomable courage—an immortality for the lowest—the vastness in humility, the kindness of the human heart, man's noblest strength—and he knows that God is nothing—nothing—but love!

Whence cometh the wonder of a moment? From sources we know not. But we do know that from obscurity and from this higher Orpheus come measures of sphere melodies (paraphrased from a passage in *Sartor Resartus*) flowing in wild, native tones, ravaging the souls of men, flowing now with thousand-fold accompaniments and rich symphonies through all our hearts, modulating and divinely leading them.

III

What is character? In how far does it sustain the soul, or the soul it? Is it a part of the soul? And then—what is the soul? Plato knows, but cannot tell us. Every new-born man knows, but no one tells us. "Nature will not be disposed of easily. No power of genius has ever yet had the smallest success in explaining existence. The perfect enigma remains." As every blind man sees the sun, so character may be the part of the soul we, the blind, can see; and then have the right to imagine that the soul is each man's share of God, and character the muscle which tries to reveal its mysteries—a kind of its first visible radiance—the right to know that it is the voice which is always calling the pragmatist a fool.

At any rate, it can be said that Emerson's character has much to do with his power upon us. Men who have known nothing of his life have borne witness to this. It is directly at the root of his substance, and affects his manner only indirectly. It gives the sincerity to the constant spiritual hopefulness we are always conscious of, and which carries with it, often, even when the expression is somber, a note of exultation in the victories of "the innate virtues" of man. And it is this, perhaps, that makes us feel his courage—not a self-courage, but a sympathetic one—courageous even to tenderness. It is the open courage of a kind heart, of not forcing opinions—a thing much needed when the cowardly, underhanded courage of the fanatic would *force* opinion. It is the courage of believing in freedom, per se, rather than of trying to force everyone to *see* that you believe in it—the courage of the willingness to be reformed, rather than of reforming—the courage teaching that sacrifice is bravery, and force, fear—the courage of righteous indignation, of stammering eloquence, of spiritual insight, a courage ever contracting or unfolding a philosophy as it grows—a courage that would make the impossible possible. Oliver Wendell Holmes says that Emerson attempted the impossible in "The Over-Soul"—"an overflow of spiritual imagination." But he (Emerson) accomplished the impossible in attempting it and still leaving it impossible. A courageous struggle to satisfy, as Thoreau says, hunger rather than the palate—the hunger of a lifetime sometimes by one meal. His essay on the pre-soul (which he did not write) treats of that part of the over-soul's influence on unborn ages, and attempts the impossible only when it stops attempting it.

Like all courageous souls, the higher Emerson soars, the more lowly he becomes. "Do you think the porter and the cook have no anecdotes, no experiences, no wonders for you? Everybody knows as much as the savant." To some, the way to be humble is to admonish the humble, not learn from them. Carlyle would have Emerson teach by more definite signs, rather than interpret his revelations, or shall we say, preach. Admitting all the inspiration and help that *Sartor Resartus* has given, in spite of its vaudeville and tragic stages, to many young men getting under way in the life of tailor or king, we believe it can be said (but very broadly said) that Emerson, either in the first or second series of essays, taken as a whole, gives, it seems to us, greater inspiration, partly because his manner is less didactic, less personally suggestive, perhaps less clearly or obviously human than Carlyle's. How direct this inspiration is, is a matter of personal viewpoint, temperament, perhaps inheritance. Augustine Birrell says he does not feel it—and he seems not to, even indirectly. Apparently "a non-sequacious author" can't inspire him, for Emerson seems to him "a little thin and vague." Is Emerson or the English climate to blame for this? He, Birrell, says a really great author dissipates all fears as to his staying-power (though fears for our staying-power, not Emerson's, is what we would like dissipated). Besides, around a really great author there are no fears to dissipate. "A wise author never allows his reader's mind to be at large, . . ." but Emerson is not a wise author. His essay on prudence has nothing to do with prudence, for to be wise and prudent he must put explanation first, and let his substance dissolve because of it. "How carefully," says Birrell again, "does a really great writer, like Dr. Newman or M. Rénan, explain to you what he is going to do, and how he is going to do it!" Personally we like the chance of having a hand in the "explaining." We prefer to look at flowers, but not through botany, for it seems that if we look at them alone, we see a beauty of Nature's poetry, a direct gift from the Divine, and if we look at botany alone, we see the beauty of Nature's intellect, a direct gift of the Divine; if we look at both together, we see nothing.

Thus it seems that Carlyle and Birrell would have it that courage and humility have something to do with "explanation"—and that it is not "a respect for all," a faith in the power of "innate virtue" to perceive by "relativeness rather than penetration" that causes Emerson to withhold explanation to a greater degree than many writers. Carlyle asks for more utility, and Birrell for more inspiration. But we like to believe that it is the height of Emerson's character, evidenced especially in his courage and humility, that shades its quality, rather than that its virtue is less—that it is his height that will make him more and more valuable and more and more within the reach of all—whether it be by utility, inspiration, or other needs of the human soul.

Cannot some of the most valuable kinds of utility and inspiration come from humility in its highest and purest forms? For is not the truest kind of humility a kind of glorified or transcendent democracy—the practicing it rather than the talking it— the not wanting to level all finite things, but the being willing to be leveled towards the infinite? Until humility produces that frame of mind and spirit in the artist, can his audience gain the greatest kind of utility and inspiration, which might be quite invisible at first? Emerson realizes the value of "the many"—that the law of averages has a divine source. He recognizes the various life-values *in reality*—not by reason of their closeness or remoteness, but because he sympathizes with men who live them, and the *majority* do. "The private store of reason is not great—would that there were a public store for man," cries Pascal. "But there is," says Emerson. "It is the universal mind, an institution congenital with the common or over-soul." Pascal is discouraged, for he lets himself be influenced by surface political and religious history, which shows the struggle of the group led by an individual rather than that of the individual led by himself—a struggle as much privately caused as privately led. The main path of all social progress has been spiritual rather than intellectual in character, but the many by-paths of individual materialism, though never obliterating the highway, have dimmed its outlines and caused travelers to confuse the colors along the road. A more natural way of freeing the congestion in the benefits of material progress will make it less difficult for the majority to recognize the true relation between the important spiritual and religious values and the less important intellectual and economic values. As the action of the intellect and universal mind becomes more and more identical, the clearer will the relation of all values become. But for physical reasons, the group has had to depend upon the individual as leaders, and the leaders, with few exceptions, restrained the universal mind—they trusted to the "private store." But now, thanks to the lessons of evolution, which Nature has been teaching men since and before the days of Socrates, the public store of reason is gradually taking the place of the once-needed leader. From the Chaldean tablet to the wireless message, this public store has been wonderfully opened. The results of these lessons, the possibilities they are offering for ever coordinating the mind of humanity, the culmination of this age-instruction, are seen today in many ways. Labor federation, suffrage extension, are two instances that come to mind among the many. In these manifestations, by reason of tradition, or the bad-habit part of tradition, the hog-mind of the few (the minority) comes in play. The possessors of this are called leaders, but even these "thick-skins" are beginning to see that the *movement* is the leader, and that they are only clerks. Broadly speaking, the effects evidenced in the political side of history have so much of the physical because the causes have been so much of the physical. As a result, the leaders, for the most part, have been under-average men, with skins, thick, wits slick, and hands quick with under-values—otherwise they would not have become leaders. But the day of leaders, as such, is gradually closing—the people are beginning to lead themselves—the public store of reason is slowly being opened—the common universal mind and the common over-soul is slowly but inevitably coming into its own. "Let a man believe in God, not in names and places and persons. Let the great soul incarnated in some poor . . . sad and simple Joan go out to service and sweep chimneys and scrub floors . . . its effulgent day beams cannot be muffled, . . ." and then, "to sweep and scrub will instantly appear supreme and beautiful actions . . . and *all* people will get brooms and mops." Perhaps, if all of Emerson—his works and his life—were to be swept away, and nothing of him but the record of the following incident remained to men—the influence of his soul would still be great. A working woman after coming from one of his lectures said: "I love to go to hear Emerson, not because I understand him, but because he looks as though he thought everybody was as good as he was." Is it not the courage—the spiritual hopefulness in his humility—that makes this story possible and true? Is it not this trait in his character that sets him above all creeds—that gives him inspired belief in the common mind and soul? Is it not this courageous universalism that gives conviction to his prophecy, and that makes his symphonies of revelation begin and end with nothing but the strength and beauty of innate goodness in man, in Nature and in God—the greatest and most inspiring theme of Concord Transcendental philosophy, as we hear it?

And it is from such a world-compelling theme and from such vantage ground that Emerson rises to almost perfect freedom of action, of thought and of soul, in any direction and to any height. A vantage ground somewhat vaster than Schelling's conception of transcendental philosophy—"a philosophy of Nature become subjective." In Concord it *includes* the objective, and becomes subjective to nothing but freedom and the absolute law. It is this underlying courage of the purest humility that gives Emerson that outward aspect of serenity which is felt to so great an extent in much of his work, especially in his codas and perorations. And within this poised strength, we are conscious of that "original authentic fire" which Emerson missed in Shelley; we are conscious of something that is not dispassionate, something that is at times almost turbulent—a kind of furious calm lying deeply in the conviction of the eventual triumph of the soul and its union with God!

Let us place the transcendent Emerson where he, himself places Milton, in Wordsworth's apostrophe: "Pure as the naked heavens, majestic, free, so didst thou travel on life's common way in cheerful Godliness."

The Godliness of spiritual courage and hopefulness—these fathers of faith rise to a glorified peace in the depth of his greater perorations. There is an "oracle" at the beginning of the *Fifth Symphony*; in those four notes lies one of Beethoven's greatest messages. We would place its translation above the relentlessness of fate knocking at the door, above the greater human message of destiny, and strive to bring it towards the spiritual message of Emerson's revelations, even to the "common heart" of Concord— the soul of humanity knocking at the door of the divine mysteries, radiant in the faith that it *will* be opened—and the human become the divine!

D. H. Lawrence (1885–1930)

When Lawrence came to write the following review of Stuart Sherman's Americans, he had just published the final version of Studies in Classic American Literature *(1923). Despite his admiration for Emerson, Lawrence spoke of him only in passing in* Studies, *and then as part of a group complaint, which included Melville, in whom Lawrence noted a likeness: "rather a tiresome New Englander of the ethical-mystical-transcendentalist sort." And so it is in this chatty, often acerbic and derisive, review of Sherman's book and its chosen subjects, published in the* Dial *(74.5, May 1923)—a rehabilitation of the Transcendentalist journal Emerson once edited, which in its later form existed until 1929—that we find Lawrence's more developed views on Emerson. Lawrence remains ambivalent, acknowledging the solidity of Emerson's reputation but wondering what he and his generation are to do with it: "Well, we're pretty sick of the ideal painters and the uplifting singers. As a matter of fact we have worked the ideal bit of our nature to death, and we shall go crazy if we can't start working from some other bit."*

Americans

D. H. Lawrence

Professor Sherman once more coaxing American criticism the way it should go.

Like Benjamin Franklin, one of his heroes, he attempts the invention of a creed that shall "satisfy the professors of all religions, and offend none."

He smites the marauding Mr. Mencken with a velvet glove, and pierces the obstinate Mr. More with a reproachful look. Both gentlemen, of course, will purr and feel flattered.

That's how Professor Sherman treats his enemies: buns to his grizzlies.

Well, Professor Sherman, being a professor, has got to be nice to everybody about everybody. What else does a professor sit in a chair of English for, except to dole out sweets?

Awfully nice, rather cloying. But there, men *are* but children of a later growth.

So much for the professor's attitude. As for his "message." He steers his little ship of Criticism most obviously between the Scylla of Mr. Mencken and the Charybdis of Mr. P. E. More. I'm sorry I never heard before of either gentleman: except that I dimly remember having read, in the lounge of a Naples hotel, a bit of an article by a Mr. Mencken, in German, in some German periodical: all amounting to nothing.

But Mr. Mencken is the Scylla of American Criticism, and hence, of American democracy. There is a verb "to menckenize," and a noun "menckenism." Apparently to *menckenize* is to manufacture jeering little gas-bomb phrases against everything deep and earnest, or high and noble, and to paint the face of corruption with phosphorus, so it shall glow. And a *menckenism* is one of the little stink-gas phrases.

Now the *nouveau riche jeune fille* of the *bourgeoisie,* as Professor Sherman puts it; in other words, the profiteers' flappers all read Mr. Mencken and swear by him: swear that they don't give a nickel for any Great Man that ever was or will be. Great Men are all a bombastical swindle. So asserts the *nouveau riche jeune fille,* on whom, apparently, American democracy rests. And Mr. Mencken "learnt it her." And Mr. Mencken got it in Germany, where all stink-gas comes from, according to Professor Sherman. And Mr. Mencken does it to poison the noble and great old spirit of American democracy, which is grandly Anglo-Saxon in origin, but absolutely American in fact.

So much for the Scylla of Mr. Mencken. It is the first essay in the book. The Charybdis of Mr. P. E. More is the last essay: to this monster the professor warbles another tune. Mr. More, author of the *Shelburne Essays,* is learned, and steeped in tradition, the very antithesis of the nihilistic stink-gassing Mr. Mencken. But alas, Mr. More is remote: somewhat haughty and supercilious at his study table. And even, alasser! with all his learning and remoteness, he hunts out the risky Restoration wits to hob-nob with on high Parnassus; Wycherley, for example; he likes his wits smutty. He even goes and fetches out Aphra Behn from her disreputable oblivion, to entertain her in public.

And there you have the Charybdis of Mr. More: snobbish, distant, exclusive, disdaining even the hero from the Marne who mends the gas bracket: and at the same time absolutely *preferring* the doubtful odour of Wycherley because it is—well, malodorous, says the professor.

Mr. Mencken: Great Men and the Great Past are an addled egg full of stink-gas.

Mr. P. E. More: Great Men of the Great Past are utterly beyond the *mobile vulgus.* Let the *mobile vulgus* (in other words, the democratic millions of America) be cynically scoffed at by the gentlemen of the Great Past, especially the naughty ones.

To the Menckenites, Professor Sherman says: Jeer not at the Great Past and at the Great Dead. Heroes are heroes still, they do not go addled, as you would try to make out, nor turn into stink-bombs. Tradition is honourable still, and will be honourable for ever, though it may be splashed like a futurist's picture with the rotten eggs of menckenism.

To the smaller and more select company of Moreites: Scorn not the horny hand of noble toil: "—the average man is, like (Mr. More) himself, at heart a mystic, vaguely hungering for a peace that diplomats cannot give, obscurely seeking the permanent amid the transitory: a poor swimmer struggling for a rock amid the flux of waters, a lonely pilgrim longing for the shadow of a mighty rock in a weary land. And if 'P. E. M.' had a bit more of that natural sympathy of which he is so distrustful, he would have perceived that what more than anything else today keeps the average man from lapsing into Yahooism is the religion of democracy, consisting of a little bundle of general principles which make him respect himself and his neighbour; a bundle of principles kindled in crucial times by an intense emotion, in which his self-interest, his petty vices, and his envy are consumed as with fire; and he sees the common weal as the mighty rock in the shadow of which his little life and personality are to be surrendered, if need be, as things negligible and transitory."

All right, Professor Sherman. All the profiteers, and shovers, and place-grabbers, and bullies, especially bullies, male and female, all that sort of gentry of the late war were, of course, outside the average. The supermen of the occasion.

The Babbitts, while they were on the make.

And as for the mighty rocks in weary lands, as far as my experience goes, they have served the pilgrims chiefly as sanitary offices and places in whose shadows men shall leave their offal and tin cans.

But there you have a specimen of Professor Sherman's "style." And the thin ends of his parabola.

The great arch is of course the Religion of Democracy, which the professor italicizes. If you want to trace the curve you must follow the course of the essays.

After Mr. Mencken and Tradition comes Franklin. Now Benjamin Franklin is one of the founders of the Religion of Democracy. It was he who invented the creed that should satisfy the professors of all religions, not of universities only, and offend none. With a deity called Providence. Who turns out to be a sort of superlative Mr. Wanamaker, running the globe as a revolving dry-goods store, according to a profit-and-loss system; the profit counted in plump citizens whose every want is satisfied: like chickens in an absolutely coyote-proof chicken-run.

In spite of this new attempt to make us like Dr. Franklin, the flesh wearies on our bones at the thought of him. The professor hints that the good old gentleman on Quaker Oats was really an old sinner. If it had been proved to us, we *might* have liked him. As it is, he just wearies the flesh on our bones. *Religion civile*, indeed.

Emerson. The next essay is called "The Emersonian Liberation." Well, Emerson is a great man still: or a great individual. And heroes are heroes still, though their banners may decay, and stink.

It is true that lilies may fester. And virtues likewise. The great Virtue of one age has a trick of smelling far worse than weeds in the next.

It is a sad but undeniable fact.

Yet why so sad, fond lover, prithee why so sad? Why should Virtue remain incorruptible, any more than anything else? If stars wax and wane, why should Goodness shine for ever unchanged? That too makes one tired. Goodness sweals and gutters, the light of the Good goes out with a stink, and lo, somewhere else a new light; a new Good. Afterwards, it may be shown that it is eternally the same Good. But to us poor mortals at the moment, it emphatically isn't.

And that is the point about Emerson and the Emersonian Liberation—save the word! Heroes are heroes still: safely dead. Heroism is always heroism. But the hero who was heroic one century, uplifting the banner of a creed, is followed the next century by a hero heroically ripping that banner to rags. *Sic transit veritas mundi.*

Emerson was an idealist: a believer in "continuous revelation," continuous inrushes of inspirational energy from the Over-Soul. Professor Sherman says: "His message when he leaves us is not, 'Henceforth be masterless,' but, 'Bear thou henceforth the sceptre of thine own control through life and the passion of life.'"

When Emerson says: "I am surrounded by messengers of God who send me credentials day by day," then all right for him. But he cozily forgot that there are many messengers. He knew only a sort of smooth-shaven Gabriel. But as far as we remember, there is Michael too: and a terrible discrepancy between the credentials of the pair of 'em. Then there are other cherubim with outlandish names, bringing very different messages than those Ralph Waldo got: Israfel, and even Mormon. And a whole bunch of others. But Emerson had a stone-deaf ear for all except a nicely aureoled Gabriel *qui n'avait pas de quoi.*

Emerson listened to one sort of message and only one. To all the rest he was blank. Ashtaroth and Ammon are gods as well, and hand out their own credentials. But Ralph Waldo wasn't having any. They could never ring *him* up. He was only connected on the Ideal phone. "We are all aiming to be idealists," says Emerson, "and covet the society of those who make us so, as the sweet singer, the orator, the ideal painter."

Well, we're pretty sick of the ideal painters and the uplifting singers. As a matter of fact we have worked the ideal bit of our nature to death, and we shall go crazy if we can't start working from some other bit. Idealism now is a sick nerve, and the more you rub on it the worse you feel afterwards. Your later reactions aren't pretty at all. Like Dostoievsky's Idiot, and President Wilson sometimes.

Emerson believes in having the courage to treat all men as equals. It takes some courage *not* to treat them so now.

"Shall I not treat all men as gods?" he cries.

If you like, Waldo, but we've got to pay for it, when you've made them *feel* that they're gods. A hundred million American godlets is rather much for the world to deal with.

The fact of the matter is, all those gorgeous inrushes of exaltation and spiritual energy which made Emerson a great man, now make us sick. They are with us a drug habit. So when Professor Sherman urges us in Ralph Waldo's footsteps, he is really driving us nauseously astray. Which perhaps is hard lines on the professor, and us, and Emerson. But it wasn't I who started the mills of God a-grinding.

I like the essay on Emerson. I like Emerson's real courage. I like his wild and genuine belief in the Over-Soul and the inrushes he got from it. But it is a museum-interest. Or else it is a taste of the old drug to the old spiritual drug-fiend in me.

We've got to have a different sort of sardonic courage. And the sort of credentials we are due to receive from the god in the shadow would have been real bones out of hell-broth to Ralph Waldo. *Sic transeunt Dei hominorum.*

So no wonder Professor Sherman sounds a little wistful, and somewhat pathetic, as he begs us to follow Ralph Waldo's trail.

Hawthorne: A Puritan Critic of Puritanism. This essay is concerned chiefly with an analysis and praise of *The Scarlet Letter.* Well, it is a wonderful book. But why does nobody give little Nathaniel a kick for his duplicity? Professor Sherman says there is nothing erotic about *The Scarlet Letter.* Only neurotic. It wasn't the sensual act itself had any meaning for Hawthorne. Only the Sin. He knew there's nothing deadly in the act itself. But if it is Forbidden, immediately it looms lurid with interest. He is not concerned for a moment with what Hester and Dimmesdale really felt. Only with their situations as Sinners. And Sin looms lurid and thrilling, when after all it is only just a normal sexual passion. This luridness about the book makes one feel like spitting. It is somewhat worked up: invented in the head and grafted on to the lower body, like some serpent of supposition under the fig-leaf. It depends so much on *coverings.* Suppose you took off the fig-leaf, the serpent isn't there. And so the relish is all two-faced and tiresome. *The Scarlet Letter* is a masterpiece, but in duplicity and half-false excitement.

And when one remembers *The Marble Faun,* all the parochial priggishness and poor-bloodedness of Hawthorne in Italy, one of the most bloodless books ever written, one feels like giving Nathaniel a kick in the seat of his poor little pants and landing him back in New England again. For the rolling, many-godded medieval and pagan world was too big a prey for such a ferret.

Walt Whitman. Walt is the high priest of the Religion of Democracy. Yet "at the first bewildering contact one wonders whether his urgent touch is of lewdness or divinity," says Professor Sherman.

"All I have said concerns you." But it doesn't. One ceases to care about so many things. One ceases to respond or to react. And at length other things come up, which Walt and Professor Sherman never knew.

"Whatever else it involves, democracy involves at least one grand salutary elementary admission, namely, that the world exists for the benefit and for the improvement of all the decent individuals in it." O Lord, how long will you submit to this Insurance Policy interpretation of the Universe! How "decent"? Decent in what way? Benefit! Think of the world's existing for people's "benefit and improvement."

So wonderful says Professor Sherman, the way Whitman identifies himself with everything and everybody: Runaway slaves and all the rest. But we no longer want to take the whole hullabaloo to our bosom. We no longer want to "identify ourselves" with a lot of other things and other people. It *is* a sort of lewdness. *Noli me tangere,* "you." I don't want "you."

Whitman's "you" doesn't get me.

We don't want to be embracing everything any more. Or to be embraced in one of Waldo's vast promiscuous armfuls. *Merci, monsieur!*

We've had enough democracy.

Professor Sherman says that if Whitman had lived "at the right place in these years of Proletarian Millennium, he would have been hanged as a reactionary member of the *bourgeoise.*" ('Tisn't my spelling.)

And he gives Whitman's own words in proof: "The true gravitation hold of liberalism in the United States will be a more universal ownership of property, general homesteads, general comforts—a vast intertwining reticulation of wealth. . . . She (Democracy) asks for men and women with occupations, well-off, owners of houses and acres, and with cash in the bank and with some craving for literature too"—so that they can buy certain books. Oh, Walt!

Allons! The road is before us.

Joaquin Miller: Poetical Conquistador of the West. A long essay with not much spirit in it, showing that Miller was a true son of the Wild and Woolly West, in so far as he was a very good imitation of other people's poetry (note the Swinburnian bit) and a rather poor assumer of other people's played-out poses. A self-conscious little "wild" man, like the rest of the "wild" men. The Wild West is a pose that pays Zane Grey today, as it once paid Miller and Bret Harte and Buffalo Bill.

A note on Carl Sandburg. That Carl is a super-self-conscious literary gent stampeding around with red-ochre blood on his hands and smeared-on soot darkening his craggy would-be-criminal brow: but that his heart is as tender as an old tomato.

Andrew Carnegie. That Andy was the most perfect American citizen Scotland ever produced, and the sweetest example of how beautifully the *Religion Civile* pays, in cold cash.

Roosevelt and the National Psychology. Theodore didn't have a spark of magnanimity in his great personality, says Professor Sherman, what a pity! And you see where it lands you, when you play at being pro-German. You go quite out of fashion.

Evolution of the Adams Family. Perfect Pedigree of the most aristocratic Democratic family. Your aristocracy is played out, my dear fellows, but don't cry about it, you've always got your Democracy to fall back on. If you don't like falling back on it of your own free will, you'll be shoved back on it by the Will of the People.

"Man is the animal that destiny cannot break."

But the Will of the People can break Man and the animal man, and the destined man, all the lot, and grind 'em to democratic powder, Professor Sherman warns us.

Allons! en-masse is before us.

But when Germany is thoroughly broken, Democracy finally collapses. (My own prophecy.)

An Imaginary Conversation with Mr. P. E. More: You've had the gist of that already.

Well there is Professor Sherman's dish of cookies which he bids you eat and have. An awfully sweet book, all about having your cookies and eating 'em. The cookies are Tradition, and Heroes, and Great Men, and $350,000,000 in your pocket. And eating 'em is Democracy, Serving Mankind, piously giving most of the $350,000,000 back again. "Oh, nobly and heroically get $350,000,000 together," chants Professor Sherman in this litany of having your cookies and eating 'em, "and then piously and munificently give away $349,000,000 again."

P. S. You can't get past Arithmetic.

Lewis Mumford (1895–1990)

*American historian, literary critic, and philosopher of technology, Mumford was
a prominent writer on the nature of cities and urban architecture. A friend of
Frank Lloyd Wright and Clarence Stein, among other architects, city planners,
and landscape designers, Mumford wrote the so-called "Renewal of Life" series in
four volumes, from the first* Technics and Civilization *(1934) to the fourth,* The
Conduct of Life *(1951, a title identical to Emerson's book from 1860). Mumford
was also a close reader of American letters and early on published* The Golden
Day *(1926, from which the following essay is drawn) and* Herman Melville: A
Study of His Life and Vision *(1929), which contributed to the positive revaluation
and recovery of Melville. While Mumford's tone and temper are very far away
from Mencken's, for example, Mumford seems highly aware of the nature and
proximity of enduring criticisms of Emerson's work. When he pairs Emerson with
Plato he says plainly, "I see no reason to qualify this hint, or apologize for the
juxtaposition"—a correspondence, we may recall that Dewey makes earlier with
similar confidence and lack of embarrassment in "Emerson—The Philosopher of
Democracy." As Santayana, Woolf, and others struggle with the nature of Emerson's
prose and its value, Mumford calmly reports in declarative sentences: "He was
the first American philosopher with a fresh doctrine: he was the first American
poet with a fresh theme: he was the first American prose writer to escape, by way
of the Elizabethan dramatists and the Seventeenth Century preachers, from the
smooth prose of Addison or the stilted periods of Johnson. He was an original, in
the sense that he was a source." From Emerson's seminal works, Mumford goes on,
"one might reconstruct the landscape and society of New England [. . .] everything
of importance in the New England scheme of things." Mumford even reframes the
critical assessment of Emerson as cool or cold, saying that we forget that his "coldness
is not that of an impotence, but of an inner intensity: it burns!"*

The Morning Star

Lewis Mumford

I

No one who was awake in the early part of the Nineteenth Century was unaware that
in the practical arrangements of life men were on the brink of a great change. The
rumble of the industrial revolution was heard in the distance long before the storm

actually broke; and before American society was completely transformed through the work of the land-pioneer and the industrial pioneer, there arose here and there over the land groups of people who anticipated the effects of this revolution and were in revolt against all its preoccupations. Some of these groups reverted to an archaic theocracy, like that of the Mormons, in which a grotesque body of beliefs was combined with an extraordinary amount of economic sagacity and statesmanship; some of them became disciples of Fourier and sought to live in cooperative colonies, which would foster men's various capacities more fully than the utilitarian community....

The period from 1830 to 1860 was in America one of disintegration and fulfillment: the new and the old, the crude and the complete, the base and the noble mingled together. Puritan fanatics like Goodyear brought to the vulcanization of rubber the same intense passion that Thoreau brought to Nature: sharp mountebanks like Barnum grew out of the same sort of Connecticut village that nourished an inspired schoolmaster like Bronson Alcott: genuine statesmen like Brigham Young organized the colonization of Utah whilst nonentities like Pierce and Buchanan governed the whole country. During this period, the old culture of the seaboard settlement had its Golden Day in the mind; the America of the migrations, on the other hand, partly because of weaknesses developed in the pioneer, partly because of the one-sided interests of the industrialist, and partly because of the volcanic eruption of the Civil War had up to 1890 little more than the boomtown optimism of the Gilded Age to justify its existence....

There were no Carlyles or Ruskins in America during this period; they were almost unthinkable. One might live in this atmosphere, or one might grapple with the White Whale and die; but if one lived, one lived without distrust, without inner complaint, and even if one scorned the ways of one's fellows, as Thoreau did, one remained among them, and sought to remedy in oneself the abuses that existed in society. Transcendentalism might criticize a fossilized past; but no one imagined that the future could be equally fossilized. The testimony is unqualified. One breathed hope, as one might breathe the heady air of early autumn, pungent with the smell of hickory fires and baking bread, as one walked through the village street.

"One cannot look on the freedom of this country, in connection with its youth," wrote Emerson in The Young American, "without a presentiment that here shall laws and institutions exist in some proportion to the majesty of Nature.... It is a country of beginnings, of projects, of vast designs and expectations. It has no past: all has an onward and prospective look." The voice of Whitman echoed Emerson through a trumpet: but that of Melville, writing in 1850, was no less sanguine and full-pulsed: "God has predestinated, mankind expects, great things from our race; and great things we feel in our souls. The rest of the nations must soon be in our rear. We are the pioneers of the world; the advance guard, sent on through the wilderness of untried things, to break a new path in the New World that is ours. In our youth is our strength; in our inexperience, our wisdom."

"Every institution is the lengthened shadow of a man." Here and there in America during its Golden Day grew up a man who cast a shadow over the landscape. They left no labor-saving machine, no discoveries, and no wealthy bequests to found a library or a hospital: what they left was something much less and much more than that—an heroic conception of life. They peopled the landscape with their own shapes. This period nourished men, as no other has done in America before or since. Up to that time, the American communities were provincial; when it was over, they had lost their base, and spreading all over the landscape, deluged with newcomers speaking strange languages and carrying on Old-World customs, they lost that essential likeness which is a necessary basis for intimate communication. The first settlement was complete: agricultural and industrial life were still in balance in the older parts of the country; and on the seas trade opened up activities for the adventurous. When Ticknor was preparing to go to Germany, in the first decade of the century, there was but one German dictionary, apparently, in New England. Within a generation, Goethe was translated, selections from the European classics were published; and importations of the Indian, Chinese and Persian classics widened the horizon of people who had known India only by its shawls, China only by its tea.... When all is reckoned ... there is nothing in the minor writers that is not pretty fully recorded by Emerson, Thoreau, Whitman, Melville, and Hawthorne. These men, as Mr. D. H. Lawrence has well said, reached a verge. They stood between two worlds. Part of their experience enabled them to bring the protestant movement to its conclusion: the critical examination of men, creeds, and institutions, which is the vital core of protestantism, could not go much further. But already, out of another part of their experience, that which arose out of free institutions planted in an unpreëmpted soil, molded by fresh contact with forest and sea and the more ingenious works of man, already this experience pushed them beyond the pit Melville fell in to, and led them towards new institutions, a new art, a new philosophy, formed on the basis of a wider past than the European, caught by his Mediterranean or Palestinian cultures, was capable of seizing....

II

All the important thinkers who shared in this large experience were born between 1800 and 1820; their best work was done by the time the Civil War came; if not beyond the reach of its hurt, they at all events could not be completely overthrown or warped by it. The leader of these minds, the central figure of them all, was Ralph Waldo Emerson. He was the first American philosopher with a fresh doctrine: he was the first American poet with a fresh theme: he was the first American prose writer to escape, by way of the Elizabethan dramatists and the Seventeenth Century preachers, from the smooth prose of Addison or the stilted periods of Johnson. He was an original, in the sense that he was a source: he was the glacier that became the white mountain torrent of Thoreau, and expanded into the serene, ample-bosomed lake of Whitman. He loses a little by this icy centrality: he must be climbed, and there is so much of him that people become satisfied with a brief glimpse, and forget that they have not reached the summit which dominates the lower peaks and platforms. His very coldness seems familiar to academic minds; and for too long they appropriated him, as one of them: they forgot that his coldness is not that of an impotence, but of an inner intensity: it burns! The outward manner of his life was mild: there are summer afternoons when from the distance Mont Blanc itself seems little more than a cone of ice-cream; and his contemporaries forgot that this sweet man carried a lash, a lash that would not merely drive the money-changers from the temple but the priests.

Emerson was a sort of living essence. The preacher, the farmer, the scholar, the sturdy New England freeholder, yes, and the shrewd Yankee peddler or mechanic, were all encompassed by him; but what they meant in actual life had fallen away from him: he represented what they stood for in eternity. With Emerson's works one might reconstruct the landscape and society of New England: a few things would be left out from Nature which Thoreau would have to supply for us—a handful of flora and fauna, and the new Irish immigrants who were already building the railroads and who finally were to take possession of Boston—but what remained would still be everything of importance in the New England scheme of things. The weaknesses of New England are there, too: its bookishness, its failure, as Margaret Fuller said of Emerson, to kiss the earth sufficiently, its impatience to assume too quickly an upright position, its too-tidy moral housekeeping. Strong or weak, Emerson was complete: in his thought the potentialities of New England were finally expressed.

It is almost impossible to sum up Emerson's doctrine, for he touched life on many sides, and what is more, he touched it freshly, so though he is a Platonist, one will not find Plato's doctrines of Art in his essay on Art; and though he was in a very derivative way a Kantian, one will not find Kant's principles at the bottom of his ethics. With most of the resources of the past at his command, Emerson achieved nakedness: his central doctrine is the virtue of this intellectual, or cultural, nakedness: the virtue of getting beyond the institution, the habit, the ritual, and finding out what it means afresh in one's own consciousness. Protestantism had dared to go this far with respect to certain minor aspects of the Catholic cult: Emerson applied the same method in a more sweeping way, and buoyed up by his faith in the future of America—a country endowed with perhaps every advantage except venerability—he asked not merely what Catholic ritual means, but all ritual, not merely what dynastic politics means but all politics; and so with every other important aspect of life. Emerson divested everything of its associations, and seized it afresh, to make what associations it could with the life he had lived and the experience he had assimilated. As a result, each part of the past came to him on equal terms: Buddha had perhaps as much to give as Christ: Hafiz could teach him as much as Shakespeare or Dante. Moreover, every fragment of present experience lost its associated values, too: towards the established hierarchy of experiences, with vested interests that no longer, perhaps, could exhibit the original power of sword or spade, he extended the democratic challenge: perhaps new experiences belonged to the summit of aristocracy, and old lines were dying out, or were already dead, leaving only empty venerated names.

Emerson saw the implications of this attempt to re-think life, and to accept only what was his. He did not shrink from them. "Nothing is at last sacred but the integrity of your own mind.... I remember an answer which when quite young I was prompted to make to a valued adviser, who was wont to importune me with the dear old doctrines of the church. On my saying, 'What have I to do with the sacredness of traditions, if I live wholly from within?' my friend suggested,—'But these impulses may be from below, not from above.' I replied, 'They do not seem to me to be such; but if I am the Devil's child, I will live then from the Devil.' No law can be sacred to me but that of my Nature."

"Life only avails, not the having lived." There is the kernel of the Emersonian doctrine of self-reliance: it is the answer which the American, in the day of his confidence and achievement, flung back into the face of Europe, where the "having lived" has always been so conspicuous and formidable. In a certain sense, this doctrine was a barbarism; but it was a creative barbarism, a barbarism that aimed to use the old buildings not as a shell, but as a quarry; neither casting them aside altogether, nor attempting wretchedly to fit a new and lush existence into the old forms. The transcendental young photographer, in Hawthorne's House of the Seven Gables, suggested that houses should be built afresh every generation, instead of lingering on in dingy security, never really fitting the needs of any family, but that which originally conceived and built it. An uncreative age is aghast at this suggestion: for the new building may be cruder than the old, the new problem may not awaken sufficient creative capacities, equal to the previous one: these are the necessary counsels of prudence, impotence.

In the heyday of the American adventure, neither Emerson nor Hawthorne was afraid. Emerson re-thought life, and in the mind he coined new shapes and images and institutions, ready to take the place of those he discarded. A building was perishable; a custom might fall into disuse; but what of it? The mind was inexhaustible; and it was only the unawakened and unimaginative practical people who did not feel that these dearly purchased trinkets might all be thrown into the melting pot and shaped over again, without a penny lost. It was not that nakedness itself was so desirable; but clothes were cheap! Why keep on piecing together and patching the old doctrines, when the supply never could run out, so long as life nourished Emersons? "We shall not always set so great a price," he exclaimed, "on a few texts, a few lives. We are like children who repeat by rote the sentences of grandames and tutors, and, as they grow older, of the men of talents and character they chance to see,—painfully recollecting the exact words they spoke; afterwards, when they come into the point of view which these had who uttered these sayings, they understand them, and are willing to let the words go; for at any time, they can use words as good when the occasion comes. . . . When we have new perceptions, we shall gladly disburden the memory of its hoarded treasures, as of old rubbish."

III

The Platonism of Emerson's mind has been overemphasized; or rather, it has been misconstrued to mean that he lived in a perpetual cloud-world. The truth is, however, that Emerson's Platonism was not a matter simply of following Plato: it was a matter of living like Plato, and achieving a similar mode of thought. Critics have too often spoken of Plato's forms as if they were merely a weak escape from the urgent problems of Fifth-Century Athens; and of Emerson's, as if they were a neurotic withdrawal from the hurly-burly of American life. They were both, in a sense, a withdrawal; but it was a withdrawal of water into a reservoir, or of grain into a bin, so that they might be available later, if they could not be effectively distributed at once. Both Plato and Emerson had mixed with the life about them and knew its concrete details: both were conscious of the purely makeshift character of existing institutions; both were aware that they were in a period of transition. Instead of busying himself with the little details of political or economic readjustment, each sought to achieve a pattern which would permit the details to fall into place, and so make possible a creative renovation. Emerson wrote about Man the Reformer; but he never belonged to any political sect or cult. The blight of Negro slavery awakened his honest anger, and his essay on the Know-nothings is an excellent diatribe; but even this great issue did not cause him to lose his perspective: he sought to abolish the white slaves who maintained that institution.

In coupling Emerson's name with Plato's I have hinted that Emerson was a philosopher; I see no reason to qualify this hint, or to apologize for the juxtaposition. He has been more or less grudgingly given such a place by current philosophic commentators, because on a superficial examination there is no originality in his metaphysics: both Plato and Kant had given an independent reality to the world of ideas, and the habit of treating existing facts as symbols is so ancient it became a shocking novelty when reemployed in our own time by Dr. Sigmund Freud. The bare metaphysical outlines of Emerson's work give no insight, however, into the body of his thought as a whole. The content of Emerson's philosophy is much richer, I think, than that of any of his contemporaries; and he is denied a high place in philosophy largely because the content is so rich that it cannot be recognized, in the attenuated twilight of academic groves, as philosophy. Hegel and Comte and Spencer, Emerson's contemporaries, had all found formulæ which led them into relations with a vast mass of concrete facts: the weakness of their several philosophies was due to severe defects of personality—they were sexually neurotic, like Comte, with his pathetic apotheosis of Clothilde, or they were querulous invalids, like Spencer, who had never been able to correct by a wider experience the original bias given to his mind by his early training as a railroad engineer. Emerson had the good fortune to live a healthy and symmetrical life: he answered Tolstoi's demand for essential greatness—he had no kinks. In him, philosophy resumed the full gamut of human experience it had known in Pythagoras and Plato.

Emerson's uniqueness, for his time, consists in the fact that he appreciated not merely the factual data of science, and the instrumental truth of scientific investigation: he also recognized the formative role of ideas, and he saw the importance of "dialectic" in placing new patterns before the mind which did not exist, ready-made, in the order of Nature. "All the facts of the animal economy, sex, nutriment, gestation, birth, growth, are symbols of the passage of the world into the soul of man, to suffer there a change, and reappear a new and higher fact." The occasion for, or the efficacy of, this passage into the soul of man was denied by the externalism of Nineteenth Century empiricism; obscurely, it was the ground for contention between religion and science, a quarrel which religion lost by holding fast to a purely superstitious empiricism. If instrumental truths are the only order of truth, all religion is a superstition, all poetry a puerility, and all art itself is a weak anticipation of photography and mechanical drawing.

Emerson's affirmation of both physics and dialectic, of both science and myth, an affirmation which justified the existence of the artist, the poet, the saint, was of prime importance; for he did not make the mistake of disdaining the order and power that science had achieved within its proper department. Emerson was a Darwinist before the Origin of Species was published, because he was familiar with the investigations which were linking together the chain of organic continuity, and he was ready to follow the facts wherever they would lead him. Agassiz, Cambridge's great man of science, accepted the facts, too; but he was afraid of them; insulated in his evangelical Christianity, he insisted that the facts did not exist in Nature but in the mind of God. Emerson was untroubled by Agassiz's reluctance: the function of "God" was perpetually being performed for him in the passage of the world into the soul of man; and there was nothing in his philosophy to make him deny an orderly sequence in Nature. For Emerson, matter and spirit were not enemies in conflict: they were phases of man's experience: matter passed into spirit and became a symbol: spirit passed into matter and gave it a form; and symbols and forms were the essences through which man lived and fulfilled his proper being. Who was there among Emerson's contemporaries in the Nineteenth Century that was gifted with such a complete vision? To withhold the name of philosopher from the man who saw and expressed this integral vision of life so clearly is to deny the central office of philosophy.

Emerson's thought does not seal the world up into a few packets, tied with a formula, and place them in a pigeonhole. In the past, it was not limited to a phase of Christianity, nor a phase of classic culture: it roamed over a much wider area, and as he himself suggested, used Plato and Proclus, not for what they were, but as so many added colors for his palette. The past for Emerson was neither a prescription nor a burden: it was rather an esthetic experience. Being no longer inevitable in America, that is, no longer something handed down with a living at Corpus Christi or a place at court, the past could be entertained freely and experimentally. It could be revalued; and the paradox of Brahma became as acceptable as the paradox that the meek shall inherit the earth.

The poet, for Emerson, was the liberator; and in that sense, he was a great poet. With him one does not feel that our "civilization nears its meridian, but rather that we are yet only at the cock-crowing and the morning star." The promise of America, of an unspotted Nature and a fresh start, had seeped into every pore of Emerson's mind. "Do not set the least value on what I do," he warns, "nor the least discredit on what I do not, as if I pretended to settle anything as true or false. I unsettle all things. No facts to me are sacred; none are profane; I simply experiment, an endless seeker, with no Past at my back. . . . Why should we import rags and relics into the new hour? . . . Nothing is secure but life, transition, the energizing spirit. No love can be bound by oath or covenant to secure it against a higher love. No truth so sublime but it may be trivial tomorrow in the light of new thoughts. People wish to be settled: only as far as they are unsettled is there any hope for them."

The vigor of this challenge, the challenge of the American wilderness, the challenge of the new American society, where the European lost the security of his past in order to gain a better stake in the future—who but can feel that this is what was distinguished and interesting in our American experience, and what was salutary, for all its incidental defects, in the dumb physical bravado of the pioneer? Two men met the challenge and carried it further: Thoreau and Whitman. They completed the Emersonian circle, carrying the potted flower of the scholar's study out into the spring sunshine, the upturned earth, and the keen air.

James Truslow Adams (1878–1949)

Adams wrote that there are "two educations"—"One should teach us how to make a living and the other how to live." Adams, who spent more than a decade at the New York Stock Exchange and thereafter worked as an independent scholar, appears to have lived the advice. From 1921 to 1926 he wrote a trilogy of New England history, the first volume of which, The Founding of New England, *won the Pulitzer Prize for History. In the following essay, published in the* Atlantic Monthly *(October 1930), Adams offers a sort of personal narrative of re-reading Emerson as an adult, and it doesn't end well: "the Emerson who evidently stirred me at sixteen leaves me cold to-day at fifty." Adams himself appears surprised by his response to the rediscovery, "by what seems to me the shallowness of the essays." When Adams comes to read the "Emerson" chapter in* A New England Group and Others *(1921), the last installment of Paul Elmer More's eleven-volume* Shelburne Essays, *which opens with the line Adams quotes below ("it becomes more and more apparent [. . .]"), the critic's opinion leaves Adams befuddled, forced to "pause" and "ponder." More did not wonder "wherein the trouble lies" with Emerson's writing; instead he noted that "a man's attitude towards it in the end will be determined by his sense of its sufficiency or insufficiency to meet the facts of experience." Adams finds Emerson's work insufficient—a "shallow doctrine" and "extremely dangerous"—yet he would "still have every youth read his Emerson." Having survived to middle age, however, Adams concludes that Emerson has not suffered enough, or at least not shown his suffering to us, and so appears to offer only a "simple optimism" that we are encouraged by Adams to outgrow.*

Emerson Re-read

James Truslow Adams

1

Except in tales of romance it is not given to us to be able to pass through postern doors or forest glades and find ourselves in lands of leisure where it is always afternoon. If one seeks the King of Elfland's Daughter it must be between the pages of a book. Nevertheless, one can change one's stage and ways of life and amplify one's days. Some months ago by a simple shift in space I so wrought a change in time that, for a while at least, I have been able without sense of haste or pressure to browse again among the books I read and marked as a boy, books which for more years than I like to count had stood untouched upon my shelves, open apparently to the reaching hand, but in reality, owing to lack of time, as remote as boyhood's days themselves.

A week ago, I picked up one of the oldest of these, oldest in possession, not in imprint—the *Essays* of Emerson. In an unformed hand there was the inscription on the flyleaf, "James Truslow Adams, 1896." I was then seventeen, and had evidently read him earlier, for at the beginning of a number of the essays, notably "Self-Reliance," are marked the dates of reading, "1895, '96, '96, '96." The volume, one of that excellent, well-printed series which in those halcyon days the National Book Company used to sell for fifty cents, is underlined and marked with marginal notes all through. The passages are not all those I should mark to-day, but at sixteen and seventeen it is clear I was reading Emerson with great enthusiasm, and again and again.

In the past few days I have gone through five volumes of his work and found the task no light one. What, I ask myself, is the trouble? It is obviously not that Emerson is not "modern," for the other evening I read aloud, to the mutual enjoyment of my wife and myself, the *Prometheus Chained* of Æschylus, which antedates Emerson by some twenty-five hundred years. I turn to Paul More's *Shelburne Essays,* Volume XI, and read the statement that "it becomes more and more apparent that Emerson, judged by an international or even by a true national standard, is the outstanding figure of American letters."

I pause and ponder. "International," even "true national," standards are high. Whom have we? Lowell as a critic? One thinks of, say, Sainte-Beuve, and a shoulder shrug for Lowell. Lowell as poet, Whittier, Longfellow, Bryant? *Exeunt omnes,* except as second-rate by world standards. The troop of current novelists and poets are much the same here as in a half-dozen other countries. Hawthorne? A very distinctive, and yet a minor voice, in the international choir. Poe? Again a minor, and scarcely distinguishable as a "national." Whitman? One thinks of Whitman five hundred years hence in world terms, and shakes one's head. The choice is narrowing fast. Is Mr. More right? Yet the Emerson who evidently so stirred me at sixteen leaves me cold to-day at fifty. It is something to be looked into. I try, at fifty, to reappraise my Emerson. I take up the volumes again to see wherein the trouble lies.

First of all it occurs to me to test him by his own appraisals of others, and I turn to his volume on *Representative Men.* The list of names is itself of considerable significance—Plato, Swedenborg, Montaigne, Shakespeare, Napoleon, Goethe. Four of these are evidently so obvious as to tell us nothing of the mind choosing them. The case is a good deal like that of the Pulitzer Jury in biography, which is forbidden to award prizes for lives of Lincoln or Washington. The essential point is, what has Emerson to say of these men?

I confess that, when after these thirty years or more I turn from reading about Emerson to reading him himself, I am rather amazed by what seems to me the shallowness of these essays. In fact, I believe that even Mr. More considers the Plato a very unsatisfactory performance. Emerson babbles of "the Franklin-like wisdom" of Socrates, and, indeed, I think we could look for as sound an essay from an intelligent undergraduate. The Shakespeare is almost equally naïve and unsatisfying, and

Emerson's final judgment is that the dramatist was merely a "master of the revels to mankind," the purveyor of "very superior pyrotechny this evening," and that the end of the record must be that with all his ability he "led an obscure and a profane life, using his genius for the public amusement." This essay throws much light on Emerson if little on Shakespeare. Nor does he show more real understanding of his other great men. He can say that Napoleon left no trace whatever on Europe, that "all passed away like the smoke of his artillery." Of Goethe's greatest poem, the *Faust,* Emerson notes mainly its "superior intelligence." One suspects that he chose these four names unconsciously because they were high in the world's record of the great, not because he understood the men or their work.

When he turns from these names, almost imposed upon him, to another of his independent choosing, it is illuminating that the one he dwells on with greatest admiration is Swedenborg. This fact is significant. For him, the Swedish mystic is "a colossal soul," the "last Father in the Church," "not likely to have a successor," compared with whom Plato is a "gownsman," whereas Lycurgus and Caesar would have to bow before the Swede. Emerson quotes from him as "golden sayings" such sentences as "in heaven the angels are advancing continually to the spring-time of their youth, so that the oldest angel appears the youngest," or "it is never permitted to any one in heaven, to stand behind another and look at the back of his head: for then the influx which is from the Lord is disturbed." Nor should we forget that entry in Emerson's *Journals* in which he noted that "for pure intellect" he had never known the equal of—Bronson Alcott!

It is true that these essays are not Emerson's best, but they were written when he was over forty years old and at the height of his fame and mental maturity, and they help us to understand our problem. They are typical products of the American mind. Conventional praise is given to the great names of Europe, with comment that indicates lack of understanding of the great currents of thought and action, while Mrs. Eddy and Brigham Young peer over the writer's shoulders. We begin to see how deeply Emerson was an American.

His national limitation is noteworthy in another important source of influence in a mature culture, that of art. Music appears to have been outside his life and consideration. Of painting he could write that, having once really seen a great picture, there was nothing for one to gain by looking at it again. In sculpture he finds a "paltriness, as of toys and the trumpery of a theater." It "is the game of a rude and youthful people, and not the manly labor of a wise and spiritual nation," and he quotes with approval Isaac Newton's remark about "stone dolls." Art is not mature unless it is "practical and moral," and addresses the uncultivated with a "voice of lofty cheer." All art should be extempore, and he utters a genuine American note in his belief that it will somehow come to us in a new form, the religious heart raising "to a divine use the railroad, the insurance office, the joint-stock company, our law, our primary assemblies, our commerce, the galvanic battery, the electric jar, the prism, and the chemist's retort." "America is a poem in our eyes; its ample geography dazzles the imagination, and it will not wait long for metres." A century later, and we realize that something more is needful for the imagination than an ample geography.

His doctrine that art should be extempore stems from his general belief that knowledge comes from intuition rather than from thought, and that wisdom and goodness are implanted in us—a fatally easy philosophy which has always appealed to the democratic masses, and which is highly flattering to their self-esteem. Wordsworth had led the romantic reaction by making us see the beauty and value in the common things of everyday life, but the philosophy of Emerson has a different ancestry. The two when joined are a perfect soil for democratic belief, and democratic laxity in mind and spirit, far as that might be from Emerson's intention and occasional statements. The more obvious inferences are dangerous, for although a cobbler's flash of insight *may* be as great as the philosopher's lifetime of thought, such is of the rarest occurrence, and preached as a universal doctrine it is a more leveling one by far than universal suffrage.

2

As the ordinary unimportant man, such as most of us are, reads Emerson, his self-esteem begins to grow and glow. "The sweetest music is not in the oratorio, but in the human voice when it speaks from its instant tones of tenderness, truth, or courage." Culture, with us, he says, "ends in headache." "Do not craze yourself with thinking, but go about your business anywhere. Life is not intellectual or critical, but sturdy." "Why all this deference to Alfred and Scanderbeg and Gustavus? As great a stake depends on your private act today as followed their public and renowned steps." "We are all wise. The difference between persons is not in wisdom but in art." "Our spontaneous action is always the best. You cannot with your best deliberation and heed come so close to any question as your spontaneous glance shall bring you whilst you rise from your bed."

There is a kernel of noble thought in all this, but it is heady doctrine that may easily make men drunk and driveling, and I think we are coming near to the heart of our problem. The preaching that we do not have to think, the doctrine of what I may term, in Emerson's phrase, "the spontaneous glance," is at the bottom of that appalling refusal to criticize, analyze, ponder, which is one of the chief characteristics of the American people to-day in all its social, political, and international affairs. Many influences have united to bring about the condition, and Emerson cannot escape responsibility for being one of them.

On the other hand, a new nation, a common man with a fleeting vision of the possibility of an uncommon life, above all the youth just starting out with ambition and hope but little knowledge or influence as yet, all need the stimulation of a belief that somehow they *are* important and that not only may their private acts and lives be as high and noble as any, but that the way is open for them to make them so. This is the one fundamental American doctrine. It is the one unique contribution America has made to the common fund of civilization. Our mines and wheat fields do not differ in kind from others. With Yankee ingenuity we have seized on the ideas of others and in many cases improved their practical applications. The ideas, however, have largely come from abroad. The use of coal as fuel, the harnessing of steam and electricity for man's use,—the foundations of our era,—originated in Europe. Even the invention of the electric light was only in part American. But the doctrine of the importance of the common man is uniquely an American doctrine. It is something different, on the one hand, from the mere awarding to him of legal rights and, on the other, from the mere career open to the talents.

It is a doctrine to which the heart of humanity has responded with religious enthusiasm. It, and not science, has been the real religion of our time, and, essentially, the doctrine is a religious and not a philosophical or scientific one, equally made up as it is of a colossal hope and a colossal illusion. This does not invalidate it. Like all religions it will have its course to run and its part to play in the moulding of man to something finer. It is one more step up, and we need not deny it merely because of the inherent falsity of that gorgeous preamble which proclaims to the world, "All men are created equal." In spite of the self-assertion of the so-called masses, that is a statement which, deep in their hearts, it is as difficult for the inferior as the superior genuinely to believe. It is an ideal, which, like every religious ideal, will be of far-reaching influence, but which must be made believable emotionally. Emerson's greatness lies in his having been the greatest prophet of this new religion, an influence that might well continue to be felt on the two classes that need the doctrine most—the common man striving to rise above the mediocre, and the youth striving to attain a courageous and independent maturity.

Another strain in Emerson, that of the poet and mystic, has also to be reckoned with in making up the man's account. His insistence upon values in life, culminating in the spiritual, is one sorely needed in the America of our day as of his. We are, perhaps, further from the ideal he drew in his "American Scholar" than were the men of his own time. His large hope has not been fulfilled. There is a delicate beauty in his spiritual outlook on life, a beauty akin to that of many an old fresco in Umbria or Tuscany. Unfortunately, there were fundamental flaws in the work of the Italian artists, flaws not of spiritual insight or of artistic craftsmanship, but of wet plaster or of wrong chemical combinations in materials, so that little by little their painting has crumbled and faded. If Emerson's mysticism led him too easily toward Swedenborg rather than toward Plato, and if the beauty of his spiritual interpretation of the universe does not carry that conviction or mould his readers as it should, may we not wonder whether there were not some fundamental flaws in the mind of the man that may explain his decreasing influence, just as in examining a wall where a few patches of dim color are all that remain of a Giotto we have to consider, not the artist's love of the Madonna, but his lack of knowledge of the mechanics of his art? Of this we shall speak presently.

The quintessence of Emersonianism is to be found in the first and second series of *Essays,* and it may be noted that it was these, as my pencilings show, which I myself read most as a boy, and of them, it was such essays as "Self-Reliance," in which the word is found in its purest form, that I read over and over. What do I find marked as I turn the old pages? "Trust thyself: every heart vibrates to that iron string." "Whoso would be a man must be a nonconformist." "Nothing at last is sacred but the integrity of your own mind." "I do not wish to expiate, but to live. My life is not an apology, but a life. It is for itself and not for a spectacle." "What I must do is all that concerns me, not what the people think." "The great man is he who in the crowd keeps with perfect sweetness the independence of solitude." "Always scorn appearances and you always may. The force of character is cumulative." "Life only avails and not the having lived." "Insist on yourself; never imitate." "Nothing can bring you peace but yourself."

This is high and worthy doctrine, the practice of which will tax a man's strength and courage to the utmost, and such sentences as the above have proved the strongest influences in the making of literally countless adolescent Americans, stimulating their ambition in the noblest fashion. Unfortunately this part of Emerson's teaching has had less influence than the other. The average American soon slips into preferring "we are all wise" to "scorn appearances." Insisting on being one's self is strenuous and difficult work anywhere, more so in America than any other country I know, thanks to social opinion, mass ideals, and psychologized advertising of national products. Emerson deserves full meed of praise for preaching the value of individualism, but it may be asked, granting that nearly all intelligent, high-minded American youths for nearly a century have, at their most idealistic stage, come under the influence of Emerson's doctrine, why has the effect of his teaching been so slight upon their later manhood? Does the fault lie in them or in the great teacher, for, in such sentences as we have quoted above, I gladly allow that the sage of Concord *was* a great teacher.

The answer, I think, is that the fault lies to a great extent in Emerson himself. His doctrine contains two great flaws, one positive, the other negative, and both as typically American as he himself was in everything. That he had no logically articulated system of thought is not his weakest point. He once said that he could not give an account of himself if challenged. Attempts have been made to prove that his thought was unified and coherent. One may accept these or not. It matters little, for it is not, and never has been, as a consistent philosopher that Emerson has influenced his readers. It has been by his trenchant aphorisms which stir the soul of the young and the not too thoughtful, and set the blood to dancing like sudden strains of martial music. It is in these, and not in any metaphysical system about which philosophers might argue, that we find the fatal flaws and influences I have mentioned.

The first, the positive one, in spite of his high doctrine of self-reliance and individualism, is that Emerson makes life too easy by his insistence on intuition and spontaneity. The style and construction of his writings deliberately emphasize the import of the aphorisms. The occasionally qualifying context sinks into insignificance and out of memory as does the stick of a rocket in the darkness of night. We see and recall only the dazzling shower of stars. If this is now and then unfair to Emerson's thought, he has himself to blame. He took no pains to bind his thought together and loved the brilliancy of his rocket-stars of "sayings." We have already quoted some of these on the point we are now discussing. All teaching is "Intuition." In "Spontaneity or Instinct" he finds "the essence of genius, the essence of virtue, and the essence of life." "It is as easy for the strong man to be strong, as it is for the weak to be weak." "All good conversation, manners, and action, come from a spontaneity which forgets usages, and makes the moment great." "No man need be perplexed by his speculations. . . . These are the soul's mumps and measles and whooping-coughs." "Our moral nature is vitiated by any interference of our will. . . . There is no merit in the matter. Either God is there or he is not there. We love characters in proportion as they are impulsive and spontaneous. The less a man thinks or knows about his virtues the better we like him." A page or two back we noted his theory of spontaneity in art and intellect.

3

This, as we have said, unless the occasional qualifications are as greatly emphasized as the sayings themselves, is extremely dangerous doctrine. Of all the youths who have read Emerson in their impressionable years, a certain proportion have subsequently retrograded in the spiritual and intellectual scale, and a certain proportion have advanced. Of the difficulty with the master felt by the latter we shall speak presently, but for the first group this doctrine of spontaneity, so emphasized by Emerson, offers all too soft a cushion upon which to recline. Act and do not think. Culture is headache. Perplexities are the soul's mumps and measles. Radiant sentence after sentence, graven with clear precision on the cameo of the mind. It has been said that, of all the sages, Emerson requires the least intellectual preparation to read. He is, indeed, in some respects, and those in which he exerts most influence, fatally easy. Fatally easy and alluring to the busy hundred-per-cent American is this doctrine of intuition and spontaneity. It is a siren voice, a soft Lydian air blown across the blue water of the mind's tropical sea. For a century the American has left the plain hard work of life to his foreign serfs. The backbreaking toil of digging trenches, laying rails, puddling iron in the furnaces, has been delegated successively to the Irish, the Italians, the Slavs. But thinking is intellectually, willing is spiritually, as backbreaking as these. The ordinary American prefers also to abandon them and to take for himself the easier task of solving the economic problems and puzzles in which he delights. Intuition and spontaneity— fatal words for a civilization which is more and more coming to depend for its very existence on clear, hard, and long-sustained "thinking-through." It is this positive flaw in Emerson's teaching that has made the effect of his really noble doctrines of so little influence upon the boys who have worshiped him this side idolatry at sixteen and then gone into the world and found every invitation to retreat from the high ground rather than to advance and other great plagues that have swept over Europe. Famine? None. Think of India and China. War? Scarcely more than one. In the Revolution only an infinitesimal part of the population was in the army for any length of time. The War of 1812 was a ripple, almost all at sea, and the deaths were negligible to the population. The Indian Wars? Skirmishes by paid troops. The Mexican War? A junket which never came home to the people. The Civil War? Yes, but even that did not come home to the whole civilian population, except in the South, as have the wars which have flowed in torrents over Europe. Compare it with the Thirty Years' War, in which, to say nothing of the rest of Europe, the population of Germany, from the ravages of the sword, famine, disease, and emigration, sank from 16,000,000 to 6,000,000, and in which of

35,000 villages in Bohemia less than 6,000 were standing at the end, and in which nine tenths of the entire population of the Palatinate disappeared. The Spanish War was a holiday affair except for a few homes. In the last Great War we lost by death a mere 126,000 as compared with 8,500,000 in the Old World. In civil life our history has been one long business boom, punctuated by an occasional panic, like a fit of indigestion for a man who continually overeats. We have never suffered like the rest of humanity, and have waxed fat without, as yet, having to consider the problems forced upon others, until we have ceased to believe in their reality. The dominant American note has thus been one of a buoyant and unthinking optimism. America is a child who has never gazed on the face of death.

Emerson somewhere speaks of "the nonchalance of boys sure of a dinner." Can any words better express the American attitude toward the universe, and, in spite of his spirituality and the somewhat faded fresco of his mysticism, does Emerson himself really give us anything deeper? Man, according to him, "is born to be rich." Economic evils trouble our sage not at all. The universe, for him, is good through and through, and "success consists in close application to the laws of the world, and, since those laws are intellectual and moral, an intellectual and moral obedience." One thinks of Jay Gould and the career of many a magnate of to-day! "In a free and just commonwealth, property rushes from the idle and imbecile, to the industrious, brave, and persevering." As I am certainly not idle (I am working on a holiday to write this), and as Americans would not admit that theirs is not a just and free commonwealth, imbecility is the only third horn of the trilemma on which to impale myself if property has not rushed toward me. "Do not skulk," the sage tells every man in "a world which exists for him." At fifty, we have found, simply, that the world does *not* exist for us. "Love and you shall be loved. All love is mathematically just, as much as the two sides of an algebraic problem." One rubs one's eyes. "There is a soul at the center of nature and over the will of every man, so that none of us can wrong the universe." Man may, he says, "easily dismiss all particular uncertainties and fears, and adjourn to the sure revelation of time the solution of his private riddles. He is sure his welfare is dear to the heart of being." Is he so sure? Alas, no longer.

4

As I think over my most recent visit to Rome, where two thousand years of human history, happiness, and suffering have left their monuments, and Heaven knows how many thousand unmarked before, I contrast it with a visit to Emerson's house at Concord on an October day many years ago. It is a charming, roomy old house, and in it Emerson was able to live with a large library and three servants on two thousand a year. In the ineffable light of an American autumn, as I saw it, it was a place of infinite peace. Concord in 1840 was an idyllic moment in the history of the race. That moment came and passed, like a baby's smile. Emerson lived in it. "In the morning," he wrote, "I awake, and find the old world, wife, babies, and mother, Concord and Boston, the dear old spiritual world, and even the dear old devil not far off."

It is true that he has very occasional qualms and doubts. He even wonders in one essay whether we must presuppose some "slight treachery and derision" in the universe. As we turn the pages, we ask ourselves with some impatience, "Did this man never really suffer?" and read that "the only thing grief has taught me, is to know how shallow it is. That, like all the rest, plays about the surface, and never introduces me into the reality, for contact with which, we would even pay the costly price of sons and lovers."

One ends. Perhaps Mr. More is right. Perhaps Emerson is the outstanding figure in American letters. Who else has expressed so magnificently the hope, and so tragically illustrated the illusion, of our unique contribution to the world? My own debt to the sage is unpayable. He was one of the great influences in my early life, as, in his highest teaching, he should be in that of every boy. It seems almost the basest of treason to write this essay, and I would still have every youth read his Emerson. But what of America? What of the hope and the illusion? A century has passed. Is no one to arise who will fuse them both in some larger synthesis, and who, inspiring youth, will not be a broken reed in maturity? Are our letters and philosophy to remain the child until the Gorgon faces of evil, disaster, and death freeze our own unlined ones into eternal stone? Is it well that the outstanding figure in American letters should be one whose influence diminishes in proportion as the minds of his readers grow in strength, breadth, and maturity? And, speaking generally, is this not true of Emerson? Does any man of steadily growing character, wealth of experience, and strength of mind find the significance and influence of Emerson for him growing as the years pass? Does he turn to him more and more for counsel, help, or solace?

There is but one answer, I think, and that is negative. Unlike the truly great, the influence of Emerson shrinks for most of us as we ourselves develop. May the cause not lie in the two flaws I have pointed out, flaws in the man as in his doctrine in spite of the serene nobility of so much of his life? If with all his wide and infinitely varied reading, noted in his *Journals,* we find his culture a bit thin and puerile, is it not because he himself trusted too much to that theory of spontaneity, of the "spontaneous glance," rather than to the harder processes of scholarship and thinking-through coherently; and if we find him lacking in depth and virility, is it not because he allowed himself to become a victim to that vast American optimism with its refusal to recognize and wrestle with the problem of evil? One turns to Æschylus and reads:—

. . . affliction knows no rest,
But rolls from breast to breast its vagrant tide.

One does not need to be a pessimist, merely human, to find here the deeper and more authentic note.

If Emerson is still the outstanding figure in American letters, is that not the equivalent of saying that America a century after the *Essays* appeared has not yet grown to mental maturity, and that the gospel it preaches is inspiring only for unformed adolescence,—of whatever age,—without having risen to a comprehension of the problems of maturity? In Europe, the past has bequeathed not only a wealth of art, but a legacy of evil borne and sorrow felt. Perhaps American letters, like American men, will not grow beyond the simple optimism and, in one aspect, the shallow doctrine of Emerson until they too shall have suffered and sorrowed. Emerson, in his weakness as in his strength, is American through and through. He could have been the product, in his entirety, of no other land, and that land will not outgrow him until it has some day passed through the fires of a suffering unfelt by him and as yet escaped by it.

William Braswell (1907–1985)

Given the relative dearth of source materials by Melville on Emerson, it seems highly serviceable to have a scholar lay out what lines of relation there are—even if, in this case, Melville's opinions of Emerson reside primarily in marginalia. And yet, despite the scarcity of first-hand remarks by Melville on Emerson, much has been written on the relationship between these two iconic figures since Braswell's article appeared in American Literature *(1937). Nevertheless, Braswell's study remains a useful outline of the main points of some textual and material facts that connect the two authors—a study from which some profitable application may be made in the course of further speculative research. After writing a dissertation at the University of Chicago entitled* Herman Melville and Christianity *(1934), Braswell published* Melville's Religious Thought, An Essay in Interpretation *(1943), and taught at Purdue University for nearly four decades. Braswell concludes his essay by saying that "Melville's criticism of Emerson seems very much what one might have expected." As a reader sets out to explore and understand this criticism, the question is: what does one expect?*

Melville as a Critic of Emerson

William Braswell

I

Because the critical remarks of one eminent author concerning another are rarely without interest, students of American literature regret that there is apparently no record of Ralph Waldo Emerson's opinion of Herman Melville.[1] That Emerson owned at least one of Melville's works is shown by the presence of *Typee* among the preserved books of his library. Yet there is no evidence that he read the volume.[2] We are more fortunate, however, in regard to our knowledge of what Melville thought of Emerson.

Until now a letter that Melville wrote to E. A. Duyckinck on March 3, 1849, has been the only generally known source from which one could learn Melville's opinion of Emerson. In the incomplete reproduction of that letter in Meade Minnigerode's *Some Personal Letters of Herman Melville and a Bibliography*,[3] one reads that Melville had recently heard Emerson lecture[4] and that he considered Emerson "more than a brilliant fellow." He had been told that Emerson was difficult to understand because of his abstruseness, but on this occasion he had found him quite clear. He jested concerning Emerson's reputed sobriety. And he made a statement that astonishes anyone familiar with the thought of the two men: he charged Emerson with insinuating "that had he lived in those days when the world was made, he might have offered some valuable suggestions." He censured Emerson on that point, whereas he himself, in his recently published *Mardi*, had shown more discontent over the universe than Emerson expressed in all his published works.[5]

On the whole, Melville wrote so capriciously of "this Plato who talks thro' his nose" that one is not surprised to discover in the manuscript of the letter his confession that he knew practically nothing about Emerson. Minnigerode's version of the letter curiously omits[6] the following important passage: "... I had only glanced at a book of his once in Putnam's store—that was all I knew of him, till I heard him lecture."[7] This statement of his unfamiliarity with Emerson's works, together with the fact that he had heard only one of Emerson's lectures, convinces one that at the time of writing the letter Melville was hardly qualified to pass judgment upon the merits of his famous contemporary. The comments on Emerson in the letter, therefore, should not be taken very seriously.

In *Pierre,* published three years after the letter was written, there is a passage which might be considered a severe condemnation of Emerson as well as the other New England Transcendentalists. In writing of "the talismanic secret" by which one reconciles "this world with his own soul," Melville says:

> Certain philosophers have time and again pretended to have found it; but if they do not in the end discover their own delusion, other people soon discover it for themselves, and so those philosophers and their vain philosophy are let glide away into practical oblivion. Plato, and Spinoza, and Goethe and many more belong to this guild of self-impostors, with a preposterous rabble of Muggletonian Scots and Yankees, whose vile brogue still the more bestreaks the stripedness of their Greek and German Neoplatonical originals.[8]

Harsh as this stricture is, one cannot but be impressed by the illustrious company in which the Transcendentalists are damned. After publishing *Pierre,* Melville apparently did not express himself in print on either Emerson or the Transcendentalists as a school.[9]

He did, however, write some comments upon Emerson which he did not mean to publish, and which have not been published until now. These appear in three volumes of Emerson's essays that Melville bought secondhand: *Essays: First Series* and *Essays: Second Series,* which he obtained in the early sixties,[10] and *The Conduct of Life,* which he obtained in 1870.[11] Judging from the markings in these books, one concludes that Melville probably did not read some of the essays; there is no evidence, for instance, that he read "Compensation," "Self-Reliance," or "The Over-Soul," which are among the sixteen unmarked essays of the thirty essays[12] contained in the three volumes. The fourteen other essays, however, are marked here and there with pencil;[13] and of these the following eight are annotated in Melville's handwriting: "Spiritual Laws," "Prudence," "Heroism," "The Poet," "Culture," "Worship," "Considerations by the Way," and "Illusions."[14] By considering the markings and annotations, one discovers some interesting facts about Melville's attitude toward Emerson. One should remember, of course, that the annotations are not to be thought of as notes for a systematic treatise on Emerson's philosophy: they are merely opinions that Melville recorded immediately after reading particular passages in Emerson's essays.

Although any grouping of these incidental observations would be arbitrary, they can be treated in a fairly coherent way under three general topics: first, comments on Emerson's ideas concerning the poet; second, praise of Emerson's views on life; and third, unfavorable criticism of Emerson's ideas concerning the problem of evil.[15]

II

The annotations on passages concerning men of letters show that Melville, like Emerson, was more concerned with thought in literature than with craftsmanship. The two men were in agreement on the timeless, universal qualities in the works of great men. In "Spiritual Laws" Emerson wrote:

> We are always reasoning from the seen to the unseen. Hence the perfect intelligence that subsists between wise men of remote ages. A man cannot bury his meaning so deep in his book, but time and like-minded men will find them. Plato had a secret doctrine, had he? What secret can he conceal from the eyes of Bacon? of Montaigne? of Kant? Therefore, Aristotle said of his works, "They are published and not published."[16]

Melville drew a line beside this passage and annotated, "Bully for Emerson!—Good." A similar idea in Emerson's "The Poet" brought forth another favorable comment. In writing of a conversation "on a recent writer of lyrics," Emerson said: "But when the question arose, whether he was not only a lyrist, but a poet, we were obliged to confess that he is plainly a contemporary, not an eternal man."[17] Melville marked heavily the words "contemporary, not an eternal man" and observed concerning them, "A noble expression, with a clear strong meaning."

He was likewise impressed by Emerson's eulogy of the poets as "liberating gods" who, with their figurative writing, open new worlds for other men. Beginning with "We are like persons who come out of a cave or cellar into the open air," Melville marked in "The Poet" the rest of the long paragraph in which that sentence appears[18] and wrote the following praise: "All this is nobly written, and proceeds from noble thinking, and a natural sympathy with greatness."

He did not agree, however, with all Emerson's statements concerning creative artists. Although he concurred in the wisdom of a man's following his peculiar bent, he opposed the view that a man's ambition and powers are commensurate. In "Spiritual Laws" he marked the following sentences as "True":

> He [each man] inclines to do something which is easy to him, and good when it is done, but which no other man can do. He has no rival. For the more truly he consults his own powers, the more difference will his work exhibit from the work of any other.

But the sentences immediately succeeding these he marked as "False":

> His ambition is exactly proportioned to his powers. The height of the pinnacle is determined by the breadth of the base. Every man has this call of the power to do somewhat unique, and no man has any other call.[19]

In connection with Melville's opinion of this passage, one recalls his writing to Duyckinck in 1850:

> Can you send me about fifty fast-writing youths.... If you can I wish you would, because since I have been here I have planned about that number of future works and can't find enough time to think about them separately.[20]

Another point upon which the two men's views conflicted is the effect upon the artist of the stimulants that are sometimes used to produce what Emerson called "animal exhilaration." After enumerating in "The Poet" several of the *"quasi-*mechanical substitutes for the true nectar" which help a man "to escape the custody of that body in which he is pent up, and of that jail-yard of individual relations in which he is enclosed," Emerson went on to affirm:

> Hence a great number of such as were professionally expressors of Beauty, as painters, poets, musicians, and actors, have been more than others wont to lead a life of pleasure and indulgence; all but the few who received the true nectar; and, as it was a spurious mode of attaining freedom, as it was an emancipation not into the heavens, but into the freedom of baser places, they were punished for that advantage they won, by a dissipation and deterioration.[21]

Melville marked this passage and wrote at the bottom of the page:

> No no no.—Titian—did he deteriorate?—Byron?—did he.—Mr E. is horribly narrow here. He has his Dardanelles for his every Marmora.[22] But he keeps nobly on, for all that!

If Emerson had had an opportunity to answer the questions in this annotation, he probably would have answered in the affirmative. He seems to have left no comment upon Titian; but he made numerous references to Byron, several of which show that although he admired that poet very much as a rhetorician, he held the not uncommon view that Byron's intellect was "depraved" and his will "perverted."[23]

In the paragraph on the harm of intoxicants to poets, Emerson went on to say:

> So the poet's habit of living should be set on a key so low and plain, that the common influences should delight him. His cheerfulness should be the gift of the sunlight; the air should suffice for his inspiration, and he should be tipsy with water.[24]

Melville annotated, "This makes the Wordsworthian poet—not the Shakespearean."[25] Although Emerson ranked Wordsworth very high,[26] he, like Melville, considered Shakespeare supreme among poets. For all his love of Shakespeare, however, he felt that the great dramatist's "profane life" and his "using his genius for the public amusement" had prevented him from filling the highest office of the poet.[27]

Melville's reaction to Emerson's argument that the poet should not indulge the senses but should become "tipsy with water" reminds one of the letter that Melville had written to Duyckinck in regard to Emerson. Here Melville replied to Duyckinck's complaint concerning Emerson's sobriety:

> Ah, my dear Sir, that's his misfortune, not his fault. His belly, Sir, is in his chest, and his brains descend down into his neck, and offer an obstacle to a draughtful of ale or a mouthful of cake....[28]

Melville's delight in conviviality is well known to all who are familiar with his life and works. The fact that he once entertained visions of paradise as a place where he might drink champagne with Hawthorne[29] sets him apart from Emerson; for although Emerson "placed wine before guests of discreet age and habit and took it with them, seldom more than one glass,"[30] he on one occasion recorded his regret that during the preceding year he had spent "say $20 in wine and liquors," only to the detriment of the drinkers, whereas that sum "would have bought a beautiful print that would have pleased for a century; or have paid a debt...."[31] The conflicting views of the two authors concerning indulgence of the senses are quite in keeping with their differences in temperament as evidenced in the austerity of Emerson's essays and poems and in the spirit of revelry in parts of Melville's novels, notably *Mardi*.

As Melville took exception to the puritanical standards of living prescribed in "The Poet," so he objected to statements made there in regard to the poet's understanding and interpretation of life. Emerson said:

> For as it is dislocation and detachment from the life of God, that makes things ugly, the poet, who reattaches things to nature and the Whole,—re-attaching even artificial things, and violations of nature, to nature, by a deeper insight,— disposes very easily of the most disagreeable facts.[32]

Melville underlined "disposes very easily of the most disagreeable facts" and commented, "So it would seem. In this sense, Mr E. is a great poet." Further on in the essay Emerson asserted concerning the poet:

> He uses forms according to the life, and not according to the form. This is true science. The poet alone knows astronomy, chemistry, vegetation, and animation, for he does not stop at these facts, but employs them as signs. He knows why the plain, or meadow of space, was strown with these flowers we call suns, and moons, and stars; why the great deep is adorned with animals, with men, and gods....[33]

Melville marked the last sentence, underscoring "He knows," and wrote, "Would some poet be pleased to tell us 'why.' Will Mr E.?" The unhappy result of Melville's search for some purpose in the universe explains his attitude toward Emerson's faith in the poet's vision. Melville agreed with Emerson that poets are "liberating gods" in that they present wise views on certain aspects of life, but he did not share Emerson's enthusiasm over the poet's ability to reconcile man to the deepest mysteries.

His criticism of Emerson on this point is related to his remarks about various opinions of Emerson concerning life in general.

III

In several instances Melville recorded a favorable opinion of Emerson's ideas about particular aspects of the individual and of society.

He was delighted by Emerson's giving veracity and honesty the first place among the virtues. In "Illusions" Emerson declared:

> I look upon the simple and childish virtues of veracity and honesty as the root of all that is sublime in character. Speak as you think, be what you are, pay your debts of all kinds. I prefer to be owned as sound and solvent, and my word as good as my bond, and to be what cannot be skipped, or dissipated, or undermined, to all the *eclat* in the universe. This reality is the foundation of friendship, religion, poetry, and art.[34]

Melville enclosed the last sentence in brackets and annotated, "True & admirable! Bravo!" for he too embodied in his writings the idea that Emerson here expressed. The necessity of being true to oneself is emphasized in the works of both men.

This fact explains the concurrence of their ideas in regard to the fundamental nature of heroism. Melville was impressed by the following passage in the *Essays*:

> Self-trust is the essence of heroism. It is the state of the soul at war, and its ultimate objects are the last defiance of falsehood and wrong, and the power to bear all that can be inflicted by evil agents. . . . Its jest is the littleness of common life. That false prudence which dotes on health and wealth is the butt and merriment of heroism.[35]

Melville drew a marginal line beside these sentences and observed, "This is noble again."[36] Besides seeing in the lives of others the truth of these remarks by Emerson, he was aware that his own struggle in the late forties and the early fifties, his most productive period, was characterized by such a heroic spirit as Emerson defined.

Personal experience served also to make him agree with Emerson that great truth is learned only through suffering. In "Considerations by the Way" Emerson wrote that we daily pray "to be conventional," saying:

> Supply, most kind gods! this defect in my address, in my form, in my fortunes, which puts me a little out of the ring: supply it, and let me be like the rest whom

I admire, and on good terms with them. But the wise gods say, No, we have better things for thee. By humiliations, by defeats, by loss of sympathy, by gulfs of disparity, learn a wider truth and humanity than that of a fine gentleman.[37]

Concerning the last sentence Melville commented, "Nothing can be truer or better said." By not writing books that would make him popular and financially prosperous, and by writing instead books containing the truth learned by just such means as "the wise gods" stipulated,[38] he himself had sacrificed the possibility of becoming "a fine gentleman."

Various other passages that Melville marked without annotating are obviously in accord with what he believed. For instance, he underlined "adversity is the prosperity of the great,"[39] and "Every man's task is his life-preserver";[40] and he heavily marked an old Persian proverb which Emerson praised:

Fooled thou must be, though wisest of the wise:
Then be the fool of virtue, not of vice.[41]

The annotations and markings referred to show quite clearly that Melville appreciated many of Emerson's opinions relative to personal integrity and fortitude. He was gratified by Emerson's argument that strong character is based upon self-reliance.

He felt, however, that Emerson went too far in his praise of self-reliance when he spoke disparagingly of the benefits to be derived from the study of foreign cultures. His attitude toward Emerson's views on traveling throws some light on that point. In writing of Americans' going to Europe for culture, Emerson queried, "You do not think you will find anything there which you have not seen at home?"[42] This statement caused Melville to observe, "Yet, possibly, Rome or Athens has something to show or suggest that Chicago has not." Since traveling had contributed much to Melville's own education, such a comment on his part seems only natural. The sights that he had seen were partly responsible for the difference between his cosmic view and that of Emerson; and it was this difference which caused Melville to write his most severe criticism of Emerson.

IV

He found a great deal to criticize in Emerson's views upon the problem of evil. Since from the time of writing *Mardi* (1849) he himself had shown great concern over the suffering and wretchedness in the universe, it is not surprising that he found fault with Emerson's relatively unperturbed attitude in regard to the matter.

In the first place, he objected to what he considered an insinuation by Emerson that man himself is responsible for the origin of his ills. In "Heroism" Emerson said:

The disease and deformity around us certify the infraction of natural, intellectual, and moral laws, and often violation on violation to breed such compound misery. A lockjaw that bends a man's head back to his heels, hydrophobia, that makes him bark at his wife and babes, insanity, that makes him eat grass; war, plague, cholera, famine, indicate a certain ferocity in nature, which, as it had its inlet by human crime, must have its outlet by human suffering.[43]

Melville marked the last part of this passage and commented:

Look squarely at this, & what is it but mere theology—Calvinism?—The brook shows the stain of the banks it has passed thro. Still, these essays are noble.

Melville's use of the word "Calvinism" indicates that he perceived in the passage evidence of Emerson's belief in the fall of man through his own agency.[44] This dissenting comment came naturally enough from one who, brought up to believe in the doctrine of the fall, had in maturity come to the conclusion that God is responsible for the presence of evil as well as for the presence of good.

Similarly Melville was perturbed, for understandable reasons, by Emerson's belief that by obeying the immutable natural laws, which Emerson thought to be at one with a Beneficent Tendency of the universe, man attains goodness, whereas by disobeying them he becomes depraved.[45] So Emerson maintained when he wrote: "it is the undisciplined will that is whipped with bad thoughts and bad fortunes."[46] This statement caused Melville to accuse Emerson again of being theological: "Jumps into the pulpit from off the tripod here," Melville annotated. Another passage concerning the punishment that a man suffers for his sins evoked a humorous comment. In "Spiritual Laws" Emerson wrote:

Our dreams are the sequel of our waking knowledge. The visions of the night bear some proportion to the visions of the day. Hideous dreams are exaggerations of the sins of the day.[47]

Melville annotated the last sentence thus: "Meaning, of course, the sins of *indigestion.*"

Like Emerson, Melville believed that man can improve his condition if he will but live by the best that is in him. Both *Redburn* and *White Jacket,* especially the latter, contain forcible argument to that effect. But Melville was not nearly so sanguine as Emerson concerning man's ability to overcome evil. He stressed much more than Emerson the fact that there is a difference between man and man. To quote Babbalanja, the philosopher in *Mardi,* some men are governed less by their "moral sense" than by their "instinctive passions," which fact makes it "easier for some men to be saints, than for others not to be sinners."[48] Babbalanja says concerning the man who is not a criminal: "That he is not bad, is not of him. Potter's clay and wax are all moulded by hands invisible. The soil decides the man."[49] Reduced to the ultimate, such a view might be held to show that Melville was a Necessitarian; but he, like Emerson, had no definite philosophical system. Suffice it here to say that he was more fully aware of the undesirable elements in human nature than Emerson was.

In an annotation already noted Melville said that if the tendency to dispose easily of disagreeable facts is a sign of poetic power, Emerson is a great poet. His dissatisfaction with Emerson's minimizing some of the harsher aspects of nature is evident in other marginal remarks. In the essay on "Prudence" Emerson declared: "The drover, the sailor, buffets it all day, and his health renews itself at as vigorous a pulse under the sleet, as under the sun of June."[50] Melville commented: "To one who has weathered Cape Horne as a common sailor what stuff all this is." The vivid description in *White Jacket* of the hardships and the danger encountered in rounding Cape Horn contains this statement concerning the Cape: "Lucky it is that it comes about midway in the homeward-bound passage, so that the sailors have time to prepare for it, and time to recover from it after it is astern."[51]

That Melville considered Emerson prejudiced in his treatment of unpleasant facts is likewise shown by an annotation upon a passage which proclaims the trustworthiness of man. "Trust men," wrote Emerson, "and they will be true to you; treat them greatly, and they will show themselves great, though they make an exception in your favor to all their rules in trade."[52] Melville observed, "God help the poor fellow who squares his life according to this." In *The Confidence-Man* (1857) Melville had written one of the severest satires ever directed at the idea that man is innately good and deserving of trust. Later works indicate that he came to hold a more favorable view of human nature, but he never found enough goodness in mankind to justify such an assumption as Emerson's.

His criticism of Emerson on these matters is merely a part of his criticism of Emerson's optimism in regard to the problem of evil. Emerson believed that evil is temporary. "Good is positive," he asserted. "Evil is merely privative, not absolute: it is like cold, which is the privation of heat."[53] Believing in a universal scheme that tends toward absolute good, Emerson made some statements that Melville thought ridiculous. In Emerson's assertion that "the first lesson of history is the good of evil"[54] Melville underlined "the good of evil" and wrote: "He still bethinks himself of his optimism—he must make that good somehow against the eternal hell itself."[55] Emerson's saying that "we use defects and deformities to a sacred purpose, so expressing our sense that the evils of the world are such only to the evil eye,"[56] caused Melville to inquire:

What does the man mean? If Mr Emerson travelling in Egypt should find the plague-spot come out on him—would he consider that an evil sight or not? And if evil, would the eye be evil because it seemed evil to his eye, or rather to his sense using the eye for instrument?

A passage in "Spiritual Laws" had a similar effect upon Melville. "The good," Emerson wrote, "compared to the evil which he [a man] sees, is as his own good to his own evil."[57] Melville annotated:

A perfectly good being, therefore, would see no evil—But what did Christ see?—He saw what made him weep.—Howard, too, the "Philanthropist" must have been a very bad man—he saw, in jails, so much evil. To annihilate all this nonsense read the Sermon on the Mount, and consider what it implies.[58]

The Sermon on the Mount was for Melville the "greatest real miracle of all religions" because it shows Christ's vivid awareness of the evil in the world and expresses his "inexhaustible . . . tenderness and loving-kindness" for mankind.[59]

The annotations upon the subject of evil help to explain the most important critical remark that Melville made concerning Emerson. In "The Poet" Melville marked the passage beginning, "Language is fossil poetry,"[60] and wrote:

> This is admirable, as many other thoughts of Mr Emerson's are. His gross and astonishing errors & illusions spring from a self-conceit so intensely intellectual and calm that at first one hesitates to call it by its right name. Another species of Mr Emerson's errors, or rather blindness, proceeds from a defect in the region of the heart.

By expressing admiration for much of Emerson, and by censuring at the same time what appeared to Melville to be intellectual smugness and an imperfect appreciation of the suffering of mankind, this comment sums up very well Melville's criticism of Emerson.[61] In spite of what the praise implies, the censure shows that between the two men's interpretations of truth there was a gulf.

V

How to account for that gulf is a problem which can be partially solved by a brief survey of certain factors in the lives of the two authors.

There is a real contrast between Emerson's long academic training and Melville's brief training. And there is a great difference between the types of people the two were associated with as young men: Melville's experiences on the high seas and on foreign soil brought him into contact with a wider variety of evils than was afforded by polite society of Boston and Cambridge. His financial failure as a novelist also taught him some bitter truth.

Yet it would be dangerous to assert that the hardships and the distress which Melville suffered were more difficult to bear than those which came to Emerson in his quiet surroundings. Mental defectiveness in one brother, temporary insanity in another, consumption that preyed upon himself and others in his family, deaths of loved ones, all caused Emerson sorrow; but they did not lessen his basic optimism.

The difference in the religious training of the two men is probably one of the chief reasons why one's outlook on life was much brighter than the other's. It is significant that Emerson was born and reared in a Unitarian world, whereas Melville spent his early years under the influence of the Reformed Theology. Emerson was taught to believe that the Deity is benevolent and that man is good. Melville was instructed in the Calvinistic views that God is a jealous God and that man is corrupt. Moreover, because of the place it gave to Christ, Melville's religious training was more emotional in effect than Emerson's. In both cases the teachings had an abiding influence.

Perhaps even more important than religious training, however, is the constitutional factor. At the age of thirty Emerson wrote in his journal:

> Men seem to be constitutionally believers and unbelievers. There is no bridge that can cross from a mind in one state to a mind in the other. All my opinions, affections, whimsies, are tinged with belief,—incline to that side. . . . But I cannot give reasons to a person of a different persuasion that are at all adequate to the force of my conviction. Yet when I fail to find the reason, my faith is not less.[62]

There is a notable contrast between this autobiographical passage and a shrewd analytical comment that Hawthorne made upon Melville. After a long talk with Melville, with whom he had conversed many times before, Hawthorne wrote in his journal in 1856:

> He can neither believe, nor be comfortable in his unbelief; and he is too honest and courageous not to try to do one or the other. If he were a religious man, he would be one of the most truly religious and reverential; he has a very high and noble nature, and [is] better worth immortality than most of us.[63]

Emerson's optimism had an unshakable basis in his intuition: physical facts and logic were secondary matters with him. Although during the early part of his career as a novelist Melville derived occasional ecstasy from intuitional thinking, he was temperamentally disposed to trust more to his understanding than to his intuition.

For that reason one might expect certain important influences from his reading. He was more affected by the arguments of skeptical philosophers than Emerson was. The attitudes of the two men toward Hume is enlightening. Emerson admitted that Hume's logic had proved invulnerable to all attacks upon it; yet he referred to Hume's arguments as "calumnies upon our nature."[64] Melville, on the other hand, said that although Hume was "the most skeptical of philosophical sceptics, yet" he was "full of that firm, creedless faith that embraces the spheres."[65]

The constitutional tastes of Emerson and Melville as well as the influences of their reading are implied in Emerson's fondness for Plotinus, who minimized the importance of evil in the universal scheme, and Melville's fondness for such works as Ecclesiastes. When praising that book, Melville wrote: "that mortal man who hath more of joy than sorrow in him, that mortal man cannot be true—not true, or undeveloped."[66] This assertion, written before Melville annotated Emerson's essays, is not unlike an opinion that he expressed some years after that experience. When writing to thank an English correspondent for a copy of Thomson's *The City of Dreadful Night, and Other Poems,* he said:

> As to the pessimism [of Thomson's poetry], although neither pessimist nor optimist myself, nevertheless I relish it in the verse, if for nothing else than as a counterpoise to the exorbitant hopefulness, juvenile and shallow, that makes such a bluster in these days, at least in some quarters.[67]

This taste for pessimism in literature helps to explain why at the very end of his life Melville read sympathetically certain passages in the works of Schopenhauer.[68] An admirer of Schopenhauer—a philosopher whom Emerson called "odious"[69]—would hardly approve of some of the ideas in Emerson's essays.

On the whole, in the light of all the facts noted concerning the two men, Melville's criticism of Emerson seems very much what one might have expected. That Melville censured Emerson's attitude toward evil is no more surprising than that he praised such qualities as Emerson's mastery of rhetoric and his love of goodness.

Notes

1 After discussing Emerson's criticism of various other novelists, John T. Flanagan says, in "Emerson as a Critic of Fiction," *Philological Quarterly*, XV, 39 (Jan., 1936): "Of Melville . . . there is no record." So far as I have been able to discover, this statement is correct.

2 I have not seen Emerson's copy of *Typee*; but Mrs. Marian E. Kent, of the Concord Antiquarian Society, has informed me by letter that it is a reprint, published in 1848, of Wiley and Putnam's Revised Edition of the novel. She says, "There are no annotations in this book, and I am unable to learn when it came into Ralph Waldo Emerson's possession."

3 (New York, 1922), pp. 32–34.

4 He heard one of the five lectures (unpublished) on "Mind and Manners in the Nineteenth Century" which Emerson delivered in Boston during Jan. and Feb., 1849. See Luther Stearns Mansfield, *Herman Melville: Author and New Yorker, 1844–1851* (an unpublished doctoral dissertation at the University of Chicago, 1936), pp. 178–179, and James Elliot Cabot, *A Memoir of Ralph Waldo Emerson* (Boston, 1899), II, 753.

5 On this point, and on other points in this article pertaining to Melville's religious thought, see William Braswell, *Herman Melville and Christianity* (an unpublished doctoral dissertation at the University of Chicago, 1934).

6 Minnigerode indicates that an omission has been made.

7 The manuscript of this letter is in the Duyckinck Collection, in the New York Public Library.

8 *Pierre*, p. 290. All references to Melville's works are to the Constable Edition (London, 1922–1924).

9 Carl Van Vechten's theory that *The Confidence-Man* is a satire on the Transcendentalists seems to me unfounded. See his article "The Later Work of Herman Melville," *Double Dealer*, III, 19 (Jan., *1922*).

10 On the verso side of the front cover of the *Essays: First Series* there is inscribed in pencil in Melville's hand, "H Melville/March 22$^\mathrm{d}$ 1862/N. Y." The other volume contains the same inscription except that the year is given as "1861" instead of "1862." It seems probable that Melville bought both books at the same time and merely made a careless error when writing the date of the year in one of them.

The copy of *Essays: First Series* labeled "New Edition" and also "Fourth Edition," was published in Boston, by James Munroe and Company, in 1847. The copy of *Essays: Second Series*, "Third Edition," was published by the same house in 1844.

Both are cheaply bound. When I examined these two volumes, they, together with Melville's copy of *The Conduct of Life,* were in the possession of Mrs. Eleanor Melville Metcalf, of Cambridge, Mass., by whose kind permission I had access to them. They are now in the Harvard College Library.

11 This volume is inscribed in Melville's hand, "H. Melville/N^{ov} 1870/N. Y." (There is the barest possibility that the third figure in the date of the year may be "9" instead of "7.") The title-page states that this copy is of both the "Author's Edition" and the "Second Edition"; the book was published in London, by Smith, Elder, and Co., in 1860.

12 This figure includes the lecture on "New England Reformers."

13 Melville marked passages in various ways: he underscored, he drew marginal lines, he used brackets and other symbols. Occasionally he marked a passage in two or three ways.

14 The six essays that are marked but not annotated are "Art," "Character," "Manners," "Power," "Wealth," and "Beauty."

15 Since no chronological development is discernible in the annotations, I have set aside the element of time in an effort to achieve more unity in considering them.

16 *Essays: First Series,* p. 131.

17 *Essays: Second Series,* pp. 9–10.

18 *Essays: Second Series,* pp. 33–34.

19 *Essays: First Series,* p. 126.

20 Minnigerode, *op. cit.,* p. 71.

21 *Essays: Second Series,* pp. 30–31.

22 *Lippincott's Gazetteer* defines the Dardenelles as "a narrow strait between Europe and Asia, connecting the Sea of Marmora and the arm of the Mediterranean known as the Aegean Sea. . . ."

23 See the *Journals of Ralph Waldo Emerson,* ed. Edward Waldo Emerson and Waldo Emerson Forbes (Boston, 1909–1914), II, 4; VII, 163, 285; VIII, 89; and *The Complete Works of Ralph Waldo Emerson* (Centenary ed.; Boston, 1903–1904), II, 355, and XII, 319.

24 *Essays: Second Series,* p. 32.

25 The paragraph preceding the one just quoted from "The Poet" also caused Melville to refer to Wordsworth. This paragraph begins: "It is a secret which every intellectual man quickly learns, that beyond the energy of his possessed and conscious intellect, he is capable of a new energy (as of an intellect doubled on itself), by an abandonment to the nature of things. . . ." Melville noted in regard to this thought, "Wordsworth, 'One impulse from a vernal wood' &c" (the quoted words are from Wordsworth's well-known poem "The Tables Turned").

26 See *Journals,* X, 68–69, where Emerson expresses his delight at Wordsworth's being acknowledged the greatest of English poets since Milton. For a good brief criticism by Emerson of Wordsworth's merits and faults, see *Works,* V, 297–298.

27 *Works,* IV, 218–219. In connection with Melville's comment on the Wordsworthian and the Shakespearean poets, it is interesting to note an opinion that Emerson expressed at the age of twenty-three. "It would seem," he wrote, that "the boisterous childhood, careless of criticism and poetry, the association of vulgar and unclean companions, were necessary to balance the towering spirit of Shakespeare, and that Mr. Wordsworth has failed of pleasing by being too much a *poet*" (in a letter to "Miss Emerson" (?), June 30, 1826; *Journals,* II, 106).

28   Minnigerode, *op. cit.,* p. 34. Viola Chittenden White, *Symbolism in Herman Melville's Writings* (an unpublished doctoral dissertation at the University of North Carolina, 1934), p. 75, points out the similarity of this conceit of Melville's and one in Burton's *Anatomy of Melancholy.*

29   During the composition of *Moby Dick* Melville wrote to Hawthorne: "If ever, my dear Hawthorne, in the eternal times that are to come, you and I shall sit down in Paradise, in some little shady corner by ourselves; and if we shall by any means be able to smuggle a basket of champagne there (I won't believe in a Temperance Heaven), and if we shall then cross our celestial legs in the celestial grass that is forever tropical, and strike our glasses and our heads together, till both musically ring in concert,—then, O my dear fellow-mortal, how shall we pleasantly discourse of all the things manifold which now so distress us,—when all the earth shall be but a reminiscence, yea, its final dissolution an antiquity" (Julian Hawthorne, *Nathaniel Hawthorne and his Wife: A Biography,* Boston, 1884, I, 402–403).

30   Edward Waldo Emerson, *Emerson in Concord: A Memoir* (Boston, 1888), pp. 154–155.

31   *Journals,* II, 468.

32   *Essays: Second Series,* p. 20.

33   *Ibid.,* p. 23.

34   *The Conduct of Life,* p. 201.

35   "Heroism," *Essays: First Series,* p. 229. The omission indicated, together with a few sentences preceding those quoted, is also marked.

36   On the preceding page he underlined: "Heroism feels and never reasons, and therefore is always right . . . ," and wrote in the margin, "Alas for the truth again!" But he erased this remark, which happens still to be discernible. Perhaps he made the erasure because he felt that the remainder of the passage sufficiently qualified the underscored words.

37   *The Conduct of Life,* p. 162. The phrase "by gulfs of disparity" is underlined. Lower on the page this sentence is also underlined: "A rich man was never insulted in his life: but this man [who becomes wise] must be stung."

38   See William Braswell, "The Satirical Temper of Melville's *Pierre,*" *American Literature,* VII, 424–426 (Jan., 1936).

39   "Worship," *The Conduct of Life,* p. 145.

40   *Ibid.,* p. 144.

41   "Illusions," *The Conduct of Life,* p. 202. At the end of his tragic life Pierre, a symbol of Melville's own spiritual life, calls himself "the fool of Truth, the fool of Virtue, the fool of Fate" (*Pierre,* p. 499).

42   "Culture," *The Conduct of Life,* p. 90.

43   *Essays: First Series,* pp. 226–227.

44   As a youth Emerson had accepted the story of Adam's entailing sin upon all mankind. On Feb. 22, 1822, Emerson wrote concerning evil: "What is its origin? The sin which Adam brought into the world and entailed upon his children" (*Journals,* I, 115). On Nov. 23 of the same year a new note appears: "it should be remembered that we wisely assume the righteousness of the Creator in placing man in a probationary state. We do not seek with vain ambition to question the abstruse and unsearchable ground of this ordination, because it is plain matter of fact that we are incompetent to the discussion" (*ibid.,* I, 195). About a year later he wrote to ask his Aunt Mary Moody Emerson a number of questions, among them: "what is the origin of evil?" (Cabot, *op. cit.,* I, 103).

But as a mature man he wrote: "We say Paradise was; Adam fell; the Golden Age, and the like. We mean man is not as he ought to be; but our way of painting this is on Time and we say *was*" (under Aug. 21, 1837, *Journals*, IV, 287). The fall of man, he observed, is "the discovery we have made that we exist" (*Works*, III, 75).

45 See Chester Eugene Jorgenson, "Emerson's Paradise under the Shadow of Swords," *Philological Quarterly*, XI, 281–282 (July, 1932).

46 "Illusions," *The Conduct of Life*, pp. 200–201.

47 *Essays: First Series*, p. 132.

48 *Mardi*, II, 156.

49 *Ibid.*, II, 251.

50 *Essays: First Series*, p. 216. Emerson, however, did not deny the ferocities of nature. In "Fate" he recorded: "But Nature is no sentimentalist,—does not cosset or pamper us. We must see that the world is rough and surly.... The cold, inconsiderate of persons, tingles your blood, benumbs your feet, freezes a man like an apple" (*Works*, VI, 6–7).

51 *White Jacket*, p. 137.

52 "Prudence," *Essays: First Series*, p. 215.

53 *Works*, I, 124.

54 "Considerations by the Way," *The Conduct of Life*, p. 157.

55 The use of "hell" here is figurative, for Melville did not believe in eternal punishment. See *Mardi*, II, 33.

56 "The Poet," *Essays: Second Series*, p. 20. To continue Emerson's passage: "In the old mythology, mythologists observe, defects are ascribed to divine natures, as lameness to Vulcan, blindness to Cupid, and the like, to signify exuberances." In this sentence Melville underlined "defects" and "signify exuberances," and in the margin he commented: "'Defects' signify 'exuberances.'—My Dear Sir!"

57 *Essays: First Series*, p. 133.

58 One can see that where Melville wrote the last sentence he had written and erased some other remark.

59 *Pierre*, pp. 289–290.

60 *Essays: Second Series*, p. 24.

61 All except three of Melville's annotations upon Emerson have been considered. For anyone who may be curious, here are those three annotations:

In "Heroism," *Essays: First Series*, p. 232, Emerson wrote: "It is told of Brutus, that when he fell on his sword, after the battle of Philippi, he quoted a line of Euripides,—'O virtue! I have followed thee through life, and I find thee at last but a shade.' I doubt not the hero is slandered by this report. The heroic soul does not sell its justice and its nobleness." Melville commented: "The meaning of the exclamation imputed to Brutus is here wrested from its obvious import. The struggle in which he was foiled was for mankind, & not for himself."

In "Worship," *The Conduct of Life*, pp. 127–128, Emerson quoted from Chaucer to show "Chaucer's extraordinary confusion of heaven and earth in the picture of Dido:—

She was so fair,
So young, so lusty, with her eyen glad,
That if that God that heaven and earthe made
Would have a love for beauty and goodness,

> And womanhede, truth, and seemliness,
> Whom should he loven but this lady sweet?
> There n' is no woman to him half so meet.

With these grossnesses, we complacently compare our own taste and decorum." Melville underlined "these grossnesses" and observed: "The idea in the quoted lines is perfect poetry—therefore very far from blasphemous or gross—as it seems to me."

In "The Poet," *Essays: Second Series,* p. 29, Emerson wrote: "As the traveller who has lost his way, throws his reins on his horse's neck, and trusts to the instinct of the animal to find his road, so must we do with the divine animal who carries us through this world." Melville annotated: "This is an original application of the thought."

62 *Journals,* III, 210.
63 Julian Hawthorne, op. cit., II, 135.
64 *Journals,* I, 292; see also *ibid.,* I, 290; *ibid., passim;* and Cabot, *op. cit.,* I, 104–105.
65 *Redburn,* p. 377.
66 *Moby Dick,* II, 181.
67 Letter to James Billson, Jan. 22, 1885, *The* [London] *Nation and the Athenaeum,* XXIX, 712 (Aug. 13, 1921).
68 See Braswell, *Herman Melville and Christianity,* chap, ix, for a discussion of some of the markings in the seven volumes of Schopenhauer that Melville owned.
69 *Works,* VIII, 138.

F. O. Matthiessen (1902–1950)

In a recent evaluation of Francis Otto Matthiessen's lasting contribution to American culture, Douglass Shand-Tucci wrote that "it is not too much to say" that his "most famous book, American Renaissance, *published in 1941 [. . .] really created the field of American literature, until then a footnote to English literature, and the allied field of American Studies generally."[1] While the title of the book anointed that mid-nineteenth century period in American letters, and gave new justification for the analytical study of it, the subtitle of that work—*Art and Expression in the Age of Emerson and Whitman—*signals Matthiessen's approach to this era and its principal agents, including Thoreau, Melville, and Hawthorne. The first of four "books" in* American Renaissance *is dedicated to Emerson and Thoreau, from which the following selections—the opening of Part I. "In the Optative Mood," and its first sub-section, "Consciousness"—are drawn. Matthiessen's method of literary criticism is so distinctive and his way of treating Emerson so influential that all of Book One should be at hand when considering his contribution to Emerson criticism. The present selection is but a "threshold" to Matthiessen's interest in Emerson's "most challenging quest for a form that would express his deepest convictions." For his own part, Matthiessen, in these initial steps and in the expanse of Book One, does the same for his treatment of a contested figure in American literature. Apparently frustrated by the limitations of existing criticism—by Henry James, Jr., Matthew Arnold, and John Dewey, among others (selections from whose work are collected in the present volume), Matthiessen aims to render new judgments that will be of service in understanding a much read but often misconstrued American author.*

In the Optative Mood

F. O. Matthiessen

'Our American literature and spiritual history are, we confess, in the optative mood.'
—EMERSON, 'The Transcendentalist' (1842)

THE PROBLEM that confronts us in dealing with Emerson is the hardest we shall have to meet, because of his inveterate habit of stating things in opposites. The representative man whom he most revered was Plato. For Plato had been able to bridge the gap between the two poles of thought, to reconcile fact and abstraction, the many and the One, society and solitude. Emerson wanted a like method for himself, but he had to confess, in words that throw a bar of light across his whole career: 'The worst feature of this double consciousness is, that the two lives, of the understanding and of the soul, which we lead, really show very little relation to each other; never meet and measure each other: one prevails now, all buzz and din; and the other prevails then, all infinitude and paradise; and, with the progress of life, the two discover no greater disposition to reconcile themselves.' Accepting thus Kant's distinction between the Reason and the Understanding, he felt himself secure in the realm of the higher laws. To-day he has been overtaken by the paradox that 'The Over-Soul' proves generally unreadable; whereas, on the level of the Understanding, which he regarded as mere appearance, his tenacious perception has left us the best intellectual history that we have of his age.

We tend to take at its face value another of his lucidly objective self-estimates: 'My contribution will be simply historical. I write anecdotes of the intellect; a sort of Farmer's Almanac of mental moods.' Philosophers have long since abandoned the futile pursuit of trying to reduce such moods into a system. But the danger now is that in the multiplicity of his conflicting statements, we shall miss the wholeness of character lying behind them. He was in reaction against the formal logic of the eighteenth century, since, he believed it not merely to confine but to distort; yet he insisted that 'we want in every man a logic, we cannot pardon the absence of it.' What he wanted could not be measured by propositions: it was to be 'a silent method,' 'the proportionate unfolding of the intuition.' In strong opposition to the usual academic dismissal of Emerson's thought, John Dewey has recognized the sustained tone through his whole production and has called him 'the one citizen of the New World fit to have his name uttered in the same breath with that of Plato.' Dwelling also on the importance of Emerson's restoration to the common man of all the rights of art and culture, which always tend to be perverted to mere sectarian and class uses, Dewey has found him the philosopher of democracy.

This estimate can be held only as Dewey made it, on the basis of a pervasive tendency. That is not to deny its being supported by a great number of such trenchant distinctions as that 'Bancroft and Bryant are historical democrats who are interested in dead or organized, but not in organizing, liberty.' When Emerson confined himself thus to observing phenomena as they were, his value can hardly be exaggerated for those who believe now in the dynamic extension of democracy on economic as well as political levels. But when he swam away into generalizations about the ideal, he showed at once the devastating consequences of the split between his Reason and his Understanding, between the two halves of his nature, which Lowell shrewdly epitomized in the seemingly offhand characterization of him as 'a Plotinus-Montaigne.' When the first half was in the ascendant, Emerson could commit himself to such remarks as that 'Money ... is, in its effects and laws, as beautiful as roses. Property keeps the accounts of the world, and is always moral. The property will be found where the labor, the wisdom and the virtue have been in nations, in classes, and (the whole life-time considered, with the compensations) in the individual also.' So staggeringly innocent an idea makes clear what Henry James, Sr., meant by speaking of Emerson as his 'unfallen friend,' who always kept astonishing him by his 'unconsciousness of evil.' The sentiments of such essays as those on 'Wealth' and 'Power', working on temperaments less unworldly than their author's, have provided a vicious reinforcement to the most ruthless elements in our economic life.

Neither the religious nor the social philosophy of Emerson is to be under detailed consideration here, but equally drastic paradoxes assert themselves in his theory and practice of art. When Henry James, Jr., wrote about him half a dozen years after his death, he took it as a sign of Emerson's 'singular power' that he was 'a striking exception to the general rule that writings live in the last resort by their form.' This fell in with the estimate that Matthew Arnold had just made, that though Emerson was neither a great poet, nor a great master of prose, nor a great philosophy-maker, he was 'the friend and aider of those who would live in the spirit.' Sixty years later such a judgment helps us not at all. We have witnessed altogether too many vague efforts to 'live in the spirit,' following in the ruck of transcendentalism and disappearing in the sands of the latest theosophy. If Emerson is judged as a writer, he will not be found to have been favored by any exceptions, since time does not grant them. At the threshold of this volume, therefore, we are faced with a different problem from those we shall encounter in its later divisions. We can hardly assess Emerson's work in the light of his theory of language and art, since there is such disproportion between this theory and any practice of it. Yet we can come at once to the major problem that the artist must solve. For Emerson made one of the most challenging quests for a form that would express his deepest convictions, and that would bring him at the same time into vital communication with his society.

Consciousness

'Peculiarities of the Present Age ... It is said to be the age of the first person singular.'

—EMERSON's *Journal* (1827)

RATHER than to give a bare formulation of Emerson's theory of expression,[2] it is more interesting to share in its development at crucial points, largely by recourse to his journal. By that means we can recapture something of his feeling of discovery as new horizons opened out. The quickest way to remind ourselves of what a different atmosphere from our own Emerson thought in is to note a remark made by Alexis de Tocqueville. Writing of the America that was just about to produce Emerson's work, the French critic began his chapter, 'Of Individualism in Democratic Countries,' by remarking, '*Individualism* is a novel expression, to which a novel idea has given birth.'[3] No wonder that Emerson believed that he was asserting a truth of cardinal importance for human development when he said in 1840: 'In all my lectures, I have taught one doctrine, namely, the infinitude of the private man.' Such a statement is the point from which any consideration of Emerson as an artist must start. For the aspect he dwelt on most was not form but content.

Shortly after the close of the Civil War he set down his 'Historic Notes of Life and Letters in New England,' his reminiscences of the transcendental era, probably the most illuminating account of the intellectual movements of our eighteen-thirties and forties which has yet been written.[4] Reconsidering that period, he found the key to it in the fact that 'the mind had become aware of itself. Men grew reflective and intellectual. There was a new consciousness. The former generations acted under the belief that a shining social prosperity was the beatitude of man, and sacrificed uniformly the citizen to the State. The modern mind believed that the nation existed for the individual, for the guardianship and education of every man. This idea, roughly written in revolutions and national movements, in the mind of the philosopher had far more precision; the individual is the world.' That consciousness, an expansion of what Tocqueville had found to be 'a new idea,' was Emerson's subject matter. Near the outset of his career (1839) he asserted, 'Ours is the Revolutionary age, when man is coming back to Consciousness.' For the full expression of such an age he kept saying that what was needed most was a great *reflective* poet.

The most immediate force behind American transcendentalism was Coleridge, who gained many ardent readers in New England following the edition of *Aids to Reflection* that was brought out in 1829 by President Marsh of the University of Vermont. The far-reaching effects of his contribution to general critical vocabulary and thus to modes of thinking can be epitomized by a few of the terms which he coined or put into renewed currency.[5] This brief exercise in semantics is another shorthand way of recalling what things were fresh for Emerson that we take for granted. We could hardly get a sharper impression of the new centers of interest for Coleridge's day than in his remark that he had found it necessary to borrow back from scholasticism *subjective* and *objective*: 'because I could not so briefly or conveniently by any more familiar terms distinguish the *percipere* from the *percipi*.' We see more of the age's drift of interest in the need that Coleridge felt to introduce *psychological*,[6] as a supplement to Hartley's borrowing of *psychology* from the German, half a century before. Other Coleridgean terms, some of which he transferred to criticism by analogy with other branches of thought, and all of which are so familiar to us that it is hard to conceive how anyone ever discussed literature without them, are *aesthetic, intuitive, idealize, intellectualize, organic, organization,* and *self-conscious.* Though Emerson was no such daring coiner as Coleridge—indeed, there has been none to equal Coleridge in the whole course of criticism in English—he participated to the full in the new processes of mind which had demanded such means of expression.

The revolution in which Emerson shared was primarily the one that was waged against the formulas of eighteenth-century rationalism in the name of the fuller resources of man. Coleridge had stressed what was to be one of Emerson's recurrent themes, 'the *all in each* of human nature,'—how a single man contains within himself, through his intuition, the whole range of experience. Coleridge, in turn, had quoted from Schelling: 'On the IMMEDIATE which dwells in every man, and on the original intuition, or absolute affirmation of it . . . all the *certainty* of our knowledge depends.' Such a doctrine of knowledge lay behind the main developments of romantic literature, and naturally made a particular appeal to isolated, provincial America. As Henry James was to remark in his study of Hawthorne, introspection, thanks to the want of other entertainment, played almost the part of a social resource for lonely men and women in New England. 'Our private theater is ourselves' might be the opening line of a lyric by Emily Dickinson as well as the drift of a passage in Emerson's journal. An even more characteristic saying for him is, 'Life consists in what a man is thinking of all day.' To his cheerful temperament, the turning of the individual upon his own inner life was a matter not for resignation but for exuberance. The possible tragic consequences of isolation, the haunted reverberations of the soul locked into its prison, though not envisaged by his optimism,[7] were the burdens of Hawthorne and Poe.

It is necessary to mark off more accurately the kind of consciousness that Emerson celebrated, if we are to understand what it was he wanted to express by saying, 'The individual is the world.' In 'Self-Reliance' he declared, 'Nothing is at last sacred but the integrity of your own mind,' a conclusion which, out of its context, may seem so extreme in its individualism as to involve finally the destruction of any valid individuality.[8] For, as John MacMurray has argued in *The Philosophy of Communism,* the 'last effort to preserve one's precious self' can lead only to the loss 'of everything that gives selfhood a positive significance.' What saved Emerson from the extremes of rugged Emersonianism was the presence not merely of egoism but also of a universal breadth in his doctrine that all souls are equal. What stirred him most deeply was not man's separateness from man, but his capacity to share directly in the divine superabundance. One of the first beliefs that he affirmed as he cut himself loose from the clergy was: 'The highest revelation is that God is in every man.'

Emerson agreed with Coleridge that the subjectivity which was the most fundamental distinction between modern and classic poetry was owing to the effect of Christianity in bending the mind inward on its own essence. He felt likewise the need for distinguishing between what he considered the true and false subjective. He was occupied with consciousness, not with self-consciousness. He wanted to study the laws of the mind, what he called throughout life the natural history of the intellect, but he always felt a repugnance to self-centered introversion. At the time when he was the target of the most direct personal attacks that were ever made upon him, after Andrews Norton had pronounced his Divinity School Address 'the latest form of Infidelity,' he wrote in his journal (1838): 'My prayer is that I may never be deprived of a fact, but be always so rich in objects of study as never to feel this impoverishment of remembering myself.' In the course of his 'Thoughts on Modern Literature' a couple of years later, he developed this distinction. He held that there was 'a pernicious ambiguity in the use of the term *subjective.*' On the one hand, it could simply mean that a man had no interest in anything save as it related to his own personality, a morbid self-indulgence. On the other hand, 'a man may say I, and never refer to himself as an individual'—such is the valid subjectivity that arises from the perception that 'there is One Mind, and that all the powers and privileges which lie in any, lie in all.' That was the beacon that Emerson believed could dispel the fogs of the romantic cultivation of the ego, for 'the great always introduce us to facts; small men introduce us always to themselves.'

Another distinction that will help disclose how much he implied by the 'integrity' of the mind is furnished in his contrast between *perception* and *notion*: 'Thoughtless people contradict as readily the statement of perceptions as of opinions, or rather much more readily; for they do not distinguish between perception and notion. They fancy that I choose to see this or that thing. But perception is not whimsical, but fatal.'[9] The doctrine hinted there is what Thoreau and Whitman also relied on. It involves a mystical acceptance of intuition as final, and demands an unswerving loyalty to its dictates. It discloses what Emerson meant by his frequent remark that he felt more kinship with the inner light of the Quakers than with any formal creed. It suggests also how his conception of consciousness extended beyond the grasp of analysis: 'There are no fixtures to men, if we appeal to consciousness. Every man supposes himself not to be fully understood; and if there is any truth in him, if he rests at last on the divine soul, I see not how it can be otherwise. The last chamber, the last closet, he must feel was never opened; there is always a residuum unknown, unanalyzable.' Again the tone conveys what Emerson discovered in himself. Similar investigations led to very different conclusions for Melville, to fluctuating ambiguity as door after door was opened onto dark truths in *Pierre*, and the last chamber was contemplated only with horror. But in Emerson, with all his alertness and receptivity, there remained what the elder Henry James found himself baffled by, a serenity that had grown from no depth of experience but seemed to be constitutional, 'like a woman's beauty or charm of manners.' Nevertheless his extension of the meaning of the inner life relates him to the dominant strain in modern art that leads from Hawthorne through the younger James to Proust, from Poe through the symbolists to Eliot.

One factor that separates Emerson's work from that of all these others, even from Hawthorne's, is that his initial preoccupation with Unitarian and transcendental thought made the origin of his conception of art almost exclusively intellectual. Those of his associates who were concerned with poetry felt the limitation in approaching it so purely through the mind. Margaret Fuller, after one of their interminable conversations, which, it must be added, she forced upon him, urged him to 'forego these tedious, tedious attempts to learn the universe by thought alone.' Thoreau seems instinctively to have agreed with a remark in Carlyle's *Characteristics*, that 'the sign of health is unconsciousness,' by which he meant that a lack of awareness of the processes of mind was the best way to realize the deeply spontaneous life. Carlyle himself grew increasingly indifferent to poetry, but he kept demanding of Emerson more concreteness in all his work. He had rejoiced in 'the sphere-music' of his friend's first book, his 'azure-colored' *Nature* (1836); but five years later he was saying of the *Essays* that they seemed like 'unembodied' voices, whereas what he wanted was 'a stalwart Yankee man ... with a coat on his back.' The image that was emerging from his impression of each successive volume, as from the second *Essays* (1844), was that of 'a *Soliloquizer* on the eternal mountain tops ... only the *man* and the stars and earth are visible.'

Emerson knew such a charge to be fundamental. When Carlyle was constructing *Past and Present* (1842), he had protested against Emerson's separating himself 'from the Fact of this Present Universe ... Surely I could wish you *returned* into your own poor nineteenth century.' He took the position that there was no use writing about things past unless they could be made things present. But that, emphatically, Emerson felt to be *his* position as well. Even when he had been a divinity student in Cambridge, he had confided to his journal, 'My business is with the living'; and now he answered the charge against his *Essays*; 'But of what you say now and heretofore respecting the remoteness of my writing and thinking from real life ... I do not know what it means. If I can at any time express the law and the ideal right, that should satisfy me without measuring the divergence from it of the last act of Congress.'

A good deal hinges on what he meant by 'real.' In lamenting, over and again, that transcendental New England was too imaginative and intellectual, lacking in male vigor and earthiness, he was painfully aware of how much he shared in its defects. He did not, like Poe, conceive his content as being 'out of space—out of time.' When he said, 'I embrace absolute life,' he did not want to escape into the empyrean. He did not want his idealism to be divorced from the material facts of his age. How deeply involved with and dependent upon its tendencies he felt himself to be can be read throughout his journals, especially during the eighteen-thirties when he was finding his way. No matter what Carlyle might judge of the result, it seemed to Emerson that he could write both about Universal Man and about man as a democratic citizen. The kind of harmony he tried to effect between the Now and the Eternal may serve to reveal why he could believe that consciousness was a subject that deserved the devotion of all his mature years.

On his way home from Europe in the fall of 1833, when asked what he meant by morals, his only answer was, 'I cannot define, and care not to define. It is man's business to observe, and the definition of moral nature must be the slow result of years, of lives, of states, perhaps of being.' But he was not at all unsure of the drift of his inner existence: 'Milton describes himself in his letter to Diodati as enamored of moral perfection. He did not love it more than I. That which I cannot yet declare has been my angel from childhood until now ... What is this they say about wanting mathematical certainty for moral truths? I have always affirmed they had it. Yet they ask me whether I know the soul immortal. No. But do I not know the Now to be eternal? ... I believe in this life ...'

No passages in Emerson are likely to stand up against searching theological analysis. He cast overboard so much ballast of tradition that his buoyant expansiveness is like one of Whitman's lines—'Purpos'd I know not whither, yet ever full of faith'; or, even more like—'All bound as is befitting each—all surely going somewhere.' In the light of a further century of scientific development no one now is apt to be very impressed by his assertion of simple correspondence between scientific laws and moral rules. Nevertheless, these sentences embrace the heart of Emerson's discovery as he turned his back on the 'pale negations' of Unitarianism, and began to utter what, after long and quiet listening to himself, he knew that he really believed. The first and recurrent upsurge of his conviction was that 'life is an ecstasy,' that the moment was an almost unbelievable miracle, which he wanted, more than anything else, to catch and to record. And the Now did not remain a figment of the mind; it was drenched with local surroundings. He could rejoice that his advantages were 'the total New England,' and the promise of American life in its first years of mature fulfilment gave him his special tone: 'Of every storied bay and cliff and plain, we will make something infinitely nobler than Salamis or Marathon. This pale Massachusetts sky, this sandy soil and raw wind, all shall nurture us. Unlike all the world before us, our own age and land shall be classic to ourselves.'

Those whose ears are attuned to the more exact and delicate verbal harmonies of *Nature* and 'The American Scholar' may find these sentences still a bit clumsy. The hackneyed 'infinitely nobler' might well have been pared away in revision. But the fact is that this passage is not by Emerson at all; it occurs in the Master's oration of Robert Bartlett of Plymouth at the Harvard Commencement of 1839. Bartlett could catch these accents because he had been listening to Emerson; and the more you read in the literature of the years just preceding Emerson's own appearance, the more you realize his dependence in turn upon a converging group of New England thinkers. You encounter especially in Channing (1780–1842), whom Emerson called 'our Bishop,' passages very close to Emerson's luminous eloquence.[10] In the same year as *Nature,* which contains in embryo nearly all his cardinal assumptions, five other books appeared in Boston with kindred views of religion.[11] And Emerson was fully cognizant of the measure in which he was simply rephrasing the position of Sampson Reed, the Swedenborgian druggist, whose little book, *Observations on the Growth of the Mind,* had been issued a decade before.

But Emerson's growth was fostered not merely by the renascence of idealistic philosophy, but likewise by his eager apprehension of the possibilities of American democracy. Only a few days after *Nature* was printed, he formulated in his journal a brief outline of literature since the Middle Ages. As he interpreted it, the line of development had tended to bring literature ever closer to the life which men know, to 'the Necessary, the Plain, the True, the Human.' He regarded that tendency in a double light. On the one hand, he spoke of its truth in transcendental terms, and found that whereas the eighteenth-century writers treated 'only of the life of common sense, the Apparent,' men like Wordsworth and Coleridge 'perceive the dependence of that on the life of the Reason, or the Real.' On the other hand, his belief in the infinitude of the private man was also a democratic doctrine. He shared in that revolution too, and held it responsible for the great extension of the scope of literature:

> What is good that is said or written now lies nearer to men's business and bosoms than of old. What is good goes now to all. What was good a century ago is written under the manifest belief that it was as safe from the eye of the common people as from the Tartars ... Tamerlane and the Buccaneers vanish before Texas, Oregon territory, the Reform Bill, the abolition of slavery and of capital punishment, questions of education, and the Reading of Reviews; and in all these all men take part. The human race have got possession, and it is all questions that pertain to their interest, outward or inward, that are now discussed, and many words leap out alive from bar-rooms, Lyceums, Committee Rooms, that escape out of doors and fill the world with their thunder.[12]

To do justice to that new interest as well as to the thinker's consciousness was the problem he set himself in trying to reconcile the claims of the One and the many, of the individual and his world. His unending concern with those claims caused his immediate response to the poet who was to declare:

> One's-self I sing, a simple separate person,
> Yet utter the word Democratic, the word En-Masse.

Notes

1 Douglass Shand-Tucci, *The Crimson Letter: Harvard, Homosexuality, and the Shaping of American Culture* (New York: St. Martin's Press, 2003), 150.

2 A thorough summary of it was made by Norman Foerster in his chapter on Emerson in *American Criticism* (1928).

3 The first English translator of *Democracy in America* (1840), which was based on Tocqueville's visit to this country in 1831–2, commented on this word: 'I adopt the expression of the original, however strange it may seem to the English ear, partly because it illustrates ... the introduction of general terms into democratic language ... and partly because I know of no English word exactly equivalent.' This is the first usage recorded by the Oxford English Dictionary. For Tocqueville's views concerning democratic language, see below in relation to Whitman, pp. 532–4.

4 Other comparable narratives which supplement Emerson's are Theodore Parker's *Experiences as a Minister* (1859) and Orestes Brownson's *The Convert* (1857).

5 I am indebted here to J. Isaacs' 'Coleridge's Critical Terminology' (*Essays and Studies by Members of the English Association,* 1936), which is a product of his work for a much-needed historical dictionary of critical terms in both literature and the fine arts.

6 His footnote to 'psychological' in his *Treatise on Method:* 'We beg pardon for the use of this *insolens verbum*; but it is one of which our language, stands in great need. We have no single term to express the Philosophy of the Human Mind: and what is worse, the Principles of that Philosophy are commonly called *Metaphysical*, a word of very different meaning.'

7 An occasional somber qualification of this appears in the period before he had found his positive gospel, for instance in 1831, shortly after his first wife had died and the year before he resigned from the pulpit: 'One of the arguments which nature furnishes us for the Immortality of the Soul is, it always seemed to me, the awful solitude in which here a soul lives. Few men communicate their highest thoughts to any person. To many they cannot, for they are unfit receivers. Perhaps they cannot to any ... Here I sit alone from month to month filled with a deep desire to exchange thoughts with a friend who does not appear. Yet shall I find, or refind, that friend.'

8 Poe carried such a thought even farther: 'My whole nature revolts at the idea that there is any being in the universe superior to myself.' He reached the desperate conclusion in *Eureka* that no one can believe 'that anything exists *greater than his own soul.*'

9 Cf. Coleridge: 'My opinion is this: that deep thinking is attainable only by a man
   of deep feeling, and all truth is a species of revelation ... It is *insolent* to *differ* from
   the public *opinion* in *opinion*, if it be only *opinion*. It is sticking up little *i by itself*,
   i against the whole alphabet. But one word with *meaning* in it is worth the whole
   alphabet together. Such is a sound argument, an incontrovertible fact.'

10 E.g. Channing's statement: 'The grand truth which pervades poetry is that the
   beautiful is not confined to the rare, the new, the distant—to scenery and modes of
   life open only to the few; but that it is poured forth profusely on the common earth
   and sky.'

11 The titles of the others, all by men who were at that time identified with the
   transcendental movement, are more formally religious than Emerson's: George
   Ripley, *Discourses on the Philosophy of Religion*; Convers Francis, *Christianity as
   a Purely Internal Principle*; Orestes Brownson, *New Views of Christianity, Society,
   and the Church*; Bronson Alcott, *Conversations with Children on the Gospels*; W. H.
   Furness, *Remarks on the Four Gospels*. It is hardly surprising that, according to his
   enemies, Andrews Norton sat in his room with the blinds drawn, and meditated on
   the forms of infidelity.

12 Many others were feeling the same promise in the air as Margaret Fuller did when
   launching *The Dial* in 1840: 'It is for dear New England that I want this review.'
   Longfellow had stressed the importance of native themes in the 'Defence of Poetry,'
   which he wrote five years before 'The American Scholar' and six years before his own
   first volume of verse. Thoreau rejoiced that he had been 'born in the most estimable
   place in all the world, and in the very nick of time.'

   A passage at the furthest extreme from Henry James' later recital of the
   liabilities encountered by an author of Hawthorne's day is this in Sylvester Judd's
   Margaret (1845): 'There are no fairies in our meadows, and no elves to spirit away
   our children. Our wells are drugged by no saint, and of St. Winifred we have
   never heard ... The Valley of the Housatonic is beautiful as the Vale of Tempe, or
   of Cashmere, and as oracular. We have no resorts for pilgrims, no shrines for the
   devout, no summits looking into Paradise. We have no traditions, legends, fables,
   and scarcely a history ... no chapels or abbeys, no broken arches or castled crags.
   You find these woods as inspiring as those of Etruria or Mamre. Robin-Good-Fellow
   is unknown, and the Devil haunts our theology, not our houses, and I see in the last
   edition of the Primer his tail is entirely abridged ... NEW ENGLAND! my birthplace,
   my chosen pilgrimage, I love it.'

Perry Miller (1905–1963)

*American intellectual historian and contributing founder of American Studies,
Miller was a counter-revisionist in his recovery of American Puritanism. Where
historians had deemed Puritans excessively authoritarian, Miller sought to expose
the tradition's implicit individualism, for example, in its protection and celebration
of conscience. In 1942, aged 37, Miller resigned his professorship at Harvard to enlist
in the US Army. After serving in the Office of Strategic Services in Britain during
World War II, he returned to Harvard and published the intellectual biography*
Jonathan Edwards *(1949). Miller's rehabilitation of Edwards, beginning with the
essay "From Edwards to Emerson" (1940), transformed Edwards' place in American
thinking, and also contributed a new approach to historiography.*[1] *In this "essay," as
Miller intentionally calls it, he "endeavors" to explore how the origins, features, and
effects of American Puritanism pertain to an analysis of Emerson's inheritance of
the tradition—how "certain basic continuities persist in a culture." In what ways,
for example, do the mystical and pantheistic aspects of American Puritanism
become part of American Transcendentalism? Was "Calvinism [...], as it were,
transcendentalized"? Miller himself offers an excellent and inspired preface to the
work, assuring us that he did not seek, with "some mystical pretension," to "argue
for a direct line of intellectual descent." Instead what we have in "From Edwards
to Emerson" is a novel reading of ideas, faith, and authority in America—an
account that lies outside the margins of "the textbooks" and "students' notebooks." In
"Emersonian Genius and the American Democracy" (*The New England Quarterly,
March 1953*), included below, Miller explores the notion of genius as Emerson
employed it and as we have largely come to understand it in his work—that is, as a
concept that left Emerson "frequently on the point of making democratic naturalism
signify an open, irreconcilable war between genius and democracy." It is part of
Miller's work in this essay to say how Emerson, while heralding the power of genius,
"did not despair of the republic."*

Emersonian Genius and the American Democracy

Perry Miller

Ralph Waldo Emerson was a poor boy, but in his community his kind of poverty
mattered little. Few of his classmates at Harvard had more money than he did, and they
made no such splurge as would cause him to feel inferior or outcast. His name was as
good as, if not better than, anybody else's. At reunions of the class of 1821, Emerson and

his fellows, without embarrassment, quietly took up a collection for their one insolvent member. In the logic of the situation, Emerson should have received the stamp and have embraced the opinions of this group—self-consciously aristocratic, not because of their wealth but because of their names and heritage, at that moment moving easily from the Federalist to the Whig party. In 1821 there could hardly be found a group of young Americans more numb to the notion that there were any stirring implications in the word "democracy."

Actually, Emerson did take their stamp and did imbibe their opinion. We know, or ought to know, that to the end of his days he remained the child of Boston; he might well have lived out his time like Dr. Holmes (whom he admired), secure in his provincial superiority, voting Whig and Republican, associating the idea of the Democratic party with vulgarity, with General Jackson and tobacco-chewing. In great part he did exactly that; for this reason he poses difficult problems for those who would see in him America's classic sage.

For reasons which only a sociological investigation might uncover, youths at Harvard College after the War of 1812 began to exhibit a weariness with life such as they fancied might become a Rochefoucauld, which, assuredly, was nothing like what the college in its Puritan days had expected of sons of the prophets. Perhaps this was their way of declaring their independence of Puritan tradition. At any rate it is exactly here that the pose of indifference commenced to be a Harvard tradition and to take its toll. But in the first days it was difficult to maintain; only a few resolute spirits really carried it off, and Emerson, of course, lost much of his Prufrock-ism in the enthusiasm of Transcendentalism. Yet not all of it—he never got rid of the fascination he early felt for this first, faint glimmer of an American sophistication; unless we remember it, we shall not understand his essays on "Culture," "Manners," "Aristocracy," or the bitterness of those who, like Parker and Ripley, had to look upon him as their leader even while hating just these aspects of him.

At the age of eighteen, in July, 1822, Emerson was bored with the prospect of another Independence Day. (At this time he also found Wordsworth crude, and what he heard of German philosophy absurd.) We Americans, he wrote his friend Hill, have marched since the Revolution "to strength, to honour, & at last to ennui." There is something immensely comic—and sad—in this spectacle of a young American of intelligence and good family, in 1822, already, overcome with lassitude. Suppose the event should prove—the disdainful youth continued—that the American experiment has rashly assumed that men can govern themselves, that it demonstrates instead "that too much knowledge, & too much liberty makes them mad?" He was already determined to flee from the oratory of the Fourth of July to the serenity of cherry trees: "I shall expend my patriotism in banqueting upon Mother Nature."

However, events and ideas in Europe were already indicating that nature was a dangerous refuge for a nice young Bostonian. In America they were soon to demonstrate just how dangerous: the crisis in Emerson's intellectual life, which he endured for the next several years, coincided with those in which the natural politician—General Andrew Jackson—rose by nature's means, certainly not those of culture, to the Democratic Presidency.

With part of his brain—a good part—Emerson reacted to the triumph of Jackson as did any Bostonian or Harvard man. He informed his new friend, Carlyle, on May 14, 1834, that government in America was becoming a "job"—he could think of no more contemptuous word—because "a most unfit person in the Presidency has been doing the worst things; and the worse he grew, the more popular." Nothing would be easier than to collect from the *Journals* enough passages about the Democratic party to form a manual of Boston snobbery. In 1868, for instance, meditating upon the already stale Transcendental thesis that beauty consists largely in expression, he thus annotated it: "I noticed, the other day, that when a man whom I had always remarked as a handsome person was venting Democratic politics, his whole expression changed, and became mean and paltry."

This was the Emerson who, in his last years, escaped as often as he could from Concord to the Saturday Club. I believe that students of Emerson get nowhere unless they realize how often Emerson wished that the cup of Transcendentalism had not been pressed to his lips. Had he been spared that, he might comfortably have regarded the Democratic party as a rabble of Irish and other unwashed immigrants, and could have refused, as for long he did refuse, to find any special virtue in democracy as a slogan.

But he could not thus protect himself; other ideas forced themselves upon him, and he was doomed to respond. He lacked the imperviousness that armored State Street and Beacon Street; intellectually he was too thin-skinned. To the friends about him, and I dare say also to himself, the reason was obvious: he was a genius. This was his burden, his fate, and the measure of his disseverance from the ethos of his clan.

He emerged into literature as the castigator of the genteel, the proper, the self-satisfied; he aligned himself with forces as disruptive of the Whig world as Jacksonianism was of the world of John Quincy Adams. He called for a stinging oath in the mouth of the teamster instead of the mincing rhetoric of Harvard and Yale graduates, who stumbled and halted and began every sentence over again. He called the scholar decent, indolent, complacent. When he cried that the spirit of the American freeman was timid, imitative, tame, he did not aim at Democrats but at the fastidious spirits who made up Boston society. He meant the corpse-cold Unitarianism of Harvard College and Brattle Street. Or at least he said that is what he meant (whether he really did or not may be argued), wherefore he seemed to uphold standards as uncouth as those of that Democrat in the White House.

The first of these, notoriously, was the standard of self-reliance, but behind it and sustaining it was the even more disturbing one of genius. Emerson had to have a flail for beating those who stammered and stuttered, and he found it in the conception of genius; he pounced upon it, and spent the rest of his life vainly struggling with its political consequences.

It is a commonplace of literary history that the cult of genius came to a special flowering in the early nineteenth century. (We cannot possibly employ the word today with a like solemnity; half the time we use it as an insult.) Wherever it prospered—whether with the Schlegels and Tieck in Germany, with Hugo and George Sand in France, with Byron and Coleridge in England—it meant revolt against convention, especially the kind of social convention that made up Harvard and Boston. "If there is any period one would desire to be born in," Emerson asked the Harvard Phi Beta Kappa, "is it not the age of Revolution?" This was precisely the sort of period many of his listeners did not want to be born in, for revolution meant Old Hickory. But to some Emerson opened alluring prospects which, he appeared to say and they wanted to hope, would have nothing to do with politics; leaving the political revolution aside, they responded to his exhortation and became, overnight if necessary, geniuses. The works of Emerson served them as a handbook; with him in one hand they learned to practice with the other the requisite gestures, much as a bride holds the cookbook while stirring the broth. But his own *Journals* show him as never quite so certain as he appeared from the outside, never entirely sure as to just what constituted genius or just how politically healthy it actually was.

Genius, he would write, consists in a trueness of sight, in such a use of words "as shows that the man was eye-witness, and not a reporter of what was told." (The early lectures are full of this idea.) Still, he had to admit at the beginning—and even more as he thought about it—that genius has methods of its own which to others may seem shocking or incoherent or pernicious. "Genius is a character of illimitable freedom." It can make greatness out of trivial material: well, Jacksonian America was trivial enough; would genius make it great? Genius unsettles routine: "Make a new rule, my dear, can you not? and tomorrow Genius shall stamp on it with starry sandal." Year after year, Emerson would tell himself—coming as near to stridency as he was capable—"To Genius everything is permitted, and not only that, but it enters into all other men's labors." Or again, he would reassure himself: "I pardon everything to it; everything is trifling before it; I will wait for it for years, and sit in contempt before the doors of that inexhaustible blessing." He was always on the lookout for genius; wherefore he sweetly greeted Whitman at the dawn of a great career, and was dismayed when this genius—who assumed that to him everything was permitted, including the attempt to make greatness out of a trivial democracy—used Emerson's endorsement in letters of gold on the back cover of the second edition of *Leaves of Grass*.

There the problem lay: it was pleasant to appeal to nature against formality, to identify religion with the blowing clover, the meteor, and the falling rain—to challenge the spectral convention in the name of the genius who lives spontaneously from nature, who has been commended, cheated, and chagrined. But who was this genius—if he wasn't Andrew Jackson, was he then Walt Whitman? Was he, whichever he was, to be permitted *everything*? An inability to spell or parse might, as in the case of genius Jones Very, be amusing; but suppose genius should find permissible or actually congenial sexual aberration or political domination? If before it all convention is trifling, must genius flaunt both monogamy and the social hierarchy? Suppose the youth did learn to affirm that a popgun is a popgun, in defiance of the ancient and honorable of the earth—and then chose as his guide to genius not the reserved sage of Concord but the indisputably greatest literary genius of the age, Goethe, or the outstanding genius in politics, Napoleon?

There were other dangerous geniuses, of course—above all, Lord Byron. He, said Andrews Norton (who clearly thought Emerson no better), was a corrupter of youth, a violator of "the unalterable principles of taste, founded in the nature of man, and the eternal truths of morality and religion." But Emerson and the New England geniuses were not too perturbed by Byron; he did indeed exhibit that love of the vast which they thought the primary discovery of their times, but, as Emerson said, in him "it is blind, it sees not its true end—an infinite good, alive and beautiful, a life nourished on absolute beatitudes, descending into nature to behold itself reflected there." The moral imperfections of geniuses—including the obscenities of Shakespeare—could likewise be exculpated. But the early nineteenth century, more acutely conscious of its peculiar identity than any age yet recorded in history, could not permit itself to tame the two greatest geniuses it had produced, the two who above all others, in the power of nature and of instinct, shattered the "over-civilized" palace of artifice. An ethic of self-reliance could not pretend that such reliers upon self as Goethe and Napoleon were blind. They were the twin "representatives of the impatience and reaction of nature against the *morgue* of conventions,—two stern realists, who, with the scholars, have severally set the axe at the root of the tree of cant and seeming, for this time, and for all time." But the point Emerson had to make, obstinately, was that if Napoleon incarnated "the popular external life and aims of the nineteenth century," then by the same token Goethe was its other half, "a man quite domesticated in the century,"—in fact, "the soul of his century."

The story of Emerson's lifelong struggle with Goethe has been often recounted. He could not give over the contest, for if Goethe had to be pronounced wicked, Emerson would become what Norton called him, an infidel. "All conventions, all tradition he rejected," says Emerson, in order to add that thus Goethe uttered "the best things about Nature that ever were said." The ancient and honorable of the earth—well, of Boston's earth—sneered that the man was immoral, but the New England geniuses dug in their heels and insisted with Margaret Fuller that Goethe was "the highest form of Nature, and conscious of the meaning she has been striving successively to unfold through those below him." Those below were demonstrably (like Andrews Norton) non-geniuses.

Life for geniuses would have been simpler could Goethe have been separated from Napoleon. But the two giants met at Erfurt—and recognized each other. (Emerson punctiliously copied into his *Journals* what Goethe said about Napoleon: it was as though he kept hitting himself with a hammer.) Emerson came back from Europe to start his brave adventure as a free-lance lecturer with a series entitled "Tests of Great Men." To judge from the notes, he spent much time explaining that Napoleon was beneath contempt: he was "the very bully of the common, & knocked down most indubitably his antagonists; he was as heavy as any six of them." Measure him against any of the tests young Emerson proposed, and Napoleon failed on every count. One test was whether a man has a good aim: "Well, Napoleon had an Aim & a Bad one." Another was whether he be in earnest: "Napoleon was no more a believer than a grocer who disposes his shop-window invitingly." The lectures held up to American admiration Luther, Washington, Lafayette, Michelangelo, Burke, Milton, Fox, but the constant moral was this (Emerson came back to it from every angle): "Of Napoleon, the strength consisted in his renunciation of all conscience. The Devil helps him." Emerson delivered this statement on January 29, 1835—eleven months after he had assured Carlyle that "a most unfit person" was President of the United States, when that person was still in office.

There is no better gauge of Emerson's progress into sophistication than the contrast between this moralistic lecture and the chapter published in 1850 in *Representative Men*—although that too has its ambiguities. No one would call it a paean of praise to Bonaparte, but still, the conscienceless devil of 1835 has become one who "respected the power of nature and fortune, and ascribed to it his superiority, instead of valuing himself, like inferior men, on his opinionativeness, and waging war with nature." But if Napoleon was now on the side of the meteor, against the timidity of scholars, what of the democracy in America? What of our own Napoleons—Jackson and Van Buren? Neither Napoleon nor they could be consigned to the Devil, for in that case there would exist in the universe of the Over-Soul a foreign, an extraneous, element, something uncontrollable; in that case, for children of the Devil to live from the Devil would be really demonic, really unnatural—as it often did seem to cultured New Englanders that Democrats lived.

There was a great temptation to identify this upsurging of democracy with nature. (Brownson was willing to risk it, but not for long; except Bancroft, hardly an American before Whitman dared—that is, after Jefferson's nature became "romantic" nature.) If the stinging clarity of a teamster's oath was worth paragraphs of Harvard prose, was not Jackson a rod of nature reproving the timid, the imitative and tame? Emerson sometimes made this identification, or almost made it; but he was still the Bostonian, ninth in a line of ministers, and by no stretching of his conception of nature could he learn to look upon the naturals who composed the Jacksonian rabble with anything but loathing. The soliloquy—the endless debate with himself—runs throughout the *Journals*; it turns upon a triangle of counterstatement: democracy raises the problem of genius; genius the problem of Napoleon and the American politician; they in turn raise the problem of democracy and of America. The pattern is not always quite so explicit, but over and over again any mention of genius is sure to be followed, within an entry or two, by a passage on democracy, the Democratic party, Napoleon. The inconclusiveness of the inner meditations makes a striking contrast to the seeming serenity of the published oracles. The art—or should we call it the artfulness?—of Emerson is nowhere more charmingly revealed than in the fashion in which he managed to separate in the *Essays* the three themes that in the *Journals* were constantly intertwined. Yet even his great ingenuity could not keep genius, Napoleon, and democracy from coming together and forming knotty passages in the *Essays*, and especially in *Representative Men*.

Surely he ought, did he respect logic, to have been like Whitman a democrat, and therefore a Democrat. Returning from Europe in 1834, having seen how monarchy and aristocracy degrade mankind, he could write:

The root and seed of democracy is the doctrine, Judge for yourself. Reverence thyself. It is the inevitable effect of that doctrine, where it has any effect (which is rare), to insulate the partisan, to make each man a state. At the same time it replaces the dead with a living check in a true, delicate reverence for superior, congenial minds. "How is the king greater than I, if he is not more just."

But the fact remained that, in the America of Jackson or of Polk, democracy in the abstract could not be dissociated from the gang of hoodlums who showed nothing more, to Emerson's view, than withering selfishness and impudent vulgarity. The boy had fled from the ranting of orators to the cherry trees; the man of 1834 sought the same comfort: "In the hush of these woods I find no Jackson placards affixed to the trees."

Yet, the literature of the new age, the revolt against "upholstery," gave a hollow sound to the names of king and lord because it voiced the forces "which have unfolded every day, with a rapidity sometimes terrific, the democratic element." Today "the Universal Man is now as real an existence as the Devil was then." At the mention of the Devil, if not of the king, Emerson must recollect himself: "I do not mean that ill thing, vain and loud, which writes lying newspapers, spouts at caucuses, and sells its lies for gold." He meant only "that spirit of love for the general good whose name this assumes." A man need not be a Transcendentalist to find this ill thing disgusting: he need only to have gone to Harvard. Viewed from this angle, there was nothing to be preferred in Abraham Lincoln over General Jackson. After the assassination, Emerson tried to atone; but in 1863 the President caused him to reflect that people of culture should not expect anything better out of the operations of universal suffrage:

> You cannot refine Mr. Lincoln's taste, extend his horizon, or clear his judgment; he will not walk dignifiedly through the traditional part of the President of America, but will pop out his head at each railroad station and make a little speech, and get into an argument with Squire A. and Judge B. He will write letters to Horace Greeley, and any editor or reporter or saucy party committee that writes to him, and cheapen himself.

In the clutch of such reflections, Emerson was frequently on the point of making democratic naturalism signify an open, irreconcilable war between genius and democracy. Genius, he said in 1847, is anthropomorphist and makes human form out of material, but America—"eager, solicitous, hungry, rabid, busy-bodied"—is without form, "has no terrible and no beautiful condensation." Had he let himself go in that direction, we could summarize him in a sentence: America's philosopher condemned America's democracy as something unnatural.

He came perilously close to this way out: he dallied with the solution that was always available for romantic theorists, that some great and natural genius, out of contempt for the herd, might master them. A man of strong will "may suddenly become the center of the movement, and compel the system to gyrate round it." Cromwell was never out of Emerson's mind. Such an actor would settle the problem, would redeem both nature and the ideal, the stability and the security of the commonwealth:

> We believe that there may be a man who is a match for events,—one who never found his match—against whom other men being dashed are broken,—one of inexhaustible personal resources, who can give you odds, and beat you.

The rest of us could even tell ourselves that we did not abdicate self-reliance should we follow such a genius: "We feed on genius."

Still, Emerson had to add, we "have a half-belief." There was always the danger that a resolution of the political question into the personality of the great man would be like trying to resolve the poetic problem into the personality of Byron. Genius has laws of its own, but in the workings of a commonwealth neither whim nor demonism should be permitted. "Politics rest on necessary foundations, and cannot be treated with levity."

Levity! There was indeed the devil. It would be levity to give way to looking down one's nose at Jackson and Lincoln, to turn from them to the great man who promised to bring mediocrity to heel. For suppose this genius should prove a demon of the only plausible devil, of levity?

Here Emerson was back again with Napoleon. Upon his mind, upon the mind of his generation, was indelibly impressed the spectacle of that meeting in Erfurt. The Goethean genius met with and subscribed to the Napoleonic. Henceforth it was impossible to lift the standard of the epicurean, civilized Goethe against the leveling thrust of Napoleon, or to rally around him against Jackson. Assuredly Napoleon was unscrupulous, selfish, perfidious, a prodigious gossip: "his manners were coarse." So was Jackson, so was Lincoln. But Napoleon fought against the enemies of Goethe: timidity, complacence, etc., etc. If Goethe had sided with Bonaparte, how then ought an American intellectual act toward the Democratic party? After all, as Emerson in "Politics" was obliged to say, "Democracy is better for us, because the religious sentiment of the present time accords better with it."

He hoped that the rhetorical balance of his famous sentence would remove his anxiety, that while the Whigs had the best men, the Democrats had the best cause. The scholar, philosopher, the man of religion, will want to vote with the Democrats, "but he can rarely accept the persons whom the so-called popular party propose to him as representatives of these liberalities." On the other hand, the conservative party was indeed timid, "merely defensive of property." No wonder that men came to think meanly of government and to object to paying their taxes: "Everywhere they think they get their money's worth, except for these."

This was a miserable prospect, an intolerable dilemma, for the author of *Nature*. Yet Emerson was never more the spokesman for nature, and never more the American, than when he added, "I do not for these defects despair of our republic." He might have mourned with Henry Adams and every disillusioned liberal, with every disgruntled businessman, that the country was going to the dogs, that there was no hope left (there being no longer hope in a compensatory Christian heaven) except in the great man, the political genius, the dictator. There was everything in Emerson's philosophy to turn him like Carlyle into a prophet of reaction and the leader-principle.

But he did not go with Carlyle; and he meant what he said, that he did not despair of the republic. Why not? Was it merely that he was stupid, or mild-mannered, or temperamentally sanguine? Was it dogmatic optimism for the sake of optimism? Perhaps it was partly for these reasons, but the play of his mind kept hope alive and vigorous by circling round and round, by drawing sustenance from, the inexhaustible power of genius. However odd, fantastic, or brutal might be the conduct of genius, it does submit to laws. Levity gets ironed out. So in society: "No forms can have any dangerous importance whilst we are befriended by the laws of things." Emerson's historical perspective was deeper, richer than that of a Cooper—great historical novelist though he was. Cooper had Natty Bumppo to give grandeur to the sordid scene of *The Pioneers,* but no philosophy of genius to sustain him once he entered into conflict with *Home as Found.* Cooper let himself dream of violent catastrophe, a devastating judgment not of Jehovah but of nature, as an ultimate solution to the ills of democracy, and prophesied it in *The Crater.* But Emerson could comprehend democracy in a larger frame of reference, as a phase of western society, and see its connection, where the *rentier* could not, with the new kind of property. Emerson could point out that it was not something a gentleman could afford to despise and then expect still to have the refuge of being a gentleman. In other words, Emerson understood the portent not alone of Goethe but of Napoleon.

For this reason, Napoleon figures in the carefully planned structure of *Representative Men* as a prologue to Goethe, as the next-to-the-last. There is some perversity—one might say almost levity—in the other choices (Swedenborg most obviously) or in the arrangement, but Emerson was pushing his way through the book to the two problems which, his genius informed him, constituted one problem: that of genius in modern society, where the bad manners of democrats would not be sufficient reason for consigning them, on that ground alone, to the limbo of levity.

Representative Men had its origins in a few simple ideas which took hold of Emerson in the 1830's, of which he was the prisoner but which, for as long as possible, he held off from publishing. The secret record of his life with these ideas is the *Journals,* but there was a public record before his fellow countrymen: the lectures, those discourses he gave for audiences and for money, out of which he mined paragraphs for what became *Essays* but which, guided by some obscure impulse, he never translated directly from the platform to the page. (From the beginning of his career as a lecturer down to his last series at Harvard in 1871, there was always a discourse on "Genius"; materials from one or another recasting of this draft found their way into "Self-Reliance," "Art," "Intellect,"—but never into a full-dress essay on genius.) With the lecture of January, 1837 (entitled "Society"), Emerson had already gone so far beyond 1835 that he could define the genius as one who has access to the universal mind and who receives its influx in wise passivity. He could employ terms he was to use throughout many subsequent lectures, but which, at least in this same and revealing language, he would never print:

> Genius is never anomalous. The greatest genius is he in whom other men own the presence of a larger portion of their common nature than is in them. And this I believe is the secret of the joy which genius gives us. Whatever men of genius say, becomes forthwith the common property of all. Why? Because the man of genius apprises us not so much of his wealth as of the commonwealth. Are his illustrations happy? So feel we [that] not *his* mind but *the* mind illustrate[s] its thoughts. A sort of higher patriotism warms us, as if one should say, "That's the way they do things in my country."

Thus early the problem took shape in his mind—never to leave it—of genius and "my country." All men share in *"the* mind," and all men are the democracy; genius must be, in some sense, a patriotic triumph. But Napoleon was a threat to the conception of a "good" genius; his American aliases, Jackson and the Democrats, were a threat to State Street. Writers are often obliged to ask themselves exactly who they are, and fear to find out that they may be the most evil of their creations. Was Emerson, in his heart of hearts, a Napoleon? If not, were the Over-Soul and all its spokesmen, all the geniuses, to be counted in the Whig column? Obviously Whiggery was no home for genius. Maybe one would have to admit that Jackson was a genius? Maybe one would have to confess—as the easiest way out—that Lincoln was a genius? Lincoln was, nominally, a Republican, but before 1865 Emerson saw him only as the creature of universal suffrage; the assassination and the rapid canonization undoubtedly helped, but Emerson was still feeling his own way and not merely moving with the times when in 1871 he told his Harvard audience, "John Brown and Abraham Lincoln were both men of genius, and have obtained this simple grandeur of utterance."

Years before he was thus able to reconcile himself to Lincoln, Emerson tried to reconcile himself to the whole panoply of genius, and the result was *Representative Men.* The value of the book is not that it invents a way out of the quandary which we now confront as terribly as did Emerson. It is not a guide for the preserving of personality against mass pressures. Too many of his terms are altered; few of us can accept his metaphysics, and many of the geniuses we admire do not seem so clearly to contribute wealth to any commonwealth. But the exhilaration of the book consists in the fact that Emerson here got his many-sided perplexity in hand, sacrificed no one aspect to any other, and wrote a book not about heroes and how to worship them, but about how an intelligent and sensitive man lives, or must learn to live, in a democratic society and era.

By calling great men not heroes but representatives, Emerson, in the most American of fashions, put them to work; the first chapter is slyly entitled "Uses of Great Men." He divides genius as a genus into subordinate species, whereupon for each type a specific set of laws can be worked out. Thus the individual genius, even when seemingly lawless, adheres to a pattern of coherence in relation to the sum total of the parts. If it be necessary—as we are compelled to recognize—that all sides of life be expressed, then each genius has a function, be he good or evil; what each incarnates we recognize as an accentuated part of ourselves—because all men are one, and any one man is all men.

Likewise, genius is fragmentary, and so deficient on several sides. Sometimes the moralizing Emerson appears to line up his great men like naughty children and to tell them wherein they all fall lamentably short of what teacher expects of them. But you forgive him some (although not all) of this didacticism not so much because he was a New Englander but because behind it lay the intense moments recorded in the *Journals,* such as that in which he had taken the very existence of such a person as the Democrat Hawthorne to signify "that in democratic America, she [nature] will not be democratized." Therefore in this book Emerson can go far—as far as clear sight can see—toward making genius democratic. The genius is great not because he surpasses but because he represents his constituency. His crimes and foibles are as much a part of the record as his triumphs and nobilities; Napoleon belongs to genius not as a child of the historical Devil whom Emerson foolishly invoked in 1835, and not even as a creation of the metaphorical devil, levity, but as a serious, real, and terrifying power in modern western civilization.

Wherefore something more should be required of the scholar, the poet, the man of religion, than timid antipathy to a blatant democracy. Napoleon was "the agent or attorney of the middle class of modern society"—of those in shops, banks, and factories who want to get rich. He represents "the Democrat, or the party of men of business, against the stationary or conservative party." And—Emerson here plunges to the bottom of his insight—"as long as our civilization is essentially one of property, of fences, of exclusiveness, it will be mocked by delusions"—against which some Bonaparte is bound to raise the cry of revolt, for which men again will die.

What Emerson most gained, I believe, by this analysis was an ability to comprehend, even while never quite reconciling himself to, the vices of democracy—whether with a small "d" or a capital "D." He did not need to blind himself by patriotic fanaticism; by the same token he did not need to despair. He could confess his mistake about Lincoln without retracting his contempt for Franklin Pierce. He could criticize his country without committing treason, without having to demand, as did an irate Cooper, that they become like himself or else go to hell. The example and the laws of genius might work, would work, even in the ranks of the Democratic party.

Of course, Emerson trusted the self-operating force of moral law more than do most of us today. Napoleon (for him read Jackson, Lincoln, the boss, the district leader) did everything a man could do to thrive by intellect without conscience. "It was the nature of things, the eternal law of the man and the world, which balked and ruined him; and the result, in a million experiments, would be the same." Emerson was fully aware of what the lesson cost: "immense armies, burned cities, squandered treasures, immolated millions of men, . . . this demoralized Europe." He did, we must confess, look upon the desolation with what seems to us smugness, we who have seen Europe infinitely more burned and demoralized; but these things are relative, and he was happy to note that out of the destruction arose a universal cry, "assez de Bonaparte."

Emerson was too often chilly. But had he been only that, *Representative Men* would have been for him the end of a theme, would have put a period to a chapter in his

Journals. It was nothing of the sort. No sooner was it published than the debate was resumed, and many of the most fascinating combinations of the triple meditation on genius, Napoleon, and democracy occur in later entries. The Civil War was for him as for others an excruciating ordeal, the more so as during the worst years he believed Lincoln the example of democratic incompetence. But in the darkest moments he never quite lost his bearings. The sanity (the chilly sanity, if you will) that sustains the essay on "Politics" and informs *Representative Men* never deserted him—the levelheadedness which is his most precious bequest to a posterity that is understandably exasperated by his unction. In 1862, although not yet respecting the President, he was able to keep the personality from obscuring the issue:

> A movement in an aristocratic state does not argue a deep cause. A dozen good fellows may have had a supper and warmed each other's blood to some act of spite or arrogance, which they talk up and carry out the next month; or one man, Calhoun or Rhett, may have grown bilious, and his grumble and fury are making themselves felt at the legislature. But in a Democracy, every movement has a deep-seated cause.

This was written by no flag-waving, tub-thumping patriot shouting, "My country right or wrong." This is no campaign orator mouthing the word "democracy" even while desecrating it by his deeds. It was written by a great American, a serious man who could finally run down the devil of politics and declare that his name is levity, who understood as well as any in what the difficult ordeal consists, that magnificent but agonizing experience of what it is to be, or to try to be, an American.

Note

1　Miller's essay first appeared in *The New England Quarterly* (December 1940) and was later featured in his still-celebrated book *Errand into the Wilderness* (1956).

Robert Frost (1874–1963)

American poet who authored the much-quoted "The Road Not Taken" (1916), winner of four Pulitzer Prizes for Poetry, Frost has occasion in the following selection to address the American Academy of Arts and Sciences who awarded him the Emerson-Thoreau Medal in 1959, remarks that were published the same year in Daedalus. *He begins by declaring: "I should like to make myself as much of an Emersonian as I can. Let me see if I can't go a long way." Frost's approach is personal, a narrative of things he finds worth knowing and remembering about Emerson told in the tone of memoir. Frost's account brims with his appreciation of Emerson's pedagogical effect: in poetry, in religion, in thinking generally. In relating his indebtedness to Emerson in matters personal and poetic, Frost conveys how untroubled he is when "accused of being Emersonian." Neither in this speech, nor elsewhere it seems, does Frost take umbrage or mount a defense. "The only reprehensible materiality is the materialism of getting lost in your own material so you can't find out yourself what it is all about." One doesn't have to be a subversive or a rebel, Frost suggests, in order to appreciate this point.*

On Emerson

Robert Frost

All that admiration for me I am glad of. I am here out of admiration for Emerson and Thoreau. Naturally on this proud occasion I should like to make myself as much of an Emersonian as I can. Let me see if I can't go a long way. You may be interested to know that I have right here in my pocket a little first edition of Emerson's poetry. His very first was published in England, just as was mine. His book was given me on account of that connection by Fred Melcher, who takes so much pleasure in bringing books and things together like that.

I suppose I have always thought I'd like to name in verse some day my four greatest Americans: George Washington, the general and statesman; Thomas Jefferson, the political thinker; Abraham Lincoln, the martyr and savior; and fourth, Ralph Waldo Emerson, the poet. I take these names because they are going around the world. They are not just local. Emerson's name has gone as a poetic philosopher or as a philosophical poet, my favorite kind of both.

I have friends it bothers when I am accused of being Emersonian, that is, a cheerful Monist, for whom evil does not exist, or if it does exist, needn't last forever. Emerson quotes Burns as speaking to the Devil as if he could mend his ways. A melancholy dualism is the only soundness. The question is: is soundness of the essence.

My own unsoundness has a strange history. My mother was a Presbyterian. We were here on my father's side for three hundred years but my mother was fresh a Presbyterian from Scotland. The smart thing when she was young was to be reading Emerson and Poe as it is today to be reading St. John Perse or T. S. Eliot. Reading Emerson turned her into a Unitarian. That was about the time I came into the world; so I suppose I started a sort of Presbyterian-Unitarian. I was transitional. Reading on into Emerson, that is into "Representative Men" until she got to Swedenborg, the mystic, made her a Swedenborgian. I was brought up in all three of these religions, I suppose. I don't know whether I was baptized in them all. But as you see it was pretty much under the auspices of Emerson. It was all very Emersonian. Phrases of his began to come to me early. In that essay on the mystic he makes Swedenborg say that in the highest heaven nothing is arrived at by dispute. Everybody votes in heaven but everybody votes the same way, as in Russia today. It is only in the second-highest heaven that things get parliamentary; we get the two-party system or the hydra-headed, as in France.

Some of my first thinking about my own language was certainly Emersonian. "Cut these sentences and they bleed," he says. I am not submissive enough to want to be a follower, but he had me there. I never got over that. He came pretty near making me an anti-vocabularian with the passage in "Monadnock" about our ancient speech. He blended praise and dispraise of the country people of New Hampshire. As an abolitionist he was against their politics. Forty per cent of them were states-rights Democrats in sympathy with the South. They were really pretty bad, my own relatives included.

> The God who made New Hampshire
> Taunted the lofty land
> With little men;—

And if I may be further reminiscent parenthetically, my friend Amy Lowell hadn't much use for them either. "I have left New Hampshire," she told me. Why in the world? She couldn't stand the people. What's the matter with the people? "Read your own books and find out." They really differ from other New Englanders, or did in the days of Franklin Pierce.

But now to return to the speech that was his admiration and mine in a burst of poetry in "Monadnock":

> Yet wouldst thou learn our ancient speech
> These the masters that can teach
> Fourscore or a hundred words
> All their vocal muse affords.
> Yet they turn them in a fashion
> Past the statesman's art and passion.
> Rude poets of the tavern hearth
> Squandering your unquoted mirth,
> That keeps the ground and never soars,

While Jake retorts and Reuben roars.
Scoff of yeoman, strong and stark,
Goes like bullet to the mark,
And the solid curse and jeer
Never balk the waiting ear.

Fourscore or a hundred is seven hundred less than my friend Ivor Richard's basic eight hundred. I used to climb on board a load of shooks (boxes that haven't been set up) just for the pleasure I had in the driver's good use of his hundred-word limit. This at the risk of liking it so much as to lose myself in mere picturesqueness. I was always in favor of the solid curse as one of the most beautiful of figures. We were warned against it in school for its sameness. It depends for variety on the tones of saying it and the situations.

I had a talk with John Erskine, the first time I met him, on this subject of sentences that may look tiresomely alike, short and with short words, yet turn out as calling for all sorts of ways of being said aloud or in the mind's ear, Horatio. I took Emerson's prose and verse as my illustration. Writing is unboring to the extent that it is dramatic.

In a recent preface to show my aversion to being interrupted with notes in reading a poem, I find myself resorting to Emerson again. I wanted to be too carried away for that. There was much of "Brahma" that I didn't get to begin with but I got enough to make me sure I would be back there reading it again some day when I had read more and lived more; and sure enough, without help from dictionary or encyclopedia I can now understand every line in it but one or two. It is a long story of many experiences that let me into the secret of:

But thou, meek lover of the good!
Find me, and turn thy back on heaven.

What baffled me was the Christianity in "meek lover of the good." I don't like obscurity and obfuscation, but I do like dark sayings I must leave the clearing of to time. And I don't want to be robbed of the pleasure of fathoming depths for myself. It was a moment for me when I saw how Shakespeare set bounds to science when he brought in the North Star, "whose worth's unknown although his height be taken." Of untold worth: it brings home some that should and some that shouldn't come. Let the psychologist take notice how unsuccessful he has to be.

I owe more to Emerson than anyone else for troubled thoughts about freedom. I had the hurt to get over when I first heard us made fun of by foreigners as the land of the free and the home of the brave. Haven't we won freedom? Is there no such thing as freedom? Well, Emerson says God

Would take the sun out of the skies
Ere freedom out of a man.

and there rings the freedom I choose.

Never mind how and where Emerson disabused me of my notion I may have been brought up to that the truth would make me free. My truth will bind you slave to me. He didn't want converts and followers. He was a Unitarian. I am on record as saying that freedom is nothing but departure—setting forth—leaving things behind, brave origination of the courage to be new. We may not want freedom. But let us not deceive ourselves about what we don't want. Freedom is one jump ahead of formal laws, as in planes and even automobiles right now. Let's see the law catch up with us very soon.

Emerson supplies the emancipating formula for giving an attachment up for an attraction, one nationality for another nationality, one love for another love. If you must break free,

> Heartily know,
> When half-gods go
> The gods arrive.

I have seen it invoked in *Harper's Magazine* to excuse disloyalty to our democracy in a time like this. But I am not sure of the reward promised. There is such a thing as getting too transcended. There are limits. Let's not talk socialism. I feel projected out from politics with lines like:

> Musketaquit, a goblin strong,
> Of shards and flints makes jewels gay;
> They lose their grief who hear his song,
> And where he winds is the day of day.
>
> So forth and brighter fares my stream,—
> Who drink it shall not thirst again;
> No darkness stains its equal gleam,
> And ages drop in it like rain.

Left to myself, I have gradually come to see what Emerson was meaning in "Give all to Love" was, Give all to Meaning. The freedom is ours to insist on meaning.

The kind of story Steinbeck likes to tell is about an old labor hero punch-drunk from fighting the police in many strikes, beloved by everybody at headquarters as the greatest living hater of tyranny. I take it that the production line was his grievance. The only way he could make it mean anything was to try to ruin it. He took arms and fists against it. No one could have given him that kind of freedom. He saw it as his to seize. He was no freedman; he was a free man. The one inalienable right is to go to destruction in your own way. What's worth living for is worth dying for. What's worth succeeding in is worth failing in.

If you have piled up a great rubbish heap of oily rags in the basement for your doctor's thesis and it won't seem to burst into flame spontaneously, come away quickly and without declaring rebellion. It will cost you only your Ph.D. union card and the respect of the union. But it will hardly be noticed even to your credit in the world. All you have to do is to amount to something anyway. The only reprehensible materiality is the materialism of getting lost in your material so you can't find out yourself what it is all about.

A young fellow came to me to complain of the department of philosophy in his university. There wasn't a philosopher in it. "I can't stand it." He was really complaining of his situation. He wasn't where he could feel real. But I didn't tell him so I didn't go into that. I agreed with him that there wasn't a philosopher in his university—there was hardly ever more than one at a time in the world—and I advised him to quit. Light out for somewhere. He hated to be a quitter. I told him the Bible says, "Quit ye, like men." "Does it," he said. "Where would I go?" Why anywhere almost. Kamchatka, Madagascar, Brazil. I found him doing well in the educational department of Rio when I was sent on an errand down there by our government several years later. I had taken too much responsibility for him when I sent him glimmering like that. I wrote to him with troubled conscience and got no answer for two whole years. But the story has a happy ending. His departure was not suicidal. I had a post card from him this Christmas to tell me he was on Robinson Crusoe's island Juan Fernandez on his way to Easter Island that it had always been a necessity for him some day to see. I would next hear from him in Chile where he was to be employed in helping restore two colleges. Two! And the colleges were universities!

No subversive myself, I think it very Emersonian of me that I am so sympathetic with subversives, rebels, runners out, runners out ahead, eccentrics, and radicals. I don't care how extreme their enthusiasm so long as it doesn't land them in the Russian camp. I always wanted one of them teaching in the next room to me so my work would be cut out for me warning the children taking my courses not to take his courses.

I am disposed to cheat myself and others in favor of any poet I am in love with. I hear people say the more they love anyone the more they see his faults. Nonsense. Love is blind and should be left so. But it hasn't been hidden in what I have said that I am not quite satisfied with the easy way Emerson takes disloyalty. He didn't know or ignored his Blackstone. It is one thing for the deserter and another for the deserted. Loyalty is that for the lack of which your gang will shoot you without benefit of trial by jury. And serves you right. Be as treacherous as you must be for your ideals, but don't expect to be kissed good-by by the idol you go back on. We don't want to look too foolish, do we? And probably Emerson was too Platonic about evil. It was a mere *Tò μή ού* that could be disposed of like the butt of a cigarette. In a poem I have called the best Western poem yet he says:

Unit and universe are round.

Another poem could be made from that, to the effect that ideally in thought only is a circle round. In practice, in nature, the circle becomes an oval. As a circle it has one center—Good. As an oval it has two centers—Good and Evil. Thence Monism versus Dualism.

Emerson was a Unitarian because he was too rational to be superstitious and too little a storyteller and lover of stories to like gossip and pretty scandal. Nothing very religious can be done for people lacking in superstition. They usually end up abominable agnostics. It takes superstition and the prettiest scandal story of all to make a good Trinitarian. It is the first step in the descent of the spirit into the material-human at the risk of the spirit.

But if Emerson had left us nothing else he would be remembered longer than the Washington Monument for the monument at Concord that he glorified with lines surpassing any other ever written about soldiers:

> By the rude bridge that arched the flood
> Their flag to April breeze unfurled
> Here once the embattled farmers stood
> And fired the shot heard round the world.

Not even Thermopylae has been celebrated better. I am not a shriner, but two things I never happen on unmoved: one, this poem on stone; and the other, the tall shaft seen from Lafayette Park across the White House in Washington.

Lionel Trilling (1905–1975)

After completing a dissertation on Matthew Arnold at Columbia University, Trilling joined the faculty, becoming the first tenured Jewish professor in the English Department. For 30 years he co-taught a course with Jacques Barzun on the interrelationship between history and literature. In Why Trilling Matters, *Adam Kirsch describes Trilling's belief that "art is the form in which the writer, and through him the reader, can face down the intolerable contradictions of history."[1] Meanwhile, Trilling is also famed for his liberalism, which entailed, as Kirsch put it: "the preservation of human difference, the ability to imagine opposing characters with equal sympathy."[2] He authored the essay collections* The Liberal Imagination *(1950),* The Opposing Self *(1955), and* Beyond Culture *(1965). The following selection is drawn from the chapter "Society and Authenticity" in Trilling's* Sincerity and Authenticity *(1972), where he considers both Emerson's sincerity and Emerson's appraisal of English sincerity, the latter mainly from a reading of* English Traits.

Society and Authenticity

Lionel Trilling

Emerson had no doubt that sincerity was the defining quality of the English character. In his *English Traits*, published in 1856, he recurs to it frequently and with vivacious admiration. Sincerity, he says, is the basis of the English national moral style. "We will not have to do with a man in a mask," he conceives the English to be saying. "Let us know the truth. Draw a straight line, hit whom and where it will." The English, Emerson tells us, are blunt in expressing what they think and they expect others to be no less so; their confidence in each other makes them unique among nations: "English believes in English. The French feel the moral superiority of this probity." And Emerson goes on to say that the superiority is not merely moral; the practical power of the English "rests on their national sincerity."

His happy surprise over the sincerity of the English makes us wonder what Emerson could have been used to in his native land, what sinister subtleties of dissimulation had been practised upon him in Concord, Massachusetts. Henry James is not exactly simple on the subject of anything that has to do with Americans, but the general tendency of his work would seem to confirm the opinion which once prevailed—how curious it now seems!—that Americans, being wholly innocent, were wholly sincere, that American sincerity was as certified as that of children, peasants, and nineteenth-century dogs. Actually, of course, Emerson's surprise at the sincerity of the English does not imply that he thought his countrymen were deficient in the trait in the sense that they were given over to duplicity. The difference between the English and Americans that Emerson was responding to was not the same as the difference between the English and the French; its nature is suggested by what Tocqueville observed of the tendency of American speech to be elaborate and abstract. Tocqueville did not suggest that Americans were being insincere in talking so. They were hiding nothing, they talked as they did because they lived in a democracy. The democratic dispensation required them to shape their speech not by the standards of a particular class or circle but by their sense of the opinion of the public, and it is this, Tocqueville says, which makes their mode of expression abstract rather than concrete, general rather than specific, periphrastic rather than direct.[3] The democratic style doesn't signify an absence of sincerity; it does, however, indicate that the personal self to which the American would wish to be true is not the private, solid, intractable self of the Englishman.

And in this respect the American self can be taken to be a microcosm of American society, which has notably lacked the solidity and intractability of English society; it is little likely to be felt by its members as being palpably *there*. The testimony on this score is one of the classic elements of nineteenth-century American cultural history. James Fenimore Cooper, Hawthorne, Henry James, all in one way or another said that American society was, in James's phrase, "thinly composed," lacking the thick, coarse actuality which the novelist, as he existed in their day, needed for the practice of his craft. It did not offer him the palpable material, the *stuff*, out of which novels were made. What came as a revelation to American visitors to England was exactly the impermeability of English society, the solidity of the composition, the thick, indubitable *thereness* which enforced upon its members a sort of primary sincerity— the free acknowledgement that in one respect, at least, they were *not* free, that their existences were bound by their society, determined by its particularities. About their being social rather than transcendent beings the English told the truth to themselves and the world. It is most engaging in Emerson that he should have taken so lively a pleasure in the moral style that followed from this avowal, for the characteristic tendency of his thought is to deny what the English affirm.[4]

The Hegelian terms which I touched on earlier bear upon the difference between the two nations. Americans, we might say—D. H. Lawrence did in effect say it fifty years ago—had moved into that historical stage of Spirit which produces the "disintegrated" or "alienated" consciousness. What defines this consciousness, according to Hegel, is its antagonism to "the external power of society"—the wish to be free of imposed social circumstances. The English belonged to an earlier historical development, in which Spirit manifests itself as the "honest soul" whose relation to society is one of "obedient service" and "inner reverence." As Hegel represents the "disintegrated consciousness," it is beyond considerations of sincerity. But the "honest soul" has sincerity as its essence. If, then, we undertake to explain in Hegelian terms the English trait to which Emerson responded so warmly, we must ascribe it to the archaic intractability of the English social organization: the English sincerity depends upon the English class structure.

And plainly this was the implicit belief of the English novelists of the nineteenth century. They would all of them appear to be in agreement that the person who accepts his class situation, whatever it may be, as a given and necessary condition of his life will be sincere beyond question. He will be sincere *and* authentic, sincere *because* authentic. Indeed, the novelists understand class to be a chief condition of personal authenticity; it is their assumption that the individual who accepts what a rubric of the Anglican catechism calls his "station and its duties" is pretty sure to have a quality of integral selfhood. Whether he be Mr. Knightley or Sam Weller or Plantagenet Palliser, the country gentleman or the cockney servant or the Prime Minister, heir of the Duke of Omnium, a man is what he is by virtue of his class membership. His sentiment of being, his awareness of his discrete and personal existence, derives from his sentiment of class.

And the converse was also true. The novelists gave judicious approval to upward social mobility so far as it could be achieved by energy and talent and without loss of probity. But they mercilessly scrutinized those of their characters who were ambitious to rise in the world, vigilant for signs of such weakening of the fabric of personal authenticity as might follow from the abandonment of an original class position. It was their presumption that such weakening was likely to occur; the names given to its evidences, to the indication of diminished authenticity, were snobbery and vulgarity.

To the general sincerity of the English which Emerson finds so pleasing there is one exception that he remarks, and with considerable asperity—these people, he says, have no religious belief and therefore nothing is "so odious as the polite bows to God" which they constantly make in their books and newspapers. No student of Victorian life will now confirm Emerson in the simplicity with which he describes the state of religious belief in England. It is true that the present indifference of the English to religion—apart from the rites of birth, marriage, and death—was already in train. By the second half of the nineteenth century the working classes of England were almost wholly alienated from the established Church and increasingly disaffected from the Nonconformist sects. It was the rare intellectual who was in any simple sense a believer. The commitment of the upper classes was largely a social propriety, and Emerson was doubtless right when he described it as cant. It is possible to say that the great Dissenting sects of the middle classes were animated as much by social and political feelings as by personal faith and doctrinal predilections. Still, when all the adverse portents have been taken into account, the fact remains that religion as a force in the life of the nation was by no means yet extinct and not even torpid, what with Low Church and High Church, Oxford Movement and the unremitting dissidence of Dissent, public trials over doctrine and private suffering over crises of belief. Christian faith was taken for granted as an element of virtue; as late as 1888, Mrs. Humphry Ward, a niece of Matthew Arnold, could scandalize the nation with her novel, *Robert Elsmere*, the history of a gifted and saintly young clergyman who finds Christian doctrine inacceptable; Gladstone himself felt called upon to review the book at enormous length.

The history of England was bound up with religion, which still exercised a decisive influence upon the nation's politics, its social and ethical style, and its intellectual culture. If there was indeed an attenuation of personal faith which gave rise to the insincerity that Emerson discerned, among the intellectual classes it had an opposite effect, making occasion for the exercise of a conscious and strenuous sincerity. The salient character-type of the Victorian educated classes was formed, we might say, in response to the loss of religious faith—the non-believer felt under the necessity of maintaining in his personal life the same degree of seriousness and earnestness that had been appropriate to the state of belief; he must guard against falling into the light-minded libertinism of the French—"You know the French . . . ," Matthew Arnold said. Perhaps the greatest distress associated with the evanescence of faith, more painful and disintegrating than can now be fully imagined, was the loss of the assumption that the universe is purposive. This assumption, which, as Freud says, "stands and falls with the religious system," was, for those who held it, not merely a comfortable idea but nothing less than a category of thought; its extirpation was a psychic catastrophe. The Victorian character was under the necessity of withstanding this extreme deprivation, which is to say, of not yielding to the nihilism it implied.

How this end might be achieved is suggested by the anecdote about George Eliot— it has become canonical—which F. W. H. Myers relates. On a rainy May evening Myers walked with his famous guest in the Fellows' Garden of Trinity College, Cambridge, and she spoke of God, Immortality, and Duty. God, she said, was inconceivable. Immortality was unbelievable. But it was beyond question that Duty was "peremptory and absolute." "Never, perhaps," Myers says, "have sterner accents affirmed the sovereignty of impersonal and unrecompensing Law. I listened and night fell; her majestic countenance turned towards me like a sybil in the gloom; it was as though she withdrew from my grasp the two scrolls of promise, and left me with the third scroll only, awful with inscrutable fate." Much as George Eliot had withdrawn from her host, she had not, we may perceive, left him with nothing. A categorical Duty—might it not seem, exactly in its peremptoriness and absoluteness, to have been laid down by the universe itself and thus to validate the personal life that obeyed it? Was a categorical Duty wholly without purpose, without *some* end in view, since it so nearly matched one's own inner imperative, which, in the degree that one responded to it, assured one's coherence and selfhood? And did it not license the thought that man and the universe are less alien to each other than they may seem when the belief in God and Immortality are first surrendered?

We cannot but be touched by Myers's little scene, and perhaps the more because we will not fail to perceive the inauthenticity in which it issues: the very hollowness of the affirmation attests to the need it was intended to satisfy. We of our time do not share that need of the Victorians. We are not under the necessity of discovering in the order of the universe, in the ineluctable duty it silently lays upon us, the validation of such personal coherence and purposiveness as we claim for ourselves. We do not ask those questions which would suggest that the validation is indeed there, needing only to be discovered; to us they seem merely factitious. But we must feel with those who were impelled to ask them.

Still, with what relief we hear the questions being brushed aside not long after they were put with such urgent hope. "The first duty in life," said one of the great figures of Victoria's reign, "The first duty in life is to be as artificial as possible." And Oscar Wilde went on: "What the second duty is no one has yet discovered."

ii

With each passing year the figure of Wilde becomes clearer and larger. Neither his posturing nor his martyrdom now obscures his intellectual significance. Its magnitude is suggested by the view expressed by both André Gide and Thomas Mann that there is a close affinity between Wilde and Nietzsche.[5] Certainly in one respect the two men are close to each other: both expressed a principled antagonism to sincerity, both spoke in praise of what they call the mask.

Wilde, of course, teases the idea of sincerity as one of the cherished attributes of Philistine respectability. Yet something more than a social polemic is being waged when he says, for example, that "all bad poetry springs from genuine feeling." He does not mean merely that most genuine feeling is dull feeling, nor even that genuine feeling needs the mediation of artifice if it is to be made into good poetry. He means that the direct conscious confrontation of experience and the direct public expression of it do not necessarily yield the truth and indeed that they are likely to pervert it. "Man is least himself," Wilde said, "when he talks in his own person. Give him a mask and he will tell you the truth." Emerson had not been deterred from his praise of English sincerity by his having given expression to the same thought in his Journal for 1840. "There is no deeper dissembler," he said, "than the sincerest man," and in the following year, "Many men can write better in a mask than for themselves." Nietzsche, whose admiration of Emerson is always an engaging surprise, says with much the same intention: "Every profound spirit needs a mask."

The mask is justified for Nietzsche by the nature of the only universe with which he is concerned—the universe of history and culture. "It seems", he says, "that all great things first bestride the earth in monstrous and frightening masks in order to inscribe themselves in the hearts of humanity with eternal demands: dogmatic philosophy was such a mask; so also was the Vedanta doctrine in Asia and Platonism in Europe." Wilde, without ranging so far, says something of similar import in the concluding sentences of his essay, "The Truth of Masks": ". . . In art there is no such thing as a universal truth. A truth in art is that whose contradictory is also true. And just as it is only in art-criticism, and through it, that we can apprehend the Platonic theory of ideas, so it is only in art-criticism, and through it, that we can realize Hegel's system of contraries. The truths of metaphysics are the truths of masks."

Irony is one of those words, like love, which are best not talked about if they are to retain any force of meaning—other such words are sincerity and authenticity—but something must be said about it in connection with Wilde and Nietzsche, for the doctrine of masks proposes the intellectual value of the ironic posture. The etymology of the word associates it directly with the idea of the mask, for it derives from the Greek word for a dissembler. It is used in a diversity of meanings,[6] of which the simplest is saying one thing when another is meant, not for the purpose of deceit and not wholly for the purpose of mockery (although this is usually implicit), but, rather, in order to establish a disconnection between the speaker and his interlocutor, or between the speaker and that which is being spoken about, or even between the speaker and himself. Hegel in his *Phenomenology* goes far towards explaining the intellectual value that irony may be supposed to have. Commenting on the extravagant histrionism of Rameau's Nephew, as he assumes an endless succession of roles or, as we may say, masks, Hegel expresses admiration for the Nephew because through his performance Spirit has been able to "pour scornful laughter on existence, on the confusion pervading the whole, and on itself as well." Hegel means, surely, that through that scornful laughter Spirit has gained a measure of freedom—the kind of freedom which we call detachment. If "existence" is responded to as if it were less than totally in earnest, Spirit is the less bound by it. It can then without sadness accept existence, and without resentment transact such business with it as is necessary. If "the whole" is seen as "confused" rather than as orderly and rational, as, in George Eliot's words, peremptory and absolute, the human relation to it need not be fixed and categorical; it can be mercurial and improvisational.

Wilde's aphorism, "The truths of metaphysics are the truths of masks," can be taken to mean that it is not the philosophical treatise but the work of art which provides the model of the process by which we gain knowledge of existence—it is the work of art which best exemplifies the detachment achieved through irony. Schiller has in mind a similar advantage for the heuristic enterprise when he says in the *Aesthetic Letters* that one of the beneficences of art is that it overcomes "the earnestness of duty and destiny." Schiller presents the "mere play" of the aesthetic experience as the activity of man's true being. "Man only plays," he says, "when he is in the fullest sense of the word a human being, and he is only fully a human being when he plays," and presumably the fullness of humanity includes the knowledge of existence. The moral earnestness with which Schiller investigates the possibility of man's liberation from the earnestness of duty and destiny must check any lingering disposition we may have to see Wilde's position as an overture to nihilism. We are further reassured on this score by the affinity between Wilde and Nietzsche, for Nietzsche's hostility to nihilism is settled and explicit.

The human autonomy which is envisioned by Schiller, Wilde, and Nietzsche is, we perceive, in essential accord with the conception of the moral life proposed by Rousseau and Wordsworth when they assigned so high a significance to the sentiment of being. Indeed, the preoccupation with being informs most speculation about the moral life throughout the nineteenth century. The intense meaning which Wordsworth gave to the word "be" became its common meaning in moral discourse. And it came commonly to be felt that *being*, which is to say the gratifying experience of the self as an entity, was susceptible to influences which either increased or diminished its force. There was a pretty clear consensus, for example, that among the things which increased the experience of self art was pre-eminent. And there was no question at all of what diminished the experience of self—the great, enemy of being was *having*. "The less you eat, drink, buy books, go to the theatre or to balls, or to the public house, and the less you think, love, theorize, sing, paint, fence, etc., the more you will be able to save and the *greater* will become your treasure which neither moth nor dust will corrupt—your *capital*. The less you *are* . . . the more you *have*. . . ." It is accumulation that robs you of being.

No one in Europe in the nineteenth century read the words I have just quoted. It is a passage from Karl Marx's *Economic and Philosophical Manuscripts*, which were written in 1844 but not published until 1932. Since then, however, they have aroused great interest because they disclose a young Marx—he was twenty-six—who may be thought different from, even at variance with, the Marx of the later agitational, polemical, and systematic writings. The mind of the young Marx is more humanistic, in the sense of being less ambitious of scientific rectitude, than that of the author of the canonical works. An index to the humanistic quality of the *Manuscripts* is the emphasis put upon alienation, and not merely the alienation of the working class but that of human beings in general, even of the middle class. Indeed, a member of the middle class might read what Marx says about alienation as having a special and direct bearing on his own bourgeois life. "The less you *are*, the less you express your life, the more you *have*, the greater is your alienated life—the greater is the saving of your alienated being. Everything which the economist takes from you in the way of life and humanity, he restores to you in the form of *money* and *wealth*. And everything which you are unable to do, your money can do for you; it can eat, drink, go to the ball and the theatre. It can acquire art, learning, historical treasures, political power, and it can travel. It *can* appropriate all these things for you ... but although it can do all this, it only *desires* to create itself, and to buy itself...."

It will readily be seen that alienation does not mean to Marx what it meant to Hegel. It is not the estrangement of the self from the self, which Hegel sees as a painful but necessary step in development. Rather, it is the transformation of the self into what is not human. Marx's concept of alienation is not wholly contained in what he says about money; but certainly money is central to it and provides the most dramatic way of representing it. In the *Manuscripts*, as later in *Capital*, Marx speaks of money as imbued with a life of its own, a devilish autonomous energy. In him, and in Engels too, there is a strong nostalgic streak which makes them always a little tender of archaic societies in which money is not dominant, and the anti-Semitism of both men has its source in the Jewish connection with money and banking. They are likely to be as anxious as any medieval or Renaissance man about the workings of the money-devil. It is Shakespeare whom Marx quotes—Goethe also, but to less effect—in support of the idea that money inverts moral values and even perception itself; he cites the speech in which Timon says that money makes "black, white; foul, fair; / Wrong, right; base, noble; old, young; coward, valiant."

Money, in short, is the principle of the inauthentic in human existence. "If I have no money for travel, I have no *need*—no real and self-realizing need—for travel. If I have a *vocation* for study but no money for it, then I have no vocation, i.e. no *effective, genuine* vocation. Conversely, if I really have *no* vocation for study but have money and the urge for it, then I have an *effective* vocation." And the section of the *Manuscripts* on money ends with these words: "Let us assume *man* to be *man*, and his relation to the world a human one. Then love can only be exchanged for love, trust for trust, etc. If you wish to enjoy art you must be an artistically cultivated person; if you wish to influence other people you must be a person who really has a stimulating and encouraging effect upon others. Every one of your relations to man and to nature must be a *specific expression* corresponding to the object of your will, of your *real individual* life."

"Let us assume *man* to be *man*, and his relation to the world a human one." It is an astounding thing to say: in no other epoch of history had it been felt necessary to make that assumption explicit. Through the nineteenth century runs the thread of anxiety that man may not be man, that his relation to the world may cease to be a human one. Marx's expression of the anxiety was of singular intensity; but one need not have been of his political persuasion to share the apprehension. The perception that being was threatened by having was characteristic of the bourgeois moralists of the age. "Culture," said Matthew Arnold, "is not a having but a being and a becoming." And Oscar Wilde, in his great essay, "The Soul of Man under Socialism," echoed Arnold: "The true perfection of man lies not in what man has but what man is." Just as over the portal of the antique world there was written the Delphic maxim, "Know thyself," just so, Wilde says, "over the portal of the new world "Be thyself" shall be written." And Ruskin said, "There is no wealth but life."

But it was of course not enough simply to set being over against having and to assert that the one is to be preferred to the other. After all, men may choose to have and yet not choose not to be. And the commitment to having could not be thought the sole cause of the diminution of the sentiment of being which the nineteenth century was aware of—there were in addition causes of an insidious, scarcely discernible kind. The word "culture" as we now use it was not yet current—the "culture" that Matthew Arnold opposed to "anarchy" of course means something else—but the idea of culture in its chief present-day meaning was rapidly becoming available: the idea, that is to say, of a unitary complex of interacting assumptions, modes of thought, habits, and styles, which are connected in secret as well as overt ways with the practical arrangements of a society and which, because they are not brought to consciousness, are unopposed in their influence over men's minds. We nowadays take the idea of culture for granted; in the nineteenth century {Hippolyte} Taine could announce it as a discovery of the age.

How much complexity and even contradiction the idea of culture can encompass is suggested by a curious passage in *English Traits*. In the first of two consecutive paragraphs, Emerson makes one of his laudatory statements about the autonomy and sincerity of the English: "They require you to be of your own opinion, and they hate the coward who cannot in practical affairs answer yes or no. They dare to displease, nay, they will let you break all the rules if you do it natively and with spirit. You must be somebody; then you may do this or that as you will." In the next paragraph, with no transition and with no apparent awareness of the contradiction, he says: "Machinery has been applied to all work and carried to such perfection that little is left for the men but to mind the engines and feed the furnaces. But the machines require punctual service, and as they never tire they prove too much for their tenders. Mines, forges, mills, breweries, railroads, steam-pump, steam-plough, drill of regiments, drill of police, rule of court and shop rule are operated to give a mechanical regularity to all the habit and action of men. A terrible machine has possessed itself of the ground, the air, the men and the women, and hardly even thought is free."

Emerson is not talking about an over-driven working class, nor about actual machine tending, which would scarcely have involved the nation as a whole. At a time to which we of today look back with nostalgia, so innocent of mechanism does it still seem, he is remarking an influence which the machine, or the idea of the machine, exerts on the conduct of life, imposing habits and modes of thought which make it ever less possible to assume that man is man, and he utters this observation in the same breath in which he speaks of the culture's characteristic demand that one "be somebody."

The anxiety about the machine is a commonplace in nineteenth-century moral and cultural thought: Marx's "Let us assume *man* to be *man*" means "Let us assume man to be not a machine." The mind is not to be a machine, not even that part of it which we call reason. The universe is not to be a machine; the thought that it might be drove Carlyle to the verge of madness. It was the mechanical principle, quite as much as the acquisitive principle—the two are of course intimately connected—which was felt to be the enemy of being, the source of inauthenticity.

The machine, said Ruskin, could make only inauthentic things, dead things; and the dead things communicated their deadness to those who used them. Nor, in his view, is it only actual machinery which produces dead objects, but any mode of making that does not permit the maker to infuse into the artefact the quality of his being. The architecture of ancient Egypt, according to Ruskin, was mechanical because "servile"— the workman carried out, not his own intention, but that of the master architect. And in the face of the settled opinion of his day Ruskin passed a similar adverse judgement upon the architecture of ancient Greece, not sparing even the sacrosanct Parthenon. Only Gothic architecture was exempt from his blame: it alone among the great styles had the quality of life. On the basis of how the nineteenth century believed the cathedrals to have been built, Ruskin was able to regard them as the embodiment both of the individual and the communal spirit—they were constructed so slowly that it was as if they grew rather than were made, fulfilling not a plan but an entelechy, reaching completion by the inherent laws of their being. Like Goethe in his famous meditation on the tower of Strasbourg, Ruskin cherished the Gothic cathedrals because they were organic. Living things made the elements of their decoration, and their structure depended upon reciprocating energies, which to the responsive eye might manifest themselves as movement.

The belief that the organic is the chief criterion of what is authentic in art and life continues, it need hardly be said, to have great force with us, the more as we become alarmed by the deterioration of the organic environment. The sense of something intervening between man and his own organic endowment is a powerful element in the modern consciousness, an overt and exigent issue in our culture. In an increasingly urban and technological society, the natural processes of human existence have acquired amoral status in the degree that they are thwarted. It is the common feeling that some inhuman force has possessed our ground and our air, our men and women and our thought, a machine more terrible than any that Emerson imagined. In many quarters, whatever can be thought susceptible of analogy to the machine, even a syllogism or a device of dramaturgy, is felt to be inimical to the authenticity of experience and being. {...}

Notes

1 Adam Kirsch, *Why Trilling Matters* (New Haven: Yale University Press, 2011), 68.
2 Ibid., 70.

3 That the mode of speech Tocqueville found characteristically American still persists is suggested by a snatch of conversation which was heard on the B.B.C. in 1969, between the Queen and the then new American Ambassador to Britain. In the course of a call being paid by the Ambassador, the Queen inquired whether he was by now settled and comfortable in his house, to which he replied: "We are still, in the residence, subject to some discomfiture and inconvenience owing to certain elements of refurbishment."

4 For an enlightening polemical discussion of Emerson's attitude to social existence, see ch. I ("The Failure of the Fathers") of Quentin Anderson's *The Imperial Self* (New York, 1971).

5 This is remarked by Richard Ellmann in the introduction to his selection of Wilde's critical writings, *The Artist as Critic* (New York and London, 1970). Gide brings the two names together in a casual and limited way in the commemoration of Wilde he wrote in 1902, but {Thomas} Mann, after expressing some anxiety about venturing on the comparison—"Of course there is something almost sacrilegious about the juxtaposition of Nietzsche and Wilde . . ."—develops it in considerable detail ("Nietzsche's Philosophy in the Light of Recent History," *Last Essays*, New York and London, 1959).

6 For a succinct explication of them, see Fowler's *Modern English Usage*.

Robert Penn Warren (1905–1989)

*Poet, novelist, and one of the founders of New Criticism, Warren is the only person to have won a Pulitzer Prize for Fiction (*All the King's Men, *(1946)), and a Pulitzer Prize for Poetry (which he was awarded twice). Early on, he was part of the poetry circle at Vanderbilt University known as the Fugitives, and later a member of the Southern Agrarians. His poem "The Briar Patch" was included in* I'll Take My Stand *(1930), an Agrarian, pro-Southern manifesto. Along with John Thibaut Purser and Cleanth Brooks (his cofounder of* The Southern Review *in 1935), Warren edited* An Approach to Literature *(1938), an anthology of American writing that did not feature anything by Emerson. In a special publication of Coleridge's* The Rime of Ancient Mariner *that included an essay by Warren and illustrations by Alexander Calder (1946), Warren inscribed the book with "all love and thanks" to "Peter and Ebie." Likewise, the following poem was published in the* New Yorker *(July 16, 1966) and dedicated to the surrealist artist, Peter Blume, and his wife, Ebie, his Connecticut friends and neighbors. In this work we seem to find Robert Penn Warren reading Ralph Waldo Emerson at 38,000 feet—perhaps a compelling image of transcendental thinking, or an appropriate vantage from which to assess Emerson's work* sub specie aeternitatis.

Homage to Emerson, On a Night Flight to New York

Robert Penn Warren

(To Peter and Ebie Blume)

I

Over Peoria we lost the sun;
The earth, by snow like sputum smeared, slides
Westward. Those fields in the last light gleam. Emerson—

The essays, on my lap, lie. A finger
Of light, in our pressurized gloom, strikes down,
Like God, to poke the page; the page glows. There is
No sin. Not even error. Night,

On the glass at my right shoulder, hisses
Like sand from a sand-blast, but
The hiss is a sound that only a dog's
Ear could catch, or the human heart. My heart

Is as abstract as an empty
Coca-Cola bottle. It whistles with speed.
It whines in that ammoniac blast caused by
The passage of stars, for,
At 38,000 feet, Emerson

Is dead right. His smile
Was sweet as he walked in the greenwood.
He walked lightly, his toes out, his body sweetly
Swaying in the dappled shade, and
His smile never withered a violet. He

Did not even know the violet's name, not having
Been introduced, but he bowed, smiling,
For he had forgiven God everything, even the violet.

II

The spider has more eyes than I have money.
I used to dream that God was a spider, or

Vice versa, but it is easier
To dream of a funnel, and you
The clear liquid being poured down it, forever.

You do not know what is beyond the little end of the funnel.

The liquid glimmers in darkness, you
Are happy, it pours easily, without fume.

All you have to do is not argue.

III

Not argue, unless, that is, you are the kind
That needs to remember something specific
In order to be, at 38,000 feet, whatever you are—and once
In New Orleans, in French Town, in

Front of the Old Absinthe House, and it
Was Saturday night, was 2 A.M., a drunk

Crip slipped, and the air was full of flying crutches,
Like a Texas tornado exploding with chicken feathers and
Split boards off busted hen-houses, and bingo!
It was prize money flat on its you-know-what, it
Was like a box of spilled spaghetti, but
I managed to reassemble everything and prop it
Against a lamp post. *Thank you,*
It said in its expensive Harvard-*cum*-cotton
Voice, then bingo!
Flat on its you-know-what, on the pavement,
And ditto the crutches. *Prithee,* the voice

Expensively said, *do not trouble yourself*
Further. This is as good a position as any
From which to watch the stars. Then added,
Until, of course, the cops come. I
Had private reasons for not wanting to be
There when the cops came. So wasn't.

Emerson thought that significance shines through everything,

And at that moment I was drunk enough to think all this
    was allegory.
If it was, it was sure-God one drunk allegory—and
Somewhere in the womb-gloom of the DC-8

A baby is crying. The cry seems to have a reality
Independent of the baby. The cry
Is like a small white worm in my brain.

It nibbles with tiny, insistent assiduity. Its teeth
Are almost too soft. Sometimes it merely tickles.

To my right, far over Kentucky, the stars are shining.

IV

If the Christmas tree at Rockefeller Center were
A billion times bigger, and you laid it
Flat down in the dark, and

With a steam roller waist-high to God and heavy as
The Rocky Mountains, flattened it out thin as paper, but
Never broke a single damned colored light bulb, and they
    were all
Blazing in the dark, that would be the way it is, but

Beyond the lights it is dark, and one night in winter, I
Stood at the end of a pier at Coney Island, while
The empty darkness howled like a dog but no wind, and
    far down
The boardwalk what must have been a cop's flashlight
Jiggled fitfully over what must have been locked store-
    fronts, then,
Of a sudden, went out. The stars were small and white,
    and I heard

The sea secretly sucking the piles of the pier with a sound
    like
An old woman sucking her teeth in the dark before she
    sleeps
The nose of the DC-8 dips, and at this point
The man sitting beside me begins, quite audibly, to recite
The multiplication table.

    Far below,
Individual lights can be seen throbbing like nerve ends.
I have friends down there, and their lives have strange shapes
Like eggs splattered on the kitchen floor. Their lives
    shine
Like oil-slicks on dark water. I love them, I think.

In a room, somewhere, a telephone keeps ringing.

V

The wind comes off the Sound, smelling
Of ice. It smells
Of fish and burned gasoline. A sheet
Of newspaper drives in the wind across
The great distance of cement that bleeds
Off into blackness beyond the red flares. The air

Shivers, it shakes like jello with
The roar of jets, oh, why

Is it you think you can hear the infinitesimal scrape
Of that newspaper as it slides over the black cement,
      forever?

The wind gouges its knuckles into my eye. No wonder
      there are tears.

VI

When you reach home tonight, you will see
That the envelope containing the policy
Of your flight insurance is waiting, unopened,
On the table. All had been in order,
In case—but can you tell me,
      Does the wild rose know your secret
      As the summer silence breathes?

Eastward, the great waters stretch in darkness.
Do you know how gulls sleep when they can't make it
      home?

      Tell me, tell me, does the wild rose—tell me, for

Tonight I shall dream of small white stars
Falling forever in darkness like dandruff, but

Now let us cross that black cement which resembles the
      Arctic ice of
Our recollections. There is the city, the sky
Glows, glows above it, and there must be

A way by which the process of living can become Truth.

Let us move toward the city. Do you think you could
      tell me
What constitutes the human bond? How often do you
      imagine
A face half in shadow, tears—
As it would seem from that muted glitter—brimming in
The eyes, but

The lips do not tremble.

Is it merely a delusion that they seem about to smile?

Jorge Luis Borges (1899–1986)

Argentine writer, poet, translator, and essayist whose works include the short story collections Ficciones *(1944) and* The Aleph *(1949). In conversations conducted in the last few decades of his life, Borges spoke openly about his admiration for Emerson—"he beams, he expands, he glows," one interlocutor writes of Borges' response to the mention of English or American literature. In a series of remarks, some of them collected below, Borges speculates how Emerson's work affected him and his writing. Speaking with Richard Burgin (1967), Rita Guibert (1968), L. S. Dembo (1969), Selden Rodman (1969), and John Biguenet and Tom Whalen (1982)—collected in* Jorge Luis Borges: Conversations—*Borges describes how Emerson is an American writer, among other American writers such as Whitman, "who meant a lot to me."[1] At one point Borges appears to add the gift of Emerson's poetry to the verse in "Another Poem of Gifts"—or perhaps he means to say his praise for Emerson is implied in that poem of indebtedness and appreciation; Emerson is explicitly mentioned in Borges' poem "Emerson" from* The Self and the Other *(El otro, el mismo, 1964), which is also included below in two translations—the first from* Jorge Luis Borges: Selected Poems *(ed. Alexander Coleman, 1999) and the second from Richard O'Connell (*National Review, *October 13, 2003). At a different time Borges and his interlocutor make reference to Emerson's notion expressed in the opening line of the essay "History": "There is one mind common to all individual men." A related passage appears in "Literary Ethics," where Emerson writes: The scholar cannot know nature and truth "until he has beheld with awe the infinitude and impersonality of the intellectual power. When he has seen, that it is not his, nor any man's, but that it is the soul which made the world, and that it is all accessible to him, he will know that he, as its minister, may rightfully hold all things subordinate and answerable to it."*

Emerson

Jorge Luis Borges

Closing the heavy volume of Montaigne,
The tall New Englander goes out
Into an evening which exalts the fields.
It is a pleasure worth no less than reading.
He walks toward the final sloping of the sun,

Toward the landscape's gilded edge;
He moves through darkening fields as he moves now
Through the memory of the one who writes this down.
He thinks: I have read the essential books
And written others which oblivion
Will not efface. I have been allowed
That which is given mortal man to know.
The whole continent knows my name.
I have not lived. I want to be someone else.

* * *

Closing the massive volume of Montaigne,
The lanky Yankee rises from his desk
And leaves his study for the golden fields
Of Concord, for a joy no less than reading.
He walks into the blazing setting sun,
Seeking to reach the landscapes' final verge;
Moving through meadows as a man might move
Through the memory of one who writes him down;
And thinks: I have read the essential books
And written others time will not efface.
I have been given more than mortal man
On earth has any right to ever know.
The continent reverberates my name.
I have not lived. Would I were born a slave.

Note

1 Jorge Luis Borges, *Jorge Luis Borges: Conversations*, ed. Richard Burgin (Jackson: University Press of Mississippi, 1998), 14–15, 45–46, 90–91, 99, 205–206.

selections from *Conversations*

Jorge Luis Borges

RICHARD BURGIN: Your writing always, from the first, had its source in other books?

BORGES: Yes, that's true. Well, because I think of reading a book as no less an experience than traveling or falling in love. I think that reading Berkeley or Shaw or Emerson, those are quite as real experiences to me as seeing London, for example. Of course I saw London through Dickens and through Chesterton and through Stevenson, no? Many people are apt to think of real life on the one side, that means toothache, headache, traveling and so on, then you have on the other side, you have imaginary life and fancy and that means the arts. But I don't think that that distinction holds water. I think that everything is a part of life. For example, today I was telling my wife, I have traveled, well, I won't say all over the world, but all over the west, no? And yet I find that I have written poems about out-of-the-way slums of Buenos Aires, I have written poems on rather drab street corners. And I have never written poems on a great subject, I mean on a famous subject. For example, I greatly enjoy New York, but I don't think I would write about New York. Maybe I'll write about some street corner, because after all so many people have done that other kind of thing.

Burgin: You wrote a poem about Emerson, though, and Jonathan Edwards and Spinoza.

Borges: That's true, yes. But in my country writing about Emerson and Jonathan Edwards is writing perhaps about rather secret characters.

Burgin: Because they're occult, almost.

Borges: Yes, more or less. I wrote a poem about Sarmiento because I had to and because I love him, but really I prefer minor characters or if not, if I write about Spinoza and Emerson or about Shakespeare and Cervantes, they are major characters, but I write about them in a way that makes them like characters out of books, rather than famous men.

* * *

RITA GUIBERT: From some of your poems, such as "Another Poem of Gifts," and "New England 1967," in which you say "And America is waiting for me at every corner," I gather that you feel affection for the United States.

BORGES: Ever since the days of my childhood, when I read Mark Twain, Bret Harte, Hawthorn, Jack London, and Edgar Allan Poe, I've been very much attached to the

United States. I still am. Perhaps I'm influenced by the fact that I had an English grandmother, and English and Spanish were spoken indiscriminately in our house when I was a boy, so much so that I wasn't even aware that they were separate languages. When I was talking to my paternal grandmother I had to speak in a manner that I afterwards discovered was called English, and when I was talking to my mother or her parents I had to talk a language that afterwards turned out to be Spanish. My affection for the United States makes me deplore the fact that many Latin Americans, and very likely many North Americans as well, admire the United States for the wrong things. For instance, when I think of the United States I visualize those New England houses, houses built of red brick, or else the sort of wooden Parthenons one sees in the South; I think of a way of life, and also of writers who have meant a lot to me. First of all I think of Whitman, Thoreau, Melville, Henry James, and Emerson. But I notice that most people admire this country for its gadgets, its supermarkets and things like paper bags—even garbage bags—and plastics. All these things are perishable, however, and are made for use, not for worship. It seems to me that we should praise or condemn the United States for quite different things. You live here, and I don't suppose you spend all your time thinking about gadgets. And perhaps the streets of New England are more typically American than the skyscrapers, or anyhow people love them more. What I'm trying to say is that it's important to see this side of America too. Although I prefer New England, when I was in New York I felt enormously proud of it, and thought to myself: "Good Lord, how well the city has turned out," just as if I'd built it myself. In my poem "Another Poem of Gifts," I praise God for many things, and among others:

> For the hard riders who, on the plains,
> Drive on the cattle and the dawn,
> For mornings in Montevideo . . .
> For the high towers of San Francisco and Manhattan Island . . .

And also for mornings in Texas, for Emerson's poetry, for the events of my life, for music, for English poetry; for my grandmother, my English grandmother, who when she was dying called us all to her side and said: "Nothing in particular is happening. I'm only an old woman who is dying very, very slowly; there's no reason for the whole house to worry about it. I have to apologize to you all." What a beautiful thing!

> For Frances Haslam, who begged her children's pardon
> For dying so slowly,
> For the minutes that precede sleep,
> For sleep and death,
> Those two hidden treasures,
> For the intimate gifts I do not mention
> For music, that mysterious form of time.

My grandmother was the wife of Colonel Borges, who was killed in action in the revolution of 1874. She had seen life on the frontier among the Indians, and had talked to their chief, Pincén. That was at Junín.

* * *

L. S. DEMBO: So for all his intellect, Averroes suffered from the same problem an illiterate gaucho did. But let me ask you something on a different subject. In an essay on Coleridge you examined the idea that all literary works are one work and that all writers are one impersonal writer.

BORGES: Yes, I got that idea from Emerson, who said they were the work of one single all-knowing or all-thinking "gentleman." The word "gentleman" is beautiful there. Because if he had written "man" it would have meant very little, but the idea of a gentleman writing, well, let's say, all Shakespeare's tragedies for him....

Dembo: Well, the word probably speaks for Emerson's own gentility.

Borges. Yes, but I don't want to blame gentility. I think it should be encouraged. At least I try to be a gentleman, though I never quite succeed in that ambition.

Dembo: In any case, what would you say is the contribution of *Ficciones* to this universal work? Is it part of traditional literature?

Borges: Oh, I think it's made of half-forgotten memories. I wonder if there is a single original line in the book. I suppose a source can be found for every line I've written, or perhaps that's what we call inventing—mixing up memories. I don't think we're capable of creation in the way that God created the world.

* * *

SELDEN RODMAN

When discussing English or American literature, Borges's whole personality changes. He beams, he expands, he glows. "You know I was brought up on English in my father's library. I was quite old when it occurred to me that poetry could be written in a language other than English."

He ordered a plate of rice, butter, and cheese, while our mouths watered at the thought of the Argentine steaks we'd soon be served. "I hate steaks," Borges said. "They are so common in this country. I can't eat more than one or two a year."

Norman {Thomas di Giovanni} said: "Borges, I heard you mention Eliot a while back—"

"Eliot is a little dry, don't you think?" Borges said. "I prefer Frost. You like Frost, Rodman?" He was glad that I preferred Frost to Eliot. He asked me how Frost looked and talked. Did I think that Frost's reserved Americanism had any kinship with Whitman's boisterous brand?

"I think Frost was a direct descendant of Emerson," I said.

"And Whitman was influenced by Emerson more than by anyone! That essay about the ideal American democrat, pioneer, truthteller, yea-sayer—with a bit of Asiatic-Indian philosophy thrown in—"

"'I greet you at the beginning of a great career,'" I quoted.

"—And how distressed Emerson was that Whitman made bit publicity out of that letter!" Borges said. "Yet why not? If Emerson didn't expect it, why did he write it? Whitman was right . . . but don't you think Whitman tries too hard, that he's really a quite unspontaneous writer?"

* * *

JOHN BIGUENET and TOM WHALEN: Literature that begets literature—some critics see this as a sign of literature being exhausted.

BORGES: No, I think that Emerson wrote that poetry comes out of poetry. Whitman thought that poetry came from experience, no? I don't think so. I think Emerson was right. I think Victor Hugo said, "Homer, of course, had his Homer." "Homer avait son Homer." I suppose he had; he lived in a literary tradition. It's like time, really, beginningless.

Joseph Blau (1909–1986)

Historian of American philosophy and philosopher of religion, a student of John Dewey's, Blau was educated and taught at Columbia, beginning undergraduate work in the 1920s and retiring from the faculty in 1977. He taught in the Philosophy Department until 1961 when he helped to found the Department of Religion. In addition to addressing how Judaism's development has been influenced by other cultures in works such as Christian Interpretation of the Cabala in the Renaissance *(1944),* The Story of Jewish Philosophy *(1962), and* Judaism in America *(1976), Blau edited* American Philosophic Addresses, 1700–1900 *(1946) and wrote* Men and Movements in American Philosophy *(1952). In* Movements, *Blau explores the history of philosophical thinking in America from the Puritans to the emergence of naturalism in figures such as Santayana and Dewey. In the following essay, delivered before the Society for the Advancement of American Philosophy on March 4, 1977, Blau offers an important corrective to the reception of Emerson's work as inimical to social and political engagement. "We concentrate our studies," Blau observes, "on the biteless passages, or those that have lost their bite, and then announce triumphantly that Emerson was toothless." At odds with much popular and conventional opinion, Blau offers compelling reasons why Emerson's work—especially the core concept "self-reliance"—is, perhaps counterintuitively, essential to social philosophy in an age, as he says, "like our own, hopelessly committed to an extreme individualism." Blau's essay forms a useful reply to the likes of John Updike who—especially in "Emersonianism" collected in this volume—complains of Emerson's "coldness and disengagement and distrust of altruism."*

Emerson's Transcendentalist Individualism
as a Social Philosophy

Joseph Blau

Much of the attention of recent students of American philosophy has been concentrated on the study of philosophers and ways of doing philosophy in the post-Civil War era. It is understandable that this should be so, for the problems of late nineteenth and twentieth century thought are still alive, still perplexing, in our own attempts at philosophic understanding. There is much, however, that is overlooked by narrowing our focus to what Max Fisch and his associates described as "classic" American philosophy, and to our own post-classic era. It may well be that some aspects of the earlier and now unfashionable philosophies and philosophers can still have resonance in our thinking if only we are willing to give these older philosophies a hearing. For this reason, this present study explores the philosophy of Ralph Waldo Emerson and reexamines his thought at the point where, it seems to me, it is still viable today, namely as a social philosophy for a society, like our own, hopelessly committed to an extreme individualism.

I

The key term with which to begin our examination, if we are to understand the increasingly social thrust of Emerson's transcendentalist individualism, is "self-reliance." Unfortunately this expression has come to be used in a sense very different from that which Emerson intended. As a result, he is too often regarded as a high-grade literary apologist for the *status quo*. An instant corrective is available to those who have read the tribute that Wendell Phillips paid him, calling him "the earthquake scholar at Concord, whose serene word, like a whisper among the avalanches, topples down superstitions and prejudices."[1] Self-reliance, for Emerson, bore no relation to what came to be called "rugged individualism." Yet Emerson's essay on "Self-Reliance" is treated, when it is mentioned at all, as if it were a high-flown *apologia* for the Carnegies, the Rockefellers, and the Harrimans of the late nineteenth-century age of the robber barons. Indeed, quite to the contrary, self-reliance is the very pivot on which Emerson's individualism transforms itself into a social philosophy of altruism.

The germ of what was to become Emerson's intuition of self-reliance may be found in a letter to his aunt, Mary Moody Emerson, dated August 17, 1827, when the young minister was only twenty four years of age. Like most of his other letters to this favorite correspondent, the letter in question ranges widely in its themes. The relevant passage (quoted in full in the note below) reads in part, "A portion of truth, bright and sublime, lives in every moment to every man."[2] Again, in 1832, when Emerson had to face the question whether he was to remain in the ministry or resign his charge, he wrote in his *Journal*, "I would be the vehicle of that divine principle that lurks within, and of which life has afforded only glimpses enough to assure me of its being."[3] After his decision to resign his ministry and the breakdown that followed this decision, while on his way to Europe, in 1833, for what, it was hoped, would be a restoration to health, he wrote the words that finally became his central message as well as furnishing him with his primary intellectual method:

> Henceforth, please God, forever I forego
> The yoke of men's opinions. I will be
> Light-hearted as a bird, and live with God.
> I find him in the bottom of my heart,
> I hear continually his voice therein.[4]

This was the message that Emerson taught others in his books and from lecture platforms for the rest of his life.

Never a doctrine, ever a method, in his hands self-reliance became an instrument of great sensitivity and enormous vitality. What he had found in the healing process of finding himself was the conviction that any person who honestly examines his own mind and his own heart and carries the examination out to its utmost limits will arrive at conclusions that are not particular, self-centered, and limited, but are universal and applicable to all of humankind. He conceived the method of self-reliance as an individual, immediate raid on ultimate, universal truth. Thought, intuitive thought, does not have to be directed toward the outer world of things to be universal; it can be directed toward the innermost world of the individual self. But in striving to reach this innermost self or soul, the individual transcends himself (herself). It is no longer his (her) finiteness that speaks the word universal, but the spark of the infinite that lies within each one. Thus Emerson's individualism was transcendentalist; it found the universal within the individual, but in the discovery it forced the individual beyond individuality to universality. The principle of self-reliance is that of respecting the guidance of the ultimate introspection gained by this transcendentalist searching.

The method of self-reliance, as Emerson practised it, superseded discursive argumentation. He was entirely honest when he answered Henry Ware's request for his arguments in support of the position he espoused in the "Divinity School Address" of 1838 with the comment that he had no "arguments"—that he did not "know what arguments mean in reference to any expression of a thought."[5] Emerson was sincere in his belief that any user of the method of transcendentalist introspection is the spiritual representative of the entire human race. The truly "representative men" are not chosen by the people's voice and suffrage. They are self-chosen by virtue of their devoted following of the universal voice within their breasts.

Emerson expressed this central insight variously in his writings. Sometimes he spoke in mystical language, easy to reject as bathos, as in the passage in his *Nature* of 1836, so cruelly and wittily caricatured by his friend Christopher P. Cranch: "Standing on the bare ground, my head bathed by the blithe air, and uplifted into infinite space—all mean egotism vanishes. I become a transparent eye-ball; I am nothing; I see all; the currents of the Universal Being circulate through me."[6] At other times, he talked in mythological terms, as in the Swedenborgian fable of the "greater man" at the beginning of his Harvard Phi Beta Kappa address of 1837, "The American Scholar."[7] At still other times, as in the essay on "Self-Reliance," Emerson tried to express his view in terms that might be understood by all, only to fall into the pit of being misunderstood by all—or almost all. For it is only in a transcendentalist sense that self-reliance can be translated as individualism. Emerson's "self-reliance" is misinterpreted and misrepresented as laissez-faire. What we want, he said, is "men of original perception and original action, who can open their eyes wider than to a nationality,"[8] and we may add *a fortiori* wider than to an individuality.

II

When Emerson combined his transcendental view of the individual as the carrier of universal truth with the relics of his traditional Christian view of the dignity of the individual as the child of God, and with his American democratic heritage of the worth of the individual as a co-equal partner in society, he produced perhaps the most thoroughgoing humanism that has ever been presented. Nowhere is this clearer than in his volume of sketches called *Representative Men*.[9] The men "profiled" by Emerson in this volume were all very unusual people of special talents and abilities whose achievements made history. They are not "representative" in the usual sense of "typical samples." Rather they are representative of the highest quality of human success, representative of the utmost that human beings have been able to achieve; representative, then, of what humankind could ideally become rather than of what humankind now is. It is worthy of notice that Emerson began the volume with a chapter called "Uses of Great Men," where he suggested that it is through the great that we can learn about ourselves, through the unusual that we can discover the potential of the ordinary.

In our usual self-centered fashion, we all tend to regard ourselves as always of a superior rightness; we "chuckle and triumph" in our opinion "over the absurdities of all the rest. Difference from me is the measure of absurdity. Not one has a misgiving of being wrong." While we engage in "this chuckle of self-gratulation," a truly representative person appears and thus aids us to overcome our petty self-centering. "Without Plato we should almost lose our faith in the possibility of a reasonable book." The great serve "to clear our eyes from egotism, and enable us to see other people and their works."

> As to what we call the masses, and common men—there are no common men. All men are at last of a size; and true art is only possible on the conviction that every talent has its apotheosis somewhere.... But heaven reserves an equal scope for every creature. Each is uneasy until he has produced his private ray unto the concave sphere and beheld his talent also in its last nobility and exaltation.[10]

Again and again Emerson points to the idea that there is progress, not in the inevitable way that the optimists of the Enlightenment anticipated, nor yet in the merely biological sense of the Evolutionists who were still to come, but in a moral sense. "The reputations of the nineteenth century will one day be quoted to prove its barbarism." This progress is not of the individual's own doing, but of the entire human race. "The genius of humanity is the real subject whose biography is written in our annals." The essence of the progress of humanity is not to be found in the study of the life of any single person, however famous. At most, the individual merely serves as "an exhibition, in some quarter, of new possibilities" for the whole of humanity. The deeper we probe into the lives of individuals the closer we come to that "elemental region wherein the individual is lost." Ultimately, insofar as the conditions can be equalized for every person, "within the limits of humane education and agency," the greatest people are those whose unique qualities enable their influence and effect to spread most widely.[11]

From these summaries, and the quotations from Emerson's own writing that have been included, it is plain that Emerson's kind of individualism did not issue in any sort of egotism, whether of the spiritual or the material economy. He recognized that the human being is a social being. Indeed, he considered that without rooting in society any person is lost. People are nothing except in relation to other people, and yet, in his sense, the essential human being is the private self. What seems paradoxical in the apposition of these two ideas is resolved, in Emerson's thought, by the belief that the private self does not exist for itself, but for the contribution that it can make to the human race. "I must have a social state and history," he wrote in *The Conduct of Life,* "or my thinking and speaking want body and basis. But to give these accessories any value, I must know them as contingent and rather showy possessions, which pass for more to the people than to me."[12] In this alternation back and forth between the sense of individuality and the sense of common humanity lies one of the most distinctive and most difficult of the Emersonian concepts. Once the position is stated, however, it can be recognized as a most appealing view for many people who wish to retain a grip on their own uniqueness and, at the same time, to hold fast to a sense of human solidarity.

III

Emerson has frequently been dismissed as a man who was not interested in politics. The statement is correct if the term be limited in meaning to the politics of parties and elections. But it is certainly incorrect to regard Emerson as non-political. It is true that he was by temperament not an activist, on most issues. During the slavery controversy, however, he was one of the handful of intellectuals who early took a firm stand. This accounts for the high praise he won from Wendell Phillips. Emerson took a moral position on the slavery issue. He spoke of the North and the South as two different levels of civilization, one democratic, the other oligarchic, which Americans have tried to hold together under a single law. This attempt had failed, he asserted, because the earlier state of society poisoned the later stage, "has poisoned politics, public morals and social intercourse in the Republic, now for many years." The time had arrived, he thought, to make the effort to extend the better state of society throughout the entire country. On moral grounds he set himself against the Gresham-like law that had been the rule in American political life, that the evil in circulation will inevitably triumph over the good. "Our whole history," he proclaimed, "appears like a last effort of the Divine Providence in behalf of the human race; and a literal, slavish following of precedents, as by a Justice of the peace, is not for those who at this hour lead the destinies of this people."[13]

Emerson refused to make his case against slavery on anything less than this moral ground. He dismissed scornfully the attempt to oppose slavery for economic reasons.

> To what purpose make more big books of these statistics? There are already mountains of facts, if any one wants them. But people do not want them. They bring their opinion into the world. If they have a comatose tendency in the brain, they are pro-slavery while they live; if of a nervous sanguineous temperament, they are abolitionists. Can you convince the shoe interest, or

the iron interest, or the cotton interest, by reading passages from Milton or Montesquieu?[14]

The Emerson who wrote these words is seldom spoken of today. We have forgotten the man of vision and courage. We concentrate our studies on the biteless passages, or those that have lost their bite, and then announce triumphantly that Emerson was toothless. He saw the slavery question as a political question as the great philosophers have always seen politics, as an aspect of man's quest for the fulfillment of humanity. His was a transcendental politics that could be carried on only by transcendental politicians—in the language of Plato, by philosopher-kings, "who can open their eyes wider than to a nationality, namely, to considerations of benefit to the human race, can act in the interest of civilization."[15]

Emerson lived at a time close enough to the foundation of the United States in a war of revolution that he lacked the fear of revolutionary action that has prevailed in America in more recent times. "I wish," he declared, "I saw in the people that inspiration which, if government would not obey the same, would leave the government behind and create on the moment the means and executors it wanted."[16] Surely the man who uttered these words was not of the Jacksonian party, and yet he was at home with the ideas of the Jacksonians in many ways. When he was still at the threshold of his new career as secular preacher and conscience of the American people, Emerson delivered at Boston, in 1839–1840, a series of lectures under the title, "The Present Age." Theodore Parker reported to Dr. Convers Francis that "It was *Democratic-Locofoco* throughout. . . . Bancroft was in ecstasies. . . . One grave, Whig-looking gentleman . . . said he could only account for his delivering such a lecture on the supposition that he wished to get a place in the Custom-House under George Bancroft."[17]

There are a number of passages in Emerson's addresses and essays that have a Jacksonian tinge. So, for example, he commented on "free trade, certainly the interest of nations," and added, "Banknotes rob the public, but are such a daily convenience that we silence our scruples and make believe they are gold."[18] Nowhere does he sound more like a Jacksonian Democrat than in his glorification of labor: "There is no interest in any country so imperative as that of labor; it covers all, the constitutions and governments exist for that—to protect and insure it to the laborer."[19] Despite such tendencies in his thought, his personal heroes among the Americans of the New England in which he lived were men who were politically affiliated with the Whig party. In one comment he suggested that, of the two parties, one had a monopoly on good causes, the other on good men[20]—and so he joined no party.

In most respects, Emerson's views were those of the political liberals of the late eighteenth century. He did, however, go beyond his immediate models in the degree to which he introduced a moral emphasis in his political thought. In a passage that, for him, was unusually specific, he wrote:

The end of all political struggle is to establish morality as the basis of all legislation. It is not free institutions, it is not a republic, it is not a democracy, that is the end—no, but only the means. Morality is the object of government . . . the government of the world is moral. . . .[21]

Legislation, governments, parties are all local and temporary. For every stage in the cultural development of the people of a territory, a different form of government may be both desirable and necessary. "The law is only a memorandum," but the grand and overarching principles of politics are eternal.[22]

Basic to Emerson's conception of the principles that apply is the notion that governments exist for the dual, though often conflicting, interest of the protection of persons and of property. The interest of persons requires the form of a democracy founded on equal rights. The interest of property calls for a form of government grounded in inequality. "Personal rights, universally the same, demand a government framed on the ratio of the census; property demands a government framed on the ratio of owners and owning."[23] The generally accepted principle of older times was that proprietors should have a larger role in the franchise than non-proprietors, but this view no longer seems self-evident. The newer tendency is to regard the interest of persons as "truly the only interest for the consideration of the State":

> that property will always follow persons; that the highest end of the government
> is the culture of men; and that if men can be educated, the institutions will share
> their improvement and the moral sentiment will write the law of the land.[24]

Emerson's politics, it is clear from these examples, both early in his life and late, is more a social philosophy than, in a strict sense, a political theory.

Two points must never be forgotten if we are to give Emerson his due as a social philosopher and not merely a phenomenon of the emergence of the "celebrity" in nineteenth-century America. The first is that, however advanced the current form of government in any country may seem to be, in the larger view it always represents a cultural lag. "The history of the State sketches in coarse outline the progress of thought, and follows at a distance the delicacy of culture, and of aspiration."[25] Political arrangements, even when claimed by their sponsors as "progressive," are always behindhand. The second point to keep in mind is that Emerson realized that his fellow Americans had to beware of the all-too-human tendency to universalize their conception of the value of the institutional arrangements that satisfy them.

> In this country we are very vain of our political institutions, which are singular
> in this, that they sprung, within the memory of living men, from the character
> and conditions of the people, which they still express with sufficient fidelity—
> and we ostentatiously prefer them to any other in history. They are not better,
> but only fitter for us.[26]

No, Ralph Waldo Emerson was not, in any way, provincial. He spoke to, and for, all the world, not merely to and for the New England heritage that he adorned or the American heritage that his essays carried to cultured circles both in the British Isles and in Continental Europe.

IV

The neo-Platonic conception of the spark of the divine within each human person which lies at the heart of Emerson's method of self-reliance, in the form of the doctrine of the universal applicability and validity of the intuitions of the innermost soul, entered into his social philosophy, or moral theory of politics, by way of the Emersonian idea that each person knows about other persons by what he (she) knows about himself (herself). The person who is, in Emerson's sense, self-reliant is the one who will be the good fellow-citizen. "Every man's nature is a sufficient advertisement to him of the character of his fellows."[27] What is right for one self-reliant person is right for all, and what is wrong for one is wrong for all. What it is proper for one to do, is proper for all, and what is improper for one is improper for all. A true community is made up of self-reliant individuals who, because they have common goals, can often agree on the means to those ends. The State does not constitute a true community because it does not rest on the foundation of such an agreement, but involves some making rules and setting goals for others. "This undertaking for another is the blunder which stands in colossal ugliness in the governments of the world. . . . Therefore all public ends look vague and quixotic beside private ones. For any laws but those which men make for themselves are laughable."[28]

The sharp distinction brought out in this quotation between the area of the "private" and that of the "State," and even of the "public," was one of the characteristic features of Emerson's social philosophy. An area of incalculability supervenes whenever individuality comes into play and wherever it flourishes. The predictability that is the essence of the law bends before the forcefulness of individuals. There is no predictable limit to the influence of persons because they are "organs of moral or supernatural force."

> Under the dominion of an idea which possesses the minds of multitudes, as civil freedom, or the religious sentiment, the powers of persons are no longer subjects of calculation. A nation of men unanimously bent on freedom or conquest can easily confound the arithmetic of statists, and achieve extravagant actions, out of all proportion to their means.[29]

To recognize this force is to have true regard for the capacities of individuals and their powers of self-transcendence.

We must also realize, however, that there is a false sort of individuality that we might call "privatism," though Emerson knew not the word. "Privatism" does not lead to self-transcendence and the negation of statistical probabilities, but rather to egotism. In some instances, "nature has secured individualism by giving the private person a high conceit of his weight in the system." There is no special type of person to whom this pestilential disease of egotism is limited.

> There are dull and bright, sacred and profane, coarse and fine egotists. It is a disease that like influenza falls on all constitutions. In the distemper known to

physicians as *chorea,* the patient sometimes turns round and continues to spin slowly on one spot. Is egotism a metaphysical variety of this malady? The man runs round a ring formed by his own talent, falls into an admiration of it, and loses relation to the world.[30]

It is difficult, indeed, for a person to discover "that there are limits to the interest which his private history has for mankind."[31] Once one has made that discovery, however, one is so much more the human being for having learned the full reach of individuality into universality.

The antidote for this egotistic, false individualism is not, in Emerson's view, politics; it is culture, education. Politics we call on when things have gone wrong. Education is the device by which we can avoid following wrong paths.

> Let us make our education brave and preventive. Politics is an after work, a poor patching. We are always a little late. The evil is done, the law is passed, and we begin the uphill agitation for repeal of that of which we ought to have prevented the enacting. We shall one day learn to supersede politics by education. What we call our root-and-branch reforms, of slavery, war, gambling, intemperance, is only medicating the symptoms. We must begin higher up, namely in Education.[32]

"All mean egotism vanishes"[33] when one becomes, by one's education, a partaker of the ages, a true aristocrat.

To be beyond egotism leads one to be social, but not always sociable, nor does a deep concern for people invariably make one popular. Truth-speaking is essential, and to speak the truth may very well bring down upon the speaker the enmity and the contempt of the people. "Popularity is for dolls. . . . There is none of the social goods that may not be purchased too dear, and mere amiableness must not take rank with high aim and self-subsistency."[34] All power is a sharing of the nature of the world, a being "made of the same stuff of which events are made." Self-reliance is the cultivation of the power that is in each of us to make oneself in the image of events, to run our course "parallel with the laws of nature."[35] To become self-reliant is to become social, not in the shallow sense of being sociable or being in society, but in the far deeper sense of oneself being society. The force of individuality is that each individual must persist in being oneself. But what this means, what one is in being oneself, depends on what one makes of oneself. The transcendental individual makes himself (herself) a medium for the expression of the universal.

Thus it is that Emersonian individualism can appear, even in our day, as an admirable, and a defensible social philosophy. Emersonian individualism is not self-centeredness, despite the apparent turning inward of the principle of self-reliance. It is a way to find within ourselves that which is universal for the sake of the betterment of the social order. Thus I can defend the view that transcendental individualism is the Emersonian road to social altruism.

Notes

1 Wendell Phillips, "The Scholar in a Republic," reprinted in *American Philosophic Addresses, 1700–1900,* (ed.) J. L. Blau (New York: Columbia University Press, 1946), p. 276.

2 "I preach half of every Sunday. When I attended church on the other half of a Sunday, and the image in the pulpit was all of clay, and not of tunable metal, I said to myself that if men would avoid that general language and general manner in which they strive to hide all that is peculiar, and would say only what was uppermost in their own minds, after their own individual manner, every man would be interesting. Everyman is a new creation, can do something best, has some intellectual modes and forms, or a character the general result of all, such as no other agent in the universe has: if he would exhibit that, it must needs be engaging, must be a curious study to every inquisitive mind. But whatever properties a man of narrow intellect feels to be peculiar he studiously hides; he is ashamed or afraid of himself, and all his communications to men are unskilful plagiarisms from the common stock of thought and knowledge, and he is of course flat and tiresome. . . . A portion of truth, bright and sublime, lives in every moment to every man." Quoted in James Elliot Cabot, A *Memoir of Ralph Waldo Emerson,* I (Boston and New York: Houghton Mifflin Co., 1877), pp. 133–134.

3 Entry of 14 July, 1832; as quoted in Cabot, *Memoir,* I, p. 156.

4 Quoted by Stuart P. Sherman in the "Introduction" to his edition of *Essays and Poems of Emerson* (New York: Harcourt, Brace & Co., 1921), p. xx.

5 R. W. Emerson to Henry Ware, Concord, October 8, 1838; text as given in Cabot, *Memoir,* II, p. 693.

6 Ralph Waldo Emerson, *Nature,* (ed.) J. L. Blau (New York: Liberal Arts Press, 1948), p. 4; see also F. DeWolfe Miller, *Christopher Pearse Cranch and his Caricatures . . .* (Cambridge, Mass.: Harvard University Press, 1951), plate 3.

7 Reprinted in J. L. Blau (ed.), *American Philosophic Addresses,* pp. 153–170; the fable on p. 154.

8 *The Complete Works of Ralph Waldo Emerson,* The Concord Edition (Boston and New York: Houghton Mifflin Co., various dates), XI, p. 282. All subsequent references to Emerson's Works will be to this edition, unless otherwise specified, and will be given by Volume and pages.

9 The full text is given in *Works,* Volume IV.

10 *Works,* IV, pp. 25, 31–32.

11 *Works,* IV, pp. 32–33, 35.

12 *Works,* VI, p. 158.

13 *Works,* XI, pp. 278–279.

14 *Works,* XI, p. 280.

15 *Works,* XI, p. 282.

16 *Works,* XI, p. 282.

17 Cabot, *Memoir,* II, pp. 400–401.

18 *Works,* XI, p. 281.

19 *Works,* XI, p. 278.

20 *Works,* III, p. 209.

21 *Works,* XI, pp. 288–289.

22 *Works*, III, p. 192.
23 *Works*, III, pp. 201–202.
24 *Works*, III, p. 204.
25 *Works*, III, p. 201.
26 *Works*, III, p. 207.
27 *Works*, III, p. 213.
28 *Works*, III, pp. 214–215.
29 *Works*, III, pp. 205–206.
30 *Works*, VI, pp. 132–133.
31 *Works*, VI, p. 135.
32 *Works*, VI, pp. 140–141.
33 Emerson, *Nature*, p. 4; or *Works*, I, p. 10.
34 *Works*, VI, pp. 162–163.
35 *Works*, VI, p. 56.

Harold Bloom (1930–)

*A leading literary critic who has taught at Yale since 1955, Bloom has devoted an
appreciable amount of scholarly attention to Emerson's place and significance in
the American literary canon. Though he is perhaps more effusive in his praise of
poet Walt Whitman, Bloom nevertheless articulates his admiration and his sense of
Emerson's achievements in* The Anatomy of Influence *(1973),* A Map of Misreading
(1975), The Western Canon *(1994), and most recently in the career-summarizing
late work* The Anatomy of Influence *(2011) in which he continues to reflect on
"what I have learned to call the American religion, our Native Strain or gnosis, of
which Emerson was the theologian and Whitman and his prodigals the Orphic
seers."[1] In the first essay below, "Emerson and Influence," a chapter from* A Map of
Misreading, *Bloom continues his study of influence, noting in his Introduction:
"Influence, as I conceive it, means that there are* no *texts, but only relationships
between* texts. These relationships depend upon a critical act, a misreading or
misprision, that one poet performs upon another," and since such acts can also
be committed by literary critics, we are in an important way prepared by Bloom
to read his "creative misreading." As a "revisionist," Bloom "strives to* see *again,
so as to* esteem *and* estimate *differently, so as to aim 'correctively.'" The second
piece, "Mr. America," is Bloom's review of John McAleer's biography* Ralph Waldo
Emerson: Days of Encounter *(1984), published in the* New York Review of Books
*(November 22, 1984). Bloom, writing "in this time of Reagan," coalesces a range
of contemporary interests in Emerson by declaring: "I think Emerson remains the
American theoretician of power—be it political, literary, spiritual, economic—
because he took the risk of exalting transition from one activity or state of mind or
kind of spiritual being to another, for its own sake."*

Mr. America

Harold Bloom

1

Emerson is a critic and essayist who based his work on observation of himself and of
American experience. He is not a transcendental philosopher. This obvious truth always
needs restating, perhaps more now than ever, when literary criticism is over-influenced
by contemporary French heirs of the German tradition of idealist or transcendental
philosophy. Emerson is the mind of our climate; he is the principal source of the
American difference in poetry and criticism and in pragmatic postphilosophy.

That is a less obvious truth, and it also needs restating, now and always. Emerson, by no means the greatest American writer, perhaps more an interior orator than a writer, is the inescapable theorist of virtually all subsequent American writing. From his moment to ours, American authors either are in his tradition, or else in a countertradition originating in opposition to him. This continues even in a time when he is not much read, such as the period between 1945 and 1965 or so. During the last twenty years, Emerson has returned, burying his undertakers. "The essays of Emerson," T. S. Eliot remarked, "are already an encumbrance," one of those judicial observations that governed the literary academy during the Age of Eliot, but now have faded into an antique charm.

Other judicial critics, including Yvor Winters and Allen Tate, sensibly blamed Emerson for everything they disliked in American literature, and even to some extent in American life. Our most distinguished living poet, Robert Penn Warren, culminated the counter traditional polemic of Eliot and Tate in his lively sequence, "Homage to Emerson, on Night-Flight to New York." Reading Emerson's essays in the "pressurized gloom" of the airliner, Warren sees the glowing page declare: "There is / No sin. Not even error." Only at a transcendental altitude can Warren's heart be abstract enough to accept the Sage of Concord, "for / At 38,000 feet Emerson / Is dead right." At ground level, Emerson "had forgiven God everything" because "Emerson thought that significance shines through everything."

Sin, error, time, history, a God external to the self, the visiting of the crimes of the fathers upon the sons: these are landmarks in the literary cosmos of Eliot and his Southern followers, and these were precisely of no interest whatsoever to Ralph Waldo Emerson. Of Emerson I am moved to say what Borges said of Oscar Wilde: he was always right. But he himself always says it better:

> That is always best which gives me to myself. The sublime is excited in me by the great stoical doctrine, obey thyself. That which shows God in me, fortifies me. That which shows God out of me, makes me a wart and a wen. There is no longer a necessary reason for my being.[2]

One might say that the Bible, Shakespeare, and Freud show us as caught in a psychic conflict, in which we need to be everything in ourselves while we go on fearing that we are nothing in ourselves. Emerson dismisses the fear, and insists upon the necessity of the single self achieving a total autonomy, of becoming its own cosmos without first having to ingest either nature or other selves. He wishes to give us to ourselves, and these days supposedly he preaches to the converted, since it is the fashion to assert that we live in a culture of narcissism, of which our smiling president is the indubitable epitome. Emerson, in this time of Reagan, should be cited upon the limitations of all American politics whatsoever:

> We might as wisely reprove the east wind, or the frost, as a political party, whose members, for the most part, could give no account of their position, but stand for the defence of those interests in which they find themselves.... A party is perpetually corrupted by personality. Whilst we absolve the association from

dishonesty, we cannot extend the same charity to their leaders. They reap the rewards of the docility and zeal of the masses which they direct. . . . Of the two great parties, which, at this hour, almost share the nation between them, I should say, that, one has the best cause, and the other contains the best men. The philosopher, the poet, or the religious man, will, of course, wish to cast his vote with the democrat, for free trade, for wide suffrage, for the abolition of legal cruelties in the penal code, and for facilitating in every manner the access of the young and the poor to the sources of wealth and power. But he can rarely accept the persons whom the so-called popular party propose to him as representatives of these liberalities.[3]

Emerson here is writing about the Democrats and the Whigs (precursors of our modern Republicans) in the early 1840s, when he still believes that Daniel Webster (foremost of "the best men") will never come to advocate the worst cause of the slaveholders. Though his politics have been categorized as "transcendental anarchism," Emerson was at once a believer in pure power and a prophet of the moral law, an apparent self-contradiction that provoked Yvor Winters in an earlier time, and President Giamatti of Yale more recently. Yet this wise inconsistency led Emerson to welcome Whitman in poetry for the same reasons he had hailed Daniel Webster in politics, until Webster's Seventh of March speech supporting the compromise of 1850, with its acceptance of the Fugitive Slave Law. Webster's speech moved Emerson to the most violent rhetoric of his life. John Jay Chapman, in a great essay on Emerson, remarked that, in his polemic against Webster, Emerson "is savage, destructive, personal, bent on death."[4] Certainly no other American politician has been so memorably denounced in public as Webster by Emerson:

> Mr. Webster, perhaps, is only following the laws of his blood and constitution. I suppose his pledges were not quite natural to him. He is a man who lives by his memory; a man of the past, not a man of faith and of hope. All the drops of his blood have eyes that look downward, and his finely developed understanding only works truly and with all its force when it stands for animal good; that is, for property.[5]

All the drops of his blood have eyes that look downward: that bitter figuration has outlived every phrase Webster himself ventured. Many modern historians defend Webster for his part in the compromise of 1850, by which California was admitted as a free state while the North pledged to honor the Fugitive Slave Law. This defense maintains that Webster helped to preserve the Union for another decade, while strengthening the ideology of Union that culminated in Lincoln. But Emerson, who had given Webster every chance, was driven out of his study and into moral prophecy by Webster's support of the Fugitive Slave Law:

> We are glad at last to get a clear case, one on which no shadow of doubt can hang. This is not meddling with other people's affairs: this is hindering other people from meddling with us. This is not going crusading into Virginia and Georgia after slaves, who it is alleged, are very comfortable where they are:—that

amiable argument falls to the ground: but this is befriending in our own State, on our own farms, a man who has taken the risk of being shot or burned alive, or cast into the sea, or starved to death, or suffocated in a wooden box, to get away from his driver: and this man who has run the gauntlet of a thousand miles for his freedom, the statute says, you men of Massachusetts shall hunt, and catch, and send back again to the dog-hutch he fled from. And this filthy enactment was made in the nineteenth century, by people who could read and write. I will not obey it, by God.[6]

As late as 1843, Emerson's love of Webster as incarnate Power had prevailed: "He is no saint, but the wild olive wood, ungrafted yet by grace." After Webster's defense of the Fugitive Slave Law, even Emerson's decorum was abandoned: "The word *liberty* in the mouth of Mr. Webster sounds like the word *love* in the mouth of a courtezan."

I suspect that Emerson's deep fury, so uncharacteristic of him, resulted partly from the violation of his own cheerfully amoral dialectics of power. The extraordinary essay "Power" in *The Conduct of Life* appears at first to worship mere force or drive as such, but the Emersonian cunning always locates power in the place of crossing over, in the moment of transition:

> In history, the great moment is, when the savage is just ceasing to be a savage, with all his hairy Pelasgic strength directed on his opening sense of beauty:— and you have Pericles and Phidias,—not yet passed over into the Corinthian civility. Everything good in nature and the world is in that moment of transition, when the swarthy juices still flow plentifully from nature, but their astringency or acridity is got out by ethics and humanity.[7]

A decade or so before, in perhaps his central essay, "Self-Reliance," Emerson had formulated the same dialectic of power, but with even more exuberance:

> Life only avails, not the having lived. Power ceases in the instant of repose; it resides in the moment of transition from a past to a new state, in the shooting of a gulf, in the darting to an aim. This one fact the world hates, that the soul *becomes*; for that for ever degrades the past, turns all riches to poverty, all reputation to a shame, confounds the saint with the rogue, shoves Jesus and Judas equally aside. Why, then, do we prate of self-reliance? Inasmuch as the soul is present, there will be power not confident but agent. To talk of reliance is a poor external way of speaking. Speak rather of that which relies, because it works and is.[8]

Magnificent, but surely even the Webster of 1850 retained his Pelasgic strength, surely even *that* Webster works and is. Emerson's cool answer would have been that Webster had failed the crossing. I think Emerson remains *the* American theoretician of power—be it political, literary, spiritual, economic—because he took the risk of exalting transition from one activity or state of mind or kind of spiritual being to another, for its own sake. American restlessness, which has been pervasive ever since, puts all stable relationships or occupations at a relatively lower estimate, because they lack the element of risk. Admittedly, I am happier when the consequence of exalting transition is Whitman's "Crossing Brooklyn Ferry" than when the Emersonian product is the first Henry Ford, but Emerson was canny enough to have prophesied both disciples. There is a great chill at the center of his cosmos, which remains ours, both the chill and the cosmos:

> But Nature is no sentimentalist,—does not cosset or pamper us. We must see that the world is rough and surly, and will not mind drowning a man or a woman; but swallows your ship like a grain of dust. The cold, inconsiderate of persons, tingles your blood, benumbs your feet, freezes a man like an apple.[9]

This is from the sublime essay, "Fate," which leads off *The Conduct of Life*, and culminates in the outrageous question: "Why should we fear to be crushed by savage elements, we who are made up of the same elements?" Elsewhere in "Fate," Emerson observes: "The way of Providence is a little rude," while in "Power" he restates the law of Compensation as: "nothing is got for nothing." Emerson too is no sentimentalist, and it is something of a puzzle how he ever got to be regarded as anything other than a rather frightening theoretician of life or of letters. But then, his personality also remains a puzzle. He was to his contemporaries the true prophet of an American kind of charisma, and founded the actual American religion, which is Protestant without being Christian. Was the man one with the essayist, or was only the wisdom uncanny in our pervasive and inescapable sage?

2

A biography of Emerson is necessarily somewhat redundant, because Emerson, like Montaigne, is almost always his own subject, though hardly in Montaigne's mode. Emerson would not have said: "I am myself the matter of my book," yet Emerson on "History" is more Emerson than history. Though he is almost never overtly autobiographical, his best lesson nevertheless is that all true subjectivity is a high but difficult achievement, while supposed objectivity is merely the failure of having become an amalgam of other selves and their opinions. Though he is in the oral tradition, his true genre was no more the lecture than it had been the sermon when he was at the Second Church in Boston, and certainly not the essay, though that is his only formal achievement, besides a double handful of strong poems.

His journals are his authentic work, and seem to me poorly represented by all available selections. Perhaps the journals simply ought not to be condensed, because Emerson's reader needs to be immersed in their flow and ebb, their own recording of the experience of the influx of insight followed by the perpetual falling back into skepticism. They move continually between a possible ecstasy and a probable shrewdness, while seeming always aware that neither demonic intensity nor worldly irony by itself can constitute wisdom.

Emerson's first twenty-seven years demonstrate a continuous striving to overcome his American Protestant heritage, without, however, wholly repudiating it. In the autumn of 1830, when he was twenty-seven and still practicing as a minister, we find the first journal entry on Self-Reliance, in which he refuses to be "a secondary man" imitating any other being. A year later (October 27, 1831) we hear the birth of Emerson's *reader's Sublime*, the notion that what moves us in the eloquence, written or oral, of another must be what is oldest in oneself. That is to say, we were not made by God, but like God himself we are part of the original Abyss:

> Were you ever instructed by a wise and eloquent man? Remember then, were not the words that made your blood run cold, that brought the blood to your cheeks, that made you tremble or delighted you,—did they not sound to you as old as yourself? Was it not truth that you knew before, or do you ever expect to be moved from the pulpit or from man by anything but plain truth. Never. It is God in you that responds to God without, or affirms his own words trembling on the lips of another.[10]

On October 28, 1832, Emerson's resignation as Unitarian minister was accepted (very reluctantly) by the Second Church, Boston. The supposed issue was the proper way of celebrating the Lord's Supper, but the underlying issue, at least for Emerson himself, was celebrating the self as God. Stephen Whicher in his superb *Emerson: An Organic Anthology* (still the best one-volume selection of Emerson) gathered together the relevant notebook texts of October 1832. We find Emerson, sustained by daemonic influx, asserting: "It is light. You don't get a candle to see the sun rise," where clearly Jesus is the candle and Emerson is the sunrise (prophetic, like so much else in early Emerson, of Nietzsche's *Zarathustra*). The most outrageous instance of an inrush of God in Emerson is the notorious and still much derided "transparent eye-ball" passage in *Nature* (1836), which is based upon a journal entry of March 19, 1835. But I give the final text, from *Nature*:

> Crossing a bare common, in snow puddles, at twilight, under a clouded sky, without having in my thoughts any occurrence of special good fortune, I have enjoyed a perfect exhilaration. I am glad to the brink of fear. . . . There I feel that nothing can befall me in life,—no disgrace, no calamity, (leaving me my eyes,) which nature cannot repair. Standing on the bare ground—my head bathed by the blithe air, and uplifted into infinite space,—all mean egotism vanishes. I become a transparent eye-ball; I am nothing; I see all; the currents of the Universal Being circulate through me; I am part or particle of God.[11]

Nature, in this passage as in the title of the little book, *Nature*, is rather perversely the wrong word, since Emerson does not mean "nature" in any accepted sense whatsoever. He means Man, and not a natural man or fallen Adam, but original Man or unfallen Adam, which is to say America, in the transcendental sense, just as Blake's Albion is the unfallen form of Man. Emerson's primal Man, to whom Emerson is joined in this epiphany, is all eye, seeing earliest, precisely as though no European, and no ancient Greek or Hebrew, had seen before him. There is a personal pathos as well, which Emerson's contemporary readers could not have known. Emerson feared blindness more than death, although his family was tubercular, and frequently died young. But there had been an episode of hysterical blindness during his college years, and its memory, however repressed, hovers throughout his work. Freud's difficult "frontier concept" of the bodily ego, which is formed partly by introjective fantasies, suggests that thinking can be associated with any of the senses or areas of the body. Emerson's fantastic introjection of the transparent eyeball as the bodily ego seems to make thinking and seeing the same activity, one that culminates in self-deification.

Emerson's power as a kind of interior orator stems from this self-deification. "Nothing is got for nothing," and perhaps the largest pragmatic consequence of being "part or particle of God" is that your need for other people necessarily is somewhat diminished. The transparent eyeball passage itself goes on to manifest an estrangement from the immediacy of other selves:

> The name of the nearest friend sounds then foreign and accidental: to be brothers, to be acquaintances, master or servant, is then a trifle and a disturbance.[12]

This passage must have hurt Emerson himself, hardly a person for whom "to be brothers" ever was "a trifle and a disturbance." The early death of his brother Charles, just four months before *Nature* was published in 1836, was one of his three terrible losses, the others being the death of Ellen Tucker, his first wife, in 1831, after little more than a year of marriage, and the death of his first born child, Waldo, in January 1842, when the boy was only five years old. Emerson psychically was preternaturally strong, but it is difficult to interpret the famous passage in his great essay, "Experience," where he writes of Waldo's death:

> An innavigable sea washes with silent waves between us and the things we aim at and converse with. Grief too will make us idealists. In the death of my son, now more than two years ago, I seem to have lost a beautiful estate,—no more. I cannot get it nearer to me. If tomorrow I should be informed of the bankruptcy of my principal debtors, the loss of my property would be a great inconvenience to me, perhaps, for many years; but it would leave me as it found me,—neither better nor worse. So it is with this calamity: it does not touch me: something which I fancied was a part of me, which could not be torn away without tearing me, nor enlarged without enriching me, falls off from me, and leaves no scar.[13]

Perhaps Emerson should have written an essay entitled "The Economic Problem of Grief," but perhaps most of his essays carry that as a hidden subtitle. The enigma of grief in Emerson, after all, may be the secret cause of his strength, of his refusal to mourn for the past. Self-reliance, the American religion he founded, converts solitude into a firm stance against history, including personal history. There is no history, only biography—this Emerson insists upon, but not in the sense that biography is a mere history of a life—and this may be why a particular biography of Emerson appears to be impossible. John McAleer's new biography sets out shrewdly to evade the Emersonian entrapment, which is that Emerson recognizes only biography, and acknowledges Emerson's own idea of biography as a record of the inner life or what one has done with one's solitude.

Such worthy practitioners of the mode as Ralph Rusk and Gay Wilson Allen worked mightily to shape the facts into a life, but were evaded by Emerson.[14] Where someone lives so formidably *from within*, he cannot be caught by chroniclers of events, public and private. McAleer instead molds his facts as a series of encounters between Emerson and all his friends and associates. Unfortunately, Emerson's encounters with others—whether his brothers, wives, children, or Transcendental and other literary colleagues—are little more revelatory of his inner life than are his encounters with events, whether it be the death of Waldo or the Civil War. All McAleer's patience, skill, and learning cannot overcome the sage's genius for solitude. A biography of Emerson becomes as baffling as a biography of Nietzsche, though the two lives have nothing in common, except of course for ideas. Nietzsche acknowledged Emerson, with affection and enthusiasm, but he probably did not realize how fully Emerson had anticipated him, particularly in unsettling the status of the self while proclaiming simultaneously a great Overself to come.

3

The critic of Emerson is little better off than the biographer, since Emerson, again like Nietzsche and remarkably also akin to Freud, anticipates his critics and does their work for them. Emerson resembles his own hero, Montaigne, in that you cannot combat him without being contaminated by him. T. S. Eliot, ruefully contemplating Pascal's hopeless contest with Montaigne, observed that fighting Montaigne was like throwing a hand grenade into a fog. Emerson, because he appropriated the position of America's spokesman, is more a climate even than an atmosphere, however misty. Attempting to write the order of the variable winds in the Emersonian climate is a hopeless task, and the best critics of Emerson, from John Jay Chapman and O. W. Firkins through Stephen Whicher to Barbara Packer and Richard Poirier, wisely decline to list his ideas of order. You track him best, as a writer and as a person, by learning the principle proclaimed everywhere in him: that which you can get from another is never instruction, but always provocation.

But what is provocation, in the life of the spirit? Emerson insisted that he called you forth only to your self, and not to any cause whatsoever. The will to power, in Emerson as afterward in Nietzsche, is reactive rather than active, receptive rather than rapacious, which is to say that it is a will to interpretation. Emerson teaches us how to interpret, according to the principle that there is no method except yourself. This is counter to any of the European modes fashionable either in his day or in our own, modes currently touching their nadir in a younger rabblement celebrating itself as having repudiated the very idea of an individual reader or an individual critic. Group criticism, like group sex, is not a new idea, but seems to revive whenever a sense of resentment dominates the aspiring clerisy. With resentment comes guilt, as though social oppressions are caused by how we read, and so we get those academic covens akin to what Emerson himself, in his 1838 journal, called "philanthropic meetings and holy hurrahs," for which read now "Marxist literary groups" and "Lacanian theory circles":

> As far as I notice what passes in philanthropic meetings and holy hurrahs there is very little depth of interest. The speakers warm each other's skin and lubricate each other's tongue, and the words flow and the superlatives thicken and the lips quiver and the eyes moisten, and an observer new to such scenes would say, Here was true fire; the assembly were all ready to be martyred, and the effect of such a spirit on the community would be irresistible; but they separate and go to the shop, to a dance, to bed, and an hour afterward they care so little for the matter that on slightest temptation each one would disclaim the meeting.[15]

My polemical aside, Emersonian in its spirit, is inspired by a sense of how Emerson would respond to the current flight from individuality in literary critical circles.

Emerson, according to President Giamatti of Yale, "was as sweet as barbed wire," a judgment recently achieved independently by John Updike.[16] Yes, and doubtless Emerson gave our politics its particular view of power as freed from all moral limitations, as Giamatti laments, but a country deserves its sages, and we deserve Emerson. He has the peculiar dialectical gift of being precursor for both the perpetual New Left of student nonstudents and the perpetual New Right of preacher nonpreachers. The American religion of self-reliance is a superb *literary* religion, but its political, economic, and social consequences, whether manifested left or right, have now helped to place us in a country where literary satire of politics is impossible, since the real thing is far more outrageous than even a satirist of genius could invent. Nathanael West presumably was parodying Calvin Coolidge in *A Cool Million*'s Shagpoke Whipple, but is this Shagpoke Whipple or President Reagan speaking?

> America is the land of opportunity. She takes care of the honest and industrious and never fails them as long as they are both. This is not a matter of opinion, it is one of faith. On the day that Americans stop believing it, on that day will America be lost.

Emerson unfortunately believed in Necessity, including "the offence of superiority in persons," and he was capable of writing passages that can help to justify Reagan's large share of the Yuppie vote, as here in "Self-Reliance":

> Then, again, do not tell me, as a good man did to-day, of my obligation to put all poor men in good situations. Are they *my* poor? I tell thee, thou foolish philanthropist, that I grudge the dollar, the dime, the cent, I give to such men as do not belong to me and to whom I do not belong. There is a class of persons to whom by all spiritual affinity I am bought and sold; for them I will go to prison, if need be; but your miscellaneous popular charities; the education at college

of fools; the building of meeting-houses to the vain end to which many now stand; alms to sots; and the thousandfold Relief Societies;—though I confess with shame I sometimes succumb and give the dollar, it is a wicked dollar, which by and by I shall have the manhood to withhold.[17]

True, Emerson meant by his "class of persons" such as his friend Henry Thoreau, his dissenting disciple, the mad poet Jones Very, and his precursor, the Reverend William Ellery Channing, which is not exactly Shagpoke Whipple, Ronald Reagan, and the Reverend Jerry Falwell. Self-Reliance translated out of the inner life and into the marketplace is difficult to distinguish from our current religion of selfishness, as set forth so sublimely in the recent grand Epiphany at Dallas. Shrewd Yankee that he was, Emerson would have shrugged off his various and dubious paternities. His spiritual elitism could only be misunderstood, but he did not much care about being misread or misused. Though he has been so oddly called "the philosopher of democracy" by so many who wished to claim him for the left, the political Emerson remains best expressed in one famous and remarkable sentence by John Jay Chapman: "If a soul be taken and crushed by democracy till it utter a cry, that cry will be Emerson."[18]

4

I return with some relief to Emerson as literary prophet, where the new McAleer biography enriches our store of anecdote, and where Emerson's effect upon all of us, *pace* Yvor Winters, seems to me again dialectical but in the end inevitable. Emerson's influence, from his day until ours, has helped to account for what I would call the American difference in literature, not only in our poetry and criticism, but even in our novels and stories, ironic since Emerson was at best uneasy about novels. This difference from European antecedents emphasizes always the repressions and recalcitrances within the self that prevent us from emerging into the courage of full expression of our own uniqueness, cultural and personal.

What is truly surprising about this influence are its depth, extent, and persistence, despite many concealments and even more evasions. Emerson does a lot more to explain most American writers than any of our writers, even Whitman or Thoreau or Dickinson or Hawthorne or Melville, serve to explain *him*. He exposes the submerged premises that inform the work of writers doubtless of more aesthetic stature than he himself achieved. The important question to ask is not "how?" but "why?" Scholarship keeps showing that "how" by demonstrating the details of Emerson's continued effect upon those who come after (though there is a great deal more to be shown). But it ought to be a function of criticism to get at that scarcely explored "why."

Emerson was controversial in his own earlier years, and then became all but universally accepted (except, of course, in the South) during his later years. This ascendancy faded during the Age of Literary Modernism (circa 1915–1945) and virtually vanished, as I remarked earlier, in the heyday of academic New Criticism or Age of Eliot (circa 1945–1965). Despite the humanistic protests of President Giamatti, and the churchwardenly mewings of John Updike, the last two decades have witnessed an Emerson revival, and I prophesy that he, rather than Marx or Heidegger, will be the guiding spirit of our imaginative literature and our criticism for some time to come. In that prophecy, "Emerson" stands for not only the theoretical position and wisdom of the historical Ralph Waldo, but for the parallels with Nietzsche, Walter Pater, and Oscar Wilde, and much of Freud as well, since Emerson's elitist vision of the higher individual is so consonant with theirs.

Like Nietzsche, Pater, Wilde, and the later Freud, Emerson is more than prepared to give up on the great masses that constitute humankind. His hope, and theirs, is that a small community of the spirit can come into existence, whether organized or not, and can continue to maintain a rational understanding of the endlessly painful interplay between culture and its inherent sorrows.

Individualism, whatever damages its American ruggedness continues to inflict on our politics and social economy, is more than ever the only hope for our imaginative lives. Emerson, who knew that the only literary and critical method was the externalization of the self, is again a necessary resource in a time beginning to weary of Gallic scientism in what are still called the humanities.

Lewis Mumford, in *The Golden Day* (1926), still is the best guide to why Emerson was and is the central influence upon American letters: "With most of the resources of the past at his command, Emerson achieved nakedness." Wisely seeing that Emerson was a Darwinian before Darwin, a Freudian before Freud, because he possessed "a complete vision" of the human potential, negative and positive, Mumford was able to make the classic formulation of Emerson's strength: "The past for Emerson was neither a prescription nor a burden: it was rather an aesthetic experience."[19] As a poem already written, the past was not a force for Emerson; it had lost power, because power for him resided only at the crossing, at the actual moment of transition.

The dangers of this repression of the past's force are evident enough, in American life as in its literature. In our political economy, we get the force of secondary repetition, Reagan as Coolidge out-Shagpoking Nathanael West's Whipple. We receive also the rhythm of ebb and flow that makes all our greater writers into crisis poets. Each of them echoes, however involuntarily, Emerson's formula for discontinuity in his weird, irrealistic essay, "Circles":

Our moods do not believe in each other. Today I am full of thoughts and can write what I please. I see no reason why I should not have the same thought, the same power of expression, tomorrow. What I write, whilst I write it, seems the most natural thing in the world; but yesterday I saw a dreary vacuity in this direction in which now I see so much; and a month hence, I doubt not, I shall wonder who he was that wrote so many continuous pages. Alas for this infirm faith, this will not strenuous, this vast ebb of a vast flow! I am God in nature; I am a weed by the wall.[20]

From God to weed and then back again; it is the cycle of Whitman from "Song of Myself" to "As I Ebb'd with the Ocean of Life," and of Emerson's and Whitman's descendants ever since. Place everything upon the nakedness of the American self, and you open every imaginative possibility from self-deification to absolute nihilism. But Emerson knew this, and saw no alternative for us, if we were to avoid the predicament of arriving too late in the cultural history of the West. Nothing is got for nothing—as he phrased it in his ironic New England law of Compensation; Emerson is not less correct now than he was a hundred and fifty years ago. On November 21, 1834, he wrote in his journal: "When we have lost our God of tradition and ceased from our God of rhetoric then may God fire the heart with his presence."[21] Our God of tradition, then and now, is as dead as Emerson and Nietzsche declared him to be. He belongs, in life, to the political clerics and the clerical politicians and, in letters, to the secondary men and women. Our God of rhetoric belongs to the academies, where he is called by the name of the Gallic Demiurge, Language. That leaves the American imagination free as always to open itself to the third God of Emerson's prayer, the god in the self.

Notes

1 Harold Bloom, *The Anatomy of Influence: Literature as a Way of Life* (New Haven: Yale University Press, 2011), 308.
2 "The Divinity School Address," in *Emerson: Essays and Lectures* (Library of America, 1983), p. 81.
3 "Politics," in *Emerson* (Library of America), p. 564.
4 *The Selected Writings of John Jay Chapman*, edited by Jacques Barzun (Anchor, 1959), p. 193.
5 Quoted by Chapman in *Selected Writings*, p. 193.
6 From the journal, Spring 1851. Included in *Emerson: An Organic Anthology*, edited by Stephen Whicher (Houghton Mifflin, 1957), p. 355.
7 "Power," in *Emerson* (Library of America), p. 980.
8 "Self-Reliance," in *Emerson* (Library of America), pp. 271–272.
9 "Fate," in Emerson (Library of America), p. 945. Subsequent passages are on p. 967 and p. 971.
10 *Emerson: An Organic Anthology*, p. 9.
11 *Emerson* (Library of America), p. 10.
12 *Emerson* (Library of America), p. 10.
13 *Emerson* (Library of America), p. 473.
14 Ralph Rusk, *The Life of Ralph Waldo Emerson* (Scribner's, 1949); Gay Wilson Allen, *Waldo Emerson* (Viking, 1981).
15 *Emerson: An Organic Anthology*, p. 87.
16 A. Bartlett Giamatti, *The University and the Public Interest* (Atheneum, 1981), p. 174. For Updike, see *The New Yorker*, June 4, 1984.
17 *Emerson: An Organic Anthology*, p. 150.
18 Chapman, *Selected Writings*, p 223.
19 Lewis Mumford, "The Morning Star," reprinted in *The Recognition of Ralph Waldo Emerson*, edited by Milton R. Konvitz (University of Michigan Press, 1972), p. 180. The previous quotation from Mumford is on p. 176.
20 *Emerson: An Organic Anthology*, p. 171.
21 *Emerson in His Journals*, ed. Joel Porte (Harvard University Press, 1982), p. 129.

Emerson and Influence

Harold Bloom

Wallace Stevens, closing the second part, *It Must Change*, of *Notes toward a Supreme Fiction*, proclaimed the "will to change, a necessitous / And present way, a presentation," that brings about "the freshness of transformation." But though this transformation "is ourselves," the Seer of Hartford was too wily not to add a customary qualification:

> And that necessity and that presentation
>
> Are rubbings of a glass in which we peer.
> Of these beginnings, gay and green, propose
> The suitable amours. Time will write them down.

Stevens died in 1955, and many suitable amours concerning various beginnings have been proposed since then. Pound, Eliot, Williams, Moore are gone, among other major figures; and Crane and Roethke were ended prematurely in a subsequent generation. Jarrell and Berryman, whose achievements were more equivocal, have taken on some of the curious lustre that attends the circumstances of such deaths. Contemporary American poetry is a more than usually elaborate panorama, replete with schools and programmes, with followers enough for all, and readers available for only a few. Even the best of our contemporary poets, whether of any grouping or of none, suffer a burden wholly appropriate to the valley of vision they hope to have chosen, a burden more important finally than the immediate sorrows of poetic over-population and the erosion of a literate audience. Peering into the glass of vision, contemporary poets confront their too-recent giant precursors staring back at them, inducing a profound anxiety that hides itself, but cannot be evaded totally. The partial evasions of this anxiety can be identified simply as the styles and strategies of contemporary verse, despite the overt manifestos to the contrary at which current poets seem more than usually adept. The anxiety of influence, a melancholy at a failure in imaginative priority, still rages like the dog-star in recent poetry, with the results that Pope observed. Poetically, call ours the Age of Sirius, the actual cultural equivalent of the fictive counter-cultural Age of Aquarius:

> The dog-star rages! nay 'tis past a doubt,
> All Bedlam, or Parnassus, is let out:
> Fire in each eye, and papers in each hand,
> They rave, recite, and madden round the land.

I write these pages after passing an educational hour watching an array of revolutionary bards, black and white, chanting on television. Their exhilarating apparent freedom from the anxiety of influence does not render even the most inchoate rhapsodes free of so necessitous a malady. Mixed into the tide of rhetoric came the recognizable detritus of the precursors, ranging from the American Sublime of Whitman to the sublime bathos of the Imamu Baraka, yet containing some surprises—of Edna Millay shining clear in a black poetess, or of Edgar Guest in a revolutionary balladeer, or of Ogden Nash in a particularly ebullient open-former.

If we move to the other extreme of contemporary achievement, say Ashbery's *Fragment* or Ammons' *Saliences*, then we confront, as readers, far more intense cases of the anxiety of influence, for Ashbery and Ammons, and a few others in their generation, have matured into strong poets. Their best work, like Robert Penn Warren's or Roethke's or Elizabeth Bishop's, begins to demand the same immense effort of the whole being to absorb and resist as is required by the strongest American poets born in the last three decades of the nineteenth century: Robinson, Frost, Stevens, Pound, Moore, Williams, Eliot, Aiken, Ransom, Jeffers, Cummings, Crane. Perhaps no single reader greatly admires all of these dozen—I do not—though the work seems to abide, admired or not. Pound and Williams primarily, Stevens more recently, Frost and Eliot now rather less so, have been the principal influences upon American poets born in the twentieth century, yet all of these twelve poets have descendants, and all of them induce massive anxieties of influence, though the Pound-Williams schools (there are clearly several) emulate their precursors by a remarkable (and damaging) overt refusal to recognize such anxieties. But poets, for three hundred years now, at least, have joined in denying these anxieties even as they more and more strongly manifest them in their poems.

The war of American poets against influence is part of our Emersonian heritage, manifested first in the great triad of "The Divinity School Address," "The American Scholar," and "Self-Reliance." This heritage can be traced in Thoreau, Whitman, Dickinson, and quite directly again in Robinson and Frost, in the architectural writings of Sullivan and Wright, in the *Essays Before a Sonata* of Charles Ives. The less direct heritage is more relevant to any brooding on the negative aspects of poetic influence, centering partly on Pound and Williams (where it is refracted through Whitman) and partly on Stevens, who disliked the very idea of influence.

This distaste is a proper characteristic of all Modern (meaning post-Enlightenment or Romantic) poets, but peculiarly so of American poets coming after our prophet (however now unhonored) Emerson. I like Charles Ives' remark upon Emerson's ambitions: "His essay on the pre-soul (which he did not write) treats of that part of the over-soul's influence on unborn ages, and attempts the impossible only when it stops attempting it." Call Emerson the over-soul, and then contemplate his influence upon American poets who had read him (like Jeffers) and those who had not, but who read him in his poetic descendants (like Crane, who read his Emerson in Whitman). It can be called the only poetic influence that counsels against itself, and against the idea of influence. Perhaps in consequence, it has been the most pervasive of American poetic influences, though partly unrecognized. In nineteenth-century America, it operated as much by negation (Poe, Melville, Hawthorne), as by discipleship (Thoreau, Very, Whitman) or by a dialectical blend of the two relations (Dickinson, Tuckerman, the Jameses).

In a Journal entry (21 July 1837) Emerson recorded an insight that made possible his three anti-influence oration-essays of 1837–1840:

> Courage consists in the conviction that they with whom you contend are no more than you. If we believed in the existence of strict *individuals*, natures, that is, not radically identical but unknown [,] immeasurable, we should never dare to fight.[1]

This striking use of "individuals" manifests Emerson's acute apprehension of the sorrows of poetic influence, even as he declines to share these sorrows. If the new poet succumbs to a vision of the precursor as the Sublime, "unknown, immeasurable," then the great contention with the dead father will be lost. We can remember such ambivalent titans of intra-textuality as the quasi-nature deity, Wordsworth, of the later nineteenth century, and in our time that Gnostic divinity, Yeats, and our own current daemon of the American Sublime, Stevens. Emerson, shrewdest of all visionaries, early perceived the accurate enemy in the path of aspiring youth: "Genius is always sufficiently the enemy of genius by over-influence."

Though we rightly blame Emerson for our capitalistic reactionaries as well as for our shamanistic revolutionaries, for the whole range that goes from Henry Ford to the Whole Earth Catalog, his own meditations forestall our observations. His broodings against influence, starting in 1837, took their origins in the great business Depression of that year. Confronting individualism in its terrible freedom, Emerson developed a characteristic antithetical notion of the individual: "Every man is an infinitely repellent orb, and holds his individual being on that condition." Most remarkably, the journal-meditations move to a great self-recognition on May 26, 1837:

> Who shall define to me an Individual? I behold with awe & delight many illustrations of the One Universal Mind. I see my being imbedded in it. As a plant in the earth so I grow in God. I am only a form of him. He is the soul of Me. I can even with a mountainous aspiring say, *I am God*, by transferring my *Me* out of the flimsy & unclean precinct of my body, my fortunes, my private will.... Yet why not always so? How came the Individual thus armed and impassioned to parricide thus murderously inclined ever to traverse & kill the divine life? Ah wicked Manichee! Into that dim problem I cannot enter. A believer in Unity, a seer of Unity, I yet behold two....[2]

The enormous split here is central in Emerson, pervades his conflicting ideas of influence, and is as relevant to contemporary poets as it was to Whitman, Robinson, Stevens, Crane, Roethke. Turning off the television set, I open the Sunday book supplement of the newspaper to behold a letter from Joyce Carol Oates, novelist, poet, critic, that replies to a reviewer:

> It is a fallacy of our time, hopefully coming to an end, that "individuals" are competitive and what one does lessens possibilities for another.... I believe that

some day . . . all this wasteful worrying about who owns what, who "owns" a portion of art, will be finished. . . . In America, we need to get back to Whitman as our spiritual father, to write novels of the kind that might have grown out of "Leaves of Grass." Whitman understood that human beings are not really in competition, excluded from one another. He knew that the role of the poet is to "transfigure" and "clarify"—and, in that way, sanctify. . . .

This moving passage, by an ambitious ephebe of Dreiser, indeed is in Whitman's tradition, and so also in Emerson's. The over-idealization of literature here is normal and necessary for *the writer in a writer*, a self constrained to deny its own selfhood. So Blake grandly noted, after reading Wordsworth, that: "This is all in the highest degree Imaginative and equal to any Poet but not Superior. I cannot think that Real Poets have any competition. None are greatest in the Kingdom of Heaven it is so in Poetry." Critics, who are people in search of images for *acts of reading*, and not of writing, have a different burden, and ought to cease emulating poets in the over-idealization of poetry.

Blake would have insisted that only the Spectre of Urthona, and not the "Real Man the Imagination" in him, experienced anxiety in reading Wordsworth, or in reading their common father, Milton. Blakean critics, like Frye, too easily join Blake in this insistence. Is this the critic's proper work, to take up the poet's stance? Perhaps there *is* a power or faculty of the Imagination, and certainly all poets *must* go on believing in its existence, yet a critic makes a better start by agreeing with Hobbes that imagination is "decaying sense" and that poetry is written by the same natural man or woman who suffers daily all the inescapable anxieties of competition. This is to say that the imagination refers not to a world of things, but rather that the consciousness of a competing poet is itself a text.

Emerson set out to excel "in Divinity," by which he meant, from the start, "eloquence," to the lasting scandal of certain American moralists from Andrews Norton to Yvor Winters, for Emerson was very much in the Oral Tradition, unlike his nearest contemporary equivalent, Nietzsche. Emerson tells his notebook, on April 18, 1824, a month before his twenty-first birthday: "I cannot dissemble that my abilities are below my ambition. . . ." But he cheerfully adds: "What we ardently love we learn to imitate" and so he hopes "to put on eloquence as a robe."[3] Certainly he did, and he learned therefore the first meaning of his idea of Self-Reliance: "Every man has his own voice, manner, eloquence. . . ." He goes on to speak of each person's "sort of love and grief and imagination and action," but these are afterthoughts. The American orator-poet requires singularity in "voice, manner, eloquence," and if he has that, he trusts he has all, or almost all.

The primary Emerson is this confident orator, who as late as 1839 can still say, in his journals, that: "It is the necessity of my nature to shed all influences." Mixed into this primary strain is a yearning *to be influenced*, but only by a Central Man who is yet to come. In 1845, a year before his Bacchic intensity-of-reaction against the Mexican War, Emerson characteristically began those expectations of a new man-god that emerged more fully in 1846. In the 1845 Journals, the tone might be called the apocalyptic wistful:

> We are candidates, we know we are, for influences more subtle and more high than those of talent and ambition. We want a leader, we want a friend whom we have not seen. In the company and fired by the example of a god, these faculties that dream and toss in their sleep would wake. Where is the Genius that shall marshal us the way that we were going? There is a vast residue, an open account ever.
>
> The great inspire us: how they beckon, how they animate, and show their legitimate power in nothing more than their power to misguide us. For the perverted great derange and deject us, and perplex ages with their fame.... This is that which the strong genius works upon; the region of destiny, of aspiration, of the unknown....

We might follow Nietzsche, Emerson's admirer, and note that as Apollo apparently represents each new poet's individuation, so Dionysus ought to be emblematic of each poet's return to his subsuming precursors. Some such realization informed Emerson's dilemma, for he believed that poetry came only from Dionysian influx, yet he preached an Apollonian Self-Reliance while fearing the very individuation it would bring. "If only he *sees*, the world will be visible enough," is one Emersonian formula carrying this individuation to the borders of a sublime solipsism. Here, expounding nature's supposed method, is a greater formula:

> His health and greatness consist in his being the channel through which heaven flows to earth, in short, in the fulness in which an ecstatical state takes place in him. It is pitiful to be an artist, when by forbearing to be artists we might be vessels filled with the divine overflowings, enriched by the circulations of omniscience and omnipresence. Are there not moments in the history of heaven when the human race was not counted by individuals, but was only the Influenced, was God in distribution, God rushing into multiform benefit? It is sublime to receive, sublime to love, but this lust of imparting as from *us,* this desire to be loved, the wish to be recognized as individuals,—is finite, comes of a lower strain.

Emerson's beautiful confusion *is* beautiful because the conflict is emotional, between equal impulses, and because it cannot be resolved. Influx would make us Bacchic, but *not* individuated poets; Self-Reliance will help make us poets, but "of a lower strain," short of ecstatic possession. Emerson's relative failure as a writer of verse ("failure" only when measured against his enormous basic aspirations) is caused by this conflict, and so is his overvaluation of poetry, *a poetry never yet written,* as he too frequently complains. He asks for a stance simultaneously Dionysiac and Self-reliant, and he does not know how this is to be attained, nor do we. I suggest that the deeper cause for his impossible demand is his inner division on the burden of influx, at once altogether to be desired and yet altogether to be resisted, if it comes to us (as it must) from a precursor no more ultimately Central than ourselves, no less a text than we are.

But this is not just the native strain in Emerson; it is the American burden. It came to him because, at the right time in our cultural history, he bravely opened himself to it, but by opening to it with so astonishing a receptivity to oppositions, he opened all subsequent American artists to the same irreconcilable acceptance of negations. Post-Emersonian American poetry, when compared to post-Wordsworthian British poetry, or post-Goethean German poetry, or French poetry after Hugo, is uniquely open to influencings, and uniquely resistant to all *ideas*-of-influence. From Whitman to our contemporaries, American poets eagerly proclaim that they reject nothing that is best in past poetry, and as desperately succumb to poetic defence mechanisms, or self-malformings, rhetorical tropes run wild, against a crippling anxiety of influence. Emerson, source of our sorrow, remains to be quarried, not so much for a remedy, but for a fuller appreciation of the malady. The crux of the matter is a fundamental question for American poets. It could be phrased: In becoming a poet, is one joining oneself to a company of others or truly becoming a solitary and single one? In a sense, this is the anxiety of *whether* one ever really *became* a poet, a double-anxiety: Did one truly join that company? Did one become truly oneself?

In his essay "Character," Emerson emphasized the fear of influence:

> Higher natures overpower lower ones by affecting them with a certain sleep. The faculties are locked up, and offer no resistance. Perhaps that is the universal law. When the high cannot bring up the low to itself, it benumbs it, as man charms down the resistance of the lower animals. Men exert on each other a similar occult power. How often has the influence of a true master realized all the tales of magic! A river of command seemed to run down from his eyes into all those who beheld him, a torrent of strong sad light, like an Ohio or Danube, which pervaded them with his thoughts and colored all events with the hue of his mind.[4]

This flood of light, which Emerson taught his descendants to fear, rather curiously ran down upon them from *his* eyes. As he himself said, in the essay "Politics": "The boundaries of personal influence it is impossible to fix, as persons are organs of moral or supernatural force."[5] Property, he cunningly added, had the same power. As eloquence, to Emerson, was identical with personal energy, eloquence was necessarily personal property, and the dialectics of energy became the dialectics also of commerce. One can say that for Emerson the imagination *was* linguistic energy.

At his most apocalyptic, as throughout the troubling year 1846, when he wrote his best poems, Emerson again denied the anxiety of influence, as here in "Uses of Great Men" from *Representative Men*:

> We need not fear excessive influence. A more generous trust is permitted. Serve the great. Stick at no humiliation. Grudge no office thou canst render. Be the

limb of their body, the breath of their mouth. Compromise thy egotism. Who cares for that, so thou gain aught wider and nobler? Never mind the taunt of Boswellism: the devotion may easily be greater than the wretched pride which is guarding its own skirts. Be another: not thyself, but a Platonist; not a soul, but a Christian; not a naturalist, but a Cartesian; not a poet, but a Shakespearian. In vain, the wheels of tendency will not stop, nor will all the forces of inertia, fear, or of love itself hold thee there. On, and forever onward![6]

Though this over-protests, it remains haunted by the unfulfillable maxim: "Never imitate." Has Emerson forgotten his own insight, that one must be an inventor to read well? Whatever "we" means, in his passage, it cannot mean what it meant in a great notebook passage behind "Self-Reliance": "We are a vision." Rather than multiply bewildering instances, of Emerson on all sides of this dark and central idea, we do him most justice by seeking his ultimate balance where always that must be sought, in his grandest essay, "Experience." Solve this, and you have Emerson-on-influence, if he can be solved at all:

> Thus inevitably does the universe wear our color, and every object fall successively into the subject itself. The subject exists, the subject enlarges; all things sooner or later fall into place. As I am, so I see; use what language we will, we can never say anything but what we are; Hermes, Cadmus, Columbus, Newton, Bonaparte are the mind's ministers. Instead of feeling a poverty when we encounter a great man, let us treat the newcomer like a travelling geologist who passes through our estate and shows us good slate, or limestone, or anthracite, in our brush pasture. The partial action of each strong mind in one direction is a telescope for the objects on which it is pointed. But every other part of knowledge is to be pushed to the same extravagance, ere the soul attains her due sphericity.[7]

The blindness of the strong, Emerson implies, necessarily constitutes insight. Is the insight of the strong also blindness? Can a soul duly spherical be enough of an *unseeing* soul to go on writing poetry? Here is the gnomic poem that introduces "Experience":

> The lords of life, the lords of life,—
> I saw them pass,
> In their own guise,
> Like and unlike,
> Portly and grim,
> Use and Surprise,
> Surface and Dream,
> Succession swift, and spectral Wrong,
> Temperament without a tongue,
> And the inventor of the game
> Omnipresent without name;—
> Some to see, some to be guessed,

They marched from east to west:
Little man, least of all,
Among the legs of his guardians tall,
Walked about with puzzled look.
Him by the hand dear Nature took,
Dearest Nature, strong and kind,
Whispered, Darling, never mind!
To-morrow they will wear another face,
The founder thou! these are thy race![8]

This is the Emerson of about 1842, and if no longer a Primary, he is not quite a Secondary Man. The lords of life (and "Life" was the first title for "Experience") are a rather dubious sevenfold to inspire any poet, and the more-than-Wordsworthian homely nurse, Nature, offers little comfort. If these are the gods, then man is sensible to be puzzled. But it all goes with a diabolically cheerful (though customarily awkward) lilt, and the indubitable prophet of our literary self-reliance seems as outrageously cheerful as ever. There aren't any good models in this procession, and man, Nature assures us, is *their* model, but we are urged to yet another mode of Self-Reliance anyway. "Ne te quaesiveris extra" ("Do not seek yourself outside yourself"), but what is it to seek yourself even within yourself? Does the essay "Experience," in giving us, as I think it does, a vision beyond skepticism, give us also any way out of the double-bind of poetic influence?

"We thrive by casualties," Emerson says, and while he means "random occurrences" he could as well have meant "losses." But these would have been casual losses, given up to "those who are powerful obliquely and not by the direct stroke." Very charmingly Emerson says of these masters that "one gets the cheer of their light without paying too great a tax." Such an influence Emerson himself hoped to be, but Thoreau and even Whitman paid a heavy tax for Emersonian light, and I suspect many contemporary Americans still pay something, whether or not they have read Emerson, since his peculiar relevance now is that we seem to read him merely by living here, in this place still somehow his, and not our own. His power over us attains an elevation in an astonishing recovery from skepticism that suddenly illuminates "Experience":

And we cannot say too little of our constitutional necessity of seeing things under private aspects. . . . And yet is the God the native of these bleak rocks. . . . We must hold hard to this poverty, however scandalous, and by more vigorous self-recoveries, after the sallies of action, possess our axis more firmly.[9]

After this, Emerson is able to give us a blithe prose-list of "the lords of life": "Illusion, Temperament, Succession, Surface, Surprise, Reality, Subjectiveness," and in accepting these he gives us also his escape from conflicting attitudes towards influence: "All I know is reception; I am and I have: but I do not get, and when I have fancied I had gotten anything, I found I did not." But there speaks the spheral man, the all-but-perfect solipsist who made Thoreau almost despair, and whom Whitman emulated only to end as a true poet in the grief-ridden palinode of "As I Ebbed With the Ocean of Life." Charles Ives, deeply under the influence of Emerson's late "Prudence," movingly remarks: "Everyone should have the opportunity of not being over-influenced." Stevens, a less candid Emersonian, is far closer to "Experience" in his ecstatic momentary victories over influence:

> I have not but I am and as I am, I am.
> ....
>   ... Perhaps,
> The man-hero is not the exceptional monster,
> But he that of repetition is most master.

Emerson says: "I am and I have," and, because he receives without self-appropriation, "I do not get." Stevens says: "I have not but I am," because he does not receive, but appropriates for himself through mastering the repetition of his own never-ending meditation upon self. Emerson is the more perfect solipsist, and yet also the more generous spirit, thus getting the better of it both ways. Stevens, the better poet but the much less transcendent consciousness, is less persuasive in proclaiming an ultimate Self-Reliance. In this, he does not differ however from all our Emersonian poets, whether voluntary like Whitman, Robinson, Frost or involuntary like Dickinson and Melville. Stevens too, who saw himself as "A new scholar replacing an older one," became another involuntary ephebe of the Supreme Fiction of our literature, Emersonian individualism, which remains our most troublesome trope.

Recoiling from the consequences of an all-repellent individualism, Emerson opted first for Dionysian influx, and later for the dominance of that other Orphic presence, Ananke, who opposed herself to the individual as his own limitations perceived under the mark of a different aesthetic, the beauty of Fate. For Emerson's was an aesthetic of *use*, a properly pragmatic American aesthetic, that came to fear imaginative entropy as the worst foe of the adverting or questing mind, seeking to make of its own utility of eloquence a vision of universal good.

What can be used can be used up; this is what Geoffrey Hartman calls "the anxiety of demand," a version of which is enacted in a fundamental Romantic genre, the crisis-lyric. Does the achieved poem give confidence that the next poem can be written? An Idealizing critic, even one of great accomplishment, evidently can believe that poets are concerned, as poets, only with the anxiety of form, and not at all with the anxieties of influence and of demand; but all form, however personalized, stems from influx, and all form, however depersonalized, shapes itself against depletion, and so seeks to meet demand. Beneath the anxiety of demand is a ghost of all precursor-obsessions: the concern that inspiration may fail, whereas the strong illusion persists that inspiration could not fail the precursor, for did he not inspire the still-struggling poet?

Emerson's inspiration never failed, in part because it never wholly came to him, or if it did then it came mixed with considerable prudence, and generally arrived in the eloquence of prose. If the anxiety-of-influence descends as a myth of the father, then we can venture that the anxiety-of-demand is likely to manifest itself through imagistic concealments of the mother or Muse. In Stevens, particularly in the late phase of *The Auroras of Autumn* and *The Rock*, the concealment is withdrawn:

> Farewell to an idea.... The mother's face,
> The purpose of the poem, fills the room....

But Stevens, for all his late bleakness, was preternaturally fecund, and did not suffer greatly from the anxiety-of-demand, nor did Emerson. Whitman did, and that sorrow still requires exploration by his readers. The anxiety induced by a vision of the imaginative father, however, is strongly Stevens', as here in the *Auroras*:

> The father sits
> In space, wherever he sits, of bleak regard.
> As one that is strong in the bushes of his eyes.
> He says no to no and yes to yes. He says yes
> To no; and in saying yes he says farewell.

This Jehovah-like affirmer, whose eyes have replaced the burning bush, is a composite figure, with Emerson and Whitman important components, since of all Stevens' precursors they most extravagantly said yes. The saying of farewell is equivocal. Stevens, more forcibly than Pound, exemplifies making it new through the freshness of transformation, and more comprehensively than Williams persuades us that the difficulties of cultural heritage cannot be overcome through evasions. Emerson, ancestor to all three, would have found in Stevens what he once had found in Whitman, a rightful heir of the American quest for a Self-Reliance founded upon a complete self-knowledge.

Contemporary American poetry, written in the large shadowings of Pound, Williams, Stevens, and their immediate progeny, is an impossibly heroic quest wholly in the Emersonian tradition, another variation on the native strain. The best of our contemporary poets show an astonishing energy of response to the sorrow of influence that forms so much of the hidden subject of their work. As heirs, sometimes unknowing, of Emerson, they receive also his heartening faith that: "Eloquence is the appropriate organ of the highest personal energy," and so they can participate also in the noblest of Emersonian conscious indulgences in the Optative Mood, the belief that influence, for a potentially strong poet, is only energy that comes from a precursor, as Emerson says, "of the same turn of mind as his own, and who sees much farther on his own way than he." On this Emersonian implicit theory of the imagination, literary energy is drawn from language and not from nature, and the influence-relationship takes place between words *and* words, and not between subjects. I am a little unhappy to find Emerson, even in one of his aspects, joining Nietzsche as a precursor of Jacques Derrida and Paul de Man, twin titans of deconstruction, and so I want to conclude by juxtaposing Derrida with Emerson on the anxiety of influence. First, Derrida:

> The concept of centered structure is in fact the concept of a freeplay based on a fundamental ground, a freeplay which is constituted upon a fundamental immobility and a reassuring certitude, which is itself beyond the reach of the freeplay. With this certitude anxiety can be mastered, for anxiety is invariably the result of a certain mode of being implicated in the game, of being caught by the game, of being as it were from the very beginning at stake in the game.

Against this, Emerson, from the essay "Nominalist and Realist":

> For though gamesters say that the cards beat all the players, though they were never so skilful, yet in the contest we are now considering, the players are also the game, and share the power of the cards.

Nietzsche, according to Derrida, inaugurated the decentering that Freud, Heidegger, Lévi-Strauss and, most subversively, Derrida himself have accomplished in the Beulah-lands of Interpretation. Though I am myself an uneasy quester after lost meanings, I still conclude I favor a kind of interpretation that seeks to restore and redress meaning, rather than primarily deconstruct meaning. To de-idealize our vision of texts is a good, but a limited good, and I follow Emerson, as against Nietzsche, in declining to make of de-mystification the principal end of dialectical thought in criticism.

Marcuse, introducing Hegel yet sounding like a Kabbalist, insists that dialectical thinking must make the absent present "because the greater part of the truth is in that which is absent." Speech and "positive" thinking are false because they are "part of a mutilated whole." A Marxist dialectician like Adorno shows us clearly what dialectical thinking is in our time; the thinker self-consciously thinks about his thinking in the very act of intending the objects of his thought. Emerson, in "Nominalist and Realist," still a genuinely startling text, simply says that: "No sentence will hold the whole truth, and the only way in which we can be just, is by giving ourselves the lie. . ." That is a wilder variety of dialectical thinking than most Post-Hegelian Europeans attempt, and Emerson is in consequence as maddening as he is ingratiating. For, in Emerson, dialectical thought does not fulfill the primary function of fighting off the idealistic drive of an expanding consciousness. Both in his Transcendental and in his Necessitarian phases, Emerson does not worry about ending in solipsism; he is only too happy to reach the transparency of solipsism whenever he can. He is very much Wittgenstein's Schopenhauerian solipsist who knows he is right in what he *means*, and who knows also that he is in error in what he *says*. The solipsism of Emerson's Transcendentalism issues finally in the supra-realism of the Necessitarianism of his last great book, the magnificent *The Conduct of Life*. Dialectical thinking in Emerson does not attempt to bring us back to the world of things and of other selves, but only to a world of language, and so its purpose is never to *negate* what is directly before us. From a European perspective, probably, Emersonian thinking is not so much dialectical as it is plain crazy, and I suspect that even Blake would have judged Emerson to be asserting that: "Without negations there is no progression," a negation being for Blake opposed to a genuinely dialectical contrary. Yet Nietzsche, who could tolerate so few of his own contemporaries, delighted in Emerson, and seems to have understood Emerson very well. And I think Nietzsche particularly understood that Emerson had come to prophesy not a de-centering, as Nietzsche had, and as Derrida and de Man are brilliantly accomplishing, but a peculiarly American *re-centering*, and with it an American mode of interpretation, one that we have begun (but only begun) to develop, from Whitman and Peirce down to Stevens and Kenneth Burke, a mode that *is* intra-textual, but that stubbornly remains logocentric, and that still follows Emerson in valorizing eloquence, the inspired voice, *over* the scene of writing. Emerson, who said he unsettled all questions, first put literature into question for us and now survives to question our questioners.

Notes

1   Ralph Waldo Emerson, *Journals and Miscellaneous Notebooks*, ed. W. H. Gilman and others (Cambridge, Mass., 1960-), V, 344–45.
2   *Journals and Notebooks*, V, 336–37.
3   *Journals and Notebooks*, II, 238, 242.
4   Ralph Waldo Emerson, *Works*, ed. E. W. Emerson (Boston, 1903–1904), III, 94.
5   *Works*, III, 205.
6   *Works*, IV, 29–30.
7   *Works*, III, 79–80.
8   *Works*, III, 43.
9   *Works*, III, 81.

Richard Rorty (1931–2007)

American philosopher, author of Philosophy and the Mirror *(1979), whose critique of analytic philosophy culminated with a new brand of pragmatism that demoted representational theories of knowledge in favor of ones that promote contingency and irony, and that thereby may lead to solidarity, as a book-title of his suggests. Rorty presented the following essay to the Bicentennial Symposium of Philosophy at the City University of New York in 1976. He aims to "understand the relations between the genteel tradition of our forebears and the highbrow culture criticism of the present," and to that end believes that "it helps to look more closely at the good and the bad senses of the term 'transcendentalism' which Santayana distinguished." Reading Rorty's remarks in tandem with Santayana's essays in the present volume will further enrich the dialogue over the perennially defined, redefined, and often contested term transcendentalism. Santayana's much-quoted description of Emerson as a "genteel" thinker in "The Genteel Tradition in American Philosophy" (1911) further refracts another crucial aspect of the inheritance of Emerson's work and Rorty's reading of the pragmatist's understanding of it.*

Professionalized Philosophy and Transcendentalist Culture

Richard Rorty

Santayana's reflections on philosophy in the new world have two singular merits. First, he was able to laugh at us without despising us—a feat often too intricate for the native-born. Second, he was entirely free of the instinctive American conviction that the westering of the spirit ends here—that whatever the ages have labored to bring forth will emerge between Massachusetts and California, that our philosophers have only to express our national genius for the human spirit to fulfill itself. Santayana saw us as one more great empire in the long parade. His genial hope was that we might enjoy the imperium while we held it. In a famous essay on American philosophy, he suggested that we were still spoiling our own fun. We wanted to retain, he said, the "agonized conscience" of our Calvinist ancestors while keeping, simultaneously if illogically, the idealistic metaphysics of their transcendentalist successors. This metaphysics embodied what he called the "conceited notion that man, or human reason, or the human distinction between good and evil, is the centre and pivot of the universe."[1] The combination of Calvinist guilt and metaphysical egoism he called "The Genteel Tradition in American Philosophy." He opposed to it what he called "America's ruling passion, the love of business"—"joy in business itself and in its further operation, in making it greater and better organized and a mightier engine in the general life." "The American Will," he said, "inhabits the sky-scraper; the American Intellect inhabits the colonial mansion. The one is the sphere of the American man; the other, at least predominantly, of the American woman. The one is all aggressive emphasis; the other is all genteel tradition."[2] The academic mind of 1911, he thought, counted as feminine in this respect: "The genteel tradition has subsisted in the academic mind for want of anything equally academic to take its place."[3]

We can afford to smile at all this, as we look about at the manly, aggressive and businesslike academics of our own time. The American academic mind has long since discovered the joy of making its own special enterprise "greater and better organized and a mightier engine in the general life." The well-funded professor, jetting home after a day spent advising men of power, is the envy of the provincial tycoon in the adjacent seat. If there is still something like a genteel tradition in American life, it cannot be identified with "the academic mind." Most academics now teach in skyscrapers. The public no longer associates our profession with epicene delicacy, but either with political violence and sexual license or with hard-nosed presidential advisors. If there is anything remotely analogous to what Santayana spoke of, it is the specifically highbrow culture—the culture which produces poems, plays and novels literary criticism and what, for want of a better term, we can call "culture criticism." Some highbrows inhabit the academy, mostly in literature departments, but they are not academic entrepreneurs. They do not get grants; they have disciples rather than research teams; they inhabit whatever mansions may still be tucked away among the academic skyscrapers. Their more businesslike colleagues treat them alternately with the deference due from tradesmen to the clergy, and the contempt the successful feel for the shabby genteel.

Where, in the busy modern academy, do we find the philosophy professors? To treat this question properly we need to look at what has been going on in philosophy since Santayana wrote, and to divide it into two periods. The period between the World Wars was one of prophecy and moral leadership—the heroic period of Deweyan pragmatism, during which philosophy played the sort of role in the country's life which Santayana could admire. The period since the Second World War has been one of professionalization, in which philosophers have quite deliberately and self-consciously abdicated such a role. In the pre-World War I period which Santayana described, philosophy defined itself by its relation to religion. In the Deweyan period, it defined itself by its relation to the social sciences. At the beginning of the professionalizing period, philosophers attempted halfheartedly to define their activity in relation to mathematics and the natural sciences. In fact, however, this period has been marked by a withdrawal from the rest of the academy and from culture—an insistence on philosophy's autonomy.

The claim that philosophy is and ought to be a technical subject, that this recent professionalization is an important good, is usually not defended directly by pointing with pride to the importance of the issues philosophers discuss or to paradigms of successful philosophical inquiry. Rather, it is defended indirectly, by pointing with scorn to the low level of argumentative rigor among the competition in the Deweyan philosophy of the thirties, in contemporary Continental philosophy, and in the culture criticism of the highbrows. Even philosophers who would like to break out of their professional isolation tend to insist that their special contribution will be in argumentative skill. It is not, they say, that philosophers know more about anything in particular, but that they have a kind of sensitivity to distinctions and presuppositions which is peculiarly their own.[4]

Since the highbrow culture critic has usurped many of the functions which traditional philosophers had fulfilled in the past, while remaining oblivious to what contemporary academic philosophers are actually doing, highbrows try to dismiss American philosophy with journalistic sneers about "irrelevance" or "scholasticism." Philosophers, in turn, try to dismiss the highbrow literary culture in the same way as Santayana dismissed the genteel tradition. They see this culture as palliating cranky hypersensitivity with aesthetic comfort, just as Santayana saw Royce and Palmer as palming the agonized conscience off with metaphysical comfort. Accusations of softness and sloppiness are exchanged for accusations of pedantry and narrowness.

When these accusations become self-conscious and explicit, they are usually offered as views about "the essence of philosophy," as if a niche in a permanent ahistorical schema of possible human activities were in danger of vacancy or of usurpation. I think that such disputes are pointless, since philosophy does not have an essence, anymore than do literature or politics. Each is what brilliant men are presently making it. There is no common standard by which to compare Royce, Dewey, Heidegger, Tarski, Carnap, and Derrida in point of "being a *real* philosopher." But although philosophy has no essence, it does have a history. Although philosophical movements cannot be seen as departures from, or returns to, True Philosophy, and although their successes are as difficult to assess as those of literary or political movements, one can sometimes say something about their grosser sociological consequences. In what follows, I want to sketch some of the things that have happened in American philosophy since Santayana wrote, and to make some predictions about the consequences of professionalization.

Santayana noted that William James had already "turned the flank" of the genteel tradition. A decade after Santayana's essay, it became clear that Dewey had consolidated James's gains and succeeded in doing what Santayana had described as finding something "equally academic to take the place" of that tradition. Dewey made the American learned world safe for the social sciences. In the early 1900s the academy had to restructure itself to make room for half a dozen new departments, and for a new sort of academic who came to inhabit them. The American academy became the privileged sanctuary of attempts to reconstruct the American social order, and American philosophy become a call for such reconstruction. The Deweyan claim that moral philosophy was not the formulation of general principles to serve as a surrogate for divine commands, but rather the application of intelligence to social problems, gave American youth a new way of looking at the meaning of their education and their lives. With the New Deal, the social scientist emerged as the representative of the academy to the public, embodying the Deweyan promise. When, during the Depression, Stalinism recruited whole battalions of highbrows, a small circle around Sidney Hook—Dewey's chief disciple—kept political morality alive among the intellectuals. Philosophers like Max Otto, Alexander Meiklejohn, and Horace Kallen offered their students the possibility that "America's ruling passion, the love of business," might be transformed into a love of social reconstruction. Having sat at their feet, a whole generation grew up confident that America would show the world how to escape both Gradgrind capitalism and revolutionary bloodshed. In the years between the wars, American philosophy not only escaped from the genteel tradition, but provided moral leadership for the country. For the first time, American philosophy professors played the sort of role which Fichte and Hegel had once played in Germany.

By the end of the Second World War, however, the great days of Deweyan philosophy and social science were over. The strenuous reformist attitude which succeeded the genteel tradition was in turn succeeded by an urge to be scientific and rigorous. Both social scientists and philosophers wanted to stop striking public attitudes and start showing that they could be as thoroughly and exclusively professional, and preferably as mathematical, as the natural scientists. American sociology, whose early stages had been satirized as the expenditure of a five-thousand-dollar grant to discover the address of a whorehouse, came to be satirized as the expenditure of a five-million-dollar grant to plot the addresses of a thousand whorehouses against a multidimensional array of socio-economic variables. American philosophy students realized that the previous generation—Dewey's pupils—had exhausted the market for celebrations of American democracy, naturalism, and social reconstruction. Nobody could remember what an idealist, a subjectivist, a transcendentalist, or even an orthodox theist looked like, so nobody was interested in hearing them criticized. New heroes were needed, and they were found among that extraordinary body of men, the emigré scholars. A young American philosopher learning phenomenology from Gurwitsch or Schuetz, or logical empiricism from Carnap or Reichenbach, was trained to think of philosophy as a rigorous discipline, a matter of cooperation in joint inquiry and the production of agreed-upon results. By the mid-fifties, the victory which the pragmatists had won on native ground over the genteel tradition seemed as remote as Emerson's victory over the Calvinists. With exacting work to be done on the structure of visual awareness or on extensional criteria of nomologicality, there seemed no time and no need to ask what had happened in philosophy before Husserl or before Russell. As logical empiricism metamorphosed into analytic philosophy, and succeeded in driving phenomenology out into the academic shadows, American philosophers' disinterest in moral and social questions became almost total. Courses in moral philosophy were, for a time, little more than elaborate epistemological sneers at the common moral consciousness. Philosophers' contact with colleagues in the social sciences became as minimal and incidental as their contacts with colleagues in literature. Dewey had predicted that philosophy would turn away from the seventeenth-century tension between mathematical physics and the world of common sense, and would take up new problems arising from the social sciences and the arts. But this prediction was completely off target. On the contrary, all the good old Cartesian problems which Dewey thought he had disposed of were brought back, restated in the formal mode of speech and surrounded by new difficulties generated by the formalism.

What Dewey had predicted for American philosophy did, however, happen elsewhere: both in Continental philosophy and in American highbrow literary culture. Attention to interpretation rather than verification—to what the arts and the "sciences of man" have in common—was the mark of the literary intellectual. One result of this—the most important result for my present purposes—was that the history of philosophy began to be taken over by the highbrows. Whereas professionalized philosophers insisted on treating the great dead philosophers as sources of hypotheses or instructive examples of conceptual confusion, the highbrows still treated them in the old-fashioned way, as heroes or villains. Dewey had still attempted to tell a great sweeping story about philosophy from Plato to himself, but philosophers in the professionalizing period distrusted such stories as "unscientific" and "unscholarly." So they are, but they also form a genre of writing which is quite indispensable. Besides the need to ask whether certain propositions asserted by Aristotle or Locke or Kant or Kierkegaard are true or were validly inferred, there is also the need to adopt an attitude towards such men, just as one must adopt an attitude towards Alcibiades and Euripides, Cromwell and Milton, Proust and Lenin. Because the writings of the great dead philosophers form a bundle of intertwined dialectical sequences, one has to have attitudes towards many of them to justify one's attitude towards the others. Nor can one's attitude towards Kant, for example, be independent of one's attitudes towards Wordsworth and Napoleon. Developing attitudes towards the mighty dead and their living rivals—dividing the pantheon into the divine and the daemonic—is the whole point of highbrow culture. The kind of name-dropping, rapid shifting of context and unwillingness to stay for an answer which this culture encourages runs counter to everything that a professionalized academic discipline stands for. Normally, the conflict between the academy and this culture can remain implicit. But in the case of philosophy it is bound to be expressed, if only because not even the most professionalized philosopher can stop seeing himself, if not as the contemporary counterpart of Plato and Kant, as at least their authorized commentator. So we have the conflict I described at the beginning of this essay—the highbrow and the academic philosopher viewing each other with equal suspicion, each harping on the vices of each other's virtues.

I want to claim that this is not a conflict which we need view with any great concern nor try to resolve. If we understand its historical background, we can live with its probable consequence that philosophy as a technical academic subject will remain as remote from highbrow culture as is paleontology or classical philology. To defend this attitude, I want to go on to say why I think that the mode of treating the great philosophers characteristic of highbrow culture is indispensable, and also why one should not confuse this culture with the genteel tradition of which Santayana was complaining. I shall try to do this by sketching the history of the emergence of highbrow culture, which seems to me as distinctively a nineteenth-century phenomenon as the New Science and the philosophical problematic which it created were seventeenth-century phenomena.[5]

Beginning in the days of Goethe and Macaulay and Carlyle and Emerson a kind of writing has developed which is neither the evaluation of the relative merits of literary productions, nor intellectual history, nor moral philosophy, nor epistemology, nor social prophecy, but all these things mingled together into a new genre. This genre is often still *called* "literary criticism," however, for an excellent reason. The reason is that in the course of the nineteenth century imaginative literature took the place of both religion and philosophy in forming and solacing the agonized conscience of the young. Novels and poems are now the principal means by which a bright youth gains a self-image. Criticism of novels is the principal form in which the acquisition of a moral character is made articulate. We live in a culture in which putting one's moral sensitivity into words is not clearly distinguishable from exhibiting one's literary sensibilities. Episodes from the history of religion and from the history of philosophy are seen as instantiating literary paradigms, rather than serving as sources of literary inspiration. The creed or the philosophical doctrine becomes the emblem of the novelist's character or the poet's image, rather than conversely. Philosophy is treated as a parallel genre to the drama or the novel or the poem, so that we speak of the epistemology common to Vaihinger and Valéry, the rhetoric common to Marlowe and Hobbes, the ethics common to E. M. Forster and G. E. Moore. What culture criticism does *not* do is to ask whether Valéry wrote more beautiful lines than Marlowe, or whether Hobbes or Moore told more truths about the good. In this form of life, the true and the good and the beautiful drop out. The aim is to understand, not to judge. The hope is that if one understands enough poems, enough religions, enough societies, enough philosophies, one will have made oneself into something worth one's own understanding.

To understand the relations between the genteel tradition of our forebears and the highbrow culture criticism of the present, it helps to look more closely at the good and the bad senses of the term "transcendentalism" which Santayana distinguished. He contrasted transcendentalist metaphysical systems, which he deplored as egotistical, with what he called "transcendentalism proper." This, he said,

> like romanticism, is not any particular set of dogmas about what things exist; it is not a system of the universe regarded as a fact.... It is a method, a point of view, from which any work, no matter what it might contain, could be approached by a self-conscious observer.... It is the chief contribution made in modern times to speculation.[6]

This transcendentalist point of view is the mark of the highbrow. It is the attitude that there is no point in raising questions of truth, goodness, or beauty, because between ourselves and the thing judged there always intervenes mind, language, a perspective chosen among dozens, one description chosen out of thousands. On one side, it is the lack of seriousness which Plato attributed to poets, the "negative capability" for which Keats praised Shakespeare. On another, it is the Sartrean sense of absurdity which Arthur Danto suggests may befall us when we give up the picture theory of language and the Platonic conception of truth as accuracy of representation. In the later Wittgenstein, it was the wry admission that anything has a sense if you give it a sense. In Heidegger, who hated it, it was the charter of the modern—of what he called "the age of the worldview." In Derrida, it is the renunciation of "the myth of the purely maternal or paternal language belonging to the lost fatherland of thought." It is crystallized in Foucault's claim that he "writes in order to have no face."

Transcendentalism in this sense, is the justification of the intellectual who has no wish to be a scientist or a professional, who does not think that intellectual honesty requires what Kuhn calls a "disciplinary matrix." It is what permits the attitude of the literary intellectual towards science which scandalizes C. P. Snow: the view of, say, quantum mechanics as a notoriously great, but quite untranslatable, poem, written in a lamentably obscure language. Transcendentalism is what gives sense to the very notion of the "highbrow"—a notion which is post-Romantic and post-Kantian. In the eighteenth century there were witty men and learned men and pious men, but there were no highbrows. Not until the Romantics did books become so various as to create readers who see what has been written as having no containing framework, no points of reference save the books one loves today but which may betray one tomorrow. Not until Kant did philosophy destroy science and theology to make room for moral faith, and not until Schiller did it seem possible that the room cleared for morality could be occupied by art. When Santayana traced "transcendentalism" (in the good sense) back to Kant, his point was that Kant's treatment of scientific truth makes science just one cultural manifestation among others. But since scientific truth has been, since the seventeenth century, the model for philosophical truth, Kant's treatment of scientific truth leads to Santayana's own aesthetic attitude towards philosophical vision. It was this sense of relativity and open possibility which Santayana thought we should admire in Emerson—the side of Emerson that resembled Whitman rather than the side that resembled Royce. It was precisely the inability to maintain this splendidly aristocratic posture which made the genteel tradition merely genteel. That tradition claimed that one could take both scientific truth and religious truth with full seriousness and weave them together into something new—transcendental philosophy—which was higher than science, purer than religion, and truer than both. This claim was what Dewey and Russell were reacting against: Dewey by social concern, and Russell by inventing something scientific and rigorous and difficult for philosophy to become. By picking these men as heroes, two major movements in American philosophy became obsessed with the danger of a form of cultural life which no longer existed. American philosophers thought of themselves as guarding against idealistic speculations, long after such speculations had ceased to be written. They called "idealist" anything they didn't like—anything outside their own discipline which breathed the faintest trust in a larger hope.

The result was that culture criticism—the sort of writing done by T. S. Eliot and Edmund Wilson, by Lionel Trilling and Paul Goodman—was hardly visible to philosophers, though little else was visible to the best of the students they were teaching. When the Deweyan period ended, the moral sense of American intellectuals began to be formed without the intervention of the philosophy professors, who assumed that any decent kid would grow up to be the same sort of pragmatic liberal as themselves. As Harold Bloom writes,

> The teacher of literature now in America, far more than the teacher of history or philosophy or religion, is condemned to teach the presentness of the past, because history, philosophy and religion have withdrawn as agents from the Scene of Instruction. . . .[7]

Whatever species of professor takes on the task of teaching the presentness of the great dead philosophers, those philosophers will be present at the Scene of Instruction as long as we have libraries. There will be a Scene of Instruction as long as there is an agonized conscience in the young. This conscience is not something which was left behind with Calvinism in the eighteenth century nor with religion generally in the nineteenth. If this conscience is not induced by one's early betrayals of one's early loves, it will nevertheless be ensured, for example, by the well-funded American academic's realization that his colleagues in Chile and Russia are presently enduring humiliation and pain to amuse the guards at their prisons. Though Santayana hoped that American culture would stop trying to solace the agonized conscience with metaphysical comfort, he did not think that conscience would go away. But American philosophers came to fear that anything which even touched upon the agonized conscience might be construed as metaphysical comfort. They reacted either by ignoring the great dead philosophers or by reinterpreting them so that they would be seen as addressing properly professional issues. The result of such reinterpretation was to obscure the presentness of the past and to separate the philosophy professors from their students and from transcendentalist culture. Whether the sort of links between transcendentalist culture and academic departments of literature which presently exist will someday be paralleled by links with philosophy departments is not terribly important. It may be that American philosophy will continue to be more concerned with developing a disciplinary matrix than with its antecedents or its cultural role. No harm will be done by this and possibly much good. The dialectical dramas which began with Plato will continue. They will be enacted; if not by people paid to teach Plato, then by others. These others may not be called "philosophers" but something else, possibly "critics." Possibly they will be given a name which would seem as odd to us as our use of "critic" would have seemed to Dr. Johnson, or our use of "philosopher" to Socrates.

This is the conclusion I wish to draw from my survey of what has happened in American philosophy since Santayana wrote. It amounts to saying that professionalized philosophy may or may not join transcendentalist culture, but that it should not try to beat it. I shall end by turning back to Santayana once again, and commending the second of the two virtues I initially attributed to him. This was his ability to avoid the conviction that America is what history has been leading up to and thus that it is up to American philosophy to express the American genius, to describe a virtue as uniquely ours as our redwoods and our rattlesnakes. This mild chauvinism was in vogue during the Deweyan period, and occasionally we still feel nostalgia for it. But, *pace* Niebuhr, Deweyan philosophy did not start from the assumption that the American and the Industrial Revolutions had, between them, rendered the agonized conscience obsolete. Nor, despite a certain amount of hopeful rhetoric from Dewey and his disciples, did it really teach that the combination of American institutions and the scientific method would produce the Good Life for Man. Its attitude was best expressed by Sidney Hook in an essay called "Pragmatism and the Tragic Sense of Life," which closes by saying, "Pragmatism . . . is the theory and practice of enlarging human freedom in a precarious and tragic world by the arts of intelligent social control. It may be a lost cause. I do not know of a better one."[8] There is indeed no better cause, and the nostalgia which philosophers in the professionalizing period have felt for the prophetic Deweyan period comes from their sense that they are not doing as much for this cause as they would like. But the defense of this cause is only incidentally a matter of formulating moral principles, and moral education is only incidentally a matter of choosing and defending a cause. Further, although America will go down in history as having done more for this cause than any of the great empires so far, there is no particular reason why a nation's philosophers, or indeed its intellectuals, need be identified in the eyes of history with the same virtues as its political and social institutions. There is no reason to think that the promise of American democracy will find its final fulfillment in America, any more than Roman law reached its fulfillment in the Roman Empire or literary culture its fulfillment in Alexandria. Nor is there much reason to think that the highbrow culture of whatever empire does achieve that fulfillment will resemble our own, or that the professors of moral philosophy then will build on principles being formulated now. Even if, through some unbelievable stroke of fortune, America survives with its freedoms intact and becomes a rallying point for the nations, the high culture of an unfragmented world need not center around anything specifically American. It may not, indeed, *center* around anything more than anything else: neither poetry, nor social institutions, nor mysticism, nor depth psychology, nor novels, nor philosophy, nor physical science. It may be a culture which is transcendentalist through and through, whose center is everywhere and circumference nowhere. In such a culture, Jonathan Edwards and Thomas Jefferson, Henry and William James, John Dewey and Wallace Stevens, Charles Peirce and Thorstein Veblen will all be present. No one will be asking which ones are the Americans, nor even, perhaps, which ones are the philosophers.

Notes

1 George Santayana, *Winds of Doctrine* (London: J. M. Dent, 1913), 214.
2 Ibid., 188.
3 Ibid., 212.
4 I develop this theme at greater length in Essay 12, below {"Philosophy in America Today"}.

5   I develop this contrast between the literary culture and the professional philosophers at greater length in Essay 8, below {"Nineteenth Century Idealism and Twentieth-Century Textualism"}.

6   Santayana, op. cit., 193–194.

7   Harold Bloom, *A Map of Misreading* (New York: Oxford University Press, 1975), 39.

8   Sidney Hook, *Pragmatism and the Tragic Sense of Life* (New York: Basic Books, 1974), 25.

John Updike (1932–2009)

Novelist, short story writer, poet, and critic, Updike won the Pulitzer Prize (twice) for his Rabbit *tetralogy (1960–1990) and contributed regularly to the* New Yorker *and the* New York Review of Books. *Updike possessed a fundamental skepticism about Emerson's status in American letters and gave pronounced public expression to it in the* New Yorker. *In "Emersonianism" (1984) he asked rhetorically, "Is there not something cloudy at the center of his reputation, something fatally faded about the works he has left us?" And in reply he suggests that "Emerson, who, so dominant and dignified a presence among his contemporaries, now clings to immortality almost because he cannot be extricated from them." Updike aims to describe the "awkwardness" in Emerson's present-day reputation: "what we like about him is not what is important, and what is important we do not much like." Unsure how to end his essay, Updike creates a satire in which he applies Emerson's lessons to his experience following the abandonment of duties: the reader is given a personal narrative that lampoons and mocks Emerson's outlook and his prose in a tone meant to convey both Updike's contempt for Emerson's ideas and the way—in life—they all seemingly resolve themselves into a series of reductio ad absurdum. Updike appears to be "the joker of an old deck of cards" he uses as a bookmark in his volume of Emerson, but to what effect? Harold Bloom viewed Updike's report, in the same year he offered it, as "churchwardenly mewings." Nearly twenty years later, in 2003, on the occasion of the bicentenary of Emerson's birth, Updike returned to the topic of Emerson's legacy in the form of a review article, "Big Dead White Male," also printed below. Of this work Stanley Cavell wrote: "[T]here appeared a couple of weeks ago in the* New Yorker *a substantial and obscurely motivated review of texts celebrating the two hundredth anniversary of the birth of Emerson, by the celebrated John Updike, who is able to, and willing to, string out a list of banal and careless criticisms of Emerson's pretensions, unwilling or unable to paraphrase subtly and accurately any of the Emersonian sentences he disparagingly cites. Whom is he protecting? What public service is he thereby performing?"[1] These are questions about the audience for Emerson's writing as much as the critics who appraise it. One might add further questions to accompany one's reading, reflecting Updike's suspicion: is Emerson honored more than read? Or, more to the consequences of Updike's worry: is honor something we grant to writers we have stopped reading?*

Emersonianism

John Updike

The critic Warner Berthoff, in his essay "American Literature: Traditions and Talents," concedes that "the American circumstance has indeed managed to yield its originating masters," then challenges himself to name them. As if slightly surprised, he responds, "I should speak at once of Melville, of Whitman, and of Emerson, who remain, in their several ways, the freshest of our writers, as well as the most provocatively intelligent; their wit, so to speak, is still the liveliest potential cause of wit in others."

One searches one's own wits, reading this. Melville and Whitman, of course. *Moby-Dick* and *Leaves of Grass*, both published in the eighteen-fifties to a reception of mockery and indifference, are American classics if any exist. Or so, at least, we feel now, having inherited our high opinion from the modernist critics of this century, who in Melville's case had to perform a considerable work of resurrection. But our received opinion, tested against the texts themselves, does seem just: the words sing, burn, and live; they have the exciting difficulty of reality itself, and the pressure and precision of things that exist. With something like rapture, each author's voice makes solid connections, and however widely their raptures range Melville and Whitman persuasively strive to give us the substance promised by their titles: grass and a whale, earth and the sea are delivered.

But Emerson? Is there not something cloudy at the center of his reputation, something fatally faded about the works he has left us? When, I ask myself, did I last read one of his celebrated essays? How much, indeed, are Emerson's works even assigned in literary courses where the emphasis is not firmly historical? I sometimes receive in the mail anthologies designed for instruction in colleges and high schools, and a check of their indices reveals little Emerson, and then often no more than one or two of his shorter poems, or a paragraph or two quoted in explication of "Walden," or a footnote explaining how the black writer Ralph Ellison's middle name came to be Waldo. *An Approach to Literature*, a massive double-column anthology edited by Cleanth Brooks, John Thibaut Purser, and Robert Penn Warren, contains not a word by Emerson, nor does Donald Hall's fifteen-hundred-page assemblage *To Read Literature*. The countercultural wave that lifted Thoreau and Whitman into renewed fashionability left Emerson scarcely touched; he was not revolutionary, or ecological, enough. Recessive, fantastical Hawthorne is an indispensable anthology presence in a way Emerson is not; even Longfellow and Whittier, it may not be reckless to say, left texts more vivid in the communal memory than the literary remains of Emerson, who, so dominant and dignified a presence among his contemporaries, now clings to immortality almost because he cannot be extricated from them.

For, however great a cause of wit he has proved or will prove to be among ourselves, he was undoubtedly in his living prime a most fertile cause of wit in others. He was a great encourager and inspirer—a center of excitement in Concord and Boston and a bestower of boldness and energy wherever he spoke. In 1842, the twenty-three-year-old Walter Whitman heard him lecture in New York: "I was simmering, simmering, simmering," the poet later said. "Emerson brought me to a boil." And when, in 1855, Whitman sent the busy Emerson a privately published sheaf of poems, a booklet in its eccentric appearance begging to be tossed aside as the work of a crank, Emerson astoundingly read it and recognized its epochal worth, as the answer to his platform prayers for a new literature and an untrammelled new consciousness. "I am not blind to the worth of the wonderful gift of 'Leaves of Grass,'" he wrote Whitman. "I find it the most extraordinary piece of wit & wisdom that America has yet contributed.... It has the best merits, namely, of fortifying & encouraging." The unstinting tone of this praise, volunteered to a stranger, is magnanimous; the terms of the praise are indicative. Emerson was too bent upon the business of encouraging and fortifying others to feel envy. His long and patient patronage of Henry David Thoreau is well known. Less well known is Emerson's kindness to the half-mad, religiously obsessed Jones Very, of Salem; for all the young man's eccentricities, Emerson not merely held frequent discourse with him but edited and saw to the publication of his *Poems and Essays* in 1839. The volatile, brilliant Margaret Fuller also presented a troublesome friendship to Emerson. "I want to see you, and still more to hear you," she wrote him in 1838. "I must kindle my torch again." She taxed him with "a certain inhospitality of soul" toward her and provoked him to address her in his journals with an imaginary rebuff that began, "You would have me love you. What shall I love?" But he fended off her appeals for more than he could provide and made something positive of their intellectual association in the so-called Hedge's Club and her editorship of the Transcendentalist magazine *The Dial.* Many others, men and women, basked in the Emerson circle at Concord; though he complains in his journals of the constant infractions upon his time, it was not only his nature but his mission to be encouraging. His address in Boston on "Man the Reformer" proclaimed a "new spirit" and called upon men to "begin the world anew." Books, he had asserted in his famous address on "The American Scholar," "are for nothing but to inspire." In his call for renewal, in his capacity for appreciation and for generating excitement, Emerson stands in catalytic relation to the classic period of America letters much as Ezra Pound does to the modernism of the early twentieth century. "A village explainer," Gertrude Stein called Pound, and the Sage of Concord was that par excellence. He lectured everywhere, and knew everybody. In New York, one of his best friends was the senior Henry James, and on his last European jaunt, in 1872, the young Henry James was one of his escorts in Paris. Twenty years earlier, having tediously travelled by railroad and steamboat to speak in St. Louis, he especially enjoyed the companionship of the Unitarian minister William Greenleaf Eliot, the grandfather of T. S. Our impression that Emerson laid benedictory hands upon all the heads of at least the Northeast American literary tradition is compounded by the fancy that Emily Dickinson is Emerson's spiritual daughter: like him, she wrote poems to bumblebees and felt herself drunk upon the intoxicating light of the divine sun. Her accomplishment proves the truth of his assertion, in "The Poet," that "day and night, house and garden, a few books, a few actions, serve as well as would all trades and all spectacles." What better encapsulation of his doctrine of "Self-Reliance" than this stanza of hers:

The soul selects her own society,
Then shuts the door;
On her divine majority
Obtrude no more.

In the two great poets Emerson's influence seems to bifurcate: his boastful all-including optimism trumpeted by Whitman, his more playful, skeptical quizzing of God and Nature carried further by the Amherst recluse.

We should not, however, imagine that all the great names of the American Renaissance obediently constellate around Emerson. Hawthorne, a year younger than he, and of the same Yankee stock, shared Concord and a long acquaintanceship with him, and lies buried in Sleepy Hollow a few paces away, but in life there was always between them a certain distance and coolness of appreciation. When the author of *The Scarlet Letter* died, in 1864, Emerson wrote in his journal;

I have found in his death a surprise & a disappointment. I thought him a greater man than any of his works betray. . . . Moreover I have felt sure of him in his neighborhood, & in his necessities of sympathy & intelligence, that I could well wait his time—his unwillingness & caprice—and might one day conquer a friendship. It would have been a happiness, doubtless to both of us, to have come into habits of unreserved intercourse. It was easy to talk with him—there were no barriers—only, he said so little, that I talked too much, & stopped only because—as he gave no indications—I feared to exceed.

Amid the quiet ghosts of Salem, Hawthorne had worked out his artistic and personal credo with no assistance from Transcendentalism; he took a generally satiric view of enthusiasm, public lectures, Unitarianism, *The Dial*, and Margaret Fuller, and remained at heart loyal to the Puritan sense of darkness, guilt, and intrinsic limitation which Emerson so exultantly wished to banish. Melville loved Hawthorne and took fire from him; he is the second great member of what we might call the anti-Emerson party. "I do not oscillate in Emerson's rainbow," he wrote. After reading some essays by "this Plato who talks through his nose," he pronounced, "To one who has weathered Cape Horn as a common sailor what stuff all this is." In that scarcely coherent voyage of rage called *The Confidence-Man* Melville planted a caricature of Emerson called Mark Winsome, who is travelling on the Mississippi with a Thoreau-like disciple called Egbert. Winsome is portrayed as "with such a preternaturally cold, gemmy glance out of his pellucid blue eye, that he seemed more a metaphysical merman than a feeling man." As "coldly radiant as a prism," Winsome spouts Plato and mocks consistency. The author, represented by his hero "the cosmopolitan," seems to find double fault with Winsome: he is too mystical and also too practical. His philosophy is unreal, yet at the same time it serves the world's base purposes. "Mystery is in the morning, and mystery in the night, and the beauty of mystery is everywhere," Winsome is made to say, "but still the plain truth remains, that mouth and purse must be filled." "Was not Seneca a usurer?" he asks. "And Swedenborg, though with one eye on the invisible, did he not keep the other on the main chance?" The disciple Egbert appears "the last person in the world that one would take for the disciple of any transcendental philosophy, though, indeed, something about his sharp nose and shaved chin seemed to hint that if mysticism, as a lesson, ever came in his way, he might, with the characteristic knack of a true New-Englander, turn even so profitless a thing to some profitable account." In the end, the two are dismissed as professors of an "inhuman philosophy"—"moonshine" suited to "frozen natures."

Emerson's first book, *Nature*—published in 1836 and the only one of his major prose writings that did not first exist in the form of public utterance—proposed some remarkable inversion of the common way of seeing things:

> Nature is the symbol of spirit. . . . The use of natural history is to give us aid in supernatural history: the use of the outer creation, to give us language for the beings and changes of the inward creation. . . . Man is conscious of a universal soul within or behind his individual life, wherein, as in a firmament, the natures of Justice, Truth, Love, Freedom, arise and shine. This universal soul, he calls Reason: it is not mine, or thine, or his, but we are its; we are its property and men. . . . That which, intellectually considered, we call Reason, considered in relation to nature, we call Spirit. Spirit is the Creator. Spirit hath life in itself. And man in all ages and countries, embodies it in his language, as the FATHER. . . . There seems to be a necessity in spirit to manifest itself in material forms; and day and night, river and storm, beast and bird, acid and alkali, preëxist in necessary Ideas in the mind of God, and are what they are by virtue of preceding affections, in the world of spirit. A Fact is the end or last issue of spirit. The visible creation is the terminus or the circumference of the invisible world.

Such thought is called Idealism, and has long roots in Plato and the Neoplatonists, in Christian metaphysics, in Berkeley and Kant and Swedenborg. Hegel, whom Emerson read only late in life, and then, without enthusiasm, made Idealism the dominant mode of nineteenth-century philosophy; it came to America through the writings of Coleridge and Carlyle and Goethe, whom Emerson did read. This way of construing reality awakens resistance in us, but a hundred and fifty years ago the men of Christendom were imbued with notions of an all-determining, circumambient invisible Power around them. Insofar as Idealism expresses the notion of repeating laws and analogies and interchanges permeating the universe, it is modern, and scientific; and Emerson was quite scientific-minded. In *Nature* he wrote:

> Not only resemblances exist in things whose analogy is obvious, as when we detect the type of the human hand in the flipper of the fossil saurus, but also in

objects wherein there is great superficial unlikeness. . . . A rule of one art, or a law of one organization, holds true throughout nature. So intimate is this Unity, that, it is easily seen, it lies under the undermost garment of nature, and betrays its source in Universal Spirit.

Except for the use of the term "spirit," this search for a Unified Field Theory is familiar enough. And Idealism does locate a real cleavage in our consciousness: "Idealism acquaints us with the total disparity between the evidence of our own being, and the evidence of the world's being." The two types of evidence, indeed, are so disparate that only moments that savor of mysticism fuse them.

> In the woods, we return to reason and faith. There I feel that nothing can befall me in life,—no disgrace, no calamity (leaving me my eyes,) which nature cannot repair. Standing on the bare ground,—my head bathed by the blithe air, and uplifted into infinite space,—all mean egotism vanishes. I become a transparent eye-ball; I am nothing; I see all; the currents of the Universal Being circulate through me; I am part or particle of God.

Now, our concern is less to explicate Emerson's philosophy than to test whether it, and the elaborations that followed from it, still might serve as the cause of wit in others. That the Idealism set forth in *Nature* served to guide Emerson himself through a productive life of exceptional serenity is a matter of biographical record. In 1871, when he was late in his sixties, he visited Northern California, descending even into the opium dens of San Francisco. A travelling companion, Professor James B. Thayer, wrote this of a trip to Yosemite:

> "How *can* Mr. Emerson," said one of the younger members of the party to me that day, "be so agreeable, all the time, without getting tired!" It was the *naïve* expression of what we all had felt. There was never a more agreeable travelling companion; he was always accessible, cheerful, sympathetic, considerate, tolerant; and there was always that same respectful interest in those with whom he talked, even the humblest, which raised them in their own estimation. One thing particularly impressed me,—the sense that he seemed to have of a certain great amplitude of time and leisure. It was the behavior of one who really *believed* in an immortal life, and had adjusted his conduct accordingly; so that, beautiful and grand as the natural objects were, among which our journey lay, they were matched by the sweet elevation of character, and the spiritual charm of our gracious friend.

Though he never again stated the tenets of Idealism at such length and with as near an approach to system as in *Nature*, they remained at the core of his thought, and all his lectures circle around the reassuring assertions that spirit is the author of matter and that our egos partake of the benign unity of Universal Being. "I have taught one doctrine," he wrote in his journals, "the infinitude of the private man."

The year after publishing *Nature*, Emerson was invited to give the annual Phi Beta Kappa oration at Harvard, since the society's first choice, a Dr. Wainwright, had declined. Emerson's address that last day of August made his fame. Oliver Wendell Holmes was present on the platform, and called it at the time "our intellectual Declaration of Independence." In it Emerson told the young scholars of his audience that "we have listened too long to the courtly muses of Europe," and that "if the single man plant himself indomitably on his instincts, and there abide, the huge world will come round to him." Not books but nature—with which America, amid many deficiencies, was well supplied—shall be the foremost shaper of these indomitable instincts. Emerson describes education by osmosis, out-of-doors:

> Thus to him, to this school-boy under the bending dome of day, is suggested, that he and it proceed from one root; one is leaf and one is flower: relation, sympathy, stirring in every vein. . . . He shall see, that nature is the opposite of the soul, answering to it part for part. One is seal, and one is print. Its beauty is the beauty of his own mind. Its laws are the laws of his own mind. . . . So much of nature as he is ignorant of, so much of his own mind does he not yet possess. And, in fine, the ancient precept, "Know thyself," and the modern precept, "Study nature," become at last one maxim.

Can this, we wonder now, and his audience then most have wondered, be true? In what sense can nature, that implacable *other* which our egos oppose, whose unheeding processes make resistance to our every effort of construction and husbandry, and whose diseases and earthquakes and oceans extinguish us with a shrug, be termed identical with our own souls? Is not a world of suffering scandalously excluded from such an equation? Emerson's next address, to the graduating seniors of the Harvard Divinity School in July of 1838, takes up again the theme of nature as the end and means of education:

> The child amidst his baubles, is learning the action of light, motion, gravity, muscular force; and in the game of human life, love, fear, justice, appetite, man, and God interact. These laws refuse to be adequately stated . . . yet we read them hourly in each other's faces, in each other's actions, in our own remorse. . . . The intuition of the moral sentiment is an insight of the perfection of the laws of the soul. These laws execute themselves. They are out of time, out of space, and not subject to circumstance. Thus; in the soul of man there is a justice whose retributions are instant and entire. . . . See how this rapid intrinsic energy worketh everywhere, righting wrongs, correcting appearances, and bringing up facts to a harmony with thoughts. Its operation in life, though slow to the senses, is, at last, as sure as in the soul. . . . Character is always known. Thefts never enrich; alms never impoverish; murder will speak out of stone walls.

Do we, in the year 1984, believe this? I suggest we do not: it is part of our received wisdom to believe that stone walls often conceal murder very well; that character is obscure and deceptive; that whatever harmony we enjoy with nature is the cruel and monstrously slow haphazard work of adaptive evolution; that our moral dispositions are bred into us by the surrounding culture; and that no great soul is shared by our own greedy egos and the ravenous natural forces at bay around us. In so believing, if Emerson is correct, we differ from all mankind hitherto, which has conceded the "facts" of indwelling moral sentiment. "These facts," he claims,

> have always suggested to man the sublime creed, that the world is not the product of manifold power, but of one will, of one mind; and that one mind is everywhere active, in each ray of the star, in each wavelet of the pool; and whatever opposes that will, is everywhere balked and baffled, because things are made so, and not otherwise. Good is positive. Evil is merely privative, not absolute: it is like cold, which is the privation of heat. All evil is so much death or nonentity. Benevolence is absolute and real. So much benevolence as a man hath, so much life hath he .... Whilst a man seeks good ends, he is strong by the whole strength of nature.

These assertions, too, we tend to doubt, though our popular arts, as recently exemplified by the *Star Wars* saga, join Emerson in proposing that a good man is naturally strengthened and evil is in the end an illusion that dissolves. To many of Emerson's audience (raised, after all, not only in the hard world but in a religious orthodoxy whose central figure was a suffering God), his optimistic cosmology must have seemed moonshine, to use Melville's word. The assertion that nature and our souls are one is a deliberate affront to our common assumptions, as is Jesus's that the meek shall inherit the earth, or Luther's that men are saved by faith alone, or Buddha's that the craving for existence and rebirth is the source of pain; such affrontive assertions mark the creation of a new religion. And Emerson certainly thought a new one was needed. He was, we must remember, a radical, whose negative views of the Christian church were considered extreme even in Transcendentalist circles. In middle life, he told a visitor, "I cannot feel interested in Christianity; it is deplorable that there should be a tendency to creeds that would take men back to the chimpanzee." Even the mild and minimal Unitarian faith—"the ice house of Unitarianism," he called it in his journals—had so strained his credence that he had resigned the ministry. He did not mince words to the Harvard Divinity School students:

> It is my duty to say to you, that the need was never greater of new revelation than now. From the views I have already expressed, you will infer the sad conviction, which I share, I believe, with numbers, of the universal decay and now almost death of faith in society.

To those moderns whose religious views have been formed by the crisis theology of Kierkegaard and Barth, which predicates a drastic condition of decay and collapse within so-called Christendom, it is a sombre sensation to apprehend, in the young life and thought of Emerson, the collapse arriving, as the geology, the paleontology, the astronomy, the Biblical criticism of the early nineteenth century pile in upon thinking men with their devastating revelations. Emerson was well aware of the historical situation: "The Puritans in England and America," he said in his Divinity School address, "found in the Christ of the Catholic Church, and in the dogmas inherited from Rome, scope for their austere piety, and their longings for civil freedom. But their creed is passing away, and none arises in its room. I think no man can go with his thoughts about him, into one of our churches, without feeling, that what hold the public worship had on men is gone, or going. It has lost its grasp on the affection of the good, and the fear of the bad. In the country, neighborhoods, half parishes are *signing off*,—to use the local term."

Yet there is, he feels, great need for *a* religion:

What greater calamity can fall upon a nation, than the loss of worship? Then all things go to decay. Genius leaves the temple to haunt the senate, or the market. Literature becomes frivolous. Science is cold. The eye of youth is not lighted by the hope of other worlds, and age is without honor. Society lives to trifles, and when men die, we do not mention them.

What is to be done, then? Emerson invokes the soul: "In the soul, then, let the redemption be sought." What does this mean, exactly? It means, I think, what Karl Barth warned against when he said, "One can *not* speak of God simply by speaking of man in a loud voice." Emerson defined "the true Christianity" to the divinity students as "a faith like Christ's in the infinitude of man." An infinitude, in Emerson's if not Jesus' terms, based upon an understanding of each man's soul as a fragment and mirror of the Universal Soul, the Over-soul, whose language is nature. A special beauty of this new religion is that, new wine though it is, it can be poured into the old bottles of the existing churches Emerson concludes with a peroration that touches upon practical concerns:

The evils of the church that now is are manifest. The question returns, What shall we do? I confess, all attempts to project and establish a Cultus with new rites and forms, seem to me vain. Faith makes us, and not we it, and faith makes its own forms. All attempts to contrive a system are as cold as the new worship introduced by the French to the goddess of Reason,—to-day, pasteboard and fillagree, and ending to-morrow in madness and murder. Rather let the breath of new life be breathed by you through the forms already existing. For, if once you are alive, you shall find they shall become plastic and new. The remedy to their deformity is, first, soul, and second, soul, and evermore, soul. . . . Two inestimable advantages Christianity has given us, first: the Sabbath, the jubilee of the whole world. . . . And secondly, the institution of preaching—the speech of man to men,—essentially the most flexible of all organs, of all forms.

And so the young divinity students of the class of 1838, shaken but, let us hope, inspired, were sent forth to take their places behind the rotten pulpits, to fill the hollow creed and exhausted forms of Christianity with the life of their own souls, somehow; the Harvard faculty did not invite Emerson to speak at Harvard again for thirty years.

Emerson had renounced his own ministry in 1832. At that time, the secular profession of lecturer was making its beginnings with such speakers as Edward Everett, Daniel Webster, and Horace Mann; within a decade Emerson was a star of the lyceum circuit. His lectures, many of which became the essays collected in two volumes in 1841 and 1844, from their titles could seem to be about anything—"History," "Heroism," "Circles," "Gifts," "Manners," "Experience"—but all were sermons of a sort on behalf of the Emersonian religion, "the speech of man to men," demonstrating in themselves and urging upon others the free and generous action of a mind open to the inspirations and evidences of the Universal Soul. They were all exhortations to be brave and bold, to trust the universe and oneself. Their supernaturalist content in general, after *Nature*, tends to fade, but is never disavowed, and is always the final recourse of the exhortation. "Let a man fall into the divine circuits, and he is enlarged" ends Emerson's disquisition on "New England Reformers." "We are escorted on every hand through life by spiritual agents, and a beneficent purpose lies in wait for us," states the short essay that also bears the title "Nature." "Nature is the incarnation of a thought, and turns to a thought again, as ice becomes water and gas. The world is mind precipitated, and the volatile essence is forever escaping again into the state of free thought. . . . Every moment instructs, and every object for wisdom is infused info every form."

Of all the essays, the one entitled "Self-Reliance" is perhaps the best known, and has entered most deeply into American thinking. It offers a curious counsel of fatalism couched in the accents of activism:

> Trust thyself: every heart vibrates to that iron string. Accept the place the divine providence has found for you, the society of your contemporaries, the connection of events. Great men have always done so, and confided themselves childlike to the genius of their age, betraying their perception that the absolutely trustworthy was seated at their heart, working through their hands, predominating in all their being.

The society of one's contemporaries, however, would seem not to be entirely acceptable, for, we learn a page later, "Society everywhere is in conspiracy against the manhood of every one of its members. . . . The virtue in most request is conformity. Self-reliance is its aversion. . . . Whoso would he a man must be a nonconformist."

Emerson had refused to conform when he resigned the ministry that his ancestors had honored, and did so furthermore at a moment, when his widowed mother and a quartet of brothers were all looking to him for stability. At the price of breaking up their Boston home, and with no financial prospects but his eventual inheritance from his recently dead young wife, Ellen, he set sail for the first of three excursions to Europe. Frail as a young man, he had developed the gift of taking it easy on himself; unlike his three brilliant brothers William, Edward, and Charles, he compiled a mediocre record at Harvard, and he outlived them all, into a ripe old age. His third European trip was undertaken as he neared seventy, in order to escape the renovation of his house in Concord, which had suffered a fire. There was something a touch cavalier about his second trip, too—nine months of lionization in England and elsewhere while his second wife, Lidian, coped in Concord with three small children and exiguous finances. Emerson's great discovery, amid the ruins of the Puritan creed, was the art of relaxation and of doing what you wanted. In "Self-Reliance" he proclaims:

> I shun father and mother and wife and brother, when my genius calls me. I would write on the lintels of the door-post, *Whim*. I hope it is somewhat better than whim at last, but we cannot spend the day in explanation.

The importunities of philanthropy—a real menace in the New England of this time, especially for the foremost proponent of Idealism—must be repelled:

> Do not tell me, as a good man did to-day, of my obligation to put all poor men in good situations. Are they *my* poor? I tell thee, thou foolish philanthropist, that I grudge the dollar, the dime, the cent, I give to such men as do not belong to me and to whom I do not belong.

A doctrine of righteous selfishness is here propounded. The Biblical injunction "Love thy neighbor as thyself" is conveniently shortened to "Love thyself":

> I must be myself. I cannot break myself any longer for you, or you. If you can love me for what I am, we shall be the happier.... I will so trust that what is deep is holy, that I will do strongly before the sun and moon whatever inly rejoices me, and the heart appoints.

As the Yippies were to say: "If it feels good, do it." Or in the nineteenth-century idiom of William Henry Vanderbilt, "The public be damned." The American Scholar being advised to "plant himself indomitably on his instincts" shades, in "Self-Reliance," into the entrepreneur; the great native creed of Rugged Individualism begins to be heard. Having derided feckless college men who lose heart if "not installed in an office within one year afterwards in the cities or suburbs of Boston," Emerson proclaims:

> A sturdy lad from New Hampshire or Vermont, who in turn tries all the professions, who *teams it, farms it, peddles*, keeps school, preaches, edits a newspaper, goes to Congress, buys a township, and so forth, in successive years, and always, like a cat, falls on his feet, is worth a hundred of these city dolls. He walks abreast with his days, and feels no shame in not "studying a profession," for he does not postpone his life, but lives already.

Emerson wished to give men courage to be, to follow their own instincts; but these instincts, he neglected to emphasize, can be rapacious. A social fabric, he did not seem quite to realize (and in the security of pre-Civil War America, in the pretty farm town of

Concord, what would insist he realize it?), exists for the protection of its members, as do the laws and inhibitions such a fabric demands. To be sure, he did not create American expansionism and our especial exploitive verve; but he did give them a blessing and a high-minded apology. Are we afraid the rich will oppress the poor? In his essay on "Compensation" Emerson assures us, "There is always some levelling circumstance that puts down the overbearing, the strong, the rich, the fortunate, substantially on the same ground with all others." Do our hearts bleed for the manacled slave? "Most suffering is only apparent," he informs us in his uncollected but fascinating essay upon "The Tragic." "A tender American girl doubts of Divine Providence whilst she reads the horrors of 'the middle passage' and they are bad enough at the mildest; but to such as she these crucifixions do not come: they come to the obtuse and barbarous, to whom they are not horrid, but only a little worse, than the old sufferings." Do the blackness and noise of the railroad and factory affront us? "Readers of poetry," Emerson says in his essay on "The Poet," "see the factory-village, and the railways, and fancy that the poetry of the landscape is broken up by these; for these works of art are not yet consecrated in their reading; but the poet sees them fall within the great Order not less than the bee-hive, or the spider's geometrical web." Are we afraid, in a land so carelessly given over to youth and its divine instincts, of growing old? No problem, says Emerson in effect, in his essay on "Circles": "Nature abhors the old, and old age seems the only disease. . . . I see no need of it. Whilst we converse with what is above us, we do not grow old, but grow young." Death, too, is eloquently fudged away: "And the knowledge that we traverse the whole scale of being, from the centre to the poles of nature, and have some stake in every possibility, lends that sublime lustre to death, which philosophy and religion have too outwardly and literally striven to express in the popular doctrine of the immortality of the soul. The reality is more excellent than the report. . . . The divine circulations never rest nor linger" ("Nature"). Are we vexed, depressed, or indignant? Emerson tells us "that there is no need of struggles, convulsions, and despairs, of the wringing of the hands and the gnashing of the teeth; that we miscreate our own evils. We interfere with the optimism of nature. . . . Nature will not have us fret and fume" ("Spiritual Laws").

Understood in relation to Emerson's basic tenets, these reassurances are not absurd. Further, amid the fading of other reassurances, they were urgently useful, and are woven into the created, inherited reality around us. The famous American pragmatism and "can do" optimism were given their most ardent and elegant expression by Emerson. His encouragements have their trace elements in the magnificent sprawl we see on all sides—the parking lots and skyscrapers, the voracious tracts of single-family homes, the heaped supermarket aisles and crowded ribbons of highway: the architectural manifestations of a nation of individuals, of wagons each hitched, in his famous phrase, to its own star. Like balloon-frame house construction—another American invention of the eighteen-forties—Emersonianism got the job done with lighter materials. In his journals he struck the constructive note: "It is greatest to believe and to hope well of the world, because he who does so, quits the world of experience, and makes the world he lives in."

And, reading Emerson, one wonders if the American style is a matter so much of energy and enterprise as of insouciance, of somewhat reckless relaxation into the random abundance of opportunities which an optimistic Nature has provided. The American accent is a drawl, and Emerson, in his collection *English Traits*, more than once marvels at the vigor and force and ruddiness of the English, as if in contrast to a languid, lazy, and pallid race he has left behind. Can it be true that, along with our sweet independence and informality, there is something desolate and phantasmal, a certain thinness of experience which goes with our thinness of civilization? As an introspective psychologist, Emerson is nowhere more original than is his baring of his own indifference. "I content myself with moderate, languid actions," he wrote in his journal of November 3, 1838. "I told J[ones] V[ery] that I had never suffered, & that I could scarce bring myself to feel a concern for the safety & life of my nearest friends that would satisfy them: that I saw clearly that if my wife, my child, my mother, should be taken from me, I should still remain whole with the same capacity of cheap enjoyment from all things." This was written before the death of his beloved five-year-old son, Waldo. After it, in his uncharacteristically sombre essay "Experience," Emerson confessed:

> Grief too will make us idealists. In the death of my son, now more than two years ago, I seem to have lost a beautiful estate,—no more. . . . It does not touch me: something which I fancied was a part of me, which could not be torn away without tearing me, nor enlarged without enriching me, falls off from me, and leaves no scar. . . . The Indian who was laid under a curse, that the wind should not blow on him, nor water flow to him, nor fire burn him, is a type of us all. The dearest events are summer-rain, and we the Para coats that shed every drop.

Which brings us back to Melville's charge of coldness, his picture of Mark Winsome "coldly radiant as a prism." "Emerson in his lifetime was accused of coldness, by Margaret Fuller and Thomas Carlyle among others, and in "Experience" addresses the issue: "The life of truth is cold, and so far mournful; but it is not the slave of tears, contritions, and perturbations. It does not attempt another's work, nor adopt another's facts. . . . I have learned that I cannot dispose of other people's facts. . . . A sympathetic person is placed in the dilemma of a swimmer among drowning men, who all catch at him, and if he give so much as a leg or a finger, they will drown him." The practical ethics of Idealism, then, turn out to be seclusion and stoicism. "We must walk as guests in nature,—not impassioned, but cool and disengaged," Emerson says in "The Tragic." Is there possibly, in this most amiable of philosophers, a preparation for the notorious loneliness and callousness and violence of American life which is mixed in with its many authentic, and indeed unprecedented, charms?

Emerson was the first American thinker to have a European influence; Carlyle sponsored him, and Matthew Arnold once said that no prose had been more influential in the nineteenth century than Emerson's. He was, in German translation, a favorite author of Friedrich Nietzsche, who copied dozens of passages into a notebook, borrowed the phrase "the gay science," and wrote of the *Essays*, "Never have I felt so much at home in a book, and in *my* home, as—I may not praise it, it is too close to me." The closeness, upon reflection, is not so strange: both were ministers' sons exultant in the liberation that came with the death of the Christian God, both were poets and rhapsodists tagged with the name of philosopher. Almost certainly, Emerson's phrase "Over-soul" influenced Nietzsche's choice of the phrase "*Übermensch*," even though "Over-soul" in the edition Nietzsche read was translated "*Die höhere Seele*," the higher soul, which is echoed by Nietzsche's talk of "the higher men." From the Over-soul to the *Übermensch* to the Supermen of Hitler's Master Race is a dreadful progression for which neither Emerson nor Nietzsche should he blamed; but Emerson's coldness and disengagement and distrust of altruism do become, in Nietzsche, a rapturous celebration of power and domination and the "'boldness' of noble races," and an exhilarated scorn of what he called "slave morality." Not just the mention of Zoroaster seems Nietzschean in this passage from "Self-Reliance":

> Welcome evermore to gods and men is the self-helping man. For him all doors are flung wide: him all tongues greet, all honors crown, all eyes follow with desire. Our love goes out to him and embraces him, because he did not need it. We solicitously and apologetically caress and celebrate him, because he held on his way and scorned our disapprobation. The gods love him because men hated him. "To the persevering mortal," said Zoroaster, "the blessed Immortals are swift."
>
> As men's prayers are a disease of the will, so are their creeds a disease of the intellect.

The essay quotes approvingly Fletcher's "Our valors are out best gods" and bluntly states, "Power is in nature the essential measure of right." Totalitarian rule, with its atrocities, offers a warped mirror in which we can recognize, distorted, Emerson's favorite concepts of genius and inspiration and whim; the totalitarian leader is a study in self-reliance gone amok, lawlessness enthroned in the place where law and debate and checks and balances should be, and with no obliging law of compensation coming to the rescue. The extermination camps are one of the things that come between us and Emerson's optimism.

Another is modern science, as it has developed. "Our approach now," my dermatologist, told me the other day, "is that nature is utterly stupid." The same chemical mechanisms, he went on to explain, will destroy as blindly as they heal, and a trend of medicine is to block the witless commands that unleash harmful reactions in the body; where, in this molecular game, can we find indication that "acid and alkali preëxist in necessary Ideas in the mind of God, and are what they are by virtue of preceding affections, in the world of spirit"?

Also we find aesthetic difficulty in a disconnected quality of Emerson's discourse which in the actual lectures must have been greatly masked and smoothed by his handsome manner and appealing baritone voice. We are left with his literary voice, which (unlike Thoreau's similar voice) seems pitched a bit over our heads, toward the back rows, and too much partakes of what he himself called "the old largeness." Knut Hamsun, in his own lectures on *The Cultural Life of Modern America*, expressed what many a student has groped to say since.

One reads all his excellent comments: one reads while awaiting a conclusion relevant to the subject itself. One awaits the third and final word that can draw a figure or cast a statue. One waits until the twentieth and final page—one waits in vain: at this point Emerson bows and departs. And the reader is left with a lapful of things said; they have not formed a picture; they are a brilliant welter of small, elegant mosaic tiles.

I myself have found that the essays melt and merge in the mind; so exciting in their broad attack and pithy sentences, they end, often, disconcertingly in air, and fail to leave an imprint of their shape. This need not have been so: one sermon of Emerson's has survived, the one he gave in the Second Church of Boston, explaining why he could not in good faith administer the Lord's Supper and therefore must resign. It moves dramatically from careful examination of the relevant Biblical and patristic texts to the speaker's own conclusions and thence to his beautifully understated but firm farewell. We remember it; its segments are articulated in a single gesture of argument. Of few of his essays can this be said. With his belief in inspiration, and what he called "*dream power*" and in patterns that all nature would conspire to express once a sufficiently pure surrender to the Over-soul was attained, Emerson read in his Concord study as his whim and his interest dictated and wrote in his celebrated journal, maintained since his college years, such quotations and paragraphs of independent thought as struck him. He assembled his lectures from this lode of intellectual treasure and, though the joinery is cunning and the language often brilliantly concrete, the net effect is somewhat jumbled and vague. We have been superbly exhorted, but to what effect? A demonstration of wit has been made, but somewhat to the stupefaction of our own wits. Modern critics, my impression is, are additionally embarrassed by the Neoplatonic, supernaturalist content of the early essays, and prefer the later, more factual considerations, and the journals themselves, where the discontinuity is overt and the tone is franker and more intimate. Yet the question is: Would the journals and even the excellent *English Traits*—the centerpiece of Mark Van Doren's *Portable Emerson*—make a major claim on our attention had they not been hoisted into prominence by the celebrated, evangelical early addresses and essays? There is this awkwardness, I believe, in Emerson's present reputation: what we like about him is not what is important, and what *is* important we do not much like. Emerson the prophet of the new American religion seems cranky and dim; what we like is the less ethereal and ministerial Emerson, the wry, observant, shrewd, skeptical man of this world. Emerson was always such, of course; as Oliver Wendell Holmes said of him, "he never let go the string of his balloon." The founder of Emersonianism was not its ideal practitioner; his extraordinary loyalty to the exasperating Bronson Alcott must have resided, it seems to me, in his awe of Alcott's great superior impracticality. Thoreau, too, appeared to Emerson a kind of saint, who, he said in the beautiful eulogy delivered at Thoreau's funeral, in 1862, "lived extempore from hour to hour, like the birds and the angels." Thoreau even worked miracles: "One day walking with a stranger who inquired, where Indian arrowheads could be found, he replied, 'Every where,' and stooping forward, picked one on the instant from the ground." More amazing still, "from a box containing a bushel or more of loose pencils, he could take up with his hands fast enough just a dozen pencils at every grasp." No such magical sureness, his self-doubting journals reveal, had been granted Emerson; he felt skeptical about his own enthusiasms, mocking himself, in the essay "Illusions," as susceptible to any new style or mythology. "I fancy that the world will be all brave and right, if dressed in these colors, which I had not thought of," he wrote. "Then at once I will daub with this new paint; but it will not stick. 'Tis like the cement which the peddler sells at the door; he makes broken crockery hold with it, but you can never buy of him a bit of the cement which will make it hold when he is gone."

So, too, the subject of these reflections. As I was reading Emerson, a hundred stimulated thoughts would besiege me, but all in the nature of paint that would not stick, of crockery coming unglued. What notes I took became scrambled; seeking to refer back to a key passage, I would find the words had quite vanished from Emerson's pages. So one morning I decided to take leave of my bookish responsibilities and work in my cellar upon some modest carpentry project that had been long left hanging. While happily, brainlessly planing away, I turned on the radio, an "educational" station to be sure, and was treated to a lengthy "Earth Mass" employing not only human voices and conventional musical instruments but tapes of howling wolves, whales conversing in their mysterious booms and groans, and the rushing sound of the Colorado River. How very Emersonian, I thought: and felt his ghost smile within me. For have we not late in this century come to believe in spite of ourselves that "the mind is One, and that nature is its correlative"? Amid all our materialism, have not sheer crowding and shared peril merged nature with our souls?

Then I had to make haste, for I was to take a train from my suburban town into Boston. I was to have a painless session at Massachusetts General Hospital, where anesthesia was first demonstrated in this country and where my dermatologist stood ready to tell me that Nature was utterly stupid. I walked down to the tracks through my own woods, and in my transcendental humor saw the oddity of owning woods at all, of legally claiming a few acres of woods which are so plainly the property of the trees themselves, and of the invisible creatures that burrow and forage among the trees and will not mark with even a minute's pause their ostensible owner's passing from this earth. Emerson, expanding his holdings in Concord, in 1844 bought fourteen acres by Walden Pond; but it was Thoreau who built a cabin and lived there, and Thoreau, who wrote the masterpiece. We possess, that is, by apprehension, not by legal fiat; the spirit does create matter, along its circumference of awareness.

Emerging from my own neglected woods, I bought at a so-called Convenient Food Mart a can of ginger ale and, after much hesitation, a bag of peanuts in the shell. Most of my life has been lived with women who find peanut shells a trial, especially those papery inner husks that elude every broom; I have associated shelling peanuts with the exercise of personal freedom ever since, as a boy, left alone to wander for an hour in the Pennsylvania city three miles from my home, I would buy a half-pound bag and eat the peanuts as I wandered, dropping the shells into what trash cans and gutters and hedges and sewer grates occurred during my irresponsible stroll. Buying and eating so whimsical a lunch as peanuts and ginger ale appeared, by the light of my recent reading, a peculiarly national opportunity and an appropriate celebration of the American insouciance that Emerson had labored to provide with a philosophical frame.

The train, I should say, was equipped with plastic windows, since younger Americans than I had been long celebrating their own insouciance and yielding to their own inspirations by tossing rocks at the windows that flew past and shattering them if they were glass. Substituted plastic solved that problem, but in time it has clouded to near-perfect opacity, so that as I hurtled to Boston the trees and houses and vistas on the way were vaguer and less to be guessed at than the shadows flickering in Plato's famous cave, the womb out of which both Emersonianism and the Gospel of St. John were born.

I arrived, still cracking peanuts, at the hospital. What better exemplifies modern-day America than a hospital! Here a true cross-section of colors and creeds, ages and classes mingles, united by our physical fallibility and our hope that science will save us. Though it was autumn, the weather in New England was still warm, so the crowd summoned to the hospital was lightly dressed, in bright colors, in sandals and jogging shorts. Nubile, merciful nurses and brisk, sage physicians moved in angelic white through the throng of the infirm and their visitors. There were limping young athletes called in from their game by some injury they would forget in a week, young women pushing delicate bug-eyed babies in strollers or lugging them on their hips, elderly couples with an air of having long harbored a single complaint between them. "Life is an ecstasy," Emerson tells us in "Illusions." "Life is sweet as nitrous oxide; and the fisherman dripping all day over a cold pond, the switchman at the railway intersection, the farmer in the field, the negro in the rice-swamp, the fop in the street, the hunter in the woods, the barrister with the jury, the belle at the ball, all ascribe a certain pleasure to their employment, which they themselves give it." Now a multitude of such as these had been fetched here, with the smells and auras of their lives and employments still on them; to be among them was happiness.

I noticed a man about my age with a bald head—not a healthy luminous baldness but the unnatural gauzy baldness that chemotherapy induces. On Emerson's advice, I checked the presumptuous motion of pity in my heart, my officious inner attempt to adopt and dispose of other people's facts; for, sitting there in the waiting lounge somewhat like a sultan, the man was not asking pity but instead was calmly wrapped in his own independent, and perhaps triumphant thoughts. I sat down myself and read—who else?—Emerson, Emerson it was my own whim to peruse in the little old uniform edition of brown leather and marbled endpapers I had bought at a church fair for five dollars and most of whose pages had never been cut. To slit these pages I used my bookmark, the joker of an old deck of cards—another whim, and yet efficient. "The way of life is wonderful," I read, "It is by abandonment." Looking up, I noticed a man in a chair opposite me reading a book also. He was reading a fanciful novel called *The Coup*, which I had once written. He was a stout cigar-smoking man who slowly turned the pages with a terrible steady frown; he was not at all my image of the Ideal Reader. Yet there he was, in front of me; who was I to doubt now that, as Emerson promised, "every proverb, every book, every byword that belongs to thee for aid or comfort, shall surely come home through open or winding passages"? And that, as the same page of

"The Over-Soul" states, "the heart in thee is the heart of all; not a valve, not a wall, not an intersection is there anywhere in nature, but one blood rolls uninterruptedly an endless circulation through all men, as the water of the globe is all one sea, and, truly seen, its tide is one." Was not this day of mine demonstrating at every emblematic turn that "a thread runs through all things; all worlds are strung on it, as beads; and men, and events, and life, come to us, only because of that thread"?

A man within unavoidable earshot was making a call on a pay phone. His side of the conversation went: Stella? Any news?" A pause, and then, "Isn't that great? It so easily could have been different. I'm so happy for him." How much, indeed, I could not help thinking, of the news we receive *is* good. "We are natural believers," Emerson says in his essay on Montaigne. "Belief consists in accepting the affirmations of the soul; unbelief, in denying them." It was Emerson's revelation that God and the self are of the same substance. He may have been wrong, too blithe on Mankind's behalf, to think that nature—what he called the "*other me*"—is possessed of optimism and always answers to our soul; but he was immensely right in implying that the prime *me*, the ego, is perforce optimistic.

Note

1   Stanley Cavell, *Little Did I Know: Excerpts from Memory* (Stanford: Stanford University Press, 2010), August 22, 2003, 158.

Big Dead White Male

John Updike

The observances this year of the two-hundredth anniversary of Ralph Waldo Emerson's birth, in 1803, have been measured but widespread: conferences were scheduled in the great man's adopted home town of Concord, Massachusetts, and, this fall, in Beijing and Rome. The year's issue of the *Journal of Unitarian Universalist History* is devoted to Emerson, a bicentennial exhibition ran at Harvard's Houghton Library from March to June, and in his birth month of May it was possible in Concord to mingle with actors playing the roles of such friends as Henry David Thoreau and the Alcott sisters and such significant relatives as his eldest daughter, Ellen, and his redoubtable aunt, Mary Moody Emerson. There were many newspaper editorials, including one in the *Times* that credited Emerson with formulating the "pernicious and currently thriving, philosophy of American individualism run amok—call it American self-absorption." The Republican tax cut, tilted toward the rich, and the Administration's us-first, go-it-alone foreign policy, not to mention the financial rapacity of Enron and Tyco executives and Wall Street mis-advisers, were all traced by the *Times* to Emerson's gospel of self-reliance.

In the world of books—the world that preserves Emerson's memory and message, now that his hypnotic baritone voice and reassuring platform presence are no more—the celebration has been restrained. The Boston firm of David R. Godine has issued a pleasing anthology, *A Year with Emerson*, edited by Richard Grossman, and with typically fine engravings by Barry Moser ($26.95). Emerson, a disbeliever in "foolish consistency" who customarily assembled his lectures from thoughts and sentences written in journals that he began keeping as a Harvard undergraduate, has always lent himself well to being excerpted. His published essays—refined and expanded versions of the lectures—can seem unduly long and, once read, slippery in the mind. The three hundred and sixty-five items assembled in this "Daybook" are drawn from letters and poems as well as from the canonized prose; while it hard to imagine even the most devout Emersonian undertaking the pious discipline of a daily reading, Grossman's arranged and annotated progress through the year hops about in lively fashion and often surprises us. Surprise was an aesthetic effect Emerson cherished, as we read in the journal entry titled "Good Writing":

> All writing should be selection in order to drop every dead word. Why do you not save out of your speech or thinking only the vital things—the spirited mot which amused or warmed you when you spoke it—because of its luck & newness. I have just been reading, in this careful book of a most intelligent & learned man, a number of flat conventional words & sentences. If a man would learn to read his own manuscript severely—becoming really a third person, & search only for what interested him, he would blot to purpose—& how every page would gain! Then all the words will be sprightly, & every sentence a surprise.

The passage sets out, in small, Emerson's priorities—spontaneity over convention, vitality over formality, luck and newness over system. Out with what is dead! But keep, along with the spirited mot, a third-person detachment. Though he averred, "I would write on the lintels of the door-post, *Whim*," he was a scrupulous and patient reviser, who extensively reworked most of his lectures for their appearance in print.

Also this spring, Princeton issued a slim volume, *Understanding Emerson: 'The American Scholar' and His Struggle for Self-Reliance*, by Kenneth S. Sacks ($29.95). Sacks, a professor of history at Brown, describes the heated intellectual context in which Emerson delivered, on August 31, 1837, the annual address before the Phi Beta Kappa Society at Harvard, a speech afterward titled "The American Scholar" and destined to become, according to Sacks, "the most famous in American academic history." It, and Emerson's address to the senior class of the Harvard Divinity School the following July, staked out his turf and made his name. Both addresses were, beneath their flowers of rhetoric, inflammatorily hostile to the host institution, from which Emerson had graduated in 1821, thirtieth in a class of fifty-nine. Harvard, in Professor Sacks's analysis, was a bastion of Unitarianism, which had become the religion of the ruling elite of Boston. Unitarianism, which in 1819 was called "the half-way house to infidelity" by a professor at the rival Andover Theological Seminary, and is now seen, with its sister the Universalist Church, as the ultimate in liberal Protestantism, by 1837 had acquired an aristocratic and conservative bias that disdained populist revivalism and, closer to home, so-called Transcendentalism, an intellectual movement derived from the mystic streak in Goethe, Wordsworth, Coleridge, and Carlyle. Emerson praised such writers for being "blood-warm" and for perceiving "the worth of the vulgar"; these were fighting words, as was his insistence on the great value of the individual person's subjectivity. According to Sacks:

> Harvard-Unitarian culture found spiritual and intellectual confirmation in empirical proof, scientific progress, and material success. Emerson acknowledged understanding derived from observation of external phenomena, but believed that the more important truths are eternal and intuitive, emerging from within. Ostensibly a struggle between the schools of Locke and Kant, after 2200 years it still pretty much came down to Aristotle versus Plato. But Emerson's scholar wasn't the elite Guardian of Plato's *Republic*, it was instead Socrates, son of a stone mason.

European Romanticism, rephrased for the American democracy, posed a revolutionary threat to a rationalist élite. At the same time, it upset Christian orthodoxy, even the attenuated Unitarian form. Emerson's Divinity School address, amid its offenses, reduced Jesus to a sublimely typical man, one who was "true to what is in you and me," alive to the "daily miracle" of "man's life," and manifesting not miracles and an impossible sanctity but "a sweet, natural goodness, a goodness like thine and mine, and that so invites thine and mine to be and to grow." To the future ministers, Emerson, having vividly sketched the dismal state of the contemporary church—"It has lost its grasp on the affection of the good, and the fear of the bad"—said, "Cast behind you all conformity, and acquaint men at first hand with Deity." He admonished them "to go alone; to refuse the good models, even those which are sacred in the imagination of men, and dare to love God without mediator or veil." That the terrain to which his auditors are released is dauntingly featureless did not curb Emerson's own delight in solitary freedom. His father, a dry conforming Unitarian clergyman, had died early, leaving little legacy of affection in his seven-year-old son's memory, and Emerson had liberated himself from a parish minister's duties, including the personally distasteful one of administering the Lord's Supper, before the age of thirty. Yet he continued supply preaching throughout the eighteen-thirties, and called his public lectures "lay sermons." His two aggressively large-minded Harvard addresses advanced his burgeoning career as a lyceum speaker, a free-ranging secular prophet.

Proper Boston resisted his message. Attending a Harvard ceremony not long after giving the Divinity School address, he noted in his journal, "The young people & the mature hint at odium, & aversion of faces to be presently encountered in society. I say no: I fear it not." Sacks relates how one Convers Francis, taking tea with a "family belonging to the straitest sect of Boston conservatism found that his hosts "abhor & abominate R. W. Emerson as a sort of mad dog: & when I defended that pure and angelic spirit ... they laughed at me with amazement." By this light, Emerson's Transcendentalism, with its claims in these two addresses that "all men have sublime thoughts," that "the active soul" is something "every man is entitled to," and that, "if the single man plant himself indomitably on his instincts, and there abide, the huge world will come round to him," formed part of the Jacksonian revolution whereby the democracy's yeomen sought to take power and responsibility from an élite of merchants and planters.

The weightiest bicentennial volume thus far has been *Emerson*, by the Harvard professor Lawrence Buell (Harvard; $29.95). A three-hundred-and-thirty-four-page rumination in seven chapters, the book has the relaxed, sometimes personal air of a graduate-student seminar rather than the clarion tones of a lecture in an undergraduate survey course. We are assumed to know something about Emerson already. The biographical facts are swiftly sketched and subjected to skeptical inquiry, the patriotic "jingoism" of his stirring ceremonial hymn beginning "By the rude bridge that arched the flood," for example, is minimized by Buell's conclusion that "Emerson's own concern was with values that stand the test of time and unite the world." Buell's repeatedly solicitous, corrective slant has the unintended effect of showing how thoroughly Emerson, who spoke to wake up the democratic masses to the powers within them, is now captive to the contentious, incestuous circles of academe. An endorsement on the back of the jacket, by Sacvan Bercovitch, the author of *The Puritan Origins of the American Self*, salutes Buell's book as "the harvest of the past half-century of Emersonian revaluations and harbinger, guide, and provocation for the next generations of Emerson scholars and critics"—as if Emerson scholars and critics, in their generations, are world enough. Buell rarely pitches his voice above classroom level. Saving type at the price of obscurity, he identifies many key quotations in "CW," specified on page xi as "*The Complete Works of Ralph Waldo Emerson*, 12 vols., Ed. Edward Waldo Emerson. Boston: Houghton-Mifflin, 1903–1904," leaving those who happen to lack that twelve-volume set from the outset of the last century to guess, often, what essay is being quoted. Such ill-equipped readers must guess, too, at the shadowy content of scholarly disputes that are second nature to the sixty-four-year-old Buell, who in his preface admits he has been mulling Emerson over since he was twenty-six.

He makes an extensive case against "a present-day literary-Americanist standpoint" that, in his view, takes too seriously the concluding peroration of "The American Scholar" ("We have listened too long to the courtly muses of Europe.... We will walk on our own feet; we will work with our own hands; we will speak our own minds.... A nation of men will for the first time exist, because each believes himself inspired by the Divine Soul which also inspires all men") and not seriously enough Emerson as a global intellectual shaped by European and Asian (Hindu, Buddhist, Persian Sufi) influences and influential in turn, abroad, with declared admirers ranging from Matthew Arnold and Friedrich Nietzsche to such outriggers as the Cuban poet-revolutionary José Marti, the Australian Charles Harpur, the Jewish Indian poet Nissim Ezekiel, and—a great catch—Marcel Proust. But who is arguing? To someone of Emerson's generation, European thought and writing was almost all there was; Puritan sermons, Benjamin Franklin's blithe compositions, the Founding Fathers' chiselled eloquence, Washington Irving's sketches, and James Fenimore Cooper's Leather-stocking Tales—all were easily overlookable by a serious American aspirant to high thought and poetry in the early nineteenth century. To Emerson, Poe, his only peer as a homegrown critical and creative mind, was "the jingle man."

In the heavily politicized world of contemporary American academic studies, nuances of emphasis loom with the menace of frontal assaults. Buell frequently sounds defensive, admitting that "Emerson's significance as a force in U.S. literary history has shrunk since the ethnic renaissances of the twentieth century, the late-century expansion of the American canon, and increasing disenchantment with the whole idea of literary canonicity." The category of "canonicity," of practical concern mostly to textbook manfacturers, distracts the celebrant from his own aesthetic reactions and evaluations. The "so-called new Americanist criticism of the last two decades," we read, "tends to see the tensions between margin and center (in particular of race, ethnicity, gender, class, and sexuality) as more central to U.S. cultural history than any supposed aesthetic mainstream. . . . No longer does it seem so self-evident that Emerson and Transcendentalism were the gateway to U.S. literary emergence." When was it self-evident? It wasn't to his contemporaries Melville and Hawthorne, who both took a satiric and suspect view of Emerson's soul-talk. "This Plato who talks thro' his nose," Melville called him, adding, "To one who has weathered Cape Horn as a common sailor what stuff all this is."

Professor Buell, while trying to give Emerson the benefit of his forty years of close and fond attention, gives evidence of having weathered many storms of political correctness. He seems, within his discourse, distracted by hectoring students and fractious fellow-faculty. Of Emerson's reluctance to join the militant abolitionists, it has to be explained that he had "initial scruples about joining what today seems a far more self-evidently righteous cause than it did to the great majority of nineteenth-century northern whites in the 1840s and 1850s." Buell pleads that "overall, Emerson's racism was certainly no greater than that of most northern white abolitionists, and far less than the average northern white." Again, Buell confides, "Nor, despite his awareness of and support for American diversity, did he cease to think of Englishness as the dominant ethnic influence in the making of America and especially of New England"—as if in 1850 any other view were possible. Bows are awkwardly made to severer theorists:

> Myra Jehlen argues that Emerson's vision of man coming into his godship through the conquest of nature reads suspiciously like an apology for westward expansion. Christopher Newfield argues that Emerson's appeal to transpersonal authorities like aboriginal self and the "orphic poet" who says the last words in *Nature* implies a forfeiture of individualism and acquiescence to dominant cultural forces that make for a parallel between Emerson's life course and the rise of corporatism in nineteenth-century America.

Buell's account of Emerson's responsiveness to intellectual women like Margaret Fuller, who believed that his "model of personal transformation" opened "the door to female liberation," is accompanied by the gratuitous disclaimer "though admiration was apt to be tinged with lingering misogynistic judgementalism." On the matter of theistic belief, Buell smilingly enlists in a collegial infidelity, with a frown for today's zealots: Emerson's frequent mention of God "is hardly calculated to appeal to the majority of university researchers who presently dominate Emerson studies. For the most part, we are a thoroughly secularized lot, all the more skeptical of God-talk given the rise of fervid evangelical power blocks at home and abroad."

A hundred years after Emerson's centennial was declared a school holiday in Concord and marked by an oration by William James and a public prayer that the spirit of Emerson inspire all present, he is put forward gingerly, apologetically, as a devalued stock on which we might still want to take a flyer. Buell was quoted in the Boston *Globe* (which reviewed his book as "scholarly natterings") as saying, "If you're looking for strong guidance, look elsewhere. But if you're looking for the courage to maintain sanity and resolution when the rest of society seems to have gone mad, Emerson may be your man." The endorsement seems excessively hedged, linking the sage's value to a presumed madness in society. Emerson was too much a realist, I think, to dismiss the workings of a society as mad, even a society like his own, passionately riven antebellum America. He pitched his palace of the Ideal on the particularities and rationale of what existed. One of Bull's few wholehearted sentences exclaims, "How many of the great essays end by propelling the reader out into the world!" Yes; Emerson wanted to encourage us, to make us fit for the world.

So *is* there anything left to say, outside the classroom, about the Sage of Concord? Some of his disciples still do excite non-academic interest: Whitman, who credited Emerson with bringing him to a boil, and who received from him a handsome endorsement, triumphantly survives, as a revolutionary versifier and celebrant of his American self. Thoreau is still read without being assigned, and lives as a patron saint of ecologists.

Though Emerson extolled Nature, centering his testament *Nature* on its manifestations and opening his Divinity School address with a lyrical evocation of the summer in progress, he was not a naturalist. He wrote about people, people in their stressed psychic anatomies, and, as he aged, people in history and society. These later, more worldly writings better suit our modern taste—more concrete, less high-flown. Mark Van Doren, in assembling the Viking *Portable Emerson* back in 1946, leaned heavily upon *English Traits* and the short biographies and omitted many of the relatively youthful philosophical essays. "For he was at his best," Van Doren wrote, "not when he was basic, not when he was trying to understand the man he was, but when he was being that man, when he was applying the ideas which that man had furnished him. He needed matter to illuminate."

Yet the later, more material and genially circumstantial Emerson is not the one whose bicentennial we celebrate. Were his surviving writings confined to those after, say, 1850, they would be remembered the way Washington Irving's travel and historical writings are, and Emerson as another Unitarian clergyman turned literary intellectual, like George Ripley. Emerson won his high place in American esteem as the rounder and proponent of a religion, one of many offshoots and modifications of Christianity—Mormonism, Shakerism, The Millerites—that flourished in the first half of the nineteenth century as Calvinism, with its baleful predestinarian God, lost its hold. Emerson's inspiring stroke of genius was to rephrase and reëmphasize the dualism of Christianity in palatable terms adapted from German philosophy and European Romanticism. On the second page of his first book, *Nature*, published in 1836 and based, we learn from Buell, on ideas in an early sermon, we read:

> Philosophically considered, the universe is composed of Nature and the Soul. Strictly speaking, therefore, all that is separate from us, all which Philosophy distinguishes as the NOT ME, that is, both nature and art, all other men and my own body must be ranked under this name, NATURE.

A year later, in "The American Scholar," the "not me" becomes the "other me" and a relation between the two entities is drawn: "The world,—this shadow of the soul, or *other me*, lies wide around. Its attractions are the keys which unlock my thoughts and make me acquainted with myself." In *Nature*'s seventh chapter, titled "Spirit," an intermediary element had appeared, on both sides of the cleavage: "The noblest ministry of nature is to stand as the apparition of God. It is the organ through which the universal spirit speaks to the individual, and strives to lead back the individual to it." The universal spirit, a striver, would seem to be God, clad in transparent robes of Kantian idealism: "Idealism saith: matter is a phenomenon, not a substance. . . . Yet, if it only deny the existence of matter, it does not satisfy the demands of the spirit. It leaves God out of me." The word "spirit" bounces from the me to the not-me and back again, yet amid this legerdemain Emerson formulates a profound and primitive fact about the human condition—"the total disparity between the evidence of our own being, and the evidence of the world's being." Consciousness creates duality. We exist, to ourselves, non-phenomenally. Our subjective existence is absolute, though indescribable. "The soul *is*," Emerson says in the essay "Compensation." "Under all this running sea of circumstance, whose waters ebb and flow with perfect balance, lies the aboriginal abyss of real Being. Essence, or God, is not a relation, or a part, but the whole. Being is the vast affirmative, excluding negation, self-balanced, and swallowing up all relations, parts and times within itself."

From the absoluteness of the "me" a great deal of religious consolation can be spun. The self is pitted against the vast physical universe as if the two were equal. From "Compensation": "The soul refuses limits, and always affirms an Optimism, never a Pessimism. . . . In the nature of the soul is the compensation for the inequalities of condition." The doctrine is tailor-made for Americans. Emerson's America was also Hawthorne's, which Henry James famously described in a cascade of negatives: "No sovereign, no court, no personal loyalty, no aristocracy, no church, no clergy, no army . . . no country gentlemen, no palaces, no castles, nor manors," and so on. In a New World so bare and barren, and faced with an overweening Nature such as the species has not encountered since prehistoric migrations, what does a person have? A self. And that is plenty, Emerson assures us. "In all my lectures," he stated in his journals, "I have taught one doctrine, the infinitude of the private man." Possessing his own infinity, a man has nothing to fear, not even (though Emerson treads light on the thin ice of personal immortality) death itself.

In essay after essay, waving aside evil as "merely privative," Emerson justifies optimism and declares a holiday for the hard-pressed American soul. Like most faiths, his makes light of the world and its usual trials. His most pessimistic essay "Experience"—that in which he declares, "I have set my heart on honesty"—proclaims the transience and shallowness of grief and love: "The great and crescive self, rooted in absolute nature, supplants all relative existence, and ruins the kingdom of mortal friendship and love. . . . We believe in ourselves, as we do not believe in others. We permit all things to ourselves, and that which we call sin in others, is experiment for us." Elsewhere he expresses a brusque impatience with charity and the clamor of worthy causes. "I must be myself," he tells us. "I cannot break myself any longer for you, or you." How well this suits our native bent! In this country, the self is not dissolved in Oriental group-think, or subordinated within medieval hierarchy. Our spiritual essence, it may be, is selfishness; certainly our art, from Whitman to the Abstract Expressionists, flaunts the naked self with a boldness rarely seen in other national cultures. Emerson is matched only by his hero Montaigne, who confessed, "The world always looks outward, I turn my gaze inward; there I fix it, and there I keep it busy. Everyone looks before him; I look within. I have no business but with myself."

A country imposed on a wilderness needs strong selves. Whether American self-assertiveness fits into today's crammed and touchy world can be debated. But Emerson, with a cobbled-together mythology, in melodious accents that sincerely feigned the old Christian reassurances, sought to instill confidence and courage in his democratic audience, and it is for this, rather than for his mellowed powers of observation and wit, that he is honored, if honored more than read. His relative neglect, a decline from a heyday of gilt-edged uniform editions and soul-stirring fireside perusal, he would have regarded philosophically. He knew how the world eats at our attention. "Experience" ends:

> We dress our garden, eat our dinners, discuss the household with our wives, and these things make no impression, are forgotten next week; but in the solitude to which every man is always returning, he has a sanity and revelations, which in his passage into new worlds he will carry with him. Never mind the ridicule, never mind the defeat: up again, old heart!

William H. Gass (1924–)

Novelist, essayist, critic, and professor of philosophy and the humanities, Gass studied at Cornell with Max Black and briefly with Ludwig Wittgenstein and wrote a dissertation entitled A Philosophical Investigation of Metaphor *(1954). He has taught at Washington University in St. Louis since 1969. In* Habitations of the Word: Essays *(1984), a collection of criticism on Joyce, Dickens, Pound, and Barthes, among others, Gass dedicates the lead essay to an engagement with Emerson's writing—more particularly, the essay form (an earlier version of the chapter appeared as "Emerson and the Essay" in the* Yale Review *(1982)). Writing in essayistic prose that both honors and innovates his subject, Gass says: the "essay induces skepticism [. . . the] essay is simply a watchful form. [. . .] Halfway between sermon and story, the essay interests itself in the narration of ideas—in their unfolding—and the conflict between philosophies or other points of view becomes a drama in its hands." That drama is interactive, as Gass later writes in* Life Sentences *(2011): "Emerson's essays build the mind that thinks them." Addressing the nature of reading Emerson, Gass recognizes the way his prose—from pulpit to lecture platform to page—can return us to our own thoughts: "beneath the reader's steady breath, we're reenacted like a play; because to live is to speak and to be spoken, just as Emerson is once again alive in me when I realize his words. He preaches: I read. I read to become the preachment. Then 'I' preach, and so 'I' listen, finding an Emerson in myself just as he did." Gass provides a penetrating sense of what Emerson means by "I also will essay to be"—where the stakes of writing and sheer existence appear codependent; and he finds a way to explain the role of Emerson's poetry, not in a judgment from on high, but rather by suggesting that "What Emerson wanted from poetry [. . .] none of this could be accomplished except in prose." And so an apparent failure becomes the condition for perceiving Emerson's accomplishment—namely, his effort to achieve his expression, to essay.*

Emerson and the Essay

William H. Gass

1

Our oblivion has been seen to . . . and unless we write as though the ear were our only page; unless upon the open slopes of some reader's understanding we send our thoughts to pasture like sheep let out to graze; unless we can jingle where we feed, sound ourselves and make our presence heard; unless ...

So you hear me read me see me begin.

I begin ... don't both of us begin? Yet as your eye sweeps over these lines—not like a wind, because not a limb bends or a letter trembles, but rather more simply— as you read do you find me here in your lap like a robe? And even if this were an oration, and we were figures in front of one another, columns perhaps, holding up the same thought, it still would not be the first time I had uttered these sentences (though I might seem to be making them up in the moment of speaking like fresh pies), for I was in another, distant, private, country-covered place when I initially constructed them, and then I whispered them above the rattle of my typing (expert and uncaring as the keys); I tried to hear them through the indifferent whirring of their manufacture as if my ear were yours, and held no such noise. My mind was book-bound and mist-mixed. Then no snow had intervened. God knows what or where I am now—now as you read. Montaigne, Lamb, Emerson, are dead. Our oblivion has been seen to ...

And what is the occasion for my writing, or your reading, other than some suggestion from a friend, a few fine books sent in the mail, an invitation to speak, an idle riffle through a few sheets of a stale review, the name Emerson, an essay, an open hour. No one can number the small signs which may revive this distant figure, a figure behind us, safely in our past (can't I confidently assume it for us both?); not even a warm hole in the air remains of all those solemn flames he lit: "Love," for instance, "The Lord's Supper," "Self-Reliance." Doesn't he dimly seem, sometimes, an Ayn Rand beforehand? and of that former earnest heat now nothing but disposed ash. Yet the shadows he casts are the shadows of an honest shade; his work remains fertile, volumes explaining him continue to appear—the progeny of his present, not his past.

Emerson is himself a man of occasions, of course, and he has considered his, and wondered whether these halls he fills like a thermos will keep his high hopes hot. He has once again gone to the lectern: that parlor pulpit and the modest phallus of the teacher. "I read the other day some verses," he will say, perhaps, or ask, "Where do we find ourselves?" (strange question!), and he knows he is up to something different and possibly enduring—a pose his immortality may assume. He is giving definition to his Being. He is waiting for himself to sail from behind a cloud.

"A lecture is a new literature," he writes. "It is an organ of sublime power, a panharmonicon for variety of note." If necessary—to exercise this organ—he will travel. Anywhere. To St. Louis. The West Coast. He is Emerson, is he not? the lapsed saint, the great energy of life itself; and he will speak when he is tired; when he is ill, frightened, nervous; he must represent the spirit even overweight, stand for unweakened resolution, unfailing courage, though faint. His public presence is the presence of his language; and the language of "Fate" or "Self-Reliance" will be formed and reformed often, just as he heard it first above the sound of his own heart, each time as though the occasion were just freshly occurring: "I read the other days some verses. ... The eye is the first circle. ..."

But life is not all eloquence and adulation: life is wiping the baby's bum; it is a bad case of croup; it is quarrels with one's spouse; it is disappointment, distraction, indignities by the dozen; it is the death of friends, wife, son, and brothers, carried off like fluff in the wind; it is alien evenings, cold stairwells, frosty sheets, lack of love; for what does the great spirit need that touches the body but the touch of the body, as oratory needs silence, and revolution peace? We are nourished by our absences and opposites; contraries quench our thirst.

Yet nature turns a dumb face toward us like a cow. When we read its wonders, we wonder whether we haven't written them ourselves. We are in ferment, but our greatness grows light like a bubble of froth. We sense that existence itself lacks substance; that it is serious in the wrong sense; that its heaviness is that of wet air. The sublime . . . ah, the sublime is far off, though we call for its coming. Yes. Life falls short—is never what it should be. Rhymes will not rescue it. Days end, and begin again, automatically. Only the clock connects them. Sullen sunshine is followed by pitiless frost, and the consequence is that we are a tick or two nearer oblivion, and the alarm for our unwaking. Emerson never tires of telling us this. "Illusion, Temperament, Succession, Surface, Surprise, Reality, Subjectiveness—these are the threads on the loom of time, these are the lords of life."

'Life'! . . . short, grand, graceless word. We partake of it, yet spread before us all like the proverbial feast, once its fruits and sweets are eaten, its vintages are drunk, the remaining bones tossed to the dogs, that same feast—life!—is carried away in a spotless cloth, as whole and unmarked as though we had never licked or torn or toothed it. What do we piss of it later but air? Our breath is just such a vacation.

Distantly we hear our children feeding on what we left and didn't leave . . . the bonbon we'd bitten not quite across, the turkey neck we had refused. Wait. Is that a song . . . ? Can it be that we have vanished, and our sons are singing . . . ?

Emerson wants us to feel our thought more literally than we phrase it. He puts face after face on the obvious to renew our recognition. How he hammers his sentences into our innocent psalm-holding hands! "That is always best which gives me to myself." He will not trouble to say once what he cannot say twice. "It is said that the world is in a state of bankruptcy. . . ." At first he adopts a threatening tone, as if something could be done about this state of the world and ourselves. "Beware when the great God lets loose a thinker on this planet." And he is full of self-admonishment. "Nothing is at last sacred but the integrity of your own mind." Because his own problems, his own resolves, are never far away. "Why should we fret and drudge? Our meat will taste tomorrow as it did yesterday, and we may at last have had enough of it."

Though read aloud and delivered repeatedly this way, the lectures become essays as if the sound of them were sunshine burning the page. At first they are addressed to crowds—in Boston or Hanover—but they always aim at the single ear, the solitary listener: the silence of the word syllabating in the silence of the reader's world—in the silence of the private house, in the hall of the whole body. "To fill the hour,—that is happiness; to fill the hour. . . ." So when Emerson gathers his talks up in books, these books are much like albums full of photographs of his former thoughts—not always well lit, unfortunately, though often gracefully, soberly, sometimes even stiffly, posed. "We live among surfaces, and the true art of life is to skate well on them." Bitter wisdom, unhappy skill, beleaguered phrase.

The full ear, full heart and hall, is fast empty; the tireless are now weary; what we thought was profundity is made of smeary surfaces like a stack of dirty plates; the noble spirit who spoke is soon horny, hungry, in need of another hall and still more redemption. The pronouns which steer Emerson's thought through the essays painfully display the problem. There is that outer, objective, commanding "you," on the one hand (stern, consoling, accusatory), the gruff, redoubtable "I," on the other, and they frequently come together in a "we"; but a "we" of what kind? Does it designate the unity of a common nature, this "we"? an illusory compound, a projection, a complicity? Does it resemble a handshake, a simple mixture, a seething mob, a complaisant copulation?

Thus we (we "we"s) say him to ourselves, press him to our inmost ear, though he seems more a stone than pillow. We are "we," "I," "you," "they," "me," moment by moment, as the pronouns pass. Still, even if we said him frequently, would that be often enough (what will it take?) to hold him like frozen smoke in the cold immortal air? Yes, unless . . . unless we can sound ourselves, reach our depths, draw them up, and make our passions heard. . . .

So I begin . . . I begin again . . . but you have put the pages down; you have drifted off in the oratory. The accident which brought you here is over. The crowds have cleared; existence calls. Diminished by curtains of sky, the sun fades where it once fell in colors through the glass; and my voice wearies of noising itself abroad like old news; courage in a dark wood fails. What will follow such a doleful "unless" like a promise, a threat?

This: the space which my speech occupied during its slender moment of aspiration will empty itself again, and unless this "unless" like a ransom note is met—I shall be gone for good. The snip of Atropos is sudden. Quick. Complete. The way the cleaning woman quits. There will be silence, an appallingly simplified silence: a walk without its footfall. There will be no more conversation, self stuffed into self like a chair; no desultory musing, no inner irrigation or any substance to the soul. If no one pronounces us. . . . If no one finds for us a voice. . . . Says: "In this refulgent summer, it has been a luxury to draw the breath of life." Well—to go wordless is to go without a soul to shit with. It is but to go.

What will any word be, then, in that simple silence, the silence of the utterly unuttered? The sum of its effects won't fat the stomach of a zero, since life essentially is what we think throughout a day; what we have said to ourselves; what we have readied ourselves to say to others: that "man is only half himself," for instance, "the other half is his expression," or that "every man should be so much an artist that he could report in conversation what had befallen him," a wish we may share among ourselves with little cost to comfort; but are these sweet notions alms now pennied out; are they a warm cup at the shelter? Where is our solace when we're told that "sleep lingers all our lifetime about our eyes, as night hovers all day in the boughs of the fir-trees"? Here we receive no idea, but a feeling seen.

"Our moods do not believe in each other," Emerson writes in a different condition, and we watch his language give terse expression to his contradictions: why is he vigorous one day, impotent another? "I am God in nature; I am a weed by the wall." Yet hearing it put precisely this way (placing an abstract and distant 'God' by a near and general 'nature,' the hard and simple 'wall' next to the low mean 'weed'—and thus making these discordancies into music) lets us know that Emerson, our determined teacher, did not want his thoughts to rattle in his readers' ears like coins in a tin cup. "The poet sees the stars because he makes them." But "'Tis the good reader that makes the good book."

Emerson's ambitions were enormous, and endangered his desires. "He burst into conclusions at a spark of evidence," Henry Seidel Canby said, accurate about Emerson's urgency, Emerson's need to be immense. He was the Horatio Alger of our youthful hopes. He would Do & Dare. He would Strive & Succeed, and drag us, unwilling as we often were, into virtuous accomplishment. He spent himself freely, but he counted his change. However lassitude might overcome his ego, Emerson's id was unaging: he would swallow the world, though little of the world could swim against the flow of all those pious, hortatory, and calamitous words which streamed forth in his voice. He sometimes seemed a grimacing spout to a drenched roof. He did fancy the idea, though: that passing through him (as if he were the categories of our consciousness) flesh would become symbol; matter would be refined like ethyl and emerge as volatile, ignitable mind.

It was an anxious exercise, nevertheless, undeniably desperate, because it risked absurdity. It risked derision. Every metaphor proves treacherous if only partly meant, and Emerson was made of oppositions and quarrelsome contrasts like a character in *Alice*. In the least likely places (that is: everywhere), his language schemed against his innocence.

It is perhaps a disagreeable comparison, but the food we eat divides itself naturally into stool and spirit; fat falls from the trimming edge to be pushed to the side of the plate; so what is the good of these splendid phenomena we are to become One with (which we're to ingest)—the "chill, grand, instantaneous night," for instance—if all one receives is the meaning, the bloodless significance? What is the good to you of my loving glance, my mouth moist with entreaty, if you never meet the lip; if we never embrace the body of the sign, and nature is metabolized without remainder?

But Emerson was always of several minds like a committee. He writes this in his journal:

May 11, 1838

Last night the moon rose behind four distinct pine-tree tops in the distant woods and the night at ten was so bright that I walked abroad. But the sublime light of night is unsatisfying, provoking; it astonishes but explains not. Its charm floats, dances, disappears, comes and goes, but palls in five minutes after you have left the house. Come out of your warm, angular house, resounding with few voices, into the chill, grand, instantaneous night, with such a Presence as a full moon in the clouds, and you are struck with poetic wonder. In the instant you leave far behind all human relations, wife, mother and child, and live only with the savages—water, air, light, carbon, lime and granite. I think of Kuhleborn. I become a moist, cold element. "Nature grows over me." Frogs pipe; waters far off tinkle; dry leaves hiss; grass bends and rustles, and I have died out of the human world and come to feel a strange, cold, aqueous, terraqueous, aerial, ethereal sympathy and existence. I sow the sun and moon for seeds.

For Emerson this is just another ordinary evening in Concord, but he hates the ordinary. It is eating up his life, and we see him strain in this passage to elevate the occasion, make it matter. The house is "resounding with few voices" (strange phrase), and the din drives him abroad. To the eye the scene is sublime, but to his mind it is boring. The sympathy he says he feels eventually, he feels at home in his study, facing the bright page with its lines of sober signs as conductible as a choir, each syllable more human than any hut; and in the ring of these words, 'aqueous,' 'terraqueous,' 'ethereal,' and 'aerial,' the sound of both the metal which makes the coin and its value as money are intimately mingled, with the sign and its sense not separate and confused as they are in the unsatisfying albeit sublime light of night, where nature grows gravely over him; and I can believe, as he sets them down ('carbon,' 'lime,' and 'granite'), and hears them singing within the chamber of his inner self, that he is one with *them*, and not the primitive elements he so carefully lists, or even the cool unstartled stars.

A night later, walking beneath a "pleasant, cloud-strewn, dim-starred sky," Emerson is considering "topics for the young men at Dartmouth," for he has his customary business to attend. Something further must be said. Something eloquent and honorable. Something which will move even its author's slow heart to a faster motion.

But only then is the orator successful when he is himself agitated & is as much a hearer as any of the assembly. In that office you may & shall (please God!) yet see the electricity part from the clouds & shine from one part of heaven to another.

So we must put our words together in a way to tempt the tongue, and entice it to pass from one round sound to another—platform to pulpit, stage to stage—until, beneath the reader's steady breath, we're reenacted like a play; because to live is to speak and to be spoken, just as Emerson is once again alive in me when I realize his words. He preaches: I read. I read to become the preachment. Then "I" preach, and so "I" listen, finding an Emerson in myself just as he did—an ear, an audience, an oracle—and so a future in the protracted shiver I am caught by when I say:

If you would know the power of character, see how much you would impoverish the world, if you could take clean out of history the life of Milton, of Shakespeare, of Plato,—these three, and cause them not to be. See you not, instantly, how much less the power of man would be? I console myself in the poverty of my present thoughts, in the paucity of great men, in the malignity and dullness of nations, by falling back on these sublime recollections, and seeing what the prolific soul could beget on actual nature;—seeing that Plato was, and Shakespeare, and Milton,—three irrefragable facts. Then I dare; I also will essay to be.

Emerson's mind and his imagination, the height of his royal aims, his loyalties, his hopes, the democratic cadence of his heart, are here. You or I read, and he is resurrected in that recitation. It matters very little that Emerson is mistaken, for what would the world lose in the loss of these three it has not already lost; what has Shakespeare meant to most men, who have not even read his name? We would mine other texts for our quotations (those of us who still quote); we would ham it up in other plays; appoint another teacher to tell us why we should forsake our bodies and forlorn the world; we would justify God's ways with Pope, and the industrious would make do glossing Aristotle and Dante and Cervantes, until we had sent them packing too, replacing everyone with Proust; but we are already a bit of dust in the wind—we friends of the Forms, lovers of the *logos*; we cannot leave a smudge on the air; we cannot pollute. Among a billion, what are a million? and for what million, dispersed like the Jews among malign dull nations, can Emerson, himself, have any meaning? And what Asian sages have shaken a hundred thousand hearts with a single sentence, and we know neither the sentence nor the sage? Do not suppose we have fallen on evil times because Shakespeare now has so little significance, Gibran more and Milton less. We cannot fall without having first attained a height. And height we have not.

You would not need to remove Plato from the world, of course, only his dialogues, as our book burnings have removed so many of the plays of Sophocles. We know little of Shakespeare's character, which seems to have been mild and agreeable enough, though we might want to wipe out Wagner's, and pretend that grand and windy music had been written by a nobler man; the lack of late Keats does not pain us past the sentences which suggest it, nor do we much miss Mozart's gray airs; but as Emerson's mind moves from what is true (that the world would be impoverished—for a few) to what is unlikely (that man would feel a loss of power as if a racing engine quit), we can *hear* how it happened; how the present was put beneath the past, power placed next to poverty in this thought of his, paucity measured against what is prolific—arrangements which argue the poet; and we can also understand what Emerson really means, because human accomplishments frequently transcend the humans who accomplish them; in fact, in time, the dross body drops away, the peevish tongue is still, greed is gone because the gut is, vanities collapse with the lungs, the long competition with the Great concludes, the very arcs of energy and impotence, of which Emerson so often complains, finally slow and cease like a swing with an empty seat, and our author is at last that; the lonely words of his work. And Emerson tries to take heart, and to become, himself, such an irrefragable fact. He will essay to be.

2

Essaying to be, Joel Porte writes in his fine book on Emerson,

> is the fundamental conceit of this greatest of American essayists. He too dares, endeavors, tries, attempts, essays . . . to create himself in the very process, in the very act, of setting words on paper or uttering them aloud. In order to exist,

he must speak, for the speech validates itself—brings into being that which is envisioned or hoped for and gives Emerson a solid platform on which to stand.[1]

Emerson had a sacred fear of the superfluous. He wished to become a Hero as his own heroes had (just as Plato, with his works, or Napoleon, through action, had become uniquely universal, or the way Shakespeare and Swedenborg were, he thought, spokesmen for the human spirit, as Goethe and Montaigne had been). He wished to be, more democratically than the elevating word 'great' suggested, a *representative man* (an honor, now, Porte's book confers upon him). To be one in a sum of simple ones, although that sum amounted to a million, was completely not to count. And not to count unthinkable . . . it was purely not to be. By means of this mathematics, 1 was equivalent to no one, and all was lost though never wagered.

As Professor Porte argues, Emerson was obsessed by the problem of the Fall. In this new clime—America—with Calvin presumably put back aboard ship and sent home to the Swiss, what one was most free from was sin; one could not blame Eve again, or any ancient crime; yet that meant that the responsibility for failure fell on us like an enemy from ambush; and if death was with us despite our sinless state, in the stalk and leaf, the blood, the flesh, real as the last rattle of the breath, then the general injustice was that for an imaginary malfeasance in a legendary age, we were to be hung tomorrow from a loop of quite unimaginary rope. Our death, too, in this case, was to be a slow prolonged closing—the squeezing to a frightened whistle of our wind. We drop from the umbilical of our birth like one condemned. The image is dismayingly familiar. And this is the illicit learning which dispels us from paradise.

"After thirty," Emerson wrote in his journal, "a man wakes up sad every morning excepting perhaps five or six until the day of his death." And he woke in Concord, in Boston, Buffalo, or Chicago, to face a new crowd, new opportunities, new uncertainties, old-fashioned fanaticism and fresh irreverence. In ancient Europe (as it seemed), and the God-ruled world from which Emerson was in the process of setting free his soul, what could be vain or pointless in the Divine Performance? However, the continent he now approached like a pilgrim seemed to be nothing but wilderness and waste, or was until Swedenborg rewrote Nature as a novel. Prodigal, abundant, vast: great grim words, and Emerson's fears were justified. These shores were longer and more indented than the lines on any palm. The country teemed with savages. Cold deep lakes lay in its glacial scratches. It offered endless vistas full of trees and creepers; beasts of all kinds were as at home here as birds in the air. Even the clouds bore the look of the land they passed over. Night came down like the shutter of a shop, and one more day was added to history, one more thistle shed to the breeze.

Nature, indeed, is prodigal to the point of embarrassment, filling the air, the deepest reaches of the sea, the whole earth, with seed. Both men and nature select by means of increase and cancel. We take many snaps and hope for a good shot. We grow thousands of flowers in order to encounter the perfect rose. Burton and Bunyan go on and on in search of virtue and a fine line. The rice we toss at the bride of course resembles the teeming hurray of sperm the groom will soon send after it. We replace the precision of the bow with the spray of the machine gun. We rain down bombs and hope something will die. The very word 'nature' becomes protean, accepting every meaning like a vase's indifferently yawning mouth. A possibility seems barely conceived and it is realized somewhere, in some tub or plot or community; for what wave has not been ordered out of the sea by now, and the beach felt its special fall; what thought, what untidy passion, what inane or selfless desire, what quirk, what constancy, has not been bitterly or beautifully expressed by this time in the long random life of the world? and Emerson's comfort could have come from that, and sometimes did so ("Man feels the blood of thousands in his body and his heart pumps the sap of all this forest of vegetation through his arteries . . ."); but the method is also wasteful and reckless and chancy and insecure, like America itself, once the Great Experiment and now just a child's play ("it runs to leaves, to suckers, to tendrils, to miscellany"): and what personal satisfaction can be derived from being a genius when that only means you were a lucky pull on the slots, a brief shower of change? so in one mood Emerson is ready to set himself against Nature, making himself up like a poem (all artifice and calculation), while in another he would grow tall with the implacable instinct of the oak; yet "our moods do not believe in each other," our moods merely watercolor the world; they will wash out.

For instance . . . it is raining everywhere within me now—in and around me now—and I can look out of a wet window at the mulberry's yellow leaves and wish my barren backyard tree were an emperor's willow; I can thereupon let fall every autumnal thought: whistle up the west wind; wish we could pot our souls like plants and remove them from the coming winter of our age to a warm protected interior life (fresh thought indeed; but freshness is only unfamiliarity); or I can celebrate the discards, in effect, and damn the hand; speak of the mulberry as if it were a tree of myth holding a hard god gnarled in its wrinkled wood; I can claim this apparently weeping world has actually reached that exultant moment when joy cries out like grief itself, and comes; and in that benevolent revision be correct; because just as philosophy turns into literature by being tied to a temperament, a tone, a style, a time of life, a rhetoric, a scaffold of categories, a schedule of rhymes; and we speak, in proper names, of Kant and Plato and Schopenhauer, of Nietzsche and Hobbes, not merely of utility, of the positive or existential, pragmatic or transcendental (terms which, like language itself, are no one's property and in sloppy general use); so for Emerson, the literary man, feelings were philosophies become atmosphere and weather (surely there are nights when we feel our eyes, like Berkeley's sleepless god, keep the world awake); a metaphysics was a metaphor made from a mood; it modeled the world for a moment, not only as it might be, but as it was in its best hour, its darkest or its last, in one kind of circumstance, in one exhausted posture, in one strong mind.

                                                                              Summer, 1841

The metamorphosis of Nature shows itself in nothing more than this, that there is no word in our language that cannot become typical to us of Nature by giving it emphasis. The world is a Dancer; it is a Rosary; it is a Torrent; it is a Boat; a Mist; a Spider's Snare; it is what you will; and the metaphor will hold, and it will give the imagination keen pleasure. Swifter than light the world converts itself into that thing you name, and all things find their right place under this new and capricious classification. . . . Call it a blossom, a rod, a wreath of parsley, a tamarisk-crown, a cock, a sparrow, the ear instantly hears and the spirit leaps to the trope. . . .

I call it a connivance, an uncombed mount of Venus, a bear pit, a turkey farm, a kettle of spit . . .

It is raining. In my heart and on the town. "How variously our passions react upon our thoughts and reasoning faculties, and change our ideas to their very opposites!" Emerson's master, Montaigne, exclaims. I call it paradise. And then the sun comes through the clouds like a melon through a wet sack. The mechanics of the mind must not be allowed to show; yet where else, if not here, may they reveal themselves, for the hero of the essay is its author in the act of thinking things out, feeling and finding a way; it is the mind in the marvels and miseries of its makings, in the *work* of the imagination, the search for form. Should we be, like Bacon, all smooth conclusion and marble floor? I am drenched beyond my skin, my bones rust like pipes, and soon the world will be wet with me and my mood. The distractions of daily life gnat and gnibble at me. Cowardice and craving defile my leafiest ideas like dogs. You turn away to listen: was that a car door? or the reluctant slide of a bureau drawer? Suddenly I sneeze upon the page and hurl an angry "god bless" after the stains.

Look upon the tempest like a pig, with perfect equanimity, Pyrrho advised his frightened, sea-thrown companions, and Montaigne, who cites him in "Apology for Raimond Sebond," reminds us of the men who interpret all things, such as the lines on their palms, ocean foam, the behavior of birds and direction of the wind, as threats and promises to them.

> Compare the life of a man enslaved to such fancies with that of a labourer following his own natural appetites, who measures things only as they actually affect his senses, without either learning or foreboding, who is never ill except when he is ill; whilst the other often has the stone in his soul before he has it in his bladder.

Our concerns collect like pigeons, and anxious men and women, such as you and I and Emerson, interpret the world in order to make a home of it, even if our image of ourselves is of Prometheus bound to a rock where an eagle feeds serenely on our liver, as Hobbes writes, devouring in the day as much as we manage to repair during the night; because our agonies are at least grand and romantic; because replenishment is equal to decay and balances the books; because then, at least, we know who and what and where we are. The world is a rain of light! Why not? Plotinus had a similar thought. "What is life," Emerson wrote, "but the angle of vision."

> Dream delivers us to dream, and there is no end to illusion. Life is a train of moods like a string of beads, and as we pass through them they prove to be many-colored lenses which paint the world their own hue, and each shows only

what lies in its focus. From the mountain you see the mountain. We animate what we can, and we see only what we animate. Nature and books belong to the eyes that see them. It depends on the mood of the man whether he shall see the sunset or the fine poem. . . . Temperament is the iron wire on which the beads are strung.

But if anyone would make a mood into a metaphor, and a metaphor into a metaphysics; if all the world's a library, or a prison, a cathedral or a stage; if the curtain rises with the first word and falls finally to God's catcalls and applause; if the fact our parents fucked to get us damns us all; if the soul is like smoke in a bottle or ghost in a machine; if the flesh is a flail or a whore on call; if—and we are serious (the body *is* a coffin), if—and we believe (the graves *will* open); then one must also be prepared to see how a mood solidifies like grease to coldly coat the pan; how feeling, in some systems, has the finality of the wound, not the evanescence of the anger which caused it; how *Angst* becomes one of the ultimate elements, memory a monument, consciousness a skeleton compressed in stone, passion a movement like molasses among the inertias of matter, and consequently how that instigating mood is no longer a momentary thing but the tantrum of eternity; for now the philosopher, the theologian, takes over from the poet like the Hyde in Jekyll, and wearily works his world out, describing the mechanisms of its perception, its hierarchies of value, the limits of our knowing and unknowing within that image, since he is at once the owner and surveyor and policeman of the dream.

I am inclined to think that it is just this lack of loyalty in Emerson, this moodiness of mind, the unfanatical hold he had on his hopes and ideals, despite the urgency of their expression, which appeals to us today (an essay like "Self-Reliance" is important only as history now, while essays like "Experience" or "Fate" are more than ever alive). Perhaps I should not employ the speaker's "we" so readily, and confess it only for myself, but it is Emerson's ability to "circle" his subject; it is the saving grace of his skepticism, that I admire; and his genuine enthusiasm for the thought he will in a moment see the other, shabby, self-serving side of.

"The universal impulse to believe," as Emerson both manifested and expressed it, was as positive in his time as it is negative in ours, because beliefs are our pestilence. Skepticism, these days, is the only intelligence. The vow of a fool—never to be led astray or again made a fool of—is our commonest resolution. Doubt, disbelief, detachment, irony, scorn, measure our disappointment, since mankind has proved even a poorer god than those which did not exist. Faith has always fallen on men like a lash, yet it has also driven them, occasionally, into an admirable selflessness. Cranks overran Concord, and Emerson was a witness to their witlessness; indeed, as Van Wyck Brooks writes, he felt obliged, in defense of toleration, to tolerate and defend them:

The vegetarians came, for whom the world was to be redeemed by bran and pumpkins; and those who would not eat rice because it was raised by slaves; and those who would not wear leather because it was stolen from animals; and those who rejected vegetables the roots of which grew downward (and food that fire had polluted). And they sat at Emerson's table and criticized or abstained. ("Tea? *I?* Butter? *I?*") They made his Thanksgiving turkey an occasion for a sermon; they lectured him over his mutton on the horrors of the shambles.[2]

But pots of poison are served at the last supper now; the crank may control an army; ideas carry bombs in their briefcases; every sector of society, every sexual preference, every whim, has its own banner, banner holder, hubbub and hoopla; every nation, race, and trade, hobby and sporting club has its own sword-rattling simplicities; there's a lie on the tip of every tongue like a bubble of spit; while the urge to permit some grand marshal of opinion to advance one's cause or determine one's fate has never been stronger, and no mind is safe which has let that yearning in its door.

Emerson, however, did not escape the beliefs of his forebears with the simple relief of the pardoned prisoner, but as one who leaves an ancestral home, with pride and gladness and regret felt together, and with the great need to replace them with others equally grand and elevating, since it was essential to have large views and strong opinions about ultimates, else you would be incomplete, low, and lack seriousness.

The crucial problem, for Emerson, Henry Nash Smith has suggested, was a choice of vocation, and the philosopher's task would naturally seem attractive to one who felt so close to Swedenborg and Plato, so freshly cut off from a preaching parent and the church. "My belief in the use of a course on philosophy is," Emerson told his classes at Harvard, "that the student shall learn to appreciate the miracle of the mind; shall learn its subtle but immense power, or shall begin to learn it. . . ." and he went on to express confidence in philosophy as the only source of truth. "When he has known the oracle he will need no priest." Characteristically, though, Emerson's confidence came from the rival he had set it against, not from philosophy itself, for he rarely thought of things in calm isolation, but in angry and anxious juxtaposition: next to God it is nothing to be a weed, yet put that weed by a wall and it is suddenly seen to be greedily alive, voracious and grasping; eventually that life will overclimb the stone; weeds will bring the wall down. To call philosophy oracular is to pay a compliment in counterfeit. The oracle's superiority to the priest is dubious indeed: both pronounce and neither reasons; often one is merely a coarse tone in the other's speech.

The essay induces skepticism. It is not altogether the fault of Montaigne. The essay is simply a watchful form. Hazlitt's thought is not shaken out like pepper on the page, nor does Lamb compose in blurts. Halfway between sermon and story, the essay interests itself in the narration of ideas—in their *unfolding*—and the conflict between philosophies or other points of view becomes a drama in its hands; systems are seen as plots and concepts as characters. Consider the description of idealists and materialists, brilliantly laid out, which Emerson furnishes us at the beginning of "The Transcendentalist."

> The idealist, in speaking of events, sees them as spirits. He does not deny the sensuous facts: by no means; but he will not see that alone. He does not deny the presence of this table, this chair, and the walls of this room, but he looks at these

things as the reverse side of the tapestry, as the *other end*, each being a sequel or completion of a spiritual fact which nearly concerns him. . . .

The materialist, secure in the certainty of sensation, mocks at fine-spun theories, at star-gazers, and dreamers, and believes that his life is solid, that he at least takes nothing for granted, but knows where he stands, and what he does. . . .

Here Emerson puts a nose to a notion, describes the personality of a proposition, outlines the habits of an ideology. The pair are reduced to sets of quirks, but at the same time humanly enlarged.

The essayist speaks one mind truly, but that is far from speaking the truth; and this lack of fanaticism, this geniality in the thinker, this sense of the social proprieties involved (the essay can be polemical but never pushy) are evidence of how fully aware the author is of the proper etiquette for meeting minds. Good manners are not merely reflections of a more refined and leisured life; they signify, here, equality and openness, a security which comes to a mind which has been released from dogmatism. If there is too much earnestness, too great a need to persuade, a want of correct convictions in the reader is implied, and therefore an *absence of community*.

November 12 [?], 1841

I own that to a witness worse than myself and less intelligent, I should not willingly put a window into my breast, but to a witness more intelligent and virtuous than I, or to one precisely as intelligent and well intentioned, I have no objection to uncover my heart. . . .

Thought must be true to its conclusions, as personal as thought is always believed to be, so that the essayist frequently begins by setting these conditions forth quite honestly, as Hazlitt does to open "On Living to One's-Self."

I never was in a better place or humour than I am at present for writing on this subject. I have a partridge getting ready for my supper, my fire is blazing on the hearth, the air is mild for the season of the year, I have had but a slight fit of indigestion to-day (the only thing that makes me abhor myself), I have three hours good before me, and therefore I will attempt it. It is as well to do it at once as to have it to do for a week to come.

It is perfectly imaginable, and no contradiction, no dishonesty, that on another occasion, the slight, fit of indigestion having become a thumping ache, the results of Hazlitt's reflections might be otherwise.

The suggestion to the reader that the essay is a converse between friends can be made into an actual invitation, as when Walter Benjamin begins:

I am unpacking my library. Yes, I am. The books are not yet on the shelves, not yet touched by the mild boredom of order. I cannot march up and down

their ranks to pass them in review before a friendly audience. You need not
fear any of that. Instead, I must ask you to join me in the disorder of crates that
have been wrenched open, the air saturated with the dust of wood, the floor
covered with torn paper, to join me among piles of volumes that are seeing
daylight again after two years of darkness, so that you may be ready to share
with me a bit of the mood—it is certainly not an elegiac mood but, rather, one
of anticipation—which these books arouse in a genuine collector. For such a
man is speaking to you, and on closer scrutiny he proves to be speaking only
about himself.

And so he is—as essayists always are. But first one must be, as Emerson saw he must
be, a self worthy to be spoken of, and a self capable of real speech.

A certain scientific or philosophical rigor is therefore foreign to the essay; ill-suited,
as when a brash young student challenges even one's most phatic observations on the
weather with demands for clarity, precision, and proof. Consequently, jargon in an
essay is like a worm in fruit; one wants to bite around the offending hunk or spit it
out. The apparatus of the scholar is generally kept hid; frequently quotations are not
even identified (we *both* know who said *that*, and anyway its origin doesn't matter).
The essayist is an amateur, a Virginia Woolf who has merely done a little reading
up; he is not out for profit (even when paid), or promotion (even if it occurs); but is
interested solely in the essay's special *art*. Meditation is the essence of it; it measures
meanings; makes maps; exfoliates. The essay is unhurried (although Bacon's aren't); it
browses among books; it enjoys an idea like a fine wine; it thumbs through things. It
turns round and round upon its topic, exposing this aspect and then that; proposing
possibilities, reciting opinions, disposing of prejudice and even of the simple truth
itself—as too undeveloped, not yet of an interesting age.

The essay is obviously the opposite of that awful object, "the article," which,
like items picked up in shops during one's lunch hour, represents itself as the latest
cleverness, a novel consequence of thought, skill, labor, and free enterprise; but never
as an activity—the process, the working, the wondering. As an article, it should be
striking of course, original of course, important naturally, yet without possessing either
grace or charm or elegance, since these qualities will interfere with the impression of
seriousness which it wishes to maintain; rather its polish is like that of the scrubbed
step; but it must appear complete and straightforward and footnoted and useful and
certain and is very likely a veritable Michelin of misdirection; for the article pretends
that everything is clear, that its argument is unassailable, that there are no soggy
patches, no illicit inferences, no illegitimate connections; it furnishes seals of approval
and underwriters' guarantees; its manners are starched, stuffy, it would wear a dress
suit to a barbecue, silk pajamas to the shower; it knows, with respect to every subject
and point of view it is ever likely to entertain, what words to use, what form to follow,
what authorities to respect; it is the careful product of a professional, and therefore it
is written as only writing can be written, even if, at various times, versions have been
given a dry dull voice at a conference, because, spoken aloud, it still sounds like writing
written down, writing born for its immediate burial in a Journal. It is a relatively recent

invention, this result of scholarly diligence, and its appearance is proof of the presence, nearby, of the Professor, the way one might, perceiving a certain sort of speckled egg, infer that its mother was a certain sort of speckled bird. It is, after all, like the essay, modest, avoiding the vices and commitments of the lengthy volume. Articles are to be worn; they make up one's dossier the way uniforms make up a wardrobe, and it is not known—nor is it clear about uniforms either—whether the article has ever contained anything of lasting value.

Like the article, the essay is born of books, as Benjamin's essay, "Unpacking My Library," points out about itself; and for every essay inspired by an event, emotion, bit of landscape, work of plastic art, there are a hundred (such as Montaigne's famous "On Some Lines of Virgil") which frankly admit it—to having an affair; because it is the words of others which most often bring the essay into being. "I myself am neither a king nor a shepherd," Hazlitt writes apropos a speech from Henry VI he's cited, "books have been my fleecy charge, and my thoughts have been my subjects." Hence the essayist is in a feminine mood at first, receptive to and fertilized by texts, hungry to quote, eager to reproduce; and often, before the essay itself is well underway in the reader's eye, its father will be briefly introduced, a little like the way a woman introduces her fiancé to her friends, confident and proud of the good impression he will make. Thus Lukács begins "Longing and Form" with a quote from *La vita nuova*, and Roland Barthes, to outdo all, opens *The Pleasures of the Text* with one in the Latin of Thomas Hobbes. It is the habit of Emerson to add these mottoes later, and to compose them himself, which is not surprising, for we do find Emerson moved by his own hand more than most.

Born of books, nourished by books, a book for its body, another for its head and hair, its syllable-filled spirit, the essay is more often than not a confluence of such little blocks and strips of text. Let me tell you, it says, what I have just read, looked up, or remembered of my reading. Horace, Virgil, Ovid, Cicero, Lucretius meet on a page of Montaigne. Emerson allows Othello and Emilia words, but in a moment asks of Jacobi, an obscure reformer and now no more than a note, a bigger speech. A strange thing occurs. Hazlitt does not quote Shakespeare but the living and the dead, the real and the fictitious, each has a part and a place. Virginia Woolf writes of Addison by writing of Macaulay writing of Addison, of whom Pope and Johnson and Thackeray have also written. On and On. In this way the essay confirms the continuity, the contemporaneity, the reality of writing. The words of Flaubert (in a letter), those of Madame Bovary (in her novel), the opinions of Gide (in his *Journal*), of Roger Fry, of Gertrude Stein, of Rilke, of Baudelaire (one can almost imagine the essay's subject and slant from this racy cast of characters), they form a new milieu—the context of citation. And what is citation but an attempt to use a phrase, a line, a paragraph, like a word, and lend it further uses, another identity, apart from the hometown it hails from?

It was inevitable that a compilation should be made of them. In my edition (the second) of the *Oxford Dictionary of Quotations*, there are 104 from Emerson, one of which is "I hate quotations," while another states that "Next to the originator of a good sentence is the first quoter of it." (Have I just now quoted Emerson, or have I quoted the *Oxford Dictionary of Quotations*?) Occasions call for quotations, qualify them, sanctify them somewhat as the Bible was—that book from which the habit stems and still draws sustenance, since the essay is, after all, a sort of secular sermon, inducing skepticism, and written by the snake.

And how they dispose themselves, these voices: inside the writer's sentences like an unbroken thread; in an isolated block upon the page, a lawn of white space around them like a house in a clearing; or in a note dropped out of the text like a piece of loose change from the author's pocket. Sometimes they stand alone like inscriptions on gates or conclude like epitaphs on tombs; they filter through a text like light through leaves or are enclosed like a hand in loving hands. Emerson's own essay "Quotation and Originality" permits me to make another point: that the essayist's subjects—in a sense always the same: other books, loneliness, love and friendship, human frailty— constantly provide a fresh challenge to thought, for if I were to write on quotation now, I should have to take into account a whole history since, not only Herman Meyer's *The Poetics of Quotation in the European Novel*, for example, but certainly Beckett's *How It Is*, which is mainly a buried quotation:

> how it was I quote before Pim with Pim after Pim how it is three parts I say it as I hear it

The essay convokes a community of writers, then. It uses any and each and all of them like instruments in an orchestra. It both composes and conducts. Texts are "plundered precisely because they are sacred, but the method, we are essay-bound to observe, is quite different from that of the Scholastics, who quoted authorities in order to acquire their imprimaturs, or from that of the scholar, who quoted in order to provide himself with a set of subjects, problems, object lessons, and other people's errors, convenient examples, confirming facts, and laboratory data. However, in the essay, most often passages are repeated out of pleasure and for praise; because the great essayist is not merely a sour quince making a face at the ideas of others, but a big belly-bumper and exclaimer aloud; the sort who is always saying, "Listen to this! Look there! Feel this touchstone! Hear that!" "By necessity, by proclivity,—and by delight, we all quote," Emerson says. You can be assured you are reading an excellent essay when you find yourself relishing the quotations as much as the text that contains them, as one welcomes the chips of chocolate in those overcelebrated cookies. The apt quotation is one of the essayist's greatest gifts, and, like the good gift, congratulates the giver. T. S. Eliot could alter our critical perceptions simply by pointing to the right place in a text. And here is Virginia Woolf, writing about an Elizabethan play, smoothing out the satin on which she'll set her gem.

> At the outset in reading an Elizabethan play we are overcome by the extraordinary discrepancy between the Elizabethan view of reality and our own. The reality to which we have grown accustomed, is, speaking roughly, based on the life and death of some knight called Smith, who succeeded his father in the family business of pitwood importers, timber merchants and coal exporters, was well known in political, temperance, and church circles, did much for the poor of Liverpool, and died last Wednesday of pneumonia while on a visit to

his son at Muswell Hill. That is the world we know. That is the reality which our poets and novelists have to expound and illuminate. Then we open the first Elizabethan play that comes to hand and read how

> I once did see
> In my young travels through Armenia
> An angry unicorn in his full career
> Charge with too swift a foot a jeweller
> That watch'd him for the treasure of his brow
> And ere he could get shelter of a tree
> Nail him with his rich antlers to the earth.
Where is Smith, we ask, where is Liverpool? And the groves
Of Elizabethan drama echo "Where?"

We should note in passing her casual choice of the "first . . . that comes to hand." We'd be naive indeed to believe that. But she is right about the manner and the tone.

We would be less than honest if we said that all was always sweetness—the page a piece of warm toast—because sometimes the quote is put there to be bitten, chewed, gnawed, spat out. Great essays have been written on vulgar errors, and Montaigne, for one, does delight in them. He is listing the various places philosophers, divers sages and divines have suggested as the likely and proper domicile for the soul—an intrinsically amusing game—when he reaches Cicero:

> The Stoics, around and within the heart;
> Erasistratus, adjoining the membrane of the epicranium;
> Empedocles, in the blood; as also
> Moses, which is the reason why he forbade the eating of the
>   blood of beasts, with which their soul is united.
> Galen believed that every part of the body has its soul.
> Strato placed it between the two eyebrows.
> *What aspect the soul bears, or where it dwells, must not be*
>   *even inquired into*, says Cicero. I gladly allow this man to use his own words;
>   for why should I mar the language of eloquence? Besides that there is small
>   gain in stealing the substance of his ideas; they are neither very frequent, nor
>   very deep, and sufficiently well known.

There is, nevertheless, a profound good humor in the way Montaigne puts most of these pages of human absurdity before us, and he is never overtaken by the unworthy feeling that these other thoughts and ingenuities and turns of phrase or sudden shifts of mood may cast a dismaying shade upon his, but rather delights in being out of the sun, because he knows that admiration is a mirror and returns a fair image. Whom would Hemingway's adolescent envy allow to take a good turn in his text?

Have we digressed, however? I hope so. For we must. What is a stroll without a stop, a calculated dawdle, coffee in a cafe we've surprised, some delicious detour down a doorway-crowded street, the indulgence of several small delays?

Yet these qualities of the essay suggest, sometimes even to the authors of essays themselves, that there is an absence of seriousness, of severity, of rigor in the writer, a fundamental failure of commitment, a basic lack of preparation even, and a withdrawal from life; because to live in books is not to live, it's often believed; since books are smooth and flat throughout, can inflict but paper cuts, and offer joys as superficially felt as ink on a thumb; then to steal from books like silver taken from a dinner table; to brood as if you were another Hamlet (though your mother's faithful and your father alive); to pass from one thought, fact, object, or attitude to another like food passed at a picnic; to set down sentences of high design on low and common matters; to worry about words when life lies dying for want of warmth, energy, and blood: all this is frivolous and enervating; it is evidence of an ambition set at "Low." Where are the essay's epic aims? its novelistic scope? its grandiose schemes and ardent explanations? Ah, no, the essay is for the amateur, all right, for the narcissist, the dilettante, for tepid souls who profess a kindly skepticism only to avoid the duties of faith, or the strenuous disciplines which define the search for truth.

Essays do not create—neither new worlds nor new philosophies. They are always written *about*; they are always either Of or On. On Reading. On Patience. Of Friendship. On the Knocking at the Gate in *Macbeth*. On and On. Out of old and often ancient texts the essayist makes another to throw like a shawl across the knees of a third. This is an activity for men? The admiration of the world is directed toward Dante or Tolstoy or Balzac or Proust, not toward Cowley or Lamb, let alone Breton or Hunt.

See if many of them aren't effeminate and sickly, full of resentment and weakness, procrastinators, passive as hens, nervous, unwed; and see if they haven't turned to the lecture and the essay because they failed in the larger roles, the finer forms, and could not get a real preacher's wind up, or populate a page with people, with passionate poetry, or with a philosophy of such profound penetration that the very body of our world— God's doll, God's Marilyn Monroe—is disclosed; then uncomfortably and inadequately redressed. After all, what do they get by on, these blue-belles of our letters; how do they succeed? They only survive on style. So if Emerson said he would "essay to be," he could not have expected to be much.

3

It is the poets, Emerson tells us, who are the liberating powers, but they do not write in the same way as the rest of us; somehow their signs sing differently, to an inward audience, as if the syllables themselves were separate singers, and the word were one tenor or soprano voice, and the line one choir. Such immaterial music is movement in its greatest purity. The mimesis that matters, for Emerson, is the one that follows the continuous transformations of nature, and thus, like Whitman, is again like nature: energetic, changeable, plentiful, and various. "The quality of the imagination is to flow, and not to freeze." It is the failure of every mysticism (and most philosophy, I'm prepared to suggest, on Emerson's behalf) to fix upon a single symbol and codify it, making of itself *"at last nothing but an excess of the organ of language."*

Not only did Emerson command us all to greatness, he demanded greatness of himself; and John Jay Chapman's remark that "Emerson seems really to have believed that if any man would only resolutely be himself, he would turn out to be as great as Shakespeare" is only somewhat overlarge. Since philosophy and theology failed as vocations, the burden of the discovery of Emerson's genius lay upon his poetry, and his poetry, as he realized with repeated anguish, was a failure: it was prose squeezed into rhymes and meters like an ungainly bumpkin into a dainty suit. Everywhere in the poems we encounter the effort to write as one inspired. We hear the expressive grunt of a marshaled strength, but we do not see the lifted bars, only the glisten of sweat on a surface of stone. We sense the desperation of his desire; but wishes have no wings but wished ones, no Pegasus to mount and then to rise with; ambition beggars us even of our bones.

In terms which seem to be always accurate, David Porter's excellent book, *Emerson and Literary Change*,[3] recounts Emerson's failures as a poet in precise and grim detail, exposing the weakness of verse after verse with almost painful completeness; nevertheless this cruel critical encounter with the poetry is necessary, not only because the poems have received much misplaced praise, and not simply because Porter can, in such a context, demonstrate effectively Emerson's own disappointment with his work, and even the accurate depths of that discontent; but especially because the strength of Emerson's essays rests, in a way, on the weakness of everything else. One hates to say they exist out of compensation, yet clearly, if Emerson was to be, he *would* have to "essay it."

When Matthew Arnold concluded that Emerson was not one of the great poets, he was still being generous, and John Morley was more nearly right when he wrote that "taken as a whole, Emerson's poetry is of that kind which springs, not from excitement of passion or feeling, but from an intellectual demand for intense and sublimated expression." Referring to an unfinished poem which Emerson initially called "The Discontented Poet, a Masque," Porter says (in something that is not quite a sentence), "The formal impoverishment of the poetry, its rigid monumentality, the stolidity of the language, the predictable gestures that failed of passion—the elements I have been at pains to point out—Emerson's recognition of these failures is latent everywhere in this plaintive poem. . . ." and then he goes on to quote Emerson in weak verse complaining of his other weak verses:

Discrowned and timid, thoughtless, worn,
The child of genius sits forlorn: . . .
A cripple of God, half true, half formed,
And by great sparks Promethean warmed.

Emerson needed room in which to achieve his effects. The words he had previously written were the source of his greatest excitement, and when they were weak, he was weakened by them. He lacked opulence, his line was already lean enough, and the local formalities of verse hobbled his thought, for he would have to swing it shut upon some rhyme before it had scarcely begun to open out; nor could he write innumerable placid stanzas like Lord Byron: instead he lost voice at the moment his entire being was calling for a closer connection between self and language.

What Emerson wanted from poetry—masses of detail to drive a moral home; strong, swift strokes as if the writer were propelling a scull, yet a slow engorgement of the line which would lead to a kind of spasm of passion in the finally completed thought, with then a gentle ebb at the end to mark the close; and consequently an effect upon the reader like similar culminations in nature—none of this could be accomplished except in prose.

The constructive posture of the self-defining self, the freedom which the crude new nation offered it, the implicit promise of democracy to exalt mankind, to praise as well as work the earth; and, above all, the gift to that emerging individual of limitless opportunity—breathing space—space for rebeginning—space to the edge of every coast—space to infinity: each required the resettlement of language on the page, an equalitarian diction, a pioneering line, the big book, the great theme; each asked for energy and optimism; each egged American authors on to annex, plunder, quote and cite, to wahoo and yawp; and none of these conditions could be realized without the lush entanglements of complete speech: the voyages of discovery, exploration, and conquest, which made it possible, the personal tone, the pied variety of voice, the ebb and flow, the strut, the brag and ballyhoo of talk; for it would take the flabbergasting virtuosities, the visionary range, the gumptious reach, the raw muscularities, the baroque vibrations, yet the flat, irregular Patersons, of prose; and nearly all the best American poets do write prose; Melville and Faulkner and James, Robinson, Thoreau, Eliot, and Frost. I mean that they remained in the service of the sentence. I mean that they sought "the poem of the idea in the poem of the words." Even Whitman, to create his extraordinary, quintessentially American poetry, had to invent a prose which would explode into verse on contact with the page. Notice what happens when we hold one such poem in the good firm grip of the paragraph:

> When I heard the learn'd astronomer, when the proofs, the figures, were ranged in columns before me, when I was shown the charts and diagrams, to add, divide, and measure them, when I sitting heard the astronomer where he lectured with much applause in the lecture-room, how soon unaccountable I became tired and sick, till rising and gliding out I wander'd off by myself, in the mystical moist night-air, and from time to time, look'd up in perfect silence at the stars.

This is not perfect, although the conclusion is clever and the rhetorical form is managed well enough, but here is Edwin Arlington Robinson in the practice of it:

> I doubt if ten men in all Tilbury Town had ever shaken hands with Captain Craig, or called him by his name, or looked at him so curiously, or so concernedly, as they had looked at ashes; but a few—say five or six of us—had found somehow

the spark in him, and we had fanned it there, choked under, like a jest in Holy Writ, by Tilbury prudence.

This sentence has a beautiful pace, and the two similes are spectacular, but is there only an inscriptional difference between poetry and prose in this instance?

This New World prose is prose which resembles talk of one kind or other: the tall tale, the loud spiel, or the sermon's moral prod; often it has the gentle swing of slow and sober reflection, the laudatory march of patriotic speech, or the unspoken assumptions of private conversation; and it is deeply marked—in theme, in pattern, rhythm, and diction—by the thumper's Bible; but there is always a point of origin, a human voice, a source in the psyche's animal squeak; and it aims at enlargement; it is always after ethical force and eloquence, like Emerson, its earliest master.

It was not America, of course, but the vision of America, the hackneyed dream, which was so spacious, so liberating, and so challenging to the writer. There was also the America the writer woke to (the towns of New England, quiet Concord, withdrawn Walden), the fields and forests as a fact; and the fact was that we were still colonists in many ways; we lived largely in little villages, our pants covered a rural seat; we worked on isolated farms; we went west in wagons which held two or three people, a straw mattress, and a dog; so that the great spaces, the small population, the wilderness, the Indians, the grizzly bears and wildcats, all combined to close us in, and a thin book could seem to open on a vast world; we were really at home in our head . . . that was our household . . . we were in violent love with the word; but this loneliness also meant we were hungry for company, for conversation, for what little could be mimic'd of the great urban (and European) ways. Had even Athens offered the orator a grander opportunity?

Emerson himself did not sprout from his native soil like the local corn, for he was full of Old World inclinations; he was the Old World gone to seed. He wanted to respect the past, yet seem wildly free, untamed and well mannered like clover in a field. He would be both above and of the people, his open, plain-folks, Yankee look a reflection from the finest glass. Our emblem and our entertainer, Emerson wished to see through common things to their uncommon core; to be all pith, yet not lack a shaping rind. His lectures, his essays, his orations, were consequently composed of planned surprise and calculated happenstance. These contradictions tore at him and shaped his style: what better banner than a flag in tatters?

It is David Porter's claim—and one I think he sustains—that "Emerson's prose *is* his power"; that his theory of poetry is really the theory of his prose; and that his view is original and radical. "He reattached language to process rather than to conclusion, to the action of the mind wonderfully finding the words adequate to its experience."

Emerson made the essay into the narrative disclosure of a thought. It became an act of thinking, but not of such thinking as had actually occurred. Real thought is gawky and ungracious; it goes in scraps, gaps, and patches, in sidles and byways, hems and haws; it is both brutal and careless, unpredictable and messy. Instead, Emerson's essays present us with an ideal process, an *ought*; yet it is, again, not one of rational confirmation; it is not the logician's order we encounter; it is the orator's: an order of revelation and response, the intertwined exfoliation of fact, feeling, and idea. In this sense, exposition becomes the narrative, and the form that of a fiction.

The unity of each essay is a unity achieved by the speaker for his audience as well as for himself, a kind of reassociation of his sensibility and theirs; so from its initiating center the mind moves out in widening rings the way it does in Emerson's first great essay, "Circles," where the sentences surround their subject, and metaphors of form control the flow of feeling.

> The life of man is a self-evolving circle, which, from a ring imperceptibly small, rushes on all sides outwards to new and larger circles, and that without end. The extent to which this generation of circles, wheel without wheel, will go, depends on the force or truth of the individual soul.

Yet the energy of the essay, like the energy of life, is always in danger of dissipation. Pages lie in unsorted heaps, full of notions which have not been extended to their complete reach. Somewhere in those piles, inferences may lie quiet now like a powerful figure hidden in clay, but where are the shaping hands, the steady intent, the attention? Where is the ardent ambition? Friends have fallen ill; one's own ailments are acting up; a relative has been disgraced; children disappoint; the sexual itch faintly remains like an old bite; yawns break apart on the face; one's oblivion has been seen like an image in an empty mirror: these distractions are the real disease.

> For it is the inert effort of each thought, having formed itself into a circular wave of circumstance . . . to heap itself on that ridge and to solidify and hem in the life.

Emerson's image beautifully resembles his dilemma, for two ideas are competing in it, and neither is the one he wants to embrace. There is, first, the conception of a course of thought (and the lecture, itself, which expresses or contains it) as spreading out in ripples like those which follow the plop of a pebble in a pool; and, second, the picture of an analogous life (and all accomplishment) growing gradually in yearlike rings to reach a crusty edge and the eventual bark of some trunk. Each variation suggests limits, and these are exactly what Emerson will stubbornly go on to deny.

> But if the soul is quick and strong it bursts over that boundary on all sides and expands another orbit on the great deep, which also runs up into a high wave, with attempt again to stop and to bind. But the heart refuses to be imprisoned; in its first and narrowest pulses it already tends outward with a vast force and to immense and innumerable expansions.

This denial, strictly speaking, makes no sense. It is quixotic. It is futile. But Emerson is not arguing for a constitutive principle here. He is recommending a directive one, an *as if*; and to act within a figure of thought rather than upon some thought itself is at least half of his transcendentalism. To fly in the face of a fact ("We grizzle every day.

I see no need of it.") is not to strike a solid wall, but to feel the fact yield, if only a bit; we can become younger by growing old the right way; limits can be overstepped, as Rilke says, so long as we respect the bounds; but only if we reject "*rest, conservatism, appropriation, inertia*" as a way of life; only if we embrace the future with the body of the present: "Why should we import rags and relics into the new hour?"

In short, to live some fictions, rather than others, improves our chances; enriches, elevates, and regulates life; allows us "to work a pitch above" our last height; and this Emerson proceeds to do in the turns his prose takes—clearsighted as a circling hawk. The essay begins with the ego perceived in the punning image of an eye ("The eye is the first circle . . ."), with the round horizon line it shapes the second; soon we encounter the "cipher," then we meet the sense, natural to space, that about every circle a larger circle can be drawn; that time, too, is endless in the ease of its addition. The energy of all things flows out in waves; round moons and planets move in rounder orbits; by the steps of ladders, by degrees, successive choirs are reached; by several stages, then, the thrones of angels. The circle is not only endless without and infinite within, it returns continuously to itself, and every opposite is seen to meet and blend, "The virtues of society are vices of the saint," he says. "One man's justice is another's injustice. . . ." This doesn't mean merely relativity; it means reciprocity. Every point upon a curve is to the right, left, and center of others. All are different. All are alike. A curve cannot be concave without being convex; every balm is someone's hurt. Point of view, perspective, position, line of sight—angle is everything. "Life is a series of surprises," he says, but we can no longer be surprised by the absence of any disciplined philosophy. He dislikes distinctions. Clarity dismays him, makes him suspicious. He dotes on degrees but damns kinds. He is dangerously devoted to the continuum. He does not want to finely, plainly *think*; scrub things clean, draw cutting lines, laboriously link. He wants to writhe.

Now, while thinking, as any essayist is, he is alive. The power of the process fills him with light. It is like that. Montaigne attests to it.

> Meditation is a powerful and ample exercise for a man who is able to search his mind and employ it vigorously. I would rather fashion my mind than furnish it. There is no exercise that is either more feeble or more strenuous, according to the nature of the mind, than that of entertaining one's thoughts. The greatest make it their profession, *for whom to live is to think* (Cicero).

(Cicero is temporarily OK to quote. But wait. The weather is changeable.)

Emerson's verbal maneuvers concluded, his listeners are sent away with their hearts a little higher in their chests, in a Dionysian mood, intoxicated by their own powers and possibilities, not by bottled artificialities, drugs, the falsehoods of gambling and war, or still further fraudulent rites.

Yet the freshly inflated soul begins immediately to leak. What porous tissues we are made of! We have scarcely gotten home, our feet wet and chilly from the snow, or our chest asweat from the deep summer heat like a heavy coat we can't remove, when our children's sneezes greet us, skinned knees bleed after waiting all day to do so. There is the bellyache and the burned-out basement bulb, the stalled car and the incontinent cat. The windows frost, the toilets sweat, the body of our spouse is one cold shoulder, and the darkness of our bedroom is soon full of the fallen shadows of our failures. Now the quiet night light whispers to us: you are unloved—unlovely—you are old. These white sheets rehearse the corpse they will cover. None of our times change. We are the same age as our essayist. Wrinkles squeeze our eyes shut, and we slide into sleep like a sailor from beneath his national flag. Tomorrow our tumescence must be resumed. Tomorrow, Emerson realizes, he must again be a genius.

Joel Porte's graceful study, by interlacing life and language, lets us see clearly many important things about Emerson, among them what a victim of entropy he was. In the most tactful way he discloses some of the strongest of Emerson's impulses, and shows us how they mix and mingle: money and sexuality, for instance, energy and the essay. My motto, my central phrase, is taken from him, and he not only seizes on the expression himself, he makes exactly the right use of it. Porte is an impressively observant reader. His understanding can slip beneath the surface of a style without scratching its features or destroying the structure of its soil. He picks up Emerson's puns, whether they are easy ones like "The eye is the first circle," or crucial ones like "I also will essay to be," or some of the more subtle which lighten Emerson's sentences with their smile, such as "In spite of all the rueful abortions that squeak and gibber in the street ..." and carries them to our attention. He does not allow the rhythm of "I also will essay" to escape him either. He notes the allusions to Hamlet's famous soliloquy in our emblematic passage; indeed, he notes the Shakespearean resonances which occur throughout those early pieces; and points out how important they are in suggesting something of Emerson's relationship to his father:

> The result seems to be, as with the paradigmatic Hamlet, a crippling habit of self-consciousness and self-questioning that threatens to paralyze the will.

The audience for these essays is not a single or a simple congregation, nor are the motives for writing—as if speaking each one—open and easy; although many have their germ in the journals, where an "I" is implicit. When we talk to ourselves, as we do in journals and diaries, we do not normally make speeches; nevertheless Emerson often addresses himself as if he were a crowd:

> May 28, 1839

> There is no history. There is only biography. The attempt to perpetuate, to fix a thought or principle, fails continually. You can only live for yourself; your action is good only whilst it is alive,—whilst it is in you. The awkward imitation of it by your child or your disciple is not a repetition of it, is not the same thing, but another thing. The new individual must work out the whole problem of science, letters and theology for himself; can owe his fathers nothing. There is no history; only biography.

Here he is already halfway to the hall. And what the hall holds. Emersons.

Who owe their fathers nothing . . . that's the destination . . . and a monetary word is used to express the moral and cultural debt he feels, and would like to cancel. *To owe our father nothing . . .* it is the impossible idea of this nation, still a child of Europe.

Two of Emerson's voices are those of the secular preacher. He wishes to speak his own mind, and thus convey his own ideas: that envy is ignorance, for instance, as he says in "Self-Reliance"; that imitation is suicide, and nonconformity a duty. Yet he also wishes to provide, as preachers do, some consolation. A little more than a week before Emerson wrote the passage quoted above (in which he is forming some of the thoughts which will comprise that famous Declaration of Everyman's Independence), Emerson puts this powerful paragraph in his journal:

May 19, 1839

> At church today I felt how unequal is this match of words against things. Cease, O thou unauthorized talker, to prate of consolation, and resignation, and spiritual joys, in neat and balanced sentences. For I know these men who sit below, and on the hearing of these words look up. Hush, quickly: for care and calamity are things to them. There is Mr. Tolman, the shoemaker, whose daughter is gone mad, and he is looking through his spectacles to hear what you can offer for his case. Here is my friend, whose scholars are all leaving him, and he knows not what to turn his hand to, next. Here is my wife, who has come to church in hope of being soothed and strengthened after being wounded by the sharp tongue of a slut in her house. Here is the stage-driver who has jaundice, and cannot get well. Here is B. who failed last week, and he is looking up. O speak things, then, or hold thy tongue.

The desire to digress is strong now, after this manifestation of Emerson's genius and good will. For the relation between the parish priest, who has the confidence of the confessional, and his congregation; the teacher, who knows a few names because she has regularly called the roll, and her raucous kids; the congressman, who is filled in on regional issues by the local pols, to his so-called constituents; the lecturer to large crowds, in distant cities sometimes—places he can't locate on a map but flies to like a thrown stone—the huckster treating a drowsy, idle, TV eye to an earache of hype; and the author to a reader, finally, the complete Anybody who has the price or the loan or the theft of your book: that difference, at every step, is prodigious, total, yet scarcely anything at all. I can write Teacher/Priest, Article/Essay, and only a slant intervenes. I can step down from the podium and take my seat. I can write, and then read what I have written. I can cease loving in order to be loved.

The essayist pretends to be wise. No scholar, no philosopher, has to pretend that. The philosopher can be mean, narrow, vindictive, suspicious, vain, small. It needn't show. "*Die Welt ist alles, was der Fall ist,*" he writes. His traffic is with Reality, not with the real; with The Case, not cases; not with anyone's hopes and fears and household tragedies. What is Substance, he asks of a man whose daughter has been abducted. Yet is the Will free, he wonders while watching the smoke rise from the ovens. O should he speak things, then, and descend toward Emerson, toward Rilke, toward the province of the poet, toward the particularities of deprivation, loss, pain? The philosopher speaks of Good, of Evil, of Duty and Desire, of Ideas, but of other people's hungers only on days off, on feast days, during festivals, when his thoughts are on things, those things which call out to Emerson, where he hovers like a kite between Mr. Tolman's unfortunate daughter and "the plight of Mankind." If the novelist and the poet probe the particular, and the philosopher deals with the Grand Design, what is left? The preacher is wise too, and carries comfort in his Bible the way the physician carries his bag, but the preacher's wisdom is the wisdom of the Church, and for him "the case" is always cautionary. Speak solidities. Emerson advises himself. But to whom? with what right? The essay has less of a place to be, and less an ear, an eye of its own to address, than a message painted on the side of a truck.

Emerson reports (the poet writes) that

It is time to be old,
To take in sail:—
The god of bounds,
Who sets to seas a shore,
Came to me in his fatal rounds,
And said: No more!

A book of poems has no electric eye which will open its covers automatically when a literate reader passes by. It is not a flytrap. Although it is presumably addressed to everyone, whether young or old, in every situation of life, it is not like an advertising sign: BUY MATTRESS BREAD! which is in a permanent state of being blurted. The command LOVE GOD! pasted on a bumper, or posted on a barn like CHEW MAIL POUCH!, awaits the accident of our passing, and then, like the beggar, threatens or entreats us. Still, we can shake our heads and go on. The bumper dwindles down another drive. In short, the sign does not cause or continue its occasion. The poet's reader, on the other hand, reaches for the poet, so to speak, and creates their encounter. Yet it would not be correct to say that Emerson's little defeatist verse was ready to adapt itself to any situation; rather it is addressed to none. His poem is, like all good poetry, quite occasionless; it is not a piece of mood music, or a set of lines to make love by.

However, when Emerson begins, so conversationally, "I read the other day some verses . . ." or more formally, "I greet you on the recommencement of our literary year," he is not beginning a talk or an address, although such a deliverance may lie in its past; he is opening an essay: something meant to be experienced, not simply heard; something meant to be understood and savored, not believed and followed; something meant to be enjoyed, admired, but not obeyed. The essay must wait its readers the way the poem does, yet it is active in establishing the conditions of its reception. The essay imagines a situation in which it would make sense to say what it will say. This is not always easy for the reader to grasp, and may take a while. "Whoever looks at the insect world, at flies, aphides, gnats, and innumerable parasites, and even at the infant mammals, must have remarked the extreme content they take in suction, which constitutes the main business of their life." Where are we, we may wonder. In the essay on "Quotation and Originality," of course, but our arena, more importantly, is the book, where we shall feed like a fly ourselves on this sweet text made up of texts.

Now—who dares call this diverting spell we've had a digression? Only those who drive one road through town and consequently miss the landscape, the local belles, the odd shops, the bandstand, and the park.

We have so far found five voices, five intentions, in our essayist: (1) the desire to talk to himself, to say "buck up, be better, stand forth, do not change your course for a little windy criticism," while (2) at the same time hoping these admonitions will offer others encouragement and solace too. Since he must speak against his hearers' weaknesses as well as his own, (3) it is essential that he become "representative," and address himself to all those men and women who may later live and chance to read him (pronounce him, I prefer to say), and confer upon him the poet's glory: the immortality of the tongue.

Like any good lecturer, however, Emerson's exchange is ultimately with his subject (4), and with those admired predecessors who have also spoken or written about it. His theme soon speaks in its own voice, and on its own terms, whether the theme is fate, Plato, Montaigne, memory, or the conduct of life. Emerson, himself, is of no importance in these moments, just as his audience, now, can do no more than "overhear" a truly transcendental conversation.

Yet can Emerson really believe what he says in these essays: that "With consistency a great soul has simply nothing to do," for instance, or "I think nothing is of any value in books excepting the transcendental and extraordinary"; since we see him regularly exaggerate his case? He becomes hyperbolic the way others grow hysterical. Overstatement creates the Oversoul, and Emerson's tight lapidary style contributes to it, for it is a style intolerant of qualification, reservation, and convolution. Nothing is less Jamesian than the hard precise bites of his mind. Although his meaning may enlarge itself in reverberating rings, his sentences themselves do not circle through a center; they do not gently wander, seep, or shower, but cover their territory by rushing from side to side, rebounding as though from rubber bumpers, hurrying out to edges, sounding alarms; so that a paragraph of them is like the knicknacknocking passage of the pinball, with its braggy totals and loud yet intermittent message, its electric enlightenment, desperate to do its business but on a downward slope and shortly out of play.

Emerson is speaking to a deeper self than he can recognize (5), and he must shout as if it were far away, and he were on a French phone. The uncertain hand slaps down its weak cards hard. So he shouts at this self which would not owe its father anything; which feels guilty about the inheritance it has from Emerson's first wife, the leisure it has therefore enjoyed, the chances this has enabled it to take; he shouts at the self which fears it cannot be the man its other ego calls for. It would reassure him mightily if the commands he issues for his own conduct could be categorical as well for the world.

Then he could hide his failure, like the fig leaf furnished by the Fall, behind a universal condition. He shouts. He shakes his fist. But he is a weed by a wall. . . .

> Society everywhere is in conspiracy against the manhood of its members. Society is a joint-stock company, in which the members agree, for the better securing of his bread to each shareholder, to surrender the liberty and culture of the eater.

Money, food, and manhood are here, in Hobbesian terms, uncomfortably connected. There is a curve in the communication. Emerson is certainly not telling his listeners that his virility is threatened, but he is telling somebody.

When Emerson lectures in Lowell or Boston or somewhere else nearby, his wife, some relatives, a few friends, will often be in the audience. He will on those occasions stand to speak in the close clutter of his life, and Emerson's sixth voice is reserved for home and household. Sometimes it breaks out angrily to say, "Take heed, this is how I feel."

> Live no longer to the expectation of these deceived and deceiving people with whom we converse. Say to them, O father, O mother, O wife, O brother, O friend, I have lived with you after appearances hitherto. Henceforward I am the truth's. . . . I shall endeavor to nourish my parents, to support my family, to be the chaste husband of one wife,—but these relations I must fill after a new and unprecedented way. I appeal from your customs. I must be myself. . . . If you are noble, I will love you, if you are not, I will not hurt you and myself by hypocritical attentions. If you are true, but not in the same truth with me, cleave to your companions; I will seek my own. . . .

The immortals are the ultimate elite, and one watches the artist in Emerson finally satisfy his need to escape our common cancellation by appealing to the only forces which could draw him safely away: the angels of order and energy. The qualities he could not give his poetry were inherent in the passionate persistence of his public themes, and in the structure of his discourse about them—a structure which was remarkably original in its spatial radiation and free rearrangements of meaning, although his bitten-off sentences surprised only through their frequency, and his rapid, epigrammatic presentation of ideas was contradicted by a somewhat halting delivery.

His final voice (7) is thus the voice of Form. It is a voice which has no sound of its own, but lives in, and directs, the others. It is not the wind, but the weathervane. It is not the force of the wind, but the rhythm of its gusts and lulls, its steady stream. It appears not in the message, but in its unfolding, as if the greatest pleasure in any gift lay in how the package was unwrapped, the beloved body unclothed, the psyche gradually discovered.

> I remember when I was a boy walking along the river, how the colours and shapes of shells used to enchant me. I would collect handfuls of them and put them in

my pockets. When I got home I could find nothing of what I had collected: nothing but wretched snails' shells. From this I learnt that composition and context are more important than the beauty of individual forms. On the shore they lay *in solidarity* with the sky and the sea.

Form is the habitat of thought, the survival of style. How we have collected these pieces of him here, where they lose their luminous elasticity and seem hard dim things!

So to his immediate audience, Emerson offers moral education and spiritual consolation; to his manifest self he brings encouragement that is much needed, and to his private self, he promises continued concealment; to his subject matter, Emerson guarantees the responsive shifts of his thought like any good dancing partner, as well as the whirling steps of the waltz of form; while to his family and friends he utters sidelong warnings, admonishments, and threats.

Though his sentences fall like single stones, the general pattern on the pond is interlaced and strong. We can cry out, in complaint: what a babble of tongues! what a scrabble of aims! what a Carroll of contradictions—this politics of push and pull—what an uncommon crowd of ears! but time after time, especially in essays like "Experience," "Montaigne," and "Fate," Emerson succeeds in putting down just the right, plurally significant note. He reaches all the ears and hence the hearts he hopes to, and among his listeners are the gods.

The customary objection to Emerson's style is that he tends to shuffle his sentences like cards, and in his late, less energetic years, he did so almost casually; but for the most part Emerson lets his exposition drift because he wants a more complex, more rhetorical, more poetic, effect; because, paradoxically, he wants to exercise a more exact control.

To survive on style is not simple, as De Quincey explains:

Rhetoric, according to its quality, stands in many degrees of relation to the permanencies of truth; and all rhetoric, like all flesh, is partly unreal, and the glory of both is fleeting. Even the mighty rhetoric of Sir Thomas Browne, or Jeremy Taylor, to whom only it has been granted to open the trumpet-stop on that great organ of passion, oftentimes leaves behind it the sense of sadness which belongs to beautiful apparitions starting out of the darkness upon the morbid eye, only to be reclaimed by darkness in the instant of their birth, or which belongs to pageantries in the clouds. But, if all rhetoric is a mode of pyrotechny, and all pyrotechnics are by necessity fugitive, yet even in these frail pomps there are many degrees of frailty. Some fireworks require an hour's duration for the expansion of their glory; others, as if formed from fulminating powder, expire in the very act of birth. Precisely on that scale of duration and of power stand the glitterings of rhetoric that are not worked into the texture, but washed on from the outside.

It is not true that Truth is permanent. That is a piety. Falsehoods both outnumber and outlast. We should reread our Montaigne and carry carefully with us what he says.

De Quincey knows the truth, though, even if he is not telling it, and puts his energies where he must. His style is so much at one, here, with his image, that it countervenes it, as if the fireworks had turned the sky dark. The comparison "as if formed from fulminating powder," we must observe, was not formed from fulminating powder.

As a public speaker, a rhetorician, Emerson was in plentiful company. There was John Grissom, who lectured on chemistry, and who tried to illustrate every point with an experiment—preferably one which went POUF!; there was Ormsby Michel, marvelous at making the sky clear and the heaven otiose, often applauded in mid-sentence, and possibly the learned astronomer of Whitman's poem; there was the tough, irascible Fanny Wright, who took the stump for abortion and the fallibility of the Bible, who stood against slavery and in favor of easy divorce (on one occasion, they tore down the platform from under her); there was John Lord, whose Beacon Lights of History were all great men: King Alfred, Muhammad, Saint Bernard; there were phrenologists like George Combe, abolitionists like Wendell Phillips, who would speak for free if he could speak against slavery and that ape Abraham Lincoln; Bayard Taylor customarily came in Arab costume and brandished a scimitar; it would be a problem to prevent Edward Everett from giving his address on the character of George Washington (some said he delivered it 135 times, or did it simply seem so?); Oliver Wendell Holmes would inevitably be witty; many, of course, were interminable; one could learn about electromagnetism from Dr. Boynton, and John B. Gough would warn of the evils of drink; for the right fee, Henry Ward Beecher might be willing to preach against avarice; then there were many under-Emersons as well, like Star King and E. P. Whipple, shades more comfortable to their crowds than the sun they took their shadow from.[4]

Audiences did not, on the whole, require eloquence or other oratorical skills from their speakers, although they often got them. From Gough they wanted vivid testimony about what alcohol could do; from John Lord, "who read his notes in a frayed, unmusical voice interrupted with a periodic Thoracic sneeze," they wanted popular history—easy and uplifting information; but Emerson was not interested in informing or entertaining his hearers, nor was he concerned to reform them, when that most often meant confirming prejudices and providing shocks and titillation. Joel Porte is especially good at defining Emerson's deepest attitudes here—both to his material and to his audience. Scholars have exhibited a curious reticence about Emerson in this regard, ignoring his imagery even when quoting his words. The following two passages from Emerson's journals bracket the problem precisely:

Feb. 4, 1841

If I judge from my own experience I should unsay all my fine things, I fear, concerning the manual labor of literary men. They ought to be released from every species of public and private responsibility. To them the grasshopper is a burden. I guard my moods as anxiously as a miser his money; for company, business, my own household chores, untune and disqualify me for writing. I think then the writer ought not to be married; ought not to have a family. I think the Roman Church with its celibate clergy and its monastic cells was right. If he must marry, perhaps he should be regarded happiest who has a shrew for a wife, a sharp-tongued notable dame who can and will assume the total economy of the house, and, having some sense that her philosopher is best in his study, suffers him not to intermeddle with her thrift.

                                                                        Dec. 1841

All writing is by the grace of God. People do not have good writing, they are so pleased with bad. In these sentences that you show me, I can find no beauty, for I see death in every clause and every word. . . . The best sepulchres, the vastest catacombs, Thebes and Cairo Pyramids are sepulchres to me. I like gardens and nurseries. Give me initiative, spermatic, prophesying, man-making words.

The action he has in mind is reciprocal. Because his words make men of men, they also make a man of Emerson, whose emotional ups and downs are sexual in a straightforward sense, it seems to me. This back-and-forth flow of the blood may be the principal psychological element in any dialectical personality. The domestic round has enfeebled his sexual life. Babies and bereavement are the dismal consequences of his romantic passions, and the ensuing daily routines, the morning-to-night disappointments, of which I have made a *leitmotif*, the drudgeries he cannot find the strength of spirit to transcend, the petty trivialities which are the very furniture of family life, distract him from his work, bedevil his mind, weaken his optimism, undermine the moral superiority of his preacherlike position, endanger the honesty of everything.

For instance: the ardents of Brook Farm have forgathered to complete their wonderland plans, and Emerson feels nothing of their fire.

And not once could I be inflamed, but sat aloof and thoughtless; my voice faltered and fell. It was not the cave of persecution which is the palace of spiritual power, but only a room in the Astor House hired for the Transcendentalists. I do not wish to remove from my present prison to a prison a little larger. I wish to break all prisons. I have not yet conquered my own house. It irks me and repents me. Shall I raise the siege of this hencoop, and march baffled away to a pretended siege of Babylon? It seems to me that so to do were to dodge the problem I am set to solve, and to hide my impotency in the thick of a crowd.

Emerson's essays are aggressive. They nettle their readers. His audiences were rarely pleased with what he said, though they had to admire him, his sincerity, his vigorous speech. Emerson's ambivalent attitude is perfectly expressed in the following dream which Joel Porte quotes and comments on quite correctly:

A droll dream last night, whereat I ghastly laughed. A congregation assembled, like some of our late Conventions, to debate the Institution of Marriage; & grave & alarming objections stated on all hands to the usage; when one speaker at last rose & began to reply to the arguments, but suddenly extended his hand & turned on the audience the spout of an engine which was copiously supplied from within the wall with water & whisking it vigorously about, up, down, right, & left, he drove all the company in crowds hither & thither & out of the house. Whilst I stood watching astonished & amused at the malice & vigor of the orator, I saw the spout lengthened by a supply of hose behind, & the man suddenly brought it round a corner & drenched me as I gazed. I woke up relieved to find myself quite dry, and well convinced that the Institution of Marriage was safe for tonight.

Porte asks, "Would it carry us beyond the bounds of simple description to call this a 'wet' dream?" It is, in fact, wet in more than one way. Much later, Porte follows this revelation of Emerson's unconscious and ambiguously hateful and amorous relation to his audience with another passage, this one a fantasy written when Emerson was only nineteen. It concerns a kind of great water organ formed from the roots and trunks of Siphar (i.e., siphon) trees, which Emerson imagines growing along the banks of a river on some Pacific island. The rise and fall of water through the tubes makes musical sounds of such beauty that the natives erect a great temple to enclose hundreds of these trees and complete the dim resonations of their notes. Six thousand gather to listen on the fatal day, and the instrument begins to emit a music which makes them mad—laughter and sorrow combine in a single embrace.

Owing to the unusual swell of the River and to some unaccountable irregularity in the ducts the pipes began to discharge their contents within the chapel. In a short time the evil became but too apparent, for the water rose in spouts from the top of the larger ducts and fell upon the multitude within. Meantime the Music swelled louder and louder, and every note was more ravishing than the last. The inconvenience of the falling water which drenched them, was entirely forgotten until finally the whole host of pipes discharged every one a volume of water upon the charmed congregation. . . . Many hundreds were immediately drowned. . . . Thenceforward there was no more use of the Siphar trees in the Pacific Islands.

The lecture is also an organ of great power (a panharmonicon, indeed), and Emerson's speech, he felt, should be a fertilizing seed. It was to have an energy which would engender energy in every listener. It was to be an example of a liberated mind which would free other minds to follow its example. In fact, what Emerson intended to do when he spoke was wipe away his audience like chalksmoke from a blackboard, and replace it with his essay, heard in their hearts like an adopted beat.

September, 1849

Today, carpets; yesterday, the aunts; the day before, the funeral of poor S.; and every day, the remembrance in the library of the rope of work which I must spin;—in this way life is dragged down and confuted. We try to listen to the hymn of gods, and must needs hear this perpetual *cock-a-doodle-doo*, and *ke-tar-kut* right under the library windows. They, the gods, ought to respect a life, you say, whose objects are their own. But steadily they throw mud and eggs at us, roll us in the dirt, and jump on us.

Time took his nights first. Soon there were only days. The youthful fever of his blood breaks, and he is restored to another illness. The dents on the bed are old and dismal signals. Porte argues it admirably, and one imagines a world of winter setting in. There is a pale cold sunlight everywhere, in all the uninvaded corners, under covers, in back of books. Snow slowly clings to the summer air like dust. Emerson has a gaze which cannot close. He complains. Between the rows of listening ears he speaks to his wife, his friends—his soul worn thin from the pacing of his passion all these years. He complains; yet as Emerson ages, he does not become an old man mad—full of lust and rage, of memories of what he might have had. Harpies do not come to hold his hand, and he does not take to drink like Dylan Thomas, or put on intemperate attitudes the way Yeats did his beggar's clothing, or collect curses to keep cleanly oiled and ready like old guns; no, he begins to husband his strength ("husband" is the wretched word), recommend restraint, suggest that it is better to save than spend.

But it is not.

To be—don't we know by now?—is to burst with energy and enterprise like a hive of bees. It is to draw from just that daily drudgery, which you contend has betrayed your genius, all its sap and substance—siphon *it* dry—and seed new sentences with life. Begin again. Oblivion is miles away and only moments off. Begin.

But his only recourse was to write, to fade when he had to—die—and then to rise once more inside us when we say, "In this refulgent summer, it has been a luxury to draw the breath of life...."

Notes

1   Joel Porte, *Representative Man, Ralph Waldo Emerson in His Time* (New York: Oxford University Press, 1979), p. 153.
2   Van Wyck Brooks, *The Life of Emerson* (New York: Literary Guild, 1932), p. 127. Brooks does well by this odd lot: "Dunkers, Muggletonians, Agrarians, Abolitionists, Groaners, Come-outers.... The Phrenologists came too, and the Mesmerists, and the Homeopathists, and the Swedenborgians. And the Rat-hole Spiritualists whose gospel came by taps in the wall and thumps in the table-drawer...."
3   David Porter, *Emerson and Literary Change* (Cambridge, Mass.: Harvard University Press, 1978).
4   A nice account of these and other speakers on the circuit can be found in Carl Bode's *The American Lyceum: Town Meeting of the Mind* (Carbondale, Ill.: Southern Illinois University Press, 1968).

John J. McDermott (1932–)

American philosopher who taught at Queens College for twenty years, and at Texas A&M University since 1977, McDermott has aimed to improve our understanding of the history of American philosophy. In addition to editing volumes of work by William James, John Dewey, and Josiah Royce, he is cofounder of the Harvard edition of James' works and correspondence. In the following essay from 1986, McDermott traces some of the intellectual history of Emerson's reception among American pragmatists C. S. Peirce, William James, George Santayana, John Dewey, and Josiah Royce. McDermott claims that Emerson's understanding of experience forms a principal point of attraction for these philosophers, and his "generalized approach to inquiry is clearly a foreshadowing of that found subsequently in James, Dewey, and Royce." Since the American intellectual tradition possesses more continuity for McDermott than some critics might believe or allow (including Santayana), it is incumbent upon readers and scholars to reconsider some of the familiar caricatures and "censorious" judgments of Emerson's thinking. For example, McDermott says: "We should not mistake Emerson's position for a flight of fancy or for the poetic stroke in the pejorative sense of that word. Emerson is a hard-headed empiricist, reminiscent of the Augustinian-Franciscan tradition for whom the world was a temporal epiphany of the eternal implications and ramifications of the eternal ideas." In this instance and others, McDermott offers us a way of thinking anew about the writing and opinions of Peirce, James, Santayana, Dewey, and Royce collected above in the present volume.

Spires of Influence: The Importance of Emerson for Classical American Philosophy

John J. McDermott

And, striving to be man, the worm
Mounts through all the spires of form.

RALPH WALDO EMERSON, *Nature*

Perhaps the title of this chapter should be "Why Emerson?" as that would better reflect how I came to write this piece. It is not so much that I have had to become convinced of the singular importance of the thought of Emerson, for the writing and teaching of Joseph Blau[1] and Robert C. Pollock[2] long ago made that clear to me. Rather the query about "Why Emerson?" proceeds from my study of the classic American philosophers, especially William James, Josiah Royce, and John Dewey. Despite their differences and disagreements, often extreme in both personal style and doctrine, these powerful and prescient philosophers did have at least one influence in common—the thought of Ralph Waldo Emerson.

Another major figure of the American classical period, George Santayana, seems to be a case apart. Santayana had an abiding interest in Emerson's thought and refers frequently to Emerson in his own writings. His judgments on Emerson vary from admiration and affection to pointed and even harsh criticism. I do not think that Emerson was a significant influence on Santayana. Nonetheless, his published assessments of Emerson at the beginning of the twentieth century are contextually interesting, especially as they contrast with those of James, Royce, and Dewey.

The remaining two major figures of the classical period, C. S. Peirce and G. H. Mead,[3] appear to be much less directly influenced by Emerson.

Parenthetically, however, we do find a text in Peirce about Emerson which is intriguing and perhaps merits further inquiry in another context. In "The Law of Mind," published in 1892, Peirce wrote:

> I may mention, for the benefit of those who are curious in studying mental biographies, that I was born and reared in the neighborhood of Concord—I mean in Cambridge—at the time when Emerson, Hedge, and their friends were disseminating the ideas that they had caught from Schelling, and Schelling from Plotinus, from Boehm, or from God knows what minds stricken with the monstrous mysticism of the East. But the atmosphere of Cambridge held many an antiseptic against Concord transcendentalism; and I am not conscious of having contracted any of that virus. Nevertheless, it is probable that some cultured bacilli, some benignant form of the disease was implanted in my soul, unawares, and that now, after long incubation, it comes to the surface, modified by mathematical conceptions and by training in physical investigation.[4]

The wary and tough-minded response of Peirce is not atypical of a philosophical assessment of Emerson. Indeed, even those philosophers who acknowledge their debt to Emerson lace their remarks with dubiety about his fundamental assumptions and unease about much of the rhetoric of his formulation. Nonetheless, James, Royce, Dewey, and Santayana, each in his own way, find it necessary to evaluate the importance of Emerson in the light of their own developing positions. Before turning to these judgments, it should be helpful if I sketch the Emersonian project in cultural and philosophical terms.

The central theme of Emerson's life and work is that of *possibility.* In an anticipation of the attitude of Martin Buber, Emerson believes that 'we are really able', that is, we and the world are continuous in an affective and nutritional way. It is human insight which is able to "animate the last fibre of organization, the outskirts of nature."[5] Emerson's persistent stress on human possibility is fed from two sources: his extraordinary confidence in the latent powers of the individual soul when related to the symbolic riches of nature and his belief that the comparatively unarticulated history of American experience could act as a vast resource for the energizing of novel and creative spiritual energy. The often oracular style of Emerson should not cloak the seriousness of his intention when he speaks of these possibilities. In this regard, the key text is found in his Introduction to the essay *Nature*.

> Our age is retrospective. It builds the sepulchres of the fathers. It writes biogra-
> phies, histories, and criticism. The foregoing generations beheld God and nature
> face to face; we, through their eyes. Why should not we also enjoy an original
> relation to the universe? Why should not we have a poetry and philosophy of
> insight and not of tradition, and a religion by revelation to us, and not the history
> of theirs? Embosomed for a season in nature, whose floods of life stream around
> and through us, and invite us, by the powers they supply, to action proportioned
> to nature, why should we grope among the dry bones of the past, or put the living
> generation into masquerade out of its faded wardrobe? The sun shines to-day
> also. There is more wool and flax in the fields. There are new lands, new men,
> new thoughts. Let us demand our own works and laws and worship.[6]

We of the twentieth century may not grasp the radical character of Emerson's invocation, standing as we do on the rubble of broken promises brought to us by the great faiths of the past, be they scientific, social, or religious. But Emerson made no such promise and cannot be accused, retroactively, of bad faith. His message was clear. We are to transform the obviousness of our situation by a resolute penetration to the liberating symbolism present in our own experience. We are not to be dependent on faith hatched elsewhere out of others' experiences, nor, above all, are we to rest on an inherited ethic whose significance is due more to longevity and authority than to the press of our own experience. Surely, Emerson's nineteenth century, which was barely able to absorb the recondite theology responsible for the transition from Presbyterianism to Unitarianism, had to blanch at his bypassing the issue entirely, while calling for a homegrown "revelation." The radical character of Emerson's position at that time was given historical credence by the reception given to his Divinity School Address, delivered two years after *Nature* and one year after "The American Scholar." Using a tone more modest than either of those, Emerson in effect told the graduating class of Harvard Divinity School that the tradition they had inherited was hollow and the Church to which they belonged "seems to totter to its fall, all life extinct."[7] As in *Nature*, he again called for a "new hope and new revelation."[8] The upshot of this address was that for nearly thirty years Emerson was unwelcome as a public figure in Cambridge.

Now, more to the point of the present discussion is Emerson's doctrine of experience and his emphasis on relations, both central concerns of the subsequent philosophical thought of James and Dewey. In his essay "The American Scholar," Emerson points to three major influences on the development of the reflective person: nature, history, and action or experience. In his discussion of the third influence, Emerson provides a microcosmic view of his fundamental philosophy. He makes it apparent that he does not accept the traditional superiority of the contemplative over the active life. Emerson tells us further that "Action is with the scholar subordinate, but it is essential. Without it he is not yet man. Without it thought can never ripen into truth."[9] It is noteworthy that accompanying Emerson's superb intellectual mastery of the great literature of the past and his commitment to the reflective life is his affirmation that "Character is higher than intellect."[10] Living is a total act, the functionary, whereas thinking is a partial act, the function. More than twenty years after the publication of "The American Scholar," Emerson reiterated his commitment to the "practical" and to the "experiential" as the touchstone of the thinking person. In his essay "Fate" he considers those thinkers for whom the central question is the "theory of the Age." In response, Emerson writes: "To me, however, the question of the times resolved itself into a practical question of the conduct of life. How shall I live? We are incompetent to solve the times."[11] The human task for Emerson is not so much to solve the times as to live them, in an ameliorative and perceptive way.

Emerson's generalized approach to inquiry is clearly a foreshadowing of that found subsequently in James, Dewey, and Royce. Too often, Emerson's anticipation of these thinkers is left at precisely that general bequest, whereby the undergoing of experience is its own mean and carries its own peculiar form of cognition.[12] What is less well known is that Emerson also anticipated the doctrine of "radical empiricism," which is central to the philosophy of James and Dewey. I do not contend that Emerson's version of relations had the same psychological or epistemological genesis[13] as that of either James or Dewey. Yet, *mutatis mutandis,* Emerson did affirm the primary importance of relations over things and he did hold to an aggressive doctrine of implication. Further, his metaphors were more allied to the language of continuity than to that of totality or finality. Finally, Emerson shared that modern assumption which began with Kant and is found repeated in James and Dewey—namely, that the known is, in some way, a function of the knower.

Emerson's attitude toward implicitness, relations, and the partially constitutive character of human inquiry helps us to understand him in other ways as well. Why, one might ask, would Emerson, a New England Brahmin, have a proletarian epistemology? That is, how could Emerson write as he did in "The American Scholar," a paean of praise to the obvious, to the ordinary? The text, as read to the audience at the Phi Beta Kappa celebration of 1837, was startling.

> I embrace the common, I explore and sit at the feet of the familiar, the low. Give me insight into to-day, and you may have the antique and future worlds. What would we really know the meaning of? The meal in the firkin; the milk in the pan; the ballad in the street; the news of the boat; the glance of the eye; the form and gait of the body; ...[14]

Emerson immediately provides the response to the rhetorical question posed above. For the "ultimate reason" why the affairs of the ordinary yield insight traces to Emerson's belief that "the sublime presence of the highest spiritual cause lurks, as always it does lurk, in these suburbs and extremities of nature."[15] His version of the world is not characterized by hierarchies, nor by fixed essences, each to be known as an object in itself. Rather he stresses the flow of our experience and the multiple implications of every event and everything for every other experience had or about to be had. Nature brings with it this rich symbolic resource, enabling all experiences, sanctioned and occasional, to retract potentially novel implications of our other experiences. The novelty is due both to the unpredictability of nature[16] and to the creative role of human imagination. Of the first Emerson writes:

> Nature hates calculators; her methods are saltatory and impulsive. Man lives by pulses; our organic movements are such; and the chemical and ethereal agents are undulatory and alternate; and the mind goes antagonizing on, and never prospers but by fits. We thrive by casualties. Our chief experiences have been casual. The most attractive class of people are those who are powerful obliquely and not by the direct stroke; men of genius, but not yet accredited; one gets the cheer of their light without paying too great a tax. Theirs is the beauty of the bird or the morning light, and not of art. In the thought of genius there is always a surprise; and the moral sentiment is well called "the newness," for it is never other; as new to the oldest intelligence as to the young child; . . .[17]

The malleability and novelty-prone capacity of nature feeds the formulating and constructive powers native to the human imagination. Emerson, like James and Dewey, sees this transaction between the open nature of nature and the "active soul" as the necessary context for meaning. In his *Journals*, Emerson writes:

> This power of imagination, the making of some familiar object, as fire or rain, or a bucket, or shovel do new duty as an exponent of some truth or general law, bewitches and delights men. It is a taking of dead sticks, and clothing about with immortality; it is music out of creaking and scouring. All opaque things are transparent, and the light of heaven struggles through.[18]

We should not mistake Emerson's position for a flight of fancy or for the poetic stroke in the pejorative sense of that word. Emerson is a hard-headed empiricist, reminiscent of the Augustinian-Franciscan tradition for whom the world was a temporal epiphany of the eternal implications and ramifications of the eternal ideas. For Emerson, "A fact is the end or last issue of spirit."[19] Such facticity, paradoxically, comes to us only on behalf of our grasping and formulating the inherent symbolic features of our life.

> We learn nothing rightly until we learn the symbolical character of life. Day creeps after day, each full of facts, dull, strange, despised things, that we cannot enough despise—call heavy, prosaic and desert. The time we seek to kill: the attention it is elegant to divert from things around us. And presently the aroused intellect finds gold and gems in one of these scorned facts—then finds that the day of facts is a rock of diamonds; that a fact is an Epiphany of God.[20]

The epiphanic, for Emerson, is not a result of human quietism. It is we who constitute these "facts" by our forging of relations. "Every new relation is a new word."[21] The making of words for Emerson, as for James, is the making of the world of meaning. Words are not simply grammatical connectors. As the embodiment of relations they do more than define. They make and remake the very fabric of our world as experienced. "The world is emblematic. Parts of speech are metaphors, because the whole of nature is a metaphor of the human mind."[22] This text mirrors the binary strands found in subsequent American philosophy: the idealist-pragmatic epistemology of James, Royce, Dewey, and Peirce, each with an original emphasis of one strand over another.

If we read the Emersonian project as one which focuses on the dialectic between the raw givenness of nature and the symbolic formulations of the human imagination, then we have a direct line of common interpretation from Emerson to the classic American philosophers. I grant that each of the American philosophers in question contexts this dialectic differently, yet even a cameo version reveals the similarity. The thought of Peirce, for example, exhibits a life-long tension between his acceptance of the irreducibly "tychistic" (i.e., chance-ridden) character of the world and of the inevitably fallibilistic character of human knowledge, and his extreme confidence in the method of science. And it is the tough-minded Peirce who writes that "without beating longer round the bush let us come to close quarters. Experience is our only teacher." And "how does this action of experience take place? It takes place by a series of surprises."[23]

The philosophy of John Dewey reflects a similar tension between a confidence in empirical method and the acknowledgment of novelty and unpredictability as indigenous to the history of nature. Dewey states that "Man finds himself living in an aleatory world; his existence involves, to put it baldly, a gamble. The world is a scene of risk; it is uncertain, unstable, uncannily unstable. Its dangers are irregular, inconstant, not to be counted upon as to their times and seasons. Although persistent, they are sporadic, episodic."[24]

Still, when faced with this extremely open and even perilous version of nature, Dewey calls upon philosophy to act as an intelligent mapping, so as to reconstruct, ameliorate, and enhance the human condition. Dewey's project is Emersonian, for the affairs of time and the activities of nature are the ground of inquiry, rather than the hidden and transcendent meaning of Being. Just as Emerson broke with the theological language of his immediate predecessors and many of his peers, so too did Dewey break with the ecstatic religious language of Emerson. This break in language should not hide from us that Dewey's understanding of the relationship which exists between nature and human life, echoes that of Emerson: always possibility, often celebration, frequently mishap and never absolute certitude.

As for an Emersonian analogue in Royce, readers of that indefatigable polymath know that cameo versions of any of his positions do not come easy. Nonetheless, Royce's long speculative trek away from the absolute and toward a theory of interpretation, ever reconstructed by the community, echoes Emerson's emphasis on the conduct of life. Royce was forced to abandon the doctrine of the absolute mind because he finally accepted the judgment of his critics that he could not account for the experience of the individual on either epistemological or metaphysical grounds.

In his last great work, *The Problem of Christianity*, Royce has come full circle and awarded to the individual the task of formulating the "real world" by virtue of the relationship between "self-interpretation" and the "community of interpretation." Emerson wrote that "we know more from nature than we can at will communicate."[25] Similarly, Royce writes that "the popular mind is deep, and means a thousand times more than it explicitly knows."[26] In my judgment, Royce's mature thought, under the influence of Peirce, structures philosophically the earlier informal approach of Emerson. Although the content is Emersonian, the following passage from Royce brings a heightened philosophical sophistication.

> Metaphysically considered, the world of interpretation is the world in which, if indeed we are able to interpret at all, we learn to acknowledge the being and the inner life of our fellow-men; and to understand the constitution of temporal experience with its endlessly accumulating sequence of significant deeds. In this world of interpretation, of whose most general structure we have now obtained a glimpse, selves and communities may exist, past and future can be defined, and the realms of the spirit may find a place which neither barren conception nor the chaotic flow of interpenetrating perceptions could ever render significant.[27]

It is with William James, however, that the Emersonian dialectic between the creative and constructive character of the human mind and the apparently intransigent character of the physical world most explicitly comes to the fore. James, like Emerson, holds to a relationship of congeniality between nature and human power. They both avoid the alternate interpretations, which, in turn, would stress either the complete objectivity of the meaning of nature or a completely subjective version in which nature has an existence only at the behest of the human, or failing that, the absolute mind. In some ways, James outdoes Emerson in his stress on the "powers" and "energies" of the individual, although we should remember that he also emphasizes "seeing and feeling the total push and pressure of the cosmos."[28]

William James is profoundly aware of these alternate versions of our situation and often evokes them in an extreme way. Two texts from *Pragmatism* stand out in this regard, and if we put them back to back, the poles of the Emersonian dialectic are thrown into bold relief.

> Woe to him whose beliefs play fast and loose with the order which realities follow in his experience: They will lead him nowhere or else make false connexions.[29]

> In our cognitive as well as in our active life we are creative. We *add*, both to the subject and to the predicate part of reality. The world stands really malleable, waiting to receive its final touches at our hands. Like the kingdom of heaven, it suffers human violence willingly. Man *engenders* truths upon it.[30]

Obviously, both of these texts cannot stand at one and the same time. James was very much aware of this conflict and continued to pose it, even though he was simultaneously working his way out of the dilemma. In an earlier entry in an unpublished notebook, he gives a reason for maintaining this conflict. "Surely nature itself and subjective construction are radically opposed, one's higher indignations are nourished by the opposition."[31] Emerson, of course, would approve of both the "indignation" and the "nourishment." It should be noted, however, that James goes beyond Emerson at this point and develops his formal doctrine of radical empiricism to mediate this "opposition." The genesis and content of James's radical empiricism is a long and complicated story, but in his conclusion to his essay on "A World of Pure Experience," James sets out the dramatic presence of the knowing self in a world both obdurate and malleable.

> There is in general no separateness needing to be overcome by an external cement; and whatever separateness is actually experienced is not overcome, it stays and counts as separateness to the end. But the metaphor serves to symbolize the fact that experience itself, taken at large, can grow by its edges. That one moment of it proliferates into the next by transitions which, whether conjunctive or disjunctive, continue the experiential tissue, cannot, I contend, be denied. Life is in the transitions as much as in the terms connected; often, indeed, it seems to be there more emphatically, as if our spurts and sallies forward were the real firing-line of the battle, were like the thin line of flame advancing across the dry autumnal field which the farmer proceeds to burn. In this line we live prospectively as well as retrospectively. It is "of" the past, inasmuch as it comes expressly as the past's continuation; it is "of" the future in so far as the future, when it comes, will have continued *it*.[32]

So much for the refractions of the Emersonian dialectic in some of the classical American philosophers. At this point, the reader may well ask why I have not cited these philosophers on this central theme in Emerson? The response, alas, is quite simple. Our philosophers did not write very much on Emerson and when they did, the focus was often on other, if related, themes. I turn now to James, Santayana, Royce, and Dewey on Emerson, directly.

II

At the age of three months, William James was visited by Ralph Waldo Emerson at the James family's home on Washington Square in New York City. This prepossessing and perhaps burdensome presence of Emerson lasted throughout most of the life of William James. In the decade following 1870, James read virtually everything Emerson wrote and at one point in 1873 made the following entry in his diary: "I am sure that an age will come when our present devotion to history, and scrupulous care for what men have done before us merely as fact, will seem incomprehensible; when acquaintance with books will be no duty, but a pleasure for odd individuals; when Emerson's philosophy will be in our bones, not our dramatic imagination."[33] Apparently, Emerson's thought had already reached the "bones" of James, for the above sentiment about the past is shared by Emerson. In "The American Scholar" he wrote that "I had better never see a book than to be warped by its attraction clean out of my own orbit and made a satellite instead of a system. The one thing in the world, of value, is the active soul."[34]

Some thirty years after his diary entry, in 1903, James was called upon to deliver the address at the centenary celebration for Emerson in Concord.[35] This occasion caused James to reread virtually all of Emerson's writings. Frankly, with regard to the question of the influence of Emerson on James, the address is disappointing. As one would expect, James is laudatory of Emerson's person and work.[36] And, as he often did in such pieces of encomium, the text is largely made up of long passages from Emerson. Despite these limitations, an important theme runs beneath the baroque prose of James and that of Emerson as selected by James. As we might expect, it is the theme of "possibility," of the hallowing of the everyday. James is struck by the radical temporality of Emerson's vision. He offers a brief collage of that attitude: "'The Deep to-day which all men scorn' receives thus from Emerson superb revindication. 'Other world! There is no other world.' All God's life opens into the individual particular, and here and now, or nowhere, is reality. 'The present hour is the decisive hour, and every day is doomsday.'"[37]

James cautions us that Emerson was no sentimentalist. The transformation of stubborn fact to an enhanced symbolic statement of richer possibility was an activity that James found very compatible with his own stress on novelty and surprise. Emerson had written, "So is there no fact, no event, in our private history, which shall not sooner or later, lose its adhesive, inert form and astonish us by soaring from our body into the empyrean."[38] On behalf of this and similar passages, James comments that Emerson "could perceive the full squalor of the individual fact, but he could also see the transfiguration."[39]

Aside from this important focus on Emerson's concern for "individuals and particulars," James's address is taken up with praise of Emerson's style as a literary artist. I note the irony here, for such praise of style is precisely what has taken up much of the commentaries on the thought of James, often to the detriment of an analysis of his serious philosophical intent. It is unfortunate that James never undertook a systematic study of Emerson, especially as directed to his notions of experience, relations, and symbol. James would have found Emerson far more "congenial"[40] and helpful than many of the other thinkers he chose to examine. A detailed study of Emerson as an incipient radical empiricist is a noteworthy task for the future.

The response of Santayana to Emerson's thought was more censorious than that of James and Dewey. On several occasions, James compared the thought of Emerson and Santayana, to the detriment of the latter. In a letter to Dickinson S. Miller, James comments on Santayana's book, *The Life of Reason*:

He is a paragon of Emersonianism—declare your intuitions, though no other man share them; . . . The book is Emerson's first rival and successor, but how different the reader's feeling! The same things in Emerson's mouth would sound entirely different. E. receptive, expansive, as if handling life through a wide funnel with a great indraught; S. as if through a pin-point orifice that emits his cooling spray outward over the universe like a nose-disinfectant from an "atomizer."[41]

We learn from a letter written by Santayana that James apparently had expressed similar sentiments to him as he had in the letter to Miller. Santayana was not pleased and in his response issues a devastating criticism of Emerson.

And you say I am less hospitable than Emerson. Of course. Emerson might pipe his wood-notes and chirp at the universe most blandly; his genius might be tender and profound and Hamlet-like, and that is all beyond my range and contrary to my purpose.... What did Emerson know or care about the passionate insanities and political disasters which religion, for instance, has so often been another name for? He could give that name to his last personal intuition, and ignore what it stands for and what it expresses in the world. It is the latter that absorbs me; and I care too much about mortal happiness to be interested in the charming vegetation of cancer-microbes in the system—except with the idea of suppressing it.[42]

Although not quite so caustic as his rebuke to James, Santayana's writings on Emerson always had a critical edge to them. In an early essay, written in 1886, Santayana comments judiciously on Emerson's optimism, which he traces more to his person than to his doctrine. Yet, Santayana's sympathetic treatment of Emerson concludes with a damaging last line: "But of those who are not yet free from the troublesome feelings of pity and shame, Emerson brings no comfort, he is a prophet of a fair-weather religion."[43]

In 1900, as a chapter in his *Interpretations of Poetry and Religion*, Santayana published his best-known essay on Emerson. This piece has been frequently cited on behalf of those who are condescending to Emerson or severely critical of him. I believe this use of Santayana's essay to be a misreading. Certainly, Santayana was more indulgent of Emerson in 1900 than he was in 1911, when he published his famous essay on "The Genteel Tradition in American Philosophy." In 1911, Santayana lumps Emerson with Poe and Hawthorne as having "a certain starved and abstract quality." Further, their collective "genius" was a "digestion of vacancy."

It was a refined labour, but it was in danger of being morbid, or tinkling, or self-indulgent. It was a play of intramental rhymes. Their mind was like an old music-box, full of tender echoes and quaint fancies. These fancies expressed their personal genius sincerely, as dreams may; but they were arbitrary fancies in comparison with what a real observer would have said in the premises. Their manner, in a word, was subjective. In their own persons they escape the mediocrity of the genteel tradition, but they supplied nothing to supplant it in other minds.[44]

In 1900, however, when Santayana addresses Emerson's thought directly, his evaluations are more favorable. Admitting of Emerson, that "at bottom he had no doctrine at all," Santayana writes that "his finer instinct kept him from doing that violence to his inspiration."[45] Santayana repeats his earlier contention that Emerson's power was not in his "doctrine" but rather in his "temperament." And that Emersonian temperament was, above all, antitradition and antiauthoritarian. Even though he was a classic instance of the "Genteel Tradition" and held many positions which were anathema to Santayana, Emerson nevertheless pleased Santayana by his refusal to professionalize and systematize his thought. Further, Santayana, with poetic sensibilities of his own, was taken with Emerson's style. He writes of Emerson: "If not a star of the first magnitude, he is certainly a fixed star in the firmament of philosophy. Alone as yet among Americans, he may be said to have won a place there, if not by the originality of this thought, at least by the originality and beauty of the expression he gave to thoughts that are old and imperishable."[46]

Still more to the point, and less known, is that Santayana shared Emerson's celebration and embracing of the "common." In 1927, as part of a chastising letter sent to Van Wyck Brooks, Santayana writes: "I therefore think that art, etc. has better soil in the ferocious 100% America than in the intelligentsia of New York. It is veneer, rouge, aestheticism, art museums, new theatres, etc. that make America impotent. The good things are football, kindness, and jazz bands."[47] It turns out that Santayana, like Whitman, learned something from Emerson.

Before examining John Dewey's essay on Emerson, I offer a brief interlude with a comment on Josiah Royce's assessment of Emerson. Although Royce was a voluminous writer[48] and ventured interpretations of an extremely wide range of problems and thinkers, he rarely spoke of Emerson. And yet, Royce thought far more of Emerson than we could have divined from his publications. In 1911, Royce delivered a Phi Beta Kappa oration in honor of William James, who had died the previous year. The theme of Royce's essay was that James was the third "representative American Philosopher." It was in Royce's opening discussion of the first two candidates that his version of Emerson emerged:

> Fifty years since, if competent judges were asked to name the American thinkers from whom there had come novel and notable and typical contributions to general philosophy, they could in reply mention only two men—Jonathan Edwards and Ralph Waldo Emerson. For the conditions that determine a fair answer to the question, "Who are your representative American philosophers?" are obvious. The philosopher who can fitly represent the contribution of his nation to the world's treasury of philosophical ideas must first be one who thinks for himself, fruitfully, with true independence, and with successful inventiveness, about problems of philosophy. And, secondly, he must be a man who gives utterance to philosophical ideas which are characteristic of some stage and of some aspect of the spiritual life of his own people. In Edwards and in Emerson, and only in these men, had these

two conditions found their fulfillment, so far as our American civilization had yet expressed itself in the years that had preceded our civil war. . . .

Another stage of our civilization—a later phase of our national ideals— found its representative in Emerson. He too was in close touch with many of the world's deepest thoughts concerning ultimate problems. Some of the ideas that most influenced him have their far-off historical origins in oriental as well as in Greek thought, and also their nearer foreign sources in modern European philosophy, but he transformed what ever he assimilated. He invented upon the basis of his personal experience, and so he was himself no disciple of the orient, or of Greece, still less of England and Germany. He thought, felt, and spoke as an American.[49]

Again, we are left with a judgment as to Emerson's importance, notably in this case as a philosopher, but without subsequent or sufficient analysis. A search through the papers and publications of Royce does not cast much more direct light on this influence of Emerson. Royce's remarks do convince me, however, that Emerson wrought more in the lives of the classical American philosophers than written evidence can sustain.

Among the centenary addresses of 1903, we find another by an American philosopher, John Dewey. This essay sets out to rescue Emerson from the condescension implied when he is described as not a philosopher. Dewey complains that "literary critics admit his philosophy and deny his literature. And if philosophers extol his keen, calm art and speak with some depreciation of his metaphysic, it is also perhaps because Emerson knew something deeper than our conventional definitions."[50] The first of Dewey's complaints is now out of date, for Emerson is taken very seriously as a literary artist. The second complaint still holds, although with important exceptions as noted above in the work of Blau and Pollock.

In Dewey's judgment, Emerson has been misread and misunderstood. He takes as Emerson's project the submitting of ideas "to the test of trial by service rendered the present and immediate experience."[51] Further, Dewey contends that Emerson's method is consistent with this experimental endeavor. "To Emerson, perception was more potent than reasoning; the deliverances of intercourse more to be desired than the chains of discourse; the surprise of reception more demonstrative than the conclusions of intentional proof."[52]

It is intriguing that Dewey, whose own style is anything but oracular, would praise this approach of Emerson. One might rather expect this indulgence from those reared in the language of the existentialists or of twentieth-century religious thinkers, such as Buber, Berdyaev, and Marcel. A closer look at Dewey's text, however, provides some source of explanation. Similar to James's emphasis, Dewey states that the locus of Emerson's inquiry is the "possibility" inherent in the experience of the "common man." Against the opinions of other commentators, Dewey holds that Emerson's "ideas are not fixed upon any Reality that is beyond or behind or in any way apart, and hence they do not have to be bent. They are versions of the Here and the Now, and flow freely."[53]

Dewey is especially sympathetic with Emerson's attempt to avoid the "apart."[54] And he is convinced that Emerson knew, as few others, of the enervating and diluting effect often had by theory on the richness of common and concrete experience. Dewey's text on this issue is crystal-clear and can be read as well as a critique for much of what passes for philosophical discourse in our own time.

> Against creed and system, convention and institution, Emerson stands for restoring to the common man that which in the name of religion, of philosophy, of art and of morality, has been embezzled from the common store and appropriated to sectarian and class use. Beyond any one we know of, Emerson has comprehended and declared how such malversation makes truth decline from its simplicity, and in becoming partial and owned, become a puzzle of and trick for theologian, metaphysician and litterateur—a puzzle of an imposed law, of an unwished for and refused goodness, of a romantic ideal gleaming only from afar, and a trick of manipular skill, of specialized performance.[55]

Dewey took Emerson's task as his own. Although his prose lacked the rhetorical flights so natural to Emerson, he too wrote out of compassion for the common man and confidence in the "possibility" inherent in every situation. By the time of Dewey's maturity, the world of New England high culture had passed. Dewey, despite being born in New England, was a child of industrial democracy. He alone of the classic American philosophers was able to convert the genius and language of Emerson to the new setting. John Dewey, proletarian by birth and style, grasped that Emerson's message was ever relevant. In the conclusion to his essay on Emerson, Dewey captures that message and carries it forward to his own time. I offer that we should do likewise.

> To them who refuse to be called "master, master," all magistracies in the end defer, for theirs is the common cause for which dominion, power and principality is put under foot. Before such successes, even the worshippers of that which to-day goes by the name of success, those who bend to millions and incline to imperialisms, may lower their standard and give at least a passing assent to the final word of Emerson's philosophy, the identity of Being, unqualified and immutable, with Character.[56]

Notes

1   *American Philosophic Addresses*, 1700–1900, ed. Joseph L. Blau (New York: Columbia University Press, 1946); *Men and Movements in American Philosophy* (Englewood Cliffs, NJ: Prentice-Hall, 1952); "Emerson's Transcendentalist Individualism as a Social Philosophy," *Review of Metaphysics* 31, no. 1 (September 1977): 80–92.
2   Robert C. Pollock, "Ralph Waldo Emerson—The Single Vision," in *American Classics Reconsidered*, ed. Harold Gardiner (New York: Scribner's, 1958), 15–58.

3 George Herbert Mead tends to speak of Emerson only in the context of Concord transcendentalism. Ironically, in lamenting the failure of the transcendentalists to develop a distinctive doctrine of American self-consciousness, Mead overlooks the powerful voice of Emerson in precisely this regard. Mead, "The Philosophies of Royce, James and Dewey in Their American Setting," *Selected Writings*, ed. Andrew J. Reck (Indianapolis: Bobbs-Merrill, 1964), 377–78.

4 Charles Sanders Peirce, *Collected Papers*, ed. Charles Hartshorne and Paul Weiss, vol. 6 (sec. 101) (Cambridge: Harvard University Press, 1934), 86–87. Peirce also was fond of quoting and mocking Emerson's poem on the Sphinx, especially the line, "Of thine eye, I am eyebeam," ibid., 1:153–54 (sec. 31), and 2:252 (sec. 404). Some unpublished material on Peirce's "boyhood impressions" of Emerson can be found in "Manuscript—296" as recorded in the *Annotated Catalogue of the Papers of Charles S. Peirce*, ed. Richard Robin (Amherst: University of Massachusetts Press, 1967), 31.

5 Ralph Waldo Emerson, "The American Scholar," in *The Complete Works of Ralph Waldo Emerson*, ed. Edward Emerson, vol. 1 (Boston: Houghton Mifflin, 1903–04), 86.

6 Ralph Waldo Emerson, *Nature*, in *The Complete Works*, 1:3.

7 Ralph Waldo Emerson, "The Divinity School Address," in *The Complete Works*, 1:135.

8 Ibid., 151.

9 Emerson, "The American Scholar," 1:95. The use of "he" and "man" in this text and in subsequent texts is to be read in the present chapter as referring as to "she" and "woman."

10 Ibid., 99.

11 Emerson, "Fate," in *The Complete Works*, 6.3. For a similar attitude, see William James, *The Varieties of Religious Experience* (New York: Longmans, Green, 1902), 489. "Knowledge about life is one thing; effective occupation of a place in life, with its dynamic currents passing through your being, is another."

12 Texts in support of this position abound in the writings of John Dewey. Among others are Dewey, *Reconstruction in Philosophy*, vol. 12 (1982) of *The Middle Works* (Carbondale: Southern Illinois University Press, 1976–83). "Experience carries principles of connection and organization within itself." And again, p. 134, "What Shakespeare so pregnantly said of nature, it is 'made better by no mean, but nature makes that mean,' becomes true of experience."

13 For a historical and philosophical treatment of the genesis of James's doctrine of radical empiricism, see John J. McDermott, "Introduction" to William James, *Essays in Radical Empiricism* (Cambridge: Harvard University Press, 1976), xi–xlviii. Dewey's doctrine of radical empiricism is best found in *The Influence of Darwinism on Philosophy and Other Essays in Contemporary Philosophy* (New York: Holt, 1910).

14 Emerson, "The American Scholar," 1:111. For a richer description of the extreme variety of audience responses to Emerson's oration of 1837, see Bliss Perry, "Emerson's Most Famous Speech," in *Ralph Waldo Emerson: A Profile*, ed. Carl Bode (New York: Hill and Wang, 1969), 52–65. Oliver Wendell Holmes heard the oration as an "intellectual Declaration of Independence," and James Russell Lowell viewed it as "our Yankee version of a lecture by Abelard, our Harvard parallel to the last public appearances of Schelling."

15 Emerson, "The American Scholar," 111.

16 Ralph Waldo Emerson, "Experience," in *The Complete Works*, 6:308 n.1. "Everything in the Universe goes by indirection. There are no straight lines."

17 Ibid., 6:68. William James holds a similar position. "Notebook" entry of 1903 as found in Ralph Barton Perry, *The Thought and Character of William James*, vol. 2 (Boston: Little, Brown, 1935), 700 (cited above, pp. 15–16).

18 *The Journals of Ralph Waldo Emerson*, vol. 9 (Boston: Houghton Mifflin, 1909–14), 277–78.

19 Emerson, *Nature*, 1:34.

20 Ralph Waldo Emerson, "Education," in *The Complete Works*, 10:132.

21 Ralph Waldo Emerson, "The Poet," in *The Complete Works*, 3:18.

22 Emerson, *Nature*, 1:32.

23 Peirce, *Collected Papers*, 1:37.

24 John Dewey, *Experience and Nature*, vol. 1 (1981) of *The Later Works* (Carbondale: Southern Illinois University Press, 1981-), 43.

25 Emerson, *Nature*, 1:31.

26 *The Letters of Josiah Royce*, ed. John Clendenning (Chicago: University of Chicago Press, 1970), 86.

27 Josiah Royce, *The Problem of Christianity* (Chicago: University of Chicago Press, 1968 [1913]), 86.

28 William James, *Pragmatism* (Cambridge: Harvard University Press, 1975), 9.

29 Ibid., 99.

30 Ibid., 123.

31 James Papers, Houghton Library, Harvard University (bMS AM 1092, box L, notebook N^2).

32 James, Essays in *Radical Empiricism*, 42.

33 Cited in Gay Wilson Allen, *William James: A Biography* (New York: Viking, 1967), 186–87.

34 Emerson, "The American Scholar," 1:89–90.

35 William James, "Address at the Emerson Centenary in Concord," in *Essays in Religion and Morality* (Cambridge: Harvard University Press, 1982), 109–15. For a contrast of James's hagiographic approach to others more critical and substantive, the reader should consult two collections of essays: *Emerson*, ed. Milton Konvitz and Stephen Whicher (Englewood Cliffs, NJ: Prentice-Hall, 1962), and *The Recognition of Ralph Waldo Emerson: Selected Criticism since 1837*, ed. Milton Konvitz (Ann Arbor: University of Michigan Press, 1972). It is striking that in the vast secondary literature on Emerson, distinctively philosophical considerations are virtually absent.

36 James was not always complimentary to Emerson. In *The Varieties of Religious Experience*, for example, he criticized Emerson for tending toward "abstraction" on the religious question (32, 56). For a discussion of James's ambivalence on Emerson, see F. O. Matthiessen, *The American Renaissance* (New York: Oxford University Press, 1941), 53–54n.

37 James, *Essays in Religion and Morality*, 114.

38 Emerson, "The American Scholar," 2:96–97.

39 James, *Essays in Religion and Morality*, 114. The potential capacity for "transfiguration" of fact as subject to human will is not a strange contention for William James, as can be seen in his own doctrine "The Will to Believe." Could it have some expressive origin in Emerson's *Nature*? "Build therefore your own world. As fast as you conform your life to the pure idea in your mind, that will unfold its

great proportions. A correspondent revolution in things will attend the influx of the spirit" (*The Complete Works*, 1:76)

40 What could be more Emersonian than James's remark in his "Sentiment of Rationality" that "the inmost nature of the reality is congenial to powers which you possess" (*The Will to Believe* [Cambridge: Harvard University Press, 1979], 73). See also *The Writings of William James*, ed. John J. McDermott (Chicago: University of Chicago Press, 1977), 331. In preparation for his "Address," James did read Emerson, "volume after volume," but came away with "a moral lesson" rather than distinctive philosophical insight. Cf. *The Letters of William James*, ed. Henry James III, 3 vols. (Boston: Atlantic Monthly Press, 1920), 190.

41 James, *Letters of William James*, 234–35. For another contrast of Emerson and Santayana, see John Crowe Ransom, "Art and Mr. Santayana," in *Santayana: Animal Faith and Spiritual Life*, ed. John Lachs (New York: Appleton-Century-Crofts, 1967), 403–04.

42 George Santayana, *The Letters of George Santayana*, ed. Daniel Cory (New York: Scribner's, 1955), 81–82.

43 George Santayana, "The Optimism of Ralph Waldo Emerson," in *George Santayana's America*, ed. James Ballowe (Urbana: University of Illinois Press, 1967), 84. Another little-known piece of Santayana is "Emerson the Poet," a centennial contribution of 1903. Although in this essay Santayana speaks of Emerson as often bland, he praises him for self-direction and a deep and unyielding sense of personal liberty. See *Santayana on America*, ed. Richard C. Lyon (New York: Harcourt, 1968), 268–83.

44 George Santayana, "The Genteel Tradition in American Philosophy," in *Winds of Doctrine* (London: Dent, 1913), 192–93.

45 George Santayana, "Emerson," in *Interpretations of Poetry and Religion* (New York: Scribner's, 1900), 218.

46 Ibid., 233.

47 Santayana, *Letters*, 225–26.

48 Ignas K. Skrupskelis, "Annotated Bibliography of the Publications of Josiah Royce," in *The Basic Writings of Josiah Royce*, ed. John J. McDermott, vol. 2 (Chicago: University of Chicago Press, 1969), 1167–226.

49 Josiah Royce, *William James and Other Essays* (New York: Macmillan, 1911), 3–4, 5–6.

50 John Dewey, "Ralph Waldo Emerson," in *Characters and Events*, vol. 1 (New York: Holt, 1929), 71.

51 Ibid., 74.

52 Ibid., 70.

53 Ibid., 75.

54 Dewey takes a similar position in *Art as Experience* (New York: Capricorn, 1958 [1934]), 11: "Theory can start with and from acknowledged works of art only when the esthetic is already compartmentalized, or only when works of art are set in a niche apart instead of being celebrations, recognized as such, of the things of ordinary experience. Even a crude experience, if authentically an experience, is more fit to give a clue to the intrinsic nature of esthetic experience than is an object already set apart from any other mode of experience."

55 Dewey, "Ralph Waldo Emerson," 75.

56 Ibid., 77.

Richard Poirier (1925–2009)

Literary and cultural critic, editor, and publisher who founded The Library of America *(in 1979) and* Raritan: A Quarterly Review *(in 1981), Poirier taught at Rutgers from 1963 to 2002. His scholarly topics included style in American literature (as in* A World Elsewhere, *1966), performance theory as it relates to artistic creation and self-constitution (as found in* The Performing Self *, 1971), and remarks on the ongoing inheritance of American literature, as disclosed in* The Renewal of Literature: Emersonian Reflections *(1987), from which the following essay is drawn. In this work, a portion from the opening of the first chapter of the book, Poirier returns our attention to the notion of genius in Emerson's writing as a topic and as a description of the work itself—that is to an appreciation of the difference between works of genius and the workings of genius. Poirier finds Emerson "an appropriate guide to the question of genius for several reasons," and saying why is at the core of Poirier's critical task. As readers we might consider, as Poirier suggests, that Emerson's own genius becomes evident in how his "writing simultaneously affirms and calls into doubt his, or anyone else's, individual authority over language." In this respect, Poirier offers another way of understanding philosophical skepticism as it is embodied and incited in Emerson's prose.*

The Question of Genius

Richard Poirier

THE CHALLENGE OF EMERSON

"The only objection to *Hamlet*," according to Emerson's *Journals* for 1841, "is that it exists." What is the best way to take this? Is it merely feisty or provocative? is it nationalistic? is it Oedipally anxious? It could be all of these and as easily none of them. Any such characterization of a remark like Emerson's would be culturally rigid and defensive, as if—the value of *Hamlet* being beyond debate—inquiry should direct itself only at motives for devaluing it. But what if such a remark is taken as seriously as I think it ought to be taken? What happens to literature if you can imagine doing without it? What happens to the reputed transactions between life and art if, apparently for the sake of life, "great" works are wished out of existence?

Such questions, which have to do with the status and, finally, the usefulness to life of literary culture, belong to the larger question of "genius," its possible nature and location. From what Emerson says about that subject, it is obvious that his position on

Hamlet is a passionately held one: for him, monumental works of art become inimical not merely to other artists but to the human vitalities that go into them. He objects to any text which purports to incorporate "genius"; and, needless to say, he is still more opposed to efforts which imbue it with moral or ethical purposes that have any kind of social or ecclesiastical derivation. The more esteemed the work or the artist has become, the greater the possibility of its also becoming dead and deadening. "For it is the inert effort of each thought, having formed itself into a circular wave of circumstance,—as, for instance, an empire, rules of an art, a local usage, a religious rite—to heap itself on that ridge, and to solidify and hem in, the life," as he remarks in "Circles."

Emerson's essential objection to *works* of genius is that they cannot in themselves ever adequately convey the *workings* of it. As he sees it, one complication in the transmission of culture is that genius is thwarted by the very shapes in which it is alleged to re-present itself. This may sound obtusely theoretical or intransigent or radical or simply weird on Emerson's part, but I think it is none of these things. He felt as if he were coping with a problem shared gregariously with the rest of us, as if, in some way or other, all of us get around to raising the question of "genius." "Genius" is a necessary idea because like the idea of God it is an abstraction a great many people want and need to believe in. And the belief depends on the fact that without it people would find it more difficult if not impossible to talk to one another about the extraordinary effects upon them of the created world. The term is useful in direct proportion to its vagueness; it conjures up something that cannot be specifically traced out; it describes things we suspect about an artist or a work but cannot know for sure. To use the word "genius" is to express a desire that human attributes should exist that are beyond human understanding.

Where is genius and whose is it? How do we find it even when we know it is there, as in Mozart's Fortieth Symphony or Balanchine's *Concerto Barocco*, or Caravaggio's *The Conversion of Saint Paul*, or *Don Quixote*? Part of the difficulty is that as we attend to such works all of us want, in a very real sense, to attribute the "genius" to ourselves, to an always imminent part of ourselves that has waited only upon the capacity for expression: in most cases a long wait. "The great poet," Emerson writes in "The Over-Soul,"

> makes us feel our own wealth, and then we think less of his compositions. His best communication to our mind is to teach us to despise all he has done. Shakespeare carries us to such a lofty strain of intelligent activity, as to suggest a wealth which beggars his own; and we then feel that the splendid works which he has created, and which in other hours we extol as a sort of self-existent poetry, take no stronger hold of real nature than the shadow of a passing traveler on the rock.

Emerson is an appropriate guide to the question of genius for several reasons. First, because, of those who address the subject, he seems to me to have the best, which is to say the most uncompromised and troubled, sense of its elusiveness. Second, because his idea of "the over-soul" persuades him that what attracts us to genius has less to do with particular works and authors than with something we want to discover in ourselves, something that resides not in the sentiments and pieties and moral values abstracted from texts, but in corporate human power. And third, because the strongest evidence for me of Emerson's own genius is that his way of writing simultaneously affirms and calls into doubt his, or anyone else's, individual authority over language, the language he himself chooses to use. He calls into doubt the very existence in language of the individual self, even while he famously affirms it.

Indeed, when he talks about the self, there is something peculiarly unsettling about his aphoristic bravado, as if the aphorisms are meant to transcend the occasion of their utterance and of our reading. "All that Adam had, all that Caesar could, you have and can do," he says at the end of *Nature*. Is anyone supposed to believe this? Should we act upon the conviction that it is true? He does not really expect us to, and his careless combination of references ought to indicate as much. Anyone who has "all that Adam had" would be utterly indifferent to all that Caesar did. And neither figure is being proposed as a model. He is dismissing both of them in favor of whatever version of their "genius" may exist in each of us, now. "Why, then," he asks a bit later in "The Over-Soul," "should I make account of Hamlet and Lear, as if we had not the soul from which they fell as syllables from the tongue?"

Classic figures and texts of the past, as Emerson invokes them, are very often objected to, rebuked, lumped together indiscriminately or, as in *Representative Men*, offered as exempla of efforts rather than of specific achievements. He wants to suggest that on behalf of all of us he is clearing the way for some forever postponed and unparalleled human performance. This, too, is how he deploys the sentences of his own writing, as if he feared being trapped by them. Within a given paragraph, he tends not to develop an argument in the direction already laid down by a previous remark but to veer away from it, as from some constraining influence. He wants always to be several steps ahead of himself. "It avails not, time nor place—distance avails not, / I am with you, you men and women of a generation, or ever so many generations hence." Whitman was to write these lines in "Crossing Brooklyn Ferry." It is an Emersonian gesture meant to transport the poet beyond any compositional occasion into some future where the poem finds itself being read, where Whitman would be the effluvium of his own writing.

It is frequently said of this Emersonian tendency—this apparent obliviousness to the present circumstance, this living into the future—that it conveys a dangerous indifference to historical and political realities, offering in their stead an illusory notion that individual freedom will someday actualize itself in a New World, a place, unlike any other in history, where there are no contrived impediments to the expression of desire. Here was a chance to give practical realizations to liberal Enlightenment hopes for individual autonomy. Superficially, therefore, it might seem as if the gaps Emerson likes to create between "genius" and the texts it is supposed to inhabit, between "genius" and the artists who are supposed to have it, or between one sentence he has written and the one that will follow it—that all this expresses his confident hope of effecting a break from inherited culture, even from the more immediate historical or cultural commitments implicit in his own uses of language. The prologue to this book, as well as my earlier *A World Elsewhere*, is meant to refute the illusion that any effort of style can radically transform history or language or effectively break the coherencies they impose upon consciousness. It seems to me apparent that Emerson himself recognized the limits of his own enterprise.

He had a tragic view of the disparity between desire and possibility, all the more so because the physical continent of America did sometimes seem like a bridge between the two. The disparity, the chasm, was enforced by the fact of language. Wherever you are, you live within its necessities, within the cultural inheritances carried in its syntax. "Build, therefore, your own world," he exhorts us at the end of *Nature* when, for a brief time, he imagined that we could learn language from "nature." But in only a very few years he would find it obvious that language had already "learned" us, so to speak; it had already taught us the words by which we can communicate to ourselves any knowledge of ourselves.

Alfred Kazin (1915–1998)

New York City–based literary critic, author of On Native Grounds *(1942), literary editor of the* New Republic, *Kazin's* An American Procession *(1984) begins with chapters entitled "The Priest Departs, the Divine Literatus Comes: Emerson" and "Things Are in the Saddle and Ride Mankind: Emerson." In 1959 he coedited* Emerson: A Modern Anthology *with the subtitle "Selections from the writings of America's first philosopher." Emerging in an age of the text-only New Critics, Kazin was decidedly interested in the context and conditions in which literature emerged. As he noted, "Criticism for me was not a theory. It was a branch of literature, a way of writing like any other, of characterization, analysis and almost physical empathy." Philip Roth eulogized him by saying "He was America's best reader of American literature in this century." Harold Laski, with* On Native Grounds *in mind, declared Kazin to be "among the best six critical minds America has had since Emerson." He was also a dedicated reader of Emerson's work as illustrated by decades worth of critical commentary and a robust set of journal reflections, selections from which are featured below. Among many thought-provoking remarks, we find his claim that "Emerson made me a Jew." Kazin's essay acknowledging the one hundred and fiftieth anniversary of Emerson's address to the Phi Beta Kappa society (1987) is also included; in it he finds reason to lament the intellectual distance between Emerson's Concord and the present-day "literary world." What if today the thinker who is "so inclusive and penetrating, with such an obvious effect as to make us 'all of one mind'" is not a writer at all, but, as Kazin suggests, a physicist? What happens to American thinking when its scholars "reflect a great sourness and introversion" and its scientists appear to be "excited and happy"?*

Where Would Emerson Find His Scholar Now?

Alfred Kazin

On August 31, 1837, the day after commencement—they don't seem to have gone in for vacations in those earnest times—the academic year at Harvard was ushered in with Ralph Waldo Emerson's address to Phi Beta Kappa on a stock topic, "The American Scholar." The meeting was held in the First Parish Church, on the exact spot where Anne Hutchinson had been examined for heresy two centuries before.

The choice of an ex-minister to address a group of future ministers was a little strange. And Emerson, thirtieth in his 1821 class of fifty-nine, had not even made Phi Beta Kappa on his own. Just as he had been chosen class poet in 1821 after six others had declined the honor, so on this occasion he was a substitute, apparently for the Reverend Dr. Jonathan Mayhew Wainwright (a future Episcopal bishop of New York), who had declined two months before.

Lucky Emerson, lucky us. The thirty-four-year-old Waldo Emerson, as he liked to call himself, was in a mood rebellious enough to make history. He had resigned the ministry of the Second Church of Boston, saying that the profession was "antiquated." "In an altered age we worship in the dead forms of our forefathers." His young wife, Ellen Tucker, had died at twenty after seventeen months of marriage. Emerson still suffered from the lung disease that was to kill two of his brothers. The year 1837 saw a severe economic depression; the ex-minister, who depended on lectures that covered popular science as well as his moral imperatives for the day, wrote in his journal, "The land stinks with suicide."

Three of Harvard's most renowned overseers—John Quincy Adams, Daniel Webster, and the Unitarian leader William Ellery Channing—were absent. Emerson, the apostate from Concord—soon to be identified with his Transcendentalist disciples—was mistrusted. His first book, *Nature*, was laughed at in Cambridge as "anonymous, unintelligible and unsold." Herman Melville's future father-in-law, Justice Lemuel Shaw, was in the audience, but not Henry David Thoreau, of the class of 1837. Thoreau's life was to be changed by Emerson, but Thoreau had simply disappeared after graduating the day before.

In his journal for July 29, Emerson had written a typically private prayer—"If the Allwise would give me light, I should write for the Cambridge men a theory of the Scholar's office." From the opening invocation—the new academic year, youth in a new country, all hopeful beginnings—it was clear to him, if not to the solemn professors, lawyers, and merchants scattered throughout the essentially clerical audience, that by "scholar" he meant not students but intellectuals—free, innovative, creative types addressing themselves to the needs of their society:

> Thus far, our holiday has been simply a friendly sign of the survival of the love of letters amongst a people too busy to give to letters any more. As such it is precious as the sign of an indestructible instinct. Perhaps the time is already come when it ought to be, and will be, something else; when the sluggard intellect of this continent will look from under its iron lids and fill the postponed expectation of the world with something better than the exertions of mechanical skill. Our day of dependence, our long apprenticeship to the learning of other lands, draws to a close. The millions that around us are rushing into life, cannot always be fed on the sere remains of foreign harvests. Events, actions arise, that must be sung, that will sing themselves.

This has been called "our intellectual Declaration of Independence" and is the most famous feature of Emerson's oration, but it was a conventional theme on such occasions. A young, new country, a new republic, was looking for a culture equal to its political aspirations. What the audience did not know, what the speaker could not foresee, was that in literature he and the absent Thoreau, to say nothing of the as yet inconceivable

Whitman and Melville, would supply this independent genius. In a particularly beautiful passage of "The American Scholar," Emerson "read with joy some of the auspicious signs of the coming days.... Instead of the sublime and beautiful; the near, the low, the common, was explored and poetized.... The literature of the poor ... the meaning of household life, are the topics of the time. It is a great stride. It is a sign,—is it not?—of new vigor, when the extremities are made active, when currents of warm life run into the hands and the feet. I ask not for the great, the remote, the romantic; what is doing in Italy or Arabia.... I embrace the common, I explore and sit at the feet of the familiar, the low. Give me insight into to-day, and you may have the antique and future worlds."

Phi Beta Kappa orators were not expected to write this well. Even in our day, when so many professors are supposed to be "reviving Emerson," they pay him the dubious compliment of turning him into one of their own—another literary critic. They do not dwell on the radiant gift of conviction, the daring and the wit with which Emerson unsettled so many minds, the unclassifiable literary gift that dazzled Nietzsche and Matthew Arnold, and gifted Americans from Justice Holmes to Edward Hopper. "I was simmering, simmering," said Whitman. "Emerson brought me to a boil." Emerson's extraordinary effect on Whitman and Thoreau, even on his admiring antagonist Herman Melville, put at the center of the Western world a literature suffused with spiritual independence in all things. The self, said Whitman, was now "miracle of miracles, beyond statement, most spiritual and vaguest of earth's dreams, yet hardest basic fact, and only entrance to all facts."

Today Americans read Emerson only in school and know him largely as an American icon. As the old lady said after seeing *Hamlet*, "It seems to be full of quotations." Emerson's original stance as a rebel at large, an intellectual liberator from formal religion, is hardly a topic for the times. The next year, 1838, he gave the Divinity School Address at Harvard, which shocked his elders because of its assertion of the individual's right to autonomy in religious belief. Emerson was not invited back to Harvard for almost thirty years. Yet sixty years after "The American Scholar," Professor William James, Emerson's truest follower, felt himself so dominated by the scientific materialism at Harvard that he affirmed his troubling, presumably neurotic, private religious inclinations in a lecture called "The Will to Believe." He admitted that it might better have been called "The Right to Believe." And James was defending his own psychological problem, without reference to deity.

Emerson in an age just beginning to veer from orthodoxy thought he had no problem. God was all within. Scorning the church, he found his real affinities with stormy prophets like Carlyle. Emerson saw that his strength as a writer lay in communing with his inner certainties, in building on the stray observations and particles of thought he caught day by day in his journal. By "scholar" he really meant the writer as thinker about everything and anything—the seer, oracle, clairvoyant, and public critic that was Emerson himself. Although an accomplished poet in an almost deliberately minor mode, Emerson needed lyric prose for his full say, for at heart he was a rhapsodist, the last American to see God face-to-face and to believe that God is all. He rejoiced in his literary idiosyncrasy, looked down on the novelists who were fascinating the nineteenth century. He was a throwback, claiming the "soul" was the one instrument of knowledge. At the most unexpected moment, as in "The American Scholar," he became illuminated, an ecstatic:

> What is nature to [the scholar]? There is never a beginning, there is never an end, to the inexplicable continuity of this web of God, but always circular power returning to itself. Therein it resembles his own spirit, whose beginning, whose ending, he never can find,—so entire, so boundless.

Emerson's starting point, a perfect self-reliance in religion, is important now only because of his genius as a writer-speaker. He had transcended the ideal boundaries and now brought a startling force and hopefulness to his call for an ideal "scholar."

> ... this original unit, this fountain of power, has been so distributed to multitudes, has been so minutely subdivided and peddled out, that it is spilled into drops, and cannot be gathered. The state of society is one in which the members have suffered amputation from the trunk, and strut about so many walking monsters,—a good finger, a neck, a stomach, an elbow, but never a man.
>
> Man is thus metamorphosed into a thing, into many things. . . . In this distribution of functions the scholar is the delegated intellect. In the right state he is *Man Thinking*. In the degenerate state, when the victim of society, he tends to become a mere thinker, or still worse, the parrot of other men's thinking.

Apparently no one hearing Emerson on August 31, 1837, protested that this was a bit exalted. Americans were accustomed to high talk about the great and appointed destiny opening up everywhere before them. And Emerson's old ministerial gift for *sursum corda*, lifting the heart, made his eloquence easy to swallow—on this occasion. After Emerson had spoken for an hour and fifteen minutes and was honored at dinner in University Hall, Charles Warren of Plymouth offered the toast: "Mr. President, I suppose you all know where the orator came from; and I suppose all know what he said. I give you—The Spirit of Concord—it makes us all of one mind."

That was untrue in 1837 and is virtually meaningless now. Emerson was invoking and already celebrating the writer as thinker, thinking about anything he cares to think about, the writer as speculative intelligence and public critic and as a writer making his point by the passion of his rhythms:

> I look upon the discontent of the literary class as a mere announcement of the fact that they find themselves not in the state of mind of their fathers, and regret the coming state as untried; as a boy dreads the water before he has learned that he can swim. If there is any period one would desire to be born in, is it not the age of Revolution; when the old and the new stand side by side and admit of being compared; when the energies of all men are searched by fear and by hope;

when the historic glories of the old can be compensated by the rich possibilities of the new era? This time, like all times, is a very good one, if we but know what to do with it.

For Emerson literature is still the greatest intellectual power. I shake my head in wonder and envy when he claims that a writer's words are fairly ranged against the indifference, torpor, pedantry, bad faith of man "in the degenerate state." If there is any thinker today so inclusive and penetrating, with such an obvious effect as to make us "all of one mind," it is surely the physicist, the last cosmologist left, and not the writers, who, whatever their talents and the considerable pleasure they give us, always look upon our lives as a "degenerate state." As the gifted John Cheever put it in fiction, "[Why, in this] half-finished civilization, in this most prosperous, equitable and accomplished world, should everyone seem so disappointed?"

The literary world is full of itself, bemused by language as theme as well as instrument, so conscious of its separation not only from the world of power but from intelligence as power that it calls daily reality "absurd." The writer as conscience has understandably been maddened by the frightful crimes of our century and by the ever-growing indifference to the outmoded, ever-weakening cry "*J'accuse!*"

Walt Whitman said that in literature "the light comes curiously from elsewhere." For many decades now literature as taught in this country, as approvable by the most influential connoisseurs, has been a light only to itself, has had to create its own light. So it was natural for modernism to become the curriculum and to dominate all judgment even of the past. For a poetry to arise increasingly witty and chic in the style of modernism, a poetry not struggling against anything, least of all itself—a kind of travel literature full of personal echoes but without a sense of tragedy. For a fiction so minimalist that you had to admire the silences in it more than the words. For a literary criticism that persuaded docile undergraduates not much given to reading anyway that literature was just performance. No one dared quote Kafka:

> Altogether, I think we ought to read only books that bite and sting us. If the book we are reading doesn't shake us awake like a blow to the skull, why bother reading it in the first place? So that it can make us happy, as you put it? Good God, we'd be just as happy if we had no books at all; books that make us happy we could, in a pinch, also write ourselves. What we need are books that hit us like a most painful misfortune, like the death of someone we loved more than ourselves. . . . A book must be the axe for the frozen sea within us.

What Emerson called "discontents of the literary class" were young people around Concord he admired for wanting to change things so completely that they seemed to have "knives in their brains." The discontents of what I should rather call the literary intelligentsia—the army of commentators and annotators forever reducing literature to their latest ideas—reflect a great sourness and introversion. The world of science, of incessant discovery and speculative intelligence, is excited and happy because there are no barriers to what it is allowed to think about. In the end, despite all our troubles, it is thinking that makes the "scholar," it is thinking that makes us happy, it is thinking that unites us with the universe. In an increasingly tyrannical world it is thinking that tells us who we are.

> These being [the scholar's] functions, it becomes him to feel all confidence in himself, and to defer never to the popular cry. He and he only knows the world. The world of any moment is the merest appearance. Some great decorum, some fetish of a government, some ephemeral trade, or war, or man, is cried up by half mankind and cried down by the other half, as if all depended on this particular up or down. The odds are that the whole question is not worth the poorest thought which the scholar has lost in listening to the controversy. Let him not quit his belief that a popgun is a popgun, though the ancient and honorable of the earth affirm it to be the crack of doom.... Success treads on every right step. For the instinct is sure that prompts him to tell his brother what he thinks.

selections from *Journals*

Alfred Kazin

September 3, 1942

I began work at the *New Republic* a month ago today. After four years of loneliness and doubt, trudging to the library and school, I feel exhilarated by being at the center of things, meeting people constantly, and as exhilarated by the money, for after three weeks [managing editor Bruce] Bliven gave me a raise when *Fortune* offered me $100 to come to work there. I couldn't see *Fortune*—yet: not that super-plush superficiality. I like the job here, though I'm a little frightened by the time one spends reading bad poetry—and other people's book reviews. I haven't much responsibility, and my job is hardly an important one. But I am learning much about the technical side of journalism, and the prejudices of journalism. I am learning much, too, about liberalism—the liberalism into which I had slid after losing my brief admiration for totalitarian Socialism. One curious effect of the job on me has been to make me lose my fear of people, my fear of writers. How much bad writing there is in the world! How different these glossy or assertive people are who come in and—shocking me by the total absence of anything like the self-consciousness I used to feel when I would come to see [Malcolm] Cowley—prove to me how silly I was, how jejune, to quake so before the little powers of the earth! When I read some of the staff here I am reminded of Emerson's wry pleasure in Andrews Norton's attack on him, anonymously printed. "How rare is good writing in the world!" . . . Meanwhile, my evenings are taken up with proofs on the book. I want so much to write in this journal and think through it about the hundred different things I study every day here. But there's so little time. . . . Yet a writer should have time for nothing so much as for a note book like this: Emerson's Savings Bank, Beethoven's Letters, Katherine Mansfield's Journals. Not [Henri Frédéric] Amiel, not the excuse, the compensation. But the working material.

July 27, 1955

The subjectivity of the transcendentalists was their way of holding on to the chief Jewish-Christian feeling: man as the child of God, man as image of truth, as a vessel appointed to receive him. *This* personal, endlessly subjective element is what Emerson saved from the tradition and made into a new tradition, unfortunately, one dependent on his genius. For unlike the old tradition, he had to keep saying, "*I* see it! *I* see it!" and his audience had to believe in the sight of his rapture. Otherwise, the whole system, so delicately made up of personal insights, of rapturous flight, of balances held together only in this man, and by him, fell apart.

Nevertheless, Emerson held firm to the tradition—in the vital sense that life makes sense, that there is a design. It is Melville who, adopting the Romantic-transcendentalism symbolism, nevertheless sees man, the "agonist," the contestant, as someone who seeks meaning, and finally despairs of it, but in the end—gives forth this profound image of the deep, the waters outside of man's ken, as in themselves they may really seem. It is this image of the sea as the great natural force, of the shroud rolling on as it rolled five thousand years ago, of the natural force and sinews of this natural element that surrounds us, in which we barely swim for our lives—it is this vision of the deep that gives the measure of Melville's greatness, for it is a vision not of the world still holding itself together in the small, secondary light of the Romantic ego, but of man seeing as far as he can—the waste of waters that does not include *him*, except as an eye to see it with.

July 23, 1957

The more I go over the events of the last few years, of the whole postwar time and starting back a little before, the more I feel how much my experience is that of a *baffled* generation—a generation brought up to ideas of radicalism, of freedom and independence and revolutionary militancy, brought down to a period more or less statist, "big," bureaucratic, reactionary. I feel that my preoccupation these last few years with Emerson and the romantics has been a way of feeling my way back to the beginnings, the spiritual fires, of the "modern" movement. And equally, that one's whole tendency for so long to "make do," to come to terms with that whole set of miserable, reactionary literary philosophers, Eliot and the Southerners, goes back to the immense and terrible defeat suffered by so many free men as a result of the 1st world war. It was then that, in answer to the threat of "chaos," there came in the new authoritarianism, in one way or another whose final horror of the modern and the free was Hitler. . . . And this, deepening in the thirties (when the free writer and the "times" diverged to the point where the free writer could be used entirely by the reactionary ultra-Slavic philosophy of communism and be deluded that he was joining it) ended in the decade of war and the next decade of state socialism everywhere. . . . The new generation, born in the '30s, is not baffled but "inside the whale" born to the comfortable slavery of the suburban culture and the permanent war state. . . .

May 31, 1962

The more I think of the professionalization and specialization that has driven the "poet" into a corner—that has made the writer ever less of a poet at all—the more I realize the aptness of Emerson's myth of the first man as the complete man, the ur-Poet, of Blake's myth of the Adamic man. Each specialization is a lopping off of the power to face the universe directly—each specialization is a progress, away from ourselves. No wonder that the "common man" today is the man who is satisfied with this specialization, with *his* specialization—the man who doesn't know any better, the man who doesn't have a "primal vision" to go back to.

No wonder that the writer constantly has this sense of a harkening back, not merely to his "primal vision," to himself as all vision, but to the connection between himself and mystery, as opposed to the modern connection between the infinitely subdividable subject as material.

In short, and oddly enough, man confronting himself as the source of vision has a sense of himself as spirit. The farther man travels from this original source of knowledge, the more materialized his view becomes. When he turns back, it is himself he can no longer recognize.

April 26, 1969

1740 hours. Protestant and Jew in American Literature. From the green, golden, towpath. RWE believes that nature is something for men to think with. It is comprehensibility (and in his case expressiveness) incarnate. It is the beginning of "natural" thinking—thinking according to nature, by the light of nature, according to the (great) book of nature. Everything is open—everything possible. There is nothing inherently different from men (witness Plato's eternal realm), only the first cause (which too lurks in nature—at the end of the labyrinth so to speak).

What has always bothered *me* in all this is the applicability and practicality of everything. There is sublimity of course, but no mystery. Whereas nothing is so obvious about the Jewish *condition* (to say nothing about the Jew's God) as its mystery. Why the Jews at all? Why do they persist? Why, without a supporting religious mystique, be a Jew at all? Why the long persistence of the Jews, the deep-felt rationality of their suffering? Mystery, not comprehensibility, like the varieties of Providence. The Jew's God is *hidden* and the Jew's fate is always mysterious. By contrast, Emerson is open, radiant, a poet of unlimited perception as possibility. Nature is not divisible. *Nature is really the mind of men disclosing itself in evidences of design all around him.*

June 3, 1974

The Jewish intellectual (our greatest son, Marx) versus *tout simple*, the Jew (Kafka) who contains all these times in himself.

The Christian idea of the future—based on the individual. The Jewish idea: the *past*, the *group*.

A Jew is someone who is always remaking his life. Renovation *endless.*

Emerson made me a Jew. What a Jew owes *Christianity* for his Judaism.

Cornel West (1953–)

Philosopher and civil rights activist, West has devoted scholarly work to the interrelationships of American pragmatism, Marxism, African-American thought, and Christian theology. In an early work "Black Theology and Marxist Thought" (1979), West sought to make evident how these "strangers" nevertheless have overlapping concerns, and therefore should "explore the possibility of promoting fundamental social amelioration together." As if to illustrate the benefits of this engagement, West's first book Prophecy Deliverance! An Afro-American Revolutionary Christianity *(1982) is aimed at revitalizing African-American liberation theology by reevaluating its significance in the light of Marxist social criticism. By the end of the decade West published* The American Evasion of Philosophy: A Genealogy of Pragmatism *(1989), a work, as he writes in the Introduction, intended to show how "the evasion of epistemology-centered philosophy—from Emerson to Rorty—results in a conception of philosophy as a form of cultural criticism in which the meaning of America is put forward by intellectuals in response to distinct social and cultural crises." Consequently, West suggests, "American pragmatism is less a philosophical tradition putting forward solutions to perennial problems in the Western philosophical conversation initiated by Plato and more a continuous cultural commentary or set of interpretations that attempt to explain American to itself at a particular historical moment." In the first chapter of* American Evasion *West addresses Emerson's seminal role in the genealogy of pragmatism's later development, a chapter that is included below. West highlights the role of "power, provocation, and personality" in Emerson's work, especially how, for West, they contribute to our understanding of history, race, politics, fate, the market, and the activities and achievements of the cultural critic (namely "to expand powers and proliferate provocations for the moral development of human personalities"). West claims that Emerson "evades modern philosophy," and in this "swerve" shows what it "means to strip the profession of philosophy of its pretense, disclose its affiliations with structures of powers (both rhetorical and political) rooted in the past, and enact intellectual practices, i.e., produce texts of various sorts and styles, that invigorate and unsettle one's culture and society." In the wake of the book's appearance, Robert S. Boynton wrote a profile appearing in the* New York Times Magazine *that described what many saw as "controversial" about West: "a young, hip black man in an old white academy; a believing Christian in a secular society; a progressive socialist in the age of triumphant capitalism; a cosmopolitan public intellectual among academic specialists" (September 15, 1991). West calls his particular inheritance of the American philosophical tradition, beginning with*

Emerson, a "prophetic pragmatism," which as he defines it "is simply an attempt to revive a grand yet flawed tradition, a rapprochement between the best of liberalism, populism and democratic socialism that takes race, class and gender seriously."

The Emersonian Prehistory of American Pragmatism

Cornel West

Mr. Emerson's authority to the imagination consists, not in his culture, not in his science, but all simply in himself in the form of his natural personality. There are scores of men of more advanced ideas than Mr. Emerson, of subtler apprehension, of broader knowledge, of deeper culture. . . . Mr. Emerson was never the least of a pedagogue, addressing your scientific intelligence, but an every way unconscious prophet, appealing exclusively to the regenerate heart of mankind, and announcing the speedy fulfillment of the hope with which it had always been pregnant. He was an American John the Baptist, proclaiming tidings of great joy to The American Israel; but like John the Baptist, he could so little foretell the form in which the predicted good was to appear, that when you went to him he was always uncertain whether you were he who should come, or another.

—Henry James, Sr.

The long shadow cast by Ralph Waldo Emerson over American pragmatism has been often overlooked and rarely examined. Yet Emerson not only prefigures the dominant themes of American pragmatism but, more important, enacts an intellectual style of cultural criticism that permits and encourages American pragmatists to swerve from mainstream European philosophy.[1] Like Friedrich Nietzsche—and deeply adored by him—Emerson is a singular and unique figure on the North Atlantic intellectual landscape who defies disciplinary classification.

Emerson lacks the patience and persistence to be a great poet. He does not have the deep sense of alienation and marginality to be a profound prophet. And he does not possess the talent for logical precision and sustained argumentation to be a rigorous philosopher.[2] Yet Emerson is more than a mediocre man of letters or a meteoric man of lectures. Rather he is a cultural critic who devised and deployed a vast array of rhetorical strategies in order to exert intellectual and moral leadership over a significant segment of the educated classes of his day. The rhetorical strategies, principally aimed at explaining America to itself,[3] weave novel notions of power, provocation, and personality into a potent and emerging American ideology of voluntaristic invulnerability and utopian possibility.

Like his contemporary (and major twentieth-century competitor) Karl Marx, Emerson is a dyed-in-the-wool romantic thinker who takes seriously the embodiment of ideals within the real, the actualization of principles in the practical—in short, some kind of inseparable link between thought and action, theory and practice.[4] Similar to Marx, Emerson focuses on the pressing concerns unleashed by the American, French, and Industrial revolutions: *the scope of human powers and the contingency of human societies.* These concerns are addressed by highlighting the willful self (or selves) up against and overcoming antecedent circumstances, or to put it in the language of social science, the relation between purposeful subjects and prevailing structures, conscious human agents and social constraints.

What distinguishes Marx and Emerson from most of their contemporaries is their stress on the dynamic character of selves and structures, the malleability of tradition and the transformative potential in human history.[5] And what separates Marx from Emerson is that the former's stress on dynamism leads toward a projection of fundamental social transformation through unavoidable class conflict, whereas Emerson's dynamic perspective results in a prescription for courageous self-reliance by means of nonconformity and inconsistency. For Marx, the major foes are class exploitation and people's lack of control of their lives; for Emerson, the principal enemies are personal stagnation and the absence of creative innovation in people's lives. Both Marx and Emerson herald self-realization and promote democracy (different versions thereof). Yet Marx's preoccupation with power, class, and social freedom leaves a tradition of historical materialist analyses, socialist ideologies, and communist parties, whereas Emerson's fascination with power, provocation, and personality bequeaths a legacy of cultural critiques, pragmatic ideologies, and reform efforts. Just as actually existing communist civilization has traduced Marx's dream of human freedom, so has present-day American civilization vulgarized Emerson's hope for personal emancipation. Yet just as Marx would be most proud of the revolutionary socialist tradition (e.g., Rosa Luxemburg, Antonio Gramsci) that sits on the margins of communist civilization, so Emerson would be most appreciative of the American pragmatist tradition (e.g., William James, John Dewey) that rests nearer to the center in American civilization. For despite an oppositional stance toward and cultural critique of American society, both Emerson and major American pragmatists fit comfortably in American civilization. The Emersonian prehistory of American pragmatism provides an initial clue as to why this is so.

Emerson on Power (and Tradition)

Most readings of Emerson accent his flight from history, his rejection of the past, his refusal of authority.[6] Emerson's obsession with the internal struggles of the "imperial" self seems to rest upon a denial of time, a usurpation of superegos, and an abundance of open space. His rapacious individualism and relentless expansionism of the self appear to be motivated by a moral faith in the possibility that goodness and greatness will emerge in the future owing to human creative powers.

Unfortunately, these influential—and often insightful—readings of Emerson hide the degree to which Emerson's perspective is infused with historical consciousness; they also conceal his seminal reflections on power. These interpretive blindnesses result, in part, from situating Emerson in the age of the American literary renaissance (along with Hawthorne, Melville, Thoreau, and Whitman) rather than relating him to the European explosions (both intellectual and social) that produced Karl Marx, John Stuart Mill, Thomas Carlyle, and Friedrich Nietzsche. We can no longer afford or justify confining Emerson to the American terrain. He belongs to that highbrow cast of North Atlantic cultural critics who set the agenda and the terms for understanding the modern world. We must not overlook the parochialism implicit in his call for American cosmopolitanism, but we can no longer view his call through present-day parochial lenses.[7]

This means principally that Emerson is neither simply a self-willed escapee from the American genteel tradition, nor a purveyor of "secular incarnation" in an imperial self, nor an American Vico who perennially remakes himself, nor the grand ideological synthesizer of American nature, the American self, and American destiny.[8] Indeed, these readings yield rich insights into Emerson. Yet they do not go far enough; that is, they do not examine the role and function of Emerson as an organic intellectual primarily preoccupied with the crisis of a moribund religious tradition, a nascent industrial order, and, most important, a postcolonial and imperialist nation unsure of itself and unsettled about its future. Not only does he create a vocation and constituency for himself—new discursive and institutional space in America for the organic intellectual—he also formulates a conception of power that enables himself and others to respond to the crises of his day. And since his response has been a, if not the, major resource for subsequent Americans facing other crises, Emerson's viewpoints must be both historically situated and historically deciphered.

A good place to begin is with Emerson's reflections on power. First, his view of power is multileveled; that is, it encompasses and distinguishes the powers of the nation, the economy, the person, tradition, and language. Second, he celebrates the possession, use, and expansion of certain kinds of power, especially transgressive acts of the literate populace that promote moral aims and personal fulfillment. Third, Emerson's perspective on power accentuates in an unprecedented manner the fluid, protean, and dynamic elements in human relations and transactions with nature. In this regard, Emerson's complex and perceptive reflections on power are guided by a profound historical consciousness.

Let us start with portions of the last section of Emerson's renowned "National Intellectual Declaration of Independence" (as Oliver Wendell Holmes dubbed it), "The American Scholar" (1837):

> If there is any period one would desire to be born in,—is it not the Age of Revolution; when the old and the new stand side by side, and admit of being compared; when the energies of all men are searched by fear and by hope; when the historic glories of the old can be compensated by the rich possibilities of the new era? This time, like all times, is a very good one, if we but know what to do with it.

> The literature of the poor, the feelings of the child, the philosophy of the street, the meaning of household life, are the topics of the time. It is a great stride. It is a sign—is it not?—of new vigor, when the extremities are made active, when currents of warm life run into the hands and the feet. I ask not for the great, the remote, the romantic; what is doing in Italy or Arabia; what is Greek art, or

Provencal minstrelsy; I embrace the common I explore and sit at the feet of the familiar the low. Give me insight into to-day and you may have the antique and future worlds.

Another sign of our times . . . is the new importance given to the single person. Everything that tends to insulate the individual—to surround him with barriers of natural respect, so that each man shall feel the world as his, and man shall treat with man as a sovereign state with a sovereign state—tends to true union as well as greatness. . . . The scholar is that man who must take up into himself all the ability of the time, all the contributions of the past, all the hopes of the future. He must be an university of knowledges. If there be one lesson more than another, which should pierce his ear, it is: The world is nothing, the man is all; in yourself is the law of all nature, and you know not yet how a globule of sap ascends; in yourself slumbers the whole of Reason; it is for you to know all, it is for you to dare all Mr. President and Gentlemen, this confidence in the unsearched might of man belongs, by all motives, by all prophecy, by all preparation, to the American Scholar.[9]

A distinctive feature of Emerson's reflections on power is that he associates a mythic self with the very content and character of America. His individualism pertains not simply to discrete individuals but, more important, to a normative and exhortative conception of the individual *as* America.[10] His ideological projection of the first new nation is in terms of a mythic self. In the passage above, this mythic self is cast as a heroic American Scholar, one who has appropriated God-like power and might and has acquired the confidence to use this power and might for "the conversion of the world."[11]

For Emerson, the powers of the nation are inseparable from the powers of rhetoric to construct "the nation" as a distinct object of discourse. For too long the identity of the country lagged behind its independence from Britain. This lag reinforced a cultural dependence, intellectual parasitism, and national inferiority complex vis-à-vis older European countries. Emerson exalts the powers of new rhetoric—the eloquent and creative weaving of myth, symbol, and narrative—in order to promote the powers of the new nation. He envisages culture as the domain wherein rhetorical powers principally deployed by intellectuals constitute "the nation" as a worthy discursive concern and consolidate "the nation" as a geographical and political entity.

Men such as they are, very naturally seek money or power; and power because it is as good as money,—the "spoils," so called, "of office." And why not? For they aspire to the highest, and this, in their sleep-walking, they dream is highest. Wake them, and they shall quit the false good, and leap to the true, and leave governments to clerks and desks. This revolution is to be wrought by the gradual domestication of the idea of Culture. The main enterprise of the world for splendor, for extent, is the upbringing of a man.

Is it not the chief disgrace in the world, not to be an unit;—not to be reckoned one character;—not to yield that peculiar fruit which each man was created to bear, but to be reckoned in the gross, in the hundred, or the thousand, of the party, the section, to which we belong; and our opinion predicted geographically, as the North, or the South? Not so, brothers and friends,—please God, ours shall not be so. We will walk on our own feet; we will work with our own hands; we will speak our own minds. The study of letters shall be no longer a name for pity, for doubt, and for sensual indulgence. The dread of man and the love of man shall be a wall of defence and a wreath of joy around all. A nation of men will for the first time exist, because each believes himself inspired by the Divine Soul which also inspires all men.[12]

Emerson's own rhetorical strategies function in a complex manner. On the one hand, his mythic conception of the exceptional individual as America provides resources for devastating critiques of the "actually existing" America. We find such criticisms scattered throughout his corpus. In a lecture at Waterville College in Maine (later Colby College) on August 11, 1841, he concluded that "we are a puny and feeble folk."[13] Just prior to his second trip to England, Emerson wrote to his friend and compatriot Margaret Fuller (then in Italy) on June 4, 1847, that the famine in Ireland "only affects potatoes, the sterility in America continues in the men."[14] In late October 1850 he noted, "My own quarrel with America, of course, was that the geography is sublime, but the men are not." The country was infected with pervasive "selfishness, fraud and conspiracy."[15] This perception was primarily in reaction to the agitation for vigorous reinforcement of the Fugitive Slave Law, the law that "has forced us all into politics."[16] In response to his early hero Daniel Webster's March 7, 1850, speech defending Henry Clay's compromise bill (including reinforcement of the Fugitive Slave Law of 1793), Emerson wrote that Webster represented "the American people just as they are, with their vast material interests, materialized intellect and low morals."[17] And in his essay "Politics" published in his *Essays, Second Series* (1844), he refused to privilege uncritically the uniqueness of the American polity.

In this country, we are very vain of our political institutions, which are singular in this, that they sprung, within the memory of living men, from the character and condition of the people, which they still express with sufficient fidelity,—and we ostentatiously prefer them to any other in history. They are not better, but only fitter for us. We may be wise in asserting the advantage in modern times of the democratic form, but to other states of society, in which religion consecrated the monarchical, that and not this was expedient. Democracy is better for us, because the religious sentiment of the present time accords better with it. Born democrats, we are nowise qualified to judge of monarchy, which, to our fathers living in the monarchical idea, was also relatively right. But our institutions, though in coincidence with the spirit of the age, have not any exemption from the practical defects which have discredited other forms. Every actual State is corrupt. Good men must not obey the laws too well. What satire on government can equal the severity of censure conveyed in the word *politic*, which now for ages has signified *cunning*, intimating that the State is a trick?[18]

Yet, on the other hand, Emerson's mythic conception of the exceptional individual as America supports an ideology of U. S. exceptionalism that posits the invulnerability and unassailability of the American way of life.

> American idea, Emancipation, appears in our freedom of intellection, in our reforms, & in our bad politics, has, of course, its sinister side, which is most felt by the drilled & scholastic. But, if followed, leads to heavenly places.[19]

Despite America's "sinister side," exceptional individuals qua America can overcome all obstacles, solve all problems, go beyond all limitations. This simple Emersonian theodicy—optimistic, moralistic, and activistic—rests upon three fundamental premises. First, it assumes that the basic nature of things, the fundamental way the world is, is congenial to and supportive of the moral aims and progress of the chosen or exceptional people, i.e., Americans. The famous first paragraphs of *Nature* (1836), his first published book-essay, proclaims this Emersonian faith.

> Our age is retrospective. It builds the sepulchres of the fathers. It writes biographies, histories, and criticism. The foregoing generations beheld God and nature face to face; we, through their eyes. Why should not we also enjoy an original relation to the universe? Why should not we have a poetry and philosophy of insight and not of tradition, and a religion by revelation to us, and not the history of theirs? Embosomed for a season in nature, whose floods of life stream around and through us, and invite us by the powers they supply, to action proportioned to nature, why should we grope among the dry bones of the past, or put the living generation into masquerade out of its faded wardrobe? The sun shines to-day also. There is more wool and flax in the fields. There are new lands, new men, new thoughts. Let us demand our own works and laws and worship.

> Undoubtedly we have no questions to ask which are unanswerable. We must trust the perfection of the creation so far, as to believe that whatever curiosity the order of things has awakened in our minds, the order of things can satisfy. Every man's condition is a solution in hieroglyphic to those inquiries he would put. He acts it as life, before he apprehends it as truth.[20]

The second Emersonian premise is that the basic nature of things, the fundamental way the world is, is itself incomplete and in flux, always the result of and a beckon to the experimental makings, workings, and doings of human beings. Language, tradition, society, nature, and the self are shot through with contingency, change, and challenge. This perception is captured most vividly in "Circles" published in his *Essays, First Series* (1841).

> Every action admits of being outdone. Our life is an apprenticeship to the truth, that round every circle another can be drawn; that there is no end in nature, but

every end is a beginning; that there is always another dawn rise on mid-noon, and under every deep a lower deep opens.

This fact, as far as it symbolizes the moral fact of the Unattainable, the flying Perfect, around which the hands of man can never meet, at once the inspirer and the condemner of every success, may conveniently serve us to connect many illustrations of human power in every department.

There are no fixtures in nature. The universe is fluid and volatile. Permanence is but a word of degrees. Our globe seen by God is a transparent law, not a mass of facts. The law dissolves the fact and holds it fluid.

In nature every moment is new; the past is always swallowed and forgotten; the coming only is sacred. Nothing is secure but life, transition, the energizing spirit. No love can be bound by oath or covenant to secure it against a higher love. No truth so sublime but it may be trivial tomorrow in the light of new thoughts. People wish to be settled; only as far as they are unsettled is there any hope for them.[21]

The third premise of Emerson's theodicy is that the experimental makings, workings, and doings of human beings have been neither adequately understood nor fully unleashed in the modern world. Furthermore, a more adequate understanding and fuller unleashing will occur when all obstacles, problems, and limitations are dwarfed by the march of giants, the actualizing of the potential of genius of individuals willing to rely on and trust themselves. For Emerson, the modern world needs self-sustaining and self-overcoming individuals who would flex their intellectual, social, political, and economic muscles in order to gain wisdom, i.e., "to see the miraculous in the common," and to build "the Kingdom of man over nature."[22] This panegyric to human power, vision, newness, and conquest is most clearly and forcefully put forward in the last paragraphs of *Nature* (1836):

At present, man applies to nature but half his force. . . . His relation to nature, his power over it, is through the understanding; as by manure; the economic use of fire, wind, water, and the mariner's needle; steam, coal, chemical agriculture; the repairs of the human body by the dentist and the surgeon. This is such a resumption of power, as if a banished King should buy his territories inch by inch, instead of vaulting at once into his throne. Meantime, in the thick darkness, there are not wanting gleams of a better light,—occasional examples of the action of man upon nature with his entire force,—with reason as well as understanding. Such examples are; the traditions of miracles in the earliest antiquity of all nations; the history of Jesus Christ; the achievements of a principle, as in religious and political revolutions, and in the abolition of the Slave-trade; the miracles of enthusiasm, as those reported of Swedenborg, Hohenlohe, and the Shakers; many obscure and yet contested facts, now arranged under the name of

Animal Magnetism; prayer; eloquence; self-healing; and the wisdom of children. These are examples of Reason's momentary grasp of the sceptre; the exertions of a power which exists not in time or space, but an instantaneous in-streaming causing power. The difference between the actual and the ideal force of man is happily figured by the schoolmen, in saying, that the knowledge of man is an evening knowledge, *vespertina cognitio*, but that of God is a morning knowledge, *matutina cognitio*.

The problem of restoring to the world original and eternal beauty, is solved by the redemption of the soul. The ruin or the blank, that we see when we look at nature, is in our own eye. . . . The reason why the world lacks unity, and lies broken and in heaps, is, because man is disunited with himself.

So shall we come to look at the world with new eyes. It shall answer the endless inquiry of the intellect,—What is truth? And of the affections,—what is good? By yielding itself passive to the educated Will. Then shall come to pass what my poet said: "Nature is not fixed but fluid. Spirit alters, moulds, makes it. The immobility or bruteness of nature, is the absence of spirit; to pure spirit, it is fluid, it is volatile, it is obedient. Every spirit builds itself a house; and beyond its house a world; and beyond its world, a heaven. Know then, that the world exists for you. For you is the phenomenon perfect. What we are, that only can we see. All that Adam had, all that Caesar could, you have and can do. Adam called his house, Heaven and Earth; Caesar called, his house, Rome; you perhaps call yours, a cobbler's trade; a hundred acres of ploughed land; or a scholar's garret. Yet line for line and point for point, your dominion is as great as theirs, though without fine names. Build, therefore, your own world."[23]

Emerson's theodicy essentially asserts three things: that "the only sin is limitation,"[24] i.e., constraints on power; that sin is overcomable; and that it is beautiful and good that sin should exist to be overcome.[25] Emerson's articulation of this theodicy led Sydney Ahlstrom to suggest "that Emerson is in fact the theologian of something we may almost term 'the American religion'" and Harold Bloom to conclude that Emerson's "truest achievement was to invent the American religion."[26]

This American religion that extols human power, vision, newness, and conquest domesticates and dilutes the devastating critiques of American civilization put forward by Emerson himself. This is so because Emerson's notion of power—the onward transitions and upward crossings achieved by human willpower—celebrates moral transgression at the expense of social revolution. Emerson is not a social revolutionary because "he believes he is already on the right track and moving towards an excellent destiny."[27] Moral transgression essentially consists for Emerson in the exercise of personal conscience against custom, law, and tradition. It rests upon a deep distrust of the masses, a profound disenchantment with the dirty affairs of politics and fervent defense of individual liberties. In this oft-quoted passage from "Politics," Emerson stakes out the vague ideological perimeters—to the left of liberalism yet scornful of socialism or progressive populism—within which most of his pragmatic legatees will reside:

> Of the two great parties, which, at this hour, almost share the nation between them, I should say, that, one has the best cause, and the other contains the best men. The philosopher, the poet, or the religious man will, of course, wish to cast his vote with the democrat, for free-trade, for wide suffrage, for the abolition of legal cruelties in the penal code, and for facilitating in every manner the access of the young and the poor to the sources of wealth and power. But he can rarely accept the persons whom the so-called popular party propose to him as representatives of these liberalities. They have not at heart the ends which give to the name of democracy what hope and virtue are in it. The spirit of our American radicalism is destructive and aimless; it is not loving; it has no ulterior and divine ends; but is destructive only out of hatred and selfishness. On the other side, the conservative party, comes of the most moderate, able, and cultivated part of the population, is timid; and merely defensive of property. It vindicates no right, it aspires to no real good, it brands no crime, it proposes no generous policy, it does not build nor write, nor cherish the arts, nor foster religion, nor establish schools, nor encourage science, nor emancipate the slave, nor befriend the poor, or the Indian or the immigrant. From neither party, when in power, has the world any benefit to expect in science, art, or humanity, at all commensurate with the resources of the nation.[28]

Similarly, Emerson's understanding of vision—in fact, much of his obsession with seeing and sight—promotes separateness over against solidarity, detachment over against association, and individual intuition over against collective action. In this most famous of passages from *Nature* (1836), we see how Emerson masterfully dissociates vision from politics, sociality, and materiality of any sort:

> Crossing a bare common, in snow puddles, at twilight, under a clouded sky, without having in my thoughts any occurrence of special good fortune, I have enjoyed a perfect exhilaration. I am glad to the brink of fear. In the woods too, a man casts off his years, as the snake his slough, and at what period soever of life, is always a child. In the woods, is perpetual youth. Within these plantations of God, a decorum and sanctity reign, a perennial festival is dressed, and the guest sees not how he should tire of them in a thousand years. In the woods, we return to reason and faith. There I feel that nothing can befall me in life,— no disgrace, no calamity (leaving me my eyes,) which nature cannot repair. Standing on the bare ground,—my head bathed by the blithe air, and uplifted into infinite space,—all mean egotism vanishes. I become a transparent eye-ball; I am nothing; I see all: the currents of the Universal Being circulate through me; I am part or particle of God. The name of the nearest friend sounds then foreign and accidental: to be brothers, to be acquaintances,—master or servant, is then a trouble and a disturbance. I am the lover of uncontained and immortal

beauty. In the wilderness, I find something more dear and connate than in streets and villages. In the tranquil landscape, and especially in the distant line of the horizon, man beholds somewhat as beautiful as his own nature.[29]

Yet this disassociation, though seductive, is deceptive, first because it implies viewing the world *sub specie aeternitatis*, yet Emerson's own dynamic "epistemology of moods" (to use Stanley Cavell's apt phrase) precludes such a viewpoint.[30] Like Hegel, Emerson acknowledges and accents the way in which what we see is mediated by what we see with and see through. Even his "transparent eye-ball" is but one horizon among others, *his* horizon which discloses a beauty *to him*. In his great essay "Experience" in *Essays, Second Series* (1844), he affirms this perceptual contextualism.

It is very unhappy, but too late to be helped, the discovery we have made, that we exist. That discovery is called the Fall of Man. Ever afterwards, we suspect our instruments. We have learned that we do not see directly, but mediately, and that we have no means of correcting these colored and distorting lenses which we are, or of computing the amount of their errors. Perhaps these subject-lenses have a creative power; perhaps there are no objects.

Thus inevitably does the universe wear our color, and every object fall successively into the subject itself. The subject exists, the subject enlarges; all things sooner or later fall into place. As I am, so I see: use what language we will, we can never see anything but what we are.

I know better than to claim any completeness for my picture, I am a fragment, and this is a fragment of me.[31]

Second, Emerson's disassociation of vision from politics, sociality, and materiality is deceptive in that his dynamic "epistemology of moods" has a teleological dimension; that is, an end and aim of seeing is to "see earliest, to see as though no one ever had seen before us."[32] This telos is not simply a strategy to deny time, reject history, and usurp authority. More important, it is symptomatic of a deep desire to conceive of time, history, and authority as commensurate with and parallel to the vast open spaces of untouched woods, virgin lands, and haunting wilderness. Emerson's notion of vision wipes the temporal slate clean not in order to stop or transcend time but in order to be at the beginning of new time, just as his exhilarating walk through the woods and wilderness locates him on the edge of new space that is on the frontier. This Emersonian quest for placement at the start of new time and space is closely linked to his mythic conception of the exceptional individual as America. As we saw earlier, this mythic individual possesses divine-like power, all-encompassing vision, and a penchant for newness in order to convert the world. Yet this conversion cannot but take the form of conquest because through an Emersonian lens there are only new selves to make, new histories to project, new authorities and traditions to undermine, and new lands and wildernesses upon which heroic energies of exceptional individuals, e.g., singular America, are to be expended. Conversion, for Emerson, is a trope for moral regeneration, which is itself a process motored by struggle, exertion of conflicting wills (within and among selves), and violence. As Michael Lopez perceptively notes,

> For Emerson, war *was* "the Father of all things." The world was "a battleground, every principle . . . A war-note." (It is difficult to comprehend Emerson's championing of the creative powers of war if one does not understand this basic aspect of his metaphysic.) In man's "lapsed estate" the crises which try his edge can appear as "the natural history of calamity" rather than that natural history of growth by which the universe proceeds and metamorphoses itself. War was within "the highest right" because it mimicked nature's tendency to "break up the old adhesions" and allow "the atoms of society to take a new order." Similarly, the incessant battle the soul waged within itself required the daily setting aside of its "dead circumstances." The task of self-conquest involved a simultaneous destruction of the self. The history of the expansion of the self is concurrently the history of its defeat.[33]

Conversion of the world and moral regeneration for individuals are related to conquest and violence not solely because Emerson devalues those peoples associated with virgin lands, cheap labor, and the wilderness—e.g., Indians, Negroes, women—but also because for Emerson land, labor, and the wilderness signify unlimited possibilities and unprecedented opportunities for moral development. As he wrote in his journals in May-June 1851:

> The absence of moral feeling in the white man is the very calamity I deplore. The captivity of a thousand Negroes is nothing to me.[34]

In this way, Emerson's "American religion" renders his moral objections and cultural criticisms of America virtually impotent and politically ineffective. More pointedly, his theodicy converges with, though it is in no way identical with, what Richard Slotkin has recently analyzed as the ideological content of the myth of the frontier.[35] This myth bifurcates both American geography and American cultural discourse into two realms: metropolis/civilization associated with scarcity, density, competition, and culture; and wilderness/savagery signifying cheap, abundant resources, usurpation of authority and tradition, and need for colonization. The ever-advancing line of demarcation between these realms is the frontier.

The distinctive features of the myth of the frontier are twofold: first, the association of progress in America with emigration outward from the metropolis; second, a faith that the frontier experience had the capacity to transform on the moral, financial, and cultural levels those who emigrated. Not only does this myth—the oldest and most central in American history—justify opposition to the Old World aristocracy of Europe and subjugation of the New World "savages" of America, i.e., Indians, Negroes, and to some extent white women; it also rationalizes the distinctive pattern of U. S. capitalist development. Imperial conquest and enslavement of New World "savages," along with the resulting cheap land, labor, and surplus capital, serve as the "invisible" basis for

American fascination with power, vision, and newness. This internal imperialism, which serves as an antidote for intense class, racial, ethnic, and religious antagonisms within the metropolis, both enables and constrains the Utopian value of migration and mobility in America.

Thus Emerson's idea of power fits well with Slotkin's analysis of the myth of the frontier. In his most explicit statement on power, he writes in "Self-Reliance":

> Life only avails, not the having lived. Power ceases in the instant of repose; it resides in the moment of transition from a past to a new state, in the shooting of the gulf, in the darting to an aim. This one fact the world hates, that the soul becomes; for that forever degrades the past, turns all riches to poverty, all reputation to a shame, confounds the Saint with the rogue, shoves Jesus and Judas equally aside. Why, then, do we prate of self-reliance? Inasmuch as the soul is present, there will be power not confident but agent. To talk of reliance is a poor external way of speaking. Speak rather of that which relies, because it works and is.[36]

Of course, Emerson's nonconformist conception of self-reliance ("and so the reliance on Property, including the reliance on governments which protect it, is the want of self-reliance")[37] resists mere ideological support of capitalist development. Yet his viewpoint also provides little substantive opposition to it. Emerson scholars have often remarked about his "omnivorous consciousness," the fact that he "fed" on books yet still starved owing to a "digestion of vacancy,"[38] and much has been made of his recorded 1840 dream of "eating" the world.[39] Hence, a simplistic link between digestion, appropriation, and imperial conquest can be made.

Yet I find the keys to both Emerson's critique of and minimal resistance to U.S. capitalist society in two often overlooked aspects of his life and writings: his guilt and shame about his inaction and impotence, and his peculiar sense of praise and thankfulness.[40] There is no doubt that Emerson believed himself to have failed to respond actively and decisively to the major events of his day, from the Cherokee Indians affair of 1835, to the revival of the Fugitive Slave Law (1850), to the Mexican War (1846), to the Civil War (1861–65). Although he seems to have never been struck by "ennui" (or lack of will), he is visibly fearful of inaction, impotence, and powerlessness. In fact, he views this anxiety as characteristic of his age.

> A new disease has fallen on the life of man . . . our torment is Unbelief, the Uncertainty as to what we ought to do. . . . A great perplexity hangs like a cloud on the brow of all cultivated persons, a certain imbecility in the best spirits, which distinguishes the period.
>
> The genius of the day does not incline to a deed, but to a beholding. It is not that men do not wish to act; they pine to be employed, but are paralyzed by the uncertainty what they should do.
>
> This *ennui*, for which we Saxons had no name,—this word of France has got a terrible significance. . . . is there less oxygen in the atmosphere? What has

checked in this age the animal spirits which gave to our forefathers their bounding pulse?[41]

For example, his infamous invective letter to President Martin Van Buren (published in the *National Intelligencer*, May 14, 1835) concerning the tragic "removal" of Cherokee Indians from Georgia left him feeling frustrated and powerless. Although he had protested, it seemed futile. In the more renowned case of George Ripley's Brook Farm, Emerson struggled with himself for months (October-December 1840) as to whether he should join the Utopian community. Yet, in the end, he refused to join. In choosing to remain "a parasite, with all the parasites on this rotten system of property,"[42] Emerson was open to joining yet knew that to do so would violate his sense of self.

> Yesterday George & Sophia Ripley, Margaret Fuller & Alcott discussed here the new social plans. I wished to be convinced, to be thawed, to be made nobly mad by the kindlings before my eye of a new dawn of human piety. But this scheme was arithmetic & comfort. . . . It was not the cave of persecution which is the palace of spiritual power, but only a room in the Astor House hired for the Transcendentalists. I do not wish to remove from my present prison to a prison a little larger. I wish to break all prisons. I have not yet conquered my own house. It irks and repents me. Shall I raise the siege of this hencoop & march baffled away to a pretended siege of Babylon? It seems to me that so to do were to dodge the problem I am set to solve, & to hide my impotency in the thick of a crowd.[43]

He seems to have felt unable to engage honestly in sustained activism with agitators or reformers.

> When a zealot comes to me & represents the importance of this Temperance Reform my hands drop—I have no excuse—I honor him with shame at my own inaction.
>
> I have been writing with some pains Essays on various matters as a sort of apology to my country for my apparent idleness.[44]

Emerson did become quite active in the abolitionist movement (though, unlike Thoreau, at relatively little risk); virtually shunned the women's movement; and became an enthusiastic proponent of the Union during the Civil War. But the internal struggle between his shortcomings as an actor and agent for social change and his vocation as cultural critic for (and of) the educated populace continued to rage.

One must also take into account Emerson's temperamental dislike of association in any form. As R. M. Gay has pointed out, what Emerson objected to in Brook Farm was not communism but organization. "At the name of a society," he wrote in 1840—significantly, to Margaret Fuller—"all my repulsions play, all my quills rise and sharpen." Yet action, in the specific environment of time and place, almost inevitably meant for Emerson "movements," participation in the work of what would now be called "pressure groups," while contemplation seemed possible only through a complete withdrawal from the busy life of the community. . . . One wonders, too, whether the precarious state of his health was not an important influence leading him to avoid the strenuous career of a reformer.[45]

There are two rather obvious explanations for this predicament. First, Emerson was simply by temperament contemplative and solitary. Institutions, organizations, movements, parties repulsed him, as they did his favorite poet, the Persian Sa'di.[46] And there is much to this view. But it fails to account for Emerson's co-founding of and vigorous participation in the *Dial* and the Hedge Club, his excitement over his membership in the prestigious Athenaeum Club in London, and his hard work as a member of the Board of Overseers of Harvard College. Second, Emerson wanted the best of two worlds—the world of bourgeois prestige, status, and influence and the world of solitude and contemplation. Engagement with zealous agitators and reformers would tip the balance. And there is some evidence for Emerson's opportunism. For instance, in his lecture "Courage" presented in Boston November 8, 1859 (less than a month after John Brown's raid on the federal arsenal at Harper's Ferry, Virginia), he called Brown "that new saint than whom none purer or more brave was ever led by love of men into conflict and death,—the new saint awaiting his martyrdom, and who, if he shall suffer [execution], will make the gallows glorious like the cross."[47] Yet he omitted these harsh and rebellious words when he published the essay in *Society and Solitude* eleven years later as a Harvard overseer and an invited lecturer in Philosophy at Harvard (selected by the new president, Charles W. Eliot, who had been strongly supported by Emerson for the presidency).

Similarly, Emerson's penchant for bourgeois respectability (despite his doctrines to the contrary) seems to have blinded him to the social misery of working people. In his second trip to England—invited by the Mechanics' Institute established by wealthy industrial capitalists to "educate" their workers—Emerson reveled in the mansions of his hosts, yet in three long months he observed little of poor people's condition, lives, or predicament. Closer to home, he seems to have had little sense of the pervasive exploitation at places like Lawrence, or any criticisms of the deplorable plight of the Irish in Boston. In three brief notes about the Irish he writes:

The poor Irishman—a wheelbarrow is his country.

I like to see our young Irish people, who arrived here in their shabby old country rags, after a few months labor drest so well & gaily. When a young Irishman after a summer's labor puts on for the first time his new coat, he puts on much much more. His good & becoming clothes set him on thinking that he must behave like people who are so drest. And silently & steadily his behavior mends.

I see with joy the Irish emigrants landing at Boston, at New York, & say to myself, there they go—to school.[48]

Even this second explanation fails to fully account for Emerson's relative inaction and minimal active opposition to American capitalist society. The missing key is Emerson's own brand of mysticism that extols receptivity, detachment, praise, and worship. This mysticism did not encourage Emerson to invest too much of himself—his time, energies, or hopes—in the immediate results of human efforts. It allows him to downplay injustice, suffering, and impotence in the world and rest content with inaction or minimal resistance to evil. His mysticism, as Santayana noted,

> allows his will and his conscience to be hypnotized by the spectacle of a necessary evolution, and lulled into cruelty by the pomp and music of a tragic show. . . . In that case the evil is not explained, it is forgotten; it is not cured, but condoned. We have surrendered the category of the better and the worse, the deepest foundation of life and reason; we have become mystics on the one subject on which, above all others, we ought to be men.[49]

Some of Emerson's mysticism is motivated by his political cynicism—his disparaging of the masses and the corruption of American political processes. He has little faith in collective political actions. At times, he writes like his admirer Nietzsche on "The Herd"—with an unabashed elitism.

> One has patience with every kind of living thing but not with the dead alive. I, at least, hate to see persons of that lumpish class who are here they know not why, & ask not whereto, but live as the larva of the ant or the bee to be lugged into the sun & then lugged back into the cell & then fed. The end of nature for such, is that they should be fatted. If mankind should pass a vote on the subject, I think they would throw them in sacks into the sea.

> The worst of charity, is, that the lives you are asked to preserve are not worth preserving. The calamity is the masses. I do not wish any mass at all, but honest men only, facultied men only, lovely & sweet & accomplished women only; and no shovel-handed Irish, & no Five Points; or Saint Gileses, or drunken crew, or mob, or stockingers, or 2 millions of paupers receiving relief, miserable factory population, or Lazzaroni, at all.

> If the government knew how, I should like to see it check, not multiply, the population. When it reaches the true law of its action, every man that is born will be hailed as essential.

> *Imbecility & Energy.* The key to the age is this thing, & that thing, & that other, as the young orators describe. I will tell you the key to all ages, Imbecility: imbecility in the vast majority of men at all times & in every man, even heroes, in all but certain eminent moments victims of mere gravitation, custom, fear, sense. This gives force to the strong, that the others have no habit of self-reliance or original action.[50]

And, in fact, subsequent American pragmatists after Emerson will be impelled either to revise his mysticism (William James), displace it with a democratic faith in common people (John Dewey), or promote a full-fledged elitism (Walter Lippmann).

Most of Emerson's mysticism rests upon his silent yet discernible sense of being jubilant and celebratory that he is alive. He discloses a sense of being contented and full of joy that he "dwells" in the house of being.[51] This mystical element in Emerson stands in stark contrast to his dominant Heraclitean side. And his mysticism, though often overlooked, functions well precisely because of its startling juxtaposition with this diametrically opposed perspective. This view of Emerson as psalmist lifting paeans of joy, praise, and thanksgiving captures but one dimension of his heterogeneous discourse. Yet, coupled with his political cynicism, it explains why the grand valorizer of human power when confronted with the relative impotence of political power from below becomes humble and even deferential to an inexplicable and mysterious Power with which humans can get in touch.

> Not thanks, not prayer seem quite the highest or truest name for our communication with the infinite,—but glad and conspiring reception,—reception that becomes giving in its turn, as the receiver is only the All-Giver in part and infancy. I cannot,—nor can any man,—speak precisely of things so sublime, but it seems to me the wit of man, his strength, his grace, his tendency, his art, is the grace and the presence of God. It is beyond explanation. When all is said and done, the rapt saint is found the only logician. Not exhortation, not argument becomes our lips, but paeans of joy and praise.[52]

This mysticism enables Emerson to affirm with unmistakable confidence that "I am *Defeated* all the time; yet to Victory I am born."[53] At the end of the line of his fervid moral voluntarism lies a vague yet comforting mysticism that discourages an engaged political activism.

EMERSON ON PROVOCATION (AND THE MARKET)

The primary aim of Emerson's life and discourse is to provoke; the principal means by which he lived, spoke, and wrote is provocation. At the "center" of his project is activity, flux, movement, and energy. It comes as no surprise that when he defines "that in us which changes not"—his conception of "unbounded substance," "ineffable cause," or "being" itself—he claims that we must

> confess that we have arrived as far as we can go. Suffice it for the joy of the universe, that we have not arrived at a wall, but at interminable oceans. Our life seems not present, so much as prospective; not for the affairs on which it is wasted, but as a hint of this vast-flowing vigor.[54]

Of course, the enshrinement of activity and energy was commonplace in the various forms of North Atlantic romanticisms. Yet what sets Emerson apart from the others is not simply his critical yet sympathetic attitude toward modern technology and market forces, but, more important, a conception of activity that was fundamentally shaped by a national environment in which the market had a more dominant presence than in other places.

For Emerson, the goal of activity is not simply domination, but also provocation; the telos of movement and flux is not solely mastery but also stimulation. Needless to say, the centrality of provocation and stimulation in a discourse is the product of and helps reproduce a market culture—that is, a market culture in which the past is effaced, the social concealed, and the future projected by the arbitrary clashing wills of individuals. Provocation and stimulation constituted rhetorical strategies of sustaining some sense of the self in the midst of the "currency wars, economic unpredictability, and high incidence of rapid financial failures and new starts" of the Jacksonian era in which Emerson emerged.[55] This material insecurity, social instability, historical fluidity, and imaginative liquidity wrought principally by market forces both enabled and constrained Emerson's valorizing of provocation. As Jean-Christophe Agnew notes in his brilliant genealogy of market culture in early modern Britain, "When freed of ritual, religious, or juridical restraints, a money medium can imbue life itself with a pervasive and ongoing sense of risk, a recurrent anticipation of gain and loss that lends to all social intercourse a pointed, transactional quality."[56]

Like the theater shunned by Emerson's Puritan ancestors, with its personal transgression of social boundaries and multiplication of identities, market forces tend to undermine authority, thwart tradition, and throw the burdens once borne by these onto the individual. Once freed from such superegos, the self can be seen to be a rather contingent, arbitrary, and instrumental affair, a mobile, performative, and protean entity perennially in process, always on an adventurous pilgrimage ("Everything good is on the highway").

> With the emergence of a placeless market, the threshold experience threatened to become coextensive with all that a deritualized commodity exchange touched. Life now resembled an infinite series of thresholds, a profusion of potential passages or opportunity costs running alongside experience as a constant reminder of the selves not taken . . . and why not, since the world was at once a market and a stage.[57]

Emerson's response to market forces is neither nostalgic nor celebratory. Unlike his good friend Thomas Carlyle, he refused to yearn for some golden age prior to the modern age; yet he also did not uncritically revel in the present. Instead, his excessively prospective perspective and exorbitantly parochial preoccupation with America enabled him to adopt the major tropes of the market culture and attempt to turn them against certain aspects of this culture.

On the one hand, Emerson—especially during his early and most fecund period—puts forward powerful moral critiques of market culture. The depression of 1837 not only adversely affected Emerson's personal fortunes but also awakened him from his complacent slumber by the "loud cracks in the social edifice."[58]

> I see a good in such emphatic and universal calamity as the times bring, that they dissatisfy me with society. . . . Society has played out its last stake; it is checkmated. Young men have no hope. Adults stand like daylaborers idle in the streets. None calleth us to labor . . . the present generation is bankrupt of principles and hope, as of property. . . . I am forced to ask if the ideal might not also be tried. Is it to be taken for granted that it is impracticable? Behold the boasted world has come to nothing. . . . Behold . . . here is the Soul erect and Unconquered still.[59]

He characterizes the emerging capitalist economy as "a system of selfishness . . . of distrust, of concealment, of superior keenness, not of giving but of taking advantage."[60] In fact, he goes as far as to claim that "there is nothing more important in the culture of man than to resist the dangers of commerce."[61] As commerce expands, he quips, "out of doors all seems a market."[62] And in his most succinct statement on the nascent capitalist order, he writes:

> This invasion of Nature by Trade with its Money, its Steam, its Railroad, threatens to upset the balance of man and establish a new Universal Monarchy more tyrannical than Babylon or Rome.

> Trade is the lord of the world nowadays—& government only a parachute to this balloon.[63]

On the other hand, Emerson projects a conception of the self that can be easily appropriated by market culture for its own perpetuation and reproduction. In fact, the well-known shift from the idealistic criticisms of the market in the early Emerson to the "realistic" apologies for the market in the later Emerson has much to do with his perceptions of the impotence of his criticisms. Again, this perceived impotence sits well with his relative political inaction.

The Emersonian self—much like the protean, mobile, performative self promoted by market forces—literally feeds off other people. It survives by means of ensuring and securing its own excitement and titillation. Nature itself becomes but a catalyst to the self's energies, a "means of arousing his interior activity."[64] Unlike reification in capitalist exchange relations that objectify and thingify persons, the aim of Emersonian provocation is to subjectify and humanize unique individuals. Mutual provocation and reciprocal stimulation are the ideal for Emersonian human relations. In the abstract, this ideal is antihierarchical, egalitarian, and democratic, for it pertains to personal relations. In the concrete, it virtually evaporates because it cannot but relate to marginal persons on the edges of dominant classes, groups, or elites. In this way, Emerson's view of a self that provokes and thrives on being provoked converges yet never fully coincides with the instrumental self engendered by market forces.

Emerson on Personality (and Race)

Emerson is the preeminent proponent of the dignity and worth of human personality. This means neither that all persons are created equal nor that every person can be as great as every other. Emerson's notion of human personality does not derive from a particular political doctrine or rest upon a theological foundation. Rather it is the starting point and ultimate aim of his project.

> In all my lectures, I have taught one doctrine, namely, the infinitude of the private man.[65]

Yet most Emerson scholars have given him too much of the benefit of the doubt regarding just how universally applicable his notion of personality was meant to be. I suggest that his ideal of the human person, though complex and profound, is inseparable from his understanding of race. This is so not simply because, as Philip Nicoloff has shown, Emerson is a typical nineteenth-century North Atlantic "mild racist."[66] Rather this is so also because Emerson understands the person as a specific mythic entity, an emerging American self or a unique variant of the North Atlantic bourgeois subject. This understanding cannot but be shot through with certain xenophobic sensibilities and racist perceptions of the time. Emerson indeed is no garden-variety racist or ranting xenophobe, yet he is a racist in the American grain in that his notion of human personality is, in part, dependent on and derived from his view of the races.

Emerson spent a significant amount of time and energy keeping up with the science of his day. His purpose seems to have been to be assured that the best knowledge available about nature buttressed and supported his idealism. An important part of his reading focused on "whence came the Negro?"[67] After his early stay in the South and his limited abolitionist activism, he writes,

> What arguments, what eloquence can avail against the power of that one word *niggers*? The man of the world annihilates the whole combined force of all the antislavery societies of the world by pronouncing it.[68]

As a youth, Emerson held a rather traditional conception of nature as a "scale of being" in which different persons, principally owing to their distinct racial endowments, fit on a hierarchical chain of faculties and talents. He records his inchoate thoughts about this only two years after he began keeping a journal:

> I believe that nobody now regards the maxim "that all men are born equal," as any thing more than a convenient hypothesis or an extravagant declamation. For the reverse is true—that all men are born unequal in personal powers and in those essential circumstances, of time, parentage, country, fortune. The least knowledge of the natural history of man adds another important particular to these; namely, what class of men he belongs to—European, Moor, Tartar,

African? Because, Nature has plainly assigned different degrees of intellect to these different races, and the barriers between are insurmountable.

This inequality is an indication that some should lead, and some should serve.

If we speak in general of the two classes Man and Beast, we say that they are separated by the distinction of reason and the want of it.

I saw ten, twenty, a hundred large lipped, lowbrowed black men in the streets who, except in the mere matter of language, did not exceed the sagacity of the elephant. Now is it true that these were created superior to this wise animal, and designed to control it? And in comparison with the highest orders of men, the Africans will stand so low as to make the difference which subsists between themselves & the sagacious beasts inconsiderable. It follows from this, that this is a distinction which cannot be much insisted on.

And if not this, what is the preeminence? Is it in the upright form, and countenance raised to heaven—fitted for command. But in this respect also the African fails. The Monkey resembles Man, and the African degenerates to a likeness of the beast. And here likewise I apprehend we shall find as much difference between the head of Plato & the head of the lowest African, as between this last and the highest species of Ape.

If therefore the distinction between the beasts and the Africans is found neither in Reason nor in figure, i.e. neither in mind or body—where then is the ground of that distinction? Is it not rather a mere name & prejudice and are not they an upper order of inferior animals?[69]

Admittedly, these reflections are made in the context of marshaling arguments against slavery, yet they do reveal the state of North Atlantic science and culture on race at the time. Similarly, in light of the central role that genius plays in his thought Emerson writes sarcastically in his journal,

I notice that Words are as much governed by Fashion as dress, both in written & spoken style. A Negro said of another today "that's a *curious genius.*"[70]

The implication here is not only that the status of genius eludes the interlocutors but also that the very word on their lips reveals the degree to which a vulgar leveling cultural process is occurring. By 1840, his doubts and questions regarding the inferiority of Africans and the necessity and desirability of their emancipation from slavery are apparent:

Strange history this of *abolition.* The Negro must be very old & belongs, one would say, to the fossil formations. What right has he to be intruding into the late & civil daylight of this dynasty of the Caucasians & Saxons? It is plain that so inferior a race must perish shortly like the poor Indians. Sarah Clarke said, "The

Indians perish because there is no place for them." That is the very fact of their inferiority. There is always place for the superior. Yet pity for these was needed, it seems, for the education of this generation in ethics. Our good world cannot learn the beauty of love in narrow circles & at home in the immense Heart, but must be stimulated by somewhat foreign & monstrous, by the simular man of Ethiopia.[71]

In his most enlightened statement of 1844, Emerson's racism is softened and his sympathy and support for Africans are visible.

When at last in a race a new principle appears, an idea, that conserves it. Ideas only save races. If the black man is feeble & not important to the existing races, not on a par with the best race, the black man must serve and be sold and exterminated. But if the black man carries in his bosom an indispensable element of a new & coming civilization, for the sake of that element no wrong nor strength nor circumstance can hurt him, he will survive & play his part. So now it seems to me that the arrival of such men as Toussaint if he is pure blood, or of Douglas if he is pure blood, outweighs all the English and American humanity. The Antislavery of the whole world is but dust in the balance, a poor squeamishness & nervousness; the might & right is here. Here is the Anti-slave. Here is Man; & if you have man, black or white is an insignificance. Why at night all men are black. . . . I say to you, you must save yourself, black or white, man or woman. Other help is none. I esteem the occasion of this jubilee to be that proud discovery that the black race can begin to contend with the white; that in the great anthem of the world which we call history, a piece of many parts & vast compass, after playing a long time a very low & subdued accompaniment they perceive the time arrived when they can strike in with force & effect & take a master's part in the music. The civilization of the world has arrived at that pitch that their moral quality is becoming indispensable, & the genius of this race is to be honoured for itself.[72]

In later allusions to black people, Emerson falls back into his earlier mode, viewing blacks as synonymous with "lowest man" who is "destined for museums like the dodo." In one of his notebooks, he writes:

The duty to our fellow man the slave
We are to assert his right in all companies
    An amiable joyous race who for ages have not been permitted to unfold their natural powers we are to befriend
    I think it cannot be maintained by any candid person that the African race have ever occupied or do promise ever to occupy any very high place in the human family. Their present condition is the strongest proof that they cannot. The Irish cannot; the American Indian cannot; the Chinese cannot. Before the energy of the Caucasian race all the other races have quailed and done obeisance.[73]

Apparently alluding to the racist arguments of the radical Theodore Parker (as in his *The Rights of Man in America*) for the abolition of slavery, Emerson acutely dissects and seems to affirm such views.

> *The Sad Side of the Negro Question.* The abolitionist (theoretical) wishes to abolish Slavery, but because he wishes to abolish the black man. He considers that it is violence, brute force, which, counter to intellectual rule, holds property in man; but he thinks the negro himself the very representative & exponent of that brute base force; that it is the negro in the white man which holds slaves. He attacks Legree, MacDuffie, & slaveholders north & south generally, but because they are the foremost negroes of the world, & fight the negro fight. When they are extinguished, & law, intellectual law prevails, it will then appear quickly enough that the brute instinct rallies and centres in the black man. He is created on a lower plane than the white, & eats men & kidnaps & tortures, if he can. The Negro is imitative, secondary, in short, reactionary merely in his successes, & there is no origination with him in mental & moral spheres.[74]

Despite Emerson's heralded shift from a "scale-of-being" view to an evolutionary perspective prompted by his reading of Robert Chambers' *Vestiges of Creation* in 1845, his belief in the doctrine of discernible racial differences and his ambivalence about the theory of the polygenetic origins of the races (though he was opposed to its use by anti-abolitionists like his good friend Louis Agassiz of Harvard) still rooted him in racist soil. Needless to say, such a perspective severely circumscribed his perception of the capacities and potentialities of non-Europeans (as well as white women).[75]

Yet the major significance of race in Emerson's reflections on human personality has to do with its relation to notions of circumstance, fate, limits—and, ultimately, history. Emerson's slow acknowledgment that there are immutable constraints on the human powers of individuals resulted primarily from his conclusions regarding the relation of persons to their racial origins and endowments. As a trope in his discourse, race signifies the circumstantial, the conditioned, the fateful—that which limits the will of individuals, even exceptional ones. In short, Emerson's sobering encounter with history—a natural history, of course—is principally mediated and motivated by his attempt to make sense of the relation of human personality to race. He writes in his journal in 1845 that he is attracted to two conceptions of "man's" history:

> One is the scientific or skeptical, and derives his origin from the gradual composition, subsidence and refining,—from the Negro, from the ape, progressive from the animalcule savages of the waterdrop, from *volvox globator*, up to the wise man of the nineteenth century.
>
> The other is the believer's, the poet's, the faithful history, always testified by the mystic and the devout, the history of the fall, of a descent from a superior and pure race, attested in actual history by the grand remains of elder ages.[76]

In both contending conceptions, race plays a major role. This is seen most clearly in the most overlooked text in Emerson's corpus, *English Traits* (1856).[77] On the one hand, History like nature is a continuous ascent from savagery to civilization motored by provocation, challenge, and conquest. This progress required that there be different races of man with some brutish, others mediocre, and still others refined. From the Negro or Indian to the Saxons, this growth and development, he claimed, is visible and undeniable; on the other hand, after a period of ebullient ascent in which the power, vision, and newness of "racial genius," i.e., especially poets, are displayed, descent sets in. The creative energies of those "racial" pioneers recede after provocation wanes, stagnation surfaces, and retrospection predominates. As Philip Nicoloff perceptively notes,

> The motives behind Emerson's affection for such a doctrine of necessitated ascent and decline are rather obvious. It was the sort of sweeping historical generality he loved. It was a view filled with poetic richness: the veneration of great sires; the semi-religious notion of an Olympian sphere of intellect in which some few men in all ages might share. More importantly, it served Emerson's unswerving but sometimes anxious confidence in America's destiny. All of America's rawness and youthful innocence, even her penchant for preposterous boasting, could thus be interpreted in her favor. America was young, Europe was old, and historical necessity would take care of the rest. The jibes of European critics could be ignored. Even the immorality of America's exuberant extermination of Indians and Mexicans could be treated with philosophical patience.[78]

Therefore Emerson's first noteworthy attempt to come to terms with history, circumstances, or fate occurs not in *The Conduct of Life* (1860) in which his classic "Fate" appears, but rather in *English Traits* (1856). In a most perplexing chapter entitled "Race," he tries to "historically" situate and condition the "genius" (power) he had earlier enshrined.

> How came such men as King Alfred, and Roger Bacon, William of Wykeham, Walter Raleigh, Philip Sidney, Isaac Newton, William Shakespeare, George Chapman, Francis Bacon, George Herbert, Henry Vane, to exist here? What made these delicate natures? Was it the air? Was it the sea? Was it the parentage? For it is certain that these men are samples of their contemporaries. The hearing ear is always found close to the speaking tongue, and no genius can long or often utter any thing which is not invited and gladly entertained by men around him.
>
> It is race, is it not? that puts the hundred millions of India under the dominion of a remote island in the north of Europe. Race avails much, if that be true which is alleged, that all Celts love unity of power, and Saxons the representative principle. Race is a controlling influence in the Jew, who for two millenniums, under every climate, has preserved the same character and employments. Race in the Negro is of appalling importance.[79]

This situating and conditioning of "genius" are complemented by "counteracting forces to race," though "race works immortally to keep its own."[80] For Emerson, to grapple with the constraints on human power, vision, and newness is to understand first and foremost the role of race in history.

Even in his canonical essay "Fate," Emerson is explicit about the centrality of race in limiting the capacities and potentialities of individual consciousness and will.

> In science, we have to consider two things: power and circumstance. . . . Once we thought, positive power was all, now we learn, that negative power, or circumstance, is half. Nature is the tyrannous circumstance, the thick skull, the sheathed snake, the ponderous, rock-like jaw; necessitated activity; violent direction; the conditions of a tool, like the locomotive, strong enough on its track, but which can do nothing but mischief off of it; or skates, which are wings on the ice, but fetters on the ground.
>
> The book of Nature is the book of Fate. . . . The face of the planet cools and dries, the races meliorate, and man is born. But when a race has lived its term, it comes no more again.

> We know in history what weight belongs to race. We see the English, French, and Germans planting themselves on every shore and market of America and Australia, and monopolizing the commerce of these countries. We like the nervous and victorious habit of our own branch of the family. We follow the step of the Jew, of the Indian, of the Negro. We see how much will has been expended to extinguish the Jew, in vain. Look at the unpalatable conclusions of Knox, in his "Fragments of Races,"—a rash and unsatisfactory writer, but charged with pungent and unforgettable truths. "Nature respects race, and not hybrids." "Every race has its own *habitat*." "Detach a colony from the race, and it deteriorates to the crab."

> Famine, typhus, frost, war, suicide, and effete races, must be reckoned calculable parts of the system of the world.

> The force with which we resist these torrents of tendency looks so ridiculously inadequate, that it amounts to little more than a criticism or a protest made by a minority of one, under compulsion of millions.

> We cannot trifle with this reality, this cropping-out in our planted gardens of the core of the world. No picture of life can have any veracity that does not admit the odious facts. A man's power is hooped in by a necessity. Thus we trace Fate, in matter, mind, and morals,—in race, in retardations of strata, and in thought and character as well.[81]

When Emerson moves toward the lord of fate, the limits of limitation, the specific examples he cites are "the instinctive and heroic races" who are "proud believers in Destiny"[82]—more pointedly,

> an imperial Saxon race, which nature cannot bear to lose, and, after cooping it up for a thousand years in yonder England, gives a hundred Englands, a hundred

Mexicos. All the bloods it shall absorb and domineer: and more than Mexicos,— the secrets of water and steam, the spasms of electricity, the ductility of metals, the chariot of the air, the ruddered balloon, are awaiting you. . . .

Very odious, I confess, are the lessons of fate. . . .

Fate involves the melioration. No statement of the Universe can have any soundness, which does not admit its ascending effort. The direction of the whole, and of the parts, is toward benefit, and in proportion to the health. Behind every individual closes organization: before him, opens liberty,—the Better, the Best. The first and worst races are dead. The second and imperfect races are dying out, or remain for the maturing of higher. In the latest race, in man, every generosity, every new perception, the love and praise he extorts from his fellows, are certificates of advance out of fate into freedom.[83]

I am suggesting neither that Emerson is an exemplary North Atlantic racist nor that his peculiar form of racism simply rationalizes Euro-American domination and extermination of Native Americans and Mexicans. In fact, his rejection of {Robert} Knox's theory of racial physiological incompatibility (hence rigid racial boundaries) and approval of racial "mixing" make Emerson a rather liberal "racist." Furthermore, Emerson's moral support for Indians and Mexican sovereignty is well known, though his organic conception of history renders this "against-the-grain" support rather impotent and innocuous. Regarding the annexation of Texas, he writes,

It is very certain that the strong British race, which has now overrun so much of this continent, must also overrun that tract, and Mexico and Oregon also, and it will in the course of ages be of small import by what particular occasions and methods it was done. It is a secular question.[84]

In *English Traits,* Emerson views the "animal vigor" of the English and their inheritance (mainly from the Normans) of an "excess of virility" as that which sustains their exercise of power and supports their capacity to provoke and be provoked by new challenges. A telling sign of decline and decay, of eclipse and ebb, is the disappearance of such vigor and virility, will and provocation.

What I am suggesting is that Emerson's conception of the worth and dignity of human personality is racially circumscribed; that race is central to his understanding of the historical circumstances which shape human personality; and that this understanding can easily serve as a defense of Anglo-Saxon imperialist domination of non-European lands and peoples. In this way, Emerson's reflections on race are neither extraneous nor superfluous in his thought. Rather they are the pillar for his later turn toward history, circumstance, fate, and limitation. As Philip Nicoloff aptly concludes,

We must insist . . . that the "transparent eye-ball" was progressively spending less and less time bathing itself in the blithe currents of universal being and more time scanning the iron pages of geological and biological history. More and more Emerson was inclined to explain the human past, present, and future in terms of some long-range destiny implicit in racial seed and the fated cycle of circumstance. The dominant concern was no longer with the possibility of private ecstasy, but rather with the endless pageant of racial man advancing irresistibly out of his "dread origin" in "the abyss" towards a ripeness of vision which, once held, could only ebb away into over-fineness and loss of power. The ability to swim well or ill with the flow of things seemed more and more to lie altogether outside the area of human volition. Nature called whom she would and in her own time.[85]

As Emerson probed the conditioned character of human will and personality, he did not move toward a tragic vision. Rather he deepened his mysticism, increased his faith in the nature of things, and adjusted himself (though never fully) to the expanding world dominance of the "imperial Saxon race." He knew this domination would not last forever, but given the golden promise of America in his day, it made little sense for him to speculate on the decline of North Atlantic civilization. So his later message was clear: the worth of human personality is grand, the will of great individuals is mighty, and the cycle of fate (symbolized by ascending and descending races) is almighty—yet it presently tilts toward the West.

EMERSON AS ORGANIC INTELLECTUAL

Emerson's dominant themes of individuality, idealism, voluntarism, optimism, amelioration, and experimentation prefigure those of American pragmatism. His complex articulation of a distinct Americanism grounded on specific interpretations of power, provocation, and personality—that is, both the content of this ideology and the way in which he presented it—deeply shaped the emergence and development of American pragmatism. Furthermore, the way in which Emerson formed a constituency constitutes a model for American pragmatists to this day.

In the previous sections I intimated that Emerson's notion of power was inextricably bound with tradition, provocation with the market, and personality with racial domination. Here I shall focus on these crucial connections and affiliations between ideas and institutions, discourses and infrastructures, intellectual practices and modes of social structuration. In fact, I suggest that it was Emerson's own sensitivity and attentiveness to these links that, in part, permitted him to swerve from the predominant epistemological concerns of European philosophers; that is, Emerson conceived of his project as a form of power, a kind of provocation, and of himself as an indomitable person whose very presence, i.e., activity, changed the world. Unlike European philosophical giants like René Descartes, John Locke, David Hume, Immanuel Kant, and G. W. F. Hegel, Emerson viewed knowledge not as a set of representations to be justified, grounded, or privileged but rather as instrumental effects of human will as it is guided by human interests, which are in turn produced by transactions with other humans and nature. He had little patience with modern philosophy, for like Pascal, Kierkegaard, and Nietzsche he rejected the epistemology-centered problematic of modern philosophy.[86] He did not rest content with the language of static substances which undergird accidental qualities, disembodied ideas that represent stationary objects, or universal mental schemes possessed by all rational subjects—a language riveted with categories derived from ossified sources. Rather Emerson preferred the language of tentative strategies, contingent functions, enabling tactics, and useful devices—mindful of the profound Wittgensteinian insight that these descriptions apply to language itself. Its character is "to flow and not to freeze."

> All language is vehicular and transitive, and is good, as ferries and horses are, for conveyance, not as farms and houses are, for homestead.[87]

Furthermore, Emerson's alternative to modern philosophy was neither to replace it with a new philosophical problematic nor to deny it by means of a strict and severe skepticism. Rather he *evades* modern philosophy; that is, he ingeniously and skillfully refuses: (1) its quest for certainty and its hope for professional, i.e., scientific, respectability; (2) its search for foundations. This distinctly American refusal is the crucible from which emerge the sensibilities and sentiments of future American pragmatists.

Instead, Emerson pursues a mode of cultural criticism which indulges in a quest for power, a perennial experimental search sustained by provocation and a hope for the enhancement and expansion of the self (viz., America). This pursuit locates Emerson at the "bloody crossroads" between weaving webs of meaning and feeling and criticizing structures of domination and exploitation ("Cut these sentences and they bleed" and "Let us answer a book of ink with a book of flesh and blood.")[88] Thus, he must create a new vocation in the open space and inaugurate (rhetorically) a new history of human freedom beyond the tyrannies (of tropes and troops) in the past. Emerson evades modern philosophy not because it is wrong, unjustified, or uninteresting, but rather because it is antiquated, anachronistic, and outdated *relative to his chosen tasks*. Like the recent European past of unfreedom, Descartes's veil of ideas is a prison, Hume's skepticism a halfway house, and Kant's dualism too debilitating. He resonates a bit with Hegel but shuns the German obsession with method which results in "committing oneself to more machinery than one had any business for."[89] Since this obsession has more to do with reproducing professional culture than with loving wisdom—(not surprisingly) the only culture capable of unifying the elites of a divided German nation until 1871—Emerson's individualism leads him to abhor it. He will not swim in a regulated pool nor allow others to imitate his stroke.

> I have been writing & speaking what were once called novelties, for twenty-five or thirty years, & have not now one disciple. Why? Not that what I said was not true; not that it has not found intelligent receivers but because it did not go from any wish in me to bring men to me, but to themselves. I delight in driving them from me. What could I do, if they came to me? They would interrupt & encumber me. This is my boast that I have no school & no follower. I should account it a measure of the impurity of insight, if it did not create independence.[90]

To evade modern philosophy means to strip the profession of philosophy of its pretense, disclose its affiliations with structures of powers (both rhetorical and political) rooted in the past, and enact intellectual practices, i.e., produce texts of various sorts and styles, that invigorate and unsettle one's culture and society. As we saw earlier, for Emerson this results in neither social revolution nor cultural upheaval but rather moral transgression based on personal integrity and individual conscience. The aim of Emersonian cultural criticism—and subsequently, most of American pragmatic thought—is to expand powers and proliferate provocations for the moral development of human personalities.

> *American Politics.* I have the belief that of all things the work of America is to make the advanced intelligence of mankind in the sufficiency of morals practical; that, since there is on every side a breaking up of the faith in the old traditions of religion of necessity, a return to the omnipotence of the moral sentiment, that in America this conviction is to be embodied in the laws, in the jurisprudence, international law, in political economy.[91]

The unconscious underside of this Emersonian aim is the setting aside of tradition and the enshrining of the market by which the Saxon race exercises imperial domination over nature and those peoples associated therewith, e.g., Indians, Mexicans, blacks, women. Emerson's evasion of modern philosophy is one of the ways in which he sets tradition aside; it also is one of the means by which he exercises his own intellectual self-reliance. He refuses to be captive to or caught up in the problematic and vocabulary of those who came before. This Emersonian refusal—both mythic and generative of new myths—sits at the core of his rhetorical strategies and the tools he deploys to create himself as an organic intellectual and to constitute a constituency over which he exercises ideological and moral leadership.

The three major historical coordinates of Emerson's career are the cultural metamorphosis of Victorian New England, the economic repercussions of a nascent industrial capitalist order, and the identity crisis of the first new nation. The cultural metamorphosis consisted of an overcoming of the "agonized conscience" of a moribund Puritanical tradition and of a creating of spontaneous self-manufactured myths to replace the cold rationalism of a stilted Unitarianism. The economic repercussions of rapid primitive capital accumulation—requiring "virgin" lands and exploiting new black, brown, red, yellow, and white labor—included panics and depressions, booms and selective prosperity. And the national identity crisis focused on the most powerful bonds of unity among citizens, namely, the realities of imperial expansion, the ideals of the democratic heritage, and the quest for individual fulfillment.

This historical context shaped Emerson's influential problematic and vocabulary. From his New England origins, he extracts a lasting concern with individual conscience linked to a conception of life as a fundamentally moral process. The emerging market operations encouraged and supported his preoccupation with contingency, flux, unpredictability, and variability. And a postcolonial yet imperialist America's need for collective self-definition prompted his own civil religion of self-reliance and self-trust. The major national events of Emerson's life were the election of Andrew Jackson (1828), the panic of 1837, the Mexican-American War (1846–48), the Civil War (1861–65), the Radical Reconstruction (1865–77), and, most important, the wholesale removal of Indians from their homelands and the making of an American industrial working class. His political response to some of these events is that of moral critique grounded in individual conscience and, at times, personal action. His silence on other events—especially the Radical Reconstruction—is in itself significant, given the direction of his thought in later years. Yet, ironically, his complex rhetoric of power (usurping tradition), provocation (both fearful of and fascinated by the market), and human personality (circumscribed by race, history, and circumstance) provides the very ingredients for varying American ideologies that legitimate and rationalize the dominant theme running through these events—the imperial expansion of the American nation principally in the interests of Saxon male elites.

The major personal events of Emerson's life—the death of his first wife, Ellen Tucker (1831), his resignation of his Unitarian church pastorate (1832), his first trip to Europe (1833), the substantial inheritance from Ellen's will that he won in a contested case before the Massachusetts Supreme Court (1834), the start of a new career of public lecturing (1834), his second marriage to Lydia Jackson (1835), the death of his brother, Charles, and publication of *Nature* (1836), the death of his son, Waldo (1842), his public support of antislavery militant John Brown (1859), his Harvard visiting lectureship (1870), the destruction of his house by fire (1872)—fanned and fueled his deep belief in moral transgression against any limits and constraints, be it the death of a loved one, the authority of the church, or the burdens of a European past, college tradition, and old forms of human enslavement. The great Emersonian refusal of "being fathered"—of being curtailed by any set of antecedent conditions or restrained circumstances—supports the expansionist sensibilities of post-colonial America, just as the grand Emersonian moralism questions the legitimacy of the conquestorial ambitions of imperial America.

This intricate interplay of rhetorically supporting American expansionism yet morally contesting its consequences for human victims is a key to Emerson's success as a public figure. This double consciousness and dual allegiance to the conqueror and the conquered, powerful and powerless, were highly attractive to a nation obsessed with underdogs yet (believed to be) destined to be the top dog of the world. Emerson's moral criticisms indeed are genuine, yet, as we saw earlier, they are politically impotent. In fact, their principal function is to expiate the "bad conscience" of moralists who acknowledge the "inevitability" of American expansionism yet who cannot accept the amoral self-image such acknowledgment seems to imply. Needless to say, the later Emerson more easily reconciles himself to such "inevitabilism" owing to his conceptions of race, history, and circumstances. Yet even the later Emerson remains a moralist with a strong doctrine of fate.

Emerson's rhetorical strategies were directed at those mildly oppositional elements of the educated portion of the petite bourgeoisie—that is, those "cultured" Saxon gentlemen (and few white women) wedded to elitist notions of individual achievement yet guided by self-images of democratic allegiance. It is no surprise that he castigates the vulgarity and crudity of the Jacksonians yet resonates with some of their democratic ideas.[92] Emerson detaches democratic ideas from Jacksonian activists, in part because he perceives them to be *parvenu* petit bourgeois reformers on the make with their own forms of greed, corruption, manipulation, and selfishness. Furthermore, he views their obsession with material prosperity and social status as symptomatic of a profound absence of moral conscience, as best exemplified in their pernicious policies of Indian removal and anti-abolitionism.[93] Emerson's hostility to the Jacksonians is also due to the fact that they were his rivals for both ideological control over the democratic national heritage and political control over the new constituency of middle-class reformers. Jackson offered them nitty-gritty activism, concrete benefits, and political involvement; Emerson, contemplative reflection, personal integrity, and individual conscience. Yet both share common rhetorics of power, expansion, and limitlessness.

Therefore the primary social base of Emerson's project consists of the mildly oppositional intelligentsia alienated from conservative moneyed interests, and "enlightened" businessmen who long for "culture" as well as profits, e.g., E. B. Phillips, president of the Michigan Southern Railroad.[94] Emerson explicitly shuns the lower class owing to their cultural narrowness and their potential for revolution.

If the wishes of the lowest class that suffer in these long streets should execute themselves, who can doubt that the city would topple in ruins.

We have had in different parts of the country mobs and moblike legislation, and even moblike judicature, which have betrayed an almost godless state of society.... There is reading, and public lecturing too, in this country, that I could recommend as medicine to any gentleman who finds the love of life too strong in him.[95]

This social location of Emerson's constituency imposes severe restrictions on the political possibilities of his project. On the one hand, the group of people with which he is aligned is dependent on the very moneyed class he is criticizing. Therefore they can bark only so loud. On the other hand, the very interests of his own group are circumscribed by their attitude toward the "mob," or working-class majority of the populace, so that any meaningful links with social movements or political organizations from below are foreclosed. Hence, one may discern Emersonian themes of self-reliance and self-sufficiency in the radical egalitarianism of Thomas Skidmore, yet one can never envision Emerson supporting Skidmore's workingmen's association.[96]

Emerson's ability to exercise moral and intellectual leadership over a small yet crucial fraction of the educated middle classes and enlightened business elites of his day principally rests upon his articulation of a refined perspective that highlights individual conscience along with political impotence, moral transgression devoid of fundamental social transformation, power without empowering the lower classes, provocation and stimulation bereft of regulated markets, and human personality disjoined from communal action. Emerson is neither a liberal nor a conservative and certainly not a socialist or even civic republican. Rather he is a petit bourgeois libertarian, with at times anarchist tendencies and limited yet genuine democratic sentiments. It is no accident that the most sustained institutional commitment of Emerson's life is a pedagogical one: to his lifelong friend Bronson Alcott's "progressive" school in Boston. In fact, he and Alcott often discussed setting up a special innovative and open college with limited enrollment and courses in Concord.[97] For Emerson, politics is not simply the clash of powers and pleasures but also another terrain on which the moral development of individuals should take place. Needless to say, his disappointment with and distrust of governments ran deep. This further reinforced his sense of political impotence.

The organic intellectual activity of Emerson serves as a useful pre-history of American pragmatism not only because he prefigures the major themes (power, provocation, personality) and crucial motifs (optimism, moralism, individualism) but also because Emerson creates a style of cultural criticism which evades modern philosophy, deploys a set of rhetorical strategies that attempt to both legitimize and criticize America, and situates his project within and among the refined and reformist elements of the middle class—the emerging and evolving class envisioned as the historical agent of the American religion.

Notes

1   The two major recent attempts to reflect upon this "swerve" are Stanley Cavell's "Thinking of Emerson" and "An Emerson Mood" in *The Senses of Walden*, 2nd ed. (San Francisco: North Point Press, 1981), pp. 123–38, 141–60; and Harold Bloom's *Agon: Towards a Theory of Revisionism* (New York: Oxford University Press, 1982), pp. 16–51, 145–78.

2   Emerson himself notes in his *Journals*, "My reasoning faculty is proportionately weak," and speaks of a "logical mode of thinking & speaking—which I do not possess, & may not reasonably hope to obtain." Instead, Emerson speaks of his "moral imagination" and of "a passionate love for the strains of eloquence." *Emerson in His Journals*, selected and edited by Joel Porte (Cambridge: Harvard University Press, 1982), pp. 45, 46. For evidence of this lack of rigor, see David Van Leer, *Emerson's Epistemology: The Argument of the Essays* (New York: Cambridge University Press, 1986).

3   "That idea which I approach & am magnetized by—is my country." *Emerson in His Journals*, p. 321.

4   If there is an overriding theme in Emerson's thought, it is encapsulated in the famous concluding words of his essay "Experience": "The true romance which the world exists to realize will be the transformation of genius into practical power." *Selected Writings of Ralph Waldo Emerson*, ed. William H. Gilman (New York: New American Library, 1965), pp. 347–48.

5   "Every man is not so much a workman in the world, as he is a suggestion of that he should be. Men walk as prophecies of the next age.... Step by step we scale this mysterious ladder: the steps are actions; the new prospect is power.... The only sin is limitation." "Circles," *Selected Writings of Ralph Waldo Emerson*, pp. 298, 299. "Society is fluid." "Politics," ibid., p. 349. "The plasticity of the tough old planet is wonderful." "Journals and Letters," ibid., p. 179.

6   The pertinent texts are John Jay Chapman, "Emerson," *Selected Writings of John Jay Chapman*, ed. Jacques Barzun (New York: Funk and Wagnalls, Minerva Press, 1968); Quentin Anderson, "The Failure of the Fathers," *The Imperial Self: An Essay in American Literary and Cultural History* (New York: Alfred A. Knopf, 1971), pp. 3–58;

O. W. Firkins, *Ralph Waldo Emerson* (Boston: Houghton Mifflin, 1915); Stephen E. Whicher, *Freedom and Fate: An Inner Life of Ralph Waldo Emerson* (Philadelphia: University of Pennsylvania Press, 1953); Joel Porte, *Representative Man: Emerson in His Time* (New York: Oxford University Press, 1979); Sherman Paul, *Emerson's Angle of Vision* (Cambridge: Harvard University Press, 1952); F. O. Matthiessen, *American Renaissance: Art and Expression in the Age of Emerson and Whitman* (New York: Oxford University Press, 1941); B. L. Packer, *Emerson's Fall: A New Interpretation of the Major Essays* (New York: Continuum, 1982).

7 Henry James makes this point when he notes the "thinness of the New England atmosphere" and "the terrible paucity of alternatives," and when he claims that Emerson's America was "not fertile in variations." "The Correspondence of Carlyle and Emerson" and "Emerson," *Henry James: The American Essays*, ed. Leon Edel (New York: Vintage, 1956), pp. 31–51, 51–76. The quotes are found on pp. 45, 56.

8 These four influential views of Emerson are put forward by George Santayana, Quentin Anderson, Harold Bloom, and Sacvan Bercovitch, respectively. See George Santayana, "The Genteel Tradition in American Philosophy," *Winds of Doctrine* (London: J. M. Dent and Sons, 1913), pp. 186–215; Quentin Anderson, *Imperial Self*, pp. 3–58; Harold Bloom, *Poetry and Repression: Revisionism from Blake to Stevens* (New Haven: Yale University Press, 1976), pp. 235–66; Sacvan Bercovitch, *The American Jeremiad* (Madison: University of Wisconsin Press, 1979), pp. 182–205.

9 Ralph Waldo Emerson, "The American Scholar," *Selected Writings of Ralph Waldo Emerson*, pp. 238, 239–40.

10 For a powerful interpretation of this idea, see Sacvan Bercovitch, "Emerson the Prophet: Romanticism, Puritanism, and Auto-American-Biography," in *Ralph Waldo Emerson*, ed. Harold Bloom (New York: Chelsea House, 1985), pp. 29–40.

11 Emerson, "The American Scholar," p. 240.

12 Ibid., pp. 236, 240

13 Quoted in Gay Wilson Allen, *Waldo Emerson* (New York: Penguin Books, 1982), p. 381.

14 Ibid., p. 495.

15 Ibid., p. 545.

16 Ibid., p. 554.

17 Ibid., p. 555. See also *Emerson in His Journals*, p. 426. Regarding the immortality of slavery, Emerson had written as early as February 2, 1835: "Let Christianity speak ever for the poor and the low. Though the voice of society should demand a defence of slavery from all its organs that service can never be expected from me. My opinion is of no worth, but I have not a syllable of all the language I have learned, to utter for the planter. If by opposing slavery I go to undermine institutions, I confess I do not wish to live in a nation where slavery exists." *Emerson in His Journals*, p. 136.

18 Ralph Waldo Emerson, "Politics," *Selected Writings of Ralph Waldo Emerson*, pp. 352–53.

19 *Emerson in His Journals*, p. 354. Note also his quip "American is the idea of emancipation" (p. 428).

20 Ralph Waldo Emerson, *Nature*, *Selected Writings of Ralph Waldo Emerson*, pp. 186–87.

21 Ralph Waldo Emerson, "Circles," *Selected Writings of Ralph Waldo Emerson*, pp. 296, 305.

22 Emerson, *Nature*, pp. 222, 223.

23 Ibid., pp. 221, 222–23.

24 Emerson, "Circles," p. 299.

25 This formulation is my Emersonian revision of Santayana's famous characterization of Calvinism: "Calvinism, essentially, asserts three things: that sin exists, that sin is punished, and that it is beautiful that sin should exist to be punished." "The Genteel Tradition in American Philosophy," p. 189.

26 Sydney E. Ahlstrom, *A Religious History of the American People* (New Haven: Yale University Press, 1972), p. 605. Bloom, *Agon*, p. 145.

27 This quote comes from Santayana's description of the typical American idealist: "Idealism in the American accordingly goes hand in hand with present contentment and with foresight of what the future very likely will actually bring. He is not a revolutionist; he believes he is already on the right track and moving towards an excellent destiny. In revolutionists, on the contrary, idealism is founded on dissatisfaction and expresses it." "Materialism and Idealism in American Life," *Character and Opinion in the United States* (1920; New York: Norton Library, 1967), p. 176.

28 Emerson, "Politics," p. 354. This vague political position can be described as a thorough libertarian view with significant though limited left substance and strong anarchist leanings.

29 Emerson, *Nature*, p. 189.

30 Cavell, "Thinking of Emerson" and "An Emerson Mood," pp. 126, 154. See also Emerson, "Experience," p. 341.

31 Emerson, "Experience," pp. 342, 344, 346.

32 Bloom, *Agon*, p. 19.

33 Michael Lopez, "Transcendental Failure: 'The Palace of Spiritual Power,'" in *Emerson: Prospect and Retrospect*, ed. Joel Porte (Cambridge: Harvard University Press, 1982), p. 140. A relevant passage from Emerson is: "I wish that war as peace shall bring out the genius of the men. . . . War, I know, is not an unmitigated evil: It is a potent alternative, tonic, magnetizer, reinforces manly power a hundred and a thousand times. I see it come as a frosty October, which shall restore intellectual and moral power to these languid and dissipated populations." *Emerson in His Journals*, p. 512. Note also his quip "Sometimes gunpowder smells good," in Allen, *Waldo Emerson*, p. 608.

34 *Emerson in His Journals*, p. 426.

35 Richard Slotkin, *The Fatal Environment: The Myth of the Frontier in the Age of Industrialization, 1800–1890* (New York: Athenaeum, 1985), pp. 33–47. Earlier crude treatments of this myth that highlight its socio-economic basis are: Bernard Smith, *Forces in American Criticism* (New York: Harcourt, Brace, 1939), pp. 95–114; V. F. Calverton, *The Liberation of American Literature* (New York: Scribner's, 1932), pp. 244–57; Ernest Marchand, "Emerson and the Frontier," *American Literature*, 3, no. 2 (May 1931), 149–74.

36 Ralph Waldo Emerson, "Self-Reliance," *Selected Writings of Ralph Waldo Emerson*, pp. 269–70.

37 Ibid., p. 278.

38 The phrase "omnivorous consciousness" comes from Anderson, *Imperial Self*, p. 58; "digestion of vacancy" is found in Santayana, "The Genteel Tradition in American Philosophy," p. 192.

39 See Lopez, "Transcendental Failure," p. 152. Emerson wrote, "I dreamed that I floated at will in the great Ether, and I saw this world floating also not far off, but diminished to the size of an apple. Then an angel took it in his hand and brought it to me and said, 'This must thou eat.' And I ate the world."

40 These important themes have been invoked in a suggestive though not thorough manner by major scholars in Emerson studies. See, for example, Stephen E. Whicher, "Emerson's Tragic Sense," in *Emerson: A Collection of Critical Essays*, ed. Milton R. Konvitz and Stephen E. Whicher (Englewood Cliffs, N. J.: Prentice-Hall, 1962), pp. 39–45; Newton Arvin, "The House of Pain: Emerson and the Tragic Sense," in ibid., pp. 46–59; George Santayana, "Emerson," in ibid., pp. 31–38.

41 Quoted in Lopez, "Transcendental Failure," pp. 130–31.

42 Quoted in Allen, *Waldo Emerson*, p. 365.

43 *Emerson in His Journals*, pp. 246, 247, 248.

44 Allen, *Waldo Emerson*, pp. 315, 363.

45 Henry Nash Smith, "Emerson's Problem of Vocation," in *Emerson: A Collection of Critical Essays*, pp. 63–64.

46 Even Emerson's active role in the abolitionist movement was radically inadequate in his own eyes. This sense surfaces in one of his notebooks: "I waked at night, and bemoaned myself, because I had not thrown myself into this deplorable question of slavery, which seems to want nothing so much as a few assured voices. But then, in hours of sanity, I recover myself, and say, God must govern His own world, and knows His way out of this pit, without my desertion of my post which has none to guard it but me. I have quite other slaves to free than those negroes—imprisoned spirits, imprisoned thoughts, far back in the brain of man. . . ." *The Journals and Miscellaneous Notebooks of Ralph Waldo Emerson*, Vol. 13, ed. Ralph H. Orth and Alfred R. Ferguson (Cambridge: Harvard University Press, 1977), p. 80.

47 Allen, *Waldo Emerson*, p. 591.

48 *Emerson in His Journals*, pp. 129, 508, 509. *Selected Writings of Ralph Waldo Emerson*, p. 178.

49 Santayana, "Emerson," p. 36.

50 *Emerson in His Journals*, pp. 157, 439. Emerson, *Selected Writings of Ralph Waldo Emerson*, p. 141.

51 This dimension of Emerson's thought is captured by the renowned Belgian Catholic mystical dramatist Maurice Maeterlinck in *On Emerson and Other Essays* (New York, 1912), p. 50: "Emerson has come to affirm simply this equal and secret grandeur of our life. He has encompassed us with silence and with wonder."

52 Quoted in Arvin, "House of Pain," p. 59.

53 *Emerson in His Journals*, p. 283.

54 Emerson, "Experience," p. 341.

55 Lopez, "Transcendental Failure," p. 141.

56 Jean-Christophe Agnew, *Worlds Apart: The Market and the Theater in Anglo-American Thought, 1550–1750* (New York: Cambridge University Press, 1986), p. 4.

57 Ibid., pp. 97–98. The Emerson quip is from "Experience," p. 336. Note also the claim of Henry James, Sr.—good friend of Emerson and father of William James—that Emerson had "no private personality." Henry James, Sr., "Mr. Emerson," *Henry James, Sr.*, ed. Giles Gunn (Chicago: American Library Association, 1974), p. 249.

58 Quoted in Allen, *Waldo Emerson*, p. 293.

59 Quoted in Michael T. Gilmore, "Emerson and the Persistence of the Commodity," in *Emerson: Prospect and Retrospect*, p. 73.

60 Ibid., p. 67.

61 Ibid., p. 68.

62 Ibid., p. 70.

63 Ibid., *Emerson in His Journals*, p. 403. For Gilmore's most recent discussion of the impact of commodity exchange on Emerson's thought, see *American Romanticism and the Marketplace* (Chicago: University of Chicago Press, 1985), pp. 18–34.

64 Quoted in Lopez, "Transcendental Failure," p. 126.

65 *Emerson in His Journals*, p. 236.

66 Philip Nicoloff, *Emerson on Race and History* (New York: Columbia University Press, 1961), p. 124.

67 *Emerson in His Journals*, p. 194.

68 Ibid., p. 338.

69 Ibid., pp. 19, 20, 21.

70 Ibid., p. 44.

71 Ibid., p. 245.

72 Ibid., p. 329.

73 *The Journals and Miscellaneous Notebooks of Ralph Waldo Emerson*, Vol. 12, ed. Linda Allardt (Cambridge: Harvard University Press, 1976), p. 152. Note also his letter to Thomas Carlyle regarding the latter's *The Nigger Question* and *Latter-Day Pamphlets* in *The Correspondence of Thomas Carlyle and Ralph Waldo Emerson, 1834–1872*, Vol. 2 (Chatto, Windus, and Picadilly, 1883), p. 192n.

74 *Selected Writings of Ralph Waldo Emerson*, pp. 159–59.

75 Two exemplary statements by Emerson regarding women are found in his essay "Woman" and his journals. "Man is the Will, and woman the sentiment. In this ship of humanity, Will is the rudder, and sentiment the sail: When woman affects to steer, the rudder is only a masked sail. When women engage in any art or trade, it is usually as a resource, not as a primary object. The life of the affections is primary to them, so that there is usually no employment or career which they will not with their own applause and that of society quit for suitable marriage. And they give entirely to their affections, set their whole fortune on the die, lose themselves eagerly in the glory of their husbands and children." Quoted in Allen, *Waldo Emerson*, pp. 559–60. "Few women are sane. They emit a coloured atmosphere, one would say, floods upon floods of coloured light, in which they walk evermore, and see all objects through this warm tinted mist which envelopes them. Men are not, to the same degree, temperamented; for there are multitudes of men who live to objects quite out of them. As to politics, to trade, to letters, or an art, unhindered by any influence of constitution." *Emerson in His Journals*, pp. 431–32.

76 Quoted in Nicoloff, *Emerson on Race and History*, p. 234.

77 In an interesting preface to this text, Howard Mumford Jones states, "Emerson was an idealist, but he was also a hardheaded Yankee, and he was never more the Yankee than when writing *English Traits*, the tone of which is so radically different from that, say, or *Nature* that if, a thousand years from now, both books were dug up and the name of the author disappeared, a cautious scholar of the thirty-first century would scarcely dare assign them to the same pen." Ralph Waldo Emerson, *English Traits*, ed. Howard Mumford Jones (Cambridge: Harvard University Press, 1966), p. xvii.

78 Nicoloff, *Emerson on Race and History*, pp. 236–37.

79 Emerson, *English Traits*, p. 30.

80 Ibid., pp. 30, 31.

81 Ralph Waldo Emerson, "Fate," *Selected Writings of Ralph Waldo Emerson*, pp. 384, 385, 386, 387, 388.

82 Ibid., p. 389.

83 Ibid., pp. 393–94, 395. These claims fly in the face of Howard Mumford Jones's apologetic statement that "in truth Emerson had no great faith in the racial theorists he read." *English Traits*, p. xx.

84 *Selected Writings of Ralph Waldo Emerson*, p. 119.

85 Nicoloff, *Emerson on Race and History*, pp. 245–46.

86 On his skepticism regarding a foundationalist epistemology, Emerson quips, "I know that the world I converse with in the city and in the farms is not the world I *think*. I observe that difference, and shall observe it. One day, I shall know the value and law of this discrepance. But I have not found that much was gained by manipular attempts to realize the world of thought. Many eager persons successively make an experiment in this way, and make themselves ridiculous." "Experience," p. 347. For a detailed treatment of Emerson's rejection of traditional epistemological perspectives, see Van Leer, *Emerson's Epistemology*, pp. 188–207. Van Leer concludes, "Emerson outlines a proto-pragmatic theory of truth that permits both general stability and local freedom, without flirting with the reifying tendency of his earlier epistemological formulations. . . . In the late essays in general and 'Fate' in particular, Emerson seems to confess his disinterest in the epistemological project so prominent up through 'Experience.'" pp. 206, 207.

87 Ralph Waldo Emerson, "The Poet," *Selected Writings of Ralph Waldo Emerson*, p. 322. For fascinating reflections on this matter, see Richard Poirier, "The Question of Genius," in *Ralph Waldo Emerson*, ed. Harold Bloom, pp. 163–86, and Poirier, *The Renewal of Literature: Emersonian Reflections* (New York: Random House, 1987), pp. 3–94, 182–223.

88 The first Emerson statement is quoted in Robert Frost's insightful "On Emerson," in *Emerson: A Collection of Critical Essays*, p. 13. {The line from "Montaigne; or, the Skeptic" reads: "Cut these words and they would bleed."} The second is from *Emerson in His Journals*, p. 257.

89 This lovely formulation comes from Stanley Cavell's comparison of Emerson with the early Heidegger—both viewed as proponents of "a kind of epistemology of moods." See "Thinking of Emerson," p. 125.

90 *Emerson in His Journals*, p. 484.

91 Ibid., p. 536.

92 Ibid., pp. 65, 125, 131. For a classic essay on the relation of Emerson's thought to Jacksonian democracy, see Perry Miller, "Emersonian Genius and the American Democracy," in *Emerson: A Collection of Critical Essays*, pp. 72–84.

93 Slotkin, *Fatal Environment*, pp. 109–58. Michael Paul Rogin, *Fathers and Children: Andrew Jackson and the Subjugation of the American Indian* (New York: Knopf, 1975).

94 Regarding this social base of Emerson's project, see Daniel Aaron, "Emerson and the Progressive Tradition," in *Emerson: A Collection of Critical Essays*, pp. 85–99; Anne C. Rose, *Transcendentalism as a Social Movement, 1830–1850* (New Haven: Yale University Press, 1981); Allen, *Waldo Emerson*, p. 630; Mary K. Cayton,

"The Making of an American Prophet: Emerson, His Audiences, and the Rise of the Culture Industry in Nineteenth-Century America," *American Historical Review*, 92, no. 3 (June 1987), 597–620.

95   Allen, *Waldo Emerson*, pp. 231, 258, 293.

96   For a recent treatment of Thomas Skidmore's democratic ideal, see Sean Wilentz, *Chants Democratic* (Oxford: Oxford University Press, 1984), pp. 182–89, 198–206. In this sense, John Dewey's famous characterization of Emerson as a philosopher of democracy requires severe qualification.

97   Allen, *Waldo Emerson*, pp. 364–65.

Charles Bernstein (1950–)

Poet, poet-critic, literary critic, and editor, Bernstein studied Wittgenstein and J. L. Austin with Stanley Cavell while at Harvard in the early 1970s, and his work at this time reflects his effort to blend analytic philosophy with avant-garde *literature. In the late 1970s, Bernstein co-edited* L=A=N=G=U=A=G=E *with Bruce Andrews, a journal that featured progressive poetry and that many regard as the beginning of the Language Poetry movement. Bernstein recalls: "We were trying to open up conversations across divides. [. . .] The journal was about dialogue not just among poets of the same generation and the same perspective, but among poets of different generations, and also with those in the other arts. [. . .] We proposed an alternative to what then dominated as* respectable poetry."[1] *Author of many books of poetry, beginning with* Asylums *(1975) up to the recent* All the Whiskey in Heaven *(2010), and many works of literary and poetic criticism, Bernstein was the cofounder and director of the Poetics Program at the University at Buffalo. The following excerpt is drawn from the middle portion of an essay in* Critical Inquiry *(1990), which is based on a presentation Bernstein gave at the "Radical Poetries/Critical Address" conference in Buffalo, April 15, 1988. He begins the essay by saying that the work functions "like a reenactment of the possibilities of performative poetics as improvistory, open-ended. [. . .] As a way to engage the relation of poetics to poetry and by implication differentiate poetics from literary theory and philosophy, although not necessarily from poetry." There is, of course, Bernstein's explicit invocation of Emerson (he asks himself with a kind of Emersonian self-consciousness if the citation is a bid to include "that kind of legitimating authority"), yet after completing the reference, Bernstein appears to continue speaking in turns, and of topics, that re-engage Emerson's own interests in the capacities and effects of language. Here we find Bernstein performing a dialogue "among poets of different generations."*

Optimism and Critical Excess (Process)

Charles Bernstein

Poetics don't explain; they redress and address.

Poetics are not supplemental but rather complementary (in the sense of giving compliments and in the sense of being additional, spilling over).

They are not directed to the unspecified world at large but rather intervene in specific contexts and are addressed to specific audiences or communities of readers.

Poetics is the continuation of poetry by other means. Just as poetry is the continuation of politics by other means.

Some tactics of poetics include hyperbole (though personally I would never exaggerate), understatement, metonomy, evasion, paranoia, aphorism, assonance, cacophony, caesura, rime, mosaic, blurring ...

Poetics makes explicit what is otherwise inexplicit and, perhaps more importantly, makes unexplicit what is otherwise explicit.

Yet, without the expectation of correctness or the assurances of closure, what ground do we have for going on, for taking positions, for speaking with assurance or conviction? What recourse is there from the inhibition of only being able to speak when you are sure about the appropriateness and propriety of what you are going to say.

Optimism is my Emersonian answer, at least today, as my mood allows (or else, more blackly disposed, I fall silent): a willingness to try, to speak up for, to propose, to make claims; enthusiasm versus the cautiousness and passivity of never advancing what is not already known; judgment versus instrumental analysis; reason not ratio.

In "The American Scholar," Emerson talks about a boy standing before water not realizing that he can swim. It's an image I find very useful in responding to questions about how people can understand poetry that hasn't already been written, that they've not learned about previously. Moreover, how can it be written?

People often ask how it's possible to make distinctions among poems that depart from certain conventional restraints. What happens is that you become aware of all kinds of other conventions. But when you don't see that second part—the new conventions—you just can't get how distinctions are to be made, how you can judge what you like from what you don't. Such a reader is like the youth in Emerson's essay, who can't imagine that the water will buoy him up. But when you jump in, of course, you discover that you can swim; if you don't sink in a panic of disbelief.

Trust your private thoughts, Emerson urges his young scholars, because they will speak the most publicly. Trust the associations that make sense to you, even if they appear out of tune or inarticulate or inconsistent: allow them to speak. "'Self-reliance is the aversion of conformity.'"

(Why do I mention Emerson here? Is it purely a rhetorical gesture to try to pull someone with that kind of legitimating authority into an otherwise ...)

One of the pleasures of poetics is to try on a paradigm—a series of related terms that characterize various poetic enterprises—and see where *it* leads you; not to lay down the line as *the* way to read poems, or even the poems considered, but a way ... For there is great pleasure in compartmentalizing, in considering various works under a single stylistic sign, in generalizing about the common features in a varied assortment of work you like and don't like.

Yet, no matter how provisionally I cast my net, the work that results seems to develop an authority of its own that belies the investigatory premise. (Or so response to various of my essays has suggested.) Here's the dark side, the ghost that haunts my optimism and turns it into a pale rider on the plains of compromise and misgiving. What started as playful considerations of possibility becomes, after the fact, an edifice of molten lead; the nimble clay dries into a stone figure removed from the process that gave birth to it.

If poetry is beyond compare (desire for what is objectively perfect, in Zukofsky's terms; a form of truth-telling, in Laura [Riding] Jackson's words) then any comparison, no matter how bracketed, risks being reductive or encapsulating or dismissive. For any mapping of poetic terrain is at the same time a mismapping, just as any positive statement (enthusiasm) can lead to a sclerotic authority that is based on the exclusionary force of the terms of engagement. This is because proposing any set of terms through which to read poems necessarily excludes other terms, other enthusiasms ("binding with briars / my joys and desires"). And no account of a poem can do justice to its many contradictory dimensions, even if the idea of contradiction is itself invoked. Criticism is necessarily insulting to the poetic work; it gives injury by its intrinsic belittling. (Laura [Riding] Jackson's relentless epistolary interventions being just the most extreme form of a commonly held view among poets.)

The idealization of the poetic as being without compare is worth contesting. I want to taint poetry if only so that you can see it better—*taint* in the sense of *staining*, giving *tint*; poetry not as transcendent but as colored: *of* the world.

I think the answer is neither to try to make more correct maps nor to abandon cartography altogether.

In the end, you don't have to choose between enthusiasm (desire unbounded by argument) and systematization (reasoning by principles).

But that doesn't mean I don't have to.

Comens has pointed to Zukofsky's distinction between tactics and strategy. In the Zukofskian sense of the local and the particular, as opposed to the general and universal, I would also advocate a pragmatics of tactics. But this would be a strategy of tactics, a method of tactics. And therefore can be criticized as a self-cancelling strategy. Except if cancelling yourself is a value.

In *The Practice of Everyday Life [Arts de faire]*, Michel de Certeau distinguishes between the strategy of power and the tactics of the dispossessed. Strategy represents a panoptic *"triumph of place over time."* One instance of the power of strategic knowledge is manifested by the historical ascent of rationality and the prerogatives of the culture of critical discourse documented by Gouldner.

A *tactic* is a calculated action determined by the absence of a proper locus [*un lieu propre:* a place of its own]. No delimitation of an exteriority . . . provides it with the condition necessary for autonomy. . . . Thus it must play on and with a terrain imposed on it and organized by the law of a foreign power. It does not have the means to *keep to itself,* at a distance, in a position of withdrawal, foresight, and self-collection: it is a maneuver "within the enemy's field of vision" . . . and within enemy territory. It does not, therefore, have the options of planning general strategy and viewing the adversary as a whole within a . . .

visible, and objectifiable space. It operates in isolated actions, blow by blow. It takes advantage of "opportunities" and depends on them, being without any base where it could stockpile its winnings, build up its own position, and plan raids. What it wins it cannot keep.

De Certeau, citing Clausewitz's theory of war, calls tactics the art of the weak. Poetics, as tactics, is also the art of the weak, or rather *poetics is "minor" philosophy*, in Gilles Deleuze and Félix Guattari's sense of "minor literature." The tactician, Clausewitz's weak strategist, uses cunning, deception, and wit. Unable to operate from entrenched positions of power, she becomes a trickster or schtick artist who turns situations around by taking advantage of opportunities, using comedy to subvert occasions, employing the know-how and make-do of "cross-cuts, fragments, cracks and lucky hits."

Sophism, says de Certeau, is the dialectics of tactics.

> As the author of a great "strategic" system, Aristotle was already very interested in the procedures of this enemy which perverted, as he saw it, the order of the truth. . . . [by] "making the worse argument seem the better" [in the words of Corax]. . . . This formula . . . is the starting point for an intellectual creativity as persistent as it is subtle, tireless . . . scattered over the terrain of the dominant order and foreign to the rules laid down and imposed by a rationality founded on established rights and property.

But isn't this just another trick of the tactician—to feign dispossession in the face of a stagnant assurance of ground. For the strategist and his "strong" philosophy, deception is not a matter of tactics but a form of self-blindness: defending territory that belongs to no one, accumulating knowledge that would have value only in use. This is as if to say that syntax makes grammar, but grammar is only a reflection of a syntax that once was. The strategist-as-grammarian is the nomad, for he possesses his home in name only: his insistence on occupation and territorial defense precludes inhabitation. The syntactician makes her home where she finds herself, where she *attends*—and that is the only possession that's worth anything, a soil in which things can grow.

But here, as in some lunatic game of Dr. Tarr and Prof. Fether, everything's gone topsy-turvy. After all, it must be admitted in evidence that a theory of poetics—even a poetics of poetics—would no longer be poetics, would, that is, relinquish its tactical advantages as underdog and assume its proper place as strategy.

A strategy of tactics would be a way to hint at the totalizing counterhegemonic project that Bruce Andrews has advanced. A way to think through, via parataxis, the relation among formal, anti-accommodationist, group-identified, cultural, regional, and gender-based poetic tactics so that they form a complementarity of critiques, projected onto an imaginary social whole in the manner of negative dialectics. That is, a social whole that can never be pictured since it is a "potentializing" formation, a "forming blank" in Arakawa and Madeline Gins's sense.

On a similar tack, I'm suggesting a syntax of motives (a sin tax on criticism) rather than a grammar of criticism, where grammar is the normative term. The motive being to provoke response and evoke company. To acknowledge. To recognize. Though surely to recognize is also to misrecognize.

You see someone's face coming out of the fog and you are propelled to make out who it is—maybe they're looking for you—and you shout out some words of recognition.

Recognition and acknowledgement are much more important motivations for me than any sort of theoretical or explanatory paradigms.

Yet to provoke is wildly different than to evoke.

Provocation is very useful, though obviously overused in many situations . . . or used by the wrong people.—If only the people who are now provoking, by and large, would stop, and the ones who are being provoked would start, it wouldn't be so bad.

Belligerence in the pursuit of justice may not be a virtue. Yet even the articulation of a variant view in a nonprovocative way is seen, by many, as provocation. There may be no way not to be provocative when you are articulating positions that go against the grain. But you can also heighten the provocation. Sometimes you may wish to do just that for explicit reasons, while other times it's just a disagreeable "personal trip," an echo of the worst traits of what you ostensibly oppose.

Belligerence produces belligerent responses. It's instructive to remember how radically Gertrude Stein's poetics refused this particular vicious circle.

The defense of belligerent provocation is that you are not mediating, or smoothing over, what you say. At the same time, there are overwhelming problems with this form of communication behavior, especially as it seems to be stereotypically male behavior. The spectrum of response from evocation to provocation is perhaps not controllable but it can be monitored. Sometimes you may want an angry response, but continually provoking angry responses stops being useful. At least in the context of poetry: in other spheres, such as foreign policy or civil rights, the dynamics are different.

Acknowledgements

Charles Altieri, "Without Consequences Is No Politics: A Response to Jerome McGann," in *Politics and Poetic Value,* ed. Robert von Hallberg (Chicago, 1987).

Bruce Andrews, "Poetry as Explanation, Poetry as Praxis," in *The Politics of Poetic Form: Poetry and Public Policy,* ed. Charles Bernstein (New York, 1990).

Bruce Comens, "From A to An: The Postmodern Twist in Louis Zukofsky," presented at the Buffalo conference.

James Clifford, *The Predicament of Culture: Twentieth-Century Ethnography, Literature, and Art* (Cambridge, Mass., 1988).

Michel de Certeau, *The Practice of Everyday Life,* trans. Steven Rendall (Berkeley, 1984).

Arthur C. Danto, "Approaching the End of Art," *The State of the Art* (New York, 1987). My discussion of Danto originally appeared in *M/E/A/N/I/N/G* 5 (1989).

Michael Davidson, *The San Francisco Renaissance: Poetics and Community at Mid-century* (New York, 1989).

Ralph Waldo Emerson, *Essays: First Series,* vol. 2 of *The Collected Works of Ralph Waldo Emerson,* ed. Joseph Slater, Alfred R. Ferguson, and Jean Ferguson Carr (Cambridge,

Mass., 1979). The citation from "Self-Reliance" is quoted in Stanley Cavell's *This New Yet Unapproachable America: Lectures after Emerson after Wittgenstein* (Albuquerque, N. Mex., 1989). Cavell discusses Emerson's "aversion" of conformity as both disobedience and conversion: contradiction as a countering of diction.

Alvin W. Gouldner, *The Future of Intellectuals and the Rise of the New Class: A Frame of Reference, Theses, Conjectures, Arguments, and an Historical Perspective on the Role of Intellectuals and Intelligentsia in the International Class Contest of the Modern Era* (New York, 1979); see especially "Thesis Six: The New Class as a Speech Community." Jeffrey Escoffier usefully discusses this work in his excellent critique of Allan Bloom and Russell Jacoby, "Pessimism of the Mind: Intellectuals, Universities and the Left," *Socialist Review* 18, no. 1 (1988). It's worth emphasizing the positive features of CCD as much as its limitations. CCD encourages freedom of critical thought, in the best sense of rationality, as opposed to ethnocentrism and knowledge by uncritical acceptance of authority. As such, CCD makes its connection to a social totality, rejecting, at least on principle, the epistemologic tyranny of vested interests.

Luce Irigaray, *This Sex Which Is Not One*, trans. Catherine Porter with Carolyn Burke (Ithaca, N.Y., 1985).

Donald Kuspit, *The Critic Is Artist: The Intentionality of Art* (Ann Arbor, Mich., 1984).

Henry David Thoreau, "Economy," and "Where I Lived, and What I Lived For," *Walden*, ed. J. Lyndon Shanley (Princeton, N.J., 1971).

Samuel Weber, *Institution and Interpretation* (Minneapolis, 1987).

Rosmarie Waldrop, "Chinese Windmills Turn Horizontally," presented at the Buffalo conference and subsequently published in *Temblor* 10 (1989).

Note

1　Charles Bernstein interview with Jay Sanders, *Bomb*, Vol. 111, Spring 2010.

Leslie Fiedler (1917–2003)

At the height of New Criticism, Fiedler, a rising literary critic, wrote skeptically of the movement in "Archetype and Signature" (1952). In 1960 his ability to stir interest and controversy was further enhanced by the publication of Love and Death in the American Novel *(1960), a six-hundred page exploration of the unique attributes of "the great American novel" coupled with an analysis of its derivation from the European narrative tradition. (By 1965 Fiedler was hired by the University at Buffalo, where his colleagues included Charles Olson, Robert Creeley, and Raymond Federman, and other illustrious poets and critics.) Among the defining features of American novels, Fiedler argues, is their incapacity to address issues of genuine human sexuality while also maintaining a pathological fixation on death. Part of his diagnosis bears an awareness of the conditions that gave rise to the writing of America's novelists—conditions that contribute both to the writing Emerson achieved, and his anxiety while writing it. As Fiedler puts it in* Love and Death: *"Merely finding a language, learning to talk in a land where there are no conventions of conversation, no special class idioms and no dialogue between classes, no continuing literary language—this exhausts the American writer. He is forever beginning, saying for the first time (without real tradition there can never be a second time) what it is like to stand alone before nature, or in a city as appallingly lonely as any virgin forest." In the following brief work, a Preface (1995), Fiedler offers a few orienting words to a book of selected Emerson quotations (the title of the collection,* Hitch Your Wagon to a Star, *is a phrase drawn from Emerson's essay "Civilization"): "What Emerson wrote was in fact neither 'prose' nor 'poetry' [. . .] yet it was precisely his blurring of the distinction between the 'poetic' and the 'non-poetic' that made possible the more subversive and uniquely American experiments of Whitman and Dickinson." If this is praise for Emerson's influence, it also courts our consideration of the ways Emerson's work was subversive on its own terms.*

Preface to *Hitch Your Wagon to a Star*

Leslie Fiedler

Ralph Waldo Emerson is, with the possible exception of Benjamin Franklin, the most quotable of all American writers. Indeed, as we read his works the gnomic sentences of which they are composed tend to detach themselves from their original contexts and live on in our heads the independent life of popular aphorisms and anonymous nursery rhymes. This is scarcely surprising, since what we first encounter as complete essays and poems were cobbled together from just such fragmentary phrases scribbled down in Emerson's journals. What is surprising is that, despite Emerson's quotability, when Keith Frome proposed compiling this collection, he found that no similar volume was in print. Yet even this is explicable in light of Emerson's declining reputation at the end of the twentieth century, at which point—for reasons more ideological than esthetic—he had almost ceased to be read outside the classroom.

On the one hand, Marxist critics charged that his pseudolibertarian credo of self-reliance was in fact just another version of the code of rugged individualism, so dear to the hearts of American imperialists and Robber Barons. On the other, the self-styled "New Critics" condemned him for having denied the reality of Evil and the fallen nature of mankind. By the 1930s, when these two attacks had peaked, I was just finding my critical voice and stance, and I found myself influenced by both sides. Consequently, in the decades since, I have published much about almost the whole range of American literature and culture, but I have never dealt at length with Emerson.

Nonetheless, when asked to write a preface for this collection, I accepted without a moment's hesitation. It occurred to me, despite our ideological differences, resonant phrases from Emerson's long unread works had continued to echo and re-echo in my head. Not only had I, at age seventeen, inscribed next to my high school graduation picture "To be great is to be misunderstood," but a quarter of a century later I had headed the chapters of my first novel with tags like "Who drinks of Cupid's nectar cup / Loveth downward and not up...."

When I tried Emerson's text, however, I found I could still not reread any of his willfully incoherent essays with ease and pleasure. I did somewhat better with the poems, although when they exceed a certain length, they, too, tend to explode into what he himself called "infinitely repellent particles." Since such centrifugal congeries of disparate images are more acceptable in rhapsodic verse than in didactic prose, I decided it was better to read even what purport to be essays as if they were poems—or rather, perhaps, anthologies of minipoems, requiring of us not belief but the willing suspension of disbelief.

There is, in any case, a good warrant for such a strategy, considering that Emerson, although he founded no continuing school of philosophy, directly inspired Walt Whitman and Emily Dickinson, whom we have come to consider our two greatest poets. Moreover, Emerson once unequivocally declared, "I am in all my theory, ethics and politics a poet." Sometimes he qualified this, writing once in a distancing third person, "He was a poet, though his singing was husky and for the most part in prose": to which James Russell Lowell was moved to add wryly, "No, 'tis not even prose."

What Emerson wrote was in fact neither "prose" nor "poetry," as defined by conventional household poets in the Victorian Era. Yet it was precisely his blurring of the distinction between the "poetic" and the "non-poetic" that made possible the more subversive and uniquely American experiments of Whitman and Dickinson. There is also a disconcerting lack of warmth in Emerson, however, that makes him unlike these eminent disciples; and of this, too, he was uneasily aware, confessing, "I was uncertain always whether I have one spark of that fire which burns in verse...." Herman Melville was certain that Emerson did *not*; in describing Mark Winsome, the wicked caricature of Emerson who appears in *The Confidence-Man*, Melville calls him "... purely and coldly radiant as a prism. It seemed as if one could almost hear him vitreously chime and ring."

Yet, however frigidly, his sentences *do* chime and ring—thus producing in some auditors at least (as Melville seems not to have realized) the state of "ecstasy" that Emerson sought to evoke in print or from the lecturer's platform. As Robert Frost, the third and latest of Emerson's poetic disciples, reminds us in quite another context, "... Ice / is also great / and would suffice."

The present collection of such icily ecstatic phrases reminds us once more of this same disconcerting fact, thus posthumously adding a peculiarly American postscript to the secular scriptures that Emerson set out to compile at the beginning of his career. "No man," he wrote at that point, "could be better occupied than in making his own bible by harkening to all those sentences which now here, now there, now in nursery rhymes, now in Hebrew, now in English bards, thrill them like the sound of a trumpet...." Let us, therefore, harken again and be thrilled.

Buffalo, New York
July 26, 1995

P. Adams Sitney (1944–)

Historian of American avant-garde cinema, Sitney cofounded Anthology Film Archives in New York in 1970, and in the same year became part of New York University's then-new doctoral program in Cinema Studies. He had recently published an article in Film Culture *(1969) that proposed a theory of "structural film," an account that both articulated an ongoing cinematic development and influenced how it was understood among critics. In 1974 he published* Visionary Film, *the first history of post-World War II American avant-garde filmmaking (revised and expanded in an edition from 2002), and subsequently devoted his career to the promotion and critical legitimacy of New American Cinema—a movement that included filmmakers such as Stan Brakhage, Jonas Mekas, Hollis Frampton, Michael Snow, Paul Sharits, among many others. Given the diversity of Emerson's influence on writers and artists—in poetry, literature, philosophy, and literary criticism—as well as musicians, political theorists, culture critics, and social activists, it may still come as a surprise to learn from Sitney of Emerson's prominent and enduring impact on American avant-garde filmmaking. The essay included below forms the Introduction to Sitney's* Eyes Upside Down: Visionary Filmmakers and the Heritage of Emerson *(2008), where he traces—in works by Gertrude Stein, John Cage, and Charles Olson—"the transmission of Emersonian aesthetics to the filmmakers" of America's cinematic avant-garde.*

Emersonian Poetics

P. Adams Sitney

The art of the first British settlers of America was literary, originating in the severe rhetoric of New England divines. Absolutely convinced of their election, and often ferociously excoriating the heresy of toleration, they theologized the very idea of America as a redemption from Europe according to God's plan and covenant. Consequently, the great flowering of American literature and painting in the first half of the nineteenth century arrived with the secularization of that rhetoric and theology. The turning point in our native tradition from an art in the service of Christian theology to an orphic theology of art may be symbolically represented by Ralph Waldo Emerson's resignation in 1832 from the Second Church of Boston (the pulpit of the author of *Magnalia Christi Americana*, Cotton Mather). In the following two years, Emerson gradually transferred the locus of his teaching from Unitarian pulpits to the public lecture halls, such as that of the Society for the Diffusion of Useful Knowledge in Boston's Masonic Temple. His essays that both predict and inform American artistic discourse retain "in the optative mode" (as he said of all of our literature) the fervor and conviction of the founding divines.

American artists—poets, composers, painters, filmmakers—have largely perpetuated Emerson's transformation of the homiletic tradition in their polemical position papers. Sometimes they have even implicitly acknowledged their awareness of that tradition, as when Charles Ives published his *Essays Before a Sonata* (1920) to accompany his "Concord Sonata." More often they have been unwitting Emersonians, or even Emersonians in spite of themselves. Gertrude Stein is an example of the former, John Cage and Charles Olson of the latter. I shall focus on them as significant figures in the transmission of Emersonian aesthetics to the filmmakers at the core of this book, although they are by no means the only exemplars that might have been chosen. They represent a sufficient variety of responses to Emerson (and his disciple Walt Whitman) to chart the array of variations on Emerson that the filmmakers will demonstrate.

Museum lectures, program notes, exhibition catalogs, interviews, and, in cinema, introductions to film screenings (since Maya Deren pioneered that mode in the late 1940s) have been the means through which American artists have continued this fundamentally oral tradition. Often they have spoken of their work with the absolutist confidence of the seventeenth century elect, and just as often have extirpated the heresies of those fellow artists who deviated from their convictions. All of Gertrude Stein's theoretical work took the form of public speeches. The tide of her most comprehensive series, *Lectures in America* (1935) attests to this. *Narration* was presented as four lectures at the University of Chicago, and she delivered "What Are Masterpieces and Why There Are So Few of Them" at Oxford. John Cage turned the lecture format into another art form, at times interweaving (on tape) at least four different lines of argument at once. Maya Deren began the practice of lecturing with her films as an economic necessity and a proselytizing tactic. Since her death in 1961, this has become a common practice for *avant-garde* filmmakers. Parallel to the oral style runs an epistolary mode (corresponding to Emerson's journals) in which public polemic takes the guise of a correspondence between artists, as in many of the polemical writings of Ezra Pound and Charles Olson. Among the filmmakers, Stan Brakhage, Hollis Frampton, Jonas Mekas, and Abigail Child are exemplars of this mode.

Throughout this book, I identify American aesthetics as Emersonian. I want to include in this sweeping claim Emerson's disciples Thoreau and Whitman, and even those such as Melville who set themselves in opposition to him, insomuch as Emerson comprehensively set out the terms of the argument and defined the terrain on which the Americanness of our native art would be determined.

Emerson himself knew that the mutually opposed artistic positions and the variety of styles, in a given nation at any one time, participate in a coherent system. Near the beginning of his essay "Art," he described the way in which the air an artist breathes "necessitates" an "ineffaceable seal on [his] work":

> [T]he new in art is always formed out of the old. The Genius of the Hour sets his ineffaceable seal on the work, and gives it an inexpressible charm for the

imagination. As far as the spiritual character of the period overpowers the artist, and finds expression in his work, so far it will retain a certain grandeur, and will represent to future beholders the Unknown, the Inevitable, the Divine. No man can quite exclude this element of Necessity from his labor. No man can quite emancipate himself from his age and country, or produce a model in which the education, the religion, the politics, usages, and arts, of his times shall have no share. Though he were never so original, never so willful and fantastic, he cannot wipe out of his work every trace of the thoughts amidst which it grew. The very avoidance betrays the usage he avoids. Above his will, and out of his sight, he is necessitated, by the air he breathes, and the idea on which he and his contemporaries live and toil, to share the manner of his times, without knowing what that manner is.[1]

Gertrude Stein virtually repeats Emerson's terms when she begins the fourth lecture of *Narration*: "After all anybody is as their land and air is. . . . It is that which makes them and the arts they make and the work they do and the way they eat and the way they drink and they way they learn and everything."[2]

It is characteristic that an avowed anti-Emersonian poet such as Charles Olson, who deliberately aligned himself with Melville's rejection of the Sage of Concord, would recast this passage in a polemical essay, ignoring its Emersonian source because he found something similar in Carl Jung's study of synchronicity and the aleatoric *Book of Changes*. But Olson was never more Emersonian and less Jungian than in asserting the prime point of his epistolary essay, that wisdom cannot be detached from poetic form:

We are ultimate when we do bend to the law. And the law is:
/ whatever is born or done this moment of time, has
the qualities of
this moment of
time /[3]

The peculiarly Emersonian inflection of this commonplace would be the invocation of Necessity or Ananke under the guise of "law."

The transformation of Necessity into a category of poetics is one of the dominant Emersonian features of American aesthetic theory that I shall emphasize in this book. Others are the primacy of the visible and the transformative value of vehicular motion.

The great ode to Ananke concludes Emerson's late essay "Fate":

I do not wonder at a snow-flake, a shell, a summer landscape, or the glory of the stars; but at the necessity of beauty under which the universe lies; that all is and must be pictorial; that the rainbow and the curve of the horizon and the arch of the blue vault are only results from the organism of the eye. . . .

Let us build altars to the Beautiful Necessity which secures that all is made of one piece; that plaintiff and defendant, friend and enemy, animal and planet, food and eater are of one kind ... to the Necessity which rudely or softly educates him to the perception that there are no contingencies; that Law rules throughout existence; a Law which is not intelligent but intelligence,—not personal nor impersonal,—it distains and passes understanding; it dissolves persons; it vivifies nature; yet solicits the pure in heart to draw on all its omnipotence.[4]

In the second half of the twentieth century, the aesthetics of the Beautiful Necessity animated the debate on the function and value of chance in making art. The expansiveness of the Emersonian heritage makes John Cage, who tirelessly sought to erase the distinctions between art and life, and Stan Brakhage, the orphic filmmaker whose poesis was a religious vocation, coequal heirs of the Beautiful Necessity, although they invoke it to opposite ends. Cage's systematic disruptions of continuous discourse often make it difficult to isolate his version of Ananke in a succinct quotation. However, the concluding paragraph of his "History of Experimental Music in America" offers the following reflection:

History is the story of original actions.... That one sees the human race is one person (all of its members parts of the same body, brothers—not in competition any more than hand is in competition with eye) enables him to see that originality is necessary, for there is no need for eye to do what hand so well does. In this way, the past and present are to be observed and each person makes what he alone must make, bringing for the whole of human society into existence a historical fact, and then, on and on, in continuum and discontinuum.[5]

In an interview with Roger Reynolds at the time of the publication of *Silence*, he restated this idea, again linking necessity to originality:

I'm devoted to the principle of originality—not originality in the egoistic sense, but originality in the sense of doing something that is necessary to do. Now, obviously the things that are necessary to do are not the things that have been done, but the ones that have not yet been done. This applies not only to other people's work, but seriously to my own work.[6]

For Brakhage, Ananke animated his vocation. He was unembarrassed by what Cage calls egoism:

OF NECESSITY I BECOME INSTRUMENT FOR THE PASSAGE OF INNER VISION THRU ALL MY SENSIBILITIES, INTO ITS EXTERNAL FORM. My most active part in their process is to increase all my sensibilities (so that all films arise out of some total area or being or full life) AND, at the given moment of possible creation to act only out of necessity. In other words, I am principally concerned with revelation. My sensibilities are art-oriented to the extent that revelation takes place, naturally, within the given historical context of specifically Western aesthetics. If my sensibilities were otherwise oriented, revelation would take another external form—perhaps a purely personal one.[7]

In the early short book *Nature* (1836), Emerson set forth a hyperbole for the primacy of the visible in his and our world. In response to it, Christopher Cranch famously caricatured him as an enormous eyeball on spindly legs:

Crossing a bare common, in snow puddles, at twilight, under a clouded sky, without having in my thoughts any occurrence of special good fortune, I have enjoyed a perfect exhilaration. . . . There I feel that nothing can befall me in life,—no disgrace, no calamity, (leaving me my eyes,) which nature cannot repair. Standing on the bare ground,—my head bathed by the blithe air, and uplifted into infinite space,—all mean egotism vanishes. I become a transparent eye-ball; I am nothing; I see all; the currents of the Universal Being circulate through me; I am part or particle of God. . . . In the tranquil landscape, and especially in the distant line of the horizon, man beholds somewhat as beautiful as his own nature.[8]

In that same book, Emerson provides a scenario for the quickening of visual experience that is central to the argument of this book, as my title suggests. I shall return to it again and again in the succeeding chapters:

The least change in our point of view, gives the whole world a pictorial air. A man who seldom rides, needs only to get into a coach and traverse his own town, to turn the street into a puppet-show. The men, the women,—talking, running, bartering, fighting,—the earnest mechanic, the lounger, the beggar, the boys, the dogs, are unrealized at once, or, at least, wholly detached from all relation to the observer, and seen as apparent, not substantial beings. What new thoughts are suggested by seeing a face of country quite familiar, in the rapid movement of the rail-road car! Nay, the most wonted objects, (make a very slight change in the point of vision,) please us most. In a camera obscura, the butcher's cart, and the figure of one of our own family amuse us. So the portrait of a well-known face gratifies us. Turn the eyes upside down by looking at the landscape through your legs, and how agreeable is the picture, though you have seen it any time these twenty years![9]

If this passage sounds familiar, it may be because Whitman so thoroughly took over its catalog of the puppet show of city life and made it his own in *Leaves of Grass*. However, before the invention of cinema it was not possible to make visual art directly following most of the cues in this catalog. We shall see the various ways in which all the filmmakers I discuss followed Emerson's suggestions without knowing the source.

For the American visual artists who inherited the exhilaration of the transparent eyeball, the dissolution of the self within a divine afflatus often entails the hypothetical silencing or disengagement of language. In particular, the temporary suspension of the substantive, name-giving activity of the mind assumed a redemptive status for the Abstract Expressionists. Furthermore, the primacy of vision always contains a dialectical moment in which visibility is effaced by whiteness. The monumental expression of that threatening void at the core of vision also can be found in Emerson's *Nature*:

> The ruin or the blank that we see when we look at nature, is in our own eye. The axis of vision is not coincident with the axis of things and so they appear not transparent but opake. The reason the world lacks unity, and lies broken and in heaps, is because man is disunited with himself.[10]

The polar stasis at the end of Poe's *Narrative of Arthur Gordon Pym* and the chapter "The Whiteness of the Whale" in *Moby-Dick* are examples of this national obsession with the "blank" (or etymologically, white) of nature that Wallace Stevens called "an ancestral theme" in "The Auroras of Autumn":

> Here, being visible is being white,
> Is being of the solid of white, the accomplishment
> Of an extremist in an exercise . . .[11]

One extremist, Gertrude Stein, absorbed Emerson through her teacher at Radcliffe College, William James, who, as Richard Poirier has shown, owed more to Emerson than he cared to acknowledge.[12] Quoting the following passage from "The Stream of Thought," the cornerstone chapter of James's *Principles of Psychology*, Poirier points to "the emphasis on action, on transitions" in both James and Emerson and the skeptical rejection of false substantives and illusionary ends in the frozen meaning of words:

> We ought to say a feeling of *and*, a feeling of *if*, a feeling of *but*, and a feeling of *by*, quite as readily as we say a feeling of *blue* or a feeling of *cold*. Yet we do not: so inveterate has our habit become of recognizing the existence of the substantive parts alone, that language almost refuses to lend itself to any other use.[13]

One might even say that Stein took this as a literary program. In the lecture "Poetry and Grammar" she discussed her reluctance to depend upon nouns in her writing:

> As I say a noun is a name of a thing, and therefore, slowly if you feel what is inside that thing you do not call it by the name by which it is known. Everybody knows that by the way they do when they are in love and a writer should always have that intensity of emotion about whatever is the object about which he writes.[14]

By dislocating syntax, she foregrounded conjunctions and prepositions in her writings of the second and third decades of the twentieth century. For example, "If I Told Him: A Completed Portrait of Picasso" (1923) lays stress on *if* and *as* in exposing the infrastructure of portraiture.[15] James's chapter "The Stream of Thought" also resonates in the thought of Stan Brakhage and Ernie Gehr, both avid readers of Stein.

In *Narration* (1935), Stein interrogated the nature of American literature, poetry, and prose, the differences between literary narratives and newspapers, and the status of an audience. Several Emersonian topoi occur in these talks. I begin with the vehicular perspective.

A sign glimpsed from a train became the exemplum of the second lecture:

Let's make our flour meal and meat in Georgia.
    This is a sign I read as we rode on a train from Atlanta to Birmingham and I wondered then and am still wondering is it poetry or is it prose let's make our flour meal and meat in Georgia, it might be poetry and it might be prose and of course there is a reason why a reason why it might be poetry and a reason why it might be prose.

Does let's make our flour meal and meat in Georgia move in various ways and very well and has that to do really to do with narrative in poetry, has it really to do with narrative at all and is it more important in poetry that a thing should move in various kinds of ways than it is in prose supposing both of them to be narrative.[16]

These "new thoughts" excited by the fast-moving perspective turn on the puns embedded in the advertising sign. Stein's method is circular; examples are displaced; later lectures suggest ways of reading earlier ones. Thus, when she distinguishes between English and American narratives in the opening lecture she offers no examples to illustrate her contention that "English literature . . . has been determined by the fact that England is an island and that the daily life on that island was a completely daily life"[17] but in a different context in the third lecture she gives her example: Defoe's *Robinson Crusoe*. Similarly, in the lecture following the description of the sign seen from a moving train, she gives an oblique clue to her reading of how it "moves in various ways":

I love my love with a b because she is peculiar. One can say this. That has nothing to do with what a newspaper does and that is the reason why that is the reason that newspapers and with it history as it mostly exists has nothing to do with anything that is living.[18]

The seeming nonsense of "I love my love with a b because she is peculiar" becomes an erotic epigram when we read "a b" as her companion and lover, Alice B. [Toklas]. Looking back to the earlier lecture with this in mind, we may note that the train was moving from A[tlanta] to B[irmingham] and the prosaic advertisement for Georgia products can be read as a call to assignation (*meat* as *meet*). This confirms Stein's definition of the American difference in literature in the opening lecture:

In the American writing the words began to have inside themselves those same words that in the English were completely quiet or very slowly moving began to have within themselves the consciousness of completely moving, they began to detach themselves from the solidity of anything, they began to excitedly feel themselves as if they were anywhere or anything, think about American writing from Emerson, Hawthorne Walt Whitman Mark Twain Henry James myself Sherwood Anderson Thornton Wilder and Dashiell Hammitt and you will see what I mean, as well as in advertising and in road signs, you will see what I mean, words left alone more and more feel that they are moving and all of it is detached and is detaching anything from anything and in this detaching and in this moving it is being in its way creating its existing. This is the real difference between English and American writing and this then can lead to anything.[19]

The play of movement and detachment here redeploys terms from Emerson's essay "The Poet," where he balances "the intellect, which delights in detachment" and "the quality of the imagination [which] is to flow."

Stein's most startling evocation of the uniqueness of the American dynamic contributes a theory of what has come to be called "hanging out" as a native posture:

I always remember during the war being so interested in one thing in seeing the American soldiers standing, standing and doing nothing standing for a long time not even talking but just standing and being watched by the whole French population and their feeling the feeling of the whole population that the American soldier standing there and doing nothing impressed them as the American soldier as no soldier could impress by doing anything. It is a much more impressive thing to anyone to see any one standing, that is not in action than acting or doing anything doing anything being a successive thing, standing not being a successive thing but being something existing. That is then the difference between narrative as it has been and narrative as it is now.[20]

These soldiers are unconsciously collective followers of Whitman, who chanted, "I lean and loaf at my ease," celebrating themselves by doing nothing. Many of the filmmakers I discuss here have been intensely aware of the excitement of doing nothing, although they may not have realized their antecedents in Stein or Whitman.

As I analyze the work of eleven filmmakers in this book, I treat images and film shots as Stein treats road signs (some of those images may even be road signs), looking at the poetry of their movement and detachment. I also point out elements in their films that might be viewed as implicit responses to themes and tropes in the major essays of Emerson and the central poems of Whitman.

The objective of Stein's *Narration* is the displacement of narrative as "a telling of what is happening in successive moments of its happening" and poetry as "an intensive calling upon the name of anything" to a modern mode of knowledge of "things moving perhaps perhaps moving in any direction," which has been the discovery of American literature.[21] Stein has reinterpreted Emerson's doctrine of the oversoul in literary terms, fashioning a new definition of *audience* from his mystical concept of the eternal One. Emerson wrote:

> We live in succession, in division, in parts, in particles. Meanwhile within man is the soul of the whole; the wise silence; the universal beauty, to which every part and particle is equally related; the eternal ONE. And this deep power in which we exist, and whose beatitude is all accessible to us, is not only self-sufficing and perfect in every hour, but the act of seeing and the thing seen, the seer and the spectacle, the subject and the object are one. . . .

> If we consider what happens in conversation, in reveries, in remorse, in times of passion, in surprises, in the instruction of dreams, wherein often we see ourselves in masquerade,—the droll disguises only magnifying and enhancing a real element, and forcing it on our distant notice,—we shall catch many hints that will broaden and lighten into knowledge of the secret of nature.[22]

In the fourth lecture, Stein comes to her definition of an audience from a darker moment of solipsism than Emerson will allow here. It is one of her versions of his earlier noncoincidence of the axes of vision and of things:

> That is to say can does anyone separate themselves from the land so they can see it and if they see it are they the audience of it or to it. If you see anything are you its audience and if you tell anything are you its audience, and is there any audience for it but the audience that sees or hears it.[23]

Still, the act of recognition that occurs in the process of writing, in which something beyond intention originates, convinces her that the apperceptive audience the writer becomes to her own writing is a model for the wider audience of readers:

> That is what mysticism is, that is what the Trinity is, that is what marriage is, the absolute conviction that in spite of knowing anything about everything about how any one is never really feeling what any other one is really feeling that after all after all three are one and two are one. One is not one because one is always two that is one is always coming to recognition of what the one who is one is writing that is telling.[24]

Her uncharacteristic evocation of theological language is itself Emersonian. In "The Over-Soul" he wrote: "In all conversation between two persons, tacit reference is made, as to a third party, to a common nature. That third party or common nature is not social; it is impersonal; is God."[25] Curiously, Stein is at her most Emersonian when she interiorizes all three parties and comes almost to identifying narrative with the Beautiful Necessity that keeps on generating the mystical marriage of reader and writer, or the trinity of reader, writer, and text. But this is the step the filmmaker Hollis Frampton will take, completing Stein, as I show when I discuss his narrative theory in chapter 7.

Since the late 1960s, John Cage has expressed his Emersonianism largely through the mediation of Emerson's first disciple, Henry David Thoreau. Cage wrote in his "Preface to 'Lecture on the Weather'": "No greater American has lived than Thoreau. Emerson called him a speaker and actor of the truth. Other great men have vision. Thoreau had none. Each day his eyes and ears were open and empty to see and hear the world he lived in. Music, he said, is continuous; only listening is intermittent."[26] Cage said he composed his *Empty Words* (1974) by "subjecting Thoreau's writings to *I Ching* chance operations to obtain a collage text." However, I understand this radical enthusiasm for Thoreau to have been primed by the Emersonian aesthetics already evident in his crucial first book, *Silence* (1961), an anthology of many of his articles and lectures since 1937, in which a sometimes chronological arrangement interacts in a thematic collage with short narrative anecdotes and interspersed parables.[27]

Stein exerted a great influence on Cage early in his career. In college he played the smart aleck, answering test questions in her style, winning thus alternately As and Fs. He quotes her in his most elaborate statement of the American uniqueness in music: "Actually America has an intellectual climate suitable for radical experimentation. We are, as Gertrude Stein said, the oldest country of the twentieth century. And I like to add: in our air way of knowing nowness."[28]

In his "Lecture on Nothing" (first delivered in 1949 or 1950 at the Abstract Expressionists' Artists' Club) he presented the core of his negative, necessitarian teaching ("I have nothing to say / and I am saying it / and that is poetry /as I need it"). He urges his listeners to think of the lecture itself as if it were a sight glimpsed from a moving vehicle:

```
                                                    Re-
gard it as something      seen          momentarily      ,        as
though          from a window      while traveling      .
If across Kansas          ,          then, of course,      Kansas
.                    Arizona                    is more interesting.
almost too interesting      ,          especially   for a New-Yorker   who is
being interested          in spite of himself      in everything.
. . .
Or you may leave it      forever          and never return to it      ,
     for we pos-sess nothing          .          Our poetry now
     is the reali-zation      that we possess   nothing
          Anything          therefore      is a delight
(since we do not      pos-ses it)    and thus      need not fear its loss
          We need not destroy the past:      it is gone;
at any moment,      it might reappear and      seem to be      and be
     the present
          Would it be a      repetition?      Only if we thought we
owned it,      but since we don't,      it is free      and so are we[29]
```

Behind this passage lie not only the aesthetics of movement from *Nature*, but also one of Emerson's most eloquent moments in his most powerful essay, "Experience": "All I know is reception; I am and I have: but I do not get, and when I fancied

I had gotten anything, I found I did not. I worship with wonder the great Fortune. My reception has been so large, that I am not annoyed by receiving this or that superabundantly."[30]

The "Lecture on Nothing" invokes as well the doctrine of the Beautiful Necessity:

> What I am calling   poetry   is often called content.
> I myself   have called   it form   .   It is the conti-
>   nuity   of a piece of music.   Continuity today,
> when it is necessary   ,   is a demonstration   of dis-
> interestedness.   That is   it is a proof   that our delight
> lies in not possessing anything   .   Each moment
> presents what happens .[31]

Charles Olson encountered Cage and felt his influence when they were both on the faculty of Black Mountain College in the 1950s. But his own relationship to Emerson owed nothing to Cage. It was profound and went back to the origins of his vocation; it has been commented upon extensively. His friend the poet Robert Duncan first noted it; Sherman Paul examined it extensively; Stephen Fredman devoted a study to it; I discussed it in my *Modernist Montage*, and Tom Clark's biography firmly established the dominant role played by Emerson's writings in Olson's undergraduate career at Wesleyan.[32] At that time, he confessed in his journal that Emerson made him feel like "an intellectual pigmy."

After Wesleyan, Olson became absorbed in the work of Herman Melville and he largely took upon himself Melville's anxiety and discomfort with Emerson. In fact, much of our direct knowledge of Melville's reaction to Emerson is the result of Olson's remarkable enacting of his own Herodotean principle: "History" is, etymologically, what one finds out for oneself; for as a young graduate student, he searched for and found much of Melville's library. He turned Melville's copy of Emerson over to his teacher, F. O. Matthiessen, who discussed the annotations in his *The American Renaissance*, and he reserved the elaborately marked Shakespeare for himself, drawing from it important points of his first book, *Call Me Ishmael*.

The gist of his Melvillean position can be gleaned from his 1958 review, "Equal, That Is, to the Real Itself":

> Melville couldn't abuse object as symbol does by depreciating it in favor of subject. Or let image lose its relational force by transferring its occurrence as allegory does. He was already aware of the complementarity of each of two pairs of how we know and present the real—image & object, and action & subject—both of which have paid off so decisively since. At this end I am thinking of such recent American painting as Pollock's, and Kline's, and some recent American narrative and verse; and at his end, his whale itself for example, what an unfolding thing it is as it sits there written 100 years off, implicit intrinsic and incident to itself.

Melville was not tempted, as Whitman was, and Emerson and Thoreau differently, to inflate the physical: take the model for the house, the house for the model, death is the open road, the soul or body is a boat, etc.[33]

This insistence on the irreducible particularity of things, one of the cornerstones of Olson's aesthetics, would seem to be a repudiation of the "transparent eye-ball" and the opacity of "the axis of things." The desire to be a disembodied eye and the fantasy of seeing through things by an Emersonian redemption of the soul are the inflations of the physical he shuns.

At the core of Olson's teaching there is an affirmation of the inescapable centrality of the poet's body, a thoroughly Whitmanian revision of Emerson. The body is forever in contact with the particularity of things so that (a) poetics must be based on the respiration patterns of the individual poet, for his words emerge "projected" from his breath; (b) the body is always in a particular locality, for which the poet must account; and (c) the body is never static; it is always in motion, dancing even when sitting down, breathing, pumping blood. Finally, (d) at each interfacing of body and things, history intervenes. The history of language, of poetry, of localities, and of the human species since the Pleistocene era become areas for the poet "to investigate for himself."

Yet for Olson, Emerson's influence is inescapable. His Herodotean definition of history is a gloss on "Self-Reliance," and Emerson's essay "History" might well be a source for his argument, in *The Special View of History*, that history itself "is the *function* of any one of us,"[34] as well as his equation of mythological and historical narratives. Emerson's essay "The Poet" plays an even more potent role behind Olson's theoretical writings. He mined it for several of his most important theoretical texts. In the most condensed statement of his poetics, "Letter to Elaine Feinstein," he responded to her inquiry about the status of imagery in his concept of the poem:

> You wld know already I'm buggy on say the Proper Noun, so much so I wld take it Pun is Rime, all from tope/type/trope, that built in is the connection, in each of us, to Cosmos, and if one taps, via psyche, plus a "true" adherence of Muse, one does reveal "Form."[35]

Packed into this sentence are several dimensions of Olson's aesthetics as he articulated them in the late 1950s and early 1960s. First of all, he stressed the poetic importance of the proper noun and of the etymology of *proper* (from *proprius*, "one's own") as the stamp of a writer's activity. Narrative, as he understood it, was the elaboration of a proper noun into a story. The trinity *tope/type/trope* (more often named by him in Greek *topos/typos/tropos*) elliptically encodes Olson's scattered claims that the poet begins in a specific place—which is always historically conditioned—and, by turning or troping through the shifting of his attention and the figuration of his language, he types a type of poem. The pun on *type* fuses the printed letters of the resulting text to its generic limitation and to the persona invoked by the poet's voice. The articulation of this situation entails the interaction of the personal history of the poet (psyche) with his language in its historical-etymological density (Muse).

We find in Emerson's "The Poet" vestiges even of Olson's aesthetic diction, as we had found Stein's use of motion and detachment:

> [T]he poet is the Namer or Language-maker, naming things sometimes after their appearance, sometimes after their essence, and giving everyone its own name and not another's, thereby rejoicing the intellect, which delights in *detachment* or boundary. The poets made all the words, and therefore language is the archives of history, and, if we must say it, a sort of tomb of the muses. . . . The etymologist finds the deadest word to have been once a brilliant picture. Language is fossil poetry.[36]

Another passage from "The Poet" may be the precursor of Olson's essay, "Against Wisdom as Such":

> But the quality of the imagination is *to flow*, and *not to freeze*. The poet did not stop at the color, or the form, but read their meaning; neither may he rest in this meaning, but he makes the same objects exponents of his new thought. Here is the difference betwixt the poet and the mystic, that the last nails a symbol to one sense, which was a true sense for a moment, but soon becomes old and false. For all symbols are fluxional; all language is *vehicular* and transitive, and is good, as ferries and horses are, for conveyance, not as farms and houses are, for homestead.[37]

"Against Wisdom as Such" attacks the mystical and cultic dimensions of Robert Duncan's work, denying the metaphor of wisdom as light, substituting instead a notion of poetic heat:

> Rhythm is time (not measure, as the pedants of Alexandria made it). The root is "rhein": *to flow*. And mastering the flow of the solid, time, we invoke others. Because we take time and *heat* it, make it serve ourselves, our, form.
>
> . . . One has to drive all nouns, the abstract most of all, back to process— to act.[38]

In his observations on the dynamics of the noun in his lecture series "The Chiasma," he comes close to Gertrude Stein's concept of American language. Clearly Whitman was on his mind:

> Why, in short, a noun is so vital is not at all that it so much differs from a verb (does not have motion) but because it is a motion which has not yet moved.
>
> . . . [Do] we not have to leave compulsions on the other side of syntax, no matter how much syntax does give us the means to indicate all stages of propulsion, including that quietist of all movements, doing nothing—contemplating a leaf of grass?

... All I want to do is to beat you into the recognition that *things*—the hard things—are, wherever, ... changeable because they are already moving, sitting down.[39]

Thus, even though there is no direct expression of the Emersonian concept of motion as a key to a new aesthetic perspective in Olson aside from that implicit in the opening of *Call Me Ishmael* ("I take SPACE to be the central fact to man born in America, from Folsom cave to now. ... Some men ride on such space, other have to fasten themselves like a tent stake to survive"[40]), his protracted reflections on naming instantiate Emerson's idea of "vehicular and transitive" language.

Perhaps because of his encounter with John Cage at Black Mountain College, chance came to play an important role in his theory of poetry. For him it was a version of the Beautiful Necessity. (In "The Poet" Emerson wrote: "The beautiful rests on the foundations of the necessary.") In *The Special View of History*, Olson lectured:

> *Coincidence* and *proximity*, because the space-time continuum is known, become determinants of *chance* and *accident* and make possible *creative success*. ... And man's order—his powers of order—are no longer separable from either those of nature or of God. The organic is one, purpose is seen to be contingent, not primordial: it follows from the chance success of the play of creative accident, it does not precede them.[41]

In reformulating the concepts of chance and purpose, he suggests that poems, or works of art generally, are the necessary consequences of an aesthetic process of natural selection rather than exclusively the willed acts of conscious individuals. The individuals respond to "instruction" by bringing the energies of their conscious and unconscious histories to the service of a "true adherence" to language. Charles Stein has written the most lucid analysis of these ideas:

> The emphasis on the inclusion of purpose and chance, accidence and necessity, form and chaos, as being *within* actual process, is the cosmological justification for Olson's "concretism," his insistence that words be treated as solid objects, and poems be treated as force fields. As events in the new cosmology are neither determined purposively nor given form by powers outside of process, so words must not be treated as if their functions could be limited by either abstract definitions or canons of usage. Similarly poems must not take models from forms extrinsic to the forms emergent in *their* emergence; symbols must not subsume the material of the work in literary reference, but must be allowed to emerge as local centers of force within the field of the poem.[42]

By *process* Stein means how the poet "must map (i.e. project) the movement of the mind in the heat or calm of composition."[43]

Olson's project suggests a possible convergence of Gertrude Stein and John Cage's positions (although that was never his intention). Her imputation of a dynamics within American language and immanent in apparent stasis and Cage's attention to the beauties of unwilled reception correspond to Olson's poetics of bounded force fields.

My insistence on the Emersonian sources of these positions is not an effort to elevate the Sage of Concord at the expense of his most lively twentieth-century heirs. Emersonian aesthetics is so radical, so diffuse, and even so contradictory that it elicits perennial refocusing. Our strongest filmmakers are less likely to attend to Emerson himself than to Stein, Cage, or Olson. When they are unmoved by any of these three and invent theoretical positions from whole cloth for themselves, they are usually reshaping a number of Emersonian stances they have absorbed from the native air they breathe.

Notes

1 Ralph Waldo Emerson, *Essays and Lectures* (New York: Library of America, 1983), pp. 431–32.

2 Gertrude Stein, *Narration* (Chicago: University of Chicago Press, 1969), p. 46.

3 Charles Olson, "Against Wisdom as Such," *The Human Universe* (New York: Grove Press, 1967), p. 70.

4 Emerson, *Essays and Lectures*, pp. 967–68.

5 John Cage, *Silence* (Middletown: Wesleyan University Press, 1961), p. 75.

6 Richard Kostelanetz, *Conversing with Cage, 2nd Edition* (New York: Routledge, 2003), p. 221.

7 Stan Brakhage, *Metaphors on Vision* (New York: *Film Culture* no. 30, 1963), pages unnumbered, fourth letter of "Margin Alien."

8 Emerson, *Essays and Lectures*, p. 10.

9 Ibid., pp. 33–34.

10 Ibid., p. 47.

11 Wallace Stevens, "The Auroras of Autumn," in *The Palm at the End of the Mind: Selected Poems and a Play*, ed. Holly Stevens (New York: Knopf, 1971), p. 308.

12 Richard Poirier, *The Renewal of Literature: Emersonian Reflections* (New Haven: Yale University Press, 1987).

13 Ibid., p. 16. From William James, *The Principles of Psychology* (New York: Dover, 1950), vol. I, pp. 245–46.

14 Gertrude Stein, "Poetry and Grammar," *Lectures in America* (New York: Random House, 1935), p. 210. Tony Tanner points to a direct Emersonian source for this rejection of nouns and sees in her use of repetition "Emerson's wisdom of wondering at the usual." Tony Tanner, *The Reign of Wonder: Naivety and Reality in American Literature* (Cambridge: Cambridge University Press, 1965), pp. 198–201.

15 See P. Adams Sitney, *Modernist Montage: The Obscurity of Vision in Cinema and Literature* (New York: Columbia University Press, 1991), pp. 151–52.

16 Stein, *Narration*, p. 16.

17 Ibid., p. 3.

18 Ibid., p. 37.

19 Ibid., p. 10.

20 Ibid., pp. 19–20.

21 Ibid., pp. 17, 25, 28.

22 Emerson, *Essays and Lectures*, p. 386.

23 Stein, *Narration*, p. 51. In an early notebook she had written another version of Emersonian blankness: "Great thinkers eyes do not turn in, they get blank or turn out to keep themselves from being disturbed." Quoted by Ulla E. Dydo, "Gertrude Stein: Composition as Meditation," in *Gertrude Stein and the Making of Literature*, ed. Shirley Neuman and Ira B. Nadel (Boston: Northeastern University Press, 1988), p. 43.

24 Stein, *Narration*, p. 57.

25 Emerson, *Essays and Lectures*, p. 390.

26 John Cage, *Empty Words: Writings '73-'78* (Middletown: Wesleyan University Press, 1973), p. 3.

27 I believe Annette Michelson was the first critic to note the importance of Emerson for Cage in her *Robert Morris* (Washington, DC: Corcoran Gallery of Art, 1969), p. 27.

28 Cage, "History of Experimental Music in America," *Silence*, p. 73.

29 Cage, *Silence*, p. 110.

30 Emerson, *Essays and Lectures*, p. 491.

31 Cage, *Silence*, p. 111.

32 Paul Sherman, *Olson's Push: Origin, Black Mountain, and Recent American Poetry* (Baton Rouge: Louisiana State University Press, 1978); Stephen Fredman, *The Grounding of American Poetry: Charles Olson and the Emersonian Tradition* (Cambridge: Cambridge University Press, 1993); Sitney, *Modernist Montage*; Tom Clark, *Charles Olson: The Allegory of a Poet's Life* (New York: Norton, 1991).

33 Charles Olson, *The Human Universe and Other Essays*, ed. Donald Allen (New York: Grove Press, 1967), p. 121.

34 Charles Olson, *The Special View of History*, ed. with intro. by Ann Charters (Berkeley: Oyez, 1970), p. 17.

35 Ibid., p. 97. See Sitney, *Modernist Montage* for an extended reading of "Letter to Elaine Feinstein."

36 Emerson, *Essays and Lectures*, pp. 456–57 (emphasis mine).

37 Ibid., 463 (emphasis mine).

38 Olson, *The Human Universe*, p. 70 (emphasis mine).

39 Charles Olson, "The Chiasma, or Lectures in the New Sciences of Man," ed. George Butterick, *Olson*, no. 10 (Fall 1978), pp. 83–84.

40 Charles Olson, *Call Me Ishmael*, (New York: Grove Press, 1947), pp. 11–12.

41 Charles Olson, *The Special View of History*, p. 49.

42 Charles Stein, *The Secret of the Black Chrysanthemum* (Barrytown: Station Hill, 1987), p. 107.

43 Ibid., p. 104.

Stanley Cavell (1926–)

Philosopher who has taught at Harvard since 1963, Cavell is the principal intellectual force of Emerson's recovery within contemporary American philosophy. Cavell's writing has expanded the range of academic fields using Emerson's work and also has revitalized international scholarly interest in it. His initial engagement with Thoreau in The Senses of Walden *(1972) was amplified by his belated discovery of Emerson, which he explores in the first of the selections below, published in* New Literary History *(1979). Throughout the 1980s and 1990s Cavell developed his radical, penetrating readings of Emerson's work—which entailed bringing Emerson into conversation with the thinking of Nietzsche, J. L. Austin, Wittgenstein, and Freud, and with the arts (including music, opera, and classical Hollywood films)—in works such as* The Senses of Walden: An Expanded Edition *(1981),* In Quest of the Ordinary: Lines of Skepticism and Romanticism *(1988),* This New Yet Unapproachable America: Lectures After Emerson After Wittgenstein *(1989),* Conditions Handsome and Unhandsome: The Constitution of Emersonian Perfectionism *(1990),* A Pitch of Philosophy: Autobiographical Exercises *(1994), and* Philosophical Passages: Wittgenstein, Emerson, Austin, Derrida *(1995), among other books and essays. In 2003 Cavell's most enduring and influential essays on Emerson were edited into the volume* Emerson's Transcendental Etudes. *The selections below are meant to show both the temporal and topical range of Cavell's engagement with Emerson's work. The second entry comes from a 1998 essay that offers a reply to the question its title pronounces; in the light of Emerson's adoption or incorporation by American pragmatists (especially among contemporary philosophers), Cavell wishes to resist—or "suspend applause" for—the apparently determined wish to anoint Emerson a "protopragmatist." The final selection highlights the initial segment of the Introduction and reprints the whole of the first chapter of* Cities of Words: Pedagogical Letters on a Register of the Moral Life *(2004), a book in which Cavell—in these specific selections and in the book generally—reconstitutes (while thinking anew about) one of his perennial courses at Harvard in which he devoted attention to the lessons of Emersonian moral perfectionism for philosophy, cinema, literature, and other arts. For instance, Cavell explains why, among other reasons, the first chapter belongs to Emerson by noting, perhaps unexpectedly for some readers, that "the primary body of Hollywood films to be adduced here may be understood as inspired by Emersonian transcendentalism." These three selections, written over the course of nearly three decades, are meant to signal different instances of representative features that pervade Cavell's work on Emerson: his recovery of Emerson in a culture that "repressed" his work; his skepticism about practitioners in American traditions of philosophy (namely, pragmatism and neopragmatism) who appear at risk of misreading Emerson; and his long-standing commitment to revealing the pedagogical significance of Emerson's writing—the way it turns us and returns us to ourselves—as readers, as writers, as humans.*

Thinking of Emerson

Stanley Cavell

[INTRODUCTORY NOTE: For a program arranged by the Division on Philosophical Approaches to Literature at the annual convention of the Modern Language Association in New York, December 1978, Professor Leo Marx invented and chaired a meeting on Emerson whose panelists were asked by him to respond to a passage from my book *The Senses of Walden* that runs this way:

> Study of *Walden* would perhaps not have become such an obsession with me had it not presented itself as a response to questions with which I was already obsessed: Why has America never expressed itself philosophically? Or has it—in the metaphysical riot of its greatest literature? Has the impulse to philosophical speculation been absorbed, or exhausted, by speculation in territory, as in such thoughts as Manifest Destiny? Or are such questions not really intelligible? They are, at any rate, disturbingly like the questions that were asked about American literature before it established itself. In rereading *Walden,* twenty years after first reading it, I seemed to find a book of sufficient intellectual scope and consistency to have established or inspired a tradition of thinking.

My response is the following essay, not quite all of which was read at the meeting. I am grateful to Leo Marx for prompting me to go further with these thoughts, and to Jay Cantor for reading the original draft and pressing me for certain clarifications. A conversation with John McNees was decisive for me in arriving at certain formulations about philosophical prose in its relation to the idea of dialogue and hence to an idea of thinking. I should in this regard also like to refer to an essay by Morse Peckham which appears as the introduction to a facsimile edition of the first printing of Emerson's *Essays* and *Essays: Second Series* (Columbus, 1969). I dedicate the present essay to the members, in the fall of 1978, of a graduate seminar at Harvard on the later writings of Heidegger.]

Thinking of Emerson, I can understand my book on *Walden* as something of an embarrassment, but something of an encouragement as well, since if what it suggests about the lack of a tradition of thinking in America is right, e.g., about how Emerson and Thoreau deaden one another's words, then my concentration on understanding Thoreau was bound to leave Emerson out. He kept sounding to me like secondhand Thoreau.

The most significant shortcoming among the places my book mentions Emerson is its accusing him of "misconceiving" Kant's critical enterprise, comparing Emerson unfavorably in this regard with Thoreau. I had been impressed by Thoreau's sentence running "The universe constantly and obediently answers to our conceptions" as in effect an elegant summary of the *Critique of Pure Reason*. When I requote that sentence later in the book, I take it beyond its Kantian precincts, adding that the universe answers whether our conceptions are mean or magnanimous, scientific or magical, faithful or treacherous, thus suggesting that there are more ways of making a habitable world—or more layers to it—than Kant's twelve concepts of the understanding accommodate. But I make no effort to justify this idea of a "world" beyond claiming implicitly that as I used the word I was making sense. The idea is roughly that moods must be taken as having at least as sound a role in advising us of reality as sense-experience has; that, for example, coloring the world, attributing to it the qualities "mean" or "magnanimous," may be no less objective or subjective than coloring an apple, attributing to it the colors red or green. Or perhaps we should say: sense-experience is to objects what moods are to the world. The only philosopher I knew who had made an effort to formulate a kind of epistemology of moods, to find their revelations of what we call the world as sure as the revelations of what we call understanding, was the Heidegger of *Being and Time*. But it was hard to claim support there without committing oneself to more machinery than one had any business for.

Now I see that I might, even ought to, have seen Emerson ahead of me, since, for example, his essay on "Experience" is about the epistemology, or say the logic, of moods. I understand the moral of that essay as contained in its late prayerful remark, "But far be from me the despair which prejudges the law by a paltry empiricism." That is, what is wrong with empiricism is not its reliance on experience but its paltry idea of experience. (This is the kind of criticism of classical empiricism leveled by John Dewey—for example, in "An Empirical Survey of Empiricisms"—who praised Emerson but so far as I know never took him up philosophically.) But I hear Kant working throughout Emerson's essay on "Experience," with his formulation of the question, "Is metaphysics possible?" and his line of answer: Genuine knowledge of (what we call) the world is for us, but it cannot extend beyond (what we call) experience. To which I take Emerson to be replying: Well and good, but then you had better be very careful what it is you understand by experience, for that might be limited in advance by the conceptual limitations you impose upon it, limited by what we know of human existence, i.e., by our limited experience of it. When, for example, you get around to telling us what we may hope for, I must know that you have experienced hope, or else I will surmise that you have not, which is to say precisely that your experience is of despair.

Emerson's "Experience" even contains a little argument, a little more explicitly with Kant, about the nature of experience in its relation to, or revelation of, the natural world. "The secret of the illusoriness [of life] is in the necessity of a succession of moods or objects. Gladly we would anchor, but the anchorage is quicksand. This onward trick of nature is too strong for us: *Pero si muove*." In the section of the *Critique of Pure Reason* entitled "Analogies of Experience," one of the last before turning to an investigation of transcendental illusion, Kant is at pains to distinguish within experience the *"subjective succession* of apprehension from the *objective succession* of appearances." The anchor he uses to keep subjectivity and objectivity from sinking one another is, as you would expect, gripped in transcendental ground, which is always, for Kant, a question of locating necessity properly, in this case the necessity, or rules, of succession in experience. (It is curious, speaking of anchoring, that one of Kant's two examples in this specific regard is that of seeing a ship move downstream.) The acceptance of Galileo's—and Western science's—chilling crisis with the Church over the motion of the earth recalls Kant's claim to have accomplished a Copernican Revolution in metaphysics; that is, understanding the configurations of the world as a function of the configurations of our own nature. Now I construe Emerson's implicit argument in the passage cited as follows. The succession of moods is not tractable by the distinction between subjectivity and objectivity Kant proposes for experience. *This* onward trick of nature is too much for us; the given bases of the self are quicksand. The fact that we are taken over by this succession, this onwardness, means that you can think of it as at once a succession of moods (inner matters) and a succession of objects (outer matters). This very evanescence of the world proves its existence to me; it *is* what vanishes from me. I guess this is not realism exactly; but it is not solipsism either.

I believe Emerson may encourage the idea of himself as a solipsist or subjectivist, for example, in such a remark, late in the same essay, as "Thus inevitably does the universe wear our color." But whether you take this to be subjective or objective depends upon whether you take the successive colors or moods of the universe to be subjective or objective. My claim is that Emerson is out to destroy the ground on which such a problem takes itself seriously, I mean interprets itself as a metaphysical fixture. The universe is as separate from me, but as intimately part of me, as one on whose behalf I contest, and who therefore wears my color. We are in a state of "romance" with the universe (to use a word from the last sentence of the essay); we do not possess it, but our life is to return to it, in ever-widening circles, "onward and onward," but with as directed a goal as any quest can have; in the present case, until "the soul attains her due sphericity." Until then, encircled, straitened, you can say the soul is solipsistic; surely it is, to use another critical term of Emerson's, partial. This no doubt implies that we do not have a universe as it is in itself. But this implication is nothing: we do not have selves in themselves either. The universe *is* what constantly and obediently answers to our conceptions. It is what *can* be all the ways we know it to be, which is to say, all the ways we can be. In "Circles" we are told: "Whilst the eternal generation of circles proceeds, the eternal generator abides. That central life . . . contains all its circles." The universe contains all the colors it wears. That it has no more than I can give it is a fact of what Emerson calls my poverty. (Other philosophers may speak of the emptiness of the self.)

The Kantian ring of the idea of the universe as inevitably wearing our color is, notwithstanding, pertinent. Its implication is that the way specifically Kant understands the generation of the universe keeps it solipsistic, still something partial, something of our, of my, making. Emerson's most explicit reversal of Kant lies in his picturing the intellectual hemisphere of knowledge as passive or receptive and the intuitive or instinctual hemisphere as active or spontaneous. Whereas for Kant the basis of the *Critique of Pure Reason* is that "concepts are based on the spontaneity of thought, sensible intuitions on the receptivity of impressions." Briefly, there is no intellectual intuition. I will come back to this.

But immediately, to imagine that Emerson could challenge the basis of the argument of the *Critique of Pure Reason*, I would have to imagine him to be a philosopher— would I not? I would have, that is to say, to imagine his writing—to take it—in such a way that it does not misconceive Kant but undertakes to engage him in dispute. I like what Matthew Arnold has to say about Emerson, but we ought no longer to be as sure as Arnold was that the great philosophical writer is one who builds a system; hence that Emerson is not such a writer on the ground that he was not such a builder. We are by now too aware of the philosophical *attacks* on system or theory to place the emphasis in defining philosophy on a product of philosophy rather than on the process of philosophizing. We are more prepared to understand as philosophy a mode of thought that undertakes to bring philosophy to an end, as, say, Nietzsche and Wittgenstein attempt to do, not to mention, in their various ways, Bacon, Montaigne, Descartes, Pascal, Marx, Kierkegaard, Carnap, Heidegger, or Austin, and in certain respects Kant and Hegel. Ending philosophy looks to be a commitment of each of the major modern philosophers; so it is hardly to be wondered at that some of them do not quite know whether what they are writing is philosophy. Wittgenstein said that what he did replaced philosophy. Heidegger said in his later period that what he was doing was thinking, or learning thinking, and that philosophy is the greatest enemy of true thinking. But to understand the attack on philosophy as itself philosophy, or undertaken in the name, or rather in the place, of philosophy, we must of course understand the attack as nevertheless internal to the act of philosophizing, accepting that autonomy. Church and State and the Academy and Poetry and the City may each suppress philosophy, but they cannot, without its complicity, replace it.

Can Emerson be understood as wishing to replace philosophy? But isn't that wish really what accounts for the poignancy, or dialectic, of Emerson's call, the year Thoreau graduated college, not for a thinker but for Man Thinking? The American Scholar is to think no longer partially, as a man following a task delegated by a society of which he is a victim, but as leading a life in which thinking is of the essence, as a man whose wholeness, say whose autonomy, is in command of the autonomy of thinking. The hitch of course is that there is no such human being. "Man in history, men in the world today are bugs, spawn" ("The American Scholar"). But the catch is that we aspire to this man, to the metamorphosis, to the human—hence that we can be guided and raised by the cheer of thinking. In claiming the office of the scholar "to cheer, to raise, and to guide men" as well as demanding that "whatsoever new verdict Reason from her inviolable seat pronounces on the passing men and events of today—this [the scholar] shall hear and promulgate," Emerson evidently requires the replacing of theology as well as of philosophy in his kind of building, his edification. We might think of this as internalizing the unended quarrel between philosophy and theology.

Whatever ways I go on to develop such thoughts are bound to be affected by the coincidence that during the months in which I was trying to get Emerson's tune into my ear, free of Thoreau's, I was also beginning to study the writing of the later Heidegger. This study was precipitated at last by a footnote of the editor of a collection of Heidegger essays, in which *The Senses of Walden* is described as in part forming an explication of Heidegger's notion of poetic dwelling (James G. Hart, in *The Piety of Thinking*). Having now read such an essay of Heidegger's as "Building Dwelling Thinking," I am sufficiently startled by the similarities to find the differences of interest and to start wondering about an account of both. I am thinking not so much of my similarities with Heidegger (I had after all profited from *Being and Time*, and it may be that that book leads more naturally to Heidegger's later work than is, I gather, sometimes supposed) but of Heidegger's with Thoreau, at least with my picture of Thoreau. The relation to Emerson was still unexpected, and hence even more startling. The title of the Heidegger collection I referred to is from a sentence of his that says: "For questioning is the piety of thinking." In the right mood, if you lay beside this a sentence of Emerson's from "Intellect" that says, "Always our thinking is a pious reception," you might well pause a moment. And if one starts digging to test how deep the connection might run, I find that one can become quite alarmed.

The principal text of Heidegger's to test here is translated as *What Is Called Thinking?* Here is a work that can be said to internalize the quarrel between philosophy and theology; that calls for a new existence from the human in relation to Being in order that its task of thinking be accomplished; a work based on the poignancy, or dialectic, of thinking about our having not yet learned true thinking, thinking as the receiving or letting be of something, as opposed to the positing or putting together of something, as this is pictured most systematically in Kant's ideas of representation and synthesis, and most radically in Nietzsche's will to power; that attempts to draw clear of Kant's subjectivity, and of the revenge upon time that Nietzsche understood us as taking. A climactic moment in Heidegger's descent into the origins of words is his understanding of the etymological entwining of thinking with the word for thanking, leading for example to an unfolding of ideas in which a certain progress of thinking is understood as a form of thanking, and originally a thanking for the gift of thinking, which means for the reception of being human. Here, if one can consider this to be something like philosophy, is something like a philosophical site within which to explore the crux in our relation to Emerson of his power of affirmation, or of his weakness for it.

We have surely known, since at least Newton Arvin (in "The House of Pain") collected the chorus of charges against Emerson to the effect that he lacked a knowledge of evil or of the sense of the tragic, that this missed Emerson's drift, that his task was elsewhere. Arvin insists, appropriately, that what Emerson gives us, what inspires us in him, "when we have cleared our minds of the cant of pessimism, is perhaps the fullest and most authentic expression in modern literature of the more-than-tragic emotion of thankfulness" (*Emerson: A Collection of Critical Essays,* ed. Konvitz and Whicher). But we might have surmised from Nietzsche's love of Emerson that no sane or mere man could have convincingly conceived "all things [to be] friendly and sacred, all events holy, all men divine" who was not aware that we may be undone by the pain of the world we make and may not make again. The more recent cant of pleasure or playfulness is no less hard to put up with. Yet a more-than-tragic emotion of thankfulness is still not the drift, or not the point. The point is the achievement not of affirmation but of what Emerson calls "the sacred affirmative" ("The Preacher"), the thing Nietzsche calls "the sacred Yes" ("Three Metamorphoses" in *Zarathustra*), the heart for a new creation. This is not an effort to move beyond tragedy—this has taken care of itself; but to move beyond nihilism, or beyond the curse of the charge of human depravity and its consequent condemnation of us to despair; a charge which is itself, Emerson in effect declares, the only depravity ("New England Reformers").

(I may interject here that the idea of thinking as reception, which began this path of reasoning, seems to me to be a sound intuition, specifically to forward the correct answer to skepticism [which Emerson meant it to do]. The answer does not consist in denying the conclusion of skepticism but in reconceiving its truth. It is true that we do not know the existence of the world with certainty; our relation to its existence is deeper—one in which it is accepted, that is to say, received. My favorite way of putting this is to say that existence is to be acknowledged.)

So the similarity of Emerson with Heidegger can be seen as mediated by Nietzsche; and this will raise more questions than it can answer. As to the question of what may look like the direction of influence, I am not claiming that Heidegger authenticates the thinking of Emerson and Thoreau; the contrary is, for me, fully as true, that Emerson and Thoreau may authorize our interest in Heidegger. Then further questions will concern the relation of the thinking of each of these writers to their respective traditions of poetry. To the figure of Hölderlin, Heidegger is indebted not alone for lessons of thought but for lessons in reading, and I suppose for the lesson that these are not different, or rather that there is ground upon which thinking and reading and philosophy and poetry meet and part. Emerson's implication in the history of the major line of American poetry is something that Harold Bloom has most concretely and I dare say most unforgettably given to us to think through. Emerson's and Thoreau's relation to poetry is inherently their interest in their own writing; they are their own Hölderlins. I do not mean their interest in what we may call their poems, but their interest in the fact that what they are building is writing, that their writing is, as it realizes itself daily under their hands, sentence by shunning sentence, the accomplishment of inhabitation, the making of it happen, the poetry of it. Their prose is a battle, using a remark of Nietzsche's, not to become poetry; a battle specifically to remain in conversation with itself, answerable to itself. (So they do write dialogues, and not monologues, after all.)

Such writing takes the same mode of relating to itself as reading and thinking do, the mode of the self's relation to itself, call it self-reliance. Then whatever is required in possessing a self will be required in thinking and reading and writing. This possessing is not—it is the reverse of—possessive; I have implied that in being an act of creation, it is the exercise not of power but of reception. Then the question is: On what terms is the self received?

The answer I give for Emerson here is a theme of his thinking that further stands it with the later Heidegger's, the thing Emerson calls "onward thinking," the thing Heidegger means in taking thinking as a matter essentially of getting ourselves "on the way."

At the beginning of "Circles" Emerson tells us he means (having already deduced one moral in considering the circular or compensatory character of every human action) to trace a further analogy (or, read a further sense; or, deduce a further moral) from the emblem of the form of a circle. Since the time of "The American Scholar" he has told us that "science is nothing but the finding of analogy," and this seems a fair enough idea of thinking. In "Circles" he invites us to think about the fact, or what the fact symbolizes, that every action admits of being outdone, that around every circle another circle can take its place. I should like to extend the invitation to think about how he pictures us as moving from one circle to another, something he sometimes thinks of as expanding, sometimes as rising. I note that there is an ambiguity in his thoughts here as between what he calls the *generating* and what he calls the *drawing* of the new circle, an ambiguity between the picturing of new circles as forming continuously or discontinuously. I will not try to resolve this ambiguity now but I will take it that the essential way of envisioning our growth, from the inside, is as discontinuous. Then my questions are: How does Emerson picture us as crossing, or rather leaping, the span from one circumference to another? What is the motive, the means of motion, of this movement? How do we go on? (In Wittgenstein's *Philosophical Investigations*, knowing how to go on, as well as knowing when to stop, is exactly the measure of our knowing, or learning, in certain of its main regions or modes—for example, in the knowledge we have of our words. Onward thinking, on the way, knowing how to go on, are of course inflections or images of the religious idea of The Way, inflections which specifically deny that there is a place at which our ways end. Were philosophy to concede such a place, one knowable in advance of its setting out, philosophy would cede its own autonomy.)

You may imagine the answer to the question how we move as having to do with power. But power seems to be the result of rising, not the cause. ("Every new prospect is power" ["Circles"].) I take Emerson's answer to be what he means by "abandonment" (ibid.). The idea of abandonment contains what the preacher in Emerson calls "enthusiasm" or the New Englander in him calls "forgetting ourselves" (ibid.), together with what he calls leaving or relief or quitting or release or shunning or allowing or deliverance, which is freedom (as in "Leave your theory as Joseph his coat in the hand of the harlot, and flee" ["Self-Reliance"]), together further with something he means by trusting or suffering (as in the image of the traveler—the conscious intellect, the intellect alone—"who has lost his way, [throwing] his reins on the horse's neck, and [trusting] to the instinct of the animal to find his road" ["The Poet"]). (Perhaps it helps if you think, as he goes on to say, that what carries us through this world is a divine animal. To spell it out, the human is the rational divine animal. It's a thought—one, by the way, which Heidegger would deny.)

This idea of abandonment gives us a way to grasp the act Emerson pictures as "[writing] on the lintels of the door-post, Whim" ("Self-Reliance"). He says he would do this after he has said that he shuns father and mother and wife and brother when his genius calls him; and he follows it by expressing the hope that it is somewhat better than whim at last. (Something has happened; it is up to us to name it, or not to. Something is wrestling us for our blessing.) Whether his writing on the lintels—his writing as such, I gather—is thought of as having the constancy of the contents of a mezuzah or the emergency of the passover blood, either way he is taking upon himself the mark of God, and of departure. His perception of the moment is taken in hope, as something to be proven only on the way, *by* the way. This departure, such setting out, is, in our poverty, what hope consists in, all there is to hope for; it is the abandoning of despair, which is otherwise our condition. (Quiet desperation Thoreau will call it; Emerson had said, silent melancholy.) Hence he may speak of perception as "not Whimsical, but fatal" (ibid.), preeminently, here, the perception of what we may call whim. Our fatality, the determination of our fate, of whether we may hope, goes by our marking the path of whim. We hope it is better than whim at last, as we hope we may at last seem something better than blasphemers; but it is our poverty not to be final but always to be leaving (abandoning whatever we have and have known): to be initial, medial, American. What the ground of the fixated conflict between solipsism and realism should give way to—or between subjectivity and objectivity, or the private and the public, or the inner and the outer—is the task of onwardness. In Heidegger: "The *thanc* means man's inmost mind, the heart, the heart's core, that innermost essence of man which reaches outward most fully and to the outermost limits" (*What Is Called Thinking?*). In Emerson: "To believe your own thought, to believe that what is true for you in your private heart, is true for all men—that is genius. Speak your latent conviction and it shall be the universal sense; for always the inmost becomes the outmost" ("Self-Reliance"). The substantive disagreement with Heidegger, shared by Emerson and Thoreau, is that the achievement of the human requires not inhabitation and settlement but abandonment, leaving. Then everything depends upon your realization of abandonment. For the significance of leaving lies in its discovery that you have settled something, that you have felt enthusiastically what there is to abandon yourself to, that you can treat the others there are as those to whom the inhabitation of the world can now be left.

What's the Use of Calling Emerson a Pragmatist?

Stanley Cavell

In general I applaud the revival of interest in John Dewey and William James, on various intellectual and political grounds, and seek to learn what is at stake for others in their revival. But I also wish to suspend applause—doubtless more a transcendentalist than a pragmatist gesture on my part—for ideas that seem to be gaining prominence within this movement, expressed by writers and thinkers I admire, according to which Emerson is to be understood as a protopragmatist and Wittgenstein as, let us say, a neopragmatist. Perhaps I will be taken as struggling merely over labels; but sometimes labels should be struggled over.

In the course of working out certain implications of the teachings of the later Wittgenstein and of J. L. Austin, I have, in more recent years, variously recurred to an idea that their sense of the ordinary or everyday in language—as goal and as procedure in philosophy—is well thought of in connection with emphases in Emerson and in Thoreau on what they call the common, the familiar, the low, the near (what Emerson means by "having the day"). As Wittgenstein increasingly was called a pragmatist (or cited for his affinities with pragmatism) I wanted to ask whether John Dewey's reputation as the spokesman, even as the provider of a metaphysics, for the common man might throw some light on the dishearteningly dark matter of the philosophical appeal to the ordinary. Naturally I have felt that the appeal to the ordinary possesses political implications that have barely been touched. Yet I have not heretofore thought that the question of Dewey's relation to that appeal's implied politics of the ordinary—which intuitively seems to mean its pertinence to the democratic ideal—demanded thematizing. In particular, I mean the intuition that the democratic bearing of the philosophical appeal to the ordinary and its methods is at least as strong as, and perhaps in conflict with, its bearing on Dewey's homologous appeal to science and what he calls its method.

To attest my good faith in this struggle over terms such as pragmatism, transcendentalism, and ordinary language philosophy, I acknowledge that if Emerson is the founder of the difference in American thinking, then later American thinkers such as Dewey and James are going to be indebted to Emerson. What I deny is that their thinking, so far as it is recognizable as something distinctly called pragmatism, captures or clarifies or retains all that is rational or moral in the Emersonian event. I quote from my title essay in *Must We Mean What We Say?*: "Wittgenstein's role in combating the idea of privacy . . . and in emphasizing the functions and contexts of language, scarcely needs to be mentioned. It might be worth pointing out that these teachings are fundamental to American pragmatism; but then we must keep in mind how different their arguments sound, and admit that in philosophy it is the sound which makes all the difference."[1] The remarks to follow may be taken as a brief gloss on that observation.

One further prefatory remark. It has been said that pragmatists wish their writing, like all good writing, to work—that is, to make a difference. But does writing (or art more generally) work in the ways that logic or technology work; and do any of these work in the way social organization works? Emerson's essay "Experience" may be understood as written to mourn the death of his young son. Freud speaks of mourning as work, something Emerson quite explicitly declares it to be; and Freud speaks in these terms also of an aspect of dreaming.[2] Does the writing of Dewey or James help us understand this idea of work? If it is a viable idea, is it less important than what they understand work to be?

I will formulate in what follows a few differences between Dewey and James, who are uncontentiously pragmatists, and Emerson and Wittgenstein, who are only contentiously so, although I know these differences may be dismissible, roughly on pragmatic grounds. I will then sketch what I consider to be my stake in these matters.

The following sentence from Dewey's *Experience and Education* is, I assume, characteristic of what makes him Dewey: "Scientific method is the only authentic means at our command for getting at the significance of our everyday experiences of the world in which we live."[3] Perhaps Emerson was wrong to identify mourning as a pervasive character of what we know as experience, and perhaps, in any case, philosophy need not regard it as part of "the significance of our everyday experiences." Yet Emerson finds a work of what he understands as mourning to be the path to human objectivity with the world, to separating the world from ourselves, from our private interests in it. That understanding offers the possibility of moral relationship. According to Wittgenstein, "Concepts . . . are the expression of our interest, and direct our interest."[4] But interest is to be distinguished from whim, something I have regarded as the task to which Emerson dedicates his writing. Does science have anything different to say about mourning? Is it supposed to? Might one say that science has its own understanding of objectivity, call that intersubjectivity? It is an understanding that neither Emerson nor Wittgenstein can assume to be in effect; the human subject has first to be discovered, as something strange to itself.

Dewey's remark about scientific method as the authentic means for getting at the significance of our everyday experiences in effect insists that the works of men, requiring human intelligence, are part of this everyday. Of some of these works Emerson writes: "In every work of genius we recognize our own rejected thoughts; they come back to us with a certain alienated majesty."[5] Do not be put off by Emerson's liberal use of "genius." For him genius is, as with Plato, something each person has, not something certain people are. Emerson's remark about genius is a kind of definition of the term: If you find the return of your thoughts to be caused by a work in this way, then you are apt, and in a sense justified, to attribute this return to the genius of the work. You might even say that this kind of reading requires what Emerson calls experimenting, something Thoreau calls "trying" people. Does what you might call science, or its philosophy, have an understanding of this use of experimentation, experimentation as provocation? Is this use less important than the understanding science requires? How do the uses get close enough even to seem to conflict—close enough, perhaps, for someone to wish to call Thoreau's use a metaphorical one?

Dewey writes that pragmatism "is the formation of a faith in intelligence, as the one and indispensable belief necessary to moral and social life."[6] Compare this with Emerson: "To believe your own thought, to believe that what is true for you in your private heart is true for all men—that is genius." Emerson expresses what he calls the ground of his hope that man is one, that we are capable of achieving our commonness, by saying that "the deeper [the scholar] dives into his privatest, secretest presentiment, to his wonder he finds, this is the most acceptable, most public, and universally true."[7] Is this route to the universal compatible with what Dewey means by science and its method? This is evidently the most privileged route he envisions to the commonness of the human species, or at least to the reform of certain groupings of them and hence to the possibility of democracy.

I realize I have been shading these comparisons between Emerson and Dewey so as to emphasize a certain air of conflict in philosophy between the appeal to science and the appeal to ordinary language. This is where I came into philosophy. The earliest papers I still use were defenses of Austin's and Wittgenstein's appeals to the ordinary, papers that were attacked as irrational for apparently denying the findings of empirical science (i.e., of Noam Chomsky's new linguistics). Like most issues in philosophy, this one was not exactly settled; rather, each side continued to feel misunderstood, each took what it needed from the exchange, and each went its way. But the issue in various ways still concerns me, perhaps because I still want to understand the source of that philosophical hostility.

The philosophical appeal to the ordinary, to words we are given in common, is inherently taken in opposition to something about my words as they stand. Hence they are in opposition to those (typically philosophers) with whom I had hitherto taken myself to be in a state of intersubjectivity. This appeal presents proposals for what we say, which, requiring something like experimentation, are trials that inherently run the risk of exasperation. The appeal challenges our commonality in favor of a more genuine commonality (surely something that characterizes Dewey's philosophical mission), but in the name of no expertise, no standing adherence to logic or to science, to nothing beyond the genius that fits me for membership in the realm of ends.

William James characteristically philosophizes off of the language of the street, which he respects and wishes to preserve, or to satisfy by clarifying the desire it expresses. This mode of philosophizing seems to me quite uncharacteristic of Dewey. In Dewey's writing, the speech of others, whose ideas Dewey wishes to correct, or rather to replace, especially the speech of children, hardly appears—as though the world into which he is drawn to intervene suffers from a well-defined lack or benightedness. Contrast this with a memorable outburst from Emerson: "Every word they say chagrins us ... and we know not where to begin to set them right."[8] Before Emerson can say what is repellent in the thoughts or noises of others, he has to discover or rediscover a language in which to say it. This turns out to require an inheritance of philosophy that gives back life to the words it has thought to own—a language in which the traditional vocabulary of philosophy is variously brought to earth, concepts such as "experience," "idea," "impression," "understanding," "reason," "universal," "necessity," or "condition." Emerson retains stretches of the vocabulary of philosophy but divests it of its old claims to mastery. This is why his writing is *difficult* in a way no other American philosopher's (save Thoreau's) has been, certainly not that of James or of Dewey. Are these different responses to language not philosophically fundamental? They seem so to me.

I suggested that I also rather cringe at the idea of thinking of Wittgenstein as a sort of pragmatist, or as having a significant pragmatist dimension to his thought. Hilary Putnam, who is more confident here than I, ends the middle of three lectures entitled *Pragmatism* identifying a central—perhaps, he says, the central—emphasis of pragmatism: its emphasis on the primacy of practice.[9]

I think we must agree that something like this emphasis is definitive for pragmatism. Then look at two passages from Wittgenstein that, I believe, are taken to suggest his affinity with pragmatism. There is, first, the always quoted passage from the *Investigations*: "If I have exhausted the grounds I have reached bedrock, and my spade is turned. Then I am inclined to say: 'This is simply what I do.'"[10] I shall not go over my own grounds for the view of this remark I have urged elsewhere, but merely repeat my conclusion, namely that this passage does not represent a call for the display of a practice at this crossroads. On the contrary, it expresses silence, the recognition that all invocable practices have been canvassed, thus preparing one, providing words, for suffering, awaiting, an inevitable crossroads in the act of teaching. The one who has reached bedrock here describes himself as "inclined to say" something, which at the same time implies that he finds the words that occur to him to be unsayable, empty, their time gone. Saul Kripke is the most prominent of those who understand that passage as equivalent to asserting a practice.

A second passage, or a pair of passages, this time from *On Certainty*,[11] have recently been taken to declare Wittgenstein's pragmatist leanings. At §422: "So I am trying to say something that sounds like pragmatism. Here I am being thwarted by a kind of *Weltanschauung*." But isn't this to say that sounding like pragmatism is not welcome but burdensome to Wittgenstein? It thwarts his making himself sufficiently clear. (I think I know just how that feels.) The previous section reads: "I am in England.— Everything around me tells me so. . . .—But might I not be shaken if things such as I don't dream of at present were to happen?" This conjunction of sections sounds like a combination expressed at §89: "One would like to say: 'Everything speaks for, and nothing against, the earth's having existed long before.' . . . Yet might I not believe the contrary after all? But the question is: What would the practical effects of this belief be?—Perhaps someone says: 'That's not the point. A belief is what it is whether it has any practical effects or not.' One thinks: It is the same adjustment of the human mind anyway." It is fairly clear that Wittgenstein is dismissing, through interpreting the fantasy of, the one who thinks that practical effects are impertinent to what it is one believes, and indeed to whether one may seriously be said to believe something. At the same time, he is casting suspicion on the introduction of the concept of "believing the contrary."

Questioning the practical effects of a belief does sound like William James, for instance in this passage from "What Pragmatism Means": "The whole function of philosophy ought to be to find out what definite difference it will make to you and me, at definite instants of our life, if this world-formula or that world-formula be the true one."[12] But Wittgenstein's passage had better not be taken to encourage James' evident faith in practicality.

Wittgenstein's case about the earth's existence long before is one in which someone has been led to forget how specialized, even how *weak*, a consideration is in question in saying, in reasonably clear circumstances, "Everything speaks for and nothing speaks against." It is perhaps enough to voice the consideration when the issue is, say, a choice to buy rather than rent a house, under circumstances in which: we already accept that we must do one or the other (that is, the basic decision to move has already been made); the length of stay is not fixed, but the family is committed to at least three years; buying, especially with help available from an institution, will almost certainly save money in the long run; it is not that much more trouble; and so, obviously, on. "Obviously" implies that there is a notable lack of enthusiasm over either prospect. If it were a great house, and an amazing bargain, where the family can at once imagine friends happily visiting, then perhaps it is smitten, and would forget the mild balancing springs of advantages and disadvantages. In other circumstances, to give "everything for and nothing against" as a conclusive reason—say for a couple living together or just going away together for a weekend—would be discouraging. (I take it that *desiring* to be or to go together is not one among other reasons for doing either but is rather the condition for anything counting as a reason, for or against.) And if one is led (for some undetermined reason) to offer so weak and summary a support for so presumably massive a structure as the existence of the earth long before, one places the ensuing, forced invocations of the practical effects of a belief in a perfectly impotent position; they are mere words. (Compare what Wittgenstein writes in the *Philosophical Investigations*: "[A] hundred reasons present themselves, each drowning the voice of the others.")[13]

One moral to draw is that, as my *Claim of Reason* claims, throughout his *Investigations* Wittgenstein is in struggle with the threat of skepticism, as Emerson is (after the big essay on *Nature*). In contrast, neither James nor Dewey seems to take the threat of skepticism seriously. This is hasty. James' treatment of the "sick soul" intersects with something I mean to capture in the concept of skepticism. But on James' account, it does not seem imaginable that *everyone* might be subject to this condition. That is, James perceives the condition as of a particular temperament, not as something coincident with the human as such, as if, as with the skeptical threat that concerns me, it is the necessary consequence of the gift of speech. Or shall we, rather than drawing a moral, lay down definitions that distinguish skeptical pragmatists from nonskeptical pragmatists? To what end? Pragmatism seems designed to refuse to take skepticism seriously, as it refuses—in Dewey's, if not always in James' case—to take metaphysical distinctions seriously.

However, I do not wish either to draw or define lines, but here merely to state differences. I know, as I said, that each of the differences I have mentioned can be rejected or reduced in significance. What is important to me is what I find to be at stake in asserting the differences.

I end by noting, against the idea of pragmatism's attention to practice, Emerson's peroration to "Experience": "I have not found that much was gained by manipular attempts to realize the world of thought. . . . Patience and patience, we shall win at the last."[14] It is hard not to take this plea of Emerson's for suffering and for waiting as pretty flatly the negation of the primacy of practice. Yet things are not so simple. Patience, as in the more obvious case of Thoreau's visible withdrawal or disinvestment from his neighbors, can be exercised aggressively, as an agent of change. Without pursuing the decisive matter of how change is to come, I will let this apparent difference of practice and patience, action and passion we might say, project a difference in the audiences (that is, in the conceptions of audience) at work in the writing of Dewey and of Emerson.

Dewey seeks to address a situation of unintelligence, which I suppose is to say, one that negates whatever predicates of intelligence a philosopher holds dearest, hence a situation that variously manifests superstition, bigotry, gullibility, and incuriousness. In a similar vein Emerson discerns a scene of what he variously calls conformity, timidity, and shame, something he describes as secret melancholy (the condition Thoreau will more famously name quiet desperation), which he perceives to characterize the lives of "the mass of men." The connection between massive unintelligence and general despair is that both are barriers to the future, to the new day whose appearance both Emerson and Dewey, in their ways, would hasten. But the ways are as different as the accompanying ideas of the future; they amount to different ideas of thinking, or reason. I once characterized the difference between Dewey and Emerson by saying that Dewey wanted to get the Enlightenment to happen in America while Emerson was in the later business of addressing the costs of the way it has happened. And again, one may deny that the differences between Enlightenment and post-Enlightenment projects are decisive enough to dislodge the idea of Emerson as a pragmatist, or perhaps take pragmatism as, in James' term, mediating between the two.

To my mind, to understand Emerson as essentially the forerunner of pragmatism is perhaps to consider pragmatism as representing more effectively or rationally what Emerson had undertaken to bring to these shores. This is the latest in the sequence of repressions of Emerson's thought by the culture he helped to found, of what is distinctive in that thought. Such a repression has punctuated Emerson's reputation from the first moment he could be said to have acquired one. So my question becomes: What is lost if Emerson's voice is lost?

In its call for intelligent action, Dewey's writing is self-evidently and famously active. And famous problems with it are, first, that you do not know what in particular he wants you to do, and second, that you do not know whether it is rational to expect the mass of men and women to exercise intelligence in their politics any more than in their religions. You might say that Dewey's writing is a wager on democracy, a wager that is rational not because of the weight of evidence that his writing will prove effective, but because it is worthy of being listened to; because there is some reason to believe that it will be listened to; and because there is no other future worth wagering on and working to achieve.

Emerson's writing, too, is a wager, not exactly of itself as the necessary intellectual preparation for a better future, but rather of itself as a present step into that future, two by two. It cannot be entered alone. ("Two . . . abreast" is the attitude between neighbors that Robert Frost advises in "Mending Wall.") Emerson writes in "Self-Reliance": "But do your work, and I shall know you."[15] Your work now, in reading him, is the reading of his page, and allowing yourself to be changed by it. I have, accordingly, wished to place Emerson's writing in a tradition of perfectionist writing that extends in the West from Plato to Nietzsche, Ibsen, Kierkegaard, Wilde, Shaw, Heidegger, and Wittgenstein. Both Dewey and Emerson are necessary for what each of them thinks of as democracy. To repress Emerson's difference is to deny that America is as transcendentalist as it is pragmatist, that it is in struggle with itself, at a level not articulated by what we understand as the political. But what Dewey calls for, other disciplines can do as well, maybe better, than philosophy. What Emerson calls for is something we do not want to hear, something about the necessity of patience or suffering in allowing ourselves to change. What discipline will call for this if philosophy does not?

Notes

1   This essay, dating from 1957, is the earliest essay of mine that I still use (Stanley Cavell, *Must We Mean What We Say?* [New York: Scribner, 1969], p. 36, n.10).

2   Ralph Waldo Emerson, "Experience," in *Essays and Lectures* (New York: Library of America, 1983), p. 473; Sigmund Freud, "Mourning and Melancholia," *Collected Papers* (New York: Basic Books, 1959), vol. 4, pp. 153–154.

3   John Dewey, *Experience and Education*, in *The Later Works*, ed. Jo Ann Boydston (Carbondale: Southern Illinois University, 1984), vol. 13, p. 59.

4   Ludwig Wittgenstein, *Philosophical Investigations*, trans. G. E. M. Anscombe (New York: Macmillan, 1951), sec. 570.

5   Emerson, "Self-Reliance," in *Essays and Lectures*, p. 259.

6   John Dewey, "The Development of American Pragmatism," in *Philosophy and Civilization* (New York: Capricorn Books, 1963), pp. 34–35.

7   Emerson, "The American Scholar," in *Essays and Lectures*, p. 64.

8   Emerson, "Self-Reliance," p. 264.

9   Hilary Putnam, *Pragmatism: An Open Question* (Cambridge: Basil Blackwell, 1995).

10 Wittgenstein, *Philosophical Investigations*, sec. 217.

11 Ludwig Wittgenstein, *On Certainty*, ed. G. E. M. Anscombe and G. H. von Wright, trans. Denis Paul and G. E. M. Anscombe (New York: Harper & Row, 1972).

12 William James, "What Pragmatism Means," in *Essays in Pragmatism*, ed. Alburey Castell (New York: Hafner Publishing Company, 1948), p. 141. Earlier, James emphasized the practical rather than definite difference.

13 Wittgenstein, *Philosophical Investigations*, sec. 478.

14 Emerson, "Experience," p. 492.

15 Robert Frost, "Mending Wall," in *The Poetry of Robert Frost*, ed. Edward Connery Lathem (New York: Holt, Rinehart and Winston, 1969), p. 33; Emerson, "Self-Reliance," p. 264.

from *Cities of Words: Pedagogical Letters on a Register of the Moral Life*

Stanley Cavell

IN THE PLACE OF THE CLASSROOM

The first of the epigraphs I have placed as guardians or guides at the entrance to this book—"I know that the world I converse with in the cities and in the farms, is not the world I *think*"—opens the concluding paragraph of Emerson's "Experience." It captures one of Kant's summary images of his colossal *Critiques*, epitomized in the *Groundwork of the Metaphysics of Morals*, namely that of the human being as regarding his existence from two standpoints, from one of which he counts himself as belonging to the world of sense (the province of the knowledge of objects and their causal laws, presided over by the human understanding), and from the other of which he counts himself as belonging to the intelligible world (the province of freedom and of the moral law, presided over by reason, transcending the human powers of knowing). But each of the thinkers and artists we will encounter in the following pages may be said to respond to some such insight of a split in the human self, of human nature as divided or double.

Emerson's variation of the insight (not unlike John Stuart Mill's) is to transfigure Kant's metaphysical division of worlds into a rather empirical (or political) division of the world, in which the way we now hold the world in bondage is contrasted with, reformed into, a future way we could help it to become (this is not exactly foreign to Kant). Plato's variation—or rather Plato's vision of which Kant's is a variation—is that the world of sense is a degraded scene or shadow of an intelligible world which can be entered only by those fit to govern the world perfectly, that is, with perfect justice. Locke's vision is between a world of nature ruled by power and violence and a world of the political created by common human consent. Ibsen's division, in *A Doll's House*, is between an incomprehensibly unjust present world and a world of freedom and reciprocity which is almost unthinkable, which only human instinct and risk can begin to divine and describe. Freud's sense of our division shows the details of the private epic in which the world we do not know we know rules the world we imagine we know. Shakespeare's late romance *The Winter's Tale* posits, in its longest act, a pastoral world of song and dance and familiar mischief which is a kind of dream of the actual world, one in which the various roles into which the arbitrariness of birth and accident have cast us—kings, princesses, merchants, clowns, peasants—are occupied by those whose natures exactly fit them for these roles, in which indeed there would be no need for "roles," since all members of such a society would know and receive pleasure and reward from their natural, and naturally modifiable, constellation of positions.

And so forth. Each of these variations provides a position from which the present state of human existence can be judged and a future state achieved, or else the present judged to be better than the cost of changing it. The very conception of a divided self and a doubled world, providing a perspective of judgment upon the world as it is, measured against the world as it may be, tends to express disappointment with the world as it is, as the scene of human activity and prospects, and perhaps to lodge the demand or desire for a reform or transfiguration of the world. So common is this pattern of disappointment and desire, in part or whole, as represented in the philosophical figures to follow here, that I think of it as the moral calling of philosophy, and name it moral perfectionism, a register of the moral life that precedes, or intervenes in, the specification of moral theories which define the particular bases of moral judgments of particular acts or projects or characters as right or wrong, good or bad.

An idea of the moral calling of philosophy as such inspires the American event in philosophy, as philosophy is discovered by Emerson. In putting Emerson first— say this is making the last first, looking back over the history of philosophy from the perspective of that re-beginning—I accordingly wish here to accent that history differently from the way it presents itself to philosophers who begin their sense of philosophy's re-beginning in the modern era with the response, in Bacon and in Descartes and in Locke, to the traumatic event of the New Science of Copernicus and Galileo and Newton, for which the basis of human knowledge of the world rather than of human conduct in that world is primary among philosophical preoccupations. It is familiar to describe modern philosophy as dominated by epistemology, the theory of knowledge, making the fields of moral philosophy and the philosophy of art and of religion secondary, even optional. My claim for Emerson's achievement is not exactly that he reverses this hierarchy but rather that he refuses the breakup of philosophy into separate fields, an eventuality fully institutionalized as philosophy becomes one discipline among others in the modern university. (Such a refusal can be understood to manifest itself in the writing of Wittgenstein and of Heidegger. But in these cases this aspect of the writing is, for reasons yet unarticulated, ignorable at will.) So that Emerson's effort to reclaim or re-begin philosophy as such on these new, perhaps intellectually inhospitable, shores ("these bleak rocks"), is precisely what keeps him from being recognized, either by friends or by enemies, as a philosopher.

The sense of disappointment with the world as a place in which to seek the satisfaction of human desire is not the same as a sense of the world as cursed, perhaps at best to be endured, perhaps as a kind of punishment for being human. This sense of existence cursed requires not merely a philosophical but a religious perspective. I do not, in what follows, take up perfectionisms based on a religious perspective, any more than I regard the perfectionism I do follow out as requiring an imagination of some ultimate human perfection. Emersonian perfectionism, on the contrary, with which I begin and to which I most often recur, specifically sets itself against any idea of ultimate perfection.

But if the world is disappointing and the world is malleable and hence we feel ourselves called upon for change, where does change begin, with the individual (with myself) or with the collection of those who make up my (social, political) world? This question seems to make good sense if we contrast Emerson or Freud with, say, Locke or Marx (who is not featured in these pages but puts in a distinct cameo appearance), but its sense is questioned as we consider what perfectionist encounters look and sound like. I would say, indeed, that it is a principal object of Emerson's thinking to urge a reconsideration of the relation ("the" relation?) of soul and society, especially as regards the sense of priority of one over the other. I take seriously, that is, Emerson's various formulations of the idea that, as he words it in "The American Scholar," "The deeper [the scholar] dives into his privatest, secretest presentiment, to his wonder he finds this is the most acceptable, most public, and universally true." By taking it seriously I mean I find it intuitively valuable enough that I am moved to work with it in making it plainer. It bears directly on what I have called the arrogance of philosophy, its claim to speak universally, to discover the bases of existence as such.

In Emerson, as in Wittgenstein's *Investigations*, I encounter the social in my every utterance and in each silence. Sometimes this means that I find in myself nothing but social, dictated thoughts (the condition Emerson opposes as "conformity," what philosophy has forever called the unexamined life); sometimes it means that I find in the social nothing but chaos (Emerson cries out, "Every word they say chagrins us"). What I conceive as the moral calling of philosophy is what I conceive the Freudian intervention in Western culture to have responded to. If I say that philosophy, as influenced by the later Wittgenstein, is therapeutically motivated, this does not mean, as some philosophers have construed it, that we are to be cured of philosophy, but that contemporary philosophy is to understand its continuity with the ancient wish of philosophy to lead the soul, imprisoned and distorted by confusion and darkness, into the freedom of the day. (A condition of philosophy is that the day not absolutely be closed to freedom, by tyranny or by poverty.) Freud perpetually distinguished his work from that of philosophy, recognizing that what he meant by the unconscious of experience and speech challenged philosophy's understanding of consciousness (I take it for granted that philosophy had no systematic understanding of the unconscious). I believe that Freud's stance against what he called philosophy has proved unfortunate both for philosophy and for psychoanalysis. It is my impression that Lacan's way of overcoming that stance only served to harden its prevalence in the United States. Perhaps those days are passing.

The sense of disappointment I find in the origin of the moral calling of philosophy is something that I have derived principally from my reading of Wittgenstein, most particularly his *Philosophical Investigations*, where the human being perpetually attacks its everyday life as intellectually lacking in certainty or fastidiousness or accuracy or immediacy or comprehensiveness and is compelled to search for an order or a system or a language that would secure a human settlement with the world that goes beyond human sense and certainty. Sometimes Wittgenstein describes or pictures this as a search or demand for the absolute, which he more generally names the metaphysical. Wittgenstein's principal contrast with the metaphysical is what he calls the ordinary or the everyday, a perpetual topic in the pages to follow here. Where Wittgenstein describes his effort in philosophy as one of "returning words from their metaphysical to their everyday use," I habitually speak of the task of accepting finitude. The attempt to satisfy the demand for the absolute makes what we say inherently private (as though we withheld the sense of our words even, or especially, from ourselves), a condition in which the good city we would inhabit cannot be constructed, since it exists only in our intelligible encounters with each other. The philosophical outlook of Deweyan pragmatism, considerably more prominent in contemporary American intellectual life, at least in American academic life, than Emersonianism, is equally devoted to discarding empty quests for the absolute. But for my taste pragmatism misses the depth of human restiveness, or say misses the daily, insistent split in the self that being human cannot, without harm to itself (beyond moments of ecstasy) escape, and so pragmatism's encouragement for me, while essential, is limited.

Wittgenstein's disappointment with knowledge is not that it fails to be better than it is (for example, immune to skeptical doubt), but rather that it fails to make us better than we are, or provide us with peace.

The sequence of texts I devote attention to—while just about all of the texts are monsters of fame—is too selective to count as a proposed canon of reading in moral philosophy, even for one register of moral thinking. The severity of selectiveness in limiting the number of principal texts to the number of weeks of the course from which this book derives was itself limited by the hope that each text could receive enough of a consecutive exposition from me to prompt and allow my reader to go on with it alone. Any sensible teacher (myself half the time) will find the pace too fast. But any fewer texts would not, it seems to me, give a sense of the magnitude and variousness of the register of moral thinking I wish to bring to attention.

I have been guided in my specific selection by two main considerations: first, to show the persistence of a family of articulations of the moral life in modern thought (say from the time of Shakespeare and, in the following generations, in the work of Milton and of Locke) that begins most famously in Western culture with the beginning of philosophy marked by Plato and Aristotle; second, to include texts that no serious (or say professional) philosophical discussion of moral reasoning would be likely to neglect, but at the same time to insist upon the pertinence of further (literary) texts that few professional philosophical discussions, or courses, would feel pressured to acknowledge. The inclusion of the films that accompany the discursive texts here is meant to help in exerting such pressure, but no professor of philosophy should be expected to feel that their omission would intellectually be much of a loss, let alone unsafe. Nor would I wish to give the impression that philosophy left to itself requires compensation by revelations within the medium of film. These films are rather to be thought of as differently configuring intellectual and emotional avenues that philosophy is already in exploration of, but which, perhaps, it has cause sometimes to turn from prematurely, particularly in its forms since its professionalization, or academization, from say the time of Kant (the first modern to show that, major philosophy can be produced by a professor, namely within a discipline that is one among other university disciplines). The implied claim is that film, the latest of the great arts, shows philosophy to be the often invisible accompaniment of the ordinary lives that film is so apt to capture (even, perhaps particularly, when the lives depicted are historical or elevated or comic or hunted or haunted).

While the wisdom in discussing a text of Emerson's first is something whose fruitfulness can only manifest itself as the sequence develops, there are reasons for it that can be given at the outset. One reason is that the primary body of Hollywood films to be adduced here may be understood as inspired by Emersonian transcendentalism. Another is that Emerson brings to philosophy dimensions of human concern that the field of philosophy, in its Anglo-American academic dispensation, in which I was trained, particularly discouraged, not to say disheartened. Matters have modified themselves to some degree over the decades since I began writing, but Emerson continues to suggest for me, for example, a remarkably apt source of paths between the Anglo-American dispensation of philosophy and the German-French.

The hard division of the philosophical mind between these dispensations has been costly to academic life, hence to intellectual life more generally, if less assessibly, in the humanities and the humanistically interested social studies in these decades. The division has served, for example, to deepen the suspicion between literary studies in America and American pedagogy in philosophy, the former so often hungrily incorporating the primarily French structuralist and post-structuralist theory that began in the late 1960s, the latter equally often holding this material in contempt. It may seem paradoxical, or irrelevant, to understand Emerson as a bridge between these philosophical dispensations since he is not widely accepted as a formidable philosophical thinker in either of them. So it figures that my fascination with Emerson has been a gift whose value I can neither renounce nor easily share.

I came late, as Emerson in his American context came late, to philosophy. This is not particular to me (merely exaggerated, as I spent the years of my life through college as a musician); it is reflected in such facts as that philosophy is not a regular part of an American high school education and that the field of American studies was formed by an association of literary study and historical study, with philosophy left, or leaving itself, out. Emerson's response, in his new world, to his irresistible want of philosophy was to include habitually in his writing any and all of the vocabulary of philosophy—from ideas and degrees of participation in ideas, to impressions as the origin of ideas, to the extinction of accident and necessity, and reason and understanding, and fate and freedom, and possibility and actuality, and theory and practice. But he often introduces terms from this vocabulary in ways that disguise their origin, hence he allows an assessment of these terms by testing whether they hold up under the pressure of ordinary speech.

When he says, in "Fate," "Ideas are in the air," can we doubt that he is invoking Plato's theory of forms at the same time that he is speaking, in 1850, of the absorbing issue of slavery, as if inquiring as to our participation in, call it our stance toward, these ideas? He goes on to follow out the literal consequence that something essential to our lives, the air we breathe, would be fatal to us but for the fact that our lungs are already filled with this air, allowing us to withstand the weight and pressure of air from above by the counterpressure of that air from within ourselves. This becomes, I take it, a parable whose moral is that the issue of slavery is a matter of life and death, for the nation and for the nation's breath, its speech, its power to understand itself, and therewith for philosophy, whose demand for freedom is incompatible with slavery. (This incompatibility may be denied, or repressed. It once helped me to assert a difference between the idea that some people may rightly be made slaves and the idea that some group of people are inherently slaves, something other than exactly human. The former idea is merely hideous. Holders of the latter idea are accursed.) A leaf I take from Emerson's essays is the sense of writing philosophy from belated America as if this locale is the remaining place where one can take philosophy by surprise, I mean with surprise at the fact that there should be such an enterprise that measures the value of our lives. The familiar recognition that famous philosophers have failed to understand their predecessors, or say to do them justice, should perhaps be seen less as a matter of a need to transcend past achievements than as an effort to discover philosophy for oneself, as if philosophy exists only in its discovery.

What impels me to such a course, risking impertinence, is that America (unless I specify otherwise, I use this term as shorthand for the United States), in refusing Emerson's bid for philosophy, has not to my mind sufficiently joined philosophically in measuring the value of our lives (unless perhaps one conceives that its literary accomplishments are its philosophy). Contemporary American philosophy has dominated the worldwide development of analytical philosophy, for which, in Quine's words, "philosophy of science is philosophy enough." It perhaps also dominates the field of moral philosophy, but with a, perhaps well-deserved, distrust of the rest of philosophy. And pragmatism, in its classical writers and in its contemporary forms, to the extent that I know them, does not, as I have suggested, seem to know what half of my life is, the half that is not subject to superstition or fanaticism or magic thinking (the traditional black beasts stalked by Enlightenment thought), but that is fraught with, let us say, disproportionate invitations to disappointment and chaos, to the sense of the public world as one in which "every word they say chagrins us."

But consider that there are no *other* words to say than the words everyone is saying. Hence each of the words at Emerson's disposal is one that he has found used in a tone or place or out of some inattentiveness or meanness that requires unswerving examination. His language is hence in continuous struggle with itself, as if he is having to translate, in his American idiom, English into English. I think Emerson is thus dramatizing a dissatisfaction with everyday language that philosophers congenitally sense. A persistent philosophical attempt to cure this dissatisfaction with the everyday is to link philosophical language with logic as in the work of Frege and Russell, initiating what has become known as analytical philosophy. When the later Wittgenstein and J. L. Austin, in a counter development of this dispensation, declare philosophy's reclamation of ordinary language, they are at the same time suggesting that logic provides not a solution to this dissatisfaction but a substitute satisfaction (which may indeed be all that is rationally attainable), and they are undertaking to demonstrate that only ordinary language is powerful enough to overcome its own inherent tendency to succumb to metaphysical denunciations of its apparent vagueness, imprecision, superstition—not overcome this once for all, but in each incidence of our intellectual and spiritual chagrin.

A sense of the struggle of language with itself forces a certain liberation in interpreting texts that seems to some to go beyond the apparent evidence of their words. Here I recall Emerson's repeated idea that serious writers write beyond themselves, or as he also puts the matter, that character (meaning our constitution and our writing) teaches above our will. So that to understand serious writing will precisely require us to question what a text asserts in order to arrive at the conviction that we are covering the ground gained in what its words actually contrive to say.

EMERSON

I spoke in the Introduction of moments of humiliation or humbling in remarriage comedy, as a prelude to overcoming the vice of snobbery. It happens that Emerson's "Self-Reliance," at the close of its opening paragraph, describes, and I would say recalls and enacts, a scene of a certain humbling, or chastening, or shaming, in particular of being humbled by the words of someone else, a scene that takes many forms in both the comedies and the melodramas we will consider.

> In every work of genius we recognize our own rejected thoughts; they come back to us with a certain alienated majesty. Great works of art have no more affecting lesson for us than this. They teach us to abide by our spontaneous impression with good-humored inflexibility then most when the whole cry of voices is on the other side. Else tomorrow a stranger will say with masterly good sense precisely what we have thought and felt all the time, and we shall be forced to take with shame our own opinion from another.

In my saying Emerson is here enacting as well as describing a scene of humbling or shaming, I mean that he is to be taken as presenting an instance of a work of genius (but what this means is a matter he will go on to examine, has already, if invisibly, begun examining in his speaking of "abiding by our impression"), in the face of which we are free to test our capacity for shame (or perhaps for congenial company, in case we know ourselves to be clear of his charge). Why has he begun with a little lesson in reading (the opening words of the essay are "I read the other day")? In particular, the idea of words presenting themselves to us with majesty is virtually a definition of the emotion of the sublime, a mode much in favor in the Romanticism which is one source of Emerson's writing, and the theory of which in recent memory was at the forefront of literary theory. (Emerson's insight that this feeling of majesty is alienated and—or because—projected out of being rejected by us, is the kind of insight I have learned to expect of Emerson.) And why does he, or where does he get the confidence to, ask us to let his work teach us, or warn us, to change our ways?

Without trying to answer at once a question that the whole of Emerson's essay is about, I can already ask you to have in mind the question whether the sound of this writing is a sound you would expect from philosophy. Serious theology, or psychoanalysis, would seem more to the point. Here again I shall not try to answer at once—but I can at least say this much by way of anticipation. I myself experienced, especially after writing a little book on Thoreau's *Walden*, a sort of cringe in trying to get back into Emerson, a recoil from what struck me as his perpetual and irritating intertwining of lyricism and cajoling. Yet I was convinced, from my experience with *Walden*, that some such mode of writing may lend itself to a systematic thoughtfulness in a way only the name of philosophy suits. And, since it is obvious that *Walden* is in conversation with Emerson's writing in every page, and since nothing before Emerson in America is philosophically ambitious and original on this scale, it is reasonable to conclude that what we have in these two writers is nothing less than the origins of the American difference in philosophical thought, as this enters into a new well of American literary ambition on these shores. I will make a perhaps smaller, if no clearer, claim for Emerson's "Self-Reliance" than that it is philosophy. I will say it calls for philosophy, intermittently by quoting or parodying undoubted and familiar philosophy. Nothing has nourished my conviction in this matter more than the number and fervor of people who have gone out of their way to deny that Emerson is capable of challenging philosophy.

The question of Emerson's powers as a philosopher has been raised about his work from early in his career and fame, from 1848 when James Russell Lowell in his recounting of American letters to his time referred to Emerson's prose as a "mist" (and because Lowell admired Emerson, he qualified his epithet by describing it as a "golden" mist). And throughout most of the century and a half since, it has continued repeatedly to be called, by admirers and detractors, something like a fog—rather discouraging attempts to read it with trust in its intellectual originality and accuracy. Why should we still be concerned with this question—of philosophicality, let's say? In today's environment, or in some regions of it, it would be acceptable to identify our age as one of post-philosophy and indeed to praise Emerson for his avoidance or transcendence of the question. I think he is to be praised—though less for avoiding the issue than for facing it in his own way. But again, if we can say that Emerson is a useful, interesting, moving, provocative writer, whose powers increase with increased attention to them, why bother about whether he is called a philosopher or something else, or nothing but a writer?

There are several reasons why it matters. First, it matters to me because I do not want a text to be denied the title of philosophy on the ground that it does not exactly take the form you might expect of philosophy. The denial of the title tends to excuse the tendency to refrain from putting much intellectual pressure on Emerson's words, to refrain from accepting the invitation of those words to get past their appearance, if I can put it so.

Second, it matters to Emerson's idea of himself, of his task, or fate, as a writer. The question whether he speaks with philosophical authority—and if not, with what authority—is an undertone, I find, of his prose throughout, connected, I cannot doubt, with the crisis in his life as a result of giving up the questionable, for him, authority of the pulpit. To give up on the question would be to give up following the way Emerson's prose questions itself. (As when, in the opening of "Self-Reliance," he describes the impressions he inscribes as merely those already rejected by the reader—leaving it open how far his own work of genius is to undo the alienation of the majesty that is the cost of the reception of other such works. The self-questioning is hence simultaneously a questioning of his audience, of those he writes for, taking the form of asking what reading is.) Third, it matters to the idea of moral perfectionism, which is somehow bound up with an idea of a philosophical way or imagination of life. Fourth, I think the ambiguity in whether or not Emerson is to be received as a philosopher may be key in working on another pervasive puzzle in the reception of Emerson, namely that he has endeared himself both to politically radical and to politically conservative temperaments.

These standing issues form a good place from which to approach the text of "Self-Reliance" more intensively, if not more consecutively. It is as familiar an American text as exists, and because for some the text, or its sound, will seem so familiar that it can seem we do not know whether we understand it at all—that it is indeed as unresistant or unsupportive as mist—I have adopted the strategy of isolating a few sentences, in pairs, torn from their contexts in that essay, in order to force us to stop over them. I adopt the strategy also because everyone knows that, but no one finds it easy to say how, the Emersonian sentence is a remarkable achievement, bearing somehow the brunt of what Emerson has to say, or to do, and often making it difficult to see how his paragraphs, let alone what he calls his Essays, hang together. I'm suggesting we don't even know what makes the sentences themselves hang together, what produces that perpetual air of understanding and not understanding, insight and obscurity.

As an introduction to the exemplary yoking of sentences I shall cite in a moment, I repeat ones I have in the past often been glad to invoke. I have in mind Emerson's saying: "The virtue most in request in society is conformity. Self-reliance is its aversion."

Immediately, as with Emerson's allusion to his own writing in speaking of returning rejected thoughts, thoughts we all have had, however bathed in mist (which we might project upon Emerson), here, in saying "Self-reliance is its aversion," he is pretty explicitly naming his own writing, as represented in his essay "Self-Reliance," as saying of itself that it is written in aversion, aversion to conformity. And since the work of the word "conformity" in its sentence is to name a virtue, a contribution to a way of life, the implication is that his writing in self-reliance exhibits or enacts a contribution to a counter way of life. "Aversion" is a striking word, not to be taken lightly as a description of his writing as such. It invokes the preacher's word once familiar to his life, that of conversion, and accordingly should raise the question whether the turning implied in conversion and aversion is to be understood as a turning away from the society that demands conformity more than as a turning toward it, as in a gesture of confrontation.

And which comes first, conformity or its aversion? Is the idea that we experience the demands of conformity, and either obey them or else find that reliance upon oneself demands, and provides in return, ways to confront those who guard and impose conformity? The demand of conformity would accordingly demand that I justify my wayward life (not at this stage criminal, but, say, critical, discomfiting), and the provision of justification, as exemplified by the self-reliance of Emerson's writing, takes the form of making myself intelligible to those concerned. (This is precisely what Thoreau stages himself as attempting to do, as he simultaneously suggests the magnitude of the task, on the opening page of *Walden*: "I . . . require of every writer, first or last, a simple and sincere account of his own life, and not merely what he has heard of other men's lives; some such account as he would send to his kindred from a distant land, for if he has lived sincerely, it must have been in a distant land to me.") Or is it the other way around—that I find myself outside, sensing a lack of justification for my existence, and interpret this as a call for conformity, showing that a rapprochement with others is something I also, other things equal, desire?

Either way, this perplexity seems particularly to mark that fateful moment of each human existence at which, given at least a minimum sense of political freedom and justice in your society, you recognize that you participate in your society's work and profit from it, you understand that you are—as liberal political theory puts the matter—asked to show your *consent* to that society, to recognize the legitimacy of its governing you. We shall see this centrally in Locke's *Second Treatise of Government* and reinterpreted in John Rawls's *A Theory of Justice*. A standing problem with this idea is that it remains unclear what it is that shows or expresses your consent. (This is a burning question for Thoreau, in *Walden* as well as in his deeply influential essay "Civil Disobedience," known to be an inspiration for both Mahatma Gandhi and Martin Luther King Jr.)

Let's put this demand as the expectation of your "taking your place" in society. And let's suppose that you do not see the place, or do not like the places you see. You may of course take on the appearance of accepting the choices, and this may present itself to you as your having adopted a state of fraudulence, a perpetual sense of some false position you have assumed, without anyone's exactly having placed you there. A mark of this stage is a sense of obscurity, to yourself as well as to others, one expression of which is a sense of compromise, of being asked to settle too soon for the world as it is, a perplexity in relating yourself to what you find unacceptable in your world, without knowing what you can be held responsible for. Do I, for example, consent to the degree of injustice we all live with? Do I know how to define my position with respect to it? Since it probably doesn't make sense for me either to assume direct responsibility for it or to deny all indirect responsibility for it, where do I stand?

I am assuming that we can all recognize such moments in our lives. They are not confined to the period between adolescence and the claims of adulthood, though they may be first encountered, and be concentrated, there. I have identified the moment as located and inhabited by the remarriage comedies as one in which moral cynicism threatens, the temptation to give up on a life more coherent and admirable than seems affordable after the compromises of adulthood come to obscure the promise and dreams of youth. The fact that the principal pair in these comedies is somewhat older than the young pairs of classical comedy provides a context in which certain ways of fulfilling earlier dreams have collapsed and a new regime must be formed to which consent can now, on reflection, be won, or wagered.

I have characterized Emerson as perceiving this state as one of my wanting (that is, lacking and desiring) justification, and understood him as perceiving our lacking the means of making ourselves intelligible (to others, to ourselves). And the depth of this crisis (if I do not miss the fact that it is a crisis) is expressed in, and by, Emerson's writing as responding to a time in which I sense as it were a lack in language itself, as if to explain myself I would have to reinvent my words. (Writing, as an allegory of aversion to conformity, to going along, getting along, inevitably raises the question of the direction of aversive turning as turning toward or away, since I crave the words I cringe from—all the words I have.)

I mean this to capture the experience of Emerson's saying, as we shall see in a moment, that conformity makes "most men," meaning most to whom he feels he is responding, "not false in a few particulars, authors of a few lies, but false in all particulars . . . So that every word they say chagrins us and we know not where to begin to set them right." I relate this to Aristotle's famous claim, at the opening of his *Politics*, that it is the gift of language that makes human beings fit for, and fated for, political association, the association that places and measures all the others. Emerson's claim of finding the language of most others depressing, let us say uncommunicative, made against the background of Aristotle's idea, which seems to me its most plausible inspiration, in effect declares that a genuine political association does not exist between him and those others; that, said otherwise, America has not yet been discovered. Then his task as a writer is to discover the terms in which it can be discovered. Then what will constitute its discovery?

I make the following fundamental assumption: What I characterized as making oneself intelligible is the interpretation moral perfectionism gives to the idea of moral reasoning, the demand for providing reasons for one's conduct, for the justification of one's life. Utilitarianism proposes a means of calculation to determine the good of an action. Kantianism proposes a principle of judgment to determine the rightness of an action. Perfectionism proposes confrontation and conversation as the means of determining whether we can live together, accept one another into the aspirations of our lives. This does not mean that perfectionism is an alternative to these other famous positions. Left to itself it may seem to make the ability to converse do too much work— what prevents us from coming to unjust agreements, or intimately talking ourselves into misdeeds? Perfectionism is the province not of those who oppose justice and benevolent calculation, but of those who feel left out of their sway, who feel indeed that most people have been left, or leave themselves out, of their sway. It is a perception, or an intuition, that Emerson articulates as most men living in "secret melancholy" and that Thoreau a few years later transcribes as "the mass of men liv[ing] lives of quiet desperation."

I put matters by contrasting utilitarianism, Kantianism, and perfectionism in terms of providing means of coming to agreement, or establishing conditions of understanding, to align them with Socrates' question to *Euthyphro* that I cited in the Introduction: "What kind of disagreement, my friend, causes hatred and anger?" Some philosophers have taken the fact of moral disagreement to show the inherent irrationality of moral argument—show it to be essentially a matter of which side has the greater power, political, rhetorical, psychological, economic. Heaven knows there are mortal conflicts of such kinds, and they often give themselves out as moral conflicts. Whereas my suggestion is that moral reasoning of the standard sorts—calculation of consequences, interpretation of motives and principles—is to be understood as obeying the moral demand for intelligibility. It is in its meeting of that demand that perfectionism counts as a moral theory (or as a dimension of any moral theory). Everything else is still open. For example, whether there are limits to the obligation to be intelligible, whether everyone isn't entitled to a certain obscurity or sense of confusion, and at some times more than others. Maybe there isn't always something to say; and there is the question of what one is to do about persisting disagreement, how far you must go in trying to resolve it—as Adam Bonner (Spencer Tracy) will put the matter to Amanda Bonner (Katharine Hepburn) in *Adam's Rib*, "I've always tried to see your point of view. But this time you've got me stumped."

Socrates' mode is important. He is clearly in disagreement with Euthyphro, as he is discussing disagreement, and I like the notation of his credibly affirming, in that circumstance, friendship with Euthyphro ("What kind of disagreement, my friend, causes hatred and anger?"). The implication is that there the context for moral argument or reasoning, one in which there is a willingness to understand and to be understood, may be difficult to maintain. A further implication I draw is that hatred and anger are not essentially irrational, but may clearly be called for. To live a moral life should not require that we become Socrateses or Buddhas or Christs, all but unprovokable. But we are asked to make even justified anger and hatred intelligible, and to be responsible for their expression in our lives, and sometimes, not always and everywhere, to put them aside.

One reason for my placing Emerson first, as a figure of the perfectionist, is the clarity and passion with which his writing tests its aspiration to honesty, to expressing all and only what it means. "Self-reliance is [conformity's] aversion" is one of Emerson's many efforts at the self-description of his writing, of the point of every word he writes. Take it this way: "Self-reliance" characterizes the manner in which his writing relates to itself, stands by itself, accounts for itself. "Conformity" characterizes the audience of this writing, the one it seeks to attract; an audience, I said earlier, from which and to which it turns, incessantly (so it is as attracted to that audience, or what it may become, as it is chagrined by it). If he believed that the audience *could not* turn to him, it would be folly for him to write as he does. As it would be folly if he believed that he was not subject to the same failings as they. (Thoreau says it this way: "I never knew . . . a worse man than myself." And "I would not [waste myself in?] preaching to a stone.") This turning is Emerson's picture of thinking, explicit in *The American Scholar*. It is manifest in the way Emerson turns words and sentences—as if you are to read them forward and backward, inside out and outside in.

Emerson's writing, in demonstrating our lack of given means of making ourselves intelligible (to ourselves, to others), details the difficulties in the way of possessing those means, and demonstrates that they are at hand. This thought, implying our need of invention and of transformation, expresses two dominating themes of perfectionism.

The first theme is that the human self—confined by itself, aspiring toward itself—is always becoming, as on a journey, always partially in a further state. This journey is described as education or cultivation. (Thoreau characteristically names his audience the student, and Emerson names it the scholar, but neither of them has in mind simply, or even primarily, people enrolled in what we call a school, but rather an aspect of their conception of the human, of any age.) Since an emphasis on cultivation is an essential feature of perfectionism, the ease with which perfectionism can be debased into a form of aestheticism or preciosity or religiosity is a measure of the ease with which perfectionism can be debased, as philosophy can be, or religion.

The second dominating theme is that the other to whom I can use the words I discover in which to express myself is the Friend—a figure that may occur as the goal of the journey but also as its instigation and accompaniment. Any moral outlook—systematically assessing the value of human existence—will accord weight to the value of friendship. But only perfectionism, as I understand it, places so absolute a value on this relationship. The presence of friendship in the films we will consider (including the sometimes drastic lack of this relation in the melodramas) is of the most specific importance in establishing them as perfectionist narratives.

We come, then, to the four pairs of excerpts from "Self-Reliance." I have arranged them as follows: The first two passages indicate how the *question of philosophy* shows itself as a determining matter of Emerson's writing. The second two suggest the role of *moral paradox* in Emerson. The next two name two narrative figures or characters whom Emerson invokes to measure his claim to authority or authorship (his disdaining of any standing authority is a measure of his claim to philosophy)—said otherwise, these figures occupy *the role of the Friend*. And the final two passages are meant as specimens of how *reading that writing* is to be accomplished.

THE QUESTION OF PHILOSOPHY

Man is timid and apologetic; he is no longer upright; he dares not say "I think," "I am," but quotes some saint or sage.

Most men have bound their eyes with one or another handkerchief, and attached themselves to some one of these communities of opinion. This conformity makes them not false in a few particulars, authors of a few lies, but false in all particulars. Their every truth is not quite true . . . so that every word they say chagrins us and we know not where to begin to set them right.

In the first extract, Emerson is invoking Descartes's fateful idea "Cogito ergo sum," "I think, therefore I am." (Don't be put off by the lack of "therefore" in Emerson's version. Descartes also leaves out the therefore in the most likely place one may encounter his idea, in the second of his six Meditations, where he writes: "*I am, I exist* is necessarily true every time that I pronounce it or conceive it in my mind.") I say Emerson is playful and serious in his repetition of Descartes because what Emerson does, in a passage that identifies quoting with a *fear of saying* ("I dare not say"), is to quote (a sage) and therefore not exactly, or exactly not, to say the thing for himself. (I do not here invoke the technical philosophical distinction between mentioning and using a signifying phrase. One reason not to do so is that there is an ordinary use of a quotation, irrelevant to logic, in which you introduce it by saying "As so-and-so aptly remarks," thus claiming your acknowledgment of the truth or aptness of the remark without taking responsibility for forming the thought. Another reason is that I take Emerson here to be questioning the flat distinction between saying and quoting. A favorite idea of Emerson's is precisely that, except in those moments when self-reliance, or coming to oneself, has overcome the necessities of conformity, one is incessantly quoting, using what Proust calls "public words.")

The implications of Emerson's strategy are various: (1) He shows himself not to have announced his own cogito (not here anyway); accordingly he shows himself to be unable or unwilling to claim and prove his own existence in that moment, hence then and there to be haunting it ("we glide ghost-like"). (2) His inability to assert the most basic facts of existence, for example the inability to name Descartes, to claim the authority of a founder of modern European philosophy, implies that America is unable to inherit and claim philosophy for itself, hence remains haunted by it. (3) If we Americans are to claim philosophy for ourselves, we will have to invent a language for it in which our existence without philosophy, or haunted by philosophy, is itself expressible philosophically. It will require a look and a sound so far unheard of, an originality not expressed in new words, as if we had to speak in tongues; we want the old words, but transfigured by our unprecedented experience of discovery, displacement, and inhabitation, of mad conflicts between the desire for freedom and the immediacy of heaven, and unending disappointment with our failings to become a new world. It will be a language, or a mode of speech, in which what we say is neither just quoted nor just said, perhaps because it is denied as well as said or because more than one thing is said.

On the second page of his essay "The Poet," Emerson says: "The highest minds of the world have never ceased to explore the double meaning, or, shall I say, the quadruple, or the centuple, or much more manifold meaning, of every sensuous fact." There is some suggestion here, no doubt, that the daring philosopher whom Emerson calls for, taking on directly the assertion of his (and our) existence, will have also to be something of a poet—the ideal of Coleridge and Wordsworth as well as of their contemporary German Romantics such as Schlegel and Tieck (the influential translators of Shakespeare into German). The process of discovering and announcing a fact is something Emerson (in "The American Scholar") calls thinking and describes in a way philosophers of our time will have difficulty recognizing as part of the work they are obliged to do: Emerson writes of a process "by which experience is converted into thought" which is a way of making the meaning of a fact public. A little later he says there is "no fact, no event, in our private history, which shall not, sooner or later, lose its adhesive, inert form, and astonish us by soaring from our body into the empyrean."

This sense of being able to speak philosophically and openly about anything and everything that happens to you is an ideal of thinking that first seemed to me possible in contemporary professional philosophy in the work of the later Wittgenstein and in that of J. L. Austin. It is what their redemption of what they call the ordinary from its rejection in much of philosophy has perhaps most importantly meant to me. Without the sense of liberation that afforded me, I do not know that I would have persisted in attempting to find a place in academic philosophy.

In the second of the two passages quoted a moment ago, Emerson specifies further characteristics of a speech that can incorporate the fatedness to quotation (to America's having come late into the world) and to the absence of a philosophical voice of America's own. (Not that America's relation to philosophy is in all respects unique. Nietzsche had his own conditions for experiencing the loss of a credible language of philosophy.) To be chagrined by every word that most men say is going to put you at odds with those men and make your common sense sound paradoxical. This is the crisis out of which moral perfectionism's aspiration takes its rise, the sense that either you or the world is wrong. For example, Emerson somewhere refers to a *casual* remark or action as a *casualty*. This may be taken as idle, cute, or perverse of him. But consider first that remarks worth calling casual (especially as an excuse) are expressions of thoughtlessness and conformity; and second that what is said is permanent, it can rarely be neutralized by a simple "Pardon me." We understand that the bustling and bumping that the human body is subject to in its daily rounds will cause some unintentional bruises, but purely unintentional words are harder to find or ignore or explain or excuse; and consider further that, unlike your unintentional actions, your as it were unintentional words may endlessly have already been taken up and repeated as they made their way amid the varied interests and accidents of others, the most ordinary perhaps affording, as in Emerson's case, a certain melancholy.

Moral Paradoxes

I shun father and mother and wife and brother when my genius calls me. I would write on the lintels of the door-post *Whim.* I hope it is somewhat better than whim at last, but we cannot spend the day in explanation.

Do not tell me, as a good man did today, of my obligation to put all poor men in good situations. Are they *my* poor? I tell thee, thou foolish philanthropist, that I grudge the dollar, the dime, the cent I give to such men as do not belong to me and to whom I do not belong.

These two instances of paradoxes are both allusions to, some might say parodies of, words reported in the Gospels as said or heard by Jesus. In the first quotation Emerson is following the injunction not to delay, for example by appealing to the obligation to bury the dead, when the King of Heaven is at hand. Yet where others will claim that this is a private appeal to faith, Emerson suggests writing "Whim" for all to see. One might feel that this shows Emerson's distrust or chagrin in response to so many ready mouthfuls of faith. But then consider that it also shows a dedication of his writing to the work of faith, to transfigured, redemptive words, which means that he cannot, in his finitude, and his distrust of the exchanges of words as they now stand in society, claim more than the existence of his own call to write otherwise. Whether it is more, whether it speaks for the world and to others, is not for him to say.

The second quotation, containing the disturbing question "Are they *my* poor?" has, you may imagine, caused hard looks and words to be sent Emerson's way. But consider that Emerson is alluding, so I claim, to Jesus' famous dismissal, or acceptance, of the poor: "The poor you have always with you." The occasion was, similarly, one in which "a good man" (a good instance of what a man is) had said to Jesus something about helping the poor. It was, namely, the occasion on which Jesus allowed Mary, the sister of Lazarus, to anoint his feet with expensive oil, and the man objecting to this gesture, instructing Jesus in the moral impropriety of this extravagance, was Judas. Does this extravagant allusion on Emerson's part alleviate his apparent harshness, or does it magnify it? Since he claims to have his own poor, and since these must be his way of referring to those for whom he spends his life writing, we will want to know on what basis he places this degree of confidence in the good of his writing, for which he claims no more than whim, betting his life that its good may prove "better than whim at last."

TWO FIGURES OF THE FRIEND

[The true man] measures you and all men and all events. You are constrained to accept his standard.*

The nonchalance of boys who are sure of a dinner, and would disdain as much as a lord to do or say aught to conciliate one, is the healthy attitude of human nature. A boy is in the parlor what the pit is in the playhouse; independent, irresponsible, looking out from his corner on such people and facts as pass by, he tries and sentences them on their merits, in the swift, summary, way of boys, as good, bad, interesting, silly, eloquent, troublesome. . . . But the man is as it were clapped into jail by his consciousness. As soon as he has once acted or spoken with *éclat* he is a committed person, watched by the sympathy or the hatred of hundreds, whose affections must now enter into his account. . . . Ah, that he could pass again into his neutrality! . . . He would utter opinions on all passing affairs, which being seen to be not private but necessary, would sink like darts into the ear of men and put them in fear.

I take both figures, the true man and the boy, to represent what Emerson calls "speaking with necessity," something I relate to Kant's demand that I speak with a "universal voice." Kant introduces the idea in accounting for the aesthetic judgment, but it seems to me to be understood, in his moral philosophy, as alluding to moral judgment, namely the application to one's conduct of the categorical imperative, which may be pictured as the universal voice speaking to me. The boy still in his neutrality is the model of an aspiration of philosophical writing, not on the ground that his judgment is always sound, but on the ground that it is always *his*, and because it concerns the basis for eventually judging usefully, fruitfully, anything and everything that passes through his world. The image of the true man is, I believe, a further development of Kantian ideas, which I will dwell on with more care in Chapter 7. But before leaving this initial sketch of Emerson's ways and means, I want at least to indicate how I see this connection with Kant.

Emerson's true man, whose "standard you are constrained to accept" is a recasting of Kant's idea, mentioned in my Introduction, of the human as having two "standpoints"

---

* The second sentence here appears in the first edition of Emerson's *Essays* but not in most of the later editions that I have consulted. I regret Emerson's whim in excising this sentence.

on his existence, which Kant also pictures as our living in two worlds—the sensuous world in which we are governed by the laws of material things, and the intelligible world in which we are free. The true man's standard is, in short, ours so far as we live adopting the standpoint of the intelligible world. (The justification for linking standard and standpoint involves my claim that "Self-Reliance" as a whole can be taken as an essay on human understanding and being misunderstood. If you take these recurrences of the idea of "standing" to be merely puns, I point to another claim of "Self-Reliance" in which Emerson declares, "I stand here for humanity," where the meaning of "standing for" as both representing something and bearing up under something is, I trust, too plain to deny. But this will come back.)

I note as a companion gesture Emerson's idea of being "constrained" by a standard as a recasting of Kant's idea of the human as "constrained" by a feeling of "ought," expressed as our recognizing and obeying the moral law, the categorical imperative. Kant pictures the origin, or what he would call the "possibility," of this feeling as a function of the human as being neither beast nor angel. This is clearly a relative of the picture of our living in two worlds, neither wholly in the sensuous world nor wholly in the intelligible world. If we lived wholly in the sensuous world, as beasts do, we would not recognize the demand of the moral law; if we lived wholly in the intelligible world, as only angels could, we would have no need of the law. Kant's constraint is that of duty, obligation, as I recognize the power of reason to overcome inclination. Emerson's constraint is that of attraction, recognizing myself as drawn, as it were, beyond my present repertory of inclination, to my unattained but attainable self. Moral reasoning is not to take me from irrational to rational choice (in the distribution of satisfactions, as in the case of moral theories that take the good as fundamental, such as that of John Stuart Mill); nor from a will corrupted by sensuous concerns to one measured and chastened by the demands of the moral law (represented by Kant and in an important sense by John Rawls, who defines an idea of right or justice in independence of a definition of the good); but to take me from confusion to (relative) clarity in seeking a world I can want.

Moral perfectionism challenges ideas of moral motivation, showing (against Kant's law that counters inclination, and against utilitarianism's calculation of benefits) the possibility of my access to experience which gives to my desire for the attaining of a self that is mine to become, the power to act on behalf of an attainable world I can actually desire.

The Nature of Reading

Character teaches above our wills.

In every work of genius we recognize our own rejected thoughts; they come back to us with a certain alienated majesty.

The idea of "character" in Emerson always (so far as I recall) refers simultaneously to something about the worth and stamp of an individual's (or human group's) difference from others and to physical traces of writing (or expression more generally). So "Character teaches above our wills" means simultaneously that writing conveys meaning beyond our intention, and quite generally that we express in every gesture more than our will accomplishes or recognizes. "In every work of genius we recognize our rejected thoughts . . . with a certain alienated majesty," as a description of the ambition Emerson harbors for his own writing, links up with Wittgenstein's saying of philosophy that what it seeks is not (as in the case of science) to teach something new and to hunt out new facts to support its claims, but rather to understand what is already before us, too obvious and pervasive to be ordinarily remarked. Wittgenstein uses as the epigraph for *Philosophical Investigations* the following, from Nestroy: "Progress generally looks much greater than it really is." This seems to me to capture (beyond the suggestion that a decisive advance may be produced by a small move) the sense of philosophy as revealing the rejected or undervalued, in which the uncovering of something obvious can create astonishment, like the relation of something casual as yielding casualties, or in Wittgenstein's *Investigations* such a remark as "I am not of the *opinion* that another has a soul." (One might equally say of such cases that progress seems smaller than it really is; in neither case are we assured of its permanence.) Philosophers like to follow Aristotle in saying that philosophy begins in wonder. My impression is that philosophers nowadays tend to associate the experience of wonder with the explanations of science rather than, as in Wittgenstein and Austin, with the recognition of our relation to things as they are, the perception of the extraordinariness of what we find ordinary (for example, beauty), and the ordinariness of what we find extraordinary (for example, violence).

Emerson's very familiarity to Americans makes him in some way the easiest and in some way the hardest to assess of the writers discussed in this book. Because I use Emerson as both a means or touchstone of interpretation and an object of interpretation, there will be many opportunities in later chapters to refine our assessment.

Acknowledgments

I began creating this anthology fifteen years ago and along the way—while writing a doctoral dissertation on Emerson (*The Fate of Embodiment*), authoring a brief intellectual biography of Emerson (*On Emerson*) and a monograph addressing his 1856 book (*Emerson's English Traits and the Natural History of Metaphor* forthcoming from Bloomsbury Academic), editing Stanley Cavell's book on Emerson (*Emerson's Transcendental Etudes*), and composing essays and articles devoted to Emerson's work—I have incurred many debts to teachers, scholars, colleagues, librarians, publishers, editors, contributors, and friends I wish to acknowledge and thank.

The prolonged research for this collection afforded me the pleasure of talking with many accomplished Emerson scholars, conversations that contributed to the richness and variety of works included here. I humbly thank the numerous scholars who upon hearing of this project not only conveyed their enthusiasm for its promise and attestation for the selections already in hand but also went further to suggest a name or text that might fit—and sometimes to offer just a hunch, something for me to follow after; very often this pursuit yielded a gratifying discovery. Some of these conversations occurred at various colloquia and conferences over the years. I extend my thanks, in particular, to the organizers, conferees, and participants at The National Endowment for the Humanities Summer Institute on Emerson "Literature, Philosophy, Democracy" in Santa Fe (2003), including Steven Affeldt, Ronald Bosco, Stanley Cavell, William Day, Richard Deming, Thomas Dumm, Russell Goodman, Timothy Gould, Joel Myerson, the late Barbara Packer, Lawrence Rhu, William Rothman, and Cornel West; the colloquium "Emerson's *Essays*" in Miami (2004); "Liberty, Language, and The Origins of American Intellectual Identity," a colloquium I directed in San Diego (2007) and for which I served as discussion leader in Louisville (2008); "Individual Liberty, Self-Reliance, and Private Property in Emerson and Mill," a colloquium for which I led discussion in San Diego (2009); "Liberty and Necessity in Emerson and Nietzsche," a colloquium I directed in Big Sky, Montana (2009); and conferences on the work of Stanley Cavell held at Loránd Eötvös University, Budapest (2004), University of Edinburgh (2008), Le Moyne College (2009), The Humanities Center at Harvard (2010), and The Johns Hopkins Humanities Center (2011).

It is my pleasure to have an occasion for more particular thanks to a few of the teachers and mentors who lent me their support during the project's lengthy development: Stanley Cavell (Harvard), the late Peter H. Hare (University at Buffalo), David D. Hall (Harvard), the late Peter J. Gomes (Harvard), Cornel West (Union Theological Seminary), John J. McDermott (Texas A & M), and Eduardo Cadava (Princeton). I offer a special thank you to John Lachs (Vanderbilt) who, recognizing the diversity, extent, and quality of the many works of criticism on Emerson, recommended that I endeavor to curate a collection from that impressive catalogue; I thank him for prompting the project and for thinking me a good candidate for its realization.

Since the headers that introduce each writer in this volume are largely fact-driven—involving specific people, places, chronologies, books, events—there was a demand for a certain reliance on the extensive and often definitive research of others, a wealth of scholarship I benefitted from as I prepared the 67 entries. Of decisive help was the editorial work of numerous scholars whose informed annotations are evident in the various collections of Emerson's writing, including *The Correspondence of Ralph Waldo Emerson and Thomas Carlyle*, Emerson's *Journals and Miscellaneous Notebooks*, *Letters*, *Complete Works*, *Early Lectures* and *Later Lectures*. Providing much-needed additional guidance was Len Gougeon's *Virtue's Hero*, Laura Dassow Walls' *Emerson's Life in Science*, and Robert Habich's *Building Their Own Waldos*, as well as the full range of biographies on Emerson by Moncure Daniel Conway (1881), George Willis Cooke (1881), Alexander Ireland (1882), Oliver Wendell Holmes (1885), James Elliot Cabot (1887), Edward Waldo Emerson (1889), Oscar W. Firkins (1915), and more recently by Ralph Rusk (1949), John McAleer (1984), Robert D. Richardson (1995) (along with his biography of William James (2006)), and Lawrence Buell (2003).

I should like to express my thanks to the authors, publishers, estates, and other rights holders who granted permission to reprint work, and I am particularly grateful to Professors Cavell, Gass, McDermott, and West for generously allowing their writing to appear in the present collection. Because of all this reinforcement, cooperation, and beneficence, the volume includes many essential works, and for that is immeasurably stronger than it otherwise would have been.

I am indebted to The Ralph Waldo Emerson Society for the 2008 Community Project Award that aided the development of the Emerson/Nietzsche colloquium. And, remarkably, since The Ralph Waldo Emerson Society also granted the 2012 Subvention Award to *Estimating Emerson*, I can thank the officers and members of the Society for its generous underwriting of the present volume.

My research was facilitated and enriched by the resources, collections, scholars, and staff at the following libraries, to which I am agreeably obliged: Vanderbilt University, University of California at Berkeley, University of Cambridge, Harvard College Library, Houghton Library, The London Library, The British Library, The Library of Congress, The New York Society Library, and The New York Public Library.

I am especially grateful to The New York Public Library for a term as Writer in Residence in the Frederick Lewis Allen Room, and to Jay Barksdale of the General Research Division, and Study Rooms Liaison, for his aid. Also at The New York Public Library, I thank Kyle R. Triplett and associates at The Brooke Russell Astor Reading Room for Rare Books and Manuscripts.

I appreciate the facilitation of John Burt, Literary Executor for the estate of Robert Penn Warren, in helping to secure rights.

For constructive remarks on an earlier draft of the manuscript, I sincerely thank Branka Arsić (Columbia) and Paul Grimstad (Yale).

I heartily thank David Mikics (University of Houston) for his meaningful support of this and other Emerson initiatives, and for his engaging mentorship.

I appreciate exacting editorial suggestions pertaining to the introduction and headers from Lorna K. Hershinow and Sheldon Hershinow.

For her scintillating and steady intellectual companionship, and for her forbearance, especially as I worked on the last stages of production, I am genuinely grateful to K. L. Evans.

And lastly, with pleasure, I extend my deepest gratitude to Haaris Naqvi, who shepherded this project and is ultimately responsible for the existence of this book.

Permissions

CPSIA information can be obtained
at www.ICGtesting.com
Printed in the USA
LVHW022145220421
685251LV00013B/563